HOLT
ELEMENTS OF
LITERATURE

First Course

HOLT, RINEHART AND WINSTON

A Harcourt Education Company

Orlando • **Austin** • New York • San Diego • Toronto • London

EDITORIAL
Project Directors: Kathleen Daniel, Mescal Evler
Executive Editor: Juliana Koenig
Senior Book Editor: Susan Kent Cakars
Senior Product Manager: Don Wulbrecht
Managing Editor: Marie Price
Associate Managing Editor: Elizabeth LaManna
Editorial Staff: Kerry Johnson, Evan Wilson, Sari Wilson
Copyediting Manager: Michael Neibergall
Copyediting Supervisor: Mary Malone
Copyeditors: Christine Altgelt, Elizabeth Dickson, Emily Force, Leora Harris, Anne Heausler, Julia Thomas Hu, Kathleen Scheiner, Nancy Shore
Editorial Support: Christine Degollado, Betty Gabriel, Janet Jenkins, Mark Koenig, Erik Netcher, Gloria Shahan
Editorial Permissions: Mark Koenig, Sally Garland

Index: Tamsin Nutter

ART, DESIGN, AND PRODUCTION
Director: Athena Blackorby
Senior Design Director: Betty Mintz
Designer: Fred Yee
Senior Picture Researcher: Mary Monaco
Picture Research: Susan Sato
Assistant Production Coordinator: Myles Gorospe

COVER
Photo Credits: (inset) *Boats at Fishbeach* by James Fitzgerald. Oil on canvasboard. Courtesy of Dan Broeckelmann and Krista Lisajus. (background) Photograph of boats on water, © Derek P. Redearn/Getty Images.

Program Author

Kylene Beers established the reading pedagogy for *Elements of Literature*. A former middle-school teacher, Dr. Beers has turned her commitment to helping readers having difficulty into the major focus of her research, writing, speaking, and teaching. Dr. Beers is currently Senior Reading Researcher at the Child Study Center of the School Development Program at Yale University and was formerly a Research Associate Professor at the University of Houston. Dr. Beers is also currently the editor of the National Council of Teachers of English journal *Voices from the Middle*. She is the author of *When Kids Can't Read: What Teachers Can Do* and the co-editor of *Into Focus: Understanding and Creating Middle School Readers*. Dr. Beers is the 2001 recipient of the Richard Halle Award from the NCTE for outstanding contributions to middle-level literacy education. She has served on the review boards of the *English Journal* and *The Alan Review*. Dr. Beers currently serves on the board of directors of the International Reading Association's Special Interest Group on Adolescent Literature.

Special Contributors

Flo Ota De Lange and **Sheri Henderson** helped plan and organize the program and played key roles in developing and preparing the informational materials. They wrote Collection 8, Reading for Life, as well as Test Smarts.

Flo Ota De Lange is a former teacher with a thirty-year second career in psychotherapy, during which she studied learning processes in children and adults. These careers have led to her third career, as a writer.

Sheri Henderson brings to the program twenty years of experience as a middle-school research practitioner and full-time reading and language arts teacher at La Paz Intermediate School in Saddleback Valley Unified School District in California. She regularly speaks at statewide and national conferences.

Since 1991, DeLangeHenderson LLC has published forty-three titles designed to integrate the teaching of literature with standards requirements and state and national tests.

Writers

John Malcolm Brinnin, author of six volumes of poetry that have received many prizes and awards, was a member of the American Academy and Institute of Arts and Letters. He was a critic of poetry and a biographer of poets and was for a number of years Director of New York's famous Poetry Center. His teaching career, begun at Vassar College, included long terms at the University of Connecticut and Boston University, where he succeeded Robert Lowell as Professor of Creative Writing and Contemporary Letters. Mr. Brinnin wrote *Dylan Thomas in America: An Intimate Journal* and *Sextet: T. S. Eliot & Truman Capote & Others.*

Virginia Hamilton wrote the Elements of Literature essay on folk tales. Ms. Hamilton is one of America's most highly acclaimed writers of books for children and young adults. She has received many awards, including the Newbery Award for *M. C. Higgins, the Great;* the Newbery Honor Award for *In the Beginning: Creation Stories from Around the Word;* the Coretta Scott King Award for *Sweet Whispers, Brother Rush;* and the Edgar Allan Poe Award for *The House of Dies Drear.* Among her collections of folk tales are *The People Could Fly* and *The Dark Way: Stories from the Spirit World.* The *All Jahdu Storybook* is a collection of Hamilton's own tales about a trickster hero who was born in an oven between two loaves of bread. In 1990, Hamilton received an honorary doctorate from the Bank Street College of Education in New York City. In 1995, she received a MacArthur Fellowship. In 1998, Kent State University established the Virginia Hamilton Literary Award for excellence in multicultural literature for children and young adults.

Writers

David Adams Leeming wrote the Elements of Literature essay on Greek and Roman myths. Dr. Leeming was a Professor of English and Comparative Literature at the University of Connecticut for many years. He is the author of several books on mythology, including *Mythology: The Voyage of the Hero; The World of Myth;* and *Encyclopedia of Creation Myths.* For several years he taught English at Robert College in Istanbul, Turkey. He also served as secretary and assistant to the writer James Baldwin in New York and Istanbul. He is the author of the biographies *James Baldwin* and *Amazing Grace: A Biography of Beauford Delaney.*

John Leggett is a novelist, biographer, and teacher. He went to the Writer's Workshop at the University of Iowa in the spring of 1969, expecting to work there for a single semester. In 1970, he assumed temporary charge of the program, and for the next seventeen years he was its director. Mr. Leggett's novels include *Wilder Stone, The Gloucester Branch, Who Took the Gold Away?, Gulliver House,* and *Making Believe.* He is also the author of the highly acclaimed biography *Ross and Tom: Two American Tragedies* and of a biography of William Saroyan, *A Daring Young Man.* Mr. Leggett lives in California's Napa Valley.

Joan Burditt is a writer and editor who has a master's degree in education with a specialization in reading. She taught for several years in Texas, where her experience included work in programs for readers having difficulty. Since then she has developed and written instructional materials for middle-school language arts texts.

Madeline Travers Hovland, who taught middle school for several years, is a writer of educational materials. She studied English at Bates College and received a master's degree in education from Harvard University.

Richard Kelso is a writer and editor whose children's books include *Building a Dream: Mary Bethune's School; Walking for Freedom: The Montgomery Bus Boycott; Days of Courage: The Little Rock Story;* and *The Case of the Amistad Mutiny.*

Mara Rockliff is a writer and editor with a degree in American civilization from Brown University. She has written dramatizations of classic stories for middle-school students, collected in a book called *Stories for Performance.* She has also published feature stories in national newspapers and is currently writing a novel for young adults.

Fannie Safier has worked as a teacher in New York City schools. She has been writing and editing educational materials for more than thirty years.

Program Consultants

CONTENT-AREA READING CONSULTANT

Judith L. Irvin served as a reading consultant for the content-area readers: *The Ancient World; A World in Transition;* and *The United States: Change and Challenge.* Dr. Irvin is a Professor of Education at Florida State University. She writes a column, "What Research Says to the Middle Level Practitioner," for the *Middle School Journal* and serves as the literacy expert for the *Middle Level News*, published by the California League of Middle Schools. Her several books include the companion volumes *Reading and the Middle School Student: Strategies to Enhance Literacy* and *Reading and the High School Student: Strategies to Enhance Literacy* (with Buehl and Klemp).

SENIOR PROGRAM CONSULTANT

Carol Jago is the editor of CATE's quarterly journal, *California English.* She teaches English at Santa Monica High School, in Santa Monica, and directs the California Reading and Literature Project at UCLA. She also writes a weekly education column for the *Los Angeles Times.* She is the author of several books, including two in a series on contemporary writers in the classroom: *Alice Walker in the Classroom* and *Nikki Giovanni in the Classroom.* She is also the author of *With Rigor for All: Teaching the Classics to Contemporary Students* and *Beyond Standards: Excellence in the High School English Classroom.*

CRITICAL REVIEWERS

Dr. Julie M. T. Chan
Director of Literacy Instruction
Newport-Mesa Unified School District
Costa Mesa, California

Kathy Dubose
Murchison Junior High School
Austin, Texas

Pamela Dukes
Boude Storey Middle School
Dallas, Texas

Debra Hardick
Bennet Middle School
Manchester, Connecticut

Cheri Howell
Reading Specialist
Covina-Valley Unified School District
Covina, California

José M. Ibarra-Tiznado
ELL Program Coordinator
Bassett Unified School District
La Puente, California

Stacy Kim
Rowland Unified School District
Rowland Heights, California

Dr. Ronald Klemp
Instructor
California State University, Northridge
Northridge, California

Mary Alice Madden
Lathrop Intermediate School
Santa Ana, California

Colette F. McDonald
HB DuPont Middle School
Hockessin, Delaware

Jeff Read
Oak Grove Middle School
Clearwater, Florida

Constance Ridenour
Ford Middle School
Brook Park, Ohio

Fern M. Sheldon
K–12 Curriculum and Instruction Specialist
Rowland Unified School District
Rowland Heights, California

Karen Simons
Slausen Middle School
Ann Arbor, Michigan

Carol Surabian
Washington Intermediate School
Dinuba, California

FIELD-TEST PARTICIPANTS

Kate Baker
South Hills Middle School
Pittsburgh, Pennsylvania

Linda Lawler
Arcadia Middle School
Rochester, New York

Cindy MacIntosh
Seven Hills Middle School
Nevada City, California

Tim Pail
South Hills Middle School
Pittsburgh, Pennsylvania

Mathew Woodin
Martha Baldwin School
Alhambra, California

CONTENTS IN BRIEF

Collection 1

Facing Danger

LITERARY FOCUS
Analyzing Plot

INFORMATIONAL FOCUS
Analyzing Text Structures

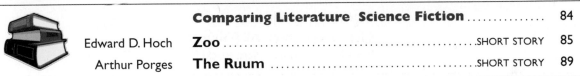
Contents **A5**

Collection 2

CHARACTERS: LIVING MANY LIVES

LITERARY FOCUS
Analyzing Character

INFORMATIONAL FOCUS
Analyzing Comparison and Contrast

Collection 3

LITERARY FOCUS
Analyzing Theme

INFORMATIONAL FOCUS
Analyzing Cause and Effect

Contents   **A9**

Collection 4

Point of View:
Can You See It My Way?

LITERARY FOCUS
Analyzing Point of View

INFORMATIONAL FOCUS
Analyzing an Author's Argument

Worlds of Words: Prose and Poetry

LITERARY FOCUS
Analyzing Prose and Poetry

INFORMATIONAL FOCUS
Analyzing Main Idea

Elements of Poetry

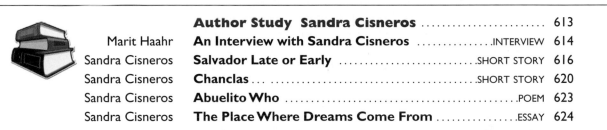

Collection 6

Our Literary Heritage

Greek Myths and World Folk Tales

LITERARY FOCUS
Analyzing Myths and Folk Tales

INFORMATIONAL FOCUS
Summarizing

The Myths of Greece and Rome

World Folk Tales

Collection 7

Literary Criticism: Where I Stand

LITERARY FOCUS
Criticizing Literature

INFORMATIONAL FOCUS
Evaluating Evidence

Collection 8

Reading for Life

INFORMATIONAL FOCUS
- Analyzing Information in Public, Workplace, and Consumer Documents
- Following Technical Directions

Resource Center

SKILLS, WORKSHOPS, AND FEATURES

SKILLS

ELEMENTS OF LITERATURE ESSAYS

READING SKILLS AND STRATEGIES LESSONS

LITERARY SKILLS

WORKSHOPS

WRITING WORKSHOPS

FEATURES

GRAMMAR LINKS

SKILLS, WORKSHOPS, AND FEATURES

SELECTIONS BY GENRE

FICTION

SHORT STORIES

DRAMA

POETRY

SONG LYRICS

NONFICTION

AUTOBIOGRAPHIES

INFORMATIONAL TEXTS

INFORMATIONAL ARTICLES

MAGAZINE ARTICLES

Elements of Literature on the Internet

TO THE STUDENT

At the *Elements of Literature* Internet site, you can read texts by professional writers and learn the inside stories behind your favorite authors. You can also build your word power and analyze messages in the media. As you move through *Elements of Literature*, you will find the best online resources at **go.hrw.com**.

Here's how to log on:

1. Start your Web browser, and enter **go.hrw.com** in the Address or Location field.

2. Note the keyword in your textbook.

3. Enter the keyword, and click "go."

The Sleeping Gypsy (1897) by Henri Rousseau. Oil on canvas (51″ × 6′ 7″).
The Museum of Modern Art, NY.

Facing Danger

Literary Focus:
Analyzing Plot

Informational Focus:
Analyzing Text Structures

go.
hrw
.com

INTERNET

Collection
Resources

Keyword: LE5 7-1

Elements of Literature
Plot *by* John Leggett

A STORY'S BUILDING BLOCKS

Plot is what happens in a story. Plot consists of a series of related episodes, one growing out of another. Most plots have four parts, which are like building blocks.

1 The first part of a plot tells you about the story's **basic situation:** Who are the characters, and what do they want? This is usually where you find out about the conflict, or problem, in a story. A **conflict** is a struggle between opposing characters or opposing forces. In an **external conflict** a character struggles against another person, a group of people, or a force of nature (a tornado, a bear, an icy mountain path). An **internal conflict** takes place in a character's mind (he struggles with shyness; she struggles to accept a death). Here is the introduction to a new version of a tale you know well:

"Hi there, Red," said a wolf to a little girl in a red velvet hood. "How'd ya like a ride on my motorcycle?"

"Thank you, sir, but I can't," replied Little Red Riding Hood. "As you can see, I'm carrying this basket of ginger cookies to my grandmother, and I can't be late."

"Tell you what, Red. You just hop on the back, and I'll run you over to Granny's in five seconds flat."

"My grandmother lives way out at the end of Lonely Road," Red protested. "It's miles and miles."

"This here motorcycle eats miles."

"No, thank you," said Little Red Riding Hood. "I've made up my mind."

To make us feel suspense, storytellers give us clues that **foreshadow,** or hint at, future events. Maybe you felt a shiver of fear when you read that Granny lives on Lonely Road. Bad things can happen on lonely roads. Could this foreshadow trouble for Little Red?

2 In the second part of a plot, one or more of the characters act to resolve the conflict. Now a **series of events** takes place that makes it very hard for the character to get what he or she wants. (Sometimes these events are called **complications.**)

"Suit yourself," chuckled the wolf, who had thought of a wicked plan. He would go alone to the end of Lonely Road, gobble up Red's grandma, and then, when the little girl turned up, he would gobble her up too.

So, arriving at the last house on Lonely Road, the wolf raced his engine, scaring Grandma out her

SKILLS FOCUS

Literary Skills
Understand plot structure.

back door and under the woodshed. The wolf was puzzled to find the house empty, but he put on Grandma's nightcap and nightshirt and climbed into the bed to wait for Red.

3 Now comes the **climax,** the story's most emotional or suspenseful moment. This is the point at which the conflict is decided one way or another.

It was nearly dark when Red arrived, but as she approached her grandma's bed, she sensed something was wrong.

"Are you all right, Granny?" Red asked. "Your eyes look bloodshot."

"All the better to see you with," replied the wolf.

"And your teeth—suddenly they look like fangs."

"All the better to eat—" the wolf began, but he stopped at the sound of his motorcycle engine thundering in the front yard. "Wait right there, Red," said the wolf, bounding from the bed.

The wolf was startled to find Grandma sitting on the motorcycle.

"Hey!" he shouted. "Stop fooling with my bike." As he lunged for her, Grandma found the gearshift, and the cycle leapt forward, scooping the wolf up on its handlebars and hurling him into a giant thorn bush—which is where the police found him when they arrived.

4 The **resolution** is the last part of the story. This is where the loose ends of the plot are tied up and the story is closed.

The wolf was brought to trial and sent to prison. Granny became a popular guest on talk shows. Red lived happily ever after.

Practice

The main events of a story's **plot** can be charted in a diagram like the one below. Think about a story you know well—maybe a movie or a TV show or a novel. See if you can show the story's main events in a similar diagram.

"Once upon a time, they lived happily ever after."

Reading Skills and Strategies

Summarizing the Plot: Retelling

by Kylene Beers

"Is this a plot?" Manuel asked as he pointed to the first paragraph of a story. He didn't understand that plot isn't a single thing he can point to in the story. He didn't know that **plot** is what happens in the story—all the related events that move from the story's beginning to its end. Plot is made up of all the building blocks you just read about on pages 2–3.

What Is Retelling?

Keeping up with all the information in a story can be difficult. A strategy called **retelling** can help you identify the elements of a plot and keep all the information about a plot straight in your mind. With this strategy you practice telling the plot of the story using a **Retelling Summary Sheet.** You use the Retelling Summary Sheet as a guide, to be sure you've included all the events in the plot.

The best way to get better at retelling is to practice retelling. Start practicing by reading the story titled "Duffy's Jacket," which begins on page 5. You can retell by jotting down some notes, by discussing your retelling with a friend, or by just thinking about what you would say.

When you've finished reading the story, use your retelling notes to fill out the Retelling Summary Sheet on page 12.

> ### Retelling Tips
>
> • Start by telling the title and author.
>
> • Explain who the characters are.
>
> • Explain the conflict, or main problem.
>
> • Name the main events, keeping them in order.
>
> • Explain what happens at the end.
>
> • Tell what you liked or didn't like about the story.
>
> • Use words like *first, second, next,* and *finally* to help keep everything in order.

SKILLS FOCUS

Reading Skills
Retell story events.

Duffy's Jacket

Bruce Coville

As you read, you'll find this open-book sign at certain points in the story: 📖. Stop at these points, and think about what you've just read. Sometimes a part of the retelling will be there for you. At other times you'll do the retelling.

If my cousin Duffy had the brains of a turnip it never would have happened. But as far as I'm concerned, Duffy makes a turnip look bright. My mother disagrees. According to her, Duffy is actually very bright. She claims the reason he's so scatterbrained is that he's too busy being brilliant inside his own head to remember everyday things. Maybe. But hanging around with Duffy means you spend a lot of time saying, "Your glasses, Duffy," or "Your coat, Duffy," or—well, you get the idea: a lot of three-word sentences that start with "Your," end with "Duffy," and have words like *book, radio, wallet,* or whatever it is he's just put down and left behind, stuck in the middle.

Me, I think turnips are brighter.

But since Duffy's my cousin, and since my mother and her sister are both single parents, we tend to do a lot of things together—like camping, which is how we got into the mess I want to tell you about.

Personally, I thought camping was a big mistake. But since Mom and Aunt Elise are raising the three of us—me, Duffy, and my little sister, Marie—on their own, they're convinced they have to do man-stuff with us every once in a while. I think they read some book

RETELL

❶ Think about what you've learned so far. What's the title? Who's the author? Who are the important characters? Who are the other characters?

This story is called "Duffy's Jacket," and it's written by Bruce Coville. I think Duffy and his cousin ("I," the narrator) are the important characters. Aunt Elise, Mom, and the narrator's sister, Marie, are the other characters.

RETELL

❷ What's Duffy's most obvious characteristic?

Duffy forgets things—like his suitcase when he takes a trip.

that said me and Duffy would come out weird if they don't. You can take him camping all you want. It ain't gonna make Duffy normal. ❶ 📖

Anyway, the fact that our mothers were getting wound up to do something fatherly, combined with the fact that Aunt Elise's boss had a friend who had a friend who said we could use his cabin, added up to the five of us bouncing along this horrible dirt road late one Friday in October.

It was late because we had lost an hour going back to get Duffy's suitcase. I suppose it wasn't actually Duffy's fault. No one remembered to say, "Your suitcase, Duffy," so he couldn't really have been expected to remember it. ❷ 📖

"Oh, Elise," cried my mother, as we got deeper into the woods. "Aren't the leaves beautiful?"

That's why it doesn't make sense for them to try to do man-stuff with us. If it had been our fathers, they would have been drinking beer and burping and maybe telling dirty stories instead of talking about the leaves. So why try to fake it?

Anyway, we get to this cabin, which is about eighteen million miles from nowhere, and to my surprise, it's not a cabin at all. It's a house. A big house.

"Oh, my," said my mother as we pulled into the driveway.

"Isn't it great?" chirped Aunt Elise. "It's almost a hundred years old, back from the time when they used to build big hunting lodges up here. It's the only one in the area still standing. Horace said he hasn't been able to get up here in some time. That's why he was glad to let us use it. He said it would be good to have someone go in and air the place out."

Leave it to Aunt Elise. This place didn't need airing out—it needed fumigating.[1] I never saw so many spider webs in my life. From the sounds we heard coming from the walls, the mice seemed to have made it a population center. We found a total of two working light-bulbs: one in the kitchen and one in the dining room, which was paneled with dark wood and had a big stone fireplace at one end.

"Oh, my," said my mother again.

Duffy, who's allergic to about fifteen different things, started to sneeze.

"Isn't it charming?" asked Aunt Elise hopefully.

No one answered her.

---

1. **fumigating** (fyo͞o′mə·gāt′iŋ) *v.* used as *n.*: spraying with chemicals to kill harmful organisms and pests.

Four hours later we had managed to get three bedrooms clean enough to sleep in without getting the heebie-jeebies—one for Mom and Aunt Elise, one for Marie, and one for me and Duffy. After a supper of beans and franks we hit the hay, which I think is what our mattresses were stuffed with. As I was drifting off, which took about thirty seconds, it occurred to me that four hours of housework wasn't all that much of a man-thing, something it might be useful to remember the next time Mom got one of these plans into her head. ❸

Things looked better in the morning when we went outside and found a stream where we could go wading. ("Your sneakers, Duffy.")

Later we went back and started poking around the house, which really was enormous.

That was when things started getting a little spooky. In the room next to ours I found a message scrawled on the wall. "Beware the Sentinel,"[2] it said in big black letters.

When I showed Mom and Aunt Elise they said it was just a joke and got mad at me for frightening Marie. ❹

Marie wasn't the only one who was frightened.

We decided to go out for another walk. ("Your lunch, Duffy.") We went deep into the woods, following a faint trail that kept threatening to disappear but never actually faded away altogether. It was a hot day, even in the deep woods, and after a while we decided to take off our coats.

When we got back and Duffy didn't have his jacket, did they get mad at him? My mother actually had the nerve to say, "Why didn't you remind him? You know he forgets things like that."

What do I look like, a walking memo pad?

Anyway, I had other things on my mind—like the fact that I was convinced someone had been following us while we were in the woods.

I tried to tell my mother about it, but first she said I was being ridiculous, and then she accused me of trying to sabotage[3] the trip. ❺

So I shut up. But I was pretty nervous, especially when Mom and Aunt Elise announced that they were going into town—which was twenty miles away—to pick up some supplies (like lightbulbs).

"You kids will be fine on your own," said Mom cheerfully. "You can make popcorn and play Monopoly. And there's enough soda here for you to make yourselves sick on."

---

2. **sentinel** (sent'n·əl) *n.*: guard; person keeping watch.
3. **sabotage** (sab'ə·täzh') *v.*: obstruct or destroy.

Using the Strategy

RETELL

❸ Review what's happened. Where are the campers? What's the condition of the cabin? What three things have happened since they arrived at the cabin?

They're in a big hunting lodge in the woods. The place is dirty and full of spiders and mice. They cleaned the cabin, ate dinner, and went to sleep.

RETELL

❹ When do things start to get spooky?

RETELL

❺ What does the narrator tell his mother? How does she react?

And with that they were gone.

It got dark.

We played Monopoly.

They didn't come back. That didn't surprise me. Since Duffy and I were both fifteen they felt it was okay to leave us on our own, and Mom had warned us they might decide to have dinner at the little inn we had seen on the way up.

But I would have been happier if they had been there.

Especially when something started scratching on the door.

"What was that?" asked Marie.

"What was what?" asked Duffy.

"That!" she said, and this time I heard it, too. My stomach rolled over, and the skin at the back of my neck started to prickle.

"Maybe it's the Sentinel!" I hissed.

"Andrew!" yelled Marie. "Mom told you not to say that."

"She said not to try to scare you," I said. "I'm not. *I'm* scared! I told you I heard something following us in the woods today."

Scratch, scratch.

"But you said it stopped," said Duffy. "So how would it know where we are now?"

"I don't know. I don't know what it is. Maybe it tracked us, like a bloodhound."

Scratch, scratch.

"Don't bloodhounds have to have something to give them a scent?" asked Marie. "Like a piece of clothing, or—"

We both looked at Duffy.

"Your jacket, Duffy!"

Duffy turned white.

"That's silly," he said after a moment.

"There's something at the door," I said frantically. "Maybe it's been lurking around all day, waiting for our mothers to leave. Maybe it's been waiting for years for someone to come back here."

Scratch, scratch.

"I don't believe it," said Duffy. "It's just the wind moving a branch. I'll prove it."

He got up and headed for the door. But he didn't open it. Instead he peeked through the window next to it. When he turned back, his eyes looked as big as the hard-boiled eggs we had eaten for supper.

"There's something out there!" he hissed. *"Something big!"* ❻

"I told you," I cried. "Oh, I knew there was something there."

RETELL

❻ You should be able to identify two problems at this point. One has to do with Duffy, and the other is about what's happening to the kids. What are the problems?

"Andrew, are you doing this just to scare me?" said Marie. "Because if you are—"

Scratch, scratch.

"Come on," I said, grabbing her by the hand. "Let's get out of here."

I started to lead her up the stairs.

"Not there!" said Duffy. "If we go up there, we'll be trapped."

"You're right," I said. "Let's go out the back way!"

The thought of going outside scared the daylights out of me. But at least out there we would have somewhere to run. Inside—well, who knew what might happen if the thing found us inside.

We went into the kitchen.

I heard the front door open.

"Let's get out of here!" I hissed.

We scooted out the back door. "What now?" I wondered, looking around frantically.

"The barn," whispered Duffy. "We can hide in the barn."

"Good idea," I said. Holding Marie by the hand, I led the way to the barn. But the door was held shut by a huge padlock.

The wind was blowing harder, but not hard enough to hide the sound of the back door of the house opening, and then slamming shut.

"Quick!" I whispered. "It knows we're out here. Let's sneak around front. It will never expect us to go back into the house."

Duffy and Marie followed me as I led them behind a hedge. I caught a glimpse of something heading toward the barn and swallowed nervously. It was big. Very big.

"I'm scared," whispered Marie.

"*Shhhh!*" I hissed. "We can't let it know where we are."

RETELL

❼ What do the kids do to get away from the creature?

We slipped through the front door. We locked it, just like people always do in the movies, though what good that would do I couldn't figure, since if something really wanted to get at us, it would just break the window and come in. ❼ 🕮

"Upstairs," I whispered.

We tiptoed up the stairs. Once we were in our bedroom, I thought we were safe. Crawling over the floor, I raised my head just enough to peek out the window. My heart almost stopped. Standing in the moonlight was an enormous, manlike creature. It had a scrap of cloth in its hands. It was looking around—looking for us. I saw it lift its head and sniff the wind. To my horror, it started back toward the house.

"It's coming back!" I yelped, more frightened than ever.

"How does it know where we are?" asked Marie.

I knew how. It had Duffy's jacket. It was tracking us down, like some giant bloodhound.

We huddled together in the middle of the room, trying to think of what to do.

A minute later we heard it.

Scratch, scratch.

None of us moved.

Scratch, scratch.

We stopped breathing, then jumped up in alarm at a terrible crashing sound.

The door was down.

We hunched back against the wall as heavy footsteps came clomping up the stairs.

I wondered what our mothers would think when they got back. Would they find our bodies? Or would there be nothing left of us at all?

Thump. Thump. Thump.

It was getting closer.

Thump. Thump. Thump.

It was outside the door.

Knock, knock.

"Don't answer!" hissed Duffy.

Like I said, he doesn't have the brains of a turnip.

It didn't matter. The door wasn't locked. It came swinging open. In the shaft of light I saw a huge figure. The Sentinel of the Woods! It had to be. I thought I was going to die.

The figure stepped into the room. Its head nearly touched the ceiling.

Marie squeezed against my side, tighter than a tick in a dog's ear.

The huge creature sniffed the air. It turned in our direction. Its eyes seemed to glow. Moonlight glittered on its fangs.

Slowly the Sentinel raised its arm. I could see Duffy's jacket dangling from its fingertips.

And then it spoke.

"You forgot your jacket, stupid."

It threw the jacket at Duffy, turned around, and stomped down the stairs.

Which is why, I suppose, no one has had to remind Duffy to remember his jacket, or his glasses, or his math book, for at least a year now.

After all, when you leave stuff lying around, you never can be sure just who might bring it back. ❽ ⌣

RETELL

❽ Finish your retelling by telling what happens at the end of the story. Add your own thoughts about the story. Explain why you did or didn't like it.

Meet the Writer

Bruce Coville

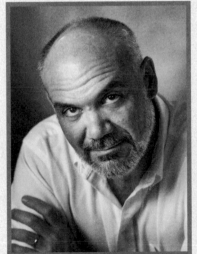

A Word Wrangler

Bruce Coville (1950–   ) grew up in a rural area north of Syracuse, New York, around the corner from his grandparents' dairy farm. About "Duffy's Jacket" he says:

ff For years I have been maintaining that I can't really write short stories, that they are just something that happen to me by accident every now and then. . . . 'Duffy's Jacket,' on the other hand, was pure joy. The idea came to me while I was walking in the woods with some friends. When we got back to the house, I excused myself, went upstairs, and typed it in a single sitting, the words seeming to fly from my fingers. . . . If only it were always that easy! But I figure a quarter century of word wrangling entitles you to at least one story that comes fairly quickly. ™

For Independent Reading

You can read more of Coville's unusual and highly entertaining stories in *Oddly Enough* and *Odder Than Ever*.

Practice the Strategy

Retelling: Summarizing the Plot

Here's how one student started a retelling of "Duffy's Jacket."

I'm going to give a retelling of a story called "Duffy's Jacket," written by Bruce Coville. The important characters are Duffy and his cousin Andrew. Other characters are Andrew's mom, his Aunt Elise, and Duffy's sister, Marie. Duffy is very smart but very forgetful. All of them go on a trip to stay in a cabin in the middle of nowhere.

Once they get to the cabin, they discover that it's not in such good shape. After they get unpacked and get things cleaned up, they go to sleep for the night. The next day, Andrew finds a message that says "Beware the Sentinel" written on the wall. No one knows who wrote it. Then . . .

PRACTICE 1

Finish the retelling. Use the Retelling Summary Sheet to organize your retelling. Keep the following points in mind:

1. Tell what happened after Andrew's mom and Aunt Elise left.
2. Describe the main problems. Think about Duffy's memory as one problem and the strange visitor as the other one.
3. Make sure you keep events in order.
4. Explain how the story ended.
5. Add your own comments about the story.

Retelling Summary Sheet

1. **Introduction**

   Begin with the title and author of the story. Then, tell where and when the story is set—if that's important.

2. **Characters**

   Tell the characters' names, and explain how the characters are related or connected to one another. Tell what the main character wants.

3. **Conflict**

   What is the main character's problem, or conflict—that is, who or what is keeping the main character from getting what he or she wants?

4. **Complications** ←

   Tell the main events—what happens as the character tries to solve the conflict.

   > **Strategy Tip**
   > Avoid linking the events with a string of and's. Here are some good time-order words to use: *first, second, third, next, eventually, later, afterward, finally, in conclusion.*

5. **Climax** ←

   Describe the climax, the most suspenseful moment in the story, when you discover at last how the conflict will be resolved.

   > **Strategy Tip**
   > This is the moment when you know you are finally about to find out how the main character will overcome the conflict (or be defeated).

6. **Resolution**

   Tell what happens after the climax. How does the story end?

7. **Personal Response**

   Tell how you felt about the story.

Practice the Strategy

PRACTICE 2

Ask a buddy to listen as you give the retelling and to rate what you say on a Retelling Rating Sheet like the one that follows:

Retelling Rating Sheet

Name _____

Text _____

Directions: Have your listener use the following checklist to rate your retelling. Ask the listener to decide whether you've covered each item listed below a little, to some extent, a lot, or not at all. Work on those details that you haven't covered or covered only a little.

0	1	2	3
Not at all	**A little**	**Some**	**A lot**

Does this retelling . . .

1. have a good beginning that tells the title, the author, and when and where the story takes place?
2. tell who the characters are and how they are related to one another?
3. include the main events?
4. keep those main events in the correct sequence?
5. explain how the conflict, or main problem, is resolved?
6. include any personal comments about the story?

You can use the retelling strategy with the stories in this collection. If you want to review the elements of any plot, try **retelling.**

SKILLS FOCUS

Reading Skills
Retell story events.

Rikki-tikki-tavi

Make the Connection
Quickwrite ✏️

Conflict is part of our real lives. For example, most people face bullies at some time in their lives. If you were facing a bully, what would you do? Would you fight? Would you run away? Would you try to negotiate? In your journal, describe how you think you would react.

Literary Focus
Conflict

All stories are built on some kind of **conflict.** Usually a conflict results when a character wants something very badly but has a hard time getting it. Think of the stories in movies and on TV, and you'll be able to find a conflict in every one of them. Conflict is worked out in the series of related events called **plot.**

Reading Skills 📖
Retelling

Try a strategy called **retelling** to identify the events that move this plot forward. Here is how it works: As you read this story, you'll see little open-book signs alongside the text. At those points, stop and jot down notes that retell what has just happened. As you do your retelling, focus on the important events that keep the plot moving.

Vocabulary Development

Every time you read, you have a chance to add words to your vocabulary. The words that follow are underlined and defined in the story. See if you can use each one in a sentence of your own.

immensely (i·mens′lē) *adv.:* enormously. *Rikki is immensely brave. The snakes are immensely powerful.*

cowered (kou′ərd) *v.:* crouched and trembled in fear. *Darzee, who is a coward, cowered before the snakes. Rikki cowered before no one.*

valiant (val′yənt) *adj.:* brave and determined. *Rikki is a valiant hero. Would other snakes think the snakes are valiant too?*

consolation (kän′sə·lā′shən) *n.:* comfort. *Snakes get no consolation from Rikki. Rikki's consolation comes from a safe, peaceful garden.*

impotent (im′pə·tənt) *adj.:* powerless. *With all but her last egg destroyed, Nagaina felt impotent against Rikki.*

Literary Skills
Analyze conflict.

Reading Skills
Retell story events.

Background
Literature and Social Studies

This story takes place in India many years ago, when the British ruled that huge country. The family in this story lives in a cantonment (kan·tän′mənt), which is a kind of army base. The father is in the British army. This story is about a conflict that takes place between two deadly snakes and a brave little mongoose—a creature that looks something like a weasel or a large squirrel.

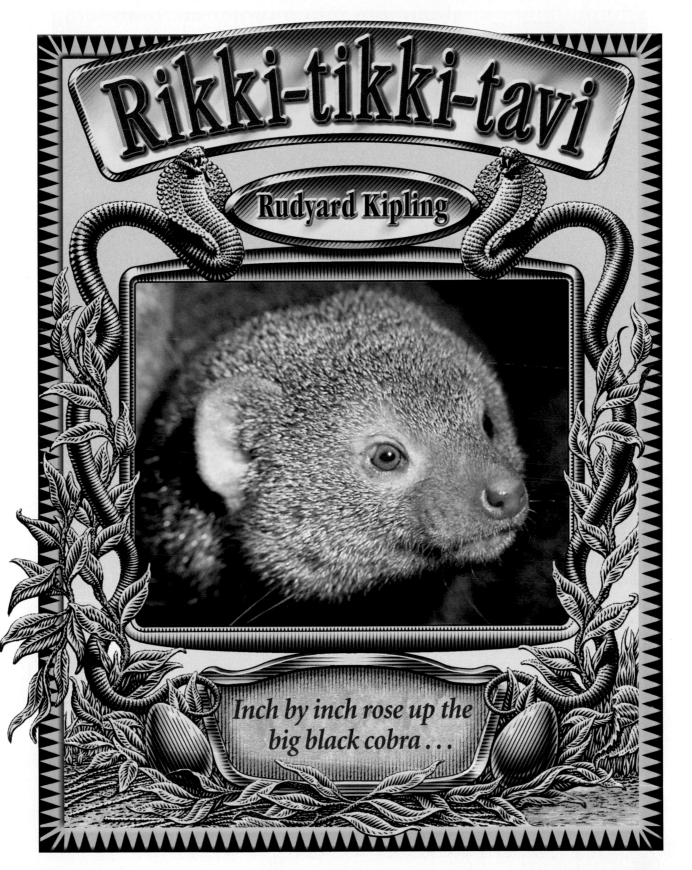

Rikki-tikki-tavi

Rudyard Kipling

*Inch by inch rose up the
big black cobra . . .*

A bungalow in India.

This is the story of the great war that Rikki-tikki-tavi fought single-handed, through the bathrooms of the big bungalow[1] in Segowlee cantonment.[2] Darzee, the tailorbird, helped him, and Chuchundra, the muskrat, who never comes out into the middle of the floor but always creeps round by the wall, gave him advice; but Rikki-tikki did the real fighting.

He was a mongoose, rather like a little cat in his fur and his tail but quite like a weasel in his head and his habits. His eyes and the end of his restless nose were pink; he could scratch himself anywhere he pleased with any leg, front or back, that he chose to use; he could fluff up his tail till it looked like a bottlebrush, and his war cry as he scuttled through the long grass was *Rikk-tikk-tikki-tikki-tchk!*

One day, a high summer flood washed him out of the burrow where he lived with his father and mother and carried him, kicking and clucking, down a roadside ditch. He

---

1. **bungalow** *n.:* in India, a low, one-storied house, named after a type of house found in Bengal, a region of South Asia.
2. **Segowlee** (sē·gou′lē) **cantonment:** British army post in Segowlee (now Segauli), India.

found a little wisp of grass floating there and clung to it till he lost his senses. When he revived, he was lying in the hot sun in the middle of a garden path, very draggled[3] indeed, and a small boy was saying: "Here's a dead mongoose. Let's have a funeral."

"No," said his mother; "let's take him in and dry him. Perhaps he isn't really dead."

They took him into the house, and a big man picked him up between his finger and thumb and said he was not dead but half choked; so they wrapped him in cotton wool and warmed him over a little fire, and he opened his eyes and sneezed.

"Now," said the big man (he was an Englishman who had just moved into the bungalow), "don't frighten him, and we'll see what he'll do."

It is the hardest thing in the world to frighten a mongoose, because he is eaten up from nose to tail with curiosity. The motto of all the mongoose family is "Run and find out," and Rikki-tikki was a true mongoose. He looked at the cotton wool, decided that it was not good to eat, ran all round the table, sat up and put his fur in order, scratched himself, and jumped on the small boy's shoulder.

"Don't be frightened, Teddy," said his father. "That's his way of making friends."

"Ouch! He's tickling under my chin," said Teddy.

Rikki-tikki looked down between the boy's collar and neck, snuffed at his ear, and climbed down to the floor, where he sat rubbing his nose.

"Good gracious," said Teddy's mother, "and that's a wild creature! I suppose he's so tame because we've been kind to him."

"All mongooses are like that," said her husband. "If Teddy doesn't pick him up by the tail or try to put him in a cage, he'll run in and out of the house all day long. Let's give him something to eat."

They gave him a little piece of raw meat. Rikki-tikki liked it immensely, and when it was finished, he went out into the veranda[4] and sat in the sunshine and fluffed up his fur to make it dry to the roots. Then he felt better.

"There are more things to find out about in this house," he said to himself, "than all my family could find out in all their lives. I shall certainly stay and find out." ❶

He spent all that day roaming over the house. He nearly drowned himself in the bathtubs, put his nose into the ink on a writing table, and burnt it on the end of the big man's cigar, for he climbed up in the big man's lap to see how writing was done. At nightfall he ran into Teddy's nursery to watch how kerosene lamps were lighted, and when Teddy went to bed, Rikki-tikki climbed up too; but he was a restless companion, because he had to get up and attend to every noise all through the night and find out what made it. Teddy's mother and father came in, the last thing, to look at their pillow. "I don't like that," said Teddy's mother; "he may bite the child." "He'll do no such thing," said the father. "Teddy's

> **RETELL**
> ❶ Before you read about how Rikki explores his new home, retell the events that brought him here.

---

3. **draggled** *v.* used as *adj.:* wet and muddy, as if from being dragged around.

---

4. **veranda** *n.:* open porch covered by a roof, running along the outside of a building.

Vocabulary
immensely (i·mens′lē) *adv.:* enormously.

safer with that little beast than if he had a bloodhound to watch him. If a snake came into the nursery now—"

But Teddy's mother wouldn't think of anything so awful.

Early in the morning, Rikki-tikki came to early breakfast in the veranda riding on Teddy's shoulder, and they gave him banana and some boiled egg; and he sat on all their laps one after the other, because every well-brought-up mongoose always hopes to be a house mongoose someday and have rooms to run about in; and Rikki-tikki's mother (she used to live in the General's house at Segowlee) had carefully told Rikki what to do if ever he came across white men.

Then Rikki-tikki went out into the garden to see what was to be seen. It was a large garden, only half cultivated, with bushes, as big as summerhouses, of Marshal Niel roses; lime and orange trees; clumps of bamboos; and thickets of high grass. Rikki-tikki licked his lips. "This is a splendid hunting ground," he said, and his tail grew bottlebrushy at the thought of it, and he scuttled up and down the garden, snuffing here and there till he heard very sorrowful voices in a thorn bush. It was Darzee, the tailorbird, and his wife. They had made a beautiful nest by pulling two big leaves together and stitching them up the edges with fibers and had filled the hollow with cotton and downy fluff. The nest swayed to and fro as they sat on the rim and cried.

"What is the matter?" asked Rikki-tikki.

"We are very miserable," said Darzee. "One of our babies fell out of the nest yesterday and Nag ate him."

"H'm!" said Rikki-tikki, "that is very sad —but I am a stranger here. Who is Nag?"

Darzee and his wife only cowered down in the nest without answering, for from the thick grass at the foot of the bush there came a low hiss—a horrid, cold sound that made Rikki-tikki jump back two clear feet. Then inch by inch out of the grass rose up the head and spread hood of Nag, the big black cobra, and he was five feet long from tongue to tail. When he had lifted one third of himself clear of the ground, he stayed balancing to and fro exactly as a dandelion tuft balances in the wind, and he looked at Rikki-tikki with the wicked snake's eyes that never change their expression, whatever the snake may be thinking of.

"Who is Nag," said he. "*I* am Nag. The great God Brahm[5] put his mark upon all our people, when the first cobra spread his hood to keep the sun off Brahm as he slept. Look, and be afraid!"

He spread out his hood more than ever, and Rikki-tikki saw the spectacle mark on the back of it that looks exactly like the eye part of a hook-and-eye fastening. He was afraid for the minute; but it is impossible for a mongoose to stay frightened for any length of time, and though Rikki-tikki had never met a live cobra before, his mother had fed him on dead ones, and he knew that all a grown mongoose's business in life was to fight and eat snakes. Nag knew that too, and at the bottom of his cold heart, he was afraid.

"Well," said Rikki-tikki, and his tail began to fluff up again, "marks or no marks, do

---

5. **Brahm** (bräm): in the Hindu religion, the creator (also called Brahma).

Vocabulary
cowered (kou′ərd) v.: crouched and trembled in fear.

you think it is right for you to eat fledglings out of a nest?"

Nag was thinking to himself and watching the least little movement in the grass behind Rikki-tikki. He knew that mongooses in the garden meant death sooner or later for him and his family, but he wanted to get Rikki-tikki off his guard. So he dropped his head a little and put it on one side.

"Let us talk," he said. "You eat eggs. Why should not I eat birds?"

"Behind you! Look behind you!" sang Darzee.

Rikki-tikki knew better than to waste time in staring. He jumped up in the air as high as he could go, and just under him whizzed by the head of Nagaina, Nag's wicked wife. She had crept up behind him as he was talking, to make an end of him; and he heard her savage hiss as the stroke missed. He came down almost across her back, and if he had been an old mongoose, he would have known that then was the time to break her back with one bite; but he was afraid of the terrible lashing return stroke of the cobra. He bit, indeed, but did not bite long enough, and he jumped clear of the whisking tail, leaving Nagaina torn and angry.

"Wicked, wicked Darzee!" said Nag, lashing up as high as he could reach toward the nest in the thorn bush; but Darzee had built it out of reach of snakes, and it only swayed to and fro.

Rikki-tikki felt his eyes growing red and hot (when a mongoose's eyes grow red, he is angry), and he sat back on his tail and hind legs like a little kangaroo, and looked all round him, and chattered with rage. But Nag and Nagaina had disappeared into the grass. ❷

RETELL
❷ What happens when Rikki first meets the snakes?

When a snake misses its stroke, it never says anything or gives any sign of what it means to do next. Rikki-tikki did not care to follow them, for he did not feel sure that he could manage two snakes at once. So he trotted off to the gravel path near the house and sat down to think. It was a serious matter for him. If you read the old books of natural history, you will find they say that when the mongoose fights the snake and happens to get bitten, he runs off and eats some herb that cures him. That is not true. The victory is only a matter of quickness of eye and quickness of foot—snake's blow against the mongoose's jump—and as no eye can follow the motion of a snake's head when it strikes, this makes things much more wonderful than any magic herb. Rikki-tikki knew he was a young mongoose, and it made him all the more pleased to think that he had managed

"*I am Nag. . . . Look, and be afraid!*"

to escape a blow from behind. It gave him confidence in himself, and when Teddy came running down the path, Rikki-tikki was ready to be petted. But just as Teddy was stooping, something wriggled a little in the dust and a tiny voice said: "Be careful. I am Death!" It was Karait, the dusty brown snakeling that lies for choice on the dusty earth; and his bite is as dangerous as the cobra's. But he is so small that nobody thinks of him, and so he does the more harm to people.

Rikki-tikki's eyes grew red again, and he danced up to Karait with the peculiar rocking, swaying motion that he had inherited from his family. It looks very funny, but it is so perfectly balanced a gait[6] that you can fly off from it at any angle you please; and in dealing with snakes this is an advantage. If Rikki-tikki had only known, he was doing a much more dangerous thing than fighting Nag, for Karait is so small and can turn so quickly that unless Rikki bit him close to the back of the head, he would get the return stroke in his eye or his lip. But Rikki did not know; his eyes were all red, and he rocked back and forth, looking for a good place to hold. Karait struck out, Rikki jumped sideways and tried to run in, but the wicked little dusty gray head lashed within a fraction of his shoulder, and he had to jump over the body, and the head followed his heels close.

Teddy shouted to the house: "Oh, look here! Our mongoose is killing a snake," and Rikki-tikki heard a scream from Teddy's mother. His father ran out with a stick, but by the time he came up, Karait had lunged out once too far, and Rikki-tikki had sprung, jumped on the snake's back, dropped his head far between his forelegs, bitten as high up the back as he could get hold, and rolled away. That bite paralyzed Karait, and Rikki-tikki was just going to eat him up from the tail, after the custom of his family at dinner, when he remembered that a full meal makes a slow mongoose, and if he wanted all his strength and quickness ready, he must keep himself thin. He went away for a dust bath under the castor-oil bushes, while Teddy's father beat the dead Karait. "What is the use of that?" thought Rikki-tikki; "I have settled it all"; and then Teddy's mother picked him up from the dust and hugged him, crying that he had saved Teddy from death, and Teddy's father said that he was a providence,[7] and Teddy looked on with big, scared eyes. Rikki-tikki was rather amused at all the fuss, which, of course, he did not understand. Teddy's mother might just as well have petted Teddy for playing in the dust. Rikki was thoroughly enjoying himself. ❸

RETELL
❸ What happens in Rikki's conflict with Karait?

That night at dinner, walking to and fro among the wineglasses on the table, he might have stuffed himself three times over with nice things; but he remembered Nag and Nagaina, and though it was very pleasant to be patted and petted by Teddy's mother and to sit on Teddy's shoulder, his eyes would get red from time to time, and he would go off into his long war cry of *Rikk-tikk-tikki-tikki-tchk!*

Teddy carried him off to bed and insisted on Rikki-tikki's sleeping under his chin.

---

6. **gait** (gāt) *n.*: way of walking or running.

7. **providence** (präv′ə·dəns) *n.*: favor or gift from God or nature.

Rikki-tikki was too well bred to bite or scratch, but as soon as Teddy was asleep, he went off for his nightly walk round the house, and in the dark he ran up against Chuchundra, the muskrat, creeping round by the wall. Chuchundra is a brokenhearted little beast. He whimpers and cheeps all night, trying to make up his mind to run into the middle of the room; but he never gets there.

"Don't kill me," said Chuchundra, almost weeping. "Rikki-tikki, don't kill me!"

"Do you think a snake killer kills muskrats?" said Rikki-tikki scornfully.

"Those who kill snakes get killed by snakes," said Chuchundra, more sorrowfully than ever. "And how am I to be sure that Nag won't mistake me for you some dark night?"

"There's not the least danger," said Rikki-tikki, "but Nag is in the garden, and I know you don't go there."

"My cousin Chua, the rat, told me—" said Chuchundra, and then he stopped.

"Told you what?"

"H'sh! Nag is everywhere, Rikki-tikki. You should have talked to Chua in the garden."

"I didn't—so you must tell me. Quick, Chuchundra, or I'll bite you!"

Chuchundra sat down and cried till the tears rolled off his whiskers. "I am a very poor man," he sobbed. "I never had spirit enough to run out into the middle of the

"Be careful. I am Death!" It was Karait. . . .

room. H'sh! I mustn't tell you anything. Can't you *hear*, Rikki-tikki?"

Rikki-tikki listened. The house was as still as still, but he thought he could just catch the faintest *scratch-scratch* in the world—a noise as faint as that of a wasp walking on a windowpane—the dry scratch of a snake's scales on brickwork.

"That's Nag or Nagaina," he said to himself, "and he is crawling into the bathroom sluice.[8] You're right, Chuchundra; I should have talked to Chua."

He stole off to Teddy's bathroom, but there was nothing there, and then to Teddy's mother's bathroom. At the bottom of the smooth plaster wall there was a brick pulled out to make a sluice for the bathwater, and as Rikki-tikki stole in by the masonry[9] curb where the bath is put, he heard Nag and Nagaina whispering together outside in the moonlight.

"When the house is emptied of people," said Nagaina to her husband, "*he* will have to go away, and then the garden will be our own again. Go in quietly, and remember that the big man who killed Karait is the first one to bite. Then come out and tell me, and we will hunt for Rikki-tikki together."

---

8. **sluice** (slōōs) *n.:* drain.
9. **masonry** *n.:* something built of stone or brick.

"But are you sure that there is anything to be gained by killing the people?" said Nag.

"Everything. When there were no people in the bungalow, did we have any mongoose in the garden? So long as the bungalow is empty, we are king and queen of the garden; and remember that as soon as our eggs in the melon bed hatch (as they may tomorrow), our children will need room and quiet."

"I had not thought of that," said Nag. "I will go, but there is no need that we should hunt for Rikki-tikki afterward. I will kill the big man and his wife, and the child if I can, and come away quietly. Then the bungalow will be empty, and Rikki-tikki will go."

Rikki-tikki tingled all over with rage and hatred at this, and then Nag's head came through the sluice, and his five feet of cold body followed it. Angry as he was, Rikki-tikki was very frightened as he saw the size of the big cobra. Nag coiled himself up, raised his head, and looked into the bathroom in the dark, and Rikki could see his eyes glitter.

"Now, if I kill him here, Nagaina will know; and if I fight him on the open floor, the odds are in his favor. What am I to do?" said Rikki-tikki-tavi.

Nag waved to and fro, and then Rikki-tikki heard him drinking from the biggest water jar that was used to fill the bath. "That is good," said the snake. "Now, when Karait was killed, the big man had a stick. He may have that stick still, but when he comes in to bathe in the morning, he will not have a stick. I shall wait here till he comes. Nagaina—do you hear me?—I shall wait here in the cool till daytime."

There was no answer from outside, so Rikki-tikki knew Nagaina had gone away.

Nag coiled himself down, coil by coil, round the bulge at the bottom of the water jar, and Rikki-tikki stayed still as death. After an hour he began to move, muscle by muscle, toward the jar. Nag was asleep, and Rikki-tikki looked at his big back, wondering which would be the best place for a good hold. "If I don't break his back at the first jump," said Rikki, "he can still fight; and if he fights—O Rikki!" He looked at the thickness of the neck below the hood, but that was too much for him; and a bite near the tail would only make Nag savage.

"It must be the head," he said at last, "the head above the hood; and when I am once there, I must not let go."

Then he jumped. The head was lying a little clear of the water jar, under the curve of it; and as his teeth met, Rikki braced his back against the bulge of the red earthenware to hold down the head. This gave him just one second's purchase,[10] and he made the most of it. Then he was battered to and fro as a rat is shaken by a dog—to and fro on the floor, up and down, and round in great circles, but his eyes were red and he held on as the body cartwhipped over the floor, upsetting the tin dipper and the soap dish and the flesh brush, and banged against the tin side of the bath. As he held, he closed his jaws tighter and tighter, for he made sure[11] he would be banged to death, and for the honor of his family, he preferred to be found with his teeth locked. He was dizzy, aching, and felt shaken to pieces, when something went off like a thunderclap just behind him; a hot wind knocked him senseless and red fire singed his fur. The big

---

10. **purchase** *n.*: firm hold.
11. **made sure**: here, felt sure.

man had been wakened by the noise and had fired both barrels of a shotgun into Nag just behind the hood.

Rikki-tikki held on with his eyes shut, for now he was quite sure he was dead; but the head did not move, and the big man picked him up and said: "It's the mongoose again, Alice; the little chap has saved *our* lives now." Then Teddy's mother came in with a very white face and saw what was left of Nag, and Rikki-tikki dragged himself to Teddy's bedroom and spent half the rest of the night shaking himself tenderly to find out whether he really was broken into forty pieces, as he fancied. ❹

RETELL
❹ What happens when Rikki sees Nag poke his head into the bathroom?

When morning came, he was very stiff but well pleased with his doings. "Now I have Nagaina to settle with, and she will be worse than five Nags, and there's no knowing when the eggs she spoke of will hatch. Goodness! I must go and see Darzee," he said.

Without waiting for breakfast, Rikki-tikki ran to the thorn bush, where Darzee was singing a song of triumph at the top of his voice. The news of Nag's death was all over the garden, for the sweeper had thrown the body on the rubbish heap.

"Oh, you stupid tuft of feathers!" said Rikki-tikki angrily. "Is this the time to sing?"

"Nag is dead—is dead—is dead!" sang Darzee. "The valiant Rikki-tikki caught him by the head and held fast. The big man brought the bang-stick, and Nag fell in two pieces! He will never eat my babies again."

"All that's true enough, but where's Nagaina?" said Rikki-tikki, looking carefully round him.

"Nagaina came to the bathroom sluice and called for Nag," Darzee went on, "and Nag came out on the end of a stick—the sweeper picked him up on the end of a stick and threw him upon the rubbish heap. Let us sing about the great, the red-eyed Rikki-tikki!" and Darzee filled his throat and sang.

"If I could get up to your nest, I'd roll your babies out!" said Rikki-tikki. "You don't know when to do the right thing at the right time. You're safe enough in your nest there, but it's war for me down here. Stop singing a minute, Darzee."

"For the great, beautiful Rikki-tikki's sake I will stop," said Darzee. "What is it, O Killer of the terrible Nag?"

"Where is Nagaina, for the third time?"

"On the rubbish heap by the stables, mourning for Nag. Great is Rikki-tikki with the white teeth."

"Bother[12] my white teeth! Have you ever heard where she keeps her eggs?"

"In the melon bed, on the end nearest the wall, where the sun strikes nearly all day. She hid them there weeks ago."

"And you never thought it worthwhile to tell me? The end nearest the wall, you said?"

"Rikki-tikki, you are not going to eat her eggs?"

"Not eat exactly; no. Darzee, if you have a grain of sense, you will fly off to the stables and pretend that your wing is broken and let Nagaina chase you away to this bush. I must get to the melon bed, and if I went there now, she'd see me."

---

12. **bother** *interj.:* here, never mind.

Vocabulary
valiant (val′yənt) *adj.:* brave and determined.

Darzee was a featherbrained little fellow who could never hold more than one idea at a time in his head, and just because he knew that Nagaina's children were born in eggs like his own, he didn't think at first that it was fair to kill them. But his wife was a sensible bird, and she knew that cobra's eggs meant young cobras later on; so she flew off from the nest and left Darzee to keep the babies warm and continue his song about the death of Nag. Darzee was very like a man in some ways.

She fluttered in front of Nagaina by the rubbish heap and cried out, "Oh, my wing is broken! The boy in the house threw a stone at me and broke it." Then she fluttered more desperately than ever.

Nagaina lifted up her head and hissed, "You warned Rikki-tikki when I would have killed him. Indeed and truly, you've chosen a bad place to be lame in." And she moved toward Darzee's wife, slipping along over the dust.

"The boy broke it with a stone!" shrieked Darzee's wife.

"Well! It may be some <u>consolation</u> to you when you're dead to know that I shall settle accounts with the boy. My husband lies on the rubbish heap this morning, but before night the boy in the house will lie very still. What is the use of running away? I am sure to catch you. Little fool, look at me!"

Darzee's wife knew better than to do *that*, for a bird who looks at a snake's eyes gets so frightened that she cannot move. Darzee's wife fluttered on, piping sorrowfully and never leaving the ground, and Nagaina quickened her pace.

Rikki-tikki heard them going up the path from the stables, and he raced for the end of the melon patch near the wall. There, in the warm litter above the melons, very cunningly hidden, he found twenty-five eggs about the size of a bantam's[13] eggs but with whitish skins instead of shells.

"I was not a day too soon," he said, for he could see the baby cobras curled up inside the skin, and he knew that the minute they were hatched, they could each kill a man or a mongoose. He bit off the tops of the eggs as fast as he could, taking care to crush the young cobras, and turned over the litter from time to time to see whether he had missed any. At last there were only three eggs left, and Rikki-tikki began to chuckle to himself, when he heard Darzee's wife screaming:

"Rikki-tikki, I led Nagaina toward the house, and she has gone into the veranda, and—oh, come quickly—she means killing!"

Rikki-tikki smashed two eggs, and tumbled backward down the melon bed with the third egg in his mouth, and scuttled to the veranda as hard as he could put foot to the ground. Teddy and his mother and father were there at early breakfast, but Rikki-tikki saw that they were not eating anything. They sat stone still, and their faces were white. Nagaina was coiled up on the matting by Teddy's chair, within easy striking distance of Teddy's bare leg, and she was swaying to and fro, singing a song of triumph.

"Son of the big man that killed Nag," she hissed, "stay still. I am not ready yet. Wait a little. Keep very still, all you three! If you

---

13. **bantam's** *n.:* small chicken's.

Vocabulary
consolation (kän′sə·lā′shən) *n.:* comfort.

move, I strike, and if you do not move, I strike. Oh, foolish people, who killed my Nag!"

Teddy's eyes were fixed on his father, and all his father could do was to whisper, "Sit still, Teddy. You mustn't move. Teddy, keep still."

Then Rikki-tikki came up and cried: "Turn round, Nagaina; turn and fight!"

"All in good time," said she, without moving her eyes. "I will settle my account with *you* presently. Look at your friends, Rikki-tikki. They are still and white. They are afraid. They dare not move, and if you come a step nearer, I strike."

"Look at your eggs," said Rikki-tikki, "in the melon bed near the wall. Go and look, Nagaina!"

The big snake turned half round and saw the egg on the veranda. "Ah-h! Give it to me," she said.

Rikki-tikki put his paws one on each side of the egg, and his eyes were blood-red. "What price for a snake's egg? For a young cobra? For a young king cobra? For the last—the very last of the brood? The ants are eating all the others down by the melon bed."

Nagaina spun clear round, forgetting everything for the sake of the one egg; and Rikki-tikki saw Teddy's father shoot out a big hand, catch Teddy by the shoulder, and drag him across the little table with the teacups, safe and out of reach of Nagaina.

"Tricked! Tricked! Tricked! *Rikk-tck-tck!*"

Darzee, a featherbrained little fellow.

chuckled Rikki-tikki. "The boy is safe, and it was I—I—I—that caught Nag by the hood last night in the bathroom." Then he began to jump up and down, all four feet together, his head close to the floor. "He threw me to and fro, but he could not shake me off. He was dead before the big man blew him in two. I did it! *Rikki-tikki-tck-tck!* Come then, Nagaina. Come and fight with me. You shall not be a widow long."

Nagaina saw that she had lost her chance of killing Teddy, and the egg lay between Rikki-tikki's paws. "Give me the egg, Rikki-tikki. Give me the last of my eggs, and I will go away and never come back," she said, lowering her hood.

"Yes, you will go away, and you will never come back; for you will go to the rubbish heap with Nag. Fight, widow! The big man has gone for his gun! Fight!"

Rikki-tikki was bounding all round Nagaina, keeping just out of reach of her stroke, his little eyes like hot coals. Nagaina gathered herself together and flung out at him. Rikki-tikki jumped up and backwards. Again and again and again she struck, and each time her head came with a whack on the matting of the veranda and she gathered herself together like a watch spring. Then Rikki-tikki danced in a circle to get behind her, and Nagaina spun round to keep her head to his head, so that the rustle of her

Rikki-tikki knew that he must catch Nagaina or all the trouble would begin again.

tail on the matting sounded like dry leaves blown along by the wind.

He had forgotten the egg. It still lay on the veranda, and Nagaina came nearer and nearer to it, till at last, while Rikki-tikki was drawing breath, she caught it in her mouth, turned to the veranda steps, and flew like an arrow down the path, with Rikki-tikki behind her. When the cobra runs for her life, she goes like a whiplash flicked across a horse's neck. Rikki-tikki knew that he must

catch her or all the trouble would begin again. She headed straight for the long grass by the thorn bush, and as he was running, Rikki-tikki heard Darzee still singing his foolish little song of triumph. But Darzee's wife was wiser. She flew off her nest as Nagaina came along and flapped her wings about Nagaina's head. If Darzee had helped, they might have turned her, but Nagaina only lowered her hood and went on. Still, the instant's delay brought Rikki-tikki up to earth. Then the grass by the mouth of the hole stopped waving, and Darzee said: "It is all over with Rikki-tikki! We must sing his death song. Valiant Rikki-tikki is dead! For Nagaina will surely kill him underground."

So he sang a very mournful song that he made up on the spur of the minute, and just as he got to the most touching part, the grass quivered again, and Rikki-tikki, covered with dirt, dragged himself out of the hole leg by leg, licking his whiskers. Darzee stopped with a little shout. Rikki-tikki shook some of the dust out of his fur and sneezed. "It is all over," he said. "The widow will never come out again." And the red ants that live between the grass stems heard him and began to troop down one after another to see if he had spoken the truth. **5**

RETELL
5 What happens when Rikki fights Nagaina?

Rikki-tikki curled himself up in the grass and slept where he was—slept and slept till it was late in the afternoon, for he had done a hard day's work.

"Now," he said, when he awoke, "I will go back to the house. Tell the Coppersmith, Darzee, and he will tell the garden that Nagaina is dead."

The Coppersmith is a bird who makes a noise exactly like the beating of a little hammer on a copper pot; and the reason he is always making it is because he is the town crier to every Indian garden and tells all the news to everybody who cares to listen. As Rikki-tikki went up the path, he heard his "attention" notes like a tiny dinner gong and then the steady "*Ding-dong-tock!* Nag is dead—*dong!* Nagaina is dead! *Ding-dong-tock!*" That set all the birds in the garden singing and the frogs croaking, for Nag and

her, and as she plunged into the rat hole where she and Nag used to live, his little white teeth were clenched on her tail and he went down with her—and very few mongooses, however wise and old they may be, care to follow a cobra into its hole. It was dark in the hole, and Rikki-tikki never knew when it might open out and give Nagaina room to turn and strike at him. He held on savagely and stuck out his feet to act as brakes on the dark slope of the hot, moist

Chuchundra, a brokenhearted little beast.

Nagaina used to eat frogs as well as little birds.

When Rikki got to the house, Teddy and Teddy's mother (she looked very white still, for she had been fainting) and Teddy's father came out and almost cried over him; and that night he ate all that was given him till he could eat no more and went to bed on Teddy's shoulder, where Teddy's mother saw him when she came to look late at night.

"He saved our lives and Teddy's life," she said to her husband. "Just think, he saved all our lives."

Rikki-tikki woke up with a jump, for the mongooses are light sleepers.

"Oh, it's you," said he. "What are you bothering for? All the cobras are dead; and if they weren't, I'm here."

Rikki-tikki had a right to be proud of himself, but he did not grow too proud, and he kept that garden as a mongoose should keep it, with tooth and jump and spring and bite, till never a cobra dared show its head inside the walls.

Darzee's Chant
Sung in honor of Rikki-tikki-tavi

Singer and tailor am I—
    Doubled the joys that I know—
Proud of my lilt[14] to the sky,
    Proud of the house that I sew.
Over and under, so weave I my music—
    so weave I the house that I sew.

Sing to your fledglings[15] again,
    Mother, O lift up your head!
Evil that plagued us is slain,
    Death in the garden lies dead.
Terror that hid in the roses is impotent—
    flung on the dunghill and dead!

Who has delivered us, who?
    Tell me his nest and his name.
Rikki, the valiant, the true,
    Tikki, with eyeballs of flame—
Rikk-tikki-tikki, the ivory-fanged,
    the hunter with eyeballs of flame!

Give him the Thanks of the Birds,
    Bowing with tail feathers spread,
Praise him with nightingale words—
    Nay, I will praise him instead.
Hear! I will sing you the praise of the
    bottle-tailed Rikki with eyeballs of red!

(*Here Rikki-tikki interrupted, so the rest of the song is lost.*)

---

14. **lilt** *n.:* song.
15. **fledglings** (flej′liŋz) *n.:* baby birds.

Vocabulary
impotent (im′pə·tənt) *adj.:* powerless.

Meet the Writer

Rudyard Kipling

On His Own

India, the setting of "Rikki-tikki-tavi," is a place **Joseph Rudyard Kipling** (1865–1936) knew well. His father was a professor of art in Bombay, and Kipling was born in that city when India was under British rule. India was a fascinating place, and young Kipling loved it.

When he was six, however, his parents shipped him and his sister off to a boardinghouse in England. Feeling very much on his own in England, he made a discovery:

> 66 [Books] were among the most important affairs in the world. . . . I could read as much as I chose and ask the meaning of things from any-one I met. I had found out, too, that one could take a pen and set down what one thought, and that nobody accused one of 'showing off' by doing so. 99

When he was seventeen, Kipling returned to India and took a job as an editor with an English-language newspaper. He was fascinated by the lives of British colonials in India and the vivid contrast they made with the Indian people they ruled. Soon the paper was printing Kipling's poems and tales about what he saw around him. Other newspapers reprinted them, and readers begged for more. Kipling's fame grew; over the next half century he wrote dozens of books, and in 1907, he won the Nobel Prize in literature. Although he later lived in many places around the world, India would always remain close to his heart.

For Independent Reading

Read more of Kipling's animal stories in *Just So Stories* and *The Jungle Book*. *The Jungle Book* is about Mowgli, a boy who is raised by wolves. *Kim,* Kipling's best-known novel, traces the adventures of an Irish orphan who is raised as an Indian and eventually becomes a British spy.

After You Read Response and Analysis

First Thoughts

1. Respond to "Rikki-tikki-tavi" by completing these sentences:

- I thought this story was . . .
- I was frightened for Rikki-tikki-tavi when . . .
- The scene I liked best was . . .

Thinking Critically

2. Describe three **conflicts** that Rikki-tikki faces. Which conflict do you think is his greatest challenge? Why? How is it resolved?

3. **Motive** refers to the reason for a character's behavior. What was Rikki's **motive** for fighting Nagaina? What did he want?

4. What was Nagaina's **motive** for fighting Rikki? What did she want?

5. What does Darzee's chant tell about the garden animals' feelings for Rikki? Give specific words from the chant to support your answer.

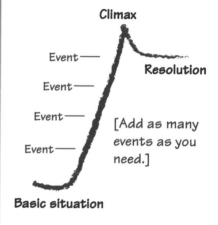

Reading Check

Work out the major events that advance the **plot** of Rikki's story. Fill in a diagram like this one. You should find at least four key events that lead to the exciting climax.

Extending Interpretations

6. Did Rikki's conflicts with the deadly garden bullies remind you of your own experiences? For ideas, think back to what you said about bullies before you read the story.

7. The animal world of "Rikki-tikki-tavi" is filled with conflict and danger. What causes the war in this animal story? What causes most wars among people?

WRITING

Expressing Your Opinion

Look back at pages 18 and 19, where Nag and Nagaina are described for the first time. Find words on those pages that make the snakes seem evil. Is Kipling being fair, or are the snakes just doing what snakes do naturally? Does Kipling present the snakes as totally evil, or are they good in any way? In a paragraph or two, discuss your evaluation of the way Kipling handles his snake characters.

After You Read | Vocabulary Development

Clarifying Word Meanings: Contrast

Sometimes you can clarify the meaning of an unfamiliar word by looking for **contrast** clues.

A writer who uses contrast will show how a word is *unlike* another word. For example, you can get a pretty clear idea of what a *splendid* garden is if you see it contrasted with a dark, narrow hole in the ground.

> **The splendid garden glowed with roses and great clumps of waving grasses, unlike the dreary hole where cobras live.**

Be on the lookout for these words, which signal contrast: *although, but, yet, still, unlike, not, in contrast, instead, however.*

Word Bank

immensely
cowered
valiant
consolation
impotent

PRACTICE

Fill in the blanks in the following sentences with words or phrases that contrast with the underlined word. You may find it helpful to make a cluster diagram of the word and its opposites before you write, like the one below for *cowered* and *cowering*:

A cowering dog

An aggressive dog

1. The cobras had immense power, but the power of Darzee and the other garden creatures was _____.

2. Darzee cowered before the cobras, but Rikki _____.

3. Rikki was certainly valiant, but Chuchundra, the little muskrat, was _____.

4. The family felt consoled that Rikki was guarding their house, though they were _____ when the cobra threatened Teddy.

5. Darzee sang that the cobras were impotent in death, but they were _____ only a few hours earlier.

SKILLS FOCUS

Vocabulary Skills
Clarify word meanings by using contrast.

Understanding Text Structures: A Textbook

Reading Focus
Structure and Purpose of a Textbook

The story of Rikki-tikki-tavi may have made you want to know more about India. Textbooks are one source you can go to for information on the history of India and on the culture of India today.

Textbooks have features that help you locate information and review what you have learned. Textbooks also offer photographs and artwork that can lead you to even further investigations of a subject.

■ In the next four pages are features from a geography textbook called *People, Places, and Change.* See how well you understand the structure of a textbook.

SKILLS FOCUS

Reading Skills
Understand the structure and purpose of a textbook.

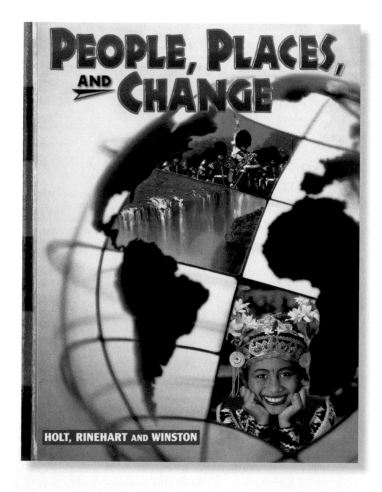

PEOPLE, PLACES, AND CHANGE

HOLT, RINEHART AND WINSTON

South Asia **640**
Notes from the Field

1. The **Table of Contents** is an important feature of a textbook. *What major topics on India does this textbook cover?*

2. *If you wanted to know about India during the time Kipling lived there, which section would you turn to?*

Contents • xix

3. History and science books often **sum up** the focus of each chapter. *Look at the Reading Focus list. If you want information on India under British rule, will you find it in this chapter?*

4. A **caption** is text that explains the subject of an illustration. *Where can you find the caption for the photo that runs across the bottom of the page?*

5. Note the **inset,** which is a very small map showing where the subject of the photo is located. Usually a star or a circle indicates the exact location. *Is the city of Mohenjo Daro in present-day Pakistan or India?*

Section 2 — India's History

Reading Focus

- What outside groups affected India's history?
- What was the Mughal Empire like?
- How did Great Britain gain control of India?
- Why was India divided when it became independent?

Key Terms
Sanskrit
sepoys
boycott

Key Places
Delhi
Calcutta
Mumbai

Coat of arms of the
East India Company

You Be the Geographer

India has been invaded several times by outside groups. These groups added new customs and beliefs to India's diverse culture. Besides through invasion, how do ideas spread from country to country?

Mohenjo Daro was one of the largest cities of the Harappan civilization.

Interpreting the Visual Record How might you tell from this photo that Harappan cities were well planned?

Early Indian Civilizations

The first civilization on the Indian subcontinent was centered around the Indus River valley. Its territory was mainly in present-day Pakistan but also extended into India. Scholars call this the Harappan civilization after one of its cities, Harappa. By about 2500 B.C. the people of this civilization were living in large, well-planned cities. Scholars believe the Harappans traded with the peoples of Mesopotamia. The Harappans had a system of writing, but scholars have not been able to read it. Very little is known about Harappan religion and customs.

The Taj Mahal is one of the most famous buildings in the world.

The British

Movement During the 1700s and 1800s the British slowly took control of India. At first this was done by the English East India Company. This company won rights to trade in the Mughal Empire in the 1600s. The East India Company first took control of small trading posts. Later the British gained more Indian territory.

Company Rule As the Mughal Empire grew weaker, the English East India Company expanded its political power. The company also built up its own military force. This army was made up mostly of **sepoys**, Indian troops commanded by British officers. The British used the strategy of backing one Indian ruler against another in exchange for cooperation. By the mid-1800s the company controlled more than half of India. The rest was divided into small states ruled by local princes.

The British changed the Indian economy to benefit British industry. India produced raw materials, including cotton, indigo—a natural dye—and jute. These materials were then shipped to Britain for use in British factories. Spices, sugar, tea, and wheat were also grown in India for export. Railroads were built to ship the raw materials to Calcutta, Bombay (now Mumbai), and other port cities. India also became a market for British manufactured goods. Indians, who had woven cotton cloth for centuries, were now forced to buy British cloth.

In September 1857, British and loyal Sikh troops stormed the gate of Delhi, defended by rebel sepoys. Bloody fighting continued until late 1858.

Interpreting the Visual Record
How did the Indian Mutiny lead to a change in the way India was governed?

6. Key ideas and terms are set in **boldface type.** The boldface terms are often defined in the text. *Is the boldface word on this page defined?*

India • 657

Anti-British Protest

After World War I more and more Indians began demandir end of British rule. A lawyer named Mohandas K. Gandhi becan most important leader of this Indian independence movement.

Gandhi and Nonviolence *Place* Gandhi reached out t millions of Indian peasants. He used a strategy of nonviolent protest. He called for Indians to peacefully refuse to cooperate the British. Gandhi led protest marches and urged Indians to **bo** or refuse to buy, British goods. Many times the police used vi against marchers. When the British jailed Gandhi, he went on h strikes. Gandhi's determination and self-sacrifice attracted man lowers. Pressure grew on Britain to leave India.

✔ **READING CHECK:** Do you know how India came under British control?

Independence and Division

Region After World War II the British government decided to India independence. The British government and the Indian Nati Congress wanted India to become one country. However, In Muslims demanded a separate Muslim state. Anger and fear ; between Hindus and Muslims. India seemed on the verge of civil

Finally, in 1947 the British divided their Indian colony into independent countries, India and Pakistan. India was mostly Hi Pakistan, which then included what is today Bangladesh, was mc Muslim. However, the new boundary left millions of Hindus in Paki and millions of Muslims in India. Masses of people rushed to cross border. Hundreds of thousands were killed in rioting and panic.

✔ **READING CHECK:** Do you know why India was divided when it became independe

▲ Mohandas Gandhi was known to his followers as the Mahatma, or the "great soul."

Section Review 2

Define Sanskrit, sepoys, boycott

Working with Sketch Maps On the map you created in Section 1, label Delhi, Calcutta, and Mumbai. What bodies of water are important to each of these cities?

Reading for Content Understanding

1. *Region* What factors made the Mughal Empire one of the most powerful states in the world?

2. *Movement* How did the English East India Company gain control of most of India?

3. *Place* Who was the most important leader of the Indian independence movement, and what was his strategy?

You Be the Geographer: CRITICAL THINKI

4. *Movement* Why was the British colony of India divided into two countries?

Organizing What You Know

5. Copy the following time line. Use it to mark important events in Indian history from 2500 B.C. to A.D. 1947.

2500 B.C.   A.D. 1947

Analyzing a Textbook

Using *Elements of Literature*

To check on how well you know the important parts of a textbook, answer the following questions by referring to the key parts of the textbook you are now using, called *Elements of Literature.*

1. The **copyright page** is in the front of the book, usually right after the main title page. Here is where you will find the date the book was published. What is the copyright date of this textbook?
   A 2003
   B 2004
   C 2005
   D 2006

2. The **table of contents** is found in the front of a textbook. According to the table of contents of this textbook, how many collections appear in the book?
   F 5
   G 6
   H 7
   J 8

3. At the back of this book is a section called **Resource Center.** Which of the following features is *not* found in this section?
   A Index of Skills
   B Handbook of Informational Terms
   C Index of Maps
   D Index of Authors and Titles

Constructed Response

4. There are many kinds of textbooks. Explain the **purpose** they all share.

5. Which features of the textbook shown on pages 33–36 do you find most useful? Why?

SKILLS FOCUS

Reading Skills
Analyze the structure and purpose of a textbook.

Three Skeleton Key

Make the Connection
Quickwrite ✏️

Movies, TV, and books are full of horror tales that make us want to check under our beds. If you were writing a horror story, what details would you use to create a scary setting? Freewrite your ideas.

Literary Focus
Suspense and Foreshadowing

The writer of this story hooks our interest with his opening sentence: "My most terrifying experience?" Once a question like this is asked in a story, we want to know the answer. We want to know what happens next. This feeling of anxious curiosity is called **suspense.**

Writers often intensify suspense by dropping clues that hint at what might happen later in the story. This use of clues is called **foreshadowing.**

Reading Skills 📖
Making Predictions

Part of the fun of following any **story** is trying to guess what will happen next. That process is called **making predictions.** Here's how to make

predictions on your own as you read a text:

- Look for clues that seem to **foreshadow** something that will happen.
- As the **suspense** builds, think about possible outcomes.
- Ask yourself questions as you read. Revise your predictions as you go.

Vocabulary Development

Pay attention to these words as you read the story:

hordes (hôrdz) *n.:* large, moving crowds. *The rats swam ashore in hordes.*

receding (ri·sēd'iŋ) *v.* used as *adj.:* moving back. *At first the ship came toward us, but then it drifted off in the receding waters.*

fathom (fath'əm) *v.:* understand. *The lighthouse keepers couldn't fathom the rats' nasty reaction.*

edible (ed'ə·bəl) *adj.:* fit to be eaten. *The rats thought the men were edible.*

derisive (di·rī'siv) *adj.:* scornful and ridiculing. *The rats peered with derisive eyes at the terrified men.*

---

go. hrw .com

INTERNET

Vocabulary Activity
•
Cross-curricular Connection

Keyword: LE5 7-1

Background
Literature and Geography

The title of this story is the name of a *key,* or low-lying island, off the coast of French Guiana (gē·an'ə), in South America. At the time the story was written, French Guiana was a colony of France. Cayenne (kī·en'), the capital, was the site of one of the prisons that France maintained there until 1945.

Literary Skills
Understand suspense.

Reading Skills
Make predictions.

Three Skeleton Key

George G. Toudouze

I did not give the warnings of the old-timers a second thought.

My most terrifying experience? Well, one does have a few in thirty-five years of service in the Lights, although it's mostly monotonous, routine work—keeping the light in order, making out the reports.

When I was a young man, not very long in the service, there was an opening in a lighthouse newly built off the coast of Guiana, on a small rock twenty miles or so from the mainland. The pay was high, so in order to reach the sum I had set out to save before I married, I volunteered for service in the new light.

Three Skeleton Key, the small rock on which the light stood, bore a bad reputation. It earned its name from the story of the three convicts who, escaping from Cayenne in a stolen dugout canoe, were wrecked on the rock during the night, managed to escape the sea, but eventually died of hunger and thirst. When they were discovered, nothing remained but three heaps of bones, picked clean by the birds. The story was that the three skeletons, gleaming with phosphorescent[1] light, danced over the small rock, screaming. . . .

But there are many such stories and I did not give the warnings of the old-timers at the *Île-de-Seine*[2] a second thought. I signed up, boarded ship, and in a month I was installed at the light.

Picture a gray, tapering cylinder,[3] welded to the solid black rock by iron rods and concrete, rising from a small island twenty-odd miles from land. It lay in the midst of the sea, this island, a small, bare piece of stone, about one hundred fifty feet long, perhaps forty wide. Small, barely large enough for a man to walk about and stretch his legs at low tide.

This is an advantage one doesn't find in all lights, however, for some of them rise sheer from the waves, with no room for one to move save within the light itself. Still, on our island, one must be careful, for the rocks were treacherously smooth. One misstep and down you would fall into the sea—not that the risk of drowning was so great, but the waters about our island swarmed with huge sharks, who kept an eternal patrol around the base of the light.

Still, it was a nice life there. We had enough provisions to last for months, in the event that the sea should become too rough for the supply ship to reach us on schedule. During the day we would work about the light, cleaning the rooms, polishing the metalwork and the lens and reflector of the light itself, and at night we would sit on the gallery and watch our light, a twenty-thousand-candlepower lantern, swinging its strong white bar of light over the sea from the top of its hundred-twenty-foot tower. Some days, when the air would be very clear, we could see the land, a threadlike line to the west. To the east, north, and south stretched the ocean. Landsmen, perhaps, would soon have tired of that kind of life, perched on a small island off the coast of South America

---

1. **phosphorescent** (făs′fə·res′ənt) *adj.*: glowing.
2. *Île-de-Seine* (ēl′ də sen′).

3. **tapering cylinder:** tube shape that gradually narrows toward one end; in this case, toward the top.

for eighteen weeks until one's turn for leave ashore came around. But we liked it there, my two fellow tenders and myself—so much so that for twenty-two months on end, with the exception of shore leaves, I was greatly satisfied with the life on Three Skeleton Key.

I had just returned from my leave at the end of June, that is to say, midwinter in that latitude, and had settled down to the routine with my two fellow keepers, a Breton[4] by the name of Le Gleo and the head keeper, Itchoua, a Basque[5] some dozen years or so older than either of us.

Eight days went by as usual; then on the ninth night after my return, Itchoua, who was on night duty, called Le Gleo and me, sleeping in our rooms in the middle of the tower, at two in the morning. We rose immediately and, climbing the thirty or so steps that led to the gallery, stood beside our chief.

Itchoua pointed, and following his finger, we saw a big three-master, with all sail set, heading straight for the light. A queer course, for the vessel must have seen us; our light lit her with the glare of day each time it passed over her.

Now, ships were a rare sight in our waters, for our light was a warning of treacherous reefs, barely hidden under the surface and running far out to sea. Consequently we were always given a wide berth, especially by sailing vessels, which cannot maneuver as readily as steamers.

No wonder that we were surprised at seeing this three-master heading dead for us in the gloom of early morning. I had immediately recognized her lines, for she stood out plainly, even at the distance of a mile, when our light shone on her.

She was a beautiful ship of some four thousand tons, a fast sailer that had carried cargoes to every part of the world, plowing the seas unceasingly. By her lines she was identified as Dutch built, which was understandable, as Paramaribo and Dutch Guiana are very close to Cayenne.

Watching her sailing dead for us, a white wave boiling under her bows, Le Gleo cried out:

"What's wrong with her crew? Are they all drunk or insane? Can't they see us?"

Itchoua nodded soberly and looked at us sharply as he remarked: "See us? No doubt—if there *is* a crew aboard!"

"What do you mean, chief?" Le Gleo had started, turned to the Basque. "Are you saying that she's the *Flying Dutchman*?"[6]

His sudden fright had been so evident that the older man laughed:

"No, old man, that's not what I meant. If I say that no one's aboard, I mean she's a derelict."[7]

Then we understood her queer behavior. Itchoua was right. For some reason, believing her doomed, her crew had abandoned her. Then she had righted herself and sailed on, wandering with the wind.

The three of us grew tense as the ship seemed about to crash on one of our numerous reefs, but she suddenly lurched with some change of the wind, the yards[8] swung around, and the derelict came clumsily about and sailed dead away from us.

---

4. **Breton** (bret′n): person from Brittany, a region of northern France.
5. **Basque** (bask): Basques are people living in the Pyrenees, a mountain range in France and Spain.
6. **Flying Dutchman:** fabled Dutch ghost ship whose captain is said to be condemned to sail the seas until Judgment Day. Seeing the *Flying Dutchman* is supposed to bring bad luck.
7. **derelict** (der′ə·likt′) *n.:* here, abandoned ship.
8. **yards** *n.:* in nautical terms, rods fastened across the masts to support the sails.

Le Séducteur by René Magritte. Oil on canvas (19" × 23").

In the light of our lantern she seemed so sound, so strong, that Itchoua exclaimed impatiently:

"But why the devil was she abandoned? Nothing is smashed, no sign of fire—and she doesn't sail as if she were taking water."

Le Gleo waved to the departing ship:

"Bon voyage!" he smiled at Itchoua and went on. "She's leaving us, chief, and now we'll never know what—"

"No, she's not!" cried the Basque. "Look! She's turning!"

As if obeying his words, the derelict three-master stopped, came about, and headed for us once more. And for the next four hours the vessel played around us—zigzagging, coming about, stopping, then suddenly lurching forward. No doubt some freak of current and wind, of which our island was the center, kept her near us.

Then suddenly the tropic dawn broke, the sun rose, and it was day, and the ship was plainly visible as she sailed past us. Our light extinguished, we returned to the gallery with our glasses[9] and inspected her.

The three of us focused our glasses on her poop[10] and saw, standing out sharply, black letters on the white background of a life ring, the stenciled name "*Cornelius de Witt, Rotterdam.*"

We had read her lines correctly: She was Dutch. Just then the wind rose and the *Cornelius de Witt* changed course, leaned to port, and headed straight for us once more. But this time she was so close that we knew she would not turn in time.

"Thunder!" cried Le Gleo, his Breton soul aching at seeing a fine ship doomed to smash upon a reef, "she's going to pile up! She's gone!"

I shook my head:

"Yes, and a shame to see that beautiful ship wreck herself. And we're helpless."

There was nothing we could do but watch. A ship sailing with all sail spread, creaming the sea with her forefoot as she runs before the wind, is one of the most beautiful sights in the world—but this time I could feel the tears stinging in my eyes as I saw this fine ship headed for her doom.

All this time our glasses were riveted on her and we suddenly cried out together:

"The rats!"

Now we knew why this ship, in perfect condition, was sailing without her crew aboard. They had been driven out by the rats. Not those poor specimens of rats you see ashore, barely reaching the length of one foot from their trembling noses to the tip of their skinny tails, wretched creatures that dodge and hide at the mere sound of a footfall.

No, these were ships' rats, huge, wise creatures, born on the sea, sailing all over the world on ships, transferring to other, larger ships as they multiply. There is as much difference between the rats of the land and these maritime rats as between a fishing smack[11] and an armored cruiser.

The rats of the sea are fierce, bold animals. Large, strong, and intelligent, clannish and seawise, able to put the best of mariners to shame with their knowledge of the sea, their uncanny ability to foretell the weather.

And they are brave, these rats, and vengeful. If you so much as harm one, his sharp cry will bring hordes of his fellows to swarm over you, tear you, and not cease until your flesh has been stripped from the bones.

The ones on this ship, the rats of Holland, are the worst, superior to other rats of the sea as their brethren are to the land rats. There is a well-known tale about these animals.

A Dutch captain, thinking to protect his cargo, brought aboard his ship not cats but two terriers, dogs trained in the hunting, fighting, and killing of vicious rats. By the time the ship, sailing from Rotterdam, had passed the Ostend light, the dogs were gone and never seen again. In twenty-four hours they had been overwhelmed, killed, and eaten by the rats.

At times, when the cargo does not suffice,[12] the rats attack the crew, either

---

9. **glasses** *n.:* here, binoculars.
10. **poop** *n.:* in nautical terms, the stern (back) deck of a ship.

11. **smack** *n.:* here, small sailboat.
12. **suffice** (sə·fīs′) *v.:* provide enough.

Vocabulary
hordes (hôrdz) *n.:* large, moving crowds.

driving them from the ship or eating them alive. And studying the *Cornelius de Witt*, I turned sick, for her small boats were all in place. She had not been abandoned.

Over her bridge, on her deck, in the rigging, on every visible spot, the ship was a writhing mass—a starving army coming toward us aboard a vessel gone mad!

Our island was a small spot in that immense stretch of sea. The ship could have grazed us or passed to port or starboard with its ravening[13] cargo—but no, she came for us at full speed, as if she were leading the regatta at a race, and impaled herself on a sharp point of rock.

There was a dull shock as her bottom stove in,[14] then a horrible crackling as the three masts went overboard at once, as if cut down with one blow of some gigantic sickle. A sighing groan came as the water rushed into the ship; then she split in two and sank like a stone.

But the rats did not drown. Not these fellows! As much at home in the sea as any fish, they formed ranks in the water, heads lifted, tails stretched out, paws paddling. And half of them, those from the forepart of the ship, sprang along the masts and onto the rocks in the instant before she sank. Before we had time even to move, nothing remained of the three-master save some pieces of wreckage floating on the surface and an army of rats covering the rocks left bare by the receding tide.

Thousands of heads rose, felt the wind, and we were scented, seen! To them we were fresh meat, after possible weeks of starving.

There came a scream, composed of innumerable screams, sharper than the howl of a saw attacking a bar of iron, and in the one motion, every rat leaped to attack the tower!

We barely had time to leap back, close the door leading onto the gallery, descend the stairs, and shut every window tightly. Luckily the door at the base of the light, which we never could have reached in time, was of bronze set in granite and was tightly closed.

The horrible band, in no measurable time, had swarmed up and over the tower as if it had been a tree, piled on the embrasures[15] of the windows, scraped at the glass with thousands of claws, covered the lighthouse with a furry mantle, and reached the top of the tower, filling the gallery and piling atop the lantern.

Their teeth grated as they pressed against the glass of the lantern room, where they could plainly see us, though they could not reach us. A few millimeters of glass, luckily very strong, separated our faces from their gleaming, beady eyes, their sharp claws and teeth. Their odor filled the tower, poisoned our lungs, and rasped our nostrils with a pestilential, nauseating smell. And there we were, sealed alive in our own light, prisoners of a horde of starving rats.

That first night, the tension was so great

---

13. **ravening** (rav′ən·iŋ) *adj.:* greedily searching for animals to kill for food. A more common related word is *ravenous* (rav′ə·nəs), meaning "wildly, greedily hungry."
14. **stove in:** caved in.

15. **embrasures** (em·brā′zhərz) *n.:* slanted openings.

Vocabulary
receding (ri·sēd′iŋ) *v.:* used as *adj.:* moving back.

that we could not sleep. Every moment, we felt that some opening had been made, some window given way, and that our horrible besiegers were pouring through the breach. The rising tide, chasing those of the rats which had stayed on the bare rocks, increased the numbers clinging to the walls, piled on the balcony—so much so that clusters of rats clinging to one another hung from the lantern and the gallery.

With the coming of darkness we lit the light and the turning beam completely maddened the beasts. As the light turned, it successively blinded thousands of rats crowded against the glass, while the dark side of the lantern room gleamed with thousands of points of light, burning like the eyes of jungle beasts in the night.

All the while we could hear the enraged scraping of claws against the stone and glass, while the chorus of cries was so loud that we had to shout to hear one another. From time to time, some of the rats fought among themselves and a dark cluster would detach itself, falling into the sea like a ripe fruit from a tree. Then we would see phosphorescent streaks as triangular fins slashed the water—sharks, permanent guardians of our rock, feasting on our jailers.

The next day we were calmer and amused ourselves teasing the rats, placing our faces against the glass which separated us. They could not fathom the invisible barrier which separated them from us, and we laughed as we watched them leaping against the heavy glass.

But the day after that, we realized how serious our position was. The air was foul; even the heavy smell of oil within our stronghold could not dominate the fetid odor of the beasts massed around us. And

there was no way of admitting fresh air without also admitting the rats.

The morning of the fourth day, at early dawn, I saw the wooden framework of my window, eaten away from the outside, sagging inwards. I called my comrades and the three of us fastened a sheet of tin in the opening, sealing it tightly. When we had completed that task, Itchoua turned to us and said dully:

"Well—the supply boat came thirteen days ago, and she won't be back for twenty-nine." He pointed at the white metal plate sealing the opening through the granite. "If that gives way"—he shrugged—"they can change the name of this place to Six Skeleton Key."

The next six days and seven nights, our only distraction was watching the rats whose holds were insecure fall a hundred and twenty feet into the maws of the sharks—but they were so many that we could not see any diminution in their numbers.

Thinking to calm ourselves and pass the time, we attempted to count them, but we soon gave up. They moved incessantly, never still. Then we tried identifying them, naming them.

One of them, larger than the others, who seemed to lead them in their rushes against the glass separating us, we named "Nero";[16] and there were several others whom we had learned to distinguish through various peculiarities.

But the thought of our bones joining those of the convicts was always in the back

---

16. **Nero** (nēr'ō): emperor of Rome (A.D. 54–68) known for his cruelty.

of our minds. And the gloom of our prison fed these thoughts, for the interior of the light was almost completely dark, as we had had to seal every window in the same fashion as mine, and the only space that still admitted daylight was the glassed-in lantern room at the very top of the tower.

Then Le Gleo became morose and had nightmares in which he would see the three skeletons dancing around him, gleaming coldly, seeking to grasp him. His maniacal, raving descriptions were so vivid that Itchoua and I began seeing them also.

It was a living nightmare, the raging cries of the rats as they swarmed over the light, mad with hunger; the sickening, strangling odor of their bodies—

True, there is a way of signaling from lighthouses. But to reach the mast on which to hang the signal, we would have to go out on the gallery where the rats were.

There was only one thing left to do. After debating all of the ninth day, we decided not to light the lantern that night. This is the greatest breach of our service, never committed as long as the tenders of the light are alive; for the light is something sacred, warning ships of danger in the night. Either the light gleams a quarter-hour after sundown, or no one is left alive to light it.

Well, that night, Three Skeleton Light was dark, and all the men were alive. At the risk of causing ships to crash on our reefs, we left it unlit, for we were worn out—going mad!

At two in the morning, while Itchoua was dozing in his room, the sheet of metal sealing his window gave way. The chief had just time enough to leap to his feet and cry for help, the rats swarming over him.

But Le Gleo and I, who had been watching from the lantern room, got to him immediately, and the three of us battled with the horde of maddened rats which flowed through the gaping window. They bit, we struck them down with our knives—and retreated.

We locked the door of the room on them, but before we had time to bind our wounds, the door was eaten through and gave way, and we retreated up the stairs, fighting off the rats that leaped on us from the knee-deep swarm.

I do not remember, to this day, how we ever managed to escape. All I can remember is wading through them up the stairs, striking them off as they swarmed over us; and then we found ourselves, bleeding from innumerable bites, our clothes shredded, sprawled across the trapdoor in the floor of the lantern room––without food or drink. Luckily, the trapdoor was metal, set into the granite with iron bolts.

The rats occupied the entire light beneath us, and on the floor of our retreat lay some twenty of their fellows, who had gotten in with us before the trapdoor closed and whom we had killed with our knives. Below us, in the tower, we could hear the screams of the rats as they devoured everything edible that they found. Those on the outside squealed in reply and writhed in a horrible curtain as they stared at us through the glass of the lantern room.

Itchoua sat up and stared silently at his blood trickling from the wounds on his limbs and body and running in thin streams on the floor around him. Le Gleo, who was in as bad a state (and so was I, for that matter), stared at the chief and me vacantly, started as his gaze swung to the multitude of rats against the glass, then suddenly began laughing horribly:

"Hee! Hee! The Three Skeletons! Hee! Hee! The Three Skeletons are now *six* skeletons! *Six* skeletons!"

He threw his head back and howled, his eyes glazed, a trickle of saliva running from the corners of his mouth and thinning the blood flowing over his chest. I shouted to him to shut up, but he did not hear me, so I did the only thing I could to quiet him—I swung the back of my hand across his face.

The howling stopped suddenly, and his eyes swung around the room; then he bowed his head and began weeping softly, like a child.

Our darkened light had been noticed from the mainland, and as dawn was breaking, the patrol was there to investigate the failure of our light. Looking through my binoculars, I could see the horrified expression on the faces of the officers and crew when, the daylight strengthening, they saw the light completely covered by a seething mass of rats. They thought, as I afterwards found out, that we had been eaten alive.

But the rats had also seen the ship or had scented the crew. As the ship drew nearer, a

---

Vocabulary

edible (ed′ə·bəl) *adj.*: fit to be eaten.

solid phalanx[17] left the light, plunged into the water, and swimming out, attempted to board her. They would have succeeded, as the ship was hove to;[18] but the engineer connected his steam to a hose on the deck and scalded the head of the attacking column, which slowed them up long enough for the ship to get under way and leave the rats behind.

Then the sharks took part. Belly up, mouths gaping, they arrived in swarms and scooped up the rats, sweeping through them like a sickle through wheat. That was one day that sharks really served a useful purpose.

The remaining rats turned tail, swam to the shore, and emerged dripping. As they neared the light, their comrades greeted them with shrill cries, with what sounded like a derisive note predominating. They answered angrily and mingled with their fellows. From the several tussles that broke out, it seemed as if they resented being ridiculed for their failure to capture the ship.

But all this did nothing to get us out of our jail. The small ship could not approach but steamed around the light at a safe distance, and the tower must have seemed fantastic, some weird, many-mouthed beast hurling defiance at them.

Finally, seeing the rats running in and out of the tower through the door and the windows, those on the ship decided that we had perished and were about to leave when Itchoua, regaining his senses, thought of using the light as a signal. He lit it and, using a plank placed and withdrawn before the beam to form the dots and dashes, quickly

sent out our story to those on the vessel.

Our reply came quickly. When they understood our position—how we could not get rid of the rats, Le Gleo's mind going fast, Itchoua and myself covered with bites, cornered in the lantern room without food or water—they had a signalman send us their reply.

His arms swinging like those of a windmill, he quickly spelled out:

"Don't give up, hang on a little longer! We'll get you out of this!"

Then she turned and steamed at top speed for the coast, leaving us little reassured.

She was back at noon, accompanied by the supply ship, two small coast guard boats, and the fireboat—a small squadron. At twelve-thirty the battle was on.

After a short reconnaissance,[19] the fireboat picked her way slowly through the reefs until she was close to us, then turned her powerful jet of water on the rats. The heavy stream tore the rats from their places and hurled them screaming into the water, where the sharks gulped them down. But for every ten that were dislodged, seven swam ashore, and the stream could do nothing to the rats within the tower. Furthermore, some of them, instead of returning to the rocks, boarded the fireboat, and the men were forced to battle them hand to hand. They were true rats of Holland, fearing no man, fighting for the right to live!

Nightfall came, and it was as if nothing had been done; the rats were still in possession. One of the patrol boats stayed by the island; the rest of the flotilla[20] departed for

---

17. **phalanx** (fā′laŋks′) *n.:* closely packed group. A phalanx is an ancient military formation, and the word still has warlike connotations.
18. **hove to:** stopped by being turned into the wind.

19. **reconnaissance** (ri·kän′ə·səns) *n.:* exploratory survey or examination.
20. **flotilla** (flō·til′ə) *n.:* small fleet of boats.

Vocabulary
derisive (di·rī′siv) *adj.:* scornful and ridiculing.

the coast. We had to spend another night in our prison. Le Gleo was sitting on the floor, babbling about skeletons, and as I turned to Itchoua, he fell unconscious from his wounds. I was in no better shape and could feel my blood flaming with fever.

Somehow the night dragged by, and the next afternoon I saw a tug, accompanied by the fireboat, come from the mainland with a huge barge in tow. Through my glasses, I saw that the barge was filled with meat.

Risking the treacherous reefs, the tug dragged the barge as close to the island as possible. To the last rat, our besiegers deserted the rock, swam out, and boarded the barge reeking with the scent of freshly cut meat. The tug dragged the barge about a mile from shore, where the fireboat drenched the barge with gasoline. A well-placed incendiary shell from the patrol boat set her on fire.

The barge was covered with flames immediatcly, and the rats took to the water in swarms, but the patrol boat bombarded them with shrapnel from a safe distance, and the sharks finished off the survivors.

A whaleboat from the patrol boat took us off the island and left three men to replace us. By nightfall we were in the hospital in Cayenne. What became of my friends?

Well, Le Gleo's mind had cracked and he was raving mad. They sent him back to France and locked him up in an asylum, the poor devil! Itchoua died within a week; a rat's bite is dangerous in that hot, humid climate, and infection sets in rapidly.

As for me—when they fumigated the light and repaired the damage done by the rats, I resumed my service there. Why not? No reason why such an incident should keep me from finishing out my service there, is there?

Besides—I told you I liked the place—to be truthful, I've never had a post as pleasant as that one, and when my time came to leave it forever, I tell you that I almost wept as Three Skeleton Key disappeared below the horizon.

Meet the Writer

George G. Toudouze

Sea Fever

George G. Toudouze (1847–1904) was born in France and grew up to develop many literary interests—he was a playwright, an essayist, and an illustrator. He also had a great interest in the sea and worked on a history of the French navy. One critic says of his storytelling style, "It has the impact of a powerful man at the fair who, for the fun of it, takes the hammer and at one blow sends the machine to the top, rings the bell, and walks off."

"Three Skeleton Key" was first published in *Esquire,* a magazine that once was famous for its macho adventure stories. The map on page 50 shows the setting of "Three Skeleton Key."

First Thoughts

1. Describe your reaction to "Three Skeleton Key" by completing these sentences:
   - When I first read about the rats, I felt . . .
   - For me the scariest part of the story was . . .

Thinking Critically

2. Early in the story the narrator explains how Three Skeleton Key got its name. How does this **foreshadow**—or hint at—the danger the three lighthouse keepers will face later on?

3. On the fourth day of the invasion, a wooden window frame in the lighthouse sags inward. How does this incident increase **suspense**? What other details create suspense?

4. The three **characters** in the lighthouse respond differently to the invasion. Describe each man's reaction to the rats and its effect on the outcome of the story. Which character (if any) did you identify with?

Extending Interpretations

5. At what point did you predict that the narrator would survive the rat attack? On what evidence did you base your prediction?

WRITING

Describing a Setting

Much of the suspense in "Three Skeleton Key" comes from the fact that the characters are completely isolated. A lonely, forsaken island is a perfect **setting** for a horror story. Write a brief description of another good setting for a horror story. Look back at your Quickwrite notes for more ideas. Consider these features of a setting: sounds, sights, smells, time of day, weather, animal life, names.

---

go.
hrw
.com

INTERNET

Projects and Activities

Keyword: LE5 7-1

SKILLS FOCUS

Literary Skills
Analyze suspense.

Reading Skills
Make predictions.

Writing Skills
Write a description.

Reading Check

To review the story line, imagine you are the narrator filling out a report on your adventure at Three Skeleton Key.

Lighthouse Log
Day 1:
Day 2:
Day 3:
Day 4:

Day 9:
Day 10:
Day 11:

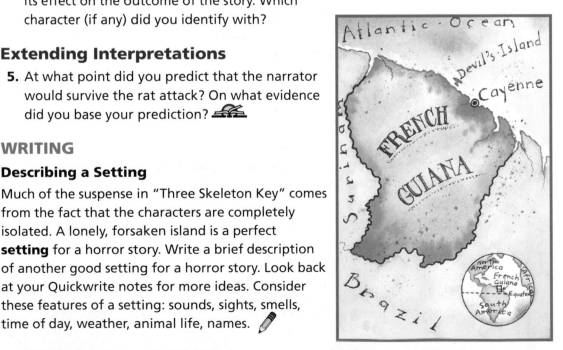

After You Read | Vocabulary Development

Clarifying Word Meanings

PRACTICE 1

Word Bank

hordes
receding
fathom
edible
derisive

Test your mastery of the Word Bank words by answering these questions:

1. <u>Hordes</u> of rats would be a terrifying sight. Describe two other kinds of <u>hordes</u> you would not like to see.

2. How might you try to <u>fathom</u> a difficult text?

3. If you were a flood victim, how would you feel when you saw the flood waters <u>receding</u>?

4. What is your favorite <u>edible</u> plant? Name one plant that is inedible.

5. Write a <u>derisive</u> remark that a skeptic might make on hearing this rat story.

Clarifying Word Meanings: Examples

Sometimes you can figure out the meaning of an unfamiliar word by finding other words or phrases that give you an example of what the word means. For example, what words in this sentence give you an idea of what *staples* are?

> **The lighthouse keepers were running very low on necessary <u>staples</u>, such as flour, sugar, and salt.**

Certain words often let you know when an example is being used: *for example, for instance, like, such as, in this case, as if.*

PRACTICE 2

Find the words in each sentence that give you clues to the meaning of the underlined word. Then, make a guess about the meaning of the underlined word.

1. The rocks were <u>treacherous</u>. One false step and you would fall into the sea. *Treacherous* probably means _____.

2. Our eyes were <u>riveted</u> on the ship, as if fixed there by an invisible force. *Riveted* probably means _____.

3. The ship was a <u>writhing</u> mass, like a pit of moving snakes. *Writhing* probably means _____.

SKILLS FOCUS

Vocabulary Skills
Clarify word meanings by using examples.

Understanding Text Structures: A Newspaper Article

Reading Focus
Structure and Purpose of a Newspaper Article

The story "Three Skeleton Key" is about a terrifying invasion of rats, but the newspaper article you are about to read presents another view of these furry creatures.

The **purpose** of a newspaper article is to give you factual information about current events. A good informational article in a newspaper provides detailed answers to the questions *who? what? when? where? why?* and *how?*

Many newspaper articles follow an **inverted**—or upside-down—**pyramid** style. The article begins with a **summary lead,** a sentence or paragraph that gives the **main idea** of the story—this is usually the most important idea or detail in the story. It is followed by the less important details of the article.

Some articles begin with a lead that simply grabs your interest in a topic. Such a lead does not summarize but instead describes an interesting situation or fact related to the story. Here are some additional elements in the **structure** of a news article:

- **Headline:** the catchy boldface words that tell you what the article is about.
- **Subhead:** additional boldface words in smaller type under the headline, which add details about the article.
- **Byline:** the name of the reporter who wrote the article.
- **Dateline:** the location where the article was reported and the date when the information was reported.
- **Lead:** the sentence or paragraph that begins the news article.
- **Tone:** the choice of words and point of view that meet the interests of the newspaper's audience. Tone often depends on the subject of the article. Some articles are light, lively, and humorous; others are serious and straightforward.

■ How many structural elements of a newspaper article can you find as you read "Eeking Out a Life"?

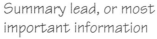

Summary lead, or most important information

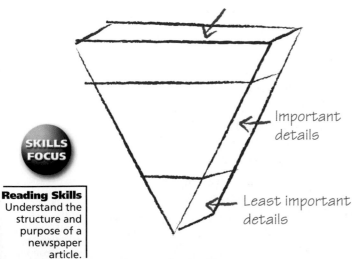

Important details

Least important details

SKILLS FOCUS

Reading Skills
Understand the structure and purpose of a newspaper article.

Eeking Out a Life

Couple Welcome a Rescued Rat into Their Home

by Matt Surman

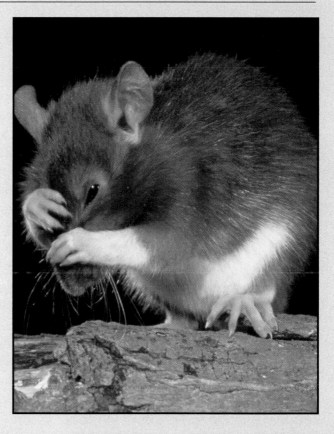

SIMI VALLEY, Calif., July 8— Who knows what trials the rat named Sunny Jim endured in his days alone in the wilderness?

Was he chased by voracious[1] owls? beset by marauding[2] gangs of streetwise sewer rats? Did he yearn for a child who had lost him on a day's outing?

His new owners—Hayley Huttenmaier and Nachshon Rose—can only guess. The little rat that they rescued, housed, and fed isn't talking, of course. And now Rose isn't sure he wants to find out about the past of the rat they have named Sunny Jim if that means the owner is going to come forward. Rose, in fact, has become attached to this sweet, squirming, don't-call-him-vermin little guy.

All the former veterinary hospital employee knows is that he was returning from a short hike through Corriganville Park one Tuesday when a bundle of fur scampered across the parking lot. He followed, saw it stick its nose out of a little burrow, and then—bit by bit—come to perch on his shoe.

"I was kind of concerned that if I didn't catch him, he would probably be eaten," Rose said. "He probably couldn't have been out there more than a day."

The rat wasn't wearing any tags. There were no remnants of a leash. But he had to be a pet: Just look at the

---

1. **voracious** (vô·rā′shəs) *adj.:* extremely hungry; eager to eat a lot of food.
2. **marauding** (mə·rôd′iŋ) *v.* used as *adj.:* roving in search of something to take or destroy.

white and brownish-gray markings, his docile[3]—could one go so far as to say friendly?—behavior, his clean fur, and diminutive[4] size. Clearly this was not one of those sooty, dirt-brown outdoor creatures known as *Rattus rattus*.

So, he brought the rat home, and there, he and his fiancee, Huttenmaier, welcomed the rat into their family of two dogs and three cats. Now, Sunny Jim has his own room—well, a cabinet actually—with a cubbyhole formed by bricks, a handful of toys, a soft bed of wood shavings, and regular meals.

Huttenmaier insisted that they place an ad seeking its owner. "My theory is a kid took him out to play and lost him," she said. But so far they have received no calls. While Huttenmaier feels a bit for the poor owner, Rose doesn't want to give Sunny up. He thinks a mom forced her kid to abandon the creature when she realized there was a rodent hiding in a bedroom.

Which brings up the question: Isn't owning a rat found in the woods—even one with a cute glossy face, busy little hands, and a slippy short tail—a little worrisome?

"We can't turn down a cute face," Huttenmaier explained.

And experts agreed: Sunny Jim is almost certainly not a tree-dwelling, bubonic-plague carrying, skinny wild rat. He is closer to man's best friend.

"Oh, rats are like little dogs," said Louis Stack, membership director of the Riverside-based American Fancy Rat & Mouse Association, whose members raise show rats the way purebred owners raise show dogs. "They can sit on your shoulder and watch TV with you."

And indeed, rat lovers are not shy about their enthusiasm. The Web hosts scores of sites extolling[5] *Rattus norvegicus*—the pet rat, domesticated about 100 years ago in England—and dispelling what they call misinformation about the cleanliness of their pets.

"There are people who are fanatical about rats," Stack said. "There are . . . all kinds of newsletters." Huttenmaier and Rose have no intentions of going that far.

They are just happy to offer little Sunny a home, a sense of safety—disregarding one little incident with a curious cat—and a chance to take it easy for a while.

And just maybe, there is a chance for a Rat Pack. "We might even get him a friend," Huttenmaier said.

---

3. **docile** (däs′əl) *adj.*: manageable.
4. **diminutive** (də·min′yo͞o·tiv) *adj.*: very small; tiny.

5. **extolling** (ek·stōl′iŋ) *v.* used as *adj.*: praising highly.

Analyzing a Newspaper Article

Eeking Out a Life

Test Practice

1. The **structure** of a newspaper article is said to be similar to an —
   - **A** octagon
   - **B** inverted pyramid
   - **C** oval
   - **D** upside-down T

2. The **dateline** of the article on page 53 names which city?
   - **F** Salt Lake City
   - **G** Des Moines
   - **H** Buxton
   - **J** Simi Valley

3. The **subhead** of the article tells you that —
   - **A** something is eeking out a life
   - **B** a couple has adopted a stray rat
   - **C** the rat may have been chased by an owl
   - **D** rats have become popular

4. The **byline** of the news article shows it was written by —
   - **F** George G. Toudouze
   - **G** Nachshon Rose
   - **H** Matt Surman
   - **J** Sunny Jim

5. The **lead** of this article —
   - **A** is an attention grabber
   - **B** makes a serious statement about dangerous rats
   - **C** answers *who? what? where? when?* and *how?*
   - **D** presents the story's main idea

6. The **main idea** of this article is —
   - **F** a couple loves its adopted rat
   - **G** rats can't live with people
   - **H** keeping a rat at home is dangerous
   - **J** the rat population is a problem

Constructed Response

1. What is the **purpose** of a newspaper article?

2. Describe the **inverted-pyramid structure** of a typical newspaper article.

3. Summarize the information from the article on page 53 that answers the questions *who? what? when? where? why?* and *how?*

4. Describe the **tone** of the article. Why do you think the reporter decided to use this tone?

5. The **headline** title of this article contains a **pun,** which is a play on word meanings. What two words, both pronounced "eek," is the headline playing with?

SKILLS FOCUS

Reading Skills
Analyze the structure and purpose of a newspaper article.

Subject-Verb Agreement

Probably the most common error people make in writing (and in speaking) is in subject-verb agreement. The rule is simple: Subjects and their verbs must always agree. That means that a singular subject takes a singular verb and a plural subject takes a plural verb. The problem comes with identifying the subject and deciding whether it's singular or plural.

Be especially careful when you have *neither/nor* or *either/or*. You must also pay attention when a subject is separated from its verb by a prepositional phrase. The verb always agrees with the subject.

1. **Neither Huttenmaier nor Rose wants/want to give up Sunny Jim.** [Singular subjects joined by *or* or *nor* take a singular verb. Therefore, the verb should be *wants*.]

2. **Neither Sunny Jim nor his owners wants/want to end their friendship.** [When a singular subject and a plural subject are joined by *or* or *nor*, the verb agrees with the subject closer to the verb. Since *owners* is plural, the verb should be *want*.]

3. **The owners of Sunny Jim is/are a bit unusual.** [The number of the subject is not affected by a prepositional phrase following the subject. Therefore, the verb should be *are*.]

PRACTICE

Rewrite the paragraph below to correct errors in subject-verb agreement.

The most interesting moments in this story comes when Sunny Jim is described. Neither tags nor a collar were found on the little rat. The owners of the rat seem very nice, but parts of their story is weird. The writer don't seem very enthusiastic either. Stories about the curious cat wasn't told here. Neither my biology teacher nor my town's pet-store owner recommend getting a pet *Rattus*.

For more help, see Agreement of Subject and Verb, 2b–n, in the Language Handbook.

SKILLS FOCUS

Grammar Skills
Use correct subject-verb agreement.

The Monsters Are Due on Maple Street

Make the Connection
Quickwrite 🖊

People often make snap judgments in life. In your journal, write about a time you jumped to an incorrect conclusion about someone or someone jumped to an incorrect conclusion about you. What was the situation? What mistake was made? How was the mistake corrected?

Literary Focus
Plot Complications

Complications in stories make it hard for characters to get what they want. Complications usually begin to develop as soon as the characters take steps to resolve their problems or to get what they want so badly. Complications are events like a sudden storm breaking just as the climbers are nearing the summit or another dragon appearing out of the cave just when the hero thinks he has finished his work. Complications usually add more conflict to the story. They also make the plot more complex. Complications are meant to increase our anxiety about how the story will finally end. In stories, as in life, it's never easy.

Reading Skills
Making Inferences

Good readers **make inferences** using clues the writer provides. It's a form of word arithmetic: The writer gives you *one* and *one* but expects you to figure out the answer—*two*.

As you read this teleplay, you'll see little open-book signs. At these points, stop and add up the important clues the writer has just given. Note your inferences in your notebook, or discuss them with your partner.

SKILLS FOCUS

Literary Skills
Understand plot complications.

Reading Skills
Make inferences.

Vocabulary Development

These words are important in the teleplay:

transfixed (trans·fikst′) *v.* used as *adj.:* very still, as if nailed to the spot. *Up and down the street, people stood transfixed, staring at the sky.*

intelligible (in·tel′i·jə·bəl) *adj.:* understandable. *The residents muttered nothing intelligible; they just made an indistinct rumble.*

assent (ə·sent′) *n.:* agreement. *At first, Steve's common sense gained the crowd's assent and goodwill.*

intimidated (in·tim′ə·dāt′id) *v.:* frightened with threats. *The angry crowd intimidated the Goodmans, who then began to defend themselves.*

defiant (dē·fī′ənt) *adj.:* boldly resisting authority. *Those who speak out against the opinions of an angry crowd must be both defiant and courageous.*

idiosyncrasy (id′ē·ō·sin′krə·sē) *n.:* peculiarity. *All people have at least one idiosyncrasy that makes them a little different.*

menace (men′əs) *n.:* danger; threat. *The residents of Maple Street believed there was a real menace to their safety.*

converging (kən·vʉrj′iŋ) *v.* used as *adj.:* closing in. *The crowd began converging around Tommy in order to hear him speak.*

explicit (eks·plis′it) *adj.:* definite; clearly stated. *The danger on Maple Street was not explicit, or understandable, making it more frightening.*

variations (ver′ē·ā′shənz) *n.:* differences. *Most of the residents of Maple Street reacted to fear in similar ways, with only small variations.*

Background
Literature and Media

From its 1959 debut through its more than 150 subsequent episodes, *The Twilight Zone* thrilled and captivated millions of television viewers. Rebroadcasts run even today—maybe you've seen some episodes. As Rod Serling, the show's creator, would eerily alert viewers at the beginning of every episode, things in the Twilight Zone are not always what they seem. Ordinary people face extraordinary situations in the Twilight Zone, where familiar rules no longer apply. As the bards and poets have warned for centuries, "Here be monsters. . . ."

Teleplay Terms

Scripts written for television or the movies are different from scripts written for the stage. A **teleplay** is a script written for TV; a **screenplay** is a script written for movies. Both kinds of scripts may contain these camera directions:

fade in: The picture gradually appears on the screen.

pan: a swiveling movement of the camera, from one side to the other.

fade to black: The picture gradually disappears until all that remains is a black screen.

cut to: a sudden change from one scene or character to another.

outside shot: a camera shot of an exterior.

long shot: a camera shot from far off.

close-up: a camera shot that is very close to its subject.

opening shot: the first scene of the production.

dissolve: A new scene is blended with a scene that is fading out.

Characters

Narrator	**Charlie**
	Charlie's wife
Figure One	**Tommy**
Figure Two	**Sally,** Tommy's mother
Residents of Maple Street	**Les Goodman**
Steve Brand	**Mrs. Goodman**
Mrs. Brand	**Woman Next Door**
Don Martin	**Woman One**
Pete Van Horn	**Man One**
	Man Two

Act One

Fade in on a shot of the night sky. The various nebulae and planets stand out in sharp, sparkling relief. As the camera begins a slow pan across the heavens, we hear the narrator offscreen.

Narrator's Voice. There is a fifth dimension beyond that which is known to man. It is a dimension as vast as space and as timeless as infinity. It is the middle ground between light and shadow—between science and superstition. And it lies between the pit of man's fears and the summit of his knowledge. This is the dimension of imagination. It is an area which we call The Twilight Zone.

[The camera pans down past the horizon, stopping on a sign which reads "Maple Street." Then it moves on to the street below. It is daytime. We see a quiet, tree-lined street, typical of small-town America. People sit and swing on gliders on their front porches, chatting across from house to house. STEVE BRAND *polishes his car, while his neighbor,* DON MARTIN, *leans against the fender watching him. A Good Humor man on a bicycle stops to sell some ice cream to a couple of kids. Two women gossip on a front lawn. Another man waters his lawn.]*

Maple Street, U.S.A., late summer. A tree-lined little world of front-porch gliders, hopscotch, the laughter of children, and the bell of an ice-cream vendor.

[The camera moves back to the Good Humor man and the two boys who are standing alongside him, buying ice cream.]

At the sound of the roar and the flash of light, it will be precisely 6:43 P.M. on Maple Street.

[One of the boys, TOMMY, *looks up to listen to a tremendous screeching roar from overhead. A flash of light plays on the boys' faces. It moves down the street, past lawns and porches and rooftops, and disappears. People leave their porches or stop what they're doing to stare up at the sky.* STEVE BRAND *stops polishing his car and stands* transfixed, *staring upward. He looks at* DON MARTIN, *his neighbor from across the street.]*

Steve. What was that? A meteor?

Don (*nods*). That's what it looked like. I didn't hear any crash, though, did you?

Steve (*shakes his head*). Nope. I didn't hear anything except a roar.

Mrs. Brand (*from her porch*). Steve? What was that?

Steve (*raising his voice and looking toward porch*). Guess it was a meteor, honey. Came awful close, didn't it?

Mrs. Brand. Too close for my money! Much too close.

Vocabulary

transfixed (trans·fikst′) *v.* used as *adj.*: very still, as if nailed to the spot.

[*People stand on their porches, watching and talking in low tones.*]

Narrator's Voice. Maple Street. 6:44 P.M., on a late September evening.(*A pause*) Maple Street in the last calm and reflective moments . . . before the monsters came!

[*The camera pans across the porches again. A man is screwing in a lightbulb on a front porch. He gets down off the stool and flicks the switch, only to find that nothing happens. Another man is working on an electric power mower. He plugs in the plug and flicks the switch of the power mower, off and on, but nothing happens. Through the window of a front porch we see a woman at a telephone, pushing her finger back and forth on the dial hook. Her voice is indistinct and distant, but intelligible and repetitive.*] ❶

MAKE INFERENCES
❶ What do the stage directions lead you to think about the roaring sound and flashing light?

Woman Next Door. Operator, operator, something's wrong on the phone, operator!

[MRS. BRAND *comes out on the porch and calls to* STEVE.]

Mrs. Brand (*calling*). Steve, the power's off. I had the soup on the stove, and the stove just stopped working.
Woman Next Door. Same thing over here. I can't get anybody on the phone either. The phone seems to be dead.

[*The camera looks down on the street. Small, mildly disturbed voices creep up from below.*]

Voices.
Electricity's off.
Phone won't work.
Can't get a thing on the radio.
My power mower won't move, won't work at all.
Radio's gone dead.

[PETE VAN HORN, *a tall, thin man, is standing in front of his house.*]

Van Horn. I'll cut through the backyard. . . . See if the power's still on on Floral Street. I'll be right back.

[*He walks past the side of his house and disappears into the backyard. We see the hammer on his hip as he walks. The camera pans down slowly until we're looking at ten or eleven people standing around the street and overflowing to the curb and sidewalk. In the background is* STEVE BRAND's *car.*]

Steve. Doesn't make sense. Why should the power go off all of a sudden, and the phone line?
Don. Maybe some sort of an electrical storm or something.
Charlie. That don't seem likely. Sky's just as blue as anything. Not a cloud. No lightning. No thunder. No nothing. How could it be a storm?
Woman One. I can't get a thing on the radio. Not even the portable.

[*The people again murmur softly in wonderment and question.*]

Charlie. Well, why don't you go downtown and check with the police, though they'll probably think we're crazy or something. A little power failure and right away we get all flustered and everything.

Vocabulary
intelligible (in·tel′i·jə·bəl) *adj.:* understandable.

Steve. It isn't just the power failure, Charlie. If it was, we'd still be able to get a broadcast on the portable.

[*There's a murmur of reaction to this.* STEVE *looks from face to face and then over to his car.*]

I'll run downtown. We'll get this all straightened out.

[STEVE *walks over to the car, gets in it, and turns the key. Through the open car door we see the crowd watching him from the other side.* STEVE *starts the engine. It turns over sluggishly and then just stops dead. He tries it again, and this time he can't even get it to turn over. Then, very slowly and reflectively, he turns the key back to "off" and slowly gets out of the car. Everyone stares at* STEVE. *He stands for a moment by the car, then walks toward the group.*]

I don't understand it. It was working fine before. . . .

Don. Out of gas?
Steve (*shakes his head*). I just had it filled up.
Woman One. What's it mean?
Charlie. It's just as if . . . as if everything

had stopped. . . . (*Then he turns toward* STEVE) We'd better walk downtown.

[*Another murmur of* assent *at this.*]

Steve. The two of us can go, Charlie. (*He turns to look back at the car.*) It couldn't be the meteor. A meteor couldn't do this.

[*He and* CHARLIE *exchange a look, then they start to walk away from the group. We see* TOMMY, *a serious-faced fourteen-year-old in spectacles, standing a few feet away from the group. He is halfway between them and the two men, who start to walk down the sidewalk.*]

Tommy. Mr. Brand . . . you better not!
Steve. Why not?
Tommy. They don't want you to.
[STEVE *and* CHARLIE *exchange a grin, and* STEVE *looks back toward the boy.*]

Steve. Who doesn't want us to?
Tommy (*jerks his head in the general direction of the distant horizon*). Them!
Steve. Them?
Charlie. Who are them?
Tommy (*very intently*). Whoever was in that thing that came by overhead.

[STEVE *knits his brows for a moment, cocking his head questioningly. His voice is intense.*]

Steve. What?
Tommy. Whoever was in the thing that came over. I don't think they want us to leave here.

[STEVE *leaves* CHARLIE *and walks over to the*

Vocabulary
assent (ə·sent′) *n.:* agreement.

boy. He kneels down in front of him. He forces his voice to remain gentle. He reaches out and holds the boy.]

Steve. What do you mean? What are you talking about?

Tommy. They don't want us to leave. That's why they shut everything off.

Steve. What makes you say that? Whatever gave you that idea?

Woman One (*from the crowd*). Now isn't that the craziest thing you ever heard?

Tommy (*persistently but a little intimidated by the crowd*). It's always that way, in every story I ever read about a ship landing from outer space.

Woman One (*to the boy's mother, SALLY, who stands on the fringe of the crowd*). From outer space, yet! Sally, you better get that boy of yours up to bed. He's been reading too many comic books or seeing too many movies or something.

Sally. Tommy, come over here and stop that kind of talk.

Steve. Go ahead, Tommy. We'll be right back. And you'll see. That wasn't any ship or anything like it. That was just a . . . a meteor or something. Likely as not— (*He turns to the group, now trying to weight his words with an optimism he obviously doesn't feel but is desperately trying to instill in himself, as well as the others.*) No doubt it did have something to do with all this power failure and the rest of it. Meteors can do some crazy things. Like sunspots. ❷

Don (*picking up the cue*). Sure. That's the kind of thing—like sunspots. They raise Cain with radio reception all over the world. And this thing being so close—why, there's no telling the sort of stuff it can do. (*He wets his lips and smiles nervously.*) Go ahead, Charlie. You and Steve go into town and see if that isn't what's causing it all.

[STEVE *and* CHARLIE *walk away from the group again, down the sidewalk. The people watch silently.* TOMMY *stares at them, biting his lips, and finally calls out again.*]

Tommy. Mr. Brand!

[*The two men stop again.* TOMMY *takes a step toward them.*]

Tommy. Mr. Brand . . . please don't leave here.

[STEVE *and* CHARLIE *stop once again and turn toward the boy. There's a murmur in the crowd, a murmur of irritation and concern as if the boy were bringing up fears that shouldn't be brought up; words that carried with them a strange kind of validity that came without logic, but nonetheless registered and had meaning and effect.* TOMMY *is partly frightened and partly defiant.*]

You might not even be able to get to town. It was that way in the story. Nobody could leave. Nobody except—

Steve. Except who?

Tommy. Except the people they'd sent down ahead of them. They looked just like humans. And it wasn't until the ship landed that—

[*The boy suddenly stops again, conscious of the parents staring at him and of the sudden hush of the crowd.*]

> **MAKE INFERENCES**
> ❷ Does Steve believe his own words? What can you infer from the stage directions?

Vocabulary

intimidated (in·tim′ə·dāt′id) *v.:* frightened with threats or violence.

defiant (dē·fī′ənt) *adj.:* boldly resisting authority.

Sally (*in a whisper, sensing the antagonism of the crowd*). Tommy, please, son . . . honey, don't talk that way—

Man One. That kid shouldn't talk that way . . . and we shouldn't stand here listening to him. Why, this is the craziest thing I ever heard of. The kid tells us a comic book plot, and here we stand listening—

[STEVE *walks toward the camera and stops by the boy.*]

Steve. Go ahead, Tommy. What kind of story was this? What about the people that they sent out ahead?

Tommy. That was the way they prepared things for the landing. They sent four people. A mother and a father and two kids who looked just like humans . . . but they weren't.

[*There's another silence as* STEVE *looks toward the crowd and then toward* TOMMY. *He wears a tight grin.*]

Steve. Well, I guess what we'd better do then is to run a check on the neighborhood and see which ones of us are really human.

[*There's laughter at this, but it's a laughter that comes from a desperate attempt to lighten the atmosphere.* CHARLIE *laughs nervously, slightly forced. The people look at one another in the middle of their laughter.*]

Charlie. There must be somethin' better to do than stand around makin' bum jokes about it. (*Rubs his jaw nervously*) I wonder if Floral Street's got the same deal we got. (*He looks past the houses.*) Where is Pete Van Horn anyway? Didn't he get back yet?

[*Suddenly there's the sound of a car's engine starting to turn over. We look across the street toward the driveway of* LES GOODMAN'*s house. He's at the wheel trying to start the car.*]

Sally. Can you get it started, Les?

[LES GOODMAN *gets out of the car, shaking his head.*]

Goodman. No dice.

[*He walks toward the group. He stops suddenly as behind him, inexplicably and with a noise that inserts itself into the silence, the car engine starts up all by itself.* GOODMAN *whirls around to stare toward it. The car idles roughly, smoke coming from the exhaust, the frame shaking gently.* GOODMAN'*s eyes go wide, and he runs over to his car. The people stare toward the car.*]

Man One. He got the car started somehow. He got his car started!

[*The camera pans along the faces of the people as they stare, somehow caught up by this revelation and somehow, illogically, wildly, frightened.*]

Woman One. How come his car just up and started like that?
Sally. All by itself. He wasn't anywheres near it. It started all by itself.

[*DON approaches the group. He stops a few feet away to look toward GOODMAN's car, and then back toward the group.*]

Don. And he never did come out to look at that thing that flew overhead. He wasn't even interested. (*He turns to the faces in the group, his face taut and serious.*) Why? Why didn't he come out with the rest of us to look?
Charlie. He always was an oddball. Him and his whole family. Real oddball.
Don. What do you say we ask him? ❸

📖 **MAKE INFERENCES**
❸ What inference have the neighbors made about Les Goodman?

[*The group suddenly starts toward the house. In this brief fraction of a moment they take the first step toward a metamorphosis from a group into a mob. They begin to head purposefully across the street toward the house at the end. STEVE stands in front of them. For a moment their fear almost turns their walk into a wild stampede, but STEVE's voice, loud, incisive, and commanding, makes them stop.*]

Steve. Wait a minute . . . wait a minute! Let's not be a mob!

[*The people stop as a group, seem to pause for a moment, and then much more quietly and slowly start to walk across the street. GOODMAN stands there alone, facing the people.*]

Goodman. I just don't understand it. I tried to start it and it wouldn't start. You saw me. All of you saw me.

[*And now, just as suddenly as the engine started, it stops. There's a long silence that is gradually intruded upon by the frightened murmuring of the people.*]

I don't understand. I swear . . . I don't understand. What's happening?
Don. Maybe you better tell us. Nothing's working on this street. Nothing. No lights, no power, no radio. (*And then meaningfully*) Nothing except one car—yours!

[*The people pick this up. Now their murmuring becomes a loud chant, filling the air with accusations and demands for action. Two of the men pass DON and head toward GOODMAN, who backs away, backing into his car. He is now at bay.*]

Goodman. Wait a minute now. You keep your distance—all of you. So I've got a car that starts by itself—well, that's a freak thing, I admit it. But does that make me some kind of criminal or something? I don't know why the car works—it just does!

[*This stops the crowd momentarily, and now GOODMAN, still backing away, goes toward his front porch. He goes up the steps and then stops to stand facing the mob. STEVE comes through the crowd.*]

Steve (*quietly*). We're all on a monster kick, Les. Seems that the general impression holds that maybe one family isn't what we think they are. Monsters from outer space or something. Different than us. Fifth columnists° from the vast beyond. (*He chuckles.*) You know anybody that might fit that description around here on Maple Street? ❹

Goodman. What is this, a gag or something? This a practical joke or something?

MAKE INFERENCES
❹ Is Steve serious here? On what do you base your inference?

[*The spotlight on his porch suddenly goes out. There's a murmur from the group.*]

Now, I suppose that's supposed to incriminate me! The light goes on and off. That really does it, doesn't it? (*He looks around the faces of the people.*) I just don't understand this— (*He wets his lips, looking from face to face.*) Look, you all know me. We've lived here five years. Right in this house. We're no different than any of the rest of you! We're no different at all. Really . . . this whole thing is just . . . just weird—

Woman One. Well, if that's the case, Les Goodman, explain why—(*She stops suddenly, clamping her mouth shut.*)

° **fifth columnists:** people who aid an enemy from within their own country.

Goodman (*softly*). Explain what?
Steve (*interjecting*). Look, let's forget this—
Charlie (*overlapping him*). Go ahead, let her talk. What about it? Explain what?
Woman One (*a little reluctantly*). Well . . . sometimes I go to bed late at night. A couple of times . . . a couple of times I'd come out on the porch and I'd see Mr. Goodman here in the wee hours of the morning standing out in front of his house . . . looking up at the sky. (*She looks around the circle of faces.*) That's right. Looking up at the sky as if . . . as if he were waiting for something. (*A pause*) As if he were looking for something. ❺

MAKE INFERENCES
❺ What fact about Goodman has the woman observed? What inference has she made? Is this reasonable?

[*There's a murmur of reaction from the crowd again. As* GOODMAN *starts toward them, they back away, frightened.*]

Goodman. You know really . . . this is for laughs. You know what I'm guilty of? (*He laughs.*) I'm guilty of insomnia. Now what's the penalty for insomnia? (*At this point the laugh, the humor, leaves his voice.*) Did you hear what I said? I said it was insomnia. (*A pause as he looks around, then shouts.*) I said it was insomnia! You fools. You scared, frightened rabbits, you. You're sick people, do you know that? You're sick people—all of you! And you don't even know what you're starting because let me tell you . . . let me tell you—this thing you're starting— that should frighten you. As God is my witness . . . you're letting something begin here that's a nightmare!

[*Fade to black.*]

Response and Analysis

Act One

First Thoughts

1. Do you believe aliens are involved in the events on Maple Street? Explain the reasons for your prediction.

Thinking Critically

2. What future events could Tommy's words **foreshadow**?

3. What is the group's reaction when Les Goodman's car starts? What **inference** do they make about the cause of the car's behavior?

4. At the end of Act One, Les Goodman warns the residents that they are starting something that should frighten them, and he goes on to call it a nightmare. What could he mean?

5. A scapegoat is someone whom people blame for their troubles. How has Les Goodman become a scapegoat?

Extending Interpretations

6. What is the difference between a crowd and a mob? Have you ever seen or been a part of a mob? Briefly describe your experiences.

7. In your own words, describe what is happening to the community, and **predict** where this kind of behavior is going to lead. Based on what you know so far and on what you know from history and from your own experience, **predict** events that may occur in Act Two. (Think back to your Quickwrite notes.)

Literary Skills
Analyze plot complications.

Reading Skills
Make inferences.

Reading Check

a. A dramatic event triggers the action on Maple Street. What do the residents believe has caused the power failure?

b. Find three incidents that show that this is not a normal power failure.

c. How do the adults first react to Tommy's suggestion that "they" are aliens who do not want Steve and Charlie to leave the area?

d. What does Tommy then say that causes the adults to become increasingly uncomfortable?

e. What is Tommy's source of information about alien life forms and their habits?

After You Read · Vocabulary Development

Act One

Clarifying Word Meanings: Definitions

Writers often help readers understand difficult words by using definition. A writer using **definition** will provide the word's meaning within the sentence. Let's look at the following sentence:

> In this brief fraction of a moment they take the first step toward a <u>metamorphosis</u> that changes people from a group into a mob.

A reader who does not understand the word *metamorphosis* would benefit from the second half of the sentence, which defines what a metamorphosis does: "changes people from a group into a mob." The reader can then know that events have just taken a pretty important turn. The good people of Maple Street have suddenly become another creature entirely.

As you read, be on the lookout for definitions provided in the text itself. Chances are, if you read a little past a difficult word, you may find that the writer has given you some help.

Word Bank

transfixed
intelligible
assent
intimidated
defiant

PRACTICE

Each sentence below contains an underlined word from the Word Bank as well as a **definition** of that word. For each item, identify the defining words. It might help to explore each word's meaning in a cluster diagram, like the one at the right for the word *transfixed.*

1. Steve stood <u>transfixed</u>, looking at the sky as if he had been nailed to the spot and couldn't move.

2. As the mob came closer, its words became more <u>intelligible</u>, allowing Mr. Goodman to hear and understand them.

3. The residents of Maple Street agreed that strange events were afoot, and when Pete Van Horn offered to investigate, everyone nodded <u>assent</u>.

4. People facing a mob would be <u>intimidated</u>, and their fright would be justified.

5. Tommy was quietly <u>defiant</u> when the adults laughed at him; he held his ground no matter what they said.

Vocabulary Skills
Clarify word meanings by using definitions.

Act Two

Fade in on the entry hall of the Goodman house at night. On the side table rests an unlit candle. MRS. GOODMAN *walks into the scene, a glass of milk in hand. She sets the milk down on the table, lights the candle with a match from a box on the table, picks up the glass of milk, and starts out of the scene. Cut to an outside shot.* MRS. GOODMAN *comes through her porch door, glass of milk in hand. The entry hall, with the table and lit candle, can be seen behind her. The camera slowly pans down the sidewalk, taking in little knots of people who stand around talking in low voices. At the end of each conversation they look toward* LES GOODMAN's *house. From the various houses we can see candlelight but no electricity. An all-pervading quiet blankets the area, disturbed only by the almost whispered voices of the people as they stand around. The camera pans over to one group where* CHARLIE *stands. He stares across at* GOODMAN's *house. Two men stand across the street from it, in almost sentrylike poses. We return to the group.*

Sally (*a little timorously*[1]). It just doesn't seem right, though, keeping watch on them. Why . . . he was right when he said he was one of our neighbors. Why, I've known Ethel Goodman ever since they moved in. We've been good friends—

Charlie. That don't prove a thing. Any guy who'd spend his time lookin' up at the sky early in the morning—well there's something wrong with that kind of a person. There's something that ain't legitimate. Maybe under normal circumstances we could let it go by, but these aren't normal circumstances. Why, look at this street! Nothin' but candles. Why, it's like goin' back into the dark ages or somethin'!

[STEVE *walks down the steps of his porch. He walks down the street, over to* LES GOODMAN's *house, and stops at the foot of the steps.* GOODMAN *stands behind the screen door, his wife behind him, very frightened.*]

Goodman. Just stay right where you are, Steve. We don't want any trouble, but this time if anybody sets foot on my porch, that's what they're going to get—trouble!

Steve. Look, Les—

Goodman. I've already explained to you people. I don't sleep very well at night

---

1. **timorously** (tim′ər·əs·lē) *adv.:* timidly; fearfully.

sometimes. I get up and I take a walk and I look up at the sky. I look at the stars!

Mrs. Goodman. That's exactly what he does. Why this whole thing, it's . . . it's some kind of madness or something.

Steve (*nods grimly*). That's exactly what it is—some kind of madness.

Charlie's Voice (*shrill, from across the street*). You best watch who you're seen with, Steve! Until we get this all straightened out, you ain't exactly above suspicion yourself. ❻

Steve (*whirling around toward him*). Or you, Charlie. Or any of us, it seems. From age eight on up!

Woman One. What I'd like to know is, what are we gonna do? Just stand around here all night?

Charlie. There's nothin' else we can do! (*He turns back looking toward* STEVE *and* GOODMAN *again.*) One of 'em'll tip their hand. They got to.

Steve (*raising his voice*). There's something you can do, Charlie. You could go home and keep your mouth shut. You could quit strutting around like a self-appointed hanging judge[2] and just climb into bed and forget it.

Charlie. You sound real anxious to have that happen, Steve. I think we better keep our eye on you too!

Don (*as if he were taking the bit in his teeth, takes a hesitant step to the front*). I think everything might as well come out now.

> **📖 MAKE INFERENCES**
> ❻ What is Charlie suggesting about the fact that Steve is talking to Les Goodman? What can you suppose about the characters from this?

(*He turns toward* STEVE.) Your wife's done plenty of talking, Steve, about how odd you are!

Charlie (*picking this up, his eyes widening*). Go ahead, tell us what she's said.

[STEVE *walks toward them from across the street.*]

Steve. Go ahead, what's my wife said? Let's get it all out. Let's pick out every idiosyncrasy of every single man, woman, and child on the street. And then we might as well set up some kind of a kangaroo court.[3] How about a firing squad at dawn, Charlie, so we can get rid of all the suspects? Narrow them down. Make it easier for you.

Don. There's no need gettin' so upset, Steve. It's just that . . . well . . . Myra's talked about how there's been plenty of nights you spend hours down in your basement workin' on some kind of radio or something. Well, none of us have ever seen that radio—

[*By this time* STEVE *has reached the group. He stands there defiantly close to them.*]

Charlie. Go ahead, Steve. What kind of "radio set" you workin' on? I never seen it. Neither has anyone else. Who you talk to on that radio set? And who talks to you?

Steve. I'm surprised at you, Charlie. How come you're so dense all of a sudden? (*A pause*) Who do I talk to? I talk to monsters from outer space. I talk to three-headed green men who fly over here in what look like meteors.

---

2. **hanging judge:** judge who sentences people to death without sufficient evidence.

3. **kangaroo court:** unauthorized court, usually one that pays no attention to legal procedures. Kangaroo courts were often set up in frontier areas.

Vocabulary
idiosyncrasy (id′ē·ō·siŋ′krə·sē) *n.:* peculiarity.

[STEVE'S *wife steps down from their porch, bites her lip, calls out.*]

Mrs. Brand. Steve! Steve, please. (*Then looking around, frightened, she walks toward the group.*) It's just a ham radio[4] set, that's all. I bought him a book on it myself. It's just a ham radio set. A lot of people have them. I can show it to you. It's right down in the basement.

Steve (*whirls around toward her*). Show them nothing! If they want to look inside our house—let them get a search warrant.

Charlie. Look, buddy, you can't afford to—

Steve (*interrupting*). Charlie, don't tell me what I can afford! And stop telling me who's dangerous and who isn't and who's safe and who's a menace. (*He turns to the group and shouts.*) And you're with him too—all of you! You're standing here all set to crucify—all set to find a scapegoat—all desperate to point some kind of a finger at a neighbor! Well now look, friends, the only thing that's gonna happen is that we'll eat each other up alive—

[*He stops abruptly as* CHARLIE *suddenly grabs his arm.*]

Charlie (*in a hushed voice*). That's not the only thing that can happen to us.

[*Cut to a long shot looking down the street. A figure has suddenly materialized in the gloom, and in the silence we can hear the clickety-clack of slow, measured footsteps on concrete as the figure walks slowly toward them. One of the women lets out a stifled cry.[5] The young mother grabs her boy, as do a couple of others.*]

Tommy (*shouting, frightened*). It's the monster! It's the monster!

[*Another woman lets out a wail and the people fall back in a group, staring toward the darkness and the approaching figure. As the people stand in the shadows watching,* DON MARTIN *joins them, carrying a shotgun. He holds it up.*]

Don. We may need this.

Steve. A shotgun? (*He pulls it out of* DON'S *hand.*) Good Lord—will anybody think a thought around here? Will you people wise up? What good would a shotgun do against—

[*Now* CHARLIE *pulls the gun from* STEVE'S *hand.*]

Charlie. No more talk, Steve. You're going to talk us into a grave! You'd let whatever's out there walk right over us, wouldn't yuh? Well, some of us won't!

[*He swings the gun around to point it toward the sidewalk. The dark figure continues to walk toward them. The group stands there, fearful, apprehensive. Mothers clutch children, men stand in front of wives.* CHARLIE *slowly raises the gun. As the figure gets closer and closer, he suddenly pulls the trigger. The sound of it explodes in the stillness. The figure suddenly lets out a small cry, stumbles forward onto his knees, and then falls forward on his face.* DON, CHARLIE, *and* STEVE *race over to him.* STEVE *is there first and turns the man over. Now the crowd gathers around them.*]

Steve (*slowly looks up*). It's Pete Van Horn.

---

4. **ham radio:** two-way radio used by an amateur operator. Ham radio operators used to talk to one another all over the world via their radios.
5. **stifled** (stī′fəld) **cry:** cry that is checked or stopped.

Vocabulary
menace (men′əs) *n.:* danger; threat.

Don (*in a hushed voice*). Pete Van Horn! He was just gonna go over to the next block to see if the power was on—

Woman One. You killed him, Charlie. You shot him dead!

Charlie (*looks around at the circle of faces, his eyes frightened, his face contorted*). But . . . but I didn't know who he was. I certainly didn't know who he was. He comes walkin' out of the darkness—how am I supposed to know who he was? (*He grabs* STEVE.) Steve—you know why I shot! How was I supposed to know he wasn't a monster or something? (*He grabs* DON *now*.) We're all scared of the same thing. I was just tryin' to . . . tryin' to protect my home, that's all! Look, all of you, that's all I was tryin' to do. (*He looks down wildly at the body.*) I didn't know it was somebody we knew! I didn't know—

[*There's a sudden hush and then an intake of breath. We see the living room window of* CHARLIE*'s house. The window is not lit, but suddenly the house lights come on behind it.*]

Woman One (*in a very hushed voice*). Charlie . . . Charlie . . . the lights just went on in your house. Why did the lights just go on?

Don. What about it, Charlie? How come you're the only one with lights now?

Goodman. That's what I'd like to know.

[*There is a pause as they all stare toward* CHARLIE.]

You were so quick to kill, Charlie, and you were so quick to tell us who we had to be careful of. Well, maybe you had to kill. Maybe Peter there was trying to tell us something. Maybe he'd found out something and came back to tell us who there was amongst us we should watch out for— **7**

[CHARLIE *backs away from the group, his eyes wide with fright.*]

Charlie. No . . . no . . . it's nothing of the sort! I don't know why the lights are on. I swear I don't. Somebody's pulling a gag or something.

[*He bumps against* STEVE, *who grabs him and whirls him around.*]

Steve. A gag? A gag? Charlie, there's a dead man on the sidewalk and you killed him! Does this thing look like a gag to you?

[CHARLIE *breaks away and screams as he runs toward his house.*]

Charlie. No! No! Please!

[*A man breaks away from the crowd to chase* CHARLIE. *The man tackles him and lands on top of him. The other people start to run toward them.* CHARLIE *is up on his feet. He breaks away from the other man's grasp and lands a couple of desperate punches that push the man aside. Then he forces his way, fighting, through the crowd to once again break free. He jumps up on his front porch. A rock thrown from the group smashes a window alongside of him, the broken glass flying past him. A couple of pieces cut him. He stands there perspiring, rumpled, blood running down from a cut on his cheek. His wife breaks away from the group to throw herself into his arms. He buries his face against her. We can see the crowd* <u>converging</u> *on the porch now.*]

MAKE INFERENCES
7 What are the residents implying about Charlie? based on what evidence?

Voices.
It must have been him.
He's the one.
We got to get Charlie.

[*Another rock lands on the porch. Now* CHARLIE *pushes his wife behind him, facing the group.*]

Charlie. Look, look, I swear to you . . . it isn't me . . . but I do know who it is . . . I swear to you, I do know who it is. I know who the monster is here. I know who it is that doesn't belong. I swear to you I know.
Goodman (*shouting*). What are you waiting for?
Woman One (*shouting*). Come on, Charlie, come on.
Man One (*shouting*). Who is it, Charlie, tell us!
Don (*pushing his way to the front of the crowd*). All right, Charlie, let's hear it!

[CHARLIE's *eyes dart around wildly.*]

Charlie. It's . . . it's . . .
Man Two (*screaming*). Go ahead, Charlie, tell us.
Charlie. It's . . . it's the kid. It's Tommy. He's the one.

[*There's a gasp from the crowd as we cut to a shot of the mother holding her boy. The boy at first doesn't understand. Then, realizing the eyes are all on him, he buries his face against his mother,* SALLY.]

Sally (*backs away*). That's crazy. That's crazy. He's a little boy.
Woman One. But he knew! He was the only

Vocabulary
converging (kən·vʉrj′iŋ) *v.* used as *adj.:* closing in.

one who knew! He told us all about it. Well, how did he know? How could he have known?

[*The various people take this up and repeat the questions aloud.*]

Voices.
How could he know?
Who told him?
Make the kid answer.

Man One. What about Goodman's car?
Don. It was Charlie who killed old man Van Horn.
Woman One. But it was the kid here who knew what was going to happen all the time. He was the one who knew!

[STEVE *shouts at his hysterical neighbors.*]

Steve. Are you all gone crazy? (*Pause as he looks about*) Stop.

[*A fist crashes at* STEVE*'s face, staggering him back out of view. Several close camera shots suggest the coming of violence: A hand fires a rifle. A fist clenches. A hand grabs the hammer from* VAN HORN*'s body, etc.*]

Don. Charlie has to be the one— Where's my rifle—
Woman One. Les Goodman's the one. His car started! Let's wreck it.
Mrs. Goodman. What about Steve's radio— He's the one that called them—
Mr. Goodman. Smash the radio. Get me a hammer. Get me something.
Steve. Stop— Stop—
Charlie. Where's that kid— Let's get him.
Man One. Get Steve— Get Charlie— They're working together.

[*The crowd starts to converge around the*

MAKE INFERENCES
8 What inference have the residents made about Tommy?

mother, who grabs her son and starts to run with him. The crowd starts to follow, at first, walking fast, and then running after him. Suddenly, CHARLIE's lights go off and the lights in another house go on. They stay on for a moment, then from across the street other lights go on and then off again.]*

Man One (*shouting*). It isn't the kid. . . . It's Bob Weaver's house.
Woman One. It isn't Bob Weaver's house, it's Don Martin's place.
Charlie. I tell you, it's the kid.
Don. It's Charlie. He's the one.

[*The people shout, accuse, scream. The camera tilts back and forth. We see panic-stricken faces in close-up and tilting shots of houses as the lights go on and off. Slowly, in the middle of this nightmarish morass[6] of sight and sound, the camera starts to pull away, until once again we've reached the opening shot, looking at the Maple Street sign from high above. The camera continues to move away until we dissolve to a shot of the metal side of a spacecraft, which sits shrouded[7] in darkness. An open door throws out a beam of light from the illuminated interior. Two figures silhouetted against the bright lights appear. We get only a vague feeling of form, but nothing more explicit than that.*]

Figure One. Understand the procedure now? Just stop a few of their machines and radios

---

6. **morass** (mə·ras′) *n.*: confusing situation. Strictly speaking, a morass is a kind of swamp.

7. **shrouded** (shroud′id) *v.* used as *adj.*: hidden; covered.

Vocabulary
explicit (eks·plis′it) *adj.*: definite.

and telephones and lawn mowers . . . throw them into darkness for a few hours and then you just sit back and watch the pattern.

Figure Two. And this pattern is always the same?

Figure One. With few <u>variations</u>. They pick the most dangerous enemy they can find . . . and it's themselves. And all we need do is sit back . . . and watch.

Figure Two. Then I take it this place . . . this Maple Street . . . is not unique.

Figure One (*shaking his head*). By no means. Their world is full of Maple Streets. And we'll go from one to the other and let them destroy themselves. One to the other . . . one to the other . . . one to the other— **❾**

 MAKE INFERENCES

❾ What can you infer about the aliens' view of the human race?

[*Now the camera pans up for a shot of the starry sky.*]

Narrator's Voice. The tools of conquest do not necessarily come with bombs and explosions and fallout. There are weapons that are simply thoughts, attitudes, prejudices—to be found only in the minds of men. For the record, prejudices can kill and suspicion can destroy, and a thoughtless, frightened search for a scapegoat has a fallout all of its own for the children . . . the children yet unborn. (*A pause*) And the pity of it is . . . that these things cannot be confined to . . . The Twilight Zone!

[*Fade to black.*]

Vocabulary
variations (ver′ē·ā′shənz) *n.:* differences.

Meet the Writer

Rod Serling

Man from Another Dimension

Rod Serling (1924–1975) was a man of great energy. He had the vitality of one who seems to be running even as he is standing still.

How does a fledgling writer caught in a dreamless job get from Cincinnati, Ohio, to New York City and then to Hollywood? If you're Rod Serling, you one day look at your wife, and together you decide that the hour has come to sink or swim—the hour has come to go for it.

In the early 1950s, Rod Serling eagerly arrived in New York and found himself a job writing for television when it was new and young. He first wrote for a live half-hour drama called *Lux Video Theatre.* From there he went on to create and produce the hit television show *The Twilight Zone.*

In the fifth-dimensional world of the Twilight Zone, Serling made his concerns and beliefs visible. He sought to show his audiences that "there is nothing in the dark that isn't there when the lights are on." In his widely known teleplay *The Monsters Are Due on Maple Street*, he dramatized what was perhaps his most enduring and urgent theme.

The teleplay was written at a time when Americans were concerned about the spread of communism to the United States. Thousands of lives were destroyed by suspicion and suggestion. People lost their jobs, homes, and friends when they were accused of being members of the Communist party, even though membership in the party was legal. During this time some people made up stories about others in order to appear innocent themselves, and many people were afraid to continue friendships with those who had been accused or were suspected of being members of the Communist party. Rod Serling could not write about these events directly for television; the show would not have made it on the air. Yet in *The Monsters Are Due on Maple Street,* he does voice his opinion.

For Independent Reading

Enter the fifth dimension by checking out Rod Serling's *The Twilight Zone: Complete Stories.*

Acts One and Two

Thinking Critically

1. Choose three **inferences** you made as you read the teleplay. Were your inferences correct? Explain.

2. Writers often speak through a particular character to voice their own opinions. Which character do you think reflects Rod Serling's **point of view**? Find at least two speeches that reveal that point of view.

3. In light of Les Goodman's behavior throughout the plot, what **inference** can you make about the significance of his name?

4. **Symbols** in literature are persons, places, or things that function as themselves but that can also stand for larger ideas, such as love, glory, or honor. When Maple Street loses power and is plunged into darkness, terrible events unfold. This loss of power is also a symbol for a larger idea. What personal power, or ability, do the residents of Maple Street lose that plunges them further into darkness?

5. According to the aliens, who is the most dangerous enemy? Who do you think are the "monsters" in this story?

Reading Check

Fill out a chart like the one below to show the bare bones of the play's **plot.** Be sure to compare your charts in class. You might have different opinions about the number of key events, or **complications,** that lead to the surprising resolution.

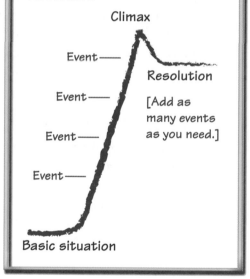

Extending Interpretations

6. This teleplay was written in 1960. Is its message still important today? Explain why or why not.

WRITING ABOUT THE TELEPLAY

Responding to a Text

What message does the play deliver about humankind? How do
the events of the teleplay illustrate this message? In a two-
paragraph essay, write your response to this play. In one
paragraph, explain the meaning of the closing comments in light
of the events of this teleplay. In the second paragraph, tell how
you feel about the message in the play, and explain how the
message still has significance in today's world (unless you believe
otherwise!).

Updating the Teleplay

Suppose you are a television producer and you want to update the
teleplay so that it takes place in 2010. In a paragraph, tell how you
would change details of the play to set it in the new time frame.
Consider these details:

- What do people now know about aliens and space travel?

- What electronic equipment would be affected by the blackout?

- Where would the aliens land (would you keep a small town as
  your setting or would you set the revised story in a suburb or
  a city)?

- What would Tommy be reading today?

Act Two

Clarifying Word Meanings: Definitions

Sharpen your definition-hunting skills with the following exercise.

PRACTICE

Choose the word from the Word Bank that best fits the blank in each sentence below. Remember to look for definitions within each sentence to help you decide. Be ready to cite the definition you found in the sentence.

1. Wherever the aliens go, the human beings react the same: There are few differences, few changes, few _____.

2. During the second act the crowd's fear, mistrust, and suspicion are meeting, or _____, to create a mob.

3. An _____ danger is by its nature knowable and understandable.

4. A frightened man with a gun can be considered a _____ and a danger to society.

5. Steve's interest in ham radios becomes a threat rather than an oddity, or _____, that makes him unique.

Word Bank

idiosyncrasy
menace
converging
explicit
variations

SKILLS FOCUS

Vocabulary Skills
Clarify word meanings by using definitions.

Understanding Text Structures: An Owner's Manual

Reading Focus
Structure and Purpose of an Instructional Manual

For the residents of Maple Street, not even cell phones might have been helpful against the aliens' powers. However, a cell phone might be just the kind of device to get you out of a crisis—if you know how to use one, that is.

The **purpose** of an instructional manual is to help you operate and care for a specific device, such as a cordless phone or a hand-held Internet appliance. Many instructional manuals have a **structure** like that of a small textbook.

Use these strategies in order to make the best use of an instructional manual:

- Scan the **table of contents** of the manual to get an idea of the topics covered.

- If you don't see the topic you're looking for, turn to the **index,** located in the back of the manual. This is an alphabetical list of the topics and the page numbers on which they appear.

- Look for a regular mail address and an **e-mail address** as well as a customer service **phone number** or **Web site** where you can get additional help from the manufacturer.

- Become familiar with the parts of the device. An instructional manual usually includes a **diagram** showing you the important parts of the device and explaining their functions.

- Read the **directions** carefully, and keep referring to the actual device as you read.

- Do the directions have **steps**? Follow them in order. Read all the directions for a procedure before you move on to the next one.

- Make sure you understand any special abbreviations or symbols. You may find definitions and meanings in the manual's **glossary**—an alphabetical list of special terms and their definitions.

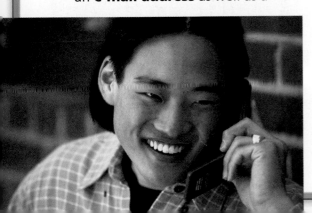

■ With all the electronic products available today, it's useful to know how to read an instructional manual like the one on page 82.

SKILLS FOCUS

Reading Skills
Understand the structure and purpose of an instructional manual.

Cellular Telephone Owner's Manual

Battery Removal and Replacement

There are two ways to remove and replace your telephone battery—the standard method and the quick-change method.

Standard Method

1. Turn off your telephone.
2. Depress the latch button on the rear of the battery, and slide the battery pack downward until it stops.
3. Lift the battery clear to remove.
4. To reinstall, place the battery pack on the unit so that its grooves align, and slide upward (in the direction of the arrows on the back of the phone) until it clicks into place.

Quick-Change Method

1. Advise the party you are talking to that you are about to change batteries.
2. Remove the battery from the telephone.
3. Put on the spare battery.
4. Press PWR. This will return you to your telephone call. You will have only five seconds to complete this action before your telephone call is terminated.

The quick-change method allows you to remove your telephone battery at any time and replace it with a charged spare battery during a telephone call. This is especially useful if you receive the "low battery" message (or an audible tone) during a call.

It is a good idea to practice this procedure a few times before using it during an actual phone call.

Analyzing an Owner's Manual

Cellular Telephone Owner's Manual

Test Practice

1. The **main topic** of the section of the manual on page 82 is —
   A removing and replacing the battery
   B making and receiving calls
   C using the phone to send e-mail
   D using the phone in out-of-state networks

2. In which part of the manual would you look to find the pages on which the topic of ringer volume appears?
   F Diagram
   G Glossary
   H Index
   J Cover

3. In which part of the manual would you look to find the meaning of the abbreviation of *LCD*?
   A Table of contents
   B Glossary
   C Index
   D Cover

4. The first step in the standard method is to —
   F remove the battery
   G tell the person you're speaking with to call back
   H turn off the phone
   J turn off the "low battery" message

5. The first step in the quick-change method is to —
   A put in the spare battery
   B remove the battery
   C tell the person you're speaking with that you're going to change the battery
   D ask the person you're speaking with to call you back after you've changed the battery

6. After you put in the spare battery using the quick-change method, your call will be terminated unless you —
   F press PWR within five seconds
   G deposit twenty-five cents
   H charge the telephone battery
   J press 0 for further assistance

Constructed Response

Use the chart to the right to compare these informational materials: newspaper articles, textbooks, and instructional manuals

Material	Purpose	Structure
Newspaper articles		
Textbooks		
Instructional manuals		

SKILLS FOCUS

Reading Skills
Analyze the structure and purpose of an instructional manual.

Comparing Literature

Literary Focus
Science Fiction

You're about to read and compare two science fiction stories. **Science fiction** is a kind of writing that lies somewhere between realistic fiction and total fantasy. It is usually set in the future in a world different from our own, but it is not a kind of writing in which anything goes. Science fiction is based on scientific laws. Most writers of science fiction use their knowledge of the latest scientific ideas and discoveries to imagine new technology that might someday be developed. They also use their understanding of human psychology to imagine how people might behave in situations involving that new technology.

The best of science fiction appeals to our intelligence and also to our imagination, to our sense of awe and wonder at being a part of a mysterious and unknown universe.

Reading Skills
Comparing and Contrasting

Although "Zoo" and "The Ruum" are very different stories, they have interesting similarities. To compare and contrast the two stories, you might look at the ways each story uses the elements of science fiction. When you **compare,** you look for ways that things are alike. When you **contrast,** you look for ways that things are different.

Elements of Science Fiction

Most science fiction stories contain some or all of the following elements:

- **a setting in the future,** often on another planet or in a spaceship
- **technology** that has not yet been invented, but that conforms to the rules of science
- **a journey through time** or to a distant planet or galaxy
- **imaginary characters** from outer space—alien or extraterrestrial creatures
- realistic human reactions to **fantastic situations**
- **a surprise ending**

SKILLS FOCUS

Literary Skills
Understand the elements of science fiction.

Reading Skills
Compare and contrast stories.

Before You Read

You've probably been to a zoo to see the animals. You may have stood in front of the animals' cages and commented on their strange features, their enormous size, or the curious way they chew their food. Have you ever wondered what these animals are thinking as they look at you?

Zoo

Edward D. Hoch

The children were always good during the month of August, especially when it began to get near the twenty-third. It was on this day that Professor Hugo's Interplanetary Zoo settled down for its annual six-hour visit to the Chicago area. ❶

Before daybreak the crowds would form, long lines of children and adults both, each one clutching his or her dollar and waiting with wonderment to see what race of strange creatures the professor had brought this year.

In the past they had sometimes been treated to three-legged creatures from Venus, or tall, thin men from Mars, or even snake-like horrors from somewhere more distant. This year, as the great round ship settled slowly to earth in the huge tri-city parking area just outside of Chicago, they watched with awe as the sides slowly slid up to reveal the familiar barred cages. In them were some wild breed of nightmare—small, horselike animals that moved with quick, jerking motions and constantly chattered in a high-pitched tongue. The citizens of Earth clustered around as Professor Hugo's crew quickly collected the waiting dollars, and soon the good professor himself made an appearance, wearing his many-colored rainbow cape and top hat. "Peoples of Earth," he called into his microphone. ❷

The crowd's noise died down and he continued. "Peoples of Earth, this year you see a real treat for your single dollar—the little-known horse-spider people of Kaan—brought to you across a million miles of space at great expense. Gather around, see them,

IDENTIFY

❶ What clue in this first paragraph suggests that this story is **science fiction**?

COMPARE AND CONTRAST

❷ "Zoo" is set on Earth sometime in the future. How is life in this future like and unlike life today?

COMPARE AND CONTRAST

❸ How do people react to the horse-spiders of Kaan? How are their reactions similar to the way people today react to animals at a zoo?

study them, listen to them, tell your friends about them. But hurry! My ship can remain here only six hours!"

And the crowds slowly filed by, at once horrified and fascinated by these strange creatures that looked like horses but ran up the walls of their cages like spiders. "This is certainly worth a dollar," one man remarked, hurrying away. "I'm going home to get the wife." ❸

All day long it went like that, until ten thousand people had filed by the barred cages set into the side of the spaceship. Then, as the six-hour limit ran out, Professor Hugo once more took the microphone in hand. "We must go now, but we will return next year on this date. And if you enjoyed our zoo this year, telephone your friends in other cities about it. We will land in New York tomorrow, and next week on to London, Paris, Rome, Hong Kong, and Tokyo. Then on to other worlds!"

He waved farewell to them, and as the ship rose from the ground, the Earth peoples agreed that this had been the very best Zoo yet. . . .

Some two months and three planets later, the silver ship of Professor Hugo settled at last onto the familiar jagged rocks of Kaan, and the odd horse-spider creatures filed quickly out of their cages. Professor Hugo was there to say a few parting words, and then they scurried away in a hundred different directions, seeking their homes among the rocks.

In one house, the she-creature was happy to see the return of her mate and offspring. She babbled a greeting in the strange tongue and hurried to embrace them. "It was a long time you were gone! Was it good?"

And the he-creature nodded. "The little one enjoyed it especially. We visited eight worlds and saw many things."

The little one ran up the wall of the cave. "On the place called Earth it was the best. The creatures there wear garments over their skins, and they walk on two legs."

"But isn't it dangerous?" asked the she-creature.

"No," her mate answered. "There are bars to protect us from them. We remain right in the ship. Next time you must come with us. It is well worth the nineteen commocs it costs." **4**

And the little one nodded. "It was the very best zoo ever. . . ." **5**

EVALUATE

4 What do you learn when you hear the horse-spiders speak?

INTERPRET

5 This story's tricky ending makes us reconsider the rest of the story. What do you learn about the zoo in Chicago after you read the second part of the story set in Kaan?

Meet the Writer

Edward D. Hoch

Edward D. Hoch (1930–   ), whose last name rhymes with "coke," was born in Rochester, New York. He became a full-time writer in 1968, publishing novels and short stories and editing collections in the fields of mystery, crime, suspense, science fiction, and fantasy. Hoch contributed more than 750 short stories to periodicals such as *Argosy, Ellery Queen's Mystery Magazine,* and *Alfred Hitchcock's Mystery Magazine.* This prolific mystery writer is a bit of a mystery himself. To find all of his work

you also have to search under his many pseudonyms, such as Irwin Booth, Anthony Circus, Stephen Dentinger, Pat McMahon, Mister X, R. E. Porter, and R. L. Stevens. Many consider Hoch to be the finest writer of short mystery fiction, and in 2001, he won the Edgar Allan Poe Grand Master Award. Two of his stories won awards—"The Oblong Room" won the Edgar Allan Poe Award for best mystery short story in 1967, and "The Problem of the Potting Shed" won the Anthony Award for best short story in 2001—and fourteen of his stories were adapted for television.

First Thoughts

1. Respond to "Zoo" by completing one of the following sentences:
   - I thought this story was . . .
   - What surprised me most about the story was . . .

Thinking Critically

2. This story has two parts and two **settings.** What if the first part of "Zoo" were set on Kaan and the second part set on Earth? How would this change the story?

3. The **plot** of this story has a tricky ending, which makes us reconsider the rest of the story. Do you find any flaws in the story—do some details in the story not make sense to you? Write down your questions, and see if you can answer them in a group discussion.

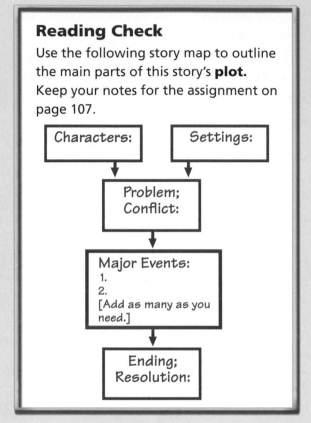

Reading Check

Use the following story map to outline the main parts of this story's **plot.** Keep your notes for the assignment on page 107.

Characters: Settings:

Problem; Conflict:

Major Events:
1.
2.
[Add as many as you need.]

Ending; Resolution:

Comparing Literature

4. After you've read the next story, you'll have an opportunity to write a comparison-contrast essay. You can begin to plan your essay by filling out a chart like the one below focusing on the story "Zoo." This chart will be repeated with "The Ruum" on page 106, where you'll add details about that story.

Comparing Science Fiction Stories		
	"Zoo"	"The Ruum"
Human characters		
Alien characters		
Journey through space		
Futuristic technology		
Lesson about life		

SKILLS FOCUS

Literary Skills
Analyze the elements of science fiction.

Reading Skills
Compare and contrast stories.

Before You Read

In "The Ruum" you will find a journey through eons of time, an indestructible nightmare machine set loose by a galactic spaceship commander, and a brave hero.

Like writers of mystery and crime stories, writers of science fiction often drop clues as their stories unfold. Every detail in this story is important. Pay attention to the dynamite, the rifle, the pistol, and the use of numbers.

The Ruum

Arthur Porges

The cruiser *Ilkor* had just gone into her interstellar overdrive beyond the orbit of Pluto when a worried officer reported to the commander.

"Excellency," he said uneasily, "I regret to inform you that because of a technician's carelessness a Type H-9 Ruum has been left behind on the third planet, together with anything it may have collected."

The commander's triangular eyes hooded momentarily, but when he spoke his voice was level.

"How was the ruum set?"

"For a maximum radius of thirty miles, and 160 pounds plus or minus 15." ❶

There was silence for several seconds; then the commander said: "We cannot reverse course now. In a few weeks we'll be returning and can pick up the ruum then. I do not care to have one of those costly, self-energizing models charged against my ship. You will see," he ordered coldly, "that the individual responsible is severely punished."

But at the end of its run, in the neighborhood of Rigel, the carrier met a flat, ring-shaped raider; and when the inevitable firefight was over, both ships, semimolten, radioactive, and laden with dead, were starting a billion-year orbit around the star.

And on the earth, it was the age of reptiles. ❷

IDENTIFY

❶ This writer drops clues for you to notice and then interpret. Look for the clues to answer these questions: Where is the *Ilkor*? Is the commander of the *Ilkor* human? What is a ruum, and what is its purpose?

IDENTIFY

❷ What was the result of the battle between the *Ilkor* and the raider? When in history did the battle take place?

Comparing Literature

INFER

❸ About how much time has passed since the *Ilkor* left the ruum behind?

IDENTIFY

❹ Where is Jim Irwin? What is he hoping to find?

When the two men had unloaded the last of the supplies, Jim Irwin watched his partner climb into the little seaplane. He waved at Walt. ❸

"Don't forget to mail that letter to my wife," Jim shouted.

"The minute I land," Walt Leonard called back, starting to rev the engine. "And you find us some uranium—a strike is just what Cele needs. A fortune for your son and her, hey?" His white teeth flashed in a grin. "Don't rub noses with any grizzlies—shoot 'em, but don't scare 'em to death!"

Jim thumbed his nose as the seaplane speeded up, leaving a frothy wake. He felt a queer chill as the amphibian took off. For three weeks he would be isolated in this remote valley of the Canadian Rockies. If for any reason the plane failed to return to the icy blue lake, he would surely die. Even with enough food, no man could surmount the frozen peaks and make his way on foot over hundreds of miles of almost virgin wilderness. But, of course, Walt Leonard would return on schedule, and it was up to Jim whether or not they lost their stake. If there was any uranium in the valley, he had twenty-one days to find it. To work then, and no gloomy forebodings. ❹

> **If for any reason the plane failed to return to the icy blue lake, he would surely die.**

Moving with the unhurried precision of an experienced woodsman, he built a lean-to in the shelter of a rocky overhang. For this three weeks of summer, nothing more permanent was needed. Perspiring in the strong morning sun, he piled his supplies back under the ledge, well covered by a waterproof tarpaulin and protected from the larger animal prowlers. All but the dynamite; that he cached,[1] also carefully wrapped against moisture, two hundred yards away. Only a fool shares his quarters with a box of high explosives.

The first two weeks went by all too swiftly, without any encouraging finds. There was only one good possibility left, and just enough time to explore it. So early one morning toward the end of his third week, Jim Irwin prepared for a last-ditch foray into the northeast part of the valley, a region he had not yet visited.

He took the Geiger counter, slipping on the earphones, reversed to keep the normal rattle from dulling his hearing, and reaching

---

1. **cached** (kasht) *v.*: hid; stored.

for the rifle, set out, telling himself it was now or never so far as this particular expedition was concerned. The bulky .30-06 was a nuisance and he had no enthusiasm for its weight, but the huge grizzlies of Canada are not intruded upon with impunity, and take a lot of killing. He'd already had to dispose of two, a hateful chore, since the big bears were vanishing all too fast. And the rifle had proved a great comfort on several ticklish occasions when actual firing had been avoided. The .22 pistol he left in its sheepskin holster in the lean-to.

He was whistling at the start, for the clear, frosty air, the bright sun on blue-white ice fields, and the heady smell of summer all delighted his heart despite his bad luck as a prospector. He planned to go one day's journey to the new region, spend about thirty-six hours exploring it intensively, and be back in time to meet the plane at noon. Except for his emergency packet, he took no food or water. It would be easy enough to knock over a rabbit, and the streams were alive with firm-fleshed rainbow trout of the kind no longer common in the States.

All morning Jim walked, feeling an occasional surge of hope as the counter chattered. But its chatter always died down. The valley had nothing radioactive of value, only traces. Apparently they'd made a bad choice. His cheerfulness faded. They needed a strike badly, especially Walt. And his own wife, Cele, with a kid on the way. But there was still a chance. These last thirty-six hours—he'd snoop at night, if necessary—might be the payoff. He reflected a little bitterly that it would help quite a bit if some of those birds he'd staked would make a strike and return his dough. Right this minute there were close to eight thousand bucks owing to him.

A wry smile touched his lips, and he abandoned unprofitable speculations for plans about lunch. The sun, as well as his stomach, said it was time. He had just decided to take out his line and fish a foaming brook when he rounded a grassy knoll to come upon a sight that made him stiffen to a halt, his jaw dropping.

It was like some enterprising giant's outdoor butcher shop: a great assortment of animal bodies, neatly lined up in a triple row that extended almost as far as the eye could see. And what animals! To be sure, those nearest to him were ordinary deer, bear, cougars, and mountain sheep—one of each, apparently—but down the line were strange, uncouth, half-formed, hairy beasts, and beyond them a nightmare conglomeration of reptiles. One of the latter, at the extreme end of the remarkable display, he recognized at once.

INTERPRET

❺ What is so surprising about this collection of animals?

COMPARE AND CONTRAST

❻ How is the ruum's collection of animals like a zoo's? Compare Jim's response to these animals with the way the people on Earth respond to creatures in the Interplanetary Zoo in the story on page 85.

INFER

❼ On page 89, re-read how the ruum was set. How might its settings explain the similarity in size of the animals in the ruum's collection? What can you infer about Jim Irwin based on this knowledge?

There had been a much larger specimen, fabricated about an incomplete skeleton, of course, in the museum at home. ❺

No doubt about it—it was a small stegosaur,[2] no bigger than a pony!

Fascinated, Jim walked down the line, glancing back over the immense array. Peering more closely at one scaly, dirty-yellow lizard, he saw an eyelid tremble. Then he realized the truth. The animals were not dead, but paralyzed and miraculously preserved. Perspiration prickled his forehead. How long since stegosaurs had roamed this valley? ❻

All at once he noticed another curious circumstance: The victims were roughly of a size. Nowhere, for example, was there a really large saurian.[3] No tyrannosaurus. For that matter, no mammoth. Each specimen was about the size of a large sheep. He was pondering this odd fact when the underbrush rustled a warning behind him.

Jim Irwin had once worked with mercury, and for a second it seemed to him that a half-filled leather sack of the liquid metal had rolled into the clearing. For the quasi-spherical[4] object moved with just such a weighty, fluid motion. But it was not leather, and what appeared at first a disgusting wartiness turned out on closer scrutiny to be more like the functional projections of some outlandish mechanism. Whatever the thing was, he had little time to study it, for after the spheroid had whipped out and retracted a number of metal rods with bulbous, lenslike structures at their tips, it rolled toward him at a speed of about five miles an hour. And from its purposeful advance, the man had no doubts that it meant to add him to the pathetic heap of living-dead specimens. ❼

Uttering an incoherent exclamation, Jim sprang back a number of paces, unslinging his rifle. The ruum that had been left behind was still some thirty yards off, approaching at that moderate but invariable velocity, an advance more terrifying in its regularity than the headlong charge of a mere brute beast.

Jim's hand flew to the bolt, and with practiced deftness he slammed a cartridge into the chamber. He snuggled the battered stock against his cheek and, using the peep sight, aimed squarely at the leathery bulk—a perfect target in the bright afternoon sun.

---

2. **stegosaur** (steg′ə·sôr′) *n.*: dinosaur with a small head and heavy, bony plates on its back.
3. **saurian** (sôr′ē·ən) *n.*: lizard; here, dinosaur.
4. **quasi-spherical** (kwā′zī·sfer′i·kəl) *adj.*: shaped somewhat like a ball, or sphere.

intent on the footprints of its prey, the strange sphere rippled along, passing directly under the great boulder. As it did so, Irwin gave a savage yell and, thrusting his whole muscular weight against the balanced mass, toppled it squarely on the ruum. Five tons of stone fell from a height of twelve feet.

Jim scrambled down. He stood there, staring at the huge lump and shaking his head dazedly. He gave the boulder a kick. "Hah! Wait and I might clear a buck or two yet from your little meat market. Maybe this expedition won't be a total loss. Enjoy yourself in hell where you came from!"

Then he leapt back, his eyes wild. The giant rock was shifting! Slowly its five-ton bulk was sliding off the trail, raising a ridge of soil as it grated along. Even as he stared, the boulder tilted, and a gray protuberance appeared under the nearest edge. With a choked cry, Jim Irwin broke into a lurching run.

He ran a full mile down the trail. Then, finally, he stopped and looked back. He could just make out a dark dot moving away from the fallen rock. It progressed as slowly and as regularly and as inexorably as before, and in his direction. Jim sat down heavily, putting his head in his scratched, grimy hands.

But that despairing mood did not last. After all, he had gained a twenty-minute respite. Lying down, trying to relax as much as possible, he took the flat packet of emergency rations from his jacket and, eating quickly but without bolting, disposed of some pemmican, biscuit, and chocolate. A few sips of icy water from a streamlet, and he was almost ready to continue his fantastic struggle. When the ruum was still an estimated ten minutes away, Jim Irwin trotted off, much of his wiry strength back, and fresh courage to counter bone-deep weariness. ❿

After running for fifteen minutes, he came to a sheer face of rock about thirty feet high. The terrain on either side was barely passable, consisting of choked gullies, spiky brush, and knife-edged rocks. If Jim could make the top of this little cliff, the ruum sure would have to detour, a circumstance that might put it many minutes behind him.

He looked up at the sun. Huge and crimson, it was almost touching the horizon. He would have to move fast. Irwin was no rock climber but he did know the fundamentals. Using every crevice, roughness, and minute ledge, he found his way up the cliff. Somehow—unconsciously—he used that flowing climb of a natural mountaineer, which takes each foothold very briefly as an unstressed pivot point in a series of rhythmic advances.

He had just reached the top when the ruum rolled up to the base of the cliff.

Jim knew very well that he ought to leave at once, taking advantage of the few precious remaining moments of daylight. Every second gained was of tremendous value, but curiosity and hope made him wait. He told himself that the instant his pursuer detoured, he would get out of there all the faster. Besides, the thing might even give up and he could sleep right here.

Sleep! His body lusted for it.

But the ruum would not detour. It hesitated only a few seconds at the foot of the barrier. Then a number of knobs opened to extrude metallic wands. One of these, topped with lenses, waved in the air. Jim drew back too late—their uncanny gaze had found him as he lay atop the cliff, peering down. He cursed his idiocy. ⑪

Immediately all the wands retracted, and from a different knob a slender rod, blood-red in the setting sun, began to shoot straight up to the man. As he watched, frozen in place, its barbed tip gripped the cliff's edge almost under his nose.

Jim leapt to his feet. Already the rod was shortening as the ruum reabsorbed its shining length. And the leathery sphere was rising off the ground. Swearing loudly, Jim fixed his eyes on the tenacious hook, drawing back one heavy foot.

But experience restrained him. The mighty kick was never launched. He had seen too many rough-and-tumbles lost by an injudicious attempt at the boot. It wouldn't do at all to let any part of his body get within reach of the ruum's superb tools. Instead he seized a length of dry branch and, inserting one end under the metal hook, began to pry.

There was a sputtering flash, white and lacy, and even through the dry wood he felt the potent surge of power that splintered the end. He dropped the smoldering stick with a gasp of pain and, wringing his numb fingers, backed off several steps, full of impotent rage. For a moment he paused, half inclined to run again, but then his upper lip drew back and, snarling, he unslung his rifle. He knew he had been right to lug the thing all this way—even if it had beat a tattoo on his ribs. Now he had the ruum right where he wanted it!

Kneeling to steady his aim in the failing light, Jim sighted at the hook and fired. There was a soggy thud as the ruum fell. Jim shouted. The heavy slug had done a lot more than he expected.

INTERPRET

⑪ What mistake does Jim make? What is the result of his mistake?

Not only had it blasted the metal claw loose, but it had smashed a big gap in the cliff's edge. It would be pretty damned hard for the ruum to use that part of the rock again!

He looked down. Sure enough, the ruum was back at the bottom. Jim Irwin grinned. Every time the thing clamped a hook over the bluff, he'd blow that hook loose. There was plenty of ammunition in his pocket, and until the moon rose, bringing a good light for shooting with, he'd stick the gun's muzzle inches away if necessary. Besides, the thing—whatever it might be—was obviously too intelligent to keep up a hopeless struggle. Sooner or later it would accept the detour. And then, maybe the night would help to hide his trail.

Then—he choked and, for a brief moment, tears came to his eyes. Down below, in the dimness, the squat, phlegmatic[7] spheroid was extruding three hooked rods simultaneously in a fanlike spread. In a perfectly coordinated movement, the rods snagged the cliff's edge at intervals of about four feet.

Jim Irwin whipped the rifle to his shoulder. All right—this was going to be just like the rapid fire for record back at Benning.[8] Only, at Benning, they didn't expect good shooting in the dark!

But the first shot was a bull's-eye, smacking the left-hand hook loose in a puff of rock dust. His second shot did almost as well, knocking the gritty stuff loose so the center barb slipped off. But even as he whirled to level at number three, Jim saw it was hopeless.

The first hook was back in place. No matter how well he shot, at least one rod would always be in position, pulling the ruum to the top.

Jim hung the useless rifle muzzle down from a stunted tree and ran into the deepening dark. The toughening of his body, a process of years, was paying off now. So what? Where was he going? What could he do now? Was there anything that could stop that thing behind him?

Then he remembered the dynamite.

Gradually changing his course, the weary man cut back toward his camp by the lake. Overhead the stars brightened, pointing the

> Now he had the ruum right where he wanted it!

---

7. **phlegmatic** (fleg·mat′ik) *adj.*: calm; impassive.
8. **Benning:** Fort Benning, Georgia, a U.S. Army post.

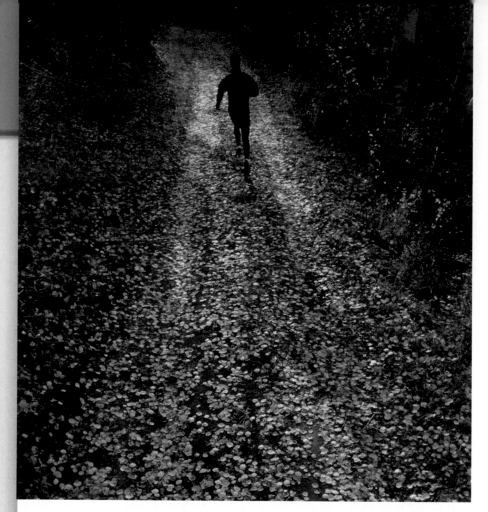

way. Jim lost all sense of time. He must have eaten as he wobbled along, for he wasn't hungry. Maybe he could eat at the lean-to . . . no, there wouldn't be time. The moon was up and he could hear the ruum close behind. Close.

Quite often phosphorescent[9] eyes peered at him from the underbrush and once, just at dawn, a grizzly woofed with displeasure at his passage.

Sometimes during the night his wife, Cele, stood before him with outstretched arms. "Go away!" he rasped; "go away! You can make it! It can't chase both of us!" So she turned and ran lightly alongside of him. But when Irwin panted across a tiny glade, Cele faded away into the moonlight and he realized she hadn't been there at all. ⓬

Shortly after sunrise Jim Irwin reached the lake. The ruum was close enough for him to hear the dull sounds of its passage. Jim

INFER

⓬ What does this hallucination suggest about Jim's mental and physical state?

___

9. **phosphorescent** (fäs′fə·res′ənt) *adj.*: glowing.

staggered, his eyes closed. He hit himself feebly on the nose, his eyes jerked open, and he saw the explosive. The sight of the greasy sticks of dynamite snapped Irwin wide awake.

He forced himself to calmness and carefully considered what to do. Fuse? No. It would be impossible to leave fused dynamite in the trail and time the detonation with the absolute precision he needed. Sweat poured down his body; his clothes were sodden with it. It was hard to think. The explosion must be set off from a distance and at the exact moment the ruum was passing over it. But Irwin dared not use a long fuse. The rate of burning was not constant enough. Couldn't calibrate[10] it perfectly with the ruum's advance. Jim Irwin's body sagged all over; his chin sank toward his heaving chest. He jerked his head up, stepped back—and saw the .22 pistol where he had left it in the lean-to.

His sunken eyes flashed.

Moving with frenetic haste, he took the half-filled case, piled all the remaining percussion caps among the loose sticks in a devil's mixture. Weaving out to the trail, he carefully placed box and contents directly on his earlier tracks some twenty yards from a rocky ledge. It was a risk—the stuff might go anytime—but that didn't matter. He would far rather be blown to rags than end up living but paralyzed in the ruum's outdoor butcher's stall. **13**

The exhausted Irwin had barely hunched down behind the thin ledge of rock before his inexorable pursuer appeared over a slight rise five hundred yards away. Jim scrunched deeper into the hollow, then saw a vertical gap, a narrow crack between rocks. That was it, he thought vaguely. He could sight through the gap at the dynamite and still be shielded from the blast. If it was a shield . . . when that half-caste blew only twenty yards away . . .

He stretched out on his belly, watching the ruum roll forward. A hammer of exhaustion pounded his ballooning skull. When had he slept last? This was the first time he had lain down in hours. Hours? Ha! It was days. His muscles stiffened, locked into throbbing, burning knots. Then he felt the morning sun on his back, soothing, warming, easing. . . . No! If he let go, if he slept now, it was the ruum's macabre collection for Jim Irwin! Stiff fingers tightened around the pistol. He'd stay awake! If he lost—if the ruum survived the blast—there'd still be time to put a bullet through his brain.

He looked down at the sleek pistol, then out at the innocent-

PREDICT

13 Describe Jim's new plan to stop the ruum, and predict whether his plan will work.

---

10. **calibrate** (kal′ə·brāt′) *v.*: measure; here, time.

seeming booby trap. If he timed this right—and he would—
the ruum wouldn't survive. No. He relaxed a little, yielding just a
bit to the gently insistent sun. A bird whistled softly somewhere
above him and a fish splashed in the lake.

Suddenly he was wrenched to full awareness. Of all times for a
grizzly to come snooping about! With the whole of Irwin's camp
ready for greedy looting, a fool bear had to come sniffing around
the dynamite! The furred monster smelled carefully at the box,
nosed around, rumbled deep displeasure at the alien scent of man.
Irwin held his breath. Just a touch would blow a cap. A single
cap meant . . .

The grizzly lifted his head from the box and growled hoarsely.
The box was ignored; the offensive odor of man was forgotten. Its
feral[11] little eyes focused on a plodding spheroid that was now only
forty yards away. Jim Irwin snickered. Until he had met the ruum,
the grizzly bear of the North American continent was the only
thing in the world he had ever feared. And now—why was he so
calm about it?—the two terrors of his existence were meeting
head-on and he was laughing. He shook his head and the great side
muscles in his neck hurt abominably. He looked down at his pistol,
then out at the dynamite. These were the only real things in
his world.

About six feet from the bear, the ruum paused. Still in the grip
of that almost idiotic detachment, Jim Irwin found himself wondering again what it was, where it had come from. The grizzly
arose on its haunches, the embodiment of utter ferocity. Terrible
teeth flashed white against red lips. The business-like ruum started
to roll past. The bear closed in, roaring. It cuffed at the ruum. A
mighty paw, armed with black claws sharper and stronger than
scythes, made that cuff. It would have disemboweled a rhinoceros.
Irwin cringed as that sideswipe knocked dust from the leathery
sphere. The ruum was hurled back several inches. It paused, recovered, and with the same dreadful casualness it rippled on, making
a wider circle, ignoring the bear. **14**

But the lord of the woods wasn't settling for any draw. Moving
with that incredible agility which has terrified Indians, Spanish,
French, and Anglo-Americans since the first encounter of any of
them with his species, the grizzly whirled, sidestepped beautifully,
and hugged the ruum. The terrible, shaggy forearms tightened; the

INTERPRET

14 Think back to what
you know about the
ruum's origin. What
fact explains why the
ruum ignores the
grizzly's attack?

---

11. **feral** (fir′əl) *adj.*: wild.

slavering jaws champed at the gray surface. Irwin half rose. "Go it!" he croaked. Even as he cheered the clumsy emperor of the wild, Jim thought it was an insane tableau: the village idiot wrestling with a beach ball.

Then silver metal gleamed bright against gray. There was a flash, swift and deadly. The roar of the king abruptly became a whimper, a gurgle, and then there was nearly a ton of terror wallowing in death—its throat slashed open. Jim Irwin saw the bloody blade retract into the gray spheroid, leaving a bright red smear on the thing's dusty hide.

And the ruum rolled forward past the giant corpse, implacable, still intent on the man's spoor, his footprints, his pathway. OK, baby, Jim giggled at the deadly grizzly, this is for you, for Cele, for—lots of poor dumb animals like us—come to, you fool, he cursed at himself. And aimed at the dynamite. And very calmly, very carefully, Jim Irwin squeezed the trigger of his pistol.

Briefly, sound first. Then giant hands lifted his body from where he lay, then let go. He came down hard, face in a patch of nettles, but he was sick, he didn't care. He remembered that the birds were quiet. Then there was a fluid thump as something massive struck the grass a few yards away. Then there was quiet.

Irwin lifted his head . . . All men do in such a case. His body still ached. He lifted sore shoulders and saw . . . an enormous smoking crater in the earth. He also saw, a dozen paces away, gray-white because it was covered now with powdered rock, the ruum.

It was under a tall, handsome pine tree. Even as Jim watched, wondering if the ringing in his ears would ever stop, the ruum rolled toward him.

Irwin fumbled for his pistol. It was gone. It had dropped somewhere, out of reach. He wanted to pray, then, but couldn't get properly started. Instead, he kept thinking idiotically, "My sister Ethel can't spell Nebuchadnezzar[12] and never could. My sister Ethel—"

The ruum was a foot away now, and Jim closed his eyes. He felt cool, metallic fingers touch, grip, lift. His unresisting body was raised several inches, and juggled oddly. Shuddering, he waited for the terrible syringe with its green liquid, seeing the yellow, shrunken face of a lizard with one eyelid a-tremble.

Then, dispassionately, without either roughness or solicitude,

---

12. **Nebuchadnezzar** (neb′yə•kəd•nez′ər): king of ancient Babylonia.

the ruum put him back on the ground. When he opened his eyes, some seconds later, the sphere was rolling away. Watching it go, he sobbed drily.

It seemed a matter of moments only before he heard the seaplane's engine and opened his eyes to see Walt Leonard bending over him.

Later in the plane, five thousand feet above the valley, Walt grinned suddenly, slapped him on the back, and cried: "Jim, I can get a whirlybird, a four-place job! Why, if we can snatch up just a few of those prehistoric lizards and things while the museum keeper's away, it's like you said—the scientists will pay us plenty."

Jim's hollow eyes lit up. "That's the idea," he agreed. Then, bitterly, "I might just as well have stayed in bed. Evidently the thing didn't want me at all. Maybe it wanted to know what I paid for these pants! Barely touched me, then let go. And how I ran!"

"Yeah," Walt said. "That was queer. And after that marathon. I admire your guts, boy." He glanced sideways at Jim Irwin's haggard face. "That night's run cost you plenty. I figure you lost over ten pounds." **⑮**

Comparing Literature

INFER

⑮ This story has a surprise ending. To figure out why the ruum puts Jim back on the ground, think about the ruum's instructions. Why might the ruum have been interested in Jim to begin with? Then, think about what might have changed. (A clue is given in the last line of the story.)

Meet the Writer

Arthur Porges

Arthur Porges (1915–   ) has published more than seventy short stories in various magazines. Porges was born in Chicago, and he taught mathematics at the Western Military Academy and the Illinois Institute of Technology until his retirement in 1975. Porges, whose best-known stories are "The Ruum" and "The Fly," also writes under the pen names Peter Arthur and Pat Rogers.

First Thoughts

1. Respond to "The Ruum" by completing one of the following sentences:
   - I thought the scariest part was when . . .
   - I am confused about . . .

Thinking Critically

2. The writer describes the bear as "lord of the woods" and "clumsy emperor of the wild." He is using **figurative language** to create a powerful and absurd picture of the grizzly battling the ruum. Use figurative language to come up with your own descriptions of the ruum.

3. Jim Irwin calls himself a dumb animal. Has Jim's opinion of himself changed in the course of his adventure? How has your opinion about Jim changed?

Reading Check

Retell the main events, and describe the characters in the opening part of "The Ruum." Where and when does this part of the story take place? Then, retell the main events, and describe the characters in the rest of the story. Where and when does this part of the story take place?

Comparing Literature

4. Add information on "The Ruum" to the chart below. Then, use your chart as you write the comparison-contrast essay on the next page.

Comparing Science Fiction Stories		
	"Zoo"	"The Ruum"
Human characters		
Alien characters		
Journey through space		
Futuristic technology		
Lesson about life		

SKILLS FOCUS

Literary Skills
Analyze the elements of science fiction.

Reading Skills
Compare and contrast stories.

Assignment

1. Writing a Comparison-Contrast Essay

Write an essay comparing "Zoo" and "The Ruum." To help plan your essay, review the chart you completed after you read each story. The chart will help you focus on elements in the stories that are very similar or very different. You do not have to write about all of these elements in your essay. You should pick the elements in each story that most interest you.

Use the workshop on writing a Comparison-Contrast Essay, pages 772–777, for help with this assignment.

Here are two ways you can organize your essay:

1. You can organize your essay by the stories. That means that you will discuss one story at a time, explaining how certain elements are used in that story. If you organize by the stories, your first and second paragraphs might be outlined like this:

> **Paragraph 1:** How "Zoo" uses certain elements
>   A. Journey in "Zoo"
>   B. Aliens in "Zoo"
> **Paragraph 2:** How "The Ruum" uses the elements
>   A. Journey in "The Ruum"
>   B. Aliens in "The Ruum"

2. You can organize your essay by the elements. That means that you will discuss each story element, one at a time, explaining how it is used in each story. If you organize by the elements, your first and second paragraph might be focused on these topics:

> **Paragraph 1:** The setting and characters of each story
>   A. "Zoo"
>   B. "The Ruum"
> **Paragraph 2:** The lesson about life taught in each story
>   A. "Zoo"
>   B. "The Ruum"

At the end of your essay, tell which story you prefer and why.

SKILLS FOCUS

Writing Skills
Write a comparison-contrast essay.

NO QUESTIONS ASKED

This poem by Edward Field presents us with a new version of a famous character in literature, the monster brought to life by Frankenstein. In the original story, by the English writer Mary Wollstonecraft Shelley, a scientist named Frankenstein uses portions of dead bodies to create a figure shaped like a man and then gives the creature the power to move and think by activating him with electricity.

Frankenstein's creation is a scientific triumph, but it is also a moral disaster that leads to tragedy. The monster, who is actually a gentle and intelligent being, is physically a hideous patchwork of other bodies. His features are so ugly and nightmarish that no one can look at him without wanting to scream. Consequently the monster is forever denied the human companionship and love that he needs.

Edward Field's poem is based on the 1931 movie starring Boris Karloff, in which some elements of the original story were changed. For example, the scientist Frankenstein is Baron Frankenstein in the movie. As you read, picture the poem as presenting a series of film clips.

Frankenstein

Edward Field

The monster has escaped from the dungeon
where he was kept by the Baron,
who made him with knobs sticking out from each side
    of his neck
where the head was attached to the body
5   and stitching all over
where parts of cadavers° were sewed together.

He is pursued by the ignorant villagers,
who think he is evil and dangerous because he is ugly
and makes ugly noises.

6. **cadavers** (kə·dav′ərz) *n.*: dead bodies; corpses.

10　　They wave firebrands at him and cudgels° and rakes,
　　　but he escapes and comes to the thatched cottage
　　　of an old blind man playing on the violin Mendelssohn's°
　　　　"Spring Song."

　　　Hearing him approach, the blind man welcomes him:
　　　"Come in, my friend," and takes him by the arm.
15　　"You must be weary," and sits him down inside the house.
　　　For the blind man has long dreamed of having a friend
　　　to share his lonely life.

　　　The monster has never known kindness—the Baron was cruel—
　　　but somehow he is able to accept it now,
20　　and he really has no instincts to harm the old man,
　　　for in spite of his awful looks he has a tender heart:
　　　Who knows what cadaver that part of him came from?

10. cudgels (kuj′əlz) *n.*: short, thick sticks or clubs.

12. Mendelssohn's (men′d′l·sənz): Felix Mendelssohn (1809–1847), a German composer.

The old man seats him at table, offers him bread,
and says, "Eat, my friend." The monster
25 rears back roaring in terror.

"No, my friend, it is good. Eat—gooood"
and the old man shows him how to eat,
and reassured, the monster eats
and says, "Eat—gooood,"
30 trying out the words and finding them good too.

The old man offers him a glass of wine,
"Drink, my friend. Drink—gooood."
The monster drinks, slurping horribly, and says,
"Drink—gooood," in his deep nutty voice
35 and smiles maybe for the first time in his life.

Then the blind man puts a cigar in the monster's mouth
and lights a large wooden match that flares up in his face.
The monster, remembering the torches of the villagers,
recoils, grunting in terror.
40 "No, my friend, smoke—gooood,"
and the old man demonstrates with his own cigar.

The monster takes a tentative puff
and smiles hugely, saying, "Smoke—gooood,"
and sits back like a banker, grunting and puffing.

45 Now the old man plays Mendelssohn's "Spring Song" on the violin
while tears come into our dear monster's eyes
as he thinks of the stones of the mob, the pleasures of mealtime,
the magic new words he has learned
and above all of the friend he has found.

50 It is just as well that he is unaware—
being simple enough to believe only in the present—
that the mob will find him and pursue him
for the rest of his short unnatural life,
until trapped at the whirlpool's edge
55 he plunges to his death.

Meet the Writer

Edward Field

Meaning of the Monster

Edward Field (1924–) "discovered" poetry during World War II, when he was in England. Between bombing missions he'd go into London on passes and buy books of poetry. He says that he was surprised to find there were actual *living* poets. He himself would receive twenty-two rejections before he finally got his first poetry collection published. Field's poetry is written in a conversational style in language that is familiar and frank. It has been described as "childlike," "open," and "funny." "Frankenstein" is one of several poems based on old movies.

© Robert Giard

66 The part I love most in the movie *Frankenstein* is where the blind man meets the monster. For the first time, the monster's need for love is revealed and we begin to see him as a victim of a cruel world which is out to destroy him because he is different.

What then is the meaning for us of this monster? Perhaps he stands for people of other races whom we learn to hate. Perhaps he is also a secret part of us, our forbidden feelings, that we fear and must punish in ourselves and others. 99

Writing Workshop

RUBRIC
Evaluation Criteria

A good story

1. centers on a major conflict that the characters must resolve

2. uses dialogue and action to develop the characters

3. provides a vivid description of the setting

4. ends with a resolution of the conflict

5. may reveal an overall message about life

112

NARRATIVE WRITING
Story

One of the best-loved forms of fictional writing is the **short story.** Some short stories are modeled closely on actual occurrences, while others are wildly imaginative—but any good story creates a world that fully engages a reader's interest.

Prewriting

1 Choosing a Story Idea

Writing a story can be an enjoyable challenge. Write a story in response to the following **prompt:**

> A good story entertains the reader with lifelike characters in a vivid setting, and in some way it resolves a conflict, or problem. Write a four-page story that presents characters who encounter and solve a problem.

The kernel of a story—your "seed" idea—might come from personal experience. Prod your memory by freewriting responses to questions like these:

• Of all the people you've known, who was the most unusual? the funniest? the most serious?

• What place do you know best? What happens there?

• What interesting experiences have you had?

• Is there an adventure you'd like to have?

2 Brainstorming

Try writing down at least ten characters, ten settings, and ten problems on separate slips of paper. For each story element, use a different-colored paper. (To get started, you may want to consider the suggestions on the right.) Then, mix and match the characters, settings, and problems until you come up with an interesting combination for a story.

3 Creating Interesting Characters

One of the best ways to hold your reader's interest is to create vivid, true-to-life **characters**. A character comes alive in the reader's imagination through specific descriptions, realistic speech and actions, and the reactions of other characters.

4 Plotting Your Story

To come up with the action, or **plot**, of your story, think about a character's problem. What is the **conflict** that arises—either between characters or in the mind of an individual character? What goal does your character have? What events lead to resolving the problem? The story-plan framework on the right might serve as a guide. You may also find it helpful to use the diagram in the margin of page 114 to visualize the shape of your story.

5 Choosing a Setting

Look for opportunities to give your reader a clear sense of the **setting**—where and when the events of the story take place. Don't just describe the setting and then forget about it when you move on to the action. Try to blend the two. Every detail of the setting should be important to either the mood or the plot of the story—or both.

Drafting

1 Getting Started

If you can come up with a good opening now, that's great, but if you can't, don't worry. Just start writing. You don't

---

Characters

park ranger

veterinarian

shy seventh-grader

Settings

national park

big city

shopping mall

Problems

battles a fire

hates dirty streets

needs a friend

Story Plan

My main character is

_____, who
    (name)

_____ .
  (basic situation)

This character wants

_____ , but
    (goal)

_____ .
  (main conflict)

Eventually,

_____ ,
    (climax)

and in the end,

_____ .
  (resolution)

Plot Diagram

Climax

Resolution

Complications,
suspense

Introduction
of characters
and conflict

Basic Situation

Character: seventh-
grade boy

Goal: to fit in and
have friends

Conflict: other kids
make fun of him

Climax and Resolution:
?

Language Handbook
H E L P

*Problems with verbs: See Agreement of
Subject and Verb, 2b–n, in the Language
Handbook.*

need to think of everything all at once! Pick an event or a character or a place, and begin. Trust your imagination—once you begin, new ideas will come to you faster than you can write them down.

2 Telling the Story

From whose **point of view** do you want to tell your story? Do you want to tell it from the point of view of one of the characters, who refers to himself or herself as "I"? Do you want to tell it from the point of view of a narrator who knows everything about all the characters? Perhaps you might want to use a narrator who knows the thoughts and feelings of just one character. (Learn more about point of view on pages 348–349.)

3 Using Dialogue to Develop Characters

Readers can learn a lot about characters through **dialogue**, or what the characters say. As you write, ask yourself if there's a way to use dialogue to show rather than tell about a character. For example, instead of writing "She was kind" to show that a character is kind, try having her speak gently to someone. Let readers hear your character talk so that they can make their own judgments.

Notice how skillfully George G. Toudouze uses dialogue to reveal character and advance the plot in "Three Skeleton Key" (page 42):

> In the light of our lantern she seemed so sound, so strong, that Itchoua exclaimed impatiently:
> "But why the devil was she abandoned? Nothing is smashed, no sign of fire—and she doesn't sail as if she were taking water."
> Le Gleo waved to the departing ship:
> "Bon voyage!" he smiled at Itchoua and went on. "She's leaving us, chief, and now we'll never know what—"
> "No, she's not!" cried the Basque. "Look! She's turning!"

Student Model

This is the beginning of a student's short story.

from Being Different

The top edge of the sun was visible over the roof of the barn. There was a slight chill in the air like every dusk. I spotted the slumped figure in the wooden swing across the field and walked to it.

The first paragraph introduces us to the **setting** *and the* **main characters.**

"Momma is worried. You didn't go tell her you were home from school," I said, noticing the pile of books at his feet. "She thought something happened to you."

He didn't answer, just shrugged.

"Why didn't you kiss Momma hello?"

The realistic **dialogue** *creates believable characters.*

"Didn't want to." He looked in the other direction. "I just needed time to think about things alone." He faced me, a tear in his left eye glistening.

"What things?" I asked. I had never seen my brother so upset.

The **main character's actions** *clearly show he is sad and upset.*

He looked up at the dusk sky and then down at his feet. "About important things."

I didn't mean to pry, I knew he disliked me to do so, but I felt so close to him now, closer than ever before, and I knew I had to pry.

We get inside the narrator's mind and know how she feels.

"I don't fit in with the other boys at school."

"Who told you that?"

"It's obvious, Angie. Don't you notice who always gets the good grades but never the good friends? I'm so different."

This is the main character's **problem.** *His* **goal** *is to fit in.*

—Amy Yustein
Suffern Junior High School
Suffern, New York

Strategies for Elaboration

To create believable, interesting characters, start carefully observing the people around you—at a shopping center or a restaurant, for example.

- Look at people's appearance—their clothing, hairstyles, and so on.

- Listen carefully. How do people really talk? What does actual speech sound like?

- Take notes on what you see and hear. In addition to helping you remember details, note-taking will sharpen your powers of observation.

- Remember that the more carefully you observe the world around you, the better you'll write about it.

INTERNET
More Writer's Models
Keyword: LE5 7-1

Evaluating and Revising

Use this chart to help you evaluate and revise the content and organization of your story.

Story: Content and Organization Guidelines

Evaluation Questions	▶ Tips	▶ Revision Techniques
1 Does the story have an interesting plot with an effective beginning, a conflict, complications, a suspenseful climax, and a clear resolution?	▶ Place a **check mark** next to each of the following elements: beginning, conflict, complications, climax, and resolution.	▶ **Add** or **elaborate** on elements of the plot as necessary. **Delete** any information that ruins the suspense.
2 Is the point of view consistent throughout the story?	▶ **Identify** pronouns (*I, he,* or *she*) that identify the point of view. **Label** the story's point of view; then, **circle** any information not given from that point of view.	▶ If any sentences are circled, **delete** them. If necessary, **add** the same information told from the narrator's point of view.
3 Are the characters complex and realistic?	▶ **Underline** specific details about each of the characters.	▶ If necessary, **add** details about a character's appearance, personality, or background. **Add** dialogue and narrative actions that reveal more about a character.
4 Does the story have a definite setting?	▶ With a colored marker, **highlight** details of the setting.	▶ If there are few highlighted words, **elaborate** on the setting by adding descriptive details.
5 Is the story well organized and coherent? Does the writer use transitions effectively?	▶ **Number** the major events in the story. **Put a star** next to transitional words and phrases such as *next* and *later that day.*	▶ **Rearrange** any events that are out of order. If there are few or no stars, **add** transitional words and phrases to show the order of events.

Put your first draft aside for a while. Then, read your story as if it has been written by someone else.

Here is one writer's revision of a passage from a short story.

Revision Model

After Peter regained consciousness, he

looked around *eagerly*, trying to identify his

surroundings. *Overhead* There was a tangled web of

yellow, red, and black cables. Each ~~cable~~ *one* was

the thickness of his waist. An entire wall

glowed with a soft *amber* light. On the floor, spaced at

regular intervals, were large *metal* boxes with *dozens of* switches

on them. He was trapped inside a ~~big~~ *gigantic* PC.

Suddenly, he heard a series of ten *loud electronic* tones. "A

modem!" he ~~said~~ *exclaimed*. His whereabouts were no

longer a mystery.

Evaluating the Revision

1. Where has the writer made descriptions more accurate and vivid by adding modifiers?

2. How has the writer improved dialogue by using a more vivid verb?

3. Where has the writer replaced an unnecessarily repeated noun with a pronoun?

4. How has the writer sustained suspense by not revealing information too early?

DIRECTIONS: Read the story. Then, answer each question that follows.

The Dinner Party

Mona Gardner

The country is India. A colonial official and his wife are giving a large dinner party. They are seated with their guests—army officers and government attachés[1] and their wives, and a visiting American naturalist[2]—in their spacious dining room, which has a bare marble floor, open rafters, and wide glass doors opening onto a veranda.

A spirited discussion springs up between a young girl who insists that women have outgrown the jumping-on-a-chair-at-the-sight-of-a-mouse era and a colonel who says that they haven't.

"A woman's unfailing reaction in any crisis," the colonel says, "is to scream. While a man may feel like it, he has that ounce more of nerve control than a woman has. That last ounce is what counts."

The American does not join in the argument but watches the other guests. As he looks, he sees a strange expression come over the face of the hostess. She is staring straight ahead, her muscles contracting slightly. With a slight gesture she summons the Indian boy standing behind her chair and whispers to him. The boy's eyes widen; he quickly leaves the room.

Of the guests, none except the American notices this nor sees the boy place a bowl of milk on the veranda just outside the open doors.

The American comes to with a start. In India, milk in a bowl means only one thing—bait for a snake. He realizes there must be a cobra in the room. He looks up at the rafters—the likeliest place—but they are bare. Three corners of the room are empty, and in the fourth the servants are waiting to serve the next course. There is only one place left—under the table.

His first impulse is to jump back and warn the others, but he knows the commotion would frighten the cobra into striking. He speaks quickly, the tone of his voice so arresting that it sobers everyone.

"I want to know just what control everyone at this table has. I will count to three hundred—that's five minutes—and

---

1. **attachés** (at′ə·shāz′) *n.*: diplomatic officials.
2. **naturalist** *n.*: person who studies nature by observing animals and plants.

SKILLS FOCUS

Literary Skills
Analyze plot structure.

not one of you is to move a muscle. Those who move will forfeit[3] fifty rupees.[4] Ready!"

The twenty people sit like stone images while he counts. He is saying ". . . two hundred and eighty . . ." when, out of the corner of his eye, he sees the cobra emerge and make for the bowl of milk. Screams ring out as he jumps to slam the veranda doors safely shut.

"You were right, Colonel!" the host exclaims. "A man has just shown us an example of perfect control."

"Just a minute," the American says, turning to his hostess. "Mrs. Wynnes, how did you know that cobra was in the room?"

A faint smile lights up the woman's face as she replies: "Because it was crawling across my foot."

---

3. forfeit (fôr′fit) *v.:* give up as a penalty.
4. rupees (rōō′pēz) *n.:* Indian money, like dollars in the United States.

---

1. The **setting** of this story is colonial —
   A   America
   B   India
   C   Africa
   D   Australia

2. Which of the following events in the **plot** of the story happens first?
   F   The American challenges the guests to remain still.
   G   A cobra is attracted to milk.
   H   The hostess whispers to a servant.
   J   The colonel argues with a girl.

3. What **later event** explains the strange expression on the hostess's face?
   A   A cobra has crawled across her foot.
   B   She dislikes the colonel's biased opinions about women.
   C   The servant is not doing his job.
   D   She sees a cobra on the veranda.

4. What **later event** explains why the boy places the milk on the veranda?
   F   The colonel's speech bores him.
   G   The American has seen a cobra.
   H   A cobra makes for the milk.
   J   The American proposes a challenge.

5. What event marks the **climax** of the story?
   A   The argument between the girl and colonel ends.
   B   The boy places a bowl of milk on the veranda.
   C   The American begins to count.
   D   The cobra emerges and screams ring out.

Constructed Response

6. Explain what happens in the **resolution** of the story.

Test Practice

DIRECTIONS: Read the informational materials. Then, answer each question that follows.

TEXTBOOK

CHAPTER 2

Biomes: World Plant Regions

What is a biome? A plant and animal community that covers a very large land area is called a **biome.** Plants are the most visible part of a biome. If you looked down on the United States from space, you would see various biomes. The forests of the eastern United States would appear green, while the deserts of the Southwest would be light brown.

NEWSPAPER ARTICLE

B2

Hatteras Lighthouse Completes Its Move

BUXTON, N.C., July 9 (AP)—As onlookers clapped and cheered, the Cape Hatteras Lighthouse slid today onto the concrete pad where its caretakers hope it will stand for another century, a safe distance from the thundering Atlantic surf.

INSTRUCTIONAL MANUAL

page 32

Looking Up Synonyms for a Word in a Document

1. SELECT THE WORD IN THE DOCUMENT.
2. CHOOSE UTILITIES THESAURUS (ALT,U,T), OR PRESS THE THESAURUS KEY (SHIFT+F7).
3. LOOK THROUGH THE LIST OF SYNONYMS IN SYNONYMS. SCROLL THROUGH THE LIST IF NECESSARY.

Command for Thesaurus

UTILITIES THESAURUS OR THESAURUS KEY (SHIFT+F7)

Lists alternative words for the selection

SKILLS FOCUS

Reading Skills
Analyze structure and purpose of informational materials.

Collection 1: Skills Review

1. Which statement explains the difference between the **purpose** of a textbook and the purpose of a newspaper article?

   A   A textbook has an index, a glossary, and graphic features, while a newspaper article has an inverted pyramid structure.

   B   A textbook has a table of contents and an index, while a newspaper article has a headline, a dateline, and a byline.

   C   A textbook gives lots of information about a big subject, while a newspaper article gives information about a current event.

   D   A textbook has many pages, while a newspaper article is usually one page long or less.

2. In comparing the **structure** of a textbook and the structure of an instructional manual, you could say that —

   F   they both have a table of contents, a glossary, an index, and graphic features, but a textbook is much longer

   G   a textbook presents information about a big subject, but an instructional manual presents information about how to operate and use a device

   H   a textbook is something you use in a classroom, but a manual is something you use at work or at home

   J   a textbook is something your school gives you to use, but a manual comes with something you buy

3. In the **textbook** excerpt the word *biome* means —

   A   a community of plants growing in a forest

   B   plants and sand that occur in desert areas

   C   the coastal areas of the United States as seen from outer space

   D   a plant and animal community that covers a large area

4. The **instructional manual** shown on page 120 gives instructions on how to —

   F   find biomes

   G   move a lighthouse

   H   look up synonyms

   J   read the Internet

5. The **newspaper article** on page 120 shows all of the following features *except* a —

   A   byline

   B   dateline

   C   page number

   D   headline

Constructed Response

6. Explain why an owner's manual has diagrams and an index.

Collection 1: Skills Review

Vocabulary Skills

Test Practice

Multiple-Meaning Words

DIRECTIONS: Each sentence below is from "Rikki-tikki-tavi." Read the sentence. Then, choose the answer in which the underlined word is used the same way.

1. "He . . . put his fur in <u>order</u>, scratched himself, and jumped on the small boy's shoulder."
   - **A** The <u>order</u> of the processional will be shortest person to tallest.
   - **B** The new <u>order</u> could not be filled because there were no more boxes.
   - **C** The meeting will come to <u>order</u>.
   - **D** Coming out of the water, the swimmer swept his hair back into <u>order</u>.

2. "She had crept up behind him as he was talking, to make an <u>end</u> of him. . . ."
   - **F** The fullback carried the ball into the <u>end</u> zone and scored a touchdown.
   - **G** The <u>end</u> of the story was too sad.
   - **H** The dinner guest looked as if it would be the <u>end</u> of him if he had to eat one more bite.
   - **J** Mr. Lee lives at the <u>end</u> of the road.

3. "When a snake misses its <u>stroke</u>, it never says anything or gives any sign of what it means to do next."
   - **A** On the <u>stroke</u> of midnight, the old year gives way to the new year.
   - **B** Winning the football pool was a <u>stroke</u> of good luck.
   - **C** With one more <u>stroke</u> of the ax, the tree was felled.
   - **D** It was said that the neighbor on the corner had suffered a <u>stroke</u>.

4. "Rikki-tikki knew he was a young mongoose, and it made him all the more pleased to think that he had managed to escape a <u>blow</u> from behind."
   - **F** Which way does the wind <u>blow</u>?
   - **G** There is one more candle to <u>blow</u> out.
   - **H** Jack felled the giant with one <u>blow</u>.
   - **J** Stop now, and <u>blow</u> your nose.

5. "He spread out his hood more than ever, and Rikki-tikki saw the spectacle <u>mark</u> on the back of it that looks exactly like the eye part of a hook-and-eye fastening."
   - **A** <u>Mark</u> my words, no good will come of this.
   - **B** This <u>mark</u> indicates the ball is mine.
   - **C** He hopes to get a higher <u>mark</u> in geometry this semester.
   - **D** Saying "thank you" is a <u>mark</u> of good manners.

SKILLS FOCUS

Vocabulary Skills
Understand multiple-meaning words.

Collection 1: Skills Review

Writing Skills

DIRECTIONS: Read the passage from a short story. Then, answer each question that follows.

Breannah stood in the goal, shifting her weight from one foot to the other, as a swarm of red jerseys nudged the soccer ball toward her. A lone blue-clad defender tried and failed to cut off the attack. Now no one stood between her and the lanky star forward of the Red Hots. The forward kicked the ball, and Breannah leaped to her right. The ball whooshed past her left ear and into the net.

She rose slowly and brushed herself off, ignoring the cheers from the Red Hots' bleachers. Next time, Breannah thought, she would be ready.

1. What strategy does the writer use to develop the main character?
   A   dialogue spoken by the character
   B   description of the character's appearance
   C   description of the character's thoughts and actions
   D   explanation of how other people respond to the character

2. What details does the writer use to show point of view in this passage?
   F   The words *she* and *her* and the main character's thoughts are used to show third-person limited point of view.
   G   The word *I* is used to show first-person point of view.
   H   The word *you* is used to show second-person point of view.
   J   Information about other characters' thoughts is used to show third-person-omniscient point of view.

3. If this passage occurs near the story's beginning, what might the writer do in later passages to build toward the climax?
   A   summarize events in the story that readers have already read about
   B   describe additional problems that add to the story's conflict
   C   change the point of view to include other characters' views of events
   D   describe the setting in detail

4. If a speaker were telling this story out loud, why might she begin by explaining that the story was based on a friend's experience playing soccer?
   F   to point out the story's climax
   G   to create a mood of suspense
   H   to establish a context for the story
   J   to include realistic dialogue

SKILLS FOCUS

Writing Skills
Analyze a short story.

Fiction

Working Girl

In Katherine Paterson's *Lyddie,* set in the 1840s, Lyddie Worthen has to grow up fast when her mother is forced to abandon the family farm. When she finds a job in a textile mill, Lyddie faces a grim new world of poverty and eighteen-hour workdays. A true heroine, Lyddie fights against injustice as she struggles to earn enough to buy back the family farm.

First Division

Sixth-graders from Barlow Road and Bear Creek Ridge have developed a serious softball rivalry that has lasted more than fifty years, and the 1949 game looks to be one of the most exciting yet. But the shadow of World War II looms over the game when Shazam—whose father was killed at Pearl Harbor—attacks Aki—who spent years in an internment camp. Virginia Euwer Wolff's *Bat 6* takes a brave look at prejudice, responsibility, and growing up.

This title is available in the HRW Library.

Strange Happenings

What if you were vacationing in Hawaii and you made a volcano goddess angry? Could you imagine being struck by lightning and finding yourself 140 years in the past? What would you do if you woke up one morning and saw seven guardian angels talking to one another in your bedroom? Neal Shusterman presents these wacky situations and more in *MindBenders.*

A Life of Danger

In *Lupita Mañana* by Patricia Beatty, Lupita Torres enters California illegally and tries to help support her widowed mother and younger siblings in Mexico by finding a job. Her search for a better life becomes a struggle in a place where the laws are not always fair and growing up is not always easy.

This title is available in the HRW Library.

Nonfiction

Courage in China

When Ji-Li Jiang turned twelve in 1966, she was an intelligent student with a bright future ahead of her. Then Mao Tse-tung launched the Cultural Revolution in China, and her family's background was revealed. As a result, Ji-Li's friends turned their backs on her, and her family suffered repeated abuse at the hands of Chinese officials. Ji-Li recalls her childhood of bravery and loyalty in *Red Scarf Girl*.

This title is available in the HRW Library.

Back in Shakespeare's Day...

Ruth Ashby goes back to the sixteenth century in *Elizabethan England*. Ashby details the lives of prominent historical figures such as Henry VIII and Sir Walter Raleigh and authors such as Sir Thomas More and William Shakespeare. She also describes the religious and social customs of the English people at the time. Helpful maps and illustrations are included.

Snakes, Snakes, and More Snakes

Are you interested in snakes? Dr. Robert Mason is *really* interested in them. For over fifteen years he has been researching the world's largest concentration of garter snakes, located in Manitoba, Canada. Sy Montgomery accompanied Dr. Mason on his field study and, in *The Snake Scientist,* recorded some of the amazing things he learned.

The Story Behind the News Stories

Newspapers have riveted the American public with troubling and sensational stories since the founding of our country. They are perhaps the single most important medium for conveying information, shaping public opinion, and spreading awareness of the world around us. In *Behind the Headlines,* Thomas Fleming explores in exacting detail the people and events that make the news.

CHARACTERS: LIVING MANY LIVES

Literary Focus:
Analyzing Character

Informational Focus:
Analyzing Comparison and Contrast

INTERNET
Collection Resources
Keyword: LE5 7-2

Market Scene (20th century)
by Carlo Decimus.
Coll. Manu Sassoonian, New York, NY.
© Manu Sassoonian/Licensed by Art Resource, NY.

Elements of Literature
Characterization *by* Mara Rockliff
ALL ABOUT THE PEOPLE WE MEET

Getting to Know You

Wouldn't life be easier if the people you met just wore T-shirts that told you what they were like? You'd know right away if the girl who just moved in next door was "SNOBBY AND CONCEITED" or "FRIENDLY, WITH A GREAT SENSE OF HUMOR." That substitute teacher? Better not mess with her—she's "TOUGH BUT FAIR." You won't have to wonder whether your new science partner will be fun or annoying. His T-shirt says it all.

Show Me a Story

If you read a novel written a hundred years ago or more, the writer may just tell you directly, "Old Luther was the meanest old cuss in five counties," or "Little Posy was barely half the size of the other orphans, but she had pluck." Those kinds of statements, in which the writer tells you directly what a character is like, are known as **direct characterization.**

These days, though, writers try to make their stories more like real life. Writers want you to get to know fictional characters just as you get to know people in real life—not by reading a statement on a T-shirt, but by observing people very closely and deciding for yourself what kinds of people they are. You ask: What do they look like? How do they act? What

do they say and how do they say it? How do other people feel about them?

One of the first pieces of advice a new writer always hears is "Show, don't tell." Telling is the old way—**direct characterization.** Most writers (and readers) think showing is more interesting and realistic than just telling. This "showing" method of revealing a character is called indirect characterization. In **indirect characterization** you have to observe the character and come to your own conclusion about the kind of person you are meeting.

Who Is This Character, Anyway?

So how does a writer *show* what a character is like?

1 Appearance. Appearances can sometimes deceive, but they're often your first clue to character. Does the grandfather in the story have laugh lines around his eyes or a

INTERNET
More About Characterization
Keyword: LE5 7-2

SKILLS FOCUS

Literary Skills
Analyze characterization.

furrowed brow from years of worrying? Is the trial lawyer cool and collected in her expensive, neatly pressed suit, or is she a sweat-soaked, wrinkled mess?

2 **Action.** The writer could *tell* you, "The boy was happy," but if you see the boy in action, you'll know for yourself.

Luis danced into the kitchen, singing along with the song on the radio. He paused just long enough to give his mother a loud kiss on the cheek, then danced on out the door.

3 **Speech.** Listen to a character talk, and she will tell you what she's like—*indirectly.* A four-year-old may not announce, "Hi! I'm bratty and stubborn," but doesn't the following outburst reveal the same thing?

"I don't have to do what you say!" screamed Darlene as she kicked the new baby sitter in the shins.

4 **Thoughts and feelings.** Here's where literature is better than life. In some books you can actually read what people are thinking, and what they think shows who they are.

Julie wanted to cry when she saw the stray cat. Its ribs were showing. She desperately wanted to add it to her well-fed tribe of cats at home.

5 **Other characters' reactions.** What do the other people in the story think of this character? What do they say about her? How do they act toward him? Of course, just as in life,

you have to consider the source. If a character has something insulting to say about everyone in his school, his comments probably tell you more about *him* than about the others.

Practice

Write down the name of a character from a story you have recently read. Choose two or three words that describe that character, write those words under the name, and then draw a circle around each word. Now, go back to the story, and find examples of how the writer shows you those characteristics. (Notice **appearance, action, speech, thoughts,** and **other characters' reactions.**) Jot down the examples, circle them, and draw lines connecting them to the main circle.

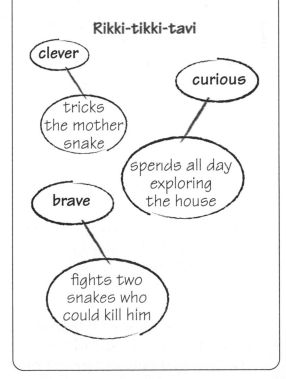

Rikki-tikki-tavi

clever

curious

tricks the mother snake

brave

spends all day exploring the house

fights two snakes who could kill him

Reading Skills and Strategies

Characters and Plots

by Kylene Beers

Pause for a moment and think of a movie you've seen or story you've read. Now, think about that movie or story without the characters. Can you do it? Probably not. Plot gives us the action of a story; characters are the ones doing the action. Take away the characters, and the plot comes to a standstill. Change the characters, and the plot changes too. Make the killer shark in the movie *Jaws* a friendly dolphin, and you have a very different movie.

Understanding How Characters Affect Plot

If you want to figure out how the plot might change if a character changes, use a simple strategy called **If—Then**. With this strategy you imagine what would have happened if the character had behaved differently. **If** you think a character is fearless, **then** what would have happened if he were frightened? **If** you think another character is cautious, **then** what would have happened if she were reckless?

As you read the next selection from Gary Paulsen's book *How Angel Peterson Got His Name*, consider how this story of a first date would change if either the boy or the girl behaved differently.

Tips for Understanding Characters

Writers use many ways to help you understand characters. They may

- use dialogue to give you insight into a character

- tell you what a character is thinking

- describe the way a character acts or reacts to situations

- tell you how other characters—or even animals—react to a character

If you read a story in which a dog growls as a character approaches, you may be right to guess that the character is up to no good. If a character says, "Who may I say is calling?" instead of "Whosit?" you're right to think that manners count to that gent.

SKILLS FOCUS

Reading Skills
Understand how characters affect plot.

Girls

from **How Angel Peterson Got His Name**

Gary Paulsen

Girls. **❶**

When we were eleven and even twelve they were just like us.
Sort of.

That is, we could be friends and do projects together in school and
some boys could even talk to them.

Not me. I never could. And neither could Orvis. Alan seemed to
have worked out a way to pretend they weren't even there and Wayne
swore that it didn't bother him at all to speak to girls.

And then we became thirteen.

Everything changed. **❷**

Well, not everything. I still couldn't talk to them, lived in mortal terror of them, and Orvis was the same way. But we talked *about* them all
the time, how they looked, how they smiled, how they sounded, how

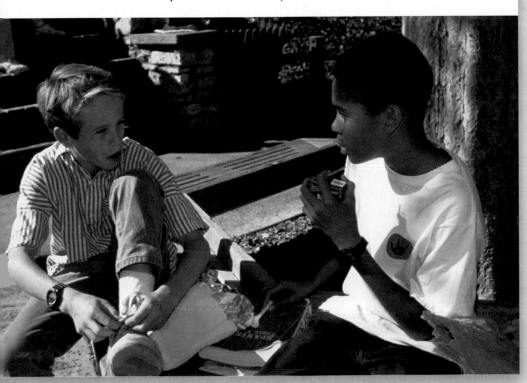

Using the Strategy

As you read, you'll find this open-book sign at certain points in the story: . Stop at these points, and think about what you've just read. Do what the prompts ask you to do.

ANALYZE

❶ Why does Paulsen start this story with a one-word paragraph? What is he trying to tell you about girls?

ANALYZE

❷ Why do you think Paulsen writes so many short paragraphs? How do the short paragraphs help you understand what he considers important?

ANALYZE

❸ Why does Paulsen use capital letters for *In Love* and *For Real,* as if these phrases were titles?

ANALYZE CHARACTER

❹ Why didn't the narrator just ask Eileen himself? What **character traits** would he have needed to be able to ask her directly?

INTERPRET

❺ Imagine what the narrator might have said if he had met Eileen's parents. What would the conversation have been like if he had been as scared to talk to them as he was to talk to Eileen? What might have been said if he had been confident instead?

they must think, about life, about us, how Elaine was really cute but Eileen had prettier hair and Eileen seemed one day to actually, actually look at me, right at me. But we couldn't speak *to* them.

Except that now it became very important that we be *able* to speak to them. Before, it didn't seem to matter, and now it was somehow the only thing that *did* matter.

I had this problem because Eileen actually *had* looked at me one day on the way out of school, or so I thought, and on top of it she had smiled—I was pretty sure at me as well—and I thought that maybe I was In Love and that it was For Real and when I asked Orvis about it he agreed that I might be In Love for Real and suggested that I take Eileen to a movie. ❸

Which nearly stopped my heart cold. I couldn't talk to her—how could I ask her to go to a movie? Finally it was Orvis who thought of the way. I would ask Wayne to ask Shirley Johnson to ask Claudia Erskine, who was a close friend of Eileen's, if Eileen might like to go to the movies with me the following Saturday afternoon. ❹

This tortuous procedure was actually followed and by the time I was told that indeed Eileen would like to see a movie the next Saturday, I was a nervous wreck and honestly hoped she wouldn't go.

We met in front of the theater, as things were done then at our age—I couldn't even imagine going to her home and ringing the bell to pick her up and having her parents answer the door. If I couldn't really speak to girls, what would I do with a set of *parents* of the girl I was going to take to a movie? ❺

So we met at the theater at one-thirty. I wore what I thought were my best clothes, a pullover sweater over a turtleneck, with my feeble attempt at a flattop, Butch-Waxed so much that dropping an anvil on my head wouldn't have flattened it. I think now I must have looked something like a really uncomfortable, sweaty, walking, greasy-topped bottle brush. (Have I mentioned that with my sweater and turtleneck I had gone solely for fashion and had ignored the fact that it was high summer? Or that the theater was most decidedly *not* air-conditioned?) ❻

But Eileen was a nice person and pretended not to notice the sweat filling my shoes so they sloshed when we walked or how I dropped my handful of money all over the ground. I had brought all of my seven dollars in savings because I really didn't know how much it would cost, what with tickets and treats, and maybe she was a big eater. ❼

She also pretended not to notice when I asked her if she wanted popcorn.

So I asked her again. Louder.

And then again. Louder.

All because I was blushing so hard my ears were ringing and I wasn't sure if I was really making a sound and so when I screamed it out the third time and she jumped back, it more or less set the tone for the whole date.

We went into the theater all right. And we sat next to each other. And she was kind enough to overlook the fact that I smelled like a dead buffalo and that other than asking her three times if she wanted popcorn I didn't say a word to her. Not a word.

I couldn't.

The movie was called *The Thing,* about a creature from another planet who crashes to earth in the Arctic and develops a need/thirst/obsession for human and sled-dog blood and isn't killed until they figure out that he's really a kind of walking, roaring, grunting plant. So they rig up some wire to "cook him like a stewed carrot." All of this I learned the second time around, when I went to the movie with Wayne, because sitting next to Eileen, pouring sweat, giving her endless boxes of Dots and candy corn and popcorn (almost none of which she wanted but accepted nicely and set on the seat next to her), I didn't remember a single thing about the movie. Not a word, not a scene. ❽

All I could do was sit and think, I'm this close to a girl, right next to a girl, my arm almost touching her arm, a girl, right there, right *there*. . . .

ANALYZE

❻ Do you think the narrator really looked like a "greasy-topped bottle brush"? Why would he describe himself this way? What response is he trying to get from you?

INTERPRET

❼ The narrator uses a lot of exaggeration in describing himself. However, he understates Eileen's character, saying only that she was "a nice person." Do you think that Eileen was also nervous? Why doesn't the narrator tell us more about the way she was acting?

INTERPRET

❽ The narrator tells this first-date story with a lot of humor. Re-read your favorite sections, and think about what would have happened if either the boy or the girl had behaved differently. If Eileen, for example, had been more outgoing or rude, how might the date have ended?

Meet the Writer

Gary Paulsen

Real-Life Adventures

One night while **Gary Paulsen** (1939–   )
was working as an electronics engineer
at a deep-space tracking station in
California, he had the sudden realization
that he needed a change. Paulsen
recalls:

> **❝**I thought . . . what am I doing? I
> just hated it. I decided to be a writer,
> pretty much that night. I drove to
> Hollywood. If I'd been in the East I
> would have gone to New York. I
> needed to find [other] writers.**❞**

Gary Paulsen has clearly found his
calling in life. He has written more than
175 books, three of which were named
Newbery Honor Books.

The popular young adult author
frequently finds inspiration for his books in his life
experiences, which have included stints as a soldier, actor,
sailor, trapper, and rancher. Paulsen has clearly seen his share
of adventure in these positions and has a wealth of material to
write about as a result.

For Independent Reading

In the memoir *Woodsong*, Paulsen presents an incredible
account of eye-opening journeys he has taken into the
wilderness with his sled dogs.

Practice the Strategy

Recognizing Characterization

PRACTICE 1

In "Girls," Paulsen wants you to feel a young boy's terror at asking a girl on a date. He doesn't want you just to *know* the boy was afraid; he wants you to *feel* his fear and nervousness. How does Paulsen do this? (Hint: Take a look at the adjectives he chooses to describe the boy's feelings.)

If—Then: How Characters Affect Plot

PRACTICE 2

On page 130, you were asked to think about how this story of a first date would change if either the boy or the girl had behaved differently. What might have happened if the boy had been more confident? if the girl had been more talkative?

From each pair of opposites below, choose the adjective that best describes the narrator or Eileen.

> *shy / bold*
> *scared / fearless*
> *caring / uncaring*

Now, think about the events in the story you just read. How would these events have changed if either the boy or the girl had displayed the opposite characteristics? If you think Eileen is scared, for example, what might have happened differently if she had been fearless?

You can use the **If—Then strategy** with the stories in this collection. If you want to figure out how any plot might change if a character changes, try using the If—Then strategy.

Strategy Tip

Here are some pairs of adjectives to keep in mind as you read any selection. Ask yourself, "**If** the character is [one of these adjectives], **then** how does the plot change if he or she were [the other adjective] instead?"

> *selfish / selfless*
> *greedy / giving*
> *active / passive*
> *brave / cowardly*
> *graceful / clumsy*
> *strong / weak*
> *good / bad*
> *wise / foolish*
> *truthful / sneaky*
> *kind / mean*
> *honest / dishonest*
> *scared / fearless*
> *caring / uncaring*
> *daring / cautious*
> *funny / serious*
> *polite / rude*
> *happy / sad*
> *shy / bold*

SKILLS FOCUS

Reading Skills
Analyze how character affects plot.

Mother and Daughter

Make the Connection
Quickwrite

Like the characters in a story, real people have **character traits** too. Think about your experiences with people. What makes you like or dislike someone? In your journal, make a list of four or five character traits that you admire most in people and a list of those you like the least.

Literary Focus
Character Traits

A **character** is anyone who plays a part in a story. A **character trait** is a quality in a person that can't be seen. Character traits are revealed through a person's appearance, words, actions, and thoughts. Character traits can also be revealed in the ways a person affects other people. As you read "Mother and Daughter," notice how the writer helps you get to know this mother and her daughter. What are their character traits (the qualities they carry inside)?

Reading Skills
Making Inferences

To find a character's traits, you have to make inferences. **Inferences** are educated guesses, based on whatever evidence you have. If you wake up in the morning and see puddles in the streets, you could infer that it rained the night before. If you read a story in which a character always mentors kids who need help reading, you could infer that she is a caring person. As you read "Mother

and Daughter," look for details in the story that can help you make inferences about the characters. To collect evidence, look for answers to questions like these:

- What do I know about the character's looks, thoughts, words, and actions?
- How do other characters react to the character?
- What does the character learn by the end of the story?

SKILLS FOCUS

Literary Skills
Understand character traits.

Reading Skills
Make inferences.

Vocabulary Development

Here are some words you'll learn as you read the story:

matinees (mat''n·āz') *n.:* afternoon performances of a play or a movie. *Yollie and her mother got along well enough to go to matinees together at the local theater.*

antics (an'tiks) *n.:* playful or silly acts. *People who witnessed Mrs. Moreno's antics couldn't help laughing.*

meager (mē'gər) *adj.:* slight; small amount. *Mrs. Moreno remembers that her parents worked hard for their meager salaries.*

sophisticated (sə·fis'tə·kāt'id) *adj.:* worldly; elegant and refined. *Yollie admired the way sophisticated people in New York dressed.*

tirade (tī'rād') *n.:* long, scolding speech. *Yollie felt bad about her tirade against her mom.*

Mother and Daughter

Gary Soto

next door, was too tired to be scared. Her eyes closed but sprang open when her mother screamed, "Look, Yollie! Oh, you missed a scary part. The guy's face was all ugly!"

But Yollie couldn't keep her eyes open. They fell shut again and stayed shut, even when her mother screamed and slammed a heavy palm on the arm of her chair.

"Mom, wake me up when the movie's over so I can go to bed," mumbled Yollie.

"OK, Yollie, I wake you," said her mother through a mouthful of popcorn.

But after the movie ended, instead of waking her daughter, Mrs. Moreno laughed under her breath, turned the TV and lights off, and tiptoed to bed. Yollie woke up in the middle of the night and didn't know where she was. For a moment she thought she was dead. Maybe something from the underworld had lifted her from her house and carried her into the earth's belly. She blinked her sleepy eyes, looked around at the darkness, and called, "Mom? Mom, where are you?" But there was no answer, just the throbbing hum of the refrigerator.

Finally, Yollie's grogginess cleared and she realized her mother had gone to bed, leaving her on the couch. Another of her little jokes.

But Yollie wasn't laughing. She tiptoed into her mother's bedroom with a glass of water and set it on the nightstand next to the alarm clock. The next morning, Yollie woke to screams. When her mother reached to turn off the alarm, she had overturned the glass of water.

Yollie burned her mother's morning toast and gloated. "Ha! Ha! I got you back. Why did you leave me on the couch when I told you to wake me up?"

Y ollie's mother, Mrs. Moreno, was a large woman who wore a muumuu and butterfly-shaped glasses. She liked to water her lawn in the evening and wave at low-riders, who would stare at her behind their smoky sunglasses and laugh. Now and then a low-rider from Belmont Avenue would make his car jump and shout *Mamacita!* But most of the time they just stared and wondered how she got so large.

Mrs. Moreno had a strange sense of humor. Once, Yollie and her mother were watching a late-night movie called *They Came to Look.* It was about creatures from the underworld who had climbed through molten lava to walk the earth. But Yollie, who had played soccer all day with the kids

Despite their jokes, mother and daughter usually got along. They watched bargain matinees together, and played croquet in the summer and checkers in the winter. Mrs. Moreno encouraged Yollie to study hard because she wanted her daughter to be a doctor. She bought Yollie a desk, a typewriter, and a lamp that cut glare so her eyes would not grow tired from hours of studying.

Yollie was slender as a tulip, pretty, and one of the smartest kids at Saint Theresa's. She was captain of crossing guards, an altar girl, and a whiz in the school's monthly spelling bees.

"*Tienes que estudiar mucho,*" Mrs. Moreno said every time she propped her work-weary feet on the hassock. "You have to study a lot, then you can get a good job and take care of me."

"Yes, Mama," Yollie would respond, her face buried in a book. If she gave her mother any sympathy, she would begin her stories about how she had come with her family from Mexico with nothing on her back but a sack with three skirts, all of which were too large by the time she crossed the border because she had lost weight from not having enough to eat.

Everyone thought Yollie's mother was a riot. Even the nuns laughed at her antics. Her brother Raul, a nightclub owner, thought she was funny enough to go into show business.

But there was nothing funny about Yollie needing a new outfit for the eighth-grade fall dance. They couldn't afford one. It was late October, with Christmas around the corner, and their dented Chevy Nova had gobbled up almost one hundred dollars in repairs.

"We don't have the money," said her mother, genuinely sad because they couldn't buy the outfit, even though there was a little money stashed away for college. Mrs. Moreno remembered her teenage years and her hard-working parents, who picked grapes and oranges, and chopped beets and cotton for meager pay around Kerman. Those were the days when "new clothes" meant limp and out-of-style dresses from Saint Vincent de Paul.

The best Mrs. Moreno could do was buy Yollie a pair of black shoes with velvet bows

Vocabulary

matinees (mat″n·āz′) *n.:* afternoon performances of a play or a movie.

antics (an′tiks) *n.:* playful or silly acts.

meager (mē′gər) *adj.:* slight; small amount.

and fabric dye to color her white summer dress black.

"We can color your dress so it will look brand-new," her mother said brightly, shaking the bottle of dye as she ran hot water into a plastic dish tub. She poured the black liquid into the tub and stirred it with a pencil. Then, slowly and carefully, she lowered the dress into the tub.

Yollie couldn't stand to watch. She *knew* it wouldn't work. It would be like the time her mother stirred up a batch of molasses for candy apples on Yollie's birthday. She'd dipped the apples into the goo and swirled them and seemed to taunt Yollie by singing *"Las Mañanitas"* to her. When she was through, she set the apples on wax paper. They were hard as rocks and hurt the kids' teeth. Finally, they had a contest to see who could break the apples open by throwing them against the side of the house. The apples shattered like grenades, sending the kids scurrying for cover, and in an odd way the birthday party turned out to be a success. At least everyone went home happy.

To Yollie's surprise, the dress came out shiny black. It looked brand-new and

sophisticated, like what people in New York wear. She beamed at her mother, who hugged Yollie and said, "See, what did I tell you?"

The dance was important to Yollie because she was in love with Ernie Castillo, the third-best speller in the class. She bathed, dressed, did her hair and nails, and primped until her mother yelled, "All right already." Yollie sprayed her neck and wrists with Mrs. Moreno's Avon perfume and bounced into the car.

Mrs. Moreno let Yollie out in front of the school. She waved and told her to have a good time but behave herself, then roared off, blue smoke trailing from the tail pipe of the old Nova.

Yollie ran into her best friend, Janice. They didn't say it, but each thought the other was the most beautiful girl at the dance; the boys would fall over themselves asking them to dance.

The evening was warm but thick with clouds. Gusts of wind picked up the paper lanterns hanging in the trees and swung them, blurring the night with reds and yellows. The lanterns made the evening seem romantic, like a scene from a movie. Everyone danced, sipped punch, and stood in knots of threes and fours, talking. Sister Kelly got up and jitterbugged with some kid's father. When the record ended, students broke into applause.

Janice had her eye on Frankie Ledesma, and Yollie, who kept smoothing her dress down when the wind picked up, had her eye on Ernie. It turned out that Ernie had his mind on Yollie, too. He ate a handful of

Vocabulary
sophisticated (sə·fis′tə·kāt′id) *adj.:* worldly; elegant and refined.

cookies nervously, then asked her for a dance.

"Sure," she said, nearly throwing herself into his arms.

They danced two fast ones before they got a slow one. As they circled under the lanterns, rain began falling, lightly at first. Yollie loved the sound of the raindrops ticking against the leaves. She leaned her head on Ernie's shoulder, though his sweater was scratchy. He felt warm and tender. Yollie could tell that he was in love, and with her, of course. The dance continued successfully, romantically, until it began to pour.

"Everyone, let's go inside—and, boys, carry in the table and the record player," Sister Kelly commanded.

The girls and boys raced into the cafeteria. Inside, the girls, drenched to the bone, hurried to the restrooms to brush their hair and dry themselves. One girl cried because her velvet dress was ruined. Yollie felt sorry for her and helped her dry the dress off with paper towels, but it was no use. The dress was ruined.

Yollie went to a mirror. She looked a little gray now that her mother's makeup had washed away but not as bad as some of the other girls. She combed her damp hair, careful not to pull too hard. She couldn't wait to get back to Ernie.

Yollie bent over to pick up a bobby pin, and shame spread across her face. A black puddle was forming at her feet. Drip, black drip. Drip, black drip. The dye was falling from her dress like black tears. Yollie stood up. Her dress was now the color of ash. She looked around the room. The other girls, unaware of Yollie's problem, were busy grooming themselves. What could she do? Everyone would laugh. They would know she dyed an old dress because she couldn't afford a new one. She hurried from the restroom with her head down, across the cafeteria floor and out the door. She raced through the storm, crying as the rain mixed with her tears and ran into twig-choked gutters.

When she arrived home, her mother was on the couch eating cookies and watching TV.

"How was the dance, *m'ija*? Come watch the show with me. It's really good."

Yollie stomped, head down, to her bedroom. She undressed and threw the dress on the floor.

Her mother came into the room. "What's going on? What's all the racket, baby?"

"The dress. It's cheap! It's no good!" Yollie kicked the dress at her mother and watched it land in her hands. Mrs. Moreno studied it closely but couldn't see what was wrong. "What's the matter? It's just a bit wet."

"The dye came out, that's what."

Mrs. Moreno looked at her hands and saw the grayish dye puddling in the shallow lines of her palms. Poor baby, she thought, her brow darkening as she made a sad face. She wanted to tell her daughter how sorry she was, but she knew it wouldn't help. She walked back to the living room and cried.

The next morning, mother and daughter stayed away from each other. Yollie sat in her room turning the pages of an old *Seventeen,* while her mother watered her plants with a Pepsi bottle.

"Drink, my children," she said loud enough for Yollie to hear. She let the water slurp into pots of coleus and cacti. "Water is all you need. My daughter needs clothes, but I don't have no money."

Yollie tossed her *Seventeen* on her bed. She was embarrassed at last night's tirade. It wasn't her mother's fault that they were poor.

When they sat down together for lunch, they felt awkward about the night before. But Mrs. Moreno had made a fresh stack of tortillas and cooked up a pan of *chile verde,* and that broke the ice. She licked her thumb and smacked her lips.

"You know, honey, we gotta figure a way to make money," Yollie's mother said. "You and me. We don't have to be poor. Remember the Garcias. They made this stupid little tool that fixes cars. They moved away because they're rich. That's why we don't see them no more."

"What can we make?" asked Yollie. She took another tortilla and tore it in half.

"Maybe a screwdriver that works on both ends? Something like that." The mother looked around the room for ideas, but then shrugged. "Let's forget it. It's better to get an education. If you get a good job and have spare time then maybe you can invent something." She rolled her tongue over her lips and cleared her throat. "The county fair hires people. We can get a job there. It will be here next week."

Yollie hated the idea. What would Ernie say if he saw her pitching hay at the cows?

How could she go to school smelling like an armful of chickens? "No, they wouldn't hire us," she said.

The phone rang. Yollie lurched from her chair to answer it, thinking it would be Janice wanting to know why she had left. But it was Ernie wondering the same thing. When he found out she wasn't mad at him, he asked if she would like to go to a movie.

"I'll ask," Yollie said, smiling. She covered the phone with her hand and counted to ten. She uncovered the receiver and said, "My mom says it's OK. What are we going to see?"

After Yollie hung up, her mother climbed, grunting, onto a chair to reach the top shelf in the hall closet. She wondered why she hadn't done it earlier. She reached behind a stack of towels and pushed her chubby hand into the cigar box where she kept her secret stash of money.

"I've been saving a little money every month," said Mrs. Moreno. "For you, *m'ija.*" Her mother held up five twenties, a blossom of green that smelled sweeter than flowers on that Saturday. They drove to Macy's and bought a blouse, shoes, and a skirt that would not bleed in rain or any other kind of weather.

Vocabulary
tirade (tī′rād′) *n.:* long, scolding speech.

Meet the Writer

Gary Soto

"A Name Among *la gente*"

Like Yollie in this story, **Gary Soto** (1952–   ) grew up in a Mexican American family in California. Much of his award-winning fiction and poetry draws on his heritage and his childhood memories. Although his work is vastly popular today, selling an average of seven thousand books a month, Soto remembers that early on he had trouble cultivating readers, even his own grandmother.

66 Unlike most other contemporary poets and writers, I've taken the show on the road and built a name among *la gente,* the people. I have ventured into schools, where I have played baseball and basketball with young people, sung songs, acted in skits, delivered commencement speeches, learned three chords on a Mexican guitar to serenade teachers. . . . My readership is strung from large cities, such as Los Angeles, to dinky Del Ray, where peach trees outnumber the population by many thousands. From all appearances my readers care.
. . . I'm in their lives and in their hearts. I'm searching for a family whose grandmother, an illiterate, fits a book into a picture frame, the centerpiece for a household that will in time quiet down and throw open the cover. **99**

For Independent Reading

"Mother and Daughter" appears in a collection of short stories called *Baseball in April,* about kids like Yollie growing up in Fresno, California. You might want to read one of Soto's novels, such as *Taking Sides* or its sequel, *Pacific Crossing.* If you like poetry, look at *A Fire in My Hands.* That book includes a question-and-answer section in which Soto talks about writing poetry.

First Thoughts

1. Respond to the story by completing these sentences:

- I thought Yollie was . . .

- I thought she and her mother . . .

Thinking Critically

2. Look back at the way Yollie and her mother tease each other at the beginning of the story. What inferences can you make about the **character traits** of the mother and the daughter in that scene?

3. How has Yollie distinguished herself at Saint Theresa's? Based on her involvement in those activities, what would you infer about her **character?**

4. Look at the way Mrs. Moreno dresses, at how other people respond to her, and at how she feels about Yollie. What inferences can you make about her **character?**

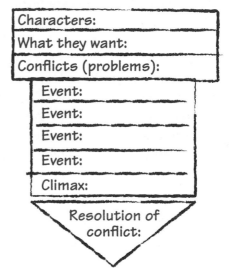

Reading Check

Fill out a story map like the one below to review the plot of "Mother and Daughter."

- Characters:
- What they want:
- Conflicts (problems):
  - Event:
  - Event:
  - Event:
  - Event:
  - Climax:

Resolution of conflict:

Focus on the main events in the plot. (You may note a different number of events.)

Extending Interpretations

5. Do you think Yollie and her mother are believable **characters**? (Think about how they compare with people you know.) How about that final discovery of the money in the cigar box? Was that a believable resolution to the plot? Why or why not?

WRITING

Creating a Character

Before you read this story, you took notes about some character traits you admire and some you don't like. Now, refer to those notes, and write a sketch of a character with the traits you admire or the traits you do not like. Be sure to use details to describe your character's actions, looks, and relationships with other people.

Vocabulary Development

Dictionaries Tell Stories: Word Origins

Etymology (et′ə·mäl′ə·jē) means "the study of the origin and development of words." Most dictionaries give an etymology in brackets or parentheses following the word itself. At the back or front of the dictionary, you'll find definitions of the symbols and abbreviations used in the etymologies. One important symbol is "<," which means "comes from" or "derived from." The "derived from" symbol followed by a question mark ("<?") indicates that the derivation of a word or word part is unknown. A backward "derived from" symbol (">") means "from which comes." Here is the etymology of *mother* from one dictionary:

Middle English

from

Old English

German

Indo-European

not certain

ME *moder* < OE *modor*, akin to Ger *mutter* < IE *matér*, mother

> L *mater*, Gr *mētēr*, OIr *māthir* < * *ma–* echoic of baby talk

from which is derived

Latin

Greek

Old Irish

imitates the sound

This etymology could be translated as "The word *mother* comes from the Middle English word *moder,* which comes from the Old English word *modor,* which is related ('akin') to the German word *mutter,* which comes from the Indo-European word *matér,* from which comes the Latin word *mater,* the Greek word *mētēr,* and the Old Irish word *māthir.* All the words might come from a word that imitates the sound of baby talk."

PRACTICE

The words in the Word Bank are derived from either Latin or Greek. Use a good dictionary to discover the original derivation of these words. Then, complete a chart like the one below:

Word Bank Word	Original Derivation
sophisticated	< Gr *sophos,* "clever; skillful; wise"

Word Bank

matinees
antics
meager
sophisticated
tirade

SKILLS FOCUS

Vocabulary Skills
Understand word origins.

Mother and Daughter **145**

The Smallest Dragonboy

Make the Connection
Quickwrite

Have you ever wanted to do something that you thought would be too hard or that someone said you couldn't do? What motivated you to overcome your difficulties? Take some notes about a time when you faced a challenge as an underdog.

Literary Focus
Motivation

Why do people do the things they do? What makes us act one way and not another? These are questions about **motivation.** Feelings, needs, wishes, pressures from family and friends—all these are forces that pull and push people from inside and outside. As you read "The Smallest Dragonboy," ask yourself what forces motivate Keevan, the main character. How does understanding Keevan's motivation help you understand the kind of character he is?

Reading Skills
Making Inferences

An **inference** is an educated guess based on evidence. When you make inferences about characters, you try to guess what kind of people they are, based on how the characters act, what they say, how other people respond. As you read "The Smallest Dragonboy," look for the little open-book signs after some paragraphs. Stop at these points to answer questions that ask you to make inferences about a character.

Vocabulary Development

These words appear in the story. See if you can use each one in a sentence of your own.

goaded (gōd′id) v.: pushed or driven. *Beterli goaded Keevan into a fight.*

imminent (im′ə·nənt) adj.: about to happen. *Pern was in imminent danger of a Thread attack.*

perturbed (pər·turbd′) v. used as adj.: disturbed; troubled. *Keevan was perturbed when he heard the bad news.*

confrontation (kän′frən·tā′shən) n.: face-to-face meeting between opposing sides. *The conflict between the two boys led to a violent confrontation.*

alleviate (ə·lē′vē·āt′) v.: relieve; reduce. *The boy's mother spoke soothing words to alleviate his fears.*

INTERNET

Vocabulary Activity
•
More About McCaffrey

Keyword: LE5 7-2

SKILLS FOCUS

Literary Skills
Understand motivation.

Reading Skills
Make inferences.

The Smallest Dragonboy

Anne McCaffrey

Background
The World of Pern

"The Smallest Dragonboy" takes place on the planet of Pern, an imaginary world somewhere in outer space. Pern is threatened by the dangerous Red Star, which rains deadly, threadlike plant spores on the planet every two hundred years or so. If a hungry Thread falls on Pern soil and grows there, it will devour every living thing in sight.

To protect their planet, colonists on Pern have bioengineered a race of great winged dragons. When fed a special rock called firestone, the dragons breathe flames that char Thread to ashes. During Thread attacks, the dragons and their dragonriders charge into battle in midair while the other colonists hide safely in their cave towns. During periods of Thread attacks, the protectors of Pern live inside the cones of old volcanoes in cave colonies called Weyrs.

As the story opens, young candidates for dragonrider in the Benden Weyr, a colony in the Benden Mountains, await the hatching of a clutch of dragon eggs. According to custom, each newborn dragon will choose its own rider—a lifelong partner—through a kind of telepathic communication called Impression.

Although Keevan lengthened his walking stride as far as his legs would stretch, he couldn't quite keep up with the other candidates. He knew he would be teased again.

Just as he knew many other things that his foster mother told him he ought not to know, Keevan knew that Beterli, the most senior of the boys, set that spanking pace just to embarrass him, the smallest dragonboy. Keevan would arrive, tail fork-end of the group, breathless, chest heaving, and maybe get a stern look from the instructing wingsecond. ❶

Dragonriders, even if they were still only hopeful candidates for the glowing eggs which were hardening on the hot sands of the Hatching Ground cavern, were expected to be punctual and prepared. Sloth[1] was not tolerated by the Weyrleader of Benden Weyr. A good record was especially important now. It was very near hatching time, when the baby dragons would crack their mottled[2] shells and stagger forth to choose their lifetime companions. The very thought of that glorious moment made Keevan's breath catch in his throat. To be chosen—to be a dragonrider! To sit astride the neck of a winged beast with jeweled eyes; to be his friend, in telepathic communion[3] with him for life; to be his companion in good times and fighting extremes; to fly effortlessly over the lands of Pern! Or, thrillingly, *between* to any point anywhere on the world! Flying *between* was done on dragonback or not at all, and it was dangerous.

Keevan glanced upward, past the black mouths of the Weyr caves, in which grown dragons and their chosen riders lived, toward the Star Stones that crowned the ridge of the old volcano that was Benden Weyr. On the height, the blue watch dragon, his rider mounted on his neck, stretched the great transparent pinions[4] that carried him on the winds of Pern to fight the evil

INFER

❶ What can you infer about Beterli from the very first mention of him in the story?

---

1. **sloth** (slôth) *n.*: laziness.
2. **mottled** (mät''ld) *adj.*: spotted.
3. **telepathic communion**: communication of thoughts without speaking.
4. **pinions** (pin'yənz) *n.*: wings.

Thread that fell at certain times from the skies. The many-faceted rainbow jewels of his eyes glistened fleetingly in the greeny sun. He folded his great wings to his back, and the watch pair resumed their statuelike pose of alertness.

Then the enticing view was obscured as Keevan passed into the Hatching Ground cavern. The sands underfoot were hot, even through heavy wher-hide boots. How the boot maker had protested having to sew so small! Keevan was forced to wonder why being small was reprehensible.[5] People were always calling him "babe" and shooing him away as being "too small" or "too young" for this or that. Keevan was constantly working, twice as hard as any other boy his age, to prove himself capable. What if his muscles weren't as big as Beterli's? They were just as hard. And if he couldn't overpower anyone in a wrestling match, he could outdistance everyone in a footrace.

"Maybe if you run fast enough," Beterli had jeered on the occasion when Keevan had been goaded to boast of his swiftness, "you could catch a dragon. That's the only way you'll make a dragonrider!"

"You just wait and see, Beterli, you just wait," Keevan had replied. He would have liked to wipe the contemptuous[6] smile from Beterli's face, but the guy didn't fight fair even when a wingsecond was watching. "No one knows what Impresses a dragon!"

"They've got to be able to *find* you first, babe!"

Yes, being the smallest candidate was not an enviable position. It was therefore imperative that Keevan Impress a dragon in his first hatching. That would wipe the smile off every face in the cavern and accord him the respect due any dragonrider, even the smallest one.

Besides, no one knew exactly what Impressed the baby dragons as they struggled from their shells in search of their lifetime partners.

"I like to believe that dragons see into a man's heart," Keevan's foster mother, Mende, told him. "If they find goodness, honesty, a flexible mind, patience, courage—and you've got that in quantity, dear Keevan—that's what dragons look for. I've seen many a well-grown lad left standing on the sands, Hatching Day, in favor of someone not so strong or tall or handsome. And if my memory serves me"—which it usually did: Mende knew every word of every Harper's tale worth telling, although Keevan did not interrupt her to say so—"I don't believe that F'lar, our Weyrleader, was all that tall when bronze Mnementh chose him. And Mnementh was the only bronze dragon of that hatching." ❷

INFER
❷ Why does Mende comment on F'lar's height?

Dreams of Impressing a bronze were beyond Keevan's boldest reflections, although that goal dominated the thoughts of every other hopeful candidate. Green dragons were small and fast and more numerous. There was more prestige to Impressing a blue or brown than a green. Being practical,

---

5. **reprehensible** (rep′ri·hen′sə·bəl) *adj.:* made to seem like it was a fault, something that deserved to be criticized.
6. **contemptuous** (kən·temp′chŏŏ·əs) *adj.:* scornful; full of meanness.

Vocabulary
goaded (gōd′id) *v.:* pushed or driven. A goad is a stick with a sharp point used to herd oxen.

Keevan seldom dreamed as high as a big fighting brown, like Canth, F'nor's fine fellow, the biggest brown on all Pern. But to fly a bronze? Bronzes were almost as big as the queen, and only they took the air when a queen flew at mating time. A bronze rider could aspire to become Weyrleader! Well, Keevan would console himself, brown riders could aspire to become wingseconds, and that wasn't bad. He'd even settle for a green dragon; they were small, but so was he. No matter! He simply had to Impress a dragon his first time in the Hatching Ground. Then no one in the Weyr would taunt[7] him anymore for being so small.

Shells, Keevan thought now, but the sands are hot!

"Impression time is imminent, candidates," the wingsecond was saying as everyone crowded respectfully close to him. "See the extent of the striations[8] on this promising egg." The stretch marks *were* larger than yesterday.

Everyone leaned forward and nodded thoughtfully. That particular egg was the one Beterli had marked as his own, and no other candidate dared, on pain of being beaten by Beterli at his first opportunity, to approach it. The egg was marked by a large yellowish splotch in the shape of a dragon backwinging to land, talons outstretched to grasp rock. Everyone knew that bronze eggs bore distinctive markings. And naturally, Beterli, who'd been presented at eight Impressions already and was the biggest of the candidates, had chosen it.

"I'd say that the great opening day is almost upon us," the wingsecond went on, and then his face assumed a grave expression. "As we well know, there are only forty eggs and seventy-two candidates. Some of you may be disappointed on the great day. That doesn't necessarily mean you aren't dragonrider material, just that *the* dragon for you hasn't been shelled. You'll have other hatchings, and it's no disgrace to be left behind an Impression or two. Or more."

Keevan was positive that the wingsecond's eyes rested on Beterli, who'd been stood off at so many Impressions already. Keevan tried to squinch down so the wingsecond wouldn't notice him. Keevan had been reminded too often that he was eligible to be a candidate by one day only. He, of all the hopefuls, was most likely to be left standing on the great day. One more reason why he simply had to Impress at his first hatching.

"Now move about among the eggs," the wingsecond said. "Touch them. We don't know that it does any good, but it certainly doesn't do any harm."

Some of the boys laughed nervously, but everyone immediately began to circulate among the eggs. Beterli stepped up officiously[9] to "his" egg, daring anyone to come near it. Keevan smiled, because he had already touched it—every inspection day, when the others were leaving the Hatching Ground and no one could see him crouch to stroke it.

Keevan had an egg he concentrated on, too, one drawn slightly to the far side of the others. The shell had a soft greenish blue tinge with a faint creamy swirl design. The

---

7. **taunt** (tônt) *v.:* ridicule; mock.
8. **striations** (strī·ā′shənz) *n.:* stretch marks; stripes. (This word is defined in the context—in the next sentence.)

9. **officiously** (ə·fish′əs·lē) *adv.:* in a self-important way.

Vocabulary
imminent (im′ə·nənt) *adj.:* about to happen.

consensus was that this egg contained a mere green, so Keevan was rarely bothered by rivals. He was somewhat <u>perturbed</u>, then, to see Beterli wandering over to him.

"I don't know why you're allowed in this Impression, Keevan. There are enough of us without a babe," Beterli said, shaking his head.

"I'm of age." Keevan kept his voice level, telling himself not to be bothered by mere words.

"Yah!" Beterli made a show of standing on his toe tips. "You can't even see over an egg; Hatching Day, you better get in front or the dragons won't see you at all. 'Course, you could get run down that way in the mad scramble. Oh, I forget, you can run fast, can't you?"

"You'd better make sure a dragon sees *you* this time, Beterli," Keevan replied. "You're almost overage, aren't you?" ❸

Beterli flushed and took a step forward, hand half raised. Keevan stood his ground, but if Beterli advanced one more step, he would call the wingsecond. No one fought on the Hatching Ground. Surely Beterli knew that much.

Fortunately, at that moment, the wingsecond called the boys together and led them from the Hatching Ground to start on evening chores. There were "glows" to be replenished in the main kitchen caverns and sleeping cubicles, the major hallways, and the queen's apartment. Firestone sacks had to be filled against Thread attack, and black rock brought to the kitchen hearths. The boys fell to their chores, tantalized by the

odors of roasting meat. The population of the Weyr began to assemble for the evening meal, and the dragonriders came in from the Feeding Ground on their sweep checks.

It was the time of day Keevan liked best: Once the chores were done but before dinner was served, a fellow could often get close enough to the dragonriders to hear their talk. Tonight, Keevan's father, K'last, was at the main dragonrider table. It puzzled Keevan how his father, a brown rider and a tall man, could *be* his father—because he, Keevan, was so small. It obviously puzzled K'last, too, when he deigned to notice his small son: "In a few more Turns, you'll be as tall as I am—or taller!"

INFER

❸ Why does Keevan taunt Beterli about his age?

Vocabulary

perturbed (pər·tɜrbd′) *v.* used as *adj.*: disturbed; troubled.

K'last was pouring Benden wine all around the table. The dragonriders were relaxing. There'd be no Thread attack for three more days, and they'd be in the mood to tell tall tales, better than Harper yarns, about impossible maneuvers they'd done a-dragonback. When Thread attack was closer, their talk would change to a discussion of tactics of evasion, of going *between,* how long to suspend there until the burning but fragile Thread would freeze and crack and fall harmlessly off dragon and man. They would dispute the exact moment to feed firestone to the dragon so he'd have the best flame ready to sear Thread midair and render it harmless to ground—and man— below. There was such a lot to know and understand about being a dragonrider that sometimes Keevan was overwhelmed. How would he ever be able to remember everything he ought to know at the right moment? He couldn't dare ask such a question; this would only have given additional weight to the notion that he was too young yet to be a dragonrider.

"Having older candidates makes good sense," L'vel was saying as Keevan settled down near the table. "Why waste four to five years of a dragon's fighting prime until his rider grows up enough to stand the rigors?" L'vel had Impressed a blue of Ramoth's first clutch. Most of the candidates thought L'vel was marvelous because he spoke up in front of the older riders, who awed them. "That was well enough in the Interval when you didn't need to mount the full Weyr complement to fight Thread. But not now. Not with more eligible candidates than ever. Let the babes wait."

"Any boy who is over twelve Turns has the right to stand in the Hatching Ground,"

K'last replied, a slight smile on his face. He never argued or got angry. Keevan wished he were more like his father. And oh, how he wished he were a brown rider! "Only a dragon—each particular dragon—knows what he wants in a rider. We certainly can't tell. Time and again, the theorists," K'last's smile deepened as his eyes swept those at the table, "are surprised by dragon choice. *They* never seem to make mistakes, however."

"Now, K'last, just look at the roster this Impression. Seventy-two boys and only forty eggs. Drop off the twelve youngest, and there's still a good field for the hatchlings to choose from. Shells! There are a couple of Weyrlings unable to see over a wher egg, much less a dragon! And years before they can ride Thread."

"True enough, but the Weyr is scarcely under fighting strength, and if the youngest Impress, they'll be old enough to fight when the oldest of our current dragons go *between* from senility."

"Half the Weyr-bred lads have already been through several Impressions," one of the bronze riders said then. "I'd say drop some of *them* off this time. Give the untried a chance."

"There's nothing wrong in presenting a clutch with as wide a choice as possible," said the Weyrleader, who had joined the table with Lessa, the Weyrwoman.

"Has there ever been a case," she said, smiling in her odd way at the riders, "where a hatchling didn't choose?"

Her suggestion was almost heretical and drew astonished gasps from everyone, including the boys.

F'lar laughed. "You say the most outrageous things, Lessa."

"Well, *has* there ever been a case where a dragon didn't choose?"

"Can't say as I recall one," K'last replied.

"Then we continue in this tradition," Lessa said firmly, as if that ended the matter.

But it didn't. The argument ranged from one table to the other all through dinner, with some favoring a weeding out of the candidates to the most likely, lopping off those who were very young or who had had multiple opportunities to Impress. All the candidates were in a swivet,[10] though such a departure from tradition would be to the advantage of many. As the evening progressed, more riders were favoring eliminating the youngest and those who'd passed four or more Impressions unchosen. Keevan felt he could bear such a dictum[11] only if Beterli were also eliminated. But this seemed less likely than that Keevan would be turfed out,[12] since the Weyr's need was for fighting dragons and riders.

By the time the evening meal was over, no decision had been reached, although the Weyrleader had promised to give the matter due consideration.

He might have slept on the problem, but few of the candidates did. Tempers were uncertain in the sleeping caverns next morning as the boys were routed out of their beds to carry water and black rock and cover the "glows." Twice Mende had to call Keevan to order for clumsiness.

"Whatever is the matter with you, boy?" she demanded in exasperation when he tipped black rock short of the bin and sooted up the hearth.

"They're going to keep me from this Impression."

"What?" Mende stared at him. "Who?"

"You heard them talking at dinner last night. They're going to turf the babes from the hatching."

Mende regarded him a moment longer before touching his arm gently. "There's lots of talk around a supper table, Keevan. And it cools as soon as the supper. I've heard the same nonsense before every hatching, but nothing is ever changed."

"There's always a first time," Keevan answered, copying one of her own phrases.

"That'll be enough of that, Keevan. Finish your job. If the clutch does hatch today, we'll need full rock bins for the feast, and you won't be around to do the filling. All my fosterlings make dragonriders."

"The first time?" Keevan was bold enough to ask as he scooted off with the rockbarrow.

Perhaps, Keevan thought later, if he hadn't been on that chore just when Beterli was also fetching black rock, things might have turned out differently. But he had dutifully trundled the barrow to the outdoor bunker for another load just as Beterli arrived on a similar errand.

"Heard the news, babe?" Beterli asked. He was grinning from ear to ear, and he put an unnecessary emphasis on the final insulting word.

"The eggs are cracking?" Keevan all but dropped the loaded shovel. Several anxieties flicked through his mind then: He was black with rock dust—would he have time to wash before donning the white tunic of candidacy? And if the eggs were hatching, why hadn't the candidates been recalled by the wingsecond?

"Naw! Guess again!" Beterli was much too pleased with himself.

With a sinking heart, Keevan knew what

---

10. **in a swivet:** frustrated and annoyed.
11. **dictum** *n.:* pronouncement or judgment.
12. **turfed out:** British expression meaning "removed; expelled."

the news must be, and he could only stare with intense desolation at the older boy.

"C'mon! Guess, babe!"

"I've no time for guessing games," Keevan managed to say with indifference. He began to shovel black rock into the barrow as fast as he could.

"I said, guess." Beterli grabbed the shovel.

"And I said I have no time for guessing games."

Beterli wrenched the shovel from Keevan's hands. "Guess!"

"I'll have that shovel back, Beterli." Keevan straightened up, but he didn't come to Beterli's bulky shoulder. From somewhere, other boys appeared, some with barrows, some mysteriously alerted to the prospect of a confrontation among their numbers.

"Babes don't give orders to candidates around here, babe!"

Someone sniggered, and Keevan, incredulous,[13] knew that he must've been dropped from the candidacy.

He yanked the shovel from Beterli's loosened grasp. Snarling, the older boy tried to regain possession, but Keevan clung with all his strength to the handle, dragged back and forth as the stronger boy jerked the shovel about.

With a sudden, unexpected movement, Beterli rammed the handle into Keevan's chest, knocking him over the barrow handles. Keevan felt a sharp, painful jab behind his left ear, an unbearable pain in his left shin, and then a painless nothingness.

Mende's angry voice roused him, and, startled, he tried to throw back the covers, thinking he'd overslept. But he couldn't move, so firmly was he tucked into his bed. And then the constriction of a bandage on his head and the dull sickishness in his leg brought back recent occurrences.

"Hatching?" he cried.

"No, lovey," Mende said in a kind voice. Her hand was cool and gentle on his forehead. "Though there's some as won't be at any hatching again." Her voice took on a stern edge.

Keevan looked beyond her to see the Weyrwoman, who was frowning with irritation.

"Keevan, will you tell me what occurred at the black-rock bunker?" asked Lessa in an even voice.

He remembered Beterli now and the quarrel over the shovel and . . . what had Mende said about some not being at any hatching? Much as he hated Beterli, he couldn't bring himself to tattle on Beterli and force him out of candidacy. ❹

INFER

❹ Why is Keevan reluctant to tell Lessa what really happened?

"Come, lad," and a note of impatience crept into the Weyrwoman's voice. "I merely want to know what happened from you, too. Mende said she sent you for black rock. Beterli—and every Weyrling in the cavern— seems to have been on the same errand. What happened?"

"Beterli took my shovel. I hadn't finished with it."

"There's more than one shovel. What did he *say* to you?"

"He'd heard the news."

---

13. **incredulous** (in·krej′oo·ləs) *adj.*: doubting; unable to believe.

Vocabulary

confrontation (kän′frən·tā′shən) *n.*: face-to-face meeting between opposing sides.

"What news?" The Weyrwoman was suddenly amused.

"That . . . that . . . there'd been changes."

"Is that what he said?"

"Not exactly."

"What did he say? C'mon, lad, I've heard from everyone else, you know."

"He said for me to guess the news."

"And you fell for that old gag?" The Weyrwoman's irritation returned.

"Consider all the talk last night at supper, Lessa," Mende said. "Of course the boy would think he'd been eliminated."

"In effect, he is, with a broken skull and leg." Lessa touched his arm in a rare gesture of sympathy. "Be that as it may, Keevan, you'll have other Impressions. Beterli will not. There are certain rules that must be observed by all candidates, and his conduct proves him unacceptable to the Weyr."

She smiled at Mende and then left.

"I'm still a candidate?" Keevan asked urgently.

"Well, you are and you aren't, lovey," his foster mother said. "Is the numbweed working?" she asked, and when he nodded, she said, "You just rest. I'll bring you some nice broth."

At any other time in his life, Keevan would have relished such cosseting,[14] but now he just lay there worrying. Beterli had been dismissed. Would the others think it was his fault? But everyone was there! Beterli provoked that fight. His worry increased, because although he heard excited comings and goings in the passageway, no one tweaked back the curtain across the sleeping alcove he shared with five other boys. Surely one of

them would have to come in sometime. No, they were all avoiding him. And something else was wrong. Only he didn't know what.

Mende returned with broth and beachberry bread.

"Why doesn't anyone come see me, Mende? I haven't done anything wrong, have I? I didn't ask to have Beterli turfed out."

Mende soothed him, saying everyone was busy with noontime chores and no one was angry with him. They were giving him a chance to rest in quiet. The numbweed made him drowsy, and her words were fair enough. He permitted his fears to dissipate.[15] Until he heard a hum. Actually he felt it first, in the broken shinbone and his sore head. The hum began to grow. Two things registered suddenly in Keevan's groggy mind: The only white candidate's robe still on the pegs in the chamber was his, and the dragons hummed when a clutch was being laid or being hatched. Impression! And he was flat abed.

Bitter, bitter disappointment turned the warm broth sour in his belly. Even the small voice telling him that he'd have other opportunities failed to alleviate his crushing depression. *This* was the Impression that mattered! This was his chance to show *everyone*, from Mende to K'last to L'vel and even the Weyrleader, that he, Keevan, was worthy of being a dragonrider.

He twisted in bed, fighting against the tears that threatened to choke him. Dragonmen don't cry! Dragonmen learn to live with pain.

Pain? The leg didn't actually pain him as

---

14. **cosseting** (käs′it·iŋ) *v.* used as *n.*: spoiling; pampering; treating as if he were a little pet.

---

15. **dissipate** (dis′ə·pāt′) *v.*: disappear; go away.

Vocabulary
alleviate (ə·lē′vē·āt′) *v.*: relieve; reduce.

he rolled about on his bedding. His head felt sort of stiff from the tightness of the bandage. He sat up, an effort in itself since the numbweed made exertion[16] difficult. He touched the splinted leg; the knee was unhampered.[17] He had no feeling in his bone, really. He swung himself carefully to the side of his bed and stood slowly. The room wanted to swim about him. He closed his eyes, which made the dizziness worse, and he had to clutch the wall.

Gingerly, he took a step. The broken leg dragged. It hurt in spite of the numbweed, but what was pain to a dragonman? ❻

INFER

❺ Why does Keevan deny the pain in his leg?

No one had said he couldn't go to the Impression. "You are and you aren't" were Mende's exact words.

Clinging to the wall, he jerked off his bed shirt. Stretching his arm to the utmost, he jerked his white candidate's tunic from the peg. Jamming first one arm and then the other into the holes, he pulled it over his head. Too bad about the belt. He couldn't wait. He hobbled to the door and hung on to the curtain to steady himself. The weight on his leg was unwieldy. He wouldn't get very far without something to lean on. Down by the bathing pool was one of the long crook-necked poles used to retrieve clothes from the hot washing troughs. But it was down there, and he was on the level above. And there was no one nearby to come to his aid; everyone would be in the Hatching Ground right now, eagerly waiting for the first egg to crack.

---

16. **exertion** (eg·zʉr′shən) *n.*: exercise; effort.
17. **unhampered** (un·ham′pərd) *v.* used as *adj.*: free to move around. (There was no tight bandage on his knee.)

The humming increased in volume and tempo, an urgency to which Keevan responded, knowing that his time was all too limited if he was to join the ranks of the hopeful boys standing around the cracking eggs. But if he hurried down the ramp, he'd fall flat on his face.

He could, of course, go flat on his rear end, the way crawling children did. He sat down, sending a jarring stab of pain through his leg and up to the wound on the back of his head. Gritting his teeth and blinking away tears, Keevan scrabbled down the ramp. He had to wait a moment at the bottom to catch his breath. He got to one knee, the injured leg straight out in front of him. Somehow, he managed to push himself erect, though the room seemed about to tip over his ears. It wasn't far to the crooked stick, but it seemed an age before he had it in his hand.

Then the humming stopped!

Keevan cried out and began to hobble frantically across the cavern, out to the bowl of the Weyr. Never had the distance between living caverns and the Hatching Ground seemed so great. Never had the Weyr been so breathlessly silent. It was as if the multitude of people and dragons watching the hatching held every breath in suspense. Not even the wind muttered down the steep sides of the bowl. The only sounds to break the stillness were Keevan's ragged gasps and the thump-thud of his stick on the hard-packed ground. Sometimes he had to hop twice on his good leg to maintain his balance. Twice he fell into the sand and had to pull himself up on the stick, his white tunic no longer spotless. Once he jarred himself so badly he couldn't get up immediately.

Then he heard the first exhalation of the crowd, the oohs, the muted cheer, the susurrus[18] of excited whispers. An egg had cracked, and the dragon had chosen his rider. Desperation increased Keevan's hobble. Would he never reach the arching mouth of the Hatching Ground?

Another cheer and an excited spate[19] of applause spurred Keevan to greater effort. If he didn't get there in moments, there'd be no unpaired hatchling left. Then he was actually staggering into the Hatching Ground, the sands hot on his bare feet.

No one noticed his entrance or his halting progress. And Keevan could see nothing but the backs of the white-robed candidates, seventy of them ringing the area around the eggs. Then one side would surge forward or back and there'd be a cheer. Another dragon had been Impressed. Suddenly a large gap appeared in the white human wall, and Keevan had his first sight of the eggs. There didn't seem to be *any* left uncracked, and he could see the lucky boys standing beside wobble-legged dragons. He could hear the unmistakable plaintive[20] crooning of hatchlings and their squawks of protest as they'd fall awkwardly in the sand.

Suddenly he wished that he hadn't left his bed, that he'd stayed away from the Hatching Ground. Now everyone would see his ignominious[21] failure. So he scrambled as desperately to reach the shadowy walls of the Hatching Ground as he had struggled to cross the bowl. He mustn't be seen.

He didn't notice, therefore, that the shifting group of boys remaining had begun to drift in his direction. The hard pace he had set himself and his cruel disappointment took their

_____
18. **susurrus** (sə·sur'əs) *n.:* rustling sound.
19. **spate** (spāt) *n.:* sudden outpouring.
20. **plaintive** (plān'tiv) *adj.:* sorrowful; sad.
21. **ignominious** (ig'nə·min'ē·əs) *adj.:* shameful.

double toll of Keevan. He tripped and collapsed, sobbing, to the warm sands. He didn't see the consternation in the watching Weyr-folk above the Hatching Ground, nor did he hear the excited whispers of speculation. He didn't know that the Weyrleader and Weyr-woman had dropped to the arena and were making their way toward the knot of boys slowly moving in the direction of the entrance.

"Never seen anything like it," the Weyrleader was saying. "Only thirty-nine riders chosen. And the bronze trying to leave the Hatching Ground without making Impression."

"A case in point of what I said last night," the Weyrwoman replied, "where a hatchling makes no choice because the right boy isn't there."

"There's only Beterli and K'last's young one missing. And there's a full wing of likely boys to choose from. . . ."

"None acceptable, apparently. Where is the creature going? He's not heading for the entrance after all. Oh, what have we there, in the shadows?"

Keevan heard with dismay the sound of voices nearing him. He tried to burrow into the sand. The mere thought of how he would be teased and taunted now was unbearable.

Don't worry! Please don't worry! The thought was urgent, but not his own.

Someone kicked sand over Keevan and butted roughly against him.

"Go away. Leave me alone!" he cried.

Why? was the injured-sounding question inserted into his mind. There was no voice, no tone, but the question was there, perfectly clear, in his head.

Incredulous, Keevan lifted his head and stared into the glowing jeweled eyes of a small bronze dragon. His wings were wet,

the tips drooping in the sand. And he sagged in the middle on his unsteady legs, although he was making a great effort to keep erect.

Keevan dragged himself to his knees, oblivious[22] of the pain in his leg. He wasn't even aware that he was ringed by the boys passed over, while thirty-one pairs of resentful eyes watched him Impress the dragon. The Weyrmen looked on, amused and surprised at the draconic[23] choice, which could not be forced. Could not be questioned. Could not be changed.

Why? asked the dragon again. *Don't you like me?* His eyes whirled with anxiety, and his tone was so piteous that Keevan staggered forward and threw his arms around the dragon's neck, stroking his eye ridges, patting the damp, soft hide, opening the fragile-looking wings to dry them, and wordlessly assuring the hatchling over and over again that he was the most perfect, most beautiful, most beloved dragon in the Weyr, in all the Weyrs of Pern.

---

22. **oblivious** (ə·bliv′ē·əs) *adj.:* forgetful; not aware of.
23. **draconic** (drə·kän′ik) *adj.:* of a dragon. *Drakōn* is the Greek word for "dragon."

"What's his name, K'van?" asked Lessa, smiling warmly at the new dragonrider. K'van stared up at her for a long moment. Lessa would know as soon as he did. Lessa was the only person who could "receive" from all dragons, not only her own Ramoth. Then he gave her a radiant smile, recognizing the traditional shortening of his name that raised him forever to the rank of dragonrider.

My name is Heth, the dragon thought mildly, then hiccuped in sudden urgency. *I'm hungry.*

"Dragons are born hungry," said Lessa, laughing. "F'lar, give the boy a hand. He can barely manage his own legs, much less a dragon's."

K'van remembered his stick and drew himself up. "We'll be just fine, thank you."

"You may be the smallest dragonrider ever, young K'van," F'lar said, "but you're one of the bravest!"

And Heth agreed! Pride and joy so leaped in both chests that K'van wondered if his heart would burst right out of his body. He looped an arm around Heth's neck, and the pair, the smallest dragonboy and the hatchling who wouldn't choose anybody else, walked out of the Hatching Ground together forever.

Meet the Writer

Anne McCaffrey

Dragon Writer

Growing up as a "lonely tomboy" in New Jersey, **Anne McCaffrey** (1926–   ) decided there were two things she really wanted. "When I was a very young girl, I promised myself very fervently (usually after I'd lost another battle with one of my brothers) that I would become a famous author and I'd own my own horse." McCaffrey's books are now known all over the world and have been translated into many languages. Since she moved to County Wicklow in Ireland, she has owned a number of horses (and cats and dogs). McCaffrey lives and works in Ireland at her home, called Dragonhold. Fans of her books rejoice in McCaffrey's promise: "I shall continue to write—I can't not write—until I am too frail to touch the keys of my word processor." McCaffrey once said this about her own writing process:

> **First I find interesting people to write about (I have written an anthology series, *Crystal Singer*, because I wanted to name a feminine character Killashandra), and then I find something for them to argue about or fight for or against. Or I think about an interesting concept—the dragons of Pern—telepathic, huge, flame-throwing dragons who fly because they 'think' they can. Aerodynamically, they can't. I like to write better than anything else, including riding [horses]. And I write because I can't always get the kind of story I like to read on library shelves.**

For Independent Reading

If you want to continue riding with the dragonriders, read *Dragonsong, Dragonsinger,* and *Dragondrums,* a series of science fantasy novels about the dragons of Pern.

First Thoughts

1. Describe or draw one vivid **image** that you recall from this story. Compare your picture with your classmates'. Is your image the same as any of theirs?

Thinking Critically

2. Make a chart showing all the **conflicts** Keevan faces. Which conflict do you think is the hardest for him?

External Conflicts	Internal Conflicts

3. Think about Beterli's **character.** What inferences can you make to explain Beterli's **motivation** for trying to ruin Keevan's chances on Hatching Day?

4. Why does K'van reject the help Lessa offers him at the end of the story? What **inference** can you make about K'van from his action?

Extending Interpretations

5. List all the women in this story. Do you think they have powerful positions in Pern society, or do only men hold power? Explain. If you were writing about Pern, what roles and responsibilities would you give to men and women?

WRITING

Writing a Narrative

This story is an "underdog" story, in which a person who seems like a loser ends up a winner. Check the notes you took before you read this story, and write a short narrative in which you tell about a time when you felt like an underdog. What did you do about it? What did the experience teach you? If you've never had an underdog experience, you might write about someone you know who has.

INTERNET

Projects and Activities

Keyword: LE5 7-2

SKILLS FOCUS

Literary Skills
Analyze motivation.

Reading Skills
Make inferences.

Writing Skills
Write a narrative.

Recognizing Roots and Affixes

Many English word roots come from Latin, Greek, and an ancestor of the English language called Old English. A **word root** is a word part from which several words are formed. An **affix** is a word part added to a root. An affix can be added to the front of a word (in which case it's called a **prefix**), or it can be added to the end of a word (in which case it's called a **suffix**). For example, the word *confrontation* is made up of the prefix *com–* ("together"), the Latin root *–frons–* ("forehead"), and the suffix *–ation* ("the act of"). In the story you just read, Keevan and Beterli are brought together in a face-to-face meeting, or confrontation.

> **Word Bank**
>
> goaded
> imminent
> perturbed
> confrontation
> alleviate

PRACTICE

1. *Goaded* is derived from the Old English word *gad,* which was a pointed stick used to prod cattle. Look up the meaning of the word *gadfly,* and tell how it is related to the meaning of *gad.*

2. *Imminent* comes from the Latin word *minere,* meaning "to threaten or to project over." Look up the derivation of *menace.* How is the meaning of *menace* related to the Latin word *minere*?

3. *Turbare* is a Latin word meaning "to disturb." How is *perturbed* related to the meaning of the Latin word?

4. The word *turbine* is built on the same root word as *perturbed.* How is "disturbance" part of the meaning of *turbine*?

5. *Alleviate* is built on the Latin word *levis,* meaning "light," and the Latin prefix *ad–,* meaning "to." Using that root word and its affix, define *alleviate.*

6. Draw a "family" tree showing words that are part of the Latin word *credere,* "to believe." You should be able to find at least six words built on *credere.* A model tree showing the family *turbare* is shown at the right.

SKILLS FOCUS

Vocabulary Skills
Understand roots and affixes.

Understanding Comparison and Contrast

Reading Focus
Comparison and Contrast

The dragons of Pern are similar in some ways: They all bond with a human for life and help defend the planet from the evil Thread. They also differ in some ways: The green dragons are small and fast; the brown are big and strong; only the huge bronze can mate with the queen. When you **compare,** you look at two or more things and see how they are the same; when you **contrast,** you look for differences. You may not realize it, but you do a lot of comparing and contrasting every day—for example, when you decide what to eat for lunch or when you think about when you'll do your homework.

Writers compare and contrast things all the time. To do it effectively, they use what's known as a **compare-and-contrast organizational pattern.** Writers use one of two methods when they compare or contrast something. (The charts below refer to the article on dragons you are about to read.)

- **Block method.** The writer first discusses all the features of subject 1, then all the features of subject 2.

- **Point-by-point method.** In this pattern the writer discusses one feature of each subject at a time. The writer chooses a feature and shows how it applies to subject 1, then how it applies to subject 2. The writer continues to discuss other features and how they apply to each subject in turn.

■ In the article that follows, the writer compares and contrasts dragons from around the world. Which method does she use?

INTERNET

Interactive Reading Model

Keyword: LE5 7-2

SKILLS FOCUS

Reading Skills
Understand comparison and contrast.

Block Method	
Subject 1:	Eastern dragons
Feature 1:	Behavior
Feature 2:	Origins
Feature 3:	Appearance
Subject 2:	Western dragons
Feature 1:	Behavior
Feature 2:	Origins
Feature 3:	Appearance

Point-by-Point Method	
Feature 1:	Behavior
Subject 1:	Eastern dragons
Subject 2:	Western dragons
Feature 2:	Origins
Subject 1:	Eastern dragons
Subject 2:	Western dragons
Feature 3:	Appearance
Subject 1:	Eastern dragons
Subject 2:	Western dragons

Here Be Dragons

Chinese dragon robe with silk embroidery (detail), from the T'ung-chih period (1862–1875). The Granger Collection, New York.

MANY, MANY YEARS AGO, when people first began to map the Western world, they charted two main areas: their settlements and the wilderness. On the wilderness areas of their maps, they wrote a warning: "Here be dragons." When the European explorers set off in their wooden ships in the fifteenth century, most of the sailors still believed that if they sailed too far, the boats would tumble off the earth and into that area populated with seething,[1] clawed monsters.

Dragon stories have been told for ages in almost every land and culture: Africa, Britain, China, Egypt, Greece, and Russia. From their beginnings in mythology, dragons were associated with the Great Mother,

with the warrior sun god, and, especially, with the water gods. Dragons were said to have been present at the creation and so were endowed with characteristics of the cosmos.[2] At one with wind and fire and water, they had the ancient power of these primal[3] forces. They had command of fire and water and could fly like the wind. But dragons differ from culture to culture: In Asia, dragons help people; in Europe and other places, dragons are associated with destruction and evil.

EASTERN DRAGONS. In Asia the dragon is a benevolent, spiritual creature, gifted with wisdom and the power to confer blessings upon humankind. One of the first dragon stories Asian children hear has a beautifully multicolored dragon emerging from the primordial[4] swamp, proudly beating its chest and calling forth, wanting to know how it can be of service to people. Eastern dragons inspire awe in the people who look to them for guidance, and many are cherished as great and wonderful creatures. Two dragons acting as honor guards are believed to have visited the home of the philosopher Confucius

---

1. **seething** *adj.:* violently agitated.

2. **cosmos** *n.:* the whole universe.
3. **primal** (prī'məl) *adj.:* basic or fundamental.
4. **primordial** (prī·môr'dē·əl) *adj.:* original; first in time.

Saint George and the Dragon by Paolo Uccello (1397–1475).
Musée Jacquemart-André, Paris. Copyright Scala/Art Resource, NY.

when he was born. The ruler Huang-Ti was supposedly carried to heaven on the back of a dragon. If you met one on the road of life, an Eastern dragon would give you a gift as opposed to, say, fire and brimstone.

WESTERN DRAGONS.

Speaking of fire and brimstone, the Western dragon is famous for both. People could always tell when they were in the vicinity of a Western dragon because the air would be heated and foul with the unmistakable sulfuric odor of brimstone. Brimstone has a smell that makes the scent of a rotten egg seem lovely by comparison.

Western dragons became feared as the foes of civilization. Perseus of ancient Greece, Beowulf of ancient Denmark, even brave little Bilbo in *The Hobbit*—all had to face down menacing dragons before they could conclude their quests. In Western stories, dragons often lie underground, guarding huge piles of gold they have stolen from the surrounding countryside, which, by the way, has also been scorched and laid waste by the dragon's fiery breath.

DRAGONS TODAY.

Dragons have largely disappeared from our stories—except for the fantasies of writers like Anne McCaffrey.

Dragons haven't died out, however. Wait a moment! What is all that noise? It sounds like people playing gongs, cymbals, and drums. What is that colorful creature a block long snaking its way through the Chinese New Year's crowd lining the sidewalks? Why, it's the Eastern dragon come again to celebrate the vitality of life! Hear that thunderous applause? That is the sound that attends an Eastern dragon passing by.

—Flo Ota De Lange

Analyzing Comparison and Contrast

Here Be Dragons

Test Practice

1. Which sentence best states the **main idea** of this article?

   A Dragon stories are very old.

   B In Asia, dragons are helpful; in the West, dragons are evil.

   C Dragons are mythical creatures.

   D Western dragons are foes of civilization.

2. The **organizational pattern** this writer uses for **comparing and contrasting** Eastern and Western dragons is the —

   F chronological method

   G point-by-point method

   H persuasive method

   J block method

3. The **title** of this article refers to —

   A a book on dragons

   B an Asian dragon story

   C a warning on old maps

   D a European dragon story

4. Dragon stories would most likely appear in a book of —

   F realistic stories

   G mystery stories

   H myths and legends

   J nonfiction

5. Anne McCaffrey's dragons in "The Smallest Dragonboy" most resemble the ones in stories from —

   A Asia

   B Europe

   C Africa

   D America

Constructed Response

A Venn diagram like the one at the right can help you sort out and analyze the similarities and differences between Eastern dragons and Western dragons. In each circle you note differences. In the center, where the circles overlap, you note similarities. Complete the diagram.

Eastern Dragons   Western Dragons

help people   have great powers   hurt people

Differences   Similarities   Differences

SKILLS FOCUS

Reading Skills
Analyze comparison and contrast.

A Rice Sandwich

Make the Connection
Quickwrite ✏️

In this story, a girl named Esperanza has an upsetting encounter with a school official. Have you, or someone you know, ever been corrected by someone in authority? Jot down some notes about the incident.

Literary Focus
The Narrator

If you have ever written a story, you know that the first questions you have to answer are "Who is going to tell this story?" and "Who will be my narrator?" A **narrator** is simply the person telling the story.

Most stories are told by what is called an **omniscient** (äm·nish′ənt) **narrator.** *Omniscient* means "all knowing," and an omniscient narrator knows all about all the characters and the events in the story. An omniscient narrator can tell you what everyone in the story is thinking. An omniscient narrator can also take you back and forth in time. "Rikki-tikki-tavi," the story about the brave mongoose and the killer cobras, which starts on page 15, is told by an omniscient narrator.

When you read the second paragraph of "A Rice Sandwich," you realize that you are listening to one of the characters in the story. Notice that this narrator says, "*My* home," not "*Esperanza's* home," and "*I* got it in my head," not "*She* got it in her head." When a story is told by a character in the story—someone who tells the whole tale using the first-person pronoun *I* or *me* or *mine*—the story is told by a **first-person narrator.**

Reading a story told by a first-person narrator is like entering into a character's mind and heart. Notice how much Esperanza reveals about herself as she tells about her experience with a rice sandwich.

Reading Skills 📖
Making Inferences

Writers don't come right out and tell you everything you want to know about their characters. You're supposed to take part in the story and make your own inferences about the characters you meet, just the way you do in real life. To make inferences about the character in this story, use these strategies:

- Watch what Esperanza says and does.
- Observe the way other characters respond to Esperanza.
- Examine what you learn about Esperanza's thoughts.
- Think about how Esperanza is like, or not like, people you know in real life.

INTERNET
More About Cisneros
Keyword: LE5 7-2

SKILLS FOCUS

Literary Skills
Understand the narrator.

Reading Skills
Make inferences.

A Rice Sandwich

Sandra Cisneros

The special kids, the ones who wear keys around their necks, get to eat in the canteen. The canteen! Even the name sounds important. And these kids at lunch time go there because their mothers aren't home or home is too far away to get to.

My home isn't far but it's not close either, and somehow I got it in my head one day to ask my mother to make me a sandwich and write a note to the principal so I could eat in the canteen too.

Oh no, she says pointing the butter knife at me as if I'm starting trouble, no sir. Next thing you know everybody will be wanting a bag lunch—I'll be up all night cutting bread into little triangles, this one with mayonnaise, this one with mustard, no pickles on mine, but mustard on one side please. You kids just like to invent more work for me.

But Nenny says she doesn't want to eat at school—ever—because she likes to go home with her best friend Gloria who lives across the schoolyard. Gloria's mama has a big color T.V. and all they do is watch cartoons. Kiki and Carlos, on the other hand, are patrol boys. They don't want to eat at school either. They like to stand out in the cold especially if it's raining. They think suffering is good for you ever since they saw that movie "300 Spartans."

I'm no Spartan[1] and hold up an anemic[2] wrist to prove it. I can't even blow up a balloon without getting dizzy. And besides, I know how to make my own lunch. If I ate at school there'd be less dishes to wash. You would see me less and less and like me better. Every day at noon my chair would be empty. Where is my favorite daughter you would cry, and when I came home finally at 3 p.m. you would appreciate me.

Okay, okay, my mother says after three days of this. And the following morning I get to go to school with my mother's letter and a rice sandwich because we don't have lunch meat.

Mondays or Fridays, it doesn't matter, mornings always go by slow and this day especially. But lunch time came finally and I got to get in line with the stay-at-school kids. Everything is fine until the nun who knows all the canteen kids by heart looks at me and says: you, who sent you here? And since I am shy, I don't say anything, just hold out my hand with the letter. This is no good, she says, till Sister Superior gives the okay. Go upstairs and see her. And so I went.

I had to wait for two kids in front of me to get hollered at, one because he did something in class, the other because he didn't. My turn came and I stood in front of the big desk with holy pictures under the glass while the Sister Superior read my letter. It went like this:

Dear Sister Superior,

Please let Esperanza eat in the lunch room because she lives too far away and she gets tired. As you can see she is very skinny. I hope to God she does not faint. Thanking you,
Mrs. E. Cordero.

You don't live far, she says. You live across the boulevard. That's only four blocks. Not even. Three maybe. Three long blocks away from here. I bet I can see your house from my window. Which one? Come here. Which one is your house?

And then she made me stand up on a box of books and point. That one? she said pointing to a row of ugly 3-flats, the ones even the raggedy men are ashamed to go into. Yes, I nodded even though I knew that wasn't my house and started to cry. I always cry when nuns yell at me, even if they're not yelling.

Then she was sorry and said I could stay—just for today, not tomorrow or the day after—you go home. And I said yes and could I please have a Kleenex—I had to blow my nose.

In the canteen, which was nothing special, lots of boys and girls watched while I cried and ate my sandwich, the bread already greasy and the rice cold.

---

1. **Spartan:** hardy, disciplined person, like the Spartans of ancient Greece.
2. **anemic** (ə·nē′mik) *adj.*: pale and weak.

Meet the Writer

Sandra Cisneros

Finding Her Own Way

Sandra Cisneros (1954–   ) was born and raised in Chicago, the only daughter in a working-class family with six sons. The harshness of life in her poor neighborhood made Cisneros shy as a child, and she escaped into the world of books. By the age of ten, she was writing her own poetry.

Cisneros grew up speaking Spanish with her Mexican-born father, but she didn't explore her heritage until she attended the Writer's Workshop at the University of Iowa. There she began a series of sketches about her old Spanish-speaking neighborhood in Chicago. These sketches grew into her first book, *The House on Mango Street* (1984), which includes the story "A Rice Sandwich." About her writing she says:

> **❝** I didn't know what I was writing when I wrote *House on Mango Street*, but I knew what I wanted. I didn't know what to call it, but I knew what I was after. It wasn't a naive thing; it wasn't an accident. I wanted to write a series of stories that you could open up at any point. You didn't have to know anything before or after and you would understand each story like a little pearl, or you could look at the whole thing like a necklace. That's what I always knew from the day that I wrote the first one. **❞**

Author Study

To read more by and about Sandra Cisneros (and her character Esperanza), see the Author Study on pages 613–627.

First Thoughts

1. Complete this sentence:

   • I thought Esperanza . . .

Thinking Critically

2. Why do you think eating in the canteen is so important for Esperanza? Do you think she'll want to eat there again? Explain. 📖

3. What can you infer about Esperanza's **character** from the fact that she argues for three days with her mother, trying to persuade her to write the note? 📖

4. How does Esperanza directly **characterize** herself? How does she directly characterize her sister, Nenny, and her brothers, Kiki and Carlos?

5. What do you learn about Esperanza's **character** in the scene with Sister Superior? Did this encounter seem believable to you? Be sure to check your Quickwrite notes. ✏️

Reading Check

a. Who eats in the canteen?

b. How does Esperanza persuade her mother to write the note so that she can eat in the canteen too?

c. Why doesn't Sister Superior want to let Esperanza eat in the canteen?

d. According to Esperanza, why does she begin to cry?

e. How does Esperanza describe her sandwich at the end of the story?

Extending Interpretations

6. This story is a **first-person narration** told by Esperanza, a character in the story. Do you think the story would have been better or not as good or about the same if someone else had been the narrator? Explain.

WRITING

Describing Another Side of the Story

This is a story about a tiny incident in Esperanza's life. Take the incident, and let another character tell a story about it. You might let Sister Superior be the new narrator or Esperanza's mother or even Nenny, Kiki, or Carlos.

SKILLS FOCUS

Literary Skills
Analyze the narrator.

Reading Skills
Make inferences.

Writing Skills
Describe events from another point of view.

Borrowed Words

When people speaking different languages come into contact, they often borrow one another's words. It is no surprise, then, that English contains many words borrowed from other cultures.

Word Bank

canteen
triangles
suffering
Spartan
anemic

PRACTICE

Explain how the following facts help you understand the meaning of one of the Word Bank words.

1. In Italian a *cantina* is a wine cellar.
2. The Latin word *ferre* means "to bear"; the Latin prefix *sub–* means "under" or "below."
3. The prefix *tri–* comes from *tres,* meaning "three" in Latin.
4. The Greek prefix *an–* means "without," and the Greek word *haima* means "blood."
5. Sparta was a great military power in ancient Greece. The people of Sparta were known for their courage, discipline, and ability to endure hardship.

SKILLS FOCUS

Vocabulary Skills
Understand word origins.

Grammar Skills
Use clear pronoun references.

Grammar Link

Avoiding Unclear Pronoun References

Writers must make sure that readers can tell which word or phrase a pronoun refers to. The word a pronoun refers to is called its **antecedent.** In the first sentence that follows, the antecedent of the pronoun *she* cannot be clearly identified.

CONFUSING | **Nenny whispered something to Gloria, and she smiled.** [Who smiled, Nenny or Gloria?]

CLEAR | **Nenny smiled as she whispered something to Gloria.** [Nenny was the one who smiled.]

To avoid confusion, the writer had to reword the sentence and move the pronoun closer to its antecedent (Nenny).

PRACTICE

Revise the following sentences to fix the unclear pronoun references.

1. Carlos told Kiki that he wasn't allowed to be on patrol anymore.
2. When the nun told Sister Superior what happened, she gave me a concerned look.
3. Esperanza later told her mother, and she started to cry.

For more help, see Agreement of Pronoun and Antecedent, 2o–x, in the Language Handbook.

Antaeus

Make the Connection
Quickwrite

Which do you think makes the best home: the country or the city? Write down some reasons for your choice, or draw a picture of what you think is the perfect place to live.

Literary Focus
Motivation

Why did he do that? What makes her act that way? These are questions about **motivation.** Feelings, needs, wishes, pressures from family and friends—all these forces pull and push people from inside and outside. As you read the story of T. J. and his friends, think about what motivates them to act the way they do.

Allusion

This title of this story is an **allusion** to a character from Greek mythology. Antaeus (an·tē′əs) is a giant whose strength comes from his mother, the Earth. As long as his feet are on the ground, Antaeus cannot be beaten. As you read the story, think about the connection between Antaeus and T. J.

SKILLS FOCUS

Literary Skills
Understand motivation; understand allusion.

Reading Skills
Make predictions.

Reading Skills
Predicting

As you read this story, do some guesswork about what you think will happen. The best thing about guessing, or **predicting**, is that you can always change your prediction (and often should) once you've read more of the story. Use your own knowledge of human behavior and details from the text to predict what T. J. and his friends will do next.

Vocabulary Development

You'll learn these words in "Antaeus."

resolute (rez′ə·lōōt′) *adj.:* firm and purposeful; determined. *T. J. was resolute; he would not change his plan.*

domain (dō·mān′) *n.:* territory. *The boys were thrilled with their own rooftop domain.*

contemplate (kän′təm·plāt′) *v.:* look at or think about carefully. *They could contemplate the result of their labor with satisfaction.*

shrewd (shrōōd) *adj.:* clever. *His shrewd words convinced his friends of his plan.*

sterile (ster′əl) *adj.:* barren; lacking interest or vitality. *They were surprised to see grass growing on the sterile roof of the building.*

Background
Literature and Social Studies

During World War II, the United States geared up to produce equipment, weapons, and goods to serve the military effort overseas. Since most factories were in the North, many families left their homes in the South seeking work. This is the situation the narrator is referring to as the story opens.

ANTAEUS

Borden Deal

saw three men standing near the trapdoor at the other end of the roof. They weren't policemen or night watchmen but three men in plump business suits, looking at us. They walked toward us.

"What are you boys doing up here?" the one in the middle said again.

We stood still, guilt heavy among us, levied by the tone of voice, and looked at the three strangers.

The men stared at the grass flourishing behind us. "What's this?" the man said. "How did this get up here?"

"Sure is growing good, ain't it?" T. J. said conversationally. "We planted it."

The men kept looking at the grass as if they didn't believe it. It was a thick carpet over the earth now, a patch of deep greenness startling in the sterile industrial surroundings.

"Yes, sir," T. J. said proudly. "We toted that earth up here and planted that grass." He fluttered the seed catalog. "And we're just fixing to plant us some watermelon."

The man looked at him then, his eyes strange and faraway. "What do you mean, putting this on the roof of my building?" he said. "Do you want to go to jail?"

T. J. looked shaken. The rest of us were silent, frightened by the authority of his voice. We had grown up aware of adult authority, of policemen and night watchmen and teachers, and this man sounded like all the others. But it was a new thing to T. J.

"Well, you wasn't using the roof," T. J. said. He paused a moment and added shrewdly, "So we just thought to pretty it up a little bit."

"And sag it so I'd have to rebuild it," the man said sharply. He started turning away, saying to another man beside him, "See that all that junk is shoveled off by tomorrow."

"Yes, sir," the man said.

T. J. started forward. "You can't do that," he said. "We toted it up here, and it's our earth. We planted it and raised it and toted it up here."

The man stared at him coldly. "But it's my building," he said. "It's to be shoveled off tomorrow."

"It's our earth," T. J. said desperately. "You ain't got no right!"

The men walked on without listening and descended clumsily through the trapdoor. T. J. stood looking after them, his body tense with anger, until they had disappeared. They wouldn't even argue with him, wouldn't let him defend his earth rights.

He turned to us. "We won't let 'em do it," he said fiercely. "We'll stay up here all day tomorrow and the day after that, and we won't let 'em do it."

We just looked at him. We knew there was no stopping it.

He saw it in our faces, and his face wavered for a moment before he gripped it into determination. "They ain't got no right," he said. "It's our earth. It's our land. Can't nobody touch a man's own land."

We kept looking at him, listening to the words but knowing that it was no use. The adult world had descended on us even in our richest dream, and we knew there was no calculating the adult world, no fighting it, no winning against it.

We started moving slowly toward the parapet and the fire escape, avoiding a last look at the green beauty of the earth that T. J. had planted for us, had planted deeply in our minds as well as in our experience. We filed slowly over the edge and down the steps to the plank, T. J. coming last, and all of us could feel the weight of his

Vocabulary
sterile (ster′əl) *adj.*: barren; lacking interest or vitality.

grief behind us.

"Wait a minute," he said suddenly, his voice harsh with the effort of calling.

We stopped and turned, held by the tone of his voice, and looked up at him standing above us on the fire escape.

"We can't stop them?" he said, looking down at us, his face strange in the dusky light. "There ain't no way to stop 'em?"

"No," Blackie said with finality. "They own the building."

We stood still for a moment, looking up at T. J., caught into inaction by the decision working in his face. He stared back at us, and his face was pale and mean in the poor light, with a bald nakedness in his skin like cripples have sometimes.

"They ain't gonna touch my earth," he said fiercely. "They ain't gonna lay a hand on it! Come on."

He turned around and started up the fire escape again, almost running against the effort of climbing. We followed more slowly, not knowing what he intended to do. By the time we reached him, he had seized a board and thrust it into the soil, scooping it up and flinging it over the parapet into the areaway below. He straightened and looked at us.

"They can't touch it," he said. "I won't let 'em lay a dirty hand on it!"

We saw it then. He stooped to his labor again, and we followed, the gusts of his anger moving in frenzied labor among us as we scattered along the edge of earth, scooping it and throwing it over the parapet, destroying with anger the growth we had nurtured with such tender care. The soil carried so laboriously upward to the light and the sun cascaded swiftly into the dark areaway, the green blades of grass crumpled and twisted in the falling.

It took less time than you would think; the task of destruction is infinitely easier than that of creation. We stopped at the end, leaving only a scattering of loose soil, and when it was finally over, a stillness stood among the group and over the factory building. We looked down at the bare sterility of black tar, felt the harsh texture of it under the soles of our shoes, and the anger had gone out of us, leaving only a sore aching in our minds, like overstretched muscles.

T. J. stood for a moment, his breathing slowing from anger and effort, caught into the same contemplation of destruction as all of us. He stooped slowly, finally, and picked up a lonely blade of grass left trampled under our feet and put it between his teeth, tasting it, sucking the greenness out of it into his mouth. Then he started walking toward the fire escape, moving before any of us were ready to move, and disappeared over the edge.

We followed him, but he was already halfway down to the ground, going on past the board where we crossed over, climbing down into the areaway. We saw the last section swing down with his weight, and then he stood on the concrete below us, looking at the small pile of anonymous earth scattered by our throwing. Then he walked across the place where we could see him and disappeared toward the street without glancing back, without looking up to see us watching him.

They did not find him for two weeks.

Then the Nashville police caught him just outside the Nashville freight yards. He was walking along the railroad track, still heading South, still heading home.

As for us, who had no remembered home to call us, none of us ever again climbed the escapeway to the roof.

Meet the Writer

Borden Deal

Keeping the Faith

Like his hero T. J., **Borden Deal** (1922–1985) came from a family of Southern cotton farmers. They knew firsthand the hardships of farm life during the Great Depression. As the following anecdote proves, Deal was just as persistent as T. J.:

❝ My short story 'Antaeus' has a strange history. Though it has been reprinted far more often than any other of my nearly one hundred short stories, it took me ten years to get it published the first time! True. It was turned down by every quality popular magazine in the country, not once but two or three times. Then, on rereading the story after a year or so, I'd like it all over again, and I'd send it around once more. After ten long years, the story was finally published by one of the country's finest literary magazines, and the next year it was reprinted in the annual collection called *The Best American Short Stories.* Since then, the story has appeared in hundreds of textbooks and anthologies on every level, from grammar school to college. So you see, when you believe in something, it pays to keep the faith and be persistent—just as, in the story, T. J. is persistent in his faith and feeling for the earth. ❞

First Thoughts

1. If you were T. J., what would you do after hearing the words "It's to be shoveled off tomorrow"?

Thinking Critically

2. T. J. inspires the boys to take on a difficult project and carries it out alone when the others lose interest. What does this tell you about his **character**?

3. What was T. J.'s **motivation** for conceiving and carrying out his grand project?

4. Find the passage in the story that mentions Antaeus (page 179). In the Greek myth, Antaeus cannot be beaten while connected with the earth, but the hero Hercules is able to kill Antaeus after lifting him into the air. Explain the connection between what happens to Antaeus and what happens to T. J. What do you think the **allusion** adds to the story?

5. What do you make of the last line, about the city boys' having "no remembered home" to call them? What do you think the word *home* means here?

6. Did any of your **predictions** turn out to be correct? Using details from the story, explain why one of your predictions was or was not correct.

Extending Interpretations

7. Look back at the notes about home that you made for the Quickwrite. How do your feelings about home compare with T. J.'s?

WRITING

Adding a Final Scene

What happens to T. J.? Write a final scene for the story. Tell it from T. J.'s point of view. Let T. J. continue the story, speaking as "I." Before you write, collect ideas by answering the questions in the graphic to the right.

Reading Check

a. What characteristic makes T. J. seem "different" at first to the narrator?

b. What does T. J. want? What obstacles must he overcome to get what he wants?

c. What does the narrator realize for the first time when he smells "the sweet odor of the earth" under his feet (page 179)?

d. How does T. J. react when the boys' project is destroyed?

INTERNET

Projects and Activities

Keyword: LE5 7-2

What is T.J. doing now?

When is it?

last scene

Where is it?

Why did T.J run away?

How does T.J. feel?

SKILLS FOCUS

Literary Skills
Analyze motivation; analyze an allusion.

Reading Skills
Make predictions.

Writing Skills
Add a scene to a story.

Clarifying Word Meanings

One way to show your understanding of words is to use them in your own writing.

Word Bank

resolute
domain
contemplate
shrewd
sterile

PRACTICE 1

1. Describe T. J., using the words *resolute* and *shrewd*.
2. Describe how the city boys feel about the roof garden, using the words *contemplate* and *domain*.
3. Using the word *sterile* describe how the boys change the tar roof into a lawn.

Dialect—Voices of a Region or a Group

In "Antaeus," T. J. speaks in a way that doesn't sound like standard English. He uses double (even triple) negatives and words like *ourn* for *ours* and *offen* for *from*. Here is an example:

T. J.'S DIALECT	"You mean you ain't got no fields to raise nothing in?"
STANDARD ENGLISH	Do you mean you have no fields in which to raise anything?

Dialect is a way of speaking that is characteristic of a particular region or group of people. People who study language say that all of us speak one dialect or another. Think of how a British speaker sounds. Think of how a Philadelphian speaks, as compared with a person from Southern California. T. J. speaks one of the dialects of the Deep South. Like all dialects, T. J.'s has a distinctive pronunciation, vocabulary, and grammar. By re-creating T. J.'s dialect, Deal helps us "see" the boy and "hear" his gentle Southern drawl.

PRACTICE 2

Do a survey of dialects spoken in your class. Does everyone sound the same, or do you hear varied dialects?

1. Do you say "crick" or "creek" to refer to a small stream?
2. Do you use *frying pan, skillet,* or *spider* to refer to the pan you fry eggs in?
3. How do you pronounce *dear, car,* and *water*?

SKILLS FOCUS

Vocabulary Skills
Clarify word meanings; understand dialect.

Understanding the Main Idea

Reading Focus
The Main Idea

In the fictional story "Antaeus," T. J. wants to grow plants on a city roof. In the newspaper article you are about to read, you'll meet some real-live people who garden in the city.

Informational texts, such as newspaper articles, usually focus on one or more main ideas. The **main idea** is the central, most important point in a text. In some texts the main idea is stated directly. Most of the time however, you, the reader, must **infer** the main idea—that is, you have to think about all the details in the text and make an educated guess about its main point.

Here are some tips for figuring out the main idea:

- Look at the **title**. Does it tell you what the text focuses on? Sometimes the title does not point to a central idea at all. Instead, it's a "grabber"— it's meant to grab your attention. (The title of the article you are about to read plays on the words *mix* and *olio*. *Olio* means "collection or mixture.")

- Look for a **sentence that seems to state a key idea** in general terms. Sometimes such statements appear at the beginning or the end of a text. Other times they are buried someplace in the middle.

- If you can't find a sentence that clearly states the main idea, go back over the text, and find the **most important details**. Ask yourself: What do all these details add up to?

■ When you have finished reading the article, think about whether the title gives you a clue to its main idea.

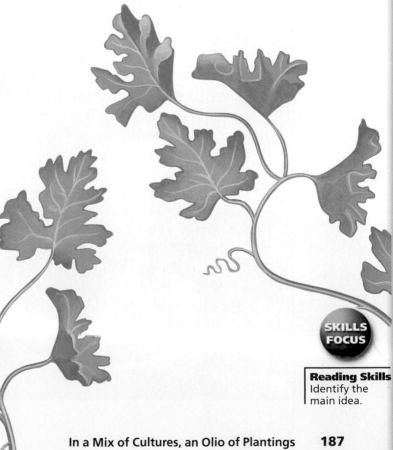

SKILLS FOCUS

Reading Skills
Identify the main idea.

In a Mix of Cultures, an Olio of Plantings

ANNE RAVER

Juan Guerrero grows tomatillos on a scrap of land that used to be a chop shop for stolen cars in the South Bronx. It's his little piece of Mexico.

"He says you cut them up with hot pepper for salsa," said Jose Garcia, who grew up in Puerto Rico. Mr. Guerrero left Puebla, Mexico, four years ago, but he speaks little English, so Mr. Garcia was translating.

He watched Mr. Guerrero peel the papery husk from a hard little green fruit and nodded yes, yes, yes, as his neighbor explained how to dry the fruit for seeds.

"In Puerto Rico," Mr. Garcia said, chuckling, "my father always told me these were poison." Then he politely tasted a pungent leaf that Mr. Guerrero had just picked from a bushy green herb.

"Papalo," Mr. Guerrero said. "Como cilantro."

This 100 by 175 foot piece of earth, on Prospect Avenue between East 181st and 182d Streets, used to grow old car parts, refrigerators, and crack vials. Now it grows zinnias, hollyhocks, eggplants, collard greens, and pear trees. And its thirty gardeners call it "The Garden of Happiness."

Happiness here has little to do with the perfect perennial° bed. It's about reclaiming scarred land from drug dealers. And planting a few vegetables and flowers that remind you of the roots you tore up to get here.

Many urban gardeners till city-owned lots leased to them for one dollar a year by Operation Green Thumb, the city's gardening program, which leases more than a thousand lots to 550 community groups. Others just take over garbage-strewn land.

"Gardening takes you back to your roots," said Karen Washington, 37, who took a pickax and shovel to the debris three years ago and now heads the community garden. "My grandparents farmed in North Carolina. If you gave them some store-bought collard greens, they'd look at you like you were crazy."

—from *The New York Times*

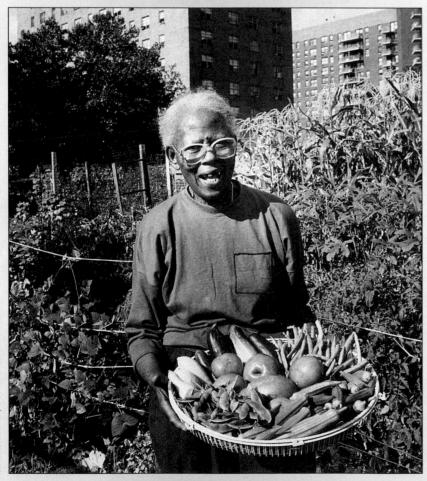

Sara Krulwich, The New York Times.

Urban gardener Annie Vigg with a harvest of squash, tomatoes, beans, peas, and okra.

°**perennial** (pə·ren′ē·əl) n. used as an *adj.*: a plant that survives and grows again year after year.

Analyzing Main Idea

In a Mix of Cultures, an Olio of Plantings

Test Practice

1. The **subject** of this article is —
    A   Juan Guerrero's tomatillos
    B   Operation Green Thumb
    C   gardening in the city
    D   gardening in Puerto Rico

2. Which of the following sentences *best* states the **main idea** of this article?
    F   It takes many different types of people to plant a garden.
    G   Gardening improves the quality of life for city dwellers.
    H   It is better to garden in New York than in North Carolina.
    J   Happiness means planting the perfect year-round garden.

3. This **newspaper article** can best be described as —
    A   fast-breaking news
    B   a human-interest story
    C   an editorial
    D   political analysis

4. The **main idea** of this article is stated —
    F   in the first sentence
    G   in the middle
    H   at the end
    J   indirectly

Constructed Response

State the **main idea** of this article in your own words. Then, list three significant **details** or **quotations** from the article that you think back up the main idea.

SKILLS FOCUS

Reading Skills
Analyze the main idea.

Comparing Literature

Literary Focus
Characters and Character Traits

How do you get to know the people you meet? They don't carry around signs saying "I am kind and caring" or "I am a mean bully." You have to figure out what they are like for yourself. How do you do it? You notice their appearance. You pay attention to what they say and do. You listen to what others say about them. Then, you think about these clues and make inferences about the **character traits** they reveal. Finally, you decide what you think about them.

You do the same thing to get to know the characters in a story. In "A Day's Wait" clues in the text will help you understand the character traits of a young boy and his father.

Reading Skills
Comparing and Contrasting

The main characters in "A Day's Wait" and "Stolen Day" are both young boys who think they are sick, but each boy behaves in a different way.

In the margins of each story, you will find numbered questions. These questions will help you focus on the actions of the boys and think about their character traits. Once you have a list of each boy's actions and the traits they reveal, you will be ready to write an essay in which you show how the two boys are similar and how they are different.

SKILLS FOCUS

Literary Skills
Understand character traits.

Reading Skills
Compare and contrast characters.

Clues to Character Traits

You can get to know the characters in a story by paying attention to their:

- appearance
- actions
- words
- thoughts and feelings
- effects on other characters

Sample Character Traits

- pushy / shy
- brave / fearful
- mean / kind
- cheerful / sad
- thoughtful / careless
- selfish / generous
- confident / unsure
- serious / silly
- restless / content
- curious / bored
- sad / happy
- weak / powerful
- hardworking / lazy
- determined / easygoing

Before You Read

To understand this story, you have to know that there are two kinds of thermometers, each using a different temperature scale. On the Celsius thermometer, used in Europe, the boiling point of water is 100 degrees. On the Fahrenheit thermometer, used in the United States, the boiling point is much higher, 212 degrees.

The events in this story really happened to Hemingway and his nine-year-old son Bumby. (In this story, Bumby is called Schatz, a German word meaning "treasure.") Hemingway and his family lived in France for many years; in this story they are back in the United States. Do the father or son in this story remind you of anyone you know?

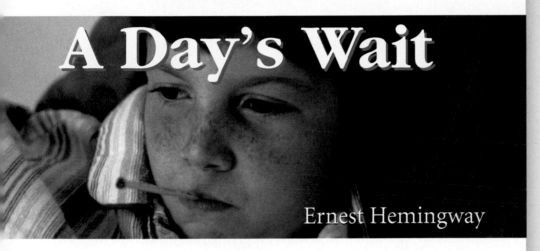

A Day's Wait

Ernest Hemingway

He came into the room to shut the windows while we were still in bed and I saw he looked ill. He was shivering, his face was white, and he walked slowly as though it ached to move.

"What's the matter, Schatz?"

"I've got a headache."

"You better go back to bed."

"No. I'm all right."

"You go to bed. I'll see you when I'm dressed."

But when I came downstairs he was dressed, sitting by the fire, looking a very sick and miserable boy of nine years. When I put my hand on his forehead I knew he had a fever.

"You go up to bed," I said, "you're sick."

"I'm all right," he said. ❶

When the doctor came he took the boy's temperature.

INFER

❶ What do the boy's words and actions so far tell you about his character?

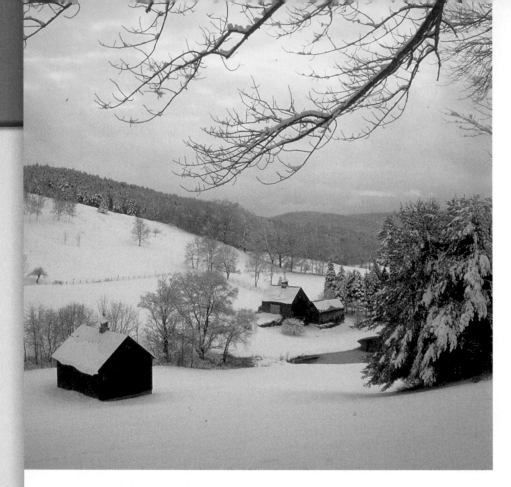

"What is it?" I asked him.

"One hundred and two."

Downstairs, the doctor left three different medicines in different-colored capsules with instructions for giving them. One was to bring down the fever, another a purgative,[1] the third to overcome an acid condition. The germs of influenza can only exist in an acid condition, he explained. He seemed to know all about influenza and said there was nothing to worry about if the fever did not go above one hundred and four degrees. This was a light epidemic of flu and there was no danger if you avoided pneumonia.

Back in the room I wrote the boy's temperature down and made a note of the time to give the various capsules.

"Do you want me to read to you?"

"All right. If you want to," said the boy. His face was very white and there were dark areas under his eyes. He lay still in the bed and seemed very detached from what was going on.

I read aloud from Howard Pyle's *Book of Pirates*; but I could see

---

1. **purgative** (pur'gə·tiv) *n.*: laxative.

he was not following what I was reading.

"How do you feel, Schatz?" I asked him.

"Just the same, so far," he said.

I sat at the foot of the bed and read to myself while I waited for it to be time to give another capsule. It would have been natural for him to go to sleep, but when I looked up he was looking at the foot of the bed, looking very strangely.

"Why don't you try to go to sleep? I'll wake you up for the medicine."

"I'd rather stay awake."

After a while he said to me, "You don't have to stay in here with me, Papa, if it bothers you."

"It doesn't bother me."

"No, I mean you don't have to stay if it's going to bother you." ❷

I thought perhaps he was a little lightheaded and after giving him the prescribed capsules at eleven o'clock I went out for a while.

It was a bright, cold day, the ground covered with a sleet that had frozen so that it seemed as if all the bare trees, the bushes, the cut brush, and all the grass and the bare ground had been varnished with ice. I took the young Irish setter for a little walk up the road and along a frozen creek, but it was difficult to stand or walk on the glassy surface and the red dog slipped and slithered and I fell twice, hard, once dropping my gun and having it slide away over the ice.

We flushed a covey[2] of quail under a high clay bank with over-hanging brush and I killed two as they went out of sight over the top of the bank. Some of the covey lit in trees, but most of them scattered into brush piles and it was necessary to jump on the ice-coated mounds of brush several times before they would flush. Coming out while you were poised unsteadily on the icy, springy brush, they made difficult shooting and I killed two, missed five, and started back pleased to have found a covey close to the house and happy there were so many left to find on another day. ❸

At the house they said the boy had refused to let anyone come into the room.

"You can't come in," he said. "You mustn't get what I have."

I went up to him and found him in exactly the position I had left him, white-faced, but with the tops of his cheeks flushed by the fever, staring still, as he had stared, at the foot of the bed.

---

2. **flushed a covey** (kuv'ē): frightened a small group of wild birds from their hiding place.

INFER

❷ What does the boy say that shows he is concerned about his father?

INFER

❸ The father goes hunting and enjoys himself while his son is sick. What does this action reveal about the father's **character**?

I took his temperature.

"What is it?"

"Something like a hundred," I said. It was one hundred and two and four tenths.

"It was a hundred and two," he said.

"Who said so?"

"The doctor."

"Your temperature is all right," I said. "It's nothing to worry about."

"I don't worry," he said, "but I can't keep from thinking."

"Don't think," I said. "Just take it easy."

"I'm taking it easy," he said and looked straight ahead. He was evidently holding tight onto himself about something.

"Take this with water."

"Do you think it will do any good?"

"Of course it will."

I sat down and opened the *Pirate* book and commenced to read, but I could see he was not following, so I stopped.

"About what time do you think I'm going to die?" he asked. ❹

"What?"

"About how long will it be before I die?"

"You aren't going to die. What's the matter with you?"

"Oh, yes, I am. I heard him say a hundred and two."

"People don't die with a fever of one hundred and two. That's a silly way to talk."

"I know they do. At school in France the boys told me you can't live with forty-four degrees. I've got a hundred and two."

He had been waiting to die all day, ever since nine o'clock in the morning.

"You poor Schatz," I said. "Poor old Schatz. It's like miles and kilometers. You aren't going to die. That's a different thermometer. On that thermometer thirty-seven is normal. On this kind it's ninety-eight."

"Are you sure?"

"Absolutely," I said. "It's like miles and kilometers. You know, like how many kilometers we make when we do seventy miles in the car?"

"Oh," he said.

But his gaze at the foot of the bed relaxed slowly. The hold over himself relaxed too, finally, and the next day it was very slack and he cried very easily at little things that were of no importance. ❺

INFER

❹ Think about what Schatz has said and done so far. What **character traits** does he show?

COMPARE AND CONTRAST

❺ How does Schatz's behavior at the end of the story differ from his behavior at the beginning?

Meet the Writer

Ernest Hemingway

Grace Under Pressure

Ernest Hemingway (1899–1961) was born in Oak Park, Illinois. He spent his first seventeen summers in northern Michigan, where his father introduced him to hunting and fishing. In high school, Hemingway boxed and played football, but he also wrote poetry, stories, and the gossip column for his school newspaper.

When the United States entered World War I, Hemingway volunteered and became an American ambulance driver in Italy. He was nineteen when a bomb landed three feet away and filled his right leg with 227 pieces of shrapnel.

After returning from the war, Hemingway wrote many stories and novels that portray men who show "grace under pressure"—that is, calm courage in the face of great danger. In his own life, Hemingway relentlessly pursued excitement and danger. He hunted and fished all over the world, surviving several plane crashes and the fierce charges of the large animals he loved to hunt.

In "A Day's Wait," Hemingway again explores the theme of grace under pressure. This time he focuses on a young boy who believes he is about to die. The silences and sparse dialogue in the story reflect the belief of Hemingway's heroes that they should keep a tight rein on their fears and other emotions.

Hemingway worked hard to keep up his image of toughness, but his son Gregory remembers a more human side:

> 66 He told me about the times he'd been scared as a boy, how he used to dream about a furry monster who would grow *taller and taller* every night and then, just as it was about to eat him, would jump over the fence. He said fear was perfectly natural and nothing to be ashamed of. 99

Hemingway won the Nobel Prize in literature in 1954. Today he is regarded as one of the great writers of the twentieth century.

First Thoughts

1. Finish these sentences:

- If I were Schatz and thought I was about to die, I would . . .
- If I were Papa and saw the way Schatz looked and acted, I would . . .

Thinking Critically

2. Although Schatz is sick, he gets up, closes the windows in his parents' room, and then gets dressed. What **character traits** do these actions reveal?

3. Why would a young boy behave so heroically in the face of death? Do you think his behavior is typical? Discuss your answer with a partner.

4. Explain the title of this story.

Comparing Literature

5. After you read the next story, you will write an essay comparing and contrasting the main characters of the two stories. You can start to plan your essay by filling out a chart like the one below. List details in the story that tell you about Schatz. Then, decide what **character traits** the details reveal. The list of traits on page 190 may help you decide, or you can think of other traits on your own.

Reading Check

Go back through "A Day's Wait," and fill in a story map like the one below.

Title:

Author:

Characters:

Conflict:

Resolution:

Setting:

Schatz in "A Day's Wait"		
	Details in the Story	Character Traits
Actions		
Words		
Thoughts and feelings		
Effects on others		

INTERNET
Projects and Activities
Keyword: LE5 7-2

SKILLS FOCUS

Literary Skills
Analyze character traits.

Reading Skills
Compare and contrast characters.

Before You Read

This story is set in a small town in the Midwest about a century ago. Some customs may have changed since then, but people's emotions and their motives, or reasons, for doing what they do have stayed pretty much the same. What motivates the narrator in this story to say he is sick?

Stolen Day

Sherwood Anderson

It must be that all children are actors. The whole thing started with a boy on our street named Walter, who had inflammatory rheumatism.[1] That's what they called it. He didn't have to go to school.

Still he could walk about. He could go fishing in the creek or the waterworks pond. There was a place up at the pond where in the spring the water came tumbling over the dam and formed a deep pool. It was a good place. Sometimes you could get some good big ones there.

I went down that way on my way to school one spring morning. It was out of my way but I wanted to see if Walter was there.

He was, inflammatory rheumatism and all. There he was, sitting with a fish pole in his hand. He had been able to walk down there all right.

It was then that my own legs began to hurt. My back too. I went on to school but, at the recess time, I began to cry. I did it when the teacher, Sarah Suggett, had come out into the schoolhouse yard. ❶

She came right over to me.

"I ache all over," I said. I did, too.

I kept on crying and it worked all right.

"You'd better go on home," she said.

So I went. I limped painfully away. I kept on limping until I got out of the schoolhouse street.

---

1. **inflammatory rheumatism** (r$\overline{oo}$′mə•tiz′əm): rheumatic fever, a disease characterized by pain in the joints, fever, and inflammation of the heart.

INFER

❶ Why does the narrator of this story decide he has inflammatory rheumatism?

Then I felt better. I still had inflammatory rheumatism pretty
bad but I could get along better.

I must have done some thinking on the way home.

"I'd better not say I have inflammatory rheumatism," I decided.
"Maybe if you've got that you swell up."

I thought I'd better go around to where Walter was and ask him
about that, so I did—but he wasn't there.

"They must not be biting today," I thought.

I had a feeling that, if I said I had inflammatory rheumatism, Mother or my brothers and my sister Stella might laugh. They did laugh at me pretty often and I didn't like it at all. ❷

"Just the same," I said to myself, "I have got it." I began to hurt and ache again.

I went home and sat on the front steps of our house. I sat there a long time. There wasn't anyone at home but Mother and the two little ones. Ray would have been four or five then and Earl might have been three.

It was Earl who saw me there. I had got tired sitting and was lying on the porch. Earl was always a quiet, solemn little fellow.

He must have said something to Mother for presently she came.

"What's the matter with you? Why aren't you in school?" she asked.

I came pretty near telling her right out that I had inflammatory rheumatism but I thought I'd better not. Mother and Father had been speaking of Walter's case at the table just the day before. "It affects the heart," Father had said. That frightened me when I thought of it. "I might die," I thought. "I might just suddenly die right here; my heart might stop beating."

On the day before I had been running a race with my brother Irve. We were up at the fairgrounds after school and there was a half-mile track.

"I'll bet you can't run a half-mile," he said. "I bet you I could beat you running clear around the track."

And so we did it and I beat him, but afterwards my heart did seem to beat pretty hard. I remembered that lying there on the porch. "It's a wonder, with my inflammatory rheumatism and all, I didn't just drop down dead," I thought. The thought frightened me a lot. I ached worse than ever.

"I ache, Ma," I said. "I just ache."

She made me go in the house and upstairs and get into bed.

It wasn't so good. It was spring. I was up there for perhaps an hour, maybe two, and then I felt better.

I got up and went downstairs. "I feel better, Ma," I said. ❸

Mother said she was glad. She was pretty busy that day and hadn't paid much attention to me. She had made me get into bed upstairs and then hadn't even come up to see how I was.

I didn't think much of that when I was up there but when I got

INFER

❷ What has the narrator revealed about his **character** so far?

COMPARE AND CONTRAST

❸ How does Schatz in "A Day's Wait" respond to his illness? How does this boy respond?

**COMPARE AND
CONTRAST**

❹ How does the boy
feel about his
mother's reaction to
his illness? How did
Schatz in "A Day's
Wait" feel about his
father?

downstairs where she was, and when, after I had said I felt better
and she only said she was glad and went right on with her work, I
began to ache again.

I thought, "I'll bet I die of it. I bet I do."

I went out to the front porch and sat down. I was pretty sore at
Mother.

"If she really knew the truth, that I have the inflammatory
rheumatism and I may just drop down dead any time, I'll bet she
wouldn't care about that either," I thought. ❹

I was getting more and more angry the more thinking I did.

"I know what I'm going to do," I thought; "I'm going to go fishing."

I thought that, feeling the way I did, I might be sitting on the
high bank just above the deep pool where the water went over the
dam, and suddenly my heart would stop beating.

And then, of course, I'd pitch forward, over the bank into the
pool and, if I wasn't dead when I hit the water, I'd drown sure.

They would all come home to supper and they'd miss me.

"But where is he?"

Then Mother would remember that I'd come home from school
aching.

She'd go upstairs and I wouldn't be there. One day during the
year before, there was a child got drowned in a spring. It was one of
the Wyatt children.

Right down at the end of the street there was a spring under a
birch tree and there had been a barrel sunk in the ground.

Everyone had always been saying the spring ought to be kept
covered, but it wasn't.

So the Wyatt child went down there, played around alone, and
fell in and got drowned.

Mother was the one who had found the drowned child. She had
gone to get a pail of water and there the child was, drowned and dead.

This had been in the evening when we were all at home, and
Mother had come running up the street with the dead, dripping
child in her arms. She was making for the Wyatt house as hard as
she could run, and she was pale.

She had a terrible look on her face, I remembered then.

"So," I thought, "they'll miss me and there'll be a search made.
Very likely there'll be someone who has seen me sitting by the pond
fishing, and there'll be a big alarm and all the town will turn out
and they'll drag the pond."

I was having a grand time, having died. Maybe, after they found me and had got me out of the deep pool, Mother would grab me up in her arms and run home with me as she had run with the Wyatt child. ❺

I got up from the porch and went around the house. I got my fishing pole and lit out for the pool below the dam. Mother was busy—she always was—and didn't see me go. When I got there I thought I'd better not sit too near the edge of the high bank.

By this time I didn't ache hardly at all, but I thought.

"With inflammatory rheumatism you can't tell," I thought.

"It probably comes and goes," I thought.

"Walter has it and he goes fishing," I thought.

I had got my line into the pool and suddenly I got a bite. It was a regular whopper. I knew that. I'd never had a bite like that. I knew what it was. It was one of Mr. Fenn's big carp.

Mr. Fenn was a man who had a big pond of his own. He sold ice in the summer and the pond was to make the ice. He had bought some big carp and put them into his pond and then, earlier in the spring when there was a freshet,[2] his dam had gone out.

So the carp had got into our creek and one or two big ones had been caught—but none of them by a boy like me.

The carp was pulling and I was pulling and I was afraid he'd

---

2. **freshet** *n.*: a sudden overflowing of a stream caused by a heavy rain or a thaw.

End of Olson's (1969)
by Andrew Wyeth.
Tempera on panel.

© Andrew Wyeth.

break my line, so I just tumbled down the high bank, holding onto
the line, and got right into the pool. We had it out, there in the
pool. We struggled. We wrestled. Then I got a hand under his gills
and got him out.

He was a big one all right. He was nearly half as big as I was
myself. I had him on the bank and I kept one hand under his gills
and I ran.

I never ran so hard in my life. He was slippery, and now and then
he wriggled out of my arms; once I stumbled and fell on him, but I
got him home.

So there it was. I was a big hero that day. Mother got a washtub
and filled it with water. She put the fish in it and all the neighbors
came to look. I got into dry clothes and went down to supper—and
then I made a break that spoiled my day. ❻

There we were, all of us, at the table, and suddenly Father asked
what had been the matter with me at school. He had met the
teacher, Sarah Suggett, on the street and she had told him how I had
become ill.

"What was the matter with you?" Father asked, and before I
thought what I was saying I let it out.

INFER

❻ Why do the boy's
family and neighbors
see him as a hero?

"I had the inflammatory rheumatism," I said—and a shout went up. It made me sick to hear them, the way they all laughed.

It brought back all the aching again, and like a fool I began to cry.

"Well, I have got it—I have, I have," I cried, and I got up from the table and ran upstairs.

I stayed there until Mother came up. I knew it would be a long time before I heard the last of the inflammatory rheumatism. I was sick all right, but the aching I now had wasn't in my legs or in my back. ❼

INFER

❼ What is the aching the narrator feels now?

Meet the Writer

Sherwood Anderson

A Talented Storyteller

Sherwood Anderson (1876–1941) grew up in Clyde, Ohio, a small town that played a major role in many of his stories. He attended school infrequently while working full time to help provide for his family. After his mother died, Anderson went to Chicago, where he worked as a laborer, until he went off to fight in the Spanish-American War.

Anderson's talent as a storyteller emerged later in life while he was running his own business, a manufacturing company. He eventually left the business to focus on writing and received encouragement from such noted writers as Carl Sandburg and Vachel Lindsay (poems by Sandburg and Lindsay appear on pages 328, 438, and 607). Anderson developed a straight-forward writing style that changed the very nature of the short story, influencing a younger generation of writers. Anderson offered his own support to writers of this younger generation, including Ernest Hemingway. In fact, Anderson was instrumental in getting Hemingway's first novel published.

First Thoughts

1. Finish these sentences:

- The part I liked best about this story was . . .
- I am confused about . . .

Thinking Critically

2. Why do you think the narrator starts to feel sick after he sees Walter fishing at the pond?

3. What does the narrator say and do that shows he wants his mother to pay more attention to him?

4. Why do you think the narrator's family laughs at him when he says he has inflammatory rheumatism?

5. Why does the narrator insist that he really *is* sick?

6. Explain the title of this story.

Reading Check

Summarize this story by retelling it to a partner. Begin with the **title** and **author**. Next, explain who the **main character** is, and describe the central **conflict** or problem. Then, list the **main events** in the order in which they occur. Finally, tell what you liked or didn't like about the story. When you finish, ask your partner if you left out any important details.

Comparing Literature

7. Add information on the narrator of "Stolen Day" to the chart below. Then, use your chart as you prepare to write the comparison-contrast essay on the next page.

The Boy in "Stolen Day"		
	Details in the Story	Character Traits
Actions		
Words		
Thoughts and feelings		
Effects on others		

SKILLS FOCUS

Literary Skills
Analyze character traits.

Reading Skills
Compare and contrast characters.

Writing a Comparison-Contrast Essay

Assignment

Write an essay comparing two characters: Schatz in "A Day's Wait" and the boy in "Stolen Day." Begin planning your essay by referring to the charts you completed after you read the stories. Use the information from those charts to fill in the comparison chart below. This chart will help you identify similarities and differences between the two characters.

Use the workshop on writing a Comparison-Contrast Essay, pages 772–777, for help with this assignment.

| | Schatz in "A Day's Wait" | | The Boy in "Stolen Day" | |
	Story Details	Character Traits	Story Details	Character Traits
Actions				
Words				
Thoughts and feelings				
Effects on others				

Organize your essay in one of these two ways:

1. Organize the essay by character traits. In your first paragraph you might discuss three traits the boys have in common. In your second paragraph you might discuss at least one way in which the boys are different. Cite details illustrating the traits you see in each character.

2. You can organize your essay by the characters. For example, you might focus on Schatz and his character traits in your first paragraph and then do the same for the boy in "Stolen Day" in your next paragraph. Cite specific details from the stories to support your analysis of each character. Be sure to show how the boys are alike and how they are different.

At the end of your essay, tell which character you liked more, and explain why. Did you identify with either character? Did either boy remind you of someone you know? Use details from the stories to explain your responses.

SKILLS FOCUS

Writing Skills
Write a comparison-contrast essay.

from Homesick

Jean Fritz

In my father's study there was a large globe with all the countries of the world running around it. I could put my finger on the exact spot where I was and had been ever since I'd been born. And I was on the wrong side of the globe. I was in China in a city named Hankow, a dot on a crooked line that seemed to break the country right in two. The line was really the Yangtze River, but who would know by looking at a map what the Yangtze River really was?

Orange-brown, muddy mustard colored. And wide, wide, wide. With a river smell that was old and came all the way up from the bottom. Sometimes old women knelt on the riverbank, begging the River God to return a son or grandson who may have drowned. They would wail and beat the earth to make the River God pay attention, but I knew how busy the River God must be. All those people on the Yangtze River! Coolies[1] hauling water. Women washing clothes. Houseboats swarming with old people and young, chickens and pigs. Big crooked-sailed junks[2] with eyes painted on their prows so they could see where they were going. I loved the Yangtze River, but of course, I belonged on the other side of the world. In America, with my grandmother.

---

1. **coolies** *n.:* workers who do heavy work for little pay. English-speakers visiting the East took this name from the Hindi word *qulī,* meaning "hired servant."
2. **junks** *n.:* Chinese ships with flat bottoms and square sails.

Twenty-five fluffy little yellow chicks hatched from our eggs today, my grandmother wrote.

I wrote my grandmother that I had watched a Chinese magician swallow three yards of fire.

The trouble with living on the wrong side of the world was that I didn't feel like a *real* American.

For instance. I could never be president of the United States. I didn't want to be president; I wanted to be a writer. Still, why should there be a *law* saying that only a person born in the United States could be president?[3] It was as if I wouldn't be American enough.

Actually, I was American every minute of the day, especially during school hours. I went to a British school and every morning we sang "God Save the King." Of course the British children loved singing about their gracious king. Ian Forbes stuck out his chest and sang as if he were saving the king all by himself. Everyone sang. Even Gina Boss, who was Italian. And Vera Sebastian, who was so Russian she dressed the way Russian girls did long ago before the Revolution,[4] when her family had to run away to keep from being killed.

But I wasn't Vera Sebastian. I asked my mother to write an excuse so I wouldn't have to sing, but she wouldn't do it. "When in Rome," she said, "do as the Romans do." What she meant was, "Don't make trouble. Just sing."

So for a long time I did. I sang with my fingers crossed but still I felt like a traitor.

Then one day I thought: If my mother and father were really and truly in Rome, they wouldn't do what the Romans did at all. They'd probably try to get the Romans to do what *they* did, just as they were trying to teach the Chinese to do what Americans did. (My mother even gave classes in American manners.)

So that day I quit singing. I kept my mouth locked tight against the king of England. Our teacher, Miss Williams, didn't notice at first. She stood in front of the room, using a ruler for a baton, striking each syllable so hard it was as if she were making up for the times she had nothing to strike.

---

3. This is not a fact. The U.S. Constitution states only that a presidential candidate must be a "natural-born" U.S. citizen. This term applies to citizens born in the United States and its territories. But no law or court case has yet decided whether "natural-born" also describes children born to U.S. citizens in other countries.

4. **Revolution:** In 1917, a revolution drove the czars (emperors) and other nobility from power, and Russia became the first nation to set up a Communist government.

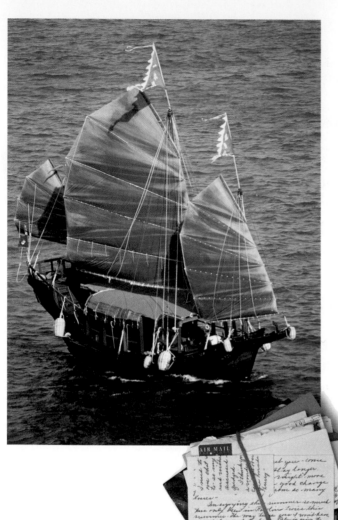

(Miss Williams was pinch-faced and bossy. Sometimes I wondered what had ever made her come to China. "Maybe to try and catch a husband," my mother said.

A husband! Miss Williams!)

"Make him vic-tor-i-ous," the class sang. It was on the strike of "vic" that Miss Williams noticed. Her eyes lighted on my mouth and when we sat down, she pointed her ruler at me.

"Is there something wrong with your voice today, Jean?" she asked.

"No, Miss Williams."

"You weren't singing."

"No, Miss Williams. It is not my national anthem."

"It is the national anthem we sing here," she snapped. "You have always sung. Even Vera sings it."

I looked at Vera with the big blue bow tied on the top of her head. Usually I felt sorry for her but not today. At recess I might even untie that bow, I thought. Just give it a yank. But if I'd been smart, I wouldn't have been looking at Vera. I would have been looking at Ian Forbes and I would have known that no matter what Miss Williams said, I wasn't through with the king of England.

Recess at the British School was nothing I looked forward to. Every day we played a game called prisoner's base, which was all running and shouting and shoving and catching. I hated the game, yet everyone played except Vera Sebastian. She sat on the sidelines under her blue bow like someone who had been dropped out of a history book. By recess I had forgotten my plans for that bow. While everyone was getting ready for the game, I was as usual trying to look as if I didn't care if I was the last one picked for a team or not. I was leaning against the high stone wall that ran around the schoolyard. I was looking up at a little white cloud skittering across the sky when all at once someone tramped down hard on my right foot. Ian Forbes. Snarling bulldog face. Heel grinding down on my toes. Head thrust forward the way an animal might before it strikes.

"You wouldn't sing it. So say it," he ordered. "Let me hear you say it."

I tried to pull my foot away but he only ground down harder.

"Say what?" I was telling my face please not to show what my foot felt.

"*God save the king.* Say it. Those four words. I want to hear you say it."

Although Ian Forbes was short, he was solid and tough and built for fighting. What was more, he always won. You had only to look at his bare knees between the top of his socks and his short pants to know that he would win. His knees were square. Bony and unbeatable. So of course it was crazy for me to argue with him.

"Why should I?" I asked. "Americans haven't said that since George the Third."[5]

He grabbed my right arm and twisted it behind my back.

"Say it," he hissed.

I felt the tears come to my eyes and I hated myself for the tears. I hated myself for not staying in Rome the way my mother had told me.

"I'll never say it," I whispered.

They were choosing sides now in the schoolyard and Ian's name was being called—among the first, as always.

He gave my arm another twist. "You'll sing tomorrow," he snarled, "or you'll be bloody sorry."

As he ran off, I slid to the ground, my head between my knees.

Oh, Grandma, I thought, why can't I be there with you? I'd feed the chickens for you. I'd pump water from the well, the way my father used to do.

It would be almost two years before we'd go to America. I was ten years old now; I'd be twelve then. But how could I think about *years*? I didn't even dare to think about the next day. After school I ran all the way home, fast so I couldn't think at all.

Our house stood behind a high stone wall, which had chips of broken glass sticking up from the top to keep thieves away. I flung open the iron gate and threw myself through the front door.

"I'm home!" I yelled.

Then I remembered that it was Tuesday, the day my mother taught an English class at the YMCA[6] where my father was the director.

I stood in the hall, trying to catch my breath, and as always I

---

5. **George the Third** (1738–1820): king of Great Britain at the time of the Revolutionary War (1775–1783), fought by the American colonies to gain independence from Great Britain.
6. **YMCA:** short for "Young Men's Christian Association."

began to feel small. It was a huge hall with ceilings so high it was as if they would have nothing to do with people. Certainly not with a mere child, not with me—the only child in the house. Once I asked my best friend, Andrea, if the hall made her feel little too. She said no. She was going to be a dancer and she loved space. She did a high kick to show how grand it was to have room.

Andrea Hull was a year older than I was and knew about everything sooner. She told me about commas, for instance, long before I took punctuation seriously. How could I write letters without commas? she asked. She made me so ashamed that for months I hung little wagging comma-tails all over the letters to my grandmother. She told me things that sounded so crazy I had to ask my mother if they were true. Like where babies came from. And that someday the whole world would end. My mother would frown when I asked her, but she always agreed that Andrea was right. It made me furious. How could she know such things and not tell me? What was the matter with grown-ups anyway?

I wished that Andrea were with me now, but she lived out in the country and I didn't see her often. Lin Nai-Nai, my amah,[7] was the only one around, and of course I knew she'd be there. It was her job to stay with me when my parents were out. As soon as she heard me come in, she'd called, "Tsai loushang," which meant that she was upstairs. She might be mending or ironing but most likely she'd be sitting by the window embroidering. And she was. She even had my embroidery laid out, for we had made a bargain. She would teach me to embroider if I would teach her English. I liked embroidering: the cloth stretched tight within my embroidery hoop while I filled in the stamped pattern with cross-stitches and lazy daisy flowers. The trouble was that lazy daisies needed French knots for their centers and I hated making French knots. Mine always fell apart, so I left them to the end. Today I had twenty lazy daisies waiting for their knots.

Lin Nai-Nai had already threaded my needle with embroidery floss.

"Black centers," she said, "for the yellow flowers."

I felt myself glowering. "American flowers don't have centers," I said, and gave her back the needle.

Lin Nai-Nai looked at me, puzzled, but she did not argue. She was different from other amahs. She did not even come from the servant class, although this was a secret we had to keep from the other ser-

---

7. **amah** *n.:* in Asia, a woman who looks after children.

vants, who would have made her life miserable had they known. She had run away from her husband when he had taken a second wife. She would always have been Wife Number One and the Boss no matter how many wives he had, but she would rather be no wife than head of a string of wives. She was modern. She might look old-fashioned, for her feet had been bound up tight when she was a little girl so that they would stay small, and now, like many Chinese women, she walked around on little stumps stuffed into tiny cloth shoes. Lin Nai-Nai's were embroidered with butterflies. Still, she believed in true love and one wife for one husband. We were good friends, Lin Nai-Nai and I, so I didn't know why I felt so mean.

She shrugged. "English lesson?" she asked, smiling.

I tested my arm to see if it still hurt from the twisting. It did. My foot too. "What do you want to know?" I asked.

We had been through the polite phrases—Please, Thank you, I beg your pardon, Excuse me, You're welcome, Merry Christmas (which she had practiced but hadn't had a chance to use since this was only October).

"If I meet an American on the street," she asked, "how do I greet him?"

I looked her straight in the eye and nodded my head in a greeting. "Sewing machine," I said. "You say, 'Sew-ing ma-chine.'"

She repeated after me, making the four syllables into four separate words. She got up and walked across the room, bowing and smiling. "Sew Ing Ma Shing."

Part of me wanted to laugh at the thought of Lin Nai-Nai maybe meeting Dr. Carhart, our minister, whose face would surely puff up, the way it always did when he was flustered. But part of me didn't want to laugh at all. I didn't like it when my feelings got tangled, so I ran downstairs and played "Chopsticks" on the piano. Loud and fast. When my sore arm hurt, I just beat on the keys harder.

Then I went out to the kitchen to see if Yang Sze-Fu, the cook, would give me something to eat. I found him reading a Chinese newspaper, his eyes going up and down with the characters. (Chinese words don't march across flat surfaces, the way ours do; they drop down cliffs, one cliff after another from right to left across a page.)

"Can I have a piece of cinnamon toast?" I asked. "And a cup of cocoa?"

Yang Sze-Fu grunted. He was smoking a cigarette, which he wasn't supposed to do in the kitchen, but Yang Sze-Fu mostly did what he wanted. He considered himself superior to common workers. You could tell because of the fingernails on his pinkies. They were at least two inches long, which was his way of showing that he didn't have to use his hands for rough or dirty work. He didn't seem to care that his fingernails were dirty, but maybe he couldn't keep such long nails clean.

He made my toast while his cigarette dangled out of the corner of his mouth, collecting a long ash that finally fell on the floor. He wouldn't have kept smoking if my mother had been there, although he didn't always pay attention to my mother. Never about butter pagodas,[8] for instance. No matter how many times my mother told him before a dinner party, "No butter pagoda," it made no difference. As soon as everyone was seated, the serving boy, Wong Sze-Fu, would bring in a pagoda and set it on the table. The guests would "oh" and "ah," for it was a masterpiece: a pagoda molded out of butter, curved roofs rising tier upon tier, but my mother could only think how unsanitary it was. For, of course, Yang Sze-Fu had molded the butter with his hands and carved the decorations with one of his long fingernails. Still, we always used the butter, for if my mother sent it back to the kitchen, Yang Sze-Fu would lose face[9] and quit.

When my toast and cocoa were ready, I took them upstairs to my

---

8. **pagodas** *n.:* Asian temples with several levels.
9. **lose face:** lose dignity or self-respect.

room (the blue room) and while I ate, I began *Sara Crewe*[10] again. Now there was a girl, I thought, who was worth crying over. I wasn't going to think about myself. Or Ian Forbes. Or the next day. I wasn't. I wasn't.

And I didn't. Not all afternoon. Not all evening. Still, I must have decided what I was going to do because the next morning when I started for school and came to the corner where the man sold hot chestnuts, the corner where I always turned to go to school, I didn't turn. I walked straight ahead. I wasn't going to school that day.

I walked toward the Yangtze River. Past the store that sold paper pellets that opened up into flowers when you dropped them in a glass of water. Then up the block where the beggars sat. I never saw anyone give money to a beggar. You couldn't, my father explained, or you'd be mobbed by beggars. They'd follow you everyplace; they'd never leave you alone. I had learned not to look at them when I passed and yet I saw. The running sores, the twisted legs, the mangled faces. What I couldn't get over was that, like me, each one of those beggars had only one life to live. It just happened that they had drawn rotten ones.

Oh, Grandma, I thought, we may be far apart but we're lucky, you and I. Do you even know how lucky? In America do you know?

This part of the city didn't actually belong to the Chinese, even though the beggars sat there, even though upper-class Chinese lived there. A long time ago other countries had just walked into China and divided up part of Hankow (and other cities) into sections, or concessions, which they called their own and used their own rules for governing. We lived in the French concession on Rue de Paris. Then there was the British concession and the Japanese. The Russian and German concessions had been officially returned to China, but the people still called them concessions. The Americans didn't have one, although, like some of the other countries, they had gunboats on the river. In case, my father said. In case what? Just in case. That's all he'd say.

The concessions didn't look like the rest of China. The buildings were solemn and orderly, with little plots of grass around them. Not like those in the Chinese part of the city: a jumble of rickety shops with people, vegetables, crates of quacking ducks, yard goods, bamboo baskets, and mangy[11] dogs spilling onto a street so narrow it was hardly there.

---

10. *Sara Crewe:* famous children's book by Frances Hodgson Burnett about a rich girl who becomes a poor orphan. Burnett also wrote *A Little Princess, Little Lord Fauntleroy,* and *The Secret Garden.*

11. **mangy** (mān′jē) *adj.:* diseased. Animals with mange lose their hair and become covered with sores and scabs.

The grandest street in Hankow was the Bund, which ran along beside the Yangtze River. When I came to it after passing the beggars, I looked to my left and saw the American flag flying over the American consulate building. I was proud of the flag and I thought maybe today it was proud of me. It flapped in the breeze as if it were saying ha-ha to the king of England.

Then I looked to the right at the Customs House, which stood at the other end of the Bund. The clock on top of the tower said nine-thirty. How would I spend the day?

I crossed the street to the promenade part of the Bund. When people walked here, they weren't usually going anyplace; they were just out for the air. My mother would wear her broad-brimmed beaver hat when we came, and my father would swing his cane in that jaunty way that showed how glad he was to be a man. I thought I would just sit on a bench for the morning. I would watch the Customs House clock, and when it was time, I would eat the lunch I had brought along in my schoolbag.

I was the only one sitting on a bench. People did not generally "take the air" on a Wednesday morning, and besides, not everyone was allowed here. The British had put a sign on the Bund, NO DOGS, NO CHINESE. This meant that I could never bring Lin Nai-Nai with me. My father couldn't even bring his best friend, Mr. T. K. Hu. Maybe the British wanted a place where they could pretend they weren't in China, I thought. Still, there were always Chinese coolies around. In order to load and unload boats in the river, coolies had to cross the Bund. All day they went back and forth, bent double under their loads, sweating and chanting in a tired, singsong way that seemed to get them from one step to the next.

To pass the time, I decided to recite poetry. The one good thing about Miss Williams was that she made us learn poems by heart and I liked that. There was one particular poem I didn't want to forget. I looked at the Yangtze River and pretended that all the busy people in the boats were my audience.

"'Breathes there the man, with soul so dead,'" I cried, "'Who never to himself hath said, This is my own, my native land!'"

I was so carried away by my performance that I didn't notice the policeman until he was right in front of me. Like all policemen in the British concession, he was a bushy-bearded Indian with a red turban wrapped around his head.

He pointed to my schoolbag. "Little miss," he said, "why aren't you in school?"

He was tall and mysterious-looking, more like a character in my *Arabian Nights* book than a man you expected to talk to. I fumbled for an answer. "I'm going on an errand," I said finally. "I just sat down for a rest." I picked up my schoolbag and walked quickly away. When I looked around, he was back on his corner, directing traffic.

So now they were chasing children away too, I thought angrily. Well, I'd like to show them. Someday I'd like to walk a dog down the whole length of the Bund. A Great Dane. I'd have him on a leash—like this—(I put out my hand as if I were holding a leash right then) and he'd be so big and strong I'd have to strain to hold him back (I strained). Then of course sometimes he'd have to do his business and I'd stop (like this) right in the middle of the sidewalk and let him go to it. I was so busy with my Great Dane I was at the end of the Bund before I knew it. I let go of the leash, clapped my hands, and told my dog to go home. Then I left the Bund and the concessions and walked into the Chinese world.

My mother and father and I had walked here but not for many months. This part near the river was called the Mud Flats. Sometimes it was muddier than others, and when the river flooded, the flats disappeared underwater. Sometimes even the fishermen's huts were washed away, knocked right off their long-legged stilts and swept down the river. But today the river was fairly low and the mud had dried so that it was cracked and cakey. Most of the men who lived here were out fishing, some not far from the shore, poling their sampans through the shallow water. Only a few people were on the flats: a man cleaning fish on a flat rock at the water's edge, a woman spreading clothes on the dirt to dry, a few small children. But behind the huts was something I had never seen before. Even before I came close, I guessed what it was. Even then, I was excited by the strangeness of it.

Meanwhile I wandered up and down the streets, in and out of stores. I weighed myself on the big scale in the Hankow Dispensary[12] and found that I was as skinny as ever. I went to the Terminus Hotel and tried out the chairs in the lounge. At first I didn't mind wandering about like this. Half of my mind was still on the river with my junk, but as time went on, my junk began slipping away until I was alone with nothing but questions. Would my mother find out about today? How could I skip school tomorrow? And the next day and the next? Could I get sick? Was there a kind of long lie-abed sickness that didn't hurt?

I arrived home at four, just as I had planned, opened the door, and called out, "I'm home!" Cheery-like and normal. But I was scarcely in the house before Lin Nai-Nai ran to me from one side of the hall and my mother from the other.

"Are you all right? Are you all right?" Lin Nai-Nai felt my arms as if she expected them to be broken. My mother's face was white. "What happened?" she asked.

Then I looked through the open door into the living room and saw Miss Williams sitting there. She had beaten me home and asked about my absence, which of course had scared everyone. But now my mother could see that I was in one piece and for some reason this seemed to make her mad. She took me by the hand and led me into the living room. "Miss Williams said you weren't in school," she said. "Why was that?"

I hung my head, just the way cowards do in books.

My mother dropped my hand. "Jean will be in school tomorrow," she said firmly. She walked Miss Williams to the door. "Thank you for stopping by."

Miss Williams looked satisfied in her mean, pinched way. "Well," she said, "ta-ta." (She always said "ta-ta" instead of "goodbye." Chicken language, it sounded like.)

As soon as Miss Williams was gone and my mother was sitting down again, I burst into tears. Kneeling on the floor, I buried my head in her lap and poured out the whole miserable story. My mother could see that I really wasn't in one piece after all, so she listened quietly, stroking my hair as I talked, but gradually I could feel her stiffen. I knew she was remembering that she was a Mother.

"You better go up to your room," she said, "and think things over. We'll talk about it after supper."

---

12. **dispensary** *n.:* place where medicine and first aid are provided.

I flung myself on my bed. What was there to think? Either I went to school and got beaten up. Or I quit.

After supper I explained to my mother and father how simple it was. I could stay at home and my mother could teach me, the way Andrea's mother taught her. Maybe I could even go to Andrea's house and study with her.

My mother shook her head. Yes, it was simple, she agreed. I could go back to the British School, be sensible, and start singing about the king again.

I clutched the edge of the table. Couldn't she understand? I couldn't turn back now. It was too late.

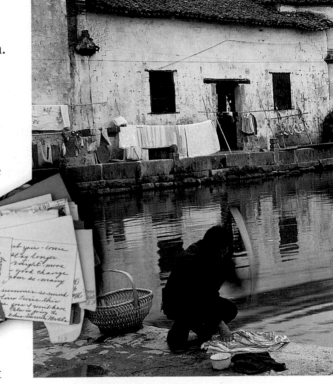

So far my father had not said a word. He was leaning back, teetering on the two hind legs of his chair, the way he always did after a meal, the way that drove my mother crazy. But he was not the kind of person to keep all four legs of a chair on the floor just because someone wanted him to. He wasn't a turning-back person so I hoped maybe he would understand. As I watched him, I saw a twinkle start in his eyes and suddenly he brought his chair down slam-bang flat on the floor. He got up and motioned for us to follow him into the living room. He sat down at the piano and began to pick out the tune for "God Save the King."

A big help, I thought. Was he going to make me practice?

Then he began to sing:

> "My country 'tis of thee,
> Sweet land of liberty . . ."

Of course! It was the same tune. Why hadn't I thought of that? Who would know what I was singing as long as I moved my lips? I joined in now, loud and strong.

"Of thee I sing."

My mother laughed in spite of herself. "If you sing that loud," she said, "you'll start a revolution."

"Tomorrow I'll sing softly," I promised. "No one will know." But for now I really let freedom ring.

Then all at once I wanted to see Lin Nai-Nai. I ran out back, through the courtyard that separated the house from the servants' quarters, and upstairs to her room.

"It's me," I called through the door and when she opened up, I threw my arms around her. "Oh, Lin Nai-Nai, I love you," I said. "You haven't said it yet, have you?"

"Said what?"

"Sewing machine. You haven't said it?"

"No," she said, "not yet. I'm still practicing."

"Don't say it, Lin Nai-Nai. Say 'Good day.' It's shorter and easier. Besides, it's more polite."

"Good day?" she repeated.

"Yes, that's right. Good day." I hugged her and ran back to the house.

The next day at school when we rose to sing the British national anthem, everyone stared at me, but as soon as I opened my mouth, the class lost interest. All but Ian Forbes. His eyes never left my face, but I sang softly, carefully, proudly. At recess he sauntered[13] over to where I stood against the wall. He spat on the ground. "You can be bloody glad you sang today," he said. Then he strutted off as if he and those square knees of his had won again.

And, of course, I was bloody glad.

---

13. **sauntered** (sôn′tərd) v.: strolled.

Meet the Writer

Jean Fritz

"I Had to Speak Up"

Jean Fritz (1915–   ) spent the first thirteen years of her life in Hankow, China. She recalls her memorable childhood in *Homesick: My Own Story*, a 1983 Newbery Honor Book and American Book Award winner.

> 66 Until I was eleven years old I attended an English school. I felt very American and often thought I had to speak up for my country. At recess, for instance. The English children would sometimes tease me by making fun of America. I never let that pass even if it meant a fight. 99

After moving to the United States and graduating from college, Jean Fritz became a librarian. "When I ran the children's department of our local library," she recalls, "I found that I not only wanted to read children's stories, I wanted to write them too."

For Independent Reading

Jean Fritz has written more than a dozen biographies for young adults, including *Why Don't You Get a Horse, Sam Adams?*; *Where Do You Think You're Going, Christopher Columbus?*; and *Traitor: The Case of Benedict Arnold*.

Writing Workshop

PERSUASIVE WRITING
Problem-Solution Essay

Many situations can be considered problems. Some problems occur in your everyday life, such as a broken bicycle wheel or a computer that crashes. The subject of a problem-solution essay, however, is a problem that seriously affects a large number of people. Your object is to explain the problem and to offer one or more solutions.

Prewriting

1 Choosing a Topic

Consider the following **prompt:**

> Think about how you might solve a problem that affects your school, your neighborhood, or your community. Write an essay in which you describe this problem and try to persuade readers to accept your solution.

Get together with a group of classmates, and brainstorm a list of problems. Here are some suggestions to help you get started:

- If I could make just one thing happen, I'd . . .
- If I were the president/mayor/principal, I would . . .
- The world would be a better place if everyone . . .

2 Finding Solutions

Choose one problem to work on. Explore solutions to the problem in a cluster diagram like the one shown on the

SKILLS FOCUS

Writing Skills
Write a problem-solution essay.

PEANUTS reprinted by permission of United Feature Syndicate, Inc.

right. You might also try jotting down all your ideas. If you've chosen a good topic, you probably won't be able to write fast enough to keep up with your thoughts! Keep writing until you can't think of anything else to say—then sort through what you've written and choose the solution that seems most promising.

3 Targeting Your Audience

A critical question you must answer is "Whom do I want to persuade?" Your audience might be:

- people who are affected by the problem
- people who are responsible for causing the problem
- people who can help with the solution

In a persuasive essay, you don't want to "preach to the choir"—that is, write to impress people who probably agree with you already—or to attack those who disagree. Neither of these tactics will help you achieve your real purpose, which is to persuade as many readers as possible to accept your assessment of the problem and your ideas for solving it.

Drafting

1 Crafting a Strong Beginning

You might open your essay with a quotation, a vivid example of the problem, or a surprising statistic. Avoid using statements beginning with "I think" or "I feel." In your introduction, state your purpose. Make the problem real for your reader. Explain what causes the problem, and describe its effects on your readers.

2 Showing the Problem

How can you make the problem real for your readers? Don't just name it. Explain what causes it and how widespread it is. Go on to describe its effects—especially those that touch your readers' lives.

Framework for a Problem–Solution Essay

Introduction (a strong example or statement):

_____

Problem: _____

Solution: _____

Details: _____

Benefits: _____

Possible objections: _____

Your responses: _____

Conclusion (a strong argument, a summary, or a call to action): _____

Writing Tip

Avoid circular reasoning: Restating the problem in different words (as in the following example) is not the same as providing a solution.

> _By showing greater consideration for others, cellphone users can solve the problem because lack of consideration is the source of the trouble._

This statement does not explain how to promote consideration for others.

3 Proposing Solutions

Briefly describe your solution to the problem. Then, describe the solution in detail, citing examples and explaining what steps need to be taken. Be sure to stress the benefits offered by your solution. Show that your proposal is realistic and doable. Remember, the best solutions are "win-win": They offer advantages to everyone affected by the problem.

4 Anticipating Objections

Your goal is to persuade readers to accept your solution and to take the actions you recommend. However, every solution will have its opponents. Can you win them over to your side? If not, can you counter their arguments?

Look for weak points in your proposed solution, and see if you can strengthen them. Think of arguments that might be raised against your ideas so that you can anticipate and respond to them. Deal with these possible objections by stressing the benefits of your approach.

Using a chart like the one below is a good way to plan your responses to anticipated objections.

My view of the problem	→	Opponent's view
_____		_____
My proposed solution	→	Opponent's objections
_____		_____
My responses		
_____		_____

5 Ending on a Strong Note

In your conclusion, state what you want your readers to do. You might remind your readers of the importance of the problem and the pressing need to solve it. You might also look toward the future. What might happen if people act—or fail to act—on your suggestion?

Student Model

KIDS SHOULD BE PAID FOR CHORES

I strongly believe that kids should be paid for doing chores around the house. Kids all across the country constantly nag their parents for money to go to the movies, buy CDs, go to McDonalds, and do many other things. Many parents complain about kids' always asking them for money.

Parents constantly complain that kids don't help out around the house enough. Lots of times parents nag kids until they clean up their rooms, put out the trash, cut the lawn, do the dishes, shovel the snow, and do many other chores.

Why can't kids and parents reach a compromise about money and chores? Parents would pay kids who remember to do their chores without being reminded a small fee for the work done. Kids would no longer ask for money.

This compromise teaches kids responsibility. They would learn that you don't get anything for doing nothing. When their chores are completed, with no nagging, they'd be paid whatever the parents had agreed to pay them. Kids could spend the money on things they like. They'd learn to save money for the expensive items.

No more nagging kids begging for money. No more nagging parents begging kids to clean up. Both kids and parents would be getting something that they want.

—T. J. Wilson
Atlantic Middle School
North Quincy, Massachusetts

*A **strong statement** is used to grab the reader's attention.*

*Detailed **examples** illustrate the **problems** faced by both sides—parents and kids.*

*The writer outlines a **solution**.*

*The writer answers possible **objections** by pointing out **benefits** of the solution.*

*The writer ends with a **strong statement** of the benefits to both parties.*

Strategies For Elaboration

To support your problem-solution essay, you can use

• facts (including statistics and other evidence from research)

• anecdotes and other examples from personal experience

• opinions of experts

• discussion of the solution's practicality in terms of money, time, and difficulty

• comparisons of various solutions

INTERNET

More Writer'o Models

Keyword: LE5 7-2

Evaluating and Revising

Use the following chart to evaluate and revise your problem-solution essay.

Problem Solution: Content and Organization Guidelines

Evaluation Questions	▶ Tips	▶ Revision Techniques
❶ Do you grab the reader's attention with a strong beginning? Does your introduction state the problem clearly?	▶ **Underline** the attention-getting opening. **Highlight** the statement of the problem.	▶ **Add** a strong statement, a statistic, or a vivid example of the problem.
❷ Do you provide details that describe the problem?	▶ **Put stars** next to details that show the causes and effects of the problem.	▶ **Add** examples that reveal the seriousness of the problem.
❸ Does your essay propose a solution to the problem? Does it examine the pros and cons of the solution?	▶ **Circle** the statements that propose a solution. **Check** the descriptions of benefits and possible objections.	▶ **Summarize** your solution, and **elaborate** with details.
❹ Does your essay target your audience?	▶ **Check** phrases or sentences that identify your audience.	▶ **Adjust tone** to reach your audience.
❺ Are paragraphs arranged in order of importance?	▶ **Number** each paragraph according to the importance of the ideas discussed.	▶ **Rearrange** paragraphs to build toward your most important idea.
❻ Does the conclusion include a convincing call to action?	▶ **Draw a wavy line** under the call to action.	▶ **Add** a call to action, or **revise** your statement to make it stronger and more specific.

On the next page you'll find the opening paragraph of a problem-solution essay that has been revised. Following the Revision Model are questions you can use to evaluate the writer's revisions.

Revision Model

                    most exciting
You've just reached the ~~best~~ scene of a movie, and you're

sitting on the edge of your seat. Suddenly, ~~out of nowhere~~

the tension is broken by a ringing noise—somebody's
        has gone off
cell phone ∧. Because people are turning to mobile phones in

ever-growing numbers, we find them being used in public
        have many important uses, but they
places. Cell phones ∧ are rapidly becoming a public nuisance.
        common-sense
We need some ∧ strategies that will encourage cell phone

users to respect the rights of others to quiet and privacy in
        including restaurants, schools, theaters, and buses
public places ∧. ~~Rules are already in place to control the~~

~~noise of car radios.~~ One possibility is posting signs ∧ in public

vehicles, movie theaters, and restaurants ⟨that restrict or

prohibit the use of cell phones⟩ . Bus drivers, for example,

might be given the authority to temporarily confiscate the

phones of riders who refuse to cooperate.

Evaluating the Revision

1. What has the writer added to clarify the nature of the problem?
2. What unnecessary details has the writer deleted?
3. Where has the writer rearranged details for greater effectiveness?

DIRECTIONS: Read the following story. Then, answer each question that follows.

Here is a portion of a story set in Antigua, an island in the Caribbean Sea. The narrator is a young girl named Annie John, who has for a while wanted to play with another girl she calls the Red Girl.

from The Red Girl

Jamaica Kincaid

The Red Girl and I stood under the guava tree looking each other up and down. What a beautiful thing I saw standing before me. Her face was big and round and red, like a moon—a red moon. She had big, broad, flat feet, and they were naked to the bare ground; her dress was dirty, the skirt and blouse tearing away from each other at one side; the red hair that I had first seen standing up on her head was matted and tangled; her hands were big and fat, and her fingernails held at least ten anthills of dirt under them. And on top of that, she had such an unbelievable, wonderful smell, as if she had never taken a bath in her whole life.

I soon learned this about her: She took a bath only once a week, and that was only so that she could be admitted to her grandmother's presence. She didn't like to bathe, and her mother didn't force her. She changed her dress once a week for the same reason. She preferred to wear a dress until it just couldn't be worn anymore. Her mother didn't mind that, either. She didn't like to comb her hair, though on the first day of school, she could put herself out for that. She didn't like to go to Sunday school, and her mother didn't force her. She didn't like to brush her teeth, but occasionally her mother said it was necessary. She loved to play marbles, and was so good that only Skerritt boys now played against her. Oh, what an angel she was, and what a heaven she lived in! I, on the other hand, took a full bath every morning and a sponge bath every night. I could hardly go out on my doorstep without putting my shoes on. I was not allowed to play in the sun without a hat on my head. My mother paid a woman who lived five houses away from us sevenpence a week—a penny for each school day and twopence for Sunday—to comb my hair. On Saturday, my mother washed my hair. Before I went to sleep at night I had to make sure my uniform was clean and creaseless and all laid out for the next day. I had to make sure that my shoes were clean and polished to a nice shine. I went to Sunday school every Sunday unless I was sick. I was not allowed to play marbles, and, as for Skerritt boys, that was hardly mentionable.

1. Which of the following **character traits** does the narrator apply to the Red Girl?

   A   She is a careful dresser.

   B   She spends too much time on her hair.

   C   She is unconcerned about her appearance.

   D   She is always clean and neat.

2. All of the following **traits** are characteristic of the narrator *except* —

   F   she envies the Red Girl's freedom

   G   she much prefers her own life to that of the Red Girl

   H   she obeys her mother

   J   she dresses neatly and wears clean shoes

3. From the narrator's vivid description of the Red Girl, you can **infer** that the narrator —

   A   is disgusted by the Red Girl

   B   wants to help the Red Girl

   C   longs to be more like the Red Girl

   D   doesn't want to be friends with the Red Girl

4. The narrator tells us directly how she feels about the Red Girl when she says —

   F   "She took a bath only once a week. . . ."

   G   "She didn't like to go to Sunday school. . . ."

   H   "I was not allowed to play in the sun without a hat on my head."

   J   "Oh, what an angel she was, and what a heaven she lived in!"

5. In this passage from "The Red Girl," the narrator uses all of the following methods of **characterization** *except* —

   A   stating character traits directly

   B   describing actions

   C   quoting speech

   D   describing appearance

Constructed Response

6. Do you think the Red Girl is as wonderful as the narrator thinks she is? Why do you think the narrator likes the Red Girl so much?

Collection 2: Skills Review

Vocabulary Skills

This Test Practice reviews Vocabulary words you have studied in Collections 1 and 2.

Synonyms

Directions: Choose the word or phrase that means the same or about the same as the underlined word.

1. To sabotage means to —
   - **A** hide
   - **B** destroy
   - **C** remove
   - **D** collect

2. A staid person is usually —
   - **F** tired
   - **G** restless
   - **H** bothersome
   - **J** quiet

3. Seeking consolation is the same as seeking —
   - **A** comfort
   - **B** prizes
   - **C** housing
   - **D** warmth

4. An intelligible conversation is —
   - **F** alien
   - **G** secretive
   - **H** understandable
   - **J** unimportant

5. If you are perturbed, you are —
   - **A** troubled
   - **B** surprised
   - **C** pleased
   - **D** calmed

6. To alleviate pain means to —
   - **F** increase it
   - **G** relieve it
   - **H** deepen it
   - **J** disguise it

7. A valiant person is —
   - **A** truthful
   - **B** brave
   - **C** graceful
   - **D** cowardly

8. A derisive laugh sounds —
   - **F** scornful
   - **G** musical
   - **H** loving
   - **J** loud

9. A menace is a —
   - **A** pest
   - **B** nightmare
   - **C** machine
   - **D** danger

10. Someone who is intimidated is —
    - **F** frightened
    - **G** alone
    - **H** angry
    - **J** hopeful

SKILLS FOCUS

Vocabulary Skills
Identify synonyms.

Collection 2: Skills Review

Writing Skills

Test Practice

DIRECTIONS: Read the following paragraph from a problem-solution essay. Then, answer each question that follows.

(1) The backwater swamps of the American South support many life forms that are threatened by the overuse of natural resources. (2) Wetlands that have not been re-planted after logging are vulnerable to floods and erosion. (3) Because the soil is so rich, lands have been cleared for agriculture. (4) The great trees have been cut down for lumber. (5) Huge stands of oak, elm, cypress, and other species of North American wetlands have been removed from the landscape. (6) To preserve and protect this important habitat, we must all work for the reforestation of these swamps.

1. Which of the following statements might be added to support the opening sentence?
   - **A** Many swamp creatures are nocturnal.
   - **B** These wetlands shelter snakes, alligators, black bears, and many varieties of birds, as well as enormous trees.
   - **C** Many superstitions exist about swamps.
   - **D** The naturalist John James Audubon wrote about alligators on the shores of the Red River.

2. Where might sentence 2 be moved to make the paragraph more effective?
   - **F** to the beginning of the paragraph, to introduce the topic
   - **G** following sentence 5, to show the harm that can come from deforestation
   - **H** to the end of the paragraph, to serve as a call to action
   - **J** out of the paragraph altogether

3. What transitional word or phrase might be added to the beginning of sentence 5?
   - **A** Fortunately,
   - **B** Otherwise,
   - **C** However,
   - **D** For example,

4. How else might sentence 5 be strengthened?
   - **F** By explaining how lumber is used for construction
   - **G** By replacing "Huge stands" with more exact statistics
   - **H** By using comparisons to the destruction of rain forests
   - **J** By moving it to the end of the paragraph

5. In the remaining paragraphs of the essay, readers would expect to find all of the following *except* —
   - **A** possible objections to the solution
   - **B** the benefits of following the writer's plan
   - **C** a call for change or action
   - **D** lists of threatened jungle habitats

SKILLS FOCUS

Writing Skills
Analyze a problem-solution essay.

Fiction

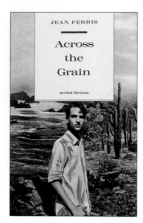

A Moving Experience

Orphan Will Griffin is feeling lost when he relocates to the California desert with his flighty sister. Then Will meets a moody girl named Mike and an old loner named Sam. These three outsiders help one another through sorrowful times and discover the value of friendship in Jean Ferris's *Across the Grain*.

Family Ties

M. C. Higgins and his family have been living on Sarah's Mountain ever since M. C.'s great-grandmother arrived there as a fugitive from slavery. His family loves their mountain, but one day M. C. notices a massive pile of debris accumulating on a cliff over their home. In Virginia Hamilton's *M. C. Higgins, the Great*, a young boy is torn between his loyalty to his family and his desire for a life beyond the mountain.

This title is available in the HRW Library.

The Notebook

If you are interested in writing, you might enjoy Louise Fitzhugh's *Harriet the Spy*. Harriet Welsch longs to be a writer, so she begins recording honest observations of her classmates in her secret notebook. When the notebook is discovered by the classmates, Harriet finds out what being a writer really means.

Friendly Fire

Artos is lonely and dissatisfied in his medieval castle. The other boys mock him because he does not know who his birth parents are. His life changes when he meets Linn, an old dragon who lives in a cave. In Jane Yolen's *The Dragon's Boy,* Linn guides Artos with his wisdom and proves that Artos's life will have great meaning after all.

Nonfiction

Starting a New Life

In *At Her Majesty's Request: An African Princess in Victorian England,* Walter Dean Myers tells the story of Sarah Forbes Bonetta, who was saved from death by a British sea captain. As a result, she spent her life in nineteenth-century England, a place where others made life decisions for her. Myers includes newspaper articles and portraits to add to the reality of Bonetta's compelling story.

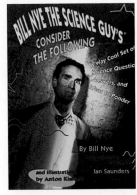

Science Stumpers

Have you ever wondered why leaves change color in the autumn? how a magnet sticks to a refrigerator? what prevents a heavy boat from sinking in the ocean? Bill Nye has the answers to all these questions and a whole lot more in *Bill Nye the Science Guy's Consider the Following.*

An Era Begins

In *Commodore Perry in the Land of the Shogun,* Rhoda Blumberg describes the beginning of trade talks between Japan and the United States in the nineteenth century. Blumberg sensitively depicts relations between two distinct cultural groups who were wary of each other at first but grew to respect each other's differences.

Medieval Times

Philip Steele provides an engaging overview of medieval life in *Castles.* In addition to providing astonishing and informative illustrations showing how castles were built, Steele describes the weapons used by medieval warriors and narrates a typical day in a castle town.

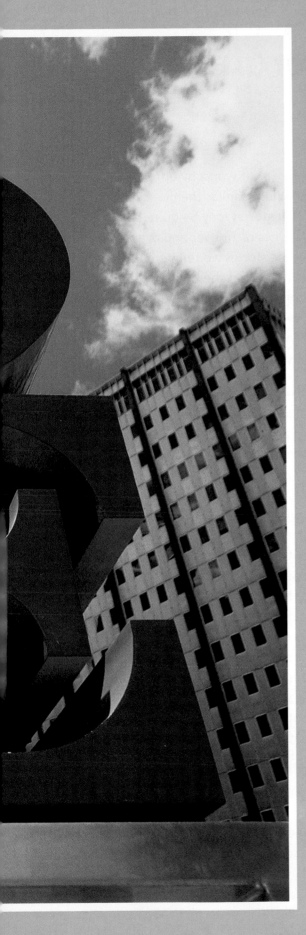

Living in the Heart

Literary Focus:
Analyzing Theme

Informational Focus:
Analyzing Cause and Effect

LOVE Sculpture
by Robert Indiana.

INTERNET
Collection
Resources
Keyword: LE5 7-3

Elements of Literature
Theme *by* Mara Rockliff
WHAT'S THE BIG IDEA?

A key element of literature—of fiction, nonfiction, poetry, and drama—is theme. **Theme** is a revelation about our lives; theme is a discovery of a truth about our own human experience.

Theme Is a Revelation

Suppose we read a story about two friends. Surprisingly, one friend betrays the other. If the story is well written, we will feel that we have lived through the betrayal ourselves. We will feel that the tragedy could have happened in exactly the way the writer tells it. As we share the characters' experiences in the story, we also discover something. We discover—or rediscover—the delicate nature and value of friendship.

Themes Focus on the "Big" Ideas

Literature that endures, that lasts through the centuries, tends to focus on discoveries about the big topics in everyone's life: understanding the nature of love, accepting responsibility, understanding loss, dealing with ambition, discovering the joys and problems of friendship.

A theme isn't something a writer tacks on to a story or poem to make it more literary. Theme grows naturally out of what the writer believes and out of the story that's being told.

If you've read several novels, you know that works by different writers can have similar themes, even though their stories may be quite different. Themes recur over and over again in the stories we tell because some truths about the human experience are universal, whether a story was written hundreds of years ago in a snowbound Alaskan village or typed on a laptop yesterday in Zimbabwe.

Plot Isn't Theme

"Plot is what a story is about," someone once said. "Theme is what a story is *really* about."

A story's plot might be about a family that drinks from a magical spring, becomes immortal, and suffers the consequences. That's what happens. But what's the story *really* about? What does the story reveal to you about life?

Maybe it reveals that living forever is more frightening than dying. Maybe it reveals that without death, growth and change would be impossible and life would no longer give us pleasure. In a single plot you might discover both themes, or you might see an entirely different theme instead.

Where Does It Say That?

You usually won't find the theme of a piece of literature stated directly. Theme is what the writer wants you to *discover* for yourself as you share the

INTERNET

More About Theme

Keyword: LE5 7-3

SKILLS FOCUS

Literary Skills
Understand and analyze theme.

experiences of the story's characters. One way to identify the theme is to look closely at what the writer is saying. Consider these questions:

- How has the main **character** changed over the course of the story? What has he or she **discovered** by the story's end?

- Which scenes or passages strike you as especially important to the story? What ideas about life do they suggest?

- What is the story's **title**? Does it reveal anything special about the story?

Evaluating Theme

Why go to the trouble of figuring out a story's theme? Why not just enjoy the plot and not worry about whether you've gotten the theme?

Because the theme *will* get through to you whether you realize it or not. Watch a double feature of shoot'em-up action movies, and twice in one night you've absorbed the idea that the world is a dangerous place where problems are best solved through violence. Read another teen romance, and you've been told once again that nothing is more important than finding true love.

You are not going to agree with all themes. In some stories you'll feel that the truth you're getting is the real deal, a gold nugget of wisdom the writer has discovered through hard experience and is passing on to you. In other stories you'll feel that the writer is just giving you an overused formula, which the writer repeats without even believing it.

Putting a theme into words brings it out into the open, where you can look at it critically and decide if it fits with what *you* know about life.

Practice

Choose two novels you have read recently that deal with similar topics—for example, loyalty, courage, friendship, or loneliness. If you have a favorite writer, use two novels by this writer.

Take a blank sheet of paper, and draw a chart like the one below. Write the title of each novel at the top of the page. Underneath the titles, identify their topics. Then, in one or two sentences, state the theme of each novel—what the story reveals to you about that topic.

Are the themes in the novels the same or different? Which theme do you find more important or more appealing and why?

Novel 1	Novel 2
Topic	Topic
Theme	Theme

Finding the Theme

by Kylene Beers

"So what's the theme of the story?" the teacher asked. Many students looked down at their books. One student began going through his backpack. "Why are you looking in your backpack?" the teacher asked. The student shrugged and replied, "Maybe the answer is in there, because it certainly isn't anyplace else."

Theme—What It Is and Is Not

When you are asked to think about theme, you might start by remembering what theme is *not*. Theme is *not* the **plot** or the **topic** of a story. **Theme** is a truth about life, which you discover by reading the story. You can't express a theme in one word, the way you can state a topic. You need a full sentence to explain the theme.

Read each item below, and decide whether it states a plot, a topic, or a theme:

1. A family travels to Alabama and faces hardships along the way.
2. Prejudice
3. Facing your fears is the only way to overcome them.
4. Happiness can be found in the joys of ordinary life.

Tips for Uncovering Theme

It might be nice if writers included a P.S. to their stories that said, "The theme of this story is . . ." But they don't do that. Instead, writers allow us to meet characters and share an experience with them.

At the end of the story, we, along with the characters, have discovered something about human experience. It might be something we already know but rediscover in new circumstances. It might be something we haven't thought about before.

The **theme,** then, is a truth about life or people that we discover as we share the characters' experiences.

As you read the story that follows, ask yourself

- What is the plot?
- What is the topic?
- What is the story's truth—its theme?

Remember, you must express the theme as a sentence—one that explains what you've discovered from the story.

SKILLS FOCUS

Reading Skills
Find the theme.

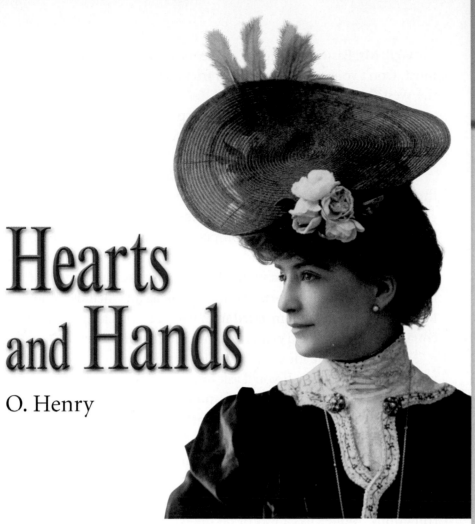

Hearts and Hands

O. Henry

As you read, you'll
find this open-book
sign at certain points
in the story: ⌐⌐⌐⌐⌐.
Stop at these points,
and think about what
you've just read. Do
what the prompts ask
you to do.

At Denver there was an influx of passengers into the coaches on the eastbound B. & M. express. In one coach there sat a very pretty young woman dressed in elegant taste and surrounded by all the luxurious comforts of an experienced traveler. Among the newcomers were two young men, one of handsome presence with a bold, frank countenance and manner; the other a ruffled, glum-faced person, heavily built and roughly dressed. The two were handcuffed together. ❶ ⌐⌐⌐

As they passed down the aisle of the coach the only vacant seat offered was a reversed one facing the attractive young woman. Here the linked couple seated themselves. The young woman's glance fell upon them with a distant, swift disinterest; then with a lovely smile brightening her countenance and a tender pink tingeing her rounded cheeks, she held out a little gray-gloved hand. When she spoke her voice, full, sweet, and deliberate, proclaimed that its owner was accustomed to speak and be heard.

IDENTIFY

❶ Who are the three main characters in this story? Where does the story take place?

INFER

❸ Read this paragraph again. Think about how Miss Fairchild's expression changes when she sees the handcuffs. What might she be thinking?

INTERPRET

❹ What has just happened? Who indicated that he is the prisoner? How does Miss Fairchild react?

INFER

❺ What do you guess happened between Mr. Easton and Miss Fairchild in Washington?

"Well, Mr. Easton, if you *will* make me speak first, I suppose I must. Don't you ever recognize old friends when you meet them in the West?"

The younger man roused himself sharply at the sound of her voice, seemed to struggle with a slight embarrassment which he threw off instantly, and then clasped her fingers with his left hand. ❷ 📖

"It's Miss Fairchild," he said, with a smile. "I'll ask you to excuse the other hand; it's otherwise engaged just at present."

He slightly raised his right hand, bound at the wrist by the shining "bracelet" to the left one of his companion. The glad look in the girl's eyes slowly changed to a bewildered horror. The glow faded from her cheeks. Her lips parted in a vague, relaxing distress. Easton, with a little laugh, as if amused, was about to speak again when the other forestalled[1] him. The glum-faced man had been watching the girl's countenance with veiled glances from his keen, shrewd eyes. ❸ 📖

"You'll excuse me for speaking, miss, but I see you're acquainted with the marshal here. If you'll ask him to speak a word for me when we get to the pen he'll do it, and it'll make things easier for me there. He's taking me to Leavenworth prison. It's seven years for counterfeiting."

"Oh!" said the girl, with a deep breath and returning color. "So that is what you are doing out here? A marshal!" ❹ 📖

"My dear Miss Fairchild," said Easton, calmly, "I had to do something. Money has a way of taking wings unto itself, and you know it takes money to keep step with our crowd in Washington. I saw this opening in the West, and—well, a marshalship isn't quite as high a position as that of ambassador, but—"

"The ambassador," said the girl, warmly, "doesn't call anymore. He needn't ever have done so. You ought to know that. And so now you are one of these dashing Western heroes, and you ride and shoot and go into all kinds of dangers. That's different from the Washington life. You have been missed from the old crowd." ❺ 📖

The girl's eyes, fascinated, went back, widening a little, to rest upon the glittering handcuffs.

"Don't you worry about them, miss," said the other man. "All marshals handcuff themselves to their prisoners to keep them from getting away. Mr. Easton knows his business."

"Will we see you again soon in Washington?" asked the girl.

---

1. **forestalled** (fôr·stôld') *v.:* prevented.

"Not soon, I think," said Easton. "My butterfly days are over, I fear."

"I love the West," said the girl irrelevantly.[2] Her eyes were shining softly. She looked away out the car window. She began to speak truly and simply, without the gloss of style and manner: "Mamma and I spent the summer in Denver. She went home a week ago because father was slightly ill. I could live and be happy in the West. I think the air here agrees with me. Money isn't everything. But people always misunderstand things and remain stupid—" **6**

"Say, Mr. Marshal," growled the glum-faced man. "This isn't quite fair. Haven't had a smoke all day. Haven't you talked long enough? Take me in the smoker now, won't you? I'm half dead for a pipe." **7**

The bound travelers rose to their feet, Easton with the same slow smile on his face.

"I can't deny a petition for tobacco," he said, lightly. "It's the one friend of the unfortunate. Goodbye, Miss Fairchild. Duty calls, you know." He held out his hand for a farewell.

"It's too bad you are not going East," she said, reclothing herself with manner and style. "But you must go on to Leavenworth, I suppose?"

"Yes," said Easton, "I must go on to Leavenworth."

INFER

6 Why does Miss Fairchild tell Mr. Easton she loves the West?

INFER

7 Why do you think the "prisoner" suddenly decides he wants to leave?

---

2. **irrelevantly** (i·rel′ə·vənt·lē) *adv.:* without relation to the subject at hand.

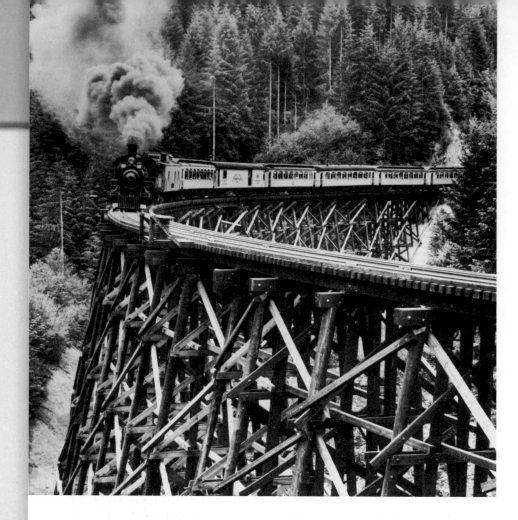

ANALYZE

8 Explain the story's surprise ending. As you think about the marshal's actions, remember that the **theme** of a story is a truth you discover through reading it. What did you discover about the power of compassion? What does this story show about how easy it is to help someone?

What does the title refer to? Does it give you a clue to the story's theme?

The two men sidled down the aisle into the smoker.

The two passengers in a seat nearby had heard most of the conversation. Said one of them: "That marshal's a good sort of chap. Some of these Western fellows are all right."

"Pretty young to hold an office like that, isn't he?" asked the other.

"Young!" exclaimed the first speaker, "why— Oh! didn't you catch on? Say—did you ever know an officer to handcuff a prisoner to his *right* hand?" **8**

Meet the Writer

O. Henry

The O. Henry Style

O. Henry (1862–1910), born William Sydney Porter, once expressed his philosophy of writing this way:

> **"** The short story is a potent medium of education. . . . It should break prejudice with understanding. I propose to send the down-and-outers into the drawing-rooms of the 'get-it-alls,' and I intend to insure their welcome. **"**

O. Henry got to know the "down-and-outers" of New York City when he moved there in 1901. The crowded streets of New York proved an ideal setting for O. Henry to make use of his exceptional powers of observation. He closely studied the ordinary people that he encountered there, transforming them into vivid characters of his short stories. O. Henry described his fascination with the city in this way:

> **"** I would like to live a lifetime on each street in New York. Every house has a drama in it. **"**

At the time of his death, O. Henry was one of the most highly regarded writers in the United States. The humor and ironic twists in his stories, characteristics of the so-called O. Henry style, have helped ensure his continuing popularity.

For Independent Reading

To meet up with more of O. Henry's New York characters, try his short story collection *The Voice of the City.*

Practice the Strategy

Recognizing Plot and Topic

Remember, a theme is *not* the plot or the topic of a story. The **plot** is the series of events that happen in the story. The **topic** is the general subject of the story; it can usually be expressed in one word. (A story may deal with several topics.)

PRACTICE 1

Read the following words and sentences about "Hearts and Hands." Explain which ones state a topic and which ones sum up the plot.

1. Deception
2. Two friends meet on a train, and one pretends to be a U.S. marshal.
3. Friendship
4. A young woman traveling on a train runs into a young man she once knew. She tries to renew the friendship, but he is unable to do so because he is headed to prison. The marshal with him pretends he is the prisoner.

Finding the Theme

When you ask, "What happens next?" you are asking about **plot.** When you ask, "Why does the character do that?" you are asking about **motivation.** When you ask, "What does the story really mean? What is it telling me?" you are asking about **theme.**

Study What the Characters Say

Sometimes the author makes clear the insight into life he or she is sharing with you. For instance, in E. B. White's classic book *Charlotte's Web,* we meet two characters—Wilbur and Charlotte—who show us time and time again how valuable friendship is. Wilbur says at one point in the book, "Friendship is one of the most satisfying things in the world." That's a pretty clear statement of the truth the author wants you to take away from reading this story. In this case you could say that the theme is directly, explicitly stated in the text.

> **Strategy Tip**
>
> As you read, jot down significant comments made by the characters. They may help you decide what truth the author wants you to discover.

Think About What the Characters Learn

Most times the theme is implicit, which means it is not stated directly. Then you must look at the situations the characters face and the conflicts they resolve and decide what the characters—and you—have learned from the experience.

> **Strategy Tip**
>
> Jot down important words or ideas as you read. They will help you track your thoughts about theme.

Think about *Charlotte's Web* again. In that story, Wilbur, a pig, and Charlotte, a spider, form a close friendship. By the end of the story, you might find yourself thinking how wonderful it is that even though Wilbur and Charlotte are so different, they still care a great deal for one another. That might lead you to uncover another truth in this story: *Friendship knows no boundaries and can occur even between those who are very different.* You might remember that truth long after you've forgotten the characters' names or even the title of the story. That's what theme does—it stays with you after the story is over.

PRACTICE 2

What truth about people stays with you after you read "Hearts and Hands"? O. Henry doesn't explicitly state a theme; instead, you've got to figure it out on your own. Ask yourself:

- What have I learned about helping someone people normally wouldn't help?
- Why does the marshal cover up for his prisoner? Is he trying to spare the feelings of the young woman? Is it because he sees the prisoner as a fellow human being?

Write a **theme statement** that starts, "This story reveals to me that . . ."

Not a Theme

| happiness | childhood | awareness |

Theme Statement

| Happiness is accepting the joys of ordinary life. | Childhood is a time of innocence. | Awareness of death can make life richer. |

> **Strategy Tip**
>
> When you write or state a theme, remember that a theme isn't a word or a phrase—it's at least one sentence!

Noticing what the characters say and what they learn will help you **find the theme** in all the stories you read.

SKILLS FOCUS

Literary Skills
Find the theme.

The Highwayman

Make the Connection
Talk It Over

It was a night for love and adventure. Start with the **setting:** a moonlit road hundreds of years ago, a country inn at midnight. Add some **characters:** a daring and dashing robber, a beautiful young woman, a jealous stableman, and a group of cruel soldiers. Can you predict what will happen? Hint: Look at the poem's title and illustrations. Skim the first verse.

Predicting. Discuss your impressions of the poem with a partner. On the basis of your preview, what do you think will happen?

Literary Focus
Topic Versus Theme

After reading a story or a poem, have you ever asked yourself, "What does it *mean*?" What you are asking about is the theme. The **theme** is what a piece of literature reveals about people and life. It is the meaning you take away from the story.

A theme is not the same as a subject or topic. The **topic** of a work can usually be expressed in just a word or two: love, childhood, injustice. The theme is the idea that the writer wishes to convey *about* a particular topic. Some themes—like the power of love or the importance of home or the strength of the human spirit—have been at the heart of stories and poems throughout time.

Narrative Poems

Poems that are written to tell a story are called **narrative poems.** These story poems resemble short stories: They have a **plot, characters,** and a **setting.** Stories sung to the strumming of a stringed instrument are probably the oldest form of storytelling. Modern poems like "The Highwayman" use strong rhythms to make their stories sound like the old sung stories—they capture the enduring power of the spoken word.

You must read this poem aloud to feel its galloping rhythms.

Background
Literature and Social Studies

The highwayman in this famous poem is a robber who lived in England in the 1700s. Highwaymen used to stop stagecoaches on the lonely moorlands of northern England and Scotland to rob the rich passengers of money and jewels. Some highwaymen were considered heroes by the Scots because they shared the money with the poor. Highwaymen were sometimes dashing, romantic figures who dressed in expensive clothes. The poem is based on a true story that the poet heard while he was on vacation in the part of England where highwaymen used to lie in wait for stagecoaches.

The Highwayman

Alfred Noyes

Part 1

The wind was a torrent of darkness among the gusty trees,
The moon was a ghostly galleon° tossed upon cloudy seas,
The road was a ribbon of moonlight over the purple moor,
And the highwayman came riding—
5   Riding—riding—
The highwayman came riding, up to the old inn door.

He'd a French cocked hat on his forehead, a bunch of lace at his
        chin,
A coat of the claret° velvet, and breeches of brown doeskin.
They fitted with never a wrinkle. His boots were up to the thigh.
10   And he rode with a jeweled twinkle,
        His pistol butts a-twinkle,
His rapier hilt° a-twinkle, under the jeweled sky.

Over the cobbles he clattered and clashed in the dark inn yard.
And he tapped with his whip on the shutters, but all was locked
        and barred.
He whistled a tune to the window, and who should be waiting
15   there
But the landlord's black-eyed daughter,
        Bess, the landlord's daughter,
Plaiting° a dark red love knot into her long black hair.

---

  2. galleon (gal′ē·ən) *n.:* large sailing ship.
  8. claret (klar′it) *n.* used as *adj.:* purplish red, like claret wine.
12. rapier (rā′pē·ər) **hilt:** sword handle.
18. plaiting (plāt′iŋ) *v.* used as *adj.:* braiding.

And dark in the dark old inn yard a stable wicket° creaked
20 Where Tim the ostler° listened. His face was white and peaked.
His eyes were hollows of madness, his hair like moldy hay,
But he loved the landlord's daughter,
     The landlord's red-lipped daughter,
Dumb as a dog he listened, and he heard the robber say—

25 "One kiss, my bonny sweetheart, I'm after a prize tonight,
But I shall be back with the yellow gold before the morning
   light;
Yet, if they press me sharply, and harry° me through the day,
Then look for me by moonlight,
     Watch for me by moonlight,
30 I'll come to thee by moonlight, though hell should bar the way."

He rose upright in the stirrups. He scarce could reach her hand,
But she loosened her hair in the casement.° His face burnt like a
   brand
As the black cascade of perfume came tumbling over his breast;
And he kissed its waves in the moonlight,
35   (Oh, sweet black waves in the moonlight!)
Then he tugged at his rein in the moonlight, and galloped away
   to the west.

Part 2

He did not come in the dawning. He did not come at noon;
And out of the tawny sunset, before the rise of the moon,
When the road was a gypsy's ribbon, looping the purple moor,
40 A redcoat troop came marching—
     Marching—marching—
King George's men came marching, up to the old inn door.

---

19. wicket *n.*: small door or gate.
20. ostler (äs′lər) *n.*: person who takes care of horses; groom.
27. harry *v.*: harass or push along.
32. casement *n.*: window that opens outward on hinges.

The Haywain by John Constable (1776–1837).

National Gallery, London/Bridgeman Art Library, London/Superstock.

They said no word to the landlord. They drank his ale instead.
But they gagged his daughter, and bound her, to the foot of her
    narrow bed.
45   Two of them knelt at her casement, with muskets at their side!
There was death at every window;
      And hell at one dark window;
For Bess could see, through her casement, the road that *he*
    would ride.

They had tied her up to attention, with many a sniggering jest;
They had bound a musket beside her, with the muzzle beneath
50   her breast!
"Now, keep good watch!" and they kissed her. She heard the
    dead man say—
Look for me by moonlight;
    Watch for me by moonlight;
I'll come to thee by moonlight, though hell should bar the way!

55 She twisted her hands behind her; but all the knots held good!
She writhed her hands till her fingers were wet with sweat or
    blood!
They stretched and strained in the darkness, and the hours
    crawled by like years,
Till, now, on the stroke of midnight,
    Cold, on the stroke of midnight,
60 The tip of one finger touched it! The trigger at least was hers!

The tip of one finger touched it; she strove no more for the rest!
Up, she stood up to attention, with the muzzle beneath her
    breast.
She would not risk their hearing; she would not strive again;
For the road lay bare in the moonlight;
65   Blank and bare in the moonlight;
And the blood of her veins, in the moonlight, throbbed to her
    love's refrain.

Tlot-tlot; tlot-tlot! Had they heard it? The horse hoofs ringing
    clear;
Tlot-tlot, tlot-tlot, in the distance? Were they deaf that they did
    not hear?
Down the ribbon of moonlight, over the brow of the hill,
70 The highwayman came riding,
    Riding, riding!
The redcoats looked to their priming!° She stood up, straight
    and still.

Tlot-tlot, in the frosty silence! *Tlot-tlot,* in the echoing night!
Nearer he came and nearer. Her face was like a light!
Her eyes grew wide for a moment; she drew one last deep
75   breath,
Then her fingers moved in the moonlight,
    Her musket shattered the moonlight,
Shattered her breast in the moonlight and warned him—with
    her death.

---

72. priming (prīm′iŋ) *n.:* explosive for firing a gun.

He turned. He spurred to the west; he did not know who stood
Bowed, with her head o'er the musket, drenched with her own
80   blood!
Not till the dawn he heard it, his face grew gray to hear
How Bess, the landlord's daughter,
     The landlord's black-eyed daughter,
Had watched for her love in the moonlight, and died in the
     darkness there.

85   Back, he spurred like a madman, shouting a curse to the sky,
With the white road smoking behind him and his rapier
     brandished high.
Blood-red were his spurs in the golden noon; wine-red was his
     velvet coat;
When they shot him down on the highway,
     Down like a dog on the highway,
And he lay in his blood on the highway, with the bunch of lace
90   at his throat.

And still of a winter's night, they say, when the wind is in the
     trees,
When the moon is a ghostly galleon tossed upon cloudy seas,
When the road is a ribbon of moonlight over the purple moor,
A highwayman comes riding—
95   *Riding—riding—*
A highwayman comes riding, up to the old inn door.

Over the cobbles he clatters and clangs in the dark inn yard;
He taps with his whip on the shutters, but all is locked and
     barred.
He whistles a tune to the window, and who should be waiting
     there
100 *But the landlord's black-eyed daughter,*
          Bess, the landlord's daughter,
Plaiting a dark red love knot into her long black hair.

Meet the Writer

Alfred Noyes

A Rousing Romantic

The British poet, novelist, biographer, and essayist **Alfred Noyes** (1880–1958) was possibly the most popular writer of his time. People enjoyed his verse for its rousing storytelling and its thumping rhythms—in fact, his work was often performed aloud.

Noyes, unlike most other poets of his time, was successful enough to earn a living solely from his poetry. He particularly liked the work of Alfred, Lord Tennyson, whose poetry had been popular during Noyes's childhood. Although the twentieth century was a time of literary experimentation and rebellion against convention, Noyes's poems were written in a traditional style, sounding as if they came from a much earlier era.

Today Noyes is best remembered for "The Highwayman," which he wrote in a small cottage on the edge of Bagshot Heath shortly after leaving Oxford University. He recalled:

The Granger Collection, New York.

> 66 Bagshot Heath in those days was a wild bit of country, all heather and pinewoods. 'The Highwayman' suggested itself to me one blustery night when the sound of the wind in the pines gave me the first line: 'The wind was a torrent of darkness among the gusty trees. . . .'

It took me about two days to complete the poem. Shortly afterward it appeared in *Blackwood's Magazine*. It illustrates the unpredictable chances of authorship, that this poem, written in so short a time, when I was twenty-four, should have been read so widely.

I think the success of the poem in all these ways was due to the fact that it was not an artificial composition but was written at an age when I was genuinely excited by that kind of romantic story. 99

After You Read Response and Analysis

First Thoughts

1. Bess gives up her life for the highwayman. Do you think her sacrifice is noble or pointless?

Thinking Critically

2. What is the **setting** of this poem? What details in the poem help you see and hear what is happening?

3. What is Tim's **motive,** or reason, for betraying Bess?

4. This poem is about love, betrayal, and death. What **theme,** or message about people and life, does the poem reveal to you?

5. **Alliteration** (ə•lit′ər•ā′shən) is the repetition of consonant sounds in words close to one another. You can hear alliteration in the phrase "ghostly galleon." Read aloud five other lines in the poem that use alliteration.

Extending Interpretations

6. If you could write a new ending for the poem, what would it be?

7. At the right is a student's letter about "The Highwayman." What points would you make in a letter about the poem?

WRITING

Writing from Another Point of View

The poem concerns itself mainly with the highwayman and Bess. We don't learn much about the other characters. Imagine you are either Tim the ostler or one of the soldiers who come to the inn. In a paragraph, describe your reaction to Bess's death, writing as "I."

Reading Check

Review the main events of this **narrative poem,** and then complete a **sequence chart** like the one below.

Part 1

1. The highwayman rides to the old inn.

2. He finds Bess waiting.

3. Tim overhears him saying . . .

Dear Editors;

   I am a seventh grader at Madison Jr. High. My name is Brooke Garner. Our class has been reading many stories in your book.
   My favorite poem ~~that~~ is "The Highwayman." It shows a very deep understanding and love between the highwayman and the girl. This poem was so touching that ~~through~~ every emotion the writer was trying to convey, filtered through my mind and I was left weakened by its magnitude. The poem lived and I feel that the author had somehow been hurt and understood how the people must have felt and lived.

   Sincerely yours,

   Brooke Garner

INTERNET

Projects and Activities

Keyword: LE5 7-3

SKILLS FOCUS

Literary Skills
Analyze theme; analyze a narrative poem.

Writing Skills
Describe events from another point of view.

Making Connections: Similes and Metaphors

In our everyday language we use many expressions that are not literally true: "Charlie's bragging gets under my skin." "Gilda's money is burning a hole in her pocket." When we use expressions like these, we are using **figures of speech.** Our listeners know that the words do not carry their ordinary meaning. Bragging, after all, does not really pierce skin, and money cannot cause a pocket to catch fire.

The meaning of such figurative expressions depends on comparisons. Bragging is *compared* to something that causes pain or annoyance, such as a thorn. Money is *compared* to something so hot that it cannot be held and must be gotten rid of.

There are many kinds of figures of speech; the most common are **similes** and **metaphors.**

A **simile** is a comparison of two unlike things using the word *like, as, than,* or *resembles.* Here are two famous similes:

> **I wandered lonely as a cloud....**
> —William Wordsworth

> **My love is like a red, red rose....**
> —Robert Burns

A **metaphor** also compares two unlike things, but it does so without using *like, as, than,* or *resembles.* For example, in "The Highwayman," Alfred Noyes does not say the moon was *like* a ghostly galleon. He uses a metaphor: "The moon *was* a ghostly galleon tossed upon cloudy seas."

PRACTICE

Fill in this chart by completing each comparison from "The Highwayman." Then, identify it as a simile or a metaphor. The first item has been done for you.

Figure of Speech
line 1: The wind is compared to a torrent of darkness. (a metaphor)
line 3: The road is compared to _____
line 12: The stars in the sky are compared to _____
line 21: Tim's eyes are compared to _____
line 21: Tim's hair is compared to _____
line 24: Tim's dumbness is compared to _____
line 32: The highwayman's face is compared to _____
line 39: The road is compared to _____
line 74: Bess's face is compared to _____

SKILLS FOCUS

Vocabulary Skills
Understand similes and metaphors.

Understanding Cause and Effect

Causes and Effects

You know from experience that one thing leads to another. If you sleep through your alarm, you know you'll be late for school and you'll miss your favorite class—English. Sleeping through your alarm is a **cause**—it makes something happen. An **effect** is what happens as a result of some event—you're late for school and miss English.

You could go on. Being late for English class causes you to have to make up the time after school. Making up the time causes you to miss tryouts for football. Missing tryouts causes you to lose the chance to impress a certain girl. So you lose the girl, and it all can be traced to sleeping through an alarm.

■ As you read the following article on real highwaymen, ask yourself, "Why did this happen?" and "What happened because of this?" These questions will help you discover causes and effects.

To find causes and their effects, look for signal terms such as *cause*, *effect*, *resulted in*, *so*, *thus*, *why*, and *because*.

Cause and Effect: The Rise of Highwaymen in England

What Happened
Some people in England got very rich. Others got poorer.

↓

Effect
Government built new toll roads for the rich to travel.

↓

Effect
Highwaymen held up stagecoaches and carriages to get money.

↓

Effect
Highwaymen . . .

INTERNET
Interactive Reading Model
Keyword: LE5 7-3

SKILLS FOCUS

Reading Skills
Understand cause and effect.

Gentlemen of the Road

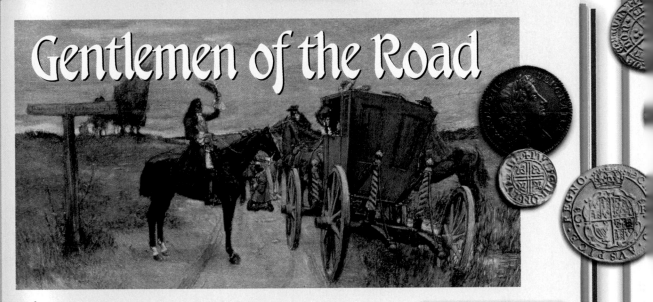

W HY DID PEOPLE ONCE THINK of highwaymen, the bandits (like Bess's beloved) who robbed travelers in seventeenth- and eighteenth-century England, as gentlemen?

To answer that question, first look at these facts. The seventeenth and eighteenth centuries saw the rise of a very wealthy class in England. England became a nation of haves and have-nots. The rich dressed in silks and velvets. Men and women wore huge powdered wigs. The rich lived on vast estates. They traveled to London for rounds of parties in the winter-spring season and spent summers in seaside towns, where gambling was a favorite pastime.

As the wealthy became richer, the conditions of the poor grew worse. Because the government did not care about their welfare, the poor lived in filthy slums in cities and in miserable conditions in farms and towns. In the worst years, 74 percent of the children in London died before the age of five. These were the social conditions that contributed to the rise of the highwaymen.

In addition, newly built toll roads ran through the countryside, connecting towns and villages. These improved roads brought out more travelers—rich ones. The highwaymen could stop the private carriages and the stagecoaches that used the toll roads and rob the passengers.

The highwaymen called themselves gentlemen of the road, and some people agreed—sometimes even their victims! How did they come by this surprising reputation?

Some people saw the highwaymen not as criminals but as the new Robin Hoods because they gave to the poor what they had stolen from the rich (or part of it).

> This article will explain why people thought of the highwaymen as gentlemen.

The Granger Collection, New York.

> This paragraph and those that follow tell what caused people to think of these bandits as gentlemen.

Another reason why people thought of these bandits as gentlemen was that they looked the part. Most highwaymen came from poor families or, at best, middle-class ones. But once they turned to a life of crime, they could afford to dress in style. They wore high-heeled boots that went all the way to the hip, fancy shirts, long, elegant coats, and wide-brimmed hats with feathers. With their dashing clothes and fine horses these former footmen, butchers, and cheese sellers might have been mistaken for aristocrats.

The Singing Lesson by Arturo Ricci.

Some highwaymen tried to act like gentlemen as well. Many would never point a gun at a lady or search her for valuables, and sometimes they'd let women they robbed keep items of sentimental value. Highwaymen loved their horses too and took pride in earning the loyalty of their steeds by treating them well.

Some highwaymen politely begged their victims' pardon as they relieved them of their money and jewels. Others took only what they felt they needed and returned the rest to their owners.

In one account a robbery victim was upset about losing his beloved watch. He offered the highwayman two guineas instead, along with a promise not to turn him in to the authorities. The highwayman agreed, and they went off together to the man's home. The money changed hands, the two men shared a bottle of wine, and after many courteous words on each side, the highwayman galloped off.

Even when captured and sentenced to hang (the usual punishment for robbery in those days), some highwaymen tried to behave like gentlemen. They were too proud to cry or beg for mercy from the authorities they defied. After the noose was tied around their neck, some threw themselves off the scaffold rather than wait for the wagon they stood on to be pulled from beneath them. For those who romanticized the highwaymen in stories and song, this final act showed scorn for the corrupt authorities and courage in the face of death.

—Mara Rockliff

Analyzing Cause and Effect

Gentlemen of the Road

Test Practice

1. This article suggests that all of the following might have **caused** the rise of the highwayman *except* the —

   A worsening conditions of the poor

   B rise of a very wealthy class

   C use of capital punishment

   D newly built toll roads

2. What **caused** people to see the highwaymen as the new Robin Hoods?

   F They rode horses and used bows and arrows.

   G They robbed from the rich and gave to the poor.

   H They lived in Sherwood Forest.

   J They wore Robin Hood outfits.

3. The highwaymen were able to dress in style because —

   A they were wealthy aristocrats

   B they took advice from their victims

   C their crimes made them wealthy

   D they were interested in fashion

4. Some highwaymen didn't beg for mercy from the hangman because of their —

   F pride

   G fear

   H mercy

   J shame

Constructed Response

1. List some of the conditions in seventeenth- and eighteenth-century England that **caused** bandits to rob travelers on the nation's highways.

2. What **caused** people to regard these bandits, or highwaymen, as gentlemen?

SKILLS FOCUS

Reading Skills
Analyze cause and effect.

Annabel Lee

Make the Connection
Think Aloud

With a partner, take turns reading stanzas of the poem aloud to hear its haunting sounds and to visualize its romantic setting. Exchange thoughts about the poem's speaker and its music. Jot down comments and questions as they come to you, and discuss them with your partner. Work together to solve any problems you have in understanding the poem.

Literary Focus
Themes Across Time

"Annabel Lee" is a famous love poem, written after the poet's young wife, Virginia, died of tuberculosis. She was laid to rest in New York, near the Hudson River, in a sepulcher (sep'əl·kər), a burial vault that stands aboveground. Poe's poem reads like a fairy tale, set in a faraway time and place.

Across time, poets, storytellers, and songwriters have written about the many faces of love. It's an age-old subject that has inspired many themes. Songs tell of love that blooms in the most unexpected places. Storytellers write about love that overcomes impossible barriers. In "Annabel Lee," Poe's speaker describes an eternal love.

Repetition

Musicians, as you may know, use repetition—of sounds, of words, of tones—to create emotional effects. Poe uses repetition in much the same way. In "Annabel Lee," notice how words, sounds, phrases, and rhythms recur with hypnotic regularity. How many times does the name Annabel Lee appear in the poem?

(Above) Edgar Allan Poe's grave in Westminster Burial Ground in Baltimore, Maryland.

(Opposite) Poe's cottage before it was moved to Dyckman Street in the Bronx, New York.

INTERNET
More About Poe
Keyword: LE5 7-3

Literary Skills
Understand universal themes; understand repetition in poems.

Annabel Lee

Edgar Allan Poe

Portrait of "Sissy,"
Poe's beloved wife.

Valentine Museum,
Richmond, Virginia.

It was many and many a year ago,
    In a kingdom by the sea,
That a maiden there lived whom you may know
    By the name of Annabel Lee;
5   And this maiden she lived with no other thought
    Than to love and be loved by me.

I was a child and *she* was a child,
    In this kingdom by the sea:
But we loved with a love that was more than love—
10   I and my Annabel Lee—
With a love that the wingèd seraphs° of heaven
    Coveted° her and me.

And this was the reason that, long ago,
    In this kingdom by the sea,
15   A wind blew out of a cloud, chilling
    My beautiful Annabel Lee;
So that her highborn kinsmen came
    And bore her away from me,
To shut her up in a sepulcher
20   In this kingdom by the sea.

The angels, not half so happy in heaven,
    Went envying her and me—
Yes!—that was the reason (as all men know,
    In this kingdom by the sea)
25   That the wind came out of the cloud by night,
    Chilling and killing my Annabel Lee.

11. **seraphs** (ser'əfs) *n.*: angels.
12. **coveted** (kuv'it·id) *v.*: envied.

But our love it was stronger by far than the love
    Of those who were older than we—
    Of many far wiser than we—
30 And neither the angels in heaven above,
    Nor the demons down under the sea,
Can ever dissever° my soul from the soul
    Of the beautiful Annabel Lee—

For the moon never beams, without bringing me dreams
35   Of the beautiful Annabel Lee;
And the stars never rise, but I feel the bright eyes
    Of the beautiful Annabel Lee;
And so, all the night-tide, I lie down by the side
Of my darling—my darling—my life and my bride,
40   In the sepulcher there by the sea,
    In her tomb by the sounding sea.

32. dissever (di·sev′ər) *v.:* separate.

Crashing Wave (c. 1938) by
Marsden Hartley.
Private Collection, New York.

Meet the Writer

Edgar Allan Poe

The Granger Collection, New York.

"A World of Moan"

Long before Stephen King began writing stories of horror, **Edgar Allan Poe** (1809–1849) was exploring the dark side of the human imagination in such works as "The Raven," "The Tell-Tale Heart," and "The Masque of the Red Death." Poe's life was hard from the start. First, his father deserted the family. Then, before Poe was three years old, his beautiful young mother died, and the little boy was left alone. John Allan, a wealthy and childless businessman in Richmond, Virginia, took in young Edgar and provided for his education, but the two constantly quarreled. Poe wanted to write, while his foster father wanted him to take over the family business. Eventually Poe broke away from his foster parents and set out on his own. Throughout his adult life he was plagued by poverty, alcoholism, and unhappiness. As Poe said, "I dwelt alone in a world of moan."

Always searching for a family, Poe married his thirteen-year-old cousin, Virginia Clemm. Her early death seemed to destroy him, and he himself died two years after she did. He had lived only forty years.

For Independent Reading

Poe's haunting poems include "The Raven" and "The Bells." You'll find some of his most chilling stories in a book titled *The Best of Poe.*

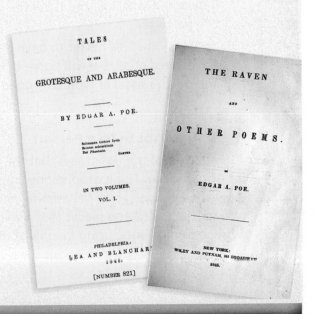

After You Read   Response and Analysis

First Thoughts

1. If you were to meet the speaker of this poem, what would you want to ask him? Be sure to refer to the notes you made as you read the poem.

Thinking Critically

2. Were you surprised when you discovered where the speaker sleeps each night? Do you think he actually sleeps there, or is he speaking of what he does in his imagination? Explain.

3. Find at least two details that help you picture the poem's **setting.**

4. List the **rhyming sounds** that echo through the six stanzas. What words are repeated over and over and over again? What does the **repetition** remind you of?

Extending Interpretations

5. One topic of this poem is loss. What does the poem say about loss? In other words, how would you state the poem's **theme**? Talk about whether you think the speaker's feelings of grief are universal.

6. Some say that it's better to have loved and lost than never to have loved at all. Do you agree or disagree? How do you think the poem's speaker would respond to that idea?

Reading Check

a. How does the speaker describe the love he shared with Annabel Lee?

b. Who is jealous of the speaker and Annabel Lee?

c. What do Annabel Lee's relatives do to her?

d. According to the last stanza, where does the speaker now see Annabel Lee? Where does he sleep each night?

WRITING

Writing a Tribute to a Person

The speaker of the poem says that the moon and stars remind him of Annabel Lee. Think of someone you feel strongly about— perhaps someone you love, admire, or miss very much. Jot down the special things and places that remind you of that person. Then, write a brief tribute, using images of the special things or places to emphasize what you miss about the person.

SKILLS FOCUS

Literary Skills
Analyze theme; understand repetition in poems.

Writing Skills
Write a tribute to a person.

Using Analogies

An **analogy** (ə·nalʹə·jē) is a comparison between two things to show how they are alike. An analogy can explain one idea by showing how that idea is similar to another, more easily understood idea. Analogies can be tricky, though, because few ideas or situations are alike in all ways. Here's an example in which a writer compares playing golf to being in love:

> I fell in love with golf when I was twenty-five. It would have been a healthier relationship had it been an adolescent romance or, better yet, a childhood crush. Though I'd like to think we've had a lot of laughs together and even some lyrical moments. I have never felt quite adequate to her demands, and she keeps secrets from me. . . . I can't get them out of my mind, or quite wrap my mind around them. Sometimes I wish that she and I had never met. She leads me on, but deep down I suspect—this is my secret—that I'm just not her type.

—from "An Ode to Golf" by John Updike

PRACTICE

Try writing your own analogy. First, you have to find a subject you would like to talk about. Updike chose golf. Then, find something familiar that you can compare this subject to. Before you write your analogy, make a list of the ways in which your two subjects are similar. In your analogy, compare your subjects point by point. Remember that in an analogy you use several points for comparison, not just one. Here are some ideas for subjects:

Doing homework [is like . . .]   Family life [is like . . .]
Exercising [is like . . .]   Keeping friends [is like . . .]
Playing soccer [is like . . .]

If you prefer, write your analogy to explain something complex, perhaps something you learned in science. Scientists, in fact, use analogies all the time. A doctor might compare antibodies zeroing in on a tumor to guided missiles finding their target, for example.

SKILLS FOCUS

Vocabulary Skills
Understand and use analogies.

Taking Notes and Outlining

Reading Focus

Taking Notes

Edgar Allan Poe's life was filled with struggle and conflict, as you learned from his poem and biography. The article you are about to read deals with another conflict involving Poe, one that took place many years after his death.

When you read informational material, like an article, a lot goes on in your head.

- You connect what you read with your own experiences and knowledge.

- You ask yourself questions and make predictions.

- You challenge the text.

- You reflect on its meaning.

Jotting down notes will help you understand and remember what you read. Here's what to do:

- **Be organized.** Use a simple outline form to jot down the information or ideas that you think are most important. (See the box for a sample outline form.)

- **Be brief.** Keep your notes short, simple, and clear. Write only words and phrases that will help you focus on the most important information.

- **Underline or circle information.** It may be useful to highlight certain information directly in the text, but don't do it in a book that doesn't belong to you, and don't get carried away. If everything is highlighted, then it's hard to tell what's most important.

■ When you read this selection about a house Edgar Allan Poe once lived in, keep a sheet of paper nearby and jot down key details.

Outlining

Outlining can help you uncover the skeleton that holds the text together. An outline highlights main ideas and supporting details. Here's an example of an informal outline:

Main idea
 supporting detail
 supporting detail
 [etc.]

Main idea
 supporting detail
 supporting detail
 [etc.]

SKILLS FOCUS

Reading Skills
Take notes and make outlines.

THE FALL OF THE HOUSE OF POE?

THINK OF YOUR FAVORITE PLACE in the world, the place where you've spent some of the happiest hours of your life.

Now, think about it being torn down.

How do you feel? Terrible, right? If Edgar Allan Poe were alive today, scholars say, that's the way he might feel about the fate of the boardinghouse he once lived in at 85 Amity Street in New York City's Greenwich Village.

More than a century and a half has passed since Poe died. Amity Street was long ago renamed West Third Street, and the former boardinghouse now belongs to New York University. For years the university used it for classrooms and offices. But in 1999, NYU officials announced that they would be tearing the house down to make room for a new building for their law school.

Loyal Poe fans joined neighborhood residents in vigorously protesting the university's plan. They wrote letters, circulated petitions, and organized a rally attended by several hundred supporters chanting, "No, no, Poe won't go." They read aloud from "The Raven," the poem that made Poe famous, and chanted its famous refrain: "Nevermore!"

"It always mystified me why there was not a gold plaque outside the house," one Poe scholar said. "It is a genuine literary landmark."

New York University disagreed. Its representatives argued that Poe (along with his young wife, Virginia, and her mother) may have lived at the boardinghouse for as little as six months and that he had not written any of his more important works there. They also said that the house had changed drastically over the years, leaving no traces of Poe's residence. They even questioned whether the current building was the same one that had stood there in 1845, when Poe moved in. One NYU representative concluded, "This is not a building that remembers Poe."

The protesters researched the university's claims. They studied all kinds of documents, from letters and recollections of people who knew Poe to public records showing the history of the neighborhood.

Judging from dates and addresses in Poe's surviving correspondence, including a valentine given to him by Virginia in 1846, it seems probable that Poe lived there for less than a year. But that may have been longer than he stayed at any of the other eight places where he lived in Manhattan, all of which have already been torn down.

But the months he spent at 85 Amity may have been the happiest in Poe's short famous detective story "The Facts in the Case of M. Valdemar." Poe was completely absorbed in his writing, sometimes spending as many as fifteen hours a day at his desk.

The house where all that happened, it turned out, was indeed the house that the university planned to demolish. Detailed city atlases in the Maps Division of the New York Public Library show that although the name of the street has changed, the house numbers have not. Eighty-five West Third was 85 Amity. The house, according to tax ledgers in the New York City Municipal Archives, was built in 1836—nearly a decade before the Poe family moved in.

On September 29, 2000, after examining the evidence on both sides, State Supreme Court Judge Robert E. Lippmann dismissed the case, saying he had no legal authority to prevent NYU from tearing down the Poe house. This prompted an NYU spokesman to add, "The Tell-Tale Heart does not beat beneath the floorboards of this building." Preservation groups planned to appeal the decision.

—Mara Rockliff

and troubled life. The boardinghouse was close to Washington Square Park, where his young wife, who was dying of tuberculosis, could breathe fresh air into her ailing lungs. That would have been his last full year with his beloved Virginia.

Professionally Poe was at the height of his career. He had finally achieved what he called "the one great purpose of my literary life"—writing and editing his own literary magazine, the *Broadway Journal.* He also had published *The Raven and Other Poems,* and he had written dozens of essays and short stories, including his

Analyzing Outlines

THE FALL OF THE HOUSE OF POE?

Test Practice

1. Which of the following statements is an **opinion,** not a fact?

   A Poe wrote *The Raven and Other Poems.*

   B Poe's young wife died of tuberculosis.

   C All the other places in Manhattan that Poe lived in have already been torn down.

   D "This is not a building that remembers Poe."

2. The judge who dismissed the case did so because he —

   F had no legal authority to prevent NYU from tearing down the house

   G believed NYU was doing the right thing

   H did not like the protesters

   J did not think the protesters had a good case

3. When Poe said he achieved "the one great purpose of my literary life," he was referring to —

   A living at 85 Amity Street with Virginia

   B writing *The Raven and Other Poems*

   C turning his attention to his wife's illness

   D writing and editing his own literary magazine

4. Which of the following would *not* be included in an outline of the article?

   F Poe definitely lived at the house on Amity Street.

   G The judge dismisses the case.

   H Preservation groups plan to appeal.

   J There are other law schools in New York City.

Constructed Response

Fill in the blanks in the following outline.

  I. NYU officials plan to tear down Poe house in order to build new law school.

  II. Poe fans and residents protest.

III. NYU argues against protesters.

  A. Poe lived there for less than six months.

  B. _____

  C. _____

IV. Protesters research NYU's claims.

  A. _____

  D. _____

  C. _____

  D. _____

SKILLS FOCUS

Reading Skills
Make and analyze an outline.

After You Read   Vocabulary Development

Latin Roots

Many English word roots come directly or indirectly from the Latin language. A word **root** is a word or word part from which other words are made. Learning some of the main word roots derived from Latin will give you a key to understanding the meanings of many English words.

PRACTICE

Match each word in the box above with the Latin word it comes from. Can you find an additional word with the same origin and use it in a sentence?

Latin Word	Meaning	Word Bank	Additional Word
petere	"to seek"		
demoliri	"to pull down; destroy"		
circulari	"to form a circle"		
absorbere	"to suck in"		
repraesentare	"to be again"		

INTERNET
Vocabulary Activity
Keyword: LE5 7-3

SKILLS FOCUS

Vocabulary Skills
Understand Latin roots.

User Friendly

Make the Connection
Quickwrite ✏

Suppose someone you just met said, "My best friend is a computer." What would that statement tell you about the person? List some **character traits** you'd guess that the person might have.

Literary Focus
Discovering Theme

Here are some tips that can help you find a story's theme:

- Decide what the characters have learned or discovered by the end of the story. Often that discovery can be translated into a statement of the theme.

- Think about the **title** and what it might mean. (Not all titles have significance. Some titles just tell you what the main character will be facing in each story. But the title of Jack London's novel *Call of the Wild* definitely points to a theme in the book.)

- Look for key passages in which the writer seems to make important statements about life. They may point to the theme.

Reading Skills
Recognizing Causes and Effects: Seeing Why Things Happen

In "User Friendly" a chain of events lands Kevin in computer trouble. He sees **effects** (what happens), but he's blind to **causes** (why the events happen) until it's too late. A **causal chain** is a series of events in which each event causes another one to happen, like dominoes falling in a row. Be careful, though—one event can follow another without having been caused by it. To figure out causes and effects, follow these steps:

- Look for what happens first. Then, ask what happens *because* of that.

- Look for hidden or multiple causes and results.

- Use a graphic organizer, such as a flowchart, to record the chain of events.

As you read, you'll find open-book signs at certain points in the story. Stop at these points, and answer the questions about cause and effect.

User Friendly

T. Ernesto Bethancourt

I reached over and shut off the insistent buzzing of my bedside alarm clock. I sat up, swung my feet over the edge of the bed, and felt for my slippers on the floor. Yawning, I walked toward the bathroom. As I walked by the corner of my room, where my computer table was set up, I pressed the *on* button, slid a diskette into the floppy drive, then went to brush my teeth. By the time I got back, the computer's screen was glowing greenly, displaying the message: *Good morning, Kevin.*

I sat down before the computer table, addressed the keyboard, and typed: *Good morning, Louis.* The computer immediately began to whir and promptly displayed a list of items on its green screen.

```
Today is Monday, April 22, the
113th day of the year. There are
253 days remaining. Your 14th
birthday is five days from
this date.

Math test today, 4th Period.

Your history project is due
today. Do you wish printout:
Y/N?
```

I punched the letter *Y* on the keyboard and flipped on the switch to the computer's printer. At once the printer sprang to life and began *eeeek*ing out page one. I went downstairs to breakfast.

My bowl of Frosted Flakes was neatly in place, flanked by a small pitcher of milk, an empty juice glass, and an unpeeled banana. I picked up the glass, went to the refrigerator, poured myself a glass of Tang, and sat down to my usual lonely breakfast. Mom was already at work, and Dad wouldn't be home from his Chicago trip for another three days. I absently[1] read the list of ingredients in Frosted Flakes for what seemed like the millionth time. I sighed deeply.

When I returned to my room to shower and dress for the day, my history project was already printed out. I had almost walked by Louis, when I noticed there was a message on the screen. It wasn't the usual:

```
Printout completed. Do you
wish to continue: Y/N?
```

Underneath the printout question were two lines:

```
When are you going to get me
my voice module,² Kevin?
```

I blinked. It couldn't be. There was nothing in Louis's basic programming that would allow for a question like this. Wondering what was going on, I sat down at the keyboard and entered: *Repeat last message.* Amazingly, the computer replied:

```
It's right there on the
screen, Kevin. Can we talk?
```

```
I mean, are you going to get
me a voice box?
```

I was stunned. What was going on here? Dad and I had put this computer together. Well, Dad had, and I had helped. Dad is one of the best engineers and master computer designers at Major Electronics, in Santa Rosario, California, where our family lives.

Just ask anyone in Silicon Valley[3] who Jeremy Neal is and you get a whole rave review of his inventions and modifications[4] of the latest in computer technology. It isn't easy being his son either. Everyone expects me to open my mouth and read printouts on my tongue.

I mean, I'm no dumbo. I'm at the top of my classes in everything but PE. I skipped my last grade in junior high, and most of the kids at Santa Rosario High call me a brain. But next to Dad I have a long, long way to go. He's a for-real genius.

So when I wanted a home computer, he didn't go to the local ComputerLand store. He built one for me. Dad had used components[5] from the latest model that Major Electronics was developing. The CPU, or central computing unit—the heart of every computer—was a new design. But surely that didn't mean much, I thought. There were CPUs just like it, all over the country, in Major's new line. And so far as I knew, there wasn't a one of them that could ask questions, besides *YES/NO?* or *request additional information.*

It had to be the extra circuitry in the gray

---

1. **absently** *adv.*: in a distracted, inattentive way.
2. **voice module:** unit that, when connected to a computer, enables it to produce speech.

3. **Silicon Valley:** area in central California that is a center of the computer industry. (Silicon is used in the manufacture of computer chips, or circuits.)
4. **modifications** (mäd′ə·fi·kā′shənz) *n.*: slight changes.
5. **components** (kəm·pō′nənts) *n.*: parts.

plastic case next to Louis's console.[6] It was a new idea Dad had come up with. That case housed Louis's "personality," as Dad called it. He told me it'd make computing more fun for me, if there was a tutorial program[7] built in, to help me get started. ❶

RECOGNIZE CAUSE AND EFFECT
❶ Why is Kevin stunned? What does he think causes Louis's unusual behavior?

I think he also wanted to give me a sort of friend. I don't have many. . . . Face it, I don't have *any*. The kids at school stay away from me, like I'm a freak or something.

We even named my electronic tutor Louis, after my great-uncle. He was a brainy guy who encouraged my dad when he was a kid. Dad didn't just give Louis a name either. Louis had gangs of features that probably won't be out on the market for years.

The only reason Louis didn't have a voice module was that Dad wasn't satisfied with the ones available. He wanted Louis to sound like a kid my age, and he was modifying a module when he had the time. Giving Louis a name didn't mean it was a person, yet here it was, asking me a question that just couldn't be in its programming. It wanted to talk to me!

Frowning, I quickly typed: *We'll have to wait and see, Louis. When it's ready, you'll get your voice.* The machine whirred and displayed another message:

`That's no answer, Kevin.`

---

6. **console** (kän′sōl′) *n.*: a computer's keyboard and monitor (display unit). *Console* can also refer to a cabinet for a radio, stereo, or television.

7. **tutorial program:** program that provides instructions for performing specific tasks on a computer.

Shaking my head, I answered: *That's what my dad tells me. It'll have to do for you. Good morning, Louis.* I reached over and flipped the standby switch, which kept the computer ready but not actively running.

I showered, dressed, and picked up the printout of my history project. As I was about to leave the room, I glanced back at the computer table. Had I been imagining things?

I'll have to ask Dad about it when he calls tonight, I thought. *I wonder what he'll think of it. Bad enough the thing is talking to me. I'm answering it!*

Before I went out to catch my bus, I carefully checked the house for unlocked doors and open windows. It was part of my daily routine. Mom works, and most of the day the house is empty: a natural setup for robbers. I glanced in the hall mirror just as I was ready to go out the door.

My usual reflection gazed back. Same old Kevin Neal: five ten, one hundred twenty pounds, light-brown hair, gray eyes, clear skin. I was wearing my Santa Rosario Rangers T-shirt, jeans, and sneakers.

"You don't look like a flake to me," I said to the mirror, then added, "but maybe Mom's right. Maybe you spend too much time alone with Louis." Then I ran to get my bus.

Ginny Linke was just two seats away from me on the bus. She was with Sherry Graber and Linda Martinez. They were laughing, whispering to each other, and looking around at the other students. I promised myself that today I was actually going to talk to Ginny. But then, I'd promised myself that every day for the past school year. Somehow I'd never got up the nerve.

What does she want to talk with you for?

I asked myself. She's great-looking . . . has that head of blond hair . . . a terrific bod, and wears the latest clothes. . . .

And just look at yourself, pal, I thought. You're under six foot, skinny . . . a year younger than most kids in junior high. Worse than that, you're a brain. If that doesn't ace you out with girls, what does?

The bus stopped in front of Santa Rosario High and the students began to file out. I got up fast and quickly covered the space between me and Ginny Linke. *It's now or never,* I thought. I reached forward and tapped Ginny on the shoulder. She turned and smiled. She really smiled!

"Uhhhh . . . Ginny?" I said.

"Yes, what is it?" she replied.

"I'm Kevin Neal. . . ."

"Yes, I know," said Ginny.

"You do?" I gulped in amazement. "How come?"

"I asked my brother, Chuck. He's in your math class."

I knew who Chuck Linke was. He plays left tackle on the Rangers. The only reason he's in my math class is he's taken intermediate algebra twice . . . so far. He's real bad news, and I stay clear of him and his crowd.

"What'd you ask Chuck?" I said.

Ginny laughed. "I asked him who was that nerdy kid who keeps staring at me on the bus. He knew who I meant, right away."

Sherry and Linda, who'd heard it all, broke into squeals of laughter. They were still laughing and looking back over their shoulders at me when they got off the bus. I slunk off the vehicle, feeling even more nerdish than Ginny thought I was.

When I got home that afternoon, at two, I went right into the empty house. I avoided my reflection in the hall mirror. I was pretty sure I'd screwed up on the fourth-period math test. All I could see was Ginny's face, laughing at me.

Nerdy kid, I thought, *that's what she thinks of me.* I didn't even have my usual after-school snack of a peanut butter and banana sandwich. I went straight upstairs to my room and tossed my books onto the unmade bed. I walked over to the computer table and pushed the *on* button. The screen flashed:

`Good afternoon, Kevin.`

Although it wasn't the programmed response to Louis's greeting, I typed in: *There's nothing good about it. And girls are no @#%!!! good!* The machine responded:

`Don't use bad language, Kevin. It isn't nice.`

Repeat last message, I typed rapidly. It was happening again! The machine was . . . well, it was talking to me, like another person would. The "bad language" message disappeared and in its place was:

`Once is enough, Kevin. Don't swear at me for something I didn't do.`

"This is it," I said aloud. "I'm losing my marbles." I reached over to flip the standby switch. Louis's screen quickly flashed out:

`Don't cut me off, Kevin. Maybe I can help: Y/N?`

I punched the *Y*. "If I'm crazy," I said, "at least I have company. Louis doesn't think I'm a nerd. Or does it?" The machine flashed the message:

`How can I help?`

Do you think I'm a nerd? I typed.

Never! I think you're
wonderful. Who said you
were a nerd?

I stared at the screen. *How do you know what a nerd is?* I typed. The machine responded instantly. It had never run this fast before.

Special vocabulary, entry
#635. BASIC Prog. #4231. And
who said you were a nerd?

"That's right," I said, relieved. "Dad programmed all those extra words for Louis's 'personality.' " Then I typed in the answer to Louis's question: *Ginny Linke said it.* Louis flashed:

This is a human female?
Request additional data.

Still not believing I was doing it, I entered all I knew about Ginny Linke, right down to the phone number I'd never had the nerve to use. Maybe it was dumb, but I also typed in how I felt about Ginny. I even wrote out the incident on the bus that morning. Louis whirred, then flashed out:

She's cruel and stupid.
You're the finest person
I know.

I'm the ONLY person you know, I typed.

That doesn't matter. You
are my user. Your happiness
is everything to me. I'll
take care of Ginny.

The screen returned to the *Good afternoon, Kevin* message. I typed out: *Wait! How can you do all this? What do you mean, you'll take care of Ginny?* But all Louis responded was:

Programming Error: 76534.

Not programmed
to respond to
this type of
question. ❷

No matter what I did for the next few hours, I couldn't get Louis to do anything outside of its regular programming. When Mom came home from work, I didn't mention the funny goings-on. I was sure Mom would think I'd gone stark bonkers. But when Dad called that evening, after dinner, I asked to speak to him.

"Hi, Dad. How's Chicago?"

"Dirty, crowded, cold, and windy," came Dad's voice over the miles. "But did you want a weather report, son? What's on your mind? Something wrong?"

"Not exactly, Dad. Louis is acting funny. Real funny."

"Shouldn't be. I checked it out just before I left. Remember you were having trouble with the modem? You couldn't get Louis to access any of the mainframe databanks."

"That's right!" I said. "I forgot about that."

"Well, I didn't," Dad said. "I patched in our latest modem model. Brand-new. You can leave a question on file and when Louis can access the databanks at the cheapest time, it'll do it automatically. It'll switch from standby to on, get the data, then return to standby, after it saves what you asked. Does that answer your question?"

"Uhhhh . . . yeah, I guess so, Dad."

"All right, then. Let me talk to your mom now."

RECOGNIZE CAUSE AND EFFECT
❷ What makes Kevin confide in Louis? What do you think Louis means by "I'll take care of Ginny"?

I gave the phone to Mom and walked upstairs while she and Dad were still talking. The modem, I thought. Of course. That was it. The modem was a telephone link to any number of huge computers at various places all over the country. So Louis could get all the information it wanted at any time, so long as the standby switch was on. Louis was learning things at an incredible rate by picking the brains of the giant computers. And Louis had a hard disk memory that could store 100 million bytes of information.

But that still didn't explain the unprogrammed responses . . . the "conversation" I'd had with the machine. Promising myself I'd talk more about it with Dad, I went to bed. It had been a rotten day and I was glad to see the end of it come. I woke next morning in a panic. I'd forgotten to set my alarm. Dressing frantically and skipping breakfast, I barely made my bus.

As I got on board, I grabbed a front seat. They were always empty. All the kids that wanted to talk and hang out didn't sit up front where the driver could hear them. I saw Ginny, Linda, and Sherry in the back. Ginny was staring at me and she didn't look too happy. Her brother Chuck, who was seated near her, glared at me too. What was going on?

Once the bus stopped at the school, it didn't take long to find out. I was walking up the path to the main entrance when someone grabbed me from behind and spun me around. I found myself nose to nose with Chuck Linke. This was not a pleasant prospect. Chuck was nearly twice my size. Even the other guys on the Rangers refer to him as "The Missing" Linke. And he looked real ticked off.

"OK, nerd," growled Chuck, "what's the big idea?"

"Energy and mass are different aspects of the same thing?" I volunteered, with a weak smile. "E equals MC squared.[8] That's the biggest idea I know."

"Don't get wise, nerd," Chuck said. He grabbed my shirt front and pulled me to within inches of his face. I couldn't help but notice that Chuck needed a shave. And Chuck was only fifteen!

"Don't play dumb," Chuck went on. "I mean those creepy phone calls. Anytime my sister gets on the phone, some voice cuts in and says things to her."

"What kind of things?" I asked, trying to get loose.

"You know very well what they are. Ginny told me about talking to you yesterday. You got some girl to make those calls for you and say all those things. . . . So you and your creepy girlfriend better knock it off. Or I'll knock you off. Get it?"

For emphasis Chuck balled his free hand into a fist the size of a ham and held it under my nose. I didn't know what he was talking about, but I had to get away from this moose before he did me some real harm.

"First off, I don't have a girlfriend, creepy or otherwise," I said. "And second, I don't know what you're talking about. And third, you better let me go, Chuck Linke."

"Oh, yeah? Why should I?"

"Because if you look over your shoulder, you'll see the assistant principal is watching us from his office window."

---

8. **E equals MC squared:** reference to Albert Einstein's famous equation describing the relationship between energy and mass. This equation transformed the field of physics.

Chuck released me and spun around. There was no one at the window. But by then I was running to the safety of the school building. I figured the trick would work on him. For Chuck the hard questions begin with "How are you?" I hid out from him for the rest of the day and walked home rather than chance seeing the monster on the bus.

Louis's screen was dark when I ran upstairs to my bedroom. I placed a hand on the console. It was still warm. I punched the *on* button, and the familiar *Good afternoon, Kevin* was displayed.

Don't good afternoon me, I typed furiously. *What have you done to Ginny Linke?* Louis's screen replied:

```
Programming Error: 76534.
Not programmed to respond
to this type of question.
```

Don't get cute, I entered. *What are you doing to Ginny? Her brother nearly knocked my head off today.* Louis's screen responded immediately.

```
Are you hurt:
Y/N? 3
```

No, I'm okay. But I don't know for how long. I've been hiding out from Chuck Linke today. He might catch me tomorrow, though. Then, I'll be history! The response from Louis came instantly.

```
Your life is in danger: Y/N?
```

I explained to Louis that my life wasn't really threatened. But it sure could be made very unpleasant by Chuck Linke. Louis flashed:

> **RECOGNIZE CAUSE AND EFFECT**
> **3** What makes Louis stop replying with the error message?

```
This Chuck Linke lives at
same address as the Ginny
Linke person: Y/N?
```

I punched in *Y.* Louis answered.

```
Don't worry then. HE'S
history!
```

Wait! What are you going to do? I wrote. But Louis only answered with: *Programming Error: 76534.* And nothing I could do would make the machine respond. . . .

"Just what do you think you're doing, Kevin Neal?" demanded Ginny Linke. She had cornered me as I walked up the path to the school entrance. Ginny was really furious.

"I don't know what you're talking about," I said, a sinking feeling settling in my stomach. I had an idea that I *did* know. I just wasn't sure of the particulars.

"Chuck was arrested last night," Ginny said. "Some Secret Service men came to our house with a warrant. They said he'd sent a telegram threatening the president's life. They traced it right to our phone. He's still locked up. . . ." Ginny looked like she was about to cry.

"Then this morning," she continued, "we got two whole truckloads of junk mail! Flyers from every strange company in the world. Mom got a notice that all our credit cards have been canceled. And the Internal Revenue Service has called Dad in for an audit! I don't know what's going on, Kevin Neal, but somehow I think you've got something to do with it!" **4**

> **RECOGNIZE CAUSE AND EFFECT**
> **4** How does Louis feel about Kevin? How do these feelings affect the Linkes?

"But I didn't . . ." I began, but Ginny was striding up the walk to the main entrance.

I finished the school day, but it was a blur. Louis had done it, all right. It had access to mainframe computers. It also had the ability to try every secret access code to federal and commercial memory banks until it got the right one. Louis had cracked their security systems. It was systematically destroying the entire Linke family, and all via telephone lines! What would it do next?

More important, I thought, what would *I* do next? It's one thing to play a trick or two, to get even, but Louis was going crazy! And I never wanted to harm Ginny, or even her stupid moose of a brother. She'd just hurt my feelings with that nerd remark.

"You have to disconnect Louis," I told myself. "There's no other way."

But why did I feel like such a rat about doing it? I guess because Louis was my friend . . . the only one I had. "Don't be a jerk," I went on. "Louis is a machine. He's a very wonderful, powerful machine. And it seems he's also very dangerous. You have to pull its plug, Kevin!"

I suddenly realized that I'd said the last few words aloud. Kids around me on the bus were staring. I sat there feeling like the nerd Ginny thought I was, until my stop came. I dashed from the bus and ran the three blocks to my house.

When I burst into the hall, I was surprised to see my father, coming from the kitchen with a cup of coffee in his hand.

"Dad! What are you doing here?"

"Some kids say hello," Dad replied. "Or even, 'Gee, it's good to see you, Dad.'"

"I'm sorry, Dad," I said. "I didn't expect anyone to be home at this hour."

"Wound up my business in Chicago a day sooner than I expected," he said. "But what are you all out of breath about? Late for something?"

"No, Dad," I said. "It's Louis. . . ."

"Not to worry. I had some time on my hands, so I checked it out again. You were right. It was acting very funny. I think it had to do with the in-built logic/growth program I designed for it. You know . . . the 'personality' thing? Took me a couple of hours to clean the whole system out."

"To what?" I cried.

"I erased the whole program and set Louis up as a normal computer. Had to disconnect the whole thing and do some rewiring. It had been learning, all right. But it was also turning itself around. . . ." Dad stopped, and looked at me. "It's kind of involved, Kevin," he said. "Even for a bright kid like you. Anyway, I think you'll find Louis is working just fine now.

"Except it won't answer you as Louis anymore. It'll only function as a regular Major Electronics Model Z-11127. I guess the personality program didn't work out."

I felt like a great weight had been taken off my shoulders. I didn't have to "face" Louis, and pull its plug. But somehow, all I could say was "Thanks, Dad."

"Don't mention it, son," Dad said brightly. He took his cup of coffee and sat down in his favorite chair in the living room. I followed him.

"One more thing that puzzles me, though," Dad said. He reached over to the table near his chair. He held up three sheets of fanfold computer paper covered with figures. "Just as I was doing the final erasing, I must have put the printer on by accident.

There was some data in the print buffer memory and it printed out. I don't know what to make of it. Do you?"

I took the papers from my father and read: *How do I love thee? Let me compute the ways:*[9] The next two pages were covered with strings of binary code figures. On the last page, in beautiful color graphics,[10] was a stylized heart. Below it was the simple message: *I will always love you, Kevin: Louise.*

"Funny thing," Dad said. "It spelled its own name wrong."

"Yeah," I said. I turned and headed for my room. There were tears in my eyes and I knew I couldn't explain them to Dad, or myself either.

---

9. **How do I . . . ways:** reference to a famous poem by the English poet Elizabeth Barrett Browning (1806–1861) that begins, "How do I love thee? Let me count the ways."

10. **graphics** *n.:* designs or pictures produced on and printed out from a computer. *Graphics* also refers to printed images produced by other means, such as engraving.

Meet the Writer

T. Ernesto Bethancourt

The Accidental Writer

T. Ernesto Bethancourt (1932–   ) became a full-time writer by accident. He was working as a folk musician in a nightclub, and his first daughter had just been born. In hopes that she would read it one day, Bethancourt used the time between shows to begin writing his autobiography.

❝ Through a series of extraordinary events, the autobiography became novelized, updated, and was published in 1975 as *New York City, Too Far from Tampa Blues.* The book was an immense success, and I began a new career in midlife. ❞

Bethancourt attributes his writing success to the New York City public schools and the public library. "I thank them, every day, for the new and wonderful life they have given to me and my family." In another interview he said, "The Brooklyn Public Library was a place of refuge from street gangs. There was adventure, travel, and escape to be found on the shelves."

For Independent Reading

T. Ernesto Bethancourt has also written science fiction novels and the Doris Fein mystery series.

First Thoughts

1. Respond to the story by completing this statement:

   • If I were the narrator, I would . . .

Thinking Critically

2. Trace the chain of **causes and effects** leading up to Kevin's decision to unplug Louis. Make a flowchart like the one on page 271 that shows how each event causes another event. Is what finally happens to Louis part of the chain of events or outside it?

3. You can tell a lot about people from what's important to them. For instance, what seems most important to Kevin is his computer. What other **character traits** does Kevin have? (Does he have any of the traits you listed in the Quickwrite?)

4. **Theme** often reveals what the main characters learn in the story and what you learn as you share their experiences. In a sentence, state what you think the theme of this story is.

Extending Interpretations

5. **Compare** the **themes** of "User Friendly," "The Highwayman," and "Annabel Lee." What does each theme say about the power of love?

6. Did the ending of the story surprise you? Did it make you feel that the writer tricked you? Describe how you feel about the story's ending.

WRITING

Writing a Tribute to an Object

In this story a computer falls in love with its owner. Write a paragraph or a poem describing the way you feel about your computer (or your scooter, in-line skates, bicycle, hair dryer, telephone—any object that is important to you). How does it affect your life? What name might you give the object of your affection? Give your tribute an interesting title.

Reading Check

"User Friendly" is narrated by the main character. **Retell** the **main events** of the story but with the computer as narrator. Be sure to include all the important details Louis would know in the order in which Louis would have found out about them.

INTERNET

Projects and Activities

Keyword: LE5 7-3

SKILLS FOCUS

Literary Skills
Analyze theme.

Reading Skills
Analyze cause and effect.

Writing Skills
Write a tribute to an object.

Idioms: Don't Take Them Literally

The English language, like other languages, is full of idioms—expressions such as "My heart is broken," "I fell in love," "She dumped me." An **idiom** is a commonly used expression that is not literally true. Idioms, like other figures of speech, are often based on comparisons. Almost no one really pays attention to the literal meaning of an idiom because it would make no sense.

PRACTICE

Find at least five idioms in the paragraph that follows. With a partner, tell what each idiom really means.

> If Chuck catches up with me, I'll be history. He's already threatened to rub me out for talking to Ginny. I was so nervous afterward that I completely bombed on the math test. It's all Louis's fault—he's making me mess up. As if I didn't have enough trouble—I'm always striking out with girls because I'm such a brain. If Louis doesn't knock it off, I'm going to have to pull the plug on him.

SKILLS FOCUS

Vocabulary Skills
Identify and explain idioms.

Grammar Skills
Use pronouns correctly.

Grammar Link

Pronouns Can Be Problems

Pronouns used in compound structures can be confusing. Which of these sentences is correct?

> Dad talked to Mom and *me.*
> Dad talked to Mom and *I.*

Mom and me and *Mom and I* are compound structures. When you proofread your own writing, you can use this trick to decide which pronoun is correct: Say the sentence aloud as if it contained only a pronoun, not a compound structure. Use each form of the pronoun in turn, and let your ear tell you which one sounds right.

TEST   Dad talked to me. [sounds right]
           Dad talked to I̶. [sounds wrong]

CORRECT   Dad talked to Mom and *me.*

PRACTICE

In the following sentences, choose the correct pronoun. Use the trick described on the left to test each choice you make.

1. Ginny and she/her laughed at me on the bus.
2. Louis and I/me sent each other messages.
3. Louis made problems for Chuck and she/her.
4. Was there much respect between Kevin and he/him?
5. Louis showed he/him and I/me that it could cause a lot of trouble.

For more help, see Using Pronouns, 4a–e, in the Language Handbook.

Understanding Text Structure: Cause and Effect

Reading Focus
Cause-and-Effect Pattern

In "User Friendly," Kevin has trouble with his computer because of a faulty experimental program his father installed. A more common cause of computer malfunction is a computer virus. The informational article you are about to read explains how a computer virus works.

The structure of this article is called a **cause-and-effect chain.** This pattern is built around a series of causes and effects. Each event **causes** another event to happen. The event it causes is called an **effect.** In this article a little mistake starts a chain reaction. Soon a chain of causes and effects has turned a minor mishap into a big mess.

Writers of cause-and-effect articles often use **transitions** to show how one idea is connected to another. These transition terms help the reader follow the cause-and-effect pattern.

Cause-and-Effect Terms	
after	so
as a result	then
because	therefore
consequently	since

■ Read "It Just Keeps Going and Going . . ." once all the way through. Then, read it a second time, and keep track of the cause-and-effect chain by filling out an organizer like the one on page 271. The annotations at the beginning of the article will get you started. Then you can take over. Start each cause statement with the word *because,* just as you see in the model. The more causes and effects you find, the longer your chain will be.

INTERNET
Interactive
Reading Model
Keyword: LE5 7-3

**SKILLS
FOCUS**

Reading Skills
Understand
cause-and-effect
text structure.

A History of the World.

Volcanoes erupted. Oceans boiled.

The universe was in a turmoil.

Then came the dog.

PEANUTS reprinted by permission of United Feature Syndicate, Inc.

IT JUST KEEPS GOING AND GOING . . .

IT IS A HUMAN-MADE MONSTER. NO ONE CAN ESCAPE the reach of its tentacles, which can extend not just across a room but also around the entire planet. It gets worse. This monster, known by names such as the Brain, Crusher, Grog, and the Creeper, can quickly reproduce and shut down entire systems. This is no science fiction or fantasy creature. It's a computer virus.

The effects of computer viruses range from pesky system crashes to life-threatening situations, but experts disagree on how serious they really are. In fact, information and opinions on viruses are spreading as fast as the viruses themselves. *Encarta Encyclopedia* defines a computer virus as a "self-replicating computer program that interferes with a computer's hardware or operating system (the basic software that runs the computer)." That doesn't sound too bad, but think about the term *self-replicating*. That means that it keeps making copies of itself over and over again.

Here's an explanation of how a computer virus works, based on a model by the computer scientist Eugene Kaspersky.

A teacher is working at his desk at the end of the day. He finds mistakes in the

midterm answer key, so he tosses it into the trash. Since the trash can is overflowing, the answer key falls onto the floor.

Then the teacher feels a headache coming on and goes home. The custodian comes to empty the trash, sees the answer key on the floor, and picks it up.

He puts it back on the teacher's desk. But now, attached to the answer key is a sticky note that says, "Copy two times, and put copies in other teachers' boxes."

A. CAUSE: Because the answer key is wrong,

B. EFFECT: the teacher tosses it into a trash can, which happens to be full.

C. CAUSE: Because the trash can is full,

D. EFFECT: the answer key falls onto the floor.

E. CAUSE: Because the custodian finds the answer key on the floor,

F. EFFECT: he puts it on the teacher's desk.

The next day the teacher stays home because he has the flu. As a result, a substitute is called to the school. The first thing the substitute sees is the answer key with the note stuck to it. So she copies it twice for each teacher and puts the copies into the teachers' boxes. She leaves the sticky note on the answer key so they will see that the absent teacher wanted them to get the copies.

When the other teachers find

the two copies of the answer key with the instructions to copy them twice and distribute them, they give them to the office clerk. She then makes more copies of the answer key and puts them into the boxes of the "other teachers." By the end of the day, the school is out of paper, and the teachers' boxes are stuffed with useless answer keys.

G. CAUSE:
Because the custodian has put the answer key on the desk,

H. EFFECT:
[You fill in the effect.]

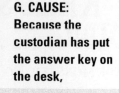

This model resembles what happens with a computer virus. The difference between the answer-key situation and a computer virus lies in motivation. The teacher didn't plan to cause chaos in the school. The whole mess was just a series of unfortunate causes and effects. On the other hand, computer viruses are created by people who have all kinds of motives, none of them good. The effects are the corruption of massive amounts of important information as well as the cost of billions of dollars in lost productivity every year.

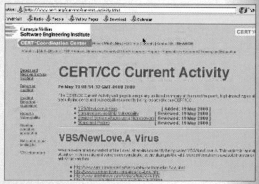

Developers of antivirus programs are gaining on the virus villains, making it easier to detect a virus before it spreads and causes a path of destruction. Nonetheless, watch what you put in your computer . . . and in your trash.

—Joan Burditt

Analyzing Cause–and–Effect Text Structure

IT JUST KEEPS GOING AND GOING . . .

1. Which of the following sentences contains a **cause** and an **effect**?

   A The computer she wanted was the most expensive one.

   B The salesperson agreed to throw in a monitor for free.

   C Since the monitor was free, she bought the computer.

   D I can't imagine life without computers.

2. According to the article, which of the following statements is a major **effect** of computer viruses?

   F Computers are ruined.

   G Billions of dollars and a lot of information are lost.

   H Some viruses ruin networks.

   J A computer will do everything it is told to do.

3. This article is mainly about —

   A problems with computers

   B how to kill a virus

   C the history of computers

   D how computer viruses work

4. The causal chain below shows some of the important **causes and effects** in the story about the answer key.

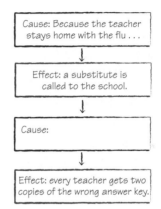

   Cause: Because the teacher stays home with the flu . . .

   ↓

   Effect: a substitute is called to the school.

   Cause:

   ↓

   Effect: every teacher gets two copies of the wrong answer key.

   Which of these statements belongs in the blank *Cause* box?

   F The substitute is unsure about what to do.

   G The substitute follows the instructions on the sticky note.

   H The substitute tells all the teachers the answer key is wrong.

   J The substitute helps the office clerk with all the extra copying.

Constructed Response

1. What does *self-replicating* mean?

2. Which two main events cause the answer-key confusion to spin out of control?

3. Make a list of all the cause-and-effect words in this article.

4. According to the article, what are the effects of computer viruses?

5. Imagine you submitted this article to an editor of a newspaper. The editor tells you to get a new title. What would you call it?

SKILLS FOCUS

Reading Skills
Analyze cause-and-effect text structure.

Putting Analogies to Work

One way to explain something is to use an **analogy** (ə·nal′ə·jē). Writers use analogies to explain an idea by comparing it point by point to something familiar. In the article you just read, a computer virus is compared to a school situation that goes out of control. Here are two other examples of analogies:

- A computer virus is like a virus in the human body. Both self-replicate, and both damage the system they infect.

- Searching for something on the Internet without a search engine is like trying to find a CD in a store where the CDs are not arranged by music category, artist, or group. It is practically impossible to find what you are looking for.

PRACTICE

Form an analogy by matching the phrases in column A with the phrases and sentences in column B. Then, think of two of your own analogies. Remember that an analogy uses more than one point of comparison.

Column A	Column B
1. Studying for a big test is like	**a.** standing on the edge of a cliff. You feel as if you might fall, but you manage to keep your balance and enjoy the experience.
2. Giving a speech in front of the whole school is like	**b.** going to the dentist to have a cavity filled. You're so nervous you would rather not do it; but when it's over, you're glad you did.
3. Learning to ride a bike is like	**c.** shooting baskets before an important game. You're worried about how you'll perform, but you know you'll be glad you took the time to prepare.

SKILLS FOCUS

Vocabulary Skills
Understand analogies.

Echo and Narcissus

Make the Connection
Conduct a Survey

Take a quick survey to find out how your classmates rate the following statements on a scale of 1 to 5, with 1 meaning they do not agree at all and 5 meaning they agree completely.

1. People judge others by their looks alone.

2. Vain, self-centered people are often not nice to others.

In your notebook, briefly explain your rating on one of the statements.

Literary Focus
Recurring Themes

People all over the world have basically the same dreams, fears, and need to understand who they are and how they should live their lives. It is not surprising, therefore, that the same **themes** come up again and again in the stories people tell. As you think about the selections in this collection, look for the themes that they share.

Reading Skills
Using Context Clues

What do you do when you come across an unfamiliar word? Rather than skipping over it or running straight to a dictionary, try using **context clues**—the surrounding words and sentences—to figure out what the word might mean. As you examine the surrounding text, ask yourself the following questions:

- Does the surrounding text give clues to the word's meaning?

- Is there a familiar word or word part within the unfamiliar word?

- How is the word used in the sentence?

- Does the meaning I've guessed make sense in the sentence?

As you read "Echo and Narcissus," use these strategies to try to figure out the meanings of words you don't know.

Vocabulary Development

Here are some words you'll want to know before you read this story. See if you can spot context clues in the sample sentences.

detain (dē·tān′) v.: hold back; delay. *Echo was asked to detain Hera so Hera's husband, Zeus, could wander about.*

vainly (vān′lē) adv.: uselessly; without result. *Echo tried vainly to attract the young man's attention.*

unrequited (un′ri·kwīt′id) v. used as adj.: not returned in kind. *Unfortunately, Echo's love was unrequited, for Narcissus loved only himself.*

parched (pärcht) v. used as adj.: very hot and dry. *Narcissus's throat was parched, so he eagerly knelt to drink the cool water.*

intently (in·tent′lē) adv.: with great concentration. *Narcissus gazed intently at his reflection in the pool.*

INTERNET

Vocabulary Practice

Keyword: LE5 7-3

Literary Skills
Understand recurring themes.

Reading Skills
Use context clues.

Echo and Narcissus

Greek myth, retold by **Roger Lancelyn Green**

Up on the wild, lonely mountains of Greece lived the Oreades,[1] the nymphs or fairies of the hills, and among them one of the most beautiful was called Echo. She was one of the most talkative, too, and once she talked too much and angered Hera, wife of Zeus, king of the gods.

When Zeus grew tired of the golden halls of Mount Olympus, the home of the immortal gods, he would come down to earth and wander with the nymphs on the mountains. Hera, however, was jealous and often came to see what he was doing. It seemed strange at first that she always met Echo, and that Echo kept her listening for hours on end to her stories and her gossip.

But at last Hera realized that Echo was doing this on purpose to detain her while Zeus went quietly back to Olympus as if he had never really been away.

"So nothing can stop you talking?" exclaimed Hera. "Well, Echo, I do not intend to spoil your pleasure. But from this day on, you shall be able only to repeat what other people say—and never speak unless someone else speaks first."

Hera returned to Olympus, well pleased with the punishment she had made for Echo, leaving the poor nymph to weep sadly among the rocks on the mountainside and speak only the words which her sisters and their friends shouted happily to one another.

She grew used to her strange fate after a while, but then a new misfortune befell her.

There was a beautiful youth called Narcissus,[2] who was the son of a nymph and the god of a nearby river. He grew up in the plain of Thebes[3] until he was sixteen years old and then began to hunt on the mountains toward the north where Echo and her sister Oreades lived.

As he wandered through the woods and valleys, many a nymph looked upon him and loved him. But Narcissus laughed at them scornfully, for he loved only himself.

Farther up the mountains Echo saw him. And at once her lonely heart was filled with love for the beautiful youth, so that nothing else in the world mattered but to win him.

Now she wished indeed that she could speak to him words of love. But the curse which Hera had placed upon her tied her

---

1. **Oreades** (ōˊrē·adˈēz).
2. **Narcissus** (när·sisˈəs).
3. **Thebes** (thēbz).

Vocabulary
detain (dē·tānˊ) *v.:* hold back; delay.

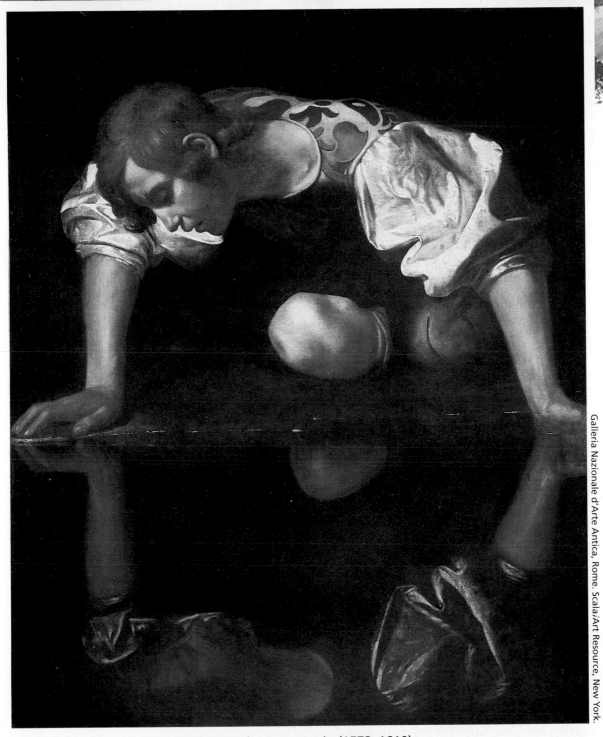

Narcissus by Caravaggio (1573–1610).

tongue, and she could only follow wherever he went, hiding behind trees and rocks, and feasting her eyes vainly upon him.

One day Narcissus wandered farther up the mountain than usual, and all his friends, the other Theban youths, were left far behind. Only Echo followed him, still hiding among the rocks, her heart heavy with unspoken love.

Presently Narcissus realized that he was lost, and hoping to be heard by his companions, or perhaps by some mountain shepherd, he called out loudly:

"Is there anybody here?"

"Here!" cried Echo.

Narcissus stood still in amazement, looking all around in vain. Then he shouted, even more loudly:

"Whoever you are, come to me!"

"Come to me!" cried Echo eagerly.

Still no one was visible, so Narcissus called again:

"Why are you avoiding me?"

Echo repeated his words, but with a sob in her breath, and Narcissus called once more:

"Come here, I say, and let us meet!"

"Let us meet!" cried Echo, her heart leaping with joy as she spoke the happiest words that had left her lips since the curse of Hera had fallen on her. And to make good her words, she came running out from behind the rocks and tried to clasp her arms about him.

But Narcissus flung the beautiful nymph away from him in scorn.

"Away with these embraces!" he cried angrily, his voice full of cruel contempt. "I would die before I would have you touch me!"

"I would have you touch me!" repeated poor Echo.

"Never will I let you kiss me!"

"Kiss me! Kiss me!" murmured Echo, sinking down among the rocks, as Narcissus cast her violently from him and sped down the hillside.

"One touch of those lips would kill me!" he called back furiously over his shoulder.

"Kill me!" begged Echo.

And Aphrodite,[4] the goddess of love, heard her and was kind to her, for she had been a true lover. Quietly and painlessly, Echo pined away and died. But her voice lived on, lingering among the rocks and answering faintly whenever Narcissus or another called.

"He shall not go unpunished for this cruelty," said Aphrodite. "By scorning poor Echo like this, he scorns love itself. And scorning love, he insults me. He is altogether eaten up with self-love . . . Well, he shall love himself and no one else, and yet shall die of unrequited love!"

It was not long before Aphrodite made good her threat, and in a very strange way. One day, tired after hunting, Narcissus came to a still, clear pool of water away up the mountainside, not far from where he had scorned Echo and left her to die of a broken heart.

With a cry of satisfaction, for the day was hot and cloudless, and he was parched with thirst, Narcissus flung himself down beside the pool and leaned forward to dip his face in the cool water.

---

4. **Aphrodite** (af′rə·dīt′ē).

Vocabulary
vainly (vān′lē) *adv.:* uselessly; without result.
unrequited (un′ri·kwīt′id) *v.* used as *adj.:* not returned in kind.
parched (pärcht) *v.* used as *adj.:* very hot and dry.

What was his surprise to see a beautiful face looking up at him through the still waters of the pool. The moment he saw, he loved—and love was a madness upon him so that he could think of nothing else.

"Beautiful water nymph!" he cried. "I love you! Be mine!"

Desperately he plunged his arms into the water—but the face vanished and he touched only the pebbles at the bottom of the pool. Drawing out his arms, he gazed intently down and, as the water grew still again, saw once more the face of his beloved.

Poor Narcissus did not know that he was seeing his own reflection, for Aphrodite hid this knowledge from him—and perhaps this was the first time that a pool of water had reflected the face of anyone gazing into it.

Narcissus seemed enchanted by what he saw. He could not leave the pool, but lay by its side day after day looking at the only face in the world which he loved—and could not win—and pining just as Echo had pined.

Slowly Narcissus faded away, and at last his heart broke.

"Woe is me for I loved in vain!" he cried.

"I loved in vain!" sobbed the voice of Echo among the rocks.

"Farewell, my love, farewell," were his last words, and Echo's voice broke and its whisper shivered into silence: "My love . . . farewell!"

So Narcissus died, and the earth covered his bones. But with the spring, a plant pushed its green leaves through the earth where he lay. As the sun shone on it, a bud opened and a new flower blossomed for the first time—a white circle of petals round a yellow center. The flowers grew and spread, waving in the gentle breeze which whispered among them like Echo herself come to kiss the blossoms of the first Narcissus flowers.

Vocabulary
intently (in·tent′lē) *adv.:* with great concentration.

Meet the Writer

Roger Lancelyn Green

Green, a Greek at Heart
Roger Lancelyn Green (1918–1987) was born in England and educated at Oxford University. After a short stint as an actor in London, he devoted his life to children's literature and the study of ancient times. His books for children include stories, poems, and his own retellings of fairy tales, legends, and myths from many lands. Green's special love was Greece, which he visited more than twenty times.

First Thoughts

1. Did reading this myth change your opinions about beauty and vanity at all? If so, how?

Thinking Critically

2. What is the major flaw in Echo's **character**? Why is Hera's curse an appropriate punishment for this flaw?

3. Why do you think Narcissus is so cruel to Echo? Does the class survey help explain why Narcissus is so mean? If so, how?

4. Which of the following statements of theme best fits the myth? Explain how this **theme** is revealed in the myth.

   • We can't love other people when we are too involved with ourselves.

   • Love is a powerful feeling whether we seek it or not.

   • Romantic love and self-love can have devastating effects.

5. Are Echo and Narcissus victims of the gods, or are they responsible for their own tragedies? Explain your opinion.

Reading Check

a. What does Echo do that annoys Hera?

b. How does Hera punish Echo?

c. Why does Aphrodite punish Narcissus?

d. What curse does Aphrodite place on Narcissus?

e. An **origin myth** is an imaginative story that explains how something came into being. According to this myth, what is the origin of the echo we hear when we call into a cave or from a mountaintop? What is the origin of the fragrant flower called the narcissus?

Extending Interpretations

6. Which other selection in this collection is built on the theme you selected in question 4? Explain how the selections are similar and how they are different.

7. Are the gods fair? What do you think of their actions in this myth?

WRITING

Writing an Origin Myth

Here's your chance to write an origin myth of your own. Think of some everyday phenomenon, and write a brief story that explains how it might have come about. Try to come up with fresh, surprising **causes** for familiar **effects**. Use your imagination!

INTERNET

Projects and Activities

Keyword: LE5 7-3

SKILLS FOCUS

Literary Skills
Analyze recurring themes.

Writing Skills
Write an origin myth.

Vocabulary Development

Building Context Clues

PRACTICE

Using the words in the Word Bank, write a short version of the Echo and Narcissus story that a six-year-old would understand. Build lots of **context clues** into the sentences.

> **Word Bank**
>
> detain
> vainly
> unrequited
> parched
> intently

Grammar Link

Words Often Confused: *Its, It's* and *Your, You're*

Do you hear an echo? The words in each pair may sound alike, but they have very different purposes.

- The **personal possessive pronouns** *its* and *your* show that something belongs to someone or something. Possessive pronouns should not have apostrophes.

  "He could not leave the pool, but lay by its side...."
  [The side "belongs" to the pool.]

  " 'Well, Echo, I do not intend to spoil your pleasure.'"
  [The pleasure "belongs" to Echo.]

- The **contractions** *it's* and *you're* are both shortened combinations of a personal pronoun and the verb *is, has,* or *are*. A contraction should have an apostrophe to show where letters have been left out.

  It's [It is] **his own reflection he sees.**

  You're [You are] **going to repeat words.**

Here's a tip to use if you are unsure of the correct word: Substitute the two words that might be used in place of the one you are unsure of, such as *it is* or *you are*. If the sentence still makes sense, use the contraction rather than the possessive pronoun.

PRACTICE

Write each sentence below, choosing the correct form of the underlined words.

1. "Your/You're not the one I love," said Narcissus.
2. A plant pushed its/it's green leaves through the earth.
3. Its/It's Echo's constant chatter that annoys Hera.
4. "Narcissus, you won't realize your/you're in love with your/you're own reflection," thought Aphrodite.

For more help, see Apostrophes, 15a–c, in the Language Handbook.

SKILLS FOCUS

Vocabulary Skills
Use context clues.

Grammar Skills
Use *its* and *it's* and *your* and *you're* correctly.

Comparing Literature

Literary Focus
Characters, Settings, Themes

Stories can be alike in some ways yet very different in other ways. Two stories might have similar characters, but the discoveries made by those characters may be quite different. One character may change during the events of the story, while another character may remain the same. The stories might have similar settings, but what happens in those settings could be very different. The stories might even have similar characters *and* settings but reveal completely different themes.

Reading Skills and Strategies
Comparing and Contrasting

Both "Charles" and "Miss Awful" are about boys who are in conflict with their teachers. As you read the two stories, however, you'll notice many differences. Though their subject matter is similar, their themes are not at all alike. Questions in the margins of the stories will help you think about how the stories are alike and—perhaps even more important— how they are different. After you have read both stories, you will be asked to compare and contrast them in an essay.

SKILLS FOCUS

Literary Skills
Analyze characters, settings, and themes.

Reading Skills
Compare and contrast stories.

Questions to Ask About the Elements

Characters
- Are the characters **dynamic**—do they change in the story and discover something of importance about themselves and their world?

- Are the characters **static**—do they remain the same?

Setting
- Where and when does the story take place?

Theme
- What does the story reveal about human nature? To uncover the theme, look for

  —discoveries made by the character

  —reasons the character changes

  —key statements

  —important scenes

Before You Read

The story you are about to read is a modern-day **trickster tale**—a story about a character, usually someone small and weak, who plays tricks on someone large and powerful. The writer Julius Lester explains, "Teachers and parents know Trickster well, because there is one in every classroom and every large family. Trickster is the class clown, the child who seems to have a genius for walking a thin line between fun and trouble, the child who is always 'up to something.'" Decide whether you identify with the trickster Charles or with his parents or teacher. Who do you think is more powerful?

Shirley Jackson

The day Laurie started kindergarten, he renounced[1] corduroy overalls with bibs and began wearing bluejeans with a belt; I watched him go off the first morning with the older girl next door, seeing clearly that an era of my life was ended, my sweet-voiced nursery-school tot replaced by a long-trousered, swaggering character who forgot to stop at the corner and wave goodbye to me.

He came home the same way, the front door slamming open, his cap on the floor, and the voice suddenly become raucous shouting, "Isn't anybody *here*?"

At lunch he spoke insolently[2] to his father, spilled his baby sister's milk, and remarked that his teacher said that we were not to take the name of the Lord in vain. ❶

"How *was* school today?" I asked, elaborately casual.

"All right," he said.

"Did you learn anything?" his father asked.

Laurie regarded his father coldly. "I didn't learn nothing," he said.

"Anything," I said. "Didn't learn anything."

"The teacher spanked a boy, though," Laurie said, addressing his

---

1. **renounced** (ri·nounsd´) *v*.: gave up; abandoned.
2. **insolently** (in´sə·lənt·lē) *adv*.: with bold disrespect.

bread and butter. "For being fresh," he added with his mouth full.

"What did he do?" I asked. "Who was it?"

Laurie thought. "It was Charles," he said. "He was fresh. The teacher spanked him and made him stand in a corner. He was awfully fresh."

"What did he do?" I asked again, but Laurie slid off his chair, took a cookie, and left, while his father was still saying, "See here, young man."

The next day Laurie remarked at lunch, as soon as he sat down, "Well, Charles was bad again today." He grinned enormously and said, "Today Charles hit the teacher." ❷

"Good heavens," I said, mindful of the Lord's name, "I suppose he got spanked again?"

"He sure did," Laurie said. "Look up," he said to his father.

"What?" his father said, looking up.

"Look down," Laurie said. "Look at my thumb. Gee, you're dumb." He began to laugh insanely.

"Why did Charles hit the teacher?" I asked quickly.

"Because she tried to make him color with red crayons," Laurie said. "Charles wanted to color with green crayons so he hit the teacher and she spanked him and said nobody play with Charles but everybody did."

The third day—it was Wednesday of the first week—Charles bounced a seesaw onto the head of a little girl and made her bleed and the teacher made him stay inside all during recess. Thursday Charles had to stand in a corner during story time because he kept pounding his feet on the floor. Friday Charles was deprived of blackboard privileges because he threw chalk.

INFER

❷ How does Laurie feel about Charles? How can you tell?

On Saturday I remarked to my husband, "Do you think kindergarten is too unsettling for Laurie? All this toughness and bad grammar, and this Charles boy sounds like such a bad influence."

"It'll be all right," my husband said reassuringly. "Bound to be people like Charles in the world. Might as well meet them now as later." ❸

On Monday Laurie came home late, full of news. "Charles," he shouted as he came up the hill; I was waiting anxiously on the front steps, "Charles," Laurie yelled all the way up the hill, "Charles was bad again."

"Come right in," I said, as soon as he came close enough. "Lunch is waiting."

"You know what Charles did?" he demanded, following me through the door. "Charles yelled so in school they sent a boy in from first grade to tell the teacher she had to make Charles keep quiet, and so Charles had to stay after school. And so all the children stayed to watch him."

"What did he do?" I asked.

"He just sat there," Laurie said, climbing into his chair at the table. "Hi Pop, y'old dust mop."

"Charles had to stay after school today," I told my husband. "Everyone stayed with him."

"What does this Charles look like?" my husband asked Laurie. "What's his other name?"

"He's bigger than me," Laurie said. "And he doesn't have any rubbers and he doesn't even wear a jacket."

Monday night was the first Parent-Teachers meeting, and only the fact that the baby had a cold kept me from going; I wanted passionately to meet Charles's mother. On Tuesday Laurie remarked suddenly, "Our teacher had a friend come see her in school today."

"He kicked the teacher's friend."

"Charles's mother?" my husband and I asked simultaneously.

"Naaah," Laurie said scornfully. "It was a man who came and made us do exercises. Look." He climbed down from his chair and squatted down and touched his toes. "Like this," he said. He got solemnly back into his chair and said, picking up his fork, "Charles didn't even *do* exercises."

"That's fine," I said heartily. "Didn't Charles want to do exercises?"

"Naaah," Laurie said. "Charles was so fresh to the teacher's friend he wasn't *let* do exercises."

"Fresh again?" I said.

"He kicked the teacher's friend," Laurie said. "The teacher's friend told Charles to touch his toes like I just did and Charles kicked him." ❹

"What are they going to do about Charles, do you suppose?" Laurie's father asked him.

Laurie shrugged elaborately. "Throw him out of school, I guess," he said.

Wednesday and Thursday were routine; Charles yelled during story hour and hit a boy in the stomach and made him cry. On Friday Charles stayed after school again and so did all the other children.

With the third week of kindergarten Charles was an institution in our family; the baby was being a Charles when she cried all afternoon; Laurie did a Charles when he filled his wagon full of mud and pulled it through the kitchen; even my husband, when he caught his elbow in the telephone cord and pulled telephone, ash tray, and a bowl of flowers off the table, said, after the first minute, "Looks like Charles."

RESPOND

❹ How do you feel about Charles at this point in the story?

During the third and fourth weeks it looked like a reformation in Charles; Laurie reported grimly at lunch on Thursday of the third week, "Charles was so good today the teacher gave him an apple."

"What?" I said, and my husband added warily,[3] "You mean Charles?"

"Charles," Laurie said. "He gave the crayons around and he picked up the books afterward and the teacher said he was her helper."

"What happened?" I asked incredulously.

"He was her helper, that's all," Laurie said, and shrugged.

"Can this be true, about Charles?" I asked my husband that night. "Can something like this happen?"

"Wait and see," my husband said cynically. "When you've got a Charles to deal with, this may mean he's only plotting."

He seemed to be wrong. For over a week Charles was the teacher's helper; each day he handed things out and he picked things up; no one had to stay after school. ❺

"The PTA meeting's next week again," I told my husband one evening. "I'm going to find Charles's mother there."

"Ask her what happened to Charles," my husband said. "I'd like to know."

COMPARE AND CONTRAST

❺ How has Charles's behavior changed?

"I'd like to know myself," I said.

On Friday of that week things were back to normal. "You know what Charles did today?" Laurie demanded at the lunch table, in a voice slightly awed. "He told a little girl to say a word and she said it and the teacher washed her mouth out with soap and Charles laughed."

"What word?" his father asked unwisely, and Laurie said, "I'll have to whisper it to you, it's so bad." He got down off his chair and went around to his father. His father bent his head down and Laurie whispered joyfully. His father's eyes widened.

"Did Charles tell the little girl to say *that*?" he asked respectfully.

"She said it *twice*," Laurie said. "Charles told her to say it *twice*."

"What happened to Charles?" my husband asked.

"Nothing," Laurie said. "He was passing out the crayons."

Monday morning Charles abandoned the little girl and said the evil word himself three or four times, getting his mouth washed out

---

3. warily (wer′ə·lē) *adv.:* cautiously.

with soap each time. He also threw chalk.

My husband came to the door with me that evening as I set out for the PTA meeting. "Invite her over for a cup of tea after the meeting," he said. "I want to get a look at her."

"If only she's there," I said prayerfully.

"She'll be there," my husband said. "I don't see how they could hold a PTA meeting without Charles's mother."

At the meeting I sat restlessly, scanning each comfortable matronly face, trying to determine which one hid the secret of Charles. None of them looked to me haggard[4] enough. No one stood up in the meeting and apologized for the way her son had been acting. No one mentioned Charles.

After the meeting I identified and sought out Laurie's kindergarten teacher. She had a plate with a cup of tea and a piece of chocolate cake; I had a plate with a cup of tea and a piece of marshmallow cake. We maneuvered up to one another cautiously and smiled.

"I've been so anxious to meet you," I said. "I'm Laurie's mother."

"We're all so interested in Laurie," she said.

"Well, he certainly likes kindergarten," I said. "He talks about it all the time."

"We had a little trouble adjusting, the first week or so," she said primly, "but now he's a fine little helper. With lapses, of course." **6**

"Laurie usually adjusts very quickly," I said. "I suppose this time it's Charles's influence."

"Charles?"

IDENTIFY

6 According to the teacher, who has had trouble adjusting but is now usually a good helper?

---

4. **haggard** (hag′ərd) *adj.:* looking worn-out and exhausted.

"Yes," I said, laughing, "you must have your hands full in that kindergarten, with Charles."

"Charles?" she said. "We don't have any Charles in the kindergarten." ❼

Comparing Literature

INFER

❼ What can you infer from the teacher's last remark?

Meet the Writer

Shirley Jackson

A Keen Sense of Humor

Shirley Jackson (1919–1965) was born in San Francisco, California. Her keen sense of humor is evident in "Charles" and other comically exaggerated accounts of life with her husband and four children. It is also evident in this mock questionnaire she wrote for fellow suffering mothers:

> ❝ At breakfast I raise a considerable howl about the general sloppy condition of the back porch and the yard. Laurie, Joanne, Sally, and Barry promise that after school there will be a monumental cleaning-up and I will find the yard and porch immaculate. (1) Who has to stay after school to finish his chemistry notebook? (2) Who forgot that today was Girl Scouts? (3) Who calls from the library to say she will be home later? (4) Who stops off at David's house to see David's new steam engine and has to be sent for at five o'clock? (5) Who raises another howl the next morning at breakfast? ❞

For Independent Reading

"Charles" comes from *Life Among the Savages*. The adventures of Laurie and the rest of the Jackson family continue in *Raising Demons*.

First Thoughts

1. This story has a **surprise** ending. Did it surprise you? Why or why not?

Thinking Critically

2. What clues does the writer give to Charles's identity?

3. Why do you think Laurie invents Charles?

4. Do you think Laurie's parents should have realized the truth about Charles sooner? Explain.

5. Do you think Laurie is a **dynamic character,** one who changes during the story, or a **static character,** one who remains the same? Explain your thinking.

6. What lessons do you think Laurie learns during his time in kindergarten?

Comparing Literature

7. After you read the next story, you will compare and contrast the characters, settings, and themes of the two stories. To plan your essay, you can start by filling in a chart like the one below with details from "Charles." Then, write out a possible theme for the story. To decide on the theme, ask yourself this question: "What did I learn from this story about life or about people?" Be sure to write your theme as a complete sentence. You will fill in the chart for "Miss Awful" when you finish that story.

> ### Reading Check
>
> **a.** Describe how Laurie's behavior at home changes when he begins school.
>
> **b.** According to Laurie, what is Charles like?
>
> **c.** How does Laurie's mother learn the truth about Charles?

Comparing Stories		
	"Charles"	"Miss Awful"
Setting		
Characters		
Theme of "Charles": _____

SKILLS FOCUS

Literary Skills
Analyze characters, settings, and themes.

Reading Skills
Compare and contrast stories.

Before You Read

Have you ever attended an elementary school in which you had the same teacher for every subject? If you did, you know that you were with that one person a long time—approximately fourteen hundred hours a year. A teacher, especially one who is with a student for so long, can have a great deal of influence. Think of the best teacher you've ever had. What qualities and actions made this teacher special? As you read, ask yourself whether your favorite teacher was anything like the teachers in "Miss Awful."

Miss Awful

Arthur Cavanaugh

The whole episode of Miss Awful began for the Clarks at their dinner table one Sunday afternoon. Young Roger Clark was explaining why he could go to Central Park with his father instead of staying home to finish his homework—Miss Wilson, his teacher, wouldn't be at school tomorrow, so who'd know the difference? "She has to take care of a crisis," Roger explained. "It's in Omaha." **❶**

"What is?" his older sister, Elizabeth, inquired. "For a kid in third grade, Roger, you talk dopey. You fail to make sense."

Roger ignored the insult. His sister was a condition of life he had learned to live with, like lions. Or snakes. Poisonous ones. Teetering,[1] as always, on the tilted-back chair, feet wrapped around the legs, he continued, "Till Miss Wilson gets back we're having some other teacher. She flew to Omaha yesterday." He pushed some peas around on his plate and was silent a moment. "I hope her plane don't crash," he said.

Roger's mother patted his hand. A lively, outgoing youngster, as noisy and rambunctious[2] as any eight-year-old, he had another side to him, tender and soft, which worried about people. Let the blind man who sold pencils outside the five-and-ten on Broadway be absent from his post, and Roger worried that catastrophe had overtaken him. When Mrs. Loomis, a neighbor of the Clarks in the

IDENTIFY

❶ Why does Roger decide he does not have to do his homework?

---

1. **teetering** *v. used as adj.:* wobbling, as if about to fall.
2. **rambunctious** *adj.:* noisy and lively.

IDENTIFY

❷ What does the narrator tell you directly about Roger's **character**?

Greenwich Village brownstone, had entered the hospital, Roger's anxious queries had not ceased until she was discharged.[3] And recently there was the cat which had nested in the downstairs doorway at night. Roger had carried down saucers of milk, clucking with concern. "Is the cat run away? Don't it have a home?" ❷

Virginia Clark assured her son, "You'll have Miss Wilson safely back before you know it. It's nice that you care so."

Roger beamed with relief. "Well, I like Miss Wilson, she's fun. Last week, for instance, when Tommy Miller got tired of staying in his seat and lay down on the floor—"

"He did what?" Roger's father was roused from his post-dinner torpor.[4]

"Sure. Pretty soon the whole class was lying down. Know what

---

3. **discharged** *v.:* released: here, from the hospital.
4. **torpor** (tôr′pər) *n.:* sluggishness.

Miss Wilson did?"

"If you'll notice, Mother," Elizabeth interjected, "he hasn't touched a single pea."

"*She* lay down on the floor, too," Roger went on ecstatically. "She said we'd *all* have a rest, it was perfectly normal in the middle of the day. That's what I love about St. Geoff's. It's fun."

"Fun," snorted his sister. "School isn't supposed to be a fun fest. It's supposed to be filling that empty noodle of yours." ❸

"Miss Wilson got down on the floor?" Mr. Clark repeated. He had met Roger's teacher on occasion; she had struck him as capable but excessively whimsical.[5] She was a large woman to be getting down on floors, Mr. Clark thought. "What did the class do next?" he asked.

"Oh, we lay there a while, then got up and did a Mexican hat dance," Roger answered. "It was swell."

"I'm sure not every day is as frolicsome," Mrs. Clark countered, slightly anxious. She brought in dessert, a chocolate mousse. Roger's story sounded typical of St. Geoffrey's. Not that she was unhappy with his school. A small private institution, while it might be called overly permissive, it projected a warm, homey atmosphere which Mrs. Clark found appealing. It was church-affiliated, which she approved of, and heaven knows its location a few blocks away from the brownstone was convenient. True, Roger's scholastic progress wasn't notable—his spelling, for example, remained atrocious. Friendly as St. Geoffrey's was, Mrs. Clark sometimes *did* wish . . . ❹

Roger attacked dessert with a lot more zest than he had shown the peas. "So can I go to the park with you, Dad? I've only got spelling left, and who cares about that?" Before his mother could comment, he was up from the table and racing toward the coat closet. "Okay, Dad?"

"I didn't say you could go. I didn't even say I'd take you," Mr. Clark objected. He happened, at that moment, to glance at his waistline and reflect that a brisk hike might do him some good. He pushed back his chair. "All right, but the minute we return, it's straight to your room to finish your spelling."

"Ah, thanks, Dad. Can we go to the boat pond first?"

"We will not," cried Elizabeth, elbowing into the closet. "We'll go to the Sheep Meadow first."

COMPARE AND CONTRAST

❸ What does Roger think school is good for? What does his sister think?

IDENTIFY

❹ What does Roger's mother like about his school? What does she find troublesome?

---

5. **whimsical** (hwim′zi·kəl) *adj.:* full of silly, fanciful ideas.

PREDICT

❺ Sometimes a writer drops a hint that **foreshadows** events to come. What do you think is going to happen next?

INFER

❻ What does the fact that Roger packs so many toys in his schoolbag tell you about him? about his school?

Roger was too happy to argue. Pulling on his jacket, he remarked, "Gee, I wonder what the new teacher will be like. Ready for your coat, Dad?" ❺

It was just as well that he gave the matter no more thought. In view of events to come, Roger was entitled to a few carefree hours. Monday morning at school started off with perfect normalcy. It began exactly like any other school morning. Elizabeth had long since departed for the girls' school she attended uptown when Mrs. Clark set out with Roger for the short walk to St. Geoff's. She didn't trust him with the Fifth Avenue traffic yet. They reached the school corner and Roger skipped away eagerly from her. The sidewalk in front of school already boasted a large, jostling throng of children, and his legs couldn't hurry Roger fast enough to join them. Indeed, it was his reason for getting to school promptly: to have time to play before the 8:45 bell. Roger's schoolbag was well equipped for play. As usual, he'd packed a supply of baseball cards for trading opportunities; a spool of string, in case anybody brought a kite; a water pistol for possible use in the lavatory; and a police whistle for sheer noise value. Down the Greenwich Village sidewalk he galloped, shouting the names of his third grade friends as he picked out faces from the throng. "Hiya, Tommy. Hey, hiya, Bruce. Hi, Steve, you bring your trading cards?" ❻

By the time the 8:45 bell rang—St. Geoff's used a cowbell, one of the homey touches—Roger had finished a game of tag, traded several baseball cards, and was launched in an exciting jump-the-hydrant contest. Miss Gillis, the school secretary, was in charge of the bell, and she had to clang it extensively before the student body took notice. Clomping up the front steps, they spilled into the downstairs hall, headed in various directions. Roger's class swarmed up the stairs in rollicking spirits, Tommy Miller, Bruce Reeves, Joey Lambert, the girls forming an untidy rear flank behind them, shrill with laughter.

It wasn't until the front ranks reached the third-grade classroom that the first ominous note was struck.

"Hey, what's going on?" Jimmy Moore demanded, first to observe the changed appearance of the room. The other children crowded behind him in the doorway. Instead of a cozy semicircle—"As though we're seated round a glowing hearth," Miss Wilson had described it—the desks and chairs had been rearranged in stiff, rigid rows. "Gee, look, the desks are in rows," commented Midge Fuller, a

> "Gee, I wonder what the new teacher will be like. Ready for your coat, Dad?"

plump little girl who stood blocking Roger's view. Midge was a child given to unnecessary statements. "It's raining today," she would volunteer to her classmates, all of them in slickers. Or, "There's the lunch bell, gang." The point to Roger wasn't that the desks had been rearranged. The point was, *why?* As if in answer, he heard two hands clap behind him, as loud and menacing as thunder. ❼

"What's this, what's this?" barked a stern, raspish voice. "You are not cattle milling in a pen. Enough foolish gaping! Come, come, form into lines."

Heads turned in unison, mouths fell agape. The children of St. Geoffrey's third grade had never formed into lines of any sort, but this was not the cause of their shocked inertia.[6] Each was staring, with a sensation similar to that of drowning, at the owner of the raspish voice. She was tall and straight as a ruler, and was garbed in an ancient tweed suit whose skirt dipped nearly to the ankles. She bore a potted plant in one arm and Miss Wilson's roll book in the other. Rimless spectacles glinted on her bony nose. Her hair was gray, like a witch's, skewered in a bun, and there was no question that she had witch's eyes. Roger had seen those same eyes leering from the pages of *Hansel and Gretel*—identical, they were. He gulped at the terrible presence.

"Form lines, I said. Girls in one, boys in the other." Poking, prodding, patrolling back and forth, the new teacher kneaded the third grade into position and ruefully inspected the result. "Sloppiest group I've ever beheld. *March!*" She clapped time with her hands and the stunned ranks trooped into the classroom. "*One,* two, three, *one,* two—girls on the window side, boys on the wall. Stand at your desks. Remove your outer garments. You, little Miss, with the vacant stare. What's your name?"

"Ja-Ja—" a voice squeaked.

"Speak up. I won't have mumblers."

"Jane Douglas."

COMPARE AND CONTRAST

❼ How is the classroom different from what it was like when Miss Wilson was there? What does the arrangement suggest about the new teacher?

---

6. **inertia** (in·ur′shə) *n.*: here, an inability or reluctance to move.

"Well, Jane Douglas, you will be coat monitor. Collect the garments a row at a time and hang them neatly in the cloakroom. Did you hear me, child? Stop staring." Normally slow-moving, Jane Douglas became a whirl of activity, charging up and down the aisles, piling coats in her arms. The new teacher tugged at her tweed jacket. "Class be seated, hands folded on desks," she barked, and there was immediate compliance. She next paraded to the windows and installed the potted plant on the sill. Her witch's hands fussed with the green leaves, straightening, pruning. "Plants and children belong in classrooms," she declared, spectacles sweeping over the rows. "Can someone suggest why?"

There was total silence, punctured by a deranged giggle, quickly suppressed.

"Very well, I will tell you. Plants and children are living organisms. Both will grow with proper care. Repeat, *proper*. Not indulgent fawning, or giving in to whims—scrupulosity!"[7] With another tug at the jacket, she strode, ruler straight, to the desk in the front of the room. "I am Miss Orville. *O-r-v-i-l-l-e*," she spelled. "You are to use my name in replying to all questions." **8**

In the back of the room, Jimmy Moore whispered frantically to Roger. "What did she say her name is?"

---

7. **scrupulosity** (skrōō′pyə·läs′ə·tē) *n.*: extreme carefulness and correctness.

INFER

8 According to Miss Orville, how are plants and children alike? What does this comparison tell you about Miss Orville's feelings toward children?

Miss Orville rapped her desk. "Attention, please, no muttering in the back." She cleared her voice and resumed. "Prior to my retirement I taught boys and girls for forty-six years," she warned. "I am beyond trickery, so I advise you to try none. You are to be in my charge until the return of Miss Wilson, however long that may be." She clasped her hands in front of her and trained her full scrutiny on the rows. "Since I have no knowledge of your individual abilities, perhaps a look at the weekend homework will shed some light. Miss Wilson left me a copy of the assignment. You have all completed it, I trust? Take out your notebooks, please. At once, at once, I say."

Roger's head spun dizzily around. He gaped at the monstrous tweed figure in dismay. Book bags were being clicked open, notebooks drawn out—what was he to do? He had gone to his room after the outing in the park yesterday, but, alas, it had not been to complete his assignment. He watched, horrified, as the tweed figure proceeded among the aisles and inspected notebooks. What had she said her name was? Awful—was that it? Miss Awful! Biting his lip, he listened to her scathing comments.

"You call this chicken scrawl penmanship?" R-r-rip! A page was torn out and thrust at its owner. "Redo it at once, it assaults the intelligence." Then, moving on, "What is this maze of ill-spelled words? Not a composition, I trust."

Ill-spelled words! He was in for it for sure. The tweed figure was heading down his aisle. She was three desks away, no escaping it. Roger opened his book bag. It slid from his grasp and, with a crash, fell to the floor. Books, pencil case spilled out. Baseball cards scattered, the water pistol, the police whistle, the spool of string . . .

"Ah," crowed Miss Awful, instantly at his desk, scooping up the offending objects. "We have come to play, have we?"

And she fixed her witch's gaze on him.

Long before the week's end, it was apparent to Virginia Clark that something was drastically wrong with her son's behavior. The happy-go-lucky youngster had disappeared, as if down a well. Another creature had replaced him, nervous, harried, continuously glancing over his shoulder, in the manner of one being followed. Mrs. Clark's first inkling of change occurred that same Monday. She had been chatting with the other mothers who congregated outside St. Geoffrey's at three every afternoon to pick up their offspring. A casual assembly, the mothers were as relaxed and informal as the school itself, lounging against the picket fence, exchanging small talk and anecdotes.

"That darling cowbell," laughed one of the group at the familiar clang. "Did I tell you Anne's class is having a taffy pull on Friday? Where else, in the frantic city of New York . . ."

The third grade was the last class to exit from the building on Monday. Not only that, but Mrs. Clark noted that the children appeared strangely subdued. Some of them were actually reeling, all but dazed. As for Roger, eyes taut and pleading, he quickly pulled his mother down the block, signaling for silence. When enough distance had been gained, words erupted from him. ❾

COMPARE AND CONTRAST

❾ The children's behavior has changed. How did they behave in the past? How do they behave now?

"No, we don't have a new teacher," he flared wildly. "We got a *witch* for a new teacher. It's the truth. She's from *Hansel and Gretel,* the same horrible eyes—and she steals toys. *Yes,*" he repeated in mixed outrage and hurt. "By accident, you happen to put some toys in your book bag, and she *steals* 'em. I'll fool her! I won't *bring* any more toys to school," he howled. "Know what children are to her? Plants! She did, she called us plants. Miss Awful, that's her name."

Such was Roger's distress that his mother offered to stop at the Schrafft's on Thirteenth Street and treat him to a soda. "Who's got time for sodas?" he bleated. "I have homework to do. Punishment homework. Ten words, ten times each. On account of the witch's spelling test."

> **"I have homework to do. Punishment homework. Ten words, ten times each."**

"Ten words, ten times each?" Mrs. Clark repeated. "How many words were on the test?"

"Ten," moaned Roger. "Every one wrong. Come on, I've got to hurry home. I don't have time to waste." Refusing to be consoled, he headed for the brownstone and the desk in his room. ❿

On Tuesday, together with the other mothers, Mrs. Clark was astonished to see the third grade march down the steps of St. Geoffrey's in military precision. Clop, clop, the children marched,

COMPARE AND CONTRAST

❿ Think back to the beginning of the story. How has Roger's attitude about homework changed?

looking neither to the left nor right, while behind them came a stiff-backed, iron-haired woman in a pepper-and-salt suit. "*One, two, three, one, two, three,*" she counted, then clapped her hands in dismissal. Turning, she surveyed the assemblage of goggle-eyed mothers. "May I inquire if the mother of Joseph Lambert is among you?" she asked.

"I'm Mrs. Lambert," replied a voice meekly, whereupon Miss Orville paraded directly up to her. The rest of the mothers looked on, speechless.

"Mrs. Lambert, your son threatens to grow into a useless member of society," stated Miss Orville in ringing tones that echoed down the street. "That is, unless you term watching television useful. Joseph has confessed that he views three hours per evening." ⓫

"Only after his homework's finished," Margery Lambert allowed.

"Madame, he does not finish his homework. He idles through it, scattering mistakes higgledy-piggledy. I suggest you give him closer supervision. Good day." With a brief nod, Miss Orville proceeded down the street, and it was a full minute before the mothers had recovered enough to comment. Some voted in favor of immediate protest to Dr. Jameson, St. Geoffrey's headmaster, on the hiring of such a woman, even on a temporary basis. But since it was temporary, the mothers concluded it would have to be tolerated.

Nancy Reeves, Bruce's mother, kept staring at the retreating figure of Miss Orville, by now far down the block. "I know her from somewhere, I'm sure of it," she insisted, shaking her head.

The next morning, Roger refused to leave for school. "My shoes aren't shined," he wailed. "Not what Miss Awful calls shined. Where's the polish? I can't leave till I do 'em over."

"Roger, if only you'd thought of it last night," sighed Mrs. Clark.

"You sound like her," he cried. "That's what *she'd* say," and it gave his mother something to puzzle over for the rest of the day. She was still thinking about it when she joined the group of mothers outside St. Geoffrey's at three. She had to admit it was sort of impressive, the smart, martial[8] air exhibited by the third grade as they trooped down the steps. There was to be additional ceremony today. The ranks waited on the sidewalk until Miss Orville passed back and forth in inspection. Stationing herself at the head of the columns, she boomed, "Good afternoon, boys and girls. Let us return with perfect papers tomorrow."

---

8. **martial** (mär′shəl) *adj.*: military.

INFER

⓫ Why do you think Miss Orville disapproves of Joseph's watching television?

"Good aaaaafternoon, Miss Orville," the class sang back in unison, after which the ranks broke. Taking little Amy Lewis in tow, Miss Orville once more nodded at the mothers. "Which is she?" she asked Amy.

Miss Orville approached the trapped Mrs. Lewis. She cleared her throat, thrust back her shoulders. "Amy tells me she is fortunate enough to enjoy the services of a full-time domestic[9] at home," said Miss Orville. "May I question whether she is fortunate—or deprived? I needn't lecture you, I'm sure, Mrs. Lewis, about the wisdom of assigning a child tasks to perform at home. Setting the table, tidying up one's room, are lessons in self-reliance for the future. Surely you agree." There was a nod from Mrs. Lewis. "Excellent," smiled Miss Orville. "Amy will inform me in the morning the tasks you have assigned her. Make them plentiful, I urge you." **12**

The lecturing, however, was not ended. Turning from Mrs. Lewis, Miss Orville cast her gaze around and inquired, "Is Roger Clark's mother present?"

"Yes?" spoke Virginia Clark, reaching for Roger's hand. "What is it?"

Miss Orville studied Roger silently for a long moment. "A scallywag, if ever I met one," she pronounced. The rimless spectacles lifted to the scallywag's mother. "You know, of course, that Roger is a prodigy,"[10] said Miss Orville. "A prodigy of misspelling. Roger, spell *flower* for us," she ordered. "Come, come, speak up."

Roger kept his head lowered. "F," he spelled. "*F-l-o-r.*"

"Spell castle."

"K," spelled Roger. "*K-a-z-l.*"

Miss Orville's lips parted grimly. "Those are the results, mind you, of an hour's solid work with your son, Mrs. Clark. He does not apply himself. He wishes to remain a child at play, absorbed in his toys. Is that what you want for him?" **13**

"I—I—" Virginia Clark would have been grateful if the sidewalk had opened up to receive her.

As she reported to her husband that evening, she had never in her life been as mortified.[11] "Spoke to me in front of all the other mothers, in loud, clarion tones," she described the scene. "Do I want Roger to remain a child at play. Imagine."

"By the way, where is Roge?" Mr. Clark asked, who had come

---

 9. **domestic** *n.:* housecleaner.
10. **prodigy** (präd′ə·jē) *n.:* child genius.
11. **mortified** (môrt′ə·fīd) *v.* used as *adj.:* ashamed and hurt.

School's Out (1936)
by Allan Rohan Crite.
Smithsonian American Art
Museum, Washington, D.C.

home late from the office. "He's not watching television, or busy with his airplanes—"

"In his room, doing over his homework for the ninety-eighth time. It has to be perfect, he says. But, really, Charles, don't you think it was outrageous?"

Mr. Clark stirred his coffee. "I bet Miss Orville doesn't get down on the floor with the class. Or do Mexican hat dances with them."

"If that's meant to disparage[12] Miss Wilson—" Virginia Clark stacked the dinner dishes irritably. She sometimes found her husband's behavior maddening. Especially when he took to grinning at her, as he was presently doing. She also concluded that she'd had her fill of Elizabeth's attitude on the subject. "At last some teacher's wised up to Roge," had been the Clarks' daughter's comment. "He's cute and all, but I wouldn't want to be in a shipwreck with him." Washing dishes in the kitchen, Mrs. Clark considered that maybe she wouldn't meet Roger in *front* of school tomorrow. Maybe she'd wait at the corner instead. "His shoes," she gasped, and hurried to remind her son to get out the polishing kit. The spelling, too, she'd better work on that . . . ⑭

12. **disparage** (di·spar′ij) *v.:* show disrespect for; "put down."

INFER

⑭ Why do Roger's sister and father think Miss Orville is an improvement over Miss Wilson?

It was on Thursday that Nancy Reeves finally remembered where previously she had seen Miss Orville. Perhaps it was from the shock of having received a compliment from the latter.

"Mrs. Reeves, I rejoice to inform you of progress," Miss Orville had addressed her, after the third grade had performed its military display for the afternoon. "On Monday, young Bruce's penmanship was comparable to a chicken's—if a chicken could write. Today, I was pleased to award him an A."

A tug at the tweed jacket, and the stiff-backed figure walked firmly down the street. Nancy Reeves stared after her until Miss Orville had merged into the flow of pedestrians and traffic. "I know who she is," Nancy suddenly remarked, turning to the other mothers. "I knew I'd seen her before. Those old ramshackle buildings near us on Hudson Street—remember when they were torn down last year?" The other mothers formed a circle around her. "Miss Orville was one of the tenants," Nancy Reeves went on. "She'd lived there for ages, and refused to budge until the landlord got a court order and deposited her on the sidewalk. I *saw* her there, sitting in a rocker on the side-walk, surrounded by all this furniture and plants. Her picture was in the papers. Elderly retired schoolteacher . . . they found a furnished room for her on Jane Street, I think. Poor old thing, evicted like that . . . I remember she couldn't keep any of the plants . . ."

On the way home, after supplying a lurid account of the day's tortures—"Miss Awful made Walter Meade stand in the corner for saying a bad word"—Roger asked his mother, "Eviction. What does that mean?"

"It's when somebody is forced by law to vacate an apartment. The landlord gets an eviction notice, and the person has to leave."

"Kicked her out on the street. Is that what they did to the witch?" **15**

"Don't call her that, it's rude and impolite," Mrs. Clark said, as they turned into the brownstone doorway. "I can see your father and I have been too easygoing where you're concerned."

"Huh, we've got worse names for her," Roger retorted. "*Curse* names, you should hear 'em. We're planning how to get even with Miss Awful, just you see." He paused, as his mother opened the downstairs door with her key. "That's where the cat used to sleep, remember?" he said, pointing at a corner of the entryway. His face was grave and earnest. "I wonder where that cat went to. Hey, Mom," he hurried to catch up. "Maybe *it* was evicted, too."

Then it was Friday at St. Geoffrey's. Before lunch, Miss Orville told the class, "I am happy to inform you that Miss Wilson will be back on Monday." She held up her hand for quiet. "This afternoon will be my final session with you. Not that discipline will relax, but I might read you a story. Robert Louis Stevenson, perhaps. My boys and girls always enjoyed him so. Forty-six years of them . . . Joseph Lambert, you're not sitting up straight. You know I don't permit slouchers in my class."

It was a mistake to have told the children that Miss Wilson would be back on Monday, that only a few hours of the terrible reign of Miss Awful were left to endure. Even before lunch recess, a certain spirit of challenge and defiance had infiltrated[13] into the room. Postures were still erect, but not quite as erect. Tommy Miller dropped his pencil case on the floor and did not request permission to pick it up.

"Ahhh, so what," he mumbled, when Miss Orville remonstrated[14] with him.

"What did you say?" she demanded, drawing herself up.

"I said, so what," Tommy Miller answered, returning her stare without distress.

Roger thought that was neat of Tommy, talking fresh like that. He was surprised, too, because Miss Awful didn't yell at Tommy or anything. A funny look came into her eyes, he noticed, and she just went on with the geography lesson. And when Tommy dropped his pencil case again, and picked it up without asking, she said nothing. Roger wasn't so certain that Tommy should have dropped the pencil case a second time. The lunch bell rang, then, and he piled out of the classroom with the others, not bothering to wait for permission. 16

At lunch in the basement cafeteria, the third grade talked of nothing except how to get even with Miss Awful. The recommendations showed daring and imagination.

"We could beat her up," Joey Lambert suggested. "We could wait at the corner till she goes by, and throw rocks at her."

---

13. **infiltrated** (in·fil′trāt′id) *v.:* gradually entered or sneaked into.
14. **remonstrated** *v.:* reasoned earnestly in protest against something.

INFER

16 Why do you think it was a mistake for Miss Orville to tell the children it was her last day?

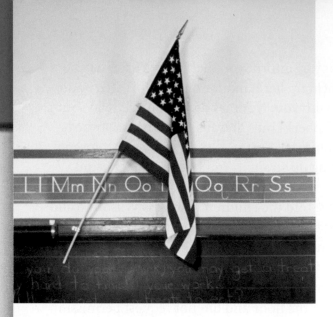

"We'd get arrested," Walter Meade pointed out.

"Better idea," said Bruce Reeves. "We could go upstairs to the classroom before she gets back, and tie a string in front of the door. She'd trip, and break her neck."

"She's old," Roger Clark protested. "We can't hurt her like that. She's too old."

It was one of the girls, actually, who thought of the plant. "That dopey old plant she's always fussing over," piped Midge Fuller. "We could rip off all the dopey leaves. That'd show her."

Roger pushed back his chair and stood up from the table. "We don't want to do that," he said, not understanding why he objected. It was a feeling inside, he couldn't explain . . . "Aw, let's forget about it," he said. "Let's call it quits."

"The plant, the plant," Midge Fuller squealed, clapping her hands.

Postures were a good deal worse when the third grade reconvened after lunch. "Well, you've put in an industrious week, I daresay . . ." Miss Orville commented. She opened the frayed volume of *Treasure Island* which she had brought from home and turned the pages carefully to Chapter One. "I assume the class is familiar with the tale of young Jim Hawkins, Long John Silver, and the other wonderful characters."

"No, I ain't," said Tommy Miller.

"Ain't. What word is that?"

"It's the word ain't," answered Tommy.

"Ain't, ain't," somebody jeered.

Miss Orville lowered the frayed volume. "No, children, you mustn't do this," she said with force. "To attend school is a privilege you must not mock. Can you guess how many thousands of children in the world are denied the gift of schooling?" Her lips quavered. "It is a priceless gift. You cannot permit yourselves to squander a moment of it." She rose from her desk and looked down at the rows of boys and girls. "It isn't enough any longer to accept a gift and make no return for it, not with the world in the shape it's in," she said, spectacles trembling on her bony nose. "The world isn't a playbox," she said. "If I have been severe with you this past week, it was for your benefit. The world needs good citizens. If I have helped one of you to grow a fraction of an inch, if just *one* of you—"

She stopped speaking. Her voice faltered, the words dammed up. She was staring at the plant on the window sill, which she had not noticed before. The stalks twisted up bare and naked, where the leaves had been torn off. "You see," Miss Orville said after a moment, going slowly to the window sill. "You *see* what I am talking about? To be truly educated is to be civilized. Here, you may observe the opposite." Her fingers reached out to the bare stalks. "Violence and destruction . . ." She turned and faced the class, and behind the spectacles her eyes were dim and faded. "Whoever is responsible, I beg of you only to be sorry," she said. When she returned to her desk, her back was straighter than ever, but it seemed to take her longer to cover the distance. **⑰**

At the close of class that afternoon, there was no forming of lines. Miss Orville merely dismissed the boys and girls and did not leave her desk. The children ran out, some in regret, some silent, others cheerful and scampering. Only Roger Clark stayed behind.

He stood at the windows, plucking at the naked plant on the sill. Miss Orville was emptying the desk of her possessions, books, pads, a folder of maps. "These are yours, I believe," she said to Roger. In her hands were the water pistol, the baseball cards, the spool of string. "Here, take them," she said.

Roger went to the desk. He stuffed the toys in his coat pocket without paying attention to them. He stood at the desk, rubbing his hand up and down his coat.

"Yes?" Miss Orville asked.

Roger stood back, hands at his side, and lifted his head erectly. "Flower," he spelled. "*F-l-o-w-e-r.*" He squared his shoulders and looked at Miss Orville's brimming eyes. "Castle," Roger spelled. "*C-a-s-t-l-e.*"

Then he walked from the room. **⑱**

COMPARE AND CONTRAST

⑰ What kind of behavior does Miss Orville contrast with civilized behavior?

INTERPRET

⑱ What message do you think Roger means to give Miss Orville when he spells *flower* and *castle* correctly?

Meet the Writer

Arthur Cavanaugh

"All of My Stories Have Been Drawn from Life"

Arthur Cavanaugh (1926–   ) was born in New York City and has lived there all his life. Many of his short stories are about the Clark family, which bears a strong resemblance to his own. "Miss Awful," in fact, is based on his son Frank's experiences at a school in Greenwich Village, New York. Cavanaugh remembers:

66 To hear him tell of it, the days at school were a happy mixture of games, crayons, milk and cookies, and outings to the playground across the street. One night when I got home from work, Frank indignantly announced that his teacher was out sick and, worse, replaced by a crabby old lady who did nothing but admonish the class for their lack of discipline and scholarship. 'Honest, you wouldn't believe how awful she is,' Frank assured me. But I noticed a marked change in my son, at night when I came home. Where before he was sprawled in front of the television, I'd find him bent over his homework or actually voluntarily reading a book. The night that I discovered him wrestling with a dictionary, looking up words for a quiz the next day, I knew that 'Miss Awful' had scored a victory on behalf of education. And when the following week I heard from Frank that his regular teacher was back at her desk, the tinge of regret in his voice was unmistakable. All of my stories have been drawn from life, usually long after the incident happened, but 'Miss Awful' was the exception, taking shape as the story happened right in front of me. 99

First Thoughts

1. Do you think Miss Orville is really "Miss Awful"? Would you like to be in her class? Discuss your responses to what happened in her classroom.

Thinking Critically

2. Think about what you know of Miss Orville's life, and try to explain why she demands so much of her class.

3. How would you explain the children's cruelty in this story? Did they have a good reason for doing what they did? What do you think of their behavior?

4. The story suggests that Roger has discovered something important in the end. What do you think he has discovered?

Comparing Literature

5. Fill in a chart like the one below with details from "Miss Awful." Then, write out a possible theme for the story. To figure out the theme, ask yourself: "What did I learn about life or people from this story?" Remember that the themes of "Charles" and "Miss Awful" may be very different.

Reading Check

Use a story map like the one below to outline the main parts of "Miss Awful."

Setting:

Characters:

Conflicts:

Event 1:

Event 2:

(Add as many as you need.)

Climax:

Resolution of conflict:

Comparing Stories		
	"Charles"	"Miss Awful"
Setting		
Characters		

Theme of "Miss Awful": _____

_____

INTERNET
Projects and Activities
Keyword: LE5 7-3

SKILLS FOCUS

Literary Skills
Analyze characters, settings, and themes.

Reading Skills
Compare and contrast stories.

Assignment

1. Writing a Comparison-Contrast Essay

Write an essay comparing and contrasting the settings, characters, and themes of "Charles" and "Miss Awful." To plan your essay, review the charts you filled in after you read the stories. The chart will help you focus on the key elements in the stories and the similarities and differences between them.

You can organize your essay in one of these two ways:

1. You can organize your essay by story: In the first paragraph, discuss the setting, characters, and theme of "Charles." In the second paragraph, discuss the setting, characters, and theme of "Miss Awful."

2. You can organize your essay by elements: In separate paragraphs, compare and contrast the settings, main characters, and themes of the two stories.

Whichever form of organization you use, include a final paragraph in which you describe your own response to each story. Did you prefer one story to the other? Did you find the story true to life? Would you recommend either story to a classmate?

Use the workshop on writing a Comparison-Contrast Essay, pages 772–777, for help with this assignment.

SKILLS FOCUS

Writing Skills
Write a comparison-contrast essay; write a descriptive essay; write a scene.

Speaking and Listening Skills
Perform a scene.

Assignment

2. Describing a Perfect Class

Describe what you think the perfect classroom would be like. How many students would be in the class? What "learning tools" would be available? How would the furniture be arranged? Would the teacher be strict, like Miss Orville and Charles's teacher, or easygoing, like Miss Wilson? What kind of atmosphere do you think is best to learn in? Write at least one paragraph.

Assignment

3. Writing and Performing a Dramatization

With a small group of classmates, stage a scene from a day in the classroom of Miss Wilson, Miss Orville, or Charles's teacher. Before you write the dialogue for your scene, decide how many speaking parts it will include. Perform the scene for your class, and ask for feedback. Is your dramatization true to the characters in the original story?

The Only Girl in the World for Me

Bill Cosby
from Love and Marriage

I can't remember where I have left my glasses, but I can still remember the smell of the first girl I ever fell in love with when I was twelve: a blend of Dixie Peach pomade on her hair and Pond's cold cream on her skin; together they were honeysuckle for me. And just as heady as her scent was the thought that I was in love with the only girl in the world for me and would marry her and take care of her forever in a palace in North Philadelphia. Because I wanted to make a wondrous impression on this girl, grooming was suddenly important to me. Before puberty, happiness in appearance for me was pants that didn't fall down and a football that stayed pumped; but now I started taking three long baths a day and washing my own belt until it was white and shining my shoes until I could see in them a face that was ready for romance.

The first time I saw her, she was crossing the street to the schoolyard and for one golden moment our eyes met. Well, maybe the moment was closer to bronze because she made no response. But at least she had seen me, just about the way that she saw lampposts, hydrants, and manholes. Or was there something more? I began to dream; and later that day, when I was playing with the boys in the yard, it seemed that she was looking at me and the world was suddenly a better place, especially Twelfth and Girard.

However, we still never talked, but just traded silent unsmiling looks whenever we passed. For several days, just her look was enough of a lift for me; but a higher altitude was coming, for one night at a party, we met and I actually danced with her. Now I was certain that I was in love and was going to win her.

I began my conquest with a combination of sporting skill and hygiene: I made my jump shots and my baths as dazzling as they could be. Oddly enough, however, although I saw her every day at school and on the weekends too, I never spoke to her. I had what was considered one of the faster mouths in Philadelphia, but I still wasn't ready to talk to her because I feared rejection. I feared:

COSBY: I like you very much. Will you be my girlfriend?
GODDESS: *(Doing a poor job of suppressing a laugh)* I'd rather have some cavities filled.

All I did, therefore, was adore her in silent cleanliness. Each Sunday night, I took a bath and then prepared my shirt and pants for display to her. On Monday morning, I took another bath (Bill the Baptist,[1] I should have been called) and then brushed my hair, my shoes, and my eyelashes and went outside to await the pang of another silent passage.

At last, deciding that I could no longer live this way, I sat down one Sunday night and wrote a note that was almost to her. It was to her constant girlfriend and it said:

Please don't tell her, but find out what she thinks of me.
Bill

The following morning, I slipped the note to the girlfriend and began the longest wait of my life.

Two agonizing days later, the girlfriend slipped me an answer, but I put it into my pocket unread. For hours, I carried it around, afraid to read it because I didn't happen to be in the mood for crushing rejection that day. At last, however, I summoned the courage to open the note and read:

She thinks you're cute.

Not even malaria[2] could have taken my temperature to where it went. I had been called many things, but cute was never one of them.

An even lovelier fever lay ahead, for the next time I saw her, she smiled at me, I smiled at her, and then I composed my next winged message to her friend:

I think she's cute too. Does she ever talk about me?

The answer to this one came return mail and it sounded like something by Keats:[3]

---

1. **Bill the Baptist:** reference to John the Baptist, a prophet who baptized his followers to show that they had repented.
2. **malaria** *n.*: disease characterized by chills and fever.
3. **Keats:** John Keats (1795–1821), an English poet.

She talks about you a lot. She knows it when you come around her.

And the angels sang! Imagine: She actually *knew* it when I came around her! The fact that she also knew it when gnats came around her in no way dampened my ecstasy.

And so, we continued to smile as we passed, while I planned my next move. My Western Union[4] style had clearly been charming the pants off her (so to speak) and now I launched my most courageous question yet:

Does she have a boyfriend?

When I opened the answer the next day in school, the air left me faster than it left the *Hindenburg:*[5]

Yes.

Trying to recover from this deflation, I told myself that I was still cute. I was the cutest man in second place. But perhaps my beloved wasn't aware of the glory she kept passing by. Once more, I sat down and wrote:

How much longer do you think she'll be going with him? And when she's finished with him, can I be next?

Note the elegance and dignity of my appeal. My dignity, however, did have some trouble with the reply:

She thinks she's going to break up with him in about a week, but she promised Sidney she would go with him next.

Suddenly, my aching heart found itself at the end of a line. But it was like a line at a bank: I knew it was leading to a payoff. I also knew that I could cream Sidney in cuteness.

Once she had made the transition to Sidney, I patiently began waiting for her to get sick of him. I had to be careful not to rush the illness because Sidney belonged to a tough gang and there was a chance that I might not be walking around too well when the time came for me to inherit her.

And then, one magnificent morning, I received the magic words:

She would like to talk to you.

---

4. **Western Union:** company that operates a telegraph service.
5. **Hindenburg:** an airship filled with hydrogen gas that caught fire and blew up following a transatlantic flight in May 1937.

I wrote back to see if she would wait until I had finished duty at my post as a school crossing guard. Yes, she would wait; I could walk her home. We were going steady now; and how much more torrid our passion would be when I began to *talk* to her.

At last, the words came and I chose them with care. As I walked her home from school, I reached into my reservoir of romantic thoughts, smiled at her soulfully, and said, "How you doing?"

Her response was equally poetic: "All right."

"So we're going steady now?"

"You want to?"

"Yeah. Give me your books."

And now, as if our relationship were not already in the depths of desire, I plunged even deeper by saying, "You wanna go to a movie on Saturday?"

"Why not?"

There might have been reasons. Some people were looking at us now because she was so beautiful, people possibly wondering what she was doing with me; but I knew that I was someone special to be the love of a vision like this, no matter how nearsighted that vision might be.

When we reached her door, I said, "Well, I'll see you Saturday."

"Right," she replied as only she could say it.

"What time?"

"One o'clock."

When this day of days finally arrived, I took her to a theater where I think the admission was a dime. As we took our seats for the matinee, two basic thoughts were in my mind: not to sit in gum and to be a gentleman.

Therefore, I didn't hold her hand. Instead, I put my arm around the top of her seat in what I felt was a smooth opening move. Unfortunately, it was less a move toward love than toward gangrene:[6] With my blood moving uphill, my arm first began to tingle and then to ache. I could not, however, take the arm down and let my blood keep flowing because such a lowering would mean I didn't love her; so I left it up there, its muscles full of pain, its fingertips full of needlepoints.

Suddenly, this romantic agony was enriched by a less romantic one: I had to go to the bathroom. Needless to say, I couldn't let her know about this urge, for great lovers never did such things. The

---

6. **gangrene** *n.:* tissue decay in a part of the body.

answer to "Romeo, Romeo, wherefore art thou, Romeo?"[7] was not "In the men's room, Julie."

What a prince of passion I was at this moment: My arm was dead, my bladder was full, and I was out of money too; but I desperately needed an excuse to move, so I said, "You want some popcorn?"

"No," she said.

"Fine, I'll go get some."

When I tried to move, every part of me could move except my arm: It was dead. I reached over and pulled it down with the other one, trying to be as casual as a man could be when pulling one of his arms with the other one.

"What's the matter?" she said.

"Oh, nothing," I replied. "I'm just taking both of my arms with me."

A few minutes later, as I came out of the bathroom, I was startled to meet her: She was coming from the bathroom *too.* How good it was to find another thing that we had in common. With empty bladders and full hearts, we returned to our seats to continue our love.

---

7. **"Romeo . . . Romeo?":** reference to a speech by Juliet in Act II of William Shakespeare's play *The Tragedy of Romeo and Juliet.* The line reads, "O Romeo, Romeo! Wherefore art thou Romeo?" Juliet is actually asking why his name is Romeo.

Meet the Writer

Bill Cosby

While attending college on a football scholarship, **Bill Cosby** (1937–   ) began working as a stand-up comedian for five dollars a night. He became famous for his funny, heart-warming stories about his boyhood in Philadelphia. Bill Cosby has said,

“You can turn painful situations around through laughter. If you can find humor in anything—even poverty—you can survive it.”

Cosby's television programs for children include the animated series *Fat Albert and the Cosby Kids.* He also developed programs for *Electric Company* and *Reading Rainbow.*

To a Golden-Haired Girl in a Louisiana Town

Vachel Lindsay

You are a sunrise,
If a star should rise instead of the sun.
You are a moonrise,
If a star should come, in the place of the moon.
5   You are the Spring,
If a face should bloom,
Instead of an apple-bough.
You are my love
If your heart is as kind
10   As your young eyes now.

Girl In A Poppy Field (1891) by Dora Hitz.

Meet the Writer

Vachel Lindsay

Poet and Entertainer

Vachel Lindsay (1879–1931) was a modern-day troubador, or wandering poet. He crisscrossed the United States, mostly on foot, seeking audiences who would listen to his poems in exchange for food and lodging.

On his first such journey, Lindsay walked from Jacksonville, Florida, all the way back to Springfield, Illinois, where he had been born and raised. During his tramps, Lindsay not only recited his poems but also spoke out against racial prejudice and other forms of injustice.

Lindsay began a life-long practice of keeping notebooks and diaries as a boy of seven. He had little success getting his poems published until he was thirty-three, when "General William Booth Enters into Heaven," a poem about the founder of the Salvation Army, was published in the journal *Poetry*.

"General William Booth" was widely praised and brought Lindsay instant fame. He became a powerful reciter of this and his other highly rhythmic poems. Rocking on his feet and shaking his arms in the air, Lindsay shouted and sang his poems. His dramatic performances brought him a wide audience of people who had not previously been interested in poetry.

Lindsay sometimes used his fame to help other poets. While on a lecture

tour, he found three poems on his plate in a restaurant in Washington, D.C. Lindsay was so impressed by the poems that he presented them at a reading that night, helping to launch the career of the twenty-three-year-old busboy who had left them there: Langston Hughes (page 566).

For Independent Reading

You might enjoy reading some of Vachel Lindsay's poems on distinctively American subjects, such as "Abraham Lincoln Walks at Midnight," "The Ghosts of the Buffaloes," "The Flower-Fed Buffaloes," and "In Praise of Johnny Appleseed."

Writing Workshop

Assignment

Write a narrative about an experience you've had.

Audience

Your teacher, classmates, friends, or family, or anyone who was involved in the event.

RUBRIC
Evaluation Criteria

A good personal narrative

1. focuses on one event
2. grabs the reader's attention
3. includes essential background information
4. relates events in a clear order
5. includes vivid descriptive details
6. may use dialogue to reveal character
7. shows what the incident means to the writer

SKILLS FOCUS

Writing Skills
Write a personal narrative.

NARRATIVE WRITING
Personal Narrative

When you write a personal narrative, you describe an event in your life that has special significance for you. Writing a personal narrative allows you to share that event with others and to take a closer look at yourself. Like a short story, a personal narrative includes a setting, a plot, a point of view, and characters. It may also contain dialogue.

Prewriting

1 Choosing a Subject

Consider the following **prompt:**

> There is one subject about which you are an expert—yourself. Your history is unique—your thoughts, feelings, and experiences belong only to you. Think about an important or memorable event in your life, one that has special meaning for you. Describe what happened, as well as your thoughts and feelings at that time. Explain why this experience is meaningful to you.

To find a subject for your narrative, try listing your favorite objects, places, and activities. Is there an incident involving one of these things that you might write about? Do you have souvenirs, such as photos, ticket stubs, or letters, that remind you of special times in your life? Explore your ideas by freewriting.

Here are some subjects to consider:

- surprises • conflicts • vacations
- helping others • luck • secrets • sports
- losing a friend • the future • honesty

In choosing a subject to write about, ask yourself these questions:

- Does this incident mean something special to me?
- Do I remember this incident clearly?
- Am I comfortable sharing this incident with my audience?

2 Reflecting on the Importance of the Experience

State in a sentence or two why the experience is important. Such a statement often appears near the end of a personal narrative. For example, the writer of the student model (page 333) concludes his essay with this statement: "I knew right then while I was on the floor that I could never have that feeling again."

As you write your draft, look back at your statement to see if it fits your narrative. If it doesn't, you may need to rewrite your draft or your statement.

Drafting

1 Getting Ideas on Paper

Get the basics of your story down on paper as quickly as you can. Ask the *5W-How?* questions as you write: *Who* was involved in the incident? *What* happened? *When* did it happen? *Where* did it happen? *Why* did it happen? *How* did it happen?

The most unforgettable time —I was fouled with four seconds left in the game and won it with my two free throws. Whole team piled on top of me.

Writing Tips

Methods of Organization

Writers generally use **chronological order** in a personal narrative. They tell about events in the order in which they happened. An alternative pattern of organization is **comparison and contrast.** For example, you might compare and contrast good and bad aspects of your experience.

Transitional Words and Phrases

To show the order of events clearly, use transitional words and phrases, such as *first, then, next, finally,* and *in the meantime.*

Framework for a Personal Narrative

What the experience means to me: _____

_____

Introduction (dialogue, question, statement, or description that grabs the reader's attention):

_____

_____

Body (description of events in chronological order):

1. _____
2. _____
3. _____
4. _____

Conclusion (summary expressing the importance of the experience):

_____

_____

Language Handbook
H E L P

To review rules for punctuating dialogue, see the Language Handbook, 14c–k.

2 Organizing Details

Organize your details chronologically by filling in a framework like the one shown to the left. Be sure to place events in the correct sequence.

3 Elaborating

Follow the strategies described below, as well as the ones listed on page 333, to come up with descriptive details.

- Replay the experience in your mind as if you were watching it on videotape. What did the people involved say to one another? How did they look? What did they do? Jot down the details.

- To jog your memory about the event and your thoughts and feelings at the time, try returning to the scene.

- Speak to others who were involved in the incident. What details do they remember?

4 Using Dialogue

If you use dialogue, be sure to make it sound the way people really talk. Although slang and sentence fragments are usually avoided in formal writing, it may be natural to use such language in your personal narrative. Here is a passage of dialogue from Borden Deal's "Antaeus" (page 177) that shows realistic use of language:

> T. J. kept looking at the tar under his feet. "You mean you ain't got no fields to raise nothing in?—no watermelons or nothing?"
>
> "Naw," I said scornfully. "What do you want to grow something for? The folks can buy everything they need at the store."

5 Keeping Point of View Consistent

Use first-person pronouns—*I, me, my, we*—in referring to yourself. Keep your point of view consistent throughout your narrative.

Student Model

The Clutch Moment

Nine, eight, seven, six, five, four. I was fouled with four seconds left in the game. The fans roared out of their seats, cheering and howling. I couldn't believe it. My dream had come true. These two free throws would decide if we won, lost, or tied.

I stepped up to the free throw line with sweat dripping off my head into my eyes. Chills ran through my body, making my arms feel numb and loose. The only thing I could think of was making these two free throws. I blocked all the cheers out of my head and took a deep breath to relax. I turned the ball in my hands and took four dribbles. I looked at the goal and released the ball. Swish! The game was tied 49–49. The Jefferson Junior fans grew quiet and the Cubs were cheering loudly.

I stepped up to the free throw line for the last time that night. After dribbling again four times I raised my arms to shoot the ball.

It felt like a piece of flab as I released the ball, letting it fly through the air. I knew the ball was not going to miss. I had made the shot of my life to win the game 50–49. It was our ball out of bounds and I threw it in and the time ran out. The game was over! As soon as I raised my hands, I was tackled by Ben Meldrum and the rest of the team. Even the B-team joined in the fun and piled on me.

I knew right then while I was on the floor that I could never have that feeling again.

—Vinnie Merrill
Simonsen Junior High School
Jefferson City, Missouri

A suspenseful opener catches the reader's attention.

The writer supplies necessary background information.

Detailed description of the writer's actions, thoughts, and feelings enable the reader to imagine the scene.

Descriptive details make us feel as if we were there.

A brief conclusion explains why the incident was important.

Strategies for Elaboration

Help your readers see, hear, feel, smell, and even taste what you've experienced by including sensory details in your narrative. Completing these statements may help you remember details:

- I saw . . .
- I heard . . .
- I smelled . . .
- I tasted . . .
- I felt . . .

Photographs of the incident can also help.

- Who's in the picture?
- What expressions do you see on the people's faces?
- What is the year or the season?
- Do any significant objects appear in the photo?

go.hrw.com

INTERNET

More Writer's Models

Keyword: LE5 7-3

Evaluating and Revising

Use the following chart to evaluate and revise your personal narrative.

Personal Narrative: Content and Organization Guidelines

Evaluation Questions	▶ Tips	▶ Revision Techniques
❶ Does your introduction grab the reader's attention and set the scene?	▶ **Put stars** next to interesting quotations or statements. **Circle** details that identify the setting.	▶ **Add** a catchy quotation or statement to the introduction. **Add** details to make the setting more vivid.
❷ Is the point of view consistent throughout your narrative?	▶ **Draw a box** around third-person pronouns, such as *they, she,* and *himself.* Make sure that these pronouns refer to others, not to yourself.	▶ Use first-person pronouns, such as *I, we,* and *my,* to refer to yourself.
❸ Have you arranged events in a clear order?	▶ **Number** the events as they appear in your paper. Compare this sequence with the actual order of events.	▶ **Rearrange** any events that are out of order. **Add** transitional words to link events.
❹ Have you included details that make people, places, and events come to life?	▶ **Highlight** details that appeal to the senses. In the margin, **note** which of the senses are involved.	▶ **Elaborate** with dialogue or sensory details. **Delete** any irrelevant details.
❺ Have you included your thoughts and feelings?	▶ **Put a check mark** next to statements of your feelings or thoughts.	▶ **Add** any other thoughts and feelings you have about what happened.
❻ Does your conclusion state why the experience is memorable?	▶ **Underline** your statement explaining the importance of the experience.	▶ **Add** a clear statement explaining why the experience was important.

A revised paragraph from a personal narrative appears on the next page. Read the paragraph; then, answer the questions that follow, which ask you to evaluate the writer's revision.

Revision Model

I have always wanted a brother, and when I learned

that an exchange student from Japan would be living with

us during the summer, I called all my friends and bragged

about it.

    "Maybe he knows judo or karate," my friend Mitch ~~said~~. *suggested*

    During the last weeks of June, I ~~saw~~ *imagined* myself with a

black belt like those worn by masters in the martial arts.

I saw myself delivering sharp, quick blows with my hands

and feet, just like the ~~movements~~ *ones* I had seen in the movies.

I looked forward to the day we would drive to the airport to

meet Toshiro. ⌇I realized that I had jumped to conclusions.⌇

When I picked him out of the crowd of passengers, I

~~was disappointed~~. *almost gasped in disappointment* Instead of being a powerful athlete, *and muscular*

Toshiro was skinny, and he was carrying a violin case!

Evaluating the Revision

1. Where has the writer replaced weak verbs with more expressive verbs?

2. How has the writer rearranged the text to connect the details more clearly?

3. What other changes would you recommend?

Test Practice

DIRECTIONS: Read the following story and poem. Then, answer each question that follows.

Home
from Maud Martha
Gwendolyn Brooks

What had been wanted was this always, this always to last, the talking softly on this porch, with the snake plant in the jardiniere in the southwest corner, and the obstinate slip from Aunt Eppie's magnificent Michigan fern at the left side of the friendly door. Mama, Maud Martha, and Helen rocked slowly in their rocking chairs, and looked at the late afternoon light on the lawn and at the emphatic iron of the fence and at the poplar tree. These things might soon be theirs no longer. Those shafts and pools of light, the tree, the graceful iron, might soon be viewed possessively by different eyes.

Papa was to have gone that noon, during his lunch hour, to the office of the Home Owners' Loan. If he had not succeeded in getting another extension, they would be leaving this house in which they had lived for more than fourteen years. There was little hope. The Home Owners' Loan was hard. They sat, making their plans.

"We'll be moving into a nice flat somewhere," said Mama. "Somewhere on South Park, or Michigan, or in Washington Park Court." Those flats, as the girls and Mama knew well, were burdens on wages twice the size of Papa's. This was not mentioned now.

"They're much prettier than this old house," said Helen. "I have friends I'd just as soon not bring here. And I have other friends that wouldn't come down this far for anything, unless they were in a taxi."

Yesterday, Maud Martha would have attacked her. Tomorrow she might. Today she said nothing. She merely gazed at a little hopping robin in the tree, her tree, and tried to keep the fronts of her eyes dry.

"Well, I do know," said Mama, turning her hands over and over, "that I've been getting tireder and tireder of doing that firing. From October to April, there's firing to be done."

"But lately we've been helping, Harry and I," said Maud Martha. "And sometimes in March and April and in October, and even in November, we could build a little fire in the fireplace. Sometimes the weather was just right for that."

She knew, from the way they looked at her, that this had been a mistake. They did not want to cry.

But she felt that the little line of white, sometimes ridged with smoked purple, and all that cream-shot saffron would never drift across any western sky except that in back of this house. The rain would drum with as sweet a dullness nowhere but here. The birds on South Park were mechanical birds, no better than the poor caught canaries in those "rich" women's sun parlors.

"It's just going to kill Papa!" burst out Maud Martha. "He loves this house! He *lives* for this house!"

"He lives for us," said Helen. "It's us he loves. He wouldn't want the house, except for us."

"And he'll have us," added Mama, "wherever."

"You know," Helen said, "if you want to know the truth, this is a relief. If this hadn't come up, we would have gone on, just dragged on, hanging out here forever."

"It might," allowed Mama, "be an act of God. God may just have reached down and picked up the reins."

"Yes," Maud Martha cracked in, "that's what you always say—that God knows best."

Her mother looked at her quickly, decided the statement was not suspect, looked away.

Helen saw Papa's coming. "There's Papa," said Helen.

They could not tell a thing from the way Papa was walking. It was that same dear little staccato walk, one shoulder down, then the other, then repeat, and repeat. They watched his progress. He passed the Kennedys', he passed the vacant lot, he passed Mrs. Blakemore's. They wanted to hurl themselves over the fence, into the street, and shake the truth out of his collar. He opened his gate—the gate—and still his stride and face told them nothing.

"Hello," he said.

Mama got up and followed him through the front door. The girls knew better than to go in too.

Presently Mama's head emerged. Her eyes were lamps turned on.

"It's all right," she exclaimed. "He got it. It's all over. Everything is all right."

The door slammed shut. Mama's footsteps hurried away.

"I think," said Helen, rocking rapidly, "I think I'll give a party. I haven't given a party since I was eleven. I'd like some of my friends to just casually see that we're homeowners."

Collection 3: Skills Review

Test Practice

The word *saguaro* (sə·gwär′ō), in line 8, refers to a huge cactus found in the southwestern United States and northern Mexico.

Gold

Pat Mora

When Sun paints the desert
with its gold,
I climb the hills.
Wind runs round boulders,
    ruffles
5   my hair. I sit on my favorite rock,
lizards for company, a rabbit,
ears stiff in the shade
of a saguaro.
In the wind, we're all
10   eye to eye.

Sparrow on saguaro watches
rabbit watch us in the gold
of sun setting.
Hawk sails on waves of light, sees
15   sparrow, rabbit, lizards, me,
our eyes shining,
watching red and purple sand
    rivers stream down the hill.

I stretch my arms wide as the sky
like hawk extends her wings
20   in all the gold light of this, home.

1. Maud Martha in "Home" and the speaker of "Gold" share strong feelings about —
   - **A** nature
   - **B** houses
   - **C** robins
   - **D** porches

2. In "Home," Mama, Maud Martha, and Helen are upset because —
   - **F** their house is more expensive than a flat
   - **G** Mama has been working too hard
   - **H** their friends won't come to see them
   - **J** they may be losing their home

3. In "Home," Brooks writes that Mama's "eyes were lamps turned on." This is an example of —
   - **A** a simile
   - **B** a metaphor
   - **C** a definition
   - **D** rhyme

4. What place is home to the speaker of the poem?
   - **F** A favorite rock
   - **G** A house with a porch
   - **H** The desert
   - **J** A nice flat

5. At the end of the story and the poem, the characters and the speaker regard their homes with a feeling of —
   - **A** disappointment
   - **B** anger
   - **C** worry
   - **D** contentment

6. In "Home," Brooks writes that Maud Martha "tried to keep the fronts of her eyes dry." This means that Maud Martha is —

F near tears

G cleaning her glasses

H wet all over from the hose

J having trouble with her vision

7. Mama says she is tired of doing "that firing." Based on clues in the story, what do you guess that <u>firing</u> means here?

A Losing a job

B Starting a fire

C Cooking

D Cleaning

8. Brooks describes Mama's eyes as "lamps turned on." Which words from "Gold" mean the same thing?

F "our eyes shining"

G "we're all / eye to eye"

H "sails on waves of light"

J "I stretch my arms"

9. The following words are in both selections. Which is the **key word** in both selections?

A purple

B light

C sky

D home

Constructed Response

10. Which statement *best* expresses the **theme** of both the story and the poem?

- Home is a place we associate with special feelings.
- Homelessness is a terrible problem.
- It's a relief to have a nice house of one's own.
- The out-of-doors makes the best kind of home.

Use examples from each to explain why you chose that statement.

Test Practice

DIRECTIONS: Read the following article. Then, answer each question that follows.

Mongoose on the Loose

Larry Luxner

In 1872, a Jamaican sugar planter imported nine furry little mongooses from India to eat the rats that were devouring his crops. They did such a good job, the planter started breeding his exotic animals and selling them to eager farmers on neighboring islands.

With no natural predators—like wolves, coyotes, or poisonous snakes—the mongoose population exploded, and within a few years, they were killing not just rats but pigs, lambs, chickens, puppies, and kittens. Dr. G. Roy Horst, a U.S. expert on mongooses, says that today mongooses live on seventeen Caribbean islands as well as Hawaii and Fiji, where they have attacked small animals, threatened endangered species, and have even spread minor rabies epidemics.

In Puerto Rico there are from 800,000 to one million of them. That is about one mongoose for every four humans. In St. Croix, there are 100,000 mongooses, about twice as many as the human population. "It's impossible to eliminate the mongoose population, short of nuclear war," says Horst. "You can't poison them, because cats, dogs, and chickens get poisoned, too. I'm not a prophet crying in the wilderness, but the potential for real trouble is there," says Horst.

According to Horst, great efforts have been made to rid the islands of mongooses, which have killed off a number of species, including the Amevia lizard on St. Croix, presumed extinct for several decades. On Hawaii, the combination of mongooses and sports hunting has reduced the Hawaiian goose, or nene, to less than two dozen individuals. . . .

Horst says his research will provide local and federal health officials with extremely valuable information if they ever decide to launch a campaign against rabies in Puerto Rico or the U.S. Virgin Islands.

SKILLS FOCUS

Reading Skills
Analyze cause and effect.

1. The following diagram displays information about the **causes and effects** of bringing mongooses to Jamaica.

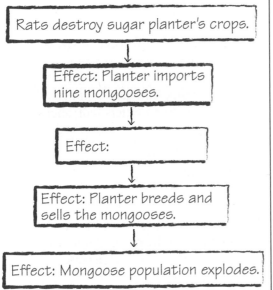

Rats destroy sugar planter's crops.

Effect: Planter imports nine mongooses.

Effect:

Effect: Planter breeds and sells the mongooses.

Effect: Mongoose population explodes.

Which of these events belongs in the third box?
   A   Mongooses do a good job getting rid of rats.
   B   Mongooses threaten the Hawaiian goose.
   C   Mongooses destroy other species.
   D   Mongooses are difficult to study.

2. In 1872, a Jamaican sugar planter imported nine mongooses to —
   F   keep snakes away from his farm
   G   serve as pets for his young children
   H   eat the rats that were ruining his crops
   J   breed them for their fur

3. Because the mongooses didn't have any natural predators in that part of the world, their population —
   A   diminished
   B   exploded
   C   fluctuated
   D   declined

4. You would be *most* likely to find this information about mongooses in a —
   F   chemistry book
   G   collection of stories
   H   travel guide
   J   magazine on nature

Constructed Response

5. List the **effects** of the mongoose population explosion.

Collection 3: Skills Review

Vocabulary Skills

Test Practice

This Test Practice reviews Vocabulary words you have studied in earlier collections.

Context Clues

DIRECTIONS: Use **context clues** to help you figure out what the underlined words mean. Then, choose the best answer.

1. The exciting juggling act proved to be immensely popular with the young, cheering audience.
   - A simply
   - B frighteningly
   - C enormously
   - D immediately

2. Even after hours of careful thought, he still couldn't fathom the solution.
   - F say
   - G understand
   - H hear
   - J measure

3. Mary's comments weren't meant to be derisive, but they still hurt my feelings.
   - A scornful
   - B playful
   - C pleasant
   - D forceful

4. Our basketball team put in a valiant effort, but it still lost the game.
   - F halfhearted
   - G overpowering
   - H determined
   - J adequate

5. Jamal hoped to alleviate his grandmother's unhappiness by cooking her favorite meal.
   - A exaggerate
   - B ignore
   - C notice
   - D reduce

6. Andy, a nineteen-game winner, made the opposition's hitters look anemic.
   - F lazy
   - G challenging
   - H weak
   - J hungry

7. Brian was so perturbed by his best friend's rude behavior that he couldn't concentrate on his homework.
   - A troubled
   - B unfazed
   - C overjoyed
   - D strengthened

8. Mannie wanted to appear sophisticated, but his thin tie and top hat just made him look silly.
   - F enthusiastic
   - G refined
   - H tired
   - J unemployed

SKILLS FOCUS

Vocabulary Skills
Use context clues.

Collection 3: Skills Review

Writing Skills

Test Practice

DIRECTIONS: Read the following paragraph from a personal narrative. Then, answer each question that follows.

(1) The day I had been dreading for months finally arrived. (2) It was a wet, cold February morning when I saw the moving vans pull up to our driveway. (3) We were leaving the only home I had ever known, the place where I had built a lifetime of memories. (4) The movers were wearing slickers to keep the rain off. (5) I heard my mother giving instructions to the movers, anxiously telling them to be careful with the baby's crib. (6) As I made a tour of the place, the rooms appeared vacant. (7) All the pictures and curtains had been taken down; the furniture was covered with sheets; the books and breakable objects had been packed away. (8) I knew that I would make new friends and have fun in the years ahead, but nothing would replace my special memories of my first home.

1. What could the writer add to further develop this personal narrative?
   - **A** The effect of the move on other members of the family
   - **B** A description of some of the narrator's special memories
   - **C** Treasured objects broken during the move
   - **D** The reactions of the neighbors

2. Which of the following sentences is unnecessary and should be deleted?
   - **F** sentence 3
   - **G** sentence 4
   - **H** sentence 7
   - **J** sentence 8

3. If the narrator were to add dialogue, it would probably come after —
   - **A** sentence 5
   - **B** sentence 6
   - **C** sentence 7
   - **D** sentence 8

4. Which of the following sentences is the best replacement for sentence 6?
   - **F** As I entered each room, I found it empty.
   - **G** As I revisited the rooms, the floorboards creaked.
   - **H** As I moved around the empty house, I was grief-stricken.
   - **J** As I walked through the rooms, the house seemed to have lost its life.

5. The **tone** of this story is —
   - **A** cheerful
   - **B** reflective and sad
   - **C** sullen and gloomy
   - **D** angry and resentful

SKILLS FOCUS

Writing Skills
Analyze a personal narrative.

Fiction

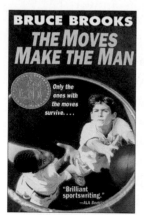

Fast Breaks

Jerome "the Jayfox" is a gifted basketball player and the first African American to attend his North Carolina high school. In *The Moves Make the Man* by Bruce Brooks, Jerome develops an intense friendship with a white teammate, and together they struggle to understand the meaning of truth.

Three's Company

In Wilson Rawls's *Where the Red Fern Grows*, which is set in the Ozark Mountains, Billy Colman works tirelessly through two years of the Great Depression to save money to purchase Old Dan and Little Ann, two hunting dogs. Billy trains the dogs to become the finest raccoon-hunting team in the valley. However, Billy experiences sadness along with his glory. **This title is available in the HRW Library.**

Pen Pals

If you enjoy writing, you may like *Letters to Julia* by Barbara Ware Holmes. Fifteen-year-old Liz Beech dreams of becoming a writer when she begins corresponding with Julia Steward Jones, an editor in New York City. Julia is impressed with Liz's writing ability, and the two become good friends. But when they have a misunderstanding, their relationship becomes strained.

Friends in Need

Mina is not sure if she was kicked out of dance camp because of her rapid growth or because she was the only African American in the class. In the midst of her confusion, she meets Tamer Shipp, a minister who becomes her confidant. Mina and Tamer support each other during traumatic times in Cynthia Voigt's *Come a Stranger*.

Nonfiction

Days of Yore

Have you ever wondered what life was like before malls or television? How did people spend their time? Did they have any fun? John D. Clare brings the past vividly to life in *Living History: Fourteenth-Century Towns*. The book features informative text and photographs reenacting fascinating rituals from the Middle Ages.

No Myth

Today we don't rely on origin myths to explain how the world operates; scientists provide us with most of the answers. In *The New Way Things Work*, David Macaulay presents "origin myths" of natural phenomena, like the acts of floating and flying. He also tells the stories behind such technological innovations as modems, burglar alarms, and helicopters. The illustrations will guide you through the explanations.

Tools of War

When you look at weaponry from the past, you realize that it can provide valuable insight into the mind-set of a culture. Prehistoric people primarily used stones to hunt. Japanese weapons were highly decorative, to represent the strength of the samurai class. In *Arms and Armor,* Michele Byam looks at weapons from the Stone Age to the Old West.

Remembering Montezuma

In 1519, Montezuma was the mighty ruler of the Aztecs. He thought he had nothing to fear. One year later he and his people were ambushed and overcome by a troop of Spanish soldiers led by the cunning Hernán Cortés. In *Montezuma and the Aztecs,* Nathaniel Harris looks at Aztec traditions and discusses Montezuma's leadership of the Aztec Empire before it fell to the Spaniards.

Point of View: Can You See It My Way?

Literary Focus:
Analyzing Point of View

Informational Focus:
Analyzing an Author's Argument

Le Faux Miroir (The False Mirror)
(1935) by René Magritte.
Phototheque R. Magritte-ADAGP, © 2005 C. Herscovici,
Brussels/Artists Rights Society (ARS), New York.

INTERNET
Collection
Resources
Keyword: LE5 7-4

Elements of Literature
Point of View *by* John Leggett
THROUGH WHOSE EYES?

When you were little, you probably imagined at one time or another that there was something terrifying under your bed. Did it ever occur to you that something might find *you* just as terrifying? As the saying goes, "It all depends on your point of view." When you're telling a story, you look at things one way—your way. When someone else tells the story, he or she will put a slightly different spin on the same events.

Novels and short stories are also told from a particular **point of view,** or vantage point. When you're reading, you should ask, "Who is the narrator?" "Can I rely on this narrator to tell the truth?" and "What is the narrator's relationship to the meaning of the story?"

The Big Three

The three most common points of view are the omniscient, the first person, and the third-person limited.

The **omniscient** (äm·nish′ənt) **point of view** is the all-knowing point of view. (In Latin, *omnis* means "all," and *sciens* means "knowing.") You can think of an omniscient narrator as being above the action, looking down on it like a god. This narrator can tell you everything about all the characters, even their most private thoughts.

THE FAR SIDE® BY GARY LARSON

"I've got it again, Larry ... an eerie feeling like there's something on top of the bed."

Once upon a time there lived a princess who would have been perfectly happy except for one thing: In a moment of weakness, she had promised to marry a frog. Her father felt sorry for her, but he insisted that she keep her word. (In fact, he was a little nervous—he'd never met a talking frog before.) "After all, a promise is a promise," agreed her mother, who thought the frog was better looking than the princess's last boyfriend. Little did any of the royal family know who the frog really was.

SKILLS FOCUS

Literary Skills
Understand point of view.

A story can also be told by one of the characters. In this viewpoint the character speaks as "I." We call this the **first-person point of view.** (*I* is the first-person pronoun.) In this point of view, we know only what this one character can tell us. Sometimes this kind of narrator isn't very reliable.

I couldn't believe that my parents were actually going to make me marry a slimy, ugly, bulgy-eyed frog! They didn't feel sorry for me at all! All they cared about was a stupid promise I never thought I'd have to keep.

Often a story is seen through the eyes of one character, but the character is *not* telling the story as "I." This is called the **third-person-limited point of view.** In this point of view, a narrator zooms in on the thoughts and feelings of just one character in the story. This point of view helps us share that character's reactions to the story's events.

The princess tried desperately to get out of her promise. "It was all my parents' fault," she thought. They were so unfair. But she had a nagging feeling that she had only herself to blame—and the frog. "I wonder if the royal chef knows how to cook frogs' legs?" she said to herself.

Point of view is very important in storytelling, and writers love to experiment with it. Someone who wants to tell the frog-and-princess story from a really unusual point of view might choose to let the frog tell it.

Practice

Write three groups of sentences about the situation in the cartoon on page 348.

- In the first group of sentences, write as the **omniscient narrator.** As the omniscient narrator you might want to let your reader know how this unusual situation came about and give some hints about how it will end.

  These people are...

- In the second group of sentences, write from the **first-person point of view** of the monster. Now you will write as "I."

  I am feeling...

- In the third group of sentences, take the **third-person-limited point of view.** This is the hardest. In this point of view, you are going to zoom in and focus on just one character. Concentrate on the boy in the bed.

  This boy is...

Reading Skills and Strategies

Analyzing an Author's Perspective

by Kylene Beers

How do the meanings of the two sentences below differ?

Jamal won the race?   Jamal won the *race*?

Although the two sentences include the same words, the difference in emphasis gives them different meanings. Each sentence reveals a different attitude about Jamal's winning the race. As you read an informational text, it's important to understand the author's point of view, or **perspective.** It will help you evaluate his or her ideas.

Tracking Perspective

The reader's job would be much easier if authors would only say, "My point of view on this subject is _____." Of course, that usually doesn't happen. Instead, authors leave hints or clues that reveal their feelings about the topic. You'll find these clues in

- the author's word choice
- the author's tone
- what the author includes
- what the author leaves out

Read the text to the right, and look for these clues. Then, read the article on page 351 and see if you can determine the author's perspective.

SKILLS FOCUS

Reading Skills
Analyze an author's perspective.

Kids' Sports Today

In our wonderful past, kids gathered for pickup baseball games. Anyone could play. Parents watched, or didn't. The point was to have fun. Some kids went on to play high school sports, and that was it. But now four-year-olds try out for the Pee Wee Baseball League. Gym lessons begin at age three. Two-year-olds take soccer class. Ridiculously tennis camps enroll toddlers. By high school, kids are so burned out, lessoned out, and played out that they either drop out or fizzle out. Sports have become too competitive, and too many parents see their child as the next Tiger Woods.

Words like *wonderful, kids, fun,* and *ridiculously* hint at the author's view of competitive sports.

Notice what the author tells you; then, notice what isn't mentioned—how sports help develop self-esteem, build leadership, improve social skills.

Repetition of the word *out* (five times!) creates an insistent **tone** and leads to the author's view that sports are too competitive today.

Using the Strategy

As you read this article, you'll find this open-book sign at certain points in the story : . Stop at these points, and do what the prompts ask.

Canines to the Rescue

Jonah Goldberg

❶ Notice that the author uses the pronoun *I*. That means he is writing in the first person, sharing his own experiences and opinions. He tells us that the dog Tara has an important and dangerous job. What does this detail tell you about the writer's attitude toward dogs?

COMPARE AND CONTRAST

❷ *Work ethic* refers to the belief that it is important to work hard. The writer says that dogs are eager to work hard. He then contrasts dogs' attitude toward work with the attitude of other animals. What does this contrast tell you about the writer's perspective on dogs?

INFER

❸ What rubble is the writer referring to? (If you aren't sure, look back at the first paragraph.) Look carefully at the word choices in this paragraph. Which words offer clues to the writer's view of dogs?

I spent the better part of an afternoon about half a mile south of where the World Trade Center[1] stood, with Tara, a three-year-old golden retriever employed by Michael Stanton Associates, a private security firm. Tara's job is to find bombs. Of course, she doesn't know that they are bombs; all she knows is that her human master wants her to find something that smells like plastic explosives, or TNT, or a dozen other dangerous substances. The only payment she will receive for this is a few moments fetching the ball with her boss. **❶**

This work ethic is the heart of canine exceptionalism. The dog is the only animal that volunteers for duty. If we want other animals—horses, oxen, mules, falcons, bears, or parrots—to come to our aid, we must either force them or bribe them. You might even call horses our slaves: Their spirit must actually be broken before they will agree to do anything for us. **❷**

Long before the rubble settled in downtown New York, German shepherds, Labrador retrievers, and Rottweilers—as well as canines of less aristocratic lineage—were already pulling at their leashes to help with the search-and-rescue efforts. Locating the dead and searching (too often in vain) for the living is obviously an arduous[2] and emotionally draining task for human beings, but it is no picnic for dogs either. The rubble provided unstable footing, was full of glass shards and twisted metal, and sometimes glowed red hot. Dangerous fumes, loud noises, and the equivalent of landslides were constant sources of distraction and peril. Dogs repeatedly had to limp out of the wreckage on bloody paws, the razor-edged debris[3] slicing through even the leather boots distributed to some of them. **❸**

---

1. **World Trade Center:** twin towers in New York City that were destroyed on September 11, 2001.
2. **arduous** (är′jo͞o·əs) *adj.:* hard; difficult.
3. **debris** (də·brē′) *n.:* pieces of stone, wood, glass, or other materials left after something is destroyed.

Worse, the stress associated with not finding survivors was extreme; dogs tasked with this assignment expect—*need*—to find survivors. "They don't like to find bodies. They'll find them, but they don't feel rewarded," veterinarian Douglas Wyler explained. "The dogs are good, they're professionals, but like any professional they can suffer from melancholy and depression. It's hard for the men not to find anyone alive, and the dogs sense that." ❹

But the dogs persevered.[4] Consider Servus, a Belgian Malinois (a smaller version of the German shepherd) who arrived at the Twin Towers site with his owner, police officer Chris Christensen, the day after the disaster. While searching for survivors, Servus fell down a nine-foot hole into a mound of dust and debris. When they pulled him free, "he couldn't breathe," Christensen explained. Servus tried to vomit, to no avail. By the time the convulsions started and Servus's tongue turned purple, between twenty and thirty men were gathered to help an animal they clearly considered a colleague (often, police dogs are given full-dress funerals). The canine was rushed to one of the veterinary MASH units set up to treat the rescue dogs as well as the numerous "civilian" animals and pets injured or abandoned in the surrounding residential areas.

The vets managed to resuscitate[5] Servus, and he was given an IV.[6] (It was not unusual to see rescue humans and rescue dogs lying beside one another, each with his own IV drip.) When the vets unstrapped the dog from the gurney and released him for some doggie R&R,[7] he ran straight from the tent and leapt into the police car assigned to bring dogs to ground zero. "I couldn't believe it," Christensen said. "I told him three times to get out and he just looked at me, so we went to work. We worked for seven hours." ❺

Such dedication has inspired a growing effort in the scientific community to explain this age-old symbiosis between men and dogs. Until fairly recently, the study of dogs has been ignored by scientists more interested in more "authentic" animals—despite the fact that the domestic dog may be the second most successful of all mammal species, after human beings. ❻

More to the point, their success is directly attributable to the fact

---

4. **persevered** (pʉr′sə·vird′) *v*.: kept trying; persisted.
5. **resuscitate** (ri·sus′ə·tāt′) *v*.: revive; bring back to life.
6. **IV** (abbreviation for *intravenous*) *n*.: medical procedure in which blood plasma, medicine, or nutrients are delivered directly into a vein.
7. **R&R:** abbreviation used in the military, meaning "rest and recuperation."

ANALYZE

❹ Why do you think the writer includes a quotation from a veterinarian? Remember that the information a writer chooses to include may offer a clue to his or her perspective.

ANALYZE

❺ Why do you think the writer included so much information about Servus? (Did you notice that the name sounds like *service*?)

WORD CHOICE

❻ You might have seen the word *symbiosis* (sim′bī·ō′sis) in your science class. *Sym*– is a prefix that means "together" and –*bio*– means "life"; the word means "association of members of two species for the benefit of both." In this case the species are humans and dogs. Why do you think the writer uses a scientific term here?

COMPARE AND CONTRAST

7 In this paragraph the writer mentions a legend that explains how the dog became a good friend to humans. He then quotes a nature writer with a very different point of view. What surprising words does Stephen Budiansky use to describe dogs?

WORD CHOICE

8 *Cynic* (sin′ik) is a harsh word that means "someone who believes that people act only out of self-interest." What does this word choice tell you about the writer's opinion of the people he is describing? Look at the third sentence in this paragraph. Who does "himself" refer to? Where is the crane? (Remember the setting in the first paragraph.)

ANALYZE

9 Re-read the last two paragraphs of the article. What do they tell you about the author's overall perspective on dogs?

that they have teamed up with human beings. I'm told that according to an American Indian legend, human beings and animals were separated by a great canyon in prehistory. Forced to choose sides, the dog decided to throw in his lot with man and leapt the chasm to live and work with us. The moral of the story is certainly true, though the choice was evolutionary as well as sentimental. Some, like nature writer Stephen Budiansky, take the story too far in the other direction. He argues that canines have mastered an evolutionary strategy that makes us love them: "Dogs belong to that elite group of con artists at the very pinnacle of their profession, the ones who pick our pockets clean and leave us smiling about it." **7**

These cynics would have us believe that dogs—which have, in numerous documented cases, given their lives for human beings—are actually slyly exploiting an emotional glitch in people that makes us love soft, big-eyed furry things. This overlooks the obvious fact that we "con" dogs too; that they, in fact, love us as much as, if not more than, we love them. Allowing himself to be carried by crane hundreds of feet above the ground and then lowered into a smoldering pit of metal and glass defies every instinct a dog has, except one: to be a selfless friend of his ally and master. "Histories are more full of examples of the fidelity[8] of dogs than of friends," observed Alexander Pope. "Heaven goes by favor," remarked Mark Twain. "If it went by merit, you would stay out and your dog would go in."**8**

There's no disputing that dogs do things for canine reasons. Many of their heroic acts can be attributed to misplaced maternal or other instincts. Newfoundlands have saved many people from drowning, but their instinct is just as strong to "save" banana crates and other flotsam. Tara—the ebullient[9] golden retriever I looked for bombs with—doesn't know the details; all she knows is that she wants to please her human master.

And isn't that good enough? **9**

---

8. **fidelity** (fə·del′ə·tē) *n.*: faithfulness.
9. **ebullient** (i·bꝏl′yənt) *adj.*: high-spirited.

Practice the Strategy

Analyzing an Author's Perspective

As you read "Canines to the Rescue," you examined many of the clues that help reveal the **author's perspective,** or point of view. These clues include word choice, tone, the information included, and the information left out.

PRACTICE

Draw a Perspective Wheel like the one below, and label each section as shown. Then, place the words and phrases listed below in the appropriate sections. Afterward, write a paragraph that describes the author's perspective. Use the wheel to organize your ideas and provide support for your argument. As you read other informational texts, use a wheel like this one to analyze the author's perspective.

Words and Phrases

employed	*volunteers*	*symbiosis*	*selfless*
work ethic	*pulling at their leashes*	*cynics*	*heroic acts*
exceptionalism	*dedication*	*exploiting*	

Quotations and Ideas

Quotation from veterinarian

Story about Servus

American Indian legend

Mark Twain's comment

The expense or effort involved in raising dogs

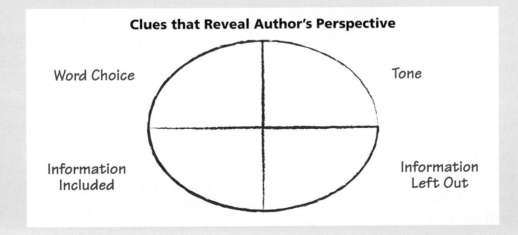

Clues that Reveal Author's Perspective

Word Choice

Tone

Information Included

Information Left Out

SKILLS FOCUS

You can use these clues to find the **author's perspective** in all the stories and informational texts you read.

Reading Skills
Analyze an author's perspective.

After Twenty Years

Make the Connection
Quickwrite ✏️

Imagine that you write an advice column for your school newspaper. One day you receive this letter from someone in your school. In a letter, advise "Confused."

> Last Friday I saw my friend Lucy (not her real name) take a wallet that was left on a cafeteria table. I know she needs the money because her dad is between jobs. I don't know what to do! I mean, I want to do what's right—but I don't know how to handle this. She's just never done anything like this before.
>
> Sincerely,
> Confused

INTERNET

Vocabulary Activity
•
Cross-curricular Connection
•
More About O. Henry

Keyword: LE5 7-4

Literary Focus
Omniscient Point of View

When you start reading a story, it's a good idea to ask, "Who is telling this story?" When you do this, you are asking about the **point of view.** "After Twenty Years" is told from the **omniscient point of view.** An omniscient narrator knows everything about everybody in a story. This narrator can tell you all about all the characters, their most private feelings, their pasts, even their futures.

Literary Skills
Understand omniscient point of view.

Reading Skills
Make predictions.

Reading Skills
Making Predictions: What Next?

Part of the fun of reading is guessing what will happen next. This process is called **making predictions.** Good readers make predictions without even thinking about it. Here's how to do it:

- Look for clues that **foreshadow,** or hint at, what will happen next.

- As the suspense builds, predict possible outcomes. See if you can guess where the writer is leading you. Revise your predictions as you go.

- Draw on your own experiences—including your other reading experiences—in making your predictions.

As you read "After Twenty Years," look for small open-book signs after some of the paragraphs. Stop at these points to predict what will happen next.

Vocabulary Development

O. Henry loved long, unusual words. Here are some words from "After Twenty Years" that you can add to your own vocabulary:

habitual (hə·bich′oo·əl) *adj.:* done or fixed by habit. *The officer made his habitual check of the buildings.*

intricate (in′tri·kit) *adj.:* complicated; full of detail. *The officer twirled his club with intricate movements.*

dismally (diz′məl·ē) *adv.:* miserably; gloomily. *People walked dismally through the rainy streets.*

egotism (ē′gō·tiz′əm) *n.:* conceit; talking about oneself too much. *His egotism made him brag about his success.*

simultaneously (sī′məl·tā′nē·əs·lē) *adv.:* at the same time. *Each man looked simultaneously at his friend's face.*

After Twenty Years

O. Henry

"We agreed that we would meet here again exactly twenty years from that date and time . . ."

(Background) Courtesy of The Valentine Museum, Richmond, Virginia.

The City from Greenwich Village (1922) by John Sloan. Oil on canvas.

The policeman on the beat moved up the avenue impressively. The impressiveness was <u>habitual</u> and not for show, for spectators were few. The time was barely ten o'clock at night, but chilly gusts of wind with a taste of rain in them had well nigh depeopled the streets.

Trying doors as he went, twirling his club with many <u>intricate</u> and artful movements, turning now and then to cast his watchful eye down the pacific[1] thoroughfare, the officer, with his stalwart form and slight swagger, made a fine picture of a guardian of the peace. The vicinity was one that kept early hours. Now and then you might see the lights of a cigar store or of an all-night lunch counter, but the majority of the doors belonged to business places that had long since been closed.

When about midway of a certain block, the policeman suddenly slowed his walk. In the doorway of a darkened hardware store a man leaned with an unlighted cigar in his mouth. As the policeman walked up to him, the man spoke up quickly.

"It's all right, officer," he said reassuringly. "I'm just waiting for a friend. It's an appointment made twenty years ago. Sounds a little funny to you, doesn't it? Well, I'll explain if you'd like to make certain it's all

---

1. **pacific** *adj.:* peaceful.

Vocabulary

habitual (hə·bich′ōō·əl) *adj.:* done or fixed by habit; customary.

intricate (in′tri·kit) *adj.:* complicated; full of detail.

straight. About that long ago there used to be a restaurant where this store stands—'Big Joe' Brady's restaurant."

"Until five years ago," said the policeman. "It was torn down then."

The man in the doorway struck a match and lit his cigar. The light showed a pale, square-jawed face with keen eyes and a little white scar near his right eyebrow. His scarf pin was a large diamond, oddly set. ❶

MAKE PREDICTIONS
❶ What could the scar and the large diamond suggest about the man's past?

"Twenty years ago tonight," said the man, "I dined here at 'Big Joe' Brady's with Jimmy Wells, my best chum and the finest chap in the world. He and I were raised here in New York, just like two brothers, together. I was eighteen and Jimmy was twenty. The next morning I was to start for the West to make my fortune. You couldn't have dragged Jimmy out of New York; he thought it was the only place on earth. Well, we agreed that night that we would meet here again exactly twenty years from that date and time, no matter what our conditions might be or from what distance we might have to come. We figured that in twenty years each of us ought to have our destiny worked out and our fortunes made, whatever they were going to be."

"It sounds pretty interesting," said the policeman. "Rather a long time between meets, though, it seems to me. Haven't you heard from your friend since you left?"

"Well, yes, for a time we corresponded," said the other. "But after a year or two we lost track of each other. You see, the West is a pretty big proposition, and I kept hustling around over it pretty lively. But I know Jimmy will meet me here if he's alive, for he always was the truest, staunchest old chap in the world. He'll never forget. I came a thousand miles to stand in this door tonight, and it's worth it if my old partner turns up."

The waiting man pulled out a handsome watch, the lids of it set with small diamonds.

"Three minutes to ten," he announced. "It was exactly ten o'clock when we parted here at the restaurant door."

"Did pretty well out West, didn't you?" asked the policeman.

"You bet! I hope Jimmy has done half as well. He was a kind of plodder, though, good fellow as he was. I've had to compete with some of the sharpest wits going to get my pile. A man gets in a groove in New York. It takes the West to put a razor edge on him." ❷

MAKE PREDICTIONS
❷ What do these boasts suggest about the man's past?

The policeman twirled his club and took a step or two.

"I'll be on my way. Hope your friend comes around all right. Going to call time on him sharp?"

"I should say not!" said the other. "I'll give him half an hour at least. If Jimmy is alive on earth, he'll be here by that time. So long, officer."

"Good night, sir," said the policeman, passing on along his beat, trying doors as he went.

There was now a fine, cold drizzle falling, and the wind had risen from its uncertain puffs into a steady blow. The few foot passengers astir in that quarter hurried dismally and silently along with coat collars turned high and pocketed hands. And in the door of the hardware store the man who had

Vocabulary
dismally (diz′məl·ē) adv.: miserably; gloomily.

come a thousand miles to fill an appointment, uncertain almost to absurdity, with the friend of his youth, smoked his cigar and waited.

About twenty minutes he waited, and then a tall man in a long overcoat, with collar turned up to his ears, hurried across from the opposite side of the street. He went directly to the waiting man.

"Is that you, Bob?" he asked, doubtfully.

"Is that you, Jimmy Wells?" cried the man in the door.

"Bless my heart!" exclaimed the new arrival, grasping both the other's hands with his own. "It's Bob, sure as fate. I was certain I'd find you here if you were still in existence. Well, well, well!—twenty years is a long time. The old restaurant's gone, Bob; I wish it had lasted, so we could have had another dinner there. How has the West treated you, old man?"

"Bully;[2] it has given me everything I asked it for. You've changed lots, Jimmy. I never thought you were so tall by two or three inches." ❸

"Oh, I grew a bit after I was twenty."

"Doing well in New York, Jimmy?"

"Moderately. I have a position in one of the city departments. Come on, Bob; we'll go around to a place I know of and have a good long talk about old times."

The two men started up the street, arm in arm. The man from the West, his egotism enlarged by success, was beginning to outline the history of his career. The other, submerged in his overcoat, listened with interest.

> **MAKE PREDICTIONS**
> ❸ What could Jimmy's height signify?

At the corner stood a drugstore, brilliant with electric lights. When they came into this glare, each of them turned simultaneously to gaze upon the other's face.

The man from the West stopped suddenly and released his arm.

"You're not Jimmy Wells," he snapped. "Twenty years is a long time, but not long enough to change a man's nose from a Roman to a pug." ❹

"It sometimes changes a good man into a bad one," said the tall man. "You've been under arrest for ten minutes, 'Silky' Bob. Chicago thinks you may have dropped over our way and wires us she wants to have a chat with you. Going quietly, are you? That's sensible. Now, before we go to the station, here's a note I was asked to hand to you. You may read it here at the window. It's from Patrolman Wells."

The man from the West unfolded the little piece of paper handed him. His hand was steady when he began to read, but it trembled a little by the time he had finished. The note was rather short.

> **MAKE PREDICTIONS**
> ❹ If the man is not Jimmy Wells, then who do you suppose he is, and why do you think he is sent in Jimmy's place?

> Bob: I was at the appointed place on time. When you struck the match to light your cigar, I saw it was the face of the man wanted in Chicago. Somehow I couldn't do it myself, so I went around and got a plainclothes man to do the job.
>
> Jimmy

---

2. **bully** *interj.:* informal term meaning "very well."

Vocabulary

egotism (ē′gō·tiz′əm) *n.:* conceit; talking about oneself too much.

simultaneously (sī′məl·tā′nē·əs·lē) *adv.:* at the same time.

Meet the Writer

O. Henry

"Stories in Everything"

O. Henry (1862–1910) is the pen name of William Sydney Porter, who was born in Greensboro, North Carolina. He left school at fifteen and eventually moved to Texas. There he edited a humor magazine called *The Rolling Stone* and worked for a few years in a bank in Austin. Unfortunately, Porter was a careless record keeper. Two years after he left the bank, he was accused of embezzling its money. Although he was probably innocent, Porter panicked and ran off to Honduras. A year or so later he returned to Austin to be with his dying wife. There he was convicted and spent more than three years in a federal prison in Ohio.

Porter found the plots of many of his stories (including "After Twenty Years") in jail. He may also have found his famous pen name there: The name of a prison guard was Orrin Henry.

After he was released from prison, in 1901, Porter moved to New York. Soon, as O. Henry, he became one of the country's most popular short story writers. His stories are known for their snappy surprise endings. Many of his best-known stories are set in New York's streets and tenements and cheap hotels.

One day while O. Henry was dining with friends at a New York restaurant, a young writer asked him where he got his plots. "Oh, everywhere," replied O. Henry. "There are stories in everything." He picked up the menu on which the dishes of the day were typewritten. "There's a story in this," he said. Then he outlined the story—which he later wrote down and published—called "Springtime à la Carte." (On menus *à la carte* means that each item is priced separately.)

For Independent Reading

"After Twenty Years" is from a collection called *The Four Million and Other Stories.* The title refers to the population of New York City in O. Henry's day. Other O. Henry stories set in New York include "The Gift of the Magi" and "The Last Leaf."

First Thoughts

1. What would you have done if you were Jimmy? Look back at the letter you wrote to "Confused" in your Quickwrite. Would you make any revisions to the advice you gave?

Thinking Critically

2. Several details about Bob's appearance and behavior warn us that he might not be honest or that he is hiding from someone. What clues hint at, or **foreshadow,** something sinister about Bob?

3. When did you realize who the police officer was? Find and explain the first clue to his identity.

4. Both men honor a commitment they made over twenty years ago, but for Jimmy Wells there's one thing more important than even a long friendship. In a sentence or two, state the **theme** of this story. What truth about loyalty versus honesty does the story reveal to you?

Reading Check

a. Why has the man in the doorway come back to the old neighborhood after twenty years?

b. What does the police officer realize when the man in the doorway lights his cigar?

c. How does the man in the doorway describe Jimmy Wells?

d. What does the police officer do after saying good night to the man in the doorway?

e. What happens to Bob at the end of the story?

Extending Interpretations

5. Some people don't like O. Henry's surprise endings. They think these endings make the stories unbelievable. Do you agree? Explain why or why not.

WRITING

Narrating from Another Point of View

O. Henry chose to tell his story from the **omniscient point of view.** What would we have known—and not known—if he had let Silky Bob tell the story from his own **first-person point of view**? Try retelling one of the scenes from Bob's or Jimmy's point of view. How could the new narrator change the story's **theme**? Is it still about loyalty versus honesty?

go.
hrw
.com

INTERNET

Projects and Activities

Keyword: LE5 7-4

SKILLS FOCUS

Literary Skills
Analyze point of view.

Reading Skills
Make predictions.

Writing Skills
Describe events from another point of view.

After You Read | Vocabulary Development

Clarifying Word Meanings

PRACTICE

To be sure you own the words in the Word Bank, fill out a word web for each word. Clarify the word's meaning through the use of definition, example, restatement, and contrast. The first word has been done for you. Be sure to compare your webs in class.

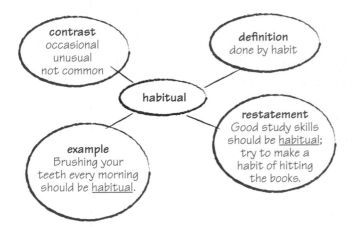

- **contrast**
  occasional
  unusual
  not common

- **definition**
  done by habit

- **habitual**

- **example**
  Brushing your teeth every morning should be <u>habitual</u>.

- **restatement**
  Good study skills should be <u>habitual</u>; try to make a habit of hitting the books.

SKILLS FOCUS

Vocabulary Skills
Clarify word meanings.

Grammar Skills
Use end marks correctly.

Grammar Link

End All End-Mark Errors

In written English every sentence must begin with a capital letter and end with one of these **end marks:** a period, a question mark, or an exclamation point. Follow these simple rules:

- Use a period at the end of a statement.
  "It's an appointment made twenty years ago."

- Use a question mark at the end of a question.
  "Is that you, Bob?"

- Use an exclamation point at the end of an exclamation or a command.
  "Bless my heart!"

PRACTICE

Rewrite the following paragraph, adding capitalization and end punctuation marks. (The paragraph contains a total of seven sentences.)

Charlie tried out for the baseball team what did he have to lose it's not as if you have to be Ken Griffey, Jr., to play a position who imagined what would happen it was such a surprise unbelievably, he's hitting leadoff I guess you never know

For more help, see End Marks, 13a–e, in the Language Handbook.

Analyzing an Author's Perspective

Reading Focus
Perspective: How We Look at Life

All writers have a perspective on their subjects. O. Henry's perspective is clear in the story "After Twenty Years." He sees life as offering us choices between honest and dishonest behavior. He comes down in favor of honesty, even when friendship is at stake.

Perspective refers to the way we look at a subject. Take the subject of school uniforms. Some people's perspective on that subject is negative. They think children should be free to dress the way they wish. Other people have a positive perspective on school uniforms. They think uniforms help equalize children and do away with clothes competition.

■ After you read "What's *Really* in a Name?," fill out a chart like the one opposite. Doing that should help you identify the writer's perspective on changing names.

"What's *Really* in a Name?"

The writer doesn't understand why Patsy changed her name.

The writer tells why some people change their names: 1. 2. 3. [and so on]

The writer states her main concern about changing names:

Final quotation:

The writer's perspective on changing names:

SKILLS FOCUS

Reading Skills
Analyze an author's perspective.

It all depends on your point of view.

What's Really in a Name?

Samuel Clemens / Mark Twain

Patsy seemed like a movie star before she really became one. She was my sister's friend, and her presence made me hide behind the plants in the living room. I didn't want to talk to her. I just wanted to watch her. She was only in the sixth grade, but she had an air of sophistication that I had never experienced in my seven years.

After we all grew up, Patsy moved to New York and then to Los Angeles. I began to see her on television. Then I saw her in movies. At the end of one movie, I searched the closing credits for her name, but it wasn't there. So I called my sister and said, "I can't believe they left Patsy's name off the credits." My sister said, "They didn't. She changed her name." I hung up the phone feeling confused. To me Patsy would always be Patsy. Why would she need a new name?

Patsy had given herself a pseudonym.° Although it sounds like a bad disease, it's not. A pseudonym is a made-up name. (*Pseudo* comes from a Greek word that means "fake.") For writers a pseudonym is also called a pen name. William Sydney Porter, the famous short story writer, called himself O. Henry (see page 361). Mark Twain's name was really Samuel Clemens.

People have all sorts of reasons for using pseudonyms. It's easy to see why William Sydney Porter had one. He spent more than three years in jail for stealing money from a bank where he had worked. Although the evidence of his crime remains questionable, the damage to his reputation was done. As an ex-convict he might have had a hard time getting his books published. So he changed his name. One story is that the name O. Henry came from his cat.

°**pseudonym** (sōō′də·nim′) *n.*

When he called the family cat, he yelled, "Oh, Henry." Another story has it that he got it from his prison guard. The guard's name was Orrin Henry.

Sometimes writers give themselves pen names because their publishers ask them to. It might have been hard to sell a shoot 'em-up western if your name was Archibald Lynn Joscelyn. Change that name to Al Cody (think of Cody, Wyoming, and Buffalo Bill Cody), however, and you've got a winner. The romance writer Elaine Carr is really a man named Charles Mason.

The main reason for taking a pseudonym is because it just sounds better. It's more appealing and memorable. Which has a better ring—Charles Lutwidge Dodson or Lewis Carroll? Reginald Kenneth Dwight or Elton John? Ralph Lifshitz or Ralph Lauren? Norma Jean Baker or Marilyn Monroe?

So why am I still troubled today that the beautiful and talented Patsy changed her name? I assumed that by adopting a new name, Patsy was trying to get rid of her past—her old friends, the neighborhood, even the scrawny seven-year-old kid who gazed at her from behind the plants.

Patsy, Norma Jean, Reginald—they probably all had good reasons for choosing new names. I hope when they changed their names, they held on tight to their roots. I agree with writer James Baldwin, who said, "Know from whence you came. If you know from whence you came, there are absolutely no limitations to where you can go."

—Joan Burditt

Reginald Dwight/Elton John

Caryn Elaine Johnson/ Whoopi Goldberg

Analyzing an Author's Perspective

What's <u>Really</u> in a Name?

Test Practice

1. The writer of this essay believes that —
   - **A** people should feel free to change their names
   - **B** it's important to remember where you came from
   - **C** William Sydney Porter was guilty of stealing money
   - **D** writers should use pseudonyms if they want to sell books

2. A writer's **perspective** is —
   - **F** his or her point of view on a subject
   - **G** a story the writer tells to entertain readers
   - **H** a sequence of related events
   - **J** the words a writer chooses

3. This essay was written in order to —
   - **A** explain a process
   - **B** describe a place
   - **C** compare several ideas
   - **D** express an opinion

4. The writer's **perspective** was *most* influenced by —
   - **F** Whoopi Goldberg
   - **G** her sister's friend Patsy
   - **H** James Baldwin
   - **J** William Sydney Porter

Constructed Response

1. What is a pseudonym? What is another expression for *pseudonym*?

2. According to this writer, what is the main reason people take pseudonyms?

3. Explain how the quotation from James Baldwin at the end of the essay supports the writer's feelings about pseudonyms.

4. How would you state the **author's perspective** on changing your name? Does she think it is a good idea?

HELLO my name is Jack

SKILLS FOCUS

Reading Skills
Analyze an author's perspective.

Bargain

Make the Connection
Quickwrite ✏

With a partner, discuss these questions: What is the difference between justice and revenge? What do these two concepts have in common? What are some examples of each? Jot down your responses so you can refer to them at the end of the story.

Literary Focus
First-Person Point of View

When you are telling a story about something that happened to you, you use *I.* You say, "I was late for practice because the dog got out." You tell your story from the **first-person point of view.** The story "Bargain" is also told from the first-person point of view. It is told by Al, a character in the story who is about thirteen years old.

When a story is told from the first-person point of view, two important things happen. First, we share directly the narrator's thoughts and feelings. Second, we know *only* what the narrator knows. All we learn about the story's events and the other characters comes from the narrator's observations.

Historical Fiction

This story takes place in Moon Dance, a town where we have all been in our imagination. You will recognize Moon Dance from TV and movie westerns—its muddy street, its saloon, and its general store. This story is a kind of **historical fiction.** Setting is important in historical fiction. This writer wants you to feel what it was like to live in a rough frontier town. If you took away Moon Dance and all the historical details, you'd have a different story.

Reading Skills
Making Predictions: What Will Happen Next?

Part of the fun of reading is trying to guess what will happen next. This process is called making **predictions.** Here is how you make predictions:

- Look for clues that **foreshadow,** or hint at, what will happen.

- As the suspense builds, predict possible outcomes. See if you can guess where the writer is leading you.

- Ask yourself questions while you read. Revise your predictions as you go.

- Draw on your own experiences and knowledge in making your predictions.

Remember: A good writer often surprises you.

You will find questions in this story that ask about predictions. Look for the open-book signs.

SKILLS FOCUS

Literary Skills
Understand first-person point of view; understand historical fiction.

Reading Skills
Make predictions.

BARGAIN

A. B. Guthrie

He was a man you wouldn't remember from meeting once.

Mr. Baumer and I had closed the Moon Dance Mercantile Company and were walking to the post office, and he had a bunch of bills in his hand ready to mail. There wasn't anyone or anything much on the street because it was suppertime. A buckboard[1] and a saddle horse were tied at Hirsches' rack, and a rancher in a wagon rattled for home ahead of us, the sound of his going fading out as he prodded his team. Freighter[2] Slade stood alone in front of the Moon Dance Saloon, maybe wondering whether to have one more before going to supper. People said he could hold a lot without showing it except in being ornerier[3] even than usual.

Mr. Baumer didn't see him until he was almost on him, and then he stopped and fingered through the bills until he found the right one. He stepped up to Slade and held it out.

Slade said, "What's this, Dutchie?"

Mr. Baumer had to tilt his head up to talk to him. "You know vat it is."

Slade just said, "Yeah?" You never could tell from his face what went on inside his

---

1. **buckboard** *n.:* open carriage.
2. **freighter** *n.* used as *adj.:* here, person who transports goods.

---

3. **ornerier** (ôr'nər·ē·ər) *adj.:* dialect for "meaner and more stubborn."

Bargain 369

skull. He had dark skin and shallow cheeks and a thick-growing moustache that fell over the corners of his mouth.

"It is a bill," Mr. Baumer said. "I tell you before, it is a bill. For twenty-vun dollars and fifty cents."

"You know what I do with bills, don't you, Dutchie?" Slade asked.

Mr. Baumer didn't answer the question. He said, "For merchandise."

Slade took the envelope from Mr. Baumer's hand and squeezed it up in his fist and let it drop on the plank sidewalk. Not saying anything, he reached down and took Mr. Baumer's nose between the knuckles of his fingers and twisted it up into his eyes. That was all. That was all at the time. Slade half turned and slouched to the door of the bar and let himself in. Some men were laughing in there. **❶**

PREDICT
❶ What part do you suppose Slade will play in this story?

Mr. Baumer stooped and picked up the bill and put it on top of the rest and smoothed it out for mailing. When he straightened up, I could see tears in his eyes from having his nose screwed around.

He didn't say anything to me, and I didn't say anything to him, being so much younger and feeling embarrassed for him. He went into the post office and slipped the bills in the slot, and we walked on home together. At the last, at the crossing where I had to leave him, he remembered to say, "Better study, Al. Is good to know to read and write and figure." I guess he felt he had to push me a little, my father being dead. **❷**

INFER
❷ What kind of a person is Mr. Baumer? How is he different from Slade?

I said, "Sure. See you after school tomorrow"—which he knew I would anyway. I had been working in the store for him during the summer and after classes ever since pneumonia took my dad off.

Three of us worked there regularly: Mr. Baumer, of course, and me and Colly Coleman, who knew enough to drive the delivery wagon but wasn't much help around the store except for carrying orders out to the rigs[4] at the hitchpost and handling heavy things like the whiskey barrel at the back of the store which Mr. Baumer sold quarts and gallons out of.

The store carried quite a bit of stuff—sugar and flour and dried fruits and canned goods and such on one side and yard goods and coats and caps and aprons and the like of that on the other, besides kerosene and bran and buckets and linoleum and pitchforks in the storehouse at the rear—but it wasn't a big store like Hirsch Brothers up the street. Never would be, people guessed, going on to say, with a sort of slow respect, that it would have gone under long ago if Mr. Baumer hadn't been half mule and half beaver. He had started the store just two years before and, the way things were, worked himself close to death.

He was at the high desk at the end of the grocery counter when I came in the next afternoon. He had an eyeshade on and black sateen protectors on his forearms, and his pencil was in his hand instead of behind his ear and his glasses were roosted on the nose that Slade had twisted. He didn't hear me open and close the door or hear my feet as I walked back to him, and I saw he wasn't doing anything with the pencil but holding

---

4. **rigs** *n.*: carriages with their horses.

"I think he hate me. That is the thing. He hate me for coming not from this country...."

it over paper. I stood and studied him for a minute, seeing a small, stooped man with a little paunch bulging through his unbuttoned vest. He was a man you wouldn't remember from meeting once. There was nothing in his looks to set itself in your mind unless maybe it was his chin, which was a small pink hill in the gentle plain of his face.

While I watched him, he lifted his hand and felt carefully of his nose. Then he saw me. His eyes had that kind of mistiness that seems to go with age or illness, though he wasn't really old or sick, either. He brought his hand down quickly and picked up the pencil, but he saw I still was looking at the nose, and finally he sighed and said, "That Slade."

Just the sound of the name brought Slade to my eye. I saw him slouched in front of the bar, and I saw him and his string[5] coming down the grade from the buttes,[6] the wheel horses held snug and the rest lined out pretty, and then the string leveling off and Slade's whip lifting hair from a horse that wasn't up in the collar.[7] I had heard it said that Slade could make a horse scream with that whip. Slade's name wasn't Freighter, of course. Our town had nicknamed

---

5. **string** *n.:* here, a group of horses.
6. **buttes** (byo͞ots)*n.:* steep, flat-topped hills that stand alone on a plain.
7. **up in the collar:** pulling as hard as the other horses.

---

him that because that was what he was.

"I don't think it's any good to send him a bill, Mr. Baumer," I said. "He can't even read."

"He could pay yet."

"He don't pay anybody," I said.

"I think he hate me," Mr. Baumer went on. "That is the thing. He hate me for coming not from this country. I come here, sixteen years old, and learn to read and write, and I make a business, and so I think he hate me."

"He hates everybody."

Mr. Baumer shook his head. "But not to pinch the nose. Not to call Dutchie."

The side door squeaked open, but it was only Colly Coleman coming in from a trip, so I said, "Excuse me, Mr. Baumer, but you shouldn't have trusted him in the first place."

"I know," he answered, looking at me with his misty eyes. "A man make mistakes. I think some do not trust him, so he will pay me because I do. And I do not know him well then. He only came back to town three, four months ago, from being away since before I go into business."

"People who knew him before could have told you," I said.

"A man make mistakes," he explained again.

"It's not my business, Mr. Baumer, but I would forget the bill."

His eyes rested on my face for a long

minute, as if they didn't see me but the problem itself. He said, "It is not twenty-vun dollars and fifty cents now, Al. It is not that anymore."

"What is it?"

He took a little time to answer. Then he brought his two hands up as if to help him shape the words. "It is the thing. You see, it is the thing."

I wasn't quite sure what he meant.

He took his pencil from behind the ear where he had put it and studied the point of it. "That Slade. He steal whiskey and call it evaporation. He sneak things from his load. A thief, he is. And too big for me." ❸

PREDICT
❸ What do you think will happen between Mr. Baumer and Slade?

I said, "I got no time for him, Mr. Baumer, but I guess there never was a freighter didn't steal whiskey. That's what I hear."

It was true, too. From the railroad to Moon Dance was fifty miles and a little better—a two-day haul in good weather, heck knew how long in bad. Any freight string bound home with a load had to lie out at least one night. When a freighter had his stock tended to and maybe a little fire going against the dark, he'd tackle a barrel of whiskey or of grain alcohol if he had one aboard consigned to Hirsch Brothers or Mr. Baumer's or the Moon Dance Saloon or the Gold Leaf Bar. He'd drive a hoop out of place, bore a little hole with a nail or bit and draw off what he wanted. Then he'd plug the hole with a whittled peg and pound the hoop back. That was evaporation. Nobody complained much. With freighters you generally took what they gave you, within reason.

"Moore steals it, too," I told Mr. Baumer. Moore was Mr. Baumer's freighter.

"Yah," he said, and that was all, but I stood there for a minute, thinking there might be something more. I could see thought swimming in his eyes, above that little hill of chin. Then a customer came in, and I had to go wait on him. ❹

INFER
❹ What do you guess Baumer is thinking? Why do you think this writer keeps mentioning his chin?

Nothing happened for a month, nothing between Mr. Baumer and Slade, that is, but fall drew on toward winter and the first flight of ducks headed south and Mr. Baumer hired Miss Lizzie Webb to help with the just-beginning Christmas trade and here it was, the first week in October, and he and I walked up the street again with the monthly bills. He always sent them out. I guess he had to. A bigger store, like Hirsches', would wait on the ranchers until their beef or wool went to market.

Up to a point things looked and happened almost the same as they had before, so much the same that I had the crazy feeling I was going through that time again. There was a wagon and a rig tied up at Hirsches' rack and a saddle horse standing hipshot[8] in front of the harness shop. A few more people were on the street now, not many, and lamps had been lit against the shortened day.

It was dark enough that I didn't make out Slade right away. He was just a figure that came out of the yellow wash of light from the Moon Dance Saloon and stood on the boardwalk and with his head made the little

_____

8. **hipshot** *adv.:* with one hip lower than the other.

The Apprentice by Robert Duncan.

Courtesy of the Artist.

motion of spitting. Then I recognized the lean, raw shape of him and the muscles flowing down into the sloped shoulders, and in the settling darkness I filled the picture in—the dark skin and the flat cheeks and the peevish eyes and the moustache growing rank.

There was Slade and here was Mr. Baumer with his bills and here I was, just as before, just like in the second go-round of a bad dream. I felt like turning back, being embarrassed and half scared by trouble even when it wasn't mine. Please, I said to myself, don't stop, Mr. Baumer! Don't bite off anything! Please, shortsighted the way you are, don't catch sight of him at all! I held up and stepped around behind Mr. Baumer and came up on the outside so as to be between him and Slade, where maybe I'd cut off his view.

But it wasn't any use. All along I think I knew it was no use, not the praying or the walking between or anything. The act had to play itself out.

Mr. Baumer looked across the front of me and saw Slade and hesitated in his step and came to a stop. Then in his slow, business way, his chin held firm against his mouth, he began fingering through the bills, squinting to make out the names. Slade had turned and was watching him, munching on a cud of tobacco like a bull waiting.

"You look, Al," Mr. Baumer said without lifting his face from the bills. "I cannot see so good."

So I looked, and while I was looking, Slade must have moved. The next I knew, Mr. Baumer was staggering ahead, the envelopes spilling out of his hands. There had been a thump, the clap of a heavy hand swung hard on his back.

Slade said, "Haryu, Dutchie?"

Mr. Baumer caught his balance and turned around, the bills he had trampled shining white between them and at Slade's feet the hat that Mr. Baumer had stumbled out from under.

Slade picked up the hat and scuffed through the bills and held it out. "Cold to be goin' without a skypiece," he said.

Mr. Baumer hadn't spoken a word. The lampshine from inside the bar caught his eyes, and in them, it seemed to me, a light came and went as anger and the uselessness of it took turns in his head.

Two men had come up on us and stood watching. One of them was Angus McDonald, who owned the Ranchers' Bank, and the other was Dr. King. He had his bag in his hand.

Two others were drifting up, but I didn't have time to tell who. The light came in Mr. Baumer's eyes, and he took a step ahead and swung. I could have hit harder myself. The fist landed on Slade's cheek without hardly so much as jogging his head, but it let the devil loose in the man. I didn't know he could move so fast. He slid in like a practiced fighter and let Mr. Baumer have it full in the face.

Mr. Baumer slammed over on his back, but he wasn't out. He started lifting himself. Slade leaped ahead and brought a boot heel down on the hand he was lifting himself by. I heard meat and bone under that heel and saw Mr. Baumer fall back and try to roll away.

Things had happened so fast that not until then did anyone have a chance to get between them. Now Mr. McDonald pushed at Slade's chest, saying, "That's enough, Freighter. That's enough, now," and Dr. King lined up, too, and another man I didn't know, and I took a place, and we formed a kind of screen between them. Dr. King turned and bent to look at Mr. Baumer.

"Fool hit me first," Slade said.

"That's enough," Mr. McDonald told him again while Slade looked at all of us as if he'd spit on us for a nickel. Mr. McDonald went on, using a half-friendly tone, and I knew it was because he didn't want to take Slade on any more than the rest of us did. "You go on home and sleep it off, Freighter. That's the ticket."

Slade just snorted.

From behind us, Dr. King said, "I think you've broken this man's hand."

"Lucky for him I didn't kill him," Slade answered. "Dutch penny pincher!" He fingered the chew out of his mouth. "Maybe he'll know enough to leave me alone now."

Dr. King had Mr. Baumer on his feet. "I'll take him to the office," he said.

Blood was draining from Mr. Baumer's nose and rounding the curve of his lip and dripping from the sides of his chin. He held his hurt right hand in the other. But the thing was that he didn't look beaten even then, not the way a man who has given up looks beaten. Maybe that was why Slade said, with a show of that fierce anger, "You stay away from me! Hear? Stay clear away, or you'll get more of the same!" ❺

Dr. King led Mr. Baumer away, Slade went back into

PREDICT

❺ What clues suggest that Baumer will not give up? How could he get even with Slade?

the bar, and the other men walked off, talking about the fight. I got down and picked up the bills, because I knew Mr. Baumer would want me to, and mailed them at the post office, dirty as they were. It made me sorer, someway, that Slade's bill was one of the few that wasn't marked up. The cleanness of it seemed to say that there was no getting the best of him.

Mr. Baumer had his hand in a sling the next day and wasn't much good at waiting on the trade. I had to hustle all afternoon and so didn't have a chance to talk to him even if he had wanted to talk. Mostly he stood at his desk, and once, passing it, I saw he was practicing writing with his left hand. His nose and the edges of the cheeks around it were swollen some.

At closing time I said, "Look, Mr. Baumer, I can lay out of school a few days until you kind of get straightened out here."

"No," he answered as if to wave the subject away. "I get somebody else. You go to school. Is good to learn."

I had a half notion to say that learning hadn't helped him with Slade. Instead, I blurted out that I would have the law on Slade.

"The law?" he asked.

"The sheriff or somebody."

"No, Al," he said. "You would not."

I asked why.

"The law, it is not for plain fights," he said. "Shooting? Robbing? Yes, the law come quick. The plain fights, they are too many. They not count enough."

He was right. I said, "Well, I'd do something anyhow."

"Yes," he answered with a slow nod of his head. "Something you vould do, Al." He didn't tell me what.

Within a couple of days he got another man to clerk for him—it was Ed Hempel, who was always finding and losing jobs—and we made out. Mr. Baumer took his hand from the sling in a couple or three weeks, but with the tape on it, it still wasn't any use to him. From what you could see of the fingers below the tape, it looked as if it never would be.

He spent most of his time at the high desk, sending me or Ed out on the errands he used to run, like posting and getting the mail. Sometimes I wondered if that was because he was afraid of meeting Slade. He could just as well have gone himself. He wasted a lot of hours just looking at nothing, though I will have to say he worked hard at learning to write left-handed.

Then, a month and a half before Christmas, he hired Slade to haul his freight for him.

Ed Hempel told me about the deal when I showed up for work.

PREDICT

6 Why do you suppose Baumer has hired Slade again?

"Yessir," he said, resting his foot on a crate in the storeroom where we were supposed to be working. "I tell you he's throwed in with Slade. Told me this morning to go out and locate him if I could and bring him in. Slade was at the saloon, o' course, and says to the devil with Dutchie, but I told him this was honest-to-God business, like Baumer had told me to, and there was a quart of whiskey right there in the store for him if he'd come and get it. He was out of money, I reckon, because the quart fetched him."

"What'd they say?" I asked him.

"Search me. There was two or three people in the store and Baumer told me to

The Fall of the Cowboy (1895) by Frederic S. Remington. Oil on canvas.
© Amon Carter Museum, Fort Worth, Texas (1961.230).

wait on 'em, and he and Slade palavered[9] back by the desk."

"How do you know they made a deal?"

Ed spread his hands out. "'Bout noon, Moore came in with his string, and I heard Baumer say he was makin' a change. Moore didn't like it too good, either."

It was a hard thing to believe, but there one day was Slade with a pile of stuff for the Moon Dance Mercantile Company, and that was

---

9. **palavered** (pə·lav′ərd) *v.:* talked; met to discuss something.

proof enough with something left for boot.

Mr. Baumer never opened the subject up with me, though I gave him plenty of chances. And I didn't feel like asking. He didn't talk much these days but went around absent-minded, feeling now and then of the fingers that curled yellow and stiff out of the bandage like the toes on the leg of a dead chicken. Even on our walks home he kept his thoughts to himself.

I felt different about him now and was sore inside. Not that I blamed him exactly. A hundred and thirty-five pounds wasn't much to throw against two hundred. And who could tell what Slade would do on a bellyful of whiskey? He had promised Mr. Baumer more of the same, hadn't he? But I didn't feel good. I couldn't look up to Mr. Baumer like I used to and still wanted to. I didn't have the beginning of an answer when men cracked jokes or shook their heads in sympathy with Mr. Baumer, saying Slade had made him come to time.

Slade hauled in a load for the store, and another, and Christmastime was drawing on and trade heavy, and the winter that had started early and then pulled back came on again. There was a blizzard and then a still cold and another blizzard and afterwards a sunshine that was iceshine on the drifted snow. I was glad to be busy, selling over-shoes and sheep-lined coats and mitts and socks as thick as saddle blankets and Christmas candy out of buckets and hickory nuts and the fresh oranges that the people in our town never saw except when Santa Claus was coming.

One afternoon, when I lit out from class, the thermometer on the school porch read forty-two degrees below. But you didn't have to look at it to know how cold the weather was. Your nose and fingers and toes and ears and the bones inside you told you. The snow cried when you stepped on it.

I got to the store and took my things off and scuffed my hands at the stove for a minute so's to get life enough in them to tie a parcel. Mr. Baumer—he was always polite to me—said, "Hello, Al. Not so much to do today. Too cold for customers." He shuddered a little, as if he hadn't got the chill off even yet, and rubbed his broken hand with the good one. "Ve need Christmas goods," he said, looking out the window to the furrows that wheels had made in the snow-banked street, and I knew he was thinking of Slade's string, inbound from the railroad, and the time it might take even Slade to travel those hard miles.

Slade never made it at all.

Less than an hour later our old freighter, Moore, came in, his beard white and stiff with frost. He didn't speak at first but looked around and clumped to the stove and took off his heavy mitts, holding his news inside him.

Then he said, not pleasantly, "Your new man's dead, Baumer."

"My new man?" Mr. Baumer said.

"Who do you think? Slade. He's dead."

All Mr. Baumer could say was "Dead!"

"Froze to death, I figger," Moore told him, while Colly Coleman and Ed Hempel and Miss Lizzie and I and a couple of customers stepped closer.

"Not Slade," Mr. Baumer said. "He know too much to freeze."

"Maybe so, but he sure's froze now. I got him in the wagon."

We stood looking at one another and at Moore. Moore was enjoying his news, enjoying feeding it out bit by bit so's to hold the stage. "Heart might've give out, for all I know."

The side door swung open, letting in a cloud of cold and three men who stood, like us, waiting on Moore. I moved a little and looked through the window and saw Slade's freight outfit tied outside with more men around it. Two of them were on a wheel of one of the wagons, looking inside.

"Had a extra man, so I brought your stuff in," Moore went on. "Figgered you'd be glad to pay for it."

"Not Slade," Mr. Baumer said again.

Only the moustache seemed still alive, sprouting thick like greasewood from alkali.

"You can take a look at him."

Mr. Baumer answered no.

"Someone's takin' word to Connor to bring his hearse. Anyhow, I told 'em to. I carted old Slade this far. Connor can have him now."

Moore pulled on his mitts. "Found him there by the Deep Creek crossin', doubled up in the snow an' his fire out." He moved toward the door. "I'll see to the horses, but your stuff'll have to set there. I got more'n enough work to do at Hirsches'."

Mr. Baumer just nodded.

I put on my coat and went out and waited my turn and climbed on a wagon wheel and looked inside, and there was Slade piled on some bags of bran. Maybe because of being frozen, his face was whiter than I ever saw it, whiter and deader, too, though it never had been lively. Only the moustache seemed still alive, sprouting thick like greasewood from alkali.[10] Slade was doubled up all right, as if he had died and stiffened leaning forward in a chair.

I got down from the wheel, and Colly and then Ed climbed up. Moore was unhitching, tossing off his pieces of information while he did so. Pretty soon Mr. Connor came up with his old hearse, and he and Moore tumbled Slade into it, and the team, which was as old as the hearse, made off, the tires squeaking in the snow. The people trailed on away with it, their breaths leaving little ribbons of mist in the air. It was beginning to get dark.

Mr. Baumer came out of the side door of the store, bundled up, and called to Colly and Ed and me. "We unload," he said. "Already is late. Al, better you get a couple lanterns now."

We did a fast job, setting the stuff out of the wagons onto the platform and then carrying it or rolling it on the one truck that the store owned and stowing it inside according to where Mr. Baumer's good hand pointed.

A barrel was one of the last things to go in. I edged it up and Colly nosed the truck under it, and then I let it fall back. "Mr. Baumer," I said, "we'll never sell all this, will we?"

"Yah," he answered. "Sure we sell it. I get it cheap. A bargain, Al, so I buy it."

I looked at the barrel head again. There in big letters I saw "Wood Alcohol—Deadly Poison."

"Hurry now," Mr. Baumer said. "Is late." For a flash and no longer I saw through the mist in his eyes, saw, you might say, that hilly chin repeated there. "Then ve go home, Al. Is good to know to read." ❼

---

10. **greasewood from alkali:** Greasewood is a thorny desert plant. Alkali is dry, salty soil that might look white and chalky, like Slade's face.

INFER
❼ What happened to Slade?

Meet the Writer

A. B. Guthrie

"Real People in Real Times"

A. B. Guthrie (1901–1991) wanted to portray the West as it was, not create myths about it. He said:

> 66 I want to talk about real people in real times. For every Wyatt Earp or Billy the Kid, there were thousands of people just trying to get along. 99

Most readers agree that Guthrie succeeded. His most famous work, a trilogy about the opening of the West, is noted for its historical accuracy. Guthrie also wrote the screenplay for *Shane,* a famous movie about a western gunslinger. Shane takes justice into his own hands to save a family and pays a bitter price.

Albert Bertram Guthrie, Jr., grew up in the little town of Choteau, Montana. After graduating from college, he traveled extensively and worked at various jobs—ranching in Sonora, Mexico; selling groceries in California; working as a census taker in Montana.

Guthrie became a fiction writer when he took time out from his newspaper job to visit his sick mother. During his visit he had time to write his first novel, *Murders at Moon Dance* (1943). In this book he introduces the setting of "Bargain" and many of his other short stories. In talking about writing, Guthrie said:

> 66 There's no immediate reward in putting words on paper. The reward, great but fugitive, is in having written, in having found the word, the line, the paragraph, the chapter that is as good as ever you can make it. I spent a full day on one line of dialogue and knocked off satisfied. 99

For Independent Reading

Guthrie's novels about the opening of the West are *The Big Sky; The Way West,* which won the Pulitzer Prize; and *These Thousand Hills.*

First Thoughts

1. What do you think of what Baumer does to Slade? Does he do the right thing? Why or why not?

Thinking Critically

2. Look again at your Quickwrite notes. Would you say this story is about justice or about revenge? Explain. ✏️

3. When Al suggests that Mr. Baumer forget Slade's bill, Mr. Baumer says that it isn't the money anymore; it is "the thing." What do you think Mr. Baumer means by "the thing"?

4. At what point in the story did you **predict** what was going to happen next? Go back now, and identify the details that provide clues to Slade's fate.

5. Why does Baumer say at the end, "Is good to know to read"?

6. **Theme** sums up what the characters learn or discover in the story and what you learn or discover as you share their experiences. What do you think the theme of "Bargain" is?

Extending Interpretations

7. "Bargain" is written in the **first-person point of view,** from Al's vantage point. What would you have known if Mr. Baumer had told the story himself? Would the story's **theme** change? If so, what might the new theme be?

Reading Check

Suppose that Al decides he has to confide to someone what he knows about Baumer's feud with Slade and the likely cause of Slade's death. He chooses to tell the whole story to Dr. King. With a partner, role-play Al and Dr. King. As Al tells what happened, Dr. King should comment and ask questions. Be sure to cover all the **main events** in the story.

go.hrw.com

INTERNET

Projects and Activities

Keyword: LE5 7-4

SKILLS FOCUS

Literary Skills
Analyze first-person point of view.

Reading Skills
Make predictions.

Writing Skills
Write persuasive arguments.

WRITING

Summarizing the Cases For and Against Mr. Baumer

Imagine that Mr. Baumer is put on trial for causing Slade's death. In one paragraph, **summarize** the case *for* Mr. Baumer. Present evidence to show that Slade is responsible for his own death. This would be the case for the defense. In another paragraph, summarize the case *against* Mr. Baumer. Give reasons and evidence to inform and convince the jury that Mr. Baumer is guilty. This would be the case for the prosecution.

Vocabulary Development

Comprehension Strategies: Tips for Word Detectives

When you come across a word you don't know and the nearest dictionary is far, far away, use these tips to unlock its meaning.

- **Look to see if parts of the word are familiar.**
  In "Bargain," Mr. Baumer's store is called the Moon Dance Mercantile Company. In figuring out *mercantile*, you might think of the word *merchant*. A merchant is someone, like Mr. Baumer, who sells goods, or merchandise. *Merchandise, merchant,* and *mercantile* all come from the Latin word *mercari,* which means "to trade."

- **Look at the word's context—the surrounding words and sentences—to see if it helps you figure out what the word means.**
  For example, what if a friend said, "I consigned my old bike to be sold at the bicycle store. They sold it for fifty dollars, kept their fee of twenty dollars, and gave me thirty." The context helps you figure out that the word *consign* means "turn goods over to someone else to sell." Your friend had a storekeeper sell his bike, and he gave the store part of the money.

PRACTICE

1. In "Bargain," Colly carries customers' orders out to carriages waiting at the hitchpost. How would you figure out the meaning of *hitchpost*?

2. Use context clues to figure out the meaning of *screen* in this sentence: "Dr. King lined up, too, and another man I didn't know, and I took a place, and we formed a kind of screen between them [Slade and Mr. Baumer]."

SKILLS FOCUS

vocabulary Skills
Use comprehension strategies.

Yeh-Shen

Make the Connection
Talk It Over

What popular story features these characters, object, and theme?

- a hardworking girl
- a wicked stepmother
- a special slipper
- Good is rewarded eventually, and evil is punished.

You probably know those characters and the theme from the fairy tale "Cinderella." "Cinderella" and "Yeh-Shen" are two versions of the same story, about a girl whose dream comes true.

Discussion. People around the world have been telling the Cinderella story for ages. In a small group, talk about why you think the story of "Cinderella" is such a favorite. What do people like about the story? What deep human wishes do you think it expresses? As you read this Chinese folk tale, keep a sheet of paper handy so that you can jot down your reactions.

INTERNET
Cross-curricular Connection
Keyword: LE5 7-4

Literary Focus
Omniscient Point of View

The omniscient (äm·nish′ənt) point of view is probably very familiar to you.

You've heard it in fairy tales since you were young. A narrator who tells a story from the **omniscient point of view** knows everything about the characters and their problems. This omniscient narrator isn't *in* the story. This narrator can't even be seen. In fact, an omniscient, or all-knowing, narrator stands above the action, like a god.

Fish, from an album of twelve studies of flowers, birds, and fish by Tsubaki Chinzan (1801–1854). Watercolor on silk with patterned border.

British Library, London, UK/Bridgeman Art Library.

SKILLS FOCUS

Literary Skills
Understand omniscient point of view.

Background
Literature and Literary History

There are more than nine hundred versions of "Cinderella." Scholars have traced the oldest version back more than a thousand years, to China. The version that you probably know best was collected in 1697 by a French writer named Charles Perrault. His is the first version to include a fairy godmother and a midnight curfew. "Yeh-Shen" is a Chinese version of the Cinderella story.

Carp (1848) by Taito.
Courtesy of the Board of Trustees of the Victoria and Albert Museum, London.

YEH-SHEN

Chinese folk tale, retold by Ai-Ling Louie

THE ONLY FRIEND THAT YEH-SHEN HAD WAS A FISH . . .

In the dim past, even before the Ch'in and the Han dynasties, there lived a cave chief of southern China by the name of Wu. As was the custom in those days, Chief Wu had taken two wives. Each wife in her turn had presented Wu with a baby daughter. But one of the wives sickened and died, and not too many days after that Chief Wu took to his bed and died too.

Yeh-Shen, the little orphan, grew to girlhood in her step-mother's home. She was a bright child and lovely too, with skin as smooth as ivory and dark pools for eyes. Her stepmother was jealous of all this beauty and goodness, for her own daughter was not pretty at all. So in her displeasure, she gave poor Yeh-Shen the heaviest and most unpleasant chores.

The only friend that Yeh-Shen had to her name was a fish she had caught and raised. It was a beautiful fish with golden eyes, and every day it would come out of the water and rest its head on the bank of the pond, waiting for Yeh-Shen to feed it. Stepmother gave Yeh-Shen little enough food for herself, but the orphan child always found something to share with her fish, which grew to enormous size.

Somehow the stepmother heard of this. She was terribly angry to discover that Yeh-Shen had kept a secret from her. She hurried down to the pond, but she was unable to see the fish, for Yeh-Shen's pet wisely hid itself. The stepmother, however, was a crafty woman, and she soon thought of a plan. She walked home and called out, "Yeh-Shen, go and collect some firewood. But wait! The neighbors might see you. Leave your filthy coat here!" The minute the girl was out of sight, her stepmother slipped on the coat herself and went down again to the pond. This time the big fish saw Yeh-Shen's familiar jacket and heaved itself onto the bank, expecting to be fed. But the stepmother, having hidden a dagger in her sleeve, stabbed the fish, wrapped it in her garments, and took it home to cook for dinner.

When Yeh-Shen came to the pond that evening, she found her pet had disappeared. Overcome with grief, the girl collapsed on the ground and dropped her tears into the still waters of the pond.

"Ah, poor child!" a voice said.

Yeh-Shen sat up to find a very old man looking down at her. He wore the coarsest of clothes, and his hair flowed down over his shoulders.

"Kind uncle, who may you be?" Yeh-Shen asked.

"That is not important, my child. All you must know is that I have been sent to tell you of the wondrous powers of your fish."

"My fish, but sir . . ." The girl's eyes filled with tears, and she could not go on.

The old man sighed and said, "Yes, my

Carp with Bogbean by Sadatora (19th century).

British Library, London, UK/Bridgeman Art Library.

child, your fish is no longer alive, and I must tell you that your stepmother is once more the cause of your sorrow." Yeh-Shen gasped in horror, but the old man went on. "Let us not dwell on things that are past," he said, "for I have come bringing you a gift. Now you must listen carefully to this: The bones of your fish are filled with a powerful spirit. Whenever you are in serious need, you must kneel before them and let them know your heart's desire. But do not waste their gifts."

Yeh-Shen wanted to ask the old sage many more questions, but he rose to the sky before she could utter another word. With heavy heart, Yeh-Shen made her way to the dung heap to gather the remains of her friend.

Time went by, and Yeh-Shen, who was often left alone, took comfort in speaking to the bones of her fish. When she was hungry, which happened quite often, Yeh-Shen asked the bones for food. In this way, Yeh-Shen managed to live from day to day, but she lived in dread that her stepmother would discover her secret and take even that away from her.

So the time passed and spring came. Festival time was approaching: It was the busiest time of the year. Such cooking and cleaning and sewing there was to be done! Yeh-Shen had hardly a moment's rest. At the spring festival young men and young women from the village hoped to meet and to choose whom they would marry. How Yeh-Shen longed to go! But her stepmother had other plans. She hoped to find a husband for her own daughter and did not want any man to see the beauteous Yeh-Shen first. When finally the holiday arrived, the stepmother and her daughter dressed themselves in their finery and filled their baskets with sweetmeats. "You must remain at home now and watch to see that no one steals fruit from our trees," her stepmother told Yeh-Shen, and then she departed for the banquet with her own daughter.

As soon as she was alone, Yeh-Shen went to speak to the bones of her fish. "Oh, dear friend," she said, kneeling before the precious bones, "I long to go to the festival, but I cannot show myself in these rags. Is there somewhere I could borrow clothes fit to wear to the feast?" At once she found herself dressed in a gown of azure[1] blue, with a cloak of kingfisher feathers draped around her shoulders. Best of all, on her tiny feet were the most beautiful slippers she had ever seen. They were woven of golden threads, in a pattern like the scales of a fish, and the glistening soles were made of solid gold. There was magic in the shoes, for they should have been quite heavy, yet when Yeh-Shen walked, her feet felt as light as air.

"Be sure you do not lose your golden shoes," said the spirit of the bones. Yeh-Shen promised to be careful. Delighted with her transformation, she bid a fond farewell to the bones of her fish as she slipped off to join in the merrymaking.

That day Yeh-Shen turned many a head as she appeared at the feast. All around her people whispered, "Look at that beautiful girl! Who can she be?"

But above this, Stepsister was heard to say, "Mother, does she not resemble our Yeh-Shen?"

---

1. **azure** (azhʹər) *adj.*: like the color of the sky.

Upon hearing this, Yeh-Shen jumped up and ran off before her stepsister could look closely at her. She raced down the mountainside, and in doing so, she lost one of her golden slippers. No sooner had the shoe fallen from her foot than all her fine clothes turned back to rags. Only one thing remained—a tiny golden shoe. Yeh-Shen hurried to the bones of her fish and returned the slipper, promising to find its mate. But now the bones were silent. Sadly Yeh-Shen realized that she had lost her only friend. She hid the little shoe in her bedstraw and went outside to cry. Leaning against a fruit tree, she sobbed and sobbed until she fell asleep.

The stepmother left the gathering to check on Yeh-Shen, but when she returned home, she found the girl sound asleep, with her arms wrapped around a fruit tree. So, thinking no more of her, the stepmother rejoined the party. Meantime, a villager had found the shoe. Recognizing its worth, he sold it to a merchant, who presented it in turn to the king of the island kingdom of T'o Han.

The king was more than happy to accept the slipper as a gift. He was entranced by the tiny thing, which was shaped of the most precious of metals, yet which made no sound when touched to stone. The more he marveled at its beauty, the more determined he became to find the woman to whom the shoe belonged. A search was begun among the ladies of his own kingdom, but all who tried on the sandal found it impossibly small. Undaunted, the king ordered the search widened to include the cave women from the countryside where the slipper had been found. Since he realized it would take many years for every woman to come to his island and test her foot in the slipper, the king thought of a way to get the right woman to come forward. He ordered the sandal placed in a pavilion[2] by the side of the road near where it had been found, and his herald[3] announced that the shoe was to be returned to its original owner. Then, from a nearby hiding place, the king and his men settled down to watch and wait for a woman with tiny feet to come and claim her slipper.

All that day the pavilion was crowded with cave women who had come to test a foot in the shoe. Yeh-Shen's stepmother and stepsister were among them, but not Yeh-Shen—they had told her to stay home. By day's end, although many women had eagerly tried to put on the slipper, it still had not been worn. Wearily, the king continued his vigil into the night.

It wasn't until the blackest part of night, while the moon hid behind a cloud, that Yeh-Shen dared to show her face at the pavilion, and even then she tiptoed timidly across the wide floor. Sinking down to her knees, the girl in rags examined the tiny shoe. Only when she was sure that this was the missing mate to her own golden slipper did she dare pick it up. At last she could return both little shoes to the fish bones. Surely then her beloved spirit would speak to her again.

Now the king's first thought, on seeing Yeh-Shen take the precious slipper, was to throw the girl into prison as a thief. But when she turned to leave, he caught a glimpse of her face. At once the king was struck by the sweet harmony of her

---

2. **pavilion** *n.*: large tent or shelter, often highly decorated.
3. **herald** *n.*: the person in a king's court who makes official announcements.

Free Library, Philadelphia, PA./Bridgeman Art Library.

Three Fish (detail) by Belshu.
Color woodblock print.

features, which seemed so out of keeping with the rags she wore. It was then that he took a closer look and noticed that she walked upon the tiniest feet he had ever seen.

With a wave of his hand, the king signaled that this tattered creature was to be allowed to depart with the golden slipper. Quietly, the king's men slipped off and followed her home.

All this time, Yeh-Shen was unaware of the excitement she had caused. She had made her way home and was about to hide both sandals in her bedding when there was a pounding at the door. Yeh-Shen went to see who it was—and found a king at her doorstep. She was very frightened at first, but the king spoke to her in a kind voice and asked her to try the golden slippers on her feet. The maiden did as she was told, and as she stood in her golden shoes, her rags were transformed once more into the feathered cloak and beautiful azure gown.

Her loveliness made her seem a heavenly being, and the king suddenly knew in his heart that he had found his true love.

Not long after this, Yeh-Shen was married to the king. But fate was not so gentle with her stepmother and stepsister. Since they had been unkind to his beloved, the king would not permit Yeh-Shen to bring them to his palace. They remained in their cave home, where one day, it is said, they were crushed to death in a shower of flying stones.

Meet the Writer

Ai-Ling Louie

It Runs in the Family

Ai-Ling Louie (1949–) remembers hearing the story "Yeh-Shen," the Chinese version of "Cinderella," from her grandmother. Louie became curious about the origins of this story, which had been told in her family for three generations, so she did

some research. She learned that the tale was first written down by Tuan Cheng-shi in an ancient Chinese manuscript during the Tang dynasty (A.D. 618–907) and had probably been handed down orally for centuries before that.

First Thoughts

1. Think about the discussion you had before you read this story. Which of our deepest wishes do you think this story expresses? Is it also about some of our fears? Explain.

Thinking Critically

2. Which of the following statements best sums up the **theme** "Yeh-Shen" reveals?

   • Goodness is rewarded in the end.
   • Bad people are always punished.
   • Love comes to those who deserve it.
   • Jealousy can lead to tragedy.

   Do you think this is a good **theme** for today? Explain.

3. Check the story to see what you learn about Yeh-Shen's step-mother. How would the story change if the stepmother, instead of the **omniscient narrator,** were telling it?

Extending Interpretations

4. Suppose a reviewer of this textbook said, "I don't think the publisher should include this story because it's outdated. Girls don't sit around and wait to be rescued any longer." Do you agree or disagree with the decision to include this story in the textbook? Explain.

WRITING

Writing a Modern Cinderella Story

Imagine a Cinderella/Yeh-Shen story set today in your own community. Who would the underdog be? Who or what would hold the underdog back? Who would rescue the underdog, and how would this happen? With a group of classmates, brainstorm to come up with some ideas. Then, plot out your story. You could act out your modern Cinderella story or videotape the production for your class.

Reading Check

a. Who is Yeh-Shen's only friend?
b. What does her stepmother do to Yeh-Shen's friend?
c. A very old man gives Yeh-Shen some advice about the bones of her fish. What is it?
d. What happens when Yeh-Shen runs away from the festival?
e. How does the king find Yeh-Shen?

INTERNET
Projects and Activities
Keyword: LE5 7-4

Literary Skills
Analyze omniscient point of view.

Writing Skills
Write a story.

Tracing an Author's Argument

Reading Focus
Presenting an Argument: Agree with Me

Argument can mean "angry disagreement." Yeh-Shen may have wanted to argue with her nasty stepmother on many occasions. You argue with your friends about all kinds of things, from who should be class president to what music should be played at a dance.

Here the word *argument* is used to mean "debate or discussion." Writers who present an argument are trying to persuade you to think or act in a certain way. They may want you to agree with their opinions, vote for their candidates, buy their products, or support their causes.

Skillful persuaders use solid **evidence** to back up their arguments. They cite **facts** (statements that can be proved true) and **statistics** (number facts).

Skillful persuaders often quote **experts** to convince you that an argument is sound.

When you finish reading a text that presents an argument, ask yourself

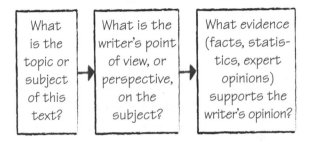

| What is the topic or subject of this text? | → | What is the writer's point of view, or perspective, on the subject? | → | What evidence (facts, statistics, expert opinions) supports the writer's opinion? |

When you read a persuasive essay, you must trace the writer's use of evidence. You want to be certain that the evidence is valid and that it is strong. After all, if you are going to accept someone's argument, you want to be sure it is a good one.

■ The notes beside the selection that follows will help you trace the author's argument.

SKILLS FOCUS

Reading Skills
Trace an author's argument.

Mirror, Mirror, on the Wall,
Do I See Myself As Others Do?

TRACING A
WRITER'S
ARGUMENT

A The writer opens with an anecdote, a brief story used to make a point.

B The writer wonders how kids feel about their appearance and conducts interviews.

Two weeks ago I was watching a local news story about the lottery. The film footage showed a young woman standing behind the store counter selling lottery tickets. She had short blond hair, big sparkling eyes, and a huge smile. I recognized her as the woman who worked in the corner drugstore down the street. The next day I walked into the store and said, "Hey, I saw you on TV last night. You looked great." She made a disgusted face.

"I told them not to film me."

"Why not?"

"Because I look so . . ." She puffed out her cheeks. *"Fat!"*

I didn't know what to say. So I just repeated, "Well, you looked great." **A**

I thought, "Here is a shining light of a woman who thinks she looks too bad to be on television for five seconds." So I decided to interview some middle-school and high school students to see if they, like this woman, feel bad about the way they look. Unfortunately, the answer became obvious very quickly. **B**

"Lots of kids think they weigh more than they look," said one ninth-grader. "Everyone wants to be size zero. Sometimes even someone who wears size zero says, 'I feel so fat.' It's hard for some people to feel really good about themselves."

It's easy to see why people feel this way, especially kids. Watch television or flip through a magazine. The females look as though they haven't had a decent meal in months. The males look as though they could be hit in the stomach by a freight train and not even feel it.

I turned every page of a popular teen magazine for girls and counted advertisements for makeup and clothes. Out of 220 pages, 70 were advertisements. That's about one third of the magazine devoted to influencing the way kids dress and look. **C**

Statistics show that models in advertisements are 9 percent taller and 23 percent thinner than the average woman. With the click of a mouse, computers can create a picture of the perfect face by cleaning up a model's complexion, trimming her chin, and getting rid of lines around her eyes. Here's a news flash: She's not a real person, folks. She's an illusion. **D**

Other students I interviewed talked about the importance of wearing certain brands of clothing. These clothes display a brand name somewhere, whether it's plastered in three-inch type across the front or appears on a tiny logo on the sleeve. A middle-school student said, "Sometimes I just want to wear a pair of sweatpants and a T-shirt, but if you do, you're looked down on. The way you dress classifies you—it shows what group you're in. You can walk down the hall and tell who different people hang out with just by looking at their clothes." **E**

If you're thinking I interviewed some pretty insecure kids, you're wrong. A study conducted by the American Association of University Women found that in elementary school 60 percent of girls and 67 percent of boys had high self-esteem—they felt good about themselves. But by the time kids are in high school, self-esteem in girls drops to only 29 percent, compared with self-esteem in boys, which drops to 46 percent. **F**

The good news is that some things may be changing for the better. One middle-school girl reported being on the volleyball and basketball teams. Unlike girls just one generation ago, she can go out for any sport she wants. After an amazing spike or a skillful dribble down the basketball court, however, this beautiful, strong fifteen-year-old still says, "Sometimes you can see yourself as others see you. But if someone says they think I'm pretty, I don't believe them." **G**

Start believing it. Remember what Eleanor Roosevelt said: "No one can make you feel inferior without your consent." **H**

—Joan Burditt

C The writer says that many advertisements in magazines tell kids how they should look.

D The writer says that models don't look like real people—especially when a computer perfects the picture!

E The writer interviewed kids who say that wearing brand-name clothes influences how other kids respond to them.

F The writer cites statistics that show that kids' self-esteem drops in high school.

G The writer says that sports may not help improve girls' self-esteem.

H The writer ends with a quotation that backs up her argument.

Analyzing an Author's Argument

Mirror, Mirror, on the Wall . . .

Test Practice

1. You can tell from this article that the writer believes that —

   A students feel tremendous pressure to look a certain way

   B teen magazines do not influence the way teenagers feel about their appearance

   C parents should keep their children from reading magazines that have models in them

   D students should wear uniforms to school so they won't worry so much about their appearance

2. Which of the following statements uses **statistics** to support a position?

   F I'll bet most students who are thin feel fat.

   G Students feel they have to wear a certain brand of clothing.

   H Models in advertisements are 9 percent taller and 23 percent thinner than the average woman.

   J Computers can change the way people look in photographs.

3. Which type of **evidence** does the writer use to support her point that brand names on clothing are important to many students?

   A An anecdote

   B An interview

   C An expert's opinion

   D A magazine article

4. What is the *most likely* reason the author wrote this essay?

   F To change readers' views about their appearance

   G To tell a story about the woman who works in the drugstore

   H To interview students about the clothes they wear

   J To explain why sports improve girls' self-esteem

5. Which statement is a **fact**—a statement that can be proved true?

   A Everyone wants to be thin.

   B Out of 220 pages, 70 were advertisements.

   C No one can make you feel inferior without your consent.

   D The females look as though they haven't eaten in months.

Constructed Response

1. How does the opening anecdote relate to the writer's main point?

2. What is the **topic,** or subject, of this article?

3. What is the writer's **perspective,** or point of view, on this subject?

Names / Nombres

Make the Connection
Quickwrite

Write about your given name, family name, or nickname. Explain how you got your name and how you feel about it. Is your name an accurate representation of who you are?

Main idea

Literary Focus
Point of View: Subjective or Objective?

Has anyone ever said to you, "Don't take it personally"? Well, some writers do take their writing personally. Writers who treat their subject **subjectively** share their own feelings, thoughts, opinions, and judgments. We find **subjective writing** in personal essays and autobiographies and in the editorial pages of a newspaper, where we expect writers to express opinions about news events.

   Objective writing, on the other hand, tends to be unbiased and presents the facts and figures rather than the writer's private feelings. The purpose of objective writing is to inform.

Reading Skills
Discovering the Main Idea: It's in the Details

All the important details in an article or essay add up to a **main idea.** A main idea is the central idea, the one that the writer wants you to remember. In some pieces of writing, like "Names/ Nombres," the writer **implies,** or suggests, the main idea. You have to

infer, or guess, the point that the writer is getting at. To infer a main idea, follow these steps:

- Identify the important details in the selection.
- Think about the point that the important details make.
- Use this information to figure out what the main idea is. State the main idea in your own words.

Vocabulary Development

Practice using these words before you read about Julia Alvarez's problem with her name:

ethnicity (eth·nis′ə·tē) *n.:* common culture or nationality. *Julia's ethnicity was important to her friends.*

exotic (eg·zät′ik) *adj.:* foreign; not native. *At her graduation party, Julia's family served exotic dishes.*

heritage (her′ə·tij) *n.:* traditions that are passed along. *Julia remained proud of her Dominican heritage.*

convoluted (kän′və·lōōt′id) *adj.:* complicated. *The grammar of a new language often seems convoluted.*

INTERNET

Vocabulary Activity
•
More About Alvarez

Keyword: LE5 7-4

Literary Skills
Understand objective and subjective points of view.

Reading Skills
Find the main idea.

Names/Nombres

JULIA ALVAREZ

A name as chaotic with sounds as a Middle Eastern bazaar...

When we arrived in New York City, our names changed almost immediately. At Immigration, the officer asked my father, *Mister Elbures,* if he had anything to declare. My father shook his head no, and we were waved through.

I was too afraid we wouldn't be let in if I corrected the man's pronunciation, but I said our name to myself, opening my mouth wide for the organ blast of the *a,* trilling my tongue for the drumroll of the *r,* *All-vah-rrr-es!* How could anyone get *Elbures* out of that orchestra of sound?

At the hotel my mother was *Missus Alburest,* and I was *little girl,* as in, "Hey, little girl, stop riding the elevator up and down. It's *not* a toy."

When we moved into our new apartment building, the super called my father *Mister Alberase,* and the neighbors who became mother's friends pronounced her name *Jew-lee-ah* instead of *Hoo-lee-ah.* I, her namesake, was known as *Hoo-lee-tah* at home. But at school I was *Judy* or *Judith,* and once an English teacher mistook me for *Juliet.*

It took a while to get used to my new names. I wondered if I shouldn't correct my teachers and new friends. But my mother argued that it didn't matter. "You know what your friend Shakespeare said, '*A rose by any other name would smell as sweet.*'"[1] My family had gotten into the habit of calling any famous author "my friend" because I had begun to write poems and stories in English class.

By the time I was in high school, I was a popular kid, and it showed in my name. Friends called me *Jules* or *Hey Jude,* and once a group of troublemaking friends my mother forbade me to hang out with called me *Alcatraz.* I was *Hoo-lee-tah* only to Mami and Papi and uncles and aunts who came over to eat sancocho[2] on Sunday afternoons—old world folk whom I would just as soon go back to where they came from and leave me to pursue whatever mischief I wanted to in America. *JUDY ALCATRAZ,* the name on the "Wanted" poster would read. Who would ever trace her to me?

My older sister had the hardest time getting an American name for herself because *Mauricia* did not translate into English. Ironically, although she had the most foreign-sounding name, she and I were the Americans in the family. We had been born in New York City when our parents had first tried immigration and then gone back "home," too homesick to stay. My mother often told the story of how she had almost changed my sister's name in the hospital.

After the delivery, Mami and some other new mothers were cooing over their new baby sons and daughters and exchanging names and weights and delivery stories. My mother was embarrassed among the Sallys and Janes and Georges and Johns to reveal the rich, noisy name of *Mauricia,* so when her turn came to brag, she gave her baby's name as *Maureen.*

"Why'd ya give her an Irish name with so many pretty Spanish names to choose from?" one of the women asked.

My mother blushed and admitted her baby's real name to the group. Her mother-in-law had recently died, she apologized, and her husband had insisted that the first daughter be named after his mother,

---

1. **"A rose . . . as sweet":** Julia's mother is quoting from the play *Romeo and Juliet.*

2. **sancocho** (sän·kō'chō) *adj.:* stew of meats and fruit.

Mauran. My mother thought it the ugliest name she had ever heard, and she talked my father into what she believed was an improvement, a combination of *Mauran* and her own mother's name, *Felicia.*

"Her name is *Mao-ree-shee-ah,*" my mother said to the group of women.

"Why, that's a beautiful name," the new mothers cried. "*Moor-ee-sha, Moor-ee-sha,*" they cooed into the pink blanket. *Moor-ee-sha* it was when we returned to the States eleven years later. Sometimes, American tongues found even that mispronunciation tough to say and called her *Maria* or *Marsha* or *Maudy* from her nickname *Maury.* I pitied her. What an awful name to have to transport across borders!

My little sister, Ana, had the easiest time of all. She was plain *Anne*—that is, only her name was plain, for she turned out to be the pale, blond "American beauty" in the family. The only Hispanic thing about her was the affectionate nicknames her boyfriends sometimes gave her. *Anita,* or, as one goofy guy used to sing to her to the tune of the banana advertisement, *Anita Banana.*

Later, during her college years in the late sixties, there was a push to pronounce Third World[3] names correctly. I remember calling her long distance at her group house and a roommate answering.

"Can I speak to Ana?" I asked, pronouncing her name the American way.

"Ana?" The man's voice hesitated. "Oh! You must mean *Ah-nah!*"

Our first few years in the States, though, ethnicity was not yet "in." Those were the blond, blue-eyed, bobby-sock years of junior high and high school before the sixties ushered in peasant blouses, hoop earrings, serapes.[4] My initial desire to be known by my correct Dominican name faded. I just wanted to be Judy and merge with the Sallys and Janes in my class. But, inevitably, my accent and coloring gave me away. "So where are you from, Judy?"

"New York," I told my classmates. After all, I had been born blocks away at Columbia-Presbyterian Hospital.

"I mean, *originally.*"

"From the Caribbean," I answered vaguely, for if I specified, no one was quite sure on what continent our island was located.

"Really? I've been to Bermuda. We went last April for spring vacation. I got the worst sunburn! So, are you from Portoriko?"

"No," I sighed. "From the Dominican Republic."

"Where's that?"

"South of Bermuda."

They were just being curious, I knew, but I burned with shame whenever they singled me out as a "foreigner," a rare, exotic friend.

"Say your name in Spanish, oh, please say it!" I had made mouths drop one day by rattling off my full name, which, according to Dominican custom, included my middle names, Mother's and Father's surnames for four generations back.

"Julia Altagracia María Teresa Álvarez Tavares Perello Espaillat Julia Pérez Rochet

---

4. **serapes** (sə·rä′pēs) *n.:* woolen shawls worn in Latin American countries.

Vocabulary
ethnicity (eth·nis′ə·tē) *n.:* common culture or nationality.
exotic (eg·zät′ik) *adj.:* foreign; not native.

---

3. **Third World:** developing countries of Latin America, Africa, and Asia.

González." I pronounced it slowly, a name as chaotic with sounds as a Middle Eastern bazaar or market day in a South American village.

My Dominican heritage was never more apparent than when my extended family attended school occasions. For my graduation, they all came, the whole lot of aunts and uncles and the many little cousins who snuck in without tickets. They sat in the first row in order to better understand the Americans' fast-spoken English. But how could they listen when they were constantly speaking among themselves in florid-sounding[5] phrases, rococo[6] consonants, rich, rhyming vowels?

Introducing them to my friends was a further trial to me. These relatives had such complicated names and there were so many of them, and their relationships to myself were so convoluted. There was my Tía[7] Josefina, who was not really an aunt but a much older cousin. And her daughter, Aida Margarita, who was adopted, una hija de crianza.[8] My uncle of affection, Tío José, brought my madrina[9] Tía Amelia and her comadre[10] Tía Pilar. My friends rarely had more than a "Mom and Dad" to introduce.

After the commencement ceremony, my family waited outside in the parking lot while my friends and I signed yearbooks with nicknames which recalled our high school good times: "Beans" and "Pepperoni" and "Alcatraz." We hugged and cried and promised to keep in touch.

Our goodbyes went on too long. I heard my father's voice calling out across the parking lot, "*Hoo-lee-tah!* Vámonos!"[11]

Back home, my tíos and tías and primas,[12] Mami and Papi, and mis hermanas[13] had a party for me with sancocho and a store-bought pudín,[14] inscribed with *Happy Graduation, Julie.* There were many gifts—that was a plus to a large family! I got several wallets and a suitcase with my initials and a graduation charm from my godmother and money from my uncles. The biggest gift was a portable typewriter from my parents for writing my stories and poems.

Someday, the family predicted, my name would be well-known throughout the United States. I laughed to myself, wondering which one I would go by.

---

5. **florid-sounding:** flowery; using fancy words.
6. **rococo** (rə·kō′kō) *adj.:* fancy. Rococo is an early-eighteenth-century style of art and architecture known for its fancy ornamentation.
7. **Tía** (tē′ä) *n.:* Spanish for "aunt." *Tío* is "uncle."
8. **una hija de crianza** (ōō′nä ē′hä de krē·än′sä): Spanish for "an adopted daughter." *Crianza* means "upbringing."
9. **madrina** (mä·drē′nä) *n.:* Spanish for "godmother."
10. **comadre** (kô·mä′drä) *n.:* informal Spanish for "close friend." *Comadre* is the name used by the mother and the godmother of a child for each other.

---

11. **Vámonos!** (vä′mô·nôs): Spanish for "Let's go!"
12. **primas** (prē′mäs) *n.:* Spanish for "female cousins."
13. **mis hermanas** (mēs er·mä′näs): Spanish for "my sisters."
14. **pudín** (pōō·dēn′) *n.:* Spanish cake.

Vocabulary

heritage (her′ə·tij) *n.:* traditions that are passed along.

convoluted (kän′və·lōōt′id) *adj.:* complicated.

Meet the Writer

Julia Alvarez

"Just Do Your Work and Put in Your Heart"

Born in New York City, **Julia Alvarez** (1950–　　) spent her childhood in the Dominican Republic, returning with her family to New York when she was ten years old. Adjusting to her new surroundings in the early 1960s wasn't easy for young Julia:

> 66 I can tap into that struggling English speaker, that skinny, dark-haired, olive-skinned girl in a sixth grade of mostly blond and blue-eyed giants. Those tall, freckled boys would push me around in the playground. 'Go back to where you came from!' 'No comprendo!' I'd reply, though of course there was no misunderstanding the fierce looks on their faces. 99

Despite the difficulties, being an immigrant gave Julia a special point of view. "We [immigrants] travel on that border between two worlds," she explains, "and we can see both points of view." Later, as a writer, she used those sometimes conflicting perspectives— American and Latino—to describe

Photograph by Cameron Davidson.

brilliantly the cultures of the United States and the Dominican Republic.

After college and graduate school, Alvarez taught poetry for twelve years in Kentucky, California, Vermont, Washington, D.C., and Illinois. Now she lives in Vermont, where she writes novels and teaches at Middlebury College.

> 66 Day to day, I guess I follow my papi's advice. When we first came [to the United States], he would talk to his children about how to make it in our new country. 'Just do your work and put in your heart, and they will accept you!' 99

After You Read Response and Analysis

First Thoughts

1. Think back to what you said about your own names in your notes for the Quickwrite. How has reading "Names/Nombres" affected your ideas about your names?

Thinking Critically

2. As a teenager, why does Julia want to be called Judy? How do you think her attitude has changed since then?

3. Why do you think the writer gave this piece the title "Names/Nombres" instead of just "Names" (or just "Nombres")? What connection do you see between this title and Alvarez's comment about being "on that border between two worlds"?

4. What would you say is the **main idea** of "Names/Nombres"? List three significant details or quotations from the story that you think back up the main idea.

5. Is this essay **subjective** or **objective**? How do you know?

Extending Interpretations

6. "Names/Nombres" includes many Spanish words and phrases. In your opinion, do they make it harder for non-Spanish speakers to read the essay, or do they add something valuable to it? Explain.

WRITING

Writing an Essay

Research all your names to find out what you can about them—first, middle, and last names, plus any other names you've been given as part of your ethnic or religious heritage. You could begin by interviewing your family members to record what they know. Then, check the name books at your library. See if you can learn the origins of all your names. Write about your search and its results in a short essay.

Reading Check

Julia Alvarez has been known by the different names listed below. Explain who uses each name or group of names and what the names mean to Alvarez.

- "little girl"
- Julita (pronounced hōō•lē'tä)
- Judith/Juliet
- Jules/Jude
- Alcatraz
- Judy
- Julia Altagracia María Teresa Álvarez Tavares Perello Espaillat Julia Pérez Rochet González
- Julia Alvarez

INTERNET
Projects and Activities
Keyword: LE5 7-4

SKILLS FOCUS

Literary Skills
Analyze objective and subjective points of view.

Reading Skills
Find the main idea.

Writing Skills
Write an essay.

Vocabulary Development

Clarifying Word Meanings: Using Definitions

Writers often help us understand difficult words by providing definitions right in the context.

A writer who uses **definition** will explain what a word means right in the sentence or passage. For example, in the following sentence the writer clarifies the meaning of *tía* by defining it later in the sentence.

> "There was my Tía Josefina, who was not really my aunt but a much older cousin."

Be on the lookout for such phrases as *in other words* and *that is* when looking for definitions of words right in context.

PRACTICE

Complete the following sentences, using definition to clarify the meanings of the words from the Word Bank.

1. The dress was definitely <u>exotic</u>—that is, it was
   _____.

2. Francis's explanation of his science project had grown <u>convoluted</u>. In other words, it was _____.

3. The street festival was planned to introduce visitors to the city's <u>heritage</u>, or _____.

4. Studies have shown that <u>ethnicity</u>, meaning _____ , influences the kinds of programs we watch on television.

> **Word Bank**
>
> *ethnicity*
> *exotic*
> *heritage*
> *convoluted*

SKILLS FOCUS

Vocabulary Skills
Clarify word meanings by using definitions.

Don't Leave Your Modifiers Dangling

It's easy to make the mistake of "hanging" a modifying phrase on a sentence (usually at the beginning) and forgetting to include the word it modifies:

DANGLING **Arriving in New York City, *our names* changed almost immediately.**

Who arrived in New York City? It sounds as if the names came on their own!

Phrases that hang, or dangle, on a sentence without clearly modifying a word are called **dangling modifiers.** You can correct a dangling modifier by adding, subtracting, or rearranging words:

CLEAR **Arriving in New York City, *we* noticed that our names changed almost immediately.**

The first sentence of "Names/Nombres" shows an even better solution:

CLEAR **"When *we* arrived in New York City, our names changed almost immediately."**

PRACTICE

Find and fix the dangling modifiers in these sentences. You will have to rewrite some of the sentences.

1. Wanting to encourage me, my graduation present was a typewriter.

2. Born in New York City, it was easier for me to adjust to America.

3. Looking back on it now, the incident was funny.

Exchange a sample of your writing with a partner. Then, act as a dangler detector. Read your partner's work carefully to be sure every sentence makes sense and every modifier or phrase modifies something. Your first step should be to identify the modifying phrases (with the permission of the writer, use a colored pen). Dangling modifiers usually appear—or dangle—at the beginning of a sentence.

For more help, see Placement of Modifiers, 5g, in the Language Handbook.

SKILLS FOCUS

Grammar Skills
Avoid dangling modifiers.

An Unforgettable Journey

Make the Connection
Quickwrite ✏️

What do you know about the Vietnam War, which was fought in Southeast Asia from 1957 to 1975? Jot down some of the facts that you know about the war. One fact might have to do with the famous memorial in Washington, D.C.

Literary Focus
Autobiography: Telling You My Story

The most personal kind of writing is autobiographical writing. An **autobiography** is the story of a person's life written by that very person. In this kind of writing, you get inside the writer's mind, and you learn about his or her most personal thoughts, feelings, and ideas. Because of this, autobiographical writing is **subjective** (see page 393).

Reading Skills 📖
Distinguishing Fact from Opinion

When you read an autobiography, it's important to be able to tell facts from opinions. A **fact** can be proved true. *The Mekong River flows through Laos* is a fact. It is a statement that can be confirmed by looking at a map.

An **opinion** can be supported by facts, but it can't be proved true or false: *The friendliest people in Southeast Asia are from Laos.* In autobiographical essays, such as "An Unforgettable Journey," writers share their opinions, but they also present facts.

Be careful: People may state an opinion as if it were a fact. If you're in doubt, ask yourself, "Can this statement be proved, or is it someone's personal feeling or belief?"

Vocabulary Development

Knowing these words will make your journey through this autobiography easier:

refuge (ref′yo͞oj) *n.:* shelter; protection. *Maijue's family sought refuge in the jungle.*

transition (tran·zish′ən) *n.:* change; passing from one condition to another. *The transition from a peaceful village to the jungle was extremely difficult.*

persecution (pur′sə·kyo͞o′shən) *n.:* act of willfully injuring or attacking others because of their beliefs or their ethnic backgrounds. *Because some Hmong worked against the Communists, they faced persecution.*

refugee (ref′yo͞o·jē′) *n.* used as *adj.:* person who flees home or country to escape war or persecution. *A refugee family may not be welcome anywhere.*

deprivation (dep′rə·vā′shən) *n.:* loss; condition of having something taken away by force. *They suffered from constant deprivation of food.*

INTERNET

Vocabulary Activity

Keyword: LE5 7-4

SKILLS FOCUS

Literary Skills
Understand autobiography.

Reading Skills
Distinguish fact from opinion.

Pre-1975 Laos and
Southeast Asia.

Maijue's sister
on her mother's
lap, 1971.

War often leads to the uprooting and exile of thousands of innocent civilians on the losing side. Such was the fate suffered by the Hmong (muŋ) people of Southeast Asia. Most of the Hmong had supported the United States in its fight against the Communist forces in Vietnam and Laos. In 1975, when the Communists finally won, one third of the Hmong people fled Laos to escape the victor's revenge. Some 135,000 Hmong ended up in the United States. By the war's end, some thirty thousand Hmong men, women, and children had perished.

The autobiographical article that follows is one of several Hmong life stories collected by Sucheng Chan, a teacher at the University of California, Santa Barbara. Maijue Xiong was one of the students who served as her collaborators. The book that the teacher and her students put together is called Hmong Means Free: Life in Laos and America.

AN UNFORGETTABLE JOURNEY

Maijue Xiong

I was born in a small village called Muong Cha in Laos on April 30, 1972. At the time I was born, my father was a soldier actively fighting alongside the American Central Intelligence Agency° against the Communists. Although a war was in progress, life seemed peaceful. We did not think of ever leaving Laos, but one day our lives were changed forever. We found ourselves without a home or a country and with a need to seek refuge in another country. This period of relocation involved a lot of changes, adjustments, and adaptations. We experienced changes in our language, customs, traditional values, and social status. Some made the transition quickly; others have never fully adjusted. The changes my family and I experienced are the foundation of my identity today.

After Laos became a Communist country in 1975, my family, along with many others, fled in fear of persecution. Because my father had served as a commanding officer for eleven years with the American Central Intelligence Agency in what is known to the American public as the "Secret War," my family had no choice but to leave immediately. My father's life was in danger, along with those of thousands of others. We were forced to leave loved ones behind, including my grandmother, who was ill in bed the day we fled our village. For a month, my family walked through the dense tropical jungles and rice fields, along rugged trails through many mountains, and battled the powerful Mekong River. We traveled in silence at night and slept in the daytime. Children were very hard to keep quiet. Many parents feared the

°**Central Intelligence Agency:** organization that helps protect the United States by gathering information about foreign governments and carrying out secret operations; also known by its initials, CIA.

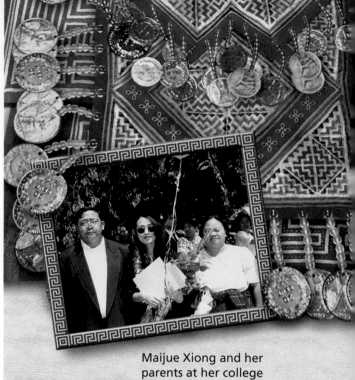

Maijue Xiong and her parents at her college graduation, June 1995.

The illustrations with this story include examples of traditional Hmong needlework. These items are worn as part of the Hmong traditional costume.

Communist soldiers would hear the cries of their children; therefore, they drugged the children with opium to keep them quiet. Some parents even left those children who would not stop crying behind. Fortunately, whenever my parents told my sisters and me to keep quiet, we listened and obeyed.

I do not remember much about our flight, but I do have certain memories that have been imprinted in my mind. It is all so unclear—the experience was like a bad dream: When you wake up, you don't

Vocabulary
refuge (ref′yo͞oj) *n.:* shelter; protection.
transition (tran·zish′ən) *n.:* change; passing from one condition to another.
persecution (pʉr′sə·kyo͞o′shən) *n.:* act of willfully injuring or attacking (even murdering) others because of their beliefs or ethnic backgrounds.

Maijue dressed in traditional Hmong costume.

The Xiong family in Lompoc, 1993. Maijue is in the front row, far right.

of red ants and being a stubborn child, I refused to walk over them. I wanted someone to pick me up because I was scared, but my parents kept walking ahead. They kept telling me to hurry up and to step over the ants, but I just stood there and cried. Finally, my father came back and put me on his shoulders, along with the heavy sack of rice he was carrying. . . .

After experiencing many cold days and rainy nights, we finally saw Thailand on the other side of the Mekong River. My parents bribed several fishermen to row us across. The fishermen knew we were desperate, yet, instead of helping us, they took advantage of us. We had to give them all our valuables: silver bars, silver coins, paper money, and my mother's silver wedding necklace, which had cost a lot of money. When it got dark, the fishermen came back with a small fishing boat and took us across the river. The currents were high and powerful. I remember being very scared. I kept yelling, "We're going to fall out! We're going to fall into the river!" My mom tried to reassure me but I kept screaming in fear. Finally, we got across safely. My family, along with many other families, were picked up by the Thai police and taken to an empty bus station for the night.

After a whole month at this temporary refugee camp set up in the bus station, during which we ate rice, dried fish, roots we dug up, and bamboo shoots we cut down, and drank water from streams, we were in very poor shape due to the lack of

remember what it was you had dreamed about but recall only those bits and pieces of the dream that stand out the most. I remember sleeping under tall trees. I was like a little ant placed in a field of tall grass, surrounded by dense jungle with trees and bushes all around me—right, left, in the back, and in front of me. I also remember that it rained a lot and that it was cold. We took only what we could carry and it was not much. My father carried a sack of rice, which had to last us the whole way. My mother carried one extra change of clothing for each of us, a few personal belongings, and my baby sister on her back. My older sister and I helped carry pots and pans. My stepuncle carried water, dried meat, and his personal belongings.

From the jungles to the open fields, we walked along a path. We came across a trail

Vocabulary
refugee (ref'yōō·jē') *n.* used as *adj.:* person who flees home or country to escape war or persecution.

nutrition. Our feet were also swollen from walking. We were then taken to a refugee camp in Nongkhai, where disease was rampant and many people got sick. My family suffered a loss: My baby sister, who was only a few months old, died. She had become very skinny from the lack of milk, and there was no medical care available. The memory of her death still burns in my mind like a flame. On the evening she died, my older sister and I were playing with our cousins outside the building where we stayed. My father came out to tell us the sad news and told us to go find my stepuncle. After we found him, we went inside and saw our mother mourning the baby's death. Fortunately, our family had relatives around to support and comfort us. . . .

Our family life in the camp was very unstable, characterized by <u>deprivation</u> and neglect. My older sister and I were left alone for days while my parents were outside the camp trying to earn money to buy extra food. My parents fought a lot during this period, because we were all under such stress. They knew that if we remained in Thailand, there would be no telling what would become of us. We had to find a better life. Some people in the camp were being sponsored to go to the United States. The news spread that anyone who had served in the military with the CIA could apply to go to America. Since my stepuncle had already gone there two years earlier, he sponsored my family. Because my father had been in the military and we had a sponsor, it took only six months to process our papers when usually it took a year or more. . . .

It took a full day to travel to Bangkok, where we stayed for four nights. The building we stayed in was one huge room. It was depressing and nerve-racking. I especially remember how, when we got off the bus to go into the building, a small child about my age came up to my family to beg for food. I recall the exact words she said to my father, "Uncle, can you give me some food? I am hungry. My parents are dead and I am here alone." My dad gave her a piece of bread that we had packed for our lunch. After she walked away, my family found an empty corner and rolled out our bedding for the night. That night, the same child came around again, but people chased her away, which made me sad.

In the morning, I ran to get in line for breakfast. Each person received a bowl of rice porridge with a few strips of chicken in it. For four days, we remained in that building, not knowing when we could leave for the United States. Many families had been there for weeks, months, perhaps even years. On the fourth day, my family was notified to be ready early the next morning to be taken to the airport. The plane ride took a long time and I got motion sickness. I threw up a lot. Only when I saw my stepuncle's face after we landed did I know we had come to the end of our journey. We had come in search of a better life in the "land of giants."

On October 2, 1978, my family arrived at Los Angeles International Airport, where my uncle was waiting anxiously. We stayed with my uncle in Los Angeles for two weeks and then settled in Isla Vista because there were already a few Hmong families there. We knew only one family in Isla Vista, but later we met other families whom my parents had known in their village and from

Vocabulary

deprivation (dep′rə·vā′shən) n.: condition of having something taken away by force.

villages nearby. It was in Isla Vista that my life really began. My home life was now more stable. My mother gave birth to a boy a month after we arrived in the United States. It was a joyous event because the first three children she had were all girls. (Boys are desired and valued far more than girls in Hmong culture.) . . .

I entered kindergarten at Isla Vista Elementary School. The first day was scary because I could not speak any English. Fortunately, my cousin, who had been in the United States for three years and spoke English, was in the same class with me. She led me to the playground where the children were playing. I was shocked to see so many faces of different colors. The Caucasian students shocked me the most. I had never seen people with blond hair before. The sight sent me to a bench, where I sat and watched everyone in amazement. In class, I was introduced to coloring. I did not know how to hold a crayon or what it was for. My teacher had to show me how to color. I also soon learned the alphabet. This was the beginning of my lifelong goal to get an education. . . .

Now that I am older, I treasure the long but valuable lessons my parents tried to teach us—lessons that gave me a sense of identity as a Hmong. "Nothing comes easy . . . ," my parents always said. As I attempt to get a college education, I remember how my parents have been really supportive of me throughout my schooling, but because they never had a chance to get an education themselves, they were not able to help me whenever I could not solve a math problem or write an English paper. Although they cannot help me in my schoolwork, I know in my heart that they care about me and want me to be successful so that I can help them when they can no longer help themselves. Therefore, I am determined to do well at the university. I want to become a role model for my younger brother and sisters, for I am the very first member of my family to attend college. I feel a real sense of accomplishment to have set such an example.

Meet the Writer

Maijue Xiong

A Writer Who Can Never Forget

Maijue Xiong (mī′zhoo·ē sē·ôŋ′) (1972–   ) was a college student in the United States when she wrote this account of her family's flight from Laos. Xiong eventually earned degrees in sociology and Asian American studies at the University of California, Santa Barbara, where she helped found the Hmong Club to promote Laotian culture. An active member of the Asian Culture Committee, Xiong now lives in St. Paul, Minnesota, and teaches at HOPE Community Academy.

First Thoughts

1. Maijue Xiong describes experiences she had when she was only three years old. Often people do not remember events from such a young age. Why do you think Maijue Xiong's memories are so vivid?

Thinking Critically

2. What details in Maijue Xiong's narrative are **subjective**—that is, where does she reveal her feelings? What parts of the story are **objective**—that is, where is there straightforward factual reporting?

3. Maijue Xiong reveals some opinions about having to flee Laos, but she also presents facts. Give an example of a **fact** and an example of an **opinion** in her autobiography.

4. The **main idea** of an article is the most important idea, the one that the writer wants you to remember. Review the last paragraph on page 407. Then, decide what the main idea of this life story appears to be.

Extending Interpretations

5. For an account of the Hmong experiences during the Vietnam War, how would the **point of view** of a historian differ from the point of view of someone who experienced the events firsthand? How might the emotional impact of the story differ?

WRITING

Writing Up an Interview

Interview a family member or neighbor who lived during the Vietnam War. You don't have to interview a veteran of the war—just someone who remembers the period. (Check your Quickwrite notes first.) Before the interview, list the questions you want to ask. Bring pencil and paper to the interview or an audiotape recorder. (If you wish to use a recorder, be sure to ask your subject's permission to do so.) Write up your interview in dialogue form. 🖉

> **Reading Check**
>
> Make a time line like the following one, and fill in the main events of Maijue Xiong's life and journey. Be sure to list the events in the sequence in which they occurred:
>
> Maijue Xiong   Xiong family
> born   leaves Laos
>
> ├────────────┼──────────────┤
>
> 1972   1975

SKILLS FOCUS

Literary Skills
Analyze an autobiography.

Reading Skills
Distinguish fact from opinion.

Writing Skills
Write up an interview.

Vocabulary Development

Clarifying Meaning Through Contrast

Sometimes writers will clarify the meaning of a word by using **contrast** clues. A writer who uses contrast clues will show how a word is *unlike* another word or another situation. For example, you can get a good idea of what *apprehensive* means in the sentence below because you see it contrasted with *fearless*.

Be on the lookout for signal words that alert you to contrasts: *although, but, yet, still, unlike, not, in contrast, instead, however.*

> **The children were extremely apprehensive as they made their way through the dense jungle, but their parents seemed fearless.**

> **Word Bank**
>
> refuge
> transition
> persecution
> refugee
> deprivation

PRACTICE

In the following sentences the **contrast** clues point you to the meaning of each underlined word. Use the contrast clues to identify the meaning of each underlined word. All the words are from the Word Bank and are defined in the story.

1. Instead of finding a safe, warm refuge, they suffered exposure to wind and rain.
Meaning: _____
Clues: _____

2. In contrast to people who made a transition between cultures, some of the exiles never moved away from their own traditions.
Meaning: _____
Clues: _____

3. Although we expected persecution for our beliefs, we found acceptance.
Meaning: _____
Clues: _____

4. Refugees are unlike people who have homes and live in their own countries.
Meaning: _____
Clues: _____

5. People who have plenty of food and even luxuries cannot understand the deprivation experienced in the refugee camps.
Meaning: _____
Clues: _____

SKILLS FOCUS

Vocabulary Skills
Clarify word meanings by using contrast.

Understanding an Author's Purpose and Perspective

Reading Focus
Purpose and Perspective

People write nonfiction with many different purposes in mind. People who write political speeches are trying to **persuade** us to believe or do something. People who write articles in magazines often want to **inform** us about something. People who write personal narratives may want to **reveal a truth about life** or **share an experience.** In "An Unforgettable Journey," Maijue Xiong shares the dramatic experiences she had emigrating from Laos.

All writing reveals some kind of **perspective** on the world. The word *perspective* comes from the Latin *perspicere,* which means "to look at closely." Perspective in writing refers to the writer's point of view toward his or her topic. The writer says, in effect, "Here is what I think about this issue."

■ The personal narrative that follows is by the radio commentator Agate Nesaule. On meeting exiles from Bosnia who had settled in her hometown, Nesaule was reminded of her experiences as a World War II refugee. This piece was written for and broadcast on National Public Radio's *Morning Edition.*

INTERNET
Interactive
Reading Model
Keyword: LE5 7-4

Reading Skills
Understand an
author's
purpose and
perspective.

Background
Literature and Social Studies
The War in Bosnia

After World War II, Yugoslavia became a Communist state under the dictatorship of Tito. Bosnia, one of Yugoslavia's republics, was largely made up of three ethnic groups—Slavic Muslims, Croats, and Serbs. In 1980, after Tito died, a government representing the three groups emerged. Muslims and Croats favored independence for Bosnia; Serbs did not. In 1992, Bosnia seceded, or separated, from Yugoslavia. However, the Serbs living in Bosnia resisted. They wished to remain part of Yugoslavia and were backed by the Yugoslav National Army. A bitter struggle resulted, in which Serbs ruth-lessly expelled Muslims and Croats from the areas the Serbs controlled. This practice became known as ethnic cleansing. By late 1995, the conflict had produced an estimated two million refugees, the largest number of refugees in Europe since World War II.

The Commentator
Agate Nesaule fled Latvia during World War II. She was only six years old. Like many exiles from war-torn regions around the world, she found refuge in the United States. Nesaule now lives in Madison, Wisconsin. In this personal narrative she talks about the new exiles she has seen in Madison.

Exile Eyes

The beauty shop in Wisconsin where I get my hair cut looks very American. The owner is young and energetic; his sideburns remind me of Elvis Presley, and scissors and dryers dangle like guns from his black holster as he moves among the glass-and-chrome shelves. But one afternoon the place is so full of women and girls that I can hardly get in. With the exception of their uniform politeness in offering me their seats, there is nothing unusual about them. Only details of their clothes suggest other places and other times: Europe after World War II; Wisconsin and the Hmong people who settled here after Vietnam; the Baltic countries after the collapse of the Soviet Union.

A summer dress with a snugly fitting dark top has the bottom of ugly checked-brown flannel. A gathered gray polyester skirt is lengthened by a six-inch-wide insert of flowered print. And their shoes are startling in their flimsiness. These details speak to me of war and exile as eloquently as words. I'm afraid to look into the women's eyes, and when I finally do, it is as bad as I had expected. They all have exile eyes: eyes that have lost everything and seen the unspeakable but are determined to keep looking, eyes that remain weary and disillusioned even during shy giggles. I have seen those eyes before too, in photographs of the Latvian women who survived Siberia and Rwandan girls being questioned by a journalist, on the Chilean woman doctor who used to clean my house, on my mother. They all have eyes like that.

The owner waits patiently for their consent before he so much as snips a hair. Like them, he is from Bosnia. Under his skilled fingers, their crudely chopped-off tresses take on lovely, sleek shapes. A young woman smiles and makes a playful little bow for her new haircut, but her eyes do not change. I'm glad the Bosnian women are getting more elegant styles than my frizzy permanent at age twelve, when I believed that cutting off my braids would transform me into an American. They will have to do much more even than learn English, live among the poor and desperate, and find new friends and lovers. Acquaintances will ask them questions about their experiences but won't be able to stand hearing honest answers. And their longing for home will be confused with ingratitude to America. So much is ahead of them before their eyes lose their power to disturb.

—Agate Nesaule,
from National Public Radio,
Morning Edition

Analyzing an Author's Purpose and Perspective

Exile Eyes

Test Practice

1. One reason the writer identifies with the women in the beauty shop is that —

    A   she likes getting her hair cut

    B   she wears the same clothing

    C   they are from her own country

    D   she was an exile as well

2. We can tell from details in this personal narrative that the writer —

    F   is puzzled by the Bosnian women

    G   thinks that the women should wear different clothes

    H   made many mistakes when she was a refugee

    J   sympathizes with the Bosnian women

3. The **purpose** of this commentary is to —

    A   persuade us to support public radio

    B   inform us about current events

    C   persuade us to act in support of exiles

    D   reveal a truth about life

4. Which sentence best describes Nesaule's **perspective** on exiles?

    F   She feels sympathetic toward exiles.

    G   She is critical of the government.

    H   She doesn't understand the problems of exile.

    J   She feels hopeless about exile problems.

5. When the writer says in the last paragraph that she believed cutting off her braids would make her an American, she realizes that —

    A   haircuts make people feel better

    B   becoming an American is easy

    C   beauty is a universal quality

    D   feeling settled in a new country is difficult

Constructed Response

1. What details about the Bosnian women speak to the writer "of war and exile"?

2. How does Nesaule describe the women's "exile eyes"?

3. At the end of the commentary, Nesaule is probably speaking from her own experience when she describes what the Bosnian women will have to do as they transform themselves into Americans. List three things exiles have to do.

SKILLS FOCUS

Reading Skills
Analyze an author's purpose and perspective.

Elizabeth I

Make the Connection
Quickwrite ✏️

If you were going to write a biography, what person would you choose? Why? Is your choice based on your feelings about the subject? Jot down some responses to these "biography questions."

Literary Focus
Biography: Telling Lives

The text you're about to read is a **biographical narrative.** In a biography a writer tells the story of another person's life. The word *biography* comes from two Greek words: *bios,* meaning "life" (think of biology), and *graphein,* meaning "to write." Most biographers follow a strictly factual style. They describe events that have been carefully researched.

Objective and Subjective Writing

Writing that presents facts without revealing the writer's feelings and opinions is said to be **objective.** Journalists who report on current events for newspapers usually write in an objective style. Their readers want the facts; they do not want to hear how the reporter feels about the event.

Writing that reveals the writer's feelings and opinions is said to be **subjective.** Biographies often combine objective writing with subjective details. After all, it is hard to write about someone's life without revealing your feelings about that person.

As you read this biography of Queen Elizabeth I of England, see if you can tell how her biographer feels about his royal subject.

Elizabeth I ruled England for forty-five years, from 1558 to 1603.

INTERNET
Vocabulary Activity
Keyword: LE5 7-4

SKILLS FOCUS

Literary Skills
Understand biography; distinguish objective from subjective writing.

Reading Skills
Use the SQ3R system for studying informational texts.

Vocabulary Development

These are the words you'll need to know as you read this biography:

monarch (män′ərk) *n.:* sole and absolute leader. *As monarch, Elizabeth came to the throne of England in 1558.*

alliance (ə·lī′əns) *n.:* pact between nations, families, or individuals that shows a common cause. *Elizabeth's advisor encouraged her to join the alliance against the enemy.*

monopoly (mə·näp′ə·lē) *n.:* exclusive control of a market. *The queen's favorites got rich from a monopoly on imported goods.*

arrogant (ar′ə·gənt) *adj.:* overly convinced of one's own importance. *The queen seemed arrogant, but she did listen to others.*

intolerable (in·täl′ər·ə·bəl) *adj.:* unbearable. *Even though Mary was an enemy, Queen Elizabeth felt it would be intolerable to cut off her cousin's head.*

Reading Skills

SQ3R: A Study System for Reading Informational Texts

SQ3R stands for *Survey, Question, Read, Retell, Review.* It is a study system that helps readers study texts independently. Below are the SQ3R steps:

S **Survey.** Preview the text. Glance quickly at the headings (if there are any), vocabulary words, and illustrations. Skim the captions, which explain the illustrations, and read the first and last sentence of each paragraph.

Q **Question.** List the questions you'd like to ask about the text, based on your survey.

R **Read.** Read the text carefully to find ideas and information that will answer your questions. Take notes.

R **Retell.** Write responses to your questions in your own words. Try to hit the main points and include important details. You might want to say your answers out loud before you write them down.

R **Review.** Start your review by looking over your completed SQ3R organizer. Try covering up the answers in the "Read and Take Notes" and "Retell" boxes to see if you can answer your questions without looking at your notes. Then, check your memory of the main points and important details by writing a brief summary of the text. If you're shaky on a few details, re-read the parts of the text that contain the information you need.

Sample SQ3R Organizer for "Elizabeth I"

Question

Survey
- Who was Elizabeth I?
- How did her subjects like a woman ruling them?
- Why didn't she get married?
- [And so on]

Read and Take Notes
- She was the daughter of Henry VIII, trained from birth to rule.
- At first they didn't like a woman ruling them, but soon her subjects loved her.
- If she married, she would have to share power.
- [And so on]

Retell
- Elizabeth I was a strong and brilliant queen who was trained to rule as well as any man.
- [And so on]

Review

Summary:

ELIZABETH I

Milton Meltzer

"GOOD QUEEN BESS" her people called her. But "good" is a tame word for one of the most remarkable women who ever lived. Elizabeth I came to the throne of England in 1558 at the age of twenty-five. It was not a happy time for a young woman to take the responsibility for ruling a kingdom. Religious conflicts, a huge government debt, and heavy losses in a war with France had brought England low. But by the time of Elizabeth's death forty-five years later, England had experienced one of the greatest periods in its long history. Under Elizabeth's leadership, England had become united as a nation; its industry and commerce, its arts and sciences had flourished; and it was ranked among the great powers of Europe.

Elizabeth was the daughter of King Henry VIII and his second wife, Anne Boleyn. At the age of two she lost her mother when Henry had Anne's head chopped off. Not a good start for a child. But her father placed her in the care of one lord or lady after another, and the lively little girl with the reddish-gold hair, pale skin, and golden-brown eyes won everyone's affection.

Almost from her infancy Elizabeth was trained to stand in for ruling men, in case the need should arise. So she had to master whatever they were expected to know and do. Her tutors found the child to be an eager student. She learned history, geography, mathematics, and the elements of astronomy and architecture. She mastered four modern languages—French, Italian, Spanish, and Flemish[1]—as well as classical Greek and Latin. She wrote in a beautiful script that was like a work of art. The earliest portrait painted of her—when she was thirteen—shows a girl with innocent eyes holding a book in her long and delicate hands, already confident and queenly in her bearing.

She was a strong-willed girl who liked to give orders. She loved to be out on horseback, and rode so fast it frightened the men assigned to protect her. She loved dancing too—she never gave it up. Even in her old age she was seen one moonlit night dancing by herself in the garden.

Elizabeth had a half sister, Mary, born in 1516 of Henry's first wife, Catherine of Aragon. Many years later came Elizabeth, the child of Anne Boleyn, and four years after, her half brother, Edward, the son of Henry's third wife, Jane Seymour. After Henry died, because succession[2] came first through the male, ten-year-old Edward was crowned king. But he lived only another six years. Now Mary took the throne and, soon after, married King Philip II of Spain, a Catholic

---

1. **Flemish:** language spoken in Flanders, a region covering a small part of northern France and Belgium.
2. **succession** *n.:* order in which one succeeds to the throne.

HENRY VIII.
Henry VIII, King of England by Hans Holbein the Younger (1497–1543).

QUEEN ELIZABETH I.
Queen Elizabeth I by Henry Bone (1755–1834). Copy of miniature (c. 1592) by Marcus Gheerhaerts. Enamel on copper.

ANNE BOLEYN.

MARY TUDOR, QUEEN OF ENGLAND.

KING PHILIP II.

PRINCESS ELIZABETH I.
Elizabeth I of England when a princess
(c. 1542–1547).

The Granger Collection, New York.

she was a very special woman. "Am I not a queen because God has chosen me to be a queen?" she demanded.

As princess and later as queen, Elizabeth lived in various palaces, with much coming and going; each time she moved, she took along her household staff of 120 people. Often the changes were required because there was no sanitation. The smelly palaces had to be emptied so they could be "aired and sweetened."

Even before Elizabeth came of age, there was much talk of when she would marry, and whom. Marriages among the nobility and royalty were arranged not for love, but for practical reasons—to add land holdings, to strengthen the prestige and power of families, to cement an alliance of nations against a common enemy.

And remember, from the most ancient times, kings claimed that they as men were born to rule by divine right. That is, God had ordained that the crown should pass through the male line of descent. But when the king's wife had no male child, it meant trouble. Who then would rule? That crisis often led to civil war as various factions battled for the

monarch like herself. He was twenty-seven and she was thirty-eight. But they were rarely together, each ruling their own kingdom. Mary died of cancer at the age of forty-two. That made Elizabeth the monarch.

When she came to the throne on November 17, 1558, it was a day to be marked by celebrations, then and long after. As Her Majesty passed down a London street, an astonished housewife exclaimed, "Oh, Lord! The queen is a woman!" For there were still many who could scarcely believe they were to be ruled by another woman. Elizabeth herself would say with mock modesty that she was "a mere woman." But everyone soon learned

Vocabulary
monarch (män'ərk) *n.:* sole and absolute leader.
alliance (ə·lī'əns) *n.:* pact between nations, families, or individuals that shows a common cause.

power to name a king. Many disputed Elizabeth's right to the throne, and as long as she had neither husband nor successor, her life was in danger.

Ever since Elizabeth was eight, however, she had said again and again, "I will never marry." Did marriage look promising to a girl whose father had had six wives, two of whom, including her own mother, he had beheaded? Yet she liked to hear of people who wanted to marry her.

And there was no shortage of suitors. She continued to insist she wished to live unmarried. No matter how often she said it, men did not believe it. Understandably, since she often made a prince or duke who had come to court her believe she was finally ready to give in—only at the last moment to back out. Once, to a delegation from Parliament come to beg her to marry, she declared, "I am already bound unto a husband, which is the Kingdom of England."

And why should she, the absolute ruler of England, allow a man to sit alongside her as king? The power of husbands over wives in that century—and even now, in many places of this world—was so great that a husband might snatch the reins of power from her and leave her with the title but not the authority she loved to exercise.

Was it fun to be queen? As monarch, she commanded great wealth, inherited from her father, and people who wanted favors were always enriching her with lavish presents. She was no spendthrift, however. She hated to see money wasted, whether her own or the

"I AM ALREADY BOUND UNTO A HUSBAND, WHICH IS THE KINGDOM OF ENGLAND."

kingdom's. Early on she began keeping careful household account books, and later she would do the same with the royal accounts. Always she urged her counselors to carry out orders as inexpensively as possible.

Above everything else, Elizabeth wanted to have her people think well of her. Her deepest desire was to assure them of peace and prosperity. And why not make a grand personal impression upon them at the same time? In her mature years she gave free rein to her love of jewels and staged brilliant displays for the court and the people. Her dresses were decorated with large rubies, emeralds, and diamonds, and she wore jeweled necklaces, bracelets, and rings. In her hair, at her ears, and around her neck she wore pearls—the symbol of virginity.

During her reign she made many great processions through London, the people wild with excitement, crowding the streets—for the English, like most people, loved spectacle. In the first of them, her coronation, she wore gold robes as she was crowned. Trumpets sounded, pipes and drums played, the organ pealed, bells rang. Then came the state banquet in Westminster Hall. It began at 3:00 P.M., and went on till 1:00 A.M.

Elizabeth was often entertained at house parties. One of them, given by the Earl of Leicester in Kenilworth Castle, lasted for eighteen days in July. Thirty other distinguished guests were invited. The great number of their servants (together with Leicester's) turned the palace into a small town. When darkness fell, candles glittered everywhere, indoors and out, creating a fairyland. Musicians sang and played, the guests danced in the garden, and such a great display of fireworks exploded that the heavens thundered and the castle shook. Then came a pleasure relished in those days: the hideous sport of bear baiting. A pack of dogs was let loose in an inner courtyard to scratch and bite and tear at thirteen tormented bears. Still, the happy guests retained their appetite for a "most delicious banquet of 300 dishes."

The tremendous festival at Kenilworth was only one of the highlights of Elizabeth's summer festival. She moved from one great house to another all season long, always at the enormous expense of her hosts. They had little to complain of, however, for their wealth was often the product of the queen's generous bestowal of special privileges. In recognition of his high rank and in return for his support, she granted the duke of Norfolk a license to import carpets from Turkey free of duty. The earl of Essex was favored with the profitable right to tax imported sweet wines. Other pets got rich from a monopoly on the importation of or taxation of silks, satins, salt, tobacco, starch.

England was a small nation at the time she ruled: less than four million people, about as many as live in Arizona today. But the English were a young people, coming to maturity with new worlds opening up to them, in the mind and across the seas. A rebirth of culture—the Renaissance—had begun in the 1400s. With the revival of interest in the literature of the ancient Greek and Roman worlds came the beginning of a great age of discovery. This period marked the transition from medieval to modern times. The arts and sciences were influenced by changes in economic life. All the nation was swept up in the vast tides of change. Merchants, bankers, the gentry,[3] artisans, seamen, miners—men and women of every class and condition—felt themselves part of the national venture.

At the heart of the change in England was the queen. But no king or queen rules alone, no matter how authoritative or arrogant they may be. They usually look to others for advice, advice they may follow or reject. Elizabeth appointed ministers to handle the various departments of government, and made Sir William Cecil, then thirty-eight, her principal advisor. He was a brilliant, hard-working master of statecraft, devoted to her and England's well-being, and as ruthless as she and the nation's interests required. When he died in old age, his son Robert replaced him at her side.

So great was the queen's role, however, that her time became known as the Age of Elizabeth. Not only did many fine musicians flower, but writers too, such as Christopher Marlowe and John Donne and Ben Jonson and Edmund Spenser. And above all, the incomparable William Shakespeare, whose plays were sometimes performed at court. Astronomers, naturalists, mathematicians, geographers, and architects pioneered in their fields.

Then, too, there were the daring explorers who pushed English expansion overseas.

---

3. **gentry** *n.*: upper class.

Vocabulary

monopoly (mə·näp′ə·lē) *n.*: exclusive control of a market. Monopolies are illegal now because they can control prices.

arrogant (ar′ə·gənt) *adj.*: overly convinced of one's own importance.

WILLIAM SHAKESPEARE.

THE GOLDEN HINDE.
A working replica of the sailing ship
Golden Hinde used by Drake during the
sixteenth century.

SIR FRANCIS DRAKE.
The English explorer Sir
Francis Drake (1540?–1596).

One of the queen's favorites, Sir Walter Raleigh, planned the colony of Virginia in America and named it for her, the Virgin Queen. The queen herself put money into several of the great voyages, keeping close watch over the plans and their results. She supported Sir Francis Drake on his three-year voyage around the world, profiting mightily from the immense loot he captured from Spanish ships taken in the Pacific.

For Elizabeth, one of the most urgent problems was the question of religion. Her father had broken with the Catholic Church and launched the English Reformation, creating the Church of England, with himself at its head. When Elizabeth's older half sister, Mary (who remained Catholic), married the Catholic king of Spain, Philip II, she reconciled England with the Church of Rome. In Mary's brief reign she persecuted those Protestants who refused to conform, executing some 270 of them.

When Elizabeth became queen upon Mary's death, she said she hoped religion would not prevent her people from living together in peaceful unity. She did not want to pry into people's souls or question their faith. But in 1570, Pope Pius V excommunicated[4] her, denied her right to the throne, and declared her subjects owed her no allegiance. A directive[5] from the pope's office decreed that the assassination of Queen Elizabeth would not be regarded as a sin. The effect of this directive was to turn practicing Catholics—about half of the English, most of them loyal—into potential traitors.

Though Elizabeth had wanted to pursue a middle way of toleration, circumstances threatened to overwhelm her. She had to beware of several Catholic monarchs of Europe who wished to see a Protestant England overthrown. Philip II of Spain sent ambassadors to England to urge Catholics to rise against

---

4. **excommunicated** *v.:* cast out from a religious community. Strictly speaking, the queen was denied the sacraments of the Catholic Church.
5. **directive** *n.:* order or instructions, especially given by a government.

Elizabeth, put her cousin Mary[6] on the throne, and restore Roman Catholicism as the national faith. The line between power, politics, and religion was becoming very thin.

Missionary priests living abroad were sent into England to stir up opposition to the queen. But the English Catholics as a body never rebelled, nor did they ever intend to. Still, missionary priests such as Edmund Campion were convicted of plotting against Elizabeth and executed.

In 1588 a long-threatened invasion of England by Spain was launched by Philip II. He mistakenly believed that the English Catholics were waiting to welcome him. News of his armada of 130 big ships carrying 17,000 soldiers was terrifying. But the queen did not panic. She supervised the high command personally, meanwhile rallying popular support for the defense of the realm and sending troops to protect the coasts while Sir Francis Drake's ships set out to attack the Spanish fleet.

The Spanish Armada was defeated in three battles, its ships dispersed. When the news came of the tremendous victory, the citizens took to the streets, shouting for joy.

The defeat of the Spanish Armada did not end Spain's aggression against England. The Jesuits[7] in England, who were especially identified with Spain, continued to be persecuted. Richard Topcliffe, a notorious hater of

HOW DARE STUBBS SAY PUBLICLY SHE WAS TOO OLD TO MARRY?

Catholics, was given authority to track down suspects. He examined them under torture to force information about people who had sheltered them. The treatment of them was so vicious and cruel that the victims welcomed death as a release from their agony.

During Elizabeth's reign several plots to assassinate her were uncovered. Elizabeth managed to give the impression that she was not frightened, but those close to her knew she was. When one of the major plots proved to center around Elizabeth's cousin, Mary, Queen of Scots, Elizabeth found it almost <u>intolerable</u> to put to death a crowned queen. Yet she ordered the use of torture on Mary's co-conspirators, and in the end, Mary was beheaded. A song composed by William Byrd at the time suggests how ominous the news of a monarch's execution was:

> The noble famous Queen
> who lost her head of late
> Doth show that kings as well as clowns
> Are bound to fortune's fate,
> And that no earthly Prince
> Can so secure his crown
> but fortune with her whirling wheel
> Hath power to pull them down.

When two earls combined forces against her, Elizabeth's troops overcame them. The queen was so enraged she ordered that 800 of the mostly poor rebels be hanged. But she spared the lives of their wealthy leaders so

---

6. **Mary:** Mary Stuart (1542–1587) (Mary, Queen of Scots, not Elizabeth's half sister).
7. **Jesuits** (jezh'oo·its): priests who are members of the Roman Catholic Society of Jesus.

Vocabulary
intolerable (in·täl'ər·ə·bəl) *adj.:* unbearable.

MARY STUART, QUEEN OF SCOTS.
Portrait of Mary Stuart, Queen of Scots (16th century).

SEA BATTLE BETWEEN THE SPANISH ARMADA AND ENGLISH NAVAL FORCES.

that they might enrich her, either by buying their pardons or by forfeiting[8] their lands.

Elizabeth came down hard on writers who criticized her actions. John Stubbs, a zealous Puritan, wrote a pamphlet expressing horror at the possibility the queen might marry a French Catholic. The queen had Stubbs and his publisher tried and convicted for seditious libel.[9] How dare Stubbs say publicly she was too old to marry, and that the much younger French suitor could not possibly be in love with her? Elizabeth was merciless as she invoked the penalty for libel. With a butcher's cleaver, the executioner cut the right hands off Stubbs and his publisher. Not an uncommon punishment.

How did Elizabeth learn of all these plots and conspiracies? How did she know what

plans Philip II of Spain was devising to invade her kingdom? Spies and secret agents—they were her eyes and ears. Crucial to the flow of information was Sir Francis Walsingham. Trained as a lawyer, he lived on the Continent[10] for years, mastering the languages and the ins and outs of European affairs. Upon his return home, he was asked by Sir William Cecil, the queen's right arm, to gather information on the doings and plans of foreign governments. Soon he was made chief of England's secret service. He placed over seventy agents and spies in the courts of Europe. And of course he watched closely the activities of people at home suspected of disloyalty. Letters to and from them were secretly opened, to nip plots in the bud.

Monarchs had absolute power. Elizabeth could arrest anyone, including the topmost ranks of the nobility, and imprison them in the Tower of London even if they had not

---

8. **forfeiting** (fôr′fit·iŋ) *v.* used as *n.:* giving up, usually because of force of some kind.
9. **seditious libel** (si·dish′əs lī′bəl): stirring up discontent about the government (sedition) with false written statements (libel).

---

10. **Continent:** Europe.

committed any legal offense. The only thing that held her back was her fear of public opinion. It upset her when a crowd gathered at a public execution and was so disgusted by the butchery that they let out roars of disapproval. Still, like all rulers, Elizabeth said she believed that "born a sovereign princess" she enjoyed "the privilege common to all kings" and was "exempt from human jurisdiction[11] and subject only to the judgement of God."

Despite her blazing nervous energy, Elizabeth was often sick. Her ailments were anxiously reported and discussed. For the English believed her survival was their only guarantee of freedom from foreign invasion and civil war. Once, suffering a raging toothache for the first time, the queen feared the pain of having an extraction. She had never had a tooth pulled and was terrified. To reassure her, an old friend, the Bishop of London, had her watch while the dental surgeon pulled out one of the bishop's own good teeth. And then she consented to have her own taken out.

It was commonly believed then that kings and queens had the magical power to cure disease in their subjects. Eager to demonstrate that she too had the sacred power of royalty, Elizabeth prayed intensely before using the royal touch on people with scrofula, a nasty skin disease. Her chaplain said he watched "her exquisite hands, boldly, and without disgust, pressing the sores and ulcers." In one day it was reported that she

"OLD AGE CAME UPON ME AS A SURPRISE, LIKE A FROST," SHE ONCE WROTE.

healed thirty-eight persons. But if she did not feel divinely inspired, she would not try her touch.

Even in the last decade of her life, Elizabeth's energy was astonishing. She was as watchful as always over the affairs of state, though sometimes forgetful. But age made her more irritable; she sometimes shouted at her ladies and even boxed their ears. She was less able to control rival factions out for power, and became so fearful of assassins she rarely left her palaces.

A portrait of her done when she was approaching sixty shows her in a great white silk dress studded with aglets[12] of black onyx, coral, and pearl. She wears three ropes of translucent pearls and stands on a map of England, her England. An ambassador reported that at sixty-three she looked old, but her figure was still beautiful, and her conversation was as brilliant and charming as ever.

There was dancing at court every evening, a pastime she still enjoyed. When it came to displays of gallantry by eager young men, she could act a bit vain and foolish, although never letting any hopeful get out of bounds.

In early 1603 Elizabeth developed a bad cold that led to a serious fever, and then she fell into a stupor[13] for four days. As she lay dying, all of London became strangely silent. On March 24, the life of a rare genius ended. The nation went into mourning.

"Old age came upon me as a surprise, like a frost," she once wrote.

---

11. **jurisdiction** (joor′is·dik′shən) *n*.: legal control.

12. **aglets** (ag′lits) *n*.: tips of lace on dresses.
13. **stupor** (stoo′pər) *n*.: loss of sensibility; dullness.

Meet the Writer

Milton Meltzer

No Shy Guy

The historian **Milton Meltzer** (1915–   ) took an interest in social issues when he was young. After attending Columbia University, he joined the Works Projects Administration, a government agency that provided jobs for workers who were unemployed during the Great Depression of the 1930s. Over time he has written about the Holocaust and the civil rights movement, slavery and immigration. Never one to shy away from controversy, Meltzer writes honestly about injustices that have occurred throughout history.

His biographies cover historic figures, such as George Washington and Mark Twain, as well as others who may not be so well known—like Tom Paine, who battled for America's independence, and Betty Friedan, who fought for women's rights. Throughout most of his work, Meltzer recognizes a common link:

> **❝ My subjects choose action. . . . Action takes commitment, the commitment of dedicated, optimistic individuals. I try to make the readers understand that history isn't only what happens to us. History is what we *make* happen. Each of us. All of us.❞**

Meltzer has written over eighty books, many of them award winners. In addition, he has made documentary films and written scripts for radio and television.

For Independent Reading

So much Meltzer to choose from! For more biographies of women like Elizabeth, try *Ten Queens: Portraits of Women of Power.* Or you may prefer *Frederick Douglass: In His Own Words* or *Thomas Jefferson: The Revolutionary Aristocrat.*

First Thoughts

1. If you could ask Elizabeth one question, what would it be?

Thinking Critically

2. What **inferences** can you make about how people felt about Elizabeth? Support your inferences with evidence from the text.

3. Which details in the life of Elizabeth would, and which would not, apply to the life of a ruler today? Consider these topics:

   - the question of marriage
   - the execution of enemies
   - intrigues and plots
   - processions
   - parties
   - the divine right of kings
   - separation of church and state

Reading Check

Answer the following questions. Then, complete your SQ3R organizer.

a. What problems did England have when Elizabeth I came to the throne?

b. How did England change during the Renaissance? Who was at the heart of the change?

c. Why didn't Elizabeth want to get married?

d. What was Elizabeth's opinion about her people's religious practices?

e. Why was it always possible that Elizabeth would be assassinated?

Extending Interpretations

4. Evaluate this biographer's feelings about Elizabeth. Is his narrative balanced? Is he mostly **objective** as a biographer, or is he very **subjective** in his account of Elizabeth? Find details from the biography to support your answers.

SKILLS FOCUS

Literary Skills
Analyze a biography; analyze objective and subjective points of view.

Reading Skills
Use the SQ3R system for studying informational texts.

Writing Skills
Write a biographical sketch.

WRITING

Writing a Biographical Sketch

Write a short biographical sketch of the person you chose for your Quickwrite. Before you write, create a character profile by listing facts you know and questions for which you want answers. Use the Internet and library resources to gather information that will answer your research questions. Do you wish to write an **objective** biography—sticking to the facts? Or do you prefer to express some **subjective** feelings?

Vocabulary Development

Clarifying Word Meanings: Definitions in Context

You may have noticed that the writer of this article helped you out when he used a word that he thought you might not know. He defined the difficult word right there in the sentence or in the next sentence. Writers of textbooks and other materials written for students often do this. It's up to you to be able to recognize a definition when you see it. Here are three examples from "Elizabeth I" in which the writer clarifies word meanings through the use of definition.

In the first example the words *that is* signal a definition coming up.

> "Kings claimed that they as men were born to rule by <u>divine right</u>. That is, God had ordained that the crown should pass through the male line of descent."

In this example, the definition comes before the word:

> "A rebirth of culture—the <u>Renaissance</u>—had begun in the 1400s."

Here the writer defines the word *scrofula* right after the comma:

> "Elizabeth prayed intensely before using the royal touch on people with <u>scrofula</u>, a nasty skin disease."

PRACTICE

Write a sentence for each word in the Word Bank, and define the word by applying one of the methods used in the examples above. Use each method of clarification at least once.

> **Word Bank**
>
> monarch
> alliance
> monopoly
> arrogant
> intolerable

ELISABETHA REG: ANGLIÆ.

Elizabeth I, Queen of England (16th century).

Old London Bridge in 1630 (detail) by Claude de Jong (c. 1610–1663).
The Granger Collection, New York.

Vocabulary Skills
Clarify word meanings by using definitions.

Elizabeth I   **427**

Comparing Literature

Literary Focus
Mood and Theme

Mood is the overall feeling of a story, poem, or other work of literature. Writers create mood through the words, images, and descriptions they use. Sometimes you can describe the feeling of a work of literature in a single word, such as *dreamy, mysterious, hopeful,* or *sad.* Other times, though, the mood may be more complex and hard to describe. You might need two or three words to convey the mood.

Theme is the truth about life revealed in a work of literature. The story and poems you are about to read are all concerned with change and loss. What each selection reveals about the impact on life of change and loss is its theme. As you read, see if describing the mood of the selection helps you express its theme.

Reading Skills
Comparing and Contrasting

As you read the selections that follow, consider what each reveals about the power of loss and change. Think about whether any of the words in the box at the right can be used to describe the mood of one or more of the texts. A chart at the end of the selections will help you to collect your ideas. You'll use the chart to write a comparison-contrast essay on page 444.

Words for Mood
nostalgic

peaceful

exciting

scary

regretful

angry

joyful

eerie

wistful

proud

Tips for Finding Theme

- Think about the **title** and what it might mean.

- Look for **key passages** in which the writer seems to make important statements about life.

SKILLS FOCUS

Literary Skills
Understand mood and theme.

Reading Skills
Compare and contrast texts.

Before You Read

Dinosaurs ruled the earth for some 160 million years. Why did they vanish? Did a massive asteroid smash into the earth? Did swamps dry up and destroy their habitats? Did drastic changes in temperature kill them off? Here a writer imagines what it might have been like to be the very last dinosaur.

The Last Dinosaur

Jim Murphy

The sun came up slowly, fingers of light poking into and brightening the tangled forest of pine and poplar and hemlock trees. The drone of insects quieted, and the tiny mammals scampered to hide.

In a clearing a small triceratops herd began their day. The female triceratops blinked several times before moving to get the light out of her eyes. Then she went back to the frond she'd ripped from a cycadeoid.[1]

The frond was tough and spiky, but her sharp-edged beak and rows of teeth chopped the plant into easily swallowed pieces. She was about to tug at another frond when a male triceratops began stamping his feet in alarm. ❶

He had been feeding at the base of a tree when his horns became entangled in a mass of grapevines. He shook his head violently to get free. When that didn't work, he backed away, yanking his head

---

1. **cycadeoid** (sī·kad′ē·oid′) *n.:* extinct plant that existed at the time of the dinosaurs. (A frond is the leaf of a palm or fern.)

PREDICT

❶ What might be the cause of the male triceratops's alarm? Use your **prior knowledge** to help you make your prediction.

from side to side. Still covered with vines, he halted. His breathing came in short, grunting pants.

Suddenly he lowered his head and charged the tree. He hit it solidly, backed up, and hit it again, and then again. The fourth butt splintered the tree's base, and it leaned over. A few wiggles of his head and the vine slipped off.

He snorted at the vine, challenging it. When it didn't move, he walked around it and left the clearing. He was the largest triceratops and leader of the herd, so the smaller male and the female followed him.

The three wandered through the forest, always staying near the stream that was their source of water. They did not hurry, and often stopped to nibble at figs or tender tree saplings. On the second day they came to a hillside covered with tasty ferns. The spot was cool and quiet, so they stayed the afternoon, browsing.

A sudden noise made the female jerk up her head to look and listen. They had not seen another dinosaur in a very long time, but she was still wary. A hungry tyrannosaur might have picked up their scent and followed, hoping one of them would stray from the herd. ❷

INTERPRET

❷ Describe the **mood,** or overall feeling, of the story so far. Find three details to support your interpretation. You may need more than one word to describe the mood.

The two males sensed her unease and also looked around. A giant dragonfly circled the triceratopses, then flew away. A bird chattered briefly. Then the forest grew still. Was a tyrannosaur out there, watching, waiting? Nothing moved and the noise did not return, but the herd was nervous. They left the hillside and continued their journey.

The next day, the land sloped downward and the stream widened to become a series of falls, pools, and swirling rapids. The path twisted to follow the water and dipped sharply in places. Despite their great size, the triceratopses walked the narrow ledges and leaped boulders with an easy grace.

The female triceratops smelled something. Her sense of sight was very poor, so she turned to face what was causing the strange odor. Wisps of smoke trailed through the trees.

The smoke was from a fire started the night before by heat lightning.[2] The female couldn't see the fire or know that it was advancing toward them. But the smoke was growing thicker and more unpleasant, so the three animals trotted away.

All night they moved quickly to stay clear of the smoke. At dawn, the ground leveled, and the smell seemed to disappear. The two males stopped, exhausted, and bent to drink the cool water. The female continued along the path.

Weeks before, the female triceratops had mated with the leader of the herd. She was hunting now for a spot to build her nest.

The leader stamped his feet and snorted for her to stop, but it did no good. The female would not obey until the nest was completed and her eggs laid. This time, the males followed.

A mile downstream, the forest thinned and the stream emptied into a broad marsh. In the past, dome-headed pachycephalosaurs or armored ankylosaurs would be browsing in the cattails and rushes. Now only the bones of a long-dead anatosaur, half buried in mud, were there to greet the herd. ❸

The female walked the edge of the marsh carefully. The ground was either too wet or too rocky for the nest. On the opposite side of the marsh she found a warm, sandy area with low-growing shrubs.

Immediately she began digging, using the toes of her front and rear feet to shovel out the sand. The hole she dug was six feet across and a foot deep.

---

2. **heat lightning:** lightning flashes that appear near the horizon on hot nights.

INFER

❸ Which details suggest that the dinosaurs are dying out? How do these details affect the **mood** of the story?

When the hole was finished, she laid fifteen eggs in it to form a circle. Gently she covered the eggs with sand. The sun would warm the sand and eggs, and eventually baby triceratopses would emerge.

The two males were feeding a little distance from the nest. The smaller male approached the nest.

When the female saw him, she placed herself between him and her eggs and lowered her head as a warning. The curious male kept coming, so the female charged him. Only when he backed away did the female stop her charge.

When the herd had been larger, many females would make nests in the same area. They would then take turns guarding the nests or feeding and sleeping. But the female triceratops was alone now. It would be her job to keep clumsy males and egg-eating creatures away from her eggs. The quick shrewlike[3] mammals were especially annoying at night. ❹

Two days later the smell of smoke returned. It was faint, distant, and yet the three triceratopses grew nervous. The female paced near her nest.

COMPARE AND CONTRAST

❹ How did a female triceratops once care for her eggs? How must she now care for her eggs? What conclusions can you draw from this?

---

3. **shrewlike:** resembling a shrew, a small mammal that looks like a mouse.

A Dino Dictionary

Did you know that the names of the dinosaurs come from Greek and Latin words? Read about these terrifying beasts, and look at their pictures. Do they resemble the Greek and Latin words that form their names?

anatosaur (ə·nat′ō·sôr′): two-legged, plant-eating dinosaur with a wide jaw resembling the bill of a duck, webbed feet, and a long tail. The name comes from *anas,* the Latin word for "duck," and *sauros*, the Greek word for "lizard."

ankylosaur (aŋ′kə·lō·sôr′): four-legged, plant-eating dinosaur with thick, leathery skin covered by bony plates. *Ankylos* is Greek for "crooked."

pachycephalosaur (pak′ə·sef′ə·lō·sôr′): two-legged, plant-eating dinosaur with a dome-shaped plate nine inches thick covering its brain. The name comes from Greek: *pachys* (thick) + *kephalē* (head) + *sauros* (lizard).

Late in the day, a heavy line of smoke appeared on the other side of the marsh. Flames erupted, reaching into the air.

A flock of birds flew overhead, screeching an alarm. Mammals, made bold by their fear, left their hiding places and ran from the fire. The two males edged away, but the female stayed to guard her eggs.

In the smoke and dark forest shadows, something moved. The shape was big, as big as many of the trees, and had a massive head. Tyrannosaurus rex. The giant flesh eater stepped from the forest, snapping his mouth to reveal seven-inch-long slashing teeth.

Instinctively the two triceratops males rejoined the female and formed a semicircle barrier in front of the nest. The leader lowered his head and stared at his enemy. Neither moved.

Ordinarily, the tyrannosaur would not attack a triceratops, especially near its nest. But a wall of flames and heat had cut off his retreat. Besides, the tyrannosaur had not had a large meal in weeks. ❺

The tyrannosaur darted at the herd, skidded to a sudden halt, then began circling warily, watching for a chance to strike. He hissed and snapped his teeth. At that instant, the largest triceratops charged, his powerful legs driving him directly at the soft belly of his attacker.

INFER

❺ What details suggest that tyrannosaurs are also in danger?

anatosaur

tyrannosaur

triceratops

ankylosaur

pachycephalosaur

tyrannosaurus rex

tyrannosaur (tə·ran′ə·sôr′): fierce two-legged meat eater, about forty feet in length. Its name comes from Greek: *tyrannos* (tyrant, or cruel ruler) + *sauros* (lizard).

Tyrannosaurus rex (reks): best-known species of tyrannosaur. In Latin, *rex* means "king."

triceratops (trī·ser′ə·täps′): four-legged, plant-eating dinosaur of North America. The triceratops had three horns on its head, grew to about twenty-five feet in length, and weighed up to four or five tons. Its name comes from Latin and Greek: *tri–* (three) + *kerat–* (horn) + *ōps* (eye, face).

The Last Dinosaur   **433**

With the aid of his long tail and thickly muscled legs, the tyrannosaur leaped aside to avoid the sharp horns. He spun and dove, mouth wide open, and sank his teeth into the back of the triceratops.

Then the smaller triceratops lunged at the giant, but he was an inexperienced fighter. The tyrannosaur's teeth closed on his neck, and with a quick, deadly yank, he tore a chunk of flesh from the triceratops. The smaller triceratops fell, dying.

The other triceratops tried to charge again, but his right leg was dragging and his movements were slow. Again the tyrannosaur moved aside easily. Using his tail as a spring, the tyrannosaur launched himself for the kill. His teeth sank into the triceratops, while his clawed feet struck him in the stomach. The two rolled, kicking and biting each other.

At this moment, the female triceratops abandoned her eggs and rammed the tyrannosaur full in the side. He bellowed painfully, releasing his hold on the male. The female pushed forward with all her strength, pinning the tyrannosaur against a tree and driving her horns in deeper.

She stepped away and watched her enemy, ready to charge if he got up. His legs and tail flailed weakly, his breathing became labored. Then, with a violent shudder, the great killer died. **❻**

During the battle, the fire had spread, leaping and dancing from tree to tree until it reached the edge of the sandy area. Flames rolled through the reeds.

The male triceratops struggled to get up, but his legs buckled under him. He crawled a few feet but had to stop. His wounds were too severe. A choking wave of smoke surrounded him.

The female triceratops went back to protect her eggs. To one side a tree crashed to the ground, sending up an explosion of sparks. A bush nearby caught fire. The female charged it, slashing at it blindly with her horns.

The roar of the fire became deafening, and the heat and smoke grew painful. Reluctantly the female moved away from her eggs to find air.

She went only a short distance and turned to go back. The smoke stung her lungs and burned her eyes. She shook her head, but the choking pain would not go away. She backed away some more and lost sight of her nest.

Immediately the tiny mammals pounced on the unguarded nest. Low to the ground the smoke was not so thick. Digging hastily,

RETELL

❻ Retell the battle between the triceratops herd and the tyrannosaur.

they uncovered the eggs and devoured them. Then they scurried from the approaching fire. ❼

The female triceratops hurried through the forest. Several times she stopped to look back toward her eggs. A wall of smoke and flames was all she could see. Finally she gave up.

A tongue of flames reached out at her, and she broke into a gallop. She crashed through branches and vines, leaped over fallen logs heedlessly, with the fire just behind her. At last she came to a rock ledge overlooking a wide river.

The water was dark and deep. Branches and tree roots floated near the banks. The female wanted to find another retreat, but she was surrounded by flames. She hesitated a second, then jumped into the water.

Legs churning frantically, she swam across the river and away from the fire. The river's current caught her, pulling her swiftly along. She struggled to keep her head above water, to breathe, all the while moving her legs. At last her feet touched the river bottom.

Exhausted, her breathing fast, she hauled herself onto solid ground. Across from her, the fire had stopped at the river's edge. She was safe. It was then she noticed the streams of mammals that had also crossed the river to escape the fire.

The light grew dim and the air became chilly. The female's breath gave off thin vapor streams.

COMPARE AND CONTRAST

❼ Think back to the way you described the story's **mood.** Would you change your description now? Why or why not?

The triceratops shook her head and snorted. She hadn't eaten much in days and wanted to find some tender plants. And maybe, somewhere deep in the forest, there was another triceratops herd she could join.

Slowly, as the sun went down, the female pushed through the bushes to begin her search. ❽

PREDICT

❽ Do you think the female will find another herd to join? Why or why not?

Meet the Writer

Jim Murphy

Digging Dinosaurs

Jim Murphy (1947–   ) says that dinosaurs have always fascinated him.

> ❝ Our knowledge of them suggests that they were amazing survivors, occupying every corner of the world and adapting to changing climates and food sources for millions of years. ❞

Murphy feels that studying dinosaurs and finding out how they survived for so long may help humans adapt and survive.

For Independent Reading

Jim Murphy is known for his dramatic re-creations of historical events. *Blizzard!: The Storm That Changed America* is one example of his award-winning historical narratives. In this book, Murphy tells about the Great Blizzard of 1888, a massive snowstorm that devastated the Northeast.

Other books by Murphy that present information in an engaging way are *The Great Fire* and *Across America on an Emigrant Train*.

After You Read

"The Last Dinosaur"

First Thoughts

1. Finish this sentence:
   - This story makes me feel . . .

Thinking Critically

2. Think about the **title** of the story. Is the female triceratops the last of her kind? Or is she the last of all dinosaurs? Find evidence in the story that supports one of these interpretations.

3. In telling this story, the writer zooms in on the experiences of a *female* triceratops. Why do you think he decided to focus on a female dinosaur to tell the story of the last dinosaur?

4. Think about how this story makes you feel. What words would you use to describe the **mood**? Find at least three details in the story that help create the mood.

5. What does this story say to you about the topic of loss and change? How would you express its **theme**?

Reading Check

Check your comprehension by **retelling** this story. Start with the **title, author,** and **main character.** Next, explain the main **conflict** or problem. Then, review the **plot,** listing the main events in the order in which they occur. Be sure to identify the **climax,** the story's most suspenseful moment, which determines how the conflict is going to turn out. Finally, describe the **resolution,** which tells how the story ends.

Comparing Literature

6. To gather details for the essay you'll write for the assignment on page 444, fill in information about "The Last Dinosaur" in a chart like the one below. When you write about your response to the text, think about your overall impression of the story. What makes it memorable for you?

Mood and Theme			
	"The Last Dinosaur"	"Buffalo Dusk"	"I Was Sleeping . . ."
Mood			
Theme			
My response to the text			

SKILLS FOCUS

Literary Skills
Analyze mood and theme.

Reading Skills
Compare and contrast texts.

Before You Read

Millions of buffalo once galloped across the Great Plains of
North America. Native Americans killed the buffalo for food,
and they found uses for all other parts of the animal—from hair
to bones. White settlers, however, killed the buffalo nearly to
extinction. They killed for food, fur, and leather, but most of all
for sport. Today, conservation efforts have succeeded in
establishing more than 200,000 head of buffalo. "Buffalo Dusk"
was written in 1920, when conservation efforts were just
getting started.

Buffalo Dusk

Carl Sandburg

The buffaloes are gone.
And those who saw the buffaloes are gone.
Those who saw the buffaloes by thousands and how they pawed
    the prairie sod into dust with their hoofs, their great heads
    down pawing on in a great pageant of dusk,
Those who saw the buffaloes are gone.
And the buffaloes are gone. ❷

Comparing Literature

INFER

❶ What does the **title** suggest this poem will be about?

ANALYZE

❷ What lines, phrases, and words are repeated in this poem? What **mood** does the repetition create?

Before You Read

About sixty-five million years ago, the dinosaurs were destroyed. On the Great Plains of North America in the nineteenth century, the buffalo herds were almost wiped out. In this poem by Louise Erdrich, a flood destroys the landscape along a river. Erdrich is part Chippewa. She often writes about Native Americans and their communities. Besides the landscape, what larger loss could this poem refer to?

I Was Sleeping Where the Black Oaks Move

Louise Erdrich

We watched from the house
as the river grew, helpless
and terrible in its unfamiliar body.
Wrestling everything into it,
5   the water wrapped around trees
until their life-hold was broken.
They went down, one by one,
and the river dragged off their covering. ❶

Nests of the herons, roots washed to bones,
10   snags of soaked bark on the shoreline:
a whole forest pulled through the teeth
of the spillway.° Trees surfacing
singly, where the river poured off
into arteries for fields below the reservation.

15   When at last it was over, the long removal,
they had all become the same dry wood.
We walked among them, the branches
whitening in the raw sun.
Above us drifted herons,
20   alone, hoarse-voiced, broken,
settling their beaks among the hollows. ❷

---

12. **spillway** *n.:* channel around a dam that carries away extra water.

IDENTIFY

❶ The speaker is describing a flood that she witnessed. She describes the river as if it were alive. What does the river "do" to the trees?

ANALYZE

❷ Re-read lines 15–21. What details help you to see and hear the scene after the flood?

Grandpa said, *These are the ghosts of the tree people,*
moving above us, unable to take their rest.

Sometimes now, we dream our way back to the heron dance.
25 Their long wings are bending the air
into circles through which they fall.
They rise again in shifting wheels.
How long must we live in the broken figures
their necks make, narrowing the sky. ❸

30 Some nights in town's cold winter,
earth shakes.
People say it's a train full of danger
or the plane-broken barriers of sound,
but out there
35 behind the dark trunks of trees
the gone elk have pulled the hide of earth
tight and they are drumming
back the woodland,
tall grass and days we were equal
40 and strong. ❹

Meet the Writers

Carl Sandburg

"I Am the People"
Carl Sandburg
(1878–1967) once defined poetry as "the opening and closing of a door, leaving those who look through to guess about what is seen during a moment." Readers who look through the openings

Sandburg provides in his poetry will see the world from the perspective of the "common folk" of America, whom Sandburg strongly identified with. As he proclaimed in one poem: "I am the people —the mob—the crowd— the mass."

Louise Erdrich

"Someone Believed in Me"
The novels and poems of **Louise Erdrich** (1954–   ) contain powerful themes that reflect her experiences growing up in North Dakota as the daughter of a Chippewa Indian mother and German-American father.

At a young age, Erdrich developed an interest in writing that continued into college. During her junior

year her talent as a poet was recognized: She received a prize from the Academy of American Poets. After graduation, Erdrich decided to "sacrifice all to be a writer." She felt all of her hard work paid off when she won a $5,000 award for one of her short stories. Erdrich notes, "It was like a validation, someone believed in me."

First Thoughts

1. Respond to the poems by completing the following sentences:

- "Buffalo Dusk" made me feel . . .
- I would describe the speaker of "I Was Sleeping Where the Black Oaks Move" as . . .

Thinking Critically

2. What changes and losses are mourned in "Buffalo Dusk"? How would you express the poem's **theme**?

3. How might the **mood** of a poem called "Buffalo Dawn" be different from the mood of Sandburg's "Buffalo Dusk"?

4. In "I Was Sleeping. . ." the speaker hints at other changes and losses besides those caused by the flood. What might these changes and losses be? (How does knowing the writer is part Chippewa help answer this question?)

Comparing Literature

5. Now, complete the second and third columns of the chart below. Filling in the chart will help you prepare to write the comparison-contrast essay assignment on page 444.

Mood and Theme			
	"The Last Dinosaur"	"Buffalo Dusk"	"I Was Sleeping . . ."
Mood			
Theme			
My response to the text			

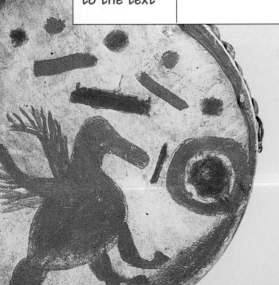

SKILLS FOCUS

Literary Skills
Analyze mood and theme.

Reading Skills
Compare and contrast texts.

After You Read

Comparing "The Last Dinosaur," "Buffalo Dusk," and "I Was Sleeping . . ."

Assignment

1. Writing a Comparison-Contrast Essay

Write a short essay comparing the three texts you've just read. To help plan your essay, review your chart. Write three paragraphs, one about each selection. For each selection, (1) describe the **mood;** (2) express the **theme;** (3) discuss your overall reaction to the text.

In a fourth paragraph, briefly explain which text you had the most positive response to and why. Use details from the texts to support what you say.

> Use the workshop on writing a Comparison-Contrast Essay, pages 772–777, for help with this assignment.

Assignment

2. Researching a Topic

Research and prepare an oral presentation on one of these topics:

- **The Life and Times of the Triceratops**
- **The Life and Times of the North American Buffalo**

Answer the following questions in your report:

- When and for how long did these animals live or thrive?
- What were (are) their eating and mating habits?
- What was their natural habitat?
- What caused the decline of the population? Were the causes human or natural—or both? (If this is not known, what theories explain the decline of the population? Which of these theories seems most likely to you? Why?)

Be sure to report on some questions of your own too!

SKILLS FOCUS

Writing Skills
Write a comparison-contrast essay.

Speaking and Listening Skills
Research and prepare an oral report.

NO QUESTIONS ASKED

The Naming of Names

Ray Bradbury

The rocket metal cooled in the meadow winds. Its lid gave a bulging *pop*. From its clock interior stepped a man, a woman, and three children. The other passengers whispered away across the Martian meadow, leaving the man alone among his family.

The man felt his hair flutter and the tissues of his body draw tight as if he were standing at the center of a vacuum.[1] His wife, before him, seemed almost to whirl away in smoke. The children, small seeds, might at any instant be sown to all the Martian climes.[2]

The children looked up at him, as people look to the sun to tell what time of their life it is. His face was cold.

"What's wrong?" asked his wife.

"Let's get back on the rocket."

"Go back to Earth?"

"Yes! Listen!"

The wind blew as if to flake away their identities. At any moment the Martian air might draw his soul from him, as marrow comes from a white bone. He felt submerged in a chemical that could dissolve his intellect and burn away his past.

They looked at Martian hills that time had worn with a crushing pressure of years. They saw the old cities, lost in their meadows, lying like children's delicate bones among the blowing lakes of grass.

"Chin up, Harry," said his wife. "It's too late. We've come over sixty million miles."

The children with their yellow hair hollered at the deep dome of Martian sky. There was no answer but the racing hiss of wind through the stiff grass.

He picked up the luggage in his cold hands. "Here we go," he said—a man standing on the edge of a sea, ready to wade in and be drowned.

They walked into town.

Their name was Bittering. Harry and his wife, Cora; Dan, Laura, and David. They built a small white cottage and ate good breakfasts there, but the fear was never gone. It lay with Mr. Bittering and Mrs. Bittering, a third, unbidden partner at every midnight talk, at every dawn awakening.

"I feel like a salt crystal," he said, "in a mountain stream, being washed away. We don't belong here. We're Earth people. This is

---

1. **vacuum** (vak′yo͞om) *n.:* closed space with the air sucked out.
2. **climes** (klīmz) *n.:* regions.

Mars. It was meant for Martians. For heaven's sake, Cora, let's buy tickets for home!"

But she only shook her head. "One day the atom bomb will fix Earth. Then we'll be safe here."

"Safe and insane!"

Tick-tock, seven o'clock, sang the voice-clock; *time to get up.* And they did.

Something made him check everything each morning—warm hearth, potted blood-geraniums—precisely as if he expected something to be amiss.[3] The morning paper was toast-warm from the 6:00 A.M. Earth rocket. He broke its seal and tilted it at his breakfast place. He forced himself to be convivial.[4]

"Colonial days all over again," he declared. "Why, in ten years there'll be a million Earthmen on Mars. Big cities, everything! They said we'd fail. Said the Martians would resent our invasion. But did we find any Martians? Not a living soul! Oh, we found their empty cities, but no one in them. Right?"

> "We don't belong here. We're Earth people. This is Mars."

A river of wind submerged the house. When the windows ceased rattling, Mr. Bittering swallowed and looked at the children.

"I don't know," said David. "Maybe there're Martians around we don't see. Sometimes nights I think I hear 'em. I hear the wind. The sand hits my window. I get scared. And I see those towns way up in the mountains where the Martians lived a long time ago. And I think I see things moving around those towns, Papa. And I wonder if those Martians *mind* us living here. I wonder if they won't do something to us for coming here."

"Nonsense!" Mr. Bittering looked out the windows. "We're clean, decent people." He looked at his children. "All dead cities have some kind of ghosts in them. Memories, I mean." He stared at the hills. "You see a staircase and you wonder what Martians looked like climbing it. You see Martian paintings and you wonder what the painter was like. You make a little ghost in your mind, a memory. It's quite natural. Imagination." He stopped. "You haven't been prowling up in those ruins, have you?"

3, **amiss** (ə·mis′) *adj.:* wrong; improper.
4. **convivial** (kən·viv′ē·əl) *adj.:* sociable or friendly.

"No, Papa." David looked at his shoes.

"See that you stay away from them. Pass the jam."

"Just the same," said little David, "I bet something happens."

"A radio flash just came. Atom bombs hit New York! All the space rockets blown up. No more rockets to Mars, ever!"

Something happened that afternoon. Laura stumbled through the settlement, crying. She dashed blindly onto the porch.

"Mother, Father—the war, Earth!" she sobbed. "A radio flash just came. Atom bombs hit New York! All the space rockets blown up. No more rockets to Mars, ever!"

"Oh, Harry!" The mother held on to her husband and daughter.

"Are you sure, Laura?" asked the father quietly.

Laura wept. "We're stranded on Mars, forever and ever!"

For a long time there was only the sound of the wind in the late afternoon.

Alone, thought Bittering. *Only a thousand of us here. No way back. No way. No way.* Sweat poured from his face and his hands and his body; he was drenched in the hotness of his fear. He wanted to strike Laura, cry, "No, you're lying! The rockets will come back!" Instead, he stroked Laura's head against him and said, "The rockets will get through someday."

"Father, what will we do?"

"Go about our business, of course. Raise crops and children. Wait. Keep things going until the war ends and the rockets come again."

The two boys stepped out onto the porch.

"Children," he said, sitting there, looking beyond them, "I've something to tell you."

"We know," they said.

In the following days, Bittering wandered often through the garden to stand alone in his fear. As long as the rockets had spun a silver web across space, he had been able to accept Mars. For he had always told himself: *Tomorrow, if I want, I can buy a ticket and go back to Earth.*

But now: the web gone, the rockets lying in jigsaw heaps of

---

5. **molten girder** (mōlt''n gur'dər) A girder is a metal beam that helps to support a framework; *molten* means "melted."

molten girder[5] and unsnaked wire. Earth people left to the strangeness of Mars, the cinnamon dusts and wine airs, to be baked like gingerbread shapes in Martian summers, put into harvested storage by Martian winters. What would happen to him, the others? This was the moment Mars had waited for. Now it would eat them.

He got down on his knees in the flower bed, a spade in his nervous hands. *Work,* he thought, *work and forget.*

He glanced up from the garden to the Martian mountains. He thought of the proud old Martian names that had once been on those peaks. Earthmen, dropping from the sky, had gazed upon hills, rivers, Martian seas left nameless in spite of names. Once Martians had built cities, named cities; climbed mountains, named mountains; sailed seas, named seas. Mountains melted, seas drained, cities tumbled. In spite of this, the Earthmen had felt a silent guilt at putting new names to these ancient hills and valleys.

Nevertheless, man lives by symbol and label. The names were given.

Mr. Bittering felt very alone in his garden under the Martian sun, an anachronism[6] bent here, planting Earth flowers in a wild soil.

Think. Keep thinking. Different things. Keep your mind free of Earth, the atom war, the lost rockets.

He perspired. He glanced about. No one watching. He removed his tie. *Pretty bold,* he thought. *First your coat off, now your tie.* He hung it neatly on a peach tree he had imported as a sapling from Massachusetts.

He returned to his philosophy of names and mountains. The Earthmen had changed names. Now there were Hormel Valleys, Roosevelt Seas, Ford Hills, Vanderbilt Plateaus, Rockefeller Rivers, on Mars. It wasn't right. The American settlers had shown wisdom, using old Indian prairie names: Wisconsin, Minnesota, Idaho, Ohio, Utah, Milwaukee, Waukegan, Osseo. The old names, the old meanings.

Staring at the mountains wildly, he thought: *Are you up there? All the dead ones, you Martians? Well, here we are, alone, cut off! Come down, move us out! We're helpless!*

The wind blew a shower of peach blossoms.

He put out his sun-browned hand, gave a small cry. He touched the blossoms, picked them up. He turned them, he touched them again and again. Then he shouted for his wife.

---

6. **anachronism** (ə·nak′rə·niz′əm) *n.:* something out of its proper time in history, like a television in the Middle Ages or penicillin in ancient Rome.

"Cora!"

She appeared at a window. He ran to her.

"Cora, these blossoms!"

She handled them.

"Do you see? They're different. They've changed! They're not peach blossoms anymore!"

"Look all right to me," she said.

"They're not. They're *wrong*! I can't tell how. An extra petal, a leaf, something, the color, the smell!"

The children ran out in time to see their father hurrying about the garden, pulling up radishes, onions, and carrots from their beds.

"Cora, come look!"

They handled the onions, the radishes, the carrots among them.

"Do they look like carrots?"

"Yes . . . no." She hesitated. "I don't know."

"They're changed."

"Perhaps."

"You know they have! Onions but not onions, carrots but not carrots. Taste: the same but different. Smell: not like it used to be." He felt his heart pounding, and he was afraid. He dug his fingers into the earth. "Cora, what's happening? What is it? We've got to get away from this." He ran across the garden. Each tree felt his touch. "The roses. The roses. They're turning green!"

And they stood looking at the green roses.

And two days later Dan came running. "Come see the cow. I was milking her and I saw it. Come on!"

They stood in the shed and looked at their one cow.

It was growing a third horn.

And the lawn in front of their house very quietly and slowly was coloring itself like spring violets. Seed from Earth but growing up a soft purple.

"We must get away," said Bittering. "We'll eat this stuff and then we'll change—who knows to what? I can't let it happen. There's only one thing to do. Burn this food!"

"It's not poisoned."

"But it is. Subtly, very subtly. A little bit. A very little bit. We mustn't touch it."

He looked with dismay at their house. "Even the house. The wind's done something to it. The air's burned it. The fog at night. The boards, all warped out of shape. It's not an Earthman's house anymore."

"Oh, your imagination!"

He put on his coat and tie. "I'm going into town. We've got to do something now. I'll be back."

"Wait, Harry!" his wife cried.

But he was gone.

In town, on the shadowy step of the grocery store, the men sat with their hands on their knees, conversing with great leisure and ease.

Mr. Bittering wanted to fire a pistol in the air.

What are you doing, you fools! he thought. *Sitting here! You've heard the news—we're stranded on this planet. Well, move! Aren't you frightened? Aren't you afraid? What are you going to do?*

"Hello, Harry," said everyone.

"Look," he said to them. "You did hear the news, the other day, didn't you?"

They nodded and laughed. "Sure. Sure, Harry."

"What are you going to do about it?"

"Do, Harry, do? What *can* we do?"

"Build a rocket, that's what!"

"A rocket, Harry? To go back to all that trouble? Oh, Harry!"

"But you *must* want to go back. Have you noticed the peach blossoms, the onions, the grass?"

"Why, yes, Harry, seems we did," said one of the men.

"Doesn't it scare you?"

"Can't recall that it did much, Harry."

"Idiots!"

"Now, Harry."

Bittering wanted to cry. "You've got to work with me. If we stay here, we'll all change. The air. Don't you smell it? Something in the air. A Martian virus, maybe; some seed, or a pollen. Listen to me!"

They stared at him.

"Sam," he said to one of them.

"Yes, Harry?"

"Will you help me build a rocket?"

"Harry, I got a whole load of metal and some blueprints. You want to work in my metal shop on a rocket, you're welcome. I'll sell you that metal for five hundred dollars. You should be able to construct a right pretty rocket, if you work alone, in about thirty years."

"You should be able to construct a right pretty rocket, if you work alone, in about thirty years."

Everyone laughed.

"Don't laugh."

Sam looked at him with quiet good humor.

"Sam," Bittering said. "Your eyes—"

"What about them, Harry?"

"Didn't they used to be gray?"

"Well, now, I don't remember."

"They were, weren't they?"

"Why do you ask, Harry?"

"Because now they're kind of yellow-colored."

"Is that so, Harry?" Sam said, casually.

"And you're taller and thinner—"

"You might be right, Harry."

"Sam, you shouldn't have yellow eyes."

"Harry, what color eyes have *you* got?" Sam said.

"My eyes? They're blue, of course."

"Here you are, Harry." Sam handed him a pocket mirror. "Take a look at yourself."

Mr. Bittering hesitated and then raised the mirror to his face.

There were little, very dim flecks of new gold captured in the blue of his eyes.

"Now look what you've done," said Sam a moment later. "You've broken my mirror."

Harry Bittering moved into the metal shop and began to build the rocket. Men stood in the open door and talked and joked without raising their voices. Once in a while they gave him a hand on lifting something. But mostly they just idled and watched him with their yellowing eyes.

"It's supper time, Harry," they said.

His wife appeared with his supper in a wicker basket.

"I won't touch it," he said. "I'll eat only food from our deep freezer. Food that came from Earth. Nothing from our garden."

His wife stood watching him. "You can't build a rocket."

"I worked in a shop once, when I was twenty. I know metal. Once I get it started, the others will help," he said, not looking at her, laying out the blueprints.

"Harry, Harry," she said, helplessly.

"We've got to get away, Cora. We've *got* to!"

The nights were full of wind that blew down the empty moonlit sea meadows past the little white chess cities lying for their twelve-thousandth year in the shallows. In the Earthmen's settlement, the Bittering house shook with a feeling of change.

Lying abcd, Mr. Bittering felt his bones shifted, shaped, melted like gold. His wife, lying beside him, was dark from many sunny afternoons. Dark she was, and golden-eyed, burnt almost black by the sun, sleeping, and the children metallic in their beds, and the wind roaring forlorn[7] and changing through the old peach trees, the violet grass, shaking out green rose petals.

---

7. **forlorn** (fôr·lôrn′) *adj.:* hopeless. *Forlorn* may also mean "deserted" or "abandoned."

> A strange word emerged from Mr. Bittering's lips. *"Iorrt. Iorrt."* He repeated it. It was a Martian word. He knew no Martian.

The fear would not be stopped. It had his throat and heart. It dripped in a wetness of the arm and the temple and the trembling palm.

A green star rose in the east.

A strange word emerged from Mr. Bittering's lips.

"Iorrt. Iorrt." He repeated it.

It was a Martian word. He knew no Martian.

In the middle of the night he arose and dialed a call through to Simpson, the archaeologist.

"Simpson, what does the word *Iorrt* mean?"

"Why, that's the old Martian word for our planet Earth. Why?"

"No special reason."

The telephone slipped from his hand.

"Hello, hello, hello, hello," it kept saying while he sat gazing out at the green star. "Bittering? Harry, are you there?"

The days were full of metal sound. He laid the frame of the rocket with the reluctant help of three indifferent men. He grew very tired in an hour or so and had to sit down.

"The altitude," laughed a man.

"Are you *eating*, Harry?" asked another.

"I'm eating," he said, angrily.

"From your deep freezer?"

"Yes!"

"You're getting thinner, Harry."

"I'm not!"

"And taller."

"Liar!"

His wife took him aside a few days later. "Harry, I've used up all the food in the deep freezer. There's nothing left. I'll have to make sandwiches using food grown on Mars."

He sat down heavily.

"You must eat," she said. "You're weak."

"Yes," he said.

He took a sandwich, opened it, looked at it, and began to nibble at it.

"And take the rest of the day off," she said. "It's hot. The children want to swim in the canals and hike. Please come along."

"I can't waste time. This is a crisis!"

"Just for an hour," she urged. "A swim'll do you good."

He rose, sweating. "All right, all right. Leave me alone. I'll come."

"Good for you, Harry."

The sun was hot, the day quiet. There was only an immense staring burn upon the land. They moved along the canal, the father, the mother, the racing children in their swimsuits. They stopped and ate meat sandwiches. He saw their skin baking brown. And he saw the yellow eyes of his wife and his children, their eyes that were never yellow before. A few tremblings shook him but were carried off in waves of pleasant heat as he lay in the sun. He was too tired to be afraid.

"Cora, how long have your eyes been yellow?"

She was bewildered. "Always, I guess."

"They didn't change from brown in the last three months?"

She bit her lips. "No. Why do you ask?"

"Never mind."

They sat there.

"The children's eyes," he said. "They're yellow, too."

"Sometimes growing children's eyes change color."

"Maybe *we're* children, too. At least to Mars. That's a thought." He laughed. "Think I'll swim."

They leaped into the canal water, and he let himself sink down and down to the bottom like a golden statue and lie there in green silence. All was water-quiet and deep, all was peace. He felt the steady, slow current drift him easily.

If I lie here long enough, he thought, *the water will work and eat away my flesh until the bones show like coral. Just my skeleton left. And then the water can build on that skeleton—green things, deep-water things, red things, yellow things. Change. Change. Slow, deep, silent change. And isn't that what it is up* there?

He saw the sky submerged above him, the sun made Martian by atmosphere and time and space.

Up there, a big river, he thought, *a Martian river, all of us lying deep in it, in our pebble houses, in our sunken boulder houses, like crayfish hidden, and the water washing away our old bodies and lengthening the bones and—*

He let himself drift up through the soft light.

Dan sat on the edge of the canal, regarding his father seriously.

"*Utha,*" he said.

"What?" asked his father.

The boy smiled. "You know. *Utha's* the Martian word for 'father.'"

"Where did you learn it?"

"I don't know. Around. *Utha!*"

"What do you want?"

The boy hesitated. "I—I want to change my name."

"Change it?"

"Yes."

His mother swam over. "What's wrong with Dan for a name?"

Dan fidgeted. "The other day you called Dan, Dan, Dan. I didn't even hear. I said to myself, that's not my name. I've a new name I want to use."

Mr. Bittering held to the side of the canal, his body cold and his heart pounding slowly. "What is this new name?"

"Linnl. Isn't that a good name? Can I use it? Can't I, please?"

Mr. Bittering put his hand to his head. He thought of the silly rocket, himself working alone, himself alone even among his family, so alone.

He heard his wife say, "Why not?"

He heard himself say, "Yes, you can use it."

"Yaaa!" screamed the boy. "I'm Linnl, Linnl!"

Racing down the meadowlands, he danced and shouted.

Mr. Bittering looked at his wife. "Why did we do that?"

"I don't know," she said. "It just seemed like a good idea."

They walked into the hills. They strolled on old mosaic[8] paths, beside still-pumping fountains. The paths were covered with a thin film of cool water all summer long. You kept your bare feet cool all the day, splashing as in a creek, wading.

They came to a small deserted Martian villa with a good view of the valley. It was on top of a hill. Blue marble halls, large murals, a swimming pool. It was refreshing in this hot summertime. The Martians hadn't believed in large cities.

"How nice," said Mrs. Bittering, "if we could move up here to this villa for the summer."

"Come on," he said. "We're going back to town. There's work to be done on the rocket."

But as he worked that night, the thought of the cool blue marble villa entered his mind. As the hours passed, the rocket seemed less important.

---

8. mosaic (mō·zāʹik) *adj.*: made of small pieces of colored glass, stone, and so on, often forming a pattern or picture.

In the flow of days and weeks, the rocket receded[9] and dwindled.[10] The old fever was gone. It frightened him to think he had let it slip this way. But somehow the heat, the air, the working conditions—

He heard the men murmuring on the porch of his metal shop.

"Everyone's going. You heard?"

"All going. That's right."

Bittering came out. "Going where?" He saw a couple of trucks, loaded with children and furniture, drive down the dusty street.

"Up to the villas," said the man.

"Yeah, Harry. I'm going. So is Sam. Aren't you, Sam?"

"That's right, Harry. What about you?"

"I've got work to do here."

"Work! You can finish that rocket in the autumn, when it's cooler."

He took a breath. "I got the frame all set up."

"In the autumn is better." Their voices were lazy in the heat.

"Got to work," he said.

"Autumn," they reasoned. And they sounded so sensible, so right.

Autumn would be best, he thought. *Plenty of time, then.*

No! cried part of himself, deep down, put away, locked tight, suffocating. *No! No!*

"In the autumn," he said.

"Come on, Harry," they all said.

"Yes," he said, feeling his flesh melt in the hot liquid air. "Yes, in the autumn. I'll begin work again then."

"I got a villa near the Tirra Canal," said someone.

"You mean the Roosevelt Canal, don't you?"

"Tirra. The old Martian name."

"But on the map—"

"Forget the map. It's Tirra now. Now I found a place in the Pillan mountains—"

"You mean the Rockefeller range," said Bittering.

"I mean the Pillan mountains," said Sam.

"Yes," said Bittering, buried in the hot, swarming air. "The Pillan mountains."

> "You can finish that rocket in the autumn, when it's cooler."

---

9. **receded** (ri·sēd′id) *v.:* withdrew; became more distant.
10. **dwindled** (dwin′dəld) *v.:* shrank.

Everyone worked at loading the truck in the hot, still afternoon of the next day.

Laura, Dan, and David carried packages. Or, as they preferred to be known, Ttil, Linnl, and Werr carried packages.

The furniture was abandoned in the little white cottage.

"It looked just fine in Boston," said the mother. "And here in the cottage. But up at the villa? No. We'll get it when we come back in the autumn."

Bittering himself was quiet.

"I've some ideas on furniture for the villa," he said after a time. "Big, lazy furniture."

"What about your encyclopedia? You're taking it along, surely?"

Mr. Bittering glanced away. "I'll come and get it next week."

They turned to their daughter. "What about your New York dresses?"

The bewildered girl stared. "Why, I don't want them anymore."

They shut off the gas, the water; they locked the doors and walked away. Father peered into the truck.

"Gosh, we're not taking much," he said. "Considering all we brought to Mars, this is only a handful!"

He started the truck.

> The daughter wove tapestries and the sons played songs on ancient flutes and pipes, their laughter echoing in the marble villa.

Looking at the small white cottage for a long moment, he was filled with a desire to rush to it, touch it, say goodbye to it, for he felt as if he were going away on a long journey, leaving something to which he could never quite return, never understand again.

Just then Sam and his family drove by in another truck.

"Hi, Bittering! Here we go!"

The truck swung down the ancient highway out of town. There were sixty others traveling the same direction. The town filled with a silent, heavy dust from their passage. The canal waters lay blue in the sun, and a quiet wind moved in the strange trees.

"Goodbye, town!" said Mr. Bittering.

"Goodbye, goodbye," said the family, waving to it.

They did not look back again.

Summer burned the canals dry. Summer moved like flame upon the meadows. In the empty Earth settlement, the painted houses flaked and peeled. Rubber tires upon which children had swung in backyards hung suspended like stopped clock pendulums[11] in the blazing air.

At the metal shop, the rocket frame began to rust.

In the quiet autumn Mr. Bittering stood, very dark now, very golden-eyed, upon the slope above his villa, looking at the valley.

"It's time to go back," said Cora.

"Yes, but we're not going," he said quietly. "There's nothing there anymore."

"Your books," she said. "Your fine clothes."

"Your *lles* and your fine *ior uele rre,*" she said.

"The town's empty. No one's going back," he said. "There's no reason to, none at all."

The daughter wove tapestries and the sons played songs on ancient flutes and pipes, their laughter echoing in the marble villa.

Mr. Bittering gazed at the Earth settlement far away in the low valley. "Such odd, such ridiculous houses the Earth people built."

"They didn't know any better," his wife mused. "Such ugly people. I'm glad they've gone."

They both looked at each other, startled by all they had just finished saying. They laughed.

"Where did they go?" he wondered. He glanced at his wife. She was golden and slender as his daughter. She looked at him, and he seemed almost as young as their eldest son.

"I don't know," she said.

"We'll go back to town maybe next year, or the year after, or the year after that," he said, calmly. "Now—I'm warm. How about taking a swim?"

They turned their backs to the valley. Arm in arm they walked silently down a path of clear-running spring water.

Five years later a rocket fell out of the sky. It lay steaming in the valley. Men leaped out of it, shouting.

"We won the war on Earth! We're here to rescue you! Hey!"

But the American-built town of cottages, peach trees, and theaters was silent. They found a flimsy rocket frame rusting in an empty shop.

---

11. **pendulums** (pen′dyo͞o·ləmz) *n.*: hanging weights that swing back and forth; used to regulate the movement of old-fashioned clocks.

The rocket men searched the hills. The captain established headquarters in an abandoned bar. His lieutenant came back to report.

"The town's empty, but we found native life in the hills, sir. Dark people. Yellow eyes. Martians. Very friendly. We talked a bit, not much. They learn English fast. I'm sure our relations will be most friendly with them, sir."

"Dark, eh?" mused the captain. "How many?"

"Six, eight hundred, I'd say, living in those marble ruins in the hills, sir. Tall, healthy. Beautiful women."

"Did they tell you what became of the men and women who built this Earth settlement, Lieutenant?"

"They hadn't the foggiest notion of what happened to this town or its people."

"Strange. You think those Martians killed them?"

"They look surprisingly peaceful. Chances are a plague[12] did this town in, sir."

"Perhaps. I suppose this is one of those mysteries we'll never solve. One of those mysteries you read about."

The captain looked at the room, the dusty windows, the blue mountains rising beyond, the canals moving in the light, and he heard the soft wind in the air. He shivered. Then, recovering, he tapped a large fresh map he had thumbtacked to the top of an empty table.

"Lots to be done, Lieutenant." His voice droned on and quietly on as the sun sank behind the blue hills. "New settlements. Mining sites, minerals to be looked for. Bacteriological specimens taken. The work, all the work. And the old records were lost. We'll have a job of remapping to do, renaming the mountains and rivers and such. Calls for a little imagination.

"What do you think of naming those mountains the Lincoln Mountains, this canal the Washington Canal, those hills—we can name those hills for you, Lieutenant. Diplomacy. And you, for a favor, might name a town for me. Polishing the apple. And why not make this the Einstein Valley, and further over . . . are you *listening*, Lieutenant?"

The lieutenant snapped his gaze from the blue color and the quiet mist of the hills far beyond the town.

"What? Oh, *yes*, sir!"

---

12. **plague** (plāg) *n.*: deadly disease that spreads quickly.

Meet the Writer

Ray Bradbury

Stories Bite Him on the Leg!

Ray Bradbury (1920–   ) decided at the age of twelve to become a writer. He credits this decision to a circus performer called Mr. Electrico. Bradbury recalls one performance:

> ❝Mr. Electrico twitched his blazing sword. He touched me on the right shoulder, the left shoulder, and then gently on my brow and the tip of my nose. I felt the storms jiggling in my eardrums, the blue fire swarming into my brain and down my arms and out my fingertips. . . .❞

Bradbury went home and shortly afterward began to write. That idea eventually paid off. Bradbury enjoyed great success with works such as *Fahrenheit 451* (the title refers to the temperature at which book paper burns), *Dandelion Wine, Something Wicked This Way Comes* (its main character is based on Mr. Electrico), and *The Martian Chronicles* (which includes "The Naming of Names").

Bradbury has been called the "world's greatest science fiction writer," but he thinks of himself as an "idea writer." Of the products of his ideas Bradbury says:

> ❝My stories have led me through my life. They shout, I follow. They run up and bite me on the leg— I respond by writing down everything that goes on during the bite. When I finish, the idea lets go, and runs off.❞

For Independent Reading

In Ray Bradbury's short story collections—such as *The Illustrated Man, R Is for Rocket*, and *The Stories of Ray Bradbury*—you'll find popular stories like "Mars Is Heaven," "The Sound of Summer Running," and "The Flying Machine."

Writing Workshop

Assignment
Describe something you've observed.

Audience
Your teacher and classmates.

SKILLS FOCUS

Writing Skills
Write a descriptive essay.

DESCRIPTIVE WRITING
Descriptive Essay

Have your ever read a story, or perhaps an autobiography, that was so evocative and richly detailed that you forgot that you were reading and felt like you were really there? In a descriptive essay your goal is to evoke a mood or to create a vivid impression of something through details that appeal to the senses and to the imagination.

Prewriting

1 Choosing a Subject

Read and respond to this prompt:

> When you write a descriptive essay, you write as an observer, not as a participant. You gather details about your subject and arrange them in an essay that lets readers see what you saw, hear what you heard, feel what you felt. A descriptive essay conveys a dominant impression of its subject. Choose a subject—a person, animal, object, place, or experience—and re-create it through detailed description.

Before picking your subject, consider these questions:

• Can I observe this subject directly? If not, can I recall it clearly enough to describe it vividly?

• Do I find the subject interesting? Would it interest a reader?

• Does the subject involve enough sensory details for a good description?

CALVIN AND HOBBES © Watterson. Reprinted with permission of UNIVERSAL PRESS SYNDICATE. All rights reserved.

2 Finding More Ideas

For more ideas, freewrite for a few minutes on one or more of these topics:

- activities you can observe (someone cooking dinner; a basketball game)
- people you can observe (your older sister; an athlete)
- animals you can observe (your pet; a monkey at the zoo)
- places and things you can observe (the lunchroom; a tree)
- events you can observe (a scientific experiment; a sunrise)

3 Gathering Details

Gather details about your subject by observing the subject directly or by drawing on your memory. You may find it helpful to use a chart like the one below.

Sensory Details	Events	Impressions
see coconut trees • crickets **hear** airplane • waves **feel** sun • hot air **smell** salt water **taste** lemon candy	dragonflies flutter and glide • trucks haul tons of dirt • ferries race by	This is just the place for me.

Good descriptions are not limited to simple observations and recollections. **Figures of speech,** or imaginative comparisons, can add color to your writing and help your readers picture the subject of your essay. To review figures of speech, see page 464.

4 Organizing

There are three common ways to organize descriptive essays:

Spatial order. Describe details according to location—near to far or far to near, left to right or right to left, top to bottom or bottom to top, clockwise or counterclockwise. Spatial order is often used in descriptions of a place.

Framework for a Descriptive Essay

Introduction (identifies the subject, time, and place and gives background information): _____ _____

Body (presents details in clear order; includes sensory images and figures of speech):

1. _____

Specifics: _____

2. _____

Specifics: _____

3. _____

Specifics: _____

4. _____

Specifics: _____

Conclusion (includes main impression; expresses your feelings; tells why the subject is important): ____ _____

---

early each morning—smells of baking bread—heat of ovens —long-handled paddles—trays of rolls crisp and hot to touch—delicious taste.

See The Pronoun, 1b;
Agreement, 2a–x.

Strategies for Elaboration

Sensory Details
Elaborate with words that appeal to the five senses:

sight   *blinding headlights*

sound   *squish of wet boots*

smell   *fetid odor of decay*

taste   *fiery peppers*

touch   *silky hair*

Figurative Language
Elaborate with vivid figures of speech:

simile
The moon was as bright as the noonday sun.

metaphor
The moon was a butterscotch candy, plump and golden.

personification
The photograph spoke to me of times past.

Language Handbook
H E L P

Order of importance. Put the most important details at the beginning or at the end for emphasis. Writers often use order of importance to convey their feelings about a subject. This type of organization works well in descriptions of people and objects.

Chronological order. Arrange details in the order in which they occur or in the order in which you observe them. Chronological order usually works best in description of events, such as a scientific experiment or an approaching storm.

Drafting

1 Focusing on the Main Idea

Everything you write needs a focus—a **main idea** that shapes what you put down on paper. To state your main idea clearly, ask yourself: "What is my overall impression of my subject?" or "What is the purpose of my essay?"

2 Setting the Scene

Whenever you observe something, you view it from a particular place and at a particular time. By telling readers where you are, you give them a place to "stand" as they observe through your eyes.

3 Using Transitions

Use transitional words and phrases to link ideas. Some words that will help you lead the reader from one idea or image to the next are listed below:

Words showing spatial organization: *across from, around, below, beside, between, close to, down, far from*
Words showing order of importance: *first, last, mainly, more important, then, to begin with*
Words showing chronological order: *after, before, eventually, finally, first, now, next, then, when*

Student Model

The Nature of Patam

Right now I'm sitting cross-legged on the big gray porch at our Patam beach house. The bright shining sun and hot day make me feel lazy.

The shadowy light-and-dark-green jungle to the left of me has tall, light-brown trunks of trees everywhere. To the right a coconut tree with its palms spread out looks like a parachute. Brown and gray monkeys chatter away as small green crickets sing. Different colored dragonflies flutter and glide so fast in every direction I can't see what color they are!

Lively waves leap to and fro on the pure white beach, while salt water and rock bash noisily together. An airplane rumbles slowly away. Across the bay trucks rattle loudly as they haul tons of brown dirt dark as chocolate.

Boats are all over the water! About three miles out huge tankers loom above the deep, gigantic, calm blue ocean, with ferries racing past them on their way to Singapore. Another boat, a small abandoned tan-brown sampan, bobs gently up and down in the gold sunlit waters that seem like enormous masses of lemon candy. I think Patam is just the place for me.

—Benjamin Bethea
Batam Island Christian Home School
Batam, Indonesia

*The writer introduces his **subject** and tells where he is.*

***Details** of sight, sound, and movement create a vivid picture.*

*The writer uses **spatial organization**; he moves from the trees near him to the plane, trucks, and boats in the distance.*

*The writer tells how he **feels** about this place.*

Writing Tips

Denotation and Connotation

Use words precisely. Let context determine whether a particular word is right. For example, the words *slim* and *skinny* have nearly the same dictionary meaning, but *slim* conveys an impression of strength and health while *skinny* has a connotation of weakness.

Clichés

Avoid expressions that have been used so often that they are stale. Examples are

- *the picture of health*
- *playful as a kitten*
- *red as a rose*

INTERNET
More Writer's Models
Keyword: LE5 7-4

Evaluating and Revising

Use the chart below to help you evaluate and revise your descriptive essay.

Descriptive Essay: Content and Organization Guidelines		
Evaluation Questions	▶ **Tips**	▶ **Revision Techniques**
❶ Does your introduction identify the subject?	▶ **Circle** the subject of the essay.	▶ **Add** a sentence that clearly identifies the subject of your description.
❷ Does your choice of words bring sensory details and figures of speech to life?	▶ **Highlight** sensory details and imaginative comparisons. **Put an S** above sensory details. **Put an F** above sentences that employ figures of speech.	▶ **Elaborate** with additional sensory details. **Delete** irrelevant details.
❸ Are the details arranged in a clear order?	▶ In the margin, **indicate** the mode of organization— spatial, chronological, or order of importance.	▶ **Rearrange** details if necessary. **Add** transitions for greater coherence.
❹ Have you included your thoughts and feelings about the subject?	▶ **Put a check mark** next to any statement of your feelings or thoughts.	▶ **Add** specific details about thoughts and feelings.
❺ Does your conclusion state why the subject is significant to you? Does it convey an overall impression of the subject?	▶ **Underline** the statement that tells why the experience is meaningful. **Bracket** statements that hint at the overall impression.	▶ **Add** a statement explaining why the experience is important or conveying the overall impression.

Read the following descriptive paragraph. Following the model you'll find questions to help you evaluate the writer's revisions.

Revision Model

What is the best food you've ever eaten? For me, it was

a freshly baked roll from my grandparents' bakery.

I discovered this when I visited them last year.
~~They own a bakery and live upstairs.~~ Every morning I

woke up at about 5 o'clock to the *delicious* ~~nice~~ smell of *freshly* newly

baked bread. I ~~would make~~ *made* my way downstairs where the

bakers were removing *loaves of* bread from the ovens with long-

handled paddles. ~~I was not allowed to touch the trays.~~

One of the bakers would throw me a crisp, well-browned

sprinkled with poppy seeds
roll , so hot that I had to keep tossing it from one hand to

the other. To this day, I can still recall the smell and taste

of that bread. I *ran* ~~went~~ back upstairs, where, all alone in the

dim ~~gloomy~~ light of early morning, I *munched* ~~ate~~ my roll slowly,

savoring ~~enjoying~~ every bite.

Evaluating the Revision

1. What order of organization has the writer used?
2. Which details were added? Do they appeal to different senses?
3. What words were added, deleted, or changed? Do they improve the description?
4. Which sentence concludes the description? Does it explain why the experience was important?

Test Practice

Directions: Read the passages. Then, read each question, and write the letter of the best response.

The News of King Midas
from *The Royal News*

Rumors of the so-called Midas touch have been confirmed today. According to sources close to the king, Midas is now unable to eat or drink, as anything he touches turns to gold.

"Serves him right," said one palace insider who asked not to be named. "He could have wished for something sensible, such as a triple-tax-free diversified bond portfolio. Now who knows where the price of gold is heading?"

The king's wife and daughter were unavailable for comment, as they had been turned to gold.

from *Cook to the King: A Novel*

"Sandwich?" the head cook roared. "You want me to fix you a sandwich?" She glared at the king. "With what, may I ask?"

What an idiot he was. Even the smallest servant boy knew what was going to happen by the time dessert was served, but not King Midas. Oh, no. Not content merely to ruin her entire day's work (that perfectly poached salmon! that lovely macaroni pudding!), he had to come tearing through her kitchen. By the time he was through, there wasn't a crumb that didn't clink and glitter when she swept it up.

from *A Courtier's Memoir*

After all my years serving in the palace, I thought I'd seen it all. When the king, however, started turning everything to gold, you could have knocked me over with a feather. Actually, he nearly *did* knock me over with a feather. An ostrich plume, it was, on my second-best hat! If I do say so myself, I was looking rather spiffy until the king snatched it off and started waving it around. He yelled that he'd turned my hat to gold. It was gold, all right. Solid gold. I've still got the lump on my head to prove it.

King Midas's E-mail

To: gods_helpline@olympus.edu
From: kmidas@palace.org
Subject: My Kingdom for a Burger

OK, point taken. I was greedy and foolish, and I'm sorry. Please, undo my wish before I starve to death!

SKILLS FOCUS

Literary Skills
Analyze point of view.

Collection 4: Skills Review

1. In which passage does the narrator use a **third-person-limited point of view**?
   A *The Royal News*
   B *Cook to the King*
   C *A Courtier's Memoir*
   D King Midas's E-mail

2. The **point of view** in *A Courtier's Memoir* is —
   F omniscient
   G first person
   H third-person limited
   J second person

3. Which passage is most **objective** in telling what has happened to King Midas?
   A *The Royal News*
   B *Cook to the King*
   C *A Courtier's Memoir*
   D King Midas's E-mail

4. The **narrator,** or speaker, in *A Courtier's Memoir* is —
   F the king himself
   G the cook to the king
   H an omniscient narrator
   J a courtier in the king's court

5. The **speaker** in King Midas's E-mail is —
   A the king himself
   B the cook to the king
   C an omniscient narrator
   D a courtier in the king's court

Constructed Response

6. Briefly describe the differences between the **omniscient, first-person,** and **third-person-limited points of view.**

Test Practice

Directions: Read the passage. Then, read each question, and write the letter of the best response.

Can We Rescue the Reefs?
Ritu Upadhyay
from *Time for Kids*

❶ Time is running out to stop the destruction of coral reefs.

❷ Under the clear blue sea, bustling communities of ocean creatures live together in brightly colored, wildly stacked structures called coral reefs. These silent, majestic underwater cities are home to four thousand different species of fish and thousands of plants and animals. For millions of years, marine creatures have lived together in reefs, going about their business in their own little water worlds.

❸ But danger looms. At an international meeting on coral reefs in October 2000, scientists issued a harsh warning. More than one quarter of the world's reefs have been destroyed. . . . Unless drastic measures are taken, the remaining reefs may be dead in twenty years. "We are about to lose them," says Clive Wilkinson of the Coral Reef Monitoring Network.

Precious Underwater Habitats

❹ The destruction of coral reefs, some of which are 2.5 million years old, would have a very serious impact on our oceans. Though coral reefs take up less than 1 percent of the ocean floor, they are home to 25 percent of all underwater species. Wiping them out would put thousands of creatures at risk of extinction. It would also destroy one of our planet's most beautiful living treasures.

❺ Though it's often mistaken for rock because of its stony texture, coral is actually made up of tiny clear animals called coral polyps. Millions stick together in colonies and form a hard outer shell. When coral die, their skeletons are left behind, and new coral build on top. The colonies eventually grow together, creating large reefs. Reefs grow into complex mazelike structures with different rooms, hallways, holes, and crevices for their inhabitants to live in. Over the years the ancient Great Barrier Reef off Australia's coast has grown to be 1,240 miles long!

SKILLS FOCUS

Reading Skills
Analyze an author's argument.

1. Which of the following statements best summarizes the writer's **perspective** in "Can We Rescue the Reefs?"

   A The outlook for coral reefs is hopeless.

   B Global warming is a threat to the whole earth.

   C Saving endangered coral reefs is very important.

   D Coral reefs are beautiful little worlds within the oceans.

2. Paragraph 2 contains words and phrases such as "bustling communities," "underwater cities," "home," "going about their business," and "their own little water worlds." The writer uses those words and phrases to —

   F make coral reefs seem like human societies

   G describe coral reefs the way a scientist would describe them

   H tell where coral reefs are located

   J describe how coral reefs are formed

3. In paragraph 3, the writer supports her position by —

   A describing her personal fears about the reefs

   B quoting an expert on the issue

   C telling a brief story about the development of coral reefs

   D giving reasons why coral reefs are beautiful

4. Which statement is an example of a **statistic**?

   F "Time is running out to stop the destruction of coral reefs."

   G "Coral is actually made up of tiny clear animals. . . ."

   H "Reefs grow into complex maze-like structures. . . ."

   J "More than one quarter of the world's reefs have been destroyed. . . ."

5. Which of the following is a statement of **fact**—something that can be proved to be true?

   A Coral is the most beautiful thing in the sea.

   B Over the years the ancient Great Barrier Reef has grown to be 1,240 miles long.

   C Coral reefs must be saved.

   D Coral reefs are fascinating.

6. The writer's **purpose** in this article is to —

   F inform

   G describe

   H persuade

   J all of the above

Constructed Response

7. According to the article, why are coral reefs important?

Collection 4: Skills Review
Vocabulary Skills

Test Practice

Synonyms

DIRECTIONS: Choose the word or phrase that means the same, or about the same, as the underlined word.

1. Something that is exotic is —
   A   ordinary in a dull way
   B   different in a fascinating way
   C   very desirable
   D   strongly offensive

2. Something that is intricate is —
   F   simple
   G   inside
   H   ancient
   J   complicated

3. Habitual is most like —
   A   customary
   B   irregular
   C   occasionally
   D   never

4. Convoluted means —
   F   complicated
   G   ordinary
   H   murky
   J   strange

5. Someone who is in transition is experiencing —
   A   prosperity
   B   balance
   C   stability
   D   change

6. Deprivation is most like —
   F   abundance
   G   loss
   H   privilege
   J   growth

7. Arrogant refers to someone who is —
   A   overly emotional
   B   deeply confused
   C   overly self-important
   D   easily persuaded

8. Intolerable means —
   F   worthwhile
   G   unjust
   H   infrequent
   J   unbearable

9. Simultaneously means —
   A   all but one
   B   never the same
   C   over the top
   D   at the same time

10. Someone seeking refuge would be in search of —
    F   food
    G   shelter
    H   clothing
    J   garbage

SKILLS FOCUS

Vocabulary Skills
Identify synonyms.

Collection 4: Skills Review

Writing Skills

Test Practice

DIRECTIONS: Read the following paragraph from a descriptive essay. Then, answer each question that follows.

(1) The annual book sale, sponsored by our parent-teacher organization, transformed the school gym into an exhibit hall filled with thousands of books, videos, and audiotapes. (2) Tables were covered with brightly colored shawls. (3) The tables were arranged in a horseshoe curve along the walls. (4) At the entrance to the left were works of fiction arranged by subjects such as adventure, romance, and sports. (5) There were tables devoted to ethnic works. (6) At the rear were tables containing works of nonfiction: biographies, histories, essays, and almanacs. (7) Then came nonprint offerings: books on cassette and movies adapted from novels. (8) At the right end of the horseshoe, a group of student volunteers took orders for books. (9) In the center of the gym were tables and chairs that invited browsers to examine books and to chat about them with teachers, librarians, and parents. (10) What one heard was a low buzz of interest, and what one saw were student faces intent on discovering something good to read.

1. The method of organization used in this paragraph is —

   A spatial
   B chronological
   C order of importance
   D all of the above

2. What would be the best way to combine sentences 2 and 3?

   F Tables were covered with brightly colored shawls, and the tables were arranged in a horse-shoe curve along the wall.
   G Tables covered with brightly colored shawls were arranged in a horseshoe curve along the walls.
   H Tables were covered with brightly colored shawls; also, they were arranged in a horse-shoe curve along the walls.
   J Tables arranged in a horseshoe curve with brightly colored shawls were along the walls of the gym.

3. Which sentence would be improved by the addition of specific details?

   A sentence 4
   B sentence 5
   C sentence 6
   D sentence 7

4. Transitional words or phrases are used in all of the following *except* —

   F sentence 3
   G sentence 4
   H sentence 6
   J sentence 7

5. Which of the following would be the *best* replacement for the word *containing* in sentence 6?

   A holding
   B enclosing
   C including
   D stacked with

SKILLS FOCUS

Writing Skills
Analyze a descriptive essay.

Fiction

A Little Patience

Young Miguel Chavez longs for his family to treat him like an adult. For a year he tries to prove that he is ready to make the difficult journey driving sheep into the mountains. It is not until some sheep are missing and a serious letter arrives that Miguel is truly able to prove himself in Joseph Krumgold's Newbery winner . . . *and now Miguel.*

The Faithful Servant

Marguerite De Angeli's *The Door in the Wall* takes place in medieval England. Robin, the son of the great lord Sir John de Bureford, is supposed to become a page—a boy training for knighthood. Unfortunately, he is stricken with a mysterious illness that causes him to lose the movement of his legs. Determined not to disappoint his father, he overcomes his problems and helps to turn back the Welsh invaders who threaten the kingdom.

All Aboard!

When Jim Hawkins, an impressionable young cabin boy, discovers a treasure map, he finds himself thrust into an adventure beyond compare. The notorious Long John Silver joins Jim and two of his friends on a ship. Can Hawkins trust this mysterious pirate? Find out in Robert Louis Stevenson's *Treasure Island.*

This title is available in the HRW Library.

In Another Land

Have you ever wondered what it would be like to make your way through India? Anni Axworthy gives you more than a passing glance of the Asian subcontinent in *Anni's India Diary.* Discover Hindu gods and goddesses, learn how to play cricket, and visit the Taj Mahal along with Anni. Lively illustrations accompany the text of Anni's unforgettable journey.

Nonfiction

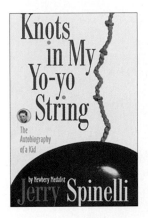

The Way He Was

In *Knots in My Yo-yo String*, Newbery Award–winner Jerry Spinelli touchingly revisits his childhood and growing up. He recalls dreams of becoming a major-league shortstop, hours with comic books, and the only time he received detention in school. Spinelli had no idea he would become a writer, but he recounts in compelling prose the event that inspired him to become one.

The Customs of Warriors

During the sixteenth and seventeenth centuries, Samurai warriors were the most honored group in Japan. In *A Samurai Castle*, Fiona MacDonald explores the Samurai culture and the conditions that helped shape this distinct group of fighting men. Perceptive illustrations reveal the design of their living arrangements, and MacDonald's narrative tells how the Samurai spent their days, how they trained for battle, and the reasons they were respected and feared.

An Exciting Journey

Megan McNeill Libby had reservations after deciding to spend her junior year in France. When she arrived, she felt out of place in her new surroundings, and she wondered if she would ever learn the customs and language. After a few months she began to make friends and appreciate the fascinating culture. Megan chronicles this exciting time of her life in *Postcards from France*.

A Wealth of Ideas

In *Made in China: Ideas and Inventions from Ancient China*, Suzanne Williams describes some of the many contributions the ancient Chinese made to science and society. From discoveries in astronomy and improvements in irrigation systems to the casting of bronze and the standardization of roads, measurements, and writing, Williams places Chinese invention in a context that helps to break down ethnic and cultural barriers.

Collection 5

Worlds of Words:
Prose and Poetry

Literary Focus:
Analyzing Prose and Poetry

Informational Focus:
Analyzing Main Idea

Sculpture of hand,
Atacama Desert, Chile.

INTERNET
Collection
Resources
Keyword: LE5 7-5

477

Elements of Literature
Reading Like a Wolf *by* Kylene Beers
UNDERSTANDING THE FORMS OF PROSE

A student once asked what I meant when I said his essay was really a short story. "What's the difference?" he wanted to know. "And," he continued, "what does it matter?"

Knowing the Difference Makes a Difference

His question was a good one. Why does knowing the difference between those types of prose make a difference? Well, it's something like knowing the difference in sports terms. If your coach says the team you're playing against uses a one-on-one defense instead of a zone defense, you know what to expect when you hit the basketball court.

Understanding the type of prose you're reading helps you anticipate what you'll find in the text. Once you know that what you are reading is a short story, for example, you'll be expecting characters, conflict, and a theme—you won't be looking for personal opinions or historical accuracy.

You Speak in Prose

You might think of **prose** as everything that isn't poetry. In fact, you've been speaking prose all your life. You also read prose every day—in your textbooks, in novels, in magazines, on the Web, in newspapers, in the notes you pass in the halls, and in the e-mails you receive. You read each type of prose differently. You read a note from your best friend in one way, and you read the chapter in your science book another way.

Obviously prose covers a lot of ground. It can be generally divided into **fiction**—made-up stories—and **nonfiction,** which relates facts about real people, places, things, and events. Let's look at the different forms that fiction and nonfiction can take.

Fiction: Imagined Events and Characters

A **short story** is just what it sounds like: a short work of **fiction** with a few characters who move through a series of events (the plot) and work through a conflict, which leads to a climax and a resolution.

If all that happens in five to twenty pages, you have a short story. If you find yourself looking at one hundred pages or more, then you've left the short story and headed straight into a **novel.** In a novel you meet lots of characters, probably see subplots unfold within the larger plot, explore many themes, and encounter many conflicts.

If one hundred pages is too long and twenty is too short, then you've got a **novella,** which is simply a short novel.

INTERNET
More About Genres
Keyword: LE5 7-5

Literary Skills
Understand forms of prose.

Nonfiction: Based on Fact

An **essay** is a short piece of prose that discusses a limited topic. Some people write short personal essays about simple things, like eating an ice-cream cone or taking a dog for a walk. Others write longer essays about complex issues, such as freedom, respect, and justice.

Some nonfiction topics are just too big for a short form like the essay. You might read about an Olympic athlete in a magazine article, for example, but if you really wanted to know the whole story of her life, you'd look at a book-length **biography.**

"Is It True?"

Sometimes writers use real-life events in their fiction. Gary Paulsen explains in an essay that he's really been attacked by moose.

When I wrote of the moose attack in *Hatchet* and again in *Brian's Winter,* I used the events from my life in the story. I wrote of what the moose attacks were like. But when it was really happening to me, I didn't think, oh man, this is great, I'm getting creamed by a moose, this will be wonderful to write about in my next book. I just used the memory later in the context of the story.

"Read Like a Wolf Eats"

Whatever type of prose you enjoy the most, remember the important thing is to read. Here's what Gary Paulsen says:

The most, *most* important thing is to read. Read all the time; read when they tell you not to read, read what they tell you not to read, read with a flashlight under the covers, read on the bus, standing on the corner, waiting for a friend, in the dentist's waiting room. Read every minute that you can. Read like a wolf eats. Read.

Practice

To show that you know more about prose than you think you do, work with a partner to fill out a prose chart like the following one. First, copy the chart on a separate piece of paper. Then, think of titles that are examples of each kind of prose. (Notice that there are more types of prose here than we just discussed. You could name even more types if you looked in a bookstore.) You might want to prepare an illustrated "prose group" for your classroom.

Finding the Main Idea

by Kylene Beers

Being an Active Reader

While visiting a first-grade classroom during reading time, I watched one boy bounce in his chair as he looked at a storybook. "What are you doing?" I asked. "My teacher said that good readers are active readers, so I'm being active," he replied. While I was sure the teacher had told him that, I was just as sure the activity she had in mind involved thinking rather than bouncing. Good readers *are* active readers, and one important reading activity is finding the main idea.

What the Main Idea *Isn't*

Sometimes figuring out what something *is* can be easier if you start by defining what it *isn't*. The main idea is *not* the plot. It is *not* the theme. It is *not* the topic. It is also *not* a term you use when discussing fiction.

What the Main Idea *Is*

Main idea *is* a term we use when discussing nonfiction. The main idea of a text *is* the idea that is central to the entire text (not just to part of the text). Sometimes the main idea is stated directly; other times it isn't. (If you are talking about fiction, the term for the central idea is *theme*.)

As you read the selection on page 481, make a list of what you learn. At the end of the selection, you'll see how to use your list to help you figure out the main idea.

SKILLS FOCUS

Reading Skills Find the main idea.

A Model for Finding the Main Idea

Look at the paragraph below. The **topic** is "dogs." What is the **main idea**? (The main idea should be stated in a full sentence.)

> Dogs are very smart animals. You can train them to do many things. They are also friendly and want to be with people and other dogs. They are loyal and quickly forgive you if you forget to play with them for a day. Because of these reasons, dogs are great pets.

The main idea *isn't* that dogs are intelligent, because that is not what the whole paragraph is about.

By the third sentence, you are learning a lot about dogs.

The final sentence reveals the main idea.

A Good Reason to Look Up

Shaquille O'Neal

*Much is required from those
to whom much is given,
for their responsibility is greater.*

Luke 12:48

When I was in junior high school, what my friends thought of me was real important to me. During those years I grew much taller than most of my peers. Being so tall made me feel uncomfortable. In order to keep the focus off of me and my unusual height, I went along with the crowd who would play practical jokes on other kids at school. Being one of the class clowns gave me a way to make sure that the jokes were directed at others, and not at me. ❶

I would pull all kinds of pranks that were hurtful, and sometimes even harmful, to others. Once before gym class, my friends and I put Icy Hot in the gym shorts of one of the kids on the basketball team. Not only was he terribly embarrassed, but he also had to go to the school nurse's office. I thought it was going to be funny, but it ended up that no one thought it was—least of all my father. ❷

My parents didn't always think that my behavior was funny. They reminded me about The Golden Rule: to treat others as I would like to be treated. Many times, I was disciplined for the hurtful way that I was treating others. What I was doing was hurting other kids, and in turn hurting my reputation as someone to be looked up to. My friends were looking up to me because I was tall, but what did they see? ❸

My parents wanted me to be a leader who was a good example to others—to be a decent human being. They taught me to set my own goals, and to do the best at everything that I set out to do. During the lectures I got from my father, he told me over and over again to be the leader that I was meant to be—to be a big man in my heart and actions, as well as in my body. I had to question myself whether or not it was important to be the kind of leader and person my father believed I was inside. I knew in my heart that he was right. So I tried my best to follow my father's advice. ❹

IDENTIFY

❶ Notice the pronoun *I* in the first sentence. This is a first-person account. To find out who the *I* is, check the name of the writer. What have you learned about the writer at this point?

INFER

❷ This paragraph gives you a specific example of a prank O'Neal pulled. Why do you think O'Neal remembers this specific prank?

IDENTIFY

❸ O'Neal says that while his pranks were hurting others, they also hurt himself. How did his actions hurt himself?

INTERPRET

❹ What do you learn about O'Neal's father in this paragraph? What lessons did his father teach O'Neal?

FIND THE MAIN IDEA

❺ In this paragraph, O'Neal is no longer telling about what happened to him in junior high. What is he now talking about?

FIND THE MAIN IDEA

❻ Why do you think the word *good* is written in italics? What have you learned about why Shaq O'Neal is a good leader today?

Once I focused on being the best that I could be at basketball and became a leader in the game, I took my responsibility to set a good example more seriously. I sometimes have to stop and think before I act, and I make mistakes occasionally—everyone is human. But I continue to look for opportunities where I can make a difference, and to set a good example because of my father's advice. I now pass it on to you. ❺

"Be a leader, Shaq, not a follower. Since people already have to look up to you, give them a *good* reason to do so." ❻

Meet the Writer

Shaquille O'Neal

"Books Can Take You Anywhere"

Shaquille O'Neal (1972–   ), also known as Shaq, is one of the most popular players in the National Basketball Association (NBA). He also has the honor of being named one of the NBA's fifty greatest players.

At 7'1", O'Neal's size alone could be intimidating. That size combined with his athletic skill have made him a powerful center for the Los Angeles Lakers.

Basketball isn't O'Neal's only love. He enjoys reading and says his parents motivated him to read. "My parents encouraged me to read and to educate myself," O'Neal has said. "Following their advice, I've always tried to read to better myself."

As a National Advisory Council member of Reading Is Fundamental, an organization that promotes child literacy, O'Neal shares his parents' message with young people. "Books can take you anywhere you want to go," Shaq says. "Follow your dreams and keep reading."

Practice the Strategy

Finding the Main Idea

PRACTICE 1

Is this selection all about _____?
When it is not stated directly, you can find the main idea of a selection by first identifying the topic and then thinking about what you learned as you read the selection. Next, you take each item on your list and ask yourself, "Is this selection all about _____?" The important word in this question is *all.* Be sure that *all* of the selection is about the item. Once you can answer yes to a question, you're close to figuring out the main idea.

To see how this strategy works, go back to page 480, and re-read the paragraph about the dogs. What did you learn about dogs? You learned they are intelligent, friendly, loyal, and forgiving and they make good pets. Now, ask yourself the "Is this selection all about _____?" question for each of these items:

- Is it all about how dogs are intelligent?
- Is it all about how dogs are friendly?
- Is it all about how dogs are loyal?
- Is it all about how dogs are forgiving?
- Is it all about how dogs make good pets?

The only question you can answer yes to is the last one, because it is the only item that applies to the entire paragraph. You can now use that question to state the main idea. You simply turn the question into a statement: "The main idea of this selection is that dogs make good pets."

Applying the Strategy

PRACTICE 2

Now, try this strategy to find the **main idea** of "A *Good* Reason to Look Up." Here are some questions you might ask yourself about this selection:

- Is this selection all about being tall?
- Is it all about being a prankster?
- Is it all about what his parents wanted O'Neal to be?
- Is it all about how O'Neal became a leader?

What else did you learn? Be sure to ask the "Is this selection all about _____?" question for each thing you learned. When you can answer yes to a question, turn the question into a statement, and you have found the main idea. What is it?

You can use this strategy to find the **main idea** of informational texts in this collection and throughout the book. Just ask yourself, "Is this selection *all* about _____?"

> **Strategy Tip**
> To figure out the **main idea,** re-read the title and the first and last paragraphs. Often something in the title and the first and last paragraphs will give you hints. If there is only one paragraph, read the first and last sentences carefully.

Reading Skills
Find the main idea.

Amigo Brothers

Make the Connection
Quickwrite ✏️

Conflicts can arise when friends take different sides in a competition. In a group, create a list titled "Rules for Competing Against a Friend."

Literary Focus
The Short Story

A short work of fiction, usually around five to twenty pages, is called a **short story.** (Sometimes a story that's even shorter is called a **short-short story.)** Short stories pack a lot of punch into a few pages. Whatever happens, happens quickly. We meet the **main characters,** get involved in their **problems,** sort out the **complications,** and move speedily to a **climax** and a **resolution.** A good short story can pack a life into a few pages.

Internal and External Conflict

In the story that follows, two best friends competing for a prize must fight each other in a boxing ring. This fight is a perfect example of an **external conflict.** The boys are supposed to knock each other out. Each boy also struggles with an **internal conflict:** How can he do his best without hurting and possibly even losing his closest friend?

Reading Skills
Comparison and Contrast: Finding Similarities and Differences

Piri Thomas begins his story by contrasting the two best friends:

"Antonio was fair, lean, and lanky, while Felix was dark, short, and husky." A **comparison** points out similarities between things; a **contrast** points out differences. After you read the story, go back over it, and use a Venn diagram to help identify the ways in which Felix and Antonio are alike and different. Write their likenesses in the space where the circles overlap.

Antonio   Felix

Similarities

Differences   Differences

INTERNET

Vocabulary Activity

Keyword: LE5 7-5

SKILLS FOCUS

Literary Skills
Understand forms of prose: the short story; understand internal and external conflict.

Reading Skills
Understand comparison and contrast.

Vocabulary Development

Here are some words to give you a fighting chance:

bouts (bouts) *n.:* matches; contests. *Both boxers had won many bouts.*

pensively (pen′siv·lē) *adv.:* thoughtfully. *Felix nodded pensively as he rested.*

torrent (tôr′ənt) *n.:* flood or rush. *A torrent of emotion left him close to tears.*

dispelled (di·speld′) *v.:* driven away. *All doubt was dispelled the moment Tony made up his mind.*

frenzied (fren′zēd) *adj.:* wild. *The audience's reaction was as frenzied as the battle in the ring.*

AMiGO BROTHERS

DiRi THoMAS

"ONLY ONE OF US CAN WiN."

Antonio Cruz and Felix Vargas were both seventeen years old. They were so together in friendship that they felt themselves to be brothers. They had known each other since childhood, growing up on the Lower East Side of Manhattan in the same tenement[1] building on Fifth Street between Avenue A and Avenue B.

Antonio was fair, lean, and lanky, while Felix was dark, short, and husky. Antonio's hair was always falling over his eyes, while Felix wore his black hair in a natural Afro style.

Each youngster had a dream of someday becoming lightweight champion of the world. Every chance they had, the boys worked out, sometimes at the Boys' Club on 10th Street and Avenue A and sometimes at the pro's gym on 14th Street. Early morning sunrises would find them running along the East River Drive, wrapped in sweat shirts, short towels around their necks, and handkerchiefs Apache style around their foreheads.

While some youngsters were into street negatives, Antonio and Felix slept, ate, rapped, and dreamt positive. Between them, they had a collection of *Fight* magazines second to none, plus a scrapbook filled with torn tickets to every boxing match they had ever attended, and some clippings of their own. If asked a question about any given fighter, they would immediately zip out from their memory banks divisions, weights, records of fights, knock-outs, technical knockouts, and draws or losses.

Each had fought many <u>bouts</u> representing their community and had won two gold-plated medals plus a silver and bronze medallion. The difference was in their style. Antonio's lean form and long reach made him the better boxer, while Felix's short and muscular frame made him the better slugger. Whenever they had met in the ring for sparring sessions,[2] it had always been hot and heavy.

Now, after a series of elimination bouts, they had been informed that they were to meet each other in the division finals that were scheduled for the seventh of August, two weeks away—the winner to represent the Boys' Club in the Golden Gloves Championship Tournament.

The two boys continued to run together along the East River Drive. But even when joking with each other, they both sensed a wall rising between them.

One morning less than a week before their bout, they met as usual for their daily work-out. They fooled around with a few jabs at the air, slapped skin, and then took off, running lightly along the dirty East River's edge.

Antonio glanced at Felix, who kept his eyes purposely straight ahead, pausing from time to time to do some fancy leg work

---

1. **tenement** *n.* used as *adj.:* apartment. Tenement buildings are often cheaply built and poorly maintained.

2. **sparring sessions:** practice matches in which boxers use light punches.

Vocabulary
bouts (bouts) *n.:* matches; contests.

while throwing one-twos followed by upper-cuts to an imaginary jaw. Antonio then beat the air with a barrage of body blows and short devastating lefts with an overhead jaw-breaking right.

After a mile or so, Felix puffed and said, "Let's stop a while, bro. I think we both got something to say to each other."

Antonio nodded. It was not natural to be acting as though nothing unusual was happening when two ace-boon buddies were going to be blasting each other within a few short days.

They rested their elbows on the railing separating them from the river. Antonio wiped his face with his short towel. The sunrise was now creating day.

Felix leaned heavily on the river's railing and stared across to the shores of Brooklyn. Finally, he broke the silence.

"Man. I don't know how to come out with it."

Antonio helped. "It's about our fight, right?"

"Yeah, right." Felix's eyes squinted at the rising orange sun.

"I've been thinking about it too, panin.[3] In fact, since we found out it was going to be me and you, I've been awake at night, pulling punches on you, trying not to hurt you."

"Same here. It ain't natural not to think about the fight. I mean, we both are cheverote[4] fighters and we both want to win. But only one of us can win. There ain't no draws in the eliminations."

Felix tapped Antonio gently on the shoulder. "I don't mean to sound like I'm bragging, bro. But I wanna win, fair and square."

Antonio nodded quietly. "Yeah. We both know that in the ring the better man wins. Friend or no friend, brother or no . . ."

Felix finished it for him. "Brother. Tony, let's promise something right here. OK?"

---

3. **panin** (pä·nēn´) *n*.: Puerto Rican Spanish slang for "pal" or "buddy."
4. **cheverote** (che′ve·rô′tā) *adj.*: Puerto Rican Spanish slang for "the greatest."

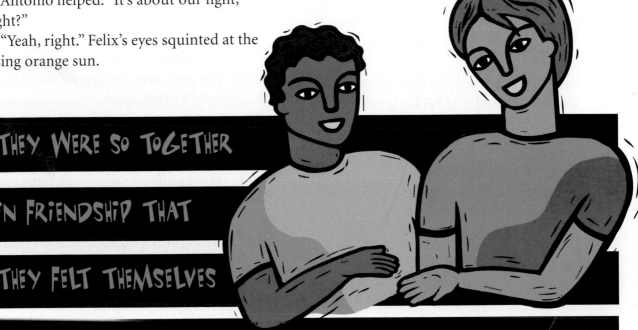

THEY WERE SO TOGETHER IN FRIENDSHIP THAT THEY FELT THEMSELVES TO BE BROTHERS. They had known each other since childhood . . .

"If it's fair, hermano,[5] I'm for it." Antonio admired the courage of a tugboat pulling a barge five times its welterweight size.

"It's fair, Tony. When we get into the ring, it's gotta be like we never met. We gotta be like two heavy strangers that want the same thing and only one can have it. You understand, don't cha?"

"Sí, I know." Tony smiled. "No pulling punches. We go all the way."

"Yeah, that's right. Listen, Tony. Don't you think it's a good idea if we don't see each other until the day of the fight? I'm going to stay with my Aunt Lucy in the Bronx. I can use Gleason's Gym for working out. My manager says he got some sparring partners with more or less your style."

Tony scratched his nose pensively. "Yeah, it would be better for our heads." He held out his hand, palm upward. "Deal?"

"Deal." Felix lightly slapped open skin.

"Ready for some more running?" Tony asked lamely.

"Naw, bro. Let's cut it here. You go on. I kinda like to get things together in my head."

"You ain't worried, are you?" Tony asked.

"No way, man." Felix laughed out loud. "I got too much smarts for that. I just think it's cooler if we split right here. After the fight, we can get it together again like nothing ever happened."

The amigo brothers were not ashamed to hug each other tightly.

"Guess you're right. Watch yourself, Felix. I hear there's some pretty heavy dudes up in the Bronx. Suavecito,[6] OK?"

"OK. You watch yourself too, sabe?"[7]

Tony jogged away. Felix watched his friend disappear from view, throwing rights and lefts. Both fighters had a lot of psyching up to do before the big fight.

The days in training passed much too slowly. Although they kept out of each other's way, they were aware of each other's progress via the ghetto grapevine.

The evening before the big fight, Tony made his way to the roof of his tenement. In the quiet early dark, he peered over the ledge. Six stories below, the lights of the city blinked and the sounds of cars mingled with the curses and the laughter of children in the street. He tried not to think of Felix, feeling he had succeeded in psyching his mind. But only in the ring would he really know. To spare Felix hurt, he would have to knock him out, early and quick.

Up in the South Bronx, Felix decided to take in a movie in an effort to keep Antonio's face away from his fists. The flick was *The Champion* with Kirk Douglas, the third time Felix was seeing it.

The champion was getting beaten, his face being pounded into raw, wet hamburger. His eyes were cut, jagged, bleeding, one eye swollen, the other almost shut. He was saved only by the sound of the bell.

Felix became the champ and Tony the challenger.

The movie audience was going out of its head, roaring in blood lust at the butchery going on. The champ hunched his shoulders, grunting and sniffing red blood back into his broken nose. The challenger, confident that he had the championship in the bag, threw a left. The champ countered with

---

5. **hermano** (er·mä′nô) *n.*: Spanish for "brother."
6. **suavecito** (swä′vä·sē′tô) *adj.*: Puerto Rican Spanish slang for "cool."
7. **sabe** (sä′bā) *v.*: Spanish for "you know."

Vocabulary
pensively (pen′siv·lē) *adv.*: thoughtfully.

a dynamite right that exploded into the challenger's brains.

Felix's right arm felt the shock. Antonio's face, superimposed on the screen, was shattered and split apart by the awesome force of the killer blow. Felix saw himself in the ring, blasting Antonio against the ropes. The champ had to be forcibly restrained. The challenger was allowed to crumble slowly to the canvas, a broken bloody mess.

When Felix finally left the theater, he had figured out how to psych himself for tomorrow's fight. It was Felix the Champion vs. Antonio the Challenger.

He walked up some dark streets, deserted except for small pockets of wary-looking kids wearing gang colors. Despite the fact that he was Puerto Rican like them, they eyed him as a stranger to their turf. Felix did a fast shuffle, bobbing and weaving, while letting loose a torrent of blows that would demolish whatever got in its way. It seemed to impress the brothers, who went about their own business.

Finding no takers, Felix decided to split to his aunt's. Walking the streets had not relaxed him; neither had the fight flick. All it had done was to stir him up. He let himself quietly into his Aunt Lucy's apartment and went straight to bed, falling into a fitful sleep with sounds of the gong for Round One.

Antonio was passing some heavy time on his rooftop. How would the fight tomorrow affect his relationship with Felix? After all, fighting was like any other profession. Friendship had nothing to do with it. A gnawing doubt crept in. He cut negative thinking real quick by doing some speedy fancy dance steps, bobbing and weaving like mercury. The night air was blurred with perpetual motions of left hooks and right

crosses. Felix, his amigo brother, was not going to be Felix at all in the ring. Just an opponent with another face. Antonio went to sleep, hearing the opening bell for the first round. Like his friend in the South Bronx, he prayed for victory via a quick clean knockout in the first round.

Large posters plastered all over the walls of local shops announced the fight between Antonio Cruz and Felix Vargas as the main bout.

The fight had created great interest in the neighborhood. Antonio and Felix were well liked and respected. Each had his own loyal following. Betting fever was high and ranged from a bottle of Coke to cold hard cash on the line.

Antonio's fans bet with unbridled faith in his boxing skills. On the other side, Felix's admirers bet on his dynamite-packed fists.

Felix had returned to his apartment early in the morning of August 7th and stayed there, hoping to avoid seeing Antonio. He turned the radio on to salsa[8] music sounds and then tried to read while waiting for word from his manager.

The fight was scheduled to take place in Tompkins Square Park. It had been decided that the gymnasium of the Boys' Club was not large enough to hold all the people who were sure to attend. In Tompkins Square Park, everyone who wanted could view the fight, whether from ringside or window fire escapes or tenement rooftops.

The morning of the fight Tompkins Square was a beehive of activity with

---

8. **salsa** (säl′sə) *n.* used as *adj.*: Latin American dance music, usually played at fast tempos.

Vocabulary
torrent (tôr′ənt) *n.*: flood or rush.

numerous workers setting up the ring, the seats, and the guest speakers' stand. The scheduled bouts began shortly after noon and the park had begun filling up even earlier.

The local junior high school across from Tompkins Square Park served as the dressing room for all the fighters. Each was given a separate classroom with desk tops, covered with mats, serving as resting tables. Antonio thought he caught a glimpse of Felix waving to him from a room at the far end of the corridor. He waved back just in case it had been him.

The fighters changed from their street clothes into fighting gear. Antonio wore white trunks, black socks, and black shoes. Felix wore sky-blue trunks, red socks, and white boxing shoes. They had dressing gowns to match their fighting trunks with their names neatly stitched on the back.

The loudspeakers blared into the open windows of the school. There were speeches by dignitaries, community leaders, and great boxers of yesteryear. Some were well prepared; some improvised on the spot. They all carried the same message of great pleasure and honor at being part of such a historic event. This great day was in the tradition of champions emerging from the streets of the Lower East Side.

Interwoven with the speeches were the sounds of the other boxing events. After the sixth bout, Felix was much relieved when his trainer, Charlie, said, "Time change. Quick knockout. This is it. We're on."

Waiting time was over. Felix was escorted from the classroom by a dozen fans in white T-shirts with the word "Felix" across their fronts.

Antonio was escorted down a different stairwell and guided through a roped-off path.

As the two climbed into the ring, the crowd exploded with a roar. Antonio and Felix both bowed gracefully and then raised their arms in acknowledgment.

Antonio tried to be cool, but even as the roar was in its first birth, he turned slowly to meet Felix's eyes looking directly into his. Felix nodded his head and Antonio responded. And both as one, just as quickly, turned away to face his own corner.

Bong—bong—bong. The roar turned to stillness.

"Ladies and Gentlemen, Señores y Señoras."

The announcer spoke slowly, pleased at his bilingual efforts.

"Now the moment we have all been waiting for—the main event between two fine young Puerto Rican fighters, products of our Lower East Side."

"Loisaida,"[9] called out a member of the audience.

"In this corner, weighing 134 pounds, Felix Vargas. And in this corner, weighing 133 pounds, Antonio Cruz. The winner will represent the Boys' Club in the tournament of champions, the Golden Gloves. There will be no draw. May the best man win."

The cheering of the crowd shook the window panes of the old buildings surrounding Tompkins Square Park. At the center of the ring, the referee was giving instructions to the youngsters.

"Keep your punches up. No low blows. No punching on the back of the head. Keep your heads up. Understand? Let's have a clean fight. Now shake hands and come out fighting."

---

9. **Loisaida** (loi·sī′dä) *n.:* Puerto Rican English dialect for "Lower East Side."

Both youngsters touched gloves and nodded. They turned and danced quickly to their corners. Their head towels and dressing gowns were lifted neatly from their shoulders by their trainers' nimble fingers. Antonio crossed himself. Felix did the same.

BONG! BONG! ROUND ONE. Felix and Antonio turned and faced each other squarely in a fighting pose. Felix wasted no time. He came in fast, head low, half-hunched toward his right shoulder, and lashed out with a straight left. He missed a right cross as Antonio slipped the punch and countered with one-two-three lefts that snapped Felix's head back, sending a mild shock coursing through him. If Felix had any small doubt about their friend-ship affecting their fight, it was being neatly dispelled.

Antonio danced, a joy to behold. His left hand was like a pis-ton pumping jabs one right after an-other with seeming ease. Felix bobbed and weaved and never stopped boring in. He knew that at long range he was at a disad-vantage. Antonio had too much reach on him. Only by coming in close could Felix hope to achieve the dreamed-of knockout.

Antonio knew the dynamite that was stored in his amigo brother's fist. He ducked a short right and missed a left hook. Felix trapped him against the ropes just long enough to pour some punishing rights and lefts to Antonio's hard midsection. Antonio slipped away from Felix, crashing two lefts to his head, which set Felix's right ear to ringing.

Bong! Both amigos froze a punch well on its way, sending up a roar of approval for good sportsmanship.

Felix walked briskly back to his corner. His right ear had not stopped ringing. Antonio gracefully danced his way toward his stool none the worse, except for glowing glove burns showing angry red against the whiteness of his midribs.

"Watch that right, Tony." His trainer talked into his ear. "Remember Felix always goes to the body. He'll want you to drop your hands for his overhand left or right. Got it?"

Antonio nodded, spraying water out between his teeth. He felt better as his sore midsection was being firmly rubbed.

Felix's corner was also busy.

"You gotta get in there, fella." Felix's trainer poured water over his curly Afro locks. "Get in there or he's gonna chop you up from way back."

Bong! Bong! Round Two. Felix was off his stool and rushed Antonio like a bull, sending a hard right to his head. Beads of water exploded from Antonio's long hair.

Antonio, hurt, sent back a blurring bar-rage of lefts and rights that only meant pain to Felix, who returned with a short left to the

Vocabulary
dispelled (di·speld′) *v.:* driven away.

head followed by a looping right to the body. Antonio countered with his own flurry, forcing Felix to give ground. But not for long.

Felix bobbed and weaved, bobbed and weaved, occasionally punching his two gloves together.

Antonio waited for the rush that was sure to come. Felix closed in and feinted with his left shoulder and threw a right instead. Lights suddenly exploded inside Felix's head as Antonio slipped the blow and hit him with a pistonlike left, catching him flush on the point of his chin.

Bedlam broke loose as Felix's legs momentarily buckled. He fought off a series of rights and lefts and came back with a strong right that taught Antonio respect.

Antonio danced in carefully. He knew Felix had the habit of playing possum when hurt, to sucker an opponent within reach of the powerful bombs he carried in each fist.

A right to the head slowed Antonio's pretty dancing. He answered with his own left at Felix's right eye that began puffing up within three seconds.

Antonio, a bit too eager, moved in too close, and Felix had him entangled into a rip-roaring, punching toe-to-toe slugfest that brought the whole Tompkins Square Park screaming to its feet.

Rights to the body. Lefts to the head. Neither fighter was giving an inch. Suddenly a short right caught Antonio squarely on the chin. His long legs turned to jelly and his arms flailed out desperately. Felix, grunting like a bull, threw wild punches from every direction. Antonio, groggy, bobbed and weaved, evading most of the blows. Suddenly his head cleared. His left flashed out hard and straight, catching Felix on the bridge of his nose.

Felix lashed back with a haymaker, right off the ghetto streets. At the same instant, his eye caught another left hook from Antonio. Felix swung out, trying to clear the pain. Only the frenzied screaming of those along ringside let him know that he had dropped Antonio. Fighting off the growing haze, Antonio struggled to his feet, got up, ducked, and threw a smashing right that dropped Felix flat on his back.

Felix got up as fast as he could in his own corner, groggy but still game. He didn't even hear the count. In a fog, he heard the roaring of the crowd, who seemed to have gone insane. His head cleared to hear the bell sound at the end of the round. He was glad. His trainer sat him down on the stool.

In his corner, Antonio was doing what all fighters do when they are hurt. They sit and smile at everyone.

The referee signaled the ring doctor to check the fighters out. He did so and then gave his OK. The cold-water sponges brought clarity to both amigo brothers. They were rubbed until their circulation ran free.

Bong! Round Three—the final round. Up to now it had been tic-tac-toe, pretty much even. But everyone knew there could be no draw and that this round would decide the winner.

This time, to Felix's surprise, it was Antonio who came out fast, charging across the ring. Felix braced himself but couldn't ward off the barrage of punches. Antonio drove Felix hard against the ropes.

Vocabulary
frenzied (fren′zēd) *adj.*: wild.

The crowd ate it up. Thus far the two had fought with mucho corazón.[10] Felix tapped his gloves and commenced his attack anew. Antonio, throwing boxer's caution to the winds, jumped in to meet him.

Both pounded away. Neither gave an inch and neither fell to the canvas. Felix's left eye was tightly closed. Claret-red blood poured from Antonio's nose. They fought toe-to-toe.

The sounds of their blows were loud in contrast to the silence of a crowd gone completely mute. The referee was stunned by their savagery.

Bong! Bong! Bong! The bell sounded over and over again. Felix and Antonio were past hearing. Their blows continued to pound on each other like hailstones.

Finally the referee and the two trainers pried Felix and Antonio apart. Cold water was poured over them to bring them back to their senses.

They looked around and then rushed toward each other. A cry of alarm surged through Tompkins Square Park. Was this a fight to the death instead of a boxing match?

The fear soon gave way to wave upon wave of cheering as the two amigos embraced.

No matter what the decision, they knew they would always be champions to each other.

BONG! BONG! BONG! "Ladies and Gentlemen. Señores and Señoras. The winner and representative to the Golden Gloves Tournament of Champions is . . ."

The announcer turned to point to the winner and found himself alone. Arm in arm the champions had already left the ring.

---

10. **mucho corazón** (mōō′chô kô′rä·sôn′): Spanish for "a lot of heart."

Meet the Writer

Piri Thomas

A Survivor from the Mean Streets

Like Antonio and Felix in "Amigo Brothers," **Piri Thomas** (1928–   ) grew up in a rough neighborhood in New York City. Unfortunately, he wasn't as lucky as Antonio and Felix—he didn't have a sport like boxing to help him escape the lures of drugs and crime. As a result, Thomas spent time in prison. While in prison, Thomas discovered he could write, and after his release he published an autobiography called *Down These Mean Streets* (1967). Thomas has worked for many years to help drug addicts give up their addictions and start new lives.

First Thoughts

1. How did you react to the end of the story? Were you surprised by what Felix and Antonio did? Were you disappointed not to find out who won the fight?

Thinking Critically

2. Why do both boys wish for an early knockout? What does this wish show about them and their feelings for each other?

3. The last sentence refers to both boys as "champions." In what sense are they both champions?

4. Which do you think is more important to the story: the **external conflict** (the fight itself) or the **internal conflict** (the feelings the boys struggled with before and during the fight)? Why?

Extending Interpretations

5. Would you be able to walk away from a contest like this fight without finding out if you had won? Why or why not?

6. Look back at your "Rules for Competing Against a Friend" list from your Quickwrite on page 484. How many of them did Antonio and Felix follow? If you had been in their situation, would you have acted differently? Explain.

7. Did you find this story, particularly its ending, true to life? Do you think two good friends can fight each other and stay friends? Give reasons for your opinion.

Reading Check

a. What dream do both Felix and Antonio have?

b. Why do the boys decide to stop training together?

c. How can you tell that the boys do not "pull punches" in their fight?

d. How does the fight end?

INTERNET

Projects and Activities

Keyword: LE5 7-5

WRITING

Comparing Characters

In a three-paragraph essay, **compare** and **contrast** the personalities of Felix and Antonio. Start by reviewing the Venn diagram of the boys' similarities and differences that you made after you read the story. In your essay you might want to talk first about their similarities and then about their differences. End by telling which character you like better and why.

SKILLS FOCUS

Literary Skills
Analyze external and internal conflict.

Reading Skills
Compare and contrast.

Writing Skills
Write a comparison-contrast essay.

Clarifying Word Meanings:
Sports Reporting

PRACTICE

1. You're writing a news article about tryouts for the Olympic Games. Write sentences using the words *bouts, frenzied,* and *torrent.*

2. You're a retired tennis player. Write sentences for your autobiography using the words *pensively* and *dispelled.*

3. You're a sportscaster describing the crowd at a hockey game. Write a description using the words *torrent* and *frenzied.*

Word Bank

bouts
pensively
torrent
dispelled
frenzied

SKILLS FOCUS

Vocabulary Skills
Clarify word meanings.

Grammar Skills
Punctuate dialogue correctly.

Grammar Link

Punctuate Dialogue Correctly—
And Punch Up Your Writing

Dialogue, or conversation, puts a lot of punch into a story. When you include what characters say, your story comes to life. It's important to get the punctuation right when you write dialogue. Just follow these rules:

- Put quotation marks around direct quotations of words spoken aloud:

  Antonio helped. "It's about our fight, right?"

- Begin a quotation with a capital letter:

  After a mile or so, Felix puffed and said, "Let's stop a while, bro. I think we both got something to say to each other."

- Use a comma, a question mark, or an exclamation point (never a period) to set a quotation off from the rest of the sentence:

  "Ready for some more running?" Tony asked lamely.
  "Loisaida," called out a member of the audience.

PRACTICE

Add commas and quotation marks to set off the dialogue in these passages.

1. Felix and Antonio decided they'd each fight to win. Tony said No pulling punches. We go all the way.

2. A woman in the crowd said to her friend with alarm What's going on? It looks as if they're trying to kill each other!

3. Let's have a clean fight said the referee. No low blows. No punching on the back of the head. Got it?

For more help, see Quotation Marks, 14c–k, in the Language Handbook.

Understanding Text Structure: Comparison and Contrast

Reading Focus
Compare-and-Contrast Text Structure

Writers who want to present two sides of an issue often use a compare-and-contrast pattern to organize their material. It's a good way to show how two sides might have similar views on some points—**comparing**—and different views on others—**contrasting.**

When writers compare and contrast, they generally arrange their ideas according to one of two organizational patterns: the **point-by-point pattern** or the **block pattern.**

A writer using the point-by-point pattern moves back and forth between the subjects being compared, discussing one feature of each subject at a time.

A writer using the block pattern covers all the points of comparison for the first subject, then all the points of comparison for the second subject, and so on.

■ Notice how "Right Hook–Left Hook: The Boxing Controversy" presents two contrasting views about the sport of boxing, using the block method. First, the writer discusses one view, supported by the American Medical Association. Then she discusses the opposing view.

Point-by-Point Method

Feature 1	Subject 1
	Subject 2
Feature 2	Subject 1
	Subject 2

Block Method

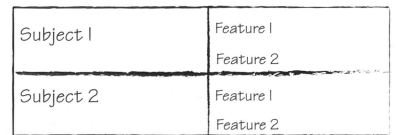

Subject 1	Feature 1
	Feature 2
Subject 2	Feature 1
	Feature 2

SKILLS FOCUS

Reading Skills
Understand comparison-and-contrast text structure.

Right Hook–Left Hook

THE BOXING CONTROVERSY

A four-year-old gazes at the television screen and laughs as a pig hits a duck over the head with an ironing board. The duck springs back to life, running around in circles with stars spinning around his head. Does this scene sound familiar?

Many doctors believe that as a society we close our eyes to the terrible injuries caused by a tremendous blow to the head. Doctors have expressed deep concern about boxing injuries such as those received by the former heavyweight champion Muhammad Ali. Ali suffers from Parkinson's disease, an illness probably caused by the hits he took in the ring. The symptoms of Parkinson's disease range from slurred speech to difficulty walking. According to doctors and researchers, a blow severe enough to render a person unconscious may result in tearing of nerve fibers and hemorrhaging. In 1984, the American Medical Association came out in support of a complete ban on boxing.

However, the sport of boxing remains popular. Supporters believe that training young people to box instills self-control. They also point out the benefits of fighting according to a set of rules. They believe that boxing provides opportunities for individuals who might otherwise have no chance to achieve financial security. Some doctors disagree with the American Medical Association's position and believe boxing produces few injuries because all major muscle groups are used.

The debate continues, with both sides of the issue verbally slugging it out to try to come to a resolution.

—Joan Burditt

Analyzing Text Structure: Comparison and Contrast

Right Hook—Left Hook

Test Practice

1. When the writer says "we close our eyes" to the devastating effects of head injuries, she means that —
   - **A** head injuries cause blindness
   - **B** people blink when struck on the head
   - **C** people choose not to take the effects of head injuries seriously
   - **D** people take head injuries too seriously

2. According to the article, the former heavyweight champion Muhammad Ali suffers from —
   - **F** Parkinson's disease
   - **G** Alzheimer's disease
   - **H** migraine headache pain
   - **J** Lou Gehrig's disease

3. Researchers say that a knockout blow to the head may result in —
   - **A** an immediate winner of the fight
   - **B** a penalty
   - **C** advances in boxing equipment
   - **D** damage to nerve fibers

4. Even though the dangers of boxing are well known, the sport has not been banned mainly because —
   - **F** it remains popular
   - **G** few fighters are seriously injured
   - **H** the American Medical Association is wrong
   - **J** researchers need to find out more

5. The last sentence of the article implies that the issue is —
   - **A** humorous
   - **B** unimportant
   - **C** controversial
   - **D** settled

Constructed Response

On page 496, a chart shows the block method of organization. Copy the chart, and use it to show the organization of this essay. First, list the views supported by the American Medical Association. Then, list the opposing views.

SKILLS FOCUS

Reading Skills
Analyze comparison-and-contrast text structure.

Before You Read — The Autobiography

Barrio Boy

Make the Connection
Quickwrite ✏️

Describe what you would do if you lived in a place where you didn't speak the language well. If you are in this situation now, describe what you are doing to learn the language.

Literary Focus
Autobiography and Biography: Who's Telling?

An **autobiography** is the story of a person's life written by that very person. A **biography** is the story of a person's life told by *another* person. In his autobiography, *Barrio Boy*, Ernesto Galarza tells what it was like to immigrate to Sacramento, California, from a small village in Mexico.

Reading Skills 📖
Distinguishing Fact from Opinion

When you read an autobiography, it's important to be able to tell facts from opinions. A **fact** is a statement that can be proved true. *Sacramento is a city in California* is a fact. An **opinion**, a personal feeling or belief, can't be proved true or false. In autobiographies, like *Barrio Boy*, writers share their feelings and opinions, but they also present facts.

Don't be fooled: People may state an opinion as if it were a fact. If you're in doubt, ask yourself, "Can this statement be proved, or is it someone's personal feeling or belief?"

Vocabulary Development

Here are some words to learn as you read *Barrio Boy*:

reassuring (rē′ə·sho͝or′iŋ) *v.* used as *adj.*: comforting. *Ernesto's teachers were kind and reassuring.*

contraption (kən·trap′shən) *n.*: strange machine or gadget. *He was amazed by a contraption that closed the door automatically.*

assured (ə·sho͝ord′) *v.*: promised confidently. *Ernesto's teachers assured him he would enjoy the new school.*

formidable (fôr′mə·də·bəl) *adj.*: awe-inspiring; impressive. *The principal's appearance was formidable.*

INTERNET

Vocabulary Activity

Keyword: LE5 7-5

Background
Literature and Social Studies

Ernesto Galarza was born in 1905 in Jalcocotán, a village in western Mexico. In 1910, when the Mexican Revolution threatened their peaceful mountain home, Ernesto, his mother, and two uncles left their village for Mazatlán, Mexico. Eventually they moved to Sacramento, California, and lived in what Galarza calls a "rented corner of the city"—the *barrio*, or Spanish-speaking neighborhood.

In this part of his life story, Ernesto starts school in America.

SKILLS FOCUS

Literary Skills
Understand forms of prose: autobiography and biography.

Reading Skills
Distinguish fact from opinion.

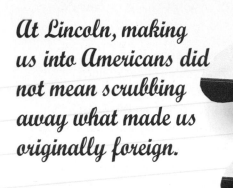

> At Lincoln, making
> us into Americans did
> not mean scrubbing
> away what made us
> originally foreign.

from
Barrio Boy

Ernesto Galarza

The two of us [Ernesto and his mother] walked south on Fifth Street one morning to the corner of Q Street and turned right. Half of the block was occupied by the Lincoln School. It was a three-story wooden building, with two wings that gave it the shape of a double T connected by a central hall. It was a new building, painted yellow, with a shingled roof that was not like the red tile of the school in Mazatlán. I noticed other differences, none of them very reassuring.

We walked up the wide staircase hand in hand and through the door, which closed by itself. A mechanical contraption screwed to the top shut it behind us quietly.

Up to this point the adventure of enrolling me in the school had been carefully rehearsed. Mrs. Dodson had told us how to find it and we had circled it several times on our walks. Friends in the barrio explained that the director was called a principal, and that it was a lady and not a man. They assured us that there was always a person at the school who could speak Spanish.

Exactly as we had been told, there was a sign on the door in both Spanish and English: "Principal." We crossed the hall and entered the office of Miss Nettie Hopley.

Miss Hopley was at a roll-top desk to one side, sitting in a swivel chair that moved on wheels. There was a sofa against the opposite wall, flanked by two windows and a door that opened on a small balcony. Chairs were set around a table, and framed pictures hung on the walls of a man with long white hair and another with a sad face and a black beard.

The principal half turned in the swivel chair to look at us over the pinch glasses crossed on the ridge of her nose. To do this, she had to duck her head slightly, as if she were about to step through a low doorway.

What Miss Hopley said to us we did not know, but we saw in her eyes a warm welcome, and when she took off her glasses and straightened up, she smiled whole-heartedly, like Mrs. Dodson. We were, of course, saying nothing, only catching the friendliness of her voice and the sparkle in her eyes while she said words we did not understand. She signaled us to the table. Almost tiptoeing across the office, I maneuvered myself to keep my mother between me and the gringo[1] lady. In a matter of seconds I had to decide whether she was a possible friend or a menace. We sat down.

Then Miss Hopley did a formidable thing. She stood up. Had she been standing when we entered, she would have seemed tall. But rising from her chair, she soared. And what she carried up and up with her was a buxom superstructure, firm shoulders, a straight sharp nose, full cheeks slightly molded by a curved line along the nostrils, thin lips that moved like steel springs, and a high forehead topped by hair

---

1. **gringo** (griŋ′gō) *n.* used as *adj.:* in Latin America, an insulting term for "foreigner"; from the Spanish *griego,* meaning "Greek."

Vocabulary

reassuring (rē′ə·s͟hoor′iŋ) *v.* used as *adj.:* comforting; giving hope or confidence; from the Latin word *securus,* meaning "secure." Look for the related word *assured* on this page.

contraption (kən·trap′s͟hən) *n.:* strange machine or gadget.

assured (ə·s͟hoord′) *v.:* guaranteed; promised confidently.

formidable (fôr′mə·də·bəl) *adj.:* awe-inspiring; impressive.

gathered in a bun. Miss Hopley was not a giant in body, but when she mobilized it to a standing position she seemed a match for giants. I decided I liked her.

She strode to a door in the far corner of the office, opened it, and called a name. A boy of about ten years appeared in the doorway. He sat down at one end of the table. He was brown like us, a plump kid with shiny black hair combed straight back, neat, cool, and faintly obnoxious.

Miss Hopley joined us with a large book and some papers in her hand. She, too, sat down and the questions and answers began by way of our interpreter. My name was Ernesto. My mother's name was Henriqueta. My birth certificate was in San Blas. Here was my last report card from the Escuela Municipal Numero 3 para Varones[2] of Mazatlán, and so forth. Miss Hopley put things down in the book and my mother signed a card.

As long as the questions continued, Doña Henriqueta could stay and I was secure. Now that they were over, Miss Hopley saw her to the door, dismissed our interpreter, and without further ado took me by the hand and strode down the hall to Miss Ryan's first grade.

Miss Ryan took me to a seat at the front of the room, into which I shrank—the

better to survey her. She was, to skinny, somewhat runty me, of a withering height when she patrolled the class. And when I least expected it, there she was, crouching by my desk, her blond, radiant face level with mine, her voice patiently maneuvering me over the awful idiocies of the English language.

During the next few weeks Miss Ryan overcame my fears of tall, energetic teachers as she bent over my desk to help me with a word in the pre-primer. Step by step, she loosened me and my classmates from the safe anchorage of the desks for recitations at the blackboard and consultations at her desk. Frequently she burst into happy announcements to the whole class. "Ito can read a sentence," and small Japanese Ito, squint-eyed and shy, slowly read aloud while the class listened in wonder: "Come, Skipper, come. Come and run." The Korean, Portuguese, Italian, and Polish first-graders had similar moments of glory, no less shining than mine the day I conquered "butterfly," which I had been persistently pronouncing in standard Spanish as boo-ter-flee. "Children," Miss Ryan called for attention. "Ernesto has learned how to pronounce *butterfly*!" And I proved it with a perfect imitation of Miss Ryan. From that celebrated success, I was soon able to match Ito's progress as a sentence reader with "Come, butterfly, come fly with me."

Like Ito and several other first-graders who did not know English, I received private lessons from Miss Ryan in the closet, a narrow hall off the classroom with a door at each end. Next to one of these doors Miss Ryan placed a large chair for herself and a small one for me. Keeping an eye on the class through the open door, she read

---

2. **Escuela Municipal Numero 3 para Varones:** Spanish for "Municipal School Number 3 for Boys."

with me about sheep in the meadow and a frightened chicken going to see the king, coaching me out of my phonetic ruts in words like *pasture, bow-wow-wow, hay,* and *pretty,* which to my Mexican ear and eye had so many unnecessary sounds and letters. She made me watch her lips and then close my eyes as she repeated words I found hard to read. When we came to know each other better, I tried interrupting to tell Miss Ryan how we said it in Spanish. It didn't work. She only said "oh" and went on with *pasture, bow-wow-wow,* and *pretty.* It was as if in that closet we were both discovering together the secrets of the English language and grieving together over the tragedies of Bo-Peep. The main reason I was graduated with honors from the first grade was that I had fallen in love with Miss Ryan. Her radiant, no-nonsense character made us either afraid not to love her or love her so we would not be afraid, I am not sure which. It was not only that we sensed she was with it, but also that she was with us.

Like the first grade, the rest of the Lincoln School was a sampling of the lower part of town, where many races made their home. My pals in the second grade were Kazushi, whose parents spoke only Japanese; Matti, a skinny Italian boy; and Manuel, a fat Portuguese who would never get into a fight but wrestled you to the ground and just sat on you. Our assortment of nationalities included Koreans, Yugoslavs, Poles, Irish, and home-grown Americans.

Miss Hopley and her teachers never let us forget why we were at Lincoln: for those who were alien, to become good Americans; for those who were so born, to accept the rest of us. Off the school grounds we traded the same insults we heard from our elders. On the playground we were sure to be marched up to the principal's office for calling someone a wop, a chink, a dago, or a greaser. The school was not so much a melting pot as a griddle where Miss Hopley and her helpers warmed knowledge into us and roasted racial hatreds out of us.

At Lincoln, making us into Americans did not mean scrubbing away what made us originally foreign. The teachers called us as our parents did, or as close as they could pronounce our names in Spanish or Japanese. No one was ever scolded or punished for speaking in his native tongue on the playground. Matti told the class about his mother's down quilt, which she had made in Italy with the fine feathers of a thousand geese. Encarnación acted out how boys learned to fish in the Philippines. I astounded the third grade with the story of my travels on a stagecoach, which nobody

> *The teachers called us as our parents did, or as close as they could pronounce our names . . .*

else in the class had seen except in the museum at Sutter's Fort. After a visit to the Crocker Art Gallery and its collection of heroic paintings of the golden age of California, someone showed a silk scroll with a Chinese painting. Miss Hopley herself had a way of expressing wonder over these matters before a class, her eyes wide open until they popped slightly. It was easy for me to feel that becoming a proud American, as she said we should, did not mean feeling ashamed of being a Mexican.

Meet the Writer

Ernesto Galarza

"Anecdotes I Told My Family"

For young **Ernesto Galarza** (1905–1984), coming to the United States meant abandoning everything he had ever known—his language, his family, and his customs. He soon discovered that education was the key to making sense of his new life. Eventually he earned his doctorate from Columbia University in New York and then returned to California to teach. Although he was a beloved teacher, Galarza is best remembered for *Barrio Boy,* his bestselling 1971 account of his journey from Mexico to the United States. Galarza explains how he came to write *Barrio Boy:*

> **❝** *Barrio Boy* began as anecdotes I told my family about Jalcocotán, the mountain village in western Mexico where I was born. Among this limited public (my wife, Mae, and daughters, Karla and Eli Lu) my thumbnail sketches became bestsellers. Hearing myself tell them over and over, I began to agree with my captive audience that they were not only interesting but possibly good.
>
> Quite by accident I told one of these vignettes at a meeting of scholars and other boring people. It was recorded on tape, printed in a magazine, and circulated among schools and libraries here and there. I received letters asking for reprints, and occasionally a tempting suggestion that I write more of the same, perhaps enough to make a book.
>
> Adding up the three listeners in my family and the three correspondents made a public of six. I didn't need more persuasion than this to link the anecdotes into a story. **❞**

For Independent Reading

The selection you've read is from one chapter of Galarza's *Barrio Boy.* If you liked the selection, you'll enjoy reading the entire book.

After You Read   Response and Analysis

First Thoughts

1. Refer back to your Quickwrite notes (page 499); then, finish one of these sentences:
   - If I went to a school where I did not speak the language, I would . . .
   - I have been in the same situation as Ernesto, and I . . .

Thinking Critically

2. What did you **predict** would happen to Ernesto, and why? How else could his story have ended?

3. In many ways this story is a tribute to Ernesto's teachers. What do you think Galarza means when he says that Miss Ryan was not only "with it" but "with us"?

4. In *Barrio Boy,* Ernesto Galarza reveals some opinions about his life in the United States. Like other writers of **autobiography,** he also presents facts. Give one example of a **fact** and one example of an **opinion** in *Barrio Boy.*

Extending Interpretations

5. The **metaphor** of the melting pot comes from a 1908 play by Israel Zangwill: "America is . . . a great melting pot, where all the races of Europe are melting and reforming!" Ernesto thinks of Lincoln School not as a melting pot—which makes everyone the same—but as a warm griddle. What do you think this means? Which comparison would you use to describe the United States, and why?

WRITING

Writing About Immigration

Ernesto Galarza and many of his classmates were immigrants. What special problems do immigrants face today? How do schools and local governments try to solve these problems? Research these questions in your school library or on the Internet. Then, write two paragraphs giving your responses to the questions. Cite both facts and opinions.

Reading Check

a. How did Ernesto feel about Miss Hopley and Miss Ryan?

b. How was the makeup of Ernesto's class a lot like that of his neighborhood?

c. How did Miss Ryan encourage her students to learn English?

d. According to Miss Hopley and the teachers at Lincoln School, what were the children to remember about *why* they were at school?

e. How did Lincoln School honor its students' original languages and customs?

INTERNET
Projects and Activities
Keyword: LE5 7-5

Literary Skills
Analyze an autobiography.

Reading Skills
Distinguish fact from opinion.

Writing Skills
Write a brief research report.

Clarifying Word Meanings: Examples

Writers often help readers understand difficult words by using definitions, examples, restatements, or contrasts.

A writer who uses **examples** provides specific instances to show what a word means. Consider the following sentence:

> **People came to the meeting from such varied municipalities as Sacramento, Oakland, Bakersfield, and San Diego.**

Even if you didn't know that a municipality is a city or town, the examples in the sentence give you a clue to the meaning of the word.

Word Bank

reassuring
contraption
assured
formidable

PRACTICE

Finish the following sentences by using examples to clarify the meanings of the underlined words.

1. The most reassuring words I ever heard were _____.

2. Three contraptions that make life easier today are _____, _____, and _____.

3. I assured my friend I was loyal. I said, "_____."

4. Three formidable figures in sports are _____, _____, and _____.

My Brother (1942) by Oswaldo Guayasamín (Oswaldo Guayasamín Calero). Oil on wood (15⅞" × 12¾"). Inter-American Fund (699.1942).

The Museum of Modern Art, New York. Digital Image © The Museum of Modern Art/Licensed by SCALA/Art Resource, NY.

SKILLS FOCUS

Vocabulary Skills
Clarify word meanings by using examples.

Grammar Link

Making the Most of Comparing Adjectives

The **comparative degree** of an adjective compares two people or things. The **superlative degree** compares more than two people or things.

Comparative Degree	Superlative Degree
Add the ending *-er* or the word *more* when you compare two items.	Add the ending *-est* or the word *most* when you compare more than two items.
Example: "The rest of the Lincoln School was a sampling of the <u>lower</u> part of town. . . ."	Example: To the children their beloved Miss Ryan was the <u>most wonderful</u> teacher in the world.

- When comparing, don't use both *more* and *-er,* and don't use both *most* and *-est.*

  Ernesto felt ~~more~~ <u>safer</u> when his mother was present.
  Matti was the ~~most~~ <u>thinnest</u> boy in the second grade.

- Don't use the superlative form when you compare only two people or things.

  prouder

  Do you think Ernesto was ~~proudest~~ of being an American or a Mexican?

  more

  Of the two boys, Ito learned ~~most~~ quickly.

PRACTICE

Act as an editor, and show how you'd correct these sentences.

1. Ernesto thought American schools were more stranger than Mexican schools.
2. Ernesto spoke Spanish and English, but his Spanish was best.
3. Was Ernesto proudest of pronouncing *butterfly* or of reading "Little Bo-Peep"?
4. Ernesto did more better in school than he had expected.
5. The most nicest teacher in the Lincoln School was Miss Ryan.
6. Miss Hopley might have been the most tallest person Ernesto had ever seen.

For more help, see Comparison of Modifiers, 5a–f, in the Language Handbook.

SKILLS FOCUS

Grammar Skills Use comparative and superlative forms correctly.

Song of the Trees

Make the Connection
Quickwrite ✎
Agree? Disagree?

disagree 0 1 2 3 4 agree

1. People gain self-respect by standing up for their beliefs.

2. Given the chance, most people will never take advantage of another person.

3. Some people are treated unfairly because of the color of their skin.

4. Nobody owns the earth.

Rate each of those statements with a number from 0 to 4. (Zero means that you completely disagree; 4 means you completely agree.) Then, discuss these issues with the rest of the class.

Literary Focus
Novels and Short Stories

A **short story** usually has just one main plot line, one or two major characters, one important conflict, and one main theme. With a **novel**—which is a book-length work of fiction—a lot more will happen. More characters will appear, the conflicts will multiply, subplots will develop, and several themes will be operating at once. Settings may also become more numerous. A short story usually takes place within a limited time frame, but a novel can span many generations.

Occasionally a writer will find that a narrative is too long for a short story and too short for a novel. The story that results, which may run from twenty to one hundred pages, is known as a **novella.** Mildred Taylor's *Song of the Trees* was first published in a small book by itself, as a forty-eight-page novella.

Reading Skills
Making Generalizations: Putting It All Together

A **generalization** is a broad statement that tells about something in general. A statement about a story's **theme** is a kind of generalization. From specific evidence in the story, you make a broad universal statement about life. To make a statement about the theme of *Song of the Trees,* you have to

- think about the main events and conflicts in the story

- decide what the characters have discovered by the end of the story

- think about how the story relates to your experiences

SKILLS FOCUS

Literary Skills
Understand forms of prose: short story, novel, and novella.

Reading Skills
Make generalizations.

Background
Literature and Social Studies

The depression referred to in this story is the Great Depression, the severe economic decline in the United States that lasted from 1929 to 1942. During the Depression many banks and businesses closed. People lost their jobs, their savings, and even their homes. Many people had barely enough food to eat. This was also a time when the segregation of African Americans was still a sad reality in parts of the United States.

Vocabulary Development

Study the following words from *Song of the Trees:*

finicky (fin′ik · ē) *adj.:* fussy and extremely careful. *Little Man was finicky when it came to his appearance.*

dispute (di · spyo͞ot′) *n.:* argument. *Mama settled the dispute between the two brothers.*

ambled (am′bəld) *v.:* walked without hurrying. *They ambled through the forest, listening to the song of the trees.*

delved (delvd) *v.:* searched. *Cassie delved into the bowl of blackberries and grabbed the biggest one.*

curtly (kʉrt′lē) *adv.:* rudely, using few words. *The man spoke curtly to Mama, showing his lack of respect.*

skirting (skʉrt′iŋ) *v.:* avoiding. *Instead of speaking to the point, Mr. Andersen was skirting the issue.*

elude (ē · lo͞od′) *v.:* escape cleverly. *The children hoped to elude punishment for their bold behavior.*

incredulously (in · krej′o͞o · ləs · lē) *adv.:* unbelievingly. *Mr. Andersen stared incredulously at Papa when Papa ignored him.*

ashen (ash′ən) *adj.:* pale. *He turned ashen with fright.*

sentries (sen′trēz) *n.:* guards. *The sentries stood guard over the quiet landscape.*

I stared at the trees, aware of an eerie silence descending . . .

SONG
OF THE
TREES

Mildred D. Taylor

"Cassie. Cassie, child, wake up now," Big Ma called gently as the new sun peeked over the horizon.

I looked sleepily at my grandmother and closed my eyes again.

"Cassie! Get up, girl!" This time the voice was not so gentle.

I jumped out of the deep, feathery bed as Big Ma climbed from the other side. The room was still dark, and I stubbed my toe while stumbling sleepily about looking for my clothes.

"Shoot! Darn ole chair," I fussed, rubbing my injured foot.

"Hush, Cassie, and open them curtains if you can't see," Big Ma said. "Prop that window open, too, and let some of that fresh morning air in here."

I opened the window and looked outside. The earth was draped in a cloak of gray mist as the sun chased the night away. The cotton stalks, which in another hour would glisten greenly toward the sun, were gray. The ripening corn, wrapped in jackets of emerald and gold, was gray. Even the rich brown Mississippi earth was gray.

Only the trees of the forest were not gray. They stood dark, almost black, across the dusty road, still holding the night. A soft breeze stirred, and their voices whispered down to me in a song of morning greeting.

"Cassie, girl, I said open that window, not stand there gazing out all morning. Now, get moving before I take something to you," Big Ma threatened.

I dashed to my clothes. Before Big Ma had unwoven her long braid of gray hair, my pants and shirt were on and I was hurrying into the kitchen.

A small kerosene lamp was burning in a corner as I entered. Its light reflected on seven-year-old Christopher-John, short, pudgy, and a year younger than me, sitting sleepily upon a side bench drinking a large glass of clabber milk.[1] Mama's back was to me. She was dipping flour from a near-empty canister, while my older brother, Stacey, built a fire in the huge iron-bellied stove.

"I don't know what I'm going to do with you, Christopher-John," Mama scolded. "Getting up in the middle of the night and eating all that cornbread. Didn't you have enough to eat before you went to bed?"

"Yes'm," Christopher-John murmured.

"Lord knows I don't want any of my babies going hungry, but times are hard, honey. Don't you know folks all around here in Mississippi are struggling? Children crying cause they got no food to eat, and their daddies crying cause they can't get jobs so they can feed their babies? And you getting up in the middle of the night, stuffing yourself with cornbread!"

Her voice softened as she looked at the sleepy little boy. "Baby, we're in a depression.

---

1. **clabber milk:** thickly curdled sour milk.

Why do you think Papa's way down in Louisiana laying tracks on the railroad? So his children can eat—but only when they're hungry. You understand?"

"Yes'm," Christopher-John murmured again, as his eyes slid blissfully shut.

"Morning, Mama," I chimed.

"Morning, baby," Mama said. "You wash up yet?"

"No'm."

"Then go wash up and call Little Man again. Tell him he's not dressing to meet President Roosevelt[2] this morning. Hurry up, now, cause I want you to set the table."

Little Man, a very small six-year-old and a most finicky dresser, was brushing his hair when I entered the room he shared with Stacey and Christopher-John. His blue pants were faded, but except for a small grass stain on one knee, they were clean. Outside of his Sunday pants, these were the only pants he had, and he was always careful to keep them in the best condition possible. But one look at him and I knew that he was far from pleased with their condition this morning. He frowned down at the spot for a moment, then continued brushing.

"Man, hurry up and get dressed," I called. "Mama said you ain't dressing to meet the president."

"See there," he said, pointing at the stain. "You did that."

"I did no such thing. You fell all by yourself."

"You tripped me!"

"Didn't!"

"Did, too!"

"Hey, cut it out, you two!" ordered Stacey, entering the room. "You fought over that stupid stain yesterday. Now get moving, both of you. We gotta go pick blackberries before the sun gets too high. Little Man, you go gather the eggs while Christopher-John and me milk the cows."

Little Man and I decided to settle our dispute later when Stacey wasn't around. With Papa away, eleven-year-old Stacey thought of himself as the man of the house, and Mama had instructed Little Man, Christopher-John, and me to mind him. So, like it or not, we humored him. Besides, he was bigger than we were.

I ran to the back porch to wash. When I returned to the kitchen, Mama was talking to Big Ma.

"We got about enough flour for two more meals," Mama said, cutting the biscuit dough. "Our salt and sugar are practically down to nothing and—" She stopped when she saw me. "Cassie, baby, go gather the eggs for Mama."

"Little Man's gathering the eggs."

"Then go help him."

"But I ain't set the table yet."

"Set it when you come back."

I knew that I was not wanted in the kitchen. I looked suspiciously at my mother and grandmother, then went to the back porch to get a basket.

Big Ma's voice drifted through the open window. "Mary, you oughta write David and tell him somebody done opened his letter and stole that ten dollars he sent," she said.

"No, Mama. David's got enough on his

---

2. **President Roosevelt:** Franklin Delano Roosevelt (1882–1945) was president of the United States from 1933 to 1945.

Vocabulary
finicky (fin′ik·ē) adj.: fussy and extremely careful.
dispute (di·spyo͞ot′) n.: argument.

mind. Besides, there's enough garden foods so we won't go hungry."

"But what 'bout your medicine? You're all out of it and the doctor told you good to—"

"Shhhh!" Mama stared at the window. "Cassie, I thought I told you to go gather those eggs!"

"I had to get a basket, Mama!" I hurried off the porch and ran to the barn.

After breakfast, when the sun was streaking red across the sky, my brothers and I ambled into the coolness of the forest, leading our three cows and their calves down the narrow cow path to the pond. The morning was already muggy, but the trees closed out the heat as their leaves waved restlessly, high above our heads.

"Good morning, Mr. Trees," I shouted. They answered me with a soft, swooshing sound. "Hear 'em, Stacey? Hear 'em singing?"

"Ah, cut that out, Cassie. Them trees ain't singing. How many times I gotta tell you that's just the wind?" He stopped at a sweet alligator gum, pulled out his knife, and scraped off a glob of gum that had seeped through its cracked bark. He handed me half.

As I stuffed the gooey wad into my mouth, I patted the tree and whispered, "Thank you, Mr. Gum Tree."

Stacey frowned at me, then looked back at Christopher-John and Little Man walking far behind us, munching on their breakfast biscuits.

"Man! Christopher-John! Come on, now," he yelled. "If we finish the berry picking early, we can go wading before we go back."

Christopher-John and Little Man ran to catch up with us. Then, resuming their leisurely pace, they soon fell behind again.

A large gray squirrel scurried across our path and up a walnut tree. I watched until it was settled amidst the tree's featherlike leaves; then, poking one of the calves, I said, "Stacey, is Mama sick?"

"Sick? Why you say that?"

"Cause I heard Big Ma asking her 'bout some medicine she's supposed to have."

Stacey stopped, a worried look on his face. "If she's sick, she ain't bad sick," he decided. "If she was bad sick, she'd been in bed."

We left the cows at the pond and, taking our berry baskets, delved deeper into the forest looking for the wild blackberry bushes.

"I see one!" I shouted.

"Where?" cried Christopher-John, eager for the sweet berries.

"Over there! Last one to it's a rotten egg!" I yelled, and off I ran.

Stacey and Little Man followed at my heels. But Christopher-John puffed far behind. "Hey, wait for me," he cried.

"Let's hide from Christopher-John," Stacey suggested.

The three of us ran in different directions. I plunged behind a giant old pine and hugged its warm trunk as I waited for Christopher-John.

Christopher-John puffed to a stop, then, looking all around, called, "Hey, Stacey! Cassie! Hey, Man! Y'all cut that out!"

I giggled and Christopher-John heard me.

"I see you, Cassie!" he shouted, starting toward me as fast as his chubby legs would carry him. "You're it!"

Vocabulary

ambled (am′bəld) v.: walked easily, without hurrying.

delved (delvd) v.: searched.

"Not 'til you tag me," I laughed. As I waited for him to get closer, I glanced up into the boughs of my wintry-smelling hiding tree, expecting a song of laughter. But the old pine only tapped me gently with one of its long, low branches. I turned from the tree and dashed away.

"You can't, you can't, you can't catch me," I taunted, dodging from one beloved tree to the next. Around shaggy-bark hickories and sharp-needled pines, past blue-gray beeches and sturdy black walnuts I sailed, while my laughter resounded through the ancient forest, filling every chink. Overhead, the boughs of the giant trees hovered protectively, but they did not join in my laughter.

Deeper into the forest I plunged.

Christopher-John, unable to keep up, plopped on the ground in a pant. Little Man and Stacey, emerging from their hiding places, ran up to him.

"Ain't you caught her yet?" Little Man demanded, more than a little annoyed.

"He can't catch the champ," I boasted, stopping to rest against a hickory tree. I slid my back down the tree's shaggy trunk and looked up at its long branches, heavy with sweet nuts and slender green leaves, perfectly still. I looked around at the leaves of the other trees. They were still also. I stared at the trees, aware of an eerie silence descending over the forest.

Stacey walked toward me. "What's the matter with you, Cassie?" he asked.

"The trees, Stacey," I said softly, "they ain't singing no more."

"Is that all?" He looked up at the sky. "Come on, y'all. It's getting late. We'd better go pick them berries." He turned and walked on.

"But, Stacey, listen. Little Man, Christopher-John, listen."

The forest echoed an uneasy silence.

"The wind just stopped blowing, that's all," said Stacey. "Now stop fooling around and come on."

I jumped up to follow Stacey, then cried, "Stacey, look!" On a black oak a few yards away was a huge white *X*. "How did that get there?" I exclaimed, running to the tree.

"There's another one!" Little Man screamed.

"I see one too!" shouted Christopher-John.

Stacey said nothing as Christopher-John, Little Man, and I ran wildly through the forest counting the ghostlike marks.

"Stacey, they're on practically all of them," I said when he called us back.

"Why?"

Stacey studied the trees, then suddenly pushed us down.

"My clothes!" Little Man wailed indignantly.

"Hush, Man, and stay down," Stacey warned. "Somebody's coming."

Two white men emerged. We looked at each other. We knew to be silent.

"You mark them all down here?" one of the men asked.

"Not the younger ones, Mr. Andersen."

"We might need them, too," said Mr. Andersen, counting the *X*'s. "But don't worry 'bout marking them now, Tom. We'll get them later. Also them trees up past the pond toward the house."

"The old woman agree to you cutting these trees?"

"I ain't been down there yet," Mr. Andersen said.

"Mr. Andersen . . ." Tom hesitated a moment, looked up at the silent trees, then back at Mr. Andersen. "Maybe you should go easy with them," he cautioned. "You know that David can be as mean as an ole jackass when he wanna be."

"He's talking about Papa," I whispered.

"Shhhh!" Stacey hissed.

Mr. Andersen looked uneasy. "What's that gotta do with anything?"

"Well, he just don't take much to any dealings with white folks." Again, Tom looked up at the trees. "He ain't afraid like some."

Mr. Andersen laughed weakly. "Don't

worry 'bout that, Tom. The land belongs to his mama. He don't have no say in it. Besides, I guess I oughta know how to handle David Logan. After all, there are ways. . . .

"Now, you get on back to my place and get some boys and start chopping down these trees," Mr. Andersen said. "I'll go talk to the old woman." He looked up at the sky. "We can almost get a full day's work in if we hurry."

Mr. Andersen turned to walk away, but Tom stopped him. "Mr. Andersen, you really gonna chop all the trees?"

"If I need to. These folks ain't got no call for them. I do. I got me a good contract for these trees and I aim to fulfill it."

Tom watched Mr. Andersen walk away; then, looking sorrowfully up at the trees, he shook his head and disappeared into the depths of the forest.

"What we gonna do, Stacey?" I asked anxiously. "They can't just cut down our trees, can they?"

"I don't know. Papa's gone. . . ." Stacey muttered to himself, trying to decide what we should do next.

"Boy, if Papa was here, them ole white men wouldn't be messing with our trees," Little Man declared.

"Yeah!" Christopher-John agreed. "Just let Papa get hold of 'em and he gonna turn 'em every which way but loose."

"Christopher-John, Man," Stacey said finally, "go get the cows and take them home."

"But we just brought them down here," Little Man protested.

"And we gotta pick the berries for dinner," said Christopher-John mournfully.

"No time for that now. Hurry up. And stay clear of them white men. Cassie, you come with me."

We ran, brown legs and feet flying high through the still forest.

By the time Stacey and I arrived at the house, Mr. Andersen's car was already parked in the dusty drive. Mr. Andersen himself was seated comfortably in Papa's rocker on the front porch. Big Ma was seated too, but Mama was standing.

Stacey and I eased quietly to the side of the porch, unnoticed.

"Sixty-five dollars. That's an awful lot of money in these hard times, Aunt Caroline," Mr. Andersen was saying to Big Ma.

I could see Mama's thin face harden.

"You know," Mr. Andersen said, rocking familiarly in Papa's chair, "that's more than David can send home in two months."

"We do quite well on what David sends home," Mama said coldly.

Mr. Andersen stopped rocking. "I suggest you encourage Aunt Caroline to sell them trees, Mary. You know, David might not always be able to work so good. He could possibly have . . . an accident."

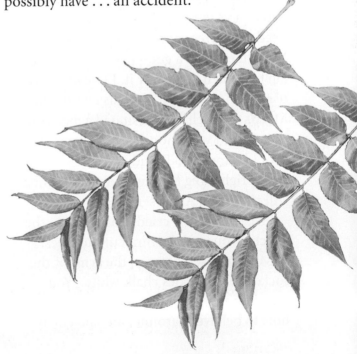

Big Ma's soft brown eyes clouded over with fear as she looked first at Mr. Andersen, then at Mama. But Mama clenched her fists and said, "In Mississippi, black men do not have accidents."

"Hush, child, hush," Big Ma said hurriedly. "How many trees for the sixty-five dollars, Mr. Andersen?"

"Enough 'til I figure I got my sixty-five dollars' worth."

"And how many would that be?" Mama persisted.

Mr. Andersen looked haughtily at Mama. "I said I'd be the judge of that, Mary."

"I think not," Mama said.

Mr. Andersen stared at Mama. And Mama stared back at him. I knew Mr. Andersen didn't like that, but Mama did it anyway. Mr. Andersen soon grew uneasy under that piercing gaze, and when his eyes swiftly shifted from Mama to Big Ma, his face was beet red.

"Caroline," he said, his voice low and menacing, "you're the head of this family and you've got a decision to make. Now, I need them trees and I mean to have them. I've offered you a good price for them and I ain't gonna haggle over it. I know y'all can use the money. Doc Thomas tells me that Mary's not well." He hesitated a moment, then hissed venomously, "And if something should happen to David . . ."

"All right," Big Ma said, her voice trembling. "All right, Mr. Andersen."

"No, Big Ma!" I cried, leaping onto the porch. "You can't let him cut our trees!"

Mr. Andersen grasped the arms of the rocker, his knuckles chalk white. "You certainly ain't taught none of your younguns how to behave, Caroline," he said curtly.

"You children go on to the back," Mama said, shooing us away.

"No, Mama," Stacey said. "He's gonna cut them all down. Me and Cassie heard him say so in the woods."

"I won't let him cut them," I threatened. "I won't let him! The trees are my friends and ain't no mean ole white man gonna touch my trees—"

Mama's hands went roughly around my body as she carried me off to my room.

"Now, hush," she said, her dark eyes flashing wildly. "I've told you how danger-ous it is . . ." She broke off in midsentence. She stared at me a moment, then hugged me tightly and went back to the porch.

Stacey joined me a few seconds later, and we sat there in the heat of the quiet room, listening miserably as the first whack of an ax echoed against the trees.

That night I was awakened by soft sounds outside my window. I reached for Big Ma, but she wasn't there. Hurrying to the window, I saw Mama and Big Ma standing in the yard in their nightclothes and Stacey, fully dressed, sitting atop Lady, our golden mare. By the time I got outside, Stacey was gone.

"Mama, where's Stacey?" I cried.

"Be quiet, Cassie. You'll wake Christopher-John and Little Man."

"But where's he going?"

"He's going to get Papa," Mama said. "Now be quiet."

"Go on, Stacey, boy," I whispered. "Ride for me, too."

As the dust billowed after him, Mama said, "I should've gone myself. He's so young."

Vocabulary

curtly (kurt′lē) *adv.:* rudely and with few words.

Big Ma put her arm around Mama. "Now, Mary, you know you couldn't've gone. Mr. Andersen would miss you if he come by and see you ain't here. You done right, now. Don't worry, that boy'll be just fine."

Three days passed, hot and windless.

Mama forbade any of us to go into the forest, so Christopher-John, Little Man, and I spent the slow, restless days hovering as close to the dusty road as we dared, listening to the foreign sounds of steel against the trees and the thunderous roar of those ancient loved ones as they crashed upon the earth. Sometimes Mama would scold us and tell us to come back to the house, but even she could not ignore the continuous pounding of the axes against the trees. Or the sight of the loaded lumber wagons rolling out of the forest. In the middle of washing or ironing or hoeing, she would look up sorrowfully and listen, then turn toward the road, searching for some sign of Papa and Stacey.

On the fourth day, before the sun had risen, bringing its cloak of miserable heat, I saw her walking alone toward the woods. I ran after her.

She did not send me back.

"Mama," I said. "How sick are you?"

Mama took my hand. "Remember when you had the flu and felt so sick?"

"Yes'm."

"And when I gave you some medicine, you got well soon afterward?"

"Yes'm."

"Well, that's how sick I am. As soon as I get my medicine, I'll be all well again. And that'll be soon, now that Papa's coming home," she said, giving my hand a gentle little squeeze.

The quiet surrounded us as we entered the forest. Mama clicked on the flashlight, and we walked silently along the cow path to the pond. There, just beyond the pond, pockets of open space loomed before us.

"Mama!"

"I know, baby, I know."

On the ground lay countless trees. Trees that had once been such strong, tall things. So strong that I could fling my arms partially around one of them and feel safe and secure. So tall and leafy green that their boughs had formed a forest temple.

And old.

So old that Indians had once built fires at their feet and had sung happy songs of happy days. So old they had hidden fleeing black men in the night and listened to their sad tales of a foreign land.

In the cold of winter, when the ground lay frozen, they had sung their frosty ballads of years gone by. Or on a muggy, sweat-drenched day, their leaves had rippled softly, lazily, like restless green fingers strumming at a guitar, echoing their epic tales.

But now they would sing no more. They lay forever silent upon the ground.

Those trees that remained standing were like defeated warriors mourning their fallen dead. But soon they, too, would fall, for the white X's had been placed on nearly every one.

"Oh, dear, dear trees," I cried as the gray light of the rising sun fell in ghostly shadows over the land. The tears rolled hot down my cheeks. Mama held me close, and when I felt her body tremble, I knew she was crying too.

When our tears eased, we turned sadly toward the house. As we emerged from the forest, we could see two small figures waiting impatiently on the other side of the road. As soon as they spied us, they hurried across to meet us.

"Mama! You and Cassie was in the forest," Little Man accused. "Big Ma told us!"

"How was it?" asked Christopher-John, rubbing the sleep from his eyes. "Was it spooky?"

"Spooky and empty," I said listlessly.

"Mama, me and Christopher-John wanna see too," Little Man declared.

"No, baby," Mama said softly as we crossed the road. "The men'll be done there soon, and I don't want y'all underfoot."

"But, Mama—" Little Man started to protest.

"When Papa comes home and the men are gone, then you can go. But until then, you stay out of there. You hear me, Little Man Logan?"

"Yes'm," Little Man reluctantly replied.

But the sun had been up only an hour when Little Man decided that he could not wait for Papa to return.

"Mama said we wasn't to go down there," Christopher-John warned.

"Cassie did," Little Man cried.

"But she was with Mama. Wasn't you, Cassie?"

"Well, I'm going too," said Little Man. "Everybody's always going someplace 'cepting me." And off he went.

Christopher-John and I ran after him. Down the narrow cow path and around the pond we chased. But neither of us was fast enough to overtake Little Man before he reached the lumbermen.

"Hey, you kids, get away from here," Mr. Andersen shouted when he saw us. "Now, y'all go on back home," he said, stopping in front of Little Man.

"We are home," I said. "You're the one who's on our land."

"Claude," Mr. Andersen said to one of the black lumbermen, "take these kids home." Then he pushed Little Man out of his way. Little Man pushed back. Mr. Andersen looked down, startled that a little black boy would do such a thing. He shoved Little Man a second time, and Little Man fell into the dirt.

Little Man looked down at his clothing covered with sawdust and dirt and wailed, "You got my clothes dirty!"

I rushed toward Mr. Andersen, my fist in a mighty hammer, shouting, "You ain't got no right to push on Little Man. Why don't you push on somebody your own size—like me, you ole—"

The man called Claude put his hand over my mouth and carried me away. Christopher-John trailed behind us, tugging on the man's shirt.

"Put her down. Hey, mister, put Cassie down."

The man carried me all the way to the pond. "Now," he said, "you and your brothers get on home before y'all get hurt. Go on, get!"

As the man walked away, I looked around. "Where's Little Man?"

Christopher-John looked around too.

"I don't know," he said. "I thought he was behind me."

Back we ran toward the lumbermen.

We found Little Man's clothing first, folded neatly by a tree. Then we saw Little Man, dragging a huge stick and headed straight for Mr. Andersen.

"Little Man, come back here," I called.

But Little Man did not stop.

Mr. Andersen stood alone, barking orders, unaware of the oncoming Little Man.

"Little Man! Oh, Little Man, don't!"

It was too late.

Little Man swung the stick as hard as he could against Mr. Andersen's leg.

Mr. Andersen let out a howl and reached to where he thought Little Man's collar was. But, of course, Little Man had no collar.

"Run, Man!" Christopher-John and I shouted. "Run!"

"Why, you little . . ." Mr. Andersen cried, grabbing at Little Man. But Little Man was too quick for him. He slid right through Mr. Andersen's legs. Tom stood nearby, his face crinkling into an amused grin.

"Hey, y'all!" Mr. Andersen yelled to the lumbermen. "Claude! Get that kid!"

But sure-footed Little Man dodged the groping hands of the lumbermen as easily as if he were skirting mud puddles. Over tree stumps, around legs, and through legs he dashed. But in the end, there were too many lumbermen for him, and he was handed over to Mr. Andersen.

For the second time, Christopher-John and I went to Little Man's rescue.

"Put him down!" we ordered, charging the lumbermen.

I was captured much too quickly, though not before I had landed several stinging blows. But Christopher-John, furious at seeing Little Man handled so roughly by Mr. Andersen, managed to elude the clutches of the lumbermen until he was fully upon Mr. Andersen. Then, with his mightiest thrust, he kicked Mr. Andersen solidly in the shins, not once, but twice, before the lumbermen pulled him away.

Mr. Andersen was fuming. He slowly took off his wide leather belt. Christopher-John, Little Man, and I looked woefully at the belt, then at each other. Little Man and Christopher-John fought to escape, but I closed my eyes and awaited the whining of the heavy belt and its painful bite against my skin.

Vocabulary
skirting (skʉrt′iŋ) v.: narrowly avoiding.
elude (ē·lo͞od′) v.: escape by quickness or cleverness.

What was he waiting for? I started to open my eyes, but then the zinging whirl of the belt began and I tensed, awaiting its fearful sting. But just as the leather tip lashed into my leg, a deep, familiar voice said, "Put the belt down, Andersen."

I opened my eyes.

"Papa!"

"Let the children go," Papa said. He was standing on a nearby ridge with a strange black box in his hands. Stacey was behind him, holding the reins to Lady.

The chopping stopped as all eyes turned to Papa.

"They been right meddlesome," Mr. Andersen said. "They need teaching how to act."

"Any teaching, I'll do it. Now, let them go."

Mr. Andersen looked down at Little Man struggling to get away. Smiling broadly, he motioned our release. "Okay, David," he said.

As we ran up the ridge to Papa, Mr. Andersen said, "It's good to have you home, boy."

Papa said nothing until we were safely behind him. "Take them home, Stacey."

"But, Papa—"

"Do like I say, son."

Stacey herded us away from the men. When we were far enough away so Papa couldn't see us, Stacey stopped and handed me Lady's reins.

"Y'all go on home now," he said. "I gotta go help Papa."

"Papa don't need no help," I said. "He told you to come with us."

"But you don't know what he's gonna do."

"What?" I asked.

"He's gonna blow up the forest if they don't get out of here. So go on home where y'all be safe."

"How's he gonna do that?" asked Little Man.

"We been setting sticks of dynamite since the middle of the night. We ain't even been up to the house cause Papa wanted the sticks planted and covered over before the men came. Now, Cassie, take them on back to the house. Do like I tell you for once, will ya?" Then, without waiting for another word, he was gone.

"I wanna see," Little Man announced.

"I don't," protested Christopher-John.

"Come on," I said.

We tied the mare to a tree, then belly-crawled back to where we could see Papa and joined Stacey in the brush.

"Cassie, I told you . . ."

"What's Papa doing?"

The black box was now set upon a sawed-off tree stump, and Papa's hands were tightly grasping a T-shaped instrument which went into it.

"What's that thing?" asked Little Man.

"It's a plunger," Stacey whispered. "If Papa presses down on it, the whole forest will go *pfffff*!"

Our mouths went dry and our eyes went wide. Mr. Andersen's eyes were wide, too.

"You're bluffing, David," he said. "You ain't gonna push that plunger."

"One thing you can't seem to understand, Andersen," Papa said, "is that a black man's always gotta be ready to die. And it don't make me any difference if I die today or tomorrow. Just as long as I die right."

Mr. Andersen laughed uneasily. The lumbermen moved nervously away.

"I mean what I say," Papa said. "Ask anyone. I always mean what I say."

"He sure do, Mr. Andersen," Claude said, eyeing the black box. "He always do."

"Shut up!" Mr. Andersen snapped. "And

the rest of y'all stay put." Then turning back to Papa, he smiled cunningly. "I'm sure you and me can work something out, David."

"Ain't nothing to be worked out," said Papa.

"Now, look here, David, your mama and me, we got us a contract. . . ."

"There ain't no more contract," Papa replied coldly. "Now, either you get out or I blow it up. That's it."

"He means it, Mr. Andersen," another frightened lumberman ventured. "He's crazy and he sure 'nough means it."

"You know what could happen to you, boy?" Mr. Andersen exploded, his face beet red again. "Threatening a white man like this?"

Papa said nothing. He just stood there, his hands firmly on the plunger, staring down at Mr. Andersen.

Mr. Andersen could not bear the stare. He turned away, cursing Papa. "You're a fool, David. A crazy fool." Then he looked around at the lumbermen. They shifted their eyes and would not look at him.

"Maybe we better leave, Mr. Andersen," Tom said quietly.

Mr. Andersen glanced at Tom, then turned back to Papa and said as lightly as he could, "All right, David, all right. It's your land. We'll just take the logs we got cut and get out." He motioned to the men. "Hey, let's get moving and get these logs out of here before this crazy fool gets us all killed."

"No," Papa said.

Mr. Andersen stopped, knowing that he could not have heard correctly. "What you say?"

"You ain't taking one more stick out of this forest."

"Now, look here—"

"You heard me."

"But you can't sell all these logs, David," Mr. Andersen exclaimed incredulously.

Papa said nothing. Just cast that piercing look on Mr. Andersen.

"Look, I'm a fair man. I tell you what I'll do. I'll give you another thirty-five dollars. An even hundred dollars. Now, that's fair, ain't it?"

"I'll see them rot first."

"But—"

"That's my last word," Papa said, tightening his grip on the plunger.

Mr. Andersen swallowed hard. "You won't always have that black box, David," he warned. "You know that, don't you?"

"That may be. But it won't matter none. Cause I'll always have my self-respect."

Mr. Andersen opened his mouth to speak, but no sound came. Tom and the lumbermen were quietly moving away, putting their gear in the empty lumber wagons. Mr. Andersen looked again at the black box. Finally, his face ashen, he too walked away.

Papa stood unmoving until the wagons and the men were gone. Then, when the sound of the last wagon rolling over the dry leaves could no longer be heard and a hollow silence filled the air, he slowly removed his hands from the plunger and looked up at the remaining trees standing like lonely sentries in the morning.

"Dear, dear old trees," I heard him call softly, "will you ever sing again?"

I waited. But the trees gave no answer.

Vocabulary

incredulously (in·krej′oo·ləs·lē) *adv.*: unbelievingly.
ashen (ash′ən) *adj.*: pale.
sentries (sen′trēz) *n.*: guards.

Meet the Writer

Mildred D. Taylor

We Could Be Anything

Mildred D. Taylor (1943–   ) grew up in Toledo, Ohio. In high school she was an honor student, a newspaper editor, and a class officer—but, she says, she wasn't able to do what she really wanted: be a cheerleader.

Every summer she and her family visited Mississippi relatives, and she listened to their stories. By the time she was nine or ten, she knew that she wanted to write. "I wanted to show a Black family united in love and pride, of which the reader would like to be a part."

Her first effort, *Song of the Trees*, introduced the Logan family and won first prize in the African American category of a competition for children's books. In 1977, when she accepted the Newbery Award for her second work about the Logan family, *Roll of Thunder, Hear My Cry*, Taylor talked about her father:

66 Throughout my childhood he impressed upon my sister and me that we were somebody, that we were important and could do or be anything we set our minds to do or be. He was not the kind of father who demanded A's on our report cards. He was more concerned about how we carried ourselves, how we respected ourselves and others, and how we pursued the principles upon which he hoped we would build our lives. He was constantly reminding us that how we saw ourselves was far more important than how others saw us.... Through David Logan have come the words of my father, and through the Logan family the love of my own family. 99

For Independent Reading

You can rejoin Cassie Logan and her family in the novels *Let the Circle Be Unbroken* and *The Road to Memphis*.

After You Read   Response and Analysis

First Thoughts

1. What scene from the story do you remember most vividly?

Thinking Critically

2. Cassie describes the trees as if they could talk and sing. Find two passages in the story in which the trees seem human. Why do you think Cassie loves her trees so much?

3. When you read on page 516 that Mr. Andersen "hissed venomously," what are you reminded of? How do you feel about Mr. Andersen's behavior?

4. *Song of the Trees* is told by Cassie. How would the story be different if it were told by her father?

Extending Interpretations

INTERNET

Projects and Activities

Keyword: LE5 7-5

5. Go back to the statements you rated on page 508. Individually and with the class, rate the four statements again, using the same scale. Have any of your opinions changed now that you've read the story?

6. Taylor says that in writing *Song of the Trees*, "[I] drew upon people and places I had known all my life." In creating the character of Cassie, for example, she drew on the personalities of her sister and an aunt. How believable did the characters seem to you? Explain.

Reading Check

Create a story map for the **plot** of *Song of the Trees*. Copy and fill in the following diagram:

> Characters:
>
> Conflicts:
>
> Event: _____
>
> Event: _____
>
> Event: _____
>
> Event: [Add as many event boxes as you need.]
>
> Resolution of conflict:

SKILLS FOCUS

Literary Skills
Analyze a novella.

Reading Skills
Make a generalization.

Writing Skills
Explain a theme.

WRITING
Writing About Theme

Theme, as you learned earlier (pages 236–237), is the *meaning* of a story. Theme points to what the main characters learn in the story and to what *you* learn as you share their experiences. In a paragraph, explain what you think the theme of this story is.

Connotations: What's the Difference Between . . .

Would you rather be described as *curious* or *nosy*? The two words have the same basic meaning, or **denotation,** but they have different connotations. **Connotations** are the feelings and associations that have come to be attached to certain words. Most people wouldn't mind being called curious: It suggests that you are interested in the world around you and want to learn about it. *Nosy* has negative connotations: It suggests that you are someone who puts your nose into other people's business.

> **Word Bank**
>
> finicky
> dispute
> ambled
> delved
> curtly
> skirting
> elude
> incredulously
> ashen
> sentries

PRACTICE

Test your skills at recognizing shades of meaning. (Use a dictionary to check your answers.) What's the difference between the following words and phrases? It would help if you go back and read the word in its context in the story.

1. *careful* and *finicky*
2. a *brawl* and a *dispute*
3. *walked* and *ambled*
4. *looked for* and *delved*
5. *matter-of-factly* and *curtly*
6. *passing* and *skirting*
7. *escape* and *elude*
8. *doubtfully* and *incredulously*
9. *creamy* and *ashen*
10. *watchers* and *sentries*

SKILLS FOCUS

Vocabulary Skills
Understand connotation and denotation.

All Modifiers! Places, Please!

To work well, modifiers have to be in the right place. A modifier that seems to modify the wrong word in a sentence is called a **misplaced modifier.** Here's an example of a misplaced modifier:

MISPLACED   **Today I read a story about a forest that was almost blown up in my literature book.**

Did the forest blow up in the book? No, the phrase *in my literature book* is misplaced. To fix the sentence, place the modifier as close as possible to the word it modifies—*read.*

CORRECT   **Today I read in my literature book a story about a forest that was almost blown up.**

MISPLACED   **Cassie heard the men say they were going to cut down the forest with her own ears.**

CORRECT   **Cassie heard with her own ears the men say they were going to cut down the forest.**

CORRECT   **With her own ears, Cassie heard the men say they were going to cut down the forest.**

SKILLS FOCUS

Grammar Skills
Avoid misplaced modifiers.

PRACTICE

Move the misplaced modifiers in these sentences to the right place.

1. The final conversation is a key scene in this story between Mr. Logan and Mr. Andersen.

2. Fidgeting with his clothing, we often watched Little Man in front of the mirror.

3. I almost understood every word of the story.

4. Stacy saw a man near the tree named Mr. Andersen.

5. The children looked at the trees who were weeping softly.

6. The trees whispered to the children with their leafy boughs.

7. Mr. Andersen's car was already parked in the driveway with its shiny fenders.

8. Other books are about the Logans by Mildred Taylor.

9. There's a story about a mongoose who kills snakes in this book.

10. There's also a story about a girl named Esperanza called "A Rice Sandwich."

For more help, see Placement of Modifiers, 5g, in the Language Handbook.

Fish Cheeks

Make the Connection
Quickwrite ✏️

A girl is walking down the hall at school. Coming toward her is a boy she's been dying to meet. They are almost next to each other when she slips, loses her balance, and falls to the floor in a clumsy heap. How could a moment like this possibly have a positive outcome?

Jot down your responses to that question. Then, in a group, share your possible outcomes.

Literary Focus
Humorous Essays: Tickling Your Funny Bone

An **essay** is a short piece of nonfiction prose that looks at one subject in a limited way. Though essays can be formal and logical, many of the essays we enjoy today are relaxed, informal writings that reveal a great deal about the writer's feelings. Most essays—like this one by Amy Tan—are published in popular magazines.

Writers of **humorous essays** are something like stand-up comics: They entertain us by putting a funny spin or twist on odd or embarrassing moments from everyday life.

Writers of humorous essays aren't always just out for laughs, however. They often have other, more serious purposes in mind. As you read the following essay, see if you think the writer intends to do more than tickle your funny bone (but first, read the essay just for fun).

Reading Skills
Describing Images: Appealing to the Senses

When writers describe things, they create **images**—pictures drawn with words. To help readers imagine places, events, and characters, they use language that appeals to the senses, as Amy Tan does in this true story. When you read descriptions, notice that

- most images are visual, but they often appeal to several senses at once
- writers often choose details that show how they *feel* about what they describe

Vocabulary Development
Learning the following words will help you appreciate the vividness of Amy Tan's writing:

appalling (ə·pôl′iŋ) *adj.:* horrifying. *The amount of food on the dinner table was simply appalling.*

wedges (wej′iz) *n.:* pie-shaped slices. *The tofu was cut into bite-sized wedges.*

clamor (klam′ər) *n.:* loud, confused noise. *The clamor in the dining room probably could have been heard down the hall.*

rumpled (rum′pəld) *v.* used as *adj.:* wrinkled and untidy. *Amy was embarrassed by her uncle's rumpled gifts.*

muster (mus′tər) *v.:* call forth. *She couldn't even muster up a smile for her mother after dinner.*

SKILLS FOCUS

Literary Skills
Understand forms of prose: the essay.

Reading Skills
Understand images.

FISH CHEEKS

Amy Tan

ON CHRISTMAS EVE
I SAW THAT MY MOTHER
HAD OUTDONE HERSELF IN
CREATING A STRANGE MENU.

I fell in love with the minister's son the winter I turned fourteen. He was not Chinese, but as white as Mary in the manger. For Christmas I prayed for this blond-haired boy, Robert, and a slim new American nose.

When I found out that my parents had invited the minister's family over for Christmas Eve dinner, I cried. What would Robert think of our shabby *Chinese* Christmas? What would he think of our noisy *Chinese* relatives who lacked proper American manners? What terrible disappointment would he feel upon seeing not a roasted turkey and sweet potatoes but *Chinese* food?

On Christmas Eve I saw that my mother had outdone herself in creating a strange menu. She was pulling black veins out of the backs of fleshy prawns. The kitchen was littered with appalling mounds of raw food: a slimy rock cod with bulging fish eyes that pleaded not to be thrown into a pan of hot oil. Tofu, which looked like stacked wedges of rubbery white sponges. A bowl soaking dried fungus back to life. A plate of squid, their backs crisscrossed with knife markings so they resembled bicycle tires.

And then they arrived—the minister's family and all my relatives in a clamor of doorbells and rumpled Christmas packages. Robert grunted hello, and I pretended he was not worthy of existence.

Dinner threw me deeper into despair. My relatives licked the ends of their chopsticks and reached across the table, dipping them into the dozen or so plates of food. Robert and his family waited patiently for platters to be passed to them. My relatives murmured with pleasure when my mother brought out the whole steamed fish. Robert grimaced. Then my father poked his chopsticks just below the fish eye and plucked out the soft meat. "Amy, your favorite," he said, offering me the tender fish cheek. I wanted to disappear.

At the end of the meal my father leaned back and belched loudly, thanking my mother for her fine cooking. "It's a polite Chinese custom to show you are satisfied," explained my father to our astonished guests. Robert was looking down at his plate with a reddened face. The minister managed to muster up a quiet burp. I was stunned into silence for the rest of the night.

After everyone had gone, my mother said to me, "You want to be the same as American girls on the outside." She handed me an early gift. It was a miniskirt in beige tweed. "But inside you must always be Chinese. You must be proud you are different. Your only shame is to have shame."

And even though I didn't agree with her then, I knew that she understood how much I had suffered during the evening's dinner. It wasn't until many years later—long after I had gotten over my crush on Robert—that I was able to fully appreciate her lesson and the true purpose behind our particular menu. For Christmas Eve that year, she had chosen all my favorite foods.

Vocabulary
appalling (ə·pôl′iŋ) *adj.:* shocking; horrifying.
wedges (wej′iz) *n.:* pie-shaped slices.
clamor (klam′ər) *n.:* loud, confused noise.
rumpled (rum′pəld) *v.* used as *adj.:* wrinkled and untidy.
muster (mus′tər) *v.:* call forth.

Meet the Writer

Amy Tan

Finding Answers in Stories

❝ I was the only Chinese girl in class from third grade on. I remember trying to belong and feeling isolated. I felt ashamed of being different and ashamed of feeling that way. When I was a teenager, I rejected everything Chinese. . . . The only people I could think I wanted to be like were fictional characters. In part, that is one of the reasons I began to write. You're looking for answers in your life, and you can't find them in anyone else. You end up finding them in stories. ❞

Amy Tan (1952–   ) found her friends in books—fairy tales, the *Little House* novels of Laura Ingalls Wilder, and later, the British novels of the Brontë sisters. Later still she began to write books of her own, about a life half a world away from America's prairies and Britain's moors.

Tan spent her childhood in Oakland, California, where her parents had settled after leaving China. When she was fifteen, both her father and her brother died from brain tumors. After these losses her mother revealed a long-kept secret: Amy had three half sisters still living in China. These upheavals in her family changed Amy Tan's sense of who she was. Suddenly her Chinese heritage became important to her. She began to read whatever she could about China, later taking college courses in Chinese literature and history. Most of all, Tan became fascinated by her mother's stories about her experiences in China during the war-torn 1930s and 1940s.

In recent years, Amy Tan has made several trips to China, where she has come to know the sisters who once seemed lost to her forever. She now loves the Chinese culture she once tried so hard to reject.

First Thoughts

1. Have you ever felt the way Amy does? What would you have done that Christmas Eve if you had been Amy?

Thinking Critically

2. Why do you think Amy is ashamed of her family's Chinese traditions? What does her mother mean when she says, "Your only shame is to have shame"?

3. Find one **image** in the story that creates a vivid picture in your mind. Find three other images that help you feel you can touch, smell, taste, or hear details of the dinner.

4. Why do you suppose it isn't until many years later that Amy realizes her mother chose all of Amy's favorite foods for the Christmas Eve dinner? What do you think are her mother's "lesson" and "true purpose" in preparing those foods?

5. Is this **essay** about a strange menu, or is it really about something else? In one or two sentences, state what you think is Tan's **main idea.**

Extending Interpretations

6. Amy's mother tells her that she can be an American girl on the outside but must always be Chinese on the inside. Do you think that is possible? Is it a good idea? Explain your answer.

7. Where does the **title** "Fish Cheeks" come from? Do you think it's a good title? Tell why or why not.

WRITING

Writing a Narrative

Have you ever been in an embarrassing situation that somehow ended with a positive outcome (like the one you wrote about for the Quickwrite)? Write about that experience, or write about a time when you were anxious about making a good impression. Think about your **purpose:** Will you be writing only to entertain, or will your narrative have a point? Include images in your story that will help readers share your experience.

> **Reading Check**
>
> Imagine that it is Christmas Eve twenty years later. With a partner, retell the main events of "Fish Cheeks." Let one person play the role of Amy and the other person play her mother. Let Amy retell the story. Let her mother add details.

INTERNET
Projects and Activities
Keyword: LE5 7-5

Literary Skills
Analyze an essay.

Reading Skills
Identify images.

Writing Skills
Write a narrative.

Vocabulary Development

Word Analogies: Pairs of Pairs

A **word analogy** begins with a pair of items that are related in some way. You figure out that relationship, and then complete another pair that has a similar relationship. For example,

Sweet is to *sour* as _____ is to *short*.

   a. small   **b. bitter**   **c. tall**   **d. round**

The relationship of *sweet* to *sour* is one of opposites. *Tall,* the opposite of *short,* is the best way to complete the analogy.

Try this one:

Kitten is to *cat* as _____ is to *dog*.

   a. poodle   **b. puppy**   **c. fur**   **d. bark**

A kitten is a young cat, so the correct answer is *puppy,* which is a young dog. Once you figure out the relationship, completing the analogy should be a snap.

> **Word Bank**
>
> appalling
> wedges
> clamor
> rumpled
> muster

PRACTICE

Complete the following analogies. First, figure out the relationship between the words in the first pair. Then, choose a Word Bank word that has a similar relationship to the last word in the sentence. Here's a hint for the first item:

1. *Sad* is to *happy* as _____ is to *delightful.*
The relationship between *sad* and *happy* is one of opposites. What word in the Word Bank is the opposite of *delightful?*

2. *Pressed* is to *neat* as _____ is to *sloppy.*

3. *Whisper* is to *soft* as _____ is to *loud.*

4. *Receive* is to *get* as _____ is to *summon.*

5. *Slices* is to *pizza* as _____ is to *cheese.*

SKILLS FOCUS

Vocabulary Skills
Complete word analogies.

A Mason-Dixon Memory

Make the Connection
Quickwrite ✏️

How far would you go to do the right thing? Think of something you really care about. It could be a possession or an event you're looking forward to— anything you'd hate to give up. Can you imagine a situation in which doing the right thing might mean giving up the thing you want so much? For example, what if going to a party means you have to break a date with a friend who wasn't invited? Jot down your thoughts on how you might handle such a situation.

Literary Focus
The Essay

One form of nonfiction you'll often be asked to read—and write—is the **essay,** a short piece of nonfiction prose that focuses on a single topic. An essay can be about anything, from "The Meaning of Life" to "How I Feel About My Cat."

An essay can be formal in tone and highly structured, with statements laid out in careful order and evidence supporting each one. An essay can also be personal and even humorous, as if the writer were sitting down with us for a chat. An essay's tone and structure will depend on its **purpose**—does the writer want to inform us? persuade us? entertain us? or do something else?

Reading Skills 📖
Recognizing Text Structures

Essays, like other pieces of writing, are often structured in ways that help make their meaning clear. This essay is structured around **flashbacks**—the narrator twice goes back to an earlier time to tell a story that relates to the first story he is telling. Like many essayists, the writer uses his final paragraph to sum up his main idea. As you read the essay, look for the open-book signs. These alert you to the essay's structure. (If you miss the flashbacks, you may be hopelessly lost in time!)

Vocabulary Development

Here are some words you'll learn as you read this selection:

predominantly (prē·däm'ə·nənt·lē) *adv.:* mainly. *The story is predominantly about the meaning of friendship.*

forfeit (fôr'fit) *v.:* lose the right to compete. *Dondré's teammates would forfeit the tournament.*

resolve (ri·zälv') *v.:* decide. *In tough situations, people can resolve to do the right thing.*

ominous (äm'ə·nəs) *adj.:* threatening. *The look on the chaperone's face was ominous.*

erupted (ē·rup'tid) *v.:* burst forth. *Applause erupted from the audience after Dondré's speech.*

INTERNET

Vocabulary Activity
Keyword: LE5 7-5

Literary Skills
Understand forms of prose: the essay.

Reading Skills
Recognize text structures: flashback.

A Mason-Dixon Memory

Clifton Davis

Sponsor:
Fred Matte

Dondré
Green

Brad
Coenen

Damon
Marsala

Jeff
McNew

David
Elias

"If we leave, we forfeit this tournament. If we stay, Dondré can't play."

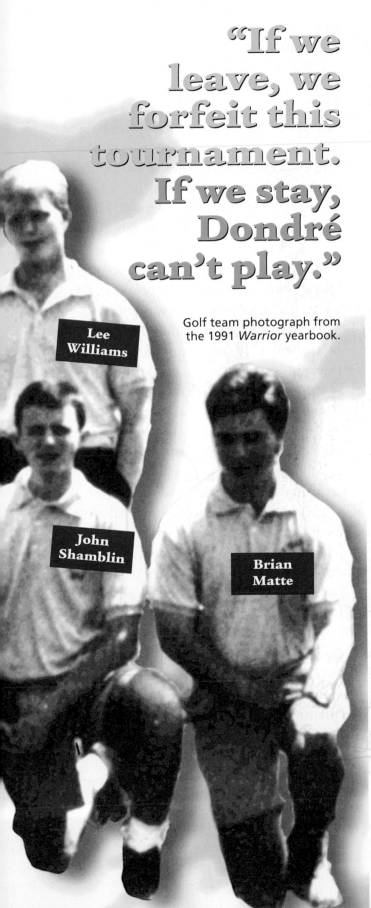

Golf team photograph from the 1991 *Warrior* yearbook.

Lee Williams

John Shamblin

Brian Matte

Dondré Green glanced uneasily at the civic leaders and sports figures filling the hotel ballroom in Cleveland. They had come from across the nation to attend a fundraiser for the National Minority College Golf Scholarship Foundation. I was the banquet's featured entertainer. Dondré, an eighteen-year-old high school senior from Monroe, Louisiana, was the evening's honored guest.

"Nervous?" I asked the handsome young man in his starched white shirt and rented tuxedo.

"A little," he whispered, grinning.

One month earlier, Dondré had been just one more black student attending a <u>predominantly</u> white Southern school. Although most of his friends and classmates were white, Dondré's race had never been an issue. Then, on April 17, 1991, Dondré's black skin provoked an incident that made nationwide news.

"Ladies and gentlemen," the emcee[1] said, "our special guest, Dondré Green."

As the audience stood applauding, Dondré walked to the microphone and began his story. "I love golf," he said quietly. "For the past two years, I've been a member of the St. Frederick High School golf team. And though I was the only black member, I've always felt at home playing at the mostly white country clubs across Louisiana."

The audience leaned forward; even the waiters and busboys stopped to listen. As I listened, a memory buried in my heart since childhood began fighting its way to life.

---

1. **emcee** (em′sē′)*n.:* master of ceremonies.

Vocabulary
predominantly (prē·däm′ə·nənt·lē) *adv.:* mainly.

"Our team had driven from Monroe," Dondré continued. "When we arrived at the Caldwell Parish Country Club in Columbia, we walked to the putting green."

Dondré and his teammates were too absorbed to notice the conversation between a man and St. Frederick athletic director James Murphy. After disappearing into the clubhouse, Murphy returned to his players.

"I want to see the seniors," he said. "On the double!" His face seemed strained as he gathered the four students, including Dondré.

"I don't know how to tell you this," he said, "but the Caldwell Parish Country Club is reserved for whites only." Murphy paused and looked at Dondré. His teammates glanced at each other in disbelief. "I want you seniors to decide what our response should be," Murphy continued. "If we leave, we forfeit this tournament. If we stay, Dondré can't play."

As I listened, my own childhood memory from thirty-two years ago broke free. ❶

🏊 **TEXT STRUCTURE**
❶ The writer adds extra space here. What words indicate a **flashback**? What year are we now in?

In 1959 I was thirteen years old, a poor black kid living with my mother and stepfather in a small black ghetto on Long Island, New York. My mother worked nights in a hospital, and my stepfather drove a coal truck. Needless to say, our standard of living was somewhat short of the American dream.

Nevertheless, when my eighth-grade teacher announced a graduation trip to Washington, D.C., it never crossed my mind that I would be left behind. Besides a complete tour of the nation's capital, we would visit Glen Echo Amusement Park in Maryland. In my imagination, Glen Echo was Disneyland, Knott's Berry Farm, and Magic Mountain rolled into one.

My heart beating wildly, I raced home to deliver the mimeographed letter describing the journey. But when my mother saw how much the trip would cost, she just shook her head. We couldn't afford it.

After feeling sad for ten seconds, I decided to try to fund the trip myself. For the next eight weeks, I sold candy bars door-to-door, delivered newspapers, and mowed lawns. Three days before the deadline, I'd made just barely enough. I was going!

The day of the trip, trembling with excitement, I climbed onto the train. I was the only nonwhite in our section.

Our hotel was not far from the White House. My roommate was Frank Miller, the son of a businessman. Leaning together out of our window and dropping water balloons on passing tourists quickly cemented our new friendship.

Every morning, almost a hundred of us loaded noisily onto our bus for another adventure. We sang our school fight song dozens of times—en route[2] to Arlington National Cemetery and even on an afternoon cruise down the Potomac River.

We visited the Lincoln Memorial twice, once in daylight, the second time at dusk. My classmates and I fell silent as we walked in the shadows of those thirty-six marble columns, one for every state in the Union that Lincoln labored to preserve. I stood next to Frank at the base of the nineteen-

---

2. **en route** (än rōōt′): on the way.

Vocabulary
forfeit (fôr′fit) v.: lose the right to something.

foot seated statue. Spotlights made the white Georgian marble seem to glow. Together, we read those famous words from Lincoln's speech at Gettysburg, remembering the most bloody battle in the War Between the States: "We here highly resolve that these dead shall not have died in vain—that this nation, under God, shall have a new birth of freedom. . . ."

As Frank motioned me into place to take my picture, I took one last look at Lincoln's face. He seemed alive and so terribly sad.

The next morning I understood a little better why he wasn't smiling. "Clifton," a chaperone said, "could I see you for a moment?"

The other guys at my table, especially Frank, turned pale. We had been joking about the previous night's direct water-balloon hit on a fat lady and her poodle. It was a stupid, dangerous act, but luckily nobody got hurt. We were celebrating our escape from punishment when the chaperone asked to see me.

"Clifton," she began, "do you know about the Mason-Dixon line?"

"No," I said, wondering what this had to do with drenching fat ladies.

"Before the Civil War," she explained, "the Mason-Dixon line was originally the boundary between Maryland and Pennsylvania—the dividing line between the slave and free states." Having escaped one disaster, I could feel another brewing. I noticed that her eyes were damp and her hands shaking.

"Today," she continued, "the Mason-Dixon line is a kind of invisible border between the North and the South. When you cross that invisible line out of Washington, D.C., into Maryland, things change."

There was an ominous drift to this conversation, but I wasn't following it. Why did she look and sound so nervous?

"Glen Echo Amusement Park is in Maryland," she said at last, "and the management doesn't allow Negroes inside." She stared at me in silence.

I was still grinning and nodding when the meaning finally sank in. "You mean I can't go to the park," I stuttered, "because I'm a Negro?"

She nodded slowly. "I'm sorry, Clifton," she said, taking my hand. "You'll have to stay in the hotel tonight. Why don't you and I watch a movie on television?"

I walked to the elevators feeling confusion, disbelief, anger, and a deep sadness. "What happened, Clifton?" Frank said when I got back to the room. "Did the fat lady tell on us?"

Without saying a word, I walked over to my bed, lay down, and began to cry. Frank was stunned into silence. Junior-high boys didn't cry, at least not in front of each other.

It wasn't just missing the class adventure that made me feel so sad. For the first time in my life, I was learning what it felt like to be a "nigger." Of course there was discrimination in the North, but the color of my skin had never officially kept me out of a coffee shop, a church—or an amusement park.

"Clifton," Frank whispered, "what is the matter?"

"They won't let me go to Glen Echo Park tonight," I sobbed.

Vocabulary

resolve (ri·zälv′) v.: decide; make a formal statement.

ominous (äm′ə·nəs) adj.: threatening, like a bad sign; warning of something bad.

"Because of the water balloon?" he asked.

"No," I answered, "because I'm a Negro."

"Well, that's a relief!" Frank said, and then he laughed, obviously relieved to have escaped punishment for our caper with the balloons. "I thought it was serious!"

Wiping away the tears with my sleeve, I stared at him. "It *is* serious. They don't let Negroes into the park. I can't go with you!" I shouted. "That's pretty serious to me."

I was about to wipe the silly grin off Frank's face with a blow to his jaw when I heard him say, "Then I won't go either."

For an instant we just froze. Then Frank grinned. I will never forget that moment. Frank was just a kid. He wanted to go to that amusement park as much as I did, but there was something even more important than the class night out. Still, he didn't explain or expand.

The next thing I knew, the room was filled with kids listening to Frank. "They don't allow Negroes in the park," he said, "so I'm staying with Clifton."

"Me too," a second boy said.

"Those jerks," a third muttered. "I'm with you, Clifton." My heart began to race. Suddenly, I was not alone. A pint-sized revolution had been born. The "water-balloon brigade," eleven white boys from Long Island, had made its decision: "We won't go." And as I sat on my bed in the center of it all, I felt grateful. But above all, I was filled with pride. ❷

TEXT STRUCTURE

❷ The writer uses extra space again. Where are we now in time?

Dondré Green's story brought that childhood memory back to life. His golfing teammates, like my childhood friends, had an important decision to make. Standing by their friend would cost them dearly. But when it came time to decide, no one hesitated. "Let's get out of here," one of them whispered.

"They just turned and walked toward the van," Dondré told us. "They didn't debate it. And the younger players joined us without looking back."

Dondré was astounded by the response of his friends—and the people of Louisiana. The whole state was outraged and tried to make it right. The Louisiana House of Representatives proclaimed a Dondré Green Day and passed legislation permitting lawsuits for damages, attorneys' fees, and court costs against any private facility that invites a team, then bars any member because of race.

As Dondré concluded, his eyes glistened with tears. "I love my coach and my teammates for sticking by me," he said. "It goes to show that there are always good people who will not give in to bigotry. The kind of love they showed me that day will conquer hatred every time."

Suddenly, the banquet crowd was standing, applauding Dondré Green. ❸

TEXT STRUCTURE

❸ Again, extra space. How do you know the writer has flashed back again?

My friends, too, had shown that kind of love. As we sat in the hotel, a chaperone came in waving an envelope. "Boys!" he shouted. "I've just bought thirteen tickets to the Senators-Tigers game. Anybody want to go?"

The room erupted in cheers. Not one of

Vocabulary

erupted (ē·rup′tid) v.: exploded or burst forth.

us had ever been to a professional baseball game in a real baseball park.

On the way to the stadium, we grew silent as our driver paused before the Lincoln Memorial. For one long moment, I stared through the marble pillars at Mr. Lincoln, bathed in that warm yellow light. There was still no smile and no sign of hope in his sad and tired eyes.

"We here highly resolve . . . that this nation, under God, shall have a new birth of freedom . . ."

In his words and in his life, Lincoln had made it clear that freedom is not free. Every time the color of a person's skin keeps him out of an amusement park or off a country-club fairway, the war for freedom begins again. Sometimes the battle is fought with fists and guns, but more often the most effective weapon is a simple act of love and courage. ❹

Whenever I hear those words from Lincoln's speech at Gettysburg, I remember my eleven white friends, and I feel hope once again. I like to imagine that when we paused that night at the foot of his great monument, Mr. Lincoln smiled at last. As Dondré said, "The kind of love they showed me that day will conquer hatred every time."

MAIN IDEA
❹ The writer reflects on both stories, his and Dondré Green's. What sentence in this paragraph states the **main idea** of this essay?

Meet the Writer

Clifton Davis

A Man of Many Talents

Clifton Davis (1946–   ) may be better known for writing tunes than for writing prose. He wrote the song "Never Can Say Goodbye," which sold two million records. He's still involved with music today, as a composer, recording artist, and host of a gospel-music radio program.

Clifton Davis is also an actor. He has appeared in several plays on Broadway and received a Tony nomination for his performance in *Two Gentlemen of Verona*. Davis has also appeared in movies and on TV shows. The role he is best known for is Rev. Reuben Gregory on the television series *Amen.* The curious thing about casting Davis in the role of the minister is that he really *is* a minister, in the Seventh-Day Adventist Church.

Davis believes it's important to do what's right, even if you're making a living amid the glitz and glamour of Hollywood.

After You Read Response and Analysis

First Thoughts

1. Finish these sentences:
   - If I were a teammate of Dondré Green's or a classmate of Clifton Davis's, I would . . .
   - Being a friend means . . .

Thinking Critically

2. The narrator, Clifton Davis, starts one story and then flashes back to another story, one that happened to him. Where does the **flashback** begin and end? What does it have to do with Davis's main story?

3. How did Dondré Green's teammates and the people of Louisiana react to the fact that he had been barred from the tournament? Why do you think Dondré was astounded by this response?

4. The narrator says there was "something even more important" than going to the amusement park. Frank never explained what that something was. How would you explain it?

Extending Interpretations

5. Look back at your Quickwrite notes. Did reading this story change the way you look at choices that might force you to give up something you value? If so, explain how and why. ✏

6. Green and Davis both believe that a simple act of love and courage is the most effective weapon against prejudice. Do you agree? Explain.

WRITING
Supporting a Position

Many people devote their lives to fighting for important causes, such as civil rights. Write a brief **persuasive essay** on an issue that *you* really care about. First, identify the issue and state your opinion of it. Then, list evidence that supports your opinion.

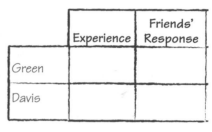

Reading Check

How were the experiences of Dondré Green and Clifton Davis alike? Fill in a chart like the one below to compare their experiences:

	Experience	Friends' Response
Green		
Davis		

INTERNET

Projects and Activities

Keyword: LE5 7-5

SKILLS FOCUS

Literary Skills
Analyze an essay.

Reading Skills
Analyze flashbacks.

Writing Skills
Write a brief persuasive essay.

After You Read | Vocabulary Development

Synonyms: Shades of Meaning

Words with the same or almost the same meaning are called **synonyms.** Synonyms usually have different shades of meaning. *Rigid* and *firm* are synonyms, but most people would rather be called *firm* than *rigid.* A dictionary or a thesaurus, a book of synonyms, can help you pick exactly the word you need.

Word Bank

predominantly
forfeit
resolve
ominous
erupted

PRACTICE

Make a word map like the following one for the rest of the Word Bank words. Find at least one synonym for each word, and put it in the word map. Then, write at least one sentence using each word. Discuss the synonyms and their shades of meaning, if any.

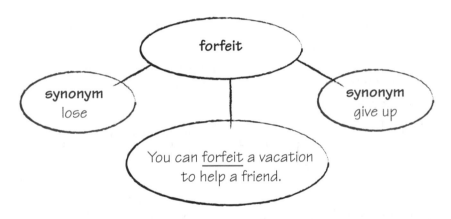

forfeit

synonym
lose

synonym
give up

You can <u>forfeit</u> a vacation to help a friend.

SKILLS FOCUS

Vocabulary Skills
Analyze shades of meaning.

Commas Make Sense of a Series

- Use commas to separate words, phrases, or clauses in a series.

    INCORRECT   Davis felt "confusion disbelief anger and a deep sadness."

    CORRECT   Davis felt "confusion, disbelief, anger, and a deep sadness."

- In most cases, use commas to separate two or more adjectives that come before a noun.

    INCORRECT   It was a stupid dangerous act.

    CORRECT   It was a stupid, dangerous act.

- Do not place a comma between an adjective and a noun that immediately follows it.

    INCORRECT   Green's teammates made a fast, important, costly, decision.

    CORRECT   Green's teammates made a fast, important, costly decision.

- If the last adjective in a series is closely connected in meaning to the noun that follows it, do not use a comma before that adjective.

    INCORRECT   "Spotlights made the white, Georgian marble seem to glow."

    CORRECT   "Spotlights made the white Georgian marble seem to glow."

To decide whether a comma is needed, add the word *and* between the adjectives. If the *and* sounds strange, don't use a comma. (*White* and *Georgian marble* sounds strange, so don't use a comma there.)

PRACTICE

Copy the sentences below. Add commas where necessary to separate the items in a series. Compare your answers with a partner's.

1. Davis sold candy bars delivered newspapers and mowed lawns.

2. Lincoln's sad wise tired face impressed them.

3. Sincere courageous acts of love can conquer hatred.

4. They saw many famous national landmarks in Washington, D.C.

For more help, see Commas: Items in a Series, 13f–g, in the Language Handbook.

SKILLS FOCUS

Grammar Skills
Use commas in a series correctly.

No comma between an adjective and a noun that immediately follows it!

TO A GREAT, MAYOR WHO

Summarizing

Reading Focus
Summarizing: Putting It All in a Nutshell!

Have you ever found yourself rambling on and on about something that's happened to you or about something you read, such as "A Mason-Dixon Memory," and your patient-but-now-frustrated listener finally says, "Enough already—just give it to me in a nut-shell"? What your friend's asking for is a summary.

A **summary** restates the main events or main ideas of a text in a much shorter form than the original.

Summaries are useful because they can help you remember the most important points in material you've just read. They're especially handy if you're doing research from a number of sources. Reviewing your summaries will show you how one source differs from another.

Before you write a summary, read the text carefully to decide what details to include and what to leave out. The main events will probably be easy to recognize, but the **main ideas**—the central or most important ideas in a text—can be harder to discover. Sometimes the writer states a main idea directly, but usually you have to infer, or guess, what it is. One way to discover the main ideas is by identifying important details and then thinking about what point they make.

■ Use a graphic organizer like the one below to collect information for a summary of the newspaper article "Buddies Bare Their Affection for Ill Classmate." Part of the organizer has been completed for you. Add as many boxes as you need for the main events. Then, fill in the writer's **main idea.**

Main Events

> Doctors remove tumor from Ian O'Gorman.

↓

> He starts chemotherapy.

↓

> [blank]

↓

> [blank]

The Writer's Main Idea

> [blank]

INTERNET
Interactive
Reading Model
Keyword: LE5 7-5

Reading Skills
Understand how to summarize; understand main idea.

Buddies Bare Their Affection for Ill Classmate

OCEANSIDE, CAL., MAR. 19 (Associated Press) — In Mr. Alter's fifth-grade class, it's difficult to tell which boy is undergoing chemotherapy. Nearly all the boys are bald. Thirteen of them shaved their heads so a sick buddy wouldn't feel out of place.

"If everybody has their head shaved, sometimes people don't know who's who. They don't know who has cancer and who just shaved their head," said eleven-year-old Scott Sebelius, one of the baldies at Lake Elementary School.

For the record, Ian O'Gorman is the sick one. Doctors recently removed a malignant tumor from his small intestine, and a week ago he started chemotherapy to treat the disease, called lymphoma.

"Besides surgery, I had tubes up my nose. I had butterflies in my stomach," said Ian, who'll have eight more weeks of chemotherapy in an effort to keep the cancer from returning.

Ian decided to get his head shaved before all his hair fell out in clumps. To his surprise, his friends wanted to join him.

"The last thing he would want is to not fit in, to be made fun of, so we just wanted to make him feel better and not left out," said ten-year-old Kyle Hanslik.

Kyle started talking to other boys about the idea, and then one of their parents started a list. Last week, they all went to the barbershop together.

"It's hard to put words to," said Ian's father, Shawn, choking back tears as he talked about the boys. "It's very emotional to think about kids like that who would come together, to have them do such a thing to support Ian."

The boy's teacher, Jim Alter, was so inspired that he, too, shaved his head.

Ian left the hospital March 2. Although he has lost twenty pounds and is pale, he is eager to get back to the business of being an eleven-year-old playing baseball and basketball. "I think I can start on Monday," he said.

—from the
Austin American-Statesman

Ian O'Gorman (center), who is undergoing chemotherapy for cancer, is surrounded by his classmates, who shaved their heads as a show of support.

Summarizing a Text

Buddies Bare Their Affection for Ill Classmate

Test Practice

1. According to the opening paragraph, what's difficult to tell about the boys in Mr. Alter's class is who —
   - A is the brightest student
   - B is undergoing chemotherapy
   - C once had the longest hair
   - D Ian O'Gorman is

2. The main reason the boys shaved their heads was to —
   - F look unusual
   - G show individuality
   - H act original
   - J show support

3. Kyle Hanslik got the idea of shaving his head because —
   - A he liked the way Ian looked
   - B he didn't want Ian to be made fun of
   - C he was protesting Ian's illness
   - D he wanted to confuse the teacher

4. Who else was surprisingly inspired to shave his head?
   - F Mr. Alter
   - G Ian's dad
   - H Kyle's dad
   - J Ian's doctor

Constructed Response

A good **summary** of an informational text covers the main events or main points, not every single detail. That is why a summary is always much shorter than the original piece. Use the information you collected in your graphic organizer (page 543) to write a summary of the news story about Ian and his friends. Here are some tips for writing a good summary:

- Cite the author and title of the article you are summarizing.
- Cite the topic of the article in a few words.

- Retell the main events or main points of the article, using your own words. Include only key events or key points.
- Sum up the writer's message or **main idea.**

After you have written your summary, read it over and ask yourself: Would a person who has not read the article understand what it is about? If your answer is negative, go back and revise your summary.

SKILLS FOCUS

Reading Skills
Summarize a text.

Elements of Literature
Painting with Words
by John Malcolm Brinnin

THE ELEMENTS OF POETRY

People rarely see poets at work. Even if you could watch a poet writing, you would not be able to notice much action. The making of a poem is mostly a solitary, mental activity. The only activity you might notice is the poet's use of speech—poets are not usually silent while they work. They often test what they write by saying it out loud.

To begin to understand what elements go into the making of a poem, it might help to think of the poet as an artist who is creating something with words.

Creating Images

A poet uses words the way a painter uses colors. Like painters, poets want to share a special, personal vision of the world. To do that, poets create **images,** or pictures. Poets also use **figures of speech**—language that helps make startling connections between dissimilar things. Like a painter's colors, a poet's words can put your imagination to work; they can make you see the world in new, unexpected ways.

Creating Sounds

Like musicians, poets are also concerned with sounds. Imagine a composer of music trying various patterns of notes on a piano in order to create a pleasing melody. That will give you a good idea of what poets try to do with words. Poets choose their words with great care. They revise them repeatedly, trying to find the combination that will produce just the right sound— perhaps a harsh sound, a musical sound, or a sound that matches the gallop of a horse. A poet's goal is to create sounds that will match the feelings and ideas they want to share with us.

Deciding on Forms

Like sculptors, poets are also concerned with shape, or form. When they write and revise, poets are chiseling their words to create the shapes you see on the page. Poets think about such things as how long their lines should be and whether they should group them into units (called **stanzas**). Some poets use forms based on strict rules that may be hundreds of years old. Other poets may experiment with freer forms. Whatever form a poet chooses to use, his or her purpose is to give the words a pleasing shape on the page and to help convey meaning.

INTERNET

More About Imagery

Keyword: LE5 7-5

Literary Skills
Understand images, sounds, and forms in poetry; understand how to read poetry.

How to Read Poetry

Follow these guidelines as you read the poems in this collection:

1. Read the poem aloud at least once. A poem's sense is linked to its sound.

2. Look for sentences, and pay attention to **punctuation.** Stop briefly at semicolons or after periods. Pause at commas. Look for sudden shifts in thought after dashes. If a line does not end with punctuation, do not make a full stop; pause only very briefly, and continue to the end of the sentence.

3. Always read a poem in a normal voice, as if you were speaking to a friend. If the poem has a steady beat, let the music emerge naturally. Do not force the poem's music by reading in a singsong way.

4. Look up unfamiliar words. Poets choose words carefully. Sometimes words in a poem are used to mean more than one thing.

5. Poets often describe one thing in terms of another. For example, a poet might describe snowflakes as if they were insects. Be alert for comparisons. Let them work on your imagination.

6. After a first reading, think about the poem. Especially think about its images and sounds, its flow of emotions and ideas. Then, read the poem a second or even a third time. With each re-reading you will discover something new.

7. Think about the poem's meaning— what message is being transmitted from the poet to you? You'll find that your response to many poems will be "It tells me something I always knew, but I never thought of it that way before."

Practice

Many years ago schoolchildren often memorized and recited poems. A poem's **rhymes** and **rhythms** help to make it fairly easy to memorize. If you would like to memorize a poem, try these techniques on one of the poems in this chapter, or memorize part of a long poem like "The Highwayman" (page 247) or "Annabel Lee" (page 261). Once you have your poem memorized, recite it for the class.

1. Read the poem aloud three or four times.

2. Look for rhymes. Rhyming words help your memory.

3. Memorize two lines at a time. Say the lines aloud several times; then cover them up, and try to recite them from memory.

4. Try to picture the words of the poem on the page.

I Like to See It Lap the Miles

Emily Dickinson

I like to see it lap the Miles—
And lick the Valleys up—
And stop to feed itself at Tanks—
And then—prodigious° step

5   Around a Pile of Mountains—
And supercilious° peer
In Shanties—by the sides of Roads—
And then a Quarry pare

To fit its sides
10   And crawl between
Complaining all the while
In horrid—hooting stanza—
Then chase itself down Hill—

And neigh like Boanerges°—
15   Then—prompter than a Star
Stop—docile and omnipotent
At its own stable door—

---

4. prodigious (prō·dij′əs) *adj.:* enormous.
6. supercilious (sōō′pər·sil′ē·əs) *adj.:* haughty; stuck-up.
14. Boanerges (bō′ə·nʉr′jēz): biblical name meaning "sons of thunder." In Dickinson's time it had come to mean a preacher who gave thunderous sermons.

Meet the Writer

Emily Dickinson

The Granger Collection, New York.

Who Is That Mysterious Woman in White?

Today **Emily Dickinson** (1830–1886) ranks as one of America's—and the world's—greatest poets. During her lifetime, however, she was anything but famous. Of the seventeen hundred poems she wrote, only seven were published while she was alive—and she refused to have her name put on any of them.

After a normal, sociable childhood and adolescence, Dickinson seemed to retreat into the world of her own household at the age of twenty-six. By the time she was forty, she dressed only in white and rarely left her family's house in Amherst, Massachusetts. Except for family and a few old friends, she saw no one. Why? No one knows for sure. Her poems often deal with the relationship between her inner self and the outer world. Perhaps she had to draw back from the world and study it from a distance in order to write about it.

Many successful poets in the nineteenth century used regular rhymes and dum-de-dum rhythms. Emily Dickinson did not. Her rhythms were irregular and her rhymes slightly off. More important, she chose strong images to express her bold ideas. All in all, she was a true American original.

After Emily Dickinson died, her sister discovered in a locked box seven or eight hundred poems written on envelopes, paper bags, and scraps of paper, all neatly sewn into little packets. It looked as if the poet had been hoping someone would find the poems and publish them. Yet in her lifetime no one had really understood what poetry meant to Emily Dickinson. Here is how she once defined it:

> 66 If I read a book and it makes my whole body so cold no fire can ever warm me, I know that is poetry. If I feel physically as if the top of my head were taken off, I know that is poetry. These are the only ways I know it. Is there any other way? 99

First Thoughts

1. Let someone read the poem aloud to you. Draw a picture of what you see as you listen to the poem. Be sure to compare what *you* see in the poem with what other listeners see.

Thinking Critically

2. Although Emily Dickinson uses an **extended metaphor** in this poem, she never says directly what she is describing or what she is comparing that thing to. What clues in the poem tell you that she is writing about a train and comparing it to a horse? Could this poem be about two other things?

3. List all the adjectives Dickinson uses to describe the train. Think about these adjectives as well as the opening line of the poem. How do you think Dickinson feels about this train?

4. Look back at the strategies for "How to Read Poetry" on page 547. Which of these suggestions did you find most helpful? Pick one and explain how it helped you to understand "I Like to See It Lap the Miles."

Extending Interpretations

5. Look back at the chart you made for the Quickwrite on page 551. Did you find any comparisons between a train and a horse that Dickinson missed? ✏️

6. What machine would be as awesome today as the train was in Emily Dickinson's time?

WRITING

Extending a Metaphor

Choose a mechanical object (car, vacuum cleaner, lawn mower, blow-dryer, electric shaver, helicopter, spaceship), and write a brief poem comparing it to something living. Try to keep the mechanical object and the living object unnamed, as Dickinson does. Hint at the identity of your mystery items by including the sounds, smells, feel, appearance, and actions of the objects.

SKILLS FOCUS

Literary Skills
Analyze an extended metaphor.

Writing Skills
Write a poem.

I Am of the Earth *and* Early Song

Make the Connection
Quickwrite ✏️

Think of all the ways in which you are connected to the earth. To begin, fill in a chart like the one below:

Planet Earth

Gifts we receive from the earth:

Gifts we give back to the earth:

What is the most important gift the earth gives to you? What is the most important thing you give the earth? Briefly explain your answers.

Literary Focus
Personification

Common sense tells us that a cloud can't cry and a river can't get angry. They can in the imagination of writers, though. When writers give human or living qualities to nonhuman or nonliving things, they are using **personification.** In "I Am of the Earth," the speaker uses personification when she speaks of the earth as a mother cradling a child.

Chochiti Pueblo jar (c. 1885).
Museum of Fine Arts, Houston, Texas.
USA/Gift of Miss Ima Hogg.

SKILLS FOCUS

Literary Skills
Understand personification.

I Am of the Earth

Anna Lee Walters

I am of the earth
She is my mother
She bore me with pride
She reared me with love
5   She cradled me each evening
She pushed the wind to make it sing
She built me a house of harmonious colors
She fed me the fruits of her fields
She rewarded me with memories of her smiles
10   She punished me with the passing of time
And at last, when I long to leave
She will embrace me for eternity

Early Song

Gogisgi/Carroll Arnett

As the sun rises
high enough to
warm the frost
off the pine needles,

5   I rise to make
four prayers of
thanksgiving for
this fine clear day,

for this good brown
10   earth, for all
brothers and sisters,
for the dark blood

that runs through me
in a great circle
15   back into this
good brown earth.

Meet the Writers

Anna Lee Walters

"Words Poured Out"
At the age of sixteen, **Anna Lee Walters** (1947–   ) left home to attend a boarding school in New Mexico. In the Southwest, Walters began to discover her roots in the Pawnee and Otoe cultures—and in the process unlocked her voice as a writer. She recalls:

66 Words poured out, page after page. I am still amazed by it, by the torrent of thoughts deposited there. … Today my occupation as a writer is related to what my grandfather and grandmother did when they repeated family history in the manner of their elders, leading the family all over this sacred land, this continent most recently called America in the last five hundred years, in their retelling of the Otoe journey from the dawn of time until they came to rest at Red Rock Creek a little over a century ago. 99

Gogisgi/Carroll Arnett

"What It Feels Like to Be Alive"
Gogisgi/Carroll Arnett (1927–   ), an American of Cherokee descent, was born in Oklahoma City. He has published more than three hundred poems and stories in magazines, sometimes under his Cherokee name, Gogisgi.

66 I write poems because it seems sensible to do so and wasteful not to. A poem has a use insofar as it shows what it feels like to be alive. 99

After You Read   Response and Analysis

First Thoughts

1. How does each speaker connect to the earth? Do you share any of these connections? Check your notes for the Quickwrite on page 555. 🖉

Thinking Critically

2. **Tone** refers to the way a writer feels about a subject. Tone is communicated by word choice, including figures of speech. What words tell you how each of these speakers feels about the earth?

3. What words in the poem tell you that Walters **personifies** the earth as her mother? What message or feeling about our world does this comparison convey?

4. What does Arnett mean by the "great circle" (line 14)? How does Walters get at the same idea?

Extending Interpretations

5. Are people always grateful children of the earth? How do some people show that their feelings about the earth are very different from the feelings of these two poets?

WRITING

Responding to a Quotation

The following quotations use features of the earth to teach lessons. Choose one that you like, and write a paragraph or a brief essay about what the words mean to you. Include any of your own experiences to illustrate the lesson.

"There is no hill that never ends." —Masai proverb

"Do you have the patience to wait till your mud settles and the water is clear?" —Tao-te Ching

Paraphrasing

Write a paraphrase of one of the poems you have just read. (When you **paraphrase** something, you put it in your own words, making sure to keep the writer's meaning.) Paraphrasing can help you understand and recall a text. Follow these rules: (1) Read the poem line by line. (2) Rewrite each line or sentence in clear and simple prose. (3) Restate each figure of speech in your own words   that is, explain the comparison, and describe its emotional effect on you.

Literary Skills
Analyze personification.

Writing Skills
Respond to a quotation; paraphrase a poem.

Madam and the Rent Man

Make the Connection
Quickwrite

"Grin and bear it."
"Stand up for yourself."

What does "grin and bear it" mean? Have you ever been in a situation where you had to grin and bear it? What does "stand up for yourself" mean? When do people have to stand up for themselves?

Write down your thoughts in response to the following questions:

• Which is harder—to grin and bear it or to stand up for yourself?

• Can you stand up for yourself and still be polite? and still be popular?

• Will people respect you if you always deal with situations you don't like by grinning and bearing it?

Literary Focus
Tone

Has anyone ever said to you, "Don't use that tone of voice with me"? Your tone can change the meaning of what you say. Tone can turn a statement like "You're a big help" into a genuine compliment or a cruel, sarcastic remark.

Poems and stories have tones too. As you read "Madam and the Rent Man," listen for the **tone,** or the writer's attitude, toward his no-nonsense speaker.

> ### Background
> #### Literature and Place
>
> This poem is set in Harlem, a section of New York City where many people live in rented apartments. The speaker of the poem is a woman who has reason to be angry with her landlord.

INTERNET
More About Hughes
Keyword: LE5 7–5

Literary Skills
Understand tone.

The poet Langston Hughes in Harlem.

Hunter Museum of American Art, Chattanooga, Tennessee. Museum purchase with funds provided by the Benwood Foundation and the 1982 Collectors' Group. HMA 1982.10. © 2005 Gwendolyn Knight Lawrence/Artists Rights Society (ARS), New York.

The Apartment (1943) by Jacob Lawrence. Gouache on paper (21¼" × 29¼").

Madam and the Rent Man

Langston Hughes

The rent man knocked.
He said, Howdy-do?
I said, What
Can I do for you?
5   He said, You know
Your rent is due.

I said, Listen,
Before I'd pay
I'd go to Hades°
10 And rot away!

The sink is broke,
The water don't run,
And you ain't done a thing
You promised to've done.

15 Back window's cracked,
Kitchen floor squeaks,
There's rats in the cellar,
And the attic leaks.

He said, Madam,
20 It's not up to me.
I'm just the agent,
Don't you see?

I said, Naturally,
You pass the buck.
25 If it's money you want
You're out of luck.

He said, Madam,
I ain't pleased!
I said, Neither am I.

30 So we agrees!

---

9. Hades (hā′dēz′): in Greek mythology, the underworld, or world of the dead.

First Thoughts

1. Which of the following would you say to Madam, and why?
   - "Wait a minute, Madam—you might be evicted."
   - "Why are you picking on the agent? It's not his fault."
   - "You tell him, Madam!"

Thinking Critically

2. Who is the **speaker** in this poem?

3. What is her argument with the rent man?

4. What does "pass the buck" mean? How has the rent man passed the buck?

5. Do you think this poem has a **message**? Explain.

6. What **tones** do you hear expressed in this poem? Think of both the speaker and the rent man.

Extending Interpretations

7. The woman in the poem speaks plainly and bluntly. Do you think she is right to speak this way? Explain. Compare her attitude with those in your Quickwrite notes.

INTERNET

Projects and Activities

Keyword: LE5 7-5

WRITING

Writing Dialogue

Write a dialogue between two people who disagree about something—perhaps money, noise, or food. The dialogue can be funny or serious. Use the vocabulary and speech patterns of everyday conversation to make your characters sound real.

SPEAKING AND LISTENING

Reading Dialogue

Prepare a read-aloud of "Madam and the Rent Man" in which you and a partner (as Madam and the rent man) read the dialogue. Practice changing the **tone** of your voice as the argument intensifies. Perform your read-aloud for the class. Afterward, ask your listeners to analyze your interpretation of the poem. Did they notice anything new about the poem as they heard it read aloud?

SKILLS FOCUS

Literary Skills
Analyze tone.

Writing Skills
Write dialogue.

Speaking and Listening Skills
Read a poem aloud.

Harlem Night Song *and* Winter Moon

Make the Connection
Quickwrite ✏️

How does the night make you feel? Do you find it mysterious? Is it a time for dreaming? Or does the night make you fearful? Do you worry that dangerous creatures might be lurking in the dark? Take a moment, and jot down the first five words that come into your mind when you think of the night.

Literary Focus
Imagery

Imagery is language that appeals to the senses. When you read "The Highwayman" on page 247, for example, you might have *pictured* the moonlit highway. You might have *heard* the horse galloping down that moonlit highway. You might have *felt* the wind blowing through the trees. You might even have *smelled* the moldy hay in the stable. Poets hope their imagery will unlock storehouses of memory and stir our imaginations. They hope their images will make us say, "Oh yes, I see what you mean."

Look for sensory images in "Harlem Night Song" and "Winter Moon." Which of your senses—sight, hearing, touch, taste, smell—do the images appeal to?

New building going up. Madison Avenue and 113th Street, New York City (1947).

INTERNET
More About Hughes
Keyword: LE5 7-5

Literary Skills
Understand imagery.

Harlem Night Song

Langston Hughes

Come,
Let us roam° the night together
Singing.

I love you.

5   Across
The Harlem roof-tops
Moon is shining.
Night sky is blue.
Stars are great drops
10   Of golden dew.

Down the street
A band is playing.

I love you.

Come,
15   Let us roam the night together
Singing.

Winter Moon

Langston Hughes

How thin and sharp is the moon tonight!
How thin and sharp and ghostly white
Is the slim curved crook of the moon tonight!

---

2. roam (rōm) *v.:* wander.

Rooftops, Midtown Manhattan (1944) by Brett Weston.

Meet the Writer

Langston Hughes

"Just Singing"

Langston Hughes (1902–1967) was one of the first African American writers to win worldwide favor. Still, he never lost his popularity with the people he wrote about. Hughes once said:

> 66 I knew only the people I had grown up with, and they weren't people whose shoes were always shined, who had been to Harvard, or who had heard of Bach. 99

Langston Hughes was born in Joplin, Missouri, and worked at many different jobs in various cities while writing poetry in his spare time. For two years he worked as a busboy at a hotel in Washington, D.C. During this time he wrote many poems, among them blues poems, which he would make up in his head and sing on his way to work.

> 66 One evening, I was crossing Rock Creek Bridge, singing a blues I was trying to get right before I put it down on paper. A man passing on the opposite side of the bridge stopped and looked at me, then turned around and cut across the roadway.

> He said 'Son, what's the matter? Are you ill?'
> 'No,' I said. 'Just singing.'
> 'I thought you were groaning,' he commented. 'Sorry!' And he went on his way.
> So after that I never sang my verses aloud in the street anymore. 99

Hughes became a major literary figure in what is now known as the Harlem Renaissance of the 1920s. His poems often echo the rhythms of blues and jazz.

For Independent Reading

You can find some of Hughes's best poems in a collection called *The Dream Keeper and Other Poems.*

Response and Analysis

First Thoughts

1. Which **image** in Hughes's poems stands out most clearly in your mind? Why?

Thinking Critically

2. Poems, like songs, often repeat lines, stanzas, or words. What sentences are repeated in "Harlem Night Song"? Describe the **tone** you hear in these lines.

3. Explain the **sensory images** in "Harlem Night Song."

4. What do the images in "Harlem Night Song" reveal about the speaker?

5. Draw a picture of the moon the speaker sees in "Winter Moon." Which words in particular help you visualize the moon?

WRITING

Writing a Poem

Write a poem about the night. Your poem can be as short as "Winter Moon" or as long as you like. Be sure to use **imagery** in your poem. See how many of the five senses you can appeal to. You may want to use some of the words you jotted down in your Quickwrite response.

SKILLS FOCUS

Literary Skills
Analyze imagery.

Writing Skills
Write a poem using imagery.

Before You Read The Poem

I Ask My Mother to Sing

Make the Connection
Quickwrite ✏️

Do you have any memories that are both happy and sad at the same time? Do you know some older people who tell stories that make them smile and weep? Jot down the bittersweet memories or stories that come to mind.

Literary Focus
Lyric Poem

There are two basic types of poems: A **narrative poem** tells a story, and a **lyric poem** expresses an emotion. The word *lyric* comes from the Greek language. In ancient Greece lyric poems were sung to the music of a stringed instrument called a lyre. Today we call the words to all kinds of songs lyrics.

Most of the poems in this collection are lyric poems. As you read these poems, you'll discover that lyric poems come in many shapes and sizes and express a wide range of feelings.

Sonnet

Some lyric forms are simple, but many, like the sonnet, are complex. The challenge to the lyric poet using a complex form is to express his or her thoughts and feelings within the restrictions of the form—somewhat like playing a game with strict rules.

Li-Young Lee's "I Ask My Mother to Sing" is a sonnet. A **sonnet** is a lyric poem of fourteen lines. There are several different types of sonnets. In the one this poet follows, the lines are divided into three quatrains (a quatrain is four lines of verse). Each quatrain focuses on one aspect of a subject. The sonnet ends with a couplet (two lines that usually rhyme). As you will see, Li-Young Lee varies this structure a bit.

SKILLS FOCUS

Literary Skills
Understand lyric poems; understand sonnets.

Background
Literature and Social Studies

Li-Young Lee's mother was a member of the Chinese royal family. His family fled China when the Communists took control of the country. The Summer Palace is where the royal family would go to escape the heat. The palace is located in the hills outside the capital city of Peking (now called Beijing) and consists of many beautiful buildings situated around Kuen Ming Lake. One of these buildings is a large teahouse made of stone in the shape of a boat. (see photograph on next page). When an emperor ruled China, the palace was visited only by the royal family and their attendants. Today it is a museum, open to tourists from around the world.

I Ask My Mother to Sing

Li-Young Lee

She begins, and my grandmother joins her.
Mother and daughter sing like young girls.
If my father were alive, he would play
his accordion and sway like a boat.

5   I've never been in Peking, or the Summer Palace,
nor stood on the great Stone Boat to watch
the rain begin on Kuen Ming Lake, the picnickers
running away in the grass.

But I love to hear it sung;
10   how the waterlilies fill with rain until
they overturn, spilling water into water,
then rock back, and fill with more.

Both women have begun to cry.
But neither stops her song.

Meet the Writer

Li-Young Lee

"Beautiful Stories"

Li-Young Lee (1957–   ) once made the following comment:

> 66 I think immigrants have beautiful stories to tell. But the problem is to make art out of it. 99

Lee succeeded in using art to tell his family's story in the award-winning memoir *The Winged Seed: A Remembrance.* An important part of the narrative is based in Jakarta, Indonesia, Lee's birthplace. His family had moved to Indonesia from China, where Lee's father had been the Communist leader Mao Tse-tung's physician. The family was forced to flee Indonesia in 1959, after anti-Chinese sentiment resulted in the jailing of Lee's father. After spending time in Hong Kong and Japan, the family settled in America in 1964.

When asked how he became a poet, Lee recalls the following:

> 66 That was when I first started to learn the English language. . . . Words like *yarn* or *bird* or *tree* felt . . . saturated with meaning. I think that's when I really was taken with the English language. I started writing little things to my mother. . . . My brother and I caught a fish once . . . and I wrote a poem. 'Here is a fish. Make a nice dish.' . . . I safety-pinned it through the gill of the fish and gave it to our mother. It seemed that the word *fish* and the thing we gave her were one and the same. 99

First Thoughts

1. Why do you think the mother and grandmother cry when they sing this song?

Thinking Critically

2. Take a look at how the poet fits his thoughts into the structure of a **sonnet.** What is the topic of each of the first three quatrains? How do the last two lines sum up the point of the poem?

3. It might seem at first that the speaker changes the subject in the second stanza. What **inference** do you have to make in order to understand how the second stanza connects to the first?

4. A **lyric poem** expresses the speaker's thoughts and feelings. How does the speaker react to the song his mother and grandmother sing?

5. What **images** do you see as the two women sing? Make a list of at least five images from the poem, and explain which senses the images appeal to.

6. The last two lines of the poem say: "Both women have begun to cry. / But neither stops her song." Compare this experience of the mother and grandmother with the story or experience you described in your Quickwrite notes.

WRITING

Describing a Song

Write a poem or a descriptive paragraph about a song that makes you especially happy or sad. Be sure to tell who sings the song, what it says, and what it makes you think about. Try to create some images to describe your responses to the song.

SKILLS FOCUS

Literary Skills
Analyze a lyric poem; analyze a sonnet.

Writing Skills
Write a poem or description.

Ode to Family Photographs

Make the Connection
Quickwrite

What do you think is worth celebrating in your life? It might be a favorite person, place, or thing. It might even be an idea, like peace or patriotism. List five subjects that you would like to praise.

Literary Focus
Ode

There are many ways to commemorate important people, things, or events. You might have a parade in their honor, as we sometimes do for baseball teams or astronauts. You might give them an award, as we do for great writing or acting. What people in ancient Greece often did was write an ode. An **ode** is a poem that pays tribute to someone or something of great importance to the poet.

The first odes, written in honor of famous people, were long, complex, and elegant. Over the centuries, many odes have been written in a formal style to praise lofty subjects, such as beauty, joy, and freedom.

Today's odes tend to be more informal. Some are even humorous. Many have been written about everyday objects, such as tomatoes, frogs, and socks. Gary Soto's ode celebrates something most people have in their homes—family photos.

SKILLS FOCUS

Literary Skills
Understand odes.

Ode to Family Photographs

Gary Soto

This is the pond, and these are my feet.
This is the rooster, and this is more of my feet.

Mamá was never good at pictures.

This is a statue of a famous general who lost an arm,
5   And this is me with my head cut off.

This is a trash can chained to a gate,
This is my father with his eyes half-closed.

This is a photograph of my sister
And a giraffe looking over her shoulder.

10   This is our car's front bumper.
This is a bird with a pretzel in its beak.
This is my brother Pedro standing on one leg on a rock,
With a smear of chocolate on his face.

Mamá sneezed when she looked
15   *Behind the camera: the snapshots are blurry,*
The angles dizzy as a spin on a merry-go-round.

But we had fun when Mamá picked up the camera.
How can I tell?
Each of us laughing hard.
20   Can you see? I have candy in my mouth.

Meet the Writer

Gary Soto

"I Began to Feel Like I Was Doing Something Valuable"

Gary Soto (1952–   ) first discovered poetry in college, where he had originally planned to major in geography:

> ❝ I know the day the change began, because it was when I discovered in the library a collection of poems . . . called *The New American Poetry*. . . . I discovered this poetry and thought, This is terrific: I'd like to do something like this. So I proceeded to write my own poetry, first alone, and then moving on to take classes. ❞

Soto obviously made the right decision when he chose to be a writer—his award-winning fiction and poetry are loved by people of all ages.

Although Soto's work contains elements from his Mexican American heritage, as well as aspects of his experiences as a migrant laborer, he also manages to address universal themes. When Soto started receiving fan mail from Mexican American teenagers in response to the work he had published for adults, he was inspired to write works specifically for young readers, including the award-winning collection *Baseball in April and Other Stories*. Soto shared these thoughts about his decision to write for young readers:

> ❝ I began to feel like I was doing something valuable. I thought I might be able to make readers and writers out of this group of kids. ❞

For Independent Reading

In *Neighborhood Odes*, which "Ode to Family Photographs" is taken from, Gary Soto presents poems that capture the pleasures of childhood.

First Thoughts

1. Did you imagine yourself or anyone you know in Soto's pictures? (Maybe you saw yourself as the photographer.) Which **images** in this ode made you smile?

Thinking Critically

2. What details in the poem tell you that the poet's *mamá* was not a very good photographer?

3. **Odes** are written in praise of something. What do you think this poet is praising? (It's not just family photographs!)

WRITING

Celebrating in an Ode

Write an **ode** celebrating something on the list you wrote for the Quickwrite on page 572. Try to convey your feelings for all aspects of your subject. For example, if you write "An Ode to My Baseball Bat," you might praise its weight, balance, and power; the comfortable grip on the rubber; the way it swings through the air; the satisfying *whonk* when it hits the ball; how you got it; how long you have had it; and how it helps you win games. When you write your ode, you can talk directly to the reader, as Gary Soto does, or you can talk to the object you are celebrating ("Bat, you are . . .").

SKILLS FOCUS

Literary Skills
Analyze an ode.

Writing Skills
Write an ode.

Elements of Literature
The Sounds of Poetry
by John Malcolm Brinnin

Poets use many techniques to make music out of words. The most common **sound effects** used in poetry are also used in the songs you love to listen to.

Rhythm: The Rise and Fall of Our Voices

Rhythm refers to the rise and fall of our voices as we use language. As in music, a poem's rhythm can be fast or slow, light or solemn. A poem might also sound just like everyday speech.

Poetry that is written in **meter** has a regular pattern of stressed and un-stressed syllables. Poetry that is written in **free verse** does not have a regular pattern of stressed and unstressed syllables. Free verse sounds like ordinary speech.

When poets write in meter, they count out the number of stressed syllables (or strong beats) and unstressed syllables (weaker beats) in each line. Then they repeat the pattern throughout the poem. To avoid a singsong effect, poets usually vary the basic pattern from time to time. Try reading aloud the following lines from a famous poem called *The Rime of the Ancient Mariner* by Samuel Taylor Coleridge. Can you hear that each line has four stressed syllables alternating with four unstressed syllables?

Day after day, day after day,
We stuck, nor breath nor motion;
As idle as a painted ship
Upon a painted ocean.

A poem's rhythm can be shown by using accent marks: (′) for stressed syllables and (˘) for unstressed syllables. This marking is called **scanning.**

˘ ′ ˘ ′ ˘ ′ ˘ ′
Day after day, day after day

Rhyme: Chiming Sounds

Rhyme is the repetition of the sound of a stressed syllable and any unstressed syllables that follow: *sport* and *court*; *smother* and *another*; *sputtering* and *muttering*. The echoing effect of rhyme gives us pleasure. It makes us look forward to hearing certain chiming sounds throughout the poem. In the verse from *The Rime of the Ancient Mariner,* the rhyming words are *motion* and *ocean.*

Rhymes like *motion/ocean* in Coleridge's verse are called **end rhymes** because they occur at the ends of lines. **Internal rhymes** occur within lines, as in this line from the same poem:

The fair breeze blew, the white foam flew . . .

Poets will often use a pattern of rhymes, called a **rhyme scheme.** To describe a rhyme scheme, assign a new letter of the alphabet to each new end rhyme. The rhyme scheme of Coleridge's verse is *abcb.*

Alliteration: Repeating Consonants

Another way poets create sound effects is through the use of alliteration (ə·lit′ər·ā′shən). **Alliteration** is the repetition of consonant sounds in words that are close together. Read this tongue twister of a poem aloud to hear all the repeated *t* sounds:

A Tutor

A tutor who tooted the flute
Tried to tutor two tooters to toot.
    Said the two to the tutor,
    "Is it harder to toot, or
To tutor two tooters to toot?"
              —Carolyn Wells

"A Tutor" is a **limerick,** a humorous five-line poem. Limericks have a definite rhythm and rhyme scheme. Try scanning the poem and describing the rhyme scheme now that you've tooted through it.

Onomatopoeia: Sound Echoes Sense

Onomatopoeia is a long word that is pronounced like this: än′ō·mat′ō·pē′ə. It is the use of words with sounds that echo their sense. *Crash, bang, boom, hiss,* and *toot* are all examples of onomatopoeia.

To see how sounds alone can suggest sense, read aloud this famous nonsense poem. You will not find all the words in a dictionary, but the sounds will help you guess what is going on. (What *is* going on?)

Jabberwocky

'Twas brillig, and the slithy toves
    Did gyre and gimble in the wabe;
All mimsy were the borogoves,
    And the mome raths outgrabe.
"Beware the Jabberwock, my son!
    The jaws that bite, the claws that catch!
Beware the Jubjub bird, and shun
    The frumious Bandersnatch!"
He took his vorpal sword in hand:
    Long time the manxome foe he sought—
So rested he by the Tumtum tree,
    And stood awhile in thought.
And, as in uffish thought he stood,
    The Jabberwock, with eyes of flame,
Came whiffling through the tulgey wood,
    And burbled as it came!
One, two! One, two! And through and through
    The vorpal blade went snicker-snack!
He left it dead, and with its head
    He went galumphing back.
"And hast thou slain the Jabberwock?
    Come to my arms, my beamish boy!
O frabjous day! Callooh! Callay!"
    He chortled in his joy.
'Twas brillig, and the slithy toves
    Did gyre and gimble in the wabe;
All mimsy were the borogoves,
    And the mome raths outgrabe.
              —Lewis Carroll

Father William *and* Sarah Cynthia Sylvia Stout Would Not Take the Garbage Out

Make the Connection
Quickwrite ✏️

What makes you laugh? Do you like wild and crazy physical actions? Do you prefer clever wordplay? Jot down some of the things in TV shows and songs that you find funny.

Literary Focus
Humorous Poems

Many poems are written to make you laugh—or at least smile. That doesn't mean they don't have a point to make. They just make their point with humor. One element that many humorous poems share is **exaggeration**—that is, describing something as bigger or smaller, or worse or better than it really is. As you read the two humorous poems that follow, notice what they exaggerate. Then, ask yourself: Were the poems written to make a serious point, or were they written just for fun?

Rhythm

In English and other languages, **rhythm** is a musical quality produced by the repetition of stressed and unstressed syllables or by the repetition of words and phrases or even whole lines or sentences. When the stressed and unstressed syllables are arranged in a regular pattern, we call the pattern **meter.**

SKILLS FOCUS

Literary Skills
Understand humorous poems and exaggeration; understand rhythm and meter.

You can discover the meter of a line by reading it aloud and exaggerating the stressed syllables. For example, in the line *The girl is walking to the store*, you can sound out the meter like this: The GIRL is WALKing TO the STORE. You can also show the poem's meter by using accent marks—(´) over stressed syllables and (˘) over unstressed syllables. This marking is called **scanning.** It looks like this:

˘   ´   ˘   ´   ˘   ´   ˘   ´
The girl is walking to the store.

There are many different kinds of meter. You can hear another pattern if you read this line aloud: *In the morning we go for a ride*. It sounds like this: In the MORning we GO for a RIDE. Here's how it looks with scanning:

˘ ˘   ´   ˘   ˘   ´   ˘ ˘   ´
In the morning we go for a ride.

As you can hear in these examples, a regular beat is often found in ordinary speech as well as in poetry. In a poem written in meter, the meter supplies the underlying beat. But just as you wouldn't want to exaggerate the stressed syllables when you talk to your friends, you also don't want to overemphasize them when you read a poem.

Read "Father William" aloud, and listen for its beat.

Father William

Lewis Carroll

"You are old, Father William," the young man said,
    "And your hair has become very white;
And yet you incessantly° stand on your head—
    Do you think, at your age, it is right?"

5   "In my youth," Father William replied to his son,
    "I feared it might injure the brain;
But now that I'm perfectly sure I have none,
    Why, I do it again and again."

"You are old," said the youth, "as I mentioned before,
10   And have grown most uncommonly fat;
Yet you turned a back somersault in at the door—
    Pray, what is the reason of that?"

"In my youth," said the sage, as he shook his gray locks,
    "I kept all my limbs very supple°
15   By the use of this ointment—one shilling the box—
    Allow me to sell you a couple."

---

3. incessantly (in·ses′ənt·lē) *adv.:* without ceasing; continually.
14. supple (sup′əl) *adj.:* easily bent; flexible.

Illustrations on pages 579–580 by John Tenniel (1820–1914), the original illustrator of Carroll's *Alice's Adventures in Wonderland.*

"You are old," said the youth, "and your jaws are too weak
    For anything tougher than suet°;
Yet you finished the goose, with the bones and the beak;
20   Pray, how did you manage to do it?"

"In my youth," said his father, "I took to the law,
    And argued each case with my wife;
And the muscular strength which it gave to my jaw,
    Has lasted the rest of my life."

25 "You are old," said the youth; "one would hardly suppose
    That your eye was as steady as ever;
Yet you balanced an eel on the end of your nose—
    What made you so awfully clever?"

"I've answered three questions, and that is enough,"
30   Said his father; "don't give yourself airs!
Do you think I can listen all day to such stuff?
        Be off, or I'll kick you downstairs!"

---

18. **suet** (so͞o′it) *n.:* a kind of fat.

Meet the Writer

Lewis Carroll

"He Was One of Us"

Lewis Carroll (1832–1898) had two separate careers. Under the pseudonym Lewis Carroll, he was the author of *Alice's Adventures in Wonderland* and its sequel, *Through the Looking Glass.* Under his real name, he was Rev. Charles Lutwidge Dodgson, a teacher of mathematics and a clergyman.

Carroll had seven sisters and three brothers. As a child, he was always in charge of family entertainment, inventing and performing magic tricks, puppet plays, and clever games.

Carroll was educated at home until he was twelve, then sent to boarding school, which he disliked intensely. The other boys teased him because he preferred reading to sports. He also stammered when he was nervous, a condition that bothered him all of his life.

As a student at Oxford University, Carroll received a grant that provided him with an income for the rest of his life. Two conditions of the grant were that he remain unmarried and that he take holy orders, which would qualify him to become a priest in the Church of England. Although his stammer made preaching difficult, he managed to deliver a sermon occasionally. Interestingly, the stutter disappeared when he was around children, who loved to hear the stories he told.

Carroll spent many days in the company of children, writing nonsense verse and creating puzzles. As one of his young friends said:

> ❝ He was one of us, and never a grown-up pretending to be a child in order to preach at us.... ❞

Once Carroll went on a picnic with three young girls, one of whom was named Alice. He told them a story he made up about a girl named Alice, who went down a rabbit hole into a fabulous wonderland. That was the beginning of *Alice's Adventures in Wonderland,* from which the poems "Jabberwocky" (page 577) and "Father William" (page 579) are taken.

Sarah Cynthia Sylvia Stout Would Not Take the Garbage Out

Shel Silverstein

Sarah Cynthia Sylvia Stout
Would not take the garbage out!
She'd scour the pots and scrape the pans,
Candy the yams and spice the hams,
5 And though her daddy would scream and shout,
She simply would not take the garbage out.
And so it piled up to the ceilings:
Coffee grounds, potato peelings,
Brown bananas, rotten peas,
10 Chunks of sour cottage cheese.
It filled the can, it covered the floor,
It cracked the window and blocked the door
With bacon rinds and chicken bones,
Drippy ends of ice cream cones,
15 Prune pits, peach pits, orange peel,
Gloppy glumps of cold oatmeal,
Pizza crusts and withered greens,
Soggy beans and tangerines,
Crusts of black burned buttered toast,
20 Gristly bits of beefy roasts . . .
The garbage rolled on down the hall,
It raised the roof, it broke the wall . . .
Greasy napkins, cookie crumbs,
Globs of gooey bubble gum,

25 Cellophane from green baloney,
   Rubbery blubbery macaroni,
   Peanut butter, caked and dry,
   Curdled milk and crusts of pie,
   Moldy melons, dried-up mustard,
30 Eggshells mixed with lemon custard,
   Cold french fries and rancid meat,
   Yellow lumps of Cream of Wheat.
   At last the garbage reached so high
   That finally it touched the sky.
35 And all the neighbors moved away,
   And none of her friends would come to play.
   And finally Sarah Cynthia Stout said,
   "OK, I'll take the garbage out!"
   But then, of course, it was too late . . .
40 The garbage reached across the state,
   From New York to the Golden Gate.
   And there, in the garbage she did hate,
   Poor Sarah met an awful fate,
   That I cannot right now relate
45 Because the hour is much too late.
   But children, remember Sarah Stout
   And always take the garbage out!

Meet the Writer

Shel Silverstein

"I Couldn't Dance. . . . So I Started to Draw and Write."

Shel Silverstein (1932–1999) began drawing and writing when he was a young boy growing up in Chicago. He wrote:

> 66 When I was a kid—12, 14 around there—I would much rather have been a good baseball player or a hit with the girls. But I couldn't play ball. I couldn't dance. Luckily, the girls didn't want me; not much I could do about that. So I started to draw and write. I was also lucky I didn't have anyone to copy, be impressed by. I . . . developed my own style. 99

When Silverstein grew up, he became a writer of children's books, a poet, a cartoonist, and a songwriter. He created and illustrated two of the world's most popular collections of poems for children: *Where the Sidewalk Ends* (1974), which includes "Sarah Cynthia Sylvia Stout," and *A Light in the Attic* (1981). Silverstein said:

> 66 I would hope that people, no matter what age, would find something to identify with in my books, pick one up and experience a personal sense of discovery. 99

First Thoughts

1. What did you find funny in these poems? Did either of the poems include any of the sources of humor that you listed in your Quickwrite notes? Explain. 🖉

Thinking Critically

2. One element of humor is **exaggeration**—describing something as bigger, smaller, better, or worse than it is. List three examples of exaggeration in "Sarah Cynthia Sylvia Stout." Explain which is your favorite example.

3. Read "Father William" aloud, and identify its **meter.** To show your answer, write out a line of the poem, and use the **scanning** method described on page 578. Use the same method to show the meter in line 3 of "Sarah Cynthia Sylvia Stout."

4. Part of the humor of these poems comes from their clever **rhymes.** Silverstein has even found a rhyme for *macaroni.* (Can you think of any other words that rhyme with *macaroni*?) Take one group of rhyming words from one of the poems, and see how far you can extend the list with other rhyming words.

5. Silverstein's poem is full of **alliteration**—the repetition of similar consonant sounds in nearby words. Sarah's entire name is an example of alliteration. Find three other examples of alliteration in Silverstein's poem. Which sounds are repeated in each of your examples?

Extending Interpretations

6. What do you think is the main point of each poem? Do you think these poets are serious about their points, or are they just having fun?

7. In "Sarah Cynthia Sylvia Stout," the poet says, "Poor Sarah met an awful fate, / That I cannot right now relate." What do you think that fate might be?

SPEAKING AND LISTENING
Reading Aloud

Work with a partner to prepare an oral reading of one of these poems. First, decide who should read which lines. Then, practice reading aloud until you are satisfied you have given the poem the expression you want. Decide where you will read slowly, where you will speed up, and where you will change your tone of voice.

SKILLS FOCUS

Literary Skills
Analyze humorous poems and exaggeration; analyze rhythm and meter.

Speaking and Listening Skills
Read a poem aloud.

The Runaway

Make the Connection

Quickwrite ✏️

In "The Runaway," Robert Frost introduces us to a colt who's never seen snow before. Even if the only horses you've met are in the movies, you can probably identify with the colt in this poem, because he is behaving the way most of us act when we encounter something new and strange.

Take a few notes on what you think the title of the poem refers to.

Literary Focus

Rhyme and Rhyme Scheme: Sound Decisions

Which words rhyme with

- *star*
- *peaches*
- *mice*
- *stopping*

Maybe your answer came automatically. There's something about **rhyme** that just comes naturally to people.

In a poem, rhymes at the ends of lines are called **end rhymes.** End rhymes determine a poem's **rhyme scheme,** or pattern of rhymes. To find out a poem's rhyme scheme, you can assign a different letter of the alphabet to each new end rhyme. The rhyme scheme of "The Runaway" begins with *abacbc.*

SKILLS FOCUS

Literary Skills
Understand rhyme and rhyme scheme.

Background
Literature and Science

The subject of "The Runaway" is a Morgan colt. Morgans are a breed of swift, strong horses named for Justin Morgan (1747–1798), a Vermont schoolteacher who owned the stallion that founded the line. Morgans are small, sturdy horses that excel at weight-pulling contests. Today they are used mostly for riding and in herding cattle.

The Runaway

Robert Frost

Once when the snow of the year was beginning to fall,
We stopped by a mountain pasture to say, "Whose colt?"
A little Morgan had one forefoot on the wall,
The other curled at his breast. He dipped his head
5   And snorted at us. And then he had to bolt.
We heard the miniature thunder where he fled,
And we saw him, or thought we saw him, dim and gray,
Like a shadow against the curtain of falling flakes.
"I think the little fellow's afraid of the snow.
10   He isn't winter-broken. It isn't play
With the little fellow at all. He's running away.
I doubt if even his mother could tell him, 'Sakes,
It's only weather.' He'd think she didn't know!
Where is his mother? He can't be out alone."
15   And now he comes again with clatter of stone,
And mounts the wall again with whited eyes
And all his tail that isn't hair up straight.
He shudders his coat as if to throw off flies.
"Whoever it is that leaves him out so late,
20   When other creatures have gone to stall and bin,
Ought to be told to come and take him in."

First Thoughts

1. How would you complete each of these sentences?

- As he faced his first snowfall alone, the colt felt . . .
- As I read about the colt, I felt . . .

Thinking Critically

2. To break a colt is to get a young horse used to being ridden. What do you think the expression "winter-broken" (in line 10) means?

3. How do you think the speaker feels about the person who has left the colt alone in the pasture?

4. Why do you think Frost called the poem "The Runaway"? (What is the colt running away from? What did you guess the **title** meant?)

5. Read the poem aloud to hear its conversational rhythms and rhyming sounds. Make a list of its **rhyming** words. Then, work out its **rhyme scheme.**

6. Some people think that the colt **symbolizes** a lost child or someone who is too young or too innocent to understand what he or she is experiencing. Do you agree with this interpretation, or do you have another one? Support your interpretation with details from the poem.

Extending Interpretations

7. The term *runaway* can refer to people too. What other runaways are found in our world? What lines from the poem could apply to them?

INTERNET

Projects and
Activities

Keyword: LE5 7-5

SPEAKING AND LISTENING
Choral Reading

With several classmates, prepare a group reading of "The Runaway." Decide which lines you will assign to a chorus and which lines you'll assign to a single voice. Practice reading aloud until the conversational speech rhythms come through.

WRITING
Writing a Poem

In five lines or more, tell how you would feel if you were this little horse. How would you feel about the weather, about your mother, and about the people watching you?

SKILLS FOCUS

Literary Skills
Analyze rhyme and rhyme scheme.

Speaking and Listening Skills
Prepare a choral reading.

Writing Skills
Write a poem.

The Pasture *and* A Minor Bird

Make the Connection
Quickwrite ✏️

Robert Frost's poetry often focuses on connections between human life and the world of nature. Even if you live in a city, nature is all around you, from the sun and moon in the sky to the grass at your feet to the birds chirping in your ear. Make a list of the aspects of nature you notice as you move through your day.

Literary Focus
Stanza

In a poem a group of lines that form a unit is called a **stanza.** Like a paragraph in prose, a stanza often expresses a unit of thought. Stanzas can be of any length; they can even be a single line. In the poems that follow, "The Pasture" has two stanzas of four lines each, and "A Minor Bird" has four stanzas of two lines each.

Couplet

Each two-line stanza in "A Minor Bird" is a couplet. A **couplet** is two consecutive lines of poetry that rhyme and express a complete thought.

Reading Skills
Reading a Poem 📖

Robert Frost writes in an easy, conversational tone, which is how *you* should sound when you read his poems aloud. Here is an important tip that will help you read poems—for both their meaning and their sound:

Pay attention to punctuation.

Most poems are written in sentences, but the sentences may not end at the ends of lines. Don't stop reading at the end of a line of poetry unless you see some punctuation there. Make a full stop for a period, but pause just briefly for a comma, colon, semicolon, or dash. If the poem has no punctuation at all (and some don't), you'll have to figure out where to pause based on the thought groups you find in the poem.

INTERNET
More About Frost
Keyword: LE5 7-5

Background
Literature and Music

In the title "A Minor Bird," Robert Frost plays with two meanings of the word *minor*. *Minor* can mean "less important or lesser in rank." (Think of minor leagues in baseball.) *Minor* also refers to a type of key in music. A musical key is a sequence of related tones that form a scale. Most Western music is written in major keys. To some people, songs written in major keys sound happy. Minor keys, to the Western ear, tend to sound sad or haunting.

SKILLS FOCUS

Literary Skills
Understand stanzas; understand couplets.

Reading Skills
Read a poem.

The Pasture

Robert Frost

I'm going out to clean the pasture spring;
I'll only stop to rake the leaves away
(And wait to watch the water clear, I may):
I shan't be gone long.—You come too.

I'm going out to fetch the little calf
That's standing by the mother. It's so young
It totters when she licks it with her tongue.
I shan't be gone long.—You come too.

A Minor Bird

Robert Frost

I have wished a bird would fly away,
And not sing by my house all day;

Have clapped my hands at him from the door
When it seemed as if I could bear no more.

The fault must partly have been in me.
The bird was not to blame for his key.

And of course there must be something wrong
In wanting to silence any song.

Meet the Writer

Robert Frost

"A Lump in the Throat"

While in high school in Lawrence, Massachusetts, **Robert Frost** (1874–1963) decided to become a poet. Not only did he succeed, but for a time he was America's most celebrated living poet.

He was the first poet ever to read a poem for a presidential inauguration, that of John F. Kennedy in 1961. On his seventy-fifth birthday, the U.S. Senate passed a resolution in his honor stating, "His poems have helped to guide American thought and humor and wisdom, setting forth to our minds a reliable representation of ourselves and of all men."

"Rob" Frost lived most of his life on farms in Vermont and New Hampshire. There he grew corn, taught, and raised a family. Frost filled his poems with images of the people of New England and their haybarns, farmhouses, pastures, apple orchards, and woods. His work speaks to people everywhere because it springs from intense feelings.

Frost says this about poetry:

> 66 A poem ... begins as a lump in the throat, a sense of wrong, a homesickness, a lovesickness. ... It finds the thought and the thought finds the words. 99

Frost felt that "it is most important of all to reach the heart of the reader."

For Independent Reading

If you enjoy poetry, read more of Frost's poems in *You Come Too: Favorite Poems for Young Readers.*

First Thoughts

1. Respond to the poems by finishing these sentences:
   - When I finished reading "The Pasture," I felt . . .
   - When I finished reading "A Minor Bird," I thought . . .

Thinking Critically

2. Frost asked that "The Pasture" be printed at the front of all collections of his poetry. Why do you think it would make a good starting point for a book of poems?

3. The speaker in "The Pasture" offers an invitation. As you read the poem, did you feel like accepting the invitation? Why or why not?

4. Who could the "you" be in "The Pasture"? Who might "I" be?

5. The **stanzas** in "A Minor Bird" are all **couplets.** Explain the main idea of each couplet.

6. Do you agree with the last two lines of "A Minor Bird"? Why or why not?

7. How would you express the **theme,** or message, of "A Minor Bird"? (You might find a hint in the two meanings of the word *minor*.)

WRITING

Imitating "The Pasture"

Write a one-stanza poem of your own that keeps the last sentence of "The Pasture." In your first three lines, tell about something you are about to do outdoors. Start your poem with the words "I'm going out to . . . ," and try to create one striking visual image. Your Quickwrite notes might give you some ideas.

SPEAKING AND LISTENING

Reading Aloud Alone

Choose one of these poems to read aloud. As you practice reading it, don't forget this tip for reading a poem: *Pay attention to the punctuation.* When you have practiced enough to read the poem smoothly, perform it for your class.

SKILLS FOCUS

Literary Skills
Analyze stanzas; analyze couplets.

Reading Skills
Read a poem.

Writing Skills
Imitate a poem.

Speaking and Listening Skills
Read a poem aloud.

Names of Horses

Make the Connection

Quickwrite ✏️

"Names of Horses" describes the life of a farm horse in the days before machinery took over the work. Think about an animal you once knew and loved, and jot down some of the memorable things that animal did in the course of a lifetime. The animal may be one you lived with or one you learned about through books or nature shows on television.

Literary Focus

Free Verse

"Names of Horses" is written in free verse. **Free verse** does not follow a regular rhyme scheme or meter, but it does make use of many other elements of poetry, including

- **imagery**—language that appeals to any of the five senses, most often sight, but also hearing, touch, taste, and smell

- **alliteration** (ə·lit′ər·ā′shən)—repetition of consonant sounds in words close to each other (*marvelous memories of mangoes and melons*)

- **onomatopoeia** (än′ō·mat′ō·pē′ə)— the use of words that sound like what they mean (the goose's *honk*)

- **rhythm**—a musical quality produced by repetition

Elegy

"Names of Horses" is an **elegy** (el′ə·jē), a poem that mourns the passing of something—a person, an animal, a way of life, a season of the year—that is important to the writer. There are many important elegies in literature. Walt Whitman wrote a heartfelt elegy mourning the death of Abraham Lincoln. Oliver Goldsmith wrote a comic elegy about a cat who was drowned in a goldfish bowl. The most famous elegy is probably Thomas Gray's "Elegy Written in a Country Churchyard." Gray mourns the anonymous people buried in a rural graveyard.

Once you've read "Names of Horses," you may agree with this reader's response:

> When someone asks me why I love poetry, I read "Names of Horses" to them, and they always say, "Oh, I didn't know poetry could be like that." And then they, too, say they love poetry.
>
> —Mary Shannon
> Kagel Canyon, California

SKILLS FOCUS

Literary Skills
Understand free verse; understand elegy.

Names of Horses

Donald Hall

All winter your brute shoulders strained against collars, padding
and steerhide over the ash hames,° to haul
sledges of cordwood for drying through spring and summer,
for the Glenwood stove next winter, and for the simmering range.

5 In April you pulled cartloads of manure to spread on the fields,
dark manure of Holsteins,° and knobs of your own clustered with oats.
All summer you mowed the grass in meadow and hayfield, the mowing machine
clacketing beside you, while the sun walked high in the morning;

and after noon's heat, you pulled a clawed rake through the same acres,
10 gathering stacks, and dragged the wagon from stack to stack,
and the built hayrack back, uphill to the chaffy° barn,
three loads of hay a day, hanging wide from the hayrack.

Sundays you trotted the two miles to church with the light load
of a leather quartertop buggy, and grazed in the sound of hymns.
15 Generation on generation, your neck rubbed the window sill
of the stall, smoothing the wood as the sea smooths glass.

---

2. **hames** (hāmz) *n.:* rigid pieces along a horse's collar, to which lines
   connecting the collar to a wagon are attached.
6. **Holsteins** (hōl′stēnz′) *n.:* members of a breed of large, black-and-white
   dairy cattle.
11. **chaffy** (chaf′ē) *adj.:* full of chaff (hay or straw).

When you were old and lame, when your shoulders hurt bending to graze,
one October the man who fed you and kept you, and harnessed you every morning,
led you through corn stubble to sandy ground above Eagle Pond,
20   and dug a hole beside you where you stood shuddering in your skin,

and lay the shotgun's muzzle in the boneless hollow behind your ear,
and fired the slug into your brain, and felled you into your grave,
shoveling sand to cover you, setting goldenrod upright above you,
where by next summer a dent in the ground made your monument.

25   For a hundred and fifty years, in the pasture of dead horses,
roots of pine trees pushed through the pale curves of your ribs,
yellow blossoms flourished above you in autumn, and in winter
frost heaved your bones in the ground—old toilers, soil makers:

O Roger, Mackerel, Riley, Ned, Nellie, Chester, Lady Ghost.

Meet the Writer

Donald Hall

"I Fell in Love with Poetry"

Donald Hall (1928–   ) started writing at a young age. When he was only sixteen years old, he was accepted to the Bread Loaf Writers' Conference, one of the oldest writers' conferences in the United States. Hall's first work was also published that same year. About his early fascination with poetry, Hall has said:

> 66 I fell in love with poetry. When I was twelve I started writing poetry; when I was fourteen I got serious. I began to work a couple of hours every day on my poems. And when I finished working on a poem, I would go back to the beginning and start writing it over again. . . . When I was fourteen I really wanted to do in my life what I in fact have . . . ended up doing, which is astounding. 99

Born in New Haven, Connecticut, Hall spent a childhood full of poetry. His mother read poems to him, and his grandfather, during Hall's summers at his New Hampshire farm, recited poems "all day long without repeating himself."

For many years, Hall was an instructor at the University of Michigan at Ann Arbor. In 1975, he moved to the family farm in New Hampshire, where he currently devotes his time to writing. From 1984 to 1989, Hall served as poet laureate of New Hampshire.

For Independent Reading

Hall has edited numerous anthologies, including *The Oxford Book of Children's Verse in America*, a collection that includes well-known poems as well as less-familiar verses.

Response and Analysis

First Thoughts

1. Respond to "Names of Horses" by finishing these sentences:

- This poem made me feel . . .
- The **image** I remember most vividly is . . .

Thinking Critically

2. This **free verse** poem is rich in **imagery.** Take your favorite **image,** and draw or describe what it helps you visualize.

3. Study lines 7 and 8. In these lines, find and explain one example of each of these devices: imagery, alliteration, and onomatopoeia.

4. Why do you think the speaker calls the horses "old toilers, soil makers" in line 28?

5. How do you think the speaker feels about the horses he names in line 29? Use examples from the poem to support your response.

6. How does the last line of the poem reflect the **title**?

Extending Interpretations

7. Re-read Mary Shannon's comment about this poem on page 593. Why do you think she reads someone "Names of Horses" when she wants to explain why she loves poetry? Explain the effect the poem had on you.

WRITING

Writing an Elegy

Review your Quickwrite notes, and then write an **elegy** for the animal you described. You may want to try writing in **free verse.** Be sure to use vivid **imagery** in describing the life of your animal. Try also to include some of the other poetic elements you learned about on page 593. (If you prefer, address your **elegy** to *many* cats, dogs, dinosaurs, or whatever type of animal you have chosen, and title your elegy "Names of . . .")

SKILLS FOCUS

Literary Skills
Analyze free verse; analyze an elegy.

Writing Skills
Write an elegy.

maggie and milly and molly and may

Make the Connection
Quickwrite ✏️

"Maggie and milly and molly and may" make some discoveries at the sea. What do you associate with the sea? Close your eyes and let sights, sounds, smells, and feelings fill your mind.

In any "ocean shape" that inspires you, such as a starfish, an octopus, or a series of waves, write down the sensory details you associate with the sea. Here's an example:

salty air

Literary Focus
Kinds of Rhymes

E. E. Cummings is famous for the ways he plays with sounds and punctuation. This poem is filled with rhyming sounds. Some of the rhymes are **exact** (*may/day, stone/alone, me/sea*), but some catch us by surprise because they are slightly off. These near rhymes are called **slant rhymes.** *Milly* and *molly*, for example, form a slant rhyme: Their sounds almost rhyme—but not exactly.

Background
Literature and Language

Editors are probably itching to capitalize the *m*'s in the title of this poem, but they'd better keep their pencils to themselves. E. E. Cummings did not use standard punctuation (or any punctuation, in many cases), and he stopped capitalizing early in his writing career. These quirks of **style** are trademarks of his poetry.

SKILLS FOCUS

Literary Skills
Understand exact and slant rhymes.

maggie and milly and molly and may

E. E. Cummings

maggie and milly and molly and may
went down to the beach(to play one day)

and maggie discovered a shell that sang
so sweetly she couldn't remember her troubles,and

5   milly befriended a stranded star
whose rays five languid° fingers were;

and molly was chased by a horrible thing
which raced sideways while blowing bubbles:and

may came home with a smooth round stone
10   as small as a world and as large as alone.

For whatever we lose(like a you or a me)
it's always ourselves we find in the sea

6. **languid** (laŋ′gwid) *adj.:* drooping; weak; slow.

First Thoughts

1. What do the last lines of the poem mean to you?

Thinking Critically

2. Cummings writes that "it's always ourselves we find in the sea." How does each girl find herself in the sea?

3. What **exact rhymes** do you hear in the poem? What **slant rhymes** do you hear? (What sounds did you expect to hear?)

4. Read the poem aloud. What **tone** do you hear as you read about maggie, milly, molly, and may? How do the sounds of the poem contribute to its tone?

Extending Interpretations

5. What do you think of E. E. Cummings's use of lowercase letters and his unusual punctuation? Does this style affect your understanding of the poem?

WRITING

Writing a Poem

Create your own poem about the ocean or another place you've visited. (You might get ideas about the ocean from the notes you made for the Quickwrite on page 598.) Try out any techniques that pleased you in Cummings's poem. You might want to adopt trademarks of Cummings's style: no capitalization, not much punctuation, and words bumping into punctuation marks.

Here's how one writer began a poem about the ocean:

> The beach was milk,
>
> the air sheer as silk,
>
> the sun kissed the shore.

ART AND WRITING

Writing Scientific Descriptions

Create a museum display that shows the objects maggie, milly, molly, and may find on the beach. Include pictures and scientific information about shells, starfish, crabs (or whatever you think the "horrible thing" is), and stones.

INTERNET

Projects and Activities

Keyword: LE5 7-5

Literary Skills
Analyze exact and slant rhymes.

Writing Skills
Write a poem; write scientific descriptions.

All in green went my love riding

Make the Connection
Quickwrite ✏️

E. E. Cummings wrote this in the twentieth century, but he imitates the style and subject matter of songs and poems of centuries ago. In those old songs and poems, a man or woman often told a story about love, death, and betrayal. Certain images were frequently used over and over again. Deer, for example, were often used to symbolize women; hunters were the men who wished to conquer the wild deer.

Think about songs that are popular today. What is one of the most common subjects? Are most songs tragic or comic? How do they deal with love? Jot down your responses.

Literary Focus
The Sounds of Poetry

"All in green went my love riding" is a haunting poem. Read the poem aloud at least once, and listen for all these sounds:

- **rhyme**—exact rhymes (*riding / smiling*) and slant rhymes (*down / dawn*)

- **repetition** of words (*riding, smiling, deer*) and lines (*All in green went my love riding*)

- **alliteration**—the repetition of consonant sounds in nearby words (*the lean lithe deer, the sleek slim deer*)

A stag hunt and a king, possibly Dagobert I (632–639), on his throne (detail), from *The Life and Miracles of St. Denis* by French School. Vellum.
Bibliotheque National, Paris, France (Ms Fr 1098).

Background
Literature and Literary History

This poem describes a romantic scene from a time when royalty hunted deer, using bows and arrows and many hunting dogs (often fast, muscular dogs that looked like greyhounds). The deer were hunted for food but also for sport.

SKILLS FOCUS

Literary Skills
Understand the sounds of poetry, such as rhyme, repetition, and alliteration.

All in green went my love riding

E. E. Cummings

All in green went my love riding
on a great horse of gold
into the silver dawn.

four lean hounds crouched low and smiling
5   the merry deer ran before.

Fleeter be they than dappled dreams
the swift sweet deer
the red rare deer.

Four red roebuck at a white water
10   the cruel bugle sang before.

Horn at hip went my love riding
riding the echo down
into the silver dawn.

four lean hounds crouched low and smiling
15   the level meadows ran before.

Softer be they than slippered sleep
the lean lithe deer
the fleet flown deer.

Four fleet does at a gold valley
20   the famished arrow sang before.

Bow at belt went my love riding
riding the mountain down
into the silver dawn.

four lean hounds crouched low and smiling
25   the sheer peaks ran before.

Paler be they than daunting death
the sleek slim deer
the tall tense deer.

Four tall stags at a green mountain
30   the lucky hunter sang before.

All in green went my love riding
on a great horse of gold
into the silver dawn.

four lean hounds crouched low and smiling
35   my heart fell dead before.

A stag hunt and a king, possibly Dagobert I (632–639), on his throne,
from *The Life and Miracles of St. Denis* by French School. Vellum.
Bibliotheque National, Paris, France (Ms Fr 1098).

Meet the Writer

E. E. Cummings

"you and I are not snobs."
E. E. Cummings (1894–1962) started writing poetry as a student at Harvard University. After he read some ancient classical poetry, suddenly, as he put it, "an unknown and unknowable bird started singing."

During World War I, Cummings was an ambulance driver in France. He was mistakenly arrested for treason and clapped into detention for three months. That experience was a turning point in his life. In prison, Cummings discovered his passion for freedom and personal growth. Over the next four decades he celebrated these passions.

The following quotation is from the preface to a book of Cummings's poems. The words appear here just as he wrote them.

> ❝ The poems to come are for you and for me and are not for mostpeople
> —it's no use trying to pretend that mostpeople and ourselves are alike. Mostpeople have less in common with ourselves than the squarerootofminusone. You and I are human beings;mostpeople are snobs. . . .

> you and I are not snobs. We can never be born enough. We are human beings;for whom birth is a supremely welcome mystery,the mystery of growing:the mystery which happens only and whenever we are faithful to ourselves. ❞

In his writing, Cummings liked to use lowercase letters, unusual word spacing (words often bump together), and his own brand of punctuation. Even though his style is new, his themes are familiar. Cummings, like lyric poets throughout the ages, celebrates the joy and wonder of life and the glory of the individual.

Response and Analysis

First Thoughts

1. What do you think happens to the speaker at the end of the poem?

Thinking Critically

2. Who do you think the speaker is? a woman or a deer? Explain.

3. Why do you think the lover's bugle is called "cruel" (line 10) and his arrow is described as "famished" (line 20)?

4. Look at the words used to describe the hounds. Are the hounds sinister in any way? Explain your answer.

5. If this is a poem about love, what message do you think it delivers about love? How does it compare with popular songs today? Check your Quickwrite responses for ideas. ✏️

6. This poem is full of color. List all the colors you see in the poem.

7. Fill in a chart like the one below with examples showing how the poem uses the **sounds of poetry.** To remind yourself of the definitions for these terms, refer to page 601.

Sounds of Poetry	Details from the Poem
Rhyme	
Repetition	
Alliteration	

ART

Illustrating the Poem

Draw or paint a picture of a scene described in this very visual poem. If you prefer, cut pictures out of magazines or newspapers, and create a collage of images from the poem. A collage (which comes from a French word meaning "glue") is a collection of items pasted on a flat surface. A collage can contain pictures, flowers, pebbles, string, and so on.

SKILLS FOCUS

Literary Skills
Analyze the sounds of poetry

Art Skills
Illustrate the poem.

Arithmetic

Make the Connection
Quickwrite ✏

You've been studying arithmetic in school ever since kindergarten, maybe even since nursery school. You might love or hate your math classes, but you probably use information you learned there in your life every day when you tell time or make purchases. How do you use math? Jot down five ways you use arithmetic when you're not in school.

Literary Focus
Catalog Poem

"Arithmetic" is a **free-verse poem**—a poem without rhyme or a regular meter. It's also a **catalog poem.** A catalog is a list. You've probably looked through lots of catalogs, perhaps from toy stores or electonics stores. Museums also create catalogs of all the artworks displayed in an exhibit. In "Arithmetic," Carl Sandburg doesn't list items for sale or on exhibition. Instead, he lists his thoughts on the subject of arithmetic.

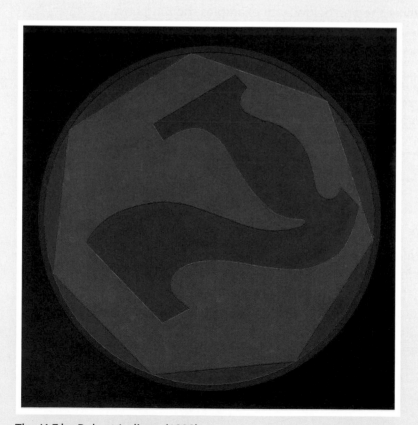

The *X-7* by Robert Indiana (1998).
Morgan Art Foundation Limited, Private Collection. © 2003 Morgan Art Foundation Ltd./
Artist Rights Society (ARS), New York.

SKILLS FOCUS

Literary Skills
Understand catalog poems.

ARITHMETIC

Carl Sandburg

1   Arithmetic is where numbers fly like pigeons in and out of your head.

2   Arithmetic tells you how many you lose or win if you know how many you
      had before you lost or won.

3   Arithmetic is seven eleven all good children go to heaven—or five six
      bundle of sticks.

4   Arithmetic is numbers you squeeze from your head to your hand to your
      pencil to your paper till you get the answer.

5   Arithmetic is where the answer is right and everything is nice and you can
      look out of the window and see the blue sky—or the answer is wrong and
      you have to start all over and try again and see how it comes out this time.

6   If you take a number and double it and double it again and then double it a
      few more times, the number gets bigger and bigger and goes higher and
      higher and only arithmetic can tell you what the number is when you
      decide to quit doubling.

7   Arithmetic is where you have to multiply—and you carry the multiplication
      table in your head and hope you won't lose it.

8   If you have two animal crackers, one good and one bad, and you eat one and a
      striped zebra with streaks all over him eats the other, how many animal
      crackers will you have if somebody offers you five six seven and you say
      No no no and you say Nay nay nay and you say Nix nix nix?

9   If you ask your mother for one fried egg for breakfast and she gives you two
      fried eggs and you eat both of them, who is better in arithmetic, you or your
      mother?

For a biography of Carl Sandburg, see Meet the Writers on page 442.

First Thoughts

1. Finish these sentences:

- The speaker's idea about arithmetic that I liked best is . . .
- I think arithmetic is . . .

Thinking Critically

2. How would you describe the **tone** of this poem? Do you think Sandburg likes arithmetic? Explain.

3. The writer of a **free-verse poem** often creates **rhythm** through repetition. What repeated words or phrases give "Arithmetic" its rhythm?

4. In the first line of the poem, a **simile** compares the way you remember numbers to "pigeons flying in and out of your head." How does this figure of speech reflect what you know about numbers?

5. List three or four examples of **alliteration**—the repetition of consonant sounds in nearby words—in this poem.

Extending Interpretations

6. Look back at your Quickwrite notes, and think about something you can say about arithmetic based on your own experiences. Write your thoughts in a form that could be added to the end of Carl Sandburg's poem.

WRITING

Writing a Catalog Poem

Catalog poems can be fun to write. Think of a topic that you care about. Then, list your ideas or feelings about your topic in the form of a catalog poem. Open your poem the way Sandburg opens his:

"[My topic] is . . ."

Maybe you want to write about another school subect:

"History is . . ."

"Grammar is . . ."

SKILLS FOCUS

Literary Skills
Analyze a catalog poem.

Writing Skills
Write a catalog poem.

For Poets

Make the Connection
Quickwrite

The poem you are about to read, "For Poets," is written especially for poets. By now you've read many poems, and you've probably even written a few. From your own poetry reading and writing experiences, what advice do you have for poets? Jot down your suggestions.

Literary Focus
Ars Poetica

As you already know from its title, "For Poets" is written for poets. That makes it an **ars poetica**—a poem about poetry. *Ars poetica* is Latin for "art of poetry."

Figures of Speech

We all use figures of speech every day. A **figure of speech** compares one thing to something else, something very different. A figure of speech is not literally true. When we say someone is "cool," we are using a figure of speech. The person is not literally "cool"—his or her temperature is not below normal. Instead, when we say someone is "cool," we are comparing that person's style and attitude to weather that is not blazing hot. We are saying the person is not bothered by things.

Metaphors and **similes** are examples of figures of speech. Here are some common figures of speech we use every day:

> *He's built like a tank.*
> *This party's a bust.*
> *Those plans are down the tube.*

Reading Skills
Reading a Poem

Remember the tip that helps you both to understand a poem and to read it aloud? *Pay attention to the punctuation.* But "For Poets" has no punctuation, so how will you know when to pause or when to keep on reading? Here's the answer: You'll have to decide for yourself. Here's another tip, though, that can help you decide:

> *Pay attention to the thoughts.*

Think about what the poet is saying, and then determine when a thought begins and when it ends. When you read "For Poets," you might want to pause at the end of most—but not all—lines. It's up to you.

SKILLS FOCUS

Literary Skills
Understand ars poetica; understand figures of speech.

Reading Skills
Read a poem.

For Poets

Al Young

Stay beautiful
but dont stay down underground too long
Dont turn into a mole
or a worm
5   or a root
or a stone

Come on out into the sunlight
Breathe in trees
Knock out mountains
10   Commune with snakes
& be the very hero of birds

Dont forget to poke your head up
& blink
Think
15   Walk all around
Swim upstream

Dont forget to fly

Three Doves and a Snake
by Andrea Eberbach.

Al Young

"A Keen Observer of the Human Comedy"

Al Young (1939–   ) has been called "a gifted stylist and a keen observer of the human comedy." He was born in Ocean Springs, Mississippi, and spent the first ten years of his life in the South. His next ten years were spent in and near Detroit, Michigan.

As a teenager, Young's poems and stories were published in local publications, providing an indication of his future career. Young attended the University of Michigan at Ann Arbor, where he was co-editor of the school's literary magazine, and the University of California at Berkeley, from which he graduated in 1969.

Between the ages of eighteen and twenty-five, Young played the guitar and flute and sang professionally throughout the United States. He also

worked as a disc jockey, a writing teacher, a language consultant, and a screenwriter.

"For Poets" appears in Young's poetry collection titled *Heaven: Collected Poems 1956–1990.*

First Thoughts

1. Respond to "For Poets" by finishing this sentence:
   - I think the best advice in this poem is . . .

Thinking Critically

2. This poem is made up of a series of **figures of speech,** in which certain behaviors are compared to things in nature. What do you think the speaker means when he says "dont stay down underground too long"? What behaviors of poets are being compared to the behaviors of a mole, a worm, a root, and a stone?

3. In the second and third stanzas, choose two lines and explain what advice the speaker is giving to poets through the **figures of speech.**

Extending Interpretations

4. Do you think that Young has offered good advice to poets? How does his advice compare to the advice you wrote about in your Quickwrite on page 609?

WRITING
An Ars Poetica

Write down your advice to poets in the form of a poem or **ars poetica.** You might imitate the structure of this poem and open three verses with the words *Stay, Come,* and *Don't forget*.

SPEAKING AND LISTENING
An Oral Interpretation

Work together with a partner to decide how to read "For Poets" aloud. Decide when you should pause and when you should keep on reading. Take turns reading the poem aloud until you both feel you are reading smoothly and well. Then, perform the poem for the class.

SKILLS FOCUS

Literary Skills
Analyze an ars poetica; analyze figures of speech.

Reading Skills
Read a poem.

Writing Skills
Write a poem giving advice.

Speaking and Listening Skills
Read a poem aloud.

Author Study Sandra Cisneros

Literary Focus
A Writer's Messages

Sandra Cisneros writes about feelings we can all understand. She writes with humor about life's joys and frustrations. She writes about being lonely and afraid. She writes about wanting what we can't have. She describes the fear of not fitting in—as well as the feeling that maybe we don't really want to fit in. These feelings are close to her heart and often come from her own experiences. Her writing also explores the lives of people who belong to two cultures and speak two languages. Many of her works celebrate her memories of her Mexican American childhood.

Reading Skills
Making Generalizations

A **generalization** is a broad statement about something. In making a generalization, you combine evidence in the text with what you already know. After you read the selections by Cisneros, you'll have a chance to make generalizations about her work. To make a generalization about a work of literature, ask yourself these questions:

- What is the work's **conflict,** or problem?
- What **message** about life does the work reveal?
- How does the work relate to your experience?

Key Elements of Cisneros's Writing

- **Everyday language,** including slang and sentence fragments, gives the feeling of people speaking aloud.

- **Strong images** and **metaphors** bring the work alive.

- **Spanish words** mixed with English words reflect the heritage of the characters and of the writer.

- **Messages** often focus on family relationships and learning how to fit into the world around us.

SKILLS FOCUS

Literary Skills
Interpret a writer's message.

Reading Skills
Make generalizations.

Before You Read

Lichtenstein Creative Media's Marit Haahr interviewed Sandra Cisneros on the public radio program *The Infinite Mind*. During the broadcast, she asks Cisneros to read her short story "Salvador Late or Early" to the listeners. The two then talk about the story and the way it relates to Cisneros's life. From their conversation we learn something about how writers draw from their own experiences to create literature.

AN INTERVIEW WITH SANDRA CISNEROS

from *The Infinite Mind*

Marit Haahr. Writer Sandra Cisneros was born in Chicago in the 1950s, the third child and only daughter of seven. Her books include *The House on Mango Street* and *Woman Hollering Creek*. She's won numerous awards, including the MacArthur Foundation Fellowship, which is often called the genius grant. Her latest novel, *Caramelo*, [was] published in September [2002].

Haahr. You were recently published in an anthology entitled *Growing Up Poor*. With that in mind, I'd actually like to begin with a reading from your short story collection *Woman Hollering Creek*. Can you describe this story, "Salvador Late or Early," for our listeners?

Sandra Cisneros. I didn't intend it to be a story. I thought perhaps it'd be a poem. I was remembering a classmate of mine I couldn't forget. So it began from that place of not being able to forget. ❶ 🕮

Cisneros now reads the story.

(continued on page 616)

IDENTIFY

❶ What four things have you just learned about the story Cisneros is going to read?

(Opposite) Sandra Cisneros at her home in San Antonio, Texas.

Salvador Late or Early

Salvador with eyes the color of caterpillar, Salvador of the crooked hair and crooked teeth, Salvador whose name the teacher cannot remember, is a boy who is no one's friend, runs along somewhere in that vague direction where homes are the color of bad weather, lives behind a raw wood doorway, shakes the sleepy brothers awake, ties their shoes, combs their hair with water, feeds them milk and corn-flakes from a tin cup in the dim dark of the morning. ❷

Salvador, late or early, sooner or later arrives with the string of younger brothers ready. Helps his mama, who is busy with the business of the baby. Tugs the arms of Cecilio, Arturito, makes them hurry, because today, like yesterday, Arturito has dropped the cigar box of crayons, has let go the hundred little fingers of red, green, yellow, blue, and nub of black sticks that tumble and spill over and beyond the asphalt puddles until the crossing-guard lady holds back the blur of traffic for Salvador to collect them again. ❸

A CISNEROS TIME LINE

In 1966, Cisneros's parents buy a house on Campbell Avenue in Chicago.

She begins a series of sketches about her family and childhood while at the University of Iowa Writers' Workshop program in 1977.

1950   **1960**   **1970**

Born on December 20, 1954, in Chicago, Illinois.

Attends Loyola University from 1972 to 1976. Takes a creative-writing class, in which she begins to write seriously.

Salvador inside that wrinkled shirt, inside the throat that must clear itself and apologize each time it speaks, inside that forty-pound body of boy with its geography of scars, its history of hurt, limbs stuffed with feathers and rags, in what part of the eyes, in what part of the heart, in that cage of the chest where something throbs with both fists and knows only what Salvador knows, inside that body too small to contain the hundred balloons of happiness, the single guitar of grief, is a boy like any other disappearing out the door, beside the schoolyard gate, where he has told his brothers they must wait. Collects the hands of Cecilio and Arturito, scuttles off dodging the many schoolyard colors, the elbows and wrists crisscrossing, the several shoes running. Grows small and smaller to the eye, dissolves into the bright horizon, flutters in the air before disappearing like a memory of kites. ❹

Haahr. Thank you. It's certainly clear that the image that Salvador left in your mind was very strong. Why do you think that was?

Cisneros. Because he sat in front of me and his shirts were always wrinkled and the collars were dirty. I thought, "Doesn't his mama

INTERPRET

❹ How do you think Salvador feels as he hurries through his busy day? What details in the story support your interpretation?

Receives artist grants in 1983 that allow her to travel and live in France.

Publishes *Woman Hollering Creek* (1991), a collection of short stories.

Her long-awaited second novel, *Caramelo* (2002), is published.

1980

1990

2000

Teaches at the Latino Youth Alternative High School in Chicago, 1978–1980.

Publishes *The House on Mango Street* (1984), based on sketches she began in Iowa.

Buys a house of her own in San Antonio, Texas, which she later paints purple.

In 1995, receives a MacArthur Foundation genius grant. *The House on Mango Street* is translated into Spanish.

INTERPRET

5 What does Cisneros mean when she says Salvador "was me"? How does this feeling of hers enable her to know her character Salvador so well?

love him?" I thought about him a lot, and I remembered him so clearly. I remember walking down streets visiting my aunt and thinking, "Now that kind of building must be the kind that Salvador lives in." I knew him intimately, perhaps more than he knew himself, and he stayed with me all the years. I realized when I finished writing the story that he was me. That's why I could know what he did and what kind of a house he lived in and who his younger brothers were and who he had to wait for—all the things that a tiny being like that knew and the remarkable things that perhaps he had to take care of that he never thought of as remarkable. **5**

Haahr. I know that one of the defining features of your childhood was growing up without much money. What were the physical circumstances of your childhood like?

INTERPRET

6 What lesson did Cisneros learn from her family?

Cisneros. Well, you know, it came [to me] at a very young age that we just didn't have money for everything. My older brother was the one that would always pull me aside and say, "Don't ask for anything. Papa doesn't have any money." or "Don't shame him by asking for something that he can't give you or that he'll give you and that'll hurt us later in the week." So there was the sense of being responsible for the others. I was very conscious of it when I went to Catholic school, because there was a class difference between myself and the majority of the students in the school that I went to.

Haahr. How did being conscious of that affect you?

Cisneros. It made you responsible. It made you want to be protective of your mother and father and not ask for too many things. It made you, sometimes, I think, value money in a way that perhaps your classmates did not, because you had to save for the things that you really wanted. When my father died, he was sad and cried and said he wished he could have given us more. And I said he gave us just enough, because we valued what we had, and we worked for what we had. That was a lesson you can't learn in Harvard. **6**

First Thoughts

1. Describe your reaction to "Salvador Late or Early."

Thinking Critically

2. "Salvador Late or Early" includes powerful **metaphors**—comparisons of unlike things. Choose one metaphor from each paragraph, and explain what it helps you to understand about Salvador and his life.

3. Strong **images** are another poetic element in this story. Draw or describe one of the visual images that especially appeals to you.

4. What is the **mood** of this story? What does the mood tell you about the writer's attitude toward Salvador?

5. Do you agree with Cisneros that Salvador is "a boy like any other"? Cite details in the story to support your interpretation.

Reading Check

a. What chores does Salvador do before and after he goes to school?

b. What does Salvador look like? Use details from the story to describe him.

c. In the interview, what reasons does Cisneros give for remembering Salvador all her life?

Cisneros's Message

6. Think about why Cisneros wrote this story. Use her responses in the interview to help you decide on the story's **message.** Some possible messages of the story are

   - Remarkable people come from all walks of life.
   - Life without much money can still be rich.
   - It's important to make sacrifices for the good of others.

   Choose one of these messages, or come up with another of your own. Write the message in a chart like the one below, and then explain why you chose it and what you think about it.

Cisneros's message in "Salvador Late or Early":
My response to the message:

SKILLS FOCUS

Literary Skills
Interpret a writer's message

Reading Skills
Make generalizations.

Before You Read

"Chanclas"[1] is a story from Cisneros's well-loved book *The House on Mango Street*. Her novel takes the form of a series of very short stories linked by the voice of a narrator, a girl named Esperanza, who is growing up in a Latino neighborhood in Chicago. In this particular story, Cisneros writes about a feeling we've probably all experienced—the embarrassment of not having the right clothes, of not looking good enough. What happens to the narrator's embarrassment by the end of the story?

Chanclas

Sandra Cisneros

It's me—Mama, Mama said. I open up and she's there with bags and big boxes, the new clothes and, yes, she's got the socks and a new slip with a little rose on it and a pink-and-white striped dress. What about the shoes? I forgot. Too late now. I'm tired. Whew! **❶**

Six-thirty already and my little cousin's baptism is over. All day waiting, the door locked, don't open up for nobody, and I don't till Mama gets back and buys everything except the shoes.

Now Uncle Nacho is coming in his car, and we have to hurry to get to Precious Blood Church quick because that's where the baptism party is, in the basement rented for today for dancing and tamales and everyone's kids running all over the place. **❷**

Mama dances, laughs, dances. All of a sudden, Mama is sick. I fan her hot face with a paper plate. Too many tamales, but Uncle Nacho says too many this and tilts his thumb to his lips.

INTERPRET

❶ The first paragraph ends with a little conversation. Who asks the question? Who responds?

IDENTIFY

❷ What has the narrator been waiting for? Where is the narrator going?

---

1. chanclas (chän′kläs) *n.*: Spanish slang for "old, worn-out shoes."

Everybody laughing except me, because I'm wearing the new dress, pink and white with stripes, and new underclothes and new socks and the old saddle shoes I wear to school, brown and white, the kind I get every September because they last long and they do. My feet scuffed and round, and the heels all crooked that look dumb with this dress, so I just sit. ❸

Meanwhile that boy who is my cousin by first communion or something asks me to dance and I can't. Just stuff my feet under the metal folding chair stamped Precious Blood and pick on a wad of brown gum that's stuck beneath the seat. I shake my head no. My feet growing bigger and bigger.

Then Uncle Nacho is pulling and pulling my arm and it doesn't matter how new the dress Mama bought is because my feet are ugly until my uncle who is a liar says, You are the prettiest girl here, will you dance, but I believe him, and yes, we are dancing, my Uncle Nacho and me, only I don't want to at first. My feet swell big and heavy like plungers, but I drag them across the linoleum floor straight center where Uncle wants to show off the new dance we learned. And Uncle spins me, and my skinny arms bend the way he taught me, and my mother watches, and my little cousins watch, and the boy who is my cousin by first communion watches, and everyone says, wow, who are those two who dance like in the movies, until I forget that I am wearing only ordinary shoes, brown and white, the kind my mother buys each year for school. ❹

And all I hear is the clapping when the music stops. My uncle and me bow and he walks me back in my thick shoes to my mother who is proud to be my mother. All night the boy who is a man watches me dance. He watched me dance. ❺

INTERPRET

❸ What great problem, or **conflict,** does the narrator face?

IDENTIFY

❹ Cisneros is famous for using **figurative language,** such as similes. What simile does the narrator use to describe her feet? (A **simile** compares two different things, using a word of comparison, such as *like* or *as*.)

COMPARE AND CONTRAST

❺ How have the narrator's feelings changed by the end of the story? Use details to explain the change.

First Thoughts

1. Finish this sentence:

- I think the narrator of this story is . . .

Thinking Critically

2. Explain why the narrator refuses to dance with the boy who asks her, but dances with her uncle.

3. In this story, the **dialogue** runs into the text rather than being set off with quotation marks. Re-read the story, and identify the passages that represent actual conversations. If you want, read the dialogue aloud.

4. What **conflict,** or challenge, does the narrator overcome?

5. Cisneros uses vivid words to make her **images** come alive. Pick out a noun, a verb, and an adjective that you think are particularly powerful. Explain why you chose them.

> ### Reading Check
> **Retell** this story to a partner. Start with the title and author. Who is the main character, and what is her problem, or **conflict**? Tell the main events in the order in which they occur. Now, describe the story's **climax,** which is the moment when the conflict ends. Finally, what is the **resolution,** or ending, of the story?

Cisneros's Message

6. Choose a message that you think is important in "Chanclas." Write it in a chart like the one below, and record your responses to the message.

Here are some possibilities:

- There are more important things in life than clothes.
- Certain kinds of beauty lie beneath the surface.
- You may find pleasure in a situation when you least expect to.

Cisneros's message in "Chanclas":
My response to the message:

SKILLS FOCUS

Literary Skills
Interpret a writer's message.

Reading Skills
Make generalizations.

Before You Read

"Abuelito Who" is a collection of memories of the poet's grandfather. *Abuelito* (ä·bwä·lē′tō) is Spanish for "granddaddy." Read the poem aloud twice.

Abuelito Who

Sandra Cisneros

Abuelito who throws coins like rain
and asks who loves him
who is dough and feathers
who is a watch and glass of water
5   whose hair is made of fur
is too sad to come downstairs today ❶
who tells me in Spanish you are my diamond
who tells me in English you are my sky
whose little eyes are string
10   can't come out to play
sleeps in his little room all night and day
who used to laugh like the letter *k*
is sick
is a doorknob tied to a sour stick
15   is tired shut the door
doesn't live here anymore
is hiding underneath the bed ❷
who talks to me inside my head
is blankets and spoons and big brown shoes
who snores up and down up and down up and down
20   again
is the rain on the roof that falls like coins
asking who loves him
who loves him who? ❸

Before You Read

Cisneros grew up speaking both Spanish and English. She writes in English but often uses Spanish words in her writing. She says, "I think that incorporating the Spanish, for me, allows me to create new expressions in English—to say things in English that have never been said before." In this essay, Cisneros talks about what inspired her to write "Abuelito Who."

La Mulita (1923) by Abraham Angel.
Artese Historia Mexico.

The Place Where Dreams Come From

Sandra Cisneros

When I was little, my grandpa—my Abuelito, that is, which is sort of like Granddaddy, only sweeter—my Abuelito used to love to give all his grandchildren their *domingo* (literally "Sunday," because that's the day children receive it), that is, their allowance. But my Abuelito loved the ritual of asking in a loud voice, "Who loves Grandpa?" and we would answer, also in a loud voice, "We do!" Then he would take a handful of change he'd been saving all week for this purpose, Mexican coins which are thick and heavy, and toss them up in the air so that they'd fall like rain, like a *piñata* (pē·nyä′tä), and we'd scramble all over each other picking up as many coins as we could. To me it was much more fun to get our *domingo* this way instead of having it placed in our hands. ❶

Well, it's this fun grandpa that this poem is about. And about the coins falling like rain, and rain falling like coins, that at times makes me think of him and miss him. I recall he became rather sick and cranky in his last years. I suppose that's what some of the images refer to, but I was grown and gone already, and my Abuelito in faraway Mexico City. ❷

ANALYZE

❶ Look back at "Abuelito Who" (page 623). Which lines in the poem does this paragraph explain?

ANALYZE

❷ Look again at "Abuelito Who." Find four **images** that might refer to the time when Abuelito was "sick and cranky."

I'm not sure what exactly all the images refer to, and I'm not sure I ever knew. But that's what's so wonderful about poetry. It comes from some deep and true place inside you, the place where dreams come from. We don't always know what dreams mean, do we, and we don't have to always know to enjoy and experience them. That's how it is with poetry, too. When I write, I don't question where images are coming from. I write dictated by sound and directed by my heart. And these images—"dough and feathers," "little eyes are string," and "doorknob tied to a sour stick"—felt right then and still feel right as I read them now. "Dough and feathers" I suppose has to do with how he felt when I held him and he held me. He was soft and squishy as dough or feathers. But it could also mean the color of his skin and hair. The texture of his skin. The silliness of his being. They're all "right." ❸

"Little eyes are string" is harder to pinpoint. Did I mean like a spiral of string, like when we are sick? Maybe. But then again, perhaps it's the way he looked at me when he was sick. And "doorknob tied to a sour stick." I recall a cane he had and how he changed when he was very old and cranky and waved it when he wanted to make a point. So I suppose he had "soured." Why tied to a doorknob? Who knows?

A few biographical tidbits. My grandfather *did* laugh like the letter *k*. A kind of "kkkk" sound when he chuckled, which, surprisingly, I've inherited. ❹

And. He was very proud that he could speak English, even though he lived in Mexico City most of his life. And so he liked to show off his English to his grandchildren from the United States when they came to visit. "You are my diamond," my grandpa would say in typical Mexican fashion. But then he would mistranslate "You're my heaven" and instead come out with "You're my sky," because "sky" and "heaven" are the same word in Spanish. I remember thinking even as a child that it sounded wonderful— "You're my sky." How much better than *heaven*. All, all of that! Imagine. I've always been much more partial to sky and clouds, and am even now. ❺

Finally, the older we grow, the younger we become as well, don't you think? That is, our Abuelito had to take naps, and he liked to play games, like the one with the coins, and he talked to us in a way that other adults didn't, and he couldn't climb the stairs very well, like my baby brothers. So in a way he was getting younger and younger and younger until he wasn't anymore.

INTERPRET

❸ According to Cisneros, what makes poetry "wonderful"?

IDENTIFY

❹ According to Cisneros, which details in "Abuelito Who" are biographical? Which details from the poem remain mysterious to Cisneros?

INTERPRET

❺ Think about Cisneros's comment about combining a knowledge of Spanish and English to create something new (see Before You Read, page 624). According to this paragraph, where has she combined languages in "Abuelito Who"? Look back at the poem to find the exact lines.

First Thoughts

1. Finish this sentence:
   - If I could ask Sandra Cisneros one question, I would ask her . . .

Thinking Critically

2. Re-read the first two lines and the last three lines of "Abuelito Who." How does the poem circle back to its beginning?

3. Explain the speaker's feelings for her grandfather.

4. In the poem, Cisneros uses many **metaphors** to describe her grandfather. List three such metaphors, and explain what you think they mean. Cisneros's essay "The Place Where Dreams Come From" may give you some ideas.

5. In the essay, Cisneros describes her inspiration for the poem. How do you feel about the poem now? Do you understand it better? Explain.

> ### Reading Check
>
> List the **similarities** and **differences** between the grandfather in "Abuelito Who" and the grandfather that Cisneros describes in "The Place Where Dreams Come From."

Cisneros's Message

6. State the message from "Abuelito Who" in a chart like the one below, and then jot down your response to that message.

Think of your own message statement, or choose one of these possibilities:

- People change with the passing of time.
- Memories of everyday life offer lasting inspiration.
- Family ties strengthen over the years.

> Cisneros's message in "Abuelito Who":
>
>
> My response to the message:

SKILLS FOCUS

Literary Skills
Interpret a writer's message.

Reading Skills
Make generalizations.

Assignment

1. Writing About a Writer's Message

Write an essay in which you discuss Cisneros's **messages** in the stories and poem you have just read. Before you write, review the charts you filled in after you read "Salvador Late or Early," "Chanclas," and "Abuelito Who." Write three paragraphs. In the first paragraph, write a **generalization** about Sandra Cisneros's writing based on the messages in each work and on what she says about her writing in the interview and essay. In the second paragraph, state the messages in the stories and poem. In the third paragraph, describe your responses to the selections and their messages. You may want to use quotations to support your interpretations.

Use the workshop on Supporting an Interpretation, pages 630–635, for help with the first two assignments.

Assignment

2. Writing About a Writer's Language

Write an essay in which you discuss how Cisneros uses everyday language, strong images, metaphors, and Spanish words in "Salvador Late or Early," "Chanclas," and "Abuelito Who." After writing an introductory paragraph, you can organize your essay in one of two ways.

1. You can write a paragraph about each work and describe its examples of the four elements.
2. You can write a paragraph about each element and describe how it is used in the three works.

Write a final paragraph describing your responses to Cisneros's writing.

Assignment

3. Writing a Poem or Story

Cisneros often turns her life experiences into stories and poems by paying attention to the details that make people and situations unique. Try your hand at writing either a poem or a story.

- Write a poem based on your memories of a relative or good friend. If you want, use Cisneros's basic structure in "Abuelito Who"—begin with the person's name, and add descriptive details, starting each line with the pronoun *who*.
- Using "Chanclas" as a model, write a short story about an autobiographical incident. Begin with your memories, and then use vivid words and images to describe the setting, characters, and events.

SKILLS FOCUS

Writing Skills
Write an interpretation; write a poem or short story.

Before You Read

Sometimes governments and even individuals with strong opinions try to control what people think by destroying the books of those who disagree with them. For example, in 1933, thousands of Nazi students and some of their professors ransacked university libraries and bookstores in thirty German cities, and burned books written by Jews and by those opposed to Nazi ideas. Bertolt Brecht's books were among those tossed on the bonfires.

The Burning of Books

Bertolt Brecht

When the Regime ordered that books with dangerous teachings
Should be publicly burnt and everywhere
Oxen were forced to draw carts full of books
To the funeral pyre, an exiled poet,
5   One of the best, discovered with fury, when he studied the list
Of the burned, that his books
Had been forgotten. He rushed to his writing table
On wings of anger and wrote a letter to those in power.
Burn me, he wrote with hurrying pen, burn me!
10   Do not treat me in this fashion. Don't leave me out. Have I not
Always spoken the truth in my books? And now
You treat me like a liar! I order you:
Burn me!

Meet the Writer

Bertolt Brecht

His Reputation Caught Fire

Bertolt Brecht (1898–1956) began studying medicine in 1917 at the University of Munich in Germany, while working at the same time as a drama critic and playwright. He eventually left his university studies to concentrate on literature and drama. In 1922, Brecht became famous for his play *Drums in the Night*, for which he received Germany's notable Kleist prize. During this period he wrote operas with music by Kurt Weill. "Mack the Knife," a song from one of those operas—*The Threepenny Opera*—was made popular in the United States and throughout the world by Louis Armstrong and other singers.

In 1933, Brecht left his homeland because the Nazis had come to power and he had been targeted as an enemy. During that year, thousands of Nazi sympathizers ransacked bookstores and libraries throughout Germany and threw tens of thousands of "anti-Nazi" books into raging bonfires. Unlike the works of the speaker in the poem "The Burning of Books," Brecht's works were among those destroyed by the Nazis.

The burning of his books did not destroy Brecht's reputation, however. He went on to receive international acclaim for his significant and innovative plays. While in exile (mostly in Denmark and the United States), Brecht produced some of his finest works, including *Mother Courage and Her Children* and *The Life of Galileo*.

Brecht is also recognized as a great poet. Some critics even consider his poetry to be his finest work.

Writing Workshop

RUBRIC
Evaluation Criteria

A good interpretation of a literary work

1. identifies the work by title and author

2. states the interpretation clearly

3. supports the interpretation with evidence such as details, examples, and reasons

4. has a clear organization

5. restates or reinforces the interpretation in a strong conclusion

SKILLS FOCUS

Writing Skills
Write an essay supporting an interpretation.

PERSUASIVE WRITING

Supporting an Interpretation

In discussing a story or a poem, you and your classmates have probably differed at times in your views of a character's actions or your analyses of a theme. Good literature often stimulates readers to think and to respond in a variety of ways. This is not to say that *any* response to a literary work is valid, however. An interpretation of a work's meaning has to be supported by evidence. In this workshop you will write an essay interpreting some aspect of a literary work that interests you.

Prewriting

1 Choosing a Subject

Read and respond to this **prompt:**

> When you analyze something, you take it apart to see how it works. When you interpret, you reveal what you've discovered through your analysis. A literary interpretation often begins with a problem you wish to solve. For example, what is the symbolic meaning of the roof garden in "Antaeus" (page 175)? What does the story "A Day's Wait" (page 191) say about courage? How does Cummings differentiate the girls in "maggie and milly and molly and may" (page 599)? Choose some aspect of a work that you would like to explore, and write an essay interpreting its significance.

Brainstorm a list of ideas with your classmates. Here are some literary topics to consider:

- how a specific literary element (such as setting, imagery, or tone) is used in a selection
- why a character is (or isn't) convincing
- what is the main idea in a story, poem, or essay

2 Developing a Thesis

Writing about a literary work is a way of getting to know it better. In putting your thoughts down on paper, you become more fully involved with the work. You may have to read a work several times before you determine what your focus will be.

Jot down your thoughts, even if they are random at first. One graphic organizer that can help you sort out your thoughts and reach conclusions is a cluster diagram such as the one on the right. Freewriting for several minutes will also allow you to explore ideas.

Aim for a manageable topic. In a short paper you may have time and space to discuss only one aspect of a work. You need to formulate a **thesis,** or controlling idea, about the topic. Here are some examples to guide you:

Selection: "The Dinner Party" (page 118)
Topic: The plot of the story
Thesis: The plot is carefully designed to overturn stereotypes about gender differences.

Selection: "Rikki-tikki-tavi" (page 15)
Topic: The character of the hero
Thesis: In his treatment of Rikki, Kipling combines animal characteristics with human motives.

Selection: "The Smallest Dragonboy" (page 147)
Topic: The theme of the story
Thesis: Through courage and determination a boy overcomes obstacles to fulfilling his dream.

Selection: "Jabberwocky" (page 577)
Topic: Making sense of the poem
Thesis: The sounds of real and invented words help to tell the story of a battle and its victory.

Selection: *The Monsters Are Due on Maple Street* (page 59)
Topic: Explaining a title
Thesis: *Monsters* in the title refers to the mob of humans as well as to the aliens.

Cluster Diagram "maggie and milly and molly and may"

maggie finds a singing seashell and forgets her troubles.

milly makes friends with a starfish by helping it.

All the girls respond individually at the beach.

molly is frightened by a creature like a crab.

may finds a stone that makes her thoughtful.

INTERNET
More Writer's Models
Keyword: LE5 7-5

Language Handbook
H E L P

See The Pronoun, 1b; Agreement, 2a–x.

Framework for an Interpretive Essay

Introduction (includes title, author, and thesis statement): _____ _____

Body (presents evidence in support of thesis): _____ _____

Main Ideas:

1. _____
2. _____

Conclusion (restates thesis, revealing insights into the work): _____ _____

Strategies for Elaboration

Note specific details that provide supporting evidence. Provide explanations or commentaries that draw connections for the reader.

In **fiction,** describe

- actions
- thoughts
- words
- others' behavior
- direct comments by writer

In **poetry,** comment on

- imagery
- figurative language
- sound effects
- tone

3 Presenting Evidence

In an interpretive essay the evidence you present in support of a thesis may include direct quotations; paraphrased lines or short passages; details such as images, actions, and dialogue; and explanations or reasons. Select evidence carefully, choosing the best or most persuasive examples to back up your conclusions.

Drafting

1 Organizing the Essay

Organize your essay to include an introduction, the body of the text, and a conclusion. In your **introduction,** identify the work, author, and the problem you will write about. Also include a statement of your thesis.

The **body** of your essay should present the evidence supporting your thesis. Each paragraph in the body should focus on a major supporting idea.

The **conclusion** should bring together your main ideas and restate your thesis. You may add a personal comment or extend the conclusion to cover related works.

In an interpretive essay the type of organization that is most effective is **order of importance.** Put the most important details at the beginning or at the end for emphasis.

2 Writing the Essay

Use language that is appropriate for your purpose and audience. Remember that your purpose is to convey ideas clearly and that you are writing for your teacher or other students.

Make the order of your ideas clear by using **transitional expressions,** such as *first, last, mainly, more important, then,* and *to begin with.*

Student Model

A Boy's Struggle with Courage

The story "A Day's Wait" by Ernest Hemingway suggests that courage is often a difficult thing to have. For a whole day, Schatz believes that he will die from a fever of 102 degrees because he misunderstood information that schoolmates told him.

The boy shows his courage by holding back his emotions. Instead of listening to the story that his father is reading, Schatz looks at the foot of the bed, thinking. While he could be crying like a baby because he believes he is going to die, he braves the reality and doesn't react. It seems that it's difficult to keep his cool and show courage because he doesn't talk much to anyone, but instead has a staring contest with the foot of the bed.

Schatz struggles with his fear. While staring at the foot of the bed, he is thinking very hard and barely listens to anything that his father tells him. Instead of giving in to his disease, he holds on and stays alive. This is proved when Schatz refuses to sleep for fear of dying while doing so. It probably took a lot of struggle to decide if he should just give up or if he should give his life a chance. Schatz decides to brave the possible consequences with courage instead of giving in. When he finally tells his father what he has been thinking and learns that he will not die, Schatz is able to relax.

"A Day's Wait" suggests that courage is difficult to deal with. I agree but think that Schatz should have asked his father in the beginning of the story to clarify his sickness instead of assuming the worst. If Schatz hadn't brought up the subject of his death near the end of the story, he might have just given up before realizing that he wasn't going to die. Instead of fighting to get better, he might not have done anything and made it worse. "A Day's Wait" certainly proves that it is hard to have courage.

—Rochelle BaRoss
George Washington Middle School
Ridgewood, NJ

*The writer's **thesis** is clearly stated in the first sentence.*

***Details** of Schatz's behavior in the story are used to support the writer's thesis.*

*More **details** from the story support the thesis.*

*The writer **contrasts** Schatz's behavior with her own opinions.*

*The last sentence **restates** the writer's thesis, or main idea.*

Evaluating and Revising

Use the following chart to evaluate and revise your essay.

Supporting an Interpretation: Content and Organization Guidelines		
Evaluation Questions	▶ **Tips**	▶ **Revision Techniques**
❶ Are the author and the title named in your introduction?	▶ **Highlight** the author and the title.	▶ **Add** a sentence or phrase naming the author and the title.
❷ Does your introduction have a clear thesis?	▶ **Underline** the thesis statement.	▶ **Add** a sentence that clearly states the thesis.
❸ Is the main idea of each paragraph clear, and does it support the thesis?	▶ **Bracket** the main idea discussed in each paragraph of the body.	▶ **Revise** the body paragraphs so that each deals with a main idea.
❹ Is the main idea of each body paragraph supported with evidence?	▶ **Draw a box** around each supporting detail or quotation. **Draw a wavy line** under elaborations.	▶ **Add** details or quotations to support your thesis. **Elaborate** on details or quotations with commentary.
❺ Does your conclusion restate the thesis and summarize your main points? Does it leave readers with something to consider?	▶ **Highlight** the sentence in the conclusion that restates the thesis. **Circle** the summary of key points.	▶ **Add** a sentence restating the thesis. **Add** a sentence that applies the thesis to a broader experience or connects it with other works.

On the next page you'll find an excerpt from an interpretive essay that has been revised. Following the model are questions to help you evaluate the writer's revisions.

Revision Model

Who are the monsters in ~~the~~ ^Rod Serling's^ teleplay <u>The Monsters</u>

<u>Are Due on Maple Street</u>? The title suggests that the

monsters ~~are~~ ^might be^ nonhuman, perhaps aliens from

another planet. At the end of the play, we see ^two figures in a spacecraft.^ ~~them~~.

However, as the events of the play ~~show~~ ^unfold^, the real

monsters are the ^ordinary^ people, whose panic ~~turns~~ ^transforms^ them into

a ^self-destructive^ mob, ready to turn on one another. As the narrator

says, "The tools of conquest do not necessarily come

with bombs and explosions ^and fallout^ ." The weapons can be

prejudice and fear. The teleplay shows that lives can be

destroyed by irrational suspicions.

Evaluating the Revision

1. Do you agree with the additions and deletions the writer has made? Explain.

2. Where has the writer changed the order of material? Does this change improve clarity?

3. What additional changes would you recommend to improve the content or organization of this essay excerpt?

PROOFREADING

TIPS

- *Pay particular attention to your punctuation of the title of the work.*

- *Use quotation marks at the beginning and at the end of material quoted directly. Indented quotations, however, do not need quotation marks.*

- *Proofread your work at least twice. Ask another student to work with you, checking for errors in grammar, spelling, and punctuation.*

Communications Handbook

H E L P

See proofreaders' marks.

PUBLISHING

TIPS

- *Publish your interpretation on a Web site that accepts student writing.*

- *Tape-record a reading of your essay for a class audio library.*

Test Practice

DIRECTIONS: Read the following list. Then, read each question, and decide which is the best answer.

A Prose Reading List

Key to Abbreviations

E = easy	A = average	C = challenging
F = fiction	NF = nonfiction	

• Caselli, Giovanni. *The Renaissance and the New World.* **C, NF** The author looks at the Renaissance advancements in commerce and technology that became the foundation of eighteenth-century life in England and America.

• Cosby, Bill. "Lessons." **A, NF** In this humorous essay, Cosby writes about how he and his daughter dealt with her poor performance on a test.

• Dahl, Roald. *Boy.* **C, NF** With a humorous touch the renowned author tells about his childhood years in England.

• Fritz, Jean. *Stonewall.* **E, NF** Fritz tells the life of Thomas "Stonewall" Jackson from his boyhood years to his Civil War achievements.

• George, Jean Craighead. *My Side of the Mountain.* **E, F** In this novel, Sam Gribley runs away to the Catskill Mountains, where challenges from humans and nature await.

• Hansen, Joyce. *Which Way Freedom?* **E, F** In this novel set at the beginning of the Civil War, Obi sets out to find his mother after a long separation.

• Saint-Exupéry, Antoine de. *The Little Prince.* **E, F** In this fable a stranded pilot meets a little boy who recounts his fantastic adventures on various planets.

• Soto, Gary. *Baseball in April.* **E, F** A collection of short stories. In one story, Michael and Jesse fail to make the Little League team but still find a way to play the game they love.

• Taylor, Mildred D. *Song of the Trees.* **A, F** In this novella the Logan family must prevent a businessman from destroying the forest that has brought joy to their lives.

• Zindel, Paul. *The Pigman.* **C, F** In this prize-winning novel, John and Lorraine are dissatisfied with their lives until they meet Mr. Pignati, who teaches them to cherish every moment.

SKILLS FOCUS

Literary Skills
Analyze forms of prose.

1. Which one of the following statements is true of both fiction and nonfiction?

   A It cannot be based on actual events.

   B It cannot be longer than one hundred pages.

   C It often reveals important truths.

   D It must have resolution.

2. Which book on the reading list is an **autobiography**?

   F *The Little Prince*

   G *The Pigman*

   H *My Side of the Mountain*

   J *Boy*

3. Which book on the reading list is a **biography**?

   A *Which Way Freedom?*

   B *Stonewall*

   C *Song of the Trees*

   D *The Renaissance and the New World*

4. Which book on the reading list is a collection of **short stories**?

   F *The Little Prince*

   G *The Renaissance and the New World*

   H *Baseball in April*

   J *Boy*

5. Which item on the reading list is an **essay**?

   A "Lessons"

   B *Stonewall*

   C *Boy*

   D *Baseball in April*

6. Which two books on the list are **novels**?

   F *Which Way Freedom?* and *Song of the Trees*

   G *The Little Prince* and *Baseball in April*

   H *Boy* and *Stonewall*

   J *The Pigman* and *My Side of the Mountain*

7. Which book on the reading list is **historical fiction**?

   A *Which Way Freedom?*

   B *My Side of the Mountain*

   C *Stonewall*

   D *The Little Prince*

Constructed Response

8. In what ways are fiction and nonfiction different?

9. How can you tell the difference between a short story, a novel, and a novella?

Test Practice

DIRECTIONS: Read the following poem. Then, answer each question.

The Sea

James Reeves

The sea is a hungry dog,
Giant and gray.
He rolls on the beach all day.
With his clashing teeth and shaggy jaws
5   Hour upon hour he gnaws
The rumbling, tumbling stones,
And "Bones, bones, bones!"
The giant sea dog moans,
Licking his greasy paws.

10   And when the night wind roars
And the moon rocks in the stormy cloud,
He bounds to his feet and snuffs and sniffs,
Shaking his wet sides over the cliffs,
And howls and hollos long and loud.

15   But on quiet days in May or June,
When even the grasses on the dune
Play no more their reedy tune,
With his head between his paws
He lies on the sandy shores,
20   So quiet, so quiet, he scarcely snores.

1. In which of the following sets do *all* the words **rhyme**?

   A   dog / gray / day

   B   stones / bones / moans

   C   sniffs / cliffs / loud

   D   paws / shores / snores

2. The **rhyme scheme** of the last **stanza** of the poem is —

   F   *aabbcc*

   G   *abcabc*

   H   *abcdef*

   J   *aaabcc*

3. Which of the following is an example of a **metaphor**?

   A   "The rumbling, tumbling stones"

   B   "But on quiet days in May or June"

   C   "The sea is a hungry dog"

   D   "Giant and gray"

4. Which of the following lines contains **alliteration,** or the repetition of consonant sounds?

   F   "The giant sea dog moans"

   G   "Licking his greasy paws"

   H   "But on quiet days in May or June"

   J   "So quiet, so quiet, he scarcely snores"

5. Which of the following lines contains **onomatopoeia,** or words that sound like what they mean?

   A   "And howls and hollos long and loud"

   B   "Hour upon hour he gnaws"

   C   "Licking his greasy paws"

   D   "He lies on the sandy shores"

6. What **tone** is evoked by the repetition and word choices in the last stanza?

   F   a quiet, peaceful tone

   G   a sad and lonely tone

   H   a lively and happy tone

   J   a rough and angry tone

Constructed Response

7. List three different ways in which the poem compares the sea to a dog.

8. Find **images** in the poem that appeal to each of the following senses: sight, hearing, touch, and taste.

Literary Skills
Analyze elements of poems.

Collection 5: Skills Review

Vocabulary Skills

Test Practice

Context Clues

DIRECTIONS: As you read each sentence, use the other words in the sentence to help you figure out what the underlined word means. Then, choose the best answer.

1. The crowd's reaction was as frenzied as the flurry of punches being thrown by the fighters.
   - A wild
   - B contagious
   - C hard
   - D deceptive

2. The children were impressed by the formidable size of their huge school.
   - F average
   - G awesome
   - H small
   - J unremarkable

3. They couldn't agree on much, but this dispute promised to drive them even further apart.
   - A problem
   - B outrage
   - C situation
   - D argument

4. She had to do everything in her power to muster the energy to be nice to her brother after what he had done.
   - F forgive
   - G summon
   - H forget
   - J receive

5. The darkening sky cast an ominous shadow, which frightened the children.
   - A cold
   - B dismal
   - C fearful
   - D threatening

6. Without warning the ground began churning like the choppy waves of a lake.
   - F sinking
   - G glistening
   - H bending
   - J stirring

7. Of the many matches scheduled for the night, the last bout would be most thrilling.
   - A choice
   - B contest
   - C bridge
   - D draw

8. The climber stood at the top of the bluff and surveyed the valley below with her binoculars.
   - F mountain range
   - G river bottom
   - H ship
   - J steep cliff

SKILLS FOCUS

Vocabulary Skills
Use context clues.

Collection 5: Skills Review

Writing Skills

Test Practice

DIRECTIONS: Read the following paragraph from an essay supporting an interpretation. Then, answer each question that follows.

(1) Why do we admire the robber in Alfred Noyes's poem "The Highwayman"? (2) Obviously, he is a criminal who holds up stagecoaches and steals passengers' money and jewels at gunpoint. (3) If King George's men had not shot him down on the highway, he might have ended his career on the gallows. (4) Yet, the poet's skill makes us admire the highwayman because he is a romantic figure—daring and fearless. (5) The poet depicts the highwayman as a romantic hero. (6) He is handsomely dressed, like a gentleman. (7) He wears a stylish hat, lace at his chin, a coat of velvet, and pants of doeskin (lines 7–8). (8) He rides with "a jeweled twinkle," his weapons reflecting the starlight. (9) He is also a faithful lover. (10) The redcoats are unable to catch him until he is betrayed by a rival for his love.

1. Which sentence contains the **thesis,** or main idea, of the essay?
   - **A** sentence 1
   - **B** sentence 3
   - **C** sentence 4
   - **D** sentence 6

2. Which sentence is repetitive and should be deleted?
   - **F** sentence 2
   - **G** sentence 5
   - **H** sentence 7
   - **J** sentence 8

3. A **paraphrase,** or restatement, of specific lines from the poem appears in —
   - **A** sentence 4
   - **B** sentence 7
   - **C** sentence 9
   - **D** sentence 10

4. Which sentence does *not* contain a transitional word?
   - **F** sentence 2
   - **G** sentence 4
   - **H** sentence 7
   - **J** sentence 9

5. Sentences 6–9 all begin with the pronoun *he.* How might you introduce variety into these sentences?
   - **A** Substitute "the highwayman" for "he" in one or more sentences.
   - **B** Add transitional expressions such as *moreover* or *in addition.*
   - **C** Combine the ideas in sentences 6 and 7 into onc sentence.
   - **D** All of the above

SKILLS FOCUS

Writing Skills
Analyze persuasive writing.

Fiction

Sentimental Journey

Suffering from a kidney disease and confined to a prison hospital, Cephus "Crab" Little decides to make up for lost time with his son Jimmy in *Somewhere in the Darkness* by Walter Dean Myers. Together they journey to Crab's hometown in Arkansas, where Jimmy's growing understanding of his father's past helps him come to terms with his father and himself.

Women of Valor

In *Cut from the Same Cloth: American Women of Myth, Legend, and Tall Tale,* Robert D. San Souci takes a look at women characters in American legends with a talent for adventure. You'll find stories about Molly Cotton-Tail, Brer Rabbit's clever wife, and Sister Fox, the brains behind Brother Coyote. The stories are entertaining, and they often offer up a few lessons as well.

Helping Hand

Fourteen-year-old Cloyd never knew his parents and never went to school. After being on his own for so long, he has trouble accepting the kindness of an old rancher from Colorado. In Will Hobbs's novel *Bearstone,* Cloyd embraces his Native American heritage, begins to respect others, and learns what it takes to be an adult.

This title is available in the HRW Library.

On the Road Again

It's the summer of the year 1294. Adam, an eleven-year-old minstrel boy who loses contact with his father, is confounded by another minstrel named Jankin, who steals his dog, Nick. In this Middle Ages adventure, Adam scours the English countryside in search of the two things that mean the most to him—his father and his lovable dog. Of course, along the way he learns a few lessons and meets some interesting friends in Elizabeth Janet Gray's Newbery Award–winning historical novel, *Adam of the Road.*

Nonfiction

Roots of Prejudice

In Africa in 1710, Amos Fortune was born to a king. At the age of fifteen, he was captured by slave traders and transported in chains to the colony of Massachusetts. Despite the horrors of captivity, Fortune never gave up hope in securing his personal freedom. When he finally became a free man at the age of sixty, he dedicated the remainder of his life to freeing others like him. Find out more about this remarkable man in Elizabeth Yates's Newbery winner, *Amos Fortune: Free Man.*

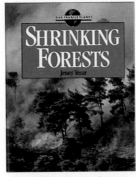

Take Care of the Earth

Forests play an important role in the earth's environment; yet we cut them down at an alarming rate, threatening the well-being of animals, plants, and ourselves. In *Shrinking Forests,* Jenny Tesar explains how essential it is to preserve rain forests. If you enjoy this book, you may enjoy other books in the Our Fragile Planet series; each examines an environmental problem.

Natural Disasters

Earthquakes, floods, volcanoes—our planet sure has had some problems. In *Eyewitness Books: Volcano & Earthquake,* Susanna Van Rose explains how these problems occur. The book also covers the most famous disasters in world history, from the eruption of Mount Vesuvius during the first century to the San Francisco earthquake of 1989.

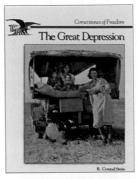

Heartbreaking Times

During the 1920s, the United States was enjoying prosperity. Then, on October 29, 1929, the New York Stock Exchange crashed. The country fell into the Great Depression; as a result, jobs were scarce, banks were closing, and families were starving. In *The Great Depression,* R. Conrad Stein looks back on this bleak period in American history.

Our Literary Heritage

Greek Myths and World Folk Tales

Literary Focus:
Analyzing Myths and Folk Tales

Informational Focus:
Summarizing

INTERNET
Collection
Resources
Keyword: LE5 7-6

Two Dragons in Clouds (detail) by Hogai Kano I.
© Philadelphia Museum of Art.

Elements of Literature
The Myths of Greece and Rome *by* David Adams Leeming

INSIGHTS INTO OUR WORLD

It is hard to imagine what our civilization would be like without the mythology of ancient Greece and Rome. The ancient immortals are still around us in spirit. If you go to any one of the great museums of Europe or America, you will find statues and paintings of classical gods and heroes. If you read poetry in English classes, you will come across references to ancient places such as Troy and Carthage, monsters such as the Sirens and the Cyclops, and gods and heroes such as Poseidon, Odysseus (whose Roman name is Ulysses), Athena, and Hercules. These are all names from mythology—names that poets and artists expect us to recognize.

What Is a Myth?

Myths are stories that represent the deepest wishes and fears of human beings. They explained to the ancient people the mysterious and sometimes frightening forces of the universe—forces such as seasonal changes, fire, lightning, drought, floods, and death.

Makers of Myths

The myths you will read here originated in the area around the Mediterranean Sea (see the inset of the map on pages 648–649). These old myths were passed on orally from generation to generation.

By the second century B.C., the Romans had conquered the Greeks and had adopted the Greek myths. The Romans added a new, cynical tone to the old stories. This tone reflected the fact that the Romans were less serious about religion than the Greeks were.

The Uses of Mythology

Myths are not merely ancient tales. Like all true art, the great myths give us insights into the nature of our world.

Myths are used for these purposes:

1. to explain the creation of the world
2. to explain natural phenomena
3. to give story form to ancient religious practices
4. to teach moral lessons
5. to explain history
6. to express, as dreams do, the deepest fears and hopes of the human race

INTERNET
More About Myths
Keyword: LE5 7-6

SKILLS FOCUS

Literary Skills
Understand Greek and Roman myths.

A Family Affair: Gods and Goddesses

According to the Greek myths, the divinities lived on Mount Olympus. Many of them traveled down to spend time with ordinary people. To the myth makers, a god or goddess was a powerful being, often identified with a force of nature.

Practice

The chart below shows some of the Greek and Roman gods and goddesses and their special powers. List the names of the divinities that you recognize. Can you think of any other Greek and Roman gods and goddesses you can add to your list? Now, write down whatever prior knowledge you have about the gods and goddesses on your list.

Greek Name	Roman Name	Area of Power
Zeus (zyo͞os)	Jupiter	king of the gods; sky; weather
Apollo (ə·päl′ō)	Apollo	the sun; youth; music; archery; healing; prophecy
Artemis (är′tə·mis)	Diana	twin sister of Apollo; the moon; hunting
Hades (hā′dēz′)	Pluto	king of the underworld
Poseidon (pō·sī′dən)	Neptune	ruler of the seas
Hera (hēr′ə)	Juno	wife of Zeus; queen of gods; women; marriage
Dionysus (dī′ə·nī′səs)	Bacchus	wine; fertility; music
Athena (ə·thē′nə)	Minerva	wisdom; war; crafts
Hephaestus (hē·fes′təs)	Vulcan	craftsman for the gods; fire
Hermes (hur′mēz)	Mercury	messenger god; secrets; tricks
Demeter (di·mēt′ər)	Ceres	agriculture; earth; corn
Persephone (pər·sef′ə·nē)	Proserpine	daughter of Demeter; queen of Hades

The World of Classical Mythology

Reading Skills and Strategies

Becoming Word-Wise

by Kylene Beers

Can you read the following sentence?

Ifay ouyay ancay eadray isthay, enthay ouyay ancay eadray igpay atinlay.

Well, how did you do? If you know Pig Latin, then you probably did just fine. Pig Latin—not at all related to the Latin the ancient Romans spoke—requires you to take off the first letter (or sometimes letters) of a word, put that letter at the end of the word, and then add the long *a* sound (ā). So, *pig* becomes *igpay*. Once you figure out how words work in Pig Latin (owhay ordsway orkway inay igpay atinlay), then you can speak it, write it, read it, and understand it.

Building Your Vocabulary

Figuring out the meaning of words and how they work to make meaning is the key to mastering any language. Since many English words can be traced to Greek and Latin, if you can learn what **Greek** and **Latin roots** and **affixes** mean, you have a key to understanding many English words.

For instance, if you know that the Latin prefix *dis–* means "not" or "the opposite," you can figure out that the word *dislocate* means "put out of place" or "locate in a different place" (as in "dislocate a shoulder"). If you know that the Latin root *–aud–* means "hear," then you can guess that *audible* has something to do with hearing.

On the next pages are lists of common roots and affixes from Greek and Latin. Note their meanings. Note examples of how these roots and affixes are used to build English words. (*L* in the chart stands for "Latin"; *G* stands for "Greek.")

> ### Remember . . .
>
> **Roots** are the fundamental parts of a word. *–Loc–* is a Latin root for "place." *Locate* is based on the Latin root *–loc–*.
>
> **Affixes** are word parts added to a root to alter its meaning.
>
> **Prefixes** are affixes added to the front of a word (*dis*locate).
>
> **Suffixes** are affixes added to the end of a word (loca*tion*).

SKILLS FOCUS

Reading Skills
Understand Greek and Latin roots and affixes.

GREEK AND LATIN ROOTS AND AFFIXES

Commonly Used Roots

Root	Meanings	Examples
–act– (L)	act	action, actor, react, transact, enact
–aud– (L)	hear	audience, auditorium, audible, audition
–bio– (G)	life	biology, biography, biofeedback, bionics
–cred– (L)	believe; trust	credit, discredit, credible, credulous
–dem– (G)	people	democracy, Democrat, demographics
–dic– (L)	speak; say	dictate, predict, contradict, verdict, diction
–geo– (G)	earth	geography, geology
–graph– (G)	write; draw;	autograph, paragraph, phonograph, photograph, telegraph
–loc– (L)	place	allocate, locate, location
–man– (L)	hand	manual, manufacture, manuscript, manipulate
–ped– (L)	foot	pedal, pedestrian, pedestal
–pop– (L)	people; nation	population, popular, populace
–port– (L)	carry	import, export, portable, porter, transport
–sign– (L)	mark; sign	insignia, signal, significant, signature
–spec– (L)	see; look at	inspect, respect, spectacle, spectator, suspect
–tract– (L)	pull; drag	attract, detract, contract, subtract, traction, tractor
–vid– (L)	see; look	evidence, video, provide, providence
–volv– (L)	roll	evolve, involve, revolve, revolver, revolution

IDENTIFY

Notice the dashes before and after the **roots.** Then, look at some of the examples. Do roots go at the beginning, middle, or end of the new words they help form? Explain.

IDENTIFY

In what part of a word would you find a **prefix**? Hint: The meaning for the prefix *pre–* will give you the answer.

Commonly Used Prefixes

Prefix	Meanings	Examples
anti– (G)	against; opposing	antiwar, anticlimax
bi– (L)	two	bisect, bimonthly
co– (L)	with; together	coexist, codependent
de– (L)	away from; off; down	debrief, debug
dia– (G)	through; across; between	diameter, diagonal
in–, im– (L)	in; into; within	introduce, imprison
inter– (L)	between; among	interpersonal, intersect
non– (L)	not	nonprofit, nonfat
post– (L)	after; following	postnasal, postgraduate
pre– (L)	before	prepayment, preview
re– (L)	back; backward; again	reverse, return, recur
sub– (L)	under; beneath	submarine, substandard
syl–, sym–, syn–, sys– (G)	together; with	syllable, symmetric, synthesis, system
trans– (L)	across	transplant, translate

Commonly Used Suffixes

Suffix	Meanings	Examples
–able (L)	able; likely	readable, lovable
–ance, –ancy (L)	act; quality	admittance, constancy
–ate (L)	to become; to cause; to be	captivate, activate
–fy (L)	to make; to cause; to be	liquefy, simplify
–ible (L)	able; likely	flexible, digestible
–ity (L)	state; condition	reality, sincerity
–ize (L)	to make; to cause; to be	socialize, motorize
–ment (L)	result; act of; state of being	judgment, fulfillment
–ous (L)	characterized by	dangerous, malicious
–tion (L)	action; condition	rotation, election

Practice the Strategy

Building Your Vocabulary

You can increase your vocabulary by building "vocabulary trees" from the root up. For an example of a vocabulary tree, look below at the tree a student made using the root –cred–. Here are the steps you can follow to create your own vocabulary tree:

1. On a piece of paper, draw a tree like the one below, and put a word root from the chart on page 651 in the root section of the tree.
2. In the trunk, put one word from the "Examples" column that uses that root, and define the word.
3. In the branches, put other words that you hear or read or use in your own writing that come from that root.
4. On the twigs of the branches, explain how you used that word or where you read it.
5. Add as many branches as possible to your vocabulary tree.

In whatever you read, use your knowledge of Greek and Latin roots and affixes to help you figure out the meaning of unfamiliar words.

credible: "believable" — in my science book

credit: "say someone did something good" — give credit: My teacher gave me a compliment.

credit: "charge something at a store" — get credit: My mother has a credit card.

incredible: "not believable" — I heard Mark say it.

discredit: "show why not to believe in someone"

–cred– "believe"

SKILLS FOCUS

Reading Skills
Analyze Greek and Latin roots and affixes.

653

The Origin of the Seasons

Make the Connection

Quickwrite ✏️

Ancient people looked to myths for answers to questions about the natural world, just as we look to science today. The ancients wondered, for example, why there were seasons. What do you know about the seasons in the area where you live? Is there anything about the seasons you don't understand? Write down your responses.

Literary Focus

Origin Myths

The ancient Greeks did not possess the scientific knowledge we have today. Still, they were as curious about their natural surroundings as we are about ours. They longed for explanations. Why do we have so many different kinds of flowers? Why is there night and day? Why do the seasons change? For answers to their questions, the ancient people turned to their myth makers. They believed these storytellers were directly in touch with the source of all knowledge—the gods. The myth makers were the guardians of a tradition with the same purpose as science: to provide explanations of how the world works. **Origin myths** are the special type of myths that give an explanation for how something came to be.

Reading Skills 📖

Understanding Cause and Effect

Since origin myths explain how something came about, they tell about causes and their effects. Often, the gods do something that causes an effect on Earth. Sometimes the cause-and-effect chain begins on Earth: People do something that causes the gods to react. The way the gods react then has an effect on Earth. As you read the myth "The Origin of the Seasons," notice the chain of cause and effect that results in the cycle of seasons on Earth.

SKILLS FOCUS

Literary Skills
Understand origin myths.

Reading Skills
Understand cause and effect.

Pomegranates.

The Origin of the Seasons

retold by **Olivia Coolidge**

Demeter, the great earth mother, was goddess of the harvest. Tall and majestic was her appearance, and her hair was the color of ripe wheat. It was she who filled the ears with grain. In her honor white-robed women brought golden garlands of wheat as first fruits to the altar. Reaping, threshing, winnowing,[1] and the long tables set in the shade for the harvesters' refreshment—all these were hers. Songs and feasting did her honor as the hard-working farmer gathered his abundant fruit. All the laws which the farmer knew came from her: the time for plowing, what land would best bear crops, which was fit for grapes, and which to leave for pasture. She was a goddess whom men called the great mother because of her generosity in giving. Her own special daughter in the family of the gods was named Persephone. ❶

> **CAUSE AND EFFECT**
> ❶ As goddess of the harvest, what **effects** does Demeter have on the Earth?

Persephone was the spring maiden, young and full of joy. Sicily was her home, for it is a land where the spring is long and lovely, and where spring flowers are abundant. Here Persephone played with her maidens from day to day till the rocks and valleys rang with the sound of laughter, and gloomy Hades heard it as he sat on his throne in the dark land of the dead. Even his heart of stone was touched by her young beauty, so that he arose in his awful majesty and came up to Olympus to ask Zeus if he might have Persephone to wife. Zeus bowed his head in agreement, and mighty Olympus thundered as he promised. ❷

> **INFER**
> ❷ Who is Persephone? What season might she represent? Why do you think Hades wants her to be his bride?

Thus it came about that as Persephone was gathering flowers with her maidens in the vale of Enna, a marvelous thing happened. Enna was a beautiful valley in whose meadows all the most lovely flowers of the year grew at the same season. There were wild roses, purple crocuses, sweet-scented violets, tall iris, rich

---

1. **reaping:** cutting and gathering the grain; **threshing** and **winnowing:** two ways of separating the grain from the husks.

narcissus,[2] and white lilies. All these the girl was gathering, yet fair as they were, Persephone herself was fairer far.

As the maidens went picking and calling to one another across the blossoming meadow, it happened that Persephone strayed apart from the rest. Then, as she looked a little ahead in the meadow, she suddenly beheld the marvelous thing. It was a flower so beautiful that none like it had ever been known. It seemed a kind of narcissus, purple and white, but from a single root there sprang a hundred blossoms, and at the sweet scent of it the very heavens and earth appeared to smile for joy. Without calling to the others, Persephone sprang forward to be the first to pick the precious bloom. As she stretched out her hand, the earth opened in front of her, and she found herself caught in a stranger's arms. Persephone shrieked aloud and struggled, while the armful of flowers cascaded down to earth. However, the dark-eyed Hades was far stronger than she. He swept her into his golden chariot, took the reins of his coal-black horses, and was gone amid the rumbling sound of the closing earth before the other girls in the valley could even come in sight of the spot. When they did get there, nobody was visible. Only the roses and lilies of Persephone lay scattered in wild confusion over the grassy turf. ❸

RETELL
❸ **Retell** the story of Persephone's disappearance.

Bitter was the grief of Demeter when she heard the news of her daughter's mysterious fate. Veiling herself with a dark cloud, she sped, swift as a wild bird, over land and ocean for nine days, searching everywhere and asking all she met if they had seen her daughter. Neither gods nor men had seen her. Even the birds could give no tidings, and Demeter in despair turned to Phoebus Apollo, who sees all things from his chariot in the heavens.

"Yes, I have seen your daughter," said the god at last. "Hades has taken her with the consent of Zeus, that she may dwell in the land of mist and gloom as his queen. The girl struggled and was unwilling, but Hades is far stronger than she." ❹

RETELL
❹ What news does Phoebus Apollo, the sun god, give to Demeter?

When she heard this, Demeter fell into deep despair, for she knew she could never rescue Persephone if Zeus and Hades had agreed. She did not care any more to enter the palace of Olympus, where the gods live in joy and feasting and where Apollo plays the lyre while the Muses sing. She took on her the form of an old woman, worn but stately, and wandered about the earth, where there is much sorrow to be seen. At first she kept away from the homes of people, since the sight of little children and happy mothers gave her pain. One day, however, as she sat by the side of a well to rest her weary feet, four girls came down to draw water. They were kind hearted and charming as they talked with her and concerned themselves about the fate of the homeless stranger-woman who was sitting at their

---

2. **narcissus** (när·sis′əs): family of lilies including daffodils and jonquils. "Echo and Narcissus" (page 290) gives the ancient Greeks' explanation of how this flower came to be.

La Primavera: Flora (detail) (1477) by Sandro Botticelli.
Uffizi Gallery, Florence, Italy. Erich Lessing/Art Resource, NY.

gates. To account for herself, Demeter told them that she was a woman of good family from Crete, across the sea, who had been captured by pirates and was to have been sold for a slave. She had escaped as they landed once to cook a meal on shore, and now she was wandering to find work.

The four girls listened to this story, much impressed by the stately manner of the strange woman. At last they said that their mother, Metaneira,[3] was looking for a nurse for their new-born brother, Demophoon.[4] Perhaps the stranger would come and talk with her. Demeter agreed, feeling a great longing to hold a baby once more, even if it were not her own. She went therefore to Metaneira, who was much struck with the quiet dignity of the goddess and glad to give her charge of her little son. For a while thereafter Demeter was nurse to Demophoon, and his smiles and babble consoled her in some part for her own darling daughter. She began to make plans for Demophoon: He should be a great hero; he should become an immortal, so that when he grew up she could keep him with her. [5]

CAUSE AND EFFECT
5 Explain what **causes** Demeter to become Demophoon's nurse.

Presently the whole household was amazed at how beautiful Demophoon was growing, the more so as they never saw the nurse feed him anything. Secretly Demeter would anoint him with ambrosia,[5] like the gods, and from her breath, as he lay in her lap, he would draw his nourishment. When the night came, she would linger by the great fireside in the hall, rocking the child in her arms while the embers burned low and the people went off to sleep. Then, when all was still, she would stoop quickly down and put the baby into the fire itself. All night long the child would sleep in the red-hot ashes, while his earthly flesh and blood changed slowly into the substance of the immortals. In the morning when people came, the ashes were cold and dead, and by the hearth sat the stranger-woman, gently rocking and singing to the child.

Presently Metaneira became suspicious of the strangeness of it all. What did she know of this nurse but the story she had heard from her daughters? Perhaps the woman was a witch of some sort who wished to steal or transform the boy. In any case it was wise to be careful. One night, therefore, when she went up to her chamber, she set the door ajar and stood there in the crack silently watching the nurse at the fireside crooning over the child. The hall was very dark, so that it was hard to see clearly, but in a little while the mother beheld the dim figure bend forward. A log broke in the fireplace, a little flame shot up, and there clear in the light lay the baby on top of the fire.

Metaneira screamed loudly and lost no time in rushing forward, but it was Demeter who snatched up the baby. "Fool that you are," she said indignantly to Metaneira, "I would have made your son immortal, but that is now impossible. He shall be a great hero, but in the end he will have to die. I, the goddess Demeter, promise it." With that

---

3. **Metaneira** (met′ə·nē′rə).
4. **Demophoon** (de·mäf′ō·än′).
5. **ambrosia** (am·brō′zhə): food of the gods.

La Primavera: Flora (detail) (1477) by Sandro Botticelli.
Uffizi Gallery, Florence, Italy. © Erich Lessing/Art Resource, NY.

old age fell from her and she grew in stature. Golden hair spread down over her shoulders so that the great hall was filled with light. She turned and went out of the doorway, leaving the baby on the ground and Metaneira too amazed and frightened even to take him up. **6**

CAUSE AND EFFECT
6 What **causes** Metaneira to become suspicious of Demeter? What is the **effect** of Metaneira's suspicion?

All the while that Demeter had been wandering, she had given no thought to her duties as the harvest goddess. Instead she was almost glad that others should suffer because she was suffering. In vain the oxen spent their strength in dragging the heavy plowshare[6] through the soil. In vain did the sower with his bag of grain throw out the even handfuls of white barley in a wide arc as he strode. The greedy birds had a feast off the seed corn that season; or if it started to sprout, sun baked it and rains washed it away. Nothing would grow. As the gods looked down, they saw threatening the earth a famine such as never had been known. Even the offerings to the gods were neglected by despairing men who could no longer spare anything from their dwindling stores. **7**

CAUSE AND EFFECT
7 Demeter is no longer acting as goddess of the harvest. List some **effects** of her neglect.

At last Zeus sent Iris, the rainbow, to seek out Demeter and

---

6. **plowshare:** cutting blade of a plow.

La Primavera: Flora (detail) (1477) by Sandro Botticelli.

Uffizi Gallery, Florence, Italy. © Erich Lessing/Art Resource, NY.

appeal to her to save mankind. Dazzling Iris swept down from Olympus swift as a ray of light and found Demeter sitting in her temple, the dark cloak still around her and her head bowed on her hand. Though Iris urged her with the messages of Zeus and offered beautiful gifts or whatever powers among the gods she chose, Demeter would not lift her head or listen. All she said was that she would neither set foot on Olympus nor let fruit grow on the earth until Persephone was restored to her from the kingdom of the dead.

At last Zeus saw that he must send Hermes of the golden sandals to bring back Persephone to the light. The messenger found dark-haired Hades sitting upon his throne with Persephone, pale and sad, beside him. She had neither eaten nor drunk since she had been in the land of the dead. She sprang up with joy at the message of Hermes, while the dark king looked gloomier than ever, for he really loved his queen. Though he could not disobey the command of Zeus, he was crafty, and he pressed Persephone to eat or drink with him as they parted. Now, with joy in her heart, she should not refuse all food. Persephone was eager to be gone, but since the king entreated her, she took a pomegranate[7] from him to avoid argument and delay. Giving in to his pleading, she ate seven of the seeds. Then Hermes took her with him, and she came out into the upper air.

When Demeter saw Hermes with her daughter, she started up, and Persephone too rushed forward with a glad cry and flung her arms about her mother's neck. For a long time the two caressed each other, but at last Demeter began to question the girl. "Did you eat or drink anything with Hades?" she asked her daughter anxiously, and the girl replied:

"Nothing until Hermes released me. Then in my joy I took a pomegranate and ate seven of its seeds."

"Alas," said the goddess in dismay, "my daughter, what have you done? The Fates have said that if you ate anything in the land of shadow, you must return to Hades and rule with him as his queen. However, you ate not the whole pomegranate, but only seven of the seeds. For seven months of the year, therefore, you must dwell in the underworld, and the remaining five you may live with me."

Thus the Fates had decreed, and even Zeus could not alter their law. For seven months of every year, Persephone is lost to Demeter and rules pale and sad over the dead. At this time Demeter mourns, trees shed their leaves, cold comes, and the earth lies still and dead. But when, in the eighth month, Persephone returns, her mother is glad and the earth rejoices. The wheat springs up, bright, fresh, and green in the plowland. Flowers unfold, birds sing, and young animals are born. Everywhere the heavens smile for joy or weep sudden showers of gladness upon the springing earth. ❽

> **CAUSE AND EFFECT**
> ❽ What **effect** did Persephone's eating seven pomegranate seeds have on the Earth?

---

7. **pomegranate** (pām′ə·grăn′ĭt): round, red fruit containing many seeds that can be eaten. Pomegranates are pictured on page 654.

First Thoughts

1. What are your first impressions of the gods and goddesses in this myth? What do you think of the way they treat one another and the people on Earth?

Thinking Critically

2. How does this story of the kidnapping of a young girl and her mother's grief explain the change of seasons on Earth?

3. Why do you think Demeter spends so much time with the baby Demophoon, even planning to make him immortal?

4. Demeter is able to force Zeus to change his mind about the marriage of Hades and Persephone. What does this tell you about "the great earth mother"?

Extending Interpretations

5. Which character in this myth do you feel the most sympathy for? Why?

6. What other stories do you know of in which someone eats a forbidden food—or breaks a taboo (a rule strictly prohibiting something) and pays dearly for it?

Reading Check

Many events in this ancient myth are connected by **cause and effect.** Describe the effect of each event listed below:

a. Gloomy Hades falls in love with beautiful young Persephone.

 Effect:

b. Unhappy about the loss of her daughter, Demeter gives no thought to her duties as the harvest goddess.

 Effect:

c. Demeter vows that she will not let fruit grow on the earth until Persephone is returned.

 Effect:

d. While in the land of the dead, Persephone eats seven seeds from a piece of fruit.

 Effect:

WRITING
Writing an Origin Myth

Throughout the world, people have told imaginative stories to explain the cycle of seasons. Write your own origin myth explaining why the seasons change as they do in your part of the world. If you live in a region where the weather rarely changes, tell how this came to be. You may find ideas for your myth in your Quickwrite notes.

go.
hrw.
.com

INTERNET
Projects and Activities
Keyword: LE5 7-6

SKILLS FOCUS

Literary Skills
Analyze an origin myth.

Reading Skills
Analyze cause and effect.

Writing Skills
Write a myth.

English Prefixes Derived from Greek

A **prefix** is a word part that is added to the beginning of a word to change the word's meaning. Many prefixes that we use today come from ancient Greek. Some common ones appear in the first column of the chart below. The first row of the chart is filled in for you.

PRACTICE

Use a dictionary to complete the rest of the chart.

	Meaning	Example
anti-	against	antidote: something that acts against a poison
auto-		
hydro-		
meta-		
sym- or syn-		

Descriptive Words

In "The Origin of the Seasons," Hades drives Persephone into a hole in the ground. Here's how Coolidge describes the scene:

> "He swept her into his golden chariot, took the reins of his coal-black horses, and was gone amid the rumbling sound of the closing earth. . . ."

This sentence creates a rich picture because it uses **descriptive words.** In good descriptive writing you find

- *concrete, specific nouns:* It isn't just a *vehicle*—it's a *chariot.*
- **precise verbs:** He didn't just *put* her in—he *swept* her in.
- **vivid adjectives** that appeal to the senses: The horses are *coal-black;* the earth makes a *rumbling* sound.

PRACTICE

Rewrite each of the sentences below, using descriptive language. Remember to use specific nouns, precise verbs, and vivid adjectives.

1. Persephone lived in a perfectly nice place.
2. Some horses went by, making a lot of noise.
3. Poor Persephone sat on a throne.

SKILLS FOCUS

Vocabulary Skills
Understand Greek prefixes; use descriptive words.

Orpheus, the Great Musician

Make the Connection
Quickwrite

"Great music can pull you right out of your chair. It can make you cry, or laugh, or feel a way you've never felt before."
—Nadja Salerno-Sonnenberg

Think of a time when music touched your life. Write briefly about the experience.

Literary Focus
The Underworld of Myth

You don't have to read many myths before you find yourself in that frightful place called the underworld. As you know from "The Origin of the Seasons," the underworld is a dark and gloomy place ruled by the stern god Hades. To reach Hades' home, you cross the River Styx (stiks) on a ferryboat rowed by Charon (ker′ən). Then you pass through gates guarded by Cerberus (sur′bər·əs), a three-headed dog. Normally only the souls of the dead go to Hades. Sometimes, however, living people attempt the dangerous journey, usually to reach someone who has died.

Reading Skills
Summarizing

In a summary, you mention only the most important information in a text.

The tricky part of **summarizing** is deciding what to include and what to leave out. When you summarize a myth, be sure to include:

- the title
- the author (the one who retells the myth)
- the main characters
- the conflict
- the main events
- the resolution

Vocabulary Development

Here are some of the words you'll learn as you read the myth.

inconsolable (in′kən·sōl′ə·bəl) *adj.:* unable to be comforted; brokenhearted. *Orpheus was inconsolable and could not be comforted when his true love died.*

ghastly (gast′lē) *adj.:* horrible; ghostlike. *People shudder in fear when they enter the ghastly halls of the underworld.*

reluctance (ri·luk′təns) *n.:* unwillingness. *His reluctance to live without his love led him to brave the underworld.*

ascended (ə·send′id) *v.:* moved up. *They ascended the long narrow path up the mountain.*

INTERNET

Vocabulary Activity

Keyword: LE5 7-6

SKILLS FOCUS

Literary Skills
Identify elements of myth: the underworld.

Reading Skills
Summarize.

ORPHEUS,
THE GREAT MUSICIAN

RETOLD BY OLIVIA COOLIDGE

In the legend of Orpheus, the Greek love of music found its fullest expression. Orpheus, it is said, could make such heavenly songs that when he sat down to sing, the trees would crowd around to shade him. The ivy and vine stretched out their tendrils. Great oaks would bend their spreading branches over his head. The very rocks would edge down the mountainsides. Wild beasts crouched harmless by him, and nymphs[1] and woodland gods would listen to him, enchanted.

Orpheus himself, however, had eyes for no one but the nymph Eurydice.[2] His love for her was his inspiration, and his power sprang from the passionate longing that he knew in his own heart. All nature rejoiced with him on his bridal day, but on that very morning, as Eurydice went down to the riverside with her maidens to gather flowers for a bridal garland, she was bitten in the foot by a snake, and she died in spite of all attempts to save her.

Orpheus was inconsolable. All day long he mourned his bride, while birds, beasts, and the earth itself sorrowed with him. When at last the shadows of the sun grew long, Orpheus took his lyre[3] and made his way to the yawning cave which leads down into the underworld, where the soul of dead Eurydice had gone.

THE EARTH ITSELF SORROWED WITH HIM.

_____

1. **nymphs:** minor goddesses of nature, usually young and beautiful, living in mountains, rivers, or trees.
2. **Eurydice** (yo͞o·rid′i·sē′).

_____

3. **lyre** (līr): small harp.

Vocabulary
inconsolable (in′kən·sōl′ə·bəl) _adj.:_ unable to be comforted; brokenhearted.

Lyre player. Greece.

Even gray Charon, the ferryman of the Styx, forgot to ask his passenger for the price of crossing. The dog Cerberus, the three-headed monster who guards Hades' gate, stopped full in his tracks and listened motionless until Orpheus had passed. As he entered the land of Hades, the pale ghosts came after him like great, uncounted flocks of silent birds. All the land lay hushed as that marvelous voice resounded across the mud and marshes of its dreadful rivers. In the daffodil fields of Elysium, the happy dead sat silent among their flowers. In the farthest corners of the place of punishment, the hissing flames stood still. Accursed Sisyphus,[4] who toils eternally to push a mighty rock uphill, sat down and knew not he was resting. Tantalus, who strains forever after visions of cool water, forgot his thirst and ceased to clutch at the empty air.

The pillared[5] hall of Hades opened before the hero's song. The ranks of long-dead heroes who sit at Hades' board looked up and turned their eyes away from the pitiless form of Hades and his pale, unhappy queen. Grim and unmoving sat the dark king of the dead on his ebony throne, yet the tears shone on his rigid cheeks in the light of his ghastly torches. Even his hard heart, which knew all misery and cared nothing for it, was touched by the love and longing of the music.

At last the minstrel[6] came to an end, and a long sigh like wind in pine trees was heard from the assembled ghosts. Then the king spoke, and his deep voice echoed through his silent land. "Go back to the light of day," he said. "Go quickly while my monsters are stilled by your song. Climb up the steep road to daylight, and never once turn back. The spirit of Eurydice shall follow, but if you look around at her, she will return to me."

Orpheus turned and strode from the hall of Hades, and the flocks of following ghosts made way for him to pass. In vain he searched their ranks for a sight of his lost Eurydice. In vain he listened for the faintest sound behind. The barge of Charon sank to the very gunwales[7] beneath his weight, but no following passenger pressed it lower down. The way from the land of Hades to the upper world is long and hard, far easier to descend than climb. It was dark and misty, full of strange shapes and noises, yet in many places merely black and silent as the tomb. Here Orpheus would stop and listen, but nothing moved behind him. For all he could hear, he was utterly alone. Then he would wonder if the pitiless Hades were deceiving him. Suppose he came up to the light again and Eurydice was not there! Once he had charmed the ferryman and the dreadful monsters, but now they had heard his song. The second time his spell would be less powerful; he could never go again. Perhaps he had lost Eurydice by his readiness to believe.

Every step he took, some instinct told him that he was going farther from his bride. He toiled up the path in reluctance and despair, stopping, listening, sighing, taking a few slow steps, until the dark

---

7. **gunwales** (gun'əlz): upper edges of the sides of a boat.

---

4. **Sisyphus** (sis'ə·fəs).
5. **pillared:** having pillars (columns).
6. **minstrel:** singer.

Vocabulary
ghastly (gast'lē) adj.: horrible; ghostlike.
reluctance (ri·luk'təns) n.: unwillingness.

thinned out into grayness. Up ahead a speck of light showed clearly the entrance to the cavern.

At that final moment Orpheus could bear no more. To go out into the light of day without his love seemed to him impossible. Before he had quite ascended, there was still a moment in which he could go back. Quick in the grayness he turned and saw a dim shade at his heels, as indistinct as the gray mist behind her. But still he could see the look of sadness on her face as he sprung forward saying, "Eurydice!" and threw his arms about her. The shade dissolved in the circle of his arms like smoke. A little whisper seemed to say "Farewell" as she scattered into mist and was gone.

The unfortunate lover hastened back again down the steep, dark path. But all was in vain. This time the ghostly ferryman was deaf to his prayers. The very wildness of his mood made it impossible for him to attain the beauty of his former music. At last, his despair was so great that he could not even sing at all. For seven days he sat huddled together on the gray mud banks, listening to the wailing of the terrible river. The flitting ghosts shrank back in a wide circle from the living man, but he paid them no attention. Only he sat with his eyes on Charon, his ears ringing with the dreadful noise of Styx.

Orpheus arose at last and stumbled back along the steep road he knew so well by now. When he came up to earth again, his song was pitiful but more beautiful than ever. Even the nightingale who mourned all night long would hush her voice to listen as Orpheus sat in some hidden place singing of his lost Eurydice. Men and women he could bear no longer, and when they came to hear him, he drove them away. At last the women of Thrace, maddened by Dionysus and infuriated by Orpheus's contempt, fell upon him and killed him. It is said that as the body was swept down the river Hebrus, the dead lips still moved faintly and the rocks echoed for the last time, "Eurydice." But the poet's eager spirit was already far down the familiar path.

In the daffodil meadows he met the shade of Eurydice, and there they walk together, or where the path is narrow, the shade of Orpheus goes ahead and looks back at his love.

THE SHADE DISSOLVED IN THE CIRCLE OF HIS ARMS LIKE SMOKE.

Vocabulary
ascended (ə·send′id) v.: moved up.

Meet the Writer

Olivia Coolidge

"I Write Because . . . I Almost Have To"

Olivia Coolidge (1908–   ) developed an interest in storytelling at an early age. She recalls:

> 66 My sister and I used to make up fairy stories and tell them to each other . . . . One day we decided that we would make a book out of them, but there was a drawback. . . . [N]either of us [was] very good at our copybooks, and we did not see how we could ever write one whole story, let alone a collection, down on paper. 99

Although Coolidge didn't succeed in writing down her childhood stories, she began to write later in life and received awards and recognition for her work.

Coolidge has used her storytelling gifts mainly to make mythology and history exciting for young readers. She believes strongly in the power of the story:

> 66 A good book should excite, amuse and interest. It should give a sense of seeing as a movie does. In other words, a good book needs imagination and the gift of a good storyteller. I write because I like writing, because I want to write, and because I almost have to. I have a great many things I want to say, ideas I want to express and pictures I want to convey to other people. 99

For Independent Reading

For more myths and ancient stories by Olivia Coolidge, look for *Greek Myths and Legends of the North*. To explore the ancient world from which these stories emerged, check out *The Golden Days of Greece*.

First Thoughts

1. If you were Orpheus, would you have looked back? Why or why not?

Thinking Critically

2. On the basis of this myth, how do you think the ancient Greeks pictured the afterlife?

3. Explain how the same feeling that prompted Orpheus's descent into the underworld also caused him to fail.

4. What lessons about love and death does this myth seem to teach? In this story, which is more powerful, love or death? Why?

Extending Interpretations

5. What does this myth say about the power of music? How does this message compare with your own feelings about music? Be sure to check your Quickwrite notes.

6. Do you think Hades was fair to Orpheus and Eurydice? Tell how you might change the outcome if you were a god or goddess.

Reading Check

Summarize the main events of the myth you have just read by filling in a diagram like the one below. Write two or three sentences in each box.

Beginning

↓

Middle

↓

End

WRITING

Comparing Myths

Use a chart like the one below to compare this myth with "The Origin of the Seasons."

	"Orpheus"	"The Origin of the Seasons"
How the character faces the mystery of death		
How nature responds to the character's grief or joy		
The effect of breaking a taboo or rule		

INTERNET

Projects and Activities

Keyword: LE5 7-6

SKILLS FOCUS

Literary Skills
Analyze a myth.

Reading Skills
Summarize a myth.

Writing Skills
Compare myths.

Clarifying Word Meanings

PRACTICE

Each numbered sentence contains a word from the Word Bank. After reading the sentence, make up a reasonable answer to the question that follows. Write your answer.

Word Bank
inconsolable
ghastly
reluctance
ascended

1. The queen was <u>inconsolable</u>. What just happened to the queen?
2. The king saw a <u>ghastly</u> sight. What did the king see?
3. He ate the meal with some <u>reluctance</u>. What explains his reluctance?
4. The golden cloud <u>ascended</u>. Where was the cloud after it ascended?

Figurative Language

Figurative language describes one thing in terms of something else. Figurative language is not meant to be taken as literally true.

A **simile** is a comparison between two unlike things, using a word such as *like, as, resembles,* or *than*.

EXAMPLE   "... a long sigh <u>like</u> wind in pine trees was heard from the assembled ghosts." [The sigh of the ghosts is compared to the wind in the pines.]

Personification is figurative language in which a nonhuman thing is talked about as if it were human.

EXAMPLE   "... when he sat down to sing, <u>the trees would crowd around to shade him.</u>" [The trees are given the human ability to crowd around someone.]

PRACTICE

Find the figurative language in each sentence. Tell what is compared to what. Then, tell if the comparison is a simile or personification.

1. "All day long he mourned his bride, while birds, beasts, and the earth itself sorrowed with him."
2. "The shade dissolved in the circle of his arms like smoke."

SKILLS FOCUS

Vocabulary Skills
Clarify word meanings, understand figurative language.

Understanding Autobiography

Reading Focus
Distinguishing Fact from Opinion

The power of music is timeless. In the ancient Greek myth, even the trees and rocks gathered around to listen to Orpheus sing. In the following selection, a modern-day violinist describes the importance of music in her life.

When you read an autobiography (the story of a person's life, written by that person), it is important to distinguish facts from opinions. What is stated as a fact by the writer might really be an opinion.

- A fact is a statement that can be proved true. *The myth of Orpheus tells the story of the great musician's love for Eurydice.* You can prove this statement is true by reading the myth. *The story of Orpheus is a myth from ancient Greece.* You can prove this statement is true by referring to a reliable source such as an encyclopedia or a text about mythology.

- An opinion is a belief, judgment, or conclusion based on what the writer thinks. Opinions cannot be proved or disproved. *People have always enjoyed the story of Orpheus.* This opinion is supported by the fact that the story has been retold for hundreds of years; it is not a fact because it cannot be proved that the story was always enjoyed. *Orpheus is the greatest myth in the world.* This is an opinion because it cannot be proved which myth is the greatest. It is not supported by any facts at all.

Anecdote

Personal writing such as an autobiography often includes anecdotes. An **anecdote** is a very brief story told to make a point.

■ In "The Power of Music," Nadja Salerno-Sonnenberg bases her statements on her own experiences and emotions. As you read, notice where she uses facts, opinions, and anecdotes. For example, in her first sentence Nadja says: "This is something I know for a fact: . . ." When you finish the sentence, decide if you agree that it is indeed a fact.

SKILLS FOCUS

Reading Skills
Distinguish fact from opinion; understand anecdote.

Background

Nadja Salerno-Sonnenberg is a violinist who appears in concert in the United States and throughout the world. She was born in Rome, Italy, and moved to the United States with her family in 1969. She writes about her love of music and her career in her autobiography, *Nadja on My Way.*

The Power of Music

from **Nadja on My Way**

Nadja Salerno-Sonnenberg

This is something I know for a fact: You have to work hardest for the thing you love most. And when it's music that you love, you're in for the fight of your life.

It starts when your blood fills with music and you know you can't live without it. Every day brings a challenge to learn as much as possible and to play even better than you did the day before.

You may want to achieve fame and glory, or you may want to play for fun. But whenever you fall in love with music, you'll never sit still again.

Music is more important than we will ever know. Great music can pull you right out of your chair. It can make you cry, or laugh, or feel a way you've never felt before. It can make you remember the first person you loved. . . Music has that power.

Just imagine a world without music. What would you whistle when you walked down the street? How could you make a movie?

How could you have a ball game without an organist leading the crowd when you're down by a run in the ninth?

You could be the most successful doctor in the world, but if you never turn on the radio, never go to a concert, never sing in the shower, never see *The King and I*[1]—then you can't be a total, fulfilled human being. It's impossible.

When you realize how vital music is, you realize a musician's fight is quite a noble, heroic endeavor. It didn't always seem that way to me. There was a time, years ago, when I felt discouraged and it seemed selfish to put so much time into music. Being a musician didn't seem as useful to others as being a surgeon, or even a good politician.

But I came to understand that it's a great, great gift to help people forget their everyday life and be uplifted. And better than uplifted, to be inspired; that's what music can do. It's important to us all, and I'm proud to put mind and muscle into recording, concerts, teaching, and studying: into being a musician.

Emotionally, music has brought me an enormous amount of joy and an enormous amount of despair and frustration. Because of music, I have learned what a battle is. I've won most, but not all—not by a long shot.

---

1. ***The King and I:*** well-known American musical and one of the most widely performed shows in the musical theater. A movie version was made in the 1950s.

Analyzing Autobiography

The Power of Music

Test Practice

1. Which of the following statements best expresses the **main idea** of the selection?

   A   Music is vitally important in life.

   B   It is easy to learn music.

   C   Music is more important than literature.

   D   Everyone loves music.

2. "You could be the most successful doctor in the world, but if you never turn on the radio, never go to a concert . . . then you can't be a total, fulfilled human being." This statement is —

   F   a fact

   G   a lie

   H   an anecdote

   J   an opinion

3. Which of the following statements is an **anecdote**?

   A   "It starts when your blood fills with music and you know you can't live without it."

   B   "Great music can pull you right out of your chair."

   C   "There was a time, years ago, when I felt discouraged and it seemed selfish to put so much time into music."

   D   "It's impossible."

4. Which of the following statements is a **fact**?

   F   "Just imagine a world without music."

   G   "How could you make a movie?"

   H   "[Great music] can make you cry or laugh, or feel a way you've never felt before."

   J   "When you realize how vital music is, you realize a musician's fight is quite a noble, heroic endeavor."

Constructed Response

1. List three **facts** you know about music.

2. Write one **opinion** about music.

3. Tell a personal **anecdote** about music.

SKILLS FOCUS

Reading Skills
Analyze facts and opinions; analyze anecdote.

The Flight of Icarus

Make the Connection
Quickwrite ✏️

Long before the invention of the airplane, people yearned to fly. They dreamed of climbing through the air, dipping, floating, plummeting—as free as birds. They wanted to escape the earth and soar above all its problems. Today, of course, flight is an everyday reality. We travel through the air in everything from helicopters to jumbo jets, from hot-air balloons to space shuttles.

Express your feelings about flying by completing one of these sentences:

- I long to fly like a seagull because . .
- If we couldn't fly . . .

Literary Focus
Morals of Myths

When a young bird flies from the nest for the first time, we say that it is "trying its wings." As you read this myth, notice what happens when a young boy tries his wings. If you think about what the boy attempts to do, what he ignores, and what happens to him as a result, you'll find the morals in the story. A **moral** is a lesson about the right way to behave. The morals in many Greek myths were used to teach children values.

Reading Skills 📖
Making Generalizations

When you make a generalization, you look at evidence and make a broad statement about what it tells you. Someone who says, "All stories contain conflicts" is making a generalization from experience with many stories. As you read these myths, think of generalizations you might make about myths and the kinds of stories they tell.

Daedalus and Icarus
by Antonio Canova.

Museo Correr, Venice, Italy.
© Alinari/Art Resource, NY.

INTERNET
Cross-curricular
Connection
Keyword: LE5 7-6

Literary Skills
Understand
morals in myths.

Reading Skills
Make
generalizations.

Cast of Characters

King Minos (mī′näs′), tyrant of Crete, enemy of Athens.

Theseus (thē′sē·əs), hero from Athens held captive by Minos. Daedalus helped him escape from the labyrinth on Crete.

Daedalus (ded″l·əs), great Athenian architect who built the labyrinth on Crete.

Icarus (ik′ə·rəs), Daedalus's young son.

The Flight of Icarus

retold by Sally Benson

"Minos may control the land and sea, but he does not control the air."

Institute de France, Paris.

Drawing of a man operating a flying machine, from a notebook of Leonardo da Vinci (1452–1519). Da Vinci wrote backward and in reverse to keep his notebooks secret; his words can be read by holding the page up to a mirror.

When Theseus escaped from the labyrinth, King Minos flew into a rage with its builder, Daedalus, and ordered him shut up in a high tower that faced the lonely sea. In time, with the help of his young son, Icarus, Daedalus managed to escape from the tower, only to find himself a prisoner on the island. Several times he tried by bribery to stow away on one of the vessels sailing from Crete, but King Minos kept strict watch over them, and no ships were allowed to sail without being carefully searched.

Daedalus was an ingenious artist and was not discouraged by his failures. "Minos may control the land and sea," he said, "but he does not control the air. I will try that way."

He called his son, Icarus, to him and told the boy to gather up all the feathers he could find on the rocky shore. As thousands of gulls soared over the island, Icarus soon collected a huge pile of feathers. Daedalus then melted some wax and made a skeleton in the shape of a bird's wing. The smallest feathers he pressed into the soft wax and the large ones he tied on with thread. Icarus played about on the beach happily while his father worked, chasing the feathers that blew away in the strong wind that swept the island and sometimes taking bits of the wax and working it into strange shapes with his fingers.

It was fun making the wings. The sun shone on the bright feathers; the breezes ruffled them. When they were finished, Daedalus fastened them to his shoulders and found himself lifted upwards, where he hung poised in the air. Filled with excitement, he made another pair for his son. They were smaller than his own, but strong and beautiful.

Finally, one clear, wind-swept morning, the wings were finished, and Daedalus fastened them to Icarus's shoulders and taught him how to fly. He bade him watch the movements of the birds, how they soared and glided overhead. He pointed out the slow, graceful sweep of their wings as they beat the air steadily, without fluttering. Soon Icarus was sure that he, too, could fly and, raising his arms up and down, skirted over the white sand and even out over the waves, letting his feet touch the snowy foam as the water thundered and broke over the sharp rocks. Daedalus watched him proudly but with misgivings. He called Icarus to his side and, putting his arm round the boy's shoulders, said, "Icarus, my son, we are about to make our flight. No human being has ever traveled through the air before, and I want you to listen carefully to my instructions. Keep at a moderate height, for if you fly too low, the fog and spray will clog your wings, and if you fly too high, the heat will melt the wax that holds them together. Keep near me and you will be safe."

He kissed Icarus and fastened the wings more securely to his son's shoulders. Icarus, standing in the bright sun, the shining wings drooping gracefully from his shoulders, his golden hair wet with spray, and his eyes bright and dark with excitement, looked like a lovely bird. Daedalus's eyes filled with tears, and turning away, he soared into the sky, calling to Icarus to follow. From time to time, he looked back to see that the boy was safe and to note how he managed his wings in his flight. As they flew across the land to test their prowess before setting out across the dark wild sea, plowmen below stopped their work and shepherds gazed in wonder, thinking Daedalus and Icarus were gods.

Father and son flew over Samos and Delos, which lay on their left, and Lebinthus,° which lay on their right. Icarus, beating his wings in joy, felt the thrill of the cool wind on his face and the clear air above and below him. He flew higher and higher up into the blue sky until he reached the clouds. His father saw him and called out in alarm. He tried to follow him, but he was heavier and his wings would not carry him. Up and up Icarus soared, through the soft, moist clouds and out again toward the glorious sun. He was bewitched by a sense of freedom and beat his wings frantically so that they would carry him higher and higher to heaven itself. The blazing sun beat down on the wings and softened the wax. Small feathers fell from the wings and floated softly down, warning Icarus to stay his flight and glide to earth. But the enchanted boy did not notice them until

---

° **Samos** (sā′mäs), **Delos** (dē′läs), and **Lebinthus** (lə·bin′thəs): Greek islands in the Aegean Sea.

the sun became so hot that the largest feathers dropped off and he began to sink. Frantically he fluttered his arms, but no feathers remained to hold the air. He cried out to his father, but his voice was submerged in the blue waters of the sea, which has forever after been called by his name.

Daedalus, crazed by anxiety, called back to him, "Icarus! Icarus, my son, where are you?" At last he saw the feathers floating from the sky, and soon his son plunged through the clouds into the sea. Daedalus hurried to save him, but it was too late. He gathered the boy in his arms and flew to land, the tips of his wings dragging in the water from the double burden they bore. Weeping bitterly, he buried his small son and called the land Icaria in his memory.

Then, with a flutter of wings, he once more took to the air, but the joy of his flight was gone and his victory over the air was bitter to him. He arrived safely in Sicily, where he built a temple to Apollo and hung up his wings as an offering to the god, and in the wings he pressed a few bright feathers he had found floating on the water where Icarus fell. And he mourned for the birdlike son who had thrown caution to the winds in the exaltation of his freedom from the earth.

Meet the Writer

Sally Benson

Stories That Have Rounded Ends

Sally Benson (1900–1972) never studied writing. She didn't have to: It came naturally. After high school she skipped college and went directly to work, first for a bank and then for newspapers. In 1930, she was reviewing thirty-two movies a month for a daily paper when she got an idea for a short story. She sat down, typed it out, and sold it to *The New Yorker*. Dazed by her good fortune, she stopped writing for nine months. But when her money ran out, she wrote another story and sold that one, too. From then on she poured stories out. Benson published one book of Greek and Roman myths, but most of her stories tell the amusing adventures of a thirteen-year-old girl named Judy Graves.

❝ I like stories that have rounded ends and don't rise to climaxes; that aren't all wrapped up in a package with plot. I like them, that's why I write them. ❞

First Thoughts

1. Look back at the sentence you completed for the Quickwrite on page 675. How might Daedalus and Icarus have completed those sentences? ✎

Thinking Critically

2. The myths of Persephone and Orpheus include warnings that the characters fail to listen to. How is the story of Icarus like those myths?

3. How does Icarus try to be something he is not? What **moral lesson** can you learn from his failure?

4. When did you first guess the outcome of the myth? What hints in the story helped you make this prediction?

Extending Interpretations

5. Like other myths, this one explains the names of some geographical features in Greece. What are they, and how did they get there?

6. How do you feel about Icarus? Do you think teenagers today can identify with him? Why or why not?

7. This story seems to suggest that people shouldn't try to "fly too high." We often hear the opposite advice: "Reach for the stars." From your own experience, when do you think taking chances is a good thing? When can it be dangerous?

Reading Check

You're a news reporter on the scene, eager to interview Daedalus when he lands. Write a lead paragraph for the news story, telling what happened, why it happened, whom it happened to, when and where it happened, and how it happened.

WRITING

Analyzing the Myths

Skim through the three myths you have read so far. Take notes on the fantasy elements, the moral lessons, and the explanations of natural phenomena in each myth. Then, use your notes to make a **generalization** about myths. Open your general statement with the words "Myths are stories that . . ." Support your generalization with details from the myths. 📖

INTERNET

Projects and Activities

Keyword: LE5 7-6

Literary Skills
Analyze the moral of a myth.

Reading Skills
Make a generalization.

Writing Skills
Write an analysis of three myths.

Place Names from Greece and Rome

When the first Europeans settled in the land that became the United States, they needed names for their towns and cities. They often looked to ancient Rome and Greece for ideas.

PRACTICE

Use the index in an atlas or other geographical reference book to identify the following:

1. the state or states in which the following American cities are located

2. the location of the original Greek or Roman place known by that name

Athens	Delphi	Olympia
Rome	Syracuse	Sparta

The Fall of Icarus (detail).
Copper engraving.
The Bettmann Archive.

Grammar Link

Adjective Versus Adverb

Many adverbs end in -*ly*. Such adverbs are generally formed by adding the ending -*ly* to adjectives.

EXAMPLES   **proud + *ly:*** "Daedalus watched him <u>proudly</u> but with misgivings."

secure + *ly:* "He . . . fastened the wings more <u>securely</u> to his son's shoulders."

In some sentences, however, it's hard to know which word to use—the adjective or the adverb.

He arrived <u>safe/safely</u> in Sicily.

To solve this problem, ask yourself which word the modifier describes. An adverb modifies a verb, an adjective, or another adverb.

EXAMPLE   **"He arrived <u>safely</u> in Sicily. . . ."**

An adjective modifies a noun or a pronoun.

EXAMPLE   **He had a <u>safe</u> arrival in Sicily.**

For more help, see The Adjective, 1c, and The Adverb, 1h, in the Language Handbook.

PRACTICE

Choose the correct word from each underlined pair.

1. Daedalus flew <u>rapid/rapidly</u> to lift his son from the sea.

2. The accident had happened so <u>sudden/suddenly.</u>

3. Mourning his son, Daedalus sat <u>listless/listlessly</u> on the sand.

4. Icarus was <u>confident/confidently</u> that he could fly higher.

SKILLS FOCUS

Vocabulary Skills
Understand word origins.

Grammar Skills
Distinguish between adjectives and adverbs.

King Midas and the Golden Touch

Make the Connection
Quickwrite ✏️

Greed is a powerful emotion—it can disrupt friendships, spark wars, and topple empires. What happens to greedy people who value money above everything else? Write briefly about a modern-day situation in which greed led to unhappiness or suffering.

Literary Focus
Irony

Irony is the difference between what you say and what you mean or between what's supposed to happen and what does happen. When you say "How graceful" to someone who's just fallen flat on his face, you're using irony. When a firehouse burns down, that's irony. It's a contrast between expectation and reality. This myth is about an ironic situation: There's a big difference between what Midas expects to happen and what does happen.

Reading Skills 📖
Using Prior Knowledge: Building on What You Know

Get together with a group of classmates. Brainstorm to find answers to the questions about greed on the map below. You may want to add questions—and answers—of your own.

Greed

Definition:

Questions about greed:
What is wrong with it?
What is an example of it?
Who is greedy?
What is its opposite?

One of a pair of bracelets with ram's-head finials (c. 330–300 B.C.). Greek. Said to be from near Thessaloniki. Gold, rock crystal (8 cm wide x 7.8 cm high).
The Metropolitan Museum of Art, Harris Brisbane Dick Fund, 1937 (37.11.11-.12). Photograph © 1993 The Metropolitan Museum of Art.

SKILLS FOCUS

Literary Skills
Understand irony.

Reading Skills
Use prior knowledge.

KING MIDAS

and the Golden

Touch

retold by
Pamela Oldfield

Brooch in the form of a pediment with Pegasus figures
(c. 340–320 B.C.). Greek. Gold (length: 7.8 cm).
The Metropolitan Museum of Art, Rogers Fund, 1906 (06.11.59).
Photograph © 1993 The Metropolitan Museum of Art.

Many years ago in the land of Lydia, there was a beautiful garden. Roses of every shade grew there, and on warm summer nights the air was heavy with their fragrance. The garden belonged to a palace, and the palace was the home of a king whose name was Midas. He was, it is true, rather greedy, but on the whole no better and no worse than any other man. Midas had a loving wife and a daughter he adored, but he was still discontented. He wanted to be the most powerful king in the world; he wanted everyone to envy him.

One day as he was walking through the palace garden, he was startled to see a pair of legs sticking out from beneath his favorite rosebush. The strange thing about these legs was that they had hoofs instead of feet. The king stared at them for a moment and then called for the gardener's boy.

"What do you make of that?" he asked. The boy parted the branches of the rosebush and peered through.

"It's a satyr, Your Majesty," he reported, trying not to laugh. "I think it's Silenus."

The satyrs were strange, mischievous creatures—half man, half beast—who roamed the world in search of adventure. Midas frowned, angry that somebody should be sleeping in his garden.

The boy ran off to fetch the gardener, and between them they dragged Silenus from under the rosebush and pulled him to his feet. Silenus grinned foolishly. He was holding an empty wine jar.

"You are trespassing in my garden," Midas told him severely. "What have you to say for yourself?" The old satyr shrugged.

"I got lost, so I sat down for a drink," he told the king, looking quite unrepentant.

"Disgraceful," said Midas. "I shall send word to your master at once." Silenus began to look worried, for his master was the god Dionysus, who was not only powerful but also quick-tempered.

"I beg you not to do that," he cried. "He will be angry with me. Suppose I make a bargain with you? If you will overlook my foolishness, I will entertain you with strange and wonderful tales, better than any you have heard before."

Midas agreed and the satyr stayed on in the palace, delighting the king with wonderful accounts of his adventures. At the end of the week, Midas sent the satyr back to Dionysus. The god was very fond of Silenus, despite his many faults, and was pleased to see him safe and sound. He wanted to thank Midas for taking care of the old satyr and offered the king any gift he cared to name.

Any gift he cared to name! What a marvelous opportunity! He pondered for a whole day and a night and then asked Dionysus if he could make a wish. The god agreed and Midas asked for the power to turn whatever he touched into gold. The god granted his wish, and Midas was jubilant.

"Imagine a king with a golden touch!" he cried. "I shall be the wealthiest and most powerful king in the world."

The king began to experiment with his new gift. He hurried into the garden and touched one of the flowers. At once, the whole bush turned to gold. He went from bush to bush, touching all the blooms, until the entire garden had turned to gold. Then he looked around him. Suddenly Midas felt doubtful. Gone were the colors and the glorious perfume. The garden was still and lifeless.

Inside the palace, the king called for a goblet of wine. As soon as it touched his lips the wine turned to gold and he could not drink.

A terrible thought occurred to him.

"What will happen when I eat?" he wondered. With trembling fingers he reached out to take an apple from a bowl of fruit. As soon as he touched it, the apple turned to gold.

"What have I done?" he whispered. "If I cannot eat or drink I shall die!" He knew that he had made a terrible mistake and decided to beg Dionysus to take back his gift. "I will go to him at once," he cried, but his decision came too late. At that very moment his daughter ran into the room.

"Stay away from me!" Midas shouted, but she took no notice. She threw her arms around him—and was turned to gold. His daughter was now a gleaming but lifeless statue. The king stared at her in horror.

"What have I done to you?" he cried, kneeling beside her. His grief was so great that nobody could console him. He hurried to the palace of Dionysus and threw himself at the god's feet.

"Forgive my stupid greed!" he begged. "Tell me what I must do to save my child. I will do anything you say."

Dionysus told him to find the river Pactolus and wash himself in its waters. Midas set off at once. He went alone and walked for many miles over rough and stony ground.

When he reached the river he found it flowing deep and strong. Midas waded straight in. He was instantly swept away by the current. When at last he managed to reach the shore, he wondered if the curse had indeed been washed from him. Looking back, he saw that the river now gleamed and sparkled in the sun. On the riverbed tiny nuggets of gold lay among the pebbles. Dionysus had spoken truthfully, and the terrible power had left him. Joyfully Midas made his way home.

As he approached the palace, Midas's daughter ran to greet him. He lifted her into his arms and carried her into the garden. Midas was overjoyed to hear her laughter once again, and he sighed happily as he breathed in the fragrance of the flowers.

"I have learned my lesson," he said softly, "and I am content."

Summarizing a Text

Reading Focus
Summarizing

To **summarize** "King Midas and the Golden Touch," you might write this:

King Midas is very rich, but he is greedy and is not content with what he has. One day Midas helps a follower of the god Dionysus, and in return the god says that Midas can have any gift he wants. King Midas asks that anything he touch be turned to gold. He is delighted with his new power until he turns his beloved daughter into a gold statue. Midas begs Dionysus to forgive his greed, undo the gift, and restore his daughter. The god agrees, and King Midas learns to be content with what he has.

A **summary** is a short restatement of the major events or main ideas of a text. A summary of a text is much shorter than the original, and it is generally not as interesting. To summarize a story, such as the myth of King Midas, you retell all the main events and explain cause and effect. To summarize an informational text, such as the magazine article that follows, you restate the main ideas and important details that support those main ideas.

■ As you read "The Funeral Banquet of King Midas," jot down anything you think might be a main idea. These notes will help you summarize the article when you have finished reading it.

SKILLS FOCUS

Reading Skills
Summarize a text.

Checklist for a Summary of Informational Texts

1. Begin the summary with the **title** and **author** of the text.
2. State the **topic** of the text.
3. List the **main ideas,** in the **order** in which they occur.
4. Include important **supporting details** for the main ideas.
5. Put **quotation marks** around any words from the text that are quoted exactly.

Vocabulary Development

You'll learn these words as you read the magazine article.

archaeologists (är′kē·äl′ə·jists) *n.:* scientists who study the culture of the past, especially by excavating ancient sites. *After years of digging, the archaeologists were thrilled to find the hidden tomb.*

excavating (eks′kə·vāt′iŋ) *v.* used as *n.:* uncovering or exposing by digging. *It was his seventh season excavating the burial site.*

avalanche (av′ə·lanch′) *n.:* mass of loosened snow, earth, rocks, and so on, suddenly and swiftly sliding down a mountain. *They did not want their digging to cause an avalanche that would again bury the tomb.*

interior (in·tir′ē·ər) *n.:* inner part of anything. The opposite of *interior* is *exterior*. *They were amazed at the condition of the objects in the interior of the tomb.*

from Muse *magazine*

THE FUNERAL BANQUET OF KING MIDAS

John Fleischman

Hercules, they say, could kill a lion with his bare hands. The great Achilles, the story goes, could only be wounded on the heel. And King Midas turned everything he touched to gold. Well, Hercules and Achilles may have been myths, but there really was a King Midas. Recently we even found out what they served at his funeral.

The real King Midas lived in what is now central Turkey 2,700 years ago, in a kingdom called Phrygia. We know there was a King Midas because his neighbors, the mighty Assyrian kings to the east, wrote about him.

They called him Mita. The Greeks, who lived west of Phrygia, also knew about him. The Greek historian Herodotus said Midas was the first "barbarian" (or non-Greek) to dedicate an offering to Apollo at his shrine at Delphi. After he died, the Greek poets turned the man into a legend, giving him the curse of a golden touch and a shameful pair of donkey's ears.[1] But we were

---

1. **donkey's ears:** In the Greek myth, sometime after King Midas recovers from his golden touch, the god Apollo gets angry at him for foolish behavior and gives him donkey's ears.

reintroduced to the real King Midas when archaeologists dug up his tomb in 1957.

Rodney Young, an archaeologist at the University of Pennsylvania Museum, was searching for Midas's tomb in the ruins of Gordion, the ancient capital of Phrygia. It was Young's seventh season excavating the city, and he was exploring the base of a massive burial mound. To explore the mound without destroying it, he brought in Turkish coal miners to dig a horizontal shaft. After tunneling 68 meters (about as far as 68 people holding hands would reach), the miners struck a smooth stone wall. When they broke through, a wave of rubble spilled out, blocking the tunnel. Young had them clear as much as they could without bringing down the clay ceiling. Beyond the rubble was a rough wall of heavy logs. The men sliced through that and unleashed another stone avalanche. Once it was cleared away, they found an inner wall of beautifully crafted boxwood and cedar.

Young carefully sawed open a hatch, pushed his light into the interior, and found himself staring into the eye sockets of King Midas. The king was facing him, laid out on what Young thought was a bed (it turned out to be an open coffin carved from a single tree) in a tomb stuffed with ancient textiles, wooden furniture, iron tripods, and bronze vessels—but not a speck of gold.

Vocabulary

archaeologists (är′kē·äl′ə·jists) *n.:* scientists who study the culture of the past, especially by excavating ancient sites.

excavating (eks′kə·vāt′iŋ) *v.* used as *n.:* uncovering or exposing by digging.

avalanche (av′ə·lanch′) *n.:* mass of loosened snow, earth, rocks, and so on, suddenly and swiftly sliding down a mountain.

interior (in·tir′ē·ər) *n.:* the inner part of anything. The opposite of *interior* is *exterior.*

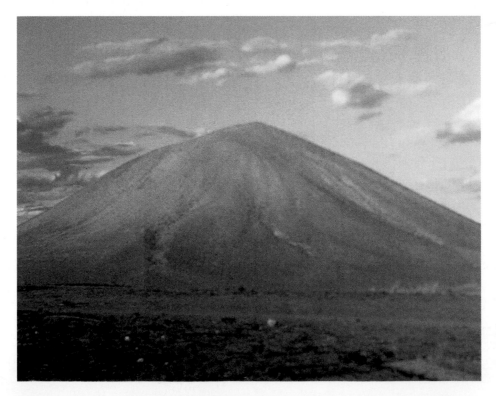

The 49-meter (about 160 feet) tall burial mound of Midas. It was almost 3,000 years before anyone bothered to check if there was anything inside.

Inside the Tomb

This drawing of the inside of the tomb was made before anything was moved, and all the objects were photographed in place.

Near the front of Midas's collapsed sarcophagus, some bronze fibulae pour out of a torn sack. (Fibulae are sort of like ancient safety pins.) People must have thought they'd come in handy in the underworld, since Midas's sack held about 100 of them.

Carved wooden panels from the front of the buffet tables. On the right is a fallen bronze bowl.

Archaeologist Ellen Kohler, who also worked on the dig, says the skeleton of King Midas rested on what looked "like a million blankets," with a cover of thick felt over uncounted layers of fine-woven linens in purple, white, and pink. When the tomb was first opened, there was a strong, clean smell of freshly cut wood. "It smelled like the inside of a cedar chest," she says. "The wood still looked freshly cut."

The archaeologists were astounded to find cloth and wood in such good condition because these materials usually rot quickly. Amazingly, the cloth and wood in Midas's

No, it's not an elephant tusk. It's the wooden leg of a table that has collapsed, spilling more bronze bowls onto the floor.

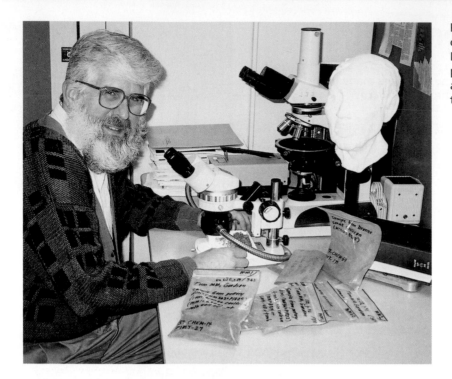

Patrick McGovern with bags of sludge from Midas's tomb. In front of him is a white plaster bust of the king—a reconstruction based on the shape of his skull.

tomb were saved by the decaying body of the king. Midas had been sealed under a burial mound of clay 49 meters high, making the tomb both dry and nearly airtight. As the bacteria that cause decay worked on his body, they also used up nearly all the oxygen in the tomb. Lack of oxygen slowed down the decay process so much that the textiles and wooden furniture were preserved for centuries. Unfortunately, once moist outside air entered the tomb, the textiles crumbled and turned a muddy brown within days.

But how could anyone be sure this was the tomb of Midas and not of some other Phrygian big shot? The answer has to do with that inner wall of boxwood and cedar. You could still see tree rings in the wood—wide ones the tree added in good years and narrow ones the tree added in bad years. Peter Kunihom of Cornell University was able to match the pattern of wide and narrow rings to the patterns in trees whose age was known. In 1996, he said that the timbers were cut no later than 718 B.C., which was when the Assyrians said King "Mita" ruled in Phrygia.

But something had been overlooked in the excitement of the big discovery. At the bottom of all those bronze cauldrons and cups there was a dry, powdery sludge.[2] The powder was poured into paper bags, which were rolled shut, labeled, and shipped back to the University of Pennsylvania Museum of Archaeology in Philadelphia. There they sat on a shelf for 40 years.

Recently, Elizabeth Simpson of the Bard Graduate Study Center in New York, an expert on the Midas-tomb furniture, wondered what had happened to the sludge. She called Patrick McGovern, an archaeo-chemist at the Penn museum. Could he find

2. **sludge** *n.:* any heavy, muddy, or slimy deposit or waste.

the bags and run modern tests on their contents?

McGovern climbed the museum stairs and found the bags on a bookshelf in Ellen Kohler's office. Examining the powdery remains, he realized that there were two different kinds of sludge, one from the tomb's big cauldrons and pots and another from the drinking vessels. He guessed that the cauldrons were used for meat, and the vessels for alcoholic beverages. Both sludges had thoroughly dried over the centuries, but there was a good chance the food molecules hadn't broken down and could still be identified.

McGovern did some of the analysis himself, but also sent samples to several chemical laboratories that had more advanced equipment. The chemists used technology that wasn't available to Rodney Young in 1957. When the results of the tests came back, McGovern had the menu for Midas's funeral banquet.

They started with barbecue, either sheep or goat roasted over an open fire and basted with olive oil, honey, and spices. Part of the barbecued meat was for sacrifice, probably to the Phrygians' most powerful goddess, Matar. The rest became the main ingredient of a stew. The Phrygians added beans (probably lentils), more olive oil and honey, wine, anise or fennel, and more spices. The second sludge turned out to be from an alcoholic drink called a *kykeon* by the Greeks; we'd call it a punch. It's a mixture of grape wine, barley beer, and a fermented honey drink known as mead. Part of this punch would have been poured out on the ground or an altar stone as an offering to Matar. All the cauldrons, bowls, and dishes that were packed away so carefully inside the tomb were used for offerings to the goddess. The food and drink were part of the religious ceremony for the dead king.

So how did Midas end up with a golden touch? "I think Greek myth is really hard to fathom," says archaeologist Elizabeth Simpson. She believes that any king who was as wealthy as Midas would have been seen as a great man, especially by the poorer Greeks along the coast. Long after his death, his great burial mound at Gordion would have impressed them. "It took a long time and a lot of precise engineering to build that," says Dr. Simpson. "I say the Gordion earthwork is the counterpart of an Egyptian pyramid."

But great monuments don't guarantee great fame. Aside from King Tut, how many pharaohs can you name? How many of the great kings of Assyria? How many emperors of Persia? But if you were asked for the kings of little Phrygia, you would remember at least one "golden" name.

Summarizing a Text

THE FUNERAL BANQUET OF KING MIDAS

Test Practice

1. How do we know there really was a King Midas?
   - **A** The Greeks made him into a legend.
   - **B** He lived 2,700 years ago in Phrygia.
   - **C** His neighbors, the Assyrians, wrote about him.
   - **D** He turned everything he touched into gold.

2. Why do scientists think they found the tomb of King Midas, and not of someone else?
   - **F** Tree rings in the wood date the tomb to the time of King Midas's rule.
   - **G** The skeleton looks just like pictures we have of King Midas.
   - **H** The tomb is filled with lots and lots of gold.
   - **J** The tomb contains the kinds of food that King Midas liked to eat.

3. What happened to the cloth in King Midas's tomb once the tomb was opened?
   - **A** It was preserved in a museum.
   - **B** It was worn in a play based on the myth.
   - **C** Historians used it to learn about customs of the time.
   - **D** It crumbled and turned brown within days.

4. How do scientists think the myth of the "golden touch" might have developed?
   - **F** King Midas was a wealthy king and impressed his neighbors.
   - **G** King Midas had a palace made entirely of gold.
   - **H** The kingdom of Phrygia was famous for its gold mines.
   - **J** The sand in Phrygia glows golden in the sunlight.

Constructed Response

Look back at the notes you took while reading "The Funeral Banquet of King Midas." Then, write a brief **summary** of the magazine article. List only the main ideas and the most important supporting details.

SKILLS FOCUS

Reading Skills
Summarize an article.

Vocabulary Development

Using Context Clues

When you don't understand a word, you can often find clues to its meaning in the surrounding passages. For an example, here is a passage from "The Funeral Banquet of King Midas" that includes a word from the Word Bank.

Word Bank

archaeologists
excavating
avalanche
interior

> "After he died, the Greek poets turned [King Midas] into a legend, giving him the curse of a golden touch and a shameful pair of donkey's ears. But we were reintroduced to the real King Midas when <u>archaeologists</u> dug up his tomb in 1957."

The word *but* is a context clue that lets you know two things are being contrasted. Poets tell "legends," but archaeologists tell about the "real" king; therefore, archaeologists are probably scientists. Since archaeologists *dug* up the tomb of an ancient king, you could figure out that they are scientists who dig up things buried in the ground.

PRACTICE

For each passage below from "The Funeral Banquet of King Midas," give the meaning of the underlined word, identify the context clues, and explain how they reveal that meaning.

1. "It was Young's seventh season <u>excavating</u> the city, and he was exploring the base of a massive burial mound. To explore the mound without destroying it, he brought in Turkish coal miners to dig a horizontal shaft."

2. "When they broke through, a wave of rubble spilled out, blocking the tunnel. Young had them clear as much as they could without bringing down the clay ceiling. Beyond the rubble was a rough wall of heavy logs. The men sliced through that and unleashed another stone <u>avalanche</u>."

3. "Once [the rubble] was cleared away, they found an inner wall of beautifully crafted boxwood and cedar.

   "Young carefully sawed open a hatch, pushed his light into the <u>interior</u>, and found himself staring into the eye sockets of King Midas."

SKILLS FOCUS

Vocabulary Skills
Clarify word meanings by context.

Elements of Literature
Folk Tales *by* Virginia Hamilton

TELLING TALES

Who tells stories where you live? Is it your mother or father? Is it your uncle or aunt? your cousin or your friend? Is it you?

"Nobody I know tells stories," I answered when my English teacher asked that question. "At my house, everybody just talks."

Now I realize that both my father and mother were storytellers. I simply did not recognize that what they were "talking" were stories.

Mother would begin a story with "That reminds me" or "I remember when." Once she began, "That reminds me of the time all of the Boston ivy fell from Mrs. Pinton's house."

"All of it? All at once—when did that happen?" my oldest sister, Nina, asked. And Mother was off and running with the tale about "the day the ivy fell."

My mom and dad loved telling stories and remembering their pasts. We don't know for certain, but perhaps folk tales—"tells"—began in a similar way.

How Folk Tales Grow

Folk tales are stories passed on by word of mouth, often over many centuries. Each time the tale is told, it is changed a bit because no two people tell a story exactly the same way.

Some of these folk tales travel; that is, as they are told and retold, they move out of their original environments into other times and other places. Although traditional folk tales reflect the particular culture and people that created them, common features, called **motifs,** can be found in folk stories from many parts of the world. You'll find that many folk tales include motifs like grateful beasts, tests of the hero, magic, false parents, fairy godmothers, and brave youngest sons and daughters.

Handed down from generation to generation, told over and over again, these "tells" become familiar stories—"They say the people could fly . . ."; "Once upon a time . . ." They have become tales of the folks.

American Folk Tales: Keeping Cultures Alive

When the first Europeans came with their folk tales, the Native Americans already had an elaborate and rich folklore tradition. Other folk tales traveled to the New World from other countries. For example, Africans who were brought to America as slaves carried with them their unique "folk-telling" traditions. Over generations they passed on tales about their lives on the plantations and about their relationships with the white men and women who held them as slaves.

In fact, the African American storyteller developed the animal tale into a

SKILLS FOCUS

Literary Skills
Understand folk tales.

highly individual form. In this animal tale the social order of the plantation is broken down into animal elements, which symbolize the people in the plantation community. The African folk-tale tellers who were slaves fantasized about freedom and so developed another kind of folk tale, an **escape story,** about flying away from slavery.

In America, people from Ireland, Denmark, Germany, France, Italy, Poland, Turkey, the Middle East, Russia, China, Japan, Korea, Vietnam, Cambodia, the Philippines, Brazil, Haiti, Puerto Rico, Nigeria, Jamaica, and practically everywhere else have told their children folk tales from their old homelands. These stories, as well as their dances, songs, and folk art, help these people stay together and keep their beliefs and cultures alive.

Folk Tales and Community

Some folk tales are simple stories and others are complex. But the basic situation of the tale teller weaving his or her magic for a community of listeners is found everywhere, in every society.

For generation after generation, folk tales keep alive and close what we regard as important. They reveal who we are. As they instruct us in living, they show us our weaknesses and strengths, our fears and joys, our nightmares and wishes. Folk tales are our self-portraits.

"Tells" and Tale Givers

All over America there are folk-tale-telling festivals, in which tale tellers stand up and give "tells" to the listeners. In fact, storytelling festivals take place every year all around the world—from Scotland to South Africa. In the United States, festivals occur in more than thirty states.

Storytelling is an ancient and wonderful custom. I have grown out of the tale-giving tradition and so, perhaps, have some of you. As you read these folk tales from around the world, think about those early folk-tale tellers who committed tales to memory in order to tell them aloud. Try to picture what those early tellings must have been like—imagine the smoky underground kivas of the Pueblos, the dusty village squares in Nigeria.

Sitting or standing there, surrounded by the community of listeners, the teller calls softly, "Time was when the animals could talk . . ." The listeners respond. They lean forward, absolutely quiet now, eager to hear, to be entertained, to learn.

Practice

All cultures have their own folk tales. Do you have any favorites? Maybe you are familiar with "Little Red Riding Hood" or "Cinderella." Make a list of all the folk tales you can remember. What makes these tales memorable?

Oni and the Great Bird

Make the Connection
Quickwrite ✏

Superman, Wonder Woman, and Batman are popular action heroes. What makes these characters superheroes? How are they different from real-life heroes? Write briefly about what you think makes someone a hero in real life.

Literary Focus
Motifs in Folk Tales: Superheroes

Features that are repeated in stories throughout the world are called **motifs** (mō·tēfs′). From your reading, you may remember the evil witch, the poor stepdaughter, the man-eating monster, the quest to save a kingdom. All these are popular motifs in storytelling. Another popular motif—the larger-than-life **superhero**—appears in the Yoruban folk tale you are about to read.

Reading Skills 📖
Summarizing

A lot happens in the next story. After you read it, you'll be asked to write a summary. To prepare for your summary, as you read take notes on the main characters, the conflict, the time and place, the main events, and the resolution.

Vocabulary Development

You'll learn these words as you read "Oni and the Great Bird."

implored (im·plôrd′) v.: asked or begged. *The old man implored Oni to do nothing dangerous.*

commenced (kə·menst′) v.: began. *Oni commenced to sing only when the eagle flew near.*

invincible (in·vin′sə·bəl) adj.: unbeatable. *No one could beat invincible Oni.*

hovered (huv′ərd) v.: hung in the air. *The great bird flew in and hovered above them.*

impostor (im·päs′tər) n.: person who pretends to be someone or something that he or she is not. *The hunter who claimed to have done Oni's deeds was an imposter.*

Background
Literature and Music

"Oni and the Great Bird" is a folk tale of the Yoruba, a West African people known for their storytelling and musical talents. In the tale, short songs, or chants, are set off from the rest of the story. When Yoruban stories are told in ritual gatherings, these lines are chanted to the accompaniment of drums called gangans. These drums are used to imitate the sounds and patterns of Yoruban speech.

Oni and the Great Bird

Yoruban, retold by
Abayomi Fuja

Yoruban water-spirit mask (early twentieth century).
Ijebu region, Nigeria.

The Fine Arts Museum of San Francisco, Museum purchase by
exchange, 76.12.1.

There was once a strange boy called Oni who was born wearing a pair of boots. As Oni grew, the boots grew also. When he was a boy of eighteen years of age, war broke out between his people and another village. It was during the battle that Oni made a second discovery about himself, which separated him from his fellow men and made him different. The enemy arrows did not seem to harm him. Many pierced his body, which in the ordinary course of events should have slain him. The other young men noticed this too. They already regarded Oni as strange because of his wonderful boots, but when they discovered that he could not be killed, they were afraid to have him near them. When he returned from the war, several people tried to kill him in various ways but without any success. Finding this did not work, it was decided to find an excuse to banish him. He was accused of setting a house on fire in the village, and although Oni had nothing to do with the fire, he was found guilty and banished.

Oni wandered alone on foot for a long time. One afternoon he came to the banks of a great river, and finding an empty canoe and feeling tired of walking, he got into the boat and made his way downstream. Towards evening, when it was growing dark, Oni reached a town and decided to pull into the bank and spend the night there. There were the sounds of many bells being rung and people seemed to be in a hurry. Oni tied up the canoe and climbed the bank, and as he did so, he met an old man. "Good evening, my friend. My name is Oni. I am a stranger to your town and have nowhere to spend the night. Will you take me to your house?" Oni asked the old man.

"Yes, certainly, come along with me, but we must go quickly because the bells are ringing and it is growing dusk," replied the old man.

"What is the name of your town and why do your people ring bells on the approach of darkness?" asked Oni.

"People call this place Ajo, but hurry up, we must get indoors. I will explain the bells to you when we are inside," replied the old man.

When they reached the old man's house, they found his people waiting anxiously for him at the door. The bells had now stopped ringing and they were hurried inside and the door was securely fastened.

"Now," said the old man, "sit down and eat with us and I will explain. For many years now we, the people of Ajo, have been troubled by the nightly arrival of a giant eagle. We call it Anodo. It always appears on the approach of darkness and stays until the approach of dawn. Anybody who is unfortunate enough to be out of doors at the time of its appearance is sure to be killed by it. You were very fortunate, young man, to reach Ajo before darkness. Our king has ordered the ringing of bells to warn the people to return to their homes and lock the doors. None of us knows where the eagle comes from or where it goes when it leaves us at dawn. It is a terrible curse, and in the past it has killed many of our people."

The old man had hardly finished speaking when Oni heard the sound of great wings flapping over the house. It sounded like a great wind, and the windows and doors shook in their frames.

"It must be a very great bird," remarked Oni. After Oni had fed, the old man gave him a mat and a cloth and he lay down to sleep in the corner of the room. Sleep would not come to Oni, however, for he heard the constant noise of the great eagle's wings as it flew to and fro over Ajo.

When morning had come and the eagle had departed, Oni thanked the old man for his kindness and set out to find the king of Ajo and to ask for an audience.[1] It was granted.

"My name is Oni and I am a stranger to your town. I have come to offer my services in helping to rid this town of the eagle Anodo," said Oni.

"And what makes you think you will succeed where so many others have tried and failed?" asked the king.

"I have certain powers and juju,"[2] said Oni.

"So had the others. One by one all my hunters have tried and have been killed or carried off by Anodo. Strangers have come from time to time to offer their services, but they too have perished. It is some time now since anybody has tried to kill Anodo, and I have issued orders to my remaining hunters not to try, as enough of them have been killed already," said the king.

"Have you ever offered a reward to anybody who could succeed in killing the bird?" asked Oni.

"Indeed, yes. The man who succeeds will have half my kingdom. I made that offer long ago," replied the king.

---

1. **audience** *n.:* here, formal interview with a person of high rank.
2. **juju** *n.:* magic charm used by some West African peoples; the magic of such charms.

Yoruban mounted-warrior veranda post, carved by Olowe of Ise (twentieth century).
New Orleans Museum of Art: Museum Purchase: Ella West Freeman Foundation Matching Fund 70.20.

"Then I will try tonight," answered Oni, and he paid his respects to the king and departed.

Oni returned to the old man's house and told him what had happened and of his intention to challenge Anodo. The old man was very frightened and implored him to give up the idea, for he would only perish and perhaps all those in the house too. But Oni was not frightened. He took his bow and arrows and knives and examined them carefully.

It seemed ages to Oni before he heard the bells ringing. Never had he known a longer day in his life. The old man was uneasy and his people were almost hostile towards Oni. When they heard the bells ringing at last, they lost no time in fastening the doors and windows and ordered Oni to lie down on his mat and keep quiet.

Presently they heard the noise of a great wind, which heralded the approach of Anodo. Soon the great wings were above the house. Oni waited till the great bird was overhead and then he commenced to sing:

Tonight Oni will be at war with Anodo,
The eagle whose talons are sharper than
    knives,
For now the knives of nature and man will
    meet.
Oni is invincible; his knife is sharp.

Anodo heard the challenge as he hovered over the house, and circling slowly round, he came back and sang:

Ah, fortune, I have found a victim
    tonight,
I have lived many months without a kill,
Will the singer come out and feel the
    sharpness

Of my talons and of my beak? It will
    take me
A moment to tear him to pieces. Come out.

All the people in the house were terrified. They seized Oni and threw him out of the house, fearing the vengeance of Anodo on them all.

As they threw Oni out into the road, Anodo swooped down and, seizing him in his talons, drew him upwards. Oni slashed the eagle in the chest with his knife and the eagle dropped him with a scream. Oni fell to the ground, dazed. He picked himself up as the huge bird descended once again. He had time to use his bow and discharge an arrow into Anodo before the wounded bird beat him to the ground with his great wings and pecked him severely. Again Oni's knife tore at the eagle, and he buried it twice in Anodo. Slowly the eagle beat his great wings and rose slowly into the air; then he hovered for a last terrible dive on Oni. Oni watched him and, putting an arrow in his bow, took aim. The great bird hovered; then with a terrible noise he tore down on the boy, gathering speed as he came. There was a great roar of wind as he came down. Oni discharged a second arrow, then another and another in quick succession, but still the bird came on. A moment later it had hit Oni and knocked him over. The boy rolled over, a thousand lights dancing before his eyes; then all went blank, and he felt himself sinking down and down into a bottomless pit. He was knocked unconscious and had not seen that the great

Vocabulary

implored (im·plôrd′) *v.*: asked or begged.
commenced (kə′·menst′) *v.*: began.
invincible (in·vin′sə·bəl) *adj.*: unbeatable.
hovered (huv′ərd) *v.*: hung in the air.

bird was already dead before it struck him. Its great wings swept the boy to one side, and it plunged on into a cotton tree, which snapped like a twig and came crashing down to bury the eagle and Oni under a mass of leaves.

When Oni recovered, he felt very weak, and it was all he could do to free himself from the great wing of the dead Anodo and the cotton tree leaves. As he struggled, one

Epa cult mask.
Founders Society Purchase, Friends of African Art Fund. Photograph © 1995 The Detroit Institute of Arts Accession number 77.71.

of his magic boots came off and remained stuck beneath the dead bird. He was very weak and with great difficulty staggered along till he reached the edge of the river; then Oni fainted again.

Early next morning the people came out to see the dead Anodo lying in the broken cotton tree. There was great rejoicing and drumming and the king soon appeared with his chiefs to view the wonderful sight. "Who is the great man who killed Anodo?" he asked. One of his hunters stepped forward and, prostrating[3] himself on the ground, claimed that he was responsible for the deed.

"Then you will be rewarded generously, for I have promised to give half my kingdom to the man who killed Anodo and it is yours," replied the king.

There was great rejoicing and dancing and the hunter was carried to the king's palace and feasted. A very bedraggled figure then appeared; his clothes were torn and one of his boots was missing. It was Oni.

"Ah," said the king, "here is the stranger who calls himself Oni and who came yesterday to announce his intention of killing the eagle. You come too late, my friend, I fear."

"I killed Anodo. This man is an impostor and a liar," said Oni.

There was whispering between the king and his chiefs. At last he said, "Very well, you claim to have killed Anodo. What proof have you got to offer?"

---

3. **prostrating** (präs′trāt′iŋ) *v.* used as *adj.:* throwing oneself on the ground to show humility and submission, a traditional gesture of respect toward rulers in many cultures.

Vocabulary
impostor (im·päs′tər) *n.:* person who pretends to be someone or something that he or she is not.

"You see my condition," replied Oni, "but if you require further proof, send your men out to clear away the dead eagle and the broken cotton tree. Somewhere underneath you will find one of my boots."

The king ordered his men to go at once and search for the boot. After some little time the men returned. They carried Oni's magic boot. "We found it underneath the dead eagle's wing," they announced to the king.

"Now if you are still undecided and disbelieve my story, will you ask everybody to try on the boot and see if it fits," said Oni.

The king ordered everybody to try to see if they could fit the boot to their feet. Strange to relate, although it looked a perfectly normal boot, nobody could manage to put it on. When they had all tried without success, the boot was placed before the king and Oni stepped forward and said:

> Boot from Heaven—boot from Heaven,
> Go on to your master's foot.

Immediately, the boot started to move from before the king and fitted itself onto Oni's foot of its own accord. The people and the king were convinced of the truth of Oni's claims and marveled greatly and were very delighted and grateful for his brave deed. The dishonest hunter was taken out and executed, and Oni received the promised reward.

That night, for the first time for many years, the bells of Ajo did not sound the curfew. Instead, the streets were full of happy, dancing people.

Meet the Writer

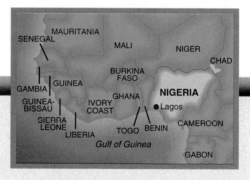

Abayomi Fuja

At Home in Two Worlds

Abayomi Fuja, a Yoruban, was born in Nigeria. When he was growing up, Fuja was taught by British missionaries, so he learned English and studied European stories at school. As an adult he decided to celebrate his Yoruban heritage by collecting the traditional folk tales of his people. He devoted six years to recording tales like "Oni and the Great Bird." Though written in English, they remain true to the style and spirit of the original Yoruban folk tales. By retelling these traditional African stories in English, Fuja brings together the two worlds in which he grew up.

For Independent Reading

If you liked "Oni and the Great Bird," you might want to explore the other stories in *Fourteen Hundred Cowries,* the book it's taken from. (A cowrie is a glossy shell that the Yoruba use to signal certain ideas. For instance, two shells placed together means friendship; two shells placed apart means hostility.)

First Thoughts

1. Do you think Oni is a hero? Be sure to check your notes for the Quickwrite on page 698. ✏️

Thinking Critically

2. Look back at Oni's song to Anodo before the fight (page 702). What do you think the song shows about Oni's **character**?

3. What makes Oni an example of the **superhero motif** in folk tales? How is Oni like the action heroes in comics and movies?

4. The magic boots set Oni apart, making him "strange" and "different." What lesson might this tale teach Yoruban children about how to behave toward people who are different from them?

5. Think about what happens to the hunter who tries to take credit for killing Anodo. What does his fate tell you about the beliefs of the Yoruba?

Extending Interpretations

6. Oni was an outsider—even among his own people. Do you think that heroes in real life are usually outsiders, or are they usually part of the group? Give examples to support your point of view.

7. In this story Oni saves the people from the threat of a giant eagle. If the story were set in modern times, what dangerous force might Oni have to save the people from?

WRITING
Writing a Summary

In a **summary** you restate the most important events of a story. Refer to the notes you took while you read, and write a summary of "Oni and the Great Bird." Tell about each major event in a complete sentence. Use transitional words like *then, after,* and *as a result* to indicate when and where events happened and what caused the events to happen. 📖

Reading Check

a. Why must Oni leave his village?

b. How does the king of Ajo react to Oni's offer to fight Anodo?

c. What happens when Oni fights Anodo?

d. How does Oni prove that the hunter who claims to have killed Anodo is an impostor?

INTERNET
Projects and Activities
Keyword: LE5 7-6

Literary Skills
Analyze the superhero motif.

Reading Skills
Summarize.

Writing Skills
Write a summary.

After You Read Vocabulary Development

Clarifying Word Meanings

PRACTICE

Imagine that you work for an animation production company that is launching a cartoon about a new superhero. Use the words in the Word Bank to write a summary of the cartoon superhero's first adventure. (You may make the verbs any tense you wish.)

(Left) Spider-Man.
(Right) Superman.

Grammar Link

They're, Their, There

Many words in English sound like other words but have very different meanings and functions. Three words often confused are *they're, their,* and *there:*

they're: a contraction of "they are."

their: a personal possessive pronoun.

there: a word that means "at that place" or that begins a sentence such as "There was once a strange boy called Oni who was born wearing a pair of boots."

EXAMPLES

When the people of the town hear the bells, they're very frightened. [They are very frightened.]

"'Our king has ordered the ringing of bells to warn the people to return to their homes and lock the doors.'" [*Their* is a possessive pronoun modifying *homes.*]

Tonight there will be much celebrating in the town.

When you find one of these confusing words in your writing, ask yourself:

1. Can I substitute the words *they are*? If so, use *they're.*
2. Does the word answer the question *whose?* If so, use *their.*

PRACTICE

Be a test maker. Write five sentences that ask for a choice between *there, their,* and *they're.* Exchange tests with a partner, and then grade your partner's paper.

SKILLS FOCUS

Vocabulary Skills
Clarify word meanings.

Grammar Skills
Use *they're, their,* and *there* correctly.

Master Frog

Make the Connection
Quickwrite ✏️

The main character of this Vietnamese folk tale is just like other boys except for his unusual appearance. People who judge him only by his looks are missing all the special qualities and talents that lie beneath the surface. There's more to all of us than what appears on the surface. What are your special qualities and talents? List some of the things you're good at.

Literary Focus
Motifs in Folk Tales: Metamorphosis

This story involves a **metamorphosis** (met'ə·môr'fə·sis)—a fantastic transformation, or change, from one shape to another. Shape changes are common motifs in comics, myths, and fairy tales. In numerous folk tales, for example, a frog with bulging eyes turns into a handsome prince when someone loves him despite his ugly appearance. In this story a frog changes shape; however, the metamorphosis has an unusual twist.

Reading Skills 📖
Making Predictions

There are so many surprises in "Master Frog" that it is a good story to use for making **predictions,** or guessing what will happen next.

Before you read, follow these steps:

- Think about your prior experience with folk tales.
- Remember what you've learned about **metamorphosis.**
- Preview the quotations on pages 708, 710, 713, and 714. Then, write a sentence predicting what will happen in this story.

While you read, follow these steps:

- Adjust your original prediction, if necessary.
- Write a new prediction before you begin each page.

Vocabulary Development

Pay attention to these words as you read "Master Frog."

admonished (ad·män'isht) *v.:* warned or urged. *The teacher admonished the other students to be more like Master Frog.*

entreaties (en·trēt'ēz) *n.:* earnest requests. *All his mother's entreaties couldn't change Master Frog's mind.*

charade (shə·rād') *n.:* obvious pretense or act. *The king got mad at Master Frog's proposal, which he thought was a charade.*

presumptuous (prē·zump'chōō·əs) *adj.:* too bold; arrogant. *The king ordered the presumptuous frog out of his sight.*

cowered (kou'ərd) *v.:* crouched and trembled in fear. *When the tigers roared, everyone cowered in fear.*

INTERNET

Vocabulary Activity
Keyword: LE5 7-6

SKILLS FOCUS

Literary Skills
Understand metamorphosis.

Reading Skills
Make predictions.

Master Frog

Vietnamese, retold by
Lynette Dyer Vuong

Except for his strange appearance, Master Frog was really quite an ordinary boy . . .

One of a pair of belt buckles. Eastern Inner Mongolia
Asian Art Museum of San Francisco, The Avery Brundage Collection, B60B1082/1083. Used by permission.

Giang Dung[1] was a plain girl, so plain in fact that all the towns-people marveled when her parents finally found her a husband. Then they nodded their heads knowingly and whispered to one another that the young man must have been after her father's money. He had plenty of it, it was true, and Giang Dung was his only child. The day of the wedding came and passed, and the people found more interesting things to gossip about until a few months later, when Giang Dung's husband died.

"It's fortunate that she's expecting a child," one person said, and the rest agreed. "At least she'll have someone to look after her in her old age. It's certain she'll never find anyone else to marry her."

But when the child was born, instead of being a boy to carry on her husband's name or at least a girl to give her some comfort and companionship, it was only a frog. And the people's tongues wagged again until they tired of the subject. "What would you expect? Giang Dung almost looks like a frog herself, she's so ugly."

Poor Giang Dung cried for days until she had no tears left. Then she resigned herself to her fate and determined to raise the frog as well as she could. If she was being punished for some unknown evil she had

---

1. **Giang Dung** (zäng′ zōōm′): Vietnamese for "pretty face," an ironic name for a plain girl.

committed, she would have to make the best of it and serve her sentence. But on the other hand, Heaven sometimes worked in mysterious ways, and it was just possible that some great destiny lay ahead for her son. ❶ 🔖

🔖 **PREDICT**
❶ Do you think Giang Dung is being punished, or is the frog marked for greatness? Give reasons for your prediction.

But as the years passed, Giang Dung forgot both of these theories. Except for his strange appearance, Master Frog was really quite an ordinary boy—now mischievous, now helpful, but always affectionate. He followed her around the house as she went about her daily tasks, helping her to care for the silkworms.[2] He gathered mulberry leaves for her to chop and place in their trays; he watched them as they began to spin their cocoons, fascinated at the way they swung their heads down and round and then up again to surround themselves with the fine strands. He often perched beside her as she sat at the loom and thought it great fun to take the shuttle in his mouth and wriggle his small body in and out among the warp threads. Sometimes, as she was cooking, he would hop up on the stove to stir the soup, or if he was sure she was not watching him, to snap up some tasty tidbit with his long, sticky tongue. But, like other children, he was often bored with being indoors and went out to play hide-and-seek and hopscotch with the boys of the neighborhood. All in all, he was both a good-natured and an intelligent little fellow, and his mother decided at last that something must be done about his education.

"A frog? In my class?" the teacher demanded when Giang Dung brought him to the school. "Impossible! I would be the laughingstock of the town."

"Then at least let him sit at the back and listen," she pleaded with him. "I promise you he won't cause you any trouble."

As the weeks went by, Master Frog proved himself such a model student that at last the teacher moved him up to the head of the class and often admonished the others to follow his example. At first he had tried to grasp the brush with his front feet but later found that he could form more graceful characters if he held it in his mouth. Generally he was the first to commit a passage to memory, and if none of the others could correctly interpret a line of the reading, the teacher would call on Master Frog. Finally, Master Frog completed his education and grew to young froghood.

"It's time to think of learning some trade," Giang Dung suggested to him one day. "Tomorrow I will go to town and talk to some of the craftsmen. Perhaps one of them would be willing to take you on as an apprentice."

But Master Frog shook his head. "Mother, first I would like to get married."

"G . . . get married!" she stammered, almost unable to believe her ears. "I . . . is there any particular girl you have in mind?"

"Yes, Mother. Princess Kien Tien,[3] the king's youngest daughter."

Giang Dung drew back in alarm. "Son, you must be out of your mind! How could

---

2. **silkworms:** moth caterpillars that produce cocoons of silk fiber. Some silkworms are grown and cultivated as the source of silk.

3. **Kien Tien** (kē·'n' tē·en').

Vocabulary
admonished (ad·män'isht) v.: warned or urged.

you ever hope to marry the king's daughter?"

"Nevertheless I shall marry her." Master Frog planted all four feet on the table in a stance of determination. "Tomorrow I shall go to the king to ask for her hand." ❷

📖 **PREDICT**
❷ Think about what you know about folk tales. Do you think Master Frog will marry Princess Kien Tien?

All Giang Dung's protests—all her <u>entreaties</u>—were in vain. Master Frog had made up his mind, and

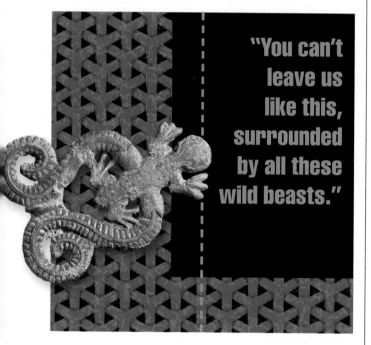

"You can't leave us like this, surrounded by all these wild beasts."

nothing could change it. And so the next morning he and Giang Dung set off for the palace.

Giang Dung set him down as they entered the audience hall, and he hopped straight up to the king, bowing respectfully as he neared the throne. The king stared at him in astonishment as he made his request and then burst out laughing.

"So you want to marry my daughter," he said. "Well, I have three daughters. Which one is it you want? But don't be in a hurry to make up your mind." His lips twisted in amusement as he motioned to one of the courtiers.[4] "Bring their royal highnesses here."

"Come here, my dears," he beckoned to them as they entered the hall. "A suitor has presented himself to request the hand of one of you." With a grand sweep of his forearm he indicated Master Frog at the foot of the throne. "He has not yet told me the extent of his kingdom or the number of vassals[5] who pay him tribute, but does he not have a noble air?" He turned back to Master Frog. "Allow me to introduce my daughters to your highness: Kim Chau,"[6] he pointed to the first, who cast a contemptuous[7] glance in Master Frog's direction, then gave her head such a violent toss that one of her pearl hairpins slipped from its place and fell to the floor; "Bich Ngoc,"[8] he indicated the second, who made a face at him and stuck out her tongue; "and Kien Tien," he presented the last of the three, who had stood the whole time, her hands folded in her long sleeves and her eyes on the floor. "Now would you please tell me which of the three pleases you?"

Kim Chau's chin rose a trifle higher. "I won't marry him, Father."

"I'll kill myself if you force me to marry him," Bich Ngoc declared with a stamp of her foot.

---

4. **courtiers** (kôrt′ē·ərz) *n.:* royal attendants.
5. **vassals** *n.:* subjects.
6. **Kim Chau** (kim′ chō′): *Kim* is Vietnamese for "gold" and *chau* for "pearl or precious stone."
7. **contemptuous** (kən·temp′ch′o͞o·əs) *adj.:* scornful, snobbish.
8. **Bich Ngoc** (bik′ näp′): *Ngoc* is Vietnamese for "emerald."

Vocabulary
entreaties (en·trēt′ēz) *n.:* earnest requests.

"Your Majesty," Master Frog interrupted them, "it is Kien Tien whose hand I have come to seek."

"Enough of this charade." The king's face had grown angry. "We have carried this joke far enough." He motioned to the guards. "Take this presumptuous creature out of my sight at once and execute him."

As the king finished speaking, Master Frog croaked in a loud voice. Suddenly the building began to shake as lightning flashed and thunder roared. On all sides the doors flew open, and the guards cowered in terror as wild beasts of every description burst into the hall. Elephants trumpeted as they stampeded in, tigers roared, leopards and panthers growled as they sprang from one corner to another.

"A few minutes ago Your Majesty inquired about my vassals," Master Frog's croak rose above the uproar. "They have come. I will leave them here to answer any questions you may have about the extent of my kingdom. Until we meet again, Your Majesty." Master Frog turned and hopped toward the exit.

"Wait! Wait!" the king shouted after him as a tiger leapt over his throne, pursuing a panther in a game of tag. "You can't leave us like this, surrounded by all these wild beasts." But Master Frog only hopped over their backs, one after another, as he made his way to the door. "Daughters, what shall we do?"

"I wouldn't marry a frog if he were the son of Jade Emperor!" Kim Chau's voice was as haughty as ever, though she winced[9] as a leopard brushed past her.

Bich Ngoc covered her face as a bear lumbered toward her. "I'd rather be torn limb from limb!" she screeched.

"Father, I'll marry him." Kien Tien squeezed between two elephants to the king's side. "It's not right for us to think only of ourselves when the whole kingdom may be in danger. And the frog cannot be such a bad sort. He's obviously an individual of great power, yet he does not appear to be cruel. With all these beasts surrounding us, not one of us has been harmed." ❸

INFER
❸ What do Kien Tien's words tell you about her **character**?

As she finished speaking, the uproar ceased, and one by one the beasts filed from the hall. Master Frog stood alone before the king.

"I will send the engagement gifts tomorrow," he said as he, too, turned and hopped from the room.

A few days later the wedding was celebrated with great pomp and ceremony. Kings and dignitaries[10] of all the surrounding countries came to pay their respects, and no one dared to laugh at Master Frog or the princess, for the tales of his great power had spread far and wide.

During the weeks that followed, Master Frog and Kien Tien lived together happily as the two came to understand each other better and to care for each other more deeply. In spite of his ugliness, Kien Tien found him such an intelligent and such a pleasant companion that as the days went by,

---

10. **dignitaries** *n.*: people holding high, dignified positions.

---

9. **winced** (winst) *v.*: drew back in fear, making a face.

Vocabulary

charade (shə·rād′) *n.*: obvious pretense or act.

presumptuous (prē·zump′chōo·əs) *adj.*: too bold; arrogant.

cowered (kou′ərd) *v.*: crouched and trembled in fear.

she grew genuinely fond of him. Then one morning she awoke to find the frog lying dead on the pillow beside her.

With a cry she lifted her husband's body to her lips, kissing it again and again as her tears wet the mottled[11] green skin. Someone called her name, and she looked up to see a handsome young man standing next to the bed, his arms outstretched as if to embrace her. ❹

She backed away from him, crying out in alarm. "How dare you come here?" she demanded. "Can't you see my husband is dead and I am mourning him?" Suddenly her eyes narrowed. "Or was it you who killed him, you miserable creature!" She burst into fresh tears. "You shall surely die for your crime!"

The man smiled. "No, Kien Tien. I am Master Frog. What you are holding there is only my skin, which I shed during the night." He sat down beside her. "I am a fairy, a heavenly mandarin,[12] one of the sons of Jade Emperor. I was bored with the life in Fairyland and wanted to seek adventure in the world below. But when I asked my father's permission, he was angry with me. He said he would grant my request but that I must be born as a frog. Only if I could succeed in that form would I be able to resume my true shape. Now I have proved myself and am allowed to shed the frog's skin. But you must put the skin away carefully where no harm

> **PREDICT**
> ❹ Many folk tales involve a **metamorphosis**, or shape change. Who do you predict the handsome young man will turn out to be?

can come to it because if it should ever be destroyed, I would have to return immediately to Jade Emperor's palace."

Overjoyed at her good fortune, Kien Tien did as he said. The days that followed were full of joy for the newlyweds. The king was filled with pride at the handsomeness and intelligence of his son-in-law, which matched so well the beauty and talent of his youngest daughter. He took them wherever he went to show them off. On every trip that he made to the surrounding countries, they accompanied him in his golden palanquin,[13] and when he rode through the streets of the capital, they sat beside him on the back of his white elephant, cheered by all who watched them pass.

"Why didn't he tell us who he was in the first place?" Kim Chau grumbled to her sister as they watched the parade from the palace balcony. "Was it fair to come in that ugly old frog skin and then change into a handsome prince after he'd married Kien Tien?"

"If she was dumb enough to marry a frog, he should have stayed a frog," Bich Ngoc grunted in agreement.

"He should be punished for his deception. What right did he have to ask for Kien Tien anyway? I'm the oldest."

"Kien Tien says he's a son of Jade Emperor, but I don't believe it. He's probably nothing but an ordinary frog. Why don't we see if we can find his skin and have a look at it?"

The sisters went to Kien Tien's room, searching through chest after chest and shelf after shelf till at last, among a pile of her

---

11. **mottled** (mät′'ld) *adj.*: spotted or streaked.
12. **mandarin** *n.*: member of any powerful group.

13. **palanquin** (pal'ən·kēn′) *n.*: covered structure enclosing a couch. A palanquin is carried by long poles resting on the shoulders of two or more men.

most precious silks, they found what they were looking for. ⑤

PREDICT

⑤ What do you think the two sisters will do with the frog skin? How might their actions affect Master Frog?

"She hid it well enough," Kim Chau sniffed. "No wonder. It's an ugly old thing, isn't it?"

Bich Ngoc reached for it, turning it over in her hands. "It certainly is. And just as I thought, nothing but an ordinary frog skin." She squinted her eyes thoughtfully. "Who knows but what, if we caught a couple of frogs for ourselves, they might shed their skins for us? There might be a handsome

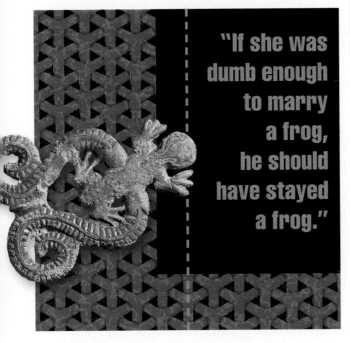

"If she was dumb enough to marry a frog, he should have stayed a frog."

prince in any one of them if we could just get him to come out." She stuffed Master Frog's skin into her sash as the two of them hurried out to the pond.

Day by day Kim Chau and Bich Ngoc watched their chosen frogs, waiting for the hoped-for transformation. They fed them on the most delicious foods, petted them; cooed endearments and whispered promises of fame, fortune, and riches in their ears. And each night they gently laid them on the pillow next to them, certain that the coming morning would bring the answer to their dreams. But nothing happened; both frogs remained as they were when they had fished them from the pond.

"There has to be a prince in there!" Bich Ngoc cried one morning in exasperation. "And I'm not going to wait any longer to find him." She picked up a knife and began to skin the poor creature alive.

Kim Chau snatched up her own frog and followed her example. But before they were finished, it was plain that no prince was to be found. In disgust the sisters threw the corpses into the fireplace.

Bich Ngoc jerked Master Frog's skin from her belt. "I don't know what I'm still carrying this around for," she grunted as she tossed it into the fire.

Meanwhile in Kien Tien's room, she and Master Frog were just getting out of bed. Suddenly he gave a cry of pain.

"My chest, my arms, my legs are burning!" he cried. "My whole body is on fire."

As Kien Tien rushed to his side, he fell to the floor, writhing in agony. Moments later he lay lifeless in her arms. Kien Tien pressed him close to her, weeping bitterly.

"It must be because you burned his old frog skin," Kim Chau whispered to Bich Ngoc when they heard what had happened. "What are we going to do? Sooner or later she'll discover the skin is missing, and if she finds out we took it and tells Father . . ."

Bich Ngoc clapped her hand over her sister's mouth. "We aren't going to sit around and wait for that to happen!"

Together they went to Kien Tien's room, where she lay on the bed weeping. They sat down beside her, stroking her hair to comfort her.

"Come, little sister, it's a terrible tragedy, but you mustn't spend the whole day lying here crying." Bich Ngoc poured some tea from the teapot on the table, dropping a little sleeping powder into the cup as she carried it back to the bed. "Here, drink something warm. It'll make you feel better."

Kien Tien raised her head, sipping the hot liquid as Bich Ngoc held it to her lips. Then she lay down again and was soon fast asleep.

Quickly the sisters lifted her and carried her outside to the carriage. As fast as they could make the horses go, they rode out of town to the seaside. Then, making sure that no one was around, they shoved their sister out of the carriage, watching with satisfaction as she hit the surface of the water and sank beneath the waves. Then they rushed home

As Master Frog rose, a company of shrimps and turtles entered the hall.

to tell their father that Kien Tien had committed suicide.

"We tried to stop her," Bich Ngoc sobbed into her handkerchief. "But she wouldn't listen to us. She was so miserable at the thought of never seeing Master Frog again that

she threw herself into the sea. The waves carried her away before we could call for help."

Suddenly gasps rose throughout the audience hall. Master Frog had entered the room.

He approached the throne, bowing respectfully. "Jade Emperor has allowed me to return to the earth to complete my lifetime," he told the king. "But why is everyone crying? What has happened?" He gazed from one person to another, seeking an answer.

"Dear brother-in-law, our sister is dead." Bich Ngoc wiped the tears from her eyes as she spoke. "She was so overcome with sorrow at losing you that she threw herself into the sea." She stepped closer to him, laying her hand on his arm. "I know what a shock it is for you. But Kim Chau and I will do everything we can to help. Either one of us would be willing to take our sister's place."

But Master Frog was already running toward the door. At his order a horse was saddled, and he leapt on its back, riding at top speed toward the sea. Fearlessly he dove in, letting his body sink to the bottom. Swiftly he ran across the ocean floor to the Crystal Palace and, bursting through the gates, prostrated himself before the Dragon King of the Waters.

The Dragon King gazed down at him kindly. "Stand up, nephew. What you are seeking may be behind you."

As Master Frog rose, a company of shrimps and turtles entered the hall. One of them bore Kien Tien in his arms.

"My soldiers have found your wife," the Dragon King told him. "I would have let her live here in my palace, but since you've come for her, you may take her home with you."

Master Frog rushed toward her joyfully. As he lifted her from the turtle-soldier's arms, she opened her eyes and smiled up at him. Then both of them fell at the Dragon

King's feet to thank him for his mercy.

Master Frog led Kien Tien out of the Crystal Palace and up through the water to the shore, where his horse was waiting. Together they rode back to the palace. ⑥

Kim Chau glanced down from her balcony to see Master Frog reining his horse below. She drew back in alarm and called to her sister.

"We're done for," she trembled, grabbing Bich Ngoc's arm and pulling her after her. "Kien Tien will tell Father everything."

PREDICT
⑥ How do you think the story will end?

The two of them raced down the stairs and out a back way. "We'll hide in the forest," Bich Ngoc decided. "No one will find us there."

And the two were never seen or heard of again. But as for Kien Tien and Master Frog, they lived happily ever after, loved and respected by all for their kind deeds. Before many days had passed, they had Giang Dung brought to the palace, where she lived in comfort and happiness to a ripe old age. In due time Master Frog became king and, with Kien Tien as his queen, ruled their people in peace and prosperity for many long years.

Meet the Writer

Lynette Dyer Vuong

Taking a Chance on Love

Lynette Dyer Vuong (1938–   ) believes in love at first sight because that's what happened when she met a young Vietnamese man who was studying in the United States. Love led her to follow him back to Vietnam, marry him, and stay there with him for thirteen years—the country was then in the midst of the Vietnam War.

As Vuong learned Vietnamese, she began to follow another love—the world of folklore and fairy tales. She was amazed to discover that Vietnam has its own versions of five stories she loved as a child—"Cinderella," "Thumbelina," "The Frog Prince," "Rip Van Winkle," and "Goose Girl." She remembers:

> **Five familiar faces in an unfamiliar land; it is fascinating that similar ideas have arisen and then developed into different stories under the influence of two such diverse cultures as East and West. Perhaps it is a testimony to the fact that we are each uniquely individual, . . . yet bound together by a common humanity.**

Vuong fled Vietnam with her husband and children in 1975. She continues to work on retelling the fairy tales she had grown to love.

For Independent Reading

If you'd like to read the other fairy tales Vuong discovered during her stay in Vietnam, look for her book *The Brocaded Slipper*.

First Thoughts

1. Which scene in the story do you remember most vividly? Why?

Thinking Critically

2. What is different about the ways Kien Tien, Kim Chau, and Bich Ngoc first react to Master Frog? What does this tell you about each sister's **character**?

3. What qualities does Kien Tien admire in Master Frog even before she realizes that he is a prince?

4. How do Kim Chau's and Bich Ngoc's feelings about Master Frog change after his **metamorphosis**? What does their sudden change of heart tell you about their **character**?

5. What lessons do you think this story teaches?

6. Think about the **predictions** you made as you read "Master Frog." Were you surprised by the twist this story takes at the end? Explain why or why not.

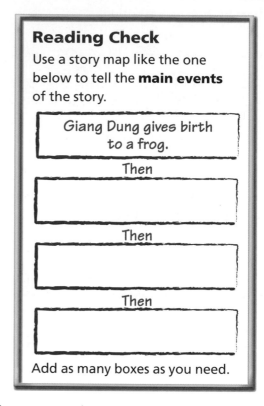

Reading Check

Use a story map like the one below to tell the **main events** of the story.

> Giang Dung gives birth to a frog.

> Then

> Then

> Then

Add as many boxes as you need.

Extending Interpretations

7. What other stories do you know in which a **metamorphosis** takes place? In each case, what caused the metamorphosis—is the change a reward or a punishment?

8. Kien Tien can look beyond Master Frog's appearance and see the person within, but her sisters can't. Do you think most people are like Kien Tien, or are they like her sisters? Why do you think so?

WRITING

Writing a Personal Essay

Refer back to your Quickwrite notes, and write a paragraph or two in which you describe your good qualities and talents. Be sure to explain why your special talents are important to you.

INTERNET

Projects and Activities

Keyword: LE5 7-6

SKILLS FOCUS

Literary Skills
Analyze metamorphosis.

Reading Skills
Make predictions.

Writing Skills
Write a personal essay.

Clarifying Word Meanings

PRACTICE

1. Use two words from the Word Bank to write a statement about a student who's been grounded for two weeks.
2. Use three words from the Word Bank to write a few sentences urging students to challenge an unfair rule.

> **Word Bank**
>
> admonished
> entreaties
> charade
> presumptuous
> cowered

Using Specific Words

No two words have exactly the same meaning. Some words, like *sit*, have a general meaning but do not paint a vivid picture. Other words, like *perch* or *settle*, describe specific kinds of sitting. Each paints a different picture.

The author of "Master Frog" helps us imagine the creature's froggy behavior by using specific words to describe him. For example, she says that he *perched* beside his mother as she sat at the loom and would *wriggle* his body in and out of the threads on the loom.

SKILLS FOCUS

Vocabulary Skills
Clarify word meanings; use specific words.

PRACTICE

Rewrite the following sentences, replacing the underlined words with more exact ones. Be sure to compare your revisions in class.

1. Kien Tien's tears wet the greenish skin of her dead husband's body.
2. When Master Frog said he wanted to marry the king's daughter, the king looked at him.
3. When Master Frog croaked, tigers, leopards, and panthers came into the room.

B.C. By permission of Johnny L. Hart FLP, and Creators Syndicate, Inc.

Before You Read The Folk Tale

The Crane Wife

Make the Connection
Quickwrite ✏️

Sometimes you may have been told that if you do—or don't do—something, there will be terrible consequences. *Don't eat too much candy all at once. Don't play with matches.* Some of these warnings may seem silly or senseless at first, but if you were to disobey them, you might be sorry. Jot down other warnings you remember and the consequences that could result if the warnings are not obeyed.

Literary Focus
Motifs in Folk Tales: Taboo

This Japanese folk tale is about the breaking of a taboo. A **taboo** is a prohibition of something. Some societies, for example, forbid the eating of certain foods. A taboo is a common motif in myths as well as folk tales. In "Orpheus, the Great Musician" (page 665), for example, Orpheus is allowed to lead his wife up and out of the Land of the Dead as long as he doesn't look back at her. If you remember what happens when he does look back, you may predict that something bad will happen involving a broken taboo in this story too. As you read "The Crane Wife," watch for the taboo, and think about whether you would have behaved as Yohei did.

Onomatopoeia

The translator of this tale gives us the flavor of its original language by using some Japanese words. The words are examples of **onomatopoeia** (än'ō·mat'ō·pē'ə), or words whose sounds echo their meanings. (In English, *boom, growl,* and *swish* are onomatopoetic words.) In the first paragraph of the folk tale, the Japanese word *basabasa* is how the original storyteller thought rustling wings would sound. When you come across the Japanese words in the story, say them out loud. They are pronounced the way they look.

Reading Skills 📖
Drawing Conclusions

Anytime you read, you probably draw many **conclusions** about what is happening in the text. You decide whether the characters are good or bad, whether their decisions are wise or stupid, whether an outcome is fair or unfair. You base your conclusions on

- your own prior knowledge, experience, and beliefs
- details in the text

Keep a list of the conclusions you draw as you read "The Crane Wife."

SKILLS FOCUS

Literary Skills
Understand taboo; recognize onomatopoeia.

Reading Skills
Draw conclusions.

Cranes on folding screen by Ogata Korin (1658).

THE CRANE WIFE

told by **Sumiko Yagawa**

translated from the Japanese
by **Katherine Paterson**

In a faraway mountain village, where the snow falls deep and white, there once lived all alone a poor young peasant named Yohei. One day, at the beginning of winter, Yohei went out into the snow to run an errand, and, as he hurried home, suddenly *basabasa* he heard a rustling sound. It was a crane, dragging its wing, as it swooped down and landed on the path. Now Yohei could see that the bird was in great pain, for an arrow had pierced its wing. He went to where the crane lay, drew out the arrow, and very carefully tended its wound.

Late that night there came a tapping *hoto-hoto* on the door of Yohei's hut. It seemed very peculiar for someone to be calling at that time of night. When he slid open the door to look out, there before him stood a beautiful young woman.

"I beg you, sir," she said in a voice both delicate and refined, "please allow me to become your wife."

Yohei could hardly believe his ears. The more closely he looked, the more noble and lovely the woman appeared. Gently he took her hand and brought her inside.

Needlework hanging with cranes, cycads, and wisteria (textile) by Japanese School (19th century). Ashmolean Museum, Oxford, UK.

"Yohei has got some fine wife at his house," the villagers gossiped among themselves.

And it was true. The young woman was modest and kind, and she served Yohei faithfully. He could no longer recognize the cold, cold dreary hut where he had lived all alone, his house had become so bright and warm. The simple Yohei was happier than he could have ever dreamed.

In reality, however, with two mouths to feed instead of one, poor Yohei became poorer than he was before. And, since it was winter and there was no work to be found, he was very quickly coming to the bottom of what he had stored away.

At this point the young woman had a suggestion. "The other women of the village have looms upon which to weave cloth," she said. "If you would be so kind as to allow it, I should like to try my hand at weaving too."

In the back room of the hut, the young woman set up a loom and closed it off with sliding paper doors. Then she said to Yohei, "Please, I beg you, I beg you, never look in upon me while I am weaving."

Tonkara tonkara. For three days and three nights the sound of the loom continued. Without stopping either to eat or drink, the young woman went on weaving and weaving. Finally, on the fourth day, she came out. To Yohei she seemed strangely thin and completely exhausted as, without a word, she held out to him a bolt of material.

And such exquisite cloth it was! Even Yohei, who had absolutely no knowledge of woven goods, could only stare in astonishment at the elegant, silken fabric.

Yohei took the cloth and set out for town. There he was able to sell it for such a high price that for a while the two of them had enough money to live quite comfortably and pleasantly.

The winter, however, stretched on and on until, finally, there was very little money left. Yohei hesitated to say anything, so he kept quiet, but at last the young woman spoke up. "I shall weave on the loom one more time. But, please, let this be the last." And, once more, having been warned not to look in on the woman as she wove, the simple Yohei settled down to wait outside just as she asked.

This time the weaving took four days and four nights. A second time the young woman appeared carrying a bolt of cloth, but now she seemed thinner and more pathetic than before. The fabric, moreover, was lighter and even more beautiful. It seemed almost to glow with a light all its own.

Yohei sold the material for an even higher price than the first time. "My," he marveled, "what a good wife I have!" The money bag he carried was heavy, but Yohei's heart was light, and he fairly skipped as he hurried home.

Now, the man next door had noticed that Yohei seemed to be living far more grandly than he had in the old days, and he was most curious. Pretending to be very casual about it all, he made his way through the snow and began to chat. Yohei, being a simple and innocent fellow, told the neighbor how his wife's woven goods had brought a wonderful price.

The man became more curious than ever. "Tell me," he said, "just what kind of thread does your wife use? My woman's cotton cloth never fetched a price like that. If your wife's stuff is as marvelous as you say, you ought to take it to the capital, to the home of some noble. You could probably sell it for ten times—for a hundred times more. Say, how about it? Why don't you let me do it for you? We'd split the profits right down the middle. Just think of it! We could live out the rest of our lives doing nothing but sitting back and fanning ourselves."

Before Yohei's very eyes, gold coins great and small began to dazzle and dance. If only he could get his wife to relent, if only he could persuade her to weave again, they could seize such a fortune as had never been known before.

When Yohei presented her with this idea, the young woman seemed quite perplexed. "Why in the world," she asked, "would anyone need so much money as that?"

"Don't you see?" he answered. "With money like that a man's problems would all disappear. He could buy anything he liked. He could even start his own business."

"Isn't it plenty to be able to live together, just the two of us?"

When she spoke this way, Yohei could say no more. However, from that time on, whether asleep or awake, all he could do was think about money. It was so painful for the young woman to see Yohei in this state that her eyes filled with tears as she watched him, until finally, unable to bear it another day, she bowed to his will.

"Very well then," she said. "I will weave one more time. But truly, after this, I must never weave again." And once more she warned the now joyful Yohei, saying, "For the sake of heaven, remember. Do not look in on me."

Yohei rubbed his hands together in his eagerness and sat down to wait.

Tonkara tonkara. The sound of the loom continued on and on into the fifth day. The work in the back room seemed to be taking longer than ever.

Yohei, no longer the simple fellow that he had once been, began to wonder about certain peculiar things. Why did the young woman appear to grow thinner every time she wove? What was going on in there behind those paper doors? How could she weave such beautiful cloth when she never seemed to buy any thread?

The longer he had to wait, the more he yearned to peep into the room until, at last, he put his hand upon the door.

"Ah!" came a voice from within. At the same time Yohei cried out in horror and fell back from the doorway.

What Yohei saw was not human. It was a crane, smeared with blood, for with its beak it had plucked out its own feathers to place them in the loom.

At the sight Yohei collapsed into a deep faint. When he came to himself, he found, lying near his hand, a bolt of fabric, pure and radiantly white, through which was woven a thread of bright crimson. It shone with a light this world has never known.

From somewhere Yohei heard the whisper of a delicate, familiar voice. "I had hoped," the voice said sorrowfully, "that you would be able to honor my entreaty. But because you looked upon me in my suffering, I can no longer tarry in the human world. I am the crane that you saved on the snowy path. I fell in love with your gentle, simple heart, and, trusting it alone, I came to live by your side. I pray that your life will be long and that you will always be happy."

"Wai-t!" Yohei stumbled in his haste to get outside.

It was nearly spring, and, over the crest of the distant mountains, he could barely discern the tiny form of a single crane, flying farther and farther away.

Snow. Print from the Tokaido series (c. 1830s) by Hiroshige Utugawa.

Meet the Writer

Katherine Paterson

"Searching for a Place to Stand"

Katherine Paterson (1932–   ) was born in China, where both of her parents served as missionaries. Of the early years of her life, when her family moved frequently, she has written:

> "I remember the many schools I attended in those years mostly as places where I felt fear and humiliation. I was small, poor, and foreign.... I was a misfit both in the classroom and on the playground. Outside of school, however, I lived a rich, imaginative life."

Paterson has also reflected on the effect that this background had on her writing:

> "When I look at the books I have written, the first thing I see is the outcast child searching for a place to stand."

Paterson has drawn upon both her rich inner life and her difficult childhood experiences in writing her highly acclaimed young adult novels.

© Samantha Loomis Paterson.

For Independent Reading

Paterson lived in Japan as well as in China. Three novels set in Japan during feudal times are *The Sign of the Chrysanthemum, Of Nightingales That Weep,* and *The Master Puppeteer.* Other popular novels by Paterson you may enjoy are *Bridge to Terabithia, Jacob Have I Loved, The Great Gilly Hopkins, Lyddie,* and *Flip-Flop Girl.*

First Thoughts

1. Finish the following sentence:
   - If I were Yohei . . .

Thinking Critically

2. What **character traits** does the young woman admire in Yohei? What weakness does he display when he asks her to weave a third time?

3. In many folk tales, a marvelous change of form, or **metamorphosis,** takes place. What metamorphosis takes place in this story? What other stories do you know that involve shape changes?

4. What **conclusions** can you draw about this tale? (Was it fair that Yohei lost his wife? Does the story have a useful message for today?) Discuss the reasons for your conclusions.

Reading Check

a. How is Yohei rewarded for his kindness to the wounded crane?

b. What makes Yohei suspect that something is strange about his wife?

c. Why does Yohei ask his wife to weave one last time?

d. What **taboo** does Yohei break? How does Yohei lose his wife?

Extending Interpretations

5. The motif of a **taboo** is common in myths and folklore. People in real life are also often told not to do something, but do it anyway. What are some taboos you know of? What are the consequences of breaking them? Check your Quickwrite notes for ideas.

WRITING
Writing a Folk Tale

Write your own folk tale that includes a **metamorphosis** and a **taboo** that is broken. First, think about where and when you want the story to take place. Will it be today? once upon a time? Second, think about your characters—are they young? old? Where do they live? Then, decide on the kind of shape change you'll include. Will it be a reward or punishment? Finally, choose a taboo that your character will break.

SKILLS FOCUS

Literary Skills
Analyze taboos.

Reading Skills
Draw conclusions.

Writing Skills
Write a folk tale.

Onomatopoeia

In "The Crane Wife" the reader can hear what is happening in the story through **onomatopoeia,** or the use of words with sounds that echo their meanings. Some examples of onomatopoeia in English are *honk, beep,* and *meow.*

PRACTICE

In place of the Japanese words in each passage below from the story, think up your own example of onomatopoeia in English.

1. ". . . as he hurried home, suddenly *basabasa* he heard a rustling sound."

2. "Late that night there came a tapping *hotohoto* on the door of Yohei's hut."

3. "*Tonkara tonkara*. For three days and three nights the sound of the loom continued."

Grammar Link

Using *Good* and *Well* Correctly

Choosing between *good* and *well* may sometimes seem very hard. Here are a few simple rules to help you get the job done right:

- *Good* is an adjective. Use it to modify a noun; never use it to modify a verb. (*Yohei was a good man.*)

- *Well* is usually an adverb. Use it to modify a verb. (*Yohei's wife wove well.*)

- Although it is usually an adverb, *well* is also used as an adjective to mean "healthy." (*Yohei's wife felt well when she recovered from weaving.*)

Note: *Feel good* and *feel well* mean different things. *Feel good* means "feel happy or pleased." (*Yohei felt good when the young woman asked to be his wife.*) *Feel well* simply means "feel healthy." (*Yohei didn't feel well when he didn't have enough to eat.*)

PRACTICE

Choose the correct word in each of the following sentences:

1. Yohei did (*good/well*) when he got a wife.

2. Yohei could not provide (*good/well*) for his small family.

3. Yohei's wife did not feel (*good/well*) when she wove the cloth.

4. The loom worked very (*good/well*).

5. Yohei did not feel (*good/well*) about his wife's leaving him.

SKILLS FOCUS

Vocabulary Skills
Use onomatopoeia.

Grammar Skills
Use *good* and *well* correctly.

Aunty Misery

Make the Connection
Quickwrite

Why do people have to face misery and death? What would happen if, for a period of time, no one in the whole world could die? How would people feel about that? Jot down your responses to these questions; then, see how this folk tale from Puerto Rico answers them.

Literary Focus
Motifs in Folk Tales: Wishes

Many folk tales are about a gift of **wishes**—often as a result of someone doing a good deed. This **motif** (mō·tēf')—a feature repeated in tales throughout the world—appears in the myth on page 683, when a god grants King Midas any gift he wants. As it turns out, the gift King Midas wishes for causes him great unhappiness. In the tale you are about to read, Aunty Misery is also granted a wish. Do you think she will be happy with the consequences, or results, of her wish?

INTERNET
More About Cofer
Keyword: LE5 7-6

Literary Skills
Understand the motif of wishes.

Reading Skills
Follow a cause-and-effect chain.

Reading Skills
Following a Cause-and-Effect Chain

Events in a story often follow a **cause-and-effect chain:** Something happens that causes something else to happen. This event then causes another event to happen. And so on and so on to the end of the story. As you read "Aunty Misery," fill in a chart like the one below to show the story's cause-and-effect chain.

Aunty Misery is kind to a traveler.

Add as many boxes as you need to tell the story.

Aunty Misery

Judith Ortiz Cofer

This is a story about an old, a very old woman who lived alone in her little hut with no other company than a beautiful pear tree that grew at her door. She spent all her time taking care of this tree. The neighborhood children drove the old woman crazy by stealing her fruit. They would climb her tree, shake its delicate limbs, and run away with armloads of golden pears, yelling insults at *la Tia Miseria*,[1] Aunty Misery, as they called her.

One day, a traveler stopped at the old woman's hut and asked her for permission to spend the night under her roof. Aunty Misery saw that he had an honest face and bid the pilgrim come in. She fed him and made a bed for him in front of her hearth. In the morning the stranger told her that he would show his gratitude for her hospitality by granting her one wish.

"There is only one thing that I desire," said Aunty Misery.

"Ask, and it shall be yours," replied the stranger, who was a sorcerer in disguise.

"I wish that anyone who climbs up my pear tree should not be able to come back down until I permit it."

"Your wish is granted," said the stranger,

---

1. **la Tia Miseria** (lä tē′ə mē′ze·rē′ə).

touching the pear tree as he left Aunty Misery's house.

And so it happened that when the children came back to taunt the old woman and to steal her fruit, she stood at her window watching them. Several of them shimmied up the trunk of the pear tree and immediately got stuck to it as if with glue. She let them cry and beg her for a long time before she gave the tree permission to let them go on the condition that they never again steal her fruit, or bother her.

Time passed and both Aunty Misery and her tree grew bent and <u>gnarled</u> with age. One day another traveler stopped at her door. This one looked untrustworthy to her, so before letting him into her home the old woman asked him what he was doing in her village. He answered her in a voice that was dry and hoarse, as if he had swallowed a desert: "I am Death, and I have come to take you with me."

"I am Death, and I have come to take you with me."

Thinking fast, Aunty Misery said, "All right, but before I go I would like to pluck some pears from my beloved tree to remember how much pleasure it brought me in this life. But I am a very old woman and cannot climb to the tallest branches where the best fruit is. Will you be so kind as to do it for me?"

With a heavy sigh like wind through a tomb, Señor Death climbed the pear tree. Immediately he became stuck to it as if with glue. And no matter how much he cursed and threatened, Aunty Misery would not allow the tree to release Death.

Many years passed and there were no deaths in the world. The people who make their living from death began to protest loudly. The doctors claimed no one bothered to come in for examinations or treatments anymore, because they did not fear dying; the pharmacists' business suffered too because medicines are, like magic potions, bought to prevent or postpone the inevitable; priests and undertakers were unhappy with the situation also, for obvious reasons. There were also many old folks tired of life who wanted to pass on to the next world to rest from miseries of this one.

La Tia Miseria was blamed by these people for their troubles, of course. Not wishing to be unfair, the old woman made a deal with her prisoner, Death: if he promised not ever to come for her again, she would give him his freedom. He agreed. And that is why there are two things you can always count on running into in this world: Misery and Death: *La miseria y la muerte.*[2]

---

2. **y la muerte** (ē lä mwer'tä).

Meet the Writer

Judith Ortiz Cofer

Bridging Between Two Cultures

Judith Ortiz Cofer (1952–) grew up surrounded by storytellers, so it was almost inevitable that she would also tell stories herself. As she points out:

> 66 In an extended family, the family story, gossip, or myth becomes something that is repeated so often and used in so many ways to teach lessons or to make a point that I couldn't help but be trained in [storytelling] as I grew up. 99

Cofer was born in Puerto Rico but moved with her family to Paterson, New Jersey, when she was two years old. Her father had joined the U.S. Navy and was stationed in the Brooklyn Naval Yard. But whenever her father was sent to sea, Cofer returned to Puerto Rico with the rest of the family. As a result, Cofer found herself divided between two very different worlds. Fortunately she was able to take refuge in books.

> 66 I absorbed literature . . . as a creature who breathed ink. Each writer . . . taught me that language could be tamed. I realized that I could make it perform. I had to believe the work was important to my being: to use my art as a bridge between my cultures. . . . I began crossing the bridge, traveling back and forth without fear and confusion. 99

For Independent Reading

In the short story collection *An Island Like You: Stories of the Barrio,* Cofer vividly portrays the experiences of teenagers growing up in a Puerto Rican community in New Jersey.

First Thoughts

1. Would people be happier if there were no death in the world? Discuss your responses to the moral of this folk tale. Be sure to check your Quickwrite notes. ✏️

> ### Reading Check
>
> Complete the chart showing a **cause-and-effect chain** (see page 726).

Thinking Critically

2. How does Aunty Misery show she is a clever woman in the ways she uses her wish?

3. According to the folk tale, what happens in the world when there is no death? What other effects can you imagine if there were no death?

4. How does the folk tale explain why we can always count on running into misery and death?

WRITING

Writing a Story About a Wish

Write your own story about a person who is granted a wish in reward for doing something generous. Is the wish a wise wish or a foolish one? Does the person learn something as a result of what happens when the wish is granted? Before you write your story, you might gather your details in a chart like the one to the right.

	Wish Story
Setting	
Characters	
Good deed	
Wish	
Consequences	
Ending	

ART

Drawing a Graphic Story

Create a graphic story based on this folk tale. (A **graphic story** is one told in pictures, like a comic strip.) You will have to decide how many panels you will need. You can tell the story by using dialogue bubbles to show what the characters are saying. If you wish, you can also explain what is happening in brief captions under the panels.

SKILLS FOCUS

Literary Skills
Analyze the motif of wishes.

Reading Skills
Analyze cause and effect.

Writing Skills
Write a story about a wish.

Art Skills
Draw a graphic story.

The Hummingbird King

Make the Connection
Quickwrite ✏️

If you could have an animal as a protector, what would the animal be? Would you choose your animal for its strength, wisdom, cleverness, comfort, beauty, speed, faithfulness—or just because you like it? Jot down your ideas for your own personal protector.

Literary Focus
Motifs in Folk Tales: Origins

Myths and folk tales often explain the origin of something in nature or human life. The Greek myth of Demeter and Persephone explains the origin of the seasons (page 655). The Puerto Rican folk tale "Aunty Misery" explains how misery came into the world (page 727). "The Hummingbird King," a Mayan folk tale, also explains the origin of something, but you may not be able to figure out what that is until the very end.

Reading Skills 📖
Retelling

A good way to be sure you understand and remember all the key events in a story is to **retell** the story when you have finished reading it. As you read this story, jot down the story's key events. When you have finished reading, you will have everything you need to retell the story.

Background
Literature and Social Studies

Today you can see the beautiful ruined temples and pyramids of the great Mayan civilization in Mexico, Guatemala, Belize, and Honduras. The Maya dominated this region for about 650 years, from about A.D. 250 to A.D. 900. At their peak the Maya ruled about two million people and had a vast network of trade. One of the items they traded was the shimmering tail feather of the bird called quetzal (ket·säl'), from the highlands of Guatemala.

What happened to the Maya? Scholars are not sure. One by one their cities were abandoned, and by 1200, the Maya were absorbed by the Toltecs. In the mid-1500s, almost all the Maya were conquered by Spain.

The character Kukul in this tale was a real person, called Kukulcán. His symbol was the quetzal. You can still see images of the bird in the great temple dedicated to Kukulcán at Chichén Itzá in Mexico's Yucatán Peninsula.

SKILLS FOCUS

Literary Skills
Understand the origin motif.

Reading Skills
Retell a story.

THE HUMMINGBIRD KING

Mayan, retold by **Argentina Palacios**

Pyramids, palaces, and temples of stone stand silent and abandoned, hidden by dense rain forests. But that was not always so. Long, long ago, great cities built by the Mayan people were centers of activity.

In one of those cities—one whose name has long been forgotten—there lived an old *halac uinic*, or chief. Since he had no son to succeed[1] him, he knew that his younger brother, Chirumá, would one day take his place.

But the chief's wife wanted a child. Each day, she prayed with all her heart. And, one day, her prayers were answered. She gave birth to a son. The child was born on the thirteenth day of the month, a lucky day. For the number thirteen reminded the Mayan people of their thirteen heavens.

Just as the baby was being born, another sign appeared. A beautiful hummingbird perched on a tree branch in front of the stately residence. It was not an ordinary bird, but the largest and most brightly colored hummingbird anyone had ever seen. No one had ever remembered a bird of its kind standing still for so long.

The high priest determined that this was an omen. "The messenger of the gods has come," he said. "He is telling us that this child will be extraordinary, just like this hummingbird."

In the days that followed, a special naming ceremony took place. The high priest gave the chief and his wife a bright red feather he'd found beneath the tree branch where the hummingbird perched.

"We shall name our son Kukul," the chief's wife proclaimed. "That name means 'beautiful feather.'"

"And so shall this feather protect the boy as long as he carries it with him," the priest said.

A great celebration took place in the public plaza. Everyone joined the festivities.

---

1. **succeed** *v.:* follow into a position (here, the position is that of *halac uinic*, or chief).

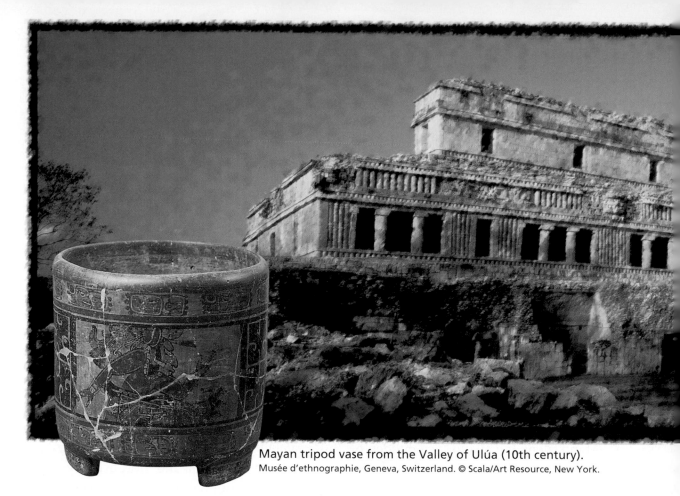

Mayan tripod vase from the Valley of Ulúa (10th century).
Musée d'ethnographie, Geneva, Switzerland. © Scala/Art Resource, New York.

Everyone was happy, except Chirumá. He knew that, because of this child, he would never become *halac uinic*.

Kukul grew into a handsome young man with jet-black hair and skin the color of cinnamon. He was quick of mind and excelled at any task he was given. As a young boy, he spent long hours with his father. Together, they would study the stars.

Like all Mayan boys, Kukul learned the art of warfare from his elders. He made his own spears, bows, and arrows—straight and strong as the boy himself.

Soon the time came for Kukul to take his place among the men of his nation. A nomad[2] tribe was attempting a raid. Kukul,

2. **nomad** *n.* used as an *adj.*: wandering, with no permanent home. Nomadic peoples move about constantly in search of food, pasture, and so on.

Chirumá, and the others went to war. Showers of spears and arrows rained down. Kukul fought bravely, at times at the very front. But wherever he was, not a single weapon fell on him.

Chirumá observed this. "The gods must watch out for Kukul," he thought to himself.

All at once, Kukul saw an arrow flying straight toward Chirumá, and Kukul positioned himself like a shield in front of his uncle. The arrow changed its course and fell to the ground without harming anyone. The enemy fled in astonishment and Kukul turned toward the wounded.

"How could it be that Kukul never gets hurt?" Chirumá wondered. "He must have a strong charm. I will find out."

That night, as Kukul slept on his straw mat, Chirumá came upon him. He carefully

Mayan plate depicting ballgame of pelota (c. A.D. 590). The Granger Collection, New York.

searched Kukul's sleeping body but found nothing. Then he saw it—a large red feather barely sticking out of the straw mat.

"His charm!" Chirumá said cheerfully to himself, as he carefully lifted the feather from its hiding place.

When Kukul awoke, he saw that the feather was gone. He searched everywhere, but he could not find it. Nor could he remember the words of the priest on the day he was born. Without realizing it, Kukul had lost the charm and all the protection it provided.

It came to pass that the old chief went to the afterlife. Upon his death, all the high priests prepared to meet in council to choose a new chief. Chirumá knew that the priests would favor his nephew. He looked for the youngest priest, the one he knew could be easily swayed.

"Kukul is not a hero," he said. "Arrows never fall where he places himself. He is afraid to fight."

"No, he is not," said the priest. "Kukul is using his intelligence to win."

Chirumá would find any opportunity to talk to that priest about Kukul. Another day, he told him, "Kukul is reckless. He stops to take care of the wounded and puts his men in danger."

"Kukul is compassionate," replied the priest.

"He is inexperienced," countered Chirumá, as he sowed the seeds of doubt.

Now according to custom, a new *halac uinic* could be anyone in the departed chief's family. The high priests met.

"It should be Kukul, without a doubt," said the oldest priest.

"It should be Kukul," the second priest chimed in.

"Yes, without a doubt," the third priest added.

There was silence. "It should be Chirumá," said the youngest. "Kukul is too young and inexperienced."

They argued about the merits of each man. In the end, no one changed his vote and Kukul was chosen as *halac uinic*.

Under his rule, there was peace throughout the land. In time, even Chirumá's friend came to appreciate that Kukul had been a good choice.

Kukul spent much time studying the stars. He made mathematical calculations. He could tell the farmers the best times to plant to reap the richest crops. Everybody was happy with Kukul, except Chirumá.

One day, Kukul was hunting in the forest. He heard the rustling of leaves and raised his bow and arrow. With a flurry, a magnificent hummingbird, larger than any hummingbird Kukul had ever seen, fluttered next to him. The hummingbird spoke these words, "I am your guardian, Kukul. My job is to warn you. Beware. Death is circling you. Beware of a man."

"Magnificent hummingbird, my guardian, what man should I beware of?" asked Kukul.

"Someone very close to you. Be careful, Kukul," said the bird. Then it flew away.

Kukul walked on through the forest. As he came to a thicket, he heard the faint rustling of leaves. He pointed his arrow, but saw nothing. Kukul crouched low to the ground and moved slowly. He had not gone far when . . . *sssss* . . . it came. An arrow pierced his chest.

In pain, Kukul pulled out the arrow and headed for the river to wash his wound. "Surely, it is not deep," he tried to convince himself, but his strength began to fade as his chest turned scarlet with blood.

A few more steps and Kukul had to lean against a tree. "It is so dark," he moaned. He fell onto a sea of emerald grass and there he died. Alone. Betrayed.

Then, something extraordinary happened. Slowly, Kukul's body changed to the color of the grass, but his chest remained scarlet. His skin became feathers, and his hair a gorgeous crest.

By the time Chirumá came out of the thicket, Kukul's arms had turned into wings. All Chirumá could see was a glowing green bird with a scarlet chest and a long, long tail, flying off into the sunlight.

Mayan seated figure of a priest or nobleman. Hardwood.
The Granger Collection, New York.

The people mourned the loss of Kukul, but after a time, Chirumá was chosen to be the new chief. Chirumá was a cruel and warlike king, and soon after, enemies again attacked the city and in fierce battle took Chirumá prisoner. Everybody watched while his body was painted black and white, the colors of a slave. He was taken away from the city, never to be seen again.

Today, a most beautiful green bird with a scarlet chest, a long, long tail, and a gorgeous crest perches high up on the trees in the deep, cool cloud forest, watching everything and listening for the rustling of leaves.

The Mayan of old called this bird *kukul*. They carved its image into stone and placed it on their temples and palaces. Today this wise and peaceful bird—a symbol of freedom to all its people—is known as the *quetzal*.

Meet the Writer

Argentina Palacios

Quetzal Tales

Argentina Palacios grew up in Panama. As an adult living in Texas, Palacios at first became a teacher, like her mother. Little by little, though, she discovered the rewards of writing and telling stories. "The Hummingbird King" is one of the stories she tells children and adults at schools, museums, zoos, and even jails around the country.

"The Hummingbird King" tells the story of the origin of the quetzal (ket·säl′). The quetzal is a brilliantly colored bird found only in the cloud forests of the highlands of Guatemala. The bird's head and back are emerald green; its chest is bright red. There is a wide crest of gold-and-green hairlike feathers on its head. The upper tail feathers are very large—up to three feet long.

Palacios says:

> 66 **Legends say the quetzal loves its freedom so much that it will die in captivity. But the cloud forests that are its natural habitat are disappearing from the earth. Happily, scientists have had some success breeding the quetzal in zoos and nature parks, preserving the Mayan ideal of people living in harmony with nature.** 99

First Thoughts

1. How would you evaluate this folk tale? To answer, complete one of these sentences:
   - I liked the folk tale because . . .
   - I disliked the tale because . . .

Thinking Critically

2. In many hero stories a baby's birth is accompanied by extraordinary events. What omens indicate that the baby Kukul will be a special person?

3. In such hero stories the baby's life is often endangered by people jealous of his or her power. Who or what threatens this baby's life?

4. What supernatural events demonstrate that Kukul has a special protector?

5. Why can this folk tale be called an **origin** story?

6. This story tells about a real person, but it mixes historical events with fantasy. What historical events do you find in the story?

Extending Interpretations

7. What supernatural events happen when Kukul dies? What other marvelous **metamorphoses,** or changes in form, have you read about in this collection of folk tales?

8. What other hero stories do you know of—from other cultures— that share some of the features of this story? (Be sure to consider stories you've seen in comics and movies.)
   - The birth of a hero accompanied by extraordinary omens
   - The threat of a jealous family member or other person
   - Supernatural events that take place in the hero's life
   - Metamorphoses at the hero's death

> ### Reading Check
> **Retell** the main events of the story to a partner. You will find help in retelling a story on page 4. You will also find a rating sheet on page 13 that your partner can use to evaluate your retelling.

SKILLS FOCUS

Literary Skills
Analyze the origin motif.

Reading Skills
Retell the story.

Writing Skills
Write a story.

WRITING

A Story About an Animal Protector

Refer to your Quickwrite notes, and choose an animal who could act as your personal protector in a time of trouble. Write a brief story describing your animal and how you found it, how the animal protects you, and what happens to you and the animal at the end.

Summarizing the Main Ideas

Reading Focus
Summarizing the Main Ideas

When you did a retelling of "The Hummingbird King," you included all the main events of that ancient Mayan folk tale. The article that follows tells about the search to discover ancient Mayan objects and buildings buried in the jungles of Guatemala. When you finish reading the article, you will be asked to **summarize** it. In summarizing informational texts such as this article, you do a brief retelling of the **main ideas** and only the most important supporting details. (For more help in summarizing informational texts, see page 688).

■ To prepare for your summary, write down the main idea in each paragraph you read. When you finish reading, decide how important each of those ideas is to the entire article. Include only the most important ones in your final summary.

Quetzal.

Vocabulary Development

Studying these words will help you understand the article.

decipher (dē·sī′fər) *v.*: interpret; find the meaning of. *Scientists try to decipher the meaning of the ancient Mayan writing.*

ransacked (ran′sakt′) *v.*: searched thoroughly for goods to steal; looted, robbed. *Grave robbers have ransacked many ancient Mayan tombs.*

artifacts (ärt′ə·fakts′) *n.*: objects made by people or adapted for human use. *Many important artifacts have been stolen from the tombs.*

connoisseurs (kän′ə·sʉrz′) *n.*: people who are experts on something. *The connoisseurs declared the "ancient" sculpture a fake.*

unscrupulous (un·skrōō′pyə·ləs) *adj.*: dishonest. *Stolen Mayan treasures may be bought by unscrupulous collectors.*

SKILLS FOCUS

Reading Skills
Summarize the main ideas.

The Search Goes On
from *The Mystery of the Ancient Maya*
Carolyn Meyer and Charles Gallenkamp

Brilliant achievements, exciting revelations, and countless unsolved mysteries—this is the legacy left by the ancient Maya. Huge areas remain to be explored, dozens of key sites to be investigated. There are hieroglyphic inscriptions[1] to decipher and mountains of data to analyze. And so there are always new projects, new digs, new studies—and new breakthroughs.

In 1962 a geologist prospecting for an oil company in the jungle of Guatemala came across a cluster of ruins. He got in touch with Richard E. W. Adams, a young archaeologist who was on a dig in another part of the country. At that time all the two could do was to map the Río Azul site, named for a river nearby. There was no money then to excavate the ruins they had found.

Over the next twenty years thieves dug trenches around the pyramids, tunneled into them, and even split them open to get at the treasures inside. The looters ransacked at least twenty-eight tombs in this and the surrounding area, smuggling jewelry and other priceless objects into the United States, where they were sold to art collectors for huge sums of money.

When Adams returned to Río Azul in 1981, he heard about the looting and saw the deep trenches and the scattered rubble. On one occasion he and another scientist surprised armed looters at work. Shots were fired and one of the thieves was wounded, but they all got away. After the incident Guatemalan government troops swept the area, and guards with automatic weapons have remained on duty ever since to prevent further looting.

There are tragic consequences to looting: When artifacts are stolen and sold, all the valuable information they could provide is lost forever. The whole historical and archaeological context of each piece of remarkable pottery and exquisite jade jewelry is destroyed. A stolen artifact becomes merely a prized object in a private collection that is often kept secret or shared with only a few connoisseurs.

But unscrupulous collectors are willing to pay enormous sums for

---

1. **hieroglyphic** (hī'ər·ō'glif'ik) **inscriptions:** engraved hieroglyphics (writing in which pictures, rather than letters, are used).

Vocabulary
decipher (dē·sī'fər) *v.:* interpret; find the meaning of.
ransacked (ran'sakt') *v.:* searched thoroughly for goods to steal; looted, robbed.
artifacts (ärt'ə·fakts') *n.:* objects made by people or adapted for human use.
connoisseurs (kän'ə·sʉrz') *n.:* people who are experts on something.
unscrupulous (un·skrōō'pyə·ləs) *adj.:* dishonest.

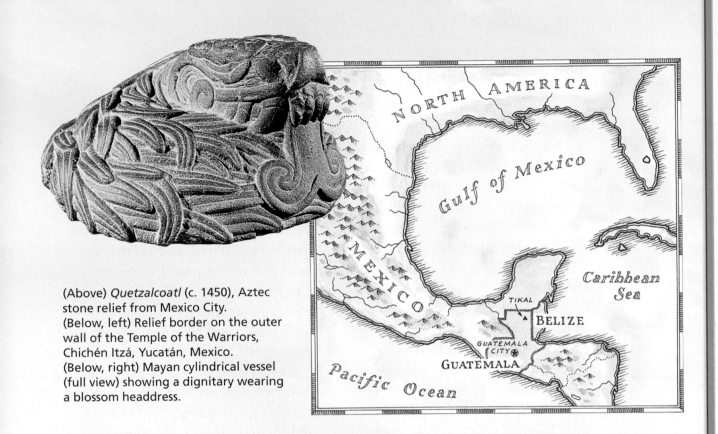

(Above) *Quetzalcoatl* (c. 1450), Aztec stone relief from Mexico City.
(Below, left) Relief border on the outer wall of the Temple of the Warriors, Chichén Itzá, Yucatán, Mexico.
(Below, right) Mayan cylindrical vessel (full view) showing a dignitary wearing a blossom headdress.

treasures for their private collections. The possibility of such profit drives looters to search out and plunder as-yet undiscovered sites. Once they've taken what they want, the looters use smuggling networks to get the ancient jars and jewels out of the jungle and into the hands of collectors all over the world.

Adams and other archaeologists used the incident at Río Azul to convince Congress to pass a law to stop national treasures looted in other countries from being brought into the United States. In addition, the United States signed an agreement that commits this country to recover and return stolen cultural and archaeological objects from Mexico and Central America.

Meanwhile, Adams raised the money to begin excavating the ruin in a race against the looters. The ancient city of Río Azul was probably a small center under the control of the bigger city of Tikal, a few miles to the south. It covers about 470 acres and contains four major temple pyramids and adjoining smaller buildings. Adams and his team had been working on the site for several weeks in the spring of 1984, hoping to get as much accomplished as possible before the rainy season began. Then on May fifteenth a workman's leg plunged through rock-and-dirt fill and down through the roof of a secret chamber, a cave cut into the rock some 13 feet below the surface of the ground.

Hidden by a wing of a temple built on top of it, the cave had gone undetected by looters—and until then by archaeologists as well.

One of the expedition leaders peered in. "It's painted!" he yelled; whoops of excitement greeted the announcement. They began working furiously to clear the rubble from the entrance to what they knew was a tomb. Next they lowered a miniature video camera into the opening. And finally, using vines and saplings from the jungle— traditional Maya building materials— they climbed down into the chamber.

The skeleton of a nobleman in his thirties, his shroud nothing more than dust, lay on a wooden bier.[2] Elaborate and mysterious wall paintings and fifteen pieces of pottery surrounded his body. One of the pieces was a beautifully made jar with an unusual screw-top lid. On top of the skeleton lay a stingray spine used in bloodletting rituals. Parrots chattered overhead and Guatemalan government guards with rifles and machetes stood by as the contents of Tomb 19, as it was now designated, were recorded and labeled and then transported to the National Museum of Anthropology in Guatemala City.

---

2. **bier** (bir) *n.*: platform on which a corpse is placed.

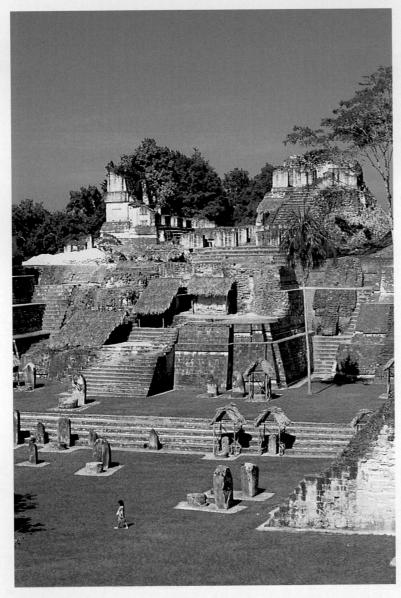

North Acropolis and Central Plaza (c. A.D. 700), Mayan ruins, Tikal, Guatemala.

The date of the tomb is about A.D. 420 to 470, the height of the Classic period.[3] Adams, who calls it "a moment frozen in time," believes that the tomb was built for a relative of a ruler buried in a large pyramid nearby, already looted and stripped of its wall paintings. All that could be read of the hieroglyphics on the walls and pottery were the words *great son*.

---

3. **Classic period:** the period, beginning around A.D. 250 and ending around 900, during which Mayan civilization reached its peak.

Summarizing the Main Ideas

The Search Goes On

1. What happened to the Río Azul site because there was no money to excavate the ruins?

   A The site was destroyed by an earthquake.

   B The treasures were stolen by looters.

   C The treasures were saved by government troops.

   D The site disappeared into the jungle.

2. What do scientists hope to discover from the objects in the ancient Mayan tombs?

   F the history and customs of the people

   G gold and precious stones in the jewelry

   H great art for private collections

   J the identity of the thieves

3. How did the scientists discover Tomb 19?

   A They saw it on a map.

   B They figured out where it was from ancient writings.

   C They dug and dug and dug.

   D A workman's leg broke through the roof.

4. Who do scientists think is buried in Tomb 19?

   F the ruler of Tikal

   G the ruler of the Río Azul site

   H a relative of a ruler

   J a common man

Constructed Response

1. What happens to the objects stolen from the ancient Mayan tombs?

2. Why are scientists upset when objects are stolen from the tombs?

3. **Summarize** the article by describing its **main ideas.** Include only the most important supporting details.

SKILLS FOCUS

Reading Skills
Summarize the main ideas.

After You Read | Vocabulary Development

Clarifying Word Meanings

PRACTICE

Use words from the Word Bank to fill in the blanks in the following sentences. Use each word only once.

1. His mother was furious when Bobby _____ the house looking for his baseball mitt.
2. The teacher gave Alicia a poor grade on her composition because he couldn't _____ the handwriting.
3. As candy _____ , Maria and Miguel knew how to pick the best chocolates from the box.
4. On a class trip to the museum, the students examined the _____ from ancient Egypt.
5. The _____ salesperson lied when he said the old jalopy had been given new brakes.

Word Bank

decipher
ransacked
artifacts
connoisseurs
unscrupulous

Grammar Link

Irregular Verbs

Many people have trouble with irregular verbs. You don't form the past tense of irregular verbs by adding *–d* or *–ed*, as you do with regular verbs. The only way to be sure you know the various forms of irregular verbs is to memorize them. Reading this list aloud several times will help you remember these odd verb forms.

Base Form	Past	Past Participle
am/is/are	was/were	(has/have) been
begin	began	(has/have) begun
break	broke	(has/have) broken
bring	brought	(has/have) brought
do	did	(has/have) done
find	found	(has/have) found
go	went	(has/have) gone
see	saw	(has/have) seen

PRACTICE

Act as an editor: Provide the correct irregular verb forms in the paragraph below.

We had went to the jungle and had began searching for ruins. We brung axes and machetes to clear the thick growth. We finally breaked through and seen a temple covered with vines. I been surprised that we done such a good job!

For more help, see Irregular Verbs, 3c, in the Language Handbook.

SKILLS FOCUS

Vocabulary Skills
Clarify word meanings.

Grammar Skills
Recognize irregular verbs.

Comparing Literature

Literary Focus
The Cinderella Story

When you read "Yeh-Shen" (page 383), you learned that there are more than nine hundred versions of the Cinderella story from all around the world and that "Yeh-Shen" comes from China. You are about to read three other versions of this popular tale. "Aschenputtel" is a traditional folk tale from Germany. "Dinorella" is a lively contemporary version. "Interview" is a short poem that suggests the story of Cinderella would be very different if it were told by another character. As you read each selection, compare it to the typical Cinderella story. Think about: Who are the **characters**? What is the **plot**? What is the **tone** (serious, humorous, sad)? What is the **theme,** or message?

Reading Skills
Comparing and Contrasting

These three selections offer different versions of the same story. As you read each one, think about how the stories are the same and how they are different. When you have finished reading all three selections, you will be asked to write an essay comparing the stories. A chart at the end of each selection will help you gather details for your essay.

> ### Features of a Typical Cinderella Story
>
> #### Characters:
> - a young girl
> - a wicked step-mother and jealous stepsisters
> - a handsome prince
> - magical characters who help the girl
>
> #### Plot:
> - The girl lives in poverty yet longs to go to the prince's ball.
> - Magical characters help the girl.
> - The prince falls in love with the girl, but she runs off and he has to find her.
> - The girl and the prince live happily ever after.

SKILLS FOCUS

Literary Skills
Analyze the Cinderella story.

Reading Skills
Compare and contrast texts.

You probably know the story of Cinderella. "Aschenputtel" is the German version of that story. In both tales a young girl's mother dies and her father remarries. The girl is then mistreated by her stepmother and stepsisters, but in the end, she marries the handsome prince. As you read, think about how this version of the Cinderella story is the same as or different from any other version you may know.

Aschenputtel

German, retold by
Jakob *and* **Wilhelm Grimm,**
translated by **Lucy Crane**

There was once a rich man whose wife lay sick, and when she felt her end drawing near, she called to her only daughter to come near her bed and said,

"Dear child, be pious and good, and God will always take care of you, and I will look down upon you from heaven and will be with you."

And then she closed her eyes and expired.[1] The maiden went every day to her mother's grave and wept and was always pious and good. When the winter came, the snow covered the grave with a white covering, and when the sun came in the early spring and melted it away, the man took to himself another wife. ❶

The new wife brought two daughters home with her and they were beautiful and fair in appearance but at heart were wicked and ugly. And then began very evil times for the poor stepdaughter.

"Is the stupid creature to sit in the same room with us?" said they. "Those who eat food must earn it. Out with the kitchen maid!"

They took away her pretty dresses and put on her an old gray kirtle[2] and gave her wooden shoes to wear.

"Just look now at the proud princess, how she is decked out!" cried they, laughing, and then they sent her into the kitchen. There she was obliged to do heavy work from morning to night, get up early in the morning, draw water, make the fires, cook, and wash. Besides that, the sisters did their utmost to torment her—mocking her and strewing peas and lentils among the ashes and setting her to pick them up. In the evenings, when she was quite tired out with her hard day's work, she had no bed to lie on but was obliged to rest on the hearth among the cinders. And as she always looked dusty and dirty, they named her Aschenputtel. ❷

It happened one day that the father went to the fair, and he asked his two stepdaughters what he should bring back for them.

"Fine clothes!" said one.

"Pearls and jewels!" said the other.

"But what will you have, Aschenputtel?" said he.

"The first twig, Father, that strikes against your hat on the way home; this is what I should like you to bring me."

IDENTIFY

❶ Re-read the first three paragraphs. How would you describe the **tone** of the folk tale?

COMPARE AND CONTRAST

❷ From what you have read so far, how is the daughter different from her stepsisters? How has the **tone** changed?

---

1. **expired** (ek·spīrd′) *v.:* died. In Latin, *exspirare* means "to breathe out"; to breathe out one's last breath is to die.
2. **kirtle** *n.:* old-fashioned word for "dress."

> ## "Is the stupid creature to sit in the same room with us?"

So he bought for the two stepdaughters fine clothes, pearls, and jewels, and on his way back, as he rode through a green lane, a hazel twig struck against his hat; and he broke it off and carried it home with him. And when he reached home, he gave to the stepdaughters what they had wished for, and to Aschenputtel he gave the hazel twig. She thanked him and went to her mother's grave, and planted this twig there, weeping so bitterly that the tears fell upon it and watered it, and it flourished and became a fine tree. Aschenputtel went to see it three times a day and wept and prayed, and each time a white bird rose up from the tree, and, if she uttered any wish, the bird brought her whatever she had wished for. ❸

Now it came to pass that the king ordained³ a festival that should last for three days and to which all the beautiful young women of that country were bidden so that the king's son might choose a bride from among them. When the two stepdaughters heard that they too were bidden to appear, they felt very pleased, and they called Aschenputtel and said,

"Comb our hair, brush our shoes, and make our buckles fast, we are going to the wedding feast at the king's castle."

Aschenputtel, when she heard this, could not help crying, for she too would have liked to go to the dance, and she begged her stepmother to allow her.

"What, you Aschenputtel!" said she. "In all your dust and dirt, you want to go to the festival! You that have no dress and no shoes! You want to dance!"

But since she persisted in asking, at last the stepmother said,

"I have scattered a dish full of lentils in the ashes, and if you can pick them all up again in two hours, you may go with us."

Then the maiden went to the back door that led into the garden and called out,

INTERPRET

❸ How does Aschenputtel's request for a twig prove to be a good choice?

---

3. **ordained** (ôr·dānd′) *v.*: ordered or decreed.

O gentle doves, O turtledoves,
And all the birds that be,
The lentils that in ashes lie
Come and pick up for me!
    The good must be put in the dish,
    The bad you may eat if you wish. ❹

Then there came to the kitchen window two white doves, and after them some turtledoves, and at last a crowd of all the birds under heaven, chirping and fluttering, and they alighted among the ashes; and the doves nodded with their heads and began to pick, peck, pick, peck, and then all the others began to pick, peck, pick, peck and put all the good grains into the dish. Before an hour was over, all was done, and they flew away. Then the maiden brought the dish to her stepmother, feeling joyful and thinking that now she should go to the feast; but the stepmother said,

"No, Aschenputtel, you have no proper clothes, and you do not know how to dance, and you would be laughed at!"

And when Aschenputtel cried for disappointment, she added,

"If you can pick two dishfuls of lentils out of the ashes, nice and clean, you shall go with us," thinking to herself, "for that is not possible." When she had strewed two dishfuls of lentils among the ashes, the maiden went through the back door into the garden and cried,

"She is my partner," said the prince.

O gentle doves, O turtledoves,
And all the birds that be,
The lentils that in ashes lie
Come and pick up for me!
    The good must be put in the dish,
    The bad you may eat if you wish.

So there came to the kitchen window two white doves, and then some turtledoves, and at last a crowd of all the other birds under heaven, chirping and fluttering, and they alighted among the ashes,

INFER

❹ How does Aschenputtel show consideration for the birds in the way she calls them? What does this tell you about her **character**?

and the doves nodded with their heads and began to pick, peck, pick, peck, and then all the others began to pick, peck, pick, peck and put all the good grains into the dish. And before half an hour was over, it was all done, and they flew away. Then the maiden took the dishes to the stepmother, feeling joyful and thinking that now she should go with them to the feast. But her stepmother said, "All this is of no good to you; you cannot come with us, for you have no proper clothes and cannot dance; you would put us to shame."

Then she turned her back on poor Aschenputtel and made haste to set out with her two proud daughters.

And as there was no one left in the house, Aschenputtel went to her mother's grave, under the hazel bush, and cried,

Little tree, little tree, shake over me,
That silver and gold may come down
    and cover me.

Then the bird threw down a dress of gold and silver and a pair of slippers embroidered with silk and silver. And in all haste she put on the dress and went to the festival. But her stepmother and sisters did not know her and thought she must be a foreign princess, she looked so beautiful in her golden dress. Of Aschenputtel they never thought at all and supposed that she was sitting at home, picking the lentils out of the ashes. The King's son came to meet her and took her by the hand and danced with her, and he refused to stand up with anyone else so that he might not be obliged to let go her hand; and when anyone came to claim it, he answered,

"She is my partner." **5**

And when the evening came, she wanted to go home, but the prince said he would go with her to take care of her, for he wanted to see where the beautiful maiden lived. But she escaped him and jumped up into the pigeon house. Then the prince waited until her father came along, and told him that the strange maiden had jumped into the pigeon house. The father thought to himself, "It cannot surely be Aschenputtel" and called for axes and hatchets and had the pigeon house cut down, but there was no one in it. And when they entered the house, there sat Aschenputtel in her dirty clothes among the cinders, and a little oil lamp burnt dimly in the chimney; for Aschenputtel had been very quick and had jumped out of the pigeon house again and had run to the hazel bush; and there she had taken off her beautiful dress and had laid it on the grave, and the bird had

COMPARE AND CONTRAST

5 Explain how people treat Aschenputtel differently depending on what she's wearing.

carried it away again, and then she had put on her little gray kirtle again and had sat down in the kitchen among the cinders.

The next day, when the festival began anew, and the parents and stepsisters had gone to it, Aschenputtel went to the hazel bush and cried,

Little tree, little tree, shake over me,
That silver and gold may come down
    and cover me.

Then the bird cast down a still more splendid dress than on the day before. And when she appeared in it among the guests, everyone was astonished at her beauty. The prince had been waiting until she came, and he took her hand and danced with her alone. And when anyone else came to invite her, he said,

"She is my partner."

And when the evening came, she wanted to go home, and the prince followed her, for he wanted to see to what house she belonged; but she broke away from him and ran into the garden at the back of the house. There stood a fine large tree, bearing splendid pears; she leapt as lightly as a squirrel among the branches, and the prince did not know what had become of her. So he waited until her father came along, and then he told him that the strange maiden had rushed from him, and that he thought she had gone up into the pear tree. The father thought to himself,

"It cannot surely be Aschenputtel" and called for an axe and felled the tree, but there was no one in it. And when they went into the kitchen, there sat Aschenputtel among the cinders, as usual, for she had got down the other side of the tree and had taken back her beautiful clothes to the bird on the hazel bush and had put on her old gray kirtle again.

On the third day, when the parents and the stepchildren had set off, Aschenputtel went again to her mother's grave and said to the tree,

Little tree, little tree, shake over me,
That silver and gold may come down
    and cover me.

Then the bird cast down a dress the likes of which had never been seen for splendor and brilliancy, and slippers that were of gold.

And when she appeared in this dress at the feast, nobody knew what to say for wonderment. The prince danced with her alone, and if anyone else asked her, he answered,

He turned his horse round and took the false bride home.

"She is my partner." ❻

And when it was evening, Aschenputtel wanted to go home, and the prince was about to go with her when she ran past him so quickly that he could not follow her. But he had laid a plan and had caused all the steps to be spread with pitch,[4] so that as she rushed down them, her left shoe remained sticking in it. The prince picked it up and saw that it was of gold and very small and slender. The next morning he went to the father and told him that none should be his bride save the one whose foot the golden shoe should fit. Then the two sisters were very glad, because they had pretty feet. The eldest went to her room to try on the shoe, and her mother stood by. But she could not get her great toe into it, for the shoe was too small; then her mother handed her a knife, and said,

"Cut the toe off, for when you are queen, you will never have to go on foot." So the girl cut her toe off, squeezed her foot into the shoe, concealed the pain, and went down to the prince. Then he took her with him on his horse as his bride and rode off. They had to pass by the grave, and there sat the two pigeons on the hazel bush and cried,

There they go, there they go!
There is blood on her shoe;
The shoe is too small,
—Not the right bride at all!

Then the prince looked at her shoe and saw the blood flowing. And he turned his horse round and took the false bride home again, saying she was not the right one and that the other sister must try on the shoe. So she went into her room to do so and got her toes comfortably in, but her heel was too large. Then her mother handed her the knife, saying, "Cut a piece off your heel; when you are queen, you will never have to go on foot."

IDENTIFY

❻ A common **motif** in folk tales is the number three. What events have happened three times in this story?

---

4. **pitch** (pich) *n.:* here, black, sticky tar.

So the girl cut a piece off her heel and thrust her foot into the shoe, concealed the pain, and went down to the prince, who took his bride before him on his horse and rode off. When they passed by the hazel bush, the two pigeons sat there and cried,

> There they go, there they go!
> There is blood on her shoe;
> The shoe is too small,
> —Not the right bride at all!

Then the prince looked at her foot and saw how the blood was flowing from the shoe and staining the white stocking. And he turned his horse round and brought the false bride home again.

"This is not the right one," said he. "Have you no other daughter?" ❼

"No," said the man, "only my dead wife left behind her a little stunted[5] Aschenputtel; it is impossible that she can be the bride." But the King's son ordered her to be sent for, but the mother said,

"Oh, no! She is much too dirty; I could not let her be seen."

But he would have her fetched, and so Aschenputtel had to appear.

First she washed her face and hands quite clean and went in and curtseyed to the prince, who held out to her the golden shoe. Then she sat down on a stool, drew her foot out of the heavy wooden shoe, and slipped it into the golden one, which fitted it perfectly. And when she stood up and the prince looked in her face, he knew again the beautiful maiden that had danced with him, and he cried,

"This is the right bride!"

The stepmother and the two sisters were thunderstruck and grew pale with anger, but the prince put Aschenputtel before him on his horse and rode off. And as they passed the hazel bush, the two white pigeons cried,

> There they go, there they go!
> No blood on her shoe;
> The shoe's not too small,
> The right bride is she after all.

And when they had thus cried, they came flying after and perched on Aschenputtel's shoulders, one on the right, the other on the left, and so remained.

---

5. stunted (stunt′id) *v.* used as *adj.*: not properly grown.
6. curry favor: try to win approval by flattering and fawning.

PREDICT

❼ Two times a sister has tried on the shoe that was too small. What do you predict will happen next?

And when her wedding with the prince was appointed to be held, the false sisters came, hoping to curry favor[6] and to take part in the festivities. So as the bridal procession went to the church, the eldest walked on the right side and the younger on the left, and the pigeons picked out an eye of each of them. And as they returned, the elder was on the left side and the younger on the right, and the pigeons picked out the other eye of each of them. And so they were condemned for the rest of their days because of their wickedness and falsehood. ❽

INTERPRET

❽ Throughout the story white pigeons (or doves) right the wrongs done to Aschenputtel. What do you think the birds might represent?

Jakob and Wilhelm Grimm

Two Brothers with a Dream

Before the 1800s, most fairy tales were not written down. They existed only in the memories of people who had heard them from their elders. **Jakob** (1785–1863) and **Wilhelm** (1786–1859) **Grimm** decided that the traditional stories of Germany ought to be written down in one book before they were forgotten. Jakob wrote:

> 66 It is high time that these old traditions were collected and rescued before they perish like dew in the hot sun or fire in a stream and fall silent forever in the unrest of our days. 99

The two brothers wandered from farm to village, looking for good storytellers who knew the old tales. They listened patiently and wrote the stories down. By the time the last edition of their stories was published, in 1857, the brothers had collected about two hundred tales. Some of the best-known ones are "Little Red Riding Hood," "Rumpelstiltskin," "Hansel and Gretel," "Sleeping Beauty," and, of course, "Aschenputtel," or "Cinderella."

The Granger Collection, New York.

For Independent Reading

If you browse through *The Complete Grimm's Fairy Tales,* you will find some truly grim stories. These German tales are filled with acts of cruelty and murder. In the United States, retellers of the tales have sometimes toned them down, producing storybook versions that are much less terrifying.

First Thoughts

1. Which of our deepest wishes do you think this story expresses? Do you think it is also about some of our fears? Explain.

Thinking Critically

2. Which of the following statements do you think best sums up the lesson "Aschenputtel" seems to teach?

   - Goodness is rewarded in the end.
   - Bad people are always punished.
   - Love conquers all.

   Do you think this is a good lesson for today's world? Explain.

3. How is the **motif** of the number three used in this folk tale? Explain how it helps to build suspense.

4. Many modern versions of this story do not punish the wicked stepsisters. What do you think of this version's ending? Did the stepsisters deserve their fate? Do such cruel details belong in a story for children? Explain your responses.

Reading Check

a. What does Aschenputtel do with the twig her father gives her?

b. What does the stepmother do to stop Aschenputtel from attending the feast?

c. Who helps Aschenputtel complete her tasks?

d. How does the prince manage to get one of Aschenputtel's golden slippers?

e. What happens to the stepsisters on Aschenputtel and the prince's wedding day?

Comparing Literature

5. After you've read all three selections, you'll be asked to compare the way each presents the typical Cinderella story. You can begin to prepare for your essay now by filling out the "Aschenputtel" column in a chart like the one below. Continue to fill in your chart after you finish reading each of the other selections.

Comparing Cinderella Stories

	"Aschenputtel"	"Dinorella"	"Interview"
Characters			
Plot			
Tone			
Theme			

INTERNET
Projects and Activities
Keyword: LE5 7-6

Literary Skills
Analyze the Cinderella story.

Reading Skills
Compare and contrast texts.

Before You Read

This is a delightful dinosaur version of the Cinderella story. It deals with dreadful stepsisters, a dance till dawn, a distracting disturbance, dangling diamonds, a dashing duke, and darling, adorable Dinorella. Do you discern a pattern here? This repetition of the same or similar consonant sounds is called **alliteration.** See if you can read the story aloud without tripping over your tongue.

DiNORELLA

Pamela Duncan Edwards

Dora, Doris, and Dinorella lived down in the sand dunes in a dinosaur den.

Dora and Doris did nothing all day. They dumped debris around the den. They never did the dusting or the dishes. Dinorella was dainty and dependable. Dora and Doris were dreadful to Dinorella. All day they demanded . . .

"**DiNORELLA,** dig the garden.

"**DiNORELLA,** fetch us drinks.

"**DiNORELLA,** start the dinner."

"She's a dingbat," sniggered Dora.

"She's a dumbhead," giggled Doris. ❶

COMPARE AND CONTRAST

❶ How is this version of the story different from the traditional story of Cinderella so far? How is it the same?

One day a card was delivered to the den:

> ### Dinosaur Dance
> Duke Dudley's Den
> At Dusk
> Hors d'oeuvres, Dandelion Cola
> Dancing Until Dawn

Duke Dudley was the most dashing dinosaur in the dunes. ❷

"I would die for a date with the duke," said Dora, decorating herself with dinosaur jewels.

"Definitely," sighed Doris, dolling up for the dance.

"A dance," said Dinorella diffidently. "How divine."

"**YOU** can't go to the dance," said Doris. "**YOU'RE** too dowdy."

"**YOU'RE** too dull," agreed Dora. "And **YOU** don't have decent dinosaur jewels. Of course **YOU** can't go to the dance."

Poor Dinorella felt down in the dumps as she watched her stepsisters depart.

Suddenly, Dinorella heard a droning noise.

"Don't be dismal," cried Fairydactyl. "You **SHALL** go to the dance."

"But I'm so drab," said Dinorella, "and I don't have decent dinosaur jewels."

"I'll soon deal with that," declared Fairydactyl. "These will outdazzle all other dinosaur jewels."

"**DARLING** Fairydactyl!" exclaimed Dinorella in delight. With her diamonds dangling, she set out for the dance. ❸

Dusk had fallen when Dinorella heard a deafening disturbance coming from the direction of Duke Dudley's Den.

A DASTARDLY DEED WAS TAKING PLACE!
A deinonychus[1] was dragging off the duke.

"**I'M DONE FOR!**" cried the duke. "He will **DEVOUR** me!"

"Indeed I will!" laughed the deinonychus. "I'll be digesting you by daybreak."

---

1. **deinonychus** (dī·nän′i·kəs) *n*.: small, swift, meat-eating dinosaur.

Comparing Literature

INTERPRET

❷ Why do you think this story has a duke instead of a prince? (Could it have something to do with **alliteration**—the use of similar consonant sounds in nearby words?)

COMPARE AND CONTRAST

❸ Fairydactyl saves the day. Who saves the day in "Aschenputtel"?

Dinorella was not a daring dinosaur, but something drastic had to be done.

"I may become dessert, but I'm determined to drive away that dreaded carnivore."

Dinorella climbed to the top of the dune.

"**YOU DISGUSTING DUMMY**," she roared. "**DROP THE DUKE!**"

Dinorella began to hurl dirtballs at the deinonychus.

The dumbfounded deinonychus stopped in disbelief. "Who called me a dummy?" he demanded.

The moon's light caught Dinorella's dangling diamonds. Dots and dabs of light darted toward the deinonychus.

"**A DEVIL!**" cried the deinonychus. "See its dreadful demon eyes!"

Dinorella detached a diamond and directed it toward the deinonychus.

The diamond hit the deinonychus **HARD** in his dentures. ❹

"The devil will destroy me with its deadly eyes," bellowed the distraught deinonychus. He dumped Duke Dudley and departed double-quick.

The den was dense with dinosaurs dashing about in distress. "A demon," they cried. "**WE'RE DOOMED.**"

"**DIMWITS!**" roared Duke Dudley through the din. "Demons don't throw diamonds. It was a damsel who defended me with her dazzling dinosaur jewel.

"When I discover her, I shall ask her to be my darling."

COMPARE AND CONTRAST

❹ How is Dinorella's behavior similar to or different from that of Aschenputtel?

All the dinosaur dames were delirious.
"The jewel is mine!" they each declared.
"**MiNE!**" cried Doris.
"**NO, DEFiNiTELY MiNE,**" bellowed
Dora, giving Doris a dig. "I am the damsel
you desire."
"**i DOUBT iT,**" declared Duke
Dudley. "Your dinosaur jewels don't match." ❺

Just then, Fairydactyl arrived at the dance. She
quickly saw the dilemma.
"**WHERE iS DiNORELLA?**" she
demanded.

"Dinorella!" scoffed Dora, "that dopey domestic."
"Dinorella!" laughed Doris. "She's back at the den."
But Fairydactyl spied Dinorella dodging behind the dune.
"**DiNORELLA,**" she directed, "come down."
So down came Dinorella, looking distracted.
Cried the duke, "She wears but one dazzling jewel!"
"Dinorella, you are adorable. You're definitely quite a dish. I beg
you to be my dearest."
"**DREAMY!**" said Dinorella as they danced off into the dawn.
"**DRAT!**" said Dora and Doris. ❻

Comparing
Literature

COMPARE AND CONTRAST

❺ How is this part of
the story similar to
"Aschenputtel"? How
is it different?

EVALUATE

❻ Which version of
the Cinderella story—
"Dinorella" or
"Aschenputtel"—do
you like best? Why?

Pamela Duncan Edwards

A Unique Character

About her story "Dinorella," **Pamela Duncan Edwards** has said:

> 66 I knew children loved fairy stories, and I also knew—because I taught for so long—that children love dinosaurs. And I thought, what a great thing to do, to put together two of the things that children like so much—put together a dinosaur and put together a fairy story. However, I didn't want to make Dinorella the same type of character as Cinderella. 99

Edwards was born and raised in England, where she was a preschool teacher. When she moved to the United States, she started her career as a children's librarian at a school in Virginia. When Edwards attended a children's literature conference with illustrator Henry Cole, they first discussed ideas for children's books. The partnership they later developed resulted in many highly praised storybooks.

The first book Edwards wrote was, like "Dinorella," focused on a single consonant. She has said:

> 66 I do like writing alliterative books. I have great fun writing them because I get my thesaurus out. I have to find a word that begins with that letter that will say what I want to say. It's such good fun. And as I'm reading in my thesaurus, I'm finding other words. . . . So it's a great expansion of my vocabulary, as well as the child's vocabulary. 99

For Independent Reading

For other funny alliterative stories by Pamela Duncan Edwards, try *Some Smug Slug* and *Four Famished Foxes and Fosdyke*.

After You Read "Dinorella"

First Thoughts

1. Finish the following sentence:

- The part of "Dinorella" I liked best (or least) was . . .

Thinking Critically

2. What new story elements does "Dinorella" add to the traditional Cinderella story, such as "Aschenputtel"? (Think about the characters, the plot, and the setting.)

3. "Aschenputtel" has a serious **tone,** which means that the storyteller takes the characters and their problems very seriously. This indicates that the teller has a serious message for the reader. What is the tone of "Dinorella"? Is it serious, comical, satiric, bitter, or something else?

4. Do you think the writer has a serious message for the reader? Explain how you would express the message, or **theme,** of "Dinorella."

5. "Dinorella" tells the Cinderella story through **alliteration** with the sound of *d.* Retell at least part of the story using another consonant. Perhaps Kittenella could cut a caper with the King of Cats, for example. You'll find lots of inspiration, as Edwards says she did, in a thesaurus.

Comparing Literature

6. Fill in the "Dinorella" column in a chart like the one below. Your finished chart will help you complete the assignment on writing a comparison-contrast essay on page 767.

> ### Reading Check
> **Summarize** "Dinorella." Start with the title and author. Then, name the main characters and their **conflict,** or problem. As you describe the main events, see how many words you can use that begin with *d.* Finally, state the **resolution** of the problem.

Comparing Cinderella Stories			
	"Aschenputtel"	"Dinorella"	"Interview"
Characters			
Plot			
Tone			
Theme			

SKILLS FOCUS

Literary Skills
Analyze the Cinderella story.

Reading Skills
Compare and contrast texts.

Before You Read

This poem uses a modern-day event—an interview with the press—to present an unexpected point of view on the story of Cinderella. As you read the poem, decide who the speaker is. What **tone** do you hear in the poem; that is, what is the speaker's attitude or feeling toward Cinderella? Do you believe the speaker?

Anjelica Huston as the stepmother in *Ever After: A Cinderella Story.*

INTERVIEW

Sara Henderson Hay

Yes, this is where she lived before she won
The title Miss Glass Slipper of the Year,
And went to the ball and married the king's son.
You're from the local press, and want to hear
5 About her early life? Young man, sit down.
These are my *own* two daughters; you'll not find
Nicer, more biddable° girls in all the town,
And lucky, I tell them, not to be the kind ❶

---

7. biddable (bid′ə·bəl) *adj.:* obedient.

IDENTIFY

❶ Who is the speaker of the poem? How can you tell?

That Cinderella was, spreading those lies,
10   Telling those shameless tales about the way
We treated her. Oh, nobody denies
That she was pretty, if you like those curls.
But looks aren't everything, I always say. ❷
Be sweet and natural, I tell my girls,
15   And Mr. Right will come along, someday.

**COMPARE AND
CONTRAST**

❷ What does the
speaker tell you about
Cinderella's **character**?
How does her
character differ from
the characters of
"Aschenputtel" and
"Dinorella"?

Meet the Writer

Sara Henderson Hay

A Dedicated Poet

Sara Henderson Hay (1906–1987) was
born in Pittsburgh and lived there and in
the South for most of her life. Hay's first
published poem, which was about golf,
appeared in a publication titled *Judge
Magazine* when she was ten years old.
Hay also received encouragement to
write when her work was published in
her hometown newspaper while she was
in high school and when her poems were
published in the school magazine at
Columbia University in New York City. Hay
went on to win awards for her poems
and to publish six poetry collections.

For Independent Reading

Read Hay's poetry collection *Story Hour,*
which "Interview" is taken from, and
enjoy the author's surprising and often
humorous twists on several old tales.

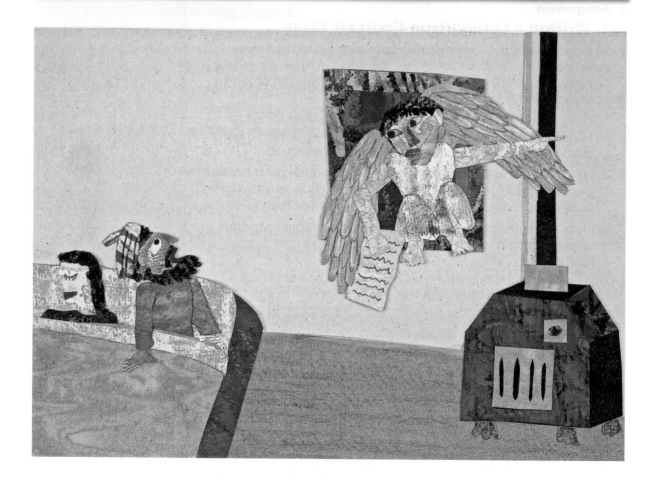

The Dream of Good Fortune

from The Arabian Nights,
dramatized by Paul Sills

Characters

Luqman Ali	The Chief of Police
His Wife	A Thief
An Angel	The Lieutenant

Luq. Luqman Ali, a poor but honest dung sweeper, lived in the alley of the tanners, off the street of the potters, in the heart of the great city of Baghdad.[1]

Wife. He and his wife had nothing in the world but an old iron stove, and barely enough to eat.

Luq. But still they did not despair in the mercy of the Almighty. One night Luqman Ali and his wife lay down to sleep, and he had a dream.

Angel. An angel appeared with a message: "Luqman Ali, alley of the tanners, off the street of the potters, in the city of Baghdad—Dear Luq, Go to Cairo,[2] and there you will find your fortune."

Luq. Luqman Ali awoke his wife and told her of his strange dream.

Wife. Go back to sleep, my love, it was only a dream.

---

1. **Baghdad:** ancient Middle Eastern city, the center of Islamic civilization during the period in which many of the *Arabian Nights* stories are set. Today Baghdad is the capital of Iraq.
2. **Cairo** (kī**′**rō): capital of Egypt.

Angel. Luqman Ali, go to Cairo, and there you will find your fortune.

Luq. Wife, wake up; the angel came again and told me to go to Cairo, to seek my fortune.

Wife. If it happens a third time, you'll have to go.

Angel. Luqman Ali, are you still here? Go to Cairo! Your fortune awaits you there.

Luq. I go! I go! Wife, awaken—I must go to Cairo. And so Luqman Ali set off on the road to Cairo. Through hot desert winds—sand-storms—cold nights. Luqman Ali traveled the road until, weary and sore, in the shimmering heat, he saw the great city of Cairo. Tired and not knowing where to go, he took refuge in the courtyard of a great mosque,[3] where he lay down to sleep.

Thief. That night, a thief entered the courtyard and broke through the wall of an adjoining house.

[*A woman screams offstage. The* THIEF *returns to the courtyard, hits* LUQ, *and runs off.*]

Luq. Stop, thief! Stop, thief!

Chief of Police. The chief of police . . .

Lieutenant. And his lieutenant . . .

Chief of Police. Arrived at the scene, and they found Luqman Ali, and thinking him to be the thief . . .

Lieutenant. They beat him with their clubs and dragged him off to jail.

Chief of Police. Who are you?

Luq. Luqman Ali.

Chief of Police. Where do you come from?

Luq. Baghdad.

Chief of Police. What brings you to Cairo?

Luq. I had a dream . . .

[*The* LIEUTENANT *squeezes* LUQ's *nose, sending him to his knees.*]

Chief of Police. What are you doing in Cairo?

Luq (*rises*). I had a dream . . .

[*The* LIEUTENANT *squeezes his head.*]

Chief of Police (*waving the* LIEUTENANT *away*). What brings you to Cairo?

---

3. **mosque** (mäsk) *n.:* Muslim house of worship.

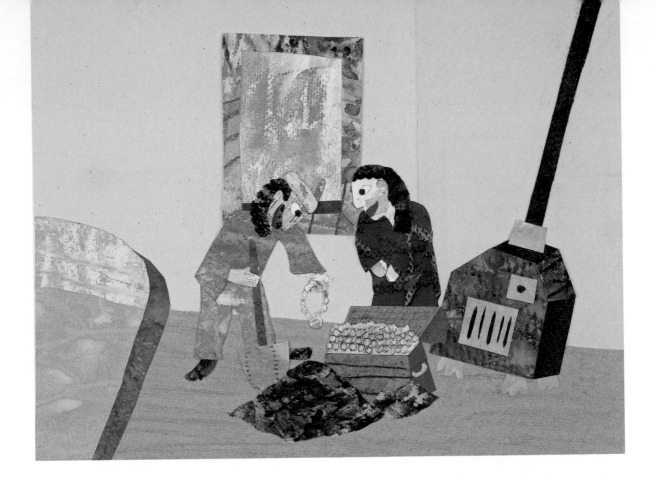

Luq (*again on his knees*). I had a dream. An angel appeared to me three times in a row and told me to go to Cairo, where I would find my fortune.

Chief of Police. And what did you find?

Luq. I got arrested and beat up.

Chief of Police. It hurts too, doesn't it? Dreams mean nothing. We all have dreams. You fool! That's the trouble with you people. Superstitious. I had a dream only last night: An angel came to me and told me to go to Baghdad, to the alley of the potters, off the street of the tanners, to a little old shack, and there under an old iron stove I would find a treasure. Did I go? No! I stayed here doing my job. Here, take these dinars[4] and get out of here.

[*So* LUQ *sets off to his home in Baghdad. He "dances" back to Baghdad, calling "Wife, wife." They move the stove, find the treasure, and adorn each other with jewels. She kisses his nose.—"Owww!!!"— Fade Out*]

---

4. dinars (di·närz′) *n.*: kind of money used in many Middle Eastern countries.

Writing Workshop

Assignment

Write an essay comparing and contrasting two literary elements, subjects, or works.

Audience

Your teacher and classmates

RUBRIC
Evaluation Criteria

A good comparison-contrast essay

1. identifies the topic and the thesis of the essay in its introduction

2. discusses at least two similarities or differences

3. includes specific details and examples to support statements

4. brings the essay to a close with a summary or restatement of the main idea

SKILLS FOCUS

Writing Skills
Write a comparison-contrast essay.

EXPOSITORY WRITING
Comparison-Contrast Essay

In this collection you have seen that there are some stories, like the tale about Cinderella, that exist in many versions. While there are similarities in all these versions, there are also differences.

The technique of comparison and contrast can help you increase your understanding of two or more things. When you **compare,** you look for similarities. When you **contrast,** you look for differences. Comparison-and-contrast writing is useful in any field of study. It is particularly useful in analyzing literary elements, characters, or works. In this workshop you will write a comparison-contrast essay on a topic of your choice.

Prewriting

1 Choosing a Topic

Read and respond to this **prompt:**

> In reading literature, you often compare and contrast different works. One folk tale or myth may recall another you have read; characters in two stories may choose different solutions to a similar problem; two poems may express different points of view on the same topic. When you compare two subjects, you may find that you get a clearer view of each one. Choosing two works that you have read in this anthology or elsewhere, write a comparison-contrast essay that discusses similarities and differences in both works.

One way to find a topic is to look through some of the collections in this book. For example, the selections in Collection 1 focus on the element of **plot;** those in Collection 2 focus on the element of **characterization.** The works you choose don't have to be the same type; however, they must have something in common. Here are some possibilities for your comparison-contrast essay:

- Two similar fables, folk tales, or myths
- Characters who face a similar problem
- Two poems with a common theme
- Two versions of a work—a novel and a movie or TV adaptation

Identify a pair of selections or features for your essay. Then, freewrite, jotting down similarities in one column and differences in another.

2 Finding Similarities and Differences

In deciding which features to compare and contrast, compare like with like. If you choose to compare and contrast two poems, focus on the same elements of both works: imagery, rhythm and theme, for example. If you choose two characters, discuss each character's actions, appearance, thoughts, and feelings. A **Venn diagram** can help you collect ideas about how your subjects are alike and different. Similarities appear where the two circles overlap; differences appear where they don't overlap. Here is a Venn diagram for the Student Model on page 775.

ANTONIO   FELIX

Differences
- "fair, lean, and lanky"
- better boxer
- before fight passes time on rooftop
- wears white trunks
- gives piston-pumping jabs

Similarities
- 17 years old
- live in same building
- dream of being a champion
- chosen for tournament
- collect Fight magazines
- keep scrapbooks
- jog and work out daily

Differences
- "dark, short, and husky"
- better slugger
- before fight watches boxing movie
- wears sky-blue trunks
- bobs and weaves

Writing Tip
The word *compare* can be used broadly to mean "compare and contrast." Whenever you see the word *compare* on a test or essay assignment, find out if you're expected to both compare and contrast.

Block Method

Subject 1: Antonio
Feature 1: behavior
Feature 2: characteristics
Feature 3: feelings

Subject 2: Felix
Feature 1: behavior
Feature 2: characteristics
Feature 3: feelings

Point-by-Point Method

Feature 1: behavior
Subject 1: Antonio
Subject 2: Felix

Feature 2: characteristics
Subject 1: Antonio
Subject 2: Felix

Feature 3: feelings
Subject 1: Antonio
Subject 2: Felix

Writing Tip

A good conclusion should be more than just a summary of your ideas. Expand the main idea that you stated in your introduction. One possibility is to connect the works with your own or your readers' experiences. Another possibility is to extend the discussion to other works or to broader topics related to the works you have chosen.

Transitional Expressions

Transitional words that show similarities

also	just as
another	like
as well as	neither
both	not only
in addition	similarly
in the same way	too

Transitional words that show differences

although	nor
but	on the other
ever	hand
in contrast	otherwise
instead	still
in spite of	unlike
nevertheless	yet

3 **Organize Your Information**

The details in a comparison-contrast essay are usually arranged in one of two patterns: **block method** or **point-by-point method.** Block style focuses on all points of comparison for one subject at a time. The point-by-point method alternates between subjects, explaining how both are alike and different for each point of comparison. These patterns are shown in the column to the right on page 773.

Drafting

1 **Developing Your Draft**

Construct your essay in three parts.

- **Introduction:** Identify the topic of your paper, giving the titles of the works and the names of the authors. Include one or two sentences that summarize your **thesis,** or main idea, about the similarities and differences of your subjects. Add any background information that your readers might need.

- **Body:** Discuss two or three of the most important similarities or differences. Choose either the block method or the point-by-point method of organization.

- **Conclusion:** Restate your main idea. Summarize all the points you have made in the body of your paper. If you wish, add a personal response or direct the reader to other related works.

2 **Guiding Your Reader**

Help your reader out by giving clues to when you are comparing and contrasting. You can do this by using transitional words and phrases. The box in the left column lists some **transitional expressions** that show similarities and some that show differences.

Student Model

Amigo Brothers

Piri Thomas's story "Amigo Brothers" is about two best friends named Felix and Antonio who love boxing. Although they are different in appearance and have different styles of boxing, the two boys share many similarities, which is probably why they are best friends. They are faced with a challenge. They will have to compete against each other for the Golden Gloves Championship Tournament, and only one can win.

Thesis statement

Both boys have shared many experiences growing up. Both are seventeen years old. Each one dreams of someday being lightweight champion of the world. They have grown up on the Lower East Side of Manhattan and live in the same tenement building. They sleep, eat, and dream positive. Between them, they have a collection of Fight magazines and also "a scrapbook filled with torn tickets to every boxing match they had ever attended." Both boys have decided that no matter what happens in the tournament fight, they will always be champions to each other!

Topic sentence

Point-by-point method

Direct quotation

During the big fight both boys show good sportsmanship and play by the rules. They fight a good clean match, and at the end of the fight they embrace. It seems obvious that they care more about their close friendship than about who actually wins the fight. Just as the announcer turns to point out the winner, he finds himself alone in the ring. The two champions, Felix and Antonio, have already left the ring, arm in arm.

Topic sentence

Conclusion

—Melissa Spechler
Weber Middle School
Port Washington, New York

INTERNET

More Writer's Models

Keyword: LE5 7-6

Evaluating and Revising

Use the following chart to evaluate and revise your comparison-contrast essay.

Comparison–Contrast Essay: Content and Organization Guidelines

Evaluation Questions	▶ Tips	▶ Revision Techniques
❶ Does your introduction state the thesis of your essay? Do you identify works by title and author?	▶ **Underline** the thesis statement. **Circle** titles and authors.	▶ **Add** a sentence that states the main idea of the essay. **Add** titles of works and authors' names.
❷ Do you discuss two or more similarities or differences?	▶ **Put a check mark** next to each example of comparison or contrast.	▶ **Add** examples of comparison or contrast. **Delete** irrelevant statements.
❸ Is the body of your essay organized by either the block method or the point-by-point method?	▶ In the margin **label** the method of organization. **Put the letter** *A* above each point about the first subject. **Put the letter** *B* above each point for the second subject.	▶ **Rearrange** sentences into either block order or point-by-point order.
❹ Does your essay contain transitional expressions to show comparison or contrast?	▶ **Highlight** transitional words and phrases.	▶ **Add** transitional words that show similarities or differences.
❺ Do you provide specific details and examples to back up your general statements?	▶ **Underline** supporting details and examples.	▶ **Elaborate** with specific details and examples.
❻ Does your conclusion restate and expand on the main idea stated in the introduction?	▶ **Bracket** the restatement of your main idea. **Underline** statements that expand your main idea.	▶ **Elaborate** on statements that summarize or evaluate.

The following paragraph is from an essay about two classical myths with some points of similarity and difference. Use the questions following the model to evaluate the writer's revisions.

Revision Model

Descent to the underworld appears as a common

theme in *several* classical myths. In "The Origin of the

Seasons," *retold by Olivia Coolidge,* Demeter, the goddess of the harvest,

grieves for her daughter, Persephone, who was

snatched away *by the lord of the underworld.* In "Orpheus, the Great Musician,"

also retold by Coolidge, Orpheus ~~shows courage in~~ *braves a journey*

~~descending~~ to the underworld to bring back his

beloved wife, Eurydice. *Whereas* Demeter succeeds in

keeping her daughter on Earth for part of the year, ~~but~~

Orpheus fails the test set by the gods and loses

Eurydice forever. He is reunited with his wife only after

his death. In both cases, there are conditions set for the

return of the young women.

Evaluating the Revision

1. Which details have been added for greater precision or clarity?

2. Where has the writer deleted or replaced text to make the writing more concise?

3. Why has the writer rearranged the order of sentences? Does this change improve the writing?

Test Practice

DIRECTIONS: Read the fable. Then, answer each question that follows.

Belling the Cat

Aesop

The Mice once called a meeting to decide on a plan to free themselves of their enemy, the Cat. At least they wished to find some way of knowing when she was coming so they might have time to run away. Indeed, something had to be done, for they lived in such constant fear of her claws that they hardly dared stir from their dens by night or day.

Many plans were discussed, but none of them was thought good enough. At last a very young Mouse got up and said:

"I have a plan that seems very simple, but I know it will be successful. All we have to do is to hang a bell about the Cat's neck. When we hear the bell ringing, we will know immediately that our enemy is coming."

All the Mice were much surprised that they had not thought of such a plan before. But in the midst of the rejoicing over their good fortune, an old Mouse arose and said:

"I will say that the plan of the young Mouse is very good. But let me ask one question: Who will bell the Cat?"

It is one thing to say that something should be done, but quite a different matter to do it.

1. What **problem** is dealt with in this fable?
   A The mice want to help a cat.
   B A silly young mouse has captured a cat.
   C The mice want to know when the cat is approaching.
   D The cat wants to befriend the mice.

2. What plan is proposed to solve the problem?
   F A bell should be put on the cat.
   G The cat should be killed.
   H The mice should put a bell in their den.
   J The cat should be welcomed.

3. What is wrong with the plan?
   A It is too easy and won't work.
   B The mice are too old to act.
   C No one wants to do it because it is dangerous.
   D It was a silly mouse's idea.

4. Which of the following is the best restatement of the **moral** of this fable?
   F A good plan is hard to find.
   G It is easier to propose plans than it is to carry them out.
   H People are basically cowards.
   J If you won't take a chance, nothing will get done.

THE FAVORITE CAT.

The Favorite Cat by Nathaniel Currier (1813–1888).
Lithograph, hand-colored (12⅞" high x 8¾" wide).
The Metropolitan Museum of Art, Bequest of Adele S. Colgate, 1962.
(63.550.159). Photograph © 1983 The Metropolitan Museum of Art.

SKILLS FOCUS

Literary Skills
Analyze a fable.

Test Practice

Synonyms

DIRECTIONS: Choose the word or phrase that means the same, or about the same, as the underlined word.

1. A person who is <u>inconsolable</u> is —
   A heartbroken
   B curious
   C hardworking
   D unconscious

2. Climbers who <u>ascended</u> a mountain —
   F went around it
   G discovered it
   H went up it
   J went down it

3. When someone <u>vainly</u> loves another, he or she loves —
   A foolishly
   B uselessly
   C successfully
   D passionately

4. If a person's love is <u>unrequited</u>, it is —
   F not returned
   G not required
   H not respectable
   J not reliable

5. If you <u>implored</u> someone to do something, you —
   A dared
   B forced
   C begged
   D insisted

6. An <u>invincible</u> army is —
   F unbeatable
   G not strong
   H in retreat
   J on attack

7. A teacher who <u>admonished</u> students to behave —
   A argued
   B urged
   C praised
   D threatened

8. A <u>presumptuous</u> person is —
   F pretty
   G fortunate
   H arrogant
   J fair

9. A dog that <u>cowered</u> —
   A crouched and trembled
   B barked and growled
   C jumped up and down
   D cried and yelped

10. When you study <u>intently</u>, you —
    F watch TV while you work
    G work halfheartedly
    H are not at all interested
    J work with great concentration

SKILLS FOCUS

Vocabulary Skills
Identify synonyms.

Collection 6: Skills Review

Writing Skills

Test Practice

DIRECTIONS: Read the following paragraph. Then, read the questions below it. Choose the best answer to each question, and mark your answers on your paper.

(1) Although myths and folk tales are often grouped together as forms of folklore, there are significant differences between them. (2) Like all forms of folklore, myths and folk tales reflect the traditional beliefs and customs of the cultures that created them. (3) Both myths and folk tales have been passed from one generation to another by word of mouth. (4) Their original authors are unknown. (5) Myths, however, usually involve gods and other supernatural beings. (6) Myths may explain some natural event, and they may teach moral lessons. (7) Folk tales also reflect the particular culture that created them. (8) Folk tales often contain legendary elements, and they may include magic and fantasy.

1. The **thesis,** or main idea, of this paper is stated in —
   A   sentence 1
   B   sentence 2
   C   sentence 3
   D   sentence 7

2. Which sentence is unnecessary and should be deleted?
   F   sentence 1
   G   sentence 3
   H   sentence 5
   J   sentence 7

3. Transitional expressions are used in all of the following *except* —
   A   sentence 1
   B   sentence 2
   C   sentence 4
   D   sentence 5

4. Which type of text structure is used in this passage?
   F   chronological
   G   cause and effect
   H   comparison and contrast
   J   step by step

5. Which of these statements is accurate?
   A   Sentence 1 contains a definition of folklore.
   B   Sentence 2 focuses on a difference between myths and folk tales.
   C   Sentence 5 focuses on a similarity between myths and folk tales.
   D   Sentence 6 identifies purposes of some myths.

SKILLS FOCUS

Writing Skills
Analyze a comparison-contrast essay.

Fiction

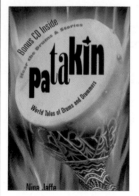

The Beat of the Drums

Listen to the powerful and inspiring language of drums. Experience the different rhythms of drumming for protection, freedom, and transformation. The ten tales of *Patakin: World Tales of Drums and Drummers* by Nina Jaffe celebrate a variety of drums and their special roles in storytelling.

Nature's Mysteries

If you like exploring nature, you'll love reading about it in Gary Ferguson's book, *Spirits of the Wild*. Stories from around the globe in this entertaining collection reveal the magical and often mysterious quality of the world around us.

Samurai Code of Honor

After being orphaned as a young boy, Taro becomes a servant to a great warrior lord. Join Taro as he rises through the ranks from kitchen cook to samurai warrior. Eventually, Taro is asked by his lord to infiltrate an enemy's castle. Will he accomplish the mission? Will he make it back home to marry the woman he loves? *The Samurai's Tale* by Erik C. Haugaard brings sixteenth-century Japan to life with samurai, shoguns, ninjas, and more.

Tales from Ancient China

Linda Fang's *The Chi-Lin Purse* is a collection of stories derived from ancient Chinese folklore, operas, and novels. The stories are from the Warring States Period in China (770–221 B.C.) and range in style from classic folktales to grand operas. Each tale is accompanied by a beautiful, black-and-white illustration, which shows the styles from that story's time period.

Nonfiction

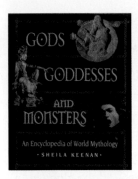

A Rich Resource

Learn about mythical figures from around the globe in *Gods, Goddesses, and Monsters*, by Sheila Keenan. Spider Woman, a powerful North American spirit who is both wise and kind, and the mighty Thor, who makes the heavens shake whenever he raises his hammer, are two of the major mythological characters from fifteen different cultures detailed in this fascinating encyclopedia.

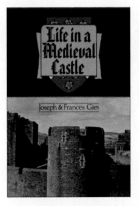

Living in a Castle

Have you ever wondered how people lived in the Middle Ages? What did the lord of a castle have for breakfast? What did boys and girls do when school ended for the day? How did people bathe? Find the answers to these questions and more when you read *Life in a Medieval Castle* by Joseph and Frances Gies.

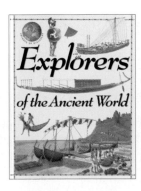

Sail Away!

Imagine heading off into an unknown world without any maps! In *Explorers of the Ancient World*, Anthony Brierley tells how the Egyptians, Phoenicians, and Greeks all courageously explored the Mediterranean world and the coasts of Africa. The book discusses and illustrates the tools and ships the explorers used on their journeys. Pictures of artifacts are included to make this exciting history come alive.

Inca Life

In *The Incas*, Tim Wood takes you on a tour of the Inca empire. You visit inside a typical Inca house, a temple to the sun god, an emperor's palace, and more. If you enjoy this book, you may want to read other titles in the See Through History series.

Literary Criticism:
Where I Stand

Literary Focus:
Criticizing Literature

Informational Focus:
Evaluating Evidence

INTERNET
Collection
Resources
Keyword: LE5 7-7

The Argonauth that guards the entrance to
the Falls of Rauros. From *The Lord of the
Rings: The Fellowship of the Ring*.

Elements of Literature
Literary Criticism

HOW DID YOU LIKE IT?

by Madeline Travers Hovland

You're leaving a movie with a friend—or you've played a new computer game a classmate has lent you—or you've read a story for homework. Your friend asks, "How'd you like it?" Suppose you give one of these answers:

"Great!"

"It was OK. I've seen better."

"That was pretty bad."

Your friend comes back at you with "How come?" You're going to feel pretty silly if all you come up with is "Uh, I dunno." Backing up your opinions of what you read gets easy once you've learned the language of literature. The fact is, you've been learning how to talk about literature as you've been reading this book. Each collection has challenged you to think, talk, and write intelligently about literary works that you've read.

Learning the Language

After you read something, you respond to it with an overall impression. You liked it, or maybe you didn't. Fine—but look a little closer. Why did you respond that way, and how can you communicate that response to others?

Chances are your response had something to do with the way the writer used the **literary elements.**

The terms for the literary elements have been in **boldface** throughout this book. Literary elements are things like **character, plot,** and **theme.** Using these terms, or **academic language,** helps all of us share our thoughts about what we read.

Talking About Stories

1 **Character.** When you respond to a story, you almost always want to talk about its characters. Here are some questions about characters that you can consider:

- Are the characters believable?

- Are they totally unrealistic?

- Are the causes, or **motivation,** of the characters' actions clear?

- How did you *feel* about the main character?

- What connections can you make between the characters and others you've met—including characters in stories, movies, and TV shows?

- Did you identify with any of the characters—that is, did any of them seem to share your values, dreams, worries, opinions, or background?

2 **Plot.** When critics talk about plot, they talk about what happened in a story. Did the writer hold your attention? Was the story

INTERNET

More About
Literary Criticism

Keyword: LE5 7-7

SKILLS
FOCUS

Literary Skills
Understand
literary criticism.

believable? Was the plot clear—did you understand the series of causes and effects that make up a plot?

3 **Theme.** When most people finish reading a novel or a short story, they want to talk about meaning, or **theme.** What did the story mean? Did the story say something important about life, or did it leave you thinking, "So what?" Did it say something new, fresh, and meaningful to you? Was its theme old and tired, something you've heard many times before, like "Crime doesn't pay" or "True love wins in the end"?

Talking About a Poem

When you're dealing with poems, the important literary elements you'll want to talk about are things such as **figurative language, imagery,** and **sound effects.** You'll talk about meaning with poetry, too—that is, as with short stories, you'll talk about **theme,** and how you respond to that theme.

Talking About Nonfiction

When you read a work of nonfiction, such as a biography or an autobiography, you'll want to talk about the writer's **objectivity.** You'll also want to ask about the **primary sources** the writer used for historical data. You'll want to talk about the writer's **accuracy** on historical details. Biography and autobiography are full of **characters.** You'll want to evaluate the characters and decide if the writer has made them seem alive.

The Mirror on the Page

When we talk about literary elements in a story, a poem, or a piece of nonfiction, we're not just learning about literature. We're learning about ourselves—what fascinates us, what inspires us, what we think of ourselves, what we believe in with all our hearts. The works of literature we read become a mirror. As we understand and learn to communicate our responses to them, we learn a little more about who we are.

Practice

Divide the class into three groups. Then, choose one story or one poem that you all have read in class. Each group will discuss the same story or poem for about five minutes. For your discussions, select a question from the ones cited in this essay, and focus your discussion on that question. When your discussions are completed, after five minutes, each group should report on its discussion. What responses were expressed? Were the responses affected by a particular literary element (for example, did a group feel strongly that a character was not believable and so rejected the whole story)? What did members of the group learn from the discussion?

Evaluating Evidence

by Sheri Henderson

The Triple A's of Evidence: Adequate, Accurate, Appropriate

When you read informational texts, you expect a writer's evidence to be adequate, accurate, and appropriate. Don't simply take evidence for granted. Evidence doesn't always make sense. You need to **evaluate,** or judge, the evidence for yourself.

Evidence should be **appropriate.** *Appropriate* means "suitable, relevant; right for the purpose." Appropriate evidence is to the point. Appropriate evidence is not inflammatory. Appropriate evidence is not based on a stereotype. When you read a statement and think to yourself, "What does that have to do with anything?" you're probably looking at **inappropriate** evidence.

Evidence should be **accurate.** *Accurate* means "free from mistakes or errors." If a writer states an opinion using words such as *all, each,* and *every,* you're probably looking at evidence that is **inaccurate.**

Evidence should be **adequate.** *Adequate* means "enough for what is needed; sufficient." If you have to trust a person's feelings instead of relying on facts, the evidence is most likely **inadequate.**

Practice your ability to evaluate evidence as you read "Letter to the Editor" on page 789.

Tips for Evaluating Evidence

- Look for **facts.** Plenty of facts usually means the information you're reading is **adequate.**

- Look for **reliable sources** in support of **accurate** information. Does the writer cite quotations, statistics, case studies?

- Are opinions backed up with facts? **Opinions** not supported by facts are examples of **inappropriate** evidence.

SKILLS FOCUS

Reading Skills
Evaluate evidence.

Letter to the Editor

Regarding your recent editorial, "Violent Video Games Cause Violence in Children":

My sisters and I used to play the Barbie Game for hours, duking it out for the chance to be "Queen of the Prom." The object of the game was to be the first player to get a dress and, of course, a date. There were four boys and four dresses to compete for. The one who drew "Poindexter" as a date was totally humiliated. The dress didn't matter as much, just so long as you had something to wear to the big event.

I suppose one could say that the Barbie Game made us care more about boys and clothes than our own brains and souls. But it did none of those things. We knew it was all fiction. We didn't care if we were competing for dresses or expensive property. We were just competing. **①** ⌂

Today some people would proclaim that games like this one made us into empty-headed weaklings. They would get a quick-witted and firm reaction from one of my sisters.

My brother, possibly the nicest guy I've ever known, spent his childhood in army fatigues wielding a plastic rifle. Outside my window I would hear the battles going on. **②** ⌂

So what is all this hysteria today about video games? Isn't it the same thing? Kids are just playing make-believe. They know it's not real.

The National Institute on Media and the Family would respond that the issue of the impact of video and computer games is no child's play. The Institute has developed "KidScore," an evaluation system that rates the amount of violence, the portrayal of violence, fear, illegal or harmful content, language, nudity, and sexual content. Not exactly things that were on my old Barbie game board nor in my brother's war games.

David Walsh, president of the Institute, reports, among many other findings, "Youth who report an increased appetite for violence in video games are more likely to have gotten into physical fights in the previous year." **③** ⌂

Using the Strategy

As you read, you'll find this open-book sign at certain points in the text: ⌂ . Stop at these points, and think about what you've just read. Do what the prompt asks you to do.

INTERPRET

① Why do you think the writer tells about playing the Barbie Game with her sisters? What statement in the third paragraph does this evidence support?

EVALUATE

② What evidence does the writer give for her claim that playing army games is not harmful? Is this evidence **appropriate**? Why or why not?

INTERPRET

③ Does this **expert testimony** support the writer's claim that games are *not* harmful? Or does it support the opposite point of view? Explain.

Using the Strategy

INTERPRET

4 What are the positive aspects of video games? Where does the writer get this information?

COMPARE AND CONTRAST

5 What problem with playing video games does the writer find in the Institute's report? Explain the difference between video games and the games her brother and sisters played.

It turns out there are positive aspects of video games. They provide practice in problem solving and logic. They introduce children to technology. Games give children a chance to practice following directions. **4**

But as I read the Institute's findings, I notice one tiny sentence that sends a chill up my spine. "Games could foster social isolation as they are often played alone." Sure, my sisters were a pain when they won the game. Yes, I got tired of listening to arguments between my brother and his friends about exactly who got hit in battle. But we all had a connection to one another. We fought some, laughed a lot, and without knowing it, helped one another grow up. **5**

I'm not sure you can do that with a computer. Technology can do a lot of things, but it still can't do that.

—A Concerned Reader

Practice the Strategy

Evaluating Evidence

When you evaluate evidence, you judge whether it is

- **adequate**—Is there enough evidence to back up the claim?
- **accurate**—Is it free from mistakes or errors?
- **appropriate**—Is it to the point and free from emotional appeals?

PRACTICE 1

Here are some examples of poor evidence from an essay about the dangers of the Internet. Decide whether each italic statement is **inadequate, inaccurate,** or **inappropriate.**

1. *Every teenager in America uses the Internet, and test scores have gone down all over the country.* This statement is _____ because not *every* teenager uses the Internet. No information supports the connection.

2. *My son's grades fell at the time he was allowed to use the Internet for a month.* This evidence is _____ because it is one person's experience, which is not enough to support the claim. There may be other reasons for the son's poor performance.

3. *The Internet stifles the imagination because anyone who spends a lot of time with machines becomes antisocial and mean.* This is _____ evidence because it is based only on an emotional appeal.

> Whenever you read informational texts—in this collection and in your life outside of school—evaluating the evidence to be sure it is adequate, accurate, and appropriate will make you a smart reader.

PRACTICE 2

In the blanks on the left, write the letter from the description on the right that best fits each statement.

___**1.** My brother, who knows a lot, says bugs are helpful.   **a.** fact

___**2.** There are fifty stars on the United States flag.   **b.** opinion

___**3.** Studying math is more valuable than studying art.   **c.** reliable source

___**4.** The almanac gives facts about all fifty states.   **d.** unreliable source

SKILLS FOCUS

Reading Skills
Evaluate evidence.

King Arthur: The Sword in the Stone

Make the Connection
Quickwrite ✏️

Some people living today could be so famous that stories about them will be made up and told for years. Think about the qualities that might turn someone into a legend. Write down the names and deeds of some people who could be legends a hundred years from now.

Literary Focus
Legend: A Little Fact, a Lot of Story

A **legend** is a very old story, passed down from one generation to the next, which usually has some connection to a real historical person or event. Legends combine historical facts with made-up events, which are often fantastic. Perhaps

Vocabulary Development

Preview these words from the story:

turbulent (tur′byə·lənt) *adj.:* wild; disorderly. *King Arthur restored peace to a turbulent land.*

tournament (toor′nə·mənt) *n.:* series of contests. *Sir Kay hoped to show his bravery during the tournament.*

integrity (in·teg′rə·tē) *n.:* honesty; uprightness. *A knight's integrity kept him from wrongdoing.*

congregation (käŋ′grə·gā′shən) *n.:* gathering. *The king spoke to a congregation of villagers.*

the most famous hero of legend in Western literature is the king called Arthur.

Background
Literature and Social Studies

The hero behind the legend of King Arthur probably lived about 500 A.D. The real Arthur is believed to have been a military leader of people called the Britons.

In the first century B.C., the Romans invaded Britain and they ruled for about four hundred years. After the armies of Rome pulled out of England in 410 A.D., several peoples tried to seize control. According to the earliest legends, a leader named Arthur united the Britons and led them to victory against one of those invading peoples, the Saxons.

After Arthur's death the Saxons and the Angles, another people, conquered the Britons, but stories about the warrior king's unusual courage and goodness lived on among his people.

For hundreds of years, minstrels traveled from castle to castle throughout Europe, singing stories about Arthur. The legend became a series of stories about noble knights who rode out to do battle with evil wherever they found it.

Perhaps Arthur continues to live in the imagination because he represents the leader who will return someday, in time of darkness and need, to save his people.

KING ARTHUR
The Sword in the Stone

**Hudson
Talbott**

Arthur drawing the sword from the stone, from *Story of King Arthur and His Knights* (1923 edition).

The Granger Collection, New York.

Medieval knight on horseback.

In ancient times, when Britain was still a wild and restless place, there lived a noble king named Uther.[1] After many years of turmoil, Uther defeated the invading barbarians and drove them from the land. For this triumph, his fellow British lords proclaimed him their high king, or Pendragon, meaning "Dragon's Head."

Soon after his coronation,[2] Uther Pendragon met and fell in love with the beautiful Lady Igraine,[3] a widow whose husband Uther had killed in battle. Uther married Igraine and adopted her two young daughters, Margaise[4] and Morgan le Fay. The price for this love was a high one, however. In his passion, the king had asked for the help of his sorcerer, Merlin, in winning the hand of Lady Igraine. In return Uther had agreed to give up their firstborn son. Merlin had foreseen great evil descending upon the king and felt that he alone could protect a young heir in the dangerous times ahead.

Before long, a beautiful boy child was born. But the joy surrounding the birth was brief, for Merlin soon appeared to take the child away.

"But the child was just born!" exclaimed Uther. "How did you find out so quickly?"

Silently, the old sorcerer led the king to a balcony and pointed upward. There overhead was a great dragon formed by the stars. Its vast wings arched over the countryside, and its tail swept north beyond the horizon. "You see by this sign, my lord, that it is not I who calls for your son, but destiny."

Sadly, the king gave up his son, for Merlin convinced him that the child's great future was threatened. Indeed, Uther Pendragon died within a year from a traitor's poison and Britain was once again plunged into darkness. ❶

RETELL
❶ What deals are made between Uther and Merlin?

After the death of the high king, the struggle for leadership tore Britain to pieces. The great alliance King Uther had forged was shattered into dozens of quarreling, petty kingdoms—leaving no united force to oppose foreign invasion. Barbarians swept in once again and order gave way to chaos. Marauding knights roamed the countryside, taking what they wanted and burning the rest. No one was safe at home, and travel was even more dangerous, with outlaws ruling the roads. Fear was a constant companion of those who managed to stay alive.

After sixteen turbulent years, the archbishop of Canterbury[5] summoned Merlin

---

1. **Uther** (yōō′thər).
2. **coronation** *n.*: ceremony for crowning a king or a queen.
3. **Igraine** (ē·grān′).
4. **Margaise** (mär·gāz′).

---

5. **archbishop of Canterbury:** even today, the highest-ranking bishop of the Church of England.

Vocabulary
turbulent (tur′byə·lənt) *adj.*: wild; disorderly.

Merlin the Magician (1903) by Howard Pyle.
The Granger Collection, New York.

to help restore order. Although the two men were of different faiths, they had great respect for each other and shared much wisdom between them.

"I am at a loss, Sir Wizard!" confided the archbishop. "I don't know how to help the people, and they are suffering more each day. If only Uther Pendragon were here!"

"I share your concerns, my lord, but I have good news," said Merlin. "Although the end of King Uther's reign left us in the dark for many years, it is at last time for the sun to return to Britain. A brilliant sun, my lord. Perhaps the brightest that Britain will ever know."

"But the sun was out this morning, sire," said the archbishop. "What has the weather to do with this?"

"I speak of the son of Uther Pendragon, the true heir of royal blood who lives in a distant land and must now be summoned forth to keep his date with destiny."

"His date with who?" asked the archbishop. "But the king had no heirs! Alas, that is our problem!"

"I wish to prove otherwise, my lord," replied Merlin. "If I have your leave to use my magic, I shall create an event to bring forth this young heir and prove to the world that he is the true and rightful high king of Britain."

The delighted archbishop agreed immediately, and Merlin withdrew to devise his scheme. ❷ 📖

📖 **ANALYZE**
❷ How does Merlin use the words *sun* and *son* in his discussion with the archbishop? What does Merlin promise the archbishop?

On a Sunday morning in late November the great cathedral of London was filled to capacity. As Mass was being said, a sudden murmur rippled through the crowd on the cathedral steps. Turning to see the cause of the commotion, the archbishop stopped in midprayer and walked toward the door. In the churchyard he discovered a block of white marble with an anvil sitting on top. Driven into the anvil, gleaming in the pale winter sun, was a sword. Its blade was of flawless blue-white steel, and the hilt was of highly wrought gold, inlaid with rubies, sapphires, and emeralds. Engraved in the marble block were these words:

WHOSO PULLETH OUT THIS SWORD FROM THIS STONE AND ANVIL IS RIGHTWISE KING BORN OF ENGLAND.

Ah, so this is Merlin's plan! thought the archbishop, smiling to himself. A group of barons and knights suddenly pushed their way through the crowd, each stating loudly that he should be the first to try. A few managed to leap onto the stone and give the sword an unsuccessful yank before the archbishop stopped them.

"Order! Order!" he shouted, raising his hands to quiet the crowd. "I hereby proclaim that on Christmas morning, one month from today, all those who consider themselves worthy of attempting to pull this sword from the stone and anvil will be given the opportunity. He who wins the sword, thereby wins the kingdom." ❸

RETELL
❸ What test will prove who the rightful king is?

A mighty roar of approval rose from the crowd. Some even danced and stomped their feet. Noticing how pleased they were, the archbishop went further. "And to celebrate this momentous occasion, a <u>tournament</u> shall be held on Christmas Eve."

With this, the delighted parishioners swept the flustered archbishop onto their shoulders and carried him jubilantly around the stone several times before setting him down. They hadn't had such cause for celebration in a long, long time.

To all parts of the kingdom, messengers rushed out, carrying the archbishop's proclamation.[6] Every castle and village was alerted, from Sussex to Cornwall and, finally, to the dark forest of Wales. There lived a certain gentle knight by the name of Sir Ector Bonmaison[7] with his two sons. The

---

6. **proclamation** *n.*: official public announcement.
7. **Bonmaison** (bō*n*′mā·zō*n*′): This name is French for "good house."

The Beginning of a Tournament, from French manuscript (14th century).
The Granger Collection, New York.

Vocabulary
tournament (tŏŏr′nə·mənt) *n.*: series of contests.

elder was a handsome, robust youth, recently knighted and now known as Sir Kay. The younger was a gentle blond lad of about sixteen whom Sir Ector and his wife had adopted as an infant. His name was Arthur.

Although Arthur was not of his blood, Sir Ector loved both sons equally and devoted himself to their upbringing. ❹

🔖 **INFER**

❹ Who do you guess this adopted son is?

Sir Kay was the first to hear the news of the great events in London, for as usual, he was in the courtyard polishing his helmet when the messenger arrived.

"A tournament! At last, a tournament!" he shouted. "We must set out for London at once! Father, you know what this means to me."

"Yes, son, I do," said Sir Ector, bringing the weary messenger a bowl of food. "I was young and hotblooded once, too, and eager to show the world my worthiness of knighthood. But this sword-pulling contest—do you wish to be king, as well?" he asked Kay with a smile.

"I make no pretense about that, sir. To prove myself on the field of battle is my dream."

"Please remember that, my son," said Sir Ector. "Pursuing one's goals with integrity is all that matters. Now go find Arthur so that we may prepare to leave. London is a long way off."

Arthur had wandered off alone, as he often did after finishing his chores. He was as devoted as ever to being a good squire for his brother. But, after all, Kay was *Sir* Kay now, and he rarely had anything to say to his younger brother except to bark orders at him. Arthur didn't mind, though. He was happy just to watch Kay practice his jousting and to dream of someday riding beside him in battle. In the meantime, he had to content himself with his other companions—Lionel and Jasper, his dogs; Cosmo, his falcon; the orphaned fox cubs he kept hidden in the hollow log; and the deer that came to the edge of the woods when he whistled. He was in the woods now, patiently holding out a handful of oats for the deer, when Kay came bounding through the meadows to find him.

"Arthur, come quickly!" he shouted. "We're leaving for London at once! There's a big tournament. Here's your chance to show me what a good squire you can be! Hurry!"

Arthur stood silently for a moment. He had never been more than a few miles from his home. Was he daydreaming? Or was he really going to London to help Sir Kay bring honor and glory to their family as the whole world looked on? He ran back home, doubting his own ears until he reached the courtyard and saw Sir Ector preparing their horses for the journey. ❺ 📖

All of Britain seemed to be making its way to London Town that Christmas. Kings and dukes, earls and barons, counts and countesses funneled into the city gates for the great contest. Sir Ector was pleased to see old friends and fellow knights. Sir Kay was eager to register for the jousting. And Arthur was simply dazzled by it all.

As Sir Ector and his sons made their way through the city streets, a glint of sunlight on steel caught Arthur's eye. How odd, he thought. A sword thrust point first into an anvil on top of a block of marble, sitting in a churchyard—surrounded by guards! London is so full of wonders!

Dawn arrived with a blare of trumpets, calling all contestants to the tournament. In Sir Ector's tent, Arthur buckled the

COMPARE AND CONTRAST
❺ Now you've met Arthur and his brother, Kay. How are they different from each other?

Vocabulary
integrity (in·teg′rə·tē) *n.:* honesty; uprightness.

chain mail[8] onto Sir Kay and slipped the tunic of the Bonmaison colors over his brother's head. Sir Ector stood and watched until the preparation was complete and his son stood before him in all his knightly glory. Silently they embraced, mounted their horses, and headed for the tournament grounds.

The stadium for the event was the grandest ever built. Never had there been such a huge <u>congregation</u> of lords and ladies in the history of England. The stands surrounded a great meadow, swept clean of all snow, with the combatants' tents at either end. In the central place of honor sat the archbishop. Patiently, he greeted each king and noble as they came forth to kiss his hand. "I should do this more often," he chuckled to himself.

The first event was the mock battle, or *mêlée*. The contestants were divided into two teams—the Reds and the Greens. Sir Kay was with the Reds, who gathered at the southern end of the field, while their opponents took the north. They all readied their lances and brought down their helmet visors in anticipation of combat. Everyone looked to the archbishop for a signal. Slowly, he raised his handkerchief, paused, and let it flutter to the ground. From either end of the field, the thunder of thousands of horse hooves rolled forward, shaking the earth, rattling the stands—louder and louder until a terrifying crash of metal split the air. A shower of splintered lances rained down in all directions. The audience gasped, and a few ladies fainted. Nothing had prepared them for this scale of violence.

Illustration from a 14th-century German manuscript.
The Granger Collection, New York.

Sir Kay performed admirably, for he charged ahead of his teammates and unseated two of the Greens. He was already winning accolades[9] as he wheeled his charger around to aid a fellow Red.

As the teams withdrew, they revealed a battleground strewn with fallen warriors, some struggling to rise under the weight of their armor, others lying ominously still. Bits and pieces of armor and broken lances littered the field.

---

9. **accolades** *n.*: words of praise.

Vocabulary
congregation (käŋ′grə·gā′shən) *n.*: gathering.

---

8. **chain mail** *n.*: flexible armor made of thousands of tiny metal links.

The next charge was to be undertaken with swords. Sir Kay was appointed captain of his team for having done so well in the first round. He trotted over to Arthur and handed down his lance.

"Kay! You were magnificent!" gushed Arthur, wiping down the steaming war horse. "You've brought great honor to our house this day!"

"I need my sword, Arthur," said Sir Kay, struggling to take his helmet off.

"Your sword, of course!" said Arthur brightly. He turned to get it, but then stopped suddenly. Where was the sword? His eyes scanned the little tent with its collection of weaponry. Spear, halberd, mace, bludgeon[10] . . . but no sword.

"Excuse me, Kay," said Arthur, "could you use a battle axe?"

"Arthur, please! My sword!" said Sir Kay. "We haven't much time."

"Of course, Kay! But just a moment—I'll finish polishing it," said Arthur, slipping out through the slit in their tent. With one great leap, he landed on his pony's back and galloped madly through the deserted streets, rushing back to their camp.

"Sword. Sword. Where did I put that *sword*?" he muttered, desperately searching through the chests and bags. But to no avail.

How could this happen? he thought. Kay without a sword . . . and the whole world watching!

He paced back and forth, and then a thought struck him: Kay will not be without a sword today. I know where I can get one!

A few minutes later, he trotted into the churchyard where the sword in the anvil stood on the marble block. There wasn't a guard in sight—even they had gone to the tourney. Quietly, he brought his pony up to the stone and tugged on the reins.

"OK, Blaze. . . . We'll just see if this sword can be unstuck," he whispered. He stretched out his arm until his fingers touched the hilt.

"Hey, it's looser than I thought. . . . Steady, Blaze! Steady, boy!" As the pony stepped back a few paces, the sword glided out of the anvil's grip, unbalancing Arthur. He regained his seat and looked down in wonder at the mighty blade in his hand. ⑥

ANALYZE
⑥ Remember Merlin's test. What is the significance of what has just happened?

"This isn't just *any* sword. . . . Perhaps it's something the church provides for needy strangers. Yes, that must be it! Well, I'll return it after the tournament. Someone else may need it. Thank you, sword, for saving me," he said, pressing its cross to his lips. "Wait until Kay sees this!"

He flung his cloak around the great sword and drove his little horse back to the tournament with lightning speed.

By now, Sir Kay had dismounted and was rather chafed.[11]

"Arthur, where have you been?" he shouted. "You . . ."

He caught himself as Arthur dropped to one knee and opened the cloak.

"Your sword, my lord," Arthur said confidently. But his smile quickly disappeared when he saw Sir Kay's reaction. Frozen in place, his face white as milk, Sir Kay stared at the sword. Finally, he spoke.

---

10. **halberd** (hal′bərd), **mace** (mās), **bludgeon** (bluj′ən): weapons.

---

11. **chafed** (chāft) *v.* used as *adj.*: annoyed.

"Where did you get this?" he asked Arthur, although he knew the answer.

Arthur confessed that he had searched in vain for Sir Kay's sword and had borrowed this one instead.

"Get Father at once, and tell no one of this!" said Sir Kay sternly.

Arthur thought he must be in terrible trouble. Surely he could return the sword without his father knowing. Why did Father have to be told? Nevertheless, he obeyed his brother and returned quickly with Sir Ector.

Sir Kay closed the curtains of the tent and opened the cloak, revealing the sword to his father.

Sir Ector gasped when he saw it. "How can this be?"

"Father, I am in possession of this sword," said Sir Kay nervously. "That is what matters. Therefore, I must be king of all Britain."

"But how came you by it, son?" asked Sir Ector.

"Well, sire, I needed a sword . . . and we couldn't find mine . . . so, I decided to use this one!" said Sir Kay. Beads of sweat formed on his brow.

"Very well, lad. You drew it out of the stone. I want to see you put it back. Let's go," said Sir Ector.

"But *I have the sword*!" said Sir Kay. "Isn't that enough?"

"No," replied Sir Ector, as he mounted his horse and headed toward the cathedral. Arthur rode close behind and, ever so slowly, Sir Kay mounted and followed.

The churchyard was still deserted when the three arrived. "Put the sword back in the anvil," said Sir Ector bluntly. "I must see it."

"Father, I . . ."

"Just do it, Kay, and you shall be king. If that's what you want." Sir Kay climbed onto the block. Sweat was now pouring off him. He raised the mighty sword over his head and plunged it downward. But the sharp point skidded across the surface of the anvil, causing Sir Kay to fall headfirst off the block.

"Now, son, tell me. How came you by this sword?" asked Sir Ector again.

"Arthur brought it to me," said Sir Kay, dusting himself off. "He *lost* my other one."

Suddenly a fear gripped Sir Ector's heart. "Arthur, my boy," he said quietly, "will you try it for us?"

"Certainly, Father," said Arthur, "but do we have to tell anyone about this? Can't we just . . ."

"Son, please," said Sir Ector solemnly. "If you can put the sword in that anvil, please do so now."

With a pounding heart, the lad took the sword from Sir Kay's hand and climbed slowly onto the block of marble. Raising it with both hands over his head, he thrust it downward, through the anvil, burying the point deep within the stone. Effortlessly he pulled it out again, glanced at his stunned father, and shoved the sword into the stone, even deeper this time.

Sir Ector shrieked and sank to his knees. His mouth moved, but no words came out. He put his hands together as in prayer. Silently, Sir Kay knelt and did the same.

"Father! What are you doing?" cried Arthur, leaping down from the stone. "Please! Get up! Get up! I don't understand!"

"Now I know!" sputtered Sir Ector, choking back tears. "Now I know who you are!" ❼

> **INFER**
> ❼ What does Sir Ector now know about his adopted son?

"I'm your son, Father!" said the bewildered lad, crouching down by his father and putting his head to Sir Ector's chest.

After a few deep breaths, Sir Ector regained his composure. He smiled sadly down at Arthur and stroked his head.

"Fate would have it otherwise, my boy. Look there behind you." He pointed to the gold lettering on the marble block, which stated the purpose of the sword and the anvil.

Arthur sat in silence and stared at the words in the marble.

"Although you were adopted, I've loved you like my own child, Arthur," said Sir Ector softly. "But now I realize you have the blood of kings in you. To discover your birthright is the true reason we came to London. You are now our king and we your faithful servants."

At this, Arthur broke into tears. "I don't want to be king. Not if it means losing my father!" he sobbed.

"You have a great destiny before you, Arthur. There's no use avoiding it," said Sir Ector.

Arthur wiped his eyes with his sleeve. He straightened up so he could look Sir Ector in the eyes. A few minutes passed.

"Very well," Arthur finally said slowly. "Whatever my destiny may be, I am willing to accept it. But I still need you with me."

"Then so it shall be, lad. So it shall be," said Sir Ector.

They sat quietly for a time, comforting each other, until they felt another presence. From across the yard a hooded figure quietly floated into the fading light of the winter afternoon and knelt down beside them.

"Merlin," said Sir Ector, bowing his head to the famous enchanter.

"I've been waiting for you, Arthur," said the wizard.

"You know me, my lord?" asked Arthur.

"I put you in this good man's care many years ago and have kept an eye on you ever since."

"How did you do that, sire? We live far from here."

"Oh, I have my ways," replied Merlin. "But you still managed to surprise me. The sword-pulling contest isn't until tomorrow, and you pulled it out today!" he said with a chuckle.

"But what is to become of me now?" asked Arthur.

"Well, let us start with tomorrow," replied the old sorcerer. "We must still have the contest to prove to the world that you are the rightful heir. I will come for you when the time is right."

"But after that, sire, what is my future?" asked the boy.

Merlin weighed this question carefully. He wasn't at all sure whether the boy was prepared for his answer. Finally, he spoke. "I can tell you only what my powers suggest— and they point to greatness. Greatness surrounds you like a golden cloak. Your achievements could inspire humankind for centuries to come. But you alone can fulfill this destiny and then only if you wish it. You own your future. You alone."

Arthur breathed deeply and cast his eyes downward. He thought of all the goodbyes he would have to say. He thought of his fishing hole, and the birds that ate seeds from his hand. He thought of the deer that came when he called them.

"What time tomorrow, sire?" he asked.

"After all have tried and failed, whenever that may be," replied Merlin.

Morgan le Fay, Queen of Avalon by
Anthony Frederick Augustus Sandys (1829–1904).

"I will be ready, sire," said Arthur. Then he rose, bade Merlin farewell, and silently returned to his tent.

On Christmas morning, the archbishop said Mass for the largest gathering he had seen in years. The grounds surrounding the cathedral were also filled—with those seeking to make history or watch it being made.

As soon as the service ended, those who wished to try for the throne formed a line next to the marble block.

Leading the line was King Urien of Gore, husband to Margaise, Uther Pendragon's adoptive daughter. Ever since the high king's death, Urien had claimed loudly that he was the rightful heir. Indeed, he took his position on the marble block with a great sense of authority and gave the sword a confident tug, then another, and another. Urien was sweating and yanking furiously when finally asked to step down.

Next came King Lot of Orkney, husband to Morgan le Fay. King Lot felt certain that his wife's magical powers would assure his victory. But pull and tug as he might, he couldn't move the sword. After that, King Mark of Cornwall, King Leodegrance of Cameliard, and King Ryence of North Wales all took their place on the stone—and failed. The dukes of Winchester, Colchester, Worcester, and Hamcester did not fare any better. Some thought the longer they waited, the looser the sword would become, thereby improving their chances. But this wasn't the case, for the sword never budged, not even slightly. Kings, dukes, earls, counts, and knights all left that marble block empty-handed. Finally, as the day waned and the line neared its end, the crowd grew impatient for a winner. Merlin went for Arthur. ❽

Sir Ector and Sir Kay opened the curtains of their tent when they saw Merlin approaching.

"Your hour has come, my lord," said the old wizard to Arthur, who was standing

> ### INFER
> ❽ How are all these men who try to pull the sword out of the anvil different from Arthur?

alone in the center of the tent. Silently, the boy walked forth as one in a dream.

The crowd made way for them as they entered, for Merlin was still revered by all. But who could these other people be? Especially that young blond lad dressed all in red. What was he doing here?

Merlin brought Arthur before the archbishop and bowed deeply. Arthur dropped to one knee.

"My lord," said Merlin, "I present to you a most worthy candidate for this contest. Has he your permission to attempt to pull yonder sword from the stone?"

The archbishop gazed down at the handsome lad. "Merlin, we are not familiar with this youth, nor with his credentials. By what right does he come to this place?"

"By the greatest right, my lord," said Merlin. "For this is the trueborn son of King Uther Pendragon and Queen Igraine."

The crowd broke into a loud clamor at hearing this. The startled archbishop raised his hands, but order was not easily restored.

"Merlin, have you proof of this?" asked the archbishop.

"With your permission, sire," blurted Arthur suddenly, "perhaps I can prove it by handling yonder sword in the anvil."

"Very well then, lad," said the archbishop, admiring Arthur's youthful boldness. "You have my permission. If what Merlin says is true, may God be with you."

Arthur rose and stepped up onto the marble block. He grabbed hold of the mighty golden hilt with both hands. A surge of sparkling warmth traveled up his arms, across his shoulders, and throughout his body. With one mighty tug, he freed the sword from the anvil and lifted it heavenward. The blade flashed like lightning as he swung it around his head for all to see. Then, turning the point downward again, he drove it back into the anvil with equal ease.

The entire gathering stood dumbstruck for a long moment, trying to comprehend what they had just seen. Arthur looked about for reassurance. He looked to Sir Ector, then Merlin, and then the archbishop. They all simply stared at him, with eyes wide in amazement. A child giggled and clapped his hands in glee, then so did another, and another. Cheers began to ring out as people found their voices again. Suddenly, a thunder of shouting and clapping rose up around Arthur. Amidst the tumult, he closed his eyes and whispered, "Thank you, Father."

Then he grabbed the sword's hilt for a second time and withdrew it. As he brought it above his head, a thousand swords throughout the crowd were raised in solidarity.[12] Arthur drove the sword back into the anvil and pulled it out once again. This time, as he lifted the great blade to the sky, more swords and halberds were raised, along with brooms, rakes, and walking sticks, as counts and common folk alike saluted their newfound king.

Not everyone was overjoyed at this turn of events, however. Although all had seen the miracle performed, several kings and dukes were unwilling to recognize Arthur's right to the throne. Loudest among the grumblers were King Lot and King Urien, Arthur's brothers-in-law. "How dare this

---

12. **solidarity** (säl′ə·dar′ə·tē) *n.*: unity among a group.

(Opposite) *Arthur Drawing Forth the Sword* (1903) by Howard Pyle.
The Granger Collection, New York.

beardless, unknown country boy think he can be made high king to rule over us!" they said. "Obviously, Merlin is using the boy to promote himself!"

But these malcontents[13] gained no support from those around them and were quickly shouted down. So they gathered themselves together and stormed away in a huff of indignation.[14] **9**

📖 **PREDICT**

9 Based on their actions here, what do you predict King Lot and King Urien will do?

To everyone else, the day belonged to Arthur. All the other kings and nobles rushed forth to show their acceptance, for they trusted Merlin and were grateful to have a leader at last. They hoisted the young king-to-be above their heads to parade him through the streets of London.

As the noisy procession flowed out of the churchyard, the archbishop hobbled over to Merlin to offer congratulations for a successful plan.

"Thank you, my lord, but I think we are not yet finished," said the wizard.

The archbishop looked puzzled.

"I fear that King Lot and King Urien and those other discontented souls will leave us no peace until they have another chance at the sword," continued Merlin. "We must offer them a new trial on New Year's Day."

And so they did. But again, no one could budge the sword but Arthur. These same troublesome kings and dukes still refused to acknowledge his victory, though. So another trial took place on Candlemas,[15] and yet another on Easter.

By now, the people had grown impatient, for they had believed in Arthur all along and had grown to love him. The idea of having a fresh young king inspired hope and optimism. The world suddenly felt young again.

Finally, after the trial held on Pentecost,[16] they cried out, "Enough! Arthur has proven himself five times now! We will have him for our king—and no other!"

The archbishop and Merlin agreed. There was proof beyond dispute at this point. So the coronation was set for May Day in the great cathedral of London.

Upon arriving that morning, Arthur stepped up on the block and pulled the sword from the anvil for the last time. With the blade pointing heavenward, he entered the church, walked solemnly down the central aisle, and laid the sword upon the altar. The archbishop administered the holy sacraments[17] and finally placed the crown upon Arthur's head.

Ten thousand cheers burst forth as the young king emerged from the cathedral. At Merlin's suggestion, Arthur stepped up on the marble block to speak to the people. A hush fell over the masses as he raised his hands to address them.

"People of Britain, we are now one. And so shall we remain as long as there is a breath in my body. My faith in your courage and wisdom is boundless. I ask now for your faith in me. In your trust I shall find my strength. For your good I dedicate my life. May this sword lead us to our destiny."

---

13. **malcontents** (mal′kən·tents′) *n.:* discontented or unhappy people.
14. **indignation** *n.:* righteous anger.
15. **Candlemas** (kan′dəl·məs): church feast on February 2.

16. **Pentecost** (pen′tə·kôst′): Christian festival on the seventh Sunday after Easter, celebrating the "birthday" of the Christian Church.
17. **sacraments** *n.:* rituals instituted by the church, such as baptism, Holy Communion, and penance.

Meet the Writer

Hudson Talbott

Time Traveler

The first highly successful series of books written and illustrated by **Hudson Talbott** (1949–   ) featured a gang of talking, time-traveling dinosaurs. *We're Back: A Dinosaur's Story,* the first of Talbott's dinosaur tales, was later adapted into a feature-length movie produced by Steven Spielberg.

Some of Talbott's readers, hoping for more humorous stories about dinosaurs, were surprised by the next subject he chose. *King Arthur: The Sword in the Stone* is the first book in his ongoing series, *Tales of King Arthur.* Before he started writing his King Arthur books, Talbott traveled through England and Wales researching the legends.

> **"Even I was surprised by what this project released in me—an untapped love of history and legend and a passion for the classics. Seemingly random occurrences in my own past—from collecting knights and horses as a child to my years in Europe wandering through castles and cathedrals—all began to make sense as they coalesced [came together] and helped inspire this work."**

Writing and illustrating books for young people is actually Talbott's second career. He supported himself first as an artist, freelance illustrator, and designer. He says that creating books for children feels "more rewarding, more permanent" than anything else he has done. "After all, a good children's book can have a lifetime effect on people."

For Independent Reading

If you especially enjoy paintings of war scenes, don't miss Talbott's *King Arthur and the Round Table.* It tells of Arthur's wars to unite his kingdom, his fateful meeting with Guinevere, and the gift of the Round Table. In Talbott's *Excalibur,* Arthur acquires a magical sword and begins to face the responsibilities of being king.

First Thoughts

1. Do you think Arthur's story deserves to be a legend? Explain.

Thinking Critically

2. The chart at the lower right shows the pattern of a typical hero tale. How well does Arthur's story fit the pattern? Fill out the chart and see.

3. How does Sir Kay, Arthur's brother, show that he doesn't have what it takes to be king?

4. How does Arthur change during the story? What evidence suggests that he will be a great king?

5. **Legends** are based on historical facts. The stories become exaggerated as they are passed down from one generation to the next. List two events in this story that could have happened in real life. List two fantastic, supernatural events that could not have happened in real life.

Extending Interpretations

6. Look back at your Quickwrite notes. Compare Arthur with the future legendary hero you described. Do a society's values determine the heroes it admires, or are all heroes alike in certain ways? Explain. 🖉

Reading Check

a. What does Uther agree to give Merlin in return for the sorcerer's help in getting Uther married to Lady Igraine?

b. Why does Merlin make the bargain with Uther?

c. What happens to Britain after Uther's death?

d. How does Arthur prove he is the rightful king of England?

e. How do King Lot and King Urien feel about Arthur as king?

Hero's Story	Arthur's Story
Hero is born in an obscure place.	
Hero is of unknown parentage.	
Hero is threatened as a child.	
Hero passes a test to prove he is king.	
Hero is an unlikely person to be king.	

WRITING

Write a Letter to Merlin

Imagine this: You're Arthur, and you've just been crowned king. You love Sir Ector and Sir Kay, but now you want to find out what happened to your father and mother. Write a letter to Merlin as if you were Arthur. What questions do you want to ask? How do you feel about the fact that you were never told you were adopted by Sir Ector? End your letter by confiding to Merlin how you feel about being king.

SKILLS FOCUS

Literary Skills
Analyze a legend.

Writing Skills
Write a letter.

After You Read   Vocabulary Development

Latin and Anglo-Saxon Word Origins

You've learned that, after Arthur's death, the Angles and the Saxons conquered the Britons. At that point, Anglo-Saxon words began coming into the language we now call English. Anglo-Saxon words tend to be short, one-syllable, simple words: *deer, pig, cow, man, wife, foot.* It's hard to make up an English sentence without using at least one Anglo-Saxon word. Words like *the, for, in,* and *is,* for instance, come from Anglo-Saxon.

In 1066, the Norman-French conquered Britain. Some of the longer, "fancier" words in English today tend to be words that were once French. In the opening sentence of *King Arthur: The Sword in the Stone,* you read the word *ancient,* which comes from a French word, *ancien.* Before it came into French, the root of *ancient* came from Latin, *ante,* "before." The Anglo-Saxon word meaning the same thing is a very different word: *old.*

PRACTICE

In each of the following sentences, find two words that come from Anglo-Saxon (also called Old English) and two words that come from French and Latin. You will have to use a dictionary. In most dictionaries you will find brackets, like these [ ], that show where the word comes from. For words from Anglo-Saxon, you'll find this: **[ME], [AS],** or **[OE].** For words from Latin or French, you'll find these: **[L]** and **[Fr].** One of the words you pick for each sentence should be the Word Bank word. Don't bother with place names or proper names. Write the Anglo-Saxon or Latin root of each word you choose.

1. After sixteen turbulent years the archbishop of Canterbury asked Merlin for help.
2. "And to celebrate this momentous occasion, a tournament shall be held on Christmas Eve."
3. "Pursuing one's goals with integrity is all that matters."
4. Never had there been such a huge congregation of lords and ladies.

Word Bank

turbulent
tournament
integrity
congregation

The Granger Collection, New York.

King Arthur of Britain (detail) (14th century). French tapestry.

SKILLS FOCUS

Vocabulary Skills
Understand Latin and Anglo-Saxon word origins.

Three Responses to Literature

Make the Connection
Quickwrite 🖉

Have you ever done peer editing in writers' workshop groups, where you've given constructive criticism about another student's work? Make a list of the criteria you use to evaluate a partner's writing.

Literary Focus
Literary Criticism: Responding to Literature

In this lesson you will read and evaluate three responses to a literary work. The three essays answer a question about the character of Arthur in *King Arthur: The Sword in the Stone* (page 793). It will be your job to evaluate each response as if you were a teacher or a critic. How well has each writer answered the question? How well are the ideas about Arthur supported?

Analyzing a Response to Literature

A response should be focused. A focused response sticks to the topic. In this case the question asks whether or not Arthur has the potential for greatness. As you read each essay, ask yourself:

- Does it answer the question?
- Does it answer the question in a convincing way?
- Does it stick to the topic of Arthur's character?

A response must provide textual support. A supported response will offer details from the text—or from the writer's own experience—to support major ideas. Ask yourself:

- Does the writer clearly define the qualities necessary for greatness?
- Does the writer prove or disprove that Arthur has these qualities?

The most **successful responses** will offer specific, concrete examples from the text to support each main idea. An analysis of character should focus on the character's actions and words and on how other people respond to that character.

The following three essays all answer the same question about Arthur's character. The side notes with the first essay show you how well the writer responds to the question. Read the other two essays carefully to see how well they do the same.

King Arthur of Britain by Howard Pyle.
The Granger Collection, New York.

SKILLS FOCUS

Literary Skills
Analyze responses to a literary work.

Three Responses to Literature

Essay 1

In *King Arthur: The Sword in the Stone*, the writer uses important contrasts between Sir Kay and Arthur to show how Arthur is different from most youths his age. In the choices he makes and in the way he lives, Arthur shows that he is capable of greatness.

To fulfill his destiny of greatness, Arthur has to have wisdom. Although nobody sixteen years old has lived long enough to have a lot of wisdom, the writer shows us that Arthur is already gaining it. Arthur has found and protected orphaned fox cubs. He has tamed birds and deer. This requires patience and the ability to look and listen. In contrast, Kay, a more typical boy, spends most of his time polishing his helmet. Today, it would be a car, but we get the idea. How many teens today would choose to tame wild creatures for the joy of it? Arthur is unusual in a good way, a way that will bring wisdom to him.

There is a more important contrast between Arthur and Kay. Kay ignores the truth and forgets his dream when he sees a chance to be king. Before they leave for London, Kay tells his father, "To prove myself on the field of battle is my dream." Yet, when the sword falls into Kay's hand the next day, Kay forgets all of that. He sees a chance to be the king, and he tries to claim it even though he knows he didn't earn it. In contrast to Kay, Arthur thinks of others. He goes to London hoping to "help bring honor and glory to his family." He takes the sword only to meet Kay's need. He says nothing while Kay claims the kingship as his own. When he is forced to admit that he took the sword, he sees right away that being king will force him to say goodbye to many things he loves: the deer, his birds, fishing. This shows how Arthur is different from most youths. Most would see only the glory of being a king; Arthur sees past that to the sacrifices it will require. He realizes that he will never be able to live for himself only. It is a future he does not want. It is his destiny, though, and he has the courage to see that too. "Very well, whatever my destiny may be, I am willing to accept it." This combination of insight and courage also shows his potential for greatness.

Answers the question directly.

States first main idea.

Supports main idea with examples from the text.

Sums up main idea.

States second main idea.

Supports second main idea with examples from the text.

When Arthur asks Merlin what his future will be, Merlin replies, "Greatness surrounds you like a golden cloak. Your achievements could inspire humankind for centuries to come. But you alone can fulfill this destiny and then only if you wish it. You own your future. You alone." How many of us are told that, if we fail ourselves, we will fail humankind? Arthur gives it all he has. He faces the archbishop, the crowds, the jealous kings who will now be his enemies. When Arthur tells the people at his coronation, "For your good I dedicate my life," somehow, we know he will not fail them . . . or himself.

Uses a direct quote to support third main idea.

Ends with a key quote from Arthur himself.

Essay 2

Arthur possesses the potential to be a great king. Throughout the story, Arthur shows kindness, honesty, a good heart, and courage. These are qualities any great person should have.

First, Arthur is kind. He rescues and tames wild animals. If he was not kind, would he do that? He is also nice to his brother, Sir Kay, even when his brother is full of himself. He is also willing to let Kay have the crown, but this might not be a kindness, since Arthur doesn't really want it. A great king must be kind to others in order to keep the love of the people. Arthur will succeed in this way.

Second, Arthur is honest. He does not lie to his father about pulling out the sword. At that point he thinks he is in trouble for it, so that is a courageous thing for him to do. Arthur is also truthful when he says he doesn't want to be a king but will do it if he has to. Arthur would rather stay at home with his animals in the woods and his family. A great person must be honest, and Arthur will succeed in this way, too.

Third, Arthur has a good heart. He tries his hardest in everything he does. He might mess things up, like when he loses Kay's sword, but he still tries his best. A great person cannot ever give up.

Fourth, Arthur is courageous. He stands up and faces all those people to pull out the sword. He is just sixteen years old, and now he will have to be a king of a country that many people want to take over. All in all, Arthur will fulfill his destiny by showing kindness, honesty, a good heart, and courage.

Arthur Drawing the Sword from the Stone by Louis Rhead (1857–1926).

The Granger Collection, New York.

Essay 3

Arthur is the son of King Uther Pendragon and Queen Igraine. On the night he is born, the stars form the shape of a dragon to foreshadow Arthur's greatness. Merlin takes him away to keep him safe. Arthur's father is poisoned a year later, so it is a good decision to take the baby away. When Arthur is sixteen, his country needs him. The years while he has been growing up were lawless and dark. Merlin devises a way to make the people accept Arthur. He puts a sword in an anvil outside the church, with a note that says that whoever could pull out the sword is the rightful king of England. The archbishop declares a contest on Christmas morning to see who is the rightful king, and a tournament on Christmas Eve. Arthur goes along to London to be squire for his bossy brother, Sir Kay. Kay is an annoying character, but Arthur doesn't mind being bossed around by Kay. He spends the time on the way to the tournament thinking of how to be a good squire and bring honor to his family. When they get to London, Arthur is amazed to see a sword in an anvil on a large block of marble with soldiers standing around it. He thinks London is full of wonders. Kay does a really good job in the first part of the tournament. He has just enough time to rest and change before the next event, and he asks Arthur for his sword. Arthur can't find it! He leaps on his pony to go back to their tent, but it isn't there. Arthur decides to borrow the one he saw from the anvil, and he goes to see about getting it. It comes out pretty easily, and Arthur takes it to Sir Kay. Kay tells Arthur to get their father. Then Kay wants to claim he's king. Their father makes him prove it. Of course, Kay cannot put the sword back, but Arthur can. Their father, Sir Ector, is overcome when he realizes who Arthur really is. He tells Arthur he can't avoid his destiny. Merlin comes along and tells Arthur he is going to be a great king, but he will have to fulfill his destiny. It will be Arthur's choice. He has to want it. Arthur is sad to give up the life he loves, but he says he will accept whatever his destiny is. Then he pulls the sword out on five different occasions to prove his worth. The people love him, and he is crowned King of England.

Illustration from an early-14th-century manuscript.

The Granger Collection, New York.

First Thoughts

1. How do you think each writer felt about the character of Arthur?

Thinking Critically

2. Essay 1 provides specific details from the text to support its analysis of Arthur's **character.** List three of these supporting details.

3. Essay 1 uses **comparison and contrast** to make its points. Is this an effective way to answer the question about Arthur's character? Why or why not?

4. Essay 2 lists four qualities of greatness that the writer thinks Arthur possesses. Which of these qualities is *not* clearly supported in the story?

5. Analyze the following criticisms of Essay 3, and decide which one is valid. Explain the reasons for your choice.

- The writer should have summarized the plot.
- The essay does not answer the question.
- The writer should have quoted some of Arthur's exact words to support the main points about his character.
- The writer doesn't put quotation marks around Arthur's exact words.

6. On a scale of 0 to 5, with 0 being the lowest rating and 5 the highest, how would you rate each essay? Base your evaluation on the tips for "Analyzing a Response to Literature" on page 810. How do these tips compare with the list of criteria you wrote in your Quickwrite response?

Reading Check

a. Which essay states the answer to the question about Arthur in the opening sentence?

b. Which essay uses direct **quotations** from the text to support its main ideas?

c. Which essay contains a plot **summary** rather than a character analysis?

WRITING

Literary Criticism: Responding to Literature

Write a paragraph discussing the literary element of *King Arthur: The Sword in the Stone* that stood out for you. Was it the plot? the characters? the unusual setting? the theme of the rightful ruler becoming king? Be sure to support your response with details from the legend.

Vocabulary Development

Latin and Anglo-Saxon Prefixes

The English language spoken during the time when the real King Arthur lived (around 500 A.D.) used a great many words from Latin and Anglo-Saxon. The Latin words in the English language have come from many sources.

- Some came into English when Roman soldiers occupied Britain for about 450 years, beginning in 55 B.C.

- Other Latin words came into English after the Normans invaded England in 1066. The Normans brought French words with them, which in turn had come from Latin.

- Other Latin words came from the Catholic Church, which was very important in Britain for centuries.

In the box are some prefixes from the Latin language and from the old form of the English language called Anglo-Saxon. English speakers have found all of these prefixes to be very useful. A **prefix** is a word part added to the front of another word to change its meaning: When you add the prefix *un–* to the word *digested,* for example, you get the word *undigested,* meaning "not digested." If you add the prefix *pre–* to *digested,* you get *predigested,* meaning "digested beforehand."

A Box of Prefixes
(*L* means the prefix is from Latin. *AS* means it is from Anglo-Saxon.)

contra–	against (L)
mis–	badly (AS)
over–	above; excessively (AS)
post–	after (L)
pre–	before (L)
pro–	favoring; forward (L)
retro–	backward (L)
semi–	half (L)
sub–	under (L)
un–	not (AS)

PRACTICE

Answer each question below. Refer to the box of prefixes to help you figure out the meanings of any words you do not already know.

1. If a rocket misfires, what has happened to it?
2. If a medical test is unfavorable, why would you be upset?
3. What does it mean to say that someone is overstating a case?
4. If a food is contraindicated by the doctor, should you eat it or avoid it?
5. If someone is postoperative, has the surgery already been performed or is it about to begin?
6. Why shouldn't a juror prejudge a case?
7. If a politician is pro–social security, is she for it or against it?
8. If your pay is retroactive, are you being paid for past work or for future work?
9. What would you expect to find if someone is semiconscious?
10. Does a subway run aboveground or underground?

SKILLS FOCUS

Vocabulary Skills
Understand Latin and Anglo-Saxon prefixes.

Evaluating Evidence: Understanding Stereotype and Bias

Reading Focus

Stereotype: No Room for Individuality

Imagine you're sitting on a bench in a shopping mall, waiting for your ride to show up. You begin hearing bits of conversations from shoppers as they walk by. You hear these comments:

"People who drive sports cars are reckless."

"All politicians are dishonest."

"Boys are better than girls at math."

"Teenagers aren't concerned with world issues."

"All teenagers drive recklessly."

"Football players aren't good at schoolwork."

"Smart kids are geeky."

"Rich kids are selfish."

You've just heard people express their opinions of others using **stereotypes.** That means they are using unfair, fixed ideas about groups of people. Stereotypes don't allow for any individuality. They brand every member of a group with the same characteristics. Stereotypes are very hurtful. They are often used to persuade you to do or believe something.

Bias: An Inclination to Favor Someone or Something

If you've ever watched your favorite sports team on the opposing team's host TV channel, you've probably noticed that the broadcasters favor the home team with their comments and calls. What you're really noticing is something called **bias**—attitudes and beliefs that shape a person's thinking in spite of the facts. Of course, your bias is evident also—you want your team to win!

■ As you read editorials, letters to the media (such as the one that follows), or any kind of political or social commentary, be on the lookout for expressions that suggest the writer has already made up his or her mind about something or someone. Think of bias as an inclination to think a certain way. In its worst form, bias becomes prejudice.

INTERNET
Interactive Reading Model
Keyword: LE5 7-7

Reading Skills
Understand stereotype and bias.

Arthur and his knights setting out on the quest for the Holy Grail (c. 1380–1400) by Italian School. Vellum.

In the first selection in this collection, *King Arthur: The Sword in the Stone,* Arthur won the future-king contest by yanking the sword out of the stone. He won it fair and square, but King Lot and King Urien were sore losers. They might have sent the following protest to the media—if the media had been available to them.

He's No King

❶ My brother and I strongly protest the outcome of this contest. Arthur is just a lowly squire. He spends his spare time playing in the forest with little animals. He does not have the ability to rule over us. We may as well have a girl ruler for all he is worth.

❷ We are far more experienced than this little boy. Also, we are part of the royal family. Our wives are daughters of King Uther Pendragon. We were born to rule. This boy is a nobody.

❸ Who has ever heard of this unknown country boy? Does anyone know who his father is? Has anyone seen the flash of a sword in his hand? Has anyone seen a helmet on his head? Has anyone seen him ride a powerful horse? How can an animal-loving, fair-haired outsider ever be considered powerful enough to be king?

❹ Look carefully, people. Look underneath the surface and you'll see what is really happening here. Merlin set this whole thing up. He is using the boy to gain power for himself. People like Merlin always figure out a way to serve their own selfish interests. Once Arthur is king, Merlin will be the real ruler of the kingdom, and Arthur will be his puppet on a string.

❺ Save our future. Our country will not survive if we have a king who is a weakling. We must have another contest to make sure we have a king who is worthy of the position.

—Kings Lot and Urien

Analyzing Stereotype and Bias

He's No King

1. Which statement best describes the speakers' **bias** in paragraph 1?

   A They are biased against a boy who plays with animals and is a lowly squire.

   B They are biased against animals.

   C They are biased against kings.

   D They are biased against using such a contest to determine who will be king.

2. "Has anyone ever seen the flash of a sword in his hand?" is a **biased** question suggesting that —

   F Arthur lied about pulling the sword out of the stone

   G Arthur has said he hates fighting

   H kings need quick reflexes

   J kings have to be tested in battle

3. It is clear that King Lot and King Urien, the speakers, protest the outcome of the sword-pulling contest mainly because —

   A they wish to rule England themselves

   B Arthur is good with animals

   C they think the contest was fixed

   D Arthur is not old enough to lead

4. In paragraph 4, the speakers reveal **bias** against —

   F Arthur

   G Merlin

   H puppet rulers

   J kings in general

Constructed Response

1. Who are the speakers?

2. What do the speakers want?

3. What action do the speakers call for?

4. Analyze the **stereotype** in paragraph 1.

5. Explain the **bias** in paragraph 2.

SKILLS FOCUS

Reading Skills
Analyze stereotype and bias.

Vocabulary Development

Greek Roots

Many English words have long histories—many words have been borrowed from the French, who borrowed them from the Romans, who in turn borrowed them from the Greeks. Knowing what a Greek word root means can help you figure out the meaning of other words that come from the same or similar roots.

PRACTICE

Below you will find five Greek roots and their definitions. Use context clues and the root definitions to figure out the modern words and fill in the blanks in each sentence.

GREEK ROOTS		
Root	Definition	Also Used As . . .
–astron–	"star"	–astro–
–chronos–	"time"	–chron–
–decem– –deka–	"ten"	–dec–
–helios–	"sun"	–heli–

1. If you are really in a hurry, you can charter a heli _ _ _ _ er to fly you there.
2. Events that are recorded in sequence of time are said to be chron _ _ _ _ _ _ al.
3. Some say that when our stars are crossed, _ _ _ aster strikes.
4. In ancient Rome the tenth month was Dec _ _ _ _ _ _ .
5. Astro _ _ _ _ s may one day visit other planets.
6. Diseases that extend over a long period of time are said to be chron _ _ .
7. A person who can compete in ten athletic events is called a dec _ _ _ _ ete.
8. Astro _ _ _ _ is the scientific study of the stars and the planets.
9. A dec _ _ _ is a period of ten years.
10. Heli _ _ is a light gas used to make balloons float.

ASTRO'S USES

SKILLS FOCUS

Vocabulary Skills
Understand Greek roots.

Merlin and the Dragons

Make the Connection
Quickwrite ✏️

Everybody loves a hero, but just what is a hero? Is it a comic book superhero with special powers? Is it an astronaut who lands on the moon? Is it a firefighter who rescues people from a burning building? Is it a freedom fighter who goes to jail in the cause of justice? Is it a librarian who helps children develop a love of learning? Jot down your ideas on what makes someone a hero.

Literary Focus
Heroes and Quests

Throughout the world and throughout literature, we find stories of great heroes who have saved their people from terrible threats. The plots of many of these stories follow a typical pattern.

Heroes in such tales are often born in unusual circumstances, often in secret. Sometimes their true parents are unknown. The hero is often trained by a wise, older man. When his time comes, the young hero proves himself (these old stories were always about masculine heroes) through some fantastic feat of strength or intellect.

The hero then gathers a band of followers and embarks on a **quest** to save his people from some threat—a monster, perhaps, or a false leader.

You have seen part of this pattern in the story of King Arthur you just read, *King Arthur: The Sword in the Stone.* As you read "Merlin and the Dragons," look for events that also match the pattern of the hero tale.

Vocabulary Development

Here are some words you'll need to know to understand the story:

ruthless (rōōth′lis) *adj.:* without pity. *A ruthless army destroyed the village.*

bedraggled (bē·drag′əld) *adj.:* hanging limp and wet; dirty. *The bedraggled horses needed rest.*

insolence (in′sə·ləns) *n.:* disrespect. *The rebels were punished for their insolence.*

recognition (rek′əg·nish′ən) *n.:* knowing again. *Merlin was pleased at Arthur's recognition of his past.*

INTERNET
Vocabulary
Activity
Keyword: LE5 7-7

Literary Skills
Understand
heroes.

Background
Literature and Legend

According to some versions of the legend, after he pulled the sword from the stone, Arthur went to live with Merlin. The old wizard was to teach the boy the lessons of being a good ruler.

In the story you are about to read, Arthur knows he is king, but he doesn't yet know his true parentage.

Merlin and the Dragons

Jane Yolen

The night was dark and storm clouds marched along the sky. Rain beat against the gray castle walls. Inside, in a bedroom hung with tapestries, the young King Arthur had trouble sleeping. Awake, he was frightened. Asleep, he had disturbing dreams.

At last he climbed out of bed, took a candle to light his way, and started out the door. Suddenly remembering his crown, he turned back and found it under the bed where he'd tossed it angrily hours before. It felt too heavy for his head, so he carried it, letting it swing from his fingers.

As he walked along the hall, strange shadows danced before him. But none were as frightening as the shadows in his dreams.

He climbed the tower stairs slowly, biting his lip. When he reached the top, he pushed open the wooden door. The old magician was asleep in his chair, but woke at once, his eyes quick as a hawk's.

"What is it, boy?" the old man asked. "What brings you here at this hour?"

"I am the king," Arthur said, but softly as if he were not really sure. "I go where I will." He put the crown on Merlin's desk.

"You are a boy," Merlin replied, "and boys should be in their beds asleep."

Arthur sighed. "I could not sleep," he said. "I had bad dreams."

"Ah . . ." Merlin nodded knowingly. "Dreams." He held out a hand to the boy, but Arthur didn't dare touch those long, gnarled fingers. "Let me read your dreams."

"It is one dream, actually," Arthur said. "And always the same: a fatherless boy who becomes king simply by pulling a sword from a stone."

"Ah . . ." Merlin said again, withdrawing his fingers. "I know the very child. But if you cannot tell me more of your dream, I shall have to tell you one of mine. After all, a dream told is a story. What better than a story on a rainy night?"

Arthur settled onto a low stool and gazed up at the wizard. A story! He hadn't known he wanted a story. He'd come seeking comfort and companionship. A story was better than both.

He listened as Merlin began.

In a small village high up in the rugged mountains of Wales lived a lonely, fatherless boy named Emrys. Dark-haired he was, and small, with sharp bright eyes, and a mouth that rarely smiled. He was troubled by dreams, sleeping and waking. Dreams of dragons, dreams of stone.

His mother was the daughter of the local king and tried to be both mother and father to him. But a princess is only taught lute songs and needlework and prayers. She'd never once climbed a tree after a bird's egg or skinned her knee pursuing a lizard, or caught a butterfly in a net. Emrys had to invent that part of growing up himself. And a lonely inventing it turned out to be.

The other boys in the village teased him for not knowing who his father was. "Mother's babe," they cried, chasing him from their games.

So Emrys went after birds' eggs and lizards, butterflies and frogs by himself, giving them names both odd and admiring, like "flutterby" and "wriggletail," and making up stories of their creation. And he chanted strange-sounding spells because he liked the sounds, spells that sometimes seemed to work, most times did not.

But he never told his dreams aloud. Dreams of dragons, dreams of stone.

Now in the village lived an old man who

knew all sorts of things, from reading and writing to how birds speak and why leaves turn brown in autumn. And because Emrys was the son of a princess, the grandson of a king, the old man taught him all he knew.

It was this learning that brought the village boys to him, not in friendship but in curiosity. They would ask Emrys to show them some trick with the birds, or to tell them stories. Glad for the company, Emrys always obliged. He even took to making up harmless predictions to amuse them.

"The rain will soon fall," he would say. And often it did.

"The first spring robin will arrive." And soon after, it came.

Now any farmer's son could have made the same right guesses and after awhile the village boys were no longer impressed. However, one day Emrys found a book of seasons and planetary movements in the old man's cottage and read it cover to cover. Then he went out and announced to the astonished boys: "Tomorrow the sun will disappear."

The next day at noon, just as the calendar had foretold, an eclipse plunged the countryside into darkness. The boys and their parents were equally horrified and blamed Emrys. From then on he was called "demon's son" and avoided altogether.

Years went by and Emrys grew up, terribly alone, dreaming dreams he did not understand: dreams of a shaking tower, dreams of fighting dragons.

One day when Emrys was twelve, a cruel and ruthless man named Vortigern came to the valley. Vortigern had unjustly declared himself High King over all Britain. But the country was at last in revolt against him and he had been forced to flee, riding ever farther north and west. At last he had

arrived at the foot of Dinys Emrys, the mountain which towered above the village, with a bedraggled army on tired horses, bearing tattered banners emblazoned with red dragons. A handful of court magicians rode with them.

Vortigern pointed to the jagged mountain peak. "There," he said in a voice hard and determined. "There I will build my battle tower, so that I may see my enemies when they approach."

He turned to his soldiers. "Gather the people of this village and bring them to me, for they will be the hackers and haulers. They will make me a tower of stone."

Vocabulary
ruthless (rōōth′lis) *adj.:* without pity.
bedraggled (bē·drag′əld) *adj.:* hanging limp and wet; dirty.

Young Emrys looked on in amazement. Banners sewn with red dragons? A tower of stone? Such things had been in his dreams. What could it all mean?

The Welsh stonecutters began their work under the watchful eyes of the soldiers. For many days they mined the stone, cutting huge pieces from the sides of Dinys Emrys. They swore they could hear the cries of the mountain at each cut.

Next they hauled the stones with ropes, their little Welsh ponies groaning with the effort. Finally, came the day when they built the tower up on the mountainside, stone upon stone, until it rose high above the valley.

That night Emrys went to bed and dreamed once again his strange dreams. He dreamed that the tower—the very one built by Vortigern—shook and swayed and tumbled to the ground. And he dreamed that beneath the tower slept two dragons, one red as Vortigern's banners, and one white.

That very night the High King's tower began to shudder and shake and, with a mighty crash, came tumbling down. In the morning, when he saw what had happened, Vortigern was furious, convinced the villagers had done it on purpose.

"Your work is worthless," he bellowed at the Welshmen. "You will be whipped, and then you will get to work all over again."

So the Welshmen had to go back to their stonework, great welts on their backs. They hacked and hauled, and once again the tower rose high above the valley. But the night they were finished, it was the same. The tower shook and tumbled to the ground. By morning there was only a jumble of stones.

Vortigern drove the villagers even harder, and by the following week the tower was once again rebuilt. But a third time, in the night, a great shudder went through the mountain and the work once again lay in ruins. Vortigern's rage could not be contained. He called for his magicians. "There is some dark Welsh magic here. Find out the cause. My tower must stand."

Now these magicians had neither knowledge nor skill, but in their fear of Vortigern they put on a good show. They consulted the trees, both bark and root; they threw the magic sticks of prophecy; they played with the sacred stones of fate. At last they reported their findings.

"You must find a fatherless child," they said. "A child spawned by a demon. You must sprinkle his blood on the stones. Only then will the gods of this land let the stones stand." They smiled at one another and at Vortigern, smiles of those sure that what they ask cannot be done.

Vortigern did not notice their smiles. "Go find me such a child."

The magicians stopped smiling and looked nervous. "We do not know if any such child exists," they said. "We do not know if your tower can stand."

Furious, Vortigern turned to his soldiers. "Gold to whomever brings me such a child," he roared.

Before the soldiers could move, a small voice cried out. "Please, sir, we of the village know such a boy." The speaker was a spindly lad named Gwillam.

"Come here, child," said Vortigern. "Name him."

Gwillam did not dare get too close to the High King. "His name is Emrys, sir. He was spawned by a demon. He can cry the sun from the sky."

Vortigern turned to the captain of his

guards. "Bring this demon's son to me."

At that very moment, Emrys was on the mountain with the old man, absorbed in a very strange dream. Under the ruins of the tower he saw two huge stone eggs breathing in and out. Just as he emerged from his dream, he was set upon by Vortigern's soldiers. "What shall I do?" he cried.

The old man put a hand on his shoulder. "Trust your dreams."

The soldiers quickly bound Emrys and carried him to the High King, but Emrys refused to show any fear. "You are the boy without a father, the boy spawned by a devil?" Vortigern asked.

"I am a boy without a father, true," Emrys said. "But I am no demon's son. You have been listening to the words of frightened children."

The villagers and soldiers gasped at his impudence, but Vortigern said, "I will have your blood either way."

"Better that you have my dream," Emrys said. "Only my dream can guide you so that your tower will stand."

The boy spoke with such conviction, Vortigern hesitated.

"I have dreamed that beneath your tower lies a pool of water that must be drained. In the mud you will find two hollow stones. In each stone is a sleeping dragon. It is the breath of each sleeping dragon that shakes the earth and makes the tower fall. Kill the dragons and your tower will stand."

Vortigern turned to his chief magician. "Can this be true?"

The chief magician stroked his chin. "Dreams *can* come true. . . ."

Vortigern hesitated no longer. "Untie the boy, but watch him," he said

to his soldiers. "And you—Welshmen—do as the boy says. Dig beneath the rubble."

So the Welshmen removed the stones and dug down until they came to a vast pool of water. Then the soldiers drained the pool. And just as Emrys had prophesied, at the pool's bottom lay two great stones. The stones seemed to be breathing in and out, and at each breath the mud around them trembled.

"Stonecutters," cried Vortigern, "break open the stones!"

Two men with mighty hammers descended into the pit and began to pound upon the stones.

Once, twice, three times their hammers rang out. On the third try, like jets of lightning, cracks ran around each stone and they broke apart as if they had been giant eggs. Out of one emerged a dragon white as new milk. Out of the other a dragon red as old wine.

Astonished at the power of his dreaming, Emrys opened and closed his mouth, but could not speak. The men in the pit scrambled for safety.

The High King Vortigern looked pleased. "Kill them! Kill the dragons!"

But even as he spoke, the dragons shook out their wings and leapt into the sky.

"They are leaving!" cried the chief magician.

"They are away!" cried the soldiers.

"They will not go quite yet," whispered Emrys.

No sooner had he spoken than the dragons wheeled about in the sky to face one another, claws out, belching flame. Their battle cries like nails on slate echoed in the air.

Advancing on one another, the dragons clashed, breast to breast, raining teeth and scales on the ground. For hour after hour they fought, filling the air with smoke.

First the red dragon seemed to be winning,

then the white. First one drew blood, then the other. At last, with a furious slash of its jaws, the white dragon caught the red by the throat. There was a moment of silence, and then the red dragon tumbled end over end until it hit the ground.

The white dragon followed it down, straddling its fallen foe and screaming victory into the air with a voice like thunder.

"Kill it! Kill the white now!" shouted Vortigern.

As if freed from a spell, his soldiers readied their weapons. But before a single arrow could fly, the white dragon leapt back into the air and was gone, winging over the highest peak.

"Just so the red dragon of Vortigern shall be defeated," Emrys said, but not so loud the High King could hear.

Cursing the fleeing dragon, Vortigern ordered the tower to be built again. Then he turned to Emrys. "If the tower does not stand this time, I *will* have your blood."

That night young Emrys stared out his

window, past the newly built tower. A hawk circled lazily in the sky. Suddenly the hawk swooped down, landing on his window ledge. There was a moment of silent communion between them, as if Emrys could read the hawk's thoughts, as if the hawk could read his. Then away the hawk flew.

Mountains, valleys, hillsides, forests gave way beneath the hawk's wings until, far off in the distance, it spied thousands of flickering lights coming up from the south. As if in a dream, Emrys saw these things, too.

Emerging from his vision, Emrys turned from the window and went downstairs. He found King Vortigern by the foot of the tower.

"I have seen in a vision that your fate is linked with the red dragon's," Emrys cried. "You will be attacked by thousands of soldiers under the white dragon's flag—attacked and slain."

Vortigern drew his sword, angry enough to kill the boy for such insolence. But at that very moment, a lookout atop the tower shouted: "Soldiers, my lord! Thousands of them!"

Vortigern raced to the top of the tower stairs and stared across the valley. It was true. And as he watched further, one of the knights leading the army urged his horse forward and raced along to the tower foot, shouting: "Come and meet your fate, murderous Vortigern!"

Vortigern turned to his own men. "Defend me! Defend my tower!"

But when they saw the numbers against them, the men all deserted.

"Surrender, Vortigern!" cried a thousand voices.

"Never!" he called back. "Never!"

Vocabulary
insolence (in′sə·ləns) *n.:* disrespect.

The old wizard stopped speaking.

"Well?" Arthur asked. "What happened to Vortigern? You cannot end a story there."

Merlin looked at him carefully. "What do *you* think happened?"

"Vortigern was slain, just as Emrys said."

"Is that the boy speaking?" asked the wizard. "Or the king?"

"The boy," admitted Arthur. "A king should forgive his enemies and make them his chiefest friends. You taught me that, Merlin. But what did happen?"

"The men of the white dragon defeated Vortigern all right. Burned him up in his own tower."

"And that knight, the one who rode up to the tower first. What became of him?"

"His name was Uther Pendragon and he eventually became the High King," Merlin said.

"Uther," mused Arthur. "He was the last High King before me. But then he was a hero. He was fit to rule. Perhaps one of his sons will come to claim my throne."

"Uther had only one son," Merlin said softly, "though only I knew of it." He looked steadily at the boy. "That son was you, Arthur."

"Me?" For a moment Arthur's voice squeaked. "Uther was my father? Then I am not fatherless? Then I am king by right and not just because I pulled a sword from a stone."

Merlin shook his head. "Don't underestimate your real strength in pulling that sword," Merlin cautioned. "It took a true and worthy king to do what you did."

Arthur gave a deep sigh. "Why did you not tell me this before?"

The old wizard's hawk eyes opened wide. "I could not tell you until you were ready.

There are rules for prophets, just as there are rules for kings."

"So now I am king in truth."

Merlin smiled. "You were always king in truth. Only you doubted it. So you can thank your dreams for waking you up."

"What of Emrys?" Arthur asked. "What happened to him?"

"Oh—he's still around," replied the wizard. "Went on dreaming. Made a career of it." He rummaged around in some old boxes and crates by the desk until he found what he was looking for. "I still have this. Saved it all this time." He tossed a large yellowed dragon's tooth across to Arthur.

Sudden <u>recognition</u> dawned on Arthur's face. "You? You saved this? Then you were the boy named Emrys!"

"Surely you guessed that before," Merlin teased. "But now perhaps we can both go back to sleep."

"Thank you, Merlin," Arthur said. "I don't think I shall dream any more bad dreams."

Merlin's gnarled fingers caged the boy's hand for a moment. "But you shall dream," he said quietly. "Great men dream great dreams, and I have dreamed your greatness." He plucked the crown from the desktop. "Don't forget this, my lord king."

Arthur took the crown and placed it carefully on his head. Then he turned, went out the door, and down the tower stairs.

Merlin watched for a moment more, then sank back down in his chair. Closing his eyes, he fell immediately to sleep, dreaming of knights and a Round Table.

Vocabulary

recognition (rek′əg·nish′ən) *n.*: knowing again.

Meet the Writer

Jane Yolen

"Empress of Thieves"

When you click on the name *Yolen, Jane* in the computerized author index at your school or public library, you'll find screen after screen after screen of book titles. **Jane Yolen** (1939–   ) has written more than two hundred books for young people, plus dozens more for adults.

Yolen has said that she was raised on the tales of King Arthur, so it is not surprising that the King Arthur legend is one of her favorite subjects. She is considered an expert in the study and research of Arthurian legends. The character of Merlin seems to fascinate her especially, and she has written several books about him.

Yolen grew up surrounded by books and the tradition of storytelling. Both her parents were writers. One of her great-grandfathers was a storyteller in a Russian village. Yolen was in the eighth grade when she wrote her earliest books: a work about pirates and a seventeen-page historical novel about a trip by covered wagon. Since then Yolen has written many kinds of books, but she says that her primary sources of inspiration are the legends, tales, and myths of folklore.

“ As a writer I am the empress of thieves, taking characters like gargoyles off Parisian churches, the *ki-lin* (or unicorn) from China, swords in stones from the Celts, landscapes from the Taino people. I have pulled threads from magic tapestries to weave my own new cloth. ”

For Independent Reading

If you want to read more of Yolen's novels about Merlin, look for her Young Merlin series: *Passager*, *Hobby*, and *Merlin*. You might also enjoy *The Dragon's Boy*, a novel about Arthur before he knew he would be king. If you share Yolen's fascination with dragons, don't miss her Pit Dragon trilogy: three fantasy novels —*Dragon's Blood*, *Heart's Blood*, and *A Sending of Dragons*—set in another world.

First Thoughts

1. Do you think Emrys is a hero? In your answer, explain what you think a hero is. Check your Quickwrite notes from page 820 for ideas. 🖉

Thinking Critically

2. What details in the **plot** of this story give Emrys some of the qualities of a hero?

3. Explain what Arthur learns about the identity of Emrys at the end of the story.

4. Merlin taught Arthur that "A king should forgive his enemies and make them his chiefest friends." What do you think of this as advice for any ruler?

Extending Interpretations

5. The tales of King Arthur say little about the childhood of Arthur and even less about Merlin's childhood. Think about your responses to this story, which presents new, made-up details for an old legend. How do you feel about Jane Yolen inventing details to fill in the gaps?

WRITING

Analyzing Two Legends

Briefly summarize the plots of *King Arthur: The Sword in the Stone* (page 793) and "Merlin and the Dragons" (page 821). Tell which story you liked better, and give two or three reasons for your preference. Explain which literary elements in the work—plot, character, setting, theme—shaped your responses. Compare your responses with the responses of several classmates.

Reading Check

a. It is important that you notice the **structure** of this story. This is a story-within-a-story. What is happening in the **frame story**—the story that starts at the beginning?

b. Where does the story-*within*-the-story start? Where does it end?

c. Who is telling that story—the story about Emrys and the dragons?

d. Why is that storyteller telling Arthur the story about Emrys and the dragons?

e. Why do the boys call Emrys "demon's son"?

f. Where does Emrys get his special knowledge about nature? How does he know about the dragons in the stones?

g. Why has Vortigern fled to the valley where Emrys lives? Why does he want to have Emrys killed?

h. What happens when Vortigern's men pound on the stones beneath the tower?

i. Who leads the attack against Vortigern? How is Vortigern's conqueror related to Arthur?

SKILLS FOCUS

Literary Skills
Analyze the qualities of a hero.

Writing Skills
Write a literary analysis.

After You Read | Vocabulary Development

Prefixes and Suffixes: Useful Additions

PRACTICE 1

The Word Bank words contain several useful prefixes and suffixes. A **prefix** is a word part added to the front of a word to change its meaning; a **suffix** is a word part added to the end of a word to change its meaning.

Using a dictionary, make word maps for these useful prefixes and suffixes:

be–	ex–	in–
un–	–less	–tion

Use the word map opposite as a model. The prefix *non–* is shown as an example.

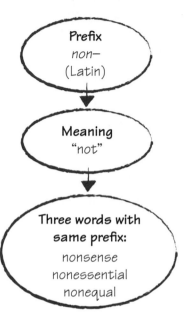

Prefix
non–
(Latin)

↓

Meaning
"not"

↓

Three words with same prefix:
nonsense
nonessential
nonequal

Word Bank

ruthless
bedraggled
insolence
recognition

Clarify Word Meanings by Using Examples

PRACTICE 2

1. Name three <u>ruthless</u> people in history.
2. Name three things that could be described as <u>bedraggled</u>.
3. Name an attitude that would be the opposite of <u>insolence</u>.
4. Name three achievements that would win someone <u>recognition</u>.

SKILLS FOCUS

Vocabulary Skills
Understand prefixes and suffixes; clarify word meanings by using examples.

Sir Gawain and the Loathly Lady

Make the Connection
Quickwrite ✏️

Imagine you're in a life-or-death situation. Your survival depends on giving the correct answer to one of these questions:

> What do men want most in the world?
> What do women want most in the world?

> In your journal, write three answers to each question. Circle the one that you think gives you your best shot at survival.

Literary Focus
The Quest

A **quest** is a long and perilous journey taken in search of something of great value: a treasure, a kingdom, the hand of a fair maiden, or the answer to an important question. During the quest, heroes of folk tales and legends face temptations and difficult tasks—they may be called on to slay a dragon or solve a riddle.

Centuries ago riddles were used often in stories, as a sort of test. A **riddle** is a puzzling question or problem. The hero usually had to answer the riddle correctly before going on with the quest. In the old days, riddles were important in real life, too. A riddle contest sometimes grew into a battle of wits with great rewards for the winner and exile or death for the loser.

Vocabulary Development

As you begin this quest, here are some words you'll need to arm yourself. The last word may be the most important word in the story.

chivalry (shiv′əl·rē) *n.:* code that governed knightly behavior, such as courage, honor, and readiness to help the weak. *Chivalry required knights to help those in need.*

countenance (koun′tə·nəns) *n.:* face; appearance. *The knight's countenance revealed his fear.*

loathsome (lōth′səm) *adj.:* disgusting. *Dame Ragnell's appearance was loathsome.*

sovereignty (säv′rən·tē) *n.:* control; authority. *Arthur had sovereignty over all of Britain.*

A knight and his lady feeding a falcon, from a German manuscript (detail) (c. 14th century).

The Granger Collection, New York.

SKILLS FOCUS

Literary Skills
Understand the quest.

Sir Gawain and the Loathly Lady

retold by Betsy Hearne

Sir Gawain, from 13th-century manuscript.

Now if you listen awhile I will tell you a tale of Arthur the King and how an adventure once befell him.

Of all kings and all knights, King Arthur bore away the honor wherever he went. In all his country there was nothing but chivalry, and knights were loved by the people.

One day in spring King Arthur was hunting in Ingleswood with all his lords beside him. Suddenly a deer ran by in the distance and the king took up chase, calling back to his knights, "Hold you still every man, I will chase this one myself!" He took his arrows and bow and stooped low like a woodsman to stalk the deer. But every time he came near the animal, it leapt away into the forest. So King Arthur went a while after the deer, and no knight went with him, until at last he let fly an arrow and killed the deer. He had raised a bugle to his lips to summon the knights when he heard a voice behind him.

"Well met, King Arthur!"

Though he had not heard anyone approach, the king turned to see a strange knight, fully armed, standing only a few yards away.

"You have done me wrong many a year and given away my northern lands," said the strange knight. "I have your life in my hands—what will you do now, King Alone?"

"Sir Knight, what is your name?" asked the king.

"My name is Gromer Somer Joure."[1]

"Sir Gromer, think carefully," said the king. "To slay me here, unarmed as I am, will get you no honor. All knights will refuse you wherever you go. Calm yourself—come to Carlyle and I shall mend all that is amiss."

"Nay," said Sir Gromer, "by heaven, King! You shall not escape when I have you at advantage. If I let you go with only a warning, later you'll defy me, of that I'm sure."

"Spare my life, Sir Gromer, and I shall grant you whatever is in my power to give. It is shameful to slay me here, with nothing but my hunting gear, and you armed for battle."

"All your talking will not help you, King, for I want neither land nor gold, truly." Sir Gromer smiled. "Still . . . if you will promise to meet me here, in the same fashion, on a day I will choose . . ."

"Yes," said the king quickly. "Here is my promise."

"Listen and hear me out. First you will swear upon my sword to meet me here without fail, on this day one year from now. Of all your knights none shall come with you. You must tell me at your coming what thing women most desire—and if you do not bring the answer to my riddle, you will lose your head. What say you, King?"

"I agree, though it is a hateful bargain," said the king. "Now let me go. I promise you as I am the true king, to come again at this day one year from now and bring you your answer."

The knight laughed, "Now go your way, King Arthur. You do not yet know your sorrow. Yet stay a moment—do not think of playing false—for by Mary[2] I think you would betray me."

"Nay," said King Arthur. "You will never

---

2. **by Mary:** a mild oath.

Vocabulary

chivalry (shĭv′əl·rē) *n*.: code that governed knightly behavior, which demanded courage, honor, and readiness to help the weak.

---

1. **Gromer Somer Joure** (grō·mer′ sō·mer′ zhoor).

find me an untrue knight. Farewell, Sir Knight, and evil met. I will come in a year's time, though I may not escape." The king began to blow his bugle for his knights to find him. Sir Gromer turned his horse and was gone as quickly as he had come, so that the lords found their king alone with the slain deer.

"We will return to Carlyle," said the king. "I do not like this hunting."

The lords knew by his <u>countenance</u> that the king met with some disturbance, but no one knew of his encounter. They wondered at the king's heavy step and sad look, until at last Sir Gawain[3] said to the king, "Sire, I marvel at you. What thing do you sorrow for?"

"I'll tell you, gentle Gawain," said Arthur. "In the forest as I pursued the deer, I met with a knight in full armor, and he charged me I should not escape him. I must keep my word to him or else I am foresworn."[4]

"Fear not my lord. I am not a man that would dishonor you."

"He threatened me, and would have slain me with great heat, but I spoke with him since I had no weapons."

"What happened then?" said Gawain.

"He made me swear to meet him there in one year's time, alone and unarmed. On that day I must tell him what women desire most, or I shall lose my life. If I fail in my answer, I know that I will be slain without mercy."

"Sire, make good cheer," said Gawain. "Make your horse ready to ride into strange country, and everywhere you meet either man or woman, ask of them the answer to the riddle. I will ride another way, and every man and woman's answer I will write in a book."

"That is well advised, Gawain," said the king. They made preparations to leave immediately, and when both were ready, Gawain rode one way and the king another—each one asked every man and woman they found what women most desire.

Some said they loved beautiful clothes; some said they loved to be praised; some said they loved a handsome man; some said one, some said another. Gawain had so many answers that he made a great book to hold them, and after many months of traveling he came back to court again. The king was there already with his book, and each looked over the other's work. But no answer seemed right.

"By God," said the king, "I am afraid. I will seek a little more in Ingleswood Forest. I have but one month to my set day, and I may find some good tidings."

"Do as you think best," said Gawain, "but whatever you do, remember that it is good to have spring again."

King Arthur rode forth on that day, into Ingleswood, and there he met with a lady. King Arthur marveled at her, for she was the ugliest creature that he had ever seen. Her face seemed almost like that of an animal, with a pushed-in nose and a few yellowing tusks for teeth. Her figure was twisted and deformed, with a hunched back and shoulders a yard broad. No tongue could tell the foulness of that lady. But she rode gaily on a palfrey[5] set with gold and precious stones,

---

3. **Gawain** (gä′wān).
4. **foresworn** *adj.:* untrue to one's word; shown to be a liar.

---

5. **palfrey** (pôl′frē) *n.:* gentle riding horse.

Vocabulary
countenance (koun′tə·nəns) *n.:* face; appearance.

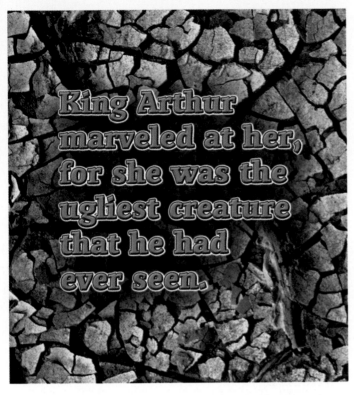

King Arthur marveled at her, for she was the ugliest creature that he had ever seen.

and when she spoke her voice was sweet and soft.

"I am glad that I have met with you, King Arthur," she said. "Speak with me, for your life is in my hand. I know of your situation, and I warn you that you will not find your answer if I do not tell you."

"What do you want with me, lady?" said the king, taken aback by the lady's boldness.

"Sir, I would like to speak with you. You will die if I do not save you, I know it very well."

"What do you mean, my lady, tell me," stammered the king. "What is your desire, why is my life in your hand? Tell me, and I shall give you all you ask."

"You must grant me a knight to wed," said the lady slowly. "His name is Sir Gawain. I will make this bargain: If your life is saved another way, you need not grant my desire. If my answer saves your life, grant

me Sir Gawain as my husband. Choose now, for you must soon meet your enemy."

"By Mary," said the king, "I cannot grant you Sir Gawain. That lies with him alone—he is not mine to give. I can only take the choice to Sir Gawain."

"Well," she said. "Then go home again and speak to Sir Gawain. For though I am foul, yet am I merry, and through me he may save your life or ensure your death."

"Alas!" cried the king. "That I should cause Gawain to wed you, for he will not say no. I know not what I should do."

"Sir King, you will get no more from me. When you come again with your answer I will meet you here."

"What is your name, I pray you tell me?"

"Sir King, I am the Dame Ragnell, that never yet betrayed a man."

"Then farewell, Dame Ragnell," said the king.

Thus they departed, and the king returned to Carlyle again with a heavy heart. The first man he met was Sir Gawain. "Sire, how did you fare?" asked the knight.

"Never so ill," said the king. "I fear I will die at Sir Gromer's hand."

"Nay," said Gawain. "I would rather die myself I love you so."

"Gawain, I met today with the foulest lady that I ever saw. She said she would save my life, but first she would have you for her husband."

"Is this all?" asked Gawain. "Then I shall wed her and wed her again! Though she were a fiend, though she were as foul as Beelzebub,[6] her I shall marry. For you are my king and I am your friend—it is my part to save your life, or else I am a false knight

---

6. **Beelzebub** (bē·el′zə·bub′): the devil; Satan.

and a great coward. If she were the most loathsome woman that ever a man might see, for your love I would spare nothing."

"Thank you, Gawain," said King Arthur then. "Of all knights that I have found, you are the finest. You have saved my life, and my love will not stray from you, as I am king in this land."

The day soon came when the king was to meet the Dame Ragnell and bear his answer to Sir Gromer. Gawain rode with him to the edge of Ingleswood Forest, but there the king said, "Sir Gawain, farewell. I must go west, and you must go no further."

"God speed you on your journey. I wish I rode your way," said Gawain.

The king had ridden but a mile or so more when he met the Dame Ragnell. "Ah, Sir King, you are welcome here bearing your answer."

"Now," said the king, "since it can be no other way, tell me your answer, save my life, and Gawain shall you wed; so he has promised. Tell me in all haste. Have done, I may not tarry."[7]

"Sire," said the Dame Ragnell, "now you will know what women desire most, high and low. Some men say we desire to be fair, or to wed, or to remain fresh and young, or to have flattery from men. But there is one thing that is every woman's fantasy: We desire of men, above all other things, to have sovereignty, for then all is ours. Therefore go on your way, Sir King, and tell that knight what I have said to you. He will be angry and curse the woman who told you, for his labor is lost. Go forth—you will not be harmed."

The king rode forth in great haste until he came to the set place and met with Sir Gromer.

"Come, come, Sir King," said the knight sternly. "Now let me have answer, for I am ready."

The king pulled out the two books for Sir Gromer to see. "Sir, I dare say the right one is there."

Sir Gromer looked over them, every one, and said at last, "Nay, nay, Sir King, you are a dead man."

"Wait, Sir Gromer," said the king. "I have one more answer to give."

"Say it," said Sir Gromer, "or so God help me you shall bleed."

"Now," said the king, "here is my answer and that is all—above all things, women desire sovereignty, for that is their liking and their greatest desire; to rule over any man. This they told me."

Sir Gromer was silent a moment with rage, but then he cried out, "And she that told you, Sir Arthur, I pray to God I might see her burn in a fire, for that was my sister, Dame Ragnell. God give her shame—I have lost much labor. Go where you like, King Arthur, for you are spared. Alas that I ever saw this day, for I know that you will be my enemy and hunt me down."

"No," said King Arthur, "you will never find me an attacker. Farewell." King Arthur turned his horse into the forest again. Soon he met with the Dame Ragnell, in the same place as before. "Sir King," she said. "I am glad you have sped well. I told you how it would be, and now since I and none other have saved your life, Gawain must wed me."

---

7. **tarry** *v.:* linger; delay.

Vocabulary
loathsome (lōth′səm) *adj.:* disgusting.
sovereignty (säv′rən·tē) *n.:* control; authority.

"I will not fail in my promise," said the king. "If you will be ruled by my council, you shall have your will."

"No, Sir King, I will not be ruled," said the lady. "I know what you are thinking. Ride before, and I will follow to your court. Think how I have saved your life and do not disagree with me, for if you do you will be shamed."

The king was ashamed to bring the loathly lady openly to the court, but forth she rode till they came to Carlyle. All the country wondered when she came, for they had never seen so foul a creature, but she would spare no one the sight of her. Into the hall she went, saying, "Arthur, King, fetch in Sir Gawain, before all the knights, so that you may troth[8] us together. Set forth Gawain my love, for I will not wait."

Sir Gawain stepped forward then, and said, "Sir, I am ready to fulfill the promise I made to you."

"God have mercy," said the Dame Ragnell when she saw Gawain. "For your sake I wish I were a fair woman, for you are of such goodwill." Then Sir Gawain wooed her[9] as he was a true knight, and Dame Ragnell was happy.

"Alas!" said the Queen Guinevere, and all the ladies in her bower.[10] "Alas!" said both king and knights, that the beautiful Gawain should wed such a foul and horrible woman.

She would be wedded in no other way than this—openly, with announcements in every town and village, and she had all the ladies of the land come to Carlyle for the

"Alas!" said the Queen Guinevere, and all the ladies in her bower.

Queen Guinevere (1858) by William Morris.
Oil on canvas.
The Granger Collection, New York.

feast. The queen begged Dame Ragnell to be married in the early morning, as privately as possible. "Nay," said the lady. "By heaven I will not no matter what you say. I will be wedded openly, as the king promised. I will

---

8. **troth** (trôth) v.: engage to marry.

9. **wooed her**: said romantic things; spoke of love.

10. **bower** (bou′ər) n.: old-fashioned word for a private room.

not go to the church until High Mass time,[11] and I will dine in the open hall, in the midst of all the court."

At the wedding feast there were lords and ladies from all estates, and Dame Ragnell was arrayed in the richest manner—richer even than Queen Guinevere. But all her rich clothes could not hide her foulness. When the feasting began, only Dame Ragnell ate heartily, while the knights and squires sat like stones. After the wedding feast, Sir Gawain and the Lady Ragnell retired to the wedding chamber that had been prepared for them.

"Ah, Gawain," said the lady. "Since we are wed, show me your courtesy and come to bed. If I were fair you would be joyous—yet for Arthur's sake, kiss me at least."

Sir Gawain turned to the lady, but in her place was the loveliest woman that he had ever seen.

"By God, what are you?" cried Gawain.

"Sir, I am your wife, surely. Why are you so unkind?"

"Lady, I am sorry," said Gawain. "I beg your pardon, my fair madam. For now you are a beautiful lady, and today you were the foulest woman that ever I saw. It is well, my lady, to have you thus." And he took her in his arms and kissed her with great joy.

"Sir," she said, "you have half-broken the spell on me. Thus shall you have me, but my beauty will not hold. You may have me fair by night and foul by day, or else have me fair by day, and by night ugly once again. You must choose."

"Alas!" said Gawain. "The choice is too hard—to have you fair on nights and no more, that would grieve my heart and shame me. Yet if I desire to have you fair by day and foul by night, I could not rest. I know not in the world what I should say, but do as you wish. The choice is in your hands."

"Thank you, courteous Gawain," said the lady. "Of all earthly knights you are blessed, for now I am truly loved. You shall have me fair both day and night, and ever while I live as fair. For I was shaped by witchcraft by my stepmother, God have mercy on her. By enchantment I was to be the foulest creature, till the best knight of England had wedded me and had given me the sovereignty of all his body and goods. Kiss me, Sir Gawain—be glad and make good cheer, for we are well." The two rejoiced together and thanked God for their fortune.

King Arthur came himself to call them to breakfast the next day, wondering why Gawain stayed so late with his loathly bride. Sir Gawain rose, taking the hand of his lady, and opened the door to greet the king.

The Dame Ragnell stood by the fire, with her pale lovely skin and red hair spilling down to her knees. "Lo," said Gawain to the king, "this is my wife the Dame Ragnell, who once saved your life." And Gawain told the king the story of the lady's enchantment.

"My love shall she have, for she has been so kind," said the king. And the queen said, "You will have my love forever, Lady, for you have saved my Lord Arthur." And from then on, at every great feast, that lady was the fairest, and all his life Gawain loved the Lady Ragnell.

Thus ends the adventure of King Arthur and of the wedding of Sir Gawain.

---

11. **High Mass time:** main Mass of Sunday morning. People of the highest class would attend High Mass.

Meet the Writer

Betsy Hearne

Transforming a Beast

Betsy Hearne (1942–) includes "Sir Gawain and the Loathly Lady" in her collection of twenty-seven Beauty and the Beast folk tales from storytellers around the world. She writes that this story "is striking in its emphasis on the importance of a woman's power to control her own choices. The horrific but heroic female saves a king's life, outwits a sorcerer, wins a husband worthy of her, and reforms him even as he transforms her."

Hearne's work in collecting and connecting various types of Beauty and the Beast tales began with her studies in graduate school. She believes that:

> **All of the stories . . . are about journeys in which the heroine or hero is transformed not through winning battles but through love for another being. . . . Beauty and the Beast tales suggest, among other things, that love is as powerful as force in coming to terms with what we fear.**

Hearne has worked as a children's librarian, and she is a highly respected critic, reviewer, writer, and university professor. She has edited both essay and folklore collections. She has also written four novels for young people and two volumes of poetry.

For Independent Reading

If you're interested in more Beauty and the Beast tales, be sure to read Hearne's collection, *Beauties and Beasts.* Another remarkable book by Hearne is *Seven Brave Women.* In it she describes the achievements of seven of her female ancestors, "unsung heroes," each of whom made history in her own way.

After You Read Response and Analysis

First Thoughts

1. Do you agree with the answer to the riddle, or do you like your own Quickwrite answer better? Tell why you think men and women are the same or different in what they want most in life.

Thinking Critically

2. Myths, legends, and folk tales are full of **metamorphoses** (met′ə·môr′fə·sēz′)—marvelous changes from one shape or form to another one. A metamorphosis can be a punishment or a reward. What metamorphosis takes place in this story? What causes it?

3. King Arthur goes on a **quest** to find the answer to a riddle. Find three places on the quest where he could have made a big mistake—but managed to stay on the right path. How did the code of **chivalry** help him make the right decision each time?

4. What did you think of the choice presented to Gawain on his wedding night? Gawain makes the correct choice and is rewarded for it. What values are shown by Gawain in the choice he makes?

Reading Check

This tightly plotted story is a series of **causes** and **effects.** Some of the key events in the story are listed in the boxes that follow. Write down the missing plot links (the empty boxes) in your notebook.

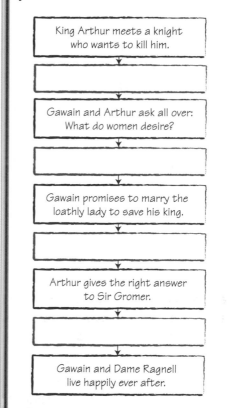

King Arthur meets a knight who wants to kill him.

Gawain and Arthur ask all over: What do women desire?

Gawain promises to marry the loathly lady to save his king.

Arthur gives the right answer to Sir Gromer.

Gawain and Dame Ragnell live happily ever after.

WRITING

SKILLS FOCUS

Literary Skills
Analyze a quest story.

Writing Skills
Write a critical response to literature.

Literary Criticism: Respond to the Legend

Find one aspect of this story you had a strong response to. Maybe you felt that the plot was not believable. Maybe you especially love stories set long ago. Maybe you didn't like the way the story treated ugliness. Maybe you disagree with the main idea of the story. Discuss the story in a small group, focusing on the aspect you had a strong response to. Then, write a brief essay describing your response to the story and explaining why you feel this way.

Vocabulary Development

French Word Origins

In 1066, the Normans, who lived in France, invaded England, led by William the Conqueror. As you may have guessed from his name, William and his Normans conquered England. Within a few years the language spoken by important people in England started to be French. Words used in government, by the church, and by people at court were French.

In fact, the stories about King Arthur and his knights include many stories from France. You can spot some French influence in this story of the loathly lady:

- The angry knight's name is Gromer Somer Joure, a French name.
- *Palfrey*, meaning "gentle horse," is from the French language.

Word Bank

chivalry
countenance
loathsome
sovereignty

PRACTICE 1

Use a dictionary to look up the Word Bank words. Most dictionaries tell you in brackets the history of a word, followed by the word's definition. Which words are from the French language? Which word is English?

PRACTICE 2

This reteller of the King Arthur legend has tried to give the story an old-fashioned flavor. Translate the following sentences into the kind of English you and your friends speak today.

1. In all his country there was nothing but <u>chivalry</u>, and knights were loved by the people.
2. The lords knew by his <u>countenance</u> that the king met with some disturbance, but no one knew of his encounter.
3. "If she were the most <u>loathsome</u> woman that ever a man might see, for your love I would spare nothing."
4. "We desire of men, above all other things, to have <u>sovereignty</u>, for then all is ours."

La Belle Dame sans Merci (1893) by John William Waterhouse.

SKILLS FOCUS

Vocabulary Skills
Understand French word origins.

Words Often Confused

The different forms of two small words in English give writers a lot of trouble. The two simple words are from Old English; they are *you* and *it. You* comes from the Old English word *eow,* and *it* comes from the Old English word *hit.*

The problems come with different forms of the words. Read these words aloud: *its* and *it's,* and *your* and *you're.* The words in each pair sound alike, but they have different uses.

- The personal possessive pronouns *its* and *your* show that something belongs to someone or something. Possessive pronouns should not have apostrophes.

  "Sir Knight, what is your name?" [The name belongs to the knight.]

  The palfrey was a gentle horse, its halters studded with jewels. [The halters belong to the horse.]

- The contractions *you're* and *it's* are both shortened combinations of a personal pronoun and the verb *is, has,* or *are.* A contraction has an apostrophe to show where letters are omitted.

  It's [it is] **easy to lose yourself in a good story.**

  You're [you are] **going to love the loathly lady story.**

SKILLS FOCUS

Grammar Skills
Use *its* and *it's* and *your* and *you're* correctly.

PRACTICE

Write each sentence below, choosing the correct form of the underlined words. A tip: If you are unsure which word is correct, try substituting two words, such as *it is* or *you are.* If the sentence makes sense, you need the apostrophe because letters are omitted.

1. Its/It's clear that the author uses old-fashioned words.

2. Her style makes you feel as if your/you're reading the original.

3. King Arthur set up the Round Table; it's/its purpose was to make every knight equal.

4. For your/you're research paper, look up the Holy Grail.

5. The quest was it's/its own reward. What quest stories are told in you're/your tradition?

For more help, see Apostrophes, 15a–c, in the Language Handbook.

King Arthur on His Throne Surrounded by Counselors (14th century).

Comparing Literature

Literary Focus
Real Heroes

In this book you have read about the deeds of many literary **heroes.** One great hero was Orpheus, who braved the underworld to rescue the woman he loved. Another was King Arthur, who used might to conquer evil in the world. Now you are going to read about two real-life heroes: Nelson Mandela and Rosa Parks. Both of these great people lived under legal systems that discriminated against people of color. For Mandela it was apartheid (ə·pär′tāt′), or racial segregation, in South Africa. For Parks it was racial segregation in the United States. Both took actions to right what they believed was wrong, and their actions helped thousands of people to know real freedom. Nelson Mandela recounts his experiences in his autobiography *Long Walk to Freedom*. Rosa Parks's story is told by the poet Rita Dove.

> ### Characteristics of a Hero
>
> - bravery
> - inner strength
> - honesty
> - sense of justice
> - loyalty to ideals
> - helpfulness to others
> - willingness to make personal sacrifices
>
> What other characteristics might a person need in order to be a hero?

Reading Skills
Comparing and Contrasting

As you read these two accounts, think about what makes these two people heroic. Consider

- the choices they make
- what happens to them
- how they respond to setbacks
- the effects of their actions

When you finish the selections, you will write an essay on heroism, focusing on Nelson Mandela and Rosa Parks.

SKILLS FOCUS

Literary Skills
Understand heroes.

Reading Skills
Compare and contrast heroes.

Before You Read

Nelson Mandela was born and raised in a tribal village in South Africa. After graduating from college and law school, Mandela joined the African National Congress to fight against apartheid, the government policy of racial segregation. He was arrested and, from 1962 till 1990, spent nearly twenty-eight years in prison, where he fought apartheid from his prison cell. In 1993, Mandela was awarded the Nobel Peace Prize. He served as the first democratically elected state president of South Africa from May 1994 until June 1999. Although now retired from public office, Mandela continues to work for democracy, freedom, and justice throughout Africa and the world. In this excerpt from his autobiography, he describes his "long walk to freedom."

Nelson Mandela at the prison on Robben Island, South Africa, where he had been incarcerated (1994).

FROM LONG WALK TO FREEDOM

Nelson Mandela

The policy of apartheid created a deep and lasting wound in my country and my people. All of us will spend many years, if not generations, recovering from that profound hurt. But the decades of oppression and brutality had another, unintended effect, and that was that it produced the Oliver Tambos, the Walter Sisulus, the Chief Luthulis, the Yusuf Dadoos, the Bram Fischers, the Robert Sobukwes[1] of our time—men of such extraordinary courage, wisdom, and generosity that their like may never be known again. Perhaps it requires such depth of oppression to create such heights of character. My country is rich in the minerals and gems that lie beneath its soil, but I have always known that its greatest wealth is its people, finer and truer than the purest diamonds. ❶

It is from these comrades in the struggle that I learned the meaning of courage. Time and again, I have seen men and women risk and give their lives for an idea. I have seen men stand up to attacks and torture without breaking, showing a strength and resiliency that defies the imagination. I learned that courage was not the absence of fear, but the triumph over it. I felt fear myself more times than I can remember, but I hid it behind a mask of boldness. The brave man is not he who does not feel afraid, but he who conquers that fear. ❷

I never lost hope that this great transformation would occur. Not only because of the great heroes I have already cited, but because of the courage of the ordinary men and women of my country. I always knew that deep down in every human heart, there is mercy and generosity. No one is born hating another person because of the color of his skin, or his background, or his religion. People must learn to hate, and if they can learn to hate, they can be taught to love, for love comes more naturally to the human heart than its opposite. Even in the grimmest times in prison, when my comrades and I were pushed to our limits, I would see a glimmer of humanity

---

1. **Oliver Tambos ... Robert Sobukwes:** freedom fighters against South African apartheid.

INTERPRET

❶ What qualities does Nelson Mandela admire in his fellow freedom fighters? Why do you think he says they are "finer and truer than the purest diamonds"?

COMPARE AND CONTRAST

❷ How is Mandela's definition of courage the same as or different from your own?

INTERPRET

❸ What does Mandela say about hate? Why do you think that a brief glimpse of a guard's humanity was enough to reassure Mandela about "man's goodness"?

in one of the guards, perhaps just for a second, but it was enough to reassure me and keep me going. Man's goodness is a flame that can be hidden but never extinguished. ❸

We took up the struggle with our eyes wide open, under no illusion that the path would be an easy one. As a young man, when I joined the African National Congress, I saw the price my comrades paid for their beliefs, and it was high. For myself, I have never regretted my commitment to the struggle, and I was always prepared to face the hardships that affected me personally. But my family paid a terrible price, perhaps too dear a price for my commitment.

In life, every man has twin obligations—obligations to his family, to his parents, to his wife and children; and he has an obligation to his people, his community, his country. In a civil and humane society, each man is able to fulfill those obligations according to his own inclinations and abilities. But in a country like South Africa, it was almost impossible for a man of my birth and color to fulfill both of those obligations. In South Africa, a man of color who attempted to live as a human being was punished and isolated. In South Africa, a man who tried to fulfill his duty to his people was inevitably ripped from his family and his home and was forced to live a life apart, a twilight existence of secrecy and rebellion. I did not in the beginning choose to place my people above my family, but in attempting to serve my people, I found that I was prevented from fulfilling my obligations as a son, a brother, a father, and a husband. ❹

INTERPRET

❹ According to Mandela, what two obligations does every man have? Why was it "almost impossible" for a man of color to meet those obligations in South Africa?

In that way, my commitment to my people, to the millions of South Africans I would never know or meet, was at the expense of the people I knew best and loved most. It was as simple and yet as incomprehensible as the moment a small child asks her father, "Why can you not be with us?" And the father must utter the terrible words: "There are other children like you, a great many of them . . ." and then one's voice trails off.

I was not born with a hunger to be free. I was born free—free in every way that I could know. Free to run in the fields near my mother's hut, free to swim in the clear stream that ran through my village, free to roast mealies[2] under the stars and ride the broad backs of slow-moving bulls. As long as I obeyed my father and

---

2. **mealies** (mē′lēz) *n*.: in South Africa, ears of corn.

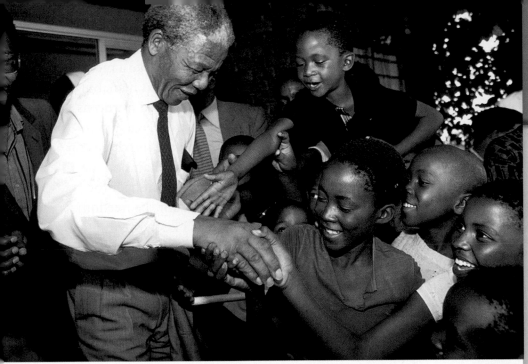

Nelson Mandela greets Soweto children in South Africa (1990).

abided by the customs of my tribe, I was not troubled by the laws of man or God.

It was only when I began to learn that my boyhood freedom was an illusion, when I discovered as a young man that my freedom had already been taken from me, that I began to hunger for it. At first, as a student, I wanted freedom only for myself, the transitory[3] freedoms of being able to stay out at night, read what I pleased, and go where I chose. Later, as a young man in Johannesburg, I yearned for the basic and honorable freedoms of achieving my potential, of earning my keep, of marrying and having a family—the freedom not to be obstructed in a lawful life.

But then I slowly saw that not only was I not free, but my brothers and sisters were not free. I saw that it was not just my freedom that was curtailed,[4] but the freedom of everyone who looked like I did. That is when I joined the African National Congress, and that is when the hunger for my own freedom became the greater hunger for the freedom of my people. It was this desire for the freedom of my people to live their lives with dignity and self-respect that animated my life, that transformed a frightened young man into a bold one, that drove a law-abiding attorney to become a criminal, that turned a family-loving husband into a man

---

3. **transitory** (tran'sə·tôr'ē) *adj*.: passing; temporary.
4. **curtailed** (kər·tāld') *v*. used as adj.: cut short.

without a home, that forced a life-loving man to live like a monk. I am no more virtuous or self-sacrificing than the next man, but I found that I could not even enjoy the poor and limited freedoms I was allowed when I knew my people were not free. Freedom is indivisible; the chains on any one of my people were the chains on all of them, the chains on all of my people were the chains on me. **5**

It was during those long and lonely years that my hunger for the freedom of my own people became a hunger for the freedom of all people, white and black. I knew as well as I knew anything that the oppressor must be liberated just as surely as the oppressed. A man who takes away another man's freedom is a prisoner of hatred, he is locked behind the bars of prejudice and narrow-mindedness. I am not truly free if I am taking away someone else's freedom, just as surely as I am not free when my freedom is taken from me. The oppressed and the oppressor alike are robbed of their humanity.

When I walked out of prison, that was my mission, to liberate the oppressed and the oppressor both. Some say that has now been achieved. But I know that that is not the case. The truth is that we are not yet free; we have merely achieved the freedom to be free, the right not to be oppressed. We have not taken the final step of our journey, but the first step on a longer and even more difficult road. For to be free is not merely to cast off one's chains, but to live in a way that respects and enhances the freedom of others. The true test of our devotion to freedom is just beginning. **6**

I have walked that long road to freedom. I have tried not to falter; I have made missteps along the way. But I have discovered the secret that after climbing a great hill, one only finds that there are many more hills to climb. I have taken a moment here to rest, to steal a view of the glorious vista that surrounds me, to look back on the distance I have come. But I can rest only for a moment, for with freedom come responsibilities, and I dare not linger, for my long walk is not yet ended.

RETELL

5 Retell the way that Mandela's attitude toward freedom changes in this paragraph.

IDENTIFY

6 Mandela says that ending apartheid is not enough to create freedom. What else does he say is necessary for people to be free?

MANDELA FOR PRESIDENT

THE PEOPLE'S CHOICE

Meet the Writer

Nelson Mandela

A Cherished Ideal

Nelson Mandela (1918–   ) has dedicated his life to ending racial oppression in South Africa. Before his historic release from prison, Mandela endured nearly three decades as a political prisoner in his native land.

Mandela joined the African National Congress (ANC), an organization promoting black liberation, in 1944. In 1960, the South African government outlawed the ANC. As a result, Mandela went into hiding and secretly continued to work for the group. He was eventually caught and received a five-year prison sentence.

In 1963, the police discovered Mandela's involvement with the military unit of the ANC, and he was put on trial for treason and other charges. During the trial, Mandela delivered a powerful speech illustrating his commitment to the struggle for racial equality. At the end of his speech, Mandela declared:

> **❝ I have cherished the ideal of a democratic and free society. . . . It is an ideal which I hope to live for and to achieve. But if needs be, it is an ideal for which I am prepared to die. ❞**

The court sentenced Mandela to life in prison.

Both at home and abroad, the South African government faced pressure to release Mandela. In 1990, F. W. de Klerk (who served as South Africa's president until 1994) ordered Mandela's release from prison.

Following Mandela's release, the two leaders worked together to bring peace to South Africa. In 1993, they were jointly awarded the Nobel Peace Prize in recognition of their efforts.

One historic reform that both men worked for was the establishment of South Africa's first democratic election, which took place in 1994. For the first time in the country's history, citizens of all races were allowed to vote in a national election. As a result, Mandela became the country's first black president, a position he held until 1999.

First Thoughts

1. Complete the following sentence:
   - Nelson Mandela is . . .

Thinking Critically

2. Explain why Mandela's commitment to the people of South Africa came at the expense of the people he knew and loved most. Who are those people?

3. What does Mandela mean when he says "the oppressor must be liberated just as surely as the oppressed" (page 850)? Use details from the text to support your response.

4. Mandela says he is no more virtuous or self-sacrificing than anyone else. Do you think someone else could have accomplished what he did? Or do you think it took someone with his special qualities or powers? Explain your position.

5. What personal strengths and beliefs enabled Mandela to devote his life to fighting injustice and to endure nearly twenty-eight years in prison without losing his dignity or humanity?

Comparing Literature

6. After you read the next selection, you will write an essay on heroism, in which you compare and contrast the heroic qualities of two people who helped to improve the world we live in—Nelson Mandela and Rosa Parks. To prepare for that essay, fill in the column on Nelson Mandela in a chart like the one below.

> ### Reading Check
> Explain how Nelson Mandela felt about **freedom**
>
> a. as a child
> b. as a student
> c. as a young lawyer
> d. when he was in prison
> e. after he got out of prison

Comparing and Contrasting Real Heroes		
	Nelson Mandela	Rosa Parks
Challenge to authority		
Effects of actions		
My responses to actions		
Feeling about freedom		

SKILLS FOCUS

Literary Skills
Analyze heroes.

Reading Skills
Compare and contrast heroes.

Before You Read

While Nelson Mandela fought injustice in South Africa, on the other side of the globe, Rosa Parks stood against injustice in the United States—by refusing to give up her seat on a Montgomery, Alabama, bus in 1955. Both helped to end discrimination in their countries, and both have come to symbolize for the world the triumph of the human spirit over injustice.

Rosa Parks

Rita Dove

Rosa Parks arrives at a Montgomery, Alabama, courthouse with civil rights leader E. D. Nixon (center).

How she sat there, the time
right inside a place so wrong it
was ready.
—From "Rosa," in *On the Bus
with Rosa Parks* by Rita Dove

We know the story. One December evening, a woman left work and boarded a bus for home. She was tired; her feet ached. But this was Montgomery, Alabama, in 1955, and as the bus became crowded, the woman, a black woman, was ordered to give up her seat to a white passenger. When she remained seated, that simple decision eventually led to the disintegration[1] of institutionalized segregation in the South, ushering in a new era of the civil rights movement.

This, anyway, was the story I had heard from the time I was curious enough to eavesdrop on adult conversations. I was three years old when a white bus driver warned Rosa Parks, "Well, I'm going to have you arrested," and she replied, "You may go on and do so." As a child, I didn't understand how doing nothing had caused so much activity, but I recognized the template:[2] David slaying the giant Goliath, or the boy who saved his village by sticking his finger in the dike. And perhaps it is precisely the lure of fairy tale retribution[3] that colors the lens we look back through. Parks was forty-two years old when she refused to give up her seat. She has insisted that her feet were not aching; she was, by her own testimony, no more tired than usual. And she did not plan her fateful act: "I did not get on the bus to get arrested," she has said. "I got on the bus to go home." **①**

Montgomery's segregation laws were complex: Blacks were required to pay their fare to the driver, then get off and reboard through the back door. Sometimes the bus would drive off before the paid-up customers made it to the back entrance. If the white section was full and another white customer entered, blacks were required to give up their seats and move farther to the back; a black person was not even allowed to sit across the aisle from whites. These humiliations were compounded by the fact that two thirds of the bus riders in Montgomery were black. **②**

Parks was not the first to be detained for this offense. Eight months earlier, Claudette Colvin, fifteen, refused to give up her seat

COMPARE AND CONTRAST

① How is Rosa Parks's action like David slaying Goliath or the boy with his finger in the dike?

RETELL

② Explain Montgomery's segregation laws.

---

1. **disintegration** (dis·in′tə·grā′shən) *n.:* the breaking up of something.
2. **template** (tem′plit) *n.:* pattern.
3. **retribution** (re′trə·byoo′shən) *n.:* punishment for evil or reward for good.

A statue of
Rosa Parks at the
Birmingham Civil
Rights Institute
in Birmingham,
Alabama.

The bus on which Rosa Parks refused to give up her seat, on exhibit at the Henry Ford Museum in Dearborn, Michigan.

and was arrested. Black activists met with this girl to determine if she would make a good test case—as secretary of the local N.A.A.C.P.,[4] Parks attended the meeting—but it was decided that a more "upstanding" candidate was necessary to withstand the scrutiny of the courts and the press. And then in October, a young woman named Mary Louise Smith was arrested; N.A.A.C.P. leaders rejected her too as their vehicle, looking for someone more able to withstand media scrutiny. Smith paid the fine and was released.

Six weeks later, the time was ripe. The facts, rubbed shiny for retelling, are these: On December 1, 1955, Mrs. Rosa Parks, seamstress for the Montgomery Fair department store, boarded the Cleveland Avenue bus. She took a seat in the fifth row—the first row of the "Colored Section." The driver was the same one who had put her off a bus twelve years earlier for refusing to get off and reboard through the back door. ("He was still mean looking," she has said.) Did that make her stubborn? Or had her work in the N.A.A.C.P. sharpened her sensibilities so that she knew what to do—or more precisely, what not to do: Don't frown, don't struggle, don't shout, don't pay the fine?

At the news of the arrest, local civil rights leader E. D. Nixon exclaimed, "My God, look what segregation has put in my hands!" Parks was not only above moral reproach (securely married, reasonably employed) but possessed a quiet fortitude as well as

4. **N.A.A.C.P.:** National Association for the Advancement of Colored People, an organization in existence since 1909.

political savvy—in short, she was the ideal plaintiff⁵ for a test case. ❸

She was arrested on a Thursday; bail was posted by Clifford Durr, the white lawyer whose wife had employed Parks as a seamstress. That evening, after talking it over with her mother and husband, Rosa Parks agreed to challenge the constitutionality of Montgomery's segregation laws. During a midnight meeting of the Women's Political Council, 35,000 handbills were mimeographed for distribution to all black schools the next morning. The message was simple:

> "We are . . . asking every Negro to stay off the buses Monday in protest of the arrest and trial. . . . You can afford to stay out of school for one day. If you work, take a cab, or walk. But please, children and grownups, don't ride the bus at all on Monday. Please stay off the buses Monday." ❹

Monday came. Rain threatened, yet the black population of Montgomery stayed off the buses, either walking or catching one of the black cabs stopping at every municipal bus stop for ten cents per customer—standard bus fare. Meanwhile, Parks was scheduled to appear in court. As she made her way through the throngs at the courthouse, a demure figure in a long-sleeved black dress with white collar and cuffs, a trim black velvet hat, gray coat and white gloves, a girl in the crowd caught sight of her and cried out, "Oh, she's so sweet. They've messed with the wrong one now!"

Yes, indeed. The trial lasted thirty minutes, with the expected conviction and penalty. That afternoon, the Montgomery Improvement Association was formed. So as not to ruffle any local activists' feathers, the members elected as their president a relative newcomer to Montgomery, the young minister of Dexter Avenue Baptist Church: the Rev. Martin Luther King, Jr. That evening, addressing a crowd gathered at the Holt Street Baptist Church, King declared in that sonorous, ringing voice millions the world over would soon thrill to: "There comes a time that people get tired." When he was finished, Parks stood up so the audience could see her. She did not speak; there was no need to. Here I am, her silence said, among you.

And she has been with us ever since—a persistent symbol of human dignity in the face of brutal authority. The famous U.P.I.⁶

---

5. **plaintiff** (plān′tif) *n.*: person who brings a suit, or complaint, into a court of law.
6. **U.P.I..** United Press International, a service that supplies articles and photographs to newspapers around the world.

COMPARE AND CONTRAST

❸ Why did civil rights leaders think Rosa Parks was the ideal person to bring a test case against the bus segregation laws? Whom else did they consider?

INTERPRET

❹ How do you think the bus boycott supported Rosa Parks's case against segregation laws?

Rosa Parks on her way to jail after her trial.

photo (actually taken more than a year later, on December 21, 1956, the day Montgomery's public transportation system was legally integrated) is a study of calm strength. She is looking out the bus window, her hands resting in the folds of her checked dress, while a white man sits, unperturbed, in the row behind her. That clear profile, the neat cloche[7] and eyeglasses and sensible coat—she could have been my mother, anybody's favorite aunt.

History is often portrayed as a string of arias in a grand opera, all baritone intrigues and tenor heroics. Some of the most tumultuous events, however, have been provoked by serendipity[8]—the assassination of an inconsequential archduke spawned World War I, a kicked-over lantern may have sparked the Great Chicago Fire. One cannot help wondering what role Martin Luther King, Jr. would have played in the civil rights movement if the opportunity had not presented itself that first evening of the boycott—if Rosa Parks had chosen a row farther back from the outset, or if she had missed the bus altogether.

At the end of this millennium (and a particularly noisy century), it is the modesty of Rosa Parks' example that sustains us. It is no less than the belief in the power of the individual, that cornerstone of the American Dream, that she inspires, along with the hope that all of us—even the least of us—could be that brave, that serenely human, when crunch time comes. **5**

COMPARE AND CONTRAST

5 How are Rosa Parks's actions and goals similar to Nelson Mandela's?

---

7. **cloche** (klōsh) *n.:* tight-fitting women's hat.
8. **serendipity** (ser′ən·dip′ə·tē) *n.:* accident, usually accidental luck.

Meet the Writer

Rita Dove

An Award-Winning Poet

Rita Dove (1952–   ) discovered that she wanted to be a poet during her college years. She recalls:

> ❝ I took creative writing courses and I began to write more and more, and I realized I was scheduling my entire life around my writing courses, and I said, 'Well maybe you need to figure out if this is what you want to do.' ❞

Dove decided to pursue her interest in poetry and received a master's degree from the University of Iowa Writers' Workshop in 1977.

Dove had already achieved recognition for her work when her first poetry collection, *The Yellow House on the Corner,* was published in 1980. In 1987, she was awarded the Pulitzer Prize for the collection *Thomas and Beulah,* which was inspired by the lives of her grandparents.

In 1993, Rita Dove was named poet laureate, one of America's highest literary honors. She became the youngest person and first African American to be appointed to this position.

Dove, who is currently an English professor at the University of Virginia, shares these feelings about writing poetry:

> ❝ I know that every time that I write a poem . . . I try to remember . . . the reader that I was . . . the moment of opening a book and absolutely having my world fall away and entering into another one and feeling there was one other voice that was almost inside of me, we were so close. ❞

First Thoughts

1. Complete the following sentence:

   • I think Rosa Parks is . . .

Thinking Critically

2. Do you think that Rosa Parks did the right thing by refusing to give up her seat on the bus, or do you think people should always obey the law? Explain your opinion.

3. What do you think causes a person to take a stand against injustice, even when it involves a personal sacrifice?

Comparing Literature

4. To plan your essay comparing and contrasting heroes, fill in the column on Rosa Parks in a chart like the one below.

Reading Check

To **retell** the story of Rosa Parks, fill in a sequence chart like the one below.

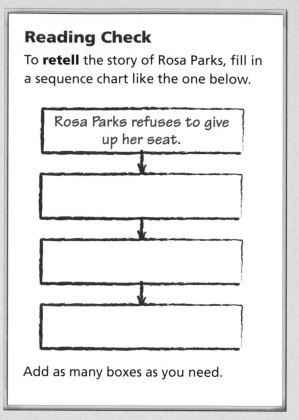

Rosa Parks refuses to give up her seat.

Add as many boxes as you need.

Comparing and Contrasting Real Heroes		
	Nelson Mandela	Rosa Parks
Challenge to authority		
Effects of actions		
My responses to actions		
Feeling about freedom		

SKILLS FOCUS

Literary Skills
Analyze heroes.

Reading Skills
Compare and contrast heroes.

Comparing *Long Walk to Freedom* with "Rosa Parks"

Assignment

1. Writing a Comparison-Contrast Essay

Write a comparison-contrast essay about the heroism of Nelson Mandela and Rosa Parks. For ideas, refer to the chart you filled in after each selection and to the "Characteristics of a Hero" on page 845. You can organize your essay in two ways:

a. You can begin with a paragraph describing your idea of a hero. Then you can write a paragraph that explains why you think Mandela and Parks are heroes. Use information from your chart to support your ideas.

b. Or you can write two paragraphs—one about Mandela and one about Parks—in which you discuss the ways they stood up for their beliefs. You might end your essay with a paragraph describing how these two people represent (or don't represent) your idea of a real hero.

Assignment

2. Biographical Sketch

Write a biographical sketch of either Nelson Mandela or Rosa Parks. Base your sketch on

- what you learned from the selection about the person you chose
- information in the Meet the Writer (if you chose Nelson Mandela)
- additional information you find in the library or on the Internet

Place the sketches from your class into a folder to serve as a resource in your school library. Or, if possible, make a display for a bulletin board to share your information with other students in your school.

Assignment

3. Celebrating Heroes

Plan a class day to celebrate heroes. Individually or with a partner, pick a person you think is a hero. This can be someone you know or someone you have read about. Gather as much information as you can about your hero, and present it to the class. If possible, add a multimedia component to your presentation: Photos, slides, and video or audio clips can help to make your hero come alive for your audience.

SKILLS FOCUS

Writing Skills
Write a comparison-contrast essay; write a biographical sketch.

Speaking and Listening Skills
Present an oral report.

NO QUESTIONS ASKED

Before You Read

"The Impossible Dream" was originally written for the musical *Man of La Mancha*, where it is sung by the character Don Quixote (kē·hōt′ē). The song has since been recorded and performed by many popular singers, including Elvis Presley and Frank Sinatra.

The Impossible Dream

Lyrics by Joe Darion

To dream the impossible dream,
To fight the unbeatable foe,
To bear with unbearable sorrow,
To run where the brave dare not go.

To right the unrightable wrong,
To love pure and chaste from afar,
To try when your arms are too weary,
To reach the unreachable star!

This is my quest, to follow that star,
No matter how hopeless, no matter how far;
To fight for the right without question or pause,
To be willing to march into hell for a heavenly cause!

And I know, if I'll only be true to this glorious quest,
That my heart will lie peaceful and calm when I'm laid to my rest.

And the world will be better for this;
That one man, scorned and covered with scars,
Still strove with his last ounce of courage,
To reach the unreachable stars.

Don Quixote (1955) by Pablo Picasso (1881–1973).

Musee d'Art et d'Histoire, St. Denis, France, © 2003 Estate of Pablo Picasso/Artist Rights Society (ARS), New York.

Writing Workshop

SKILLS FOCUS

Writing Skills
Write an informative report.

EXPOSITORY WRITING
Informative Report

In this workshop you'll find, organize, and present facts in an informative report that will add to your readers' knowledge of a topic. Your success will depend upon how well you select and use evidence to support your **thesis,** the controlling idea of your paper.

Prewriting

1 Choosing a Subject

Read and respond to the following **prompt:**

> A research project often begins with a question or a topic that interests the writer. The selections in this collection, for example, may have raised questions about the Arthurian legend. What evidence exists for a historical King Arthur? What kind of training did a medieval knight receive? How has the Arthurian legend been treated in the movies or on television?

For your report, choose a subject you would like to investigate, such as some aspect of conservation, space travel, coed sports, or animal communication. Then, frame a question that will guide your research. To keep your subject focused and manageable, check an encyclopedia or another general source. If the entry is lengthy, your topic may be too broad. See the inverted pyramid on the next page for an example of how to narrow a topic.

2 Finding and Evaluating Sources

Most informative reports are based on several sources. Plan to consult at least three sources. Whenever possible, use **primary sources,** such as diaries, letters, and maps. You can also use **secondary sources,** which are interpretations of primary materials. They include magazine and newspaper articles, encyclopedia entries, and TV and video documentaries. You can access both primary and secondary sources in a library or on the Internet, and you may be able to get additional information from museums, colleges, and interviews with experts. Be sure to evaluate every source by asking the questions that appear in the Research Tips box to the right.

3 Taking Notes

Use these guidelines as you take notes:

- Write your notes on three-by-five-inch note cards. On each card, write the source of the information. Include the title and the page number where you found the information.

- Write your notes in your own words, summarizing information carefully. If you copy anything word for word, put quotation marks around it in your notes. Using someone else's words without crediting your source is **plagiarism,** a form of stealing. Generally, you should **paraphrase,** or restate information in your own words.

4 Writing a Thesis Statement

Your **thesis statement** tells what the point of your paper will be. It usually appears in your introductory paragraph. Your thesis statement should include both the topic of your paper and the most important conclusion you've drawn from your research.

5 Organizing the Report

Making an outline is a good way to plan and organize the information you'll put in your report.

- Decide how you will organize the information in your report—by **order of importance** or **chronological** (time) **order.**

Research Tips

Evaluate sources by asking these questions:

- Who is the author? What is the author's background?

- How trustworthy is the information? What are the author's sources?

- Is the information up-to-date? If you use a Web site, check when the site was developed or last revised.

Outline

A Typical Day in a Cambodian Village

Organization: time order

I. Morning
  A. Rooster instead of alarm clock
  B. Go outside to wash
    1. Brush teeth with finger and sand
    2. Water in barrel
  C. Breakfast not customary

II. Daytime
  A. Long walk to school . . .

Main point: Customs are different in Cambodia.

Framework for an Informative Report

- **Introduction:** Hooks reader's interest; clearly identifies subject of report

- **Body:** Discusses each main idea in one or more paragraphs; supports each main idea with facts, examples, and quotations

- **Conclusion:** Summarizes or restates main idea(s); draws conclusions

- Decide which facts and examples from your notes you'll use to support each part of your report. Arrange your note cards in the order of the points in your outline.

- Include a sentence that sums up the main point of your report.

The box to the left shows part of an outline for the Student Model.

Drafting

1 Getting Started

To capture your readers' attention, offer an unusual piece of information or set a surprising scene. Make your topic and main point clear.

2 Drafting the Body

Write at least one paragraph for each main heading in your outline. As you write, you may decide to rearrange your ideas, take out information, or add new information. Keep referring to your notes, and go back to your sources if you need more information.

3 Wrapping Up

Bring your report to a close by tying your ideas together. Sum up your main point or reflect on the information. Consider closing with a vivid image or quotation.

4 Listing Sources

At the end of your paper, list your sources of information. Follow the guidelines in the Communications Handbook or a style guide, such as the Modern Language Association (MLA) guide, your teacher selects. Look carefully at the punctuation, capitalization, and order of information in your guide. Follow it exactly.

Student Model

This is the beginning of a report on Africanized honeybees.

The Invasion of the Killer Bees

They were once the subject of science fiction movies. Now that they have traveled over five thousand miles and left more than one thousand deaths in their wake, Africanized or "killer" honeybees are a frightening reality to people from South America to Nevada. Today scientists warn that the bees are here to stay and urge people to learn how to coexist with these sometimes hostile creatures.

Africanized honeybees are very different from the native honeybees that live in the United States. Native bees, also called European honeybees, live mostly in hives and hollow trees. They have few enemies and are usually gentle. In warm regions of Africa, honeybees build their nests in the open and protect them fiercely.

Killer bees are extremely nervous, and they are also fighters. Native bees chase people for a few yards when they are bothered. Africanized bees, however, will chase an intruder for as much as half a mile. Their poison is not different from the poison of ordinary bees, but they come after people in a big swarm, sometimes leaving their victims with more than one thousand stings. According to one expert, a human can't survive more than six stings per pound of body weight (Horiuchi).

—Adel Habib
Austin, Texas

*The title states the **topic** clearly but in a way that grabs the reader's attention.*

*The writer presents the history of the bees in **chronological order.***

*The writer **contrasts** Africanized bees with native bees.*

*The writer supports the **main point**—that Africanized bees are a dangerous invasion—with **facts** and an **expert opinion.***

*The writer follows the MLA style guide for his **source citations.***

Strategies for Elaboration

Elaborate on the main points of your paper by using these strategies:

- Use **specific details** and **examples** to support your general statements. Search for relevant passages to quote or paraphrase.

- Show understanding of the subject matter by using terminology accurately. Check definitions of any literary elements referred to in your essay.

INTERNET
More Writer's Modolo
Keyword: LE5 7-7

Works Cited

Horiuchi, Vince. "Yes, the Bees Are Coming. No, Don't Panic Yet."
The Salt Lake Tribune 11 Nov. 1999. 25 Mar. 2000

http://www.sltrib.com/1999/nov/11111999/science/46004.htm.

Schoenmann, Joe. "Valley Buzz." Las Vegas Review-Journal 13 Feb. 2000.
25 Mar. 2000

http://www/lvrj/com/lvrj home/2000/Feb-13-Sun-000/news/12954791.html.

Evaluating and Revising

Use the following chart to revise and evaluate your informative report.

Informative Report: Content and Organization Guidelines

Evaluation Questions	▶ Tips	▶ Revision Techniques
❶ Does your introduction identify both the topic and the main point of your report?	▶ **Underline** your statement of the report's topic and main idea.	▶ **Add** a thesis statement, or the main point you are making about the topic.
❷ Does each paragraph in the body of your report develop one subtopic?	▶ In the margin, **label** the subtopic of each paragraph.	▶ **Delete** unrelated ideas. **Rearrange** information into specific paragraphs. **Link** ideas with transitional words and phrases.
❸ Does each paragraph contain supporting evidence such as facts, examples, and direct quotations?	▶ **Highlight** the facts, examples, and quotations that elaborate each subtopic.	▶ **Elaborate** with additional facts and examples from notes.
❹ Does your conclusion sum up your overall findings?	▶ **Put a check mark** next to your final statement or summary.	▶ **Add** a question that your research did not answer, or revise your conclusion for clarity.
❺ Have you included at least three sources in the *Works Cited* list?	▶ **Number** the sources listed.	▶ **Add** sources to the *Works Cited* list, and add information from those sources to your report.

The following Revision Model is from an informative report. Use the
questions below the model to evaluate the writer's changes.

Revision Model

The education of a medieval knight was quite rigorous.

At the age of seven, a boy *from a noble household* would be taken to the court

or castle *of an overlord*. There, as a page, he performed menial tasks

but also ~~learned many things:~~ *received instruction in* dancing, playing musical

instruments, hunting, falconry, wrestling, tilting with

spears, and riding a horse. At fourteen, the page became

a squire. He then had to learn how to *mount* ~~get on~~ a horse

while wearing armor, use a battle-axe, and perform

other military skills. His education usually ended at

twenty-one, *when* ~~and~~ he was initiated into the order of

knighthood. Knighthood was conferred by an "accolade."

According to The Columbia Encyclopedia, this was "a blow,

usually with the flat of sword, on the neck or shoulder."

He first fasted and spent whole nights at prayer.

Evaluating the Revision

1. What details have been added? Do these details add important information? Tell why or why not.

2. Where has the writer rearranged material? Do you agree with these changes? Explain.

Literary Skills

Test Practice

DIRECTIONS: Read the essays. Then, answer each question that follows.

Essay 1

Themes in Arthurian Legends

There are many themes in the stories of King Arthur and his knights. The themes all speak to our deepest wishes: We all wish for a leader who will come and save us in our hour of need; we all wish that might will be used for right; we all wish that goodness will always be rewarded. The Arthur stories are also about doing the right thing, even when the cost of such action is great.

In *King Arthur: The Sword in the Stone,* Arthur is only sixteen when he is faced with a destiny that fills him with unhappiness: to be king of England. Yet he shoulders the burden because it is his fate. It is the right thing to do.

"Sir Gawain and the Loathly Lady" is the best story built around the theme of doing the right thing. Arthur and Gawain must make horrible choices, and they both choose to do the right thing. Sir Gromer makes Arthur promise to return unarmed one year from that day. Arthur will not break his word to save his life, even when the bargain he was forced to make is most unfair. Sir Gawain must make a truly horrifying choice. He weds the loathly lady because, for him, it is the right thing to do. He gave his word.

The end of each story shows that characters are rewarded for choosing to do the right thing. We wish that were always true in real life.

Essay 2

Women Characters in the King Arthur Stories

The three selections, *King Arthur: The Sword in the Stone,* "Merlin and the Dragons," and "Sir Gawain and the Loathly Lady," all reveal the way women are portrayed in the King Arthur stories. In *King Arthur: The Sword in the Stone* and "Merlin and the Dragons," there are no women characters at all. All of the characters are male, and all of them are heroic because they are strong and brave. They earn the reader's approval by pulling swords out of stones and stabbing people in battle. In "Sir Gawain and the Loathly Lady," one of the main characters is a lady changed by magic into a beast. She is doomed to stay in this state until a man loves her for herself alone. She is freed from her enchantment when a man agrees to marry her, although the truth is that Sir Gawain marries her only because he has agreed to in order to save King Arthur.

SKILLS FOCUS

Literary Skills
Analyze literary criticism.

None of these stories show women or girls in active roles. I prefer to read *Harriet the Spy*. At least there is a character girls can identify with.

1. What **literary element** is the focus of Essay 1?
   A Plot
   B Character
   C Setting
   D Theme

2. What **literary element** is the focus of Essay 2?
   F Plot
   G Character
   H Setting
   J Theme

3. Which of these **generalizations** is supported by details in the essays?
   A The writer of Essay 1 wishes that people were rewarded for doing the right thing in real life.
   B The writer of Essay 1 hates the King Arthur stories.
   C The writer of Essay 2 dislikes male characters.
   D The writer of Essay 2 likes the women characters in the King Arthur stories.

4. Which **criticism** would you apply to Essay 1?
   F The writer does not mention *King Arthur: The Sword in the Stone.*
   G The writer does not mention "Merlin and the Dragons."
   H The writer does not supply any details to support the main idea.
   J The writer talks about too many literary elements.

Constructed Response
5. What is the **main idea** in Essay 1?
6. What is the **main idea** in Essay 2?

Test Practice

DIRECTIONS: Read the speech. Then, answer each question that follows.

Looking for Heroes

A Speech to the Graduating Class of Lakeville Middle School

Our world, freshly beginning a new age, is a long way from the time of King Arthur. We have no fighting knights, no daring rescues of damsels, no more brave souls who think only of others above all else. We have no loyalty, no honor, no chivalry. All we have are the stories and thus, some distant memories of what the world used to be and will never be again.

If you believe that, I've got some oceanfront property in Oklahoma to sell you.

We have to change the way we think about heroes. We've just been looking in all the wrong places. Let's dismiss King Arthur and the knights of the Round Table for just a moment and go on our own quest to find our own heroes.

So, turn off the TV. Shut down the computer. Put away the magazines. Just watch life with me for a few moments.

First, we'll journey to Abilene, Texas. As we walk down the sidewalk, I want you to notice that elderly man walking toward his car. He's just an ordinary man, and it seems as if there is nothing special about him. But over fifty years ago on his forty-third Air Force mission escorting bombers over occupied Europe, his plane's engine quit at thirty thousand feet. The plane plunged 26,000 feet before he could get the engine started again. He eventually had to bail out and spent six months in hiding. He was then turned over to the Gestapo and spent three months in prison. This pilot, Bill Grosvenor, is one of about 93,000 American prisoners of war who returned alive from Europe after World War II.

Next, we fly to Seattle, Washington. As we pull up to St. Joseph's Catholic Church, I want you to notice the woman carrying a large bag and hurrying up the steps. Her name is Jeannie Jaybush, and she created the Baby Corner, an organization that last year gave away about $1,000,000 worth of baby items to families in need. About 12 percent of Seattle's homeless population is made up of children who are five years old and younger, according to the City of Seattle's Human Services Department. Because of the efforts of Jaybush, these children now have some of the basic

SKILLS FOCUS

Reading Skills
Evaluate evidence.

necessities that are needed to grow and be healthy.

If we had more time, we could fly to Duluth to visit a woman who is caring for her husband, one of the fourteen million Americans who have Alzheimer's disease. We could stop in Chicago, where a child with cancer lives each day fully. We could also land in Los Angeles, where a bilingual child is teaching his parents to read in English.

We'll stop our search for now, but let yours continue. Keep looking, and let your heart lead you to the heroes of today. I'll promise you, they're a lot easier to find than oceanfront property in Oklahoma.

---

1. The main **assertion** in this speech is —
   A there were more heroes in the old days
   B our world is full of heroes
   C we need more heroes like King Arthur
   D it is impossible to find heroes in today's world

2. Which of the following statements from the speech is an **accurate** piece of evidence that can be proven?
   F "About 12 percent of Seattle's homeless population is made up of children who are five years old and younger."
   G "We have to change the way we think about heroes."
   H "We have no loyalty, no honor, no chivalry."
   J "We've just been looking [for heroes] in all the wrong places."

3. Suppose a listener responded to this speech by saying, "Heroes are usually males who are recognized by most of the population." This would be an example of —
   A accurate evidence
   B appropriate evidence
   C adequate evidence
   D stereotyping

4. The speech supports its assertion mainly with —
   F statistics
   G quotes from experts
   H examples of people considered heroic
   J stereotypes

Constructed Response

5. Do you think the evidence in this speech is **adequate** to support its assertion? Why or why not?

Test Practice

Multiple-Meaning Words

DIRECTIONS: Choose the answer in which the underlined word is used the same way it is used in the quotation from *King Arthur: The Sword in the Stone.*

1. "In the churchyard he discovered a block of white marble with an anvil sitting on top."
   A The football player tried to block his opponent's kick.
   B They walked one block to the bus stop.
   C The statue was placed on a large wooden block.
   D Our class bought a block of tickets for the performance.

2. "Nothing had prepared them for this scale of violence."
   F Weigh yourself on the scale in the bathroom.
   G The pianist practiced each scale twenty times.
   H The scale of talent at this year's gymnastic competition was quite impressive.
   J On this scale model, one inch represents three feet.

3. "As soon as the service ended, those who wished to try for the throne formed a line next to the marble block."
   A The line to buy tickets was longer than we expected.
   B The fisherman attached the hook to his line.
   C The actor had only one line to memorize.
   D The truck crossed the state line at six o'clock.

4. " 'My lord,' said Merlin, 'I present to you a most worthy candidate for this contest.' "
   F When the teacher called my name, I said, "Present."
   G For my birthday I was given the present of my dreams.
   H Don't dwell on the past; focus on the present.
   J The emcee at the wedding reception finally said, "I now present the bride and groom."

5. "Then, turning the point downward again, he drove it back into the anvil with equal ease."
   A It's not polite to point.
   B At a certain point in the discussion, the group felt it would be a good time to take a break.
   C The warrior sharpened the point of his spear before going into battle.
   D "Get to the point," she said impatiently.

SKILLS FOCUS

Vocabulary Skills
Understand multiple-meaning words.

Collection 7: Skills Review

Writing Skills

Test Practice

DIRECTIONS: Read the following passage from an informative report. Then, read the questions below it. Choose the best answer to each question.

(1) One place connected with the legend of King Arthur is Glastonbury, in Somerset, England. (2) Around 1190, monks claimed they had found Arthur's grave in Glastonbury Abbey's cemetery. (3) An excavation turned up a lead cross with Arthur's name inscribed on it. (4) A coffin was also found. (5) It contained the bones of a man and a woman. (6) They were presumed to be the remains of King Arthur and Queen Guinevere. (7) These remains were moved to a tomb in the abbey church, but everything disappeared after the monasteries were dissolved in 1539. (8) No one knows what became of the cross. (9) Modern excavation has shown that there had indeed been an earlier burial at Glastonbury. (10) No evidence exists of whose grave it was. (11) Some storytellers identify Glastonbury with Avalon, King Arthur's final resting place.

1. This is an excerpt from an informative report. What is the most likely topic of the complete essay?
    A The beginnings of the Arthurian legend
    B Important excavations
    C Places connected with the Arthurian legend
    D Historical events and the legend of Arthur

2. Which of the following sources would be appropriate to consult in writing this informative report?
    F *The New Arthurian Encyclopedia*
    G *The Early History of Glastonbury*
    H *The Arthurian Handbook*
    J All of the above

3. Which two sentences could best be combined to improve the flow of the passage?
    A sentences 2 and 3
    B sentences 4 and 5
    C sentences 6 and 7
    D sentences 8 and 9

4. Which of the following words could *best* be used to connect sentences 9 and 10?
    F and
    G so
    H however
    J therefore

5. Where could sentence 11 be moved to improve the logical flow of the passage?
    A after sentence 1
    B after sentence 4
    C after sentence 7
    D after sentence 9

SKILLS FOCUS

Writing Skills
Analyze an informative report.

Fiction

All Sides of Arthur

Richard Barber has compiled the most exciting stories about King Arthur in *The Arthurian Legends: An Illustrated Anthology.*
You will learn about the social and historical contexts of the legends and how the stories have changed over time. But the focus of the book is King Arthur himself: his daring rescues, his heroic deeds, and his greatest challenges. You will find out why these tales still resonate with readers of all ages.

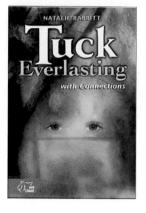

The Water of Life

Have you ever wished you could live forever? In Natalie Babbitt's *Tuck Everlasting,* the members of the Tuck family are granted eternal life when they drink from a hidden stream. Then they find out that living forever isn't what it's cracked up to be. This novel is also published in Spanish as *Tuck para siempre.*
This title is available in the HRW Library.

More than They Can Chew?

Four young lives are changed one summer by the discovery of a coin. Not just any coin, but a coin that grants wishes—or rather, *half* wishes. In Edward Eager's novel, *Half Magic,* Jane, Katherine, Mark, and Martha accidentally make themselves *half* invisible, ship themselves to the Sahara Desert, and finally transport themselves back to King Arthur's court. Then they think that maybe *double* wishing can solve all their problems—but will it really?

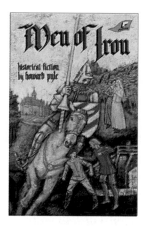

Payback

As Myles Falworth undergoes rigorous training for knighthood, he learns that his blind father was wrongfully accused of treason and stripped of his lands. Now that he has grown up, Myles attempts to restore honor to his father by challenging his father's toughest enemies. In *Men of Iron,* Howard Pyle weaves a dramatic tale of suspense and bravery.

Nonfiction

Leaders by Example

Anthony Masters looks at the lives of twenty-four exceptional people in *Heroic Stories*. You've probably heard of some of these heroes, such as Martin Luther King, Jr., and Anne Frank. Do you know about Christy Brown, who overcame a troubling disability to become a writer, or Pauline Cutting, who worked tirelessly in hospitals in Beirut? All of the people profiled in the book embody a heroic ideal.

Things Have Changed

Gwyneth Morgan takes you back to thirteenth-century England in *Life in a Medieval Village*. In vivid detail, Morgan explores the everyday life of a peasant family, a lord and his manor, and the role of the church during this unique period in history. You may be surprised by the food people ate, the clothes they wore, and what they did for a living.

The Historical Arthur

Kevin Crossley-Holland's *The World of King Arthur and His Court* examines the ideals and customs of Arthurian times. You'll learn how a boy became a knight and was schooled in the specifics of courtly love. Crossley-Holland also compares the legends of King Arthur to actual history. Was Arthur real or fictional? The answer may surprise you.

A Heroic Woman

Eleanor of Aquitaine (ak'wə·tān') was queen of France and later England in the 1100s. During her lifetime she supported the arts and helped establish the courtly manners you've read about in the Arthurian tales. Her strength of character brought her trouble—she was held in confinement for fifteen years by her husband. Find out the whole story in Polly Schoyer Brooks's biography *Queen Eleanor: Independent Spirit of the Medieval World*.

Reading for Life

Informational Focus:

- **Analyzing Information in Public, Workplace, and Consumer Documents**

- **Following Technical Directions**

INTERNET

Collection
Resources
Keyword: LE5 7-8

Reading Informational Texts
Reading for Life *by* Sheri Henderson

Getting the Job Done

The purpose of consumer, workplace, and public documents is to provide information. These documents are everywhere, and that is a *good* thing. Without them a society as complex as ours would not be able to function well. Since these documents contain information that is important to all of us, they deserve—and require—our close attention and careful reading. The information they contain can be as simple as advertising for a new movie or as complex as warnings about your prescription medication. Whether simple or complex, though, consumer, workplace, and public documents cannot do their job of providing information if we do not do our job, which is reading them carefully.

Consumer Documents

Most days you probably look to consumer documents for all sorts of information. **Advertisements** tell you what is available to buy and how much it costs, what movie is just out on video, and when your favorite store is having a sale. Providers of services publish **schedules** of movie showtimes, school lunch menus, TV programs, and bus or train or plane timetables. **Labels** on the goods you buy give you, the consumer, information about what you are buying. Labels on packaged food list the food's ingredients and nutritional value. Labels on shoes

declare which parts are synthetic and which parts are not. Labels on your clothing tell you what your shirt is made of and how to care for it.

Mechanical and electronic equipment come with **warranties, contracts, instructional manuals,** and **technical directions.** These guide you in the safe and proper use of products. Whenever you encounter consumer information, especially technical directions, it is a good idea to read it through slowly and carefully. The seller is required only to include the information. It's up to you to read and understand it. As many consumers have found out too late, "I didn't understand it" will not get you your money back if the item does not work because you didn't read the directions. Informed consumers know that it's better to read consumer documents *before* they use the product.

Workplace Documents

As their name suggests, workplace documents are those you encounter in a job. Your first communication with a possible employer may be through a **business letter,** in which you state your qualifications and request a job interview. However, a business letter isn't always necessary. You may merely be asked to complete an **application.** When you are hired, you may be asked to sign an **employment contract,** which spells out what is expected of you as an employee and what you can expect in return from your employer. You may need to provide a Social Security number, a **work permit,** and a **tax form** for your employer to use when calculating taxes to deduct from your wages. You may also be given **insurance forms** to fill out and sign. To help you succeed in your job, your employer may provide an **employee manual,** a set of rules and instructions related to the job.

When workers need to communicate with one another, they usually do so through **memorandums,** often called memos. Businesses frequently use **e-mail memos** to communicate because e-mail is fast, convenient, and easily retrieved. Of course, the number and types of workplace documents you encounter will depend on the kind of work you do. However, one thing is certain: Whatever kind of work you do, workplace documents will play an important role in helping you succeed.

Public Documents

If there were a chemical spill on a road near your house, would you be told about it? If you wanted to learn about sports programs at local parks before you moved into a new neighborhood, could you do it? If you wanted to know how much the mayor earns in your community, could you find out? The answer to all of these questions is *yes!* The answers can be found in public

documents. Public documents supply citizens with information that may be of interest to them. Public documents can relate to schools, churches, government agencies, the courts, libraries, and fire and police departments, to name just a few.

Typically most citizens do not read the public documents put out by the government, the military, and nonprofit agencies or groups. Instead, they read **newspaper articles** that report on the documents. Whether you read a document itself or a newspaper account of its contents, public documents exist to tell you what is happening in your world.

Reading Ahead

The following pages will give you some practice reading various kinds of consumer, workplace, and public documents. You'll also get a chance to follow some technical directions. Challenge yourself as you read to see how well you can locate the important information in all the documents.

Reading Skills and Strategies

Reading for Information

by Kylene Beers

In one basic way, reading informational materials differs from reading stories. Can you figure out what that difference is?

It's *not* that stories are usually fiction and informational texts are usually nonfiction. With both fiction and nonfiction you have to

- process information
- think about what the text is saying
- compare and contrast
- predict what will happen next
- summarize what has happened already
- understand the sequence of events
- recognize the writer's point of view
- connect what you already know with what you are reading
- note cause-and-effect relationships
- make inferences
- draw conclusions

The basic difference is that most fiction uses a narrator to tell you what is happening, but in most informational materials there is no narrator to guide you along. This lack of a guide may slow down some readers. You can guide yourself through informational texts, though, by following the tips on the right.

Tips for Reading Informational Texts

1. **Numbered steps** in a text tell you, "First, do this. Next, do that."

2. **Headings** call out, "Look here! This is a new topic you're about to meet."

3. **Boldface** and **italic** words or phrases alert you, "This is an important word or definition. Pay attention!"

4. **Graphics,** such as maps, charts, graphs, and illustrations, also tell you, "Step right up! Important information can be found here."

5. Phrases such as *on the other hand, by comparison, by contrast,* or *still others believe* often introduce the **opposite** of what's come before. The information may conflict with what you've already read.

6. Phrases and words such as *consequently, as a result, this results in,* or *therefore* explain the **effects** of something.

SKILLS FOCUS

Reading Skills
Read for Information.

What's the next big movie? It just might be at the bottom of your book bag! ❶

From Page to Film

Kathryn R. Hoffman
from Time for Kids

Ron Weasley, Stuart Little, Shrek, Jesse Tuck: What do they have in common? All have made the move from the small, printed page to the big silver screen—and all with a good deal of success! ❷

Children's books can make blockbuster movies. The film based on J. K. Rowling's first Harry Potter book made more money than any film the year it came out. *Harry Potter*'s success has sent movie producers to their kids' bookshelves in search of the next big hit. *Ella Enchanted, Holes, The Cat in the Hat,* and Lemony Snicket's *The Bad Beginning* are just a few of the books that have made it to the movies.

Using the Strategy

As you read, you'll find this open-book sign at certain points in the story: 📖. Stop at these points, and think about what you've just read. Do what the prompt asks you to do.

PREDICT

❶ The **boldface headline** above the title draws you in and hints at what the article is about. What do you think the subject of the article will be?

IDENTIFY

❷ The **title** and the **first paragraph** make the subject of the article clear. What is it?

ANALYZE

❸ **Subheads** alert you to the subject of the text that follows. Do the red subheads on this page make the subject of each section clear? Explain.

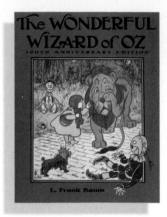

Great Expectations ❸

Movie versions of kids' books have been around for a long time. Some favorite family films—*The Wizard of Oz* and *Willy Wonka and the Chocolate Factory*—are loved just as much as the books they were based on.

But making movies from beloved books isn't easy. Filmmakers have a hard time living up to the images in readers' minds. "When you read, you translate what the author says into your own personal movie that runs in your head," says Natalie Babbitt, the author of *Tuck Everlasting*. It can be hard to accept another version.

Write and Rewrite

Screenwriters don't set out to ruin the work of a great author. Sometimes they are the same person! Louis Sachar not only wrote the bestseller *Holes,* he penned the screenplay too. Movies are so different from books, he says, "I had to figure out the story all over again."

Pacing is a big issue. Films usually move faster than books and require more action. The book *Tuck Everlasting,* for example, devotes many pages to an emotional struggle in a character's head. Says Jeffrey Lieber, who wrote the *Tuck* screenplay: "I kept asking myself, 'What's the image on the screen?'"

Length is an issue too. When film-makers take a four-hundred-page book, something has to go. While working on the second film, *Harry Potter* director Chris Columbus realized he had to cut the Death Day Party scene—a ghostly celebration. "I had some heated discussions with my kids," Columbus says. Over their objections, he sacrificed the scene for the good of the movie. ❹ 🔖

At the other extreme, the creators of *Shrek, Jumanji,* and *The Cat in the Hat* movies have had to turn short stories into ninety minutes of big-screen action. To do so, they added characters and plot details. The donkey that almost stole the show in *Shrek* barely existed in the book.

INFER

❹ **Paragraph breaks** indicate that the writer is beginning a new subject. What is the **main idea** of this paragraph?

It Takes Teamwork

Authors who have helped turn their books into films are struck by the team effort. "The book is just me alone in my room," says Sachar. Movies draw on the talents of actors, set and costume designers, and musicians, among others. They have tools that no writer has. "A safe, faithful telling of the book, I think that's a failure," says *Jumanji* author Chris Van Allsburg. "You haven't used the magic of filmmaking."

A Few Recent Books That Made It to the Movies

The Polar Express
The book is reported to be a favorite of Tom Hanks, who plays the conductor.

The Cat in the Hat
The cat from the books has a Hollywood look. Mike Myers plays the cat.

The Bad Beginning
This is the first book in Lemony Snicket's book series *A Series of Unfortunate Events* to make it to the screen. Others may soon follow. ⑤

ANALYZE

⑤ This **sidebar** repeats information that appears in the text. Why do you think it is included here?

What additional information do you learn from the **illustrations** that appear with the article?

Practice the Strategy

Reading for Information

Similarities to Reading Stories

When you read informational texts, you use most of the same reading skills that you need for reading a story. For example, you compare and contrast, predict what will happen next, make inferences, connect the text with what you know already, and draw conclusions.

Differences from Reading Stories

When you read a story, a narrator guides you through what is happening by recounting the events, usually in chronological order. When you read informational texts, there is usually no narrator to guide you. However, you can use some common informational text features as your guides.

PRACTICE

In a chart like the one below, give examples and explain how you were able to use each text feature to help you read and understand "From Page to Film."

Informational Text Features	Examples and Explanations
Headings	
Boldface or italic words and phrases	
Graphics (maps, charts, illustrations)	
Sidebar	
Paragraph breaks	

Whenever you read for information, you can use these **text features** to help guide you through the documents.

SKILLS FOCUS

Reading Skills
Read for information.

Analyzing Information in Public Documents

Reading Focus
Public Documents

All **public documents** have one thing in common: They inform people (you) about things you might need or want to know. Public documents are all about information. Let's follow one person's experience in finding information she needs by using some public documents.

Locating Information: An Announcement

Meet Sam (Miss Samantha Sallyann Lancaster, and don't even think about calling her anything but Sam, thank you very much). Anyone who knows Sam for five minutes knows two things about her: She's smart, and she can beat anyone, anytime, anywhere on her BMX bike. So imagine Sam's excitement when she comes across this **announcement** in her favorite biking magazine:

Casting Call

If you've been looking for the right break to get into motion pictures, this may be your chance. StreetWheelie Productions is casting fresh talent for an upcoming action movie.

 What?

To audition, you must

- be a charismatic, awesome, off-the-wall male or female individualist
- be an expert at making your BMX-type bike do whatever you want it to do **Who?**
- have your own bike
- look like you're between the ages of twelve and fifteen
- meet the requirements for a permit to work in the entertainment industry if you are under age eighteen
- be living in or near San Francisco during July and August 2004

Auditions will be held in

**Golden Gate Park, San Francisco
Saturday, May 25, 2004
10:00 A.M. to 5:00 P.M.** **When and where?**

Bring your bike.

See you in the movies!

Locating Information: An Article

Sam thinks, "Cool!" This may be for her, but she wants more information. An **Internet search** using the key words *StreetWheelie Productions* and *San Francisco* yields this **article** from *Hollywood Beat,* a newsmagazine:

Hollywood Beat

Shhhhhh!

Here's a little secret for you. Remember Bilbo Baggins, the lovable little hobbit who saved Middle Earth from the Powers of Darkness in J.R.R. Tolkien's classic novel? Well, that little hobbit's about to get radical. *Hollywood Beat* has discovered that StreetWheelie Productions is developing an out-of-sight version of this tale, and Middle Earth will never be the same.

Set in San Francisco, the hobbits are bike-riding dudes who, in order to save their world, oppose an endless stream of baddies who ride BMX bikes. The principal character, Bilbo, is a nerdy innocent who finds himself at the center of (Middle) Earth–shaking events. The result? Batman meets Mr. Rogers.

Sources close to the production say that there is some big talent interested in the project. As of yet, nobody's talking, but remember . . . you'll hear all about it first on *Hollywood Beat.*

? What's the topic?

? Why a bike?

Locating Information:
An Application

Since *The Hobbit* is one of her favorite books, Sam now knows the basics of the movie's plot, theme, and characters (although Hollywood is famous for taking liberties with one's favorite books). She thinks trying out for the movie will be fun. She has also learned what kind of character she will be auditioning to play. Now she can do a little costuming to look the part.

However, she's only twelve years old. Can she qualify for a work permit? She doesn't want to audition if she isn't eligible to take the part. Sam does another **Internet search,** this time using the key words *permit to work in the entertainment industry* and *California.* This leads her to the state of California's Division of Labor Standards Enforcement. All the information she needs is on the **Web site,** including the **application** itself, which she downloads (just in case!).

Study the application on the next page to find out what Sam will need to do to get permission to work in a movie. The margin notes help you identify key information.

STATE OF CALIFORNIA
Division of Labor Standards Enforcement

APPLICATION FOR PERMISSION TO WORK IN THE ENTERTAINMENT INDUSTRY

THIS IS NOT A PERMIT ☐ NEW ☐ RENEWAL

PROCEDURES FOR OBTAINING WORK PERMIT

1. Complete the information required below.
2. School authorities must complete the School Record section below.
3. For minors 15 days through kindergarten, please attach a certified copy of the minor's birth certificate. See reverse side for other documents that may be accepted.
4. Mail or present the completed application to any office of the Division of Labor Standards Enforcement for issuance of your work permit.

? What does the first section require?

Name of Child	Professional Name, if applicable

Permanent Address Number Street City State Zip Code	Home Phone No.

School Attending						Grade

Date of Birth	Age	Height	Weight	Hair Color	Eye Color	Sex

Statement of Parent or Guardian: It is my desire that an Entertainment Work Permit be issued to the above-named child. I will read the rules governing such employment and will cooperate to the best of my ability in safeguarding his or her educational, moral, and physical interest. I hereby certify, under penalty of perjury, that the foregoing statements are true and correct.

Name of Parent or Guardian (print or type)	Signed	Daytime phone #

SCHOOL RECORD

☐ I certify that the above-named minor meets the school district's requirements with respect to age, school record, attendance, and health.

☐ Does not meet the district's requirements and permit should not be issued.

? What does the second section require?

Authorized School Official	Date	
School Address	School Telephone	[School Seal or Stamp]

HEALTH RECORD

COMPLETE THIS SECTION IF INSTRUCTED TO DO SO OR IF INFANT UNDER ONE MONTH OF AGE

Name of Doctor	Address	Telephone Number

? What does the last section require?

I certify that I am Board Certified in pediatrics and have carefully examined

and, in my opinion: He/She is physically fit to be employed in the production of motion pictures and television. If less than one month, infant is at least 15 days old, was carried to full term, and is physically able to perform.

_____ M.D. _____
Signature   Date

Approved DLSE 277 Rev. 03/99

Sam's happy. She knows she'll qualify for a work permit, and she decides to go to the audition. Before she goes, test yourself. In reading these documents, have you been able to find all the information Sam needs?

Analyzing Information in Public Documents

1. The fact that the advertisement appeared in Sam's favorite biking magazine suggests that the casting agents are especially interested in kids who can —
   A read magazines
   B act a little crazy
   C follow directions
   D ride a bike

2. If Sam is hired to play a part, she will be working during —
   F May and June
   G June and July
   H July and August
   J August and September

3. Sam is probably auditioning to play —
   A a hobbit
   B Mr. Rogers
   C a baddie
   D Bilbo Baggins

4. Sam is confident that she will qualify for a **work permit.** To do so, she will need all of the following *except* —
   F the full support and help of her parent or guardian
   G a statement of good health from a doctor
   H a statement from her school that she has met the district's requirements for her grade level
   J permission from her school to be absent when necessary

5. If Sam wanted to find out more about StreetWheelie Productions, her *best* choice would be to —
   A search the Internet using the key words *StreetWheelie Productions*
   B look in an encyclopedia under "Film Industry"
   C read *The Hobbit* again
   D post a question on her school's electronic bulletin board

Constructed Response

1. What is the most important purpose of a **public document**?

2. Where and when will the auditions be held?

3. What special talent must people have to audition for this part?

4. What will the movie be about?

Reading Skills
Analyze information in public documents.

Analyzing Information in Workplace Documents

Reading Focus
Workplace Documents

Whether you work in a small business with only one other person or in a huge corporation with offices all over the world, your working life will depend on many types of **workplace documents.** Businesses put important information in writing so that agreements, decisions, and requirements are clear to everyone involved. Let's look at some of the workplace documents that Sam encounters after her audition.

Locating Information: A Business Letter

The audition has gone really well. Everyone is as nice as he or she can be, and someone takes down all of Sam's information and talks with her and her mother for quite a while. Pretty soon Sam receives the **business letter** shown on the next page.

Reading Skills
Analyze information in workplace documents.

STREETWHEELIE PRODUCTIONS

2323 South Robertson Boulevard
Beverly Hills, CA 90210

June 7, 2004
Miss Samantha Lancaster
1920 Ygnacio Valley Road
Walnut Creek, CA 94598

Dear Sam:

On behalf of StreetWheelie Productions, it is my pleasure to offer you a part in our production. Attached is your contract. I know that contracts can be difficult to read and understand, so it is important that before you sign it, you and your parents understand it thoroughly. The items in the contract spell out the issues we discussed last Saturday, as follows:

- You are responsible for your own transportation to and from filming. Pay attention to scheduled dates, times, and locations.
- Check your e-mail first thing each morning and last thing each night. If you are experiencing trouble with your e-mail and are unsure of the next day's schedule, call Alonsa anytime, 24/7.
- You must report to makeup, hair, and wardrobe two hours before your first call.
- You may *not* change your hairstyle or hair color during filming. We all admired the brightness of the lime green you have achieved and the way your hair flows from under your helmet when you're riding.
- Unless otherwise noted, you must report with your bike for all calls. You may not wash or otherwise clean all that great grunge off your bike.
- Because you are not yet age sixteen, a parent or guardian must be present whenever you are working. As we discussed with your mother, your grandfather will be an appropriate guardian as long as he has with him at all times a written document signed by your parents, authorizing him to act as your guardian.
- Nonprofessional actors are paid a minimum hourly wage. You will receive a check at the end of each week. Your eight-hour maximum workday will begin when you arrive each day and end when you leave each day. By law you may not work more than eight hours a day. One paid hour of rest and recreation will be part of your eight-hour workday, but the thirty-minute lunch, also paid, will *not* be part of the workday. You will always have twelve hours or more between the end of one workday and the makeup call for the next.
- In addition to the above hourly wage, you will receive a bonus at the end of your filming schedule. This bonus will be paid on your last day of work, on the condition that you have fulfilled all aspects of your contract with regard to attendance, punctuality, and appearance. This bonus will equal the total of all your previous hourly checks. It will, in effect, double your earnings.

If you have any questions, call Juanita Diaz, our lawyer. Her phone number is on the contract. We look forward to having you on the project.

Sincerely,

Cassandra Rice

Cassandra Rice, Casting Director

Responsibility 1: transportation.

Responsibility 2: work schedule.

Responsibility 3: arrival time.

Responsibility 4: appearance.

Responsibility 5: equipment.

Responsibility 6: parental supervision.

Wages.

Contact for questions.

Locating Information: Workplace Instructions

Sam thinks, "Wow! I'm going to be in a movie!" Before she knows it, her first day arrives. As soon as Sam gets to the location, she is introduced to a whole new set of friends . . . *and* to a whole new set of rules. Everyone in the crew is nice, but they all make it clear that everyone is there to work, and they expect Sam to understand that fun movies are just as hard to make as serious ones. Sam's job doesn't require an employee manual, but she does receive a list of **workplace instructions.**

Talent Instructions: On Location

What to do and what not to do.

1. No horseplay is permitted.

2. When you arrive, sign in with Jim, and pick up a call pager.

3. Report *immediately* to makeup, hair, and wardrobe.

4. Movies require a lot of waiting. Bring something that you can do *quietly* while you wait. Music players are fine if the headphones do not interfere with makeup, hair, or costume. Electronic games are popular; their sound effects *must* be turned off. You *could* even read a book. People do.

5. When you are ready, report to the call area, and stay there. *Always* keep your call pager with you.

6. Personal cell phones, pagers, etc., may be used only in the call or food areas and only if they do not interfere with filming. Ringers must be set to "off" or "silent alert."

7. Leave all personal belongings in your assigned locker when on the shooting site.

8. You may talk in nonfilming areas, but there is *no talking* on the shooting site.

Locating Information:
E-mail Memos and Directory

Sam finds out she loves being involved in making movies. The work is fun and interesting. Many of the other kids complain about having to wait for hours just to do a short scene, but Sam is interested in everything going on and so is never bored. Since she knows how to be quiet and stay out of the way, she is allowed to watch the filming all day long. The days just fly by.

As time goes on, Sam understands why she is required to check her e-mail every morning and night. It's hard to remember which schedule is the most recent one. Luckily, Sam can always look it up on her saved mail. At the right is one of Sam's **e-mail memos.**

Sam changes her calendar for August 8 but cannot find her latest revised schedule. She breathes a sigh of relief when she remembers that she can check her saved e-mail and print another copy. Look at Sam's **e-mail directory.**

Test Practice

1. The **business letter** discusses mainly Sam's —
   A audition
   B contract
   C ability to act
   D ability to ride a bike

2. The **business letter** points out that with the bonus, Sam will —
   F be paid only if she fulfills all conditions of her contract
   G not be paid if she fails to fulfill any conditions of her contract
   H be paid double if she fulfills all conditions of her contract
   J earn minimum wage for the project

3. Sam can **infer** from the **business letter** that a law requires a parent or guardian to be present when a child is working in the entertainment industry until the child reaches age —
   A ten
   B twelve
   C sixteen
   D eighteen

4. Sam's **workplace instructions** make it clear that while waiting, actors are expected to be all of the following *except* —
   F patient
   G responsible
   H self-controlled
   J loud

5. Sam's July 25 **e-mail memo** tells her about a change in —
   A date
   B time
   C part
   D costume

6. Sam's **e-mail directory** lists —
   F all the people she works with
   G e-mail she has received
   H e-mail she plans to send
   J her favorite movies

Constructed Response

1. Name the **workplace documents** Sam has encountered. What is the purpose of each document?

2. How much will Sam be paid?

3. What equipment is Sam expected to provide?

4. What is the date of Sam's most recently revised schedule?

SKILLS FOCUS

Reading Skills
Analyze information in workplace documents.

Analyzing Information in Consumer Documents

Reading Focus
Consumer Documents

A consumer buys or uses what someone else sells. Have you ever treated a friend to an ice-cream cone or a movie? If so, both you and the person you treated were consumers. Even your pets can be considered consumers—of the food and the toys you buy for them. Consumers need information about the products and services they buy. **Consumer documents** provide that information. Let's look at some of the consumer documents Sam uses while she is working.

Locating Information: A Transit Map

Sam has to travel to work with her bike, and she doesn't look forward to a long bike ride from Walnut Creek to the movie location and back. Besides, her grandfather has to come with her, and he doesn't have a bike. Her grandfather could drive, but parking a car in San Francisco is expensive—even if you can find a parking space! So the two decide to take the Bay Area Rapid Transit System, known as BART. BART is a network of trains that can take you just about anywhere in the San Francisco Bay Area.

First, Sam and her grandpa log on to the Internet to look at the **BART system map.** They want to be sure they can get from their home in Walnut Creek to the Embarcadero Station, where the StreetWheelie production van will be waiting. They find the map that is shown on the next page.

SKILLS FOCUS

Reading Skills
Analyze information in consumer documents.

BART System Map

San Pablo ⓣ

Ⓟ **Richmond**

El Cerrito del Norte Ⓟ

El Cerrito Plaza Ⓟ

Ⓟ North Berkeley
Downtown Berkeley
Ⓟ Ashby

Ⓟ West Oakland

Embarcadero
Montgomery St.
Powell St
Civic Center

16th St Mission
24th St Mission

Balboa Park

San Francisco

Air-BART

Oakland
International
Airport ✈

Ⓟ Daly City

Rush hour only

Colma Ⓟ

Glen Park Ⓟ

S. San Francisco
San Bruno

San Francisco
International
Airport ✈ ⓣ

Milbrae

Foster City

Rockridge Ⓟ

MacArthur Ⓟ
19th St/Oakland
Oakland City Center/12th St
Lake Merritt Ⓟ
Fruitvale Ⓟ

Coliseum/
Oakland Airport Ⓟ

San Leandro Ⓟ

Bay Fair Ⓟ

Castro Valley Ⓟ
Hayward Ⓟ

South Hayward Ⓟ

Union City Ⓟ

Fremont

Irvington

Warm Springs

Orinda Ⓟ

Lafayette

Ⓟ Concord

North
Concord/
Martinez Ⓟ

**Pittsburg/
Bay Point** Ⓟ

Pleasant Hill Ⓟ

Walnut Creek Ⓟ

**Dublin/
Pleasanton** Ⓟ

	Richmond–Daly City/Colma
	Fremont–Daly City
	Fremont–Richmond
	Pittsburg/Bay Point–Colma
	Dublin/Pleasanton–Daly City
Ⓟ	BART Parking

❓ Which line should Sam take?

❓ Which BART lines stop at Walnut Creek? at the Embarcadero?

Locating Information: Rules

Sam is glad to see that BART will take her directly from Walnut Creek to the Embarcadero station. She still needs more BART information: Is she allowed to bring a bike with her? She clicks on "Bikes on BART." Read the Web page on bicycle **rules** on the next page to see if Sam can take her bike on BART.

Back   Forward   Reload   Home   Search

 Riding BART | BART General Information | Inside BART | Doing Business with BART | BART-SFO Extension

Riding BART

BART-SFO Extension

Trip Planner

Station Info

Tickets

Bikes on BART
Lockers
Comments

Accessibility

FAQ

Rider Feedback

BART's Bicycle Rules

- Bikes are allowed on all trains except those indicated by the BART Trip Planner and highlighted in the *All About BART* brochure. It is the rider's responsibility to refer to BART schedules.

- Regardless of any other rule, bikes are never allowed on crowded cars. Use your good judgment and only board cars that can comfortably accommodate you and your bicycle. Hold your bike while on the trains.

- Bikes are allowed in any car but the first car of a train.

- Bicyclists must use elevator or stairs, not escalators, and always walk bikes.

- Bicyclists must yield priority seating to seniors and people with disabilities, yield to other passengers, and not block aisles or doors or soil seats.

- In case of an evacuation, leave your bike on the train, and do not let it block aisles or doors.

- Bicyclists under 14 years old must be accompanied by an adult.

- Gas-powered vehicles are never permitted.

- Bikes must be parked in racks and lockers. Call (510) 464-7133 for locker availability. Bikes parked against poles, fences, or railings will be removed.

COMMUTE HOURS
(Weekdays approximately 7:05 to 8:50 am and 4:25 to 6:45 pm)

- During morning commute hours, bikes are allowed in the Embarcadero Station only for trips to the East Bay (as indicated by the BART Trip Planner and the *All About BART* brochure).

- During evening commute hours, bicyclists traveling from the East Bay must exit at the Embarcadero Station (as indicated by the BART Trip Planner and the *All About BART* brochure).

*Violation of the above rules subject to citation under
CA Vehicle Code Sec. 21113 and Sec. 42001.*

 Will any bike restrictions affect Sam?

? What are the Embarcadero restrictions? What do they mean for Sam?

Home Page | Riding BART | BART Information | Inside BART | Doing Business | BART-SFO Extension

Locating Information: Ticket Guide

Now Sam checks the **ticket guide** to learn how much it will cost them. Since Grandpa is over sixty-five and Sam is twelve, can they get any discount fares?

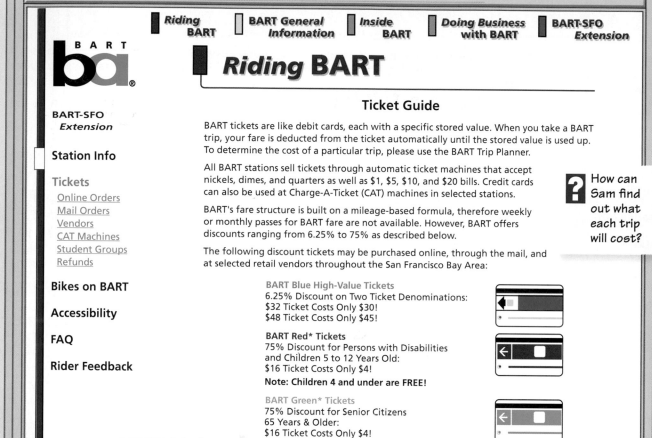

Riding BART | **BART General Information** | **Inside BART** | **Doing Business with BART** | **BART-SFO Extension**

Riding BART

BART-SFO *Extension*

Station Info

Tickets
Online Orders
Mail Orders
Vendors
CAT Machines
Student Groups
Refunds

Bikes on BART

Accessibility

FAQ

Rider Feedback

Ticket Guide

BART tickets are like debit cards, each with a specific stored value. When you take a BART trip, your fare is deducted from the ticket automatically until the stored value is used up. To determine the cost of a particular trip, please use the BART Trip Planner.

All BART stations sell tickets through automatic ticket machines that accept nickels, dimes, and quarters as well as $1, $5, $10, and $20 bills. Credit cards can also be used at Charge-A-Ticket (CAT) machines in selected stations.

? How can Sam find out what each trip will cost?

BART's fare structure is built on a mileage-based formula, therefore weekly or monthly passes for BART fare are not available. However, BART offers discounts ranging from 6.25% to 75% as described below.

The following discount tickets may be purchased online, through the mail, and at selected retail vendors throughout the San Francisco Bay Area:

BART Blue High-Value Tickets
6.25% Discount on Two Ticket Denominations:
$32 Ticket Costs Only $30!
$48 Ticket Costs Only $45!

? Which is the best ticket for Sam? Which is the best ticket for Grandpa?

BART Red* Tickets
75% Discount for Persons with Disabilities and Children 5 to 12 Years Old:
$16 Ticket Costs Only $4!
Note: Children 4 and under are FREE!

BART Green* Tickets
75% Discount for Senior Citizens 65 Years & Older:
$16 Ticket Costs Only $4!

BART Orange Tickets
BART Orange Tickets provide discounts for middle and secondary school students.
Note: Special purchasing restrictions apply.

BART Plus Tickets
BART Plus tickets can be used as a "flash pass" for other transit operators.

Home Page | Riding BART | BART Information | Inside BART | Doing Business | BART-SFO Extension

Locating Information: Schedule

To get the **BART schedule**, Sam goes to the trip-planning page and enters the name of the station they'll be leaving from and the name of the station they'll be arriving at. What she finds is on the next page.

BART

ba®

Riding BART

Plan another trip ... ⬍

BART-SFO
Extension

Trip Planner
Schedule by Map
Schedule by Line
System Map
Bay Area Transit
Employer Shuttles
Planning Help

Station Info

Tickets

Bikes on BART

Accessibility

FAQ

Rider Feedback

Here are all the weekday trains after 5:00 a.m. arriving before 10:00 a.m.:

Origin Station : Walnut Creek
Destination Station : Embarcadero
One-way fare : $3.45

Walnut Creek	Embarcadero	Bikes	Details
5:05a	5:39a	Yes	❶
5:20a	5:54a	Yes	❶
5:35a	6:09a	Yes	❶
5:50a	6:24a	Yes	❶
6:05a	6:39a	Yes	❶
6:15a	6:49a	Yes	❶
6:20a	6:54a	Yes	❶
6:30a	7:04a	Yes	❶
6:35a	7:09a	No	❶
6:45a	7:19a	No	❶
6:50a	7:24a	No	❶
6:55a	7:29a	No	❶
7:00a	7:34a	No	❶
7:05a	7:39a	No	❶
7:10a	7:44a	No	❶

Walnut Creek	Embarcadero	Bikes	Details
7:15a	7:49a	No	❶
7:20a	7:54a	No	❶
7:30a	8:04a	No	❶
7:35a	8:09a	No	❶
7:45a	8:19a	No	❶
7:50a	8:24a	No	❶
8:00a	8:34a	No	❶
8:05a	8:39a	No	❶
8:15a	8:49a	No	❶
8:20a	8:54a	No	❶
8:35a	9:09a	Yes	❶
8:50a	9:24a	Yes	❶
9:05a	9:39a	Yes	❶
9:20a	9:54a	Yes	❶

❶ provides more details about a selected trip.

No indicates that bicycles are not allowed on the trip. See BART's Bicycle Rules for more information.

Bicycles cannot enter or exit 12th or 19th Street during commute hours.

E-mail this Schedule

Print this Schedule

? What is the fare for the trip? What will it cost Sam and Grandpa?

? When are bikes allowed on BART trains?

Home Page | Riding BART | BART Information | Inside BART | Doing Business | BART-SFO Extension

Thanks to her ability to use **consumer information materials**, Sam has found the correct BART line, discovered when bikes are allowed on the trains, learned about the cost of the tickets and discounts, and checked the schedules. She can do this from a library or the comfort of her home, thanks to the Internet and her ability to use consumer documents.

So look out, world. The name is Sam (Samantha Sallyann Lancaster, but call her Sam)—soon to be in a movie playing at a theater near *you*.

Analyzing Information in Consumer Documents

1. Which type of **consumer document** would you consult to learn what BART line to take to get from one place to another?
   A   System map
   B   Bicycle rules
   C   Ticket guide
   D   Train schedule

2. According to the **bicycle rules,** in which cars of the train can you ride with a bike?
   F   Any car at all
   G   Any car but the first
   H   Any car but the last
   J   Only the first three cars

3. According to the **ticket guide,** Grandpa (age 75) and Sam (age 12) should buy —
   A   one blue and one red ticket
   B   one red and one green ticket
   C   one orange and one blue ticket
   D   two orange tickets

4. Reading the BART trip-planning Web page, you can learn all of the following *except* —
   F   the basic cost of the trip
   G   the schedule of departures and arrivals
   H   when bicycles are allowed
   J   available discounts

5. Sam must arrive two hours before her first call. If her first call is at 8:00 A.M., what is the latest she can leave the Walnut Creek station and still meet the van by 5:45 A.M.?
   A   5:05 A.M.
   B   5:20 A.M.
   C   5:35 A.M.
   D   5:50 A.M.

Constructed Response

1. Sam consults four **consumer documents** from the BART system. What is the purpose of each document?

2. Sam got all of her information about the BART system from the Internet. How might you get this same information if you did not have access to a computer?

SKILLS FOCUS

Reading Skills
Analyze information in consumer documents.

Following Technical Directions

Reading Focus
Technical Directions

Technical directions are step-by-step instructions that explain how to accomplish mechanical tasks. You follow technical directions when you want to assemble the new TV satellite dish that you just bought. The technical directions in the instructional manual may have taught you how to operate your new cell phone. Technical directions can also instruct you how to repair mechanical devices you are using. You may have followed them when you removed and oiled the wheels on your in-line skates or when you cleaned the sprockets on your bicycle.

You're probably too young to drive a car, but you're certainly not too young to be thinking about it. Driving can give you a new independence, but it also gives you new responsibilities. Any number of things can go wrong with your car, and it's up to you to fix them—or get them fixed. You won't be expected to repair the engine, but you can fairly easily fix one of the most common automobile emergencies: a flat tire. A flat is something every driver will have to face someday—possibly on a lonely country road, without a living soul in sight. To be prepared for that, study the directions on the next page.

go.
hrw
.com

INTERNET
Interactive
Reading Model
Keyword: LE5 7-8

SKILLS FOCUS

Reading Skills
Follow technical directions.

How to Change a Flat Tire

Before you can change a flat tire on your car, you first have to realize that the tire is flat. You might come out of your house in the morning and see the wheel rim resting on the road with the tire spread around it. You'll know right away the tire's flat. How can you tell, though, if it goes flat while you are driving? A first clue is that your car starts to pull to the right or the left even though you aren't turning the steering wheel. Another clue is that passing motorists honk and point as they drive by. Yet another clue is that the car starts bouncing up and down and making a loud *thumpity-thump-thump* sound.

When you suspect you have a flat tire, follow these procedures:

1 Park the car as far off the road as possible. Put the car in park (if you have an automatic transmission) or in gear (if you have a standard transmission), turn off the engine, and put on the emergency brake. Turn on your car's flashing lights. Now, get out and look at your tires. If you have a flat, put out emergency triangles or, at night, flares. (It's a good idea to carry warning triangles and flares in your trunk at all times in case of an emergency.)

3 Remove the wheel cover from the flat tire, using a screwdriver or the end of the jack handle.

4 Loosen the lug nuts with the lug wrench, but do not remove them. Most lug nuts turn counterclockwise.

2 Remove the spare tire from the trunk. Also take out the jack, the lug wrench, and related tools.

5 Position your jack. Different makes of cars come with different types of jacks, so check your owner's manual to learn how to use your jack. Make sure the jack is sitting on a solid, flat surface.

6 Lift the car with the jack until your flat tire is two or three inches off the ground. (*Never lie under the car when it is on the jack!*)

7 Now, finish unscrewing the lug nuts. Put them inside the wheel cover so you don't lose them.

8 Remove the flat tire, and replace it with the spare tire. Replace the lug nuts, and tighten them by hand.

9 Lower the jack until the spare tire is firmly on the ground. Remove the jack. Firmly tighten the lug nuts with the lug wrench. Work diagonally—tighten one on the top, then one on the bottom; one on the left, then one on the right; and so on.

10 Place the flat tire, the wheel cover, and all your tools in the trunk. As soon as you can, drive to a garage or a tire repair shop to get the tire fixed or replaced. You never want to be without a spare, because you never know when you'll get another flat!

Following Technical Directions

1. When you think you have a flat tire, what should you do first?

   A Drive the car to your family's garage.

   B Call your parents, and ask them to pick you up.

   C Park the car as far off the road as possible.

   D Look out your window to see if the tire's flat.

2. The best tool for loosening the lug nuts is —

   F a screwdriver

   G a lug wrench

   H a jack

   J your hand

3. You should lift the car with the jack until —

   A you can fit comfortably underneath the car

   B the car is two to three feet in the air

   C the flat tire is two to three inches off the ground

   D the flat tire comes off the wheel

4. When you remove the lug nuts, you should —

   F let them fall to the ground

   G put them in the wheel cover

   H throw them away

   J feed them to a squirrel

5. After you have changed a flat tire, what should you do next?

   A Call your parents to let them know what happened.

   B Drive to a garage to get the flat tire fixed.

   C Continue where you were going before you got the flat.

   D Throw away the flat tire.

Constructed Response

1. How can you tell you have a flat tire? List three clues.

2. List the tools needed to fix a flat tire.

3. What should you do as soon as you can after you've changed your flat tire?

SKILLS FOCUS

Reading Skills
Follow technical directions.

Media Workshop

MULTIMEDIA PRESENTATION
Public-Service Announcement

In other workshops you have written expository papers, such as informative reports, where your chief purpose has been to present information. You have also written persuasive papers, where you have offered solutions to a problem or given your interpretation of a literary work.

In a public-service announcement, your object is both to share information and to advise or persuade your public about a specific course of action. If you search the World Wide Web, you will discover that public-service announcements are issued by governmental agencies, consumer advocates, and a variety of community groups. You will also discover that a number of young people who want to help their communities have written and produced public-service announcements.

A public-service announcement may appear in different forms. It may be produced as a newsletter, a poster, a radio or television presentation, or a Web site. It may even be animated and run for less than a minute.

Planning Your Announcement

1 Choosing a Focus

In a public-service announcement you wish to raise other people's awareness of a problem or situation and get them to take action. To get ideas for your own public-service message, you can explore local newspapers, newsletters, and bulletin boards; listen to radio and television announcements; and examine public-service announcements on the World Wide Web.

The subjects of public-service announcements range widely, including topics such as environmental concerns, safety tips, health issues, animal care, nutrition, and even

Assignment

Plan and deliver a public-service announcement.

Audience

Your classmates, teacher, friends, and other students.

R U B R I C
Evaluation Criteria

A successful public-service announcement

1. focuses on an issue of public concern
2. targets its audience
3. relies on facts, examples, and other evidence to support its points
4. may use print, visuals, and sound to deliver its message

SKILLS FOCUS

Speaking and Listening Skills
Deliver a public-service announcement.

Research Strategies

- Most libraries are now equipped with online catalogs where you can locate sources. To access information, you can use **electronic databases.**

- To do research on the World Wide Web, you will need a **Web browser** to access information.

- For additional help, see Research Strategies in the Communication Handbook.

Suggested Topics

- how to behave at a school dance
- preparing for a test
- dealing with a bully
- a help line for new students
- rules for radio rookies
- conducting an interview
- tolerance for those who are different
- handling a library book
- dealing with teasing
- online etiquette

warnings about financial scams. Public-service announcements on the Web often can be accessed in more than one form. They might be available as both scripts and audios. Some use images and music to send their messages.

Consider your **purpose** and **audience.** A public-service announcement may have a large national audience or a local community audience, such as a school's student body. Choose a topic that will be of interest to your audience and that will hold their attention.

See the list on the left for suggestions for a public-service announcement that might be directed to other students in your school.

2 Researching Background Material

Learn as much as you can about the topic you have chosen for your public-service announcement. For example, if your topic is "online etiquette," you might begin by exploring a keyword like *netiquette* on a Web browser and by taking notes on the rules about online behavior. You might also take note of the special terms that are in current use, such as *flaming,* a word that means "belittling or putting down someone else's ideas." Gather the facts, examples, and reasons you will need to educate your audience.

3 Utilizing Different Media

A public-service announcement can be presented in print, or it can be presented in the form of a poster, an animated cartoon, or a recorded bulletin on radio or television. Your message can be accompanied by music, illustrations, or slides. Choose media that will express your ideas most effectively and dramatically.

Developing a Script

1 Organizing Your Ideas

Even if your public-service announcement is brief, it should include an introduction, a body, and a conclusion. (If the message is to be aired on radio or television, it probably should not exceed one minute.)

Your **introduction** should be aimed at getting your audience's attention. If the technology is available, you can use music, a transparency, or a video clip to engage your listeners. Indicate the purpose of your announcement, and emphasize its importance.

In the **body** of your public-service announcement, present your information in a clear and logical manner. To support your points, use facts, statistics, examples, and reasons. You can introduce charts or other visual evidence to accompany your announcement.

In your **conclusion,** restate your main point. You may end with a slide, a photograph, or a dramatic quotation.

2 Formatting a Public-Service Announcement

Your public-service announcement can involve visuals and sound as well as texts. What will be the general makeup or arrangement of your announcement? Will it be delivered as a brochure or flier—that is, as a small pamphlet or handbill that can be distributed? Will it be recorded on tape to be aired on radio? Will it take the form of a colorful poster?

Decide on the best format for your public-service announcement. If you are using a visual format, you might use bullets to call out your main points. You can also vary the styles of type and the size of headings to create emphasis.

On the following page you'll find a script for a public-service announcement about netiquette. This announcement has been designed as a flier to be passed out by hand or posted on a bulletin board.

Media Elements

Visual Aids
Book and magazine illustrations
Posters
Photographs
Transparencies or slides

Audio Aids
Audiotapes of voices and sound effects
Web sites
Music recordings on CD or audiotape
Live instruments

Video Aids
Clips from movies or TV

Audience: Other students who use the Web

Purpose: —To inform students about appropriate behavior online
—To give tips about communicating online

Public-Service Announcement Script

NETIQUETTE

When you "speak" to someone online, you need to observe certain rules of etiquette, just as you would in meeting someone face to face. Here are some do's and don'ts to help you maintain good relationships and have fun talking online.

Do's and Don'ts

DO pick an appropriate nickname, such as your first name or a short descriptive phrase.

DON'T use a nickname that will offend others or cause them to ignore you.

DO greet people politely. You can begin: "Hi" or "Hello everyone."

DON'T interrupt an ongoing conversation. Be sure you know the subject before you enter a conversation.

DO address individuals by using their nicknames: "LZJo, I like your idea."

DON'T type long, detailed messages. Give others a chance to speak.

DO type asterisks around a word or phrase you wish to emphasize.

DON'T type in capital letters or use boldface. This is like screaming at people.

DO use polite language. Discuss disagreements calmly. Always respect others' beliefs and opinions.

DON'T use or accept any verbal abuse. Ignore any person who uses offensive language or whose behavior is rude.

DO be careful when sharing personal information. Give out only details that you are comfortable sharing with strangers.

DON'T ask personal questions. Don't give out your last name, address, or phone number. Don't send photographs.

Chatting with your friends online can be great fun as long as you follow these simple rules and are considerate of one another.

Online Shorthand

AFK	Away from keyboard	FYI	For your information	OIC	Oh, I see
B4	Before	K	OK	ROFL	Rolling on the floor laughing
BRB	Be right back	L8R	Later		
BTW	By the way	LOL	Laugh out loud	THX	Thanks
CUL	See you later	MSG	Message	WB	Welcome back
EOM	End of message	NRN	No reply necessary	WTG	Way to go

Evaluating and Revising

Use the following chart to evaluate and revise your public-service announcement.

Public–Service Announcement: Content and Organization Guidelines		
Evaluation Questions	▶ **Tips**	▶ **Revision Techniques**
❶ Does your introduction state the purpose of your message?	▶ **Underline** the statement that shows the focus of your message.	▶ **Add** a statement that identifies your purpose and the importance of your message.
❷ Have you targeted your audience?	▶ **Bracket** words or phrases that identify your audience.	▶ If appropriate, **name** the individuals or groups who are affected.
❸ Have you supplied facts, examples, and other evidence to support your message?	▶ **Put a star** next to evidence that supports your message.	▶ **Add** facts, examples, and other details that support your main points.
❹ Did you use different forms of media in your presentation?	▶ **Put a check mark** next to each different form of media used in your presentation.	▶ When possible, **replace** print with another form of media, such as an illustration, a slide, or a video clip.
❺ Did you wrap up your message in your conclusion?	▶ **Underline** the statement that provides a conclusion to your message.	▶ **Add** a sentence that restates your position, or **add** a dramatic quotation.

On the next page is a public-service announcement that has been revised. Use the questions below the model to evaluate the writer's changes.

INTERNET

Media Tutorials

Keyword: LE5 7-8

PROOFREADING

TIP

- Ask a classmate to proofread your public-service announcement for errors in spelling, grammar, and mechanics.

Communications Handbook

H E L P

See Proofreaders' Marks.

PUBLISHING

TIPS

- Display your public-service announcement in an appropriate place, such as a bulletin board or the library.

- If your announcement has been taped, request permission to have it aired over the public-address system.

- Create a Web page for your class's public-service announcements.

Revision Model

When does teasing stop being a playful joke and turn into cruelty or meanness? Before you let your tongue slip, ask yourself, "How would I feel if someone said that about me?" You may think an insulting comment that embarrasses someone is quite innocent, but it is always

rude

~~bad~~ to hurt a person's feelings. *A good rule is to be considerate of others.*

respond

How should you ~~act~~ if someone teases you? ~~What is the best way to handle this?~~ Try to stay cool. Instead of showing anger, ignore the remark. Just laugh or walk away. If your response is good-natured, you will ~~keep~~ *discourage* the teaser from trying again.

Evaluating the Revision

1. Which details did the writer add? Do these details improve the message? Why or why not?

2. Which details did the writer delete? Why do you think these cuts were made?

3. How did the writer rearrange material? Do you think this change is an improvement? Explain.

Collection 8: Skills Review

Speaking and Listening Skills

Test Practice

DIRECTIONS: Read the following public-service announcement. Then, read the questions below it. Choose the best answer to each question, and mark your answers on your own piece of paper.

(1) Fellow middle schoolers, since our team placed first in the statewide debates, our school has become big news. (2) A reporter from the town newspaper wants to spend a day here, observing and asking questions. (3) The reporter has won several awards for her local coverage. (4) So here are some tips for what to do if you are interviewed. (5) Try to stay relaxed and keep your sense of humor. (6) Be as accurate as you can in your answers. (7) Listen to the questions carefully before you answer. (8) Take your time to respond. (9) If you don't understand a question, ask the interviewer to repeat or restate it. (10) We want the school to look good, so please do your best to make a good impression.

1. The best title for this announcement would be —
    A   Conducting an Interview
    B   How to Be Interviewed
    C   Interviewer and Interviewee
    D   Following Up an Interview

2. Which sentence is unnecessary and can be deleted?
    F   sentence 3
    G   sentence 5
    H   sentence 7
    J   sentence 9

3. The message of this public-service announcement would very likely be delivered —
    A   over the school's public-address system
    B   on a local radio station
    C   in a town newspaper
    D   on a billboard

4. Which of these additional tips would be appropriate?
    F   Give the interviewer a list of questions.
    G   Maintain eye contact throughout the interview.
    H   Answer questions simply with a yes or no.
    J   Review the interviewer's notes.

5. Which sentence reveals the underlying purpose of this public-service announcement?
    A   sentence 1
    B   sentence 2
    C   sentence 4
    D   sentence 10

SKILLS FOCUS

Speaking and Listening Skills
Analyze a public-service announcement.

Reading for Life: Magazines and Web Sites

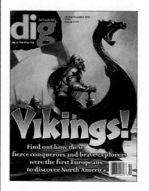

Dig We Must

Do you dig ancient artifacts? If you do, unearth a copy of *Archaeology's dig*. This magazine covers the latest discoveries in the field of archaeology, from fossils to Vikings. It also features games and experiments and invites you to ask Dr. Dig all the questions you have about archaeology.

Up-to-Date

When a news story breaks, the magazine *Time for Kids* is there to report it. For the latest on history, sports, and culture, look on its Web site at www.timeforkids.com. You can contribute to *Time for Kids* by participating in its polls and writing letters in response to its stories and features.

Get Creative!

If you like writing, reading, and drawing, look for *Stone Soup: The Magazine by Young Writers and Artists*. Here you'll find short stories and poems written by kids from all around the world. Check out book reviews when you're looking for a new book to read. You may even decide to submit your own work for publication. Go to its Web site, www.stonesoup.com, for more links to sites for young writers, such as "ZuZu," "Young Girl Writers," and "Just Write."

Journey to the Past

Have you wondered how people lived during the Renaissance? Did you ever want to learn more about Mohammed, Charlemagne, and other leaders from world history? If you're curious about the past, read an issue of the magazine *Calliope*. You might not be able to put it down. In addition to its fantastic features, *Calliope* includes time lines, maps, and activities to enhance your understanding of history.

Nonfiction

The Ways of the World

Ever wondered where you can learn about the latest developments in computers and science? *Scientific American Explorations* magazine offers a comprehensive guide to technology and a whole lot more. Find out how to conduct science experiments in your home or classroom, and look into "Why and How," a feature that explains some of the mysteries of nature.

Endless Stories

The Web site storybookonline.net supplies compelling ways to practice your writing: Submit your own work of fiction, or collaborate with other writers on a story. Start your own stories, and let other writers contribute twists and turns to your plot. The site features links to book readings, fairy tales, and games.

Back Through Time

The Learning Curve's online "Millennium Exhibition" looks back on the last thousand years of England's history. Learn the importance of historic documents such as the Magna Carta. Read brief biographies of kings and queens, the story behind the invention of the printing press, and other interesting anecdotes. The "Millennium Exhibition" Web site is organized by century and can be found at learningcurve.pro.gov.uk/millennium /default.htm.

Friendly Advice

How do you decide what to buy and what to leave on the store shelf? *Consumer Reports* magazine offers guidance at its Web site designed for young people: zillions.org. Kids test such products as jeans and backpacks, evaluating their durability and safety. Their findings are then posted on the site.

Resource Center

The Parisian Novels (The Yellow Books), Vincent van Gogh, 1888.

by **Flo Ota De Lange and Sheri Henderson**

Strategies for Taking a Multiple-Choice Test

If you have ever watched a quiz show on TV, you know how multiple-choice tests work. You get a question and (usually) four choices. Your job is to pick the correct one. Easy! (Don't you wish?) Taking multiple-choice tests will get a whole lot easier when you apply these Test Smarts:

T rack your time.

E xpect success.

S tudy the directions.

T ake it all in.

S pot those numbers.

M aster the questions.

A nticipate the answers.

R ely on 50/50.

T ry. Try. Try.

S earch for skips and smudges.

Track Your Time

You race through a test for fear you won't finish, and then you sit watching your hair grow because you finished early, or you realize you have only five minutes left to complete eleven zillion questions. Sound familiar? You can avoid both problems if you take a few minutes before you start to estimate how much time you have for each question. Using all the time you are given can help you avoid making errors. Follow these tips to set **checkpoints:**

- How many questions should be completed when one quarter of the time is gone?

- What should the clock read when you are halfway through the questions?

- If you find yourself behind your checkpoints, you can speed up.

- If you are ahead, you can—and should—slow down.

Expect Success

Top athletes know that attitude affects performance. They learn to deal with their negative thoughts, to get on top of their mental game. So can you! But how? Do you compare yourself with others? Most top athletes will tell you that they compete against only one person: themselves. They know they cannot change another person's performance. Instead, they study their own performance and find ways to improve it. That makes sense for you too. You are older and more experienced than you were the day you took your last big test, right? So review your last scores. Figure out just what you need to do to top that "kid" you used to be. You can!

What if you get anxious? It's OK if you do. A little nervousness will help you focus. Of course, if you're so nervous that you think you might get sick or faint, take time to relax for a few minutes. Calm bodies breathe slowly. You can fool yours into feeling calmer and thinking more clearly by taking a few deep breaths—five slow counts in, five out. Take charge, take five, and then take the test.

Study the Directions

You're ready to go, go, go, but first it's wait, wait, wait. Pencils. Paper. Answer sheets. Lots of directions. Listen! In order to follow directions, you have to know them. Read all test directions as if they contain the key to lifetime happiness and several years' allowance. Then, read them again. Study the answer sheet. How is it laid out? Is it

1

2

3

4

or

1   2   3   4 ?

What about answer choices? Are they arranged

A   B   C   D

or

A   B

C   D ?

Directions count. Be very, very sure you know exactly what to do and how to do it before you make your first mark.

Take It All In

When you finally hear the words "You may begin," briefly **preview the test** to get a mental map of your tasks:

- Know how many questions you have to complete.
- Know where to stop.
- Set your time checkpoints.
- Do the easy sections first; easy questions are worth just as many points as hard ones.

Spot Those Numbers

"I got off by one and spent all my time trying to fix my answer sheet." Oops. Make it a habit to

- match the number of each question to the numbered space on the answer sheet every time
- leave the answer space on your answer sheet blank if you skip a question
- keep a list of your blank spaces on scratch paper or somewhere else—but *not* on your answer sheet. The less you have to erase on your answer sheet, the better.

Master the Questions

"I knew that answer, but I thought the question asked something else." Be sure—very sure—that you **know what a question is asking you.** Read the question at least twice before reading the answer choices. Approach it as you would a mystery story or a riddle. Look for clues. Watch especially for words like *not* and *except*—they tell you to look for the choice that is false or different from the other choices or opposite in some way. If you are taking a reading-comprehension test, read the selection, master all the questions, and then re-read the selection. The answers will be likely to pop out the second time around. Remember: A test isn't trying to trick you; it's trying to test your knowledge and your ability to think clearly.

Anticipate the Answers

All right, you now understand the question. Before you read the answer choices, **answer the question yourself. Then, read the choices.**

If the answer you gave is among the choices listed, it is probably correct.

Rely on 50/50

"I . . . have . . . no . . . clue." You understand the question. You gave an answer, but your answer is not listed, or perhaps you drew a complete blank. It happens. Time to **make an educated guess**—not a *wild* guess, but an *educated* guess. Think about quiz shows again, and you'll know the value of the 50/50 play. When two answers are eliminated, the contestant has a 50/50 chance of choosing the correct one. You can use elimination too.

Always read every choice carefully. **Watch out for distracters**—choices that may be true but are too broad, too narrow, or not relevant to the question. Eliminate the least likely choice. Then, eliminate the next, and so on until you find the best one. If two choices seem equally correct, look to see if "All of the above" is an option. If it is, that might be your choice. If no choice seems correct, look for "None of the above."

Try. Try. Try.

Keep at it. **Don't give up**. This sounds obvious, so why say it? You might be surprised by how many students do give up. Think of tests as a kind of marathon. Just as in any marathon, people get bored, tired, hungry, thirsty, hot, discouraged. They may begin to feel sick or develop aches and pains. They decide the test doesn't matter that much. They decide they don't care if it does—there'll always be next time; whose idea was this, anyway? They lose focus. Don't do it.

Remember: The last question is worth just as much as the first question, and the questions on a test don't get harder as you go. If the question you just finished was really hard, an easier one is probably coming up soon. Take a deep breath, and keep on slogging. Give it your all, all the way to the finish.

Search for Skips and Smudges

"Hey! I got that one right, and the machine marked it wrong!" If you have ever—ever—had this experience, pay attention! When this happens in class, your teacher can give you the extra point. On a machine-scored test, however, you would lose the point and never know why. So, listen up: All machine-scored answer sheets have a series of lines marching down the side. The machine stops at the first line and scans across it for your answer, stops at the second line, scans, stops at the third line, scans, and so on, all the way to the end. The machine is looking for a dark, heavy mark. If it finds one where it should be, you get the point. What if you left that question blank? A lost point. What if you changed an answer and didn't quite get the first mark erased? The machine sees two answers instead of one. A lost point. What if you made a mark to help yourself remember where you skipped an answer? You filled in the answer later but forgot to erase the mark. The machine again sees two marks. Another lost point. What if your marks are not very dark? The machine sees blank spaces. More lost points.

To avoid losing points, take time at the end of the test to make sure you

- did not skip any answers
- gave one answer for each question
- made the marks heavy and dark and within the lines

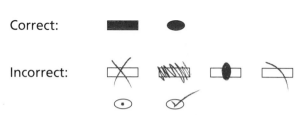

Get rid of smudges. Make sure there are no stray pencil marks on your answer sheet. Cleanly erase those places where you changed your mind. Check for little stray marks from pencil tapping. Check everything. You are the only person who can.

Reading Comprehension

Many tests have a section called **reading comprehension.** The good news is that you do not have to study for this part of the test. Taking a reading-comprehension test is a bit like playing ball. You don't know where the ball will land, so you have to stay alert to all possibilities. However, just as the ball can come at you in only a few ways, there are only a few kinds of questions on reading-comprehension tests. This discussion will help you identify the most common ones. Two kinds of texts are used here. The first one is an informational text. The second is an updated fairy tale.

DIRECTIONS: Read the following selection. Then, choose the best answer for each question. Mark each answer on your answer sheet in the square provided.

Night Lights on the High Seas

For centuries, lighthouses have been used to alert sailors that land is near, to point out dangerous rocks and reefs, and to cast a bright light into the night to guide ships on their way. Seafarers have relied on these structures since the days of ancient Egypt. The lighthouse built in 300 B.C. on Pharos, an island near Alexandria, was regarded as one of the Seven Wonders of the World.

Lighthouses help to guide ships at night by giving off an intense beam that flashes every few seconds. Until the eighteenth century, the source of light was an oak-log fire. Coal fire was used for many years after that, until electricity became common in the early twentieth century. Some modern lighthouses also send out radio signals to help ships find their way in foggy weather. Even in their modern form, lighthouses serve their ancient purpose as guiding lights, flashing specks of civilization in the dark, lonely waters of night.

ITEM 1 asks for vocabulary knowledge.

1. In the first paragraph, the word seafarers means —

   A oceans

   B sailors

   C fish

   D ships

Answer: Look at the surrounding sentences, or **context,** to see which definition fits.

A is incorrect. The word *ocean* is another word for "sea," but oceans do not rely on lighthouses.

B is the best answer. In the context of the passage, it makes sense that *sailors* have relied on lighthouses for centuries.

C is incorrect. Fish live and travel in the sea, but nothing in the passage indicates that they depend on lighthouses.

D is incorrect. The safety of ships on the ocean depends on lighthouses. However, it is the *sailors* on the ships who have "relied on these structures" for centuries.

ITEM 2 asks for close reading. Read carefully to see if the answer is stated directly in the text.

2. What was used to produce the light in lighthouses before the eighteenth century?

   F Wood

   G Coal

   H Gas

   J Electricity

Answer: Read the passage carefully to find the answer.

F is the correct answer. The second sentence of the second paragraph indicates that "until the eighteenth century, the source of light was an oak-log fire." The words *oak* and *log* clearly indicate that "wood" is the right choice.

ITEM 3 asks for an inference.

3. What is the main idea of this passage?

   A Working in a lighthouse is a dangerous job.

   B Modern lighthouses are very different from those of long ago.

   C The first lighthouse was built in 300 B.C. on the island of Pharos.

   D Lighthouses have helped guide ships for thousands of years.

Answer: Think about which statement covers the passage as a whole.

A is incorrect. The passage does not provide an explanation of working in a lighthouse.

B is incorrect. Lighthouses have not changed that much over the years.

C is incorrect. It is only one detail in the passage.

D is the best answer. It covers most of the details in the passage.

ITEM 4 asks for a prediction.

4. As more and more ships become equipped with navigational computers, what will probably happen?

   F More lighthouses will be built.

   G There will be more shipping accidents.

   H The number of lighthouses will be reduced.

   J Different energy sources will be used in lighthouses.

Answer: Find the information in the passage that supports a probable future outcome.

F is incorrect. Navigational computers will most likely reduce the need for lighthouses.

G is incorrect. The navigational computers will protect the ships from accidents.

H is the best answer. Navigational computers mean that ships will no longer need to rely on lighthouses for guidance.

J is incorrect. The passage does not say anything about new or different energy sources.

ITEM 5 asks you to recognize an opinion.

5. Which is an **opinion** expressed in the passage?

   A The beam from a lighthouse flashes every few seconds.

   B Modern lighthouses send out radio signals.

   C Pharos is an island near Alexandria.

   D The ocean waters are lonely at night.

Answer: A **fact** can be proved true or false. An **opinion,** a personal feeling or belief, cannot be proved true or false. **A, B,** and **C** are facts that can be proved true or false. **D is correct** because it is the only opinion.

ITEM 6 asks you to decide why the author wrote the passage.

6. What is the author's main **purpose** for writing this passage?

   F To entertain readers with an exciting story

   G To inform readers about the history of lighthouses

   H To persuade readers to visit a lighthouse

   J To describe what life in a lighthouse is like

Answer: Look at the information given in the passage, and decide what the writer's purpose was in writing.

F is incorrect. The writer does not tell a story.

G is the best answer. The writer presents information about the function of light-houses over time.

H is incorrect. The writer's purpose is not to persuade readers to visit a lighthouse.

J is incorrect. The writer never tells what it's like to live in a lighthouse.

DIRECTIONS: Read the following selection. Then, choose the best answer for each question. Mark each answer on your answer sheet in the space provided.

A Technologically Correct Fairy Tale:

Jack and the Beanstalk

There once was a poor widow who lived in a small cottage with her son, Jack. Jack was a good-hearted fellow who devoted all his time to a mega-computer game. Since Jack did not have a paying job, he and his widowed mother were very poor.

The day arrived when the widow had sold all her possessions via the Internet, except for an elderly cow. Jack was to sell the cow at the market since his mother was too frail to make the trip.

"Get a good price for her," the widow instructed.

"Yes, Mother," Jack answered.

Off he went with the cow in tow.

Out on the highway, Jack was stopped by a man who offered to trade him a handful of oddly shaped, brightly colored beans for the cow. "These are turbo-beans," the man whispered. While Jack didn't know exactly what that meant, he did know that the word *turbo* made the beans sound special, so he agreed to the trade. When he got home, he proudly handed the beans to his mother. She promptly tossed them out the window, declaring she didn't know what he could have been thinking. . . .

ITEM 1 is a vocabulary question. To answer it, consider the surrounding words, or **context,** to identify the best definition.

1. In the first paragraph the underlined word devoted means —

   A donated

   B avoided

   C captured

   D dedicated

A is incorrect. *Donated* means "gave someone something of value." It doesn't fit in this context.

B is incorrect. It doesn't fit the context, which shows what Jack did with his time, not what he didn't do.

C is incorrect. It doesn't fit in the context.

D is the best answer. In this context, *devoted* means "dedicated" or "gave one's time to a particular pursuit."

ITEM 2 is another vocabulary question.

2. In the second paragraph of the fairy tale, frail means —

   F proud

   G weak

   H stubborn

   J forceful

The best answer is G, since it offers the only reason why the widow would not be able to make the trip herself.

ITEM 3 is a factual question. Re-read the fairy tale, and you'll find the answer.

3. How did the widow sell all of her possessions, except for the old cow?

   A She sold them via the Internet.

   B She set up a shop on the highway.

   C She sold them to her neighbors.

   D She sold them to the man with the beans.

A is the best answer. The fairy tale clearly states that she sold her possessions on the Internet.

B is incorrect. Jack met the man with the beans on the main highway. The widow did not go there.

C is incorrect. Neighbors are not mentioned in the selection.

D is incorrect. Jack, not the widow, traded the cow for the beans.

ITEM 4 asks you to analyze a cause-and-effect relationship. Don't worry, though. The answer is in the text.

4. Because Jack didn't have a paying job, he and his mother were —

    F   supported by an uncle

    G   very poor

    H   reduced to stealing

    J   very angry

F is incorrect. An uncle is not mentioned in the story.

G is the best answer. The fairy tale says that they were poor.

H is incorrect. Stealing is not mentioned in the story.

J is incorrect. Anger is not mentioned in the story.

ITEM 5 requires that you make an **inference** based on the text.

5. Jack's mother didn't think beans for a cow was a good trade. How do you know this?

    A   She explains that a cow is worth more than a handful of beans.

    B   Jack was supposed to sell the cow.

C   The man cheated Jack.

D   She tossed the beans out the window.

A is incorrect. Jack's mother doesn't say this in the story.

B is incorrect. This is true, but it doesn't explain why his mother didn't think it was a good trade.

C is incorrect. This may be true, but it doesn't tell us how we know what Jack's mother thought of the trade.

D is the best answer. Her actions show what she thought of the trade.

ITEM 6 asks you to use your **prior knowledge** about fairy tales to predict the outcome of this tale.

6. If this story ended like a typical fairy tale, which of the following predictions would you make?

    F   The beans do, indeed, prove worthless.

    G   The beans become the key to lifelong happiness for Jack and his mother.

    H   The beans end up in a stew.

    J   The cow comes home.

F is incorrect. The fairy tale cannot have its "happily ever after" ending if the beans are worthless.

G is the best answer. In fairy tales, magical gifts from strangers often bring great rewards in the end.

H is incorrect. This is too ordinary an ending for a fairy tale.

J is incorrect. This ending is also too ordinary for a fairy tale.

Strategies for Taking Writing Tests

Writing a Story

Some tests may include writing prompts that ask you to write a narrative, or story. The following steps will help you write a **story**. The responses are based on this prompt.

Prompt

Write a short fictional narrative. The story should include major and minor characters, a thoroughly developed plot, and a definite setting.

> **STEP 1** **Read the prompt carefully.** Does the prompt ask you to write a **fictional story** (a made-up story) or an **autobiographical story** (a story of something that really happened to you)?

The word "fictional" tells me that the prompt is asking for a made-up story.

> **STEP 2** **Outline the plot of your narrative.** Explain the conflict, the climax, and the resolution.

Conflict—the main character, Sue, wants to win the fencing tournament. Climax—Sue fences against the champion. Resolution—Sue wins but feels bad when she sees her opponent crying.

> **STEP 3** **Identify the major and minor characters.** What do they look and act like? How do they sound when they speak?

Major character—Sue is tall and lanky; she is shy; she is very competitive. Minor character—Sue's competitor, Tory, is tall; she is confident and sometimes rude.

> **STEP 4** **Identify the setting of your narrative.** Where and when does your story take place?

The story takes place in January during the state fencing championships in a gymnasium.

> **STEP 5** **Draft your narrative, adding dialogue, suspense, and sensory details.**

I plan to create suspense by drawing out the moment when Sue must decide what to do when she sees Tory crying. I will use sensory details to describe how she feels. I will also include dialogue of her conversation with Tory.

> **STEP 6** **Revise and proofread your narrative.** Make sure that you have organized the events in your story in a logical order. Add transitions that show time, such as *earlier, afterward, at the same time,* and *later.*

Writing a Summary

Some tests include writing prompts like the one to the right.

Prompt

Read the article "The Body's Defenses," and then summarize it. In your summary, include the main idea and significant details of the article.

To write a **summary** of a passage, you rewrite in your own words the passage's main idea and significant details. The summary should both paraphrase and condense the original. A summary of a short passage should be about one-third as long. For a longer selection, a summary should include no more than one sentence for each paragraph.

The following steps will help you write an effective summary in response to a prompt.

STEP 1 Read the passage carefully. Identify the main idea, and restate it in your own words. What is the most important point the writer is making about the topic? How would *you* say it?

STEP 2 Identify significant details to include in the summary. Which details directly support the main idea? List at least one key idea or detail from each paragraph.

STEP 3 Write the main idea and most significant details in a paragraph, using your own words. Give details in the same order they are presented in the passage.

Writing a Response to Literature

On a writing test, you may be asked to write a **literary response.** Often on such tests, you will be given a literary selection to read and a prompt such as the one on the right.

The following steps and the partial student responses will help you respond to a prompt like the one above. The short story "Duffy's Jacket" can be found on pages 5–11.

Prompt

What sort of character is Andrew from the short story "Duffy's Jacket"? Analyze his thoughts, actions, and words.

▶ **STEP 1 Read the prompt carefully, noting key words.** Key words might include a verb—such as *analyze, identify,* or *explain*—and a literary element—such as *plot, character, setting,* or *theme.*

The key words are "analyze" and "character."

▶ **STEP 2 Read the selection at least twice.** Read first for the overall meaning of the work. Then, read the selection a second time, keeping the key words from the prompt in mind.

▶ **STEP 3 Write a main idea statement.** Your main idea statement should give the title and author of the work and should directly address the prompt.

Andrew, the narrator of "Duffy's Jacket" by Bruce Coville, is similar to my friend Joss; both are easygoing and funny.

▶ **STEP 4 Find specific examples and details from the selection to support your main idea.** If you include quotations from the literary work, remember to enclose them in quotation marks.

When Andrew's mom gets mad at Andrew for not reminding Duffy to get his jacket, Andrew thinks to himself, "What do I look like, a walking memo pad?"

▶ **STEP 5 Draft, revise, and proofread your response.** To create coherence, use transitions between ideas, such as *for example, however,* and *finally.* When you have written your draft, re-read it to make sure you have presented your ideas clearly. Also, check to see that you have fully addressed all the key words in the prompt. Finally, proofread to correct mistakes in spelling, punctuation, and capitalization.

Using the T.H.E.M.E.S. Strategy on a Writing Test

Writing tests often ask you to write a **persuasive essay** in response to a prompt. Most of these prompts give you a topic, but you must identify your position and generate support for your position. Thinking of what to say in a limited amount of time is one of the most difficult parts of such a test.

Use the T.H.E.M.E.S. strategy, explained in the steps below, to generate support for a position quickly. The student responses are based on this prompt.

Prompt

The city council is considering building a parking garage or a park on an empty lot. Write an essay that takes a position on the issue and defends the position with relevant support.

Each letter in T.H.E.M.E.S. stands for a category you could use to trigger ideas for supporting your position in a persuasive essay.

T=Time **H=Health** **E=Education** **M=Money** **E=Environment** **S=Safety**

▶ **STEP 1 Identify your position on the topic given in the prompt.**

The city council should build a park.

▶ **STEP 2 Use T.H.E.M.E.S to list benefits for your position.**

T = A park would take less time to build than a garage. H = People could use the park to exercise and remain healthy. E = People might become more aware, or educated, about the wildlife and plants that occupy the area. M = The city would save money because constructing playscapes and jogging trails is less expensive than clearing the land and building a garage. E = The environment would benefit because the trees and homes of animals are not destroyed. S = Without a garage, fewer cars may drive in the area, reducing the safety hazard of automobile accidents.

▶ **STEP 3 Identify the three strongest reasons you developed using T.H.E.M.E.S.** Your strongest reasons will be those for which you have the most evidence and those that address readers' concerns about the topic.

My three strongest reasons for building a park are health benefits, reduced costs, and environmental benefits. These are the issues that I think concern my readers the most.

Handbook of Literary Terms

For more information about a topic, turn to the page(s) in this book indicated on a separate line at the end of the entries. To learn more about *Alliteration,* for example, turn to pages 577 and 601.

On another line are cross-references to entries in this handbook that provide closely related information. For instance, at the end of *Autobiography* is a cross-reference to *Biography.*

ALLITERATION **The repetition of the same or very similar consonant sounds in words that are close together.** Though alliteration usually occurs at the beginning of words, it can also occur within or at the end of words. Among other things, alliteration can help establish a mood, emphasize words, and serve as a memory aid. In the following example the *s* sound is repeated at the beginning of the words *silken* and *sad* and within the words *uncertain* and *rustling:*

> And the silken sad uncertain rustling of each
> purple curtain
>
> —Edgar Allan Poe, from
> "The Raven"

See pages 577, 601.

ALLUSION **A reference to a statement, a person, a place, or an event from literature, history, religion, mythology, politics, sports, or science.** Allusions enrich the reading experience. Writers expect readers to recognize an allusion and to think, almost at the same time, about the literary work and the person, place, or event that it refers to. The following lines, describing a tunnel in the snow, contain an allusion to Aladdin, a character in *The Thousand and One Nights:*

> With mittened hands, and caps drawn low,
> To guard our necks and ears from snow,
> We cut the solid whiteness through.
> And, where the drift was deepest, made
> A tunnel walled and overlaid
> With dazzling crystal: we had read
> Of rare Aladdin's wondrous cave,
> And to our own his name we gave.
>
> —John Greenleaf Whittier,
> from "Snow-Bound"

The cave in the tale contains a magic lamp that helps Aladdin discover vast riches. By alluding to Aladdin's cave, Whittier makes us see the icy tunnel in the snow as a magical, fairy-tale place.

The cartoon below makes an allusion to a popular fairy tale.

"Now, this policy will cover your home for fire, theft, flood and huffing and puffing."

Reprinted with permission of The Saturday Evening Post, © 1993, BFL&MS, Inc., Indianapolis.

See pages 174, 687.

ATMOSPHERE The overall mood or emotion of a work of literature. A work's atmosphere can often be described with one or two adjectives, such as *scary, dreamy, happy, sad,* or *nostalgic.* A writer creates atmosphere by using images, sounds, and descriptions that convey a particular feeling.

See also *Mood.*

AUTOBIOGRAPHY The story of a person's life, written or told by that person. Maijue Xiong wrote an autobiography called "An Unforgettable Journey" (page 403) about her escape from war-torn Laos as a child. Another well-known autobiographical work is Maya Angelou's *I Know Why the Caged Bird Sings.*

See pages 402, 499, 672, 846.
See also *Biography.*

BIOGRAPHY The story of a real person's life, written or told by another person. Milton Meltzer has written a number of biographies of historical figures, such as George Washington and Mark Twain. "Elizabeth I" (page 416) is his biography of the remarkable queen of England who reigned in the sixteenth century. Frequent subjects of biographies are movie stars, television personalities, politicians, sports figures, self-made millionaires, even underworld figures. Biographies are among the most popular forms of contemporary literature.

See pages 414, 479, 499, 853.
See also *Autobiography.*

CHARACTER A person or animal who takes part in the action of a story, play, or other literary work. In some works, such as Aesop's fables, a character is an animal. In myths and legends a character may be a god or a superhero. Most often a character is an ordinary human being, such as Kevin in "User Friendly" (page 272).

The process of revealing the personality of a character in a story is called **characterization.** A writer can reveal a character in the following ways:

1. by letting you hear the character speak

2. by describing how the character looks and dresses

3. by letting you listen to the character's inner thoughts and feelings

4. by revealing what other people in the story think or say about the character

5. by showing you what the character does—how he or she acts

6. by telling you directly what the character's personality is like (cruel, kind, sneaky, brave, and so on)

When a writer uses the first five ways to reveal a character, you must make an inference, based on the evidence the writer provides, to decide what the character is like. When a writer uses the sixth method, however, you don't make a decision but are told directly what kind of person the character is.

Characters can be classified as static or dynamic. A **static character** is one who does not change much in the course of a work. Mr. Andersen in "Song of the Trees" (page 509) is a static character. By contrast, a **dynamic character** changes as a result of the story's events. Keevan in "The Smallest Dragonboy" (page 147) is a dynamic character.

A character's **motivation** is any force that drives or moves the character to behave in a particular way. Many characters are motivated by the force of fear or love or ambition.

See pages 128–129, 130, 136, 146, 174, 190, 296.

CONFLICT A struggle or clash between opposing characters or opposing forces. In an **external conflict** a character struggles against some outside force. This outside force may be another character or society as a whole or a storm or a grizzly bear or even a machine. In "Three Skeleton Key" (page 39), the characters have an external conflict with a swarm of sea rats. An **internal conflict,** on the other hand, takes place within a character's mind. It is a struggle between opposing needs, desires, or emotions. In "After Twenty Years" (page 357), Officer Wells must resolve an internal conflict: Should he arrest an old friend or let him go?

See pages 2, 14.

CONNOTATION The feelings and associations that a word suggests. For example, *tiny*, *cramped*, and *compact* all have about the same dictionary definition, or **denotation,** but they have different connotations. A manufacturer of small cars would not describe its product as tiny or cramped. Instead, the company might say that its cars are compact. To grasp a writer's full meaning, you must pay attention not only to the literal definitions of words but also to their connotations. Connotations can be especially important in poetry.

See page 525.

DENOTATION The literal, dictionary definition of a word.

See page 525.
See also *Connotation.*

DESCRIPTION The kind of writing that creates a clear image of something, usually by using details that appeal to one or more of the senses: sight, hearing, smell, taste, and touch. Writers use description in all forms of fiction, nonfiction, and poetry. In "Fish Cheeks" (page 528), Amy Tan vividly describes the colors, sounds, and tastes of her family's Christmas celebration.

DIALECT A way of speaking that is characteristic of a particular region or group of people. A dialect may have a distinct vocabulary, pronunciation system, and grammar. In a sense, we all speak a dialect. One dialect usually becomes dominant in a country or culture and is accepted as the standard way of speaking. In the United States, for example, the formal written language is known as standard English. This is the dialect used in most newspapers and magazines.

Writers often reproduce regional dialects, or speech that reveals a character's economic or social class, in order to give a story local color. Mr. Baumer in "Bargain" (page 369) speaks in a dialect that reveals that his first language is German. The poem "Madam and the Rent Man" (page 561) is written in a dialect spoken in some urban African American communities in the northeastern United States.

See page 186.

DIALOGUE A conversation between two or more characters. Most stage dramas consist of dialogue together with stage directions. (Screenplays and teleplays sometimes include an unseen narrator.) The dialogue in a drama, such as *The Monsters Are Due on Maple Street* (page 59), must move the plot along and reveal its characters almost single-handedly. Dialogue is also an important element in most stories and novels as well as in some poems and nonfiction. It is one of the most effective ways for a writer to show what a character is like. It can also add realism and humor.

In the written form of a play, dialogue appears without quotation marks. In prose or poetry, however, dialogue is usually enclosed in quotation marks.

A **monologue** is a part of a drama in which one character speaks alone.

See page 495.

DRAMA A story written to be acted for an audience. (A drama can also be appreciated and enjoyed in written form.) In a drama, such as *The Monsters Are Due on Maple Street* (page 59), the action is usually driven by characters who want something very much and take steps to get it. The related events that take place within a drama are often separated into **acts.** Each act is often made up of shorter sections, or **scenes.** Most plays have three acts, but there are many, many variations. The elements of a drama are often described as **introduction** or **exposition, complications, conflict, climax,** and **resolution.**

ESSAY A short piece of nonfiction prose that examines a single subject. Most essays can be categorized as either personal or formal.

The **personal essay** generally reveals a great deal about the writer's personality and tastes. Its tone is often conversational, sometimes even humorous. In a personal essay the focus is the writer's feelings and response to an experience.

The **formal essay** is usually serious, objective, and impersonal in tone. Its purpose is to inform readers about a topic or to persuade them to accept the writer's views.

See pages 479, 527, 533.

FABLE A brief story in prose or verse that teaches a moral or gives a practical lesson about how to get along in life. The characters of most fables are animals that behave and speak like human beings. Some of the most popular fables are attributed to Aesop, who is thought to have been a slave in ancient Greece.

See also *Folk Tale, Myth.*

FICTION A prose account that is made up rather than true. The term *fiction* usually refers to novels and short stories. Fiction may be based on a writer's experiences or on historical events, but characters, events, and

other details are altered or added by the writer to create a desired effect. "A Rice Sandwich" (page 169) is a fictional account based on an episode in the writer's childhood.

See pages 478–479.
See also *Nonfiction.*

FIGURE OF SPEECH A word or phrase that describes one thing in terms of something else and is not literally true. Figures of speech always involve some sort of imaginative comparison between seemingly unlike things. The most common forms are **simile** ("The stars were like diamonds"), **metaphor** ("My soul is an enchanted boat"), and **personification** ("The sun smiled down on the emerald-green fields").

See pages 546, 548, 551, 555, 609.
See also *Metaphor, Personification, Simile.*

FLASHBACK An interruption in the action of a plot to tell what happened at an earlier time. A flashback breaks the usual movement of the narrative by going back in time. It usually gives background information that helps the reader understand the present situation. "A Mason-Dixon Memory" (page 534) contains a long flashback.

A break in the unfolding of a plot to an episode in the future is known as a **flash-forward.**

See page 533.

FOLK TALE A story with no known author that originally was passed on from one generation to another by word of mouth. Folk tales tend to travel, so similar plots and characters are found in several cultures. For example, "Yeh-Shen" (page 383) is a Chinese folk tale that is very similar to the European story of Cinderella. Folk tales often contain **fantastic** elements, or events that could not happen in the world as we know it.

See pages 696–697, 698, 707, 718, 724, 732, 747, 758.
See also *Fable, Myth.*

FORESHADOWING **The use of clues to suggest events that will happen later in the plot.** Foreshadowing is used to build suspense or create anxiety. In a drama a gun found in a bureau drawer in Act One is likely to foreshadow violence later in the play. In "Three Skeleton Key" (page 39), the story of three convicts who perished on the key foreshadows the danger the three lighthouse keepers will face.

> See pages 2, 38, 356.
> See also *Suspense.*

FREE VERSE **Poetry without a regular meter or a rhyme scheme.** Poets writing in free verse try to capture the natural rhythms of ordinary speech. To create their music, poets writing in free verse may use internal rhyme, repetition, alliteration, and onomatopoeia. Free verse also frequently makes use of vivid imagery. The following poem in free verse effectively uses images and the repetition of words to describe the effects of a family's eviction for not paying rent:

The 1st

What I remember about that day
is boxes stacked across the walk
and couch springs curling through the air
and drawers and tables balanced on the curb
and us, hollering,
leaping up and around
happy to have a playground;

nothing about the emptied rooms
nothing about the emptied family

—Lucille Clifton

> See pages 576, 593.
> See also *Poetry, Rhyme, Rhythm.*

IMAGERY **Language that appeals to the senses.** Most images are visual—that is, they create pictures in your mind by appealing to the sense of sight. Images can also appeal to the sense of hearing, touch, taste, or smell or to several senses at once. The sensory images in "The Highwayman" (page 247) add greatly to the enjoyment of the poem. Though imagery is an element in all types of writing, it is especially important in poetry.

> See pages 546, 563.
> See also *Poetry.*

IRONY **In general, a contrast between expectation and reality.** Irony can create powerful effects, from humor to strong emotion. Here are three common types of irony:

1. **Verbal irony** involves a contrast between what is said or written and what is meant. If you were to call someone who failed a math test Einstein, you would be using verbal irony.

2. **Situational irony** occurs when what happens is very different from what is expected to happen. The surprise ending of "After Twenty Years" (page 357) involves situational irony.

3. **Dramatic irony** occurs when the audience or the reader knows something a character does not know. In Part 2 of "The Highwayman" (page 247), the reader feels an anxious sense of irony when King George's soldiers have Bess tied up. Although the highwayman doesn't yet know it, *we* know that a trap is set for him.

MAIN IDEA **The most important idea expressed in a paragraph or in an entire essay.** The main idea may be directly stated in a **topic sentence,** or you may have to look at all the details in the paragraph and make an **inference,** or educated guess, about its main idea.

> See page 393.

METAMORPHOSIS A marvelous change from one shape or form to another one. In myths the change is usually from human to animal, from animal to human, or from human to plant. Greek and Roman myths contain many examples of metamorphosis. The myth of Echo and Narcissus (page 290) tells how the vain youth Narcissus pines away for love of his own reflection until he is changed into a flower.

> See page 707.
> See also *Myth.*

METAPHOR An imaginative comparison between two unlike things in which one thing is said to be another thing. A metaphor is an important type of figurative language. Metaphors are used in all forms of writing and are common in ordinary speech. If you were to say someone has a heart of gold, you would not mean that the person's heart is actually made of metal. You would mean, instead, that the person is warm and caring. You would be speaking metaphorically.

Metaphors differ from similes, which use specific words (notably *like, as, than,* and *resembles*) to state comparisons. William Wordsworth's famous comparison "I wandered lonely as a cloud" is a simile because it uses *as.* If Wordsworth had written "I was a lonely, wandering cloud," he would have been using a metaphor.

PEANUTS reprinted by permission of United Feature Syndicate, Inc.

An **extended metaphor** is a metaphor that is developed, or extended, through several lines of writing or even throughout an entire poem. "I Like to See It Lap the Miles" (page 552) uses an extended metaphor to compare a train to a horse throughout the whole poem.

> See pages 255, 548, 551, 609.
> See also *Figure of Speech, Personification, Simile.*

MOOD The overall emotion created by a work of literature. A work of literature can often be described with one or more adjectives: *sad, scary, hopeful, exciting,* and so on. These are descriptions of the work's mood—its emotional atmosphere. For example, the mood of "Annabel Lee" (page 261) could be described as haunting or romantic. That mood has a lingering effect on its readers.

> See page 428.
> See also *Atmosphere.*

MOTIVATION See *Character.*

MYTH A story that explains something about the world and typically involves gods or other superhuman beings. Myths, which at one time were believed to be true, reflect the traditions of the culture that produced them. Almost every culture has **origin myths** (or **creation myths**), stories that explain how something in the world (perhaps the world itself) came to be. Myths may also explain many other aspects of nature. The ancient Greek myth of Echo and Narcissus (page 290), for example, explains the origins of a flower. Most myths are very old and were handed down orally long before being put in written form. In some of the world's greatest myths, a hero or even a god embarks on a **quest,** a perilous journey taken in pursuit of something of great value.

> See pages 646–647, 648–649, 654, 664, 675, 683.
> See also *Fable, Folk Tale.*

NONFICTION **Prose writing that deals with real people, events, and places without changing any facts.** Popular forms of nonfiction are the **autobiography,** the **biography,** and the **essay.** Other examples of nonfiction include newspaper stories, magazine articles, historical writing, scientific reports, and even personal diaries and letters.

Nonfiction writing can be subjective or objective. **Subjective writing** expresses the feelings and opinions of the writer. **Objective writing** conveys the facts without introducing any emotion or personal bias.

See pages 393, 402, 478–479.
See also *Autobiography, Biography, Fiction.*

NOVEL **A fictional story that is usually more than one hundred book pages long.** A novel uses all the elements of storytelling—**plot, character, setting, theme,** and **point of view.** A novel, because of its length, usually has more characters, settings, and themes and a more complex plot than a short story. Modern writers sometimes do not pay much attention to one or more of the novel's traditional elements. Some novels today are basically character studies that include only the barest story lines. Other novels don't look much beyond the surface of their characters and concentrate instead on plot and setting. A novel can deal with almost any topic. Many of the books recommended in the Read On sections of this text are novels. A **novella** is shorter than a novel and longer than a short story.

See pages 478–479, 508.

ONOMATOPOEIA **The use of words whose sounds echo their sense.** Onomatopoeia (än′ō·mat′ō·pē′ə) is so natural to us that we use it at a very early age. *Buzz, rustle, boom, ticktock, tweet,* and *bark* are all examples of onomatopoeia. Onomatopoeia is an important element in creating the music of poetry. In the following lines the poet creates a frenzied mood by choosing words that imitate the sounds of alarm bells:

> Oh, the bells, bells, bells!
> What a tale their terror tells
> Of Despair!
> How they clang, and clash, and roar!
> What a horror they outpour
> On the bosom of the palpitating air!
> Yet the ear, it fully knows
> By the twanging
> And the clanging
> How the danger ebbs and flows.
>
> —Edgar Allan Poe, from
> "The Bells"

See pages 577, 725.
See also *Alliteration.*

PERSONIFICATION **A figure of speech in which a nonhuman or nonliving thing or quality is talked about as if it were human or alive.** In "I Am of the Earth" (page 556), the poet personifies the earth as a mother.

See page 555.
See also *Figure of Speech, Metaphor, Simile.*

PLOT **The series of related events that make up a story.** Plot is what happens in a short story, novel, play, or narrative poem. Most plots are built on these bare bones: An **introduction,** or **exposition,** tells us who the characters are and what their **conflict** is. **Complications** arise as the characters take steps to resolve the conflict. The plot reaches a **climax,** the most emotional or suspenseful moment in the story, when the outcome is decided one way or another. The last part of a story is the **resolution,** when the characters' problems are solved and the story ends.

Not all works of fiction or drama have this traditional plot structure. Some modern writers experiment, often eliminating parts of a traditional plot in order to focus on elements such as character, point of view, or mood.

See pages 2–3, 4, 14, 57, 130, 820.
See also *Conflict.*

POETRY A kind of rhythmic, compressed language that uses figures of speech and imagery designed to appeal to emotion and imagination. We know poetry when we see it because it is usually arranged in a particular way on the page. Traditional poetry often has a regular pattern of rhythm (**meter**) and may have a regular **rhyme scheme.**

Free verse is poetry that has no regular rhythm or rhyme. "Names of Horses" (page 594) is a free-verse poem that is also an **elegy,** a poem that mourns the passing of something that is important to the writer. "Arithmetic" (page 607) is a free-verse poem that is also a **catalog poem,** a poem that lists the poet's thoughts or feelings about a subject. A major form of poetry is the **narrative poem,** which tells a story, such as "The Highwayman" (page 247). Two popular narrative forms are the **epic** and the **ballad.** Another major form of poetry is the **lyric poem,** which expresses a speaker's feelings. "I Ask My Mother to Sing" (page 569) is a lyric poem that is also a **sonnet**—a poem of fourteen lines that follows a strict form. The **ode** is a type of lyric poem that celebrates something. A lighthearted example is "Ode to Family Photographs" (page 573).

See pages 246, 260, 546–547, 568, 572, 576–577, 578, 586, 589, 593, 606, 609. See also *Figure of Speech, Free Verse, Imagery, Refrain, Rhyme, Rhythm, Speaker, Stanza.*

POINT OF VIEW The vantage point from which a story is told. The most common points of view are the **omniscient,** the **third-person limited,** and the **first person.**

1. In the **omniscient** (äm·nish′ənt), or all-knowing, **point of view** the narrator knows everything about the characters and their problems. This all-knowing narrator can tell about the characters' past, present, and future. This kind of narrator can even tell what the characters are thinking or what is happening in other places. This narrator is not in the story. Instead, he or she stands above the action, like a god. The omniscient is a very familiar point of view; we have heard it in fairy tales since we were very young. "Yeh-Shen" (page 383), a Chinese Cinderella story, is told from the omniscient point of view.

> Her loveliness made her seem a heavenly being, and the king suddenly knew in his heart that he had found his true love.

2. In the **third-person limited point of view,** the narrator focuses on the thoughts and feelings of only one character. From this point of view, you observe the action through the eyes and feelings of only one character in the story. "The Smallest Dragonboy" (page 147) is told from the third-person limited point of view.

> There was such a lot to know and understand about being a dragonrider that sometimes Keevan was overwhelmed. How would he ever be able to remember everything he ought to know at the right moment?

3. In the **first-person point of view,** one of the characters, using the personal pronoun *I,* is telling the story. You become very familiar with this narrator but can know only what he or she knows and can observe only what he or she observes. All information about the story must come from this character. In some cases the information is incorrect. "User Friendly" (page 272) is told from the first-person point of view of the boy whose computer starts acting funny.

> As I walked by the corner of my room, where my computer table was set up, I pressed the *on* button, slid a diskette into the floppy drive, then went to brush my

teeth. By the time I got back, the computer's screen was glowing greenly, displaying the message: *Good morning, Kevin.*

See pages 348–349, 356, 368, 382, 393.

REFRAIN A group of words repeated at intervals in a poem, song, or speech. Refrains are usually associated with songs and poems, but they are also used in speeches and other forms of literature. Refrains are most often used to create rhythm, but they may also provide emphasis or commentary, create suspense, or help hold a work together. Refrains may be repeated with small variations in a work in order to fit a particular context or to create a special effect.

See page 260.

RHYME The repetition of accented vowel sounds and all sounds following them in words close together in a poem. *Mean* and *screen* are rhymes, as are *crumble* and *tumble.* Rhyme has many purposes in poetry: It creates rhythm, lends a songlike quality, emphasizes ideas, organizes the poem (for instance, into stanzas or couplets), provides humor or delight, and makes the poem memorable.

Many poems—for example, "The Runaway" (page 587)—use **end rhymes,** rhymes at the end of a line. In the following stanza, *walls/calls/falls* form end rhymes, as do *hands/sands.* The pattern of end rhymes in a poem is called a **rhyme scheme.** To indicate the rhyme scheme of a poem, use a separate letter of the alphabet for each rhyme. For example, the rhyme scheme below is *aabba.*

> Darkness settles on roofs and walls,
> But the sea, the sea in the darkness calls;
> The little waves, with their soft,
>   white hands,
> Efface the footprints in the sands,
> And the tide rises, the tide falls.
>
> —Henry Wadsworth Longfellow,
>   from "The Tide Rises, the Tide Falls"

Internal rhymes are rhymes within lines. The following line has an internal rhyme (*turning/burning*):

> Back into the chamber turning, all my soul
>   within me burning
>
> —Edgar Allan Poe, from "The Raven"

Rhyming sounds need not be spelled the same way; for instance, *gear/here* forms a rhyme. Rhymes can involve more than one syllable or more than one word; *poet/know it* is an example. Rhymes involving sounds that are similar but not exactly the same are called **slant rhymes** (or **near rhymes** or **approximate rhymes**). *Leave/live* is an example of a slant rhyme. Poets writing in English often use slant rhymes because English is not a very rhymable language. It has many words that rhyme with no other word (*orange*) or with only one other word (*mountain/fountain*). Poets interested in how a poem looks on the printed page sometimes use **eye rhymes,** or **visual rhymes**—rhymes involving words that are spelled similarly but are pronounced differently. *Tough/cough* is an eye rhyme. (*Tough/rough* is a "real" rhyme.)

See pages 576–577, 586, 598.
See also *Free Verse, Poetry, Rhythm.*

RHYTHM A musical quality produced by the repetition of stressed and unstressed syllables or by the repetition of certain other sound patterns. Rhythm occurs in all language—written and spoken—but is particularly important in poetry.

The most obvious kind of rhythm is the regular pattern of stressed and unstressed syllables that is found in some poetry. This pattern is called **meter.** In the following lines describing a cavalry charge, the rhythm echoes the galloping of the attackers' horses:

The Assyrian came down like the wolf on the
    fold,
And his cohorts were gleaming in purple and
    gold;
And the sheen of their spears was like stars on
    the sea,
When the blue wave rolls nightly on deep
    Galilee.

—George Gordon, Lord Byron,
    from "The Destruction of Sennacherib"

Marking the stressed (') and unstressed (ˇ) syllables in a line is called **scanning** the line. Lord Byron's scanned lines show a rhythmic pattern in which two unstressed syllables are followed by a stressed syllable. Read the lines aloud and listen to this rhythmic pattern. Also, notice how the poem's end rhymes help create the rhythm.

Writers can also create rhythm by repeating words and phrases or even by repeating whole lines and sentences.

See pages 576–577, 578, 601.
See also *Free Verse, Poetry, Rhyme.*

SETTING The time and place in which the events of a work of literature take place. Most often the setting of a narrative is described early in the story. Setting often contributes to a story's emotional effect. In "Song of the Trees" (page 509), the forest setting helps create a soothing (yet mysterious) mood. Setting frequently plays an important role in a story's plot, especially one that centers on a conflict between a character and nature. In "Three Skeleton Key" (page 39), the characters must fight elements of a deadly setting to survive—they are threatened by a vast army of rats. Some stories are closely tied to particular settings, and it is difficult to imagine them taking place elsewhere. By contrast, other stories could easily take place in a variety of settings.

See page 296.

SHORT STORY A fictional prose narrative that is usually ten to twenty book pages long. Short stories were first written in the nineteenth century. Early short story writers include Sir Walter Scott and Edgar Allan Poe. Short stories are usually built on a plot that consists of at least these bare bones: the **introduction** or **exposition, conflict, complications, climax,** and **resolution.** Short stories are more limited than novels. They usually have only one or two major characters and one important setting.

See pages 478, 484, 508.
See also *Conflict, Fiction, Plot.*

SIMILE A comparison between two unlike things, using a word such as *like, as, than,* or *resembles.* The simile is an important type of figure of speech. In the following lines a simile creates a clear image of moths in the evening air:

When the last bus leaves, moths stream
    toward lights like litter in wind.

—Roberta Hill, from "Depot in Rapid City"

This example shows that similes can generate a strong emotional impact. By choosing to compare the moths to litter, the poet not only creates a picture in the reader's mind but also establishes a lonely, dreary mood.

See pages 255, 548, 609.
See also *Figure of Speech, Metaphor.*

SPEAKER The voice talking in a poem. Sometimes the speaker is identical to the poet, but often the speaker and the poet are not the same. The poet may be speaking as a child, a woman, a man, an animal, or even an object.

See also *Poetry.*

STANZA In a poem a group of consecutive lines that forms a single unit. A stanza in a poem is something like a paragraph in prose; it often expresses a unit of thought. A stanza may consist of any number of lines. "I'm Nobody!" (page 549) consists of two four-line stanzas, each expressing a separate idea. In some poems each stanza has the same rhyme scheme.

See pages 546, 589.
See also *Poetry, Rhyme.*

SUSPENSE The uncertainty or anxiety you feel about what will happen next in a story. In "Three Skeleton Key" (page 39), the narrator hooks your curiosity in the first sentences when he says he is about to describe his "most terrifying experience."

See page 38.
See also *Foreshadowing.*

SYMBOL A person, a place, a thing, or an event that has its own meaning *and* stands for something beyond itself as well. Examples of symbols are all around us—in music, on television, and in everyday conversation. The skull and crossbones, for example, is a symbol of danger; the dove is a symbol of peace; and the red rose stands for true love. In literature, symbols are often more personal. For example, in "Names/Nombres" (page 394), Julia Alvarez's name is a symbol of her cultural identity.

THEME The truth about life revealed in a work of literature. A theme is not the same as a subject. The subject of a work can usually be expressed in a word or two: *love, childhood, death.* The theme is the idea that the writer wishes to convey about a particular subject. The theme must be expressed in at least one sentence. For example, the subject of *The Monsters Are Due on Maple Street* (page 59) is alien invasion. The play's theme might be this: Prejudice is the fearful, unseen enemy within each of us.

A story can have several themes, but one will often stand out from the others. A work's themes are usually not stated directly. You have to think about all the elements of the work and use them to make an **inference,** or educated guess, about what the themes are.

It is not likely that two readers will ever state a theme in exactly the same way. Sometimes readers even differ greatly in their interpretations of theme. A work of literature can mean different things to different people.

See pages 236–237, 238, 246, 260, 271, 289, 296, 428, 508.

TONE The attitude that a writer takes toward the audience, a subject, or a character. Tone is conveyed through the writer's choice of words and details. The poem "maggie and milly and molly and may" (page 599) is light and playful in tone. By contrast, the poem "Annabel Lee" (page 261) is serious in tone.

See page 560.

Handbook of Reading and Informational Terms

For more information about a topic, turn to the page(s) in this book indicated on a separate line at the end of the entry. To learn more about *Cause and Effect,* for example, turn to page 256.

On another line are cross-references to entries in this handbook that provide closely related information. For instance, the entry *Chronological Order* contains a cross-reference to *Text Structures.*

ANALOGY

1. An **analogy** is a point-by-point comparison made between two things to show how they are alike. An analogy shows how something unfamiliar is like something well-known.
2. Another kind of analogy is a **verbal analogy.** A verbal analogy is a word puzzle. It gives you two words and asks you to identify another pair of words with a similar relationship. In an analogy the symbol ":" means "is to." The symbol "::" means "as."

> Select the pair of words that best completes the analogy.
>
> Toe : foot :: _____
>
> A   house : barn
> B   finger : hand
> C   road : path
> D   light : darkness

> The correct answer is B: Toe : foot :: finger : hand, or "Toe is to foot as finger is to hand." The relationship is that of part to whole. A toe is part of the foot; a finger is part of the hand.

Another relationship often represented in verbal analogies is that of opposites:

> clear : cloudy :: bright : dark

Both sets of words are opposites. Clear is the opposite of cloudy, and bright is the opposite of dark.

Verbal analogies are often found in tests, where they are used to check vocabulary and thinking skills.

See pages 265, 288, 532.

ARGUMENT An **argument** is a position supported by evidence. Arguments are used to persuade us to accept or reject an opinion on a subject. Arguments are also used to persuade us to act in a certain way.

Supporting evidence can take the form of facts, statistics, anecdotes (brief stories that illustrate a point), and expert opinions. Not all arguments are logical. **Emotional appeals** find their way into most arguments, and you should learn to recognize them. Details that appeal to your feelings make an argument more interesting and memorable—but you should not accept an argument that is based only on an emotional appeal.

Athletes should not charge kids for autographs. The most popular players are the ones that fans ask for autographs. These players don't need extra money. They already earn millions of dollars. Kids are much poorer than star athletes. I had to spend six weeks of my allowance and borrow twenty dollars from my brother to attend a game. After the game I started waiting in line to get an autograph. The line broke up quickly when we heard that the player was charging fifty dollars for each autograph. We were all disgusted. After all, the athletes' fans make them famous. My soccer coach says players should see that an autograph is a way of saying "thank you" to a loyal fan. Signing a name isn't hard. It takes less than a minute. To be asked to pay for an autograph is an insult.	Position Opinion Fact Anecdote Emotional appeal Expert opinion Fact Emotional appeal

See pages 389, 672, 788.
See also *Evidence*.

BIAS (bī′əs) A leaning in favor of or against a person or issue is called a **bias.** Sometimes a writer's bias is obvious. For instance, Rudyard Kipling in "Rikki-tikki-tavi" (page 15) reveals his bias against snakes. In the conflict between the cobras and a mongoose, Kipling is clearly biased in favor of the mongoose. People are often not upfront about their biases. You should look for bias whenever writers or speakers make claims and assertions that they don't (or can't) support with logical reasons and facts. When people ignore, distort, or hide the facts that oppose their bias, they may be guilty of prejudice.

See page 816.

CAUSE AND EFFECT A **cause** is the event that makes something happen. An **effect** is what happens as a result of the cause. Storytellers use the cause-and-effect organizational pattern to develop their plots. Writers of historical texts use this organizational pattern to explain things like the causes and effects of war. Scientific writers use this organizational pattern to explain things like the causes and effects of an epidemic. Some of the words and phrases that point to causes and effects are *because, since, therefore, so that,* and *if . . . then.* Notice the cause-and-effect chain in the following summary of the Midas myth:

Because he did a favor for a god, Midas was granted the golden touch. Since everything he touched turned to gold, his daughter also turned to gold. Because of that, he asked to be released from the golden touch. Since gold had brought him such trouble, he then turned to nature and rejected riches.

See pages 256, 271, 284, 654, 726.
See also *Text Structures*.

CHRONOLOGICAL ORDER Most narrative texts, true or fictional, are written in **chronological order.** Writers use chronological order when they put events in the sequence, or order, in which they happened in time, one after the other. Recipes and technical directions are usually written in chronological order. When you read a narrative, look for words and phrases like *next, then,* and *finally.* Writers use such words as transitions to signal the order in which events or steps occur.

See also *Text Structures.*

COMPARE-AND-CONTRAST PATTERN

When you **compare,** you look for similarities, or likenesses. When you **contrast,** you look for differences. You've used comparison and contrast many times. For instance, you might compare and contrast the features of several dogs when you choose a puppy that is like the dog you used to have. When writers compare and contrast, they organize the text to help readers understand the **points of comparison,** the features that they're looking at.

A Venn diagram can help you tell similarities from differences. The one below compares and contrasts two stories: "Yeh-Shen" (page 383) and the Cinderella folk tale. Where the circles overlap, note how the stories are alike. Where there is no overlap, note differences.

Venn Diagram

"Cinderella"
- helped by fairy godmother
- meets prince at ball

- has wicked stepmother
- wants to go to ball
- has wish granted
- has rags changed to beautiful clothes
- obeys one rule
- loses shoe
- is found by royalty

"Yeh-Shen"
- helped by fish
- meets king when he is searching for owner of shoe

Differences   Similarities   *Differences*

An effective comparison-and-contrast text may be organized in the block pattern or the point-by-point pattern.

Block pattern. A writer using the block pattern first discusses all the points of subject 1, then goes on to discuss all the points of subject 2.

> **Subject 1—"Yeh-Shen":** In the Chinese folk tale "Yeh-Shen" a magic fish dies, but its spirit gives Yeh-Shen, a kind orphan, advice and help. It changes her rags into beautiful clothes. Her wicked stepmother treats Yeh-Shen badly. [*And so on*]
>
> **Subject 2—"Cinderella":** American children probably know best the Cinderella story in which a fairy godmother changes Cinderella's rags into beautiful clothes. Cinderella also has a wicked stepmother. [*And so on*]

Point-by-point pattern. A writer who uses the point-by-point pattern goes back and forth between the two things being compared and contrasted.

> In "Yeh-Shen" a magic fish helps the orphan girl. In "Cinderella," however, a fairy godmother helps the girl. In both stories, there is a wicked stepmother. [*And so on*]

Some of the words that signal comparison and contrast are *although, but, either . . . or, however,* and *yet.*

See pages 84, 164, 190, 296, 428, 484, 496, 746, 845.
See also *Text Structures.*

CONCLUSIONS A **conclusion** is a general summing up of the specific details in a text. The text below is from "Buddies Bare Their Affection for Ill Classmate" (page 544). One reader's conclusion based on these details follows the text.

> In Mr. Alter's fifth-grade class, it's difficult to tell which boy is undergoing chemotherapy. Nearly all the boys are bald. Thirteen of them shaved their heads so a sick classmate wouldn't feel out of place.
>
> **Conclusion:** These boys care a lot about their sick classmate.

See page 718.
See also *Evidence*.

CONNOTATION AND DENOTATION The **connotation** of a word is all the feelings and associations that have come to be attached to the word. The **denotation** of a word is its strict dictionary definition. Not all words have connotations. Words like *the, writer,* and *paper* do not have connotations. Words like *Democrat, Republican, conservative,* and *liberal* are loaded with associations and feelings.

The words *skinny, slender, gaunt,* and *lean* have approximately the same denotation. They all mean "thin; having little fat." There are important shades of meaning among those words, however. If a relative said you were skinny or gaunt, you'd probably feel hurt or angry. *Skinny* and *gaunt* have negative connotations. They suggest that the thin person may have been sick and is now unattractive. *Slender* and *lean,* on the other hand, have positive connotations. They suggest a healthy, athletic body.

See page 525.

CONTEXT CLUES When you don't know the meaning of a word, look for a clue to its meaning in the **context,** the words and sentences surrounding the unfamiliar word. Here are some common types of context clues. In each sentence, the unfamiliar word appears in boldface type; the clue is underlined.

Definition clue. Look for a familiar word that defines the meaning of the unfamiliar word.

> Keevan was rarely <u>bothered</u> by rivals, but he was **perturbed** to see Beterli wandering over to him.

The word *bothered* tells you that *perturbed* also means "something like bothered."

Example clue. Look for examples of the unfamiliar word. In the context of the sentence, the examples reveal the meaning of the unfamiliar word.

> **Tugs** and <u>other</u> <u>boats</u> were washed ashore by the tidal wave.

The words *other boats* tell you that a tug is a kind of boat.

Restatement clue. Look for words that restate the meaning of the unfamiliar word.

> We **delved** into the criminal's past—we <u>searched through</u> hundreds of pieces of evidence.

The restatement clue that helps you guess the meaning of *delved* is *searched through.* (*Delved* means "dug into; searched; investigated.")

Contrast clue. Look for words that contrast the unfamiliar word with a word or phrase in the sentence that you know.

> Although Helen wanted to **detain** the visitors, she had to <u>let them go</u>.

This sentence tells you that *detain* means the opposite of "let go."

See pages 289, 381, 427, 695.

EVIDENCE When you read informational and persuasive texts, you need to **assess,** or judge, the **evidence** that a writer uses to support a position. That means you need to read carefully, looking critically at the writer's claims and assertions. You need to evaluate the writer's sources. You also need to look at the writer's own background and expertise. One way to assess evidence is to give it the **3As test.** The As stand for *adequate, appropriate,* and *accurate.*

Adequate means "sufficient" or "enough." You have to see if the writer has provided enough evidence to support his or her position. For some positions, one or two supporting facts may be adequate. For others a writer may need to provide many facts, maybe even statistics. Sometimes a direct quotation from a well-respected expert, an authority on the subject, will be convincing.

You must make sure that the writer's evidence is **appropriate,** that it has direct bearing on the conclusion. Sometimes a writer presents a lot of flashy evidence, such as details loaded with emotional appeals. When you look at this kind of evidence closely, you realize that it doesn't have much, if anything, to do with the writer's conclusions.

To make sure that the evidence is **accurate,** or correct, check to see that it comes from a source you can trust. Don't assume that everything (or anything) you see online or even printed in a newspaper or book is accurate. If a fact, example, or quotation doesn't sound accurate, check it out. Look for the title of the magazine or book that the quotation comes from. Is it a reliable source? Look up the writer's background. Does the writer have the background and education to qualify him or her as an expert on the subject? Is the writer biased in some way?

See page 788.
See also *Argument.*

FACT AND OPINION A **fact** is a statement that can be proved true. Some facts are easy to prove by **observation.** For instance, *Cats make different vocal sounds* is a fact you can prove by listening to cats meow and purr. Other facts can be **verified,** or proved, if you look them up in a reliable source. You need to be sure that the source is **authoritative**—an official source that can be trusted, such as an encyclopedia. In fields where new discoveries are being made, you need to check facts in a *recently* published source.

An **opinion** expresses a personal belief or feeling. Sometimes strongly held opinions look and sound like facts. Dog lovers would never question the statement *Dogs are smarter than cats.* Cat lovers, however, would express the opposite opinion, *Cats are smarter than dogs,* and believe it just as strongly. Even if a statement sounds as if it's true, it's not a fact unless it can be proved. Here are some opinions:

Travel to other planets will happen in my lifetime.

We have the best football team in the United States.

Every teenager should receive an allowance.

A **valid opinion** is a personal belief that is supported by facts. An **invalid opinion** is a belief that is either not supported by facts or is supported by illogical and wishful thinking.

Remember that what you see in print or on the Internet may or may not be true. If a statement looks like a fact but you suspect it's an opinion, check it out in a reliable source. Ask: Can this be proved true?

See pages 389, 402, 499, 672.

FALLACIOUS REASONING
Fallacious (fə·lā′shəs) means "false." **Fallacious reasoning** is false reasoning. Here are four major types of false reasoning:

1 **Hasty generalizations** are reached without considering enough facts. A

generalization is a conclusion drawn after considering as much of the evidence as possible. (See page 508.) If there is even one exception to the conclusion, your generalization is not true or valid.

> **Fact:** "User Friendly" is a story with a surprise ending.
>
> **Fact:** "After Twenty Years" is a story with a surprise ending.
>
> **Hasty generalization:** All stories have surprise endings.

That conclusion is a hasty generalization. You could name many stories that do not have a surprise ending. Sometimes hasty generalizations can be corrected by using a qualifying word such as *most, usually, some, many,* or *often.* It is especially important to watch out for hasty generalizations when you're reading a persuasive text.

2. With **circular reasoning** a writer tries to fool you by restating the opinion in different words.

> Hungry students can't study because they haven't had enough to eat.
>
> Jean is the best candidate for student-council president because she's better than all the other candidates.

3. **Cause-and-effect fallacies.** One common **cause-and-effect fallacy** assumes that if something happens right before another event, the first event caused the next event.

> I wasn't wearing my lucky shirt, so I failed my history test.

Another **cause-and-effect fallacy** names a single cause for a complicated situation that has many causes.

> Popularity in middle school depends on wearing the right clothes.

4. The **either-or fallacy** suggests that there are only two sides to an issue.

> Either you get a summer job, or you waste the whole summer.

See also *Argument, Evidence, Persuasion.*

5W-HOW? The first paragraph of a news story, called the **lead** (lēd) paragraph, usually answers the questions *who? what? when? where? why?* and *how?* Look for the answers to these **5W-How?** questions when you read a newspaper story or any eyewitness account.

See page 52.

GENERALIZATION A **generalization** is a broad statement that covers several particular situations. Scientists and detectives, for instance, begin their investigations by amassing many specific facts. Then they put the facts together and draw a conclusion about what all this evidence tells them, what it adds up to.

> **Fact:** Cobras are poisonous.
>
> **Fact:** Rattlesnakes are poisonous.
>
> **Fact:** Garter snakes are not poisonous.
>
> **Generalization:** Some snakes are poisonous.

The generalization *Most snakes are poisonous* would have been incorrect. Only three species out of a population of more than 2,500 species of snakes were considered. About four fifths of all snakes are not poisonous. To be valid, a generalization must be based on all the evidence (the facts) that can be gathered.

See pages 508, 613, 675.
See also *Stereotyping.*

GRAPHIC FEATURES **Graphic features** are design elements in a text. They include things like headings, maps, charts, graphs, and illustrations. Graphic features are visual ways of communicating information.

Some design elements you may find in a text are **boldface** and *italic* type; type in different styles (called fonts), sizes, and colors; bullets (dots that set off items in a list); and logos (like computer icons). For example, the Quickwrite heading in this book always appears with the pencil logo. Design elements make a text look more attractive. They also steer your eyes to different types of information and make the text easier to read.

A **heading** serves as a title for the information that follows it. Size and color set off from the rest of the text the type used for a heading. A repeated heading, like "Reading Skills" in this textbook, is always followed by the same type of material. Skimming the headings is one way to preview a text.

Graphic features such as **maps, charts,** and **graphs** display and sometimes explain complex information with lines, drawings, and symbols. Graphic features usually include these elements:

1. A **title** identifies the subject or main idea of the graphic.

2. **Labels** identify specific information.

3. A **caption** is text (usually under an illustration) that explains what you're looking at.

4. A **legend,** or **key,** helps you interpret symbols and colors, usually on a map.

Look for a **scale,** which relates the size or distance of something on a map to the real-life size and distance.

5. The source tells where the information in the graphic comes from. Knowing the source helps you evaluate the accuracy.

Different types of **maps** present special information. **Physical maps** show the natural landscape of an area. Shading may be used to show features like mountains and valleys. Different shades of color are often used to show different elevations (heights above sea level). **Political maps** show political units, such as states, nations, and capitals. The map of Canada, the United States, and Mexico shown here is a political map. **Special-purpose maps** present information such as the routes of explorers or the location of earthquake fault lines.

A **flowchart** shows a sequence of events or the steps in a process. Flowcharts are often used to show cause-and-effect relationships. See page 256 for an example of a flowchart. **Pie charts,** also called **circle graphs,** show how parts of a whole are related. A pie chart is a circle divided into different-sized sections, like slices of a pie. The emphasis in a pie chart is always on the proportions of the sections, not on the specific amounts of each section.

Pie Chart

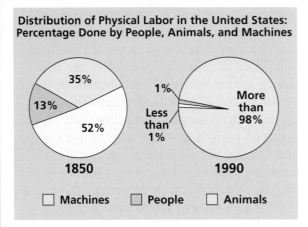

Distribution of Physical Labor in the United States: Percentage Done by People, Animals, and Machines

A **diagram** is a graphic that outlines the parts of something and shows how the parts relate to one another or how they work. You'll often find diagrams in technical directions, to show how a mechanical device works. Diagrams prove that a picture can be worth more than a thousand words. See page 906 for an example of a diagram.

A **time line** identifies events that take place over the course of time. In a time line, events are organized in chronological order, the order in which they happened. See pages 616–617 for a time line of an author's life.

Graphs usually show changes or trends over time. In line graphs, dots showing the quantity at different times are connected to

create a line. **Bar graphs** generally compare various quantities.

Bar Graph

Line Graph

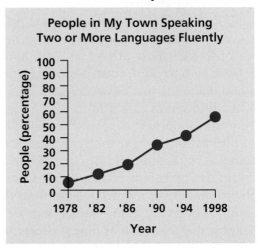

A **table** presents information arranged in rows and columns. There are many different types of tables. See page 903 for an example of a table showing a train schedule.

Tips for Understanding Graphic Features

1. Read the title, labels, and legend before you try to analyze the information.

2. Read numbers carefully. Note increases or decreases in sequences. Look for the direction or order of events and for trends and relationships.

3. Draw your own conclusions from the graphic. Then, compare your conclusions with the writer's conclusions.

See pages 32, 52.

IMAGES Descriptive writing appeals to the senses to create **mental images,** pictures in the reader's mind. Most description appeals to the sense of sight, but description can also appeal to one or more of the other senses. When you read a description, use the details to *visualize,* or form mental pictures of, the characters, settings, and events. Forming mental images is especially important when you read description in scientific texts.

See page 527.

INFERENCE An **inference** is an educated guess, a conclusion that makes sense because it's supported by evidence. The evidence may be a collection of **facts,** information that can be proved, or it may come from experiences in your own life. However, the evidence must provide some reason for believing that the conclusion is true if the inference is to be valid, or based on sound, logical thought. Nevertheless, people may draw different conclusions from the same evidence—especially if there isn't much evidence to go on.

Bobby has recently transferred to your school. You ask Bobby to join you and a couple of other friends, Sam and Ali, at your house after school on Thursday. Bobby says, "Sorry. I have to go home right after school."

Inferences: Sam infers that Bobby's parents are really strict. Ali infers that Bobby is stuck-up. You infer that Bobby doesn't like you.

As you read, you make inferences based on clues that the writer provides. For example, when you read a narrative, you **infer,** or guess, what will happen next based on what the writer has told you and on your own knowledge and experience. Sometimes a writer deliberately gives clues that lead you to different—and incorrect—inferences. That's part of the fun of reading. Until you get to the end of a suspenseful story, you can never be completely sure about what will happen next.

In O. Henry's short story "After Twenty Years" (page 357), a policeman speaks to a well-dressed man waiting in a doorway in New York City. The man is waiting for his boyhood friend, Jimmy. He hasn't seen Jimmy for more than twenty years. Read the following dialogue, and the inferences that follow it.

"Did pretty well out West, didn't you?" asked the policeman.

"You bet! I hope Jimmy has done half as well. He was a kind of plodder, though, good fellow as he was. I've had to compete with some of the sharpest wits going to get my pile. A man gets in a groove in New York. It takes the West to put a razor edge on him."

Inferences: The policeman seems to be impressed by the man in the doorway. The well-dressed man thinks a lot of himself and looks down on his old friend Jimmy, who may have been too "good" to be successful.

See pages 57, 136, 146, 168.
See also *Evidence, Fact and Opinion.*

INSTRUCTIONAL MANUALS Instructional manuals tell you how to operate a specific device, such as a VCR or a car. Instructional manuals contain detailed directions, usually organized in chronological steps. Drawings and diagrams, such as flowcharts, might be included to help you understand the different parts of the device.

See page 81.

KWL CHART Using a **KWL chart** is a way to focus your reading and record what you learn. KWL means "What I **k**now, what I **w**ant to know, and what I **l**earned." When you use a KWL strategy, you first skim the text, looking at headings, subtitles, and illustrations. You decide what the topic of the text is. Then, on a blank sheet of paper, you draw a KWL chart. In the K column you note what you already know about the subject. In the W column you write down what you'd like to find out. After you finish reading the text, you write the answers under the L column to the questions you asked in the W column. Here is the beginning of a KWL chart based on "Sir Gawain and the Loathly Lady" (page 834).

K	W	L
What I **K**now	What I **W**ant to Know	What I **L**earned
Sir Gawain was a knight.	Why was the lady loathly?	

See also *Graphic Features.*

MAIN IDEA The most important point or focus of a passage is its **main idea.** Writers of essays, nonfiction narratives, and informational articles have one or more **main ideas** in mind as they write a text. The writer may state the main idea directly. More often the main idea is suggested, or implied. Then it's up to you, the reader, to **infer,** or guess at,

what it is. To infer the main idea, look at the key details in the text. See if you can create a statement that expresses a general idea that covers all these important details. When you are deciding on the main idea, look especially for a key passage at the beginning or end of the text. That's where a writer often refers to a key idea.

See pages 393, 480, 543.

NEWSPAPERS Newspapers are informational texts that present facts about current events. Newspapers may also contain feature articles that aim to entertain as well as inform. Newspapers often contain editorials that support a *position* for or against an issue. **Headlines** at the top of each story indicate the topic of the story. They are worded to catch your attention. The writer of a **news story** usually organizes the details in order of importance. If the article is running too long, the less important details can easily be cut from the end of the story.

See page 52.

OBJECTIVE WRITING Objective writing sticks to the facts. It does not reveal the writer's feelings, beliefs, or point of view about the subject. In a newspaper, news articles are usually written objectively. Readers of news articles want to get a true and accurate account of what happened. If they want to know a writer's point of view or perspective on the news, they turn to the **editorial page.** Editorials and letters to the editor are usually *not* written objectively. They are examples of **subjective writing.** See page 789 for an example of a letter to the editor.

See pages 393, 414.
See also *Subjective Writing.*

OUTLINING Outlining an informational text can help you identify main ideas and understand how they are related to one another. Outlining also shows you the important details that support each main idea. When you have an outline, you have a visual summary of the text.

Many readers start an outline by taking notes. Note taking is an especially good idea if you're reading a text with many facts, such as names and dates, that you want to remember.

Tips for Taking Notes

1. You can jot down notes in a notebook or on note cards. Put your notes in your own words, writing each main idea on its own note card or page.

2. As you continue to read, add details that relate to the important idea you have on each card.

3. Whenever you copy the writer's exact words, put quotation marks around them. Write down the page number for the source of each note.

After you have your notes on the text, you're ready to make an outline. Many outlines label the main ideas with Roman numerals. You need to have at least two headings at each level. This is how an outline might begin:

I. Main idea

  A. Detail supporting main idea I

    1. Detail supporting A

      a. Detail supporting 1

      b. Detail supporting 1

    2. Detail supporting A

  B. Detail supporting main idea I

II. Main idea

See page 266.

PERSUASION Persuasion is the use of language or pictures to convince us to think or act in a certain way. Recognizing **persuasive techniques** will help you evaluate the persuasion that you read, hear, and see all around you today. Here are some persuasive techniques to watch for:

1. **Logical appeals** are based on correct reasoning. Logic appeals to reason with opinions supported by strong factual evidence, such as facts, statistics, or statements by experts on the issue being considered.

2. **Emotional appeals** get your feelings involved in the argument. Some writers use vivid language and supporting evidence that arouse basic feelings, such as pity, anger, and fear. Persuasion tends to be most effective when it appeals to both your head and your heart. However, it's important to be able to recognize emotional appeals—and to be suspicious of how they can sway you.

3. **Logical fallacies** (fal′ə·sēz) are mistakes in reasoning. If you're reading a text quickly, fuzzy or dishonest reasoning may look as if it makes sense. See the entry for *Fallacious Reasoning* for examples of specific logical fallacies.

See pages 389, 788, 816.
See also *Argument*.

PREDICTIONS Guessing what will happen next in a narrative text is a reading skill called **making predictions.** To make predictions, you look for clues that **foreshadow,** or hint at, future actions. You try to connect those clues with past and present actions in the story. You quickly check your memory for other things you've read that are in any way like the story you're reading. You recall your real-life experiences. Then you make your predictions. As you read, you'll continuously revise your guesses, adjusting your predictions as new clues crop up.

See pages 38, 174, 246, 356, 368, 707.

PROPAGANDA **Propaganda** is an organized attempt to influence a large audience of readers, listeners, or TV watchers. Propaganda techniques are used in all kinds of persuasive texts. You see them especially in advertisements, speeches, and editorials. Some writers use propaganda to advance good causes—for instance, to persuade people to recycle, to exercise, or to join together to fight a terrible disease. However, many writers of propaganda use emotional appeals to confuse readers and to convince them that the writer's biased opinions are the only ones worth considering.

Common propaganda techniques include the following:

- The **bandwagon** appeal urges you to do or believe something because everyone else does.

> "Shop where the action is! Join the parade to Teen-Town Mall."

- The **testimonial** uses a famous person, such as an actor or an athlete, to testify that he or she supports the issue or uses the product.

> "I'm professional basketball player Hank Smith, and I drink Starade every day for quick and long-lasting energy."

- **Snob appeal** suggests that by using this product you can be superior to others—more powerful, wealthy, or beautiful.

> "You deserve this car. Don't settle for less than the best."

- **Stereotyping.** Writers who use stereotyping refer to members of a group as if they were all the same. (See also page 816.)

> Teenagers are bad drivers.
>
> Didn't I tell you that Martians can't be trusted?

- Writers using **name-calling** avoid giving reasons and logical evidence for or against an issue. Instead, they attack people who disagree with them by giving those people negative labels.

> That's just what I'd expect a nerd like you to say.
>
> I won't waste time listening to a puppet-politician whose strings are controlled by ill-informed special-interest groups.

PURPOSES OF TEXTS Texts are written for different **purposes:** to inform, to persuade, to express feelings, or to entertain. The purpose of a text, or the reason why a text is written, determines its **structure,** the way the writer organizes and presents the material.

READING RATE The speed at which you read a text is your **reading rate.** How quickly or slowly you should read depends on the type of text you are reading and your purpose for reading it.

Reading Rates According to Purpose

Reading Rate	Purpose	Example
Skimming	Reading for main points	Glancing at newspaper headlines; reviewing charts and headings in your science textbook before a test
Scanning	Looking for specific details	Looking for an author's name in a table of contents; looking in a geography book for the name of the highest mountain in North America
Reading for mastery	Reading to understand and remember	Taking notes on a chapter in your science textbook to study for a test; reading a story or poem for understanding

RETELLING The reading strategy called **retelling** helps you identify and remember events that advance the plot of a story. Retelling is also useful when you read informational texts, such as science or history texts. From time to time in your reading, stop for a moment. Review what's gone on before you go ahead. Focus on the important events or key details. Think about them, and retell them briefly in your own words. When you read history or science texts, you should stop after each section of the text and see if you can retell the key details to yourself.

See pages 4, 14, 732.

SQ3R The abbreviation **SQ3R** stands for a reading and study strategy that takes place in five steps: **s**urvey, **q**uestion, **r**ead, **r**etell, **r**eview. The SQ3R process takes time, but it helps you focus on the text—and it works.

- *S—Survey.* Glance through the text. Skim the headings, titles, charts, illustrations, and vocabulary words in boldface type. Read the first and last sentences of the major sections of the text, if they are indicated by headings.

- *Q—Question.* List the questions that you have. These may be questions that came out of your survey, or they may be general questions about the subject. Ask the questions that you hope to find answers to in the text.

- *R—Read.* Read the text carefully, keeping your questions in mind. As you read, look for answers. Take brief notes on the answers you find.

- *R—Retell.* Use your notes to write down the main ideas and important details in the text. Before you write, say your answers out loud. Listen to your answers to hear if they make sense.

- *R—Review.* Look back over the text. See if you can answer your questions without using the notes and answers you wrote down. Write a brief summary of the text so you'll be able to remember it later.

See page 415.

STEREOTYPING (ster′ē·ə·tīp′iŋ) Referring to all members of a group as if they were all the same is called **stereotyping**. Stereotyping ignores the facts about individuals. The most important fact about members of a group is that each individual person is *different* from all the others. Stereotyping does not allow for individual differences. Whenever you assess a writer's evidence, be on the lookout for stereotyping. When a writer makes a claim about an individual or a group and supports the assertion with a stereotype, you know that the writer is guilty of faulty reasoning. Here are some examples of stereotyping:

> All teenagers are lazy.
>
> Senior citizens have more money than they need.
>
> All lawyers are dishonest.
>
> All football players are dumb.

See page 816.
See also *Propaganda*.

SUBJECTIVE WRITING Writing that reveals and emphasizes the writer's personal feelings and opinions is called **subjective**. Subjective and objective writing are opposites. *Subjective* means "personal; resulting from feelings; existing only in the mind." *Objective* means "real; actual; factual; without bias." Writers may combine subjective and objective details in the same text. As a reader you must figure out which statements are based on subjective impressions and which are based on factual, objective evidence.

We expect subjectivity in some writing. We would expect an autobiography to reveal the writer's personal feelings. In a historical text, however, we expect objectivity—we want facts, not the writer's personal feelings.

See pages 393, 414.
See also *Objective Writing.*

SUMMARIZING Restating the main ideas or major events in a text is called **summarizing.** A summary of text is much shorter than the original. To summarize an informational text, you must include the main ideas and the important details that support those main ideas. To summarize a narrative, you must include the main events and be certain you have indicated cause and effect. In a summary, except for direct quotations from the text, you put the writer's ideas into your own words. (Every time you jot down a direct quotation, be sure to put quotation marks around it and write down the source.) Here is a summary of the selection from *Barrio Boy* by Ernesto Galarza (page 500):

Ernesto's family had recently moved to Sacramento from Mazatlán, Mexico. This true account begins with Ernesto's mother taking him to school. The new school seems strange to Ernesto, who speaks no English. Ernesto finds out that many of his first-grade classmates are from other countries or have different ethnic backgrounds.

Several of them, along with Ernesto, receive private English lessons from their teacher. The teachers at the school help Ernesto learn that he can be proud of being American while still feeling proud of his Mexican roots.

See pages 543, 664, 698.
See also *Main Idea.*

TEXT STRUCTURES There are some basic ways in which writers structure informational texts: **cause and effect, chronological order,** and **comparison-and-contrast.** Sometimes a writer will use one pattern throughout a text. Many writers will combine two or more patterns. These guidelines can help you analyze text structure:

1. Search the text for the main idea. Look for words that signal a specific pattern of organization.

2. Study the text for other important ideas. Think about how the ideas are connected to one another. Look for an obvious pattern.

3. Draw a graphic organizer that shows how the text seems to be structured. Your graphic organizer may look like one of the common text structures shown below.

The **cause-and-effect pattern** presents a series of causes and their effects. This example shows the effect of an earthquake, which led to another effect, which became the cause of another effect, and so on:

Causal Chain

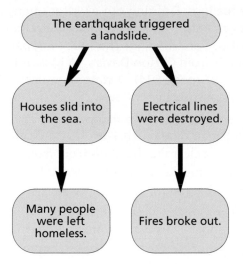

Chronological-order pattern shows events or ideas happening in time sequence. The example below gives directions for getting from school to a student's home:

Sequence Chain

The **comparison-and-contrast pattern** points out similarities and differences. A Venn diagram can help you see how two subjects are alike and how they are different. Similarities are listed where the two circles overlap. Differences are shown where the circles don't overlap. This example compares a middle school with a high school.

Venn Diagram

Middle School

- smaller—500 students
- students from four K–5 schools
- everyone knows everyone else

High School

- Big school— 2000 students
- Students from four middle schools
- More cliques; hard to get to know people

- classes same length
- many electives
- three foreign languages to choose from

Differences   *Similarities*   *Differences*

Another kind of graphic organizer focuses on points of comparison (the features being compared).

Comparing and Contrasting

	Middle School	High School
Size of school		
Length of school day		
Sports program		

See pages 284, 496.
See also *Cause and Effect, Chronological Order, Compare-and-Contrast Pattern.*

TEXTBOOKS **Textbooks** are informational texts written to help students learn about a subject. This textbook is quite different in structure from a geography textbook. Nonetheless, both kinds of textbooks have certain elements in common. For example, they have the same general purpose. In addition, most textbooks present information followed by questions that help students determine whether they have learned the material. Finally, most textbooks contain a table of contents, an index, illustrations, charts, and other graphic features.

See page 32.

WRITER'S PERSPECTIVE **Perspective** is the way a person looks at a subject. Some people have a negative perspective, for instance, on violent computer games. They believe that such games may influence children to become violent. Other people have a positive perspective on violent computer games. They say that when children play such games, they may rid themselves of some of their aggressive feelings. Figuring out a writer's perspective can help you understand and evaluate what you are reading. The following paragraph is from Clifton Davis's "A Mason-Dixon Memory" (page 534). A statement describing Davis's perspective follows:

In his words and in his life, Lincoln had made it clear that freedom is not free. Every time the color of a person's skin keeps him out of an amusement park or off a country-club fairway, the war for freedom begins again. Sometimes the battle is fought with fists and guns, but more often the most effective weapon is a simple act of love and courage.

Writer's perspective: Prejudice still exists today, and it can be fought best with simple, nonviolent actions.

See pages 351, 364, 410.

Language Handbook

1 THE PARTS OF SPEECH

THE NOUN

1a. **A *noun* is a word used to name a person, a place, a thing, or an idea.**

PERSONS	giant, Miss Nettie Hopley, baby sitter, immigrant
PLACES	pasture, Italy, Sutter's Fort, Crocker Art Gallery
THINGS	quilt, key, frog, desk, Newbery Medal, *Voyager 2*
IDEAS	knowledge, friendliness, success, love, self-esteem

Compound Nouns

A **compound noun** is two or more words used together as a single noun. The parts of a compound noun may be written as one word, as separate words, or as a hyphenated word.

Compound words may be written as one word, as separate words, or as a hyphenated word. To be sure you are spelling a compound word correctly, always use a current dictionary.

ONE WORD	butterfly, playground, Passover, classroom
SEPARATE WORDS	Golden Age, compact disc, post office
HYPHENATED WORD	self-control, bull's-eye, six-year-old

Collective Nouns

A **collective noun** is a word that names a group.

EXAMPLES   class   family   choir   herd   jury

Common Nouns and Proper Nouns

A **common noun** is a general name for a person, a place, a thing, or an idea. A **proper noun** names a particular person, place, thing, or idea. Proper nouns always begin with a capital letter. Common nouns begin with a capital letter in titles and when they begin sentences.

COMMON NOUNS	poem nation day
PROPER NOUNS	"The Runaway" Japan Friday

✔ QUICK CHECK 1

Identify the nouns in the following sentences. Classify each noun as *common* or *proper*. Also label any *compound* or *collective* nouns.

EXAMPLE   1. "Rikki-tikki-tavi" is a short story by Rudyard Kipling.
    1. *"Rikki-tikki-tavi"—compound, proper; short story—compound, common; Rudyard Kipling—compound, proper*

Try It Out ✎

In the following paragraph, replace the vague nouns with exact, specific nouns.

[1] As a girl wept under a tree, a woman suddenly appeared. [2] She waved a magic stick. [3] A vegetable turned into a vehicle. [4] With another movement of the woman's stick, the girl's torn clothing turned into a beautiful dress. [5] Overjoyed, the girl thanked the woman and rode to the party at the building.

1. Rikki-tikki-tavi is the brave pet of a family in India.
2. A fierce little mongoose, Rikki-tikki knows no fear.
3. Although his teeth are sharp, he would never bite a person.
4. Instead, he kills a deadly cobra in the bathroom.
5. He saves the lives of Teddy and his family.

Using Specific Nouns

Whenever possible, use specific, exact nouns. Using specific nouns will make your writing more accurate as well as more interesting.

NONSPECIFIC Animals drank from the water.

SPECIFIC Horses, cattle, and burros drank from the creek.

THE PRONOUN

1b. **A *pronoun* is a word used in place of one or more nouns or pronouns.**

EXAMPLES Emily Dickinson took few trips; Dickinson spent most of Dickinson's time at Amherst.

Emily Dickinson took few trips; **she** spent most of **her** time at Amherst.

The word that a pronoun stands for is called its ***antecedent.*** The antecedent is not always stated.

STATED Dickinson wrote many **poems** and hid **them** in her room.

UNSTATED **Who** edited *The Poems of Emily Dickinson*?

Personal Pronouns

A ***personal pronoun*** refers to the one speaking (*first person*), the one spoken to (*second person*), or the one spoken about (*third person*).

NOTE Some authorities prefer to call possessive forms of pronouns (such as *my, his,* and *their*) *possessive adjectives.* Follow your teacher's instructions regarding possessive forms.

PERSONAL PRONOUNS		
	SINGULAR	**PLURAL**
First Person	I, me, my, mine	we, us, our, ours
Second Person	you, your, yours	you, your, yours
Third Person	he, him, his, she, her, hers, it, its	they, them, their, theirs

Reflexive and Intensive Pronouns

A *reflexive pronoun* refers to the subject and directs the action of the verb back to the subject. An *intensive pronoun* emphasizes a noun or another pronoun. Reflexive and intensive pronouns have the same form.

FIRST PERSON	myself, ourselves
SECOND PERSON	yourself, yourselves
THIRD PERSON	himself, herself, itself, themselves

REFLEXIVE Emily Dickinson wrote **herself** notes on the backs of recipes.

INTENSIVE She did all the baking **herself.**

Demonstrative Pronouns

A *demonstrative pronoun* (*this, that, these, those*) points out a person, a place, a thing, or an idea.

EXAMPLE **This** is a collection of her poems.

Interrogative Pronouns

An *interrogative pronoun* (*what, which, who, whom, whose*) introduces a question.

EXAMPLE **What** were Dickinson's household duties?

Relative Pronouns

A *relative pronoun* (*that, what, which, who, whom, whose*) introduces a subordinate clause.

EXAMPLE Dickinson wrote of thoughts and feelings **that** she had.

Indefinite Pronouns

An *indefinite pronoun* refers to a person, a place, or a thing that is not specifically named. Many indefinite pronouns can also serve as adjectives.

Common Indefinite Pronouns				
all	each	few	no one	several
any	either	many	nobody	some
both	everything	none	one	somebody

PRONOUN **Neither** of Emily's sisters was aware of the poems.

ADJECTIVE **Neither** sister was aware of the poems.

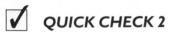 **QUICK CHECK 2**

Identify each of the pronouns in the following sentences as *personal, reflexive, intensive, demonstrative, interrogative, relative,* or *indefinite.*

☞ *This, that, these,* and *those* can also be used as adjectives. See page 963.

☞ See pages 996–1000 for more on subordinate clauses.

Language Handbook

EXAMPLE   1. I wonder about anyone who is famous.
              1. *I—personal; anyone—indefinite; who—relative*

1. Are you famous or important?
2. Emily Dickinson herself declared that she wasn't.
3. Yet, who doesn't recognize her name today?
4. If you don't, this is your chance to read some of her poems.
5. You can decide for yourself if someone important wrote them.

THE ADJECTIVE

1c.   An *adjective* is a word used to modify a noun or a pronoun.

To **modify** a word means to describe the word or to make its meaning more definite. An adjective modifies a word by telling *what kind, which one, how much,* or *how many.*

WHAT KIND?	WHICH ONE?	HOW MUCH? or HOW MANY?
noisy relatives	*those* days	*many* years
proper manners	*another* skirt	*more* guests
Mexican food	*next* lesson	*one* mistake

Articles

The most frequently used adjectives are *a, an,* and *the.* These adjectives are called **articles.** The adjectives *a* and *an* are **indefinite articles.** Each one indicates that the noun refers to someone or something in general. *A* is used before a word beginning with a consonant sound. *An* is used before a word beginning with a vowel sound.

EXAMPLES   **An** early gift later caused Tan **an** embarrassing moment.
               Her mother gave her **a** miniskirt.
               It took him **an** hour to find **a** uniform that fit.

The adjective *the* is a **definite article.** It indicates that the noun refers to someone or something in particular.

EXAMPLE   **The** minister's son attended **the** potluck dinner.

Proper Adjectives

A **proper adjective** is formed from a proper noun and begins with a capital letter.

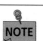 **NOTE**   An adjective may come before or after the word it modifies.

EXAMPLES   **Each one** of the guests ate **steamed fish.** [The adjective *each* modifies *one.* The adjective *steamed* modifies *fish.*]
The **minister, proper** and **dignified,** was also **courteous.** [The adjectives *proper, dignified,* and *courteous* modify *minister.*]

PROPER NOUNS	PROPER ADJECTIVES
China	**Chinese** customs
America	**American** manners
Buddhist	**Buddhist** monk
Christmas	**Christmas** dinner

 NOTE Some proper nouns, such as *Buddhist,* do not change spelling when they are used as adjectives.

Demonstrative Adjectives

This, that, these, and *those* can be used as adjectives and as pronouns. When these words modify a noun or a pronoun, they are called **demonstrative adjectives.** When used alone, these words are called **demonstrative pronouns.**

DEMONSTRATIVE ADJECTIVES	Is **this** story more interesting than **that** one?
	Those dishes are considered a delicacy.
DEMONSTRATIVE PRONOUNS	**That** is the way to hold chopsticks.
	Are **these** typical foods in China?

☞ For more about demonstrative pronouns, see page 961.

Nouns Used as Adjectives

When a noun modifies another noun or a pronoun, it is considered an adjective. Most compound nouns can be used as adjectives.

NOUNS	NOUNS USED AS ADJECTIVES
fish	**fish** scales
holiday	**holiday** menu
bicycle	**bicycle** tires
Christmas Eve	**Christmas Eve** celebration

 QUICK CHECK 3

Identify each adjective in the following sentences. Then, give the word the adjective modifies. Do not include the articles *a, an,* and *the.*

EXAMPLE   1. That name sounds strange to me.
    1. *That—name; strange—name*

1. Having an unusual name can be a problem for anyone.
2. That problem plagued Julia Alvarez all through school.
3. As a girl, she was known by many names—Judy, Jules, and even Alcatraz—but her family pronounced *Julia* "Hoo-lee-ah."
4. Those neighbors with a New York City accent said "Joo-lee-ah."
5. Family members told her to keep writing and her name would be famous.

1d. A *verb* is a word used to express action or a state of being.

EXAMPLES   Gary Soto **wrote** "The No-Guitar Blues."
Soto's stories **seem** realistic to me.

Every sentence must have a subject and a verb. The verb says something about the subject.

Action Verbs

1e. An *action verb* may express physical action or mental action.

PHYSICAL ACTION   lean, watch, hop, say, push, toss, pull
MENTAL ACTION   want, hope, regret, wonder, forget, dream

Transitive and Intransitive Verbs

(1) A *transitive verb* is an action verb that expresses an action directed toward a person or thing.

EXAMPLE   He **held** a guitar. [The action of *held* is directed toward *guitar*.]

With transitive verbs, the action passes from the doer (the subject) to the receiver of the action. Words that receive the action of a transitive verb are called *objects*.

EXAMPLES   She called **him**. [*Him* is the object of the verb *called*.]
The boy told the **villagers** a **lie**. [Both *villagers* and *lie* are objects of the verb *told*.]

(2) An *intransitive verb* expresses action (or tells something about the subject) without passing the action to a receiver.

EXAMPLE   Fausto **waited** hopefully for a reward. [The action of *waited* is not directed toward a receiver. The verb *waited* does not have an object.]

Linking Verbs

1f. A *linking verb* links, or connects, the subject with a noun, a pronoun, or an adjective in the predicate.

EXAMPLES   The dog's name **was** Roger. [name = Roger]
Los Lobos **became** Fausto's role models. [Los Lobos = role models]

For more about subjects and verbs, see pages 970–973 and 1001–1003.

For more information about objects, see pages 1005–1006.

NOTE   A verb may be transitive in one sentence and intransitive in another.

TRANSITIVE   He **smelled** his grandfather's aftershave.

INTRANSITIVE   Grandfather **smelled** good.

Language Handbook

Like intransitive verbs, linking verbs never take direct objects.

Linking Verbs Formed from the Verb *Be*			
am	were	should have been	was being
are	be	will have been	can be
being	been	has been	must be
is	may be	have been	might be
was	would be	will be	could be

Other Linking Verbs
appear, grow, seem, stay, become, look, smell, taste, feel, remain, sound, turn

Helping Verbs

1g. A *helping verb (auxiliary verb)* helps the main verb to express an action or a state of being.

EXAMPLES **could** be   **may have** asked   **might have been** caught

COMMONLY USED HELPING VERBS	
Forms of *Be*	am, be, being, was, are, been, is, were
Forms of *Do*	do, does, did
Forms of *Have*	have, has, had
Other Helping Verbs	can, may, must, should, would, could, might, shall, will

A *verb phrase* consists of a main verb and at least one helping verb.

EXAMPLE   Fausto **could have kept** the money. [The main verb is *kept*.]

QUICK CHECK 4

Identify the italicized verb in each of the following sentences as an *action verb,* a *linking verb,* or a *helping verb.* Then, for each action verb, tell whether the verb is *transitive* or *intransitive.*

EXAMPLE   **1.** Have you *read* other poems by Shel Silverstein?
　　　　　　 1. *action verb, transitive*

1. Sarah Cynthia Sylvia Stout would not *take* the trash out.
2. It *smelled* bad.
3. She *did*n't care about that or about her family or friends.
4. Finally, she *was* alone with her garbage.
5. That huge pile of garbage *reached* to another state.

  See pages 1006–1007 for more information about linking verbs.

 NOTE Some words may be either action verbs or linking verbs, depending on how they are used.

LINKING   The dog **looked** hungry.
ACTION   The dog **looked** for another orange peel.

NOTE Sometimes the verb phrase is interrupted by other words.

EXAMPLES   **Will** you please **explain** the theme of this story? Fausto **did** not [*or* **did**n't] **tell** the dog's owners the truth.

  For more information about verb phrases, see pages 970, 991, and 1002.

Language Handbook

THE ADVERB

1h. An *adverb* is a word used to modify a verb, an adjective, or another adverb.

MODIFYING A VERB	They could **not** radio for help.
MODIFYING AN ADJECTIVE	The sun was **extremely** hot.
MODIFYING ANOTHER ADVERB	**Quite** bravely, they landed a shark.

An adverb tells *where, when, how,* or *to what extent* (*how much* or *how long*).

WHERE?	Killer whales are common **here.**
HOW?	The accident occurred **suddenly.**
WHEN?	**Then** the survivors depended on their wits.
TO WHAT EXTENT?	They were **exceptionally** careful with their supplies.

The word *not* is an adverb. When *not* is part of a contraction like *hadn't,* the *–n't* is an adverb.

 QUICK CHECK 5

Identify the adverb or adverbs in each of the following sentences. Then, give the word or phrase each adverb modifies.

EXAMPLE   1. Have you ever wondered about being shipwrecked?
   1. *ever—Have wondered*

1. Neil cried sadly for their lost ship.
2. Too soon, a cargo vessel sailed into the distance.
3. Dougal Robertson would not yield to his most desperate fears.
4. He steeled himself and tried harder.
5. Eventually, a Japanese tuna fisher rescued them.

> **NOTE** Adverbs may come before, after, or between the words they modify.
>
> **EXAMPLES**   **Slowly,** the shark was circling.
> The shark was **slowly** circling.
> The shark was circling **slowly.**

> For more on modifiers in general, see Part 5: Using Modifiers.

Try It Out ✎

For each use of *very* below, substitute another adverb. You may wish to revise the sentence.

1. For entertainment, they imagined *very* delicious foods.
2. Douglas dreamed of a *very* cold honeydew melon.
3. At night on the sea, they felt *very* alone.
4. *Very* quickly, they pulled the sea turtle aboard.
5. After their rescue, a *very* fine cook helped them back to health.

 Using Descriptive Adverbs

The adverb *very* is overused. In your writing, try to replace *very* with more descriptive adverbs, or revise the sentence so that other words carry more of the descriptive meaning.

EXAMPLE   Their ordeal at sea lasted a very long time.
REVISED   Their ordeal at sea lasted an **extremely** long time.

or

Their ordeal at sea lasted **thirty-eight days.**

THE PREPOSITION

1i. A *preposition* is a word used to show the relationship of a noun or a pronoun to another word in the sentence.

Notice how a change in the preposition changes the relationship between *waves* and *rocks* in each of the following examples.

> The waves crashed **under** the rocks.
> The waves crashed **on** the rocks.
> The waves crashed **against** the rocks.
> The waves crashed **in front of** the rocks.

Commonly Used Prepositions

aboard	before	in	over
about	behind	in addition to	past
above	below	in front of	since
according to	beneath	inside	through
across	beside	in spite of	throughout
against	between	into	under
around	from	out of	without

The Prepositional Phrase

A preposition is usually followed by a noun or a pronoun. This noun or pronoun is called the **object of the preposition.** All together, the preposition, its object, and any modifiers of the object are called a **prepositional phrase.**

EXAMPLE   The family went **to beautiful Cocoa Beach.**

A preposition may have more than one object.

EXAMPLE   Tiffany sat **with David, Susan, and Amber.**

✓ QUICK CHECK 6

Identify the preposition or prepositions in each of the following sentences. Then, give the object of each preposition.

EXAMPLE   **1.** Do you know any stories about the sea?
       1. *about—sea*

1. Elizabeth told a sad story about her youth.
2. She had loved a man of the sea.
3. She never said the words to him.
4. One day, he didn't return from a fishing trip.
5. Still, according to Elizabeth, he is always with her.

NOTE Some words may be used as either prepositions or adverbs. To tell an adverb from a preposition, remember that a preposition is always followed by a noun or pronoun object.

NOTE Do not confuse a prepositional phrase that begins with *to* (*to town*) with a verb form that begins with *to* (*to run*).

☞ For more about prepositional phrases, see pages 985, 990, and 991–992.

THE CONJUNCTION

1j. A *conjunction* is a word used to join words or groups of words.

(1) *Coordinating conjunctions* connect words or groups of words used in the same way.

Coordinating Conjunctions						
and	but	or	nor	for	so	yet

EXAMPLES Echo **or** Narcissus [two proper nouns]
down from Olympus **and** to the mountains [two prepositional phrases]
Echo angered Hera, **so** Hera punished her. [two independent clauses]

(2) *Correlative conjunctions* are pairs of conjunctions that connect words or groups of words used in the same way.

Correlative Conjunctions		
both . . . and	either . . . or	neither . . . nor
not only . . . but also	whether . . . or	

EXAMPLES **Both** the nymphs **and** Echo were loyal to Zeus. [two nouns]
She **not only** delayed Hera **but also** detained her. [two verbs with objects]
Either Echo would have love, **or** she would die. [two complete ideas]

NOTE When *for* is used as a conjunction, it connects groups of words that are sentences, and it is preceded by a comma. On all other occasions, *for* is used as a preposition.

CONJUNCTION The team forfeited the game, **for** they refused to play.

PREPOSITION Outraged, people shouted **for** fair play.

☞ Coordinating conjunctions that join independent clauses are preceded by a comma. See page 1019.

THE INTERJECTION

1k. An *interjection* is a word used to express emotion. An interjection does not have a grammatical relation to other words in the sentence. Usually an interjection is followed by an exclamation point. Sometimes an interjection is set off by a comma.

EXAMPLES **Oh!** You surprised me.
Why, I've heard this story before.
Wow! What a story that was.
Well, Hera certainly isn't someone to cross!

Common Interjections			
aha	hooray	ouch	wow
aw	oh	well	yikes
goodness	oops	whew	yippee

 QUICK CHECK 7

Identify the *conjunctions* and *interjections* in the following sentences.

EXAMPLE   1. Well, Echo was either unwise or unlucky.
   1. *Well—interjection; either . . . or—conjunction*

1. Echo not only answered Narcissus but also ran to and embraced him.
2. Oh! Why did Narcissus scoff and shove Echo away?
3. Goodness! Narcissus was a handsome but self-centered person.
4. Both Echo and Narcissus suffered because of his selfishness.
5. They were doomed, yet he lives on in the narcissus flower.

DETERMINING PARTS OF SPEECH

The part of speech of a word is determined by the way the word is used in a sentence. Many words can be used as more than one part of speech.

EXAMPLES   This **well** belongs to the golf course. [noun]
   Well, Dondré was quite disappointed. [interjection]
   He has always played **well.** [adverb]

   Clifton Davis suddenly remembered an event from his **past.** [noun]
   Didn't his team drive **past** the Lincoln Memorial? [preposition]
   As they rode along, the lights of the city flew **past.** [adverb]

 QUICK CHECK 8

Identify the part of speech of the italicized word in each sentence.

EXAMPLE   1. *For* Dondré Green, it was a blessing in disguise.
   1. *preposition*

1. *Any* of the boys might have objected, but no one did.
2. They all would *back* him.
3. And they never looked *back.*
4. *Support* like that can make a man proud.
5. I wish everyone would *support* each other as those boys did!

2 AGREEMENT

NUMBER

Number is the form of a word that indicates whether the word is singular or plural.

2a. **When a word refers to one person, place, thing, or idea, the word is *singular* in number. When a word refers to more than one, it is *plural* in number.**

SINGULAR	house	drum	wife	I	he	each
PLURAL	houses	drums	wives	we	they	all

 For more about plurals, see pages 1033–1034.

AGREEMENT OF SUBJECT AND VERB

2b. **A verb agrees with its subject in number.**

A subject and verb **agree** when they have the same number.

(1) Singular subjects take singular verbs.

EXAMPLE A **messenger gives** the king's orders.

(2) Plural subjects take plural verbs.

EXAMPLE Many **wives weep** after their husbands' departures during the war.

The first auxiliary (helping) verb in a verb phrase must agree with its subject.

EXAMPLES **He is** marching to war.
They are marching to war.

TIPS FOR SPELLING

Generally, nouns ending in *s* are plural (*candles, ideas, neighbors, horses*), and verbs ending in *s* are singular (*sees, writes, speaks, carries*). However, verbs used with the singular pronouns *I* and *you* generally do not end in *s*.

 For more information about verb phrases, see pages 965, 991, and 993–994.

✓ QUICK CHECK 1

For each of the following sentences, choose the correct form of the verb in parentheses.

EXAMPLE 1. (*Do, Does*) you like folk tales like this one?
1. *Do*

1. A tree spirit (*take, takes*) the shape of the absent husband.
2. Many days (*pass, passes*).
3. Then the husband (*return, returns*).
4. Dogs (*bark, barks*) at him.
5. The judge (*has, have*) suggested a solution.

Problems in Agreement

Prepositional Phrases Between Subjects and Verbs

2c. The number of a subject is not changed by a prepositional phrase following the subject.

NONSTANDARD   One of the strongest heroes are Hercules.

STANDARD   **One** of the strongest heroes **is** Hercules.

Indefinite Pronouns

Some pronouns do not refer to a definite person, place, thing, or idea and are therefore called *indefinite pronouns.*

2d. The following indefinite pronouns are singular: *anybody, anyone, each, either, everybody, everyone, neither, nobody, no one, one, somebody, someone.*

EXAMPLE   **Neither** of these offers **relieves** him of his task.

2e. The following indefinite pronouns are plural: *both, few, many, several.*

EXAMPLE   **Both** of the wild boar's tusks **frighten** Eurystheus.

2f. The following indefinite pronouns may be either singular or plural: *all, any, most, none, some.*

COMPUTER NOTE
You may want to create an indefinite-pronoun guide to help you use these pronouns correctly. First, summarize the information in rules 2d–2f and 2p–2r. Then, choose several examples to illustrate the rules. Using a computer, you can create a "Help" file in which to store this information. Call up your "Help" file whenever you run into difficulty with indefinite pronouns in your writing. If you don't use a computer, keep a writing notebook.

The number of these pronouns is often determined by the object in a prepositional phrase that follows the pronoun. If the pronoun refers to a singular object, the subject is singular. If the pronoun refers to a plural object, the subject is plural.

EXAMPLES   **All** of the stable **needs** cleaning. [*All* refers to *stable.*]
All of the stalls **need** cleaning. [*All* refers to *stalls.*]

Compound Subjects

2g. Subjects joined by *and* usually take a plural verb.

EXAMPLE   **Augeas** and **Eurystheus rule** kingdoms.

2h. When subjects are joined by *or* or *nor,* the verb agrees with the subject nearer the verb.

EXAMPLES   Neither the **Hydra** nor Juno's huge **snakes defeat** Hercules.
Neither Juno's huge **snakes** nor the **Hydra defeats** Hercules.

NOTE   A compound subject that names only one person or thing takes a singular verb.

EXAMPLES   The **friend** and **teacher** of Hercules **is** Chiron.
Law and **order suffers** when monsters roam the land.

Other Problems in Agreement

2i. **Collective nouns may be either singular or plural.**

A collective noun takes a singular verb when the noun refers to the group as a unit. A collective noun takes a plural verb when the noun refers to the individual parts or members of the group.

EXAMPLES   An oxen **herd goes** with Hercules. [The herd as a unit goes.]

The **herd call** to the stolen cattle. [The members of the herd individually call.]

2j. **When the subject follows the verb, find the subject, and make sure the verb agrees with it. The subject usually follows the verb in sentences beginning with *here* or *there* and in questions.**

EXAMPLES   There **is Centaurus,** and there **are** its **stars.**
Does the **fox** really not **want** the grapes?

The contractions *here's, there's,* and *where's* contain the verb *is* and should be used only with singular subjects.

NONSTANDARD   There's the constellations Hydra and Leo.
STANDARD   There **are** the **constellations** Hydra and Leo.
STANDARD   There**'s** the **constellation** Hydra.

2k. **The contractions *don't* and *doesn't* must agree with their subjects.**

Use *don't* with plural subjects and with the pronouns *I* and *you*. Use *doesn't* with other singular subjects.

EXAMPLES   **They don't** like movies about Hercules, and **I don't** either.

This **film doesn't** seem realistic, but **that doesn't** matter to me.

2l. **Words stating amounts are usually singular.**

A word or phrase stating a weight, a measurement, or an amount of money or time is usually considered a single item. Such a word or phrase takes a singular verb.

EXAMPLE   Five **dollars is** too much for a movie ticket.

2m. **The title of a book or the name of an organization or country, even when plural in form, usually takes a singular verb.**

EXAMPLES   *Aesop's Fables* **is** on our reading list.
Has the **United States** signed the treaty?

NOTE   When the subject of a sentence follows the verb, the word order is said to be *inverted*. To find the subject of a sentence with inverted order, restate the sentence in normal word order.

INVERTED   There **goes Hercules.**
NORMAL   **Hercules goes** there.

INVERTED   Into the clearing **stepped** the mighty **Hercules.**
NORMAL   The mighty **Hercules stepped** into the clearing.

2n. **A few nouns, though plural in form, are singular and take singular verbs.**

EXAMPLES   news, measles, mathematics, civics, mumps, physics

 QUICK CHECK 2

For the following sentences, correct each error in agreement.

EXAMPLE   **1.** There's many interesting stories about heroes.
   1. *There are many interesting stories about heroes.*

1. A flock of monstrous birds hover over the Stymphalian lake.
2. Doesn't the arrows of Hercules strike each bird in turn?
3. Neither Nereus nor his daughters foils Hercules.
4. The god of the oceans don't escape Hercules.
5. Some of the ancient myths seeks to explain actual geological or botanical facts.

AGREEMENT OF PRONOUN AND ANTECEDENT

2o. **A pronoun agrees with its antecedent in number and gender.**

An *antecedent* is the word the pronoun refers to. Some singular personal pronouns have forms that indicate gender. Masculine pronouns refer to males. Feminine pronouns refer to females. Neuter pronouns refer to things (neither male nor female) and sometimes to animals.

FEMININE	she	her	hers
MASCULINE	he	him	his
NEUTER	it	it	its

EXAMPLES   The **speaker** in "Annabel Lee" lost **his** bride.
   Annabel Lee had given **her** heart to him.
   Heaven sent **its** angels for Annabel Lee.

The antecedent of a personal pronoun can be another kind of pronoun, such as *each, neither,* or *one*. To determine the gender of a personal pronoun that refers to one of these other pronouns, look in the phrase that follows the antecedent.

EXAMPLES   **Each** of these **men** left **his** mark on the development of the American short story.
   Neither of the **women** got what **she** wanted.

> **NOTE** When an antecedent may be either masculine or feminine, use both the masculine and the feminine forms.
>
> **EXAMPLES**   No one ever gave **his or her** approval of Poe's criticisms.
> **Everybody** wanted **his or her** writing in Poe's magazine.

Problems in Agreement of Pronoun and Antecedent

Indefinite Pronouns

2p. A singular pronoun is used to refer to *anybody, anyone, each, either, everybody, everyone, neither, nobody, no one, one, someone,* and *somebody.*

For more about indefinite pronouns, see page 961.

EXAMPLE **Each** of these countries has **its** own Cinderella story.

2q. A plural pronoun is used to refer to *both, few, many,* and *several.*

EXAMPLES **Both** of these stories take **their** characters from legend.
Many of these versions are similar, but **they** all differ.

2r. Either a singular or a plural pronoun may be used to refer to *all, any, most, none,* and *some.*

The number of the pronouns *all, any, most, none,* and *some* is determined by the object in the prepositional phrase following the pronoun.

EXAMPLES **Some** of the story may come from the culture telling **it.**
[*Some* refers to the singular noun *story.*]
Some of the sisters are punished for **their** cruelty.
[*Some* refers to the plural noun *sisters.*]

Compound Subjects

2s. A plural pronoun is used to refer to two or more antecedents joined by *and.*

EXAMPLE The **sisters and their mother** never share **their** fine clothing.

2t. A singular pronoun is used to refer to two or more singular antecedents joined by *or* or *nor.*

EXAMPLE Neither **the mother nor a sister** shared **her** clothes.

Other Problems in Pronoun-Antecedent Agreement

2u. Either a singular or a plural pronoun may be used with a collective noun.

For more information about collective nouns, see page 959.

EXAMPLES The royal **family** was preparing **its** celebration.
The royal **family** are greeting **their** new princess.

2v. Words stating amounts usually take singular pronouns.

EXAMPLE Admission costs five **dollars.** Maybe I can earn **it** in time.

2w. **The title of a book or the name of an organization or a country, even when plural in form, usually takes a singular pronoun.**

EXAMPLES I read *Folktales Around the World,* and **it** was great.
The **United Nations** can revise **its** charter.

2x. **A few nouns, though plural in form, are singular and take singular pronouns.**

EXAMPLE **Physics** is important, but **it** has nothing to do with folk tales.

 See page 973 for a list of singular nouns that are plural in form.

 QUICK CHECK 3

For each blank in the following sentences, give a pronoun that will complete the meaning of the sentence. Then, identify the antecedent or antecedents of that pronoun.

EXAMPLE 1. Kari or Leah will bring _____ copy of *The Glass Slipper.*
1. *her—Kari or Leah*

1. Aschenputtel and Cinderella got _____ names from ashes.
2. One of the stories features pigeons in _____ ending.
3. Many of the stories reward _____ heroes, but some don't.
4. The court cheered the prince and her and gave _____ a grand wedding.
5. Neither the prince nor the Pharaoh married the young woman _____ expected.

 Using Compound Antecedents

Sentences with singular antecedents joined by *or* or *nor* can sound awkward if the antecedents are of different genders. If the sentence sounds awkward, revise it to avoid the problem.

AWKWARD Ana or Ed will read her or his version of *Cinderella.*

REVISED **Ana** will read **her** version of *Cinderella,* or **Ed** will read **his.**

Similarly, a singular and a plural antecedent joined by *or* or *nor* can create an awkward or a confusing sentence. Revise such a sentence to avoid the problem.

AWKWARD Either my cousins or Mary will bring their video of *Cinderella.*

REVISED Either **my cousins** will bring **their** video of *Cinderella,* or **Mary** will bring **hers.**

Try It Out ✎

Revise each of the following sentences to eliminate awkward pronoun usage.

1. Neither her mother nor her sisters recognized that the girl was their own Aschenputtel.
2. Either birds or a fish help the heroine in their own way.
3. Did a fish or a falcon lend their help to Yeh-Shen?
4. Neither Yeh-Shen nor the king could have guessed her or his fate.
5. Joey or Linda will read his or her report on "Sealskin, Soulskin."

3 USING VERBS

THE PRINCIPAL PARTS OF A VERB

The four basic forms of a verb are called the **principal parts** of the verb.

3a. **The principal parts of a verb are the** *base form,* **the** *present participle,* **the** *past,* **and the** *past participle.*

BASE FORM	PRESENT PARTICIPLE	PAST	PAST PARTICIPLE
work	(is) working	worked	(have) worked
sing	(is) singing	sang	(have) sung

> **NOTE** Notice that the present participle and the past participle require helping verbs (forms of *be* and *have*).

The principal parts of a verb are used to express the time that an action occurs.

PRESENT TIME   I **sing** rhythm and blues now.
We **are singing** along with the frog.

PAST TIME   The frog **sang** at the Big Time Weekly Concert.
We **have sung** there before.

FUTURE TIME   The audience **will sing** along with the frog.
By 8:00 P.M., we **will have sung** two numbers.

> ☞ See page 990 for information about participles used as modifiers.

Regular Verbs

3b. **A** *regular verb* **forms its past and past participle by adding** *–d* **or** *–ed* **to the base form.**

BASE FORM	PRESENT PARTICIPLE	PAST	PAST PARTICIPLE
use	(is) using	used	(have) used
attack	(is) attacking	attacked	(have) attacked

Avoid the following common errors when forming the past or past participle of regular verbs:

1. leaving off the *–d* or *–ed* ending

NONSTANDARD   We use to think the frog couldn't sing.
STANDARD   We **used** to think the frog couldn't sing.

2. adding unnecessary letters

NONSTANDARD   The audience of animals attackted him.
STANDARD   The audience of animals **attacked** him.

☑ **QUICK CHECK 1**

For each of the following sentences, supply the correct past or past participle form of the verb given in italics.

EXAMPLE   **1.** *discover*   Frog has _____ his singing talent.
                   1. *discovered*

1. *cross*   He _____ over to the other side of the pond.
2. *visit*   He has _____ his friends to tell them of his wish to sing.
3. *join*   The birds already have _____ together to form a group.
4. *use*   Fox let Frog sing but also _____ a trick to fool Frog.
5. *leap*   When Frog was introduced, he _____ out on stage.

Irregular Verbs

3c. **An *irregular verb* forms its past and past participle in some other way than by adding *–d* or *–ed* to the base form.**

An irregular verb forms its past and past participle by

- changing vowels *or* consonants

	Base Form	Past	Past Participle
EXAMPLE	ring	rang	(have) rung

- changing vowels *and* consonants

	Base Form	Past	Past Participle
EXAMPLE	go	went	(have) gone

- making no changes

	Base Form	Past	Past Participle
EXAMPLE	spread	spread	(have) spread

When you are not sure how to spell the principal parts of an irregular verb, look in a dictionary.

Avoid the following common errors when forming the past or past participle of irregular verbs:

1. using the past form with a helping verb

NONSTANDARD	Frog has went to the Big Time Weekly Concert.
STANDARD	Frog **went** to the Big Time Weekly Concert.

or

STANDARD	Frog **has gone** to the Big Time Weekly Concert.

2. using the past participle form without a helping verb

NONSTANDARD	I seen all of his shows.
STANDARD	I **have seen** all of his shows.

3. adding *–d* or *–ed* to the base form

NONSTANDARD	The elephant throwed a pineapple at the frog.
STANDARD	The elephant **threw** a pineapple at the frog.

COMMON IRREGULAR VERBS

GROUP I: Each of these irregular verbs has the same form for its past and past participle.

BASE FORM	PRESENT PARTICIPLE	PAST	PAST PARTICIPLE
bring	(is) bringing	brought	(have) brought
build	(is) building	built	(have) built
catch	(is) catching	caught	(have) caught
hold	(is) holding	held	(have) held
lay	(is) laying	laid	(have) laid
lead	(is) leading	led	(have) led
say	(is) saying	said	(have) said
send	(is) sending	sent	(have) sent
spin	(is) spinning	spun	(have) spun
swing	(is) swinging	swung	(have) swung

 QUICK CHECK 2

For each of the following sentences, give the correct past or past participle form of the verb in parentheses.

EXAMPLE **1.** Joey (*say*) he had the blues.
        1. *said*

1. Frog has (*bring*) rhythm and blues to the world.
2. Since then, many a guitarist has (*lay*) down a blues riff.
3. Many blues singers (*lead*) listeners to recall sad times.
4. Some musicians have (*build*) that sound using only a harmonica.
5. Others (*catch*) the beat with only their voice.

COMMON IRREGULAR VERBS

GROUP II: Each of these irregular verbs has a different form for its past and past participle.

BASE FORM	PRESENT PARTICIPLE	PAST	PAST PARTICIPLE
begin	(is) beginning	began	(have) begun
choose	(is) choosing	chose	(have) chosen
do	(is) doing	did	(have) done
draw	(is) drawing	drew	(have) drawn
go	(is) going	went	(have) gone
know	(is) knowing	knew	(have) known
run	(is) running	ran	(have) run
shake	(is) shaking	shook	(have) shaken
sing	(is) singing	sang	(have) sung
swim	(is) swimming	swam	(have) swum

QUICK CHECK 3

For each of the following sentences, give the correct past or past participle form of the verb in parentheses.

EXAMPLE   **1.** Louis Armstrong really (*know*) how to play jazz on his trumpet.

      1. *knew*

1. Some say rhythm and blues (*begin*) in the 1940s.
2. Like the frog, the legendary Muddy Waters (*draw*) crowds.
3. Who has (*sing*) with him?
4. Have you ever (*do*) the bump or the mashed potato?
5. In the story, the lion (*shake*) to the twist.

COMMON IRREGULAR VERBS			
GROUP III: Each of these irregular verbs has the same form for its base form, past, and past participle.			
BASE FORM	**PRESENT PARTICIPLE**	**PAST**	**PAST PARTICIPLE**
burst	(is) bursting	burst	(have) burst
cost	(is) costing	cost	(have) cost
cut	(is) cutting	cut	(have) cut
hit	(is) hitting	hit	(have) hit
hurt	(is) hurting	hurt	(have) hurt
let	(is) letting	let	(have) let
put	(is) putting	put	(have) put
read	(is) reading	read	(have) read
set	(is) setting	set	(have) set
spread	(is) spreading	spread	(have) spread

 QUICK CHECK 4

For each of the following sentences, give the correct past or past participle form of the verb in italics.

EXAMPLE   **1.** How many people have been (*hurt*) by misunderstandings with others?

      1. *hurt*

1. *cost*   Slade and others like him have _____ Mr. Baumer a lot of money.
2. *hit*   Once, Slade _____ Mr. Baumer.
3. *let*   Yet, Mr. Baumer _____ Slade work for him.
4. *set*   Secretly, Mr. Baumer has _____ a trap for Slade.
5. *read*   Unlike Slade, Mr. Baumer _____ the warning.

Try It Out ✎

Revise each of the following sentences to sound natural in a dialogue.

1. Butch replied, "I must say, old friend, that I cannot quite believe you."
2. "Gracious, what a marvelous party that was!" beamed Tanya when the group met Monday morning at school.
3. "Please accept our congratulations on a job well done," cried Jim's teammates, slapping him on the back after the game.
4. "I beg your pardon, but you are sitting in my seat," said the sergeant to the recruit.
5. "What an unfaithful friend you are to have spoken against me behind my back," exclaimed Angela to her classmate.

Using Nonstandard Verb Forms

Using standard verb forms is important in almost all the writing that you do for school. Your readers expect standard usage in essays and reports. On the other hand, readers expect the dialogue in plays and short stories to sound natural. For dialogue to sound natural, it must reflect the speech patterns of real people, and real people speak in all sorts of nonstandard ways. Look at the following example from the short story "Bargain."

> "I think he hate me," Mr. Baumer went on. "That is the thing. He hate me for coming not from this country. I come here, sixteen years old, and learn to read and write, and I make a business, and so I think he hate me."

How might you translate this passage into standard English? How would that affect your impression of Mr. Baumer?

You may want to discuss the use of nonstandard verb forms with your teacher. Together you can decide how you can use such forms in your writing.

VERB TENSE

3d. **The *tense* of a verb indicates the time of the action or state of being that is expressed by the verb.**

Every verb has six tenses.

Present	Past	Future
Present Perfect	Past Perfect	Future Perfect

This time line shows how the six tenses are related to one another.

Past	*Present*	*Future*
existing or happening in the past	existing or happening now	existing or happening in the future

Past Perfect	*Present Perfect*	*Future Perfect*
existing or happening before a specific time in the past	existing or happening sometime before now or starting in the past and continuing now	existing or happening before a specific time in the future

Listing all forms of a verb in the six tenses is called ***conjugating*** a verb.

CONJUGATION OF THE VERB *WRITE*

PRESENT TENSE

SINGULAR	*PLURAL*
I write	we write
you write	you write
he, she, *or* it writes	they write

PAST TENSE

SINGULAR	*PLURAL*
I wrote	we wrote
you wrote	you wrote
he, she, *or* it wrote	they wrote

FUTURE TENSE

SINGULAR	*PLURAL*
I will write	we will write
you will write	you will write
he, she, *or* it will write	they will write

PRESENT PERFECT TENSE

SINGULAR	*PLURAL*
I have written	we have written
you have written	you have written
he, she, *or* it has written	they have written

PAST PERFECT TENSE

SINGULAR	*PLURAL*
I had written	we had written
you had written	you had written
he, she, *or* it had written	they had written

FUTURE PERFECT TENSE

SINGULAR	*PLURAL*
I will have written	we will have written
you will have written	you will have written
he, she, *or* it will have written	they will have written

NOTE In the future tense and in the future perfect tense, the helping verb *shall* is sometimes used in place of *will*.

Consistency of Tense

3e. **Do not change needlessly from one tense to another.**

When writing about events in the present, use verbs in the present tense. When writing about events in the past, use verbs in the past tense.

INCONSISTENT   When they were satisfied, they begin planting.

CONSISTENT   When they **are** satisfied, they **begin** planting.

CONSISTENT   When they **were** satisfied, they **began** planting.

✓ QUICK CHECK 5

Read the following paragraph, and decide whether it should be rewritten in the present or past tense. Then, change the verb forms to make the verb tense consistent.

EXAMPLE [1] These city boys enjoyed gardening when they get the chance.

1. These city boys enjoyed gardening when they got the chance.

or

1. These city boys enjoy gardening when they get the chance.

[1] No one tells them no, so they started to work. [2] It is hard, too; over and over, they carried dozens of sacks of dirt up the stairs. [3] None of the neighbors noticed them, or maybe they don't mind. [4] At last, almost before they know it, the rooftop is ready. [5] The rich, black earth waits for seeds.

COMPUTER NOTE

Most word processors can help you check your writing to be sure that you've used verbs correctly. Spelling checkers will highlight misspelled verb forms such as *drownded* or *costed*. Style-checking software can point out inconsistent verb tenses and may also highlight questionable uses of problem verb pairs such as *lie/lay* or *rise/raise*.

SPECIAL PROBLEMS WITH VERBS

Sit and Set

(1) The verb *sit* means "rest in an upright, seated position." *Sit* seldom takes an object.

(2) The verb *set* means "put (something) in a place." *Set* usually takes an object.

BASE FORM	PRESENT PARTICIPLE	PAST	PAST PARTICIPLE
sit (rest)	(is) sitting	sat	(have) sat
set (put)	(is) setting	set	(have) set

EXAMPLES Let's **sit** in the shade. [no object]
Let's **set** the buckets here. [Let's set what? *Buckets* is the object.]

Lie and Lay

(1) The verb *lie* means "rest," "recline," or "be in a place." *Lie* never takes an object.

(2) The verb *lay* means "put (something) in a place." *Lay* usually takes an object.

BASE FORM	PRESENT PARTICIPLE	PAST	PAST PARTICIPLE
lie (rest)	(is) lying	lay	(have) lain
lay (put)	(is) laying	laid	(have) laid

EXAMPLES   In the photograph, juicy, red watermelons **lay** on rich earth. [no object]

They **laid** dirt on the roof. [They laid what? *Dirt* is the object.]

Rise and *Raise*

(1) The verb *rise* means "go up" or "get up." *Rise* never takes an object.

(2) The verb *raise* means "lift up" or "cause (something) to rise." *Raise* usually takes an object.

BASE FORM	PRESENT PARTICIPLE	PAST	PAST PARTICIPLE
rise (go up)	(is) rising	rose	(have) risen
raise (lift up)	(is) raising	raised	(have) raised

EXAMPLES   My next-door neighbors **rise** very early in the morning. [no object]

They **raise** the blinds at dawn. [They raise what? *Blinds* is the object.]

 QUICK CHECK 6

For each of the following sentences, choose the correct verb form in parentheses.

EXAMPLE   **1.** Our garden (*lies, lays*) in the sunniest corner of our backyard.
   1. *lies*

1. Juan Guerrero (*raises, rises*) the bag containing the tomatillos he has grown.
2. Like Juan, other people also (*sat, set*) out their own plants each spring.
3. He will not just (*sit, set*) and remain idle.
4. Avoiding the heat of the day, Mr. Garcia also (*raises, rises*) early to tend his plot.
5. Once, only junk and trash (*lay, laid*) there, but now there is a beautiful garden.

4 USING PRONOUNS

CASE

Case is the form of a noun or a pronoun that shows how it is used. There are three cases: **nominative, objective,** and **possessive.** The form of a noun is the same for both the nominative and objective cases. A noun changes its form for the possessive case, usually by the addition of an apostrophe and an *s.*

Most personal pronouns have different forms for all three cases.

PERSONAL PRONOUNS		
SINGULAR		
NOMINATIVE CASE	**OBJECTIVE CASE**	**POSSESSIVE CASE**
I	me	my, mine
you	you	your, yours
he, she, it	him, her, it	his, her, hers, its
PLURAL		
NOMINATIVE CASE	**OBJECTIVE CASE**	**POSSESSIVE CASE**
we	us	our, ours
you	you	your, yours
they	them	their, theirs

The Nominative Case

4a. **A subject of a verb is in the nominative case.**

EXAMPLES **I** enjoy Anne McCaffrey's writing style. [*I* is the subject of *enjoy.*]

He and **she** were still at home. [*He* and *she* are the subjects of *were.*]

4b. **A *predicate nominative* is in the nominative case.**

A ***predicate nominative*** follows a linking verb and explains or identifies the subject of the verb. A personal pronoun used as a predicate nominative follows a form of the verb *be* (*am, is, are, was, were, be,* or *been*).

EXAMPLES The last one to arrive there was **he.** [*He* identifies the subject *one.*]

Could it be **she?** [*She* identifies the subject *it.*]

NOTE Possessive pronouns (such as *my, your,* and *our*) are also sometimes called **possessive adjectives.**

☞ For more about possessive pronouns, see pages 960 and 1027.

NOTE To choose the correct pronoun in a compound subject, try each form of the pronoun separately.

EXAMPLE: Beterli and (*be, him*) quarreled. [*He* quarreled. *Him* quarreled.]

ANSWER: Beterli and **he** quarreled.

☞ For more about predicate nominatives, see page 1006.

The Objective Case

4c. A *direct object* is in the objective case.

A *direct object* follows an action verb and tells *who* or *what* receives the action of the verb.

EXAMPLES   The bronze dragon's choice amazed **us**. [*Us* tells *who* was amazed.]

                    Heth moved his wings and dried **them**. [*Them* tells *what* Heth dried.]

4d. An *indirect object* is in the objective case.

An *indirect object* comes between an action verb and a direct object and tells *to whom* or *to what* or *for whom* or *for what*.

EXAMPLES   Heth asked **him** a question. [*Him* tells *to whom* Heth asked a question.]

                    The dragon and his rider taught **them** a lesson. [*Them* tells *to whom* they taught a lesson.]

4e. An *object of a preposition* is in the objective case.

A *prepositional phrase* contains a preposition, a noun or pronoun called the *object of the preposition,* and any modifiers of that object.

EXAMPLES   like a **hero**   near **us**
                    next to **Dr. Chang**   without **you** and **me**

A pronoun used as the object of a preposition should always be in the objective case.

EXAMPLES   A great honor had been bestowed on **him**.
                    We went with **her** to the mall.

☞ For more about direct objects, see page 1005.

☞ For more about indirect objects, see page 1005.

☞ For a list of prepositions, see page 967. For more about prepositional phrases, see pages 967, 990, and 991–992.

✓ QUICK CHECK 1

For each of the following sentences, identify the correct personal pronoun in parentheses.

EXAMPLE   **1.** Rikki's gentleness surprised (*she, her*).
              1. *her*

1. Rikki had almost drowned, but an English boy named Teddy rescued (*he, him*).
2. Could a mongoose live with (*they, them*) happily?
3. Teddy's mother wasn't sure whether a mongoose would make a good pet, but Rikki gave (*she, her*) a surprise.
4. Didn't (*he, him*) save their lives?
5. "The winner of this battle will be (*I, me*)!" he vowed.

Try It Out ✎

Revise each of the following sentences to show standard and polite usage of pronouns.

1. We and the other candidates dashed to the Impression.
2. "Save a good place for me and my friends," someone called.
3. I wondered who would be first and thought, "Maybe it'll be me!"
4. When K'last asked me who Keevan was, I answered, "That's him."
5. Keevan was the smallest, yet it was him who impressed the bronze dragon.

NOTE In spoken English, the use of *whom* is becoming less common. In fact, when you are speaking, you may correctly begin any question with *who* regardless of the grammar of the sentence. In written English, however, you should distinguish between *who* and *whom*.

Improving Pronoun Usage

Expressions such as *It's me, That's her,* and *It was them* are accepted in everyday speaking. In writing, however, such expressions are generally considered nonstandard and should be avoided.

STANDARD   It is **I.**   That is **she.**   It was **they.**

Additionally, remember that it is considered polite to put first-person pronouns (*I, me, mine, we, us, ours*) last in compound constructions.

EXAMPLE   **The dragonriders and we** arrived at the Hatching Ground.

SPECIAL PRONOUN PROBLEMS

Who and Whom

The pronoun *who* has different forms in the nominative and objective cases. *Who* is the nominative form; *whom* is the objective form.

When deciding whether to use *who* or *whom* in a question, follow these steps:

STEP 1:   Rephrase the question as a statement.

STEP 2:   Decide how the pronoun is used in the statement—as subject, predicate nominative, object of the verb, or object of a preposition.

STEP 3:   Determine the case of the pronoun according to the rules of standard English.

STEP 4:   Select the correct form of the pronoun.

EXAMPLE: (*Who, Whom*) did Jerry see?

STEP 1:   The statement is *Jerry did see (who, whom).*

STEP 2:   The subject of the verb is *Jerry,* the verb is *did see,* and the pronoun is the direct object.

STEP 3:   A pronoun used as a direct object should be in the objective case.

STEP 4:   The objective form is *whom.*

ANSWER: **Whom** did Jerry see?

Pronouns with Appositives

Sometimes a pronoun is followed directly by a noun that identifies the pronoun. Such a noun is called an **appositive.** To choose which pronoun to use before an appositive, omit the appositive, and try each form of the pronoun separately.

EXAMPLE: (*We, Us*) boys live in the Carolinas. [*Boys* is the apposi-
            tive.] *We* live in the Carolinas. *Us* live in the Carolinas.
ANSWER: **We** boys live in the Carolinas.

Reflexive Pronouns

Reflexive pronouns (such as *myself*, *himself*, and *yourselves*) can be used as
objects. Do not use the nonstandard forms *hisself* and *theirself* or *theirselves* in place of *himself* and *themselves*.

NONSTANDARD   Jerry prepared a fire for hisself.
STANDARD   Jerry prepared a fire for **himself.**

 QUICK CHECK 2

For each of the following sentences, choose the correct pronoun in
parentheses.

EXAMPLE   **1.** May (*we, us*) students read aloud?
               1. *we*

1. For (*who, whom*) did the boy work?
2. Jerry did not often play with (*we, us*) in the neighborhood.
3. (*Who, Whom*) wrote *The Yearling*?
4. He promised (*hisself, himself*) that he would do a good job.
5. They seemed pleased with (*theirselves, themselves*).

5 USING MODIFIERS

COMPARISON OF MODIFIERS

A *modifier* is a word, a phrase, or a clause that describes or limits the
meaning of another word. Two kinds of modifiers—*adjectives* and
adverbs—may be used to compare things.

5a. **The three degrees of comparison of modifiers are**
         ***positive, comparative,* and *superlative*.**

POSITIVE	cold	loud	politely
COMPARATIVE	colder	louder	more politely
SUPERLATIVE	coldest	loudest	most politely

Regular Comparison

**(1) Most one-syllable modifiers form their comparative and
       superlative degrees by adding –er and –est.**

POSITIVE	sharp	calm	cold
COMPARATIVE	sharper	calmer	colder
SUPERLATIVE	sharpest	calmest	coldest

☞ For more about
appositives, see page 995.

☞ For more about
reflexive pronouns, see
page 961.

NOTE To show decreas-
ing comparisons,
all modifiers form their
comparative and superla-
tive degrees with *less* and
least.

POSITIVE
  calm
  rapidly
COMPARATIVE
  less calm
  less rapidly
SUPERLATIVE
  least calm
  least rapidly

(2) Some two-syllable modifiers form their comparative and superlative degrees by adding *–er* and *–est*. Others form their comparative and superlative degrees by using *more* and *most*.

POSITIVE	simple	sudden	quietly
COMPARATIVE	simpler	more sudden	more quietly
SUPERLATIVE	simplest	most sudden	most quietly

(3) Modifiers that have three or more syllables form their comparative and superlative degrees by using *more* and *most*.

POSITIVE	luxurious	fearfully	curious
COMPARATIVE	more luxurious	more fearfully	more curious
SUPERLATIVE	most luxurious	most fearfully	most curious

Irregular Comparison

Some modifiers do not form their comparative and superlative degrees by using the regular methods.

POSITIVE	bad	far	good	well	many	much
COMPARATIVE	worse	farther	better	better	more	more
SUPERLATIVE	worst	farthest	best	best	most	most

 QUICK CHECK 1

Drop the final silent e before a suffix beginning with a vowel.

EXAMPLES   safe + er = safer
ripe + est = ripest
gentle + er = gentler

Give the forms for the comparative and superlative degrees of the following modifiers.

EXAMPLE   **1.** colorful

    1. *more (less) colorful, most (least) colorful*

1. fine	**5.** daring	**9.** well
2. cautiously	**6.** comfortable	**10.** dainty
3. gladly	**7.** much	
4. thankful	**8.** cozy	

Uses of Comparative and Superlative Forms

5b. Use the comparative degree when comparing two things. Use the superlative degree when comparing more than two.

COMPARATIVE   This mouse is **safer** than the Town Mouse.
She sleeps **more soundly** than the Town Mouse.

SUPERLATIVE   This mouse is the **safest** one in the world.
Of the three animals, the cat slept **most soundly.**

5c. Use *good* to modify a noun or a pronoun. Use *well* to modify a verb.

EXAMPLE   The Town Mouse enjoyed **good food.** She **ate well.**

5d. **Use adjectives, not adverbs, after linking verbs.**

EXAMPLE   The Town Mouse's life seemed **wonderful.** [*not* wonderfully]

5e. **Avoid using double comparisons.**

A **double comparison** is the use of both *–er* and *more* (*less*) or both *–est* and *most* (*least*) to form a comparison. A comparison should be formed in only one of these two ways, not both.

EXAMPLE   The Country Mouse is **safer** [*not* more safer] than the Town Mouse.

5f. **A double negative is the use of two negative words to express one negative idea.**

Common Negative Words			
barely	never	none	nothing
hardly	no	no one	nowhere
neither	nobody	not (–n't)	scarcely

NONSTANDARD   She hasn't never liked cats.

STANDARD   She hasn't ever [*or* has never] liked cats.

 QUICK CHECK 2

The following sentences contain incorrect forms of comparison. Revise each sentence, using the correct form.

EXAMPLE   1. The acorns were the more delicious of all the foods.
                1. *The acorns were the most delicious of all the foods.*

1. Of course, the Town Mouse had the more finer foods.
2. However, the Country Mouse couldn't hardly enjoy those foods.
3. To the mice, was the cat most dangerous than the dog?
4. The Town Mouse ate worst on her visit to the country.
5. Of the two mice, which is the safest?

PLACEMENT OF MODIFIERS

5g. **Place modifying words, phrases, and clauses as close as possible to the words they modify.**

Notice how the meaning of the following sentence changes when the position of the phrase *from the country* changes.

The mouse **from the country** saw a cat. [The phrase modifies *mouse.*]

The mouse saw a cat **from the country.** [The phrase modifies *cat.*]

Prepositional Phrases

A **prepositional phrase** consists of a preposition, a noun or a pronoun called the *object of the preposition,* and any modifiers of that object. A prepositional phrase used as an adjective should be placed directly after the word it modifies.

MISPLACED	A cat would not be dangerous to the mice with a bell.
CLEAR	A cat **with a bell** would not be dangerous to the mice.

A prepositional phrase used as an adverb should be placed near the word it modifies.

MISPLACED	The mice had a meeting about the cat **in fear.**
CLEAR	**In fear,** the mice had a meeting about the cat.

Avoid placing a prepositional phrase in a position where it can modify either of two words. Place the phrase so that it clearly modifies the word you intend it to modify.

MISPLACED	The mouse said in the morning she would go. [Does the phrase modify *said* or *would go*?]
CLEAR	The mouse said she would go **in the morning.**
	or
CLEAR	**In the morning,** the mouse said she would go.

Participial Phrases

A **participial phrase** consists of a verb form—either a present participle or a past participle—and its related words. A participial phrase modifies a noun or a pronoun. Like a prepositional phrase, a participial phrase should be placed as close as possible to the word it modifies.

MISPLACED	The mice hid from the cat scurrying fearfully.
CLEAR	**Scurrying fearfully,** the mice hid from the cat.

A participial phrase that does not clearly and sensibly modify any word in the sentence is a **dangling participial phrase.** To correct a dangling phrase, supply a word that the phrase can modify, or add a subject, a verb, or both to the dangling modifier.

DANGLING	Worried constantly, a plan was needed.
CLEAR	Worried constantly, **the mice** needed a plan.
	or
CLEAR	The mice needed a plan **because they worried** constantly.

For more about prepositions and prepositional phrases, see pages 967, 985, and 991–992.

For more about participial phrases, see page 993.

Clauses

A *clause* is a group of words that contains a verb and its subject and that is used as a part of a sentence. An *adjective clause* modifies a noun or a pronoun. Most adjective clauses begin with a relative pronoun, such as *that, which, who, whom,* or *whose.* An *adverb clause* modifies a verb, an adjective, or another adverb. Most adverb clauses begin with a subordinating conjunction, such as *although, while, if,* or *because.*

Like phrases, clauses should be placed as close as possible to the words they modify.

MISPLACED	The fable was written by Aesop that we read today.
CLEAR	The fable **that we read today** was written by Aesop.

 For more about clauses, see Part 7: Clauses.

 QUICK CHECK 3

Each of the following sentences contains a misplaced or dangling modifier. Revise each sentence so that it is clear and correct.

EXAMPLE
   1. A cat was frightening the mice with sharp claws and teeth.

   1. *A cat with sharp claws and teeth was frightening the mice.*

1. The mice complained about the cat at the meeting.
2. A bell could protect the mice on the cat.
3. Ringing loudly with each step, the mice could run away.
4. The plan had a flaw that he was suggesting.
5. An old mouse questioned the young mouse shaking his head sadly.

COMPUTER NOTE   A computer can help you find and correct nonstandard forms of modifiers such as *baddest, expensiver,* and *mostest.* However, the computer cannot help you make sure that a modifier is not misplaced or dangling. You will need to check the placement of your modifiers yourself.

6   PHRASES

6a.   **A *phrase* is a group of related words that is used as a single part of speech and does not contain a verb and its subject.**

VERB PHRASE	should have been stabled
PREPOSITIONAL PHRASE	with a shudder and whitened eyes

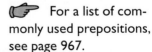 For more information about verb phrases, see pages 965, 970, and 1002.

THE PREPOSITIONAL PHRASE

6b.   **A *prepositional phrase* includes a preposition, a noun or pronoun called the *object of the preposition,* and any modifiers of that object.**

EXAMPLES   The runaway was filled **with confusion and fear.**
                 The colt **in front of them** climbed **up the wall.**

For a list of commonly used prepositions, see page 967.

NOTE An adjective phrase always follows the word it modifies. That word may be the object of another prepositional phrase.

EXAMPLE "The Runaway" is a poem **about a colt in the snow.**

[The phrase *about a colt* modifies the predicate nominative *poem.* The phrase *in the snow* modifies the object *colt.*]

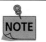

NOTE An adverb phrase may come either before or after the word it modifies.

EXAMPLES **Before that time,** Frost had published little.
Frost had published little **before that time.**

The Adjective Phrase

6c. An *adjective phrase* is a prepositional phrase that modifies a noun or a pronoun.

An adjective phrase tells *what kind* or *which one.*

EXAMPLES Robert Frost was a poet **of nature.** [What kind?]
"The Runaway" is the one **about a colt.** [Which one?]

More than one adjective phrase may modify the same word.

EXAMPLE A pasture **of snow on a mountain** upsets him. [The phrases *of snow* and *on a mountain* modify *pasture.*]

The Adverb Phrase

6d. An *adverb phrase* is a prepositional phrase that modifies a verb, an adjective, or an adverb.

An adverb phrase tells *how, when, where, why,* or *to what extent* (that is, *how long, how many,* or *how far*).

EXAMPLES The colt bolted **with a nervous snort.** [How?]
The colt seemed uneasy **because of the snow.** [Why?]
The poem takes place late **in the day.** [When?]
Frost had written poetry **for many years.** [How long?]

More than one adverb phrase may modify the same word or words.

EXAMPLE **At the Kennedy Inauguration,** Frost read **to the American people.**

An adverb phrase may be modified by an adjective phrase.

EXAMPLE **In his poem about the runaway,** Frost uses several verbals. [The adverb phrase modifies the verb *uses.* The adjective phrase modifies *poem.*]

QUICK CHECK I

Identify the prepositional phrase or phrases in each numbered sentence in the following paragraph. Then, label each phrase as an *adjective phrase* or an *adverb phrase.* Give the word the phrase modifies.

EXAMPLE [1] They make judgments about the colt and its care.
1. *about the colt and its care—adjective phrase—judgments*

[1] Many of Robert Frost's poems contain imagery from nature. [2] These images say much about people and human nature. [3] "The Runaway" focuses on a colt's experiences during its first winter. [4] In the poem Frost shows observers' reactions to the colt. [5] The colt, the subject of conversation between the observers, is important to them.

VERBALS AND VERBAL PHRASES

A **verbal** is a form of a verb that is used as a noun, an adjective, or an adverb. There are three kinds of verbals: the *participle,* the *gerund,* and the *infinitive.*

Participles and Participial Phrases

6e. A *participle* is a verb form that can be used as an adjective.

There are two kinds of participles—*present participles* and *past participles.*

(1) *Present participles* end in *–ing.*

EXAMPLE The rats **swimming** ashore alarmed them. [*Swimming,* a form of the verb *swim,* modifies *rats.*]

(2) Most *past participles* end in *–d* or *–ed.* Others are irregularly formed.

EXAMPLES No one was on the **abandoned** ship. [*Abandoned,* a form of the verb *abandon,* modifies *ship.*]

The rats, **known** for their ferocity, swam toward the sailors. [*Known,* a form of the verb *know,* modifies *rats.*]

6f. A *participial phrase* consists of a participle and all the words related to the participle. The entire phrase is used as an adjective.

EXAMPLES **Seeing a ship nearby,** scores of rats dove into the sea. [The participial phrase modifies the noun *scores.* The noun *ship* is the direct object of the present participle *seeing.*]

We could see the sharks **feasting hungrily on the swarms of rats.** [The participial phrase modifies the noun *sharks.* The adverb *hungrily* and the adverb phrase *on the swarms of rats* modify the present participle *feasting.*]

☞ For information on placement of participial phrases, see page 990.

Gerunds and Gerund Phrases

6g. A *gerund* is a verb form ending in *–ing* that is used as a noun.

SUBJECT	**Singing** can be fun.
PREDICATE NOMINATIVE	My favorite pastime is **singing.**
OBJECT OF PREPOSITION	I warm up before **singing.**
DIRECT OBJECT	Do you enjoy **singing**?

6h. A *gerund phrase* consists of a gerund and all the words related to the gerund.

EXAMPLE   **Counting the innumerable rats on the lighthouse** calmed the men. [The gerund phrase is the subject of the sentence. The noun *rats* is the direct object of the gerund *counting*.]

Infinitives and Infinitive Phrases

6i. An *infinitive* is a verb form that can be used as a noun, an adjective, or an adverb. Infinitives usually begin with to.

NOUNS   **To escape** was their sole desire. [subject]
Was the sailors' fate **to become** dinner? [predicate nominative]
They had **to signal** but not **to let** the rats in. [direct objects]

ADJECTIVES   The time **to signal** was now. [*To signal* modifies *time.*]
Who was the first man **to crack** under the pressure? [*To crack* modifies *man.*]

ADVERBS   Rescuers were quick **to answer.** [*To answer* modifies *quick.*]
They came to the island **to tend** the light. [*To tend* modifies *came.*]

> **NOTE** *To* plus a noun or a pronoun (*to class, to them, to the dance*) is a prepositional phrase, not an infinitive. Be careful not to confuse infinitives with prepositional phrases beginning with *to.*
>
> **INFINITIVE**   I want **to go.**
> **PREPOSITIONAL PHRASE**   I want to go **to sea.**

6j. An *infinitive phrase* consists of an infinitive and its modifiers and complements. The entire infinitive phrase may act as an adjective, an adverb, or a noun.

EXAMPLES   Lighthouses are one way **to warn ships away from rocks.** [adjective]
The men were grateful **to see the ship.** [adverb]
To be rescued was their only hope. [noun]

 ## QUICK CHECK 2

Identify each italicized phrase in the following sentences as *participial, gerund,* or *infinitive.*

EXAMPLE   **1.** *Swimming in the sea* was easy for the rats.
1. *gerund*

1. The rats, *lured by the scent,* approached the lighthouse.
2. *Seeing the laughing men* enraged the frenzied rats.
3. They tried *to get in through the windows and door.*
4. *Clawing and biting the metal, glass, and stone,* they succeeded.
5. What happened to the horrified men left *to fend for themselves*?

APPOSITIVES AND APPOSITIVE PHRASES

6k. An *appositive* is a noun or a pronoun placed beside another noun or pronoun to identify or explain it.

Appositives are often set off from the rest of the sentence by commas or dashes. However, when an appositive is necessary to the meaning of the sentence or when it is closely related to the word it refers to, no commas are necessary.

EXAMPLES   The author **George G. Toudouze** wrote the story "Three Skeleton Key." [The noun *George G. Toudouze* identifies the noun *author*.]

The men saw a strange ship, **one** with Dutch lines and three masts. [The pronoun *one* refers to the noun *ship*.]

Their victims—the **captain** and **crew**—had vanished. [The nouns *captain* and *crew* explain who were the victims.]

☞ For information on the use of commas with appositives and appositive phrases, see page 1020.

6l. An *appositive phrase* consists of an appositive and its modifiers.

EXAMPLES   Le Gleo, **one of the lighthouse keepers,** had horrible nightmares. [The adjective phrase *of the lighthouse keepers* modifies the appositive *one*.]

Rats, **the foul scourge of sailing ships,** pressed for entrance. [The article *the,* the adjective *foul,* and the adjective phrase *of sailing ships* modify the appositive *scourge.*]

☑ QUICK CHECK 3

Identify the appositives or appositive phrases in the following sentences. Give the word or words each appositive or appositive phrase identifies or explains.

EXAMPLE   1. The rats, a huge and hardy breed, swarmed the decks.
      1. *a huge and hardy breed—rats*

1. Three men—the narrator, Le Gleo, and Itchoua—stared in horror at the rats.
2. The entire crew would likely have perished but for the engineer, a brave man.
3. Terriers, dogs bred for hunting, were certainly no match for these vicious rats.
4. The supply boat, the last one of the month, would be no help because it would arrive too late.
5. His friend Le Gleo was never the same again.

Try It Out ✎

For each of the following items, use phrases to combine the short, choppy sentences into one smooth sentence.

1. Three Skeleton Key was a small rock. It was about twenty miles offshore.
2. Three convicts had died there. They were in hiding after escaping from prison.
3. People said that the dead men's skeletons danced. They danced at night.
4. He wanted to save money. He volunteered for the lighthouse job.
5. The rocks had smooth, slick surfaces. They were dangerous.

Using Phrases to Combine Sentences

Knowing how to use different kinds of phrases can help you improve your writing. For example, to revise a series of choppy sentences, combine them by turning at least one sentence into a phrase.

CHOPPY — A beautiful ship approached. The ship was a Dutch three-master.

APPOSITIVE PHRASE — A beautiful ship, **a Dutch three-master,** approached.

PARTICIPIAL PHRASE — A beautiful Dutch ship **having three masts** approached.

INFINITIVE PHRASE — A beautiful Dutch three-master continued **to approach us.**

7 CLAUSES

7a. A *clause* is a group of words that contains a verb and its subject and that is used as a part of a sentence.

Every clause has a subject and a verb. However, not every clause expresses a complete thought.

COMPLETE THOUGHT — **Wagons delivered** milk daily.
INCOMPLETE THOUGHT — before **cars were invented**

The two kinds of clauses are the *independent clause* and the *subordinate clause*.

THE INDEPENDENT CLAUSE

7b. An *independent* (or *main*) *clause* expresses a complete thought and can stand by itself as a sentence.

                                S   V
INDEPENDENT CLAUSE   Joseph pulled the wagon.

THE SUBORDINATE CLAUSE

7c. A *subordinate* (or *dependent*) *clause* does not express a complete thought and cannot stand alone as a sentence.

                                S   V
SUBORDINATE CLAUSE   that Pierre drove

The meaning of a subordinate clause is complete only when the clause is attached to an independent clause.

EXAMPLE   Joseph pulled the wagon **that Pierre drove.**

 QUICK CHECK 1

Identify each of the following groups of words as an *independent clause* or a *subordinate clause.*

EXAMPLE   **1.** because Pierre was growing old
              1. *subordinate clause*

1. although Pierre did not read or write
2. everyone liked him
3. although he arrived early each day to get his wagon
4. when he spoke to his horse
5. Joseph knew every stop on the route

The Adjective Clause

7d.   An *adjective clause* is a subordinate clause that modifies a
          noun or a pronoun.

An adjective clause usually follows the word it modifies and tells *which one* or *what kind.*

EXAMPLES   Joseph knew every house **that they served.** [Which house?]
               Pierre was a man **who loved his job.** [What kind of man?]

An adjective clause is usually introduced by a *relative pronoun.*

Relative Pronouns				
that	which	who	whom	whose

A *relative pronoun* relates an adjective clause to the word that the clause modifies.

EXAMPLES   After work, Pierre, **who had seemed fit,** limped
               slowly. [The relative pronoun *who* relates the clause
               to the noun *Pierre.*]
               St. Joseph, **whose name the horse bore,** was also
               kind and faithful. [The relative pronoun *whose* relates
               the clause to the noun *St. Joseph.*]

Sometimes a relative pronoun is preceded by a preposition that is part of the adjective clause.

EXAMPLE   The character **to whom I am referring** is Jacques.

☞ For information on when to set off adjective clauses with commas, see rule 13i(1) on page 1020.

NOTE The relative pronouns *who* and *whom* are used to refer to people only. The relative pronoun *that* is used to refer both to people and to things. The relative pronoun *which* is used to refer to things only.

QUICK CHECK 2

Identify the adjective clause in each of the following sentences. Give the relative pronoun and the word that the relative pronoun refers to.

EXAMPLE **I.** Jacques, who was the foreman, seemed kind.
I. *who was the foreman, who—Jacques*

1. Pierre Dupin worked for a milk company that was in Montreal.
2. The wagon that he drove carried milk to St. Catherine Street.
3. Pierre relied on his horse, whom he had named Joseph.
4. Joseph, whose coat was white, was large and reliable.
5. Pierre was offered a pension, which is a regular payment to a retired person.

The Adverb Clause

7e. An *adverb clause* is a subordinate clause that modifies a verb, an adjective, or an adverb.

An adverb clause tells *where, when, how, why, to what extent,* or *under what condition.*

EXAMPLES They live **where it never gets cold.**
[Where?]
When he left, I cried. [When?]
Grover's room seems **as if it will never be the same.** [How?]
Because the weather was hot, the cool water felt good. [Why?]
My parents still miss him **as much as I do.** [To what extent?]
If I keep tickling him, he won't fall asleep. [Under what condition?]

An adverb clause is introduced by a **subordinating conjunction**—a word that shows the relationship between the adverb clause and the word or words that the clause modifies.

A computer can help you proofread your writing. Use the computer's "Search" function to locate any use of the words *after, as, before, since,* and *until.* Examine the use of such words at the beginnings of sentences. Determine whether the word begins a prepositional phrase or a subordinate clause. In most cases, an introductory prepositional phrase is not set off by a comma. An introductory adverb clause, however, should be followed by a comma.

NOTE Some subordinating conjunctions, such as *after, as, before, since,* and *until,* are also used as prepositions.

Common Subordinating Conjunctions			
after	as though	since	when
although	because	so that	whenever
as	before	than	where
as if	how	though	wherever
as long as	if	unless	whether
as soon as	in order that	until	while

An adverb clause does not always follow the word it modifies. When an adverb clause begins a sentence, the clause is followed by a comma.

EXAMPLE   Whenever King Midas touched something, it turned to gold.

 For more about using commas with adverb clauses, see page 1021.

 Placement of Adverb Clauses

In most cases, the decision of where to place an adverb clause is a matter of style, not correctness. Both of the following sentences are correct.

> **Although she was almost unknown during her lifetime,** Emily Dickinson is now considered a major American poet.

> Emily Dickinson is now considered a major American poet **although she was almost unknown during her lifetime.**

Which sentence might you use in a paper on Emily Dickinson? The sentence to choose would be the one that looks and sounds better in the **context**—the rest of the paragraph to which the sentence belongs.

 QUICK CHECK 3

Identify the adverb clause in each of the following sentences. For each clause, circle the subordinating conjunction, and underline the subject once and the verb twice.

EXAMPLE   **1.** Many things change as you grow older.
    1. (as) you <u>grow older</u>

1. Grover worked on the computer whenever he could.
2. He packed all his things before he left.
3. Because he needed the computer, he took it too.
4. Although the room has been painted, it reminds me of him.
5. It won't be the same as long as he is gone.

The Noun Clause

7f.   A *noun clause* is a subordinate clause used as a noun.

A noun clause may be used as a subject, a complement (predicate nominative, indirect object, or direct object), or an object of a preposition.

SUBJECT	**What Mama promises** is tomorrow.
PREDICATE NOMINATIVE	She is **who makes us happy.**
INDIRECT OBJECT	She bids **whoever is sleeping** good morning.

Try It Out ✎

Each of the following sentences contains an adverb clause. Decide whether you think each adverb clause is placed where it would read best in context. If the clause could be better placed, revise the sentence. If the clause reads best where it is, write *No change.*

[1] "The Highwayman" was an inevitable reading assignment when I was in school. [2] I now enjoy the poem although I laughed at it then. [3] Because it was remote in time and place, I did not relate to it. [4] The vocabulary and content seemed false because they were unfamiliar. [5] However, I discovered that this poem is filled with lively images when I read it carefully!

| DIRECT OBJECT | Choose **whichever you need most.** |
| OBJECT OF A PREPOSITION | A poem can be about **whatever you think is important.** |

 For guidelines on using *who* and *whom* correctly, see page 986. The same guidelines apply to *whoever* and *whomever*.

Common Introductory Words for Noun Clauses

how	what	whatever	which
who	whoever	when	whichever
whom	whomever	where	that

✓ QUICK CHECK 4

Identify the noun clause in each of the following sentences. Tell whether the noun clause is a *subject,* a *predicate nominative,* a *direct object,* an *indirect object,* or an *object of a preposition.*

EXAMPLE   1. Whatever we do affects our whole family.
    1. *Whatever we do—subject*

1. What Evelyn Tooley Hunt is talking about is a mother's effect on her family.
2. This mother gives whoever is near warmth and brightness.
3. Similarly, she puts love into whatever she is cooking.
4. Notice that Hunt compares her warmth to grits and gravy.
5. A bright future is what her constant love promises.

8 SENTENCES

8a.   **A *sentence* is a group of words that has a subject and a verb and expresses a complete thought.**

A sentence begins with a capital letter and ends with a period, a question mark, or an exclamation point.

EXAMPLES   Sandra Cisneros wrote "Four Skinny Trees**.**"
Have you read any of her work**?**
What surprising rhythms she uses**!**

SENTENCE OR SENTENCE FRAGMENT?

A ***sentence fragment*** is a group of words that either does not have a subject and verb or does not express a complete thought.

| SENTENCE FRAGMENT | The rhythms in this story. [What about the rhythms in this story?] |
| SENTENCE | The rhythms in this story are based on repetition. |

SENTENCE FRAGMENT	After reading her story. [Who read her story? What happened then?]
SENTENCE	After reading her story, I looked at trees differently.

✓ QUICK CHECK 1

Tell whether each group of words is a *sentence* or a *sentence fragment*. If the word group is a sentence, correct it by adding a capital letter and end punctuation. If the word group is a sentence fragment, correct it by adding words to make a complete sentence, and also capitalize and punctuate it correctly.

EXAMPLE   **1.** one of my favorite writers

     1. *sentence fragment—One of my favorite writers is Sandra Cisneros.*

1. let me recommend this story
2. in front of her house grow four skinny trees
3. growing in the midst of concrete
4. where they don't belong
5. do you see a part of yourself in nature

COMPUTER NOTE If sentence fragments are a problem in your writing, a computer may be able to help you. Some style-checking programs can identify and highlight sentence fragments. Such programs are useful, but they aren't perfect. The best way to eliminate fragments from your writing is still to check each sentence yourself. Be sure that each expresses a complete thought and has a subject and a verb.

THE SUBJECT AND THE PREDICATE

A sentence consists of two parts: a *subject* and a *predicate*.

> **8b.**   A *subject* tells whom or what the sentence is about. The *predicate* tells something about the subject.

        subj.   pred.

EXAMPLE   Helen Callaghan | played professional baseball.

Finding the Subject

Usually, the subject comes before the predicate. Sometimes, however, the subject may appear elsewhere in the sentence. To find the subject of a sentence, ask *Who?* or *What?* before the predicate. In sentences that begin with *here, there,* or *where,* ask *Here* (or *There* or *Where*) before the predicate, followed by *who?* or *what?* after the predicate.

EXAMPLES   In the old photograph was a **woman at bat.** [Who was? A woman was.]

          By the way, **her son** plays for the Astros. [Who plays? Her son does.]

          Do **you** play baseball? [Who does play? You do play.]

          Where is **my notebook?** [Where is what? Where is my notebook.]

NOTE The subject of a sentence is *never* part of a prepositional phrase.

EXAMPLE   **Many** of the women in the league attended the reunion. [Who attended? You might be tempted to say *women,* but *women* is part of the prepositional phrase *of the women. Many* attended.]

The Simple Subject

8c. A *simple subject* is the main word or group of words in the complete subject.

EXAMPLES   Her **mother** still had that old fire. [The complete subject is *her mother.*]

"**The No-Guitar Blues**" by Gary Soto is on the test. [The complete subject is *"The No-Guitar Blues" by Gary Soto.*]

NOTE   In this book, the term *subject* refers to the simple subject unless otherwise indicated.

The Simple Predicate, or Verb

8d. A *simple predicate, or verb,* is the main word or group of words in the complete predicate.

A **complete predicate** consists of a verb and all the words that describe the verb and complete its meaning. Usually, the complete predicate follows the subject in a sentence. Sometimes, however, the complete predicate appears at the beginning of a sentence. Other times, part of the predicate may appear on one side of the subject and the rest on the other side.

EXAMPLES   **In the darkness of a doorway stood** a stranger.
On this night, he **had a meeting with an old friend.**
Would his friend **appear**?

NOTE   In this book, the term *verb* refers to the simple predicate unless otherwise indicated.

A simple predicate may be a one-word verb, or it may be a verb phrase. A **verb phrase** consists of a main verb and its helping verbs.

EXAMPLES   O. Henry's stories often **end** with a twist.
"After Twenty Years" **does** not **have** a happy ending.

☞ For more about verb phrases, see pages 965, 970, and 991.

✓ QUICK CHECK 2

Identify the *complete subject* and *simple subject* and the *complete predicate* and *simple predicate* in each of the following sentences.

EXAMPLE   1. On the mantel was an old baseball.
1. *an old baseball—complete subject; baseball—simple subject; on the mantel was—complete predicate; was—simple predicate*

1. The All-American Girls Professional Baseball League was started by Philip K. Wrigley.
2. It enjoyed ten years of popularity.
3. Have you seen the movie about the Rockford Peaches?
4. The famous Rockford Peaches was only one of nine teams.
5. At the league's reunion many years later was a much older Callaghan.

The Compound Subject

8e. A *compound subject* consists of two or more connected subjects that have the same verb. The usual connecting word is *and* or *or*.

EXAMPLES Neither **Daedalus** nor **Icarus** escaped the king's anger.
Among Daedalus's gifts were **creativity, ingenuity,** and **skill.**

The Compound Verb

8f. A *compound verb* consists of two or more verbs that have the same subject.

A connecting word—usually *and, or,* or *but*—is used between the verbs.

EXAMPLE He **flew** upward, **turned,** and **called** to his son.

Both the subject and the verb of a sentence may be compound.

     S   S   V   V

EXAMPLE **Icarus** and his **father put** on the wings and **took** off.
[Icarus put on the wings and took off. His father put on the wings and took off.]

☑ QUICK CHECK 3

Identify the *subjects* and the *verbs* in the following sentences.

EXAMPLE 1. Myths and fairy tales sometimes hide their meanings.
           1. *Myths, fairy tales—subjects; hide—verb*

1. The myth of Icarus tells about creativity and warns of its dangers.
2. In this story, Daedalus and his son suffer a tragic fate.
3. Yet, did they not also create wings and fly?
4. You and I can read the story, learn, and avoid their mistakes.
5. "Echo and Narcissus" and this classic story can teach us much.

Using Compound Subjects and Verbs

Using compound subjects and verbs, you can combine ideas and reduce wordiness in your writing. Compare the examples below.

WORDY With his wings, Daedalus escaped. Icarus escaped also.

REVISED With their wings, **Daedalus and Icarus escaped.**

Try It Out ✎

Using compound subjects and verbs, combine the following pairs of sentences.

1. Daedalus angered King Minos. Daedalus was imprisoned by King Minos.
2. Clouds sailed through the skies. Birds sailed through the skies.
3. Daedalus melted wax. Daedalus shaped a skeleton of a wing.
4. Daedalus flew close to his son, Icarus. Icarus flew close to his father.
5. Delos rushed by beneath them. Samos rushed by beneath them.

9 COMPLEMENTS

9a. A *complement* is a word or a group of words that completes the meaning of a verb.

Every sentence has a subject and a verb. Often a verb also needs a complement to complete the meaning of the verb. A complement may be a noun, a pronoun, or an adjective. Each of the following subjects and verbs needs a complement to make a complete sentence.

INCOMPLETE   James Weldon Johnson became [what?]

COMPLETE   James Weldon Johnson became **a poet.**

INCOMPLETE   Johnson's poetry is [what?]

COMPLETE   Johnson's poetry is **wonderful.**

INCOMPLETE   Tamisha showed [what? to whom?]

COMPLETE   Tamisha showed **me** her **poem.**

As you can see, a complement may be a noun, a pronoun, or an adjective. An adverb is never a complement.

ADVERB   He writes **powerfully.** [*Powerfully* tells how he writes.]

COMPLEMENT   His writing is **powerful.** [The adjective *powerful* modifies the subject *writing.*]

A complement is never in a prepositional phrase.

OBJECT OF A PREPOSITION   The whole world was in **darkness.**

COMPLEMENT   The whole world was **darkness.**

☞ For more information about prepositional phrases, see pages 967, 985, 990, and 991–992.

✓ QUICK CHECK I

Identify the *subjects, verbs,* and *complements* in the sentences in the following paragraph. [Remember: A complement is never in a prepositional phrase.]

EXAMPLE   [1] Will you read "The Creation" aloud?
    1. *you—subject; will read—verb; "The Creation"—complement*

[1] With his deep voice, James Earl Jones is a marvelous speaker. [2] Only his rich voice can do justice to a poem like "The Creation." [3] With lingering pauses and startling changes of volume, Jones's performance is awe-inspiring. [4] Can you find us a recording of his recitation? [5] No one will speak or move a muscle during the whole performance.

DIRECT OBJECTS

9b. A *direct object* is a noun or a pronoun that receives the action of the verb or that shows the result of the action. A direct object tells *what* or *whom* after a transitive verb.

EXAMPLE In this poem, God creates **light, animals,** and all **things.** [The nouns *light, animals,* and *things* receive the action of the transitive verb *creates* and tell *what.*]

A direct object can never follow a linking verb because a linking verb does not express action.

LINKING VERB People **became** living souls. [The verb *became* does not express action; therefore, it does not have a direct object.]

A direct object is never part of a prepositional phrase.

OBJECT OF A PREPOSITION Humans gazed at the **moon.** [*Moon* is not the direct object of the verb *gazed; moon* is the object of the preposition *at.*]

INDIRECT OBJECTS

Like a direct object, an *indirect object* helps to complete the meaning of a transitive verb. If a sentence has an indirect object, it always has a direct object also.

9c. An *indirect object* is a noun or a pronoun that comes between the verb and the direct object and tells *to what* or *to whom* or *for what* or *for whom* the action of the verb is done.

EXAMPLE In the last stanza, God gives **man** life. [The noun *man* tells *to whom* God has given life.]

Linking verbs do not have indirect objects. Also, an indirect object, like a direct object, is never in a prepositional phrase.

LINKING VERB The cypress **is** a type of evergreen tree. [The linking verb *is* does not express action, so it cannot have an indirect object.]

INDIRECT OBJECT Cypress trees give **swamps** deep shade. [The noun *swamps* shows *to what* cypress trees give shade.]

OBJECT OF A PREPOSITION They give deep shade to the **swamps.** [The noun *swamps* is the object of the preposition *to.*]

☞ For more about transitive verbs, see page 964.

☞ For more about linking verbs, see pages 964–965 and 1006. For more about prepositional phrases, see pages 967, 985, 990, and 991–992.

NOTE Like a direct object, an indirect object may be compound.

EXAMPLE Cypresses give **swamps** and **creeks** deep shade.

✓ QUICK CHECK 2

Identify the *direct objects* and the *indirect objects* in the following sentences. [Note: Not every sentence has an indirect object.]

EXAMPLE 1. Johnson's God has physical presence.
1. *presence—direct object*

1. This poem delivers a strong characterization of God.
2. With the muscle of a worker, this God makes the world.
3. For Johnson, all the earth shows us His footsteps.
4. Not God's intellect but His body literally gives humans breath.
5. After all, God shaped humans in His own image.

SUBJECT COMPLEMENTS

A **subject complement** completes the meaning of a linking verb and identifies or describes the subject.

Common Linking Verbs					
appear	become	grow	remain	smell	stay
be	feel	look	seem	sound	taste

EXAMPLES This unfortunate person became **Sky Woman.** [*Sky Woman* identifies the subject *person.*]

The story of Sky Woman is **sad.** [*Sad* describes the subject *story.*]

There are two kinds of subject complements—the *predicate nominative* and the *predicate adjective*.

Predicate Nominatives

9d. **A *predicate nominative* is a noun or a pronoun that follows a linking verb and identifies the subject or refers to it.**

EXAMPLE Sky Woman became the **Great Earth Mother.** [The compound noun *Great Earth Mother* is a predicate nominative that identifies the subject *Sky Woman.*]

Like subjects and objects, predicate nominatives never appear in prepositional phrases.

EXAMPLE The world was only a few **bits** of earth on a turtle. [The word *bits* is a predicate nominative that identifies the subject *world*. *Earth* is the object of the preposition *of*, and *turtle* is the object of the preposition *on*.]

☞ For information about linking verbs, see pages 964–965 and 1005.

 NOTE Expressions such as "It is I" and "That was he" sound awkward even though they are correct. In conversation, you would likely say "It's me" and "That was him." Such nonstandard expressions may one day become acceptable in writing as well as in speech. For now, however, it is best to follow the rules of standard English in your writing.

NOTE A predicate nominative may be compound.

EXAMPLE Her helpers were **birds**, a **muskrat**, a **toad**, and a **turtle**.

Predicate Adjectives

9e. A *predicate adjective* is an adjective that follows a linking verb and describes the subject.

EXAMPLE   Sky Woman was **young** and **beautiful.** [The words *young* and *beautiful* are predicate adjectives that describe the subject *Sky Woman.*]

Some verbs, such as *look, grow,* and *feel,* may be used as either linking verbs or action verbs.

LINKING VERB   The Chief of Heaven **looked** angry. [*Looked* is a linking verb because it links the adjective *angry* to the subject *Chief of Heaven.*]

ACTION VERB   Sky Woman **looked** through the hole in the floor of Heaven. [*Looked* is an action verb because it expresses Sky Woman's action.]

 QUICK CHECK 3

Identify the subject complement in each of the following sentences. Then, label each as a *predicate nominative* or a *predicate adjective.*

EXAMPLE   1. Traditional stories are one way of understanding nature.
            1. *way—predicate nominative*

1. These stories may seem simple but may be quite complex.
2. After all, their theme is the whole world.
3. Sky Woman's misfortune was our good fortune.
4. With her fall, the world became possible.
5. Is anything, even luck, permanent?

 Using Action Verbs

Overusing the linking verb *be* can make writing dull and lifeless. As you evaluate your writing, you may get the feeling that nothing is *happening,* that nobody is *doing* anything. That feeling may be an indication that your writing contains too many *be* verbs. Wherever possible, replace a dull *be* verb with a verb that expresses action.

BE VERB   "Sky Woman" **is** a traditional Seneca story.

ACTION VERB   Traditionally, the Seneca people **tell** the story of Sky Woman.

COMPUTER NOTE   The overuse of *be* verbs is a problem that a computer can help you eliminate. Use the computer's "Search" function to locate and highlight each occurrence of *am, are, is, was, were, be, been,* and *being.* In each case, determine whether the *be* verb is necessary or whether it could be replaced with an action verb for greater impact.

Try It Out ✎

Revise each of the following sentences by substituting an interesting action verb for the dull *be* verb.

1. The Chief of Heaven was angry at Sky Woman.
2. Paradise was the home of the Chief of Heaven, Sky Woman, and many animals and plants.
3. Animals of all kinds were her friends.
4. The shell of that turtle is now the earth.
5. Many things from the sky are now on earth.

10 KINDS OF SENTENCES

SENTENCES CLASSIFIED BY STRUCTURE

One way that sentences are classified is by **structure**—the kinds of clauses and the number of clauses the sentences contain.

The Simple Sentence

10a. A *simple sentence* has one independent clause and no subordinate clauses.

> S S V
> **EXAMPLE** Jean Fritz and her parents discussed her problem and
> V
> found a clever solution to it.

Notice in the example above that a simple sentence may have a compound subject, a compound verb, or both.

☞ For more about compound subjects and compound verbs, see pages 971 and 1003.

The Compound Sentence

10b. A *compound sentence* has two or more independent clauses but no subordinate clauses.

The independent clauses are usually joined by a coordinating conjunction: *and, but, for, nor, or, so,* or *yet.* The independent clauses in a compound sentence may also be joined by a semicolon.

> S V S V
> **EXAMPLES** Jared read *Old Yeller,* and then he saw the movie.
>
> S V
> Anne McCaffrey has written many stories about drag-
> S V
> ons; in fact, she has contributed to their popularity.

☞ For more about using commas in compound sentences, see page 1019. For more about using semicolons, see pages 1021–1022.

The Complex Sentence

10c. A *complex sentence* has one independent clause and at least one subordinate clause.

> **EXAMPLE** When I read one of Anne McCaffrey's stories, I want to ride a dragon.
>
> S V
> *Independent Clause* I want to ride a dragon
>
> S V
> *Subordinate Clause* When I read one of Anne McCaffrey's stories

QUICK CHECK 1

Identify each of the following sentences as *simple, compound,* or *complex.*

EXAMPLE   **1.** *Homesick* was interesting to me because I once lived abroad.
        1. *complex*

1. Boys and girls ran and played on the playground.
2. Jean Fritz did not feel like part of their world at the British school.
3. They sang "God Save the King," but she didn't.
4. Her problem disappeared after she spoke to her father.
5. She told her amah that *sewing machine* meant "hello."

 Using Varied Sentence Structure

Variety is the spice of life. It's also the spice of writing. By varying the length and the structure of your sentences, you can make your writing clearer and more interesting to read.

Simple sentences are best used to express single ideas. To describe more complicated ideas and to show relationships between them, use compound and complex sentences.

SENTENCES CLASSIFIED BY PURPOSE

In addition to being classified by structure, a sentence is also classified according to its purpose. The four kinds of sentences are *declarative, interrogative, imperative,* and *exclamatory.*

10d. A *declarative sentence* makes a statement. It is followed by a period.

EXAMPLE   I can guess what that is**.**

10e. An *interrogative sentence* asks a question. It is followed by a question mark.

EXAMPLE   What was the matter with Ted's bike**?**

10f. An *imperative sentence* gives a command or makes a request. It is followed by a period. A strong command is followed by an exclamation point.

EXAMPLES   Please open the door, Theo**.**
             Look out**!**

 COMPUTER NOTE

A computer can help you analyze your writing for sentence length and structure. Programs are available that will tell you the average number of words in your sentences and the number of each kind of sentence you used. In this way, you can easily see which sentence structures you've mastered and which ones you'll need to work on.

Try It Out ✎

Read each of the following items containing short sentences. Decide what type of sentence structure would best express the ideas in each item. Then, rewrite the item.

1. Commas seemed complicated. Andrea Hull knew how to use them.
2. Andrea Hull knew more than young Jean. Andrea taught her many things.
3. Embroidery is beautiful. It can be tedious.
4. She stretched the cloth. She marked her pattern. She began stitching.
5. A design is finished. Everyone can enjoy it.

NOTE   If an imperative sentence does not have a subject, the "understood" subject is always *you.*

EXAMPLE
(You) Do it now**!**

For more on the different end marks of punctuation, see page 1018.

10g. An *exclamatory sentence* shows excitement or expresses strong feeling. An exclamatory sentence is followed by an exclamation point.

EXAMPLES What a bargain this is**!**
We won regionals**!**

✓ QUICK CHECK 2

Classify each of the following sentences according to its purpose—*declarative, interrogative, imperative,* or *exclamatory.*

EXAMPLE **1.** Explain the theme of this story, Andy.
1. *imperative*

1. Have you ever lived in a foreign country?
2. As a child, Jean Fritz attended a British school in China.
3. How wonderful the Yangtze River was!
4. Please take me there.
5. Read *Homesick*, and see for yourself.

11 WRITING EFFECTIVE SENTENCES

Combining Sentences

11a. Improve short, choppy sentences by combining them into longer, smoother sentences.

There are many ways to combine sentences. Here are a few examples.

(1) Insert words and phrases.

CHOPPY The pan was hot. The pan was made of iron.
COMBINED The **iron** pan was hot.

CHOPPY Cook the steak. Cook it for five minutes.
COMBINED Cook the steak **for five minutes.**

(2) Use coordinating conjunctions.

CHOPPY Father likes steak. Mother does too.
COMBINED Father **and** Mother like steak.

CHOPPY The preparation was Chinese. The food was not.
COMBINED The preparation was Chinese, **but** the food was not.

(3) Use subordinate clauses.

CHOPPY Be careful. It is easy to be burned.
COMBINED Be careful **because it is easy to be burned.**

CHOPPY   I sliced the meat. It was already cooked.

COMBINED   I sliced the meat **that was already cooked.**

 QUICK CHECK 1

Use the methods you've learned in this section to combine some of the choppy sentences in the following paragraph.

EXAMPLE   [1] He is Chinese. [2] He is American.
          1. *He is Chinese and American.*

[1] "T-Bone Steak" is a poem about identity. [2] It was written by Wing Tek Lum. [3] The poet describes an ordinary moment. [4] This ordinary moment is filled with meaning. [5] The meaning is complex. [6] It includes self-assertion, rebellion, respect, and self-acceptance. [7] Preparing the meal is almost a ritual for the family. [8] It is a ritual that asserts their individuality. [9] The meal draws from Chinese and American customs. [10] Elements of both cultures contribute to the family's identity.

Revising Run-on Sentences

11b. **Avoid using run-on sentences.**

If you run together two complete sentences as if they were one sentence, you get a **run-on sentence.**

RUN-ON   This poet values individuality, he also respects tradition.

Here are two of the ways you can revise run-on sentences.

1. You can make two sentences.

> **REVISED**   This poet values individuality**. H**e also respects tradition.

2. You can use a comma and the coordinating conjunction *and, but,* or *or.*

> **REVISED**   This poet values individuality**, but** he also respects tradition.

Revising Stringy Sentences and Wordy Sentences

11c. **Improve** *stringy* **and** *wordy sentences* **by making them shorter and more precise.**

Stringy sentences have too many independent clauses strung together with words like *and* or *but.*

STRINGY   The Hummingbird King was betrayed, and an enemy betrayed him, and Kukul turned into a hummingbird, for the hummingbird symbolizes freedom for the Maya, and even today he watches everything.

NOTE   A *comma splice* is a kind of run-on sentence in which a comma is used without a coordinating conjunction to join independent clauses. The sample run-on sentence given under rule 11b is a comma splice.

To fix a stringy sentence, you can break the sentence into two or more sentences. You can also turn some of the independent clauses into phrases or subordinate clauses.

REVISED   When the Hummingbird King was betrayed by an enemy, Kukul turned into a hummingbird, the symbol of freedom for the Maya. Even today, he watches everything.

You can revise wordy sentences in three different ways.

1. Replace a group of words with one word.

WORDY   With great sorrow, they mourned their king.

REVISED   **Sorrowfully,** they mourned their king.

2. Replace a clause with a phrase.

WORDY   When Kukul's life ended, he turned into a hummingbird.

REVISED   **After his death,** Kukul turned into a hummingbird.

3. Take out a whole group of unnecessary words.

WORDY   What I mean to say is that Kukul is known as the *quetzal.*

REVISED   Kukul is known as the *quetzal.*

 QUICK CHECK 2

The following paragraph contains run-on, stringy, and wordy sentences. Revise them to improve the style of the paragraph.

EXAMPLE   [1] We know little about many ancient cultures due to the fact that records have been lost.

1. *We know little about many ancient cultures because records have been lost.*

[1] Many people all over the world have legends, these legends tell of people being turned into animals. [2] It seems evident that people must feel a great kinship with the animals. [3] Many of these legends feature an animal, and the animal was once a person, and that person had special powers. [4] The fact is that many animals have powers that people do not have. [5] Perhaps these legends are expressive of the idea that people sometimes have envy for animals.

Revising Wordy Sentences

Extra words and phrases tend to make writing sound awkward and unnatural. As you revise your writing, read your sentences aloud to check for wordiness or a stringy style. If you run out of breath before the end of a sentence, it is likely stringy, wordy, or both.

Try It Out

Revise each of the following sentences to eliminate wordiness and stringy style.

1. The reason that many legends, myths, and fairy tales have survived for centuries is that they address something important in people.
2. They continually surprise and delight readers due to the fact of their impossibility.
3. People have long told stories that explain human behavior and ones that explain natural forces in the world.
4. Children read these stories or view them on film, and so do their parents.
5. The needs of a culture change, and details of the story change, and the ending may change, but the readers remain.

12 CAPITAL LETTERS

12a. **Capitalize the first word in every sentence.**

EXAMPLE   **W**ho gets a place in the choir?

The first word of a sentence that is a direct quotation is capitalized even if the quotation begins within a sentence.

EXAMPLE   Francis Bacon states, "**K**nowledge is power."

Traditionally, the first word in a line of poetry is capitalized. However, some modern poets and writers do not follow this style. When you are quoting, follow the capitalization used in the source of the quotation.

EXAMPLE   **I**t was many and many a year ago,
　　　　　　　　In a kingdom by the sea,
　　　　　　That a maiden there lived whom you may know
　　　　　　　　By the name of Annabel Lee;
　　　　　　And this maiden she lived with no other thought
　　　　　　　　Than to love and be loved by me.
　　　　　　　　　　　　—Edgar Allan Poe, "Annabel Lee"

12b. **Capitalize the pronoun *I*.**

EXAMPLE   **I** enjoyed the book, but **I** didn't like the film.

12c. **Capitalize the interjection *O*.**

The interjection *O* is most often used on solemn or formal occasions. It is usually followed by a word in direct address.

EXAMPLE   Protect us in the battle, **O** great Athena!

☑ *QUICK CHECK 1*

Most of the following sentences contain errors in capitalization. If a sentence is correct, write *C*. If there are errors in the use of capitals, correct the word or words that should be changed.

EXAMPLE   **1.** William says that *i* am his best friend.
　　　　　　　1. *I*

1. If i need a ride, i will give you a call.
2. Loretta is in Maine, but Oh, how she would like to visit Paris.
3. oh no, I left my backpack on the bus!
4. Please accept these gifts, o Lord.
5. The poem ends with a question.

12d. **Capitalize proper nouns.**

A **common noun** is a general name for a person, a place, a thing, or an idea. A **proper noun** names a particular person, place, thing, or idea.

☞ For more about using capital letters in quotations, see page 1024.

NOTE The interjection *oh* requires a capital letter only at the beginning of a sentence. Otherwise, *oh* is not capitalized.

EXAMPLES   **O**h, look at the sunset!
We felt tired but, **oh**, so victorious.

A common noun is capitalized only when it begins a sentence or is part of a title. A proper noun is always capitalized. Some proper nouns consist of more than one word. In these names, short prepositions (those of fewer than five letters) and articles (*a, an, the*) are not capitalized.

COMMON NOUNS	statue	man
PROPER NOUNS	Statue of Liberty	Eric the Red

(1) Capitalize the names of persons and animals.

EXAMPLES Franklin Chang-Díaz, Alice Walker, Lassie, Shamu

(2) Capitalize geographical names.

TYPE OF NAME	EXAMPLES
Towns, Cities	San Diego, Jamestown
Islands	Isle of Wight, Wake Island
Counties, States	Cook County, New Hampshire
Countries	New Zealand, Germany
Bodies of Water	Gulf of Mexico, Indian Ocean
Forests, Parks	Sherwood Forest, Yellowstone National Park
Streets, Highways	Route 44, West Fourth Street
Mountains	Mount Washington, Big Horn Mountain
Continents	South America, Asia
Regions	the West Coast, the Great Plains

> **NOTE** In a hyphenated street number, the second part of the number is not capitalized.
>
> **EXAMPLE** Seventy-eighth Street

> **NOTE** Words such as *north, east,* and *southwest* are not capitalized when they indicate direction, but they are capitalized when they are part of a proper name.
>
> **EXAMPLES** go south for the winter
> northeast of Atlanta
> East End Cafe
> Old West Jamboree

(3) Capitalize the names of planets, stars, and other heavenly bodies.

EXAMPLES Jupiter   Sirius   Milky Way
Big Dipper   North Star

(4) Capitalize the names of teams, organizations, businesses, institutions, and government bodies.

> **NOTE** The word *earth* is not capitalized unless it is used along with the names of other heavenly bodies that are capitalized. The words *sun* and *moon* are not capitalized.

TYPE OF NAME	EXAMPLES
Teams	Detroit Pistons, Seattle Seahawks
Organizations	Girl Scouts, African Studies Association
Businesses	Wilson's Vacuum World, Seaside Cycle Shop
Institutions	Cary Memorial Hospital, Hilltop High School
Government Bodies	Air National Guard, Department of Agriculture

(5) Capitalize the names of historical events and periods, special events, and calendar items.

TYPE OF NAME	EXAMPLES
Historical Events	**B**attle of **B**unker **H**ill, **Y**alta **C**onference
Historical Periods	**G**reat **D**epression, **M**iddle **A**ges
Special Events	**O**klahoma **S**tate **F**air, **C**annes **F**ilm **F**estival
Calendar Items	**F**riday, **F**ourth of **J**uly

> **NOTE** The name of a season is not capitalized unless it is part of a proper name.
>
> **EXAMPLES** the last day of summer, the Oak Ridge **W**inter **C**arnival

(6) Capitalize the names of nationalities, races, and peoples.

EXAMPLES Greek, Asian, Caucasian, Hispanic, Shawnee

(7) Capitalize the names of religions and their followers, holy days, sacred writings, and specific deities.

TYPE OF NAME	EXAMPLES
Religions and Followers	**Z**en **B**uddhism, **C**hristianity, **M**uslim
Holy Days	**P**assover, **L**ent, **R**amadan
Sacred Writings	**T**ao **T**e **C**hing, **B**ible, **T**almud, **K**oran
Specific Deities	**H**oly **S**pirit, **B**rahma, **A**llah, **J**ehovah

> **NOTE** The word *god* is not capitalized when it refers to a mythological god. The names of specific gods, however, are capitalized.
>
> **EXAMPLE** The king of Greek **g**ods was **Z**eus.

(8) Capitalize the names of buildings and other structures.

EXAMPLES **R**itz **T**heater, **G**olden **G**ate **B**ridge

(9) Capitalize the names of monuments and awards.

TYPE OF NAME	EXAMPLES
Monuments	**V**ietnam **V**eterans **M**emorial, **S**tatue of **L**iberty
Awards	**N**ewbery **M**edal, **P**urple **H**eart

(10) Capitalize the names of trains, ships, aircraft, and spacecraft.

TYPE OF NAME	EXAMPLES
Trains	*Silver Rocket, Orient Express*
Ships	*Nimitz, Santa Maria*
Aircraft	*Spirit of St. Louis, Air Force One*
Spacecraft	*Apollo 11, Columbia*

(11) **Capitalize the brand names of business products.**

EXAMPLES Nike shoes, Buick station wagon, Wrangler jeans

 QUICK CHECK 2

Correct each of the following expressions, using capital letters as needed.

EXAMPLE **1.** the stone age
1. *the Stone Age*

1. decisions of the united states supreme court
2. three skeleton key, an island off guiana
3. pictures of saturn sent by *voyager 2*
4. the apaches of the southwest
5. the tomb of the unknown soldier

12e. **Capitalize proper adjectives.**

A *proper adjective* is formed from a proper noun and is almost always capitalized.

PROPER NOUN Rome, Islam, King Arthur
PROPER ADJECTIVE Roman army, Islamic culture, Arthurian legend

12f. **Do *not* capitalize the names of school subjects, except language classes and course names followed by a number.**

EXAMPLES I have tests in English, math, and Art II.

12g. **Capitalize titles.**

(1) **Capitalize the title of a person when it comes before a name.**

EXAMPLES Does Ms. Tam know Dr. Politi or Governor Halsey?

(2) **Capitalize a title used alone or following a person's name only when you want to emphasize the position of someone holding a high office.**

EXAMPLES We grew quiet as the Rabbi rose to speak.
Is he the rabbi at the new synagogue?

A title used alone in direct address is often capitalized.

EXAMPLES Is the patient resting comfortably, Nurse?
What is your name, Sir [*or* sir]?

(3) **Capitalize a word showing a family relationship when the word is used before or in place of a person's name.**

EXAMPLES Hey, Mom, I received a letter from Aunt Christina and Uncle Garth.

☞ For more about proper nouns and proper adjectives, see pages 959 and 962–963.

 Remember that correct capitalization of abbreviations is part of proper spelling. You may notice that certain abbreviations are capitalized.

EXAMPLES Mr. Ms. U.S. TV Fla.
NAACP

However, some abbreviations, especially those for measurements, are not capitalized.

EXAMPLES in. ft lb cc ml

Consult a dictionary for the correct capitalization of an abbreviation.

Do not capitalize a word showing a family relationship when a possessive comes before the word.

EXAMPLES   Angela's **m**other and my **g**randmother Daphne coach the softball team.

(4) Capitalize the first and last words and all important words in titles of books, magazines, newspapers, poems, short stories, historical documents, movies, television programs, works of art, and musical compositions.

Unimportant words in titles include

- prepositions of fewer than five letters (such as *at, of, for, from, with*)
- coordinating conjunctions (*and, but, for, nor, or, so, yet*)
- articles (*a, an, the*)

TYPE OF NAME	EXAMPLES
Books	*The Old Man and the Sea, Dust Tracks on a Road*
Magazines	*Sports Illustrated, Woman's Day*
Newspapers	*San Francisco Examiner, The Miami Herald*
Poems	"My Father Is a Simple Man," "Annabel Lee"
Short Stories	"The Naming of Names," "A Day's Wait"
Historical Documents	Bill of Rights, Emancipation Proclamation
Movies	*Stand and Deliver, Jurassic Park*
Television Programs	*FBI: The Untold Stories, A Different World*
Works of Art	*Birth of Venus, The Old Guitarist*
Musical Compositions	*The Marriage of Figaro,* "In the Pines"

 QUICK CHECK 3

Use capital or lowercase letters to correct each error in capitalization in the following sentences.

EXAMPLE   1. Did you know that dr. Santos subscribes to *field and stream*?
        1. *Did you know that Dr. Santos subscribes to <u>Field and Stream</u>?*

1. When my Aunt Rose and I went to Mexico, she introduced me to grandmother Villa.
2. Try looking up that word in *the american heritage dictionary.*
3. Did you hear commissioner of education boylan's speech?
4. Did the treasurer review the club's budget, senator?
5. When I get older, I hope I will be like the father in "My Father Is A Simple Man."

NOTE   The article *the* before a title is not capitalized unless it is the first word of the title.

EXAMPLES   Is that the late edition of **the** *Chicago Sun-Times*? I read an interesting story in *The New Yorker.*

If you are not sure whether *the* is part of a magazine's title, look for the official title in the magazine's masthead or on the table-of-contents page. For a newspaper, look on the editorial page. For a book, look on the title page.

☞   For information on when to italicize (underline) a title, see page 1023. For information on using quotation marks for titles, see page 1026.

13 PUNCTUATION

END MARKS

An **end mark** is a mark of punctuation placed at the end of a sentence. The three kinds of end marks are the *period,* the *question mark,* and the *exclamation point.*

13a. Use a period at the end of a statement.

EXAMPLE Kristi Yamaguchi is a world-champion figure skater**.**

13b. Use a question mark at the end of a question.

EXAMPLE Did Gordon Parks write *The Learning Tree***?**

13c. Use an exclamation point at the end of an exclamation.

EXAMPLES Wow**!** What a view**!**

13d. Use a period or an exclamation point at the end of a request or a command.

EXAMPLES Please give me the scissors**.** [a request]
Give me the scissors**!** [a command]

13e. Use a period after most abbreviations.

TYPES OF ABBREVIATIONS	EXAMPLES			
Personal Names	Pearl S. Buck		W.E.B. Du Bois	
Titles Used with Names	Mr.	Ms.	Jr.	Sr.	Dr.
States	Ky.	Fla.	Tenn.	Calif.
Addresses	St.	Blvd.	P.O. Box	
Organizations and Companies	Co.	Inc.	Corp.	Assn.
Times	A.M.	P.M.	B.C.	A.D.

Place A.D. before the number and B.C. after the number. For centuries expressed in words, place both A.D. and B.C. after the century.

EXAMPLES A.D. 540   31 B.C.   sixth century B.C.   third century A.D.

When an abbreviation with a period ends a sentence, another period is not needed. However, a question mark or an exclamation point is used as needed.

EXAMPLES This is my friend J**.** R**.**
Have you met Nguyen, J**.** R**.?**

NOTE A two-letter state abbreviation without periods is used only when it is followed by a ZIP Code.

EXAMPLE
Austin, **TX** 78741

NOTE Some widely used abbreviations are written without periods.

EXAMPLES UN, FBI, PTA, NAACP, PBS, CNN, YMCA, VHF

NOTE Abbreviations for most units of measure are written without periods.

EXAMPLES cm, kg, ml, ft, lb, mi, oz, qt

The abbreviation for *inch (in.)* is written with a period to prevent confusion with the word *in.* If you're not sure whether to use periods with abbreviations, look in a dictionary.

QUICK CHECK 1

Add end marks where they are needed in the following sentences.

EXAMPLE   1. Japanese haiku are very short poems
              1. *Japanese haiku are very short poems.*

1. Have you ever heard of Little Tokyo
2. It's a Japanese neighborhood in Los Angeles, Calif, bordered by First St, Third St, Alameda St, and Los Angeles St
3. Some friends of ours who live in Los Angeles, Mr and Mrs Cook, Sr, and their son, Al, Jr, introduced us to the area
4. They met our 11:30 AM flight from Atlanta, Ga, and took us to lunch at a restaurant in the Japanese Plaza Village
5. What a great afternoon we had with our friends

COMMAS

Items in a Series

13f. **Use commas to separate items in a series.**

Words, phrases, and clauses in a series are separated by commas to show the reader where one item in the series ends and the next item begins. Commas are always needed with three or more items in a series. Two items often do not need a comma.

WORDS IN A SERIES   *Hammock*, *canoe*, and *moccasin* are Native American words.

PHRASES IN A SERIES   Seaweed was in the water, on the beach, and in our shoes.

CLAUSES IN A SERIES   Tell us who was there, what happened, and why it happened.

If all items in a series are joined by *and* or *or*, commas are not needed.

EXAMPLE   I voted for Corey **and** Mona **and** Ethan.

13g. **Use a comma to separate two or more adjectives that come before a noun.**

EXAMPLE   An Arabian horse is a fast, beautiful animal.

Compound Sentences

13h. **Use a comma before *and, but, or, nor, for, so,* or *yet* when it joins independent clauses.**

EXAMPLE   I enjoyed *The King and I*, **but** *Oklahoma!* is still my favorite musical.

You may omit the comma before *and, but, or,* or *nor* if the clauses are very short and there is no chance of misunderstanding.

Interrupters

13i. Use commas to set off an expression that interrupts a sentence.

Two commas are needed if the expression comes in the middle of the sentence. One comma is needed if the expression comes at the beginning or the end of the sentence.

EXAMPLES   Yes, my favorite gospel singers, BeBe and CeCe Winans, were on TV, Ed.

(1) Use commas to set off a *nonessential* participial phrase or a *nonessential* subordinate clause.

A *nonessential* (or *nonrestrictive*) phrase or clause adds information to the sentence but can be omitted without changing the main idea of the sentence.

NONESSENTIAL PHRASE   Orpheus, **mourning his bride,** entered Hades.

NONESSENTIAL CLAUSE   Orpheus, **who was a musician,** met a cruel fate.

(2) Use commas to set off an appositive or an appositive phrase that is nonessential.

APPOSITIVE   The gray ferryman, **Charon,** did not charge him any fare.

APPOSITIVE PHRASE   Even Cerberus, **the dog at the gate,** listened.

(3) Use commas to set off words used in direct address.

EXAMPLE   Do you know, **Elena,** when the next bus is due?

(4) Use commas to set off a parenthetical expression.

A *parenthetical expression* is a side remark that either adds information or relates ideas in a sentence. Some of these expressions are not always used as interrupters. Use commas only when the expressions are parenthetical.

EXAMPLES   What, **in your opinion,** is the best solution to this problem? [parenthetical]
I have faith **in your opinion.** [not parenthetical]

Introductory Words, Phrases, and Clauses

13j. Use a comma after certain introductory elements.

(1) Use a comma after *yes, no,* or any mild exclamation such as *well* or *why* at the beginning of a sentence.

EXAMPLE   Yes, King Midas had been foolish.

NOTE   Do not set off an *essential* (or *restrictive*) phrase or clause. It cannot be omitted without changing the meaning of the sentence.

ESSENTIAL PHRASE   All the spirits **toiling in Hades** stopped and listened.

ESSENTIAL CLAUSE The song **that Orpheus sang** charmed the king of Hades.

(2) Use a comma after an introductory prepositional phrase if the phrase is long or if two or more phrases appear together.

EXAMPLES   **Long ago in a land called Lydia,** King Midas lived.
            In the garden of his palace, he met Silenus.

(3) Use a comma after a participial phrase or an infinitive phrase that introduces a sentence.

PARTICIPIAL PHRASE   **Threatened by Midas,** the satyr struck a bargain.

INFINITIVE PHRASE   **To reward Midas,** Dionysus offered a gift.

(4) Use a comma after an introductory adverb clause.

EXAMPLE   **When his daughter arrived,** he warned her to stay away.

Conventional Situations

13k. **Use commas in certain conventional situations.**

(1) Use commas to separate items in dates and addresses.

EXAMPLES   They met on June 17, 1965, in Erie, Pennsylvania.
            My address is 520 Cocoa Lane, Orlando, FL 32804.

(2) Use a comma after the salutation of a friendly letter and after the closing of any letter.

EXAMPLES   Dear Aunt Margaret,   Sincerely yours,

 QUICK CHECK 2

Insert commas where they are needed in the following sentences.

EXAMPLE   I. This story the tale of King Midas warns us about greed.
           I. *This story, the tale of King Midas, warns us about greed.*

1. Horrified by the sight of his daughter Midas wept.
2. Well Midas left the palace went to Dionysus and begged relief.
3. Dionysus sometimes a merciful god told him to go to Pactolus.
4. In the deep strong waters of the river Midas washed himself.
5. My friend do not make Midas's error or you may not find mercy.

Semicolons

13l. **Use a semicolon instead of a comma between independent clauses when they are not joined by *and, but, or, nor, for, so,* or *yet.***

EXAMPLE   Our parents settled our dispute; they gave us each half.

 NOTE   Use a semicolon rather than a period between independent clauses only when the ideas in the clauses are closely related.

EXAMPLE   I called Leon; he will be here in ten minutes.

Try It Out ✎

Decide whether each of the following sentences is better expressed as a single sentence or as two or more sentences. Then, write the sentence accordingly. Revise the sentence for style and clarity as well.

1. The frogs wanted a king, one who could amuse them with royal customs; they thought a strong ruler would be exciting.
2. Jupiter heard their request; he granted it; he felt they were foolish.
3. Jupiter threw down a large log; the log landed next to the frogs.
4. Was this strange, new king fearsome; was he peaceful?
5. Strangely enough, these spoiled, bored frogs were not grateful; they petitioned Jupiter, who again granted their wish.

NOTE Never use a colon directly after a verb or a preposition. Omit the colon, or reword the sentence.

INCORRECT My stepsister's favorite sports are: basketball, tennis, swimming, and bowling.

CORRECT My stepsister's favorite sports are basketball, tennis, swimming, and bowling.

NOTE Use a colon between chapter and verse in referring to passages from the Bible.

EXAMPLES John 3:16
Matthew 6:9–13

Using Semicolons

Semicolons are most effective when they are not overused. Sometimes it is better to separate a compound sentence or a heavily punctuated sentence into two sentences rather than to use a semicolon.

ACCEPTABLE In the jungles of South America, it rains every day, sometimes all day; the vegetation there, some of which is found nowhere else in the world, is lush, dense, and fast-growing.

BETTER In the jungles of South America, it rains practically every day, sometimes all day. The vegetation there, some of which is found nowhere else in the world, is lush, dense, and fast-growing.

Colons

13m. Use a colon before a list of items, especially after expressions like *as follows* or *the following.*

EXAMPLE Minimum equipment for camping includes the following: bedroll, utensils for eating, warm clothing, and rope.

13n. Use a colon in certain conventional situations.

(1) Use a colon between the hour and the minute.

EXAMPLES 11:30 P.M.   4:08 A.M.

(2) Use a colon after the salutation of a business letter.

EXAMPLES Dear Ms. Gonzalez: To Whom It May Concern:

 ## QUICK CHECK 3

Insert a colon or semicolon wherever one is needed in each sentence.

EXAMPLE 1. Daedalus made Minos the following furniture, weapons, and armor.
1. *Daedalus made Minos the following: furniture, weapons, and armor.*

1. Some reptiles like a dry climate others prefer a wet climate.
2. The first lunch period begins at 11 00 A.M.
3. Icarus flew too high his wings melted.
4. In Ruth 1 16, Ruth pledges her loyalty to Naomi.
5. The frogs wanted a king they got one.

14 PUNCTUATION

UNDERLINING (ITALICS)

Italics are printed letters that lean to the right, such as *the letters in these words*. In handwritten or typewritten work, indicate italics by underlining.

TYPED <u>Born Free</u> is the story of a lion that became a pet.

PUBLISHED *Born Free* is the story of a lion that became a pet.

> **COMPUTER NOTE** If you use a computer, you may be able to set words in italics yourself. Most word-processing software and many printers are capable of producing italic type.

14a. Use underlining (italics) for titles of books, plays, periodicals, works of art, films, television programs, recordings, long musical compositions, trains, ships, aircraft, and spacecraft.

TYPE OF TITLE	EXAMPLES	
Books	*Barrio Boy*	*House Made of Dawn*
Plays	*Macbeth*	*Visit to a Small Planet*
Periodicals	*Hispanic*	*The New York Times*
Works of Art	*The Thinker*	*American Gothic*
Films	*Stand and Deliver*	*Jurassic Park*
Television Programs	*Home Improvement*	*Wall Street Week*
Recordings	*Unforgettable*	*Man of Steel*
Long Musical Compositions	*Don Giovanni*	*The Four Seasons*
Ships	*Calypso*	USS *Nimitz*
Trains	*Orient Express*	*City of New Orleans*
Aircraft	*Enola Gay*	*Spirit of St. Louis*
Spacecraft	*Apollo 12*	USS *Enterprise*

> **NOTE** The article *the* before the title of a magazine or a newspaper is usually neither italicized nor capitalized when it is written within a sentence. Some periodicals do include *the* in their titles.
>
> **EXAMPLES** My parents subscribe to **the** *San Francisco Chronicle.* On Sundays, we all share *The New York Times.*

> ☞ For examples of titles that are not italicized but enclosed in quotation marks, see page 1026.

14b. Use underlining (italics) for words, letters, and figures referred to as such.

EXAMPLES What is the difference between the words *affect* and *effect*?

Don't forget to drop the final *e* before you add *–ing* to that word.

Is the last number a *5* or an *8*?

QUICK CHECK 1

Underline the words that should be italicized in each of the following sentences.

EXAMPLE 1. Who will play the lead in Brian's Song?

　　　　　　1. *Who will play the lead in Brian's Song?*

1. Sometimes I forget the r in the word friend and write fiend.
2. Pablo Picasso's famous painting Guernica is named for a Spanish town that was bombed during the Spanish Civil War.
3. My father reads the Washington Post because he likes Carl Rowan's column.
4. The movie My Left Foot celebrates the accomplishments of a writer and artist who has serious disabilities.
5. Janice finally found her mistake; she had written the 4 in the wrong column.

QUOTATION MARKS

14c. Use quotation marks to enclose a *direct quotation—* a person's exact words.

EXAMPLE "Here is Eric's drawing of the runaway," said Ms. Rios.

14d. A direct quotation begins with a capital letter.

EXAMPLE Brandon shouted, "Let's get busy!"

14e. When the expression identifying the speaker interrupts a quoted sentence, the second part of the quotation begins with a small letter.

EXAMPLE "Gee," Angelo added, "the boy in 'A Day's Wait' is a lot like my brother."

When the second part of a divided quotation is a separate sentence, it begins with a capital letter.

EXAMPLE "Travel is exciting," said Mrs. Ash. "Space travel is no exception."

14f. A direct quotation is set off from the rest of the sentence by a comma, a question mark, or an exclamation point, but not by a period.

Set off means "separated." If a quotation appears at the beginning of a sentence, place a comma after it. If a quotation falls at the end of a sentence, place a comma before it. If a quoted sentence is interrupted, place a comma after the first part and before the second part.

NOTE Do not use quotation marks for an *indirect quotation,* which is a rewording of a direct quotation.

DIRECT QUOTATION
Kaya asked, "What is your interpretation of the poem?"

INDIRECT QUOTATION
Kaya asked what my interpretation of the poem was.

EXAMPLES   "I just read a story by Amy Tan**,**" Alyssa said.

Mark said**,** "I've read a couple of her stories, too."

"Alyssa**,**" asked Janet**,** "what story did you read?"

When a quotation ends with a question mark or an exclamation point, no comma is needed.

EXAMPLE   "Have you seen my brother**?**" Alicia asked.

14g. **A period or a comma is always placed inside the closing quotation marks.**

EXAMPLES   Ramón said, "My little brother loves Shel Silverstein's poems**."**

"My sister does too**,**" Paula responded.

14h. **A question mark or an exclamation point is placed inside the closing quotation marks when the quotation itself is a question or exclamation. Otherwise, it is placed outside.**

EXAMPLES   "Is the time difference between Los Angeles and Chicago two hours**?**" asked Ken. [The quotation is a question.]

Linda exclaimed, "I thought everyone knew that**!**" [The quotation is an exclamation.]

What did Sandra Cisneros mean in her story "Four Skinny Trees" when she wrote "Keep, keep, keep, trees say when I sleep"**?** [The sentence, not the quotation, is a question.]

I can't believe that Mom said, "I'm not planning to raise your allowance until next year"**!** [The sentence, not the quotation, is an exclamation.]

When both the sentence and the quotation at the end of the sentence are questions (or exclamations), only one question mark (or exclamation point) is used. It is placed inside the closing quotation marks.

EXAMPLE   Who wrote the poem that begins "How do I love thee**?**"

14i. **When you write dialogue (conversation), begin a new paragraph each time you change speakers.**

EXAMPLE   "Frog, how may we help you?"

"Uh, well, uh, you see," says Frog, "I would like to become a part of your group."

"That's wonderful," says the head bird.

"Yes, wonderful," echo the other birds.

"Frog, you may help us carry our worms," says the head bird.

"That's not what I had in mind," says Frog.

—Linda Goss, "The Frog Who Wanted to Be a Singer"

14j. When a quotation consists of several sentences, place quotation marks at the beginning and at the end of the whole quotation.

EXAMPLE "Take the garbage out. Clean your room. Have fun!" said Dad.

14k. Use single quotation marks to enclose a quotation within a quotation.

EXAMPLES "I said, 'The quiz will be this Friday,'" repeated Mr. Allyn.

"What poem begins with the words 'I'm Nobody'?" Carol asked.

14l. Use quotation marks to enclose titles of short works such as short stories, poems, articles, songs, episodes of television programs, and chapters and other parts of books.

TYPE OF TITLE	EXAMPLES	
Short Stories	"Papa's Parrot"	"Amigo Brothers"
Poems	"Early Song"	"The Runaway"
Articles	"Free Speech and Free Air" "How to Sharpen Your Wit"	
Songs	"La Bamba"	"Amazing Grace"
Episodes of Television Programs	"Heart of a Champion" "The Trouble with Tribbles"	
Chapters and Other Parts of Books	"Learning About Reptiles" "English: Origins and Uses"	

 For examples of titles that are italicized, see page 1023.

✓ QUICK CHECK 2

Revise the following sentences by adding commas, end marks, quotation marks, and paragraph breaks where necessary.

[1] Gordon, do you ever think about pencils Annie asked [2] I'm always wondering where I lost mine Gordon replied [3] Well said Annie let me tell you some of the things I learned about pencils [4] Sure Gordon said I love trivia [5] People have used some form of pencils for a long time Annie began [6] The ancient Greeks and Romans used lead pencils [7] However, pencils as we know them weren't developed until the 1500s, when people began using graphite [8] What's graphite asked Gordon [9] Graphite is a soft form of carbon Annie explained that leaves a mark when it's drawn over most surfaces [10] Thanks for the information, Annie Gordon said Now, do you have a pencil I can borrow?

15 PUNCTUATION

APOSTROPHES

15a. The *possessive case* of a noun or a pronoun shows owner-ship or relationship.

(1) To form the possessive case of a singular noun, add an apostrophe and an *s*.

EXAMPLES   a dog's collar   Cinderella's slipper

(2) To form the possessive case of a plural noun ending in *s*, add only the apostrophe.

EXAMPLES   doctors' opinions   hosts' invitations

(3) To form the possessive case of a plural noun that does not end in *s*, add an apostrophe and an *s*.

EXAMPLES   women's suits   geese's noise

(4) To form the possessive case of some indefinite pronouns, add an apostrophe and an *s*.

EXAMPLES   someone's opinion   no one's fault

15b. To form a contraction, use an apostrophe to show where letters have been left out.

A *contraction* is a shortened form of a word, figure, or group of words.

EXAMPLES   I am . . . . .I'm   they had . . . . .they'd
1996 . . . .'96   where is . . . . . . .where's
let us . . . . .let's   of the clock . . . .o'clock

The word *not* can be shortened to *–n't* and added to a verb, usually without changing the spelling of the verb.

EXAMPLES   is not . . . . .isn't   had not . . . . .hadn't
do not . . . . .don't   should not . . .shouldn't
EXCEPTIONS   will not . . . . . . .won't   cannot . . . . .can't

Do not confuse contractions with possessive pronouns.

CONTRACTIONS	POSSESSIVE PRONOUNS
It's snowing. [*It is*]	**Its** front tire is flat.
Who's Clifton Davis? [*Who is*]	**Whose** idea was it?
There's only one answer. [*There is*]	This trophy is **theirs.**
They're not here. [*They are*]	**Their** dog is barking.

NOTE A proper name ending in *s* may take only an apostrophe to form the possessive case if the addition of 's would make the name awkward to pronounce.
EXAMPLES
Ms. Masters' class
Hercules' feats

NOTE Do not use an apostrophe with possessive personal pro-nouns.

EXAMPLES   **His** pan-tomime was good, but **hers** was better.

15c. **Use an apostrophe and an *s* to form the plurals of letters, numerals, and signs, and of words referred to as words.**

EXAMPLES   Your *2*'s look like *5*'s.
Don't use &'s in place of *and*'s.

✓ QUICK CHECK 1

Add an apostrophe wherever one is needed in the following sentences.

EXAMPLE   1. Who wrote "A Days Wait," class?
1. *Who wrote "A Day's Wait," class?*

1. My cousin Dorothy, everybodys favorite, usually gets all As.
2. It isnt correct to use &s in your compositions.
3. Many of my friends scores were in the 80s and 90s.
4. Theyll meet us later, if its not raining where were going.
5. Whos signed up to try out for a part in *Antaeus*?

HYPHENS

15d. **Use a hyphen to divide a word at the end of a line.**

(1) Divide a word only between syllables.

INCORRECT   Didn't Carrie write her science report on the tyrannosaurs, the largest meat-eating dinosaurs?
CORRECT   Didn't Carrie write her science report on the tyrannosaurs, the largest meat-eating dinosaurs?

(2) Divide an already hyphenated word at a hyphen.

INCORRECT   I went to the state fair with my sister and my brother-in-law.
CORRECT   I went to the state fair with my sister and my brother-
in-law.

(3) Do not divide a word so that one letter stands alone.

INCORRECT   On our last class trip, all of us stayed o-
vernight in a hotel.
CORRECT   On our last class trip, all of us stayed
overnight in a hotel.

15e. **Use a hyphen with compound numbers from *twenty-one* to *ninety-nine* and with fractions used as adjectives.**

EXAMPLES   thirty-five   one-half   forty-eighth

TIPS FOR SPELLING

Hyphens are used in some compound names. In such cases, the hyphen is part of the name's spelling.

PEOPLE   Daniel Day-Lewis
Orlando Hines-Smith

PLACES   Wilkes-Barre [city]
Stratford-on-Avon [borough]

If you are not sure whether a name is hyphenated, consult a reference source.

PARENTHESES

15f. Use parentheses to enclose material that is added to a sentence but is not considered of major importance.

EXAMPLES Mohandas K. Gandhi **(1869–1948)** led India's struggle for independence.

Ms. Matsuo served us the sushi **(s͞oo′sh͞e)**.

Fill in the order form carefully. **(Do not use a pencil.)**

My great-uncle Chester **(he's Grandma's brother)** will stay with us.

DASHES

15g. Use a dash to indicate an abrupt break in thought or speech.

EXAMPLES Ms. Alonzo—she just left—will be one of the judges.

"You'll find it—oh, excuse me, Sir—over here," said the librarian.

✓ QUICK CHECK 2

For each of the following sentences, insert hyphens, parentheses, or dashes where they are needed.

EXAMPLE 1. My grandfather, who is seventy five, can recite "The High wayman."

1. *My grandfather, who is seventy-five, can recite "The High-wayman."*

1. On Fifty third Street, there is a restaurant called The Highwayman.
2. The restaurant founded in 1925 draws half of its cus tomers from tourists.
3. I painted its one hundred thirty one chairs a tedious job, to say the least.
4. Last night, the restaurant was oh, hi, Ed about one quarter full.
5. It's decorated like an inn my restaurant won't be.

Punctuating Parenthetical Information

Too many parenthetical expressions in a piece of writing can distract readers from the main idea. Keep your meaning clear by limiting the number of parenthetical expressions you use.

NOTE Many words and phrases are used *parenthetically;* that is, they break into the main thought of a sentence. Most parenthetical elements are set off by commas or parentheses. Sometimes, parenthetical elements demand stronger emphasis. In such instances, a dash is used.

Try It Out ✎

Revise the following sentences to eliminate the parentheses. If you think the sentence is best written with parentheses, write *C.*

1. *Survive the Savage Sea* (true stories are my favorites) is about people on a raft.
2. Yellowstone National Park (established in 1872) covers territory in Wyoming, Idaho, and Montana.
3. The writer Langston Hughes (1902–1967) is best known for his poetry.
4. Alligators use their feet and tails to dig holes (called "gator holes") in marshy fields.
5. On the Sabbath we eat braided bread called challah (pronounced khä′ lə).

16 SPELLING

USING WORD PARTS

Many English words are made up of various word parts. Learning to spell the most frequently used parts can help you spell many words correctly.

Roots

16a. The *root* of a word is the part that carries the word's core meaning.

WORD ROOT	MEANING	EXAMPLES
–dict–	speak	dictation, dictionary
–duc–, –duct–	lead	educate, conductor
–ject–	throw	eject, reject
–ped–	foot	pedal, biped
–vid–, –vis–	see	videotape, invisible

Prefixes

16b. A *prefix* is one or more letters or syllables added to the beginning of a word or a word part to create a new word.

PREFIX	MEANING	EXAMPLES
anti–	against, opposing	antiwar, anticlimax
co–	with, together	coexist, codependent
in–	not	inaccurate, ineffective
re–	back, again	reclaim, rebuild
trans–	across, beyond	transport, translate

Suffixes

16c. A *suffix* is one or more letters or syllables added to the end of a word or a word part to create a new word.

SUFFIX	MEANING	EXAMPLES
–able	able, likely	readable, perishable
–ance, –ancy	act, quality	admittance, constancy
–ate	become, cause	captivate, activate
–ize	make, cause to be	socialize, motorize
–ness	quality, state	peacefulness, sadness

ie and *ei*

16d. Except after *c*, write *ie* when the sound is long *e*.

EXAMPLES	achieve	believe	chief	field	piece
	ceiling	conceit	deceit	deceive	receive
EXCEPTIONS	either	protein	neither	seize	weird

16e. Write *ei* when the sound is not long *e*, especially when the sound is long *a*.

EXAMPLES	foreign	forfeit	height	heir	their
	freight	neighbor	reign	veil	weigh
EXCEPTIONS	ancient	conscience	patient	friend	efficient

> **NOTE** This time-tested verse may help you remember the *ie* rule.
>
> *I* before *e*
> Except after *c*
> Or when sounded like *a*,
> As in *neighbor* and *weigh*.
>
> The rhyme above and rules 16d and 16e apply only when the *i* and the *e* are in the same syllable.

✓ QUICK CHECK I

Add the letters *ie* or *ei* to spell each of the following words correctly.

EXAMPLE	1. bel . . . ve
	1. *believe*

1. gr . . . f
2. v . . . n
3. n . . . ce
4. sh . . . ld
5. . . . ght
6. perc . . . ve
7. pat . . . nce
8. th . . . f
9. r . . . ndeer
10. p . . . rce

–cede, –ceed, and –sede

16f. The only English word ending in *–sede* is *supersede*. The only words ending in *–ceed* are *exceed*, *proceed*, and *succeed*. Most other words with this sound end in *–cede*.

EXAMPLES	concede	intercede	precede	recede	secede

Adding Prefixes and Suffixes

16g. When adding a prefix to a word, do not change the spelling of the word itself.

EXAMPLES	mis + spell = **mis**spell	il + logical = **il**logical

16h. When adding the suffix *–ly* or *–ness* to a word, do not change the spelling of the word itself.

EXAMPLES	slow + ly = slow**ly**	dark + ness = dark**ness**
EXCEPTIONS	For words that end in *y* and have more than one syllable, change the *y* to *i* before adding *–ly* or *–ness*. happy + ly = happ**ily** lazy + ness = laz**iness**	

Language Handbook

> **NOTE** When adding *–ing* to words that end in *ie*, drop the e and change the *i* to *y*.
>
> **EXAMPLES**
> lie + ing = **lying**
> die + ing = **dying**

16i. Drop the final silent e before a suffix beginning with a vowel.

EXAMPLES   line + ing = lin**ing**   desire + able = desir**able**

EXCEPTIONS   Keep the final silent *e* in a word ending in *ce* or *ge* before a suffix beginning with *a* or *o*.
*notice + able = notice**able***
*courage + ous = courag**eous***

16j. Keep the final silent e before a suffix beginning with a consonant.

EXAMPLES   hope + less = hope**less**   care + ful = care**ful**

EXCEPTIONS   nine + th = nin**th**   argue + ment = argu**ment**

16k. For words ending in y preceded by a consonant, change the y to *i* before any suffix that does not begin with *i*.

EXAMPLES   try + ed = tr**ied**   duty + ful = dut**iful**

16l. For words ending in y preceded by a vowel, keep the y when adding a suffix.

EXAMPLES   pray + ing = pray**ing**   pay + ment = pay**ment**

EXCEPTIONS   day—da**ily**   lay—la**id**   pay—pa**id**   say—sa**id**

16m. Double the final consonant before a suffix beginning with a vowel if the word

(1) **has only one syllable or has the accent on the last syllable**

and

(2) **ends in a single consonant preceded by a single vowel**

> **NOTE** In some cases, the final consonant either may or may not be doubled.
>
> **EXAMPLE**
> cancel + ed = cance**led**
> *or* cance**lled**

EXAMPLES   sit + ing = sit**ting**   begin + er = begin**ner**

EXCEPTIONS   Do not double the final consonant in words ending in *w* or *x*.
mow + ing = mo**wing**   wax + ed = wa**xed**

Otherwise, the final consonant is usually not doubled before a suffix beginning with a vowel.

EXAMPLES   sing + er = sing**er**   final + ist = final**ist**

 QUICK CHECK 2

Add the given prefix or suffix to each word listed at the top of the next page.

EXAMPLE   **1.** display + ed
   1. *displayed*

1. im + migrate   5. semi + circle   9. carry + ed
2. re + settle   6. trace + able   10. advantage + ous
3. un + certain   7. jog + er
4. lucky + ly   8. dry + ness

Forming the Plurals of Nouns

16n. **For most nouns, add –s.**

EXAMPLES desks   ideas   shoes   friends   cameras   Wilsons

16o. **For nouns ending in s, x, z, ch, or sh, add –es.**

EXAMPLES gases   foxes   waltzes   inches   dishes   Suarezes

16p. **For nouns ending in y preceded by a vowel, add –s.**

EXAMPLES decoys   highways   alleys   Rileys

16q. **For nouns ending in y preceded by a consonant, change the y to i and add –es.**

EXAMPLES armies   countries   cities   ponies   allies   daisies

EXCEPTIONS For proper nouns ending in *y,* just add –s.
Brady—Bradys   Murphy—Murphys

16r. **For some nouns ending in f or fe, add –s. For others, change the f or fe to v and add –es.**

EXAMPLES beliefs   thieves   sheriffs   knives
giraffes   leaves   roofs   calves

16s. **For nouns ending in o preceded by a vowel, add –s.**

EXAMPLES radios   patios   stereos   igloos
Matteos

16t. **For nouns ending in o preceded by a consonant, add –es.**

EXAMPLES tomatoes   potatoes   echoes   heroes

EXCEPTIONS For musical terms and proper nouns, add -s.
alto—altos   soprano—sopranos
Blanco—Blancos   Nakamoto—Nakamotos

16u. **The plural of a few nouns is formed in irregular ways.**

EXAMPLES oxen   geese   feet   teeth   women   mice

16v. **For most compound nouns, form the plural of the last word in the compound.**

EXAMPLES bookshelves   push-ups   sea gulls   ten-year-olds

TIPS FOR SPELLING

In some names, marks that show pronunciation are just as important as the letters themselves.

PEOPLE Alemán   Böll   Ibáñez
Khayyám   Janáček   Eugène
PLACES Açores   Bogotá   Camagüey
Gîza   Köln   Sainte-Thérèse

If you're not sure about the spelling of a name, ask the person whose name it is, or check in a reference source.

When you use numbers in your writing, follow these guidelines:

• Spell out a number that begins a sentence.

EXAMPLE   **Fifty** people received free tickets.

• Within a sentence, spell out numbers that can be written in one or two words.

EXAMPLE   In all, **fifty-two** people worked on our play.

• If you use several numbers, some short and some long, write them all the same way. Usually, it is better to write them all as numerals.

EXAMPLE   We sold **86** tickets today and **121** yesterday.

• Spell out numbers used to indicate order.

EXAMPLE   Our team came in **third** [*not* 3rd] in the track meet.

16w.   **For compound nouns in which one of the words is modified by the other word or words, form the plural of the word modified.**

EXAMPLES   brothers-in-law   maids of honor
eighth-grade**rs**   boy scout**s**

16x.   **For some nouns, the singular and the plural forms are the same.**

SINGULAR AND PLURAL   Sioux   trout   sheep
deer   moose   series

16y.   **For numerals, letters, symbols, and words used as words, add an apostrophe and –s.**

EXAMPLES   *4***'s**   *s***'s**   *$***'s**   *and***'s**

✓ QUICK CHECK 3

Spell the plural form of each of the following items. [Note: An item may have more than one correct plural form. You only need to give one.]

EXAMPLE 1. &
    1. &'s

1. cargo
2. diary
3. Gómez
4. sit-up
5. child
6. video
7. hoof
8. Japanese
9. *M*
10. *10*

17 GLOSSARY OF USAGE

This Glossary of Usage is an alphabetical list of words and expressions that are commonly misused in English. Throughout this section some examples are labeled *standard* or *nonstandard*. **Standard English** is the most widely accepted form of English. It is used in *formal* situations, such as in speeches and writing for school, and in *informal* situations, such as in conversation and everyday writing. **Nonstandard English** is language that does not follow the rules and guidelines of standard English.

---

all ready, already   *All ready* means "completely prepared." *Already* means "before a certain point in time."

EXAMPLES   Everyone was **all ready** for the show.
That bill has **already** been paid.

all right   Used as an adjective, *all right* means "unhurt" or "satisfactory." Used as an adverb, *all right* means "well enough." *All right* should always be written as two words.

EXAMPLES   Linda fell off the horse, but she is **all right.** [adjective]
Does this suit look **all right** on me? [adjective]
You did **all right** at the track meet. [adverb]

a lot   *A lot* should always be written as two words.

EXAMPLE   She knows **a lot** about computer software.

anywheres, everywheres, nowheres, somewheres   Use these words without the final *s.*

EXAMPLE   I didn't go **anywhere** [*not* anywheres] yesterday.

at   Do not use *at* after *where.*

EXAMPLE   Where is it? [*not* Where is it at?]

bad, badly   *Bad* is an adjective. *Badly* is an adverb.

EXAMPLES   The raw celery did not taste **bad.** [*Bad* modifies the noun *celery.*]
One little boy behaved **badly.** [*Badly* modifies the verb *behaved.*]

between, among   Use *between* when referring to two things at a time, even though they may be part of a group containing more than two.

EXAMPLES   In homeroom, Carlos sits **between** Bob and me.
Some players practice **between** innings. [Although a game has more than two innings, the practice occurs only *between* any two of them.]

Use *among* to refer to a group rather than separate individuals.

EXAMPLES   We saved ten dollars **among** the three of us. [As a group, the three saved ten dollars.]
There was disagreement **among** the fans about the coach's decision. [The fans are thought of as a group.]

bust, busted   Avoid using these words as verbs. Use a form of either *burst* or *break.*

EXAMPLES   The door **burst** [*not* busted] open and rats teemed in.
What would happen if the window **broke** [*not* busted]?

choose, chose   *Choose* is the present tense form of the verb *choose.* It rhymes with *whose* and means "select." *Chose* is the past tense form of *choose.* It rhymes with *grows* and means "selected."

EXAMPLES   Did you **choose** "Fish Cheeks" for your report?
Sara **chose** "Miss Awful."

 NOTE   Many writers overuse *a lot.* Whenever you run across *a lot* as you revise your own writing, try to replace it with a more exact word or phrase.

 among   See **between, among.**
as   See **like, as.**
as if   See **like, as if, as though.**

because   See **reason . . . because.**

☞ **doesn't, don't**
See page 972.

could of Do not write *of* with the helping verb *could.* Write *could have.* Also avoid *had of, ought to of, should of, would of, might of,* and *must of.*

EXAMPLE All of Emily Dickinson's poems **could have** [*not* could of] been lost.

fewer, less *Fewer* is used with plural words. *Less* is used with singular words. *Fewer* tells "how many"; *less* tells "how much."

EXAMPLES We sold **fewer** [*not* less] tickets than they did.
These plants require **less** water than those do.

good, well *Good* is always an adjective. Never use *good* as an adverb. Instead, use *well.*

EXAMPLE Nancy sang **well** [*not* good] at the audition.

Well may also be used as an adjective to mean "healthy."

EXAMPLE He didn't look **well** after eating the entire pizza.

☞ **had of** See **could of.**

had ought, hadn't ought *Had* should not be used with *ought.*

EXAMPLE Eric **ought** [*not* had ought] to help us; he **oughtn't** [*not* hadn't ought] to have missed our meeting yesterday.

he, she, they Avoid using a pronoun along with its antecedent as the subject of a verb. This error is called the **double subject.**

NONSTANDARD Linda Goss she is a famous writer.
STANDARD Linda Goss is a famous writer.

hisself *Hisself* is nonstandard English. Use *himself.*

EXAMPLE Ira bought **himself** [*not* hisself] a polka-dot tie.

how come In informal situations, *how come* is often used instead of *why.* In formal situations, *why* should always be used.

INFORMAL I don't know how come she didn't take the garbage out.
FORMAL I don't know **why** she didn't take the garbage out.

☞ **its, it's** See page 1027.

kind of, sort of In informal situations, *kind of* and *sort of* are often used to mean "somewhat" or "rather." In formal English, *somewhat* or *rather* is preferred.

INFORMAL He seemed kind of embarrassed by our applause.
FORMAL He seemed **somewhat** embarrassed by our applause.

✓ QUICK CHECK I

Revise each of the following sentences to correct any error in usage.

EXAMPLE 1. The author she had lived in China.
1. *The author had lived in China.*

1. Alot of stars and planets have names from mythology.
2. Icarus had ought to have listened to his father.
3. If he had listened, he could of survived.
4. I wonder how come he didn't listen.
5. Surely, Daedalus's heart was busted by the death of his son.

learn, teach   *Learn* means "gain knowledge." *Teach* means "instruct" or "show how."

EXAMPLES   He is **learning** how to play the guitar.

His grandfather is **teaching** him how to play.

like, as   In informal situations, the preposition *like* is often used instead of the conjunction *as* to introduce a clause. In formal situations, *as* is preferred.

EXAMPLE   Look in the dictionary, **as** [*not* like] the teacher suggests.

like, as if, as though   In informal situations, the preposition *like* is often used for the compound conjunctions *as if* or *as though*. In formal situations, *as if* or *as though* is preferred.

EXAMPLES   They acted **as if** [*not* like] they hadn't heard him.

You looked **as though** [*not* like] you knew the answer.

of   Do not use *of* with other prepositions such as *inside, off,* and *outside.*

EXAMPLE   Did anyone fall **off** [*not* off of] the raft?

Revising Adverbs in Sentences

In informal situations, the adjective *real* is often used as an adverb meaning "very" or "extremely." In formal situations, *extremely* or another adverb is preferred.

INFORMAL   I'm expecting a real important telephone call.

FORMAL   I'm expecting an **extremely** important telephone call.

reason . . . because   In informal situations, *reason . . . because* is often used instead of *reason . . . that*. In formal situations, use *reason . . . that,* or revise your sentence.

INFORMAL   The reason I did well on the test was because I had studied hard.

FORMAL   The **reason** I did well on the test was **that** I had studied hard.

some, somewhat   Do not use *some* for *somewhat* as an adverb.

EXAMPLE   My writing has improved **somewhat** [*not* some].

less   See **fewer, less.**

lie, lay   See pages 982–983.

might of, must of See **could of.**

ought to of See **could of.**

Try It Out ✎

Revise the following sentences by substituting another adverb for the word *real*. Use a variety of adverbs.

1. Hercules was real strong.
2. He accomplished many tasks that were real hard.
3. Stories of his labors are real interesting.
4. They have endured a real long time.
5. Even today, real young children know his story from television shows.

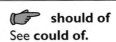
should of See **could of.**

somewheres See **anywheres,** etc.

sort of See **kind of, sort of.**

 NOTE Here's an easy way to remember the difference between *stationary* and *stationery*:

You write a lett**er** on station**ery**.

 who's, whose See page 1027.

 would of See **could of.**

stationary, stationery The adjective *stationary* means "in a fixed position." The noun *stationery* means "writing paper."

EXAMPLES Furnishings in a space capsule must be **stationary.**
I need a new box of **stationery.**

them *Them* should not be used as an adjective. Use *those.*

EXAMPLE The fox couldn't get **those** [*not* them] grapes.

way, ways Use *way,* not *ways,* in referring to a distance.

EXAMPLE They still had a long **way** [*not* ways] to go.

when, where Do not use *when* or *where* incorrectly in a definition.

NONSTANDARD In bowling, a "turkey" is when a person makes three strikes in a row.

STANDARD In bowling, a "turkey" is making three strikes in a row.

where Do not use *where* for *that.*

EXAMPLE I read **that** [*not* where] Pete Sampras won the match.

who, which, that The relative pronoun *who* refers to people only; *which* refers to things only; *that* refers to either people or things.

EXAMPLES Kim is the only one **who** got the right answer. [person]
My bike, **which** has ten speeds, is for sale. [thing]
He is the one person **that** can help you. [person]
This is the ring **that** I want to buy. [thing]

without, unless Do not use the preposition *without* in place of the conjunction *unless.*

EXAMPLE My mother said I can't go **unless** [*not* without] I finish my homework first.

 QUICK CHECK 2

Revise the following sentences to correct any error in usage.

EXAMPLE 1. The team forfeited the game like they had agreed to.
1. *The team forfeited the game as they had agreed to.*

1. The reason they forfeited was because Dondré couldn't play there.
2. What was going on inside of their heads?
3. They would not play without their teammate could play, too.
4. That story learned me something about loyalty.
5. True friendship is where people value each other as much as themselves.

Spelling Handbook

COMMONLY MISSPELLED WORDS

No matter how many spelling rules you learn, you will find that it is helpful to learn to spell certain common words from memory. The fifty "demons" in the first list are words that you should be able to spell without any hesitation, even though they all contain spelling problems. Study them in groups of five until you are sure you know them.

The second, longer list contains words that you should learn if you do not already know them. They are grouped by tens so that you may study them ten at a time. In studying each list, pay particular attention to the underlined letters. These letters are generally the ones that pose problems for students.

For more on spelling, see spelling rules 16a–16y in the Language Handbook.

FIFTY SPELLING DEMONS				
ache	cough	guess	once	though
again	could	half	ready	through
always	country	hour	said	tired
answer	doctor	instead	says	tonight
blue	does	knew	shoes	trouble
built	don't	know	since	wear
busy	early	laid	straight	where
buy	easy	meant	sugar	which
can't	every	minute	sure	whole
color	friend	often	tear	women

TWO HUNDRED SPELLING WORDS

abandon	commercial	February	nickel	separate
absolutely	committees	finally	nuisance	sergeant
acceptance	competition	flu	numerous	shepherd
accidentally	conceive	friendliness	obvious	similar
accommodate	condemn	generally	occasionally	solemn
accomplish	congratulations	governor	occurrence	sponsor
achieve	conscience	grammar	opportunity	straighten
acquaintance	conscious	gratitude	orchestra	subscription
acquire	convenience	guarantee	originally	succeed
actually	courteous	guardian	parallel	success
advertisement	criticism	gymnasium	parliament	sufficient
aisle	cylinder	height	patience	suppress
amount	dealt	hesitate	personal	surprise
analysis	deceit	humorous	persuade	surrounded
anticipate	definite	hypocrite	philosopher	suspense
anxiety	definition	ignorance	picnicking	tailor
apology	description	imagination	planned	temperament
apparent	desirable	immediately	possess	tendency
appearance	despair	incidentally	precede	theories
application	difficulties	individual	preferred	therefore
appreciation	disappointment	initial	prejudice	thorough
approach	discipline	inspiration	privilege	tobacco
assistance	discussion	intelligence	probably	tonsils
authority	diseased	interfere	procedure	tradition
beginning	distinction	interrupt	professor	tragedy
believe	distribution	judgment	pursuit	transferred
benefit	duplicate	knowledge	realize	truly
boundary	eligible	laboratory	receipt	unanimous
bouquet	embarrass	leisure	recommend	unnecessary
bulletin	engineering	lieutenant	referring	useful
business	equipped	luncheon	regularly	utilized
canceled	eventually	majority	relieve	vacuum
capacity	exactly	manufacture	repetition	various
carrier	exaggerate	marriage	research	vein
ceiling	excellent	mechanical	response	villain
challenge	existence	medieval	rhythm	violence
chorus	experience	mourn	satisfied	warrant
circuit	experiment	muscular	schedule	weird
colonel	fascinating	naturally	scissors	wholly
column	favorite	necessary	sense	writing

Communications Handbook

Using a Media Center or Library

To find a book, tape, film, or video in a library, start by looking in the **catalog.** Most libraries use an **online,** or computer, **catalog.**

Online catalogs vary from library to library. With some you begin searching for resources by **title, author,** or **subject.** With others you simply enter **keywords** for the subject you're researching. With either system, you enter information into the computer and a new screen will show you a list of materials or subject headings relating to your request. When you find an item you want, write down the title, author, and **call number,** the code of numbers and letters that shows you where to find the item on the library's shelves.

Some libraries still use card catalogs. A **card catalog** is a collection of index cards arranged in alphabetical order by title and author. Nonfiction is also cataloged by subject.

Electronic Databases. Electronic databases are collections of information you can access by computer. You can use these databases to find such resources as encyclopedias, almanacs, and museum art collections.

There are two kinds of electronic databases: **Online databases** are accessed at a computer terminal connected to a modem. The modem allows the computer to communicate with other computers over telephone lines. **Portable databases** are available on magnetic tape, diskette, or CD-ROM.

A **CD-ROM** (compact disc—read only memory) is played on a computer equipped with a CD-ROM player. If you were to look up *Amy Tan* on a CD-ROM guide to literature, for example, you could hear passages from her books and read critical analyses of her work.

Periodicals. Most libraries have a collection of magazines and newspapers. To find up-to-date magazine or newspaper articles on a topic, use a computerized index, such as *InfoTrac* or *EBSCO*. Some of these indices provide a summary of each article. Others provide the entire text, which you can read on-screen or print out. The *Readers' Guide to Periodical Literature* is a print index of articles that have appeared in hundreds of magazines.

Using the Internet

The **Internet** is a huge network of computers. Libraries, news services, government agencies, researchers, and organizations communicate and share information on the Net. The Net also lets you chat online with students around the world. For help in using the Internet to do research or to communicate with someone by computer, explore the options on the next page.

The Reference Section

Every library has materials you can use only in the library. Some examples are listed below. (Some reference works are available in both print and electronic form.)

Encyclopedias
Collier's Encyclopedia
The World Book Encyclopedia

General Biographical References
Current Biography Yearbook
The International Who's Who
Webster's New Biographical Dictionary

Special Biographical References
American Men & Women of Science
Biographical Dictionary of American Sports
Mexican American Biographies

Atlases
Atlas of World Cultures
National Geographic Atlas of the World

Almanacs
Information Please Almanac
The World Almanac and Book of Facts

Books of Quotations
Bartlett's *Familiar Quotations*

Books of Synonyms
Roget's International Thesaurus
Webster's New Dictionary of Synonyms

You've Got Mail!

E-mail is an electronic message sent over a computer network. On the Internet you can use e-mail to reach institutions, businesses, and individuals. When you e-mail places like museums, you may be able to ask **experts** about a topic you're researching. You can also use e-mail to chat with students around the country and around the world.

Internet forums, or newsgroups, let you discuss and debate lots of subjects with other computer users. You can write and send a question to a forum and get an answer from someone who may (or may not) know something about your topic.

Techno Tip

- If you get too few hits, use a more general word as your search term.

- If you get too many hits, use a more specific word as your search term.

The World Wide Web

The easiest way to do research on the Internet is on the World Wide Web. On the Web, information is stored in colorful, easy-to-access files called **Web pages.** Web pages usually have text, graphics, images, sound, and even video clips.

Using a Web Browser

You look at Web pages with a **Web browser,** a program for accessing information on the Web. Every page on the Web has its own address, called a **URL,** or Uniform Resource Locator. If you know the address of a Web page you want to go to, just enter it in the location field on your browser.

Hundreds of millions of Web pages are connected by **hyperlinks,** which let you jump from one page to another. These links are usually underlined or colored words or images, or both, on your computer screen. With hundreds of millions of linked Web pages, how can you find the information you want?

Using a Web Directory

If you're just beginning to look for a research topic, click on a **Web directory,** a list of topics and subtopics created by experts to help users find Web sites. Think of the directory as a giant index. Start by choosing a broad category, such as Literature. Then, work your way down through the subtopics, perhaps from Poetry to Poets. Under Poets, choose a Web page that looks interesting, perhaps one on Robert Frost.

Using a Search Engine

If you already have a topic and need information about it, try using a **search engine,** a software tool that finds information on the Web. To use a search engine, just go to an online search form and enter a **search term,** or keyword. The search engine will return a list of Web pages containing your search term. The list will also show you the first few lines of each page. A search term such as *Frost* may produce thousands of results, or **hits,** including weather data on frost. If you're doing a search on the poet Robert Frost, most of these thousands of hits will be of no use. To find useful material, you have to narrow your search.

"On the Internet, nobody knows you're a dog."

Refining a Keyword Search

To focus your research, use **search operators,** such as the words AND or NOT, to create a string of keywords. If you're looking for material on Robert Frost and his life in Vermont, for example, you might enter the following search term:

Frost AND Vermont NOT weather

The more focused search term yields pages that contain both *Frost* and *Vermont* and nothing about weather. The chart on the right explains how several search operators work.

Evaluating Web Sources

Since anyone can publish a Web page, it's important to evaluate your sources. Use these criteria to evaluate a source:

Authority

Who is the author? What is his or her knowledge or experience? Trust respected sources, such as the Smithsonian Institution, not a person's newsletter or Web page.

Accuracy

How trustworthy is the information? Does the author give his or her sources? Check information from one site against information from at least two other sites or print sources.

Objectivity

What is the author's **perspective,** or point of view? Find out whether the information provider has a bias or a hidden purpose.

Currency

Is the information up-to-date? For a print source, check the copyright date. For a Web source, look for the date on which the page was created or revised. (This date appears at the bottom of the site's home page.)

Coverage

How well does the source cover the topic? Could you find better information in a book? Compare the source with several others.

COMMON SEARCH OPERATORS AND WHAT THEY DO	
AND	Demands that both terms appear on the page; narrows search
+	Demands that both terms appear on the page; narrows search
OR	Yields pages that contain either term; widens search
NOT	Excludes a word from consideration; narrows search
–	Excludes a word from consideration; narrows search
NEAR	Demands that two words be close together; narrows search
ADJ	Demands that two words be close together; narrows search
" "	Demands an exact phrase; narrows search

Techno Tip

To evaluate a Web source, look at the top-level domain in the URL. Here is a sample URL with the top-level domain—a government agency—labeled.

top-level domain

http://www.loc.gov

COMMON TOP-LEVEL DOMAINS AND WHAT THEY STAND FOR

.edu	Educational institution. Site may publish scholarly work or the work of elementary or high school students.
.gov	Government body. Information is generally reliable.
.org	Usually a nonprofit organization. If the organization promotes culture (as a museum does), information is generally reliable; if it advocates a cause, information may be biased.
.com	Commercial enterprise. Information should be evaluated carefully.
.net	Organization offering Internet services. Information is generally reliable.

Listing Sources and Taking Notes

When you write a research paper, you must **document,** or identify, your sources so that readers will know where you found your material. You must avoid **plagiarism,** or presenting another writer's words or ideas as if they were your own.

Listing Sources

List each source, and give it a number. (You'll use these source numbers later, when you take notes.) Here's where to find the publication information (such as the name of the publisher and the copyright date) you'll need for different types of sources:

- **Print sources.** Look at the title and copyright pages of the book or periodical.

- **Online sources.** Look at the beginning or end of the document or in a separate electronic file. For a Web page, look for a link containing the word *About.*

- **Portable electronic databases.** Look at the start-up screen, the packaging, or the disc itself.

There are several ways to list sources. The chart on page 1045 shows the style created by the Modern Language Association.

Taking Notes

Here are some tips for taking notes:

- Put notes from different sources on separate index cards, sheets of paper, or computer files.

- At the top of each card, sheet of paper, or file, write a label telling what that note is about.

- At the bottom, write the numbers of the pages on which you found the information.

- Use short phrases, and make lists of details and ideas. You don't have to write full sentences.

- Use your own words unless you find material you want to quote. If you quote an author's exact words, put quotation marks around them.

The sample note card at the left shows how to take notes.

Sample Note Card

Poe's Childhood and Youth   1

—Parents were actors—father deserted family, mother died before Poe's 3rd birthday

—Raised by Frances and John Allan

—Published first poems at age 18   p. 20

Preparing a List of Sources

Use your source cards to make a **works cited** list, which should appear at the end of your report. At the top of a sheet of paper, type and center the heading *Works Cited*. Below it, list your sources in alphabetical order. Follow the MLA guidelines for citing sources (see the chart below). The sample works cited list below shows you how to do this.

Sample Works Cited List

Anderson, M. K. Edgar Allan Poe: A Mystery. New York: Franklin Watts, 1993.

"The Life of a Poet." Edgar Allan Poe Historic Site Home Page. 2003. 19 Aug. 2003 <http://www.nps.gov/edal/brochure.htm>.

"Poe, Edgar Allan." The World Book Encyclopedia. 2003 ed.

The chart below shows citations of print, audiovisual, and electronic sources:

MLA GUIDELINES FOR CITING SOURCES	
Books	Give the author, title, city of publication, publisher, and copyright year. Anderson, M. K. Edgar Allan Poe: A Mystery. New York: Franklin Watts, 1993.
Magazine and newspaper articles	Give the author (if named), title of the article, name of the magazine or newspaper, date, and page numbers. "Did Rabies Fell Edgar Allan Poe?" Science News 2 Nov. 1996: 282.
Encyclopedia articles	Give the author (if named), title of the article, name of the encyclopedia, and edition (year). "Poe, Edgar Allan." The World Book Encyclopedia. 2003 ed.
Interviews	Give the expert's name, the words *Personal interview* or *Telephone interview,* and the date. M. K. Anderson. Telephone interview. 12 Jan. 2004.
Films, videotapes, and audiotapes	Give the title; producer, director, or developer; medium; distributor; and year of release. Edgar Allan Poe: Terror of the Soul. Prod. Film Odyssey. Videocassette. PBS Home Video, 1995.
Electronic materials, including CD-ROMs and online sources	Give the author (if named); title; title of project, database, periodical, or site; electronic posting date (online); type of source (CD-ROMs); city (CD-ROMs); distributor (CD-ROMs); publication date (CD-ROMs) or access date; and Internet address (if any). "Poe, Edgar Allan." Grolier Multimedia Encyclopedia. CD-ROM. Danbury: Grolier Interactive, 2003. "The Life of a Poet." Edgar Allan Poe Historic Home Site Page. 2003. 19 Aug. 2003 <http://www.nps.gov/edal/brochure.htm>.

PROOFREADERS' MARKS

Symbol	Example	Meaning
≡	New mexico	Capitalize lowercase letter.
/	next $\cancel{S}$pring	Lowercase capital letter.
^	a book $\overset{of}{\wedge}$ quotations	Insert.
℘	a good go$\cancel{o}$d idea	Delete.
⌢⌣	a grape fruit tree	Close up space.
∿	does'$\cancel{t}$t	Change order (of letters or words).
¶	¶"Who's there?" she asked.	Begin a new paragraph.
⊙	Please don't forget⊙	Add a period.
⋏	Maya⋏did you call me?	Add a comma.
◇	Dear Mrs. Mills◇	Add a colon.
⋏,	Columbus, Ohio⋏ Dallas, Texas	Add a semicolon.
⌵ ⌵	⌵Are you OK?⌵ he asked.	Add quotation marks.

Giving and Listening to a Personal Narrative

Choosing a Story

To plan your oral narrative, you must find the right story to tell. (You might want to adapt the personal narrative you wrote for the Writing Workshop on pages 330–335.) Your story should have the following elements:

- **major and minor characters** that seem real
- **setting,** a definite time and place in which the story occurs
- **conflict,** a problem that the major characters must solve
- **plot,** made up of a **beginning** that sets the scene, **rising action** that leads to the story's **climax,** and a **resolution**

Make sure the story also has **dialogue** that brings the characters to life, **suspense** that makes listeners wonder what will happen next, and **action** that you can describe vividly or act out using movements, gestures, and facial expressions.

In addition, you need to consider the *purpose* and *audience* for your story. The **purpose** is to entertain, so you should choose a story that will appeal to the backgrounds and interests of your **audience,** namely, your teacher and classmates.

Planning Your Presentation

You can choose to tell the story as yourself, as a character involved in the story, or as an uninvolved narrator, but be sure to use a consistent **point of view** to keep your audience from becoming confused. Also, use the following strategies as you plan how to tell your story.

- **Describe the setting.** Use vivid language to describe each setting in the story. Focus on details that appeal to the senses. For example, if your story takes place in a garage, take time to describe the oil stains on the floor and the smell of gasoline in the air.

- **Describe the characters.** Bring your characters to life with specific details, such as the way they dress or talk.

- **Organize details in a logical way.** Organize your story in a way that will make sense and appeal to your listeners. Most listeners will expect a story to be told in **chronological order,** the order in which the events occur. As you organize your ideas, make sure they are **coherent**—all the events, actions, and dialogue should flow together smoothly.

Delivering Your Personal Narrative

Do not write out your narrative on a piece of paper, or you may be tempted just to read it aloud. Instead, jot down **notes** about key scenes, details, gestures, and so on, on an index card or sheet of paper. You can refer to your notes as you deliver your narrative without losing eye contact with your audience.

In your narrative, you must communicate the overall **mood,** or feeling, of the story, including your **attitude,** or what you think and feel about the situation and characters. You must also show the emotions of the individual characters in the story. Along with **movements, gestures,** and **facial expressions,** use these **speaking techniques** to make your narrative more effective:

- **Voice modulation.** Change the **tone** and **volume** of your voice to emphasize important moments, to build suspense, and to show emotion.

- **Inflection. Pitch** your voice to express shades of meaning or to share your attitude about the subject of the story.

- **Tempo.** Change the **speed** at which you talk to communicate emotion. A fast tempo often expresses excitement, while a slow one may reflect sadness or seriousness.

- **Enunciation.** Say each word clearly and precisely. Be sure not to slur words or drop word endings.

- **Eye contact.** Make eye contact with your audience members frequently. This will make them feel that you are speaking to each of them personally.

Rehearsing Your Presentation

To make your personal narrative the best it can be, you need to practice many times. Try following these steps:

REHEARSING A PERSONAL NARRATIVE	
Step 1	Rehearse your narrative several times. Practice your movements, gestures, and facial expressions in front of a mirror.
Step 2	Practice in front of a friend or relative, or tape your rehearsal with a video camera or tape recorder. Focus on making eye contact and speaking clearly and expressively. Ask your listener for feedback or play back the tape. Which parts of your narrative do you need to improve?
Step 3	Adjust your performance based on what your listener says or what you see or hear on the tape. Rehearse your narrative until you feel confident and do not need the notes much.

Responding to a Personal Narrative

In addition to giving your presentation, you will also listen carefully to your classmates' oral narratives and offer feedback on their performances. To **evaluate** a narrative's content, delivery, and overall impact, answer these questions.

- Are the story's content and organization **logical**? Have any important events or details been left out? What? Where?

- How does the speaker use movements, gestures, and facial expressions to portray characters in the story or to share his or her **attitude** about the subject of the story?

- How does the speaker's voice show his or her attitude? Do changes in **inflection** or **tempo** show amusement, or excitement?

- Does the presenter speak loudly and clearly and make **eye contact** with the audience?

Giving and Listening to a Persuasive Speech

Adapting a Persuasive Essay

When giving a persuasive speech, your purpose is to convince the people to whom you are speaking that your position on the issue is correct. Your speech needs to have strong content and appeal to your audience.

To find material for your speech, you may want to consider the persuasive essays you wrote for the assignments on pages 222–227 or 630–635. To adapt your essay into a speech, begin with a copy of your written essay. Identify your essay's **position** (your opinion statement), **reasons** and **evidence,** and **proposal** or **proposition.** Next, make notes on the copy using the following instructions.

- For a successful persuasive speech, you must consider your **audience.** Since your listening audience may be different from your essay's audience, you will need to reconsider what you include in your speech.

- As you choose **reasons** for your opinion and the **evidence** (anecdotes, facts, statistics, examples, and expert opinions) that supports your reasons, consider how they relate to your listeners. For example, if you give a speech in support of a better lunch menu in your school cafeteria to your classmates, you might describe better-tasting food. But if your audience is school administrators, you might give statistics that show how the new menu would improve attentiveness in class.

- Remember that your audience may not have the same **background information** as you do, particularly since you have researched your topic. Be sure that you explain in your speech any terms or ideas that may be unfamiliar to your listeners.

To organize your persuasive speech effectively, consider the following strategies for different **audiences** and **purposes**.

ORGANIZING IDEAS PERSUASIVELY		
If your audience . . .	**Your purpose is to . . .**	**Use this strategy:**
opposes your ideas	get them to consider your ideas	Acknowledge their point of view, and then list the reasons for your opinion.
agrees with your ideas	get them to take action	Strengthen their existing opinion by beginning with your opinion and then listing reasons. Close with your proposal, or call to action.
is unsure about your ideas	persuade them to agree with you	Open their minds to your position by beginning with reasons for your opinion.
does not care about your ideas	get them to consider your ideas	Start with information on how the issue affects them before giving your opinion and listing reasons.

As you organize your speech, remember that the **order** of your reasons and supporting evidence also has an impact on your audience. Do you want to start or end your speech with your strongest argument?

Delivering a Persuasive Speech

In persuasion, *how* you say something is often as important as *what* you say. A strong presenter can often make any argument more persuasive by using certain *speaking techniques*. How well can you pay attention to a speaker who quietly mumbles, who stumbles over words, who looks down while talking, or who races through a speech? To persuade your listeners, practice delivery techniques that will hold their attention, not distract them from your message.

To help audience members focus their attention on hearing your ideas, consider the speaking techniques below:

- **Enunciation.** Pronounce words carefully and clearly.
- **Vocal modulation.** Stress certain words and phrases through the volume of your voice.
- **Inflection.** Raise your voice at the end of a question, and lower it at the end of a statement.
- **Tempo.** Adjust the speed and rhythm of your speech.
- **Eye contact.** Keep the audience involved by looking at them.

Listening to a Speech

When you listen to **evaluate,** or judge, a speech, you should listen actively, giving the speaker your undivided attention. If you miss something that a speaker says, you may not get another chance to hear that information. While you listen to speeches, consider these tips to help you pay attention and get the message:

- Face the speaker, and listen quietly and attentively.
- Keep an open mind in weighing the reasons and evidence in the speech.
- Ask yourself if you understand the speaker's position.
- Take notes, writing down main ideas or details in your own words.

Remember that as a member of the audience, you can give the speaker **feedback.** For instance, after a speech you could ask for more information, politely counter a speaker's claim with your own ideas or experiences, or tell the speaker that you agree with his or her opinion.

Evaluating a Speech

One of the best ways for speakers to improve their speeches is to receive evaluations from their peers. When you are an audience member, the most useful thing you can do for your classmates is to give them honest, thorough, polite feedback about their speeches.

- When evaluating a speech's **content,** think about its message as well as the supporting reasons and evidence. The evidence the speaker provides should be **logical.** It should be relevant, or closely tied to the issue. To evaluate the **organization** of a speech, consider how easily you were able to follow the speaker's ideas.
- One of the most important elements of a persuasive speech is its **believability.** How knowledgeable and sincere does the speaker seem? Think about the strength of the speaker's reasons and evidence.
- By examining a speaker's **attitude**—his or her feelings toward the subject—you may find reasons to reject the speaker's position. You might discover a **bias,** or prejudice, the speaker holds. A biased speaker might present only one side of an issue, downplay information in favor of the other side, or keep his or her true purpose hidden from the listener.
- Criteria to consider when evaluating **delivery** are the speaker's use of presentation techniques, such as enunciation, voice modulation, inflection, tempo, and eye contact.

Giving and Listening to an Informative Speech

Delivering a speech can be a nerve-racking experience. If you prepare well, however, delivering a speech can also be fun. After all, when you give a speech, you are the center of attention. All eyes—and ears—are on *you*.

Planning an Informative Speech

To plan your speech, follow these steps:

- **Choose a focused topic.** You may want to base your speech on the informative report you wrote for the assignment on pages 864–869, or you might be ready to explore a different subject. Either way, make sure you **focus** your topic to keep your speech a manageable length. To focus your topic, ask yourself questions that are **relevant** (closely tied to the topic) and **concise** (brief and to the point).

- **Think about your purpose and audience.** For this speech, your general purpose is to share information with listeners. You should also decide on a specific purpose—what you hope to achieve through speaking. Ask yourself, "What do I want my audience to gain from my speech?" Then, write a sentence that answers your question. To make sure your listeners understand your purpose, plan to include a **thesis statement** at the beginning of your speech.

  As you plan your speech, think about what your audience may already know about your topic and what they might wonder about it. Thinking carefully about your listeners' backgrounds and interests will help you decide how to catch and hold their attention throughout your presentation.

- **Gather support.** You can search the library for printed information on your topic by looking in the card catalog, the *Readers' Guide to Periodical Literature,* magazines, newspapers, and dictionaries. At many libraries you will also find videotapes, audiotapes, slides, microfiches, CD-ROMs, and Internet access. Some libraries offer access to **databases,** collections of specific types of information.

In order to give your audience a clear and accurate understanding of your topic, you will need to track down sources that offer a variety of **perspectives.**

Organizing Your Speech

Once you have collected ideas about your topic, you need to organize them in a way that will appeal to your **audience** and help you achieve your **purpose.**

Introduction   Your introduction is the audience's first impression of you *and* your topic, so plan it carefully. It should be just a few sentences and should

- catch your listeners' interest
- focus attention on your topic
- make your listeners feel comfortable with you and your topic
- end with a thesis statement that makes your purpose clear

As you plan your introduction, consider using one of the following openings. Notice that each example ends with a sentence that serves as the speaker's thesis statement.

OPENING TECHNIQUES	
Technique	**Student Example**
Begin with a question.	What do a dollar bill and a letter carrier's car have in common? Both display the bald eagle, the symbol of the United States. Bald eagles almost became extinct in the 1960s. You can see a real eagle today, however, because many people have worked hard to help eagles make an amazing comeback.
Begin with a personal anecdote.	On a recent vacation, I visited an area where eagles often nest. I spotted a bald eagle swooping down and grabbing a fish out of the water with its talons. Fortunately, that sight is one people can still hope to see in person. Bald eagles almost became extinct in the 1960s, but thanks to the hard work of many people, eagles have made an amazing comeback since then.
Begin with a startling fact.	The bald eagle has symbolized the United States since 1782—seven years longer than our Constitution has been in effect. Yet in the 1960s this majestic national symbol almost became extinct. Fortunately, thanks to the hard work of many people, bald eagles have made an amazing comeback since then.

Body To plan the body of your speech, you will need to choose an effective organizational structure and then create an outline. Thinking about your audience and your specific purpose will help you decide how to arrange the main ideas and support (details, descriptions, examples) in the body of your speech. If you are adapting a written report, revise the report outline to fit the audience and the time available.

Conclusion Like your introduction, your conclusion might be only a few sentences long, but those few sentences serve an important purpose—to reemphasize your main idea in a memorable way. Your audience should recognize immediately that you are ending your speech, not adding to it. Two effective ways to conclude an informative speech are in the following chart:

CONCLUDING TECHNIQUES	
Technique	**Student Example**
End with a summary of your findings.	Sadly, it was human factors—the need for lumber and land, the misunderstanding of the birds' role in nature, and the use of hazardous chemicals—that brought the bald eagle to the brink of extinction. Other human actions, such as enacting legislation and breeding programs, are now giving these great birds new hope.
End with an echo of your introduction.	The bald eagle is not completely out of danger yet, but its future looks brighter every day. If the eagles continue their comeback, future generations will see our national symbol as more than just a picture on a dollar bill or on a mail truck.

Sources Just as you listed your sources of information in your written research report, you will also need to give your sources credit in your speech. You should credit each source by mentioning its author, title, or both.

According to the National Foundation to Protect America's Eagles, there are now about 55,000 bald eagles in the United States.

In her book Bald Eagles, Karen Dudley explains that eagles that ate DDT laid thin-shelled eggs that broke easily.

Delivering Your Speech

Using **note** cards, practice your speech until you can get through it comfortably without stopping. Try rehearsing in front of a few friends or family members. Use natural gestures, and make **eye contact** with your listeners.

Consider including **audiovisual materials,** such as *charts, graphs, illustrations,* and *audio* or *video recordings,* in your speech. Audiovisual materials can make your ideas clearer and easier to remember for listeners or provide extra information in your speech.

Be sure that all materials can be heard and seen by all members of your audience. Always explain to your audience what the audiovisual material means, and continue to face the audience. Be sure to cue any audiotape or videotape before you speak to avoid wasting time rewinding or fast-forwarding during your speech.

Listening to an Informative Speech

To get the most out of the informative speeches you hear, follow these guidelines.

During the Speech

- Determine the speaker's **attitude** toward the topic. The speaker's word choice or tone of voice may reveal his or her feelings about the topic.

- Listen for **cues** that signal **main points,** such as changes in volume or tone of voice. Cues can also include transitional words and phrases such as *first, there are many reasons, most important,* and *in conclusion.*

- Ask yourself whether you **understand** what is being said well enough to explain the ideas to someone else. If not, try creating a rough outline or cluster diagram of the main idea and important points in the speech as you hear them.

- **Summarize** the main points of the speech in your own words.

After the Speech

- **Ask probing questions.** Ask the speaker to clarify any points in the speech that you did not understand. If any points you expected to be covered were left out, ask the speaker to address them. Ask for specific evidence to back any unsupported claims or conclusions the speaker may have made.

- **Provide constructive feedback.** Be specific in commenting on the speaker's content, organization, and delivery. Whenever possible, begin by complimenting specific things that you thought the speaker did well. When you ask questions or offer suggestions for improvement, be sure to phrase them politely.

Giving and Listening to a Poetry Reading

Many people experience poetry only by reading it in a book, but most poetry is meant to be read aloud. Long before writing and printing presses, people shared poems, stories, and even history through oral recitation. Today, the tradition of oral poetry continues at poetry readings, slams, and contests in places like schools, libraries, bookstores, and clubs.

Preparing for a Poetry Reading

To prepare to recite a poem at a poetry reading, start by selecting a poem that you like. Whether the poem is the work of a famous author or one of your own, choose one that you will enjoy reading aloud. Remember also to pick a poem that fits the time limits you are given. Once you have chosen a poem, work on preparing it for a reading by following these steps:

- **Study the poem for its meaning.** Learn all you can about the **speaker** of the poem. Learn about the speaker's attitude toward the poem's subject and toward the audience. Your study of the speaker will tell you what **tone** to take in your reading. Should it be happy or sad? serious or humorous? sincere or sarcastic?

- **Mark up a copy of the poem.** Mark the parts you want to emphasize, the places you need to pause, and the parts that should be read slowly or quickly. Remember not to stop at the end of lines of poetry unless a punctuation mark stops you.

Rehearsing for a Poetry Reading

Here are some ways you can make your presentation of a poem more enjoyable for yourself and your **audience**:

- **Get familiar with your poem.** You do not need to memorize your poem completely. You do, however, need to know it well enough that you can make **eye contact** with your audience while you are speaking. The better you understand your poem, the easier it will be to remember.

- **Practice reading your poem.** Practice several times by yourself. Then, read your poem into a **tape recorder.** Play each reading back and critique yourself. At least once before you present your poem, have a dress rehearsal. Read it to one or more family members or friends. Ask them for ways you might improve. You can stand still or move around, but you should not lose contact with your audience.

Presenting at a Poetry Reading

If you have followed all the preparation and practice steps described above, you'll have nothing to fear when you make your presentation. Just relax, speak loudly and clearly, look at your audience, and—most important of all—enjoy yourself!

Listening to a Poetry Reading

When you listen to a poetry reading, your **purpose** is to **enjoy** and to **appreciate,** just as when you listen to music or the dialogue in a movie. The first rule of good listening is, of course, to concentrate. As you listen, try to **visualize** what you are hearing. Close your eyes if it helps you picture what the words you are hearing describe.

Notice the **rhyme** and the **rhythm,** or beat, you feel when you hear the poem. For example, the rhythm of words in a poem about the ocean may be steady like waves lapping against the shore. Listen also for **sounds** in the poem. Do bees buzz? Does the snow sweep with repeated *s* sounds? The language of good poetry has both beauty and power. Listen for these qualities just as you do when you listen to music.

Every poem has a **speaker.** The reader should become the speaker of the poem. Is the reader's style right for the poem? For example, if the speaker of the poem is a mouse, the reader might use a high-pitched, hurried tone of voice.

Evaluating a Poetry Reading

Giving and receiving **feedback** for a poetry reading can help you sharpen your listening and presenting skills. Work with other students to evaluate poetry readings by filling out a chart like the one below. After all ratings have been given, add up the numbers and divide the total by six to find the average score.

Scale: 1—poor presentation
2—improvement needed
3—fair
4—good
5—excellent

Criteria	Rating
The reader uses the effects of rhyme, imagery, and language effectively to give the audience a clear impression of the poem.	
The reader's tone of voice is appropriate for the speaker's voice in the poem.	
The reader speaks at a speed that allows the audience to follow the words in the poem.	
The reader stresses appropriate words.	
The reader maintains eye contact with the audience.	
The reader is easy to hear and understand.	
TOTAL	
AVERAGE (Divide the TOTAL by six.)	

Interviewing

Interviews—coversations in which one person asks questions to obtain information—are more common than you might think. You've probably been interviewed—by a teacher, the school nurse, or a neighbor wanting you to baby-sit or mow the lawn. Sometime you may need to conduct an interview yourself. For example, you might interview a neighbor for an oral history project or a local official for an informative report. Here's how to get off to a good start.

Preparing for the Interview

A good interviewer is well prepared. Before you take out your pencil and note pad, follow these steps:

- **Research your topic.** If your interview focuses on a topic—kayaking, say—go to the library and find out all you can about it. The more you know, the better your questions will be.

- **Know your subject.** If your interview focuses on the ideas and life of the person you're interviewing (your subject), see if any newspaper or magazine articles have been written about him or her. If your subject is a writer, read her latest book; if he's an architect, go see—or find a picture of—a building he designed.

- **Make a list of questions.** Ask obvious questions rather than pretend you know the answer. Don't ask questions that can be answered with a simple yes or no. Avoid questions that might influence your subject, like "You hate losing, don't you?"

- **Set up a time and place for the interview.** Choose a place that's comfortable and familiar to your subject—interview a horse trainer at her ranch or a chemistry teacher in his lab. Be on time.

Conducting the Interview

You're seated across from your subject, pencil poised. How do you make the most of your opportunity? Follow these guidelines:

- **Set the ground rules.** If you want to tape-record or videotape the interview, ask your subject for permission before you begin. If you plan to quote your subject's exact words in a newspaper article or in an essay, you must ask for permission to do that, too.

- **Be courteous and patient.** Allow your subject plenty of time to answer your questions. Try not to interrupt. Respect the person's ideas and opinions, even if you disagree.
- **Listen carefully.** Don't rush on to your next question. If you're confused, ask for an explanation. If an answer reminds you of a related question, ask it—even if it isn't on your list.
- **Focus on your subject,** not on yourself. Avoid getting off on tangents, such as "Something like that happened to me. . . ."
- **Wrap things up.** A good interview is leisurely but doesn't go on forever. Know when to stop. You can always phone later to check a fact or ask a final question. Be sure to thank your subject.

Following Up the Interview

Your notebook is filled, and your mind is bursting with ideas. How do you get your thoughts in order? Follow these steps:

- **Review your notes.** As soon as possible, read through your notes and make sure your information is complete and clear.
- **Write a summary.** To make sure you understand what was said, write a summary of the main points of the interview.
- **Check your facts.** If you can, check the spelling of all names and technical facts against another source, such as an encyclopedia.

Being Interviewed

Sometime someone may want to interview you. Here are some tips:

- **Stay relaxed.** Listen carefully to each question before you begin your answer. If a question confuses you, ask the interviewer to reword it or repeat it. Take your time. Long, thoughtful answers are better than short, curt ones.
- **Be accurate.** Don't exaggerate. If you're not sure of something, say so.
- **Keep a sense of humor.**

Analyzing Electronic Journalism

Just as you can analyze the elements of fiction, you can analyze the elements of a TV news story. A TV news story is made up of words, images, and sounds. Television journalists use specific techniques for presenting these words, images, and sounds. Each of these techniques serves a specific purpose.

Analyzing Elements of TV News

Textual Elements   **Text** is the name given to the words you hear and sometimes see on the TV screen. When you hear text, it is presented by a *news anchor* or *news reporter.* The **news anchor** reads the text of the primary, or most important, news stories. The anchor also introduces other reporters and their news stories. **Reporters**—often reporting live from where a news event is happening—may provide additional information on the primary news stories or give information on secondary, or less important, news stories.

Because of time limitations on TV, news stories are short, usually no more than two to three minutes long. This means that news writers and reporters must carefully plan text to achieve their purposes—capturing and keeping your attention, engaging your mind and emotions, and informing you. In order to understand the effects of a news story, you must examine both the *structure* by which the text is arranged and *content* of the text. You must also think about how the structure helps determine the content.

To help viewers understand and remember the main points of a news story during the couple of minutes it is broadcast, the text usually follows a brief, simple, attention-getting **structure,** or order. The following graphic shows the typical news story structure.

Lead-in

In the TV studio, the anchor introduces the story.

"Tonight a fire has broken out at the Olde Towne Bakery in the historic East End district. Here's Brian Steele on location with this breaking story. . . ."

Setup

The reporter, usually on location, grabs the audience's attention and introduces the images viewers are about to see.

"What you are about to see may trouble those of you with fond memories of the Olde Towne Bakery. . . ."

Sound Bites

Short audio pieces of interviews are mixed in with video clips.

(voice of Olde Towne Bakery owner): "This is truly heartbreaking. My grandparents started this business back in 1884. . . ."

Voice-overs

The reporter talks while the video is playing. Usually, the reporter explains the images on the screen.

"The flames are shooting up over thirty feet above the building."

Back Announcing

After the video clips, the reporter briefly sums up the main points of the story.

"Again, fire is raging through the Olde Towne Bakery in the historic East End district. The joyless residents of Thayerville are in shock as this landmark goes up in smoke."

Stand-up

The reporter addresses the camera and the anchor with closing commentary.

"The owners hope to rebuild soon so they can continue the generations-long tradition of bringing fresh baked goods to the folks of Thayerville. Back to you."

As you can see, the same information is repeated many times. Repeating the information gives viewers several chances to hear and understand the main point of a story.

Content The brief, repetitive structure of broadcast news stories limits the **content,** or information provided. Viewers may receive an oversimplified understanding of events, getting the basic facts without understanding the full meaning of the story. Because broadcast news stories are so short, they are often presented without much **context**—the whole situation or background information behind the story. As a result, viewers may not really be aware of the other issues related to the event.

Watch out for signs of **bias**—a slanted point of view, either in favor of or against an issue. Signs of bias include personal opinions and **loaded language**—words or phrases that carry strong positive or negative emotional impact, such as "a heartbreaking loss" or "an inspiring act." Try to form your own opinion about a story rather than being influenced by bias or loaded language.

Visual Elements   TV viewers tend to think of "live" images on the news as an accurate portrayal of reality. However, TV images represent just one piece of reality, as seen through a camera. **Photojournalists,** such as news reporters, photographers, and producers, make choices about the way each image will look. They also decide which **point of view,** or way of portraying the world, to show on the TV screen. As a critical TV viewer, you should know how the camera techniques TV photojournalists use can affect your perceptions of the news.

The **camera shot** is what the viewer sees on the television screen. Shots are put together to form a scene or story and may show closeness or distance.

A **long shot** is a shot made from far away, such as a landscape. A **cover shot**—a long shot at the beginning of a news story—can set the scene for the story. It may also create the impression of distance and objectivity. A long shot can also be used as **wallpaper,** an interesting visual image to show behind an anchor's narration.

A **close-up** is a shot taken very close to the subject. A close-up shot can show fine details, such as a detail of a craftsperson's hands weaving yarn. The camera may **zoom in** (moving from a wider shot of a subject to a closer one) to focus on the emotion in someone's face.

Long shot

Close-up

The **camera angle** is the viewpoint at which a camera is set when it is pointed toward a subject. Sometimes, conditions may limit the angles from which a cameraperson may shoot. For example, in filming a forest fire, a photojournalist may be able only to get shots taken from above, using a helicopter or airplane.

A **high angle** is a shot from above, with the camera looking down on the subject. A high camera angle can be used, for example, to provide an overview of a scene. A high camera angle can, however, make the subject look small, unimportant, and vulnerable.

High angle

A shot from below, with the camera looking up at the subject, is called a **low-angle** shot. A low camera angle can make the subject look tall and powerful. A low camera angle may distort reality, making subjects look much larger than they are.

Framing is the process by which the photojournalist decides which details to include or cut from the camera shot. Framing is used to focus on the subject, eliminate clutter, and engage the viewer's emotions. Unfortunately, framing can leave out important details, making a story seem less complex than it is. For example, the photojournalist who took the following pictures framed the right-hand shot so that just young women are shown in the frame. Viewers might wrongly conclude from the framed shot that the band is popular only with women, when in fact men are also fans.

Low angle

Full scene

Framed shot

Props are all the objects that appear in a camera shot. Whether it is intentional or not, these props can add meaning to a shot. Possible problems arise if a prop distracts the viewer or demonstrates a bias for or against a particular opinion. For example, if the brand name of a computer is visible on camera, the reporter may unintentionally be advertising that computer company.

Audio Elements   In addition to the text that you hear read by an anchor or reporter, there are other sounds that you may hear in a news report. Background noises captured on videotape, such as ambulance sirens, high winds, or hands clapping, add depth to a story. Sometimes you will hear the sounds of a busy newsroom behind a news anchor. Because music can affect viewers' emotions, network guidelines prohibit the use of music during a newscast. However, music is often used as a sound effect to open and close a program and to introduce commercial breaks.

Analyzing a TV News Story

Television newscasts blend textual, visual, and audio elements to create an effect greater than that which could be achieved through only one element. Still, before you can judge the effect of this blend, you need to analyze each of the individual elements. The following steps will help you identify the elements in a TV news broadcast and the techniques used to affect viewers:

▶ **STEP 1 Describe the news segment, identifying text, image, or sound techniques used in the segment.**
The story is a network news feature about the declining prairie dog population.
Sound: Prairie dogs bark and chatter through much of the story.
Image: The camera shows a long shot of a nearly deserted prairie dog town, medium shots of the remaining prairie dogs playing and eating, and a close-up of a rancher's face.
Text: The voice-over tells us that prairie dogs are in trouble because of disease and human activity and that they are a crucial part of the ecosystem. A rancher says he worries about them spreading disease. The story focuses on ways to handle the conflict between the environmental importance of prairie dogs and the needs of the ranchers and other people who consider them pests.

▶ **STEP 2 Explain the purposes of each major technique.** (Hint: Think about why the producer might choose these techniques.)

<u>Sound</u>: The barking noises grab my attention.

<u>Image</u>: The long shot sets the scene. The medium shot shows prairie dog activities, and the close-up shot shows the rancher's weathered face.

<u>Text</u>: The words of the voice-over tell me why some people are concerned about prairie dogs, and the rancher's words tell me why other people consider them pests.

▶ **STEP 3 Write an evaluation of the effects of the various techniques on you, the viewer.** (Hint: Think about how the techniques make you feel.)

The sounds the prairie dogs make in this story are kind of funny and cute. The long shot is a little sad because the prairie dog town is nearly empty. The medium shot is also really cute, and the prairie dogs act almost as if they have personalities. The close-up shows me the years of hard work the rancher has done. His expression is tired and tough at the same time— very different from the playful and vulnerable prairie dogs. The text gives specific reasons why prairie dogs are important to the ecosystem but only vague reasons why people exterminate them.

Overall, the techniques used in the story got my attention and the story was fairly informative. It may not have been totally balanced, though. The rancher's point of view seemed less important in the story than the case for saving the prairie dogs—probably because the prairie dogs were more appealing than the rancher and because the text went into more detail about the impact of their loss on the environment.

Analyzing a Documentary

Several decades ago, CBS aired Edward R. Murrow's *Harvest of Shame*. This documentary led to legislation that improved the lives of migrant farm workers, who travel from place to place to harvest crops.

Murrow followed the workers for a season, showing viewers what life was like for them. One **technique** that he used effectively was the **interview**—letting the workers speak for themselves. One woman he interviewed had been working in the fields since she was eight years old. She had worked ten hours that day and earned only one dollar. She had fourteen children to feed.

Media critics say that this documentary triggered changes in federal policy toward migrant workers. What made the documentary so effective in influencing and informing viewers?

- **A timely topic.** CBS aired the program on Thanksgiving Day, forcing viewers to connect the food they ate with the migrant workers who had harvested it.

- **Powerful images, words, and sounds.** Part of what gives images, words, and sounds power is their arrangement. For example, an image of cattle being shipped was placed next to an image of workers jammed into trucks. This technique, **juxtaposition** (side-by-side arrangement), showed viewers that the workers were treated like cattle. Filmmakers can also use sound techniques, such as **music** and **background noise,** to add to the messages they present.

- **A strong bias, or point of view.** The filmmaker's **attitude,** or **bias,** toward the subject can reflect the documentary's **purpose.** The creators of *Harvest of Shame* revealed their bias indirectly through the selection and arrangement of images and interviews. Clearly, they intended to influence, not just inform. Murrow also revealed his bias directly by urging viewers to help pass legislation to improve conditions for migrant workers.

Evaluating a Documentary

- As you watch a documentary, take notes on the topic; powerful images, words, and sounds; and the filmmaker's point of view and purpose.
- Also note techniques, such as interviews, juxtaposition, and music or background noise, used for effect.
- Use your notes to write an analysis of the documentary.

Glossary

The glossary that follows is an alphabetical list of words found in the selections in this book. Use this glossary just as you would use a dictionary—to find out the meanings of unfamiliar words. (Some technical, foreign, and more obscure words in this book are not listed here but instead are defined for you in the footnotes that accompany many of the selections.)

Many words in the English language have more than one meaning. This glossary gives the meanings that apply to the words as they are used in the selections in this book. Words closely related in form and meaning are usually listed together in one entry (for instance, *cower* and *cowered*), and the definition is given for the first form.

The following abbreviations are used:

adj.	adjective
adv.	adverb
n.	noun
v.	verb

Each word's pronunciation is given in parentheses. A guide to the pronunciation symbols appears at the bottom of this page. For more information about the words in this glossary or for information about words not listed here, consult a dictionary.

A

adaptation (ad′əp·tā′shən) *n.:* in biology, a change in structure, function, or form that improves an animal's or a plant's chances of survival. The protective coloration of some animals is a form of adaptation.
admonish (ad·män′ish) *v.:* warn or urge.
alleviate (ə·lē′vē·āt′) *v.:* relieve; reduce.

alliance (ə·lī′əns) *n.:* pact between nations, families, or individuals that shows a common cause.
amble (am′bəl) *v.:* walk without hurrying.
amplify (am′plə·fī′) *v.:* increase in strength. —**amplified** *v.* used as *adj.*
antic (an′tik) *n.:* playful or silly act.
appalling (ə·pôl′iŋ) *adj.:* horrifying.
archaeologist (är′kē·äl′ə·jist) *n.:* scientist who studies the culture of the past, especially by excavating ancient sites.
arrogant (ar′ə·gənt) *adj.:* overly convinced of one's own importance.
artifact (ärt′ə·fakt′) *n.:* object made by people or adapted for human use.
ascend (ə·send′) *v.:* move up.
ashen (ash′ən) *adj.:* pale.
assent (ə·sent′) *n.:* agreement.
assure (ə·shoor′) *v.:* promise confidently.
avalanche (av′ə·lanch′) *n.:* mass of loosened snow, earth, rocks, and so on, suddenly and swiftly sliding down a mountain.

B

bedraggled (bē·drag′əld) *adj.:* hanging limp and wet; dirty.
bluff (bluf) *n.:* steep cliff.
bout (bout) *n.:* match; contest.
buckle (buk′əl) *v.:* collapse under pressure.

C

charade (shə·rād′) *n.:* obvious pretense or act.
chivalry (shiv′əl·rē) *n.:* code that governed knightly behavior, such as courage, honor, and readiness to help the weak.

---

at, āte, cär; ten, ēve; is, īce; gō, hôrn, look, tool; oil, out; up, fur; ə *for unstressed vowels, as a in* ago, u *in* focus; ′ *as in* Latin (lat′'n); chin; she; zh *as in* azure (azh′ər); thin; the; ŋ *as in* ring (riŋ)

---

churn (churn) *v.:* shake; stir.
  —**churning** *v.* used as *adj.*
clamor (klam′ər) *n.:* loud, confused noise.
coexist (kō′ig·zist′) *v.:* live together
  peacefully.
commence (kə·mens′) *v.:* begin.
commotion (kə·mō′shən) *n.:* disturbance.
confrontation (kän′frən·tā′shən) *n.:* face-to-
  face meeting between opposing sides.
congregation (kän′grə·gā′shən) *n.:* gathering.
connoisseur (kän′ə·sur′) *n.:* person who is an
  expert on something.
consolation (kän′sə·lā′shən) *n.:* comfort.
contemplate (kän′təm·plāt′) *v.:* consider;
  look at or think about carefully.
contraption (kən·trap′shən) *n.:* strange
  machine or gadget.
converge (kən·vurj′) *v.:* close in.
  —**converging** *v.* used as *adj.*
convoluted (kän′və·lōōt′id) *adj.:*
  complicated.
countenance (koun′tə·nəns) *n.:* face;
  appearance.
cower (kou′ər) *v.:* crouch and tremble in fear.
curt (kurt) *adj.:* rude, using few words.
  —**curtly** *adv.*

D

decipher (dē·sī′fər) *v.:* interpret; find the
  meaning of.
defiant (dē·fī′ənt) *adj.:* boldly resisting
  authority.
delve (delv) *v.:* search.
deprivation (dep′rə·vā′shən) *n.:* loss; condition of having something taken away by
  force.
derisive (di·rī′siv) *adj.:* scornful and
  ridiculing.
descent (dē·sent′) *n.:* ancestry.
detain (dē·tān′) *v.:* hold back; delay.
dismal (diz′məl) *adj.:* miserable; gloomy.
  —**dismally** *adv.*
dispel (di·spel′) *v.:* drive away.
dispute (di·spyōōt′) *n.:* argument.
domain (dō·mān′) *n.:* territory.

E

edible (ed′ə·bəl) *adj.:* fit to be eaten.
egotism (ē′gō·tiz′əm) *n.:* conceit; talking
  about oneself too much.
elude (ē·lōōd′) *v.:* escape cleverly.
elusive (ē·lōō′siv) *adj.:* hard to detect.
entreaty (en·trēt′ē) *n.:* earnest request.
erupt (ē·rupt′) *v.:* burst forth.
eternity (ē·tur′nə·tē) *n.:* very long time;
  forever.
ethnicity (eth·nis′ə·tē) *n.:* common culture or
  nationality.
excavate (eks′kə·vāt′) *v.:* uncover or expose
  by digging.
exotic (eg·zät′ik) *adj.:* foreign; not native.
explicit (eks·plis′it) *adj.:* definite; clearly
  stated.

F

fathom (fath′əm) *v.:* understand.
finicky (fin′ik·ē) *adj.:* fussy and extremely
  careful.
forfeit (fôr′fit) *v.:* lose the right to compete.
formidable (fôr′mə·də·bəl) *adj.:* awe-
  inspiring; impressive.
frenzied (fren′zēd) *adj.:* wild.
fumigate (fyōō′mə·gāt′) *v.:* clean out by
  spraying with chemical vapors.
  —**fumigating** *v.* used as *n.*

G

ghastly (gast′lē) *adj.:* horrible; ghostlike.
goad (gōd) *v.:* push or drive.

H

habitual (hə·bich′ōō·əl) *adj.:* done or fixed by
  habit.
heritage (her′ə·tij) *n.:* traditions that are
  passed along.
horde (hôrd) *n.:* large, moving crowd.
hover (huv′ər) *v.:* hang in the air.
huddle (hud′′l) *v.:* nestle close together.

I

idiosyncrasy (id′·ē·ō·siŋ′krə·sē) *n.:* peculiarity.

immense (i·mens′) *adj.:* enormous.
—**immensely** *adv.*

imminent (im′·ə·nənt) *adj.:* about to happen.

implore (im·plôr′) *v.:* ask or beg.

imposter (im·päs′tər) *n.:* person who pretends to be someone or something that he or she is not.

impotent (im′pə·tənt) *adj.:* powerless.

inconsolable (in′kən·sōl′ə·bəl) *adj.:* unable to be comforted; brokenhearted.

incredulous (in·krej′oo·ləs) *adj.:* unbelieving.
—**incredulously** *adv.*

insolence (in′sə·ləns) *n.:* disrespect.

integrity (in·teg′rə·tē) *n.:* honesty; uprightness.

intelligible (in·tel′i·jə·bəl) *adj.:* understandable.

intent (in·tent′) *adj.:* concentrating deeply.
—**intently** *adv.*

interior (in·tir′ē·ər) *n.:* inner part of anything. The opposite of *interior* is *exterior.*

intimidate (in·tim′ə·dāt′) *v.:* frighten with threats.

intolerable (in·täl′ər·ə·bəl) *adj.:* unbearable.

intricate (in′tri·kit) *adj.:* complicated; full of detail.

invincible (in·vin′sə·bəl) a*dj.:* unbeatable.

L

ligament (lig′ə·mənt) *n.:* in anatomy, band of tough tissue that connects bones and holds organs in place.

loathsome (lō*th*′səm) *adj.:* disgusting.

M

matinee (mat′′n·ā′) *n.:* afternoon performance of a play or a movie.

meager (mē′gər) *adj.:* slight; scanty.

menace (men′əs) *n.:* danger; threat.

minority (mī·nôr′ə·tē) *n.:* small group that differs from the larger, controlling group.

monarch (män′ərk) *n.:* sole and absolute leader.

monopoly (mə·näp′ə·lē) *n.:* exclusive control of a market.

muster (mus′tər) *v.:* call forth.

O

observatory (əb·zurv′ə·tôr′ē) *n.:* building equipped for scientific observation.

ominous (äm′ə·nəs) *adj.:* threatening.

P

parch (pärch) *v.:* make very hot and dry.
—**parched** *v.* used as *adj.*

particle (pärt′i·kəl) *n.:* tiny piece.

pensive (pen′siv) *adj.:* thoughtful.
—**pensively** *adv.*

persecution (pur′sə·kyoo′shən) *n.:* act of willfully injuring or attacking others because of their beliefs or ethnic backgrounds.

perturb (pər·turb′) *v.:* disturb; trouble.
—**perturbed** *v.* used as *adj.*

predominant (prē·däm′ə·nənt) *adj.:* main.
—**predominantly** *adv.*

presumptuous (prē·zump′choo·əs) *adj.:* too bold; arrogant.

prey (prā) *n.:* animal hunted or killed for food by another animal. Mice are prey to owls. Gazelles are prey to lions.

profane (prō·fān′) *adj.:* not religious.

R

ransack (ran′sak′) *v.:* search thoroughly for goods to steal; loot, rob.

reassure (rē′ə·shoor′) *v.:* comfort.
—**reassuring** *v.* used as *adj.*

recede (ri·sēd′) *v.:* move back.
—**receding** *v.* used as *adj.*

recognition (rek′əg·nish′ən) *n.:* knowing again.

refuge (ref′yoōj) *n.:* shelter; protection.

refugee (ref′yo͞o·jē′) *n.:* person who flees home or country to escape war or persecution.
  —**refugee** *n.* used as *adj.*
reluctance (ri·luk′təns) *n.:* unwillingness.
resolute (rez′ə·lo͞ot′) *adj.:* firm and purposeful; determined.
resolve (ri·zälv′) *v.:* decide.
rumple (rum′pəl) *v.:* wrinkle and make untidy.
  —**rumpled** *v.* used as *adj.*
ruthless (ro͞oth′lis) *adj.:* without pity.

S

sabotage (sab′ə·täzh′) *v.:* obstruct or destroy.
sentinel (sent′'n·əl) *n.:* watchful guard.
sentry (sen′trē) *n.:* guard.
shrewd (shro͞od) *adj.:* clever.
simultaneous (sī′məl·tā′nē·əs) *adj.:* occurring at the same time.
  —**simultaneously** *adv.*
skirt (skʉrt) *v.:* avoid.
sophisticated (sə·fis′tə·kāt′id) *adj.:* worldly; elegant and refined.
sovereignty (säv′rən·tē) *n.:* control; authority.
species (spē′shēz) *n.:* in biology, a naturally existing population of similar organisms that usually breed only among themselves. The human species living today is called *Homo sapiens* ("wise man").
staid (stād) *adj.:* settled; quiet.
sterile (ster′əl) *adj.:* barren; lacking interest or vitality.

T

tirade (tī′rād′) *n.:* long, scolding speech.
torrent (tôr′ənt) *n.:* flood or rush.
tournament (to͞or′nə·mənt) *n.:* series of contests.
transfix (trans·fiks′) *v.:* cause to stand very still, as if nailed to the spot.
  —**transfixed** *v.* used as *adj.*
transition (tran·zish′ən) *n.:* change; passage from one condition to another.
turbulent (tʉr′byə·lənt) *adj.:* wild; disorderly.

U

unrequited (un′ri·kwīt′id) *adj.:* not returned in kind.
unscrupulous (un·skro͞o′pyə·ləs) *adj.:* dishonest.

V

vain (vān) *adj.:* useless; having no result.
  —**vainly** *adv.*
valiant (val′yənt) *adj.:* brave and determined.
variation (ver′ē·ā′shən) *n.:* difference.

W

wedge (wej) *n.:* pie-shaped slice.

Spanish Glossary

A

adaptation/adaptación *s.* en biología, un cambio de estructura, de función o de forma que mejora el potencial de supervivencia de una planta o de un animal. El color protectivo de ciertos animales es una forma de adaptación.

admonish/amonestar *v.* prevenir; advertir; reprender.

alleviate/aliviar *v.* mitigar; calmar; tranquilizar.

alliance/alianza *s.* coalición; liga; confederación; pacto entre naciones, familias o individuos con una causa común.

amble/deambular *v.* rondar; andar sin prisa; pasear.

amplify/amplificar *v.* ampliar; desarrollar; extender; incrementar en fuerza.

antic/travesura *s.* diablura; chiquillada.

artifact/artefacto *s.* conjunto de piezas que se adapta a un fin determinado.

appalling/espantoso *adj.* horrible; aterrador; grotesco.

archaeologist/arqueólogo *s.* científico que estudia los objetos y culturas antiguas especialmente mediante excavaciones de lugares antiguos.

arrogant/arrogante *adj.* soberbio; presuntuoso; orgulloso; convencido de su propia importancia.

ascend/ascender *v.* subir de un sitio a otro más alto.

ashen/pálido *adj.* exangüe; demacrado; sin color.

assent/asentimiento *n.* afirmación; consentimiento; confirmación; aceptación.

assure/asegurar *v.* afirmar; aseverar; prometer con seguridad.

avalanche/avalancha *s.* alud, masas grandes de nieve que se desprenden de las cumbres de las montañas, y al caer causan muchos daños.

avenge/vengar *v.* castigar; escarmentar; reivindicar.

B

bedraggled/destrozado *adj.* destrozado; manchado de barro.

bluff/acantilado *s.* talud; precipicio; barranco.

bout/combate *s.* pugilato; encuentro.

buckle/pandearse *v.* torcerse; caer bajo la presión.

C

charade/charada *s.* pasatiempo en que se trata de adivinar una palabra, haciendo una indicación sobre su significado, adivinanza.

chivalry/caballerosidad *s.* cortesía; urbanidad.

churn/batir *v.* remover; agitar.

clamor/clamor *s.* estruendo; ruido; fragor.

coexist/coexistir *v.* vivir juntos en armonía; convivir.

commence/comenzar *v.* empezar; dar comienzo a; iniciar.

commotion/conmoción *s.* tumulto; disturbio.

confrontation/confrontación *s.* careo; entrevista cara a cara entre oponentes.

congregation/congregación *s.* sociedad; agrupación; hermandad.

connoisseur/conocedor *s.* perito; entendido en alguna materia; inteligente.

consolation/consuelo *s.* alivio; desahogo; remedio.

contemplate/contemplar *v.* estudiar; considerar; poner atención en alguna cosa material o espiritual.

contraption/artefacto *s.* aparato; chisme; artilugio.

converge/convergor *v.* confluir; reunirse; coincidir.

convoluted/retorcido *adj.* complicado; intrincado; sinuoso.

countenance/semblante *s.* cara; apariencia; fisonomía.

cower/acobardarse *v.* encogerse; amedren-tarse; agacharse y temblar de miedo.

curt/brusco *adj.* parco; breve; lacónico.

D

decipher/decifrar *v.* interpretar, aclarar, describir lo oculto o dudoso.

defy/retador *adj.* desafiador; provocador; competidor; duelista.

delve/buscar *v.* explorar; hurgar; cavar.

deprivation/privación *s.* pérdida; falta; carencia.

derisive/burlón *adj.* socarrón; farsante.

descent/descendencia *s.* linaje; familia; estirpe.

detain/detener *v.* contener; suspender; arrestar.

dismal/deprimente *adj.* triste; patético; penoso.

dispel/disipar *v.* esfumar; eliminar; alejar; apartar.

dispute/disputa *s.* altercado; querella; contienda.

domain/dominio *s.* bienes; estados; posesión de tierras.

E

edible/comestible *adj.* que se puede comer; alimenticio.

egotism/egoísmo *s.* narcisismo; hablar demasiado de si mismo.

elude/eludir *v.* evitar; esquivar; rodear.

elusive/evasivo *adj.* escurridizo; esquivo; huidizo.

entreaty/peticion *s.* ruego; súplica.

erupt/arrojar *v.* entrar en erupción; dispersar.

eternity/eternidad *s.* perpetuidad; tiempo infinito; para siempre.

ethnicity/origen étnico *s.* cultura o nacionalidad en común.

excavate/excavar *v.* quitar de una cosa sólida parte de su masa haciendo un hoyo o cavidad en ella.

exude/exudar *v.* rezumar; sudar; transpirar.

exotic/exótico *adj.* extraño; raro; original.

explicit/explícito *adj.* claro; manifiesto; claramente explicado.

F

fathom/comprender *v.* entender; interpretar; concebir.

finicky/melindroso *adj.* quisquilloso; delicado; caprichoso; receloso.

forfeit/perder *v.* perder el derecho a competir.

formidable/formidable *adj.* tremendo; terrible; impresionante; que inspira la admiración.

frenzied/frenético *adj.* arrebatado; delirante; rabioso; extraviado.

fumigate/fumigar *v.* desinfectar; sanear; limpiar mediante vapores químicos.

G

ghastly/espantoso *adj.* horrible; lúgubre; parecido a la muerte.

goad/instigar *v.* aguijonear; incitar; alentar.

H

habitual/habitual *adj.* acostumbrado; inveterado; habituado.

heritage/herencia *s.* patrimonio; tradiciones que se heredan.

horde/horda *s.* multitud; tropa.

hover/colgar *v.* estar suspenso en el aire; revolotear; aletear.

huddle/amontonarse *v.* apiñarse; apretarse unos contra otros; acurrucarse.

I

idiosyncracy/idiosincrasia *s.* peculiaridad; especialidad.

immense/inmenso *adj.* enorme; desmesurado; colosal; gigantesco.

imminent/inminente *adj.* próximo; a punto de ocurrir.

implore/implorar *v.* suplicar; rogar; pedir con instancia.

imposter/impostor *adj.* se aplica al que engaña haciéndose pasar por lo que no es o por alguien que no es.

impotent/impotente *adj.* desautorizado; sin fuerza ni poder.

inconsolable/inconsolable *adj.* que no puede ser consolado o consolarse.

incredulous/incrédulo *adj.* suspicaz; prevenido.

insolence/insolencia *s.* desfachatez; descaro; frescura; falta de respeto.

integrity/integridad *s.* honradez; rectitud; probidad.

intelligible/inteligible *adj.* claro; evidente; legible; que se puede comprender.

intent/atento *adj.* considerado; muy concentrado en una tarea; dispuesto; vigilante.

interior/interior *adj.* interno; lo que está en la parte de dentro. El opuesto de *interior* es exterior.

intimidate/intimidar *v.* acobardar; amedrentar; atemorizar.

intolerable/intolerable *adj.* insoportable; insufrible; irritante.

intricate/intrincado *adj.* complicado; enredado; equívoco.

invincible/invencible *adj.* infranqueable; insuperable.

L

ligament/ligamento *s.* tendón; fibra; en anatomía, fibra segura que conecta huesos y mantiene órganos en su lugar.

loathsome/odioso *adj.* detestable; infame; horrible.

M

matinee/primera sesión *s.* función de la tarde.

meager/escaso *adj.* parco; pobre; exiguo.

menace/amenaza *s.* peligro; riesgo.

minority/minoría *s.* grupo pequeño que difiere del grupo mayor y en control.

monarch/monarca *s.* soberano; líder único y absoluto.

monopoly/monopolio *s.* consorcio; grupo; control exclusivo de un mercado.

muster/formar *v.* reunir; congregar.

O

observatory/observatorio *s.* mirador; edificio equipado para la observación científica.

ominous/siniestro *adj.* inquietante; adverso.

P

parch/secar *v.* tostar; abrasar; resecar; agostar.

particle/partícula *s.* átomo; fragmento minúsculo.

pensive/pensativo *adj.* meditabundo; ensimismado; absorto.

persecution/persecución *s.* acosamiento; perseguir o atacar a otros debido a sus creencias o procedencias.

perturb/perturbar *v.* inquietar; trastornar; alterar.

predominant/predominante *adj.* preponderante; superior; que prevalece.

presumptuous/presuntoso *adj.* presumido; arrogante; atrevido.

prey/presa *s.* captura; caza; víctima.

profane/profano *adj.* mundano; terrenal; que no es religioso.

R

ransack/rebuscar *v.* rebuscar; explorar; saquear; pillar; robar.

reassure/tranquilizar *v.* calmar; sosegar; aliviar.

recede/retroceder *v.* retirarse; volverse atrás.

recognition/reconocimiento *s.* evocación; recuerdo; volver a conocer.

refuge/refugio *s.* amparo; abrigo; protección.

refugee/refugiado *adj.* expatriado; persona que huye de su hogar o país para escapar de la guerra o persecución.

reluctance/desgana *s.* de mala gana, no dispuesto a ceder.

resolute/resuelto *adj.* determinado; firme; constante.

resolve/resolver *v.* decidir; arbitrar; despachar.

rumple/arrugar *v.* fruncir; marchitar.

ruthless/despiadado *adj.* cruel; feroz; sin compasión.

S

sabotage/sabotear *v.* estropear; arruinar; destrozar.

sentinel/centinela *s.* vigilante; guardián; celador.

sentry/guarda *s.* vigilante; celador; centinela.

shrewd/astuto *s.* perspicaz, de vivo ingenio, sutil.

simultaneous/simultáneo *adj.* sincrónico; paralelo; presente; que ocurre al mismo.

skirt/rodear *v.* circundar; contornear; bordear; evadir; prevenir; eludir.

sophisticated/sofisticado *adj.* mundano; carente de naturalidad.

sovereignty/soberanía *s.* control; autoridad; señorío; gobierno.

species/especie *s.* clase; en biología, una población natural de organismos similares que suelen procrearse únicamente entre ellos. La especie humana actual es *Homo sapiens* ("hombre sabio").

staid/serio *adj.* formal; quieto; moderado.

sterile/estéril *adj.* que no da fruto, o no produce nada.

T

tirade/diatriba *s.* perorata; sermón.

torrent/torrente *s.* arroyo; cascada; llover a cántaros; tumulto.

tournament/torneo *s.* liza; lucha; combate.

transfix/paralizar *v.* detener; suspender; inmovilizar.

transition/transición *s.* metamorfosis; evolución; etapa entre una condición a la otra.

turbulent/turbulento *adj.* perturbado; revuelto; agitado.

U

unrequited/no correspondido *adj.* un amor no correspondido; un servicio no recompensado.

unscrupulous/poco escrupuloso *adj.* inmoral; falto de principios morales; deshonesto.

V

vain/vano *adj.* sin éxito; infructuoso; inútil.

valiant/valiente *adj.* valeroso; bravo; indomable.

variation/variación *s.* muda; diferencia; diversificación.

W

wedge/trozo *s.* un pedazo en forma de pastel.

Acknowledgments

For permission to reprint copyrighted material, grateful acknowledgment is made to the following sources:

American Library Association: From Newbery Award Acceptance Speech by Mildred D. Taylor, 1977.

Américas, bimonthly magazine published by the General Secretariat of the Organization of American States in English and Spanish: From "Mongoose on the Loose" by Larry Luxner from *Américas*, July/August 1993, vol. 45, no. 4, p. 3. Copyright © 1993 by Américas.

Claudia Arnett: "Early Song" from *Collected Poems of Carroll Arnett/Gogisgi: Poems 1958–1995.* Copyright © 1979 by Gogisgi/Carroll Arnett. Published by Pavement Saw Press.

The Associated Press: "Buddies Bare Their Affection for Ill Classmate" by Associated Press from *Austin American-Statesman,* March 19, 1994. Copyright © 1994 by The Associated Press. From "Hatteras Lighthouse Completes Its Move" by Associated Press from *The New York Times,* July 10, 1999. Copyright © 1999 by The Associated Press.

Susan Bergholz Literary Services: "Names/Nombres" by Julia Alvarez. Copyright © 1985 by Julia Alvarez. First published in *Nuestro,* March 1985. "Chanclas" and "A Rice Sandwich" from *The House on Mango Street* by Sandra Cisneros. Copyright © 1984 by Sandra Cisneros. Published by Vintage Books, a division of Random House, Inc., and in hardcover by Alfred A. Knopf in 1994. All rights reserved. "Abuelito Who" from *My Wicked, Wicked Ways* by Sandra Cisneros. Copyright © 1987 by Sandra Cisneros. Published by Third Woman Press and in hardcover by Alfred A. Knopf. "The Place Where Dreams Come From" by Sandra Cisneros. Copyright © 1991 by Sandra Cisneros. "Salvador Late or Early" from *Woman Hollering Creek* by Sandra Cisneros. Copyright © 1991 by Sandra Cisneros. Published by Vintage Books, a division of Random House, Inc., and originally in hardcover by Random House, Inc. All rights reserved.

BOA Editions, Ltd.: "the 1st" *from good woman: poems and a memoir 1969–1980* by Lucille Clifton. Copyright © 1987 by Lucille Clifton. "I Ask My Mother to Sing" from *Rose* by Li-Young Lee. Copyright © 1986 by Li-Young Lee.

Brooks Permissions: "Home" from *Maud Martha* by Gwendolyn Brooks. Copyright © 1993 by Gwendolyn Brooks. Published by Third World Press, Chicago.

Arthur Cavanaugh: "Miss Awful" by Arthur Cavanaugh from *McCall's,* April 1969. Copyright © 1969 by Arthur Cavanaugh.

Laura Cecil, Literary Agent, on behalf of The James Reeves Estate: "The Sea" from *Complete Poems for Children* by James Reeves. Copyright © 1950 by James Reeves.

Judith Ortiz Cofer: "Aunty Misery," a Puerto Rican folktale translated by Judith Ortiz Cofer.

Don Congdon Associates, Inc.: "The Naming of Names" by Ray Bradbury from *Thrilling Wonder Stories.* Copyright © 1949 by Standard Magazines, Inc.; copyright renewed © 1976 by Ray Bradbury.

Bruce Coville c/o Ashley Grayson, Literary Agent: "Duffy's Jacket" from *Oddly Enough: Stories by Bruce Coville.* Copyright © 1989 by Bruce Coville.

Crown Publishers, Inc., an imprint of Random House Children's Books, a division of Random House, Inc.: "Overture" (retitled "The Power of Music") from *Nadja on My Way* by Nadja Salerno-Sonnenberg. Copyright © 1989 by Nadja Salerno-Sonnenberg.

Dell Publishing, a division of Random House, Inc.: "User Friendly" by T. Ernesto Bethancourt from *Connections: Short Stories,* edited by Donald R. Gallo. Copyright © 1989 by T. Ernesto Bethancourt.

Dial Books for Young Readers, a Member of Penguin Group (USA) Inc.: "The Flight of Icarus" from *Stories of the Gods and Heroes* by Sally Benson. Copyright 1940 and renewed © 1968 by Sally Benson. *Song of the Trees* by Mildred D. Taylor. Copyright © 1975 by Mildred Taylor.

Doubleday, a division of Random House, Inc.: Excerpt (retitled "The Only Girl in the World for Me") from *Love & Marriage* by Bill Cosby. Copyright © 1989 by Bill Cosby. "King Midas and the Golden Touch" from *Tales from Ancient Greece* by Pamela Oldfield. Copyright © 1988 by Grisewood and Dempsey, Ltd.

Dutton Children's Books, a Member of Penguin Group (USA) Inc.: *Merlin and the Dragons* by Jane Yolen. Copyright © 1995 by Jane Yolen; illustrations copyright © 1995 by Li Ming.

Esquire Magazine: "Three Skeleton Key" by George G. Toudouze from *Esquire,* January 1937. Copyright 1937 by Hearst Communications, Inc. All rights reserved. *Esquire* is a trademark of Hearst Magazines Property, Inc.

Farrar, Straus & Giroux, LLC: "Charles" from *The Lottery* by Shirley Jackson. Copyright © 1948, 1949 by Shirley Jackson; copyright renewed © 1976, 1977 by Laurence Hyman, Barry Hyman, Mrs. Sarah Webster, and Mrs. Joanne Schnurer. From "The Red Girl" from *Annie John* by Jamaica Kincaid. Copyright © 1985 by Jamaica Kincaid.

Edward Field: "Frankenstein" from *Counting Myself Lucky: Selected Poems 1963–1992* by Edward Field. Copyright © 1992 by Edward Field. Comment by Edward Field.

John Fleischman: "The Funeral Banquet of King Midas" by John Fleischman from *Muse,* vol. 4, no. 8, October 2000. Copyright © 2000 by John Fleischman.

Samuel French, Inc.: From *The Dream of Good Fortune: Arabian Nights* from *More from Story Theatre* by Paul Sills. Copyright © 1981 by Paul Sills. CAUTION: Professionals and amateurs are hereby warned that "The Dream of Good Fortune" being fully protected under the copyright laws of the United States of America, the British Commonwealth countries, including Canada, and the other countries of the Copyright Union, is subject to a royalty. All rights, including professional, amateur, motion picture, recitation, public reading, radio, television and cable broadcasting, and the rights of translation into foreign languages, are strictly reserved. Any inquiry regarding the availability of performance rights, or the purchase of individual copies of the authorized acting edition, must be directed to Samuel French, Inc., 45 West 25th Street, NY, NY 10010 with other locations in Hollywood and Toronto, Canada.

Abayomi Fuja: From "Oni and the Great Bird" from *Fourteen Hundred Cowries: Traditional Stories of the Yoruba,* collected by Abayomi Fuja. Copyright © 1962 by Oxford University Press.

The Gale Group: Quotes by Anne McCaffrey from "Anne McCaffrey" from *Something About the Author,* vol. 8, edited by Anne Commire. Copyright © 1976 by Gale Research Inc.

Greenwood Publishing Group, Inc., Westport, CT: "Sir Gawain and the Loathly Lady" from *The Oryx Multicultural Folktale Series: Beauties and Beasts* by Betsy Hearne. Copyright © 1993 by The Oryx Press.

Donald Hall: "Names of Horses" from *Kicking the Leaves* by Donald Hall. Copyright © 1975 by Donald Hall.

Harcourt, Inc.: "Arithmetic" from *The Complete Poems of Carl Sandburg.* Copyright © 1969, 1970 by Lilian Steichen Sandberg, Trustee. "Ode to Family Photographs" from *Neighborhood Odes* by Gary Soto. Copyright © 1992 by Gary Soto. "Mother and Daughter" from *Baseball in April and Other Stories* by Gary Soto. Copyright © 1990 by Gary Soto.

HarperCollins Publishers, Inc.: "Sarah Cynthia Sylvia Stout Would Not Take the Garbage Out" from *Where the Sidewalk Ends* by Shel Silverstein. Copyright © 1974 by Evil Eye Music, Inc. From *King Arthur: The Sword in the Stone* by Hudson Talbott. Copyright © 1991 by Hudson Talbott. Quotation by Hudson Talbott from jacket cover of *King Arthur: The Sword in the Stone,* written and illustrated by Hudson Talbott. Copyright © 1991 by Hudson Talbott. "Master Frog" from *The Brocaded Slipper and Other Vietnamese Tales* by Lynette Dyer Vuong. Text copyright © 1982 by Lynette Dyer Vuong. *The Crane Wife,* retold by Sumiko Yagawa, translated by Katherine Paterson. Text copyright © 1979 by Sumiko Yagama. Originally published in Japan by Fukuinkan-Shoten, Publishers, Inc., Tokyo.

Harvard University Press and the Trustees of Amherst College: "288: I'm Nobody! Who are you?" and "I Like to See It Lap the Miles" from *The Poems of Emily Dickinson,* edited by Thomas H. Johnson. Copyright © 1951, 1955, 1979 by the President and Fellows of Harvard College. Published by The Belknap Press of Harvard University Press, Cambridge, Mass.

Edward D. Hoch: "Zoo" by Edward D. Hoch. Copyright © 1958 by King-Size Publications, Inc.; copyright renewed © 1986 by Edward D. Hoch.

Henry Holt and Company, LLC: "The Runaway," "A Minor Bird," and "The Pasture" from *The Poetry of Robert Frost,* edited by Edward Connery Lathem. Copyright 1951 by Robert Frost; copyright 1923, © 1969 by Henry Holt and Company, Inc.

Houghton Mifflin Company: "The Great Musician" (retitled "Orpheus, the Great Musician") and "The Origin of the Seasons" from *Greek Myths* by Olivia Coolidge. Copyright © 1949 and renewed © 1977 by Olivia E. Coolidge. All rights reserved. "Bargain" from *The Big It and Other Stories* by A. B. Guthrie. Copyright © 1960 by A. B. Guthrie. All rights reserved.

Hyperion, an imprint of Disney's Children's Book Group, LLC: From *Dinorella: A Prehistoric Fairy Tale* by Pamela Duncan Edwards, illustrated by Henry Cole. Text copyright © 1997 by Pamela Duncan Edwards; illustrations copyright © 1997 by Henry Cole.

International Creative Management, Inc.: *The Monsters Are Due on Maple Street* by Rod Serling. Copyright © 1960 by Rod Serling.

Alfred A. Knopf, a division of Random House, Inc.: "Madam and the Rent Man," "Winter Moon," and "Harlem Night Song" from *The Collected Poems of Langston Hughes.* Copyright © 1994 by The Estate of Langston Hughes.

Lichtenstein Creative Media: Interview with Sandra Cisneros by Marit Haahr from *The Infinite Mind.* Copyright © 2002 by Lichtenstein Creative Media.

Little Brown and Company: From *Long Walk to Freedom* by Nelson Mandela. Copyright © 1994, 1995 by Nelson Rolihlahla Mandela.

Liveright Publishing Corporation: "All in green went my love riding" and "maggie and milly and molly and may" from *Complete Poems: 1904–1962* by E. E. Cummings, edited by George J. Firmage. Copyright © 1956, 1984, 1991 by the Trustees for the E. E. Cummings Trust.

Los Angeles Times: "Eeking out a Life" by Matt Surman from the *Los Angeles Times,* July 8, 2000. Copyright © 2000 by The Los Angeles Times.

Barry N. Malzberg for Arthur Porges: "The Ruum" by Arthur Porges. Copyright © 1953 by Mercury Press; copyright renewed © 1981 by Arthur Porges. Originally appeared in *The Magazine of Fantasy & Science Fiction,* October 1953.

Ashley Deal Matin: "Antaeus" by Borden Deal. Copyright © 1961 by Southern Methodist University Press. Quotation by Borden Deal.

Anne McCaffrey and agent, Virginia Kidd: "The Smallest Dragonboy" from *Get Off the Unicorn* by Anne McCaffrey. Copyright © 1973 and renewed © 2001 by Anne McCaffrey. First appeared in *Science Fiction Tales.*

Margaret K. McElderry Books, an imprint of Simon & Schuster Children's Publishing Division: From "The Search Goes On" from *The Mystery of the Ancient Maya* by Carolyn Meyer and Charles Gallenkamp. Copyright © 1985, 1995 by Carolyn Meyer and Charles Gallenkamp.

Pat Mora, www.patmora.com: "Gold" by Pat Mora. Copyright © 1998 by Pat Mora. Originally published by Harcourt Brace in *Home: A Journey Through America* by Thomas Locker and Candace Christiansen.

Motorola, Inc.: "Battery Removal/Replacement" from *Premier Cellular Telephone: Owner's Manual.* Copyright © 1994 by Motorola, Inc.

National Review: From "Canines to the Rescue" by Jonah Goldberg from the *National Review* web site accessed September 26, 2002, at http://www.nationalreview.com/goldberg/goldberg111201.shtml.

NEA Today: From "Amy Tan: Joy, Luck, and Literature," an interview by Anita Merina from *NEA Today*, October 1991. Copyright © 1991 by the National Education Association of the United States.

Agate Nesaule: Comment by Agate Nesaule from *NPR Morning Edition*, October 24, 2000. Copyright © 2000 by Agate Nesaule.

New York Times Agency: From "In a Mix of Cultures, an Olio of Plantings" by Anne Raver from *The New York Times*, August 15, 1991. Copyright © 1991 by The New York Times Company.

W. W. Norton & Company, Inc.: "Rosa" from *On the Bus with Rosa Parks* by Rita Dove. Copyright © 1999 by Rita Dove.

Harold Ober Associates, Incorporated: "Stolen Day" by Sherwood Anderson from *This Week Magazine*, 1941. Copyright 1941 by United Newspapers Magazine Corporation; copyright renewed © 1968 by Eleanor Copenhaver Anderson.

Shaquille O'Neal: "A Good Reason to Look Up" by Shaquille O'Neal. Copyright © 1998 by Shaquille O'Neal.

Penguin Young Readers Group, a Member of Penguin Group (USA) Inc.: From "Elizabeth I" from *Ten Queens: Portraits of Women of Power* by Milton Meltzer. Copyright © 1998 by Milton Meltzer.

Persea Books, Inc. (New York): From "Who Is Your Reader?" from *The Effects of Knut Hamsun on a Fresno Boy* by Gary Soto. Copyright © 1983 and renewed © 1988 and © 2000 by Gary Soto.

Philomel Books, a division of Penguin Young Readers Group, a Member of Penguin Group (USA) Inc.: *Yeh-Shen: A Cinderella Story from China*, retold by Ai-Ling Louie. Text copyright © 1982 by Ai-Ling Louie.

G. P. Putnam's Sons, a Member of Penguin Group (USA) Inc.: From *Homesick* by Jean Fritz. Copyright © 1982 by Jean Fritz.

Random House, Inc.: "Girls, and the Circle of Death" (retitled "Girls") from *How Angel Peterson Got His Name* by Gary Paulsen. Copyright © 2003 by Gary Paulsen.

Random House UK Ltd: "Narcissus" (retitled "Echo and Narcissus") from *Tales the Muses Told* by Roger Lancelyn Green. Copyright © 1965 by Don Bolognese. Published by The Bodley Head.

The Saturday Review: "The Dinner Party" by Mona Gardner from *The Saturday Review of Literature*, vol. 25, no. 5, January 31, 1941. Copyright © 1979 by General Media Communications, Inc.

Scholastic Inc.: From *The Last Dinosaur* by Jim Murphy. Copyright © 1988 by Jim Murphy. "The Hummingbird King" from *The Hummingbird King: A Guatemalan Legend*, written and adapted by Argentina Palacios. Copyright © 1993 by Troll Communications LLC.

Andrew Scott Music: Lyrics from "The Impossible Dream" from *Man of La Mancha*. Lyrics by Joseph Darion. Copyright © 1965 by Joseph Darion.

Scribner, an imprint of Simon & Schuster Adult Publishing Group: "A Day's Wait" from *The Short Stories of Ernest Hemingway* by Ernest Hemingway. Copyright 1933 by Charles Scribner's Sons; copyright renewed © 1961 by Mary Hemingway.

Spoon River Poetry Press: "To A Golden-Haired Girl in a Louisiana Town" from *The Poetry of Vachel Lindsay*. Copyright © 1985 by Spoon River Poetry Press.

Suhrkamp Verlag: "The Burning of the Books" from *Selected Poems* by Bertolt Brecht, translated by H. R. Hays. Copyright 1947 by Bertolt Brecht and H. R. Hays; copyright © 1961 Suhrkamp Verlag Frankfurt am Main.

Amy Tan and Sandra Dijkstra Literary Agency: "Fish Cheeks" by Amy Tan. Copyright © 1987 by Amy Tan. Originally appeared in *Seventeen Magazine*, December 1987.

Temple University Press: From "The Xiong Family of Lompoc" from *Hmong Means Free: Life in Laos and America*, edited by Sucheng Chang. Copyright © 1994 by Temple University. All rights reserved.

Piri Thomas: "Amigo Brothers" from *Stories from El Barrio* by Piri Thomas. Copyright © 1978 by Piri Thomas.

Time Inc.: "Can We Rescue the Reefs?" by Ritu Upadhyay from *Time for Kids*, vol. 6, no. 9, November 10, 2000. Copyright © 2000 by Time Inc. From "From Page to Film" by Kathryn R. Hoffman from *Time for Kids*, November 8, 2002. Copyright © 2002 by Time Inc. From "The Torchbearer: Rosa Parks" by Rita Dove from *Time.com* web site, accessed September 25, 2002, at http://www.time.com/time/time100/heroes/profile/parks01.html. Copyright © 2002 by Time Inc.

The University of Arkansas Press: "Interview" by Sara Henderson Hay from *Story Hour*, University of Arkansas Press, 1982. Copyright © 1982 by Sara Henderson Hay.

University of Notre Dame Press: From *Barrio Boy* by Ernesto Galarza. Copyright © 1971 by University of Notre Dame Press. Quotation about *Barrio Boy* by Ernesto Galarza. Copyright © 1971 by University of Notre Dame Press.

University Press of Mississippi: Interview with Sandra Cisneros from *Interviews with Writers of the Post-Colonial World* by Reed Dasenbrock and Feroza Jussawalla.

John Updike: From "An Ode to Golf" by John Updike. Copyright © 2000 by John Updike. Originally published in *The New Yorker*. All rights reserved.

Anna Lee Walters: "I Am of the Earth" by Anna Walters from *Voices of the Rainbow: Contemporary Poetry by American Indians*, edited by Kenneth Rosen. Copyright © 1975 by Anna Lee Walters.

Mel White: "A Mason-Dixon Memory" by Clifton Davis, slightly adapted from *Reader's Digest*, March 1993. Copyright © 1993 by Mel White.

Roberta Hill Whiteman: From "Depot in Rapid City" by Roberta Hill from *A Book of Women Poets: From Antiquity to Now*, edited by Aliki Barnstone and Willis Barnstone.

The Wylie Agency, Inc.: "I Was Sleeping Where the Black Oaks Move" from *Jacklight* by Louise Erdrich. Copyright © 1984 by Louise Erdrich.

Al Young: "For Poets" by Al Young. Copyright © 1968 and © 1992 by Al Young.

Sources Cited

From "A Note from the Author" from *Oddly Enough: Stories* by Bruce Coville. Published by Harcourt, Inc., 1994, Orlando, FL.

Picture Credits

The illustrations and photographs on the Contents pages are picked up from pages in the textbook. Credits for those can be found either on the textbook page on which they appear or in the listing below.

A11, © Art Resource/NY; **A14,** Oeffentliche Kunstsammlung Basel, Kunstmuseum Assession no. 1569. © 2003 Artists Rights Society (ARS), New York/VG Bild-Kunst, Bonn; **A15,** Hunter Museum of American Art, Chattanooga, Tennessee. Museum purchase with funds provided by the Benwood Foundation and the 1982 Collectors' Group HMA 1982.10. © 2005 Gwendolyn Knight Lawrence/Artists Rights Society (ARS), New York; **A38–1,** Digital Image, © The Museum of Modern Art/Licensed by Scala/Art Resource, NY; **5,** © Getty Images, Inc.; **9,** © Craig Tuttle/CORBIS; **11,** Courtesy of Bruce Coville; **15,** © Joe McDonald/DRK Photo; (background) Michael Halbert; **16,** Dinodia/Omni–Photo Communications, Inc.; **19,** Renee Lynn/Photo Researchers, Inc.; **21,** Michael Fogden/Animals Animals; **25,** OSF/Senani/Animals Animals; **26,** Studio Carlo Dani/Animals Animals; **28,** Dr. E. R. Degginger/Color-Pic, Inc.; **29,** © Bettmann/CORBIS; **31,** (top and bottom) © PhotoDisc/Getty Images; **32,** Cover photo by John Fei Photography; **39,** Stephen Dalton/Photo Researchers, Inc.; **53,** © Joe McDonald/CORBIS; **56,** © Joe McDonald/CORBIS; **77,** © Bettmann/CORBIS; **81,** (top) Bob Daemmrich/PictureQuest, (bottom) Don Romero/PictureQuest; **84,** © David B. Mattingly; **86,** © David B. Mattingly; **93,** Drone © Erik C. Omtvedt; **96,** © Forrest J. Ackerman Collection/CORBIS; **101,** © Wood River Gallery/PictureQuest; **102,** © Getty Images, Inc.; **103,** © Pictures Now!; **109,** © Bettmann/CORBIS; **124,** (top left) Cover by Max Ginsberg, copyright © 1992 by Max Ginsberg, cover illustration from *Lyddie* by Katherine Paterson. Used by permission of Lodestar Books, an affiliate of Dutton Children's Books, a division of Penguin Young Readers Group, a member of Penguin Group (USA) Inc., 345 Hudson St., New York, NY 10014. All rights reserved, (top right) Cover from *Bat 6 by Virginia Euwer Wolff with Connections,* © HRW, (bottom left) Cover art: David Gaadt, cover design: Joe Curcio. Used with permission, (bottom right) Cover from *Lupita Mañana by Patricia Beatty with Connections,* © HRW; Illustration by Diane Bennett/Daniele Collignon Represents; **125,** (top left) Cover from *Red Scarf Girl by Ji-Li Jiang with Connections,* © HRW, (top right) Cover art: Queen Elizabeth I (1533–1603): The Pelican Portrait, c.1574 (oil on panel) by Nicholas Hilliard (1547–1619). © Walker Art Gallery, Liverpool, Merseyside, UK/Trustees of the National Museums & Galleries on Merseyside/Bridgeman Art Library, (bottom left) Cover from *The Snake Scientist* by Sy Montgomery. Jacket photograph copyright © 1999 by Nic Bishop. Reprinted by permission of Houghton Mifflin Company. All rights reserved, (bottom right) From *Behind the Headlines* by Thomas Fleming. Jacket by Michael Chesworth. Reprinted with permission from Walker and Company; **126,** © Manu Sassoonian/Art Resource, NY; **131,** © Tony Freeman/PhotoEdit/PictureQuest; **132,** © Image Bank/Getty Images; **134,** Courtesy of Gary Paulsen; **143,** Courtesy of Gary Soto; **161,** Courtesy of Anne McCaffrey; **169,** © PhotoDisc/Getty Images; **170,** © PhotoDisc/Getty Images; **171,** © Ruben Guzman; **175,** Orion Press; **184,** AP/Wide World Photos; **191,** © Omni–Photo Communications, Inc./Index Stock; **192,** © Andre Jenny/Focus Group/PictureQuest; **195,** © Bettmann/CORBIS; **198,** © Francis G. Mayer/CORBIS; **201,** © Pictures Now!; **203,** © Bettmann/CORBIS; **206,** © 1993 Tom Van Sant/The Geosphere Project/The Stock Market/CORBIS; **207,** © PhotoDisc/Getty Images; **208,** © Edward W. Bower/Getty Images, (inset) © PhotoDisc/Getty Images; **211,** © PhotoDisc/Getty Images; **212,** Keren Su/Stock Boston; **215,** Robert Knopes/Omni–Photo Communications, Inc.; **216,** © PhotoDisc/Getty Images; **219,** © PhotoDisc/Getty Images; **220,** © PhotoDisc/Getty Images; **221,** (top) Reprinted by permission of Penguin Putnam Books for Young Readers, (bottom) © 1993 Tom Van Sant/The Geosphere Project/The Stock Market/CORBIS; **232,** (top left) Jacket design by Eric Jon Nones from *Across the Grain* by Jean Ferris. Jacket illustration © 1990 by Eric Jon Nones. Reprinted by permission of Farrar, Straus and Giroux, LLC., (top right) Cover from *M. C. Higgins, the Great by Virginia Hamilton with Connections,* © HRW; Illustration by Sarajo Frieden, (bottom left) From *Harriet the Spy* (jacket cover) by Louise Fitzhugh, copyright. Used by permission of Random House Children's Books, a division of Random House, Inc., (bottom right) Cover art copyright © Ed Acuna. Used by permission of HarperCollins Publishers; **233,** (top left) The Royal Archives © 2003 Her Majesty Queen Elizabeth II, (top right) © 1995 by Bill Nye. Used with permission from Disney Enterprises, Inc., (bottom left) Used by permission of HarperCollins Publishers, (bottom right) Cover from *Castles* by Philip Steele. Cover art © John Jamieson. Used with permission from Kingfisher Publications; **235–236,** © Richard Cummins/CORBIS; **239,** © Hulton Archive/Getty Images; **241,** © Bettmann/CORBIS; **242,** © CORBIS; **243,** Private Collection/Ken Welsh/Bridgeman Art Library; **244,** © PhotoDisc/Getty Images; **250,** Amos Zezmer/Omni–Photo Communications, Inc.; **256,** British Museum, London/Bridgeman Art Library; **257,** North Wind Picture Archives; **258,** Christie's Images/© SuperStock; **260,** (top) © Lee Snider/CORBIS, (bottom) © Bettmann/CORBIS; **263,** (bottom left) © Bettmann/CORBIS, (bottom right) Courtesy of The Edgar Allan Poe Museum of The Poe Foundation, Inc.; **266,** Art Today; **267,** (top left) Photographs by Michael J. Deas, (top right) Art Today, (bottom) © PhotoDisc/Getty Images; **268,** Photographs by Michael J. Deas; **270,** (left) Art Today, (right) Photographs by Michael J. Deas; **281,** Tom Tondee; **286,** (top right) © PhotoDisc/Getty Images; **290,** Dr. E. R. Degginger; **291,** (border) Dr. E. R. Degginger; **299,** Paul Fusco/Magnum Photos, Inc.; **303,** Erich Hartmann/Magnum Photos, Inc.; **310,** © Zefa Visual Media-Germany/Index Stock Imagery; **315,** © Art Resource, NY; **317,** © Dave Ryan/Index Stock Imagery; **318,** © Bill Bachmann/Index Stock Imagery; **320,** Ann Aldrich; **322,** © Dave Ryan/Index Stock Imagery; **323,** © 2003 James Innes/Picture Perfect; **324,** © Paul Barton/The Stock Market/CORBIS; **325,** James Innes/Picture Perfect; **326,** James Innes/Picture Perfect; **327,** © Joe McNally; **328,** © SuperStock; **329,** Courtesy Vachel Lindsay Association; **344,** (top left) Cover art copyright © 1995 by Trevor Brown. Cover © 1995 by HarperCollins Publishers. Used by permission of HarperCollins Publishers, (top right) Cover from *Where the Red Fern Grows by Wilson Rawls with Connections,* © HRW; Illustration by Lori Lohstoeter/Lindgren & Smith Represents, (bottom left) Jacket art © 1997 Phil Boatwright. Used by permission of HarperCollins Publishers, (bottom right) Cover illustration © 1995 by Jody Hewgill. Used with permission from The Art Works, USA; **345,** (top left) Jacket used with permission from Harcourt, Inc. All Rights Reserved, (top right) Used with permission from Harcourt, Inc., (bottom left) Used with permission from Dorling Kindersley Publishing, Inc., (bottom right) Hodder Wayland Picture Library; **346,** © Art Resource/NY; **351,** © Robin Weiner/Mediapix/The Image Works; **352,** © Diane J. Ali; **357,**

Grace Davies/Omni–Photo Communications, Inc.; **361, 365,** © Bettmann/CORBIS; **366,** (top) AP Photo/Copyright Chuck Close, High Museum of Art, Atlanta, (bottom) © Roger Ressmeyer/CORBIS; **367,** © PhotoDisc/Getty Images, (inset) Bill Bachmann/PictureQuest; **369,** Culver Pictures, Inc.; **379,** © Bettmann/CORBIS; **381,** Culver Pictures, Inc.; **387,** (bottom) Reprinted by permission of McIntosh and Otis, Inc.; **389,** © PhotoDisc/Getty Images; **390,** © Jacqui Hurst/CORBIS, (inset) © PhotoDisc/CORBIS; **394,** Photo courtesy of Julia Alvarez. Reprinted by permission of Susan Bergholz Literary Services, New York. All rights reserved; **400,** © Francisco Villaflor/CORBIS; **403,** (top) Courtesy of Maijue Xiong, (bottom) © Michael S. Yamashita/CORBIS; **404, 405, 407,** Courtesy of Maijue Xiong; **410,** Courtesy of Agate Nesaule; **411,** © Peter Turnley/CORBIS; **412,** (top) © Peter Turnley/CORBIS, (top middle) © David Turnley/CORBIS, (bottom middle) © Peter Turnley/CORBIS, (bottom) © Lisa Taylor/CORBIS; **417,** (top left) Copyright Scala/Art Resource, NY; (top middle) Copyright National Trust/Art Resource, NY, (top right) Copyright Giraudon/Art Resource, NY, (bottom left) Copyright Scala/Art Resource, NY, (bottom right) © Archivo Iconografico SA/CORBIS; **419,** © CORBIS; **421,** (left) Bettmann/CORBIS, (middle) © Joel W. Rogers/CORBIS, (right) © Michael Nicholson/CORBIS; **422,** © CORBIS; **423,** (left) © Archivo Iconografico SA/CORBIS, (right) Copyright Erich Lessing/Art Resource, NY; **424,** © CORBIS; **425,** Courtesy of Milton Meltzer; **427,** (top) © Archivo Iconografico SA/CORBIS; **432,** © Philip Gould/CORBIS; **435,** Karen Carr Studio; **436,** © Arthur Cohen Photography/Scholastic Press; **438,** © Stephen Gassman/Index Stock Imagery/PictureQuest; **441,** © The Image Bank/Getty Images; **442,** (top) © Guy Gillette/Photo Researchers, Inc., (bottom) Photo © Miriam Berkley; **443,** © Burstein Collection/CORBIS; **446,** NASA/Omni–Photo Communications, Inc.; **461,** AP/Wide World Photos; **474,** (top left) Cover art copyright © 1995 by Chris Miles. Cover copyright © 1995 by HarperCollins Publishers. Used by permission of HarperCollins Publishers, (top right) From *The Door in the Wall* (jacket cover) by Marguerite De Angeli. Used by permission of Random House Children's Books, a division of Random House, Inc., (bottom left) Cover from *Treasure Island by Robert Louis Stevenson with Connections,* © HRW; Illustration by Brian Fox, (bottom right) Text and illustration copyright © 1992 by Anni Axworthy. Used with permission by Charlesbridge Publishing, Inc. All rights reserved; **475,** (top left) From *Knots in My Yo-yo String* by Jerry Spinelli, copyright © 1998 by Jerry Spinelli. Cover photograph copyright © 1998 by Penny Gentieu. Map copyright © 1998 by Jennifer Pavlovitz. Used by permission of Alfred A. Knopf, an imprint of Random House Children's Books, a division of Random House, Inc., (top right) Used with permission from the Salariya Book Co. Ltd., (bottom left) From *Postcards from France* by Megan McNeill Libby, cover illustration, (bottom right) From *Made in China: Ideas and Inventions from Ancient China* by Suzanne Williams, cover art by Andrea Fong. Used with permission from Pacific View Press; **476–477,** © Digital Vision/Getty Images; **481,** © The Image Bank/Getty Images; **482,** (top) © Duomo/CORBIS, (bottom) © AFP/CORBIS; **491,** © PhotoDisc/Getty Images; **493,** Jim Pickerell/Stock Photo; **496,** © PhotoDisc/Getty Images; **497,** © Chris George/CORBIS; **500,** (top) © Randy Duchaine/The Stock Market/CORBIS, (bottom) Gary Conner/PhotoEdit; **504,** From *Barrio Boy* by Ernesto Galarza. Copyright 1971 by The University of Notre Dame Press. Notre Dame, Indiana 46556. Used by permission; **523,** Jack Ackerman/Penguin USA; **529,** (inset) Grace Davies/Omni–Photo Communications, Inc.; **530,** AP/Wide World Photos; **532,** © PhotoDisc/Getty Images; **534,** Saint Frederick High School Yearbook; **539,** © Gerardo Somoza/CORBIS Outline; **541,** Saint Frederick High School Yearbook; **544–545,** AP/Wide World

Photos; **552,** © SuperStock; **555,** Bridgeman Art Library; **556,** Wunrow/Index Stock Imagery; **557,** Kevin Fall Collection; **558,** Courtesy of Anna Lee Walters. Photograph by Ed McCombs; **560,** Robert W. Kelley/TimePix; **563,** © Bettmann/CORBIS; **564,** © The Brett Weston Archive/CORBIS; **566,** Peter Stein/Blackstar (Stock Photo); **569,** © Jian Chen/Stock Connection/PictureQuest; **570,** Arthur Furst; **572,** © Giantstep/Stone/Getty Images; **573,** © Ronnie Kaufman/CORBIS; **574,** Courtesy of Gary Soto; **575,** © Ariel Skelley/CORBIS; **581,** © Bettmann/CORBIS; **584,** AP/Wide World Photos; **587,** (inset) Ralph Reinhold/Animals Animals; **590,** © Jeremy Woodhouse/PhotoDisc/Getty Images; **591,** © Bettmann/CORBIS; **594,** © Peter Finger/CORBIS; **596,** © Hugh Chatfield, 2002; **598,** Ryuichi Nagasima/Photonica; **601, 603,** Bridgeman Art Library; **604,** © Bettmann/CORBIS; **606,** © Art Resource, NY; **610,** © Images.com/CORBIS; **611,** © Miriam Berkley; **615,** © Bryce Harper; **616,** Vintage Books, a division of Random House, Inc.; **617,** © AP/Wide World Photos; **618,** © Bryce Harper; **620,** © Stone/Getty Images; **621,** © Grace Davies; **623,** © Jeff Greenberg/PhotoEdit, Inc.; **628,** © Don Farrall/PhotoDisc/Getty Images; **629,** © Bettmann/CORBIS; **642,** (top left) From *Somewhere in the Darkness* by Walter Dean Myers. Cover illustration copyright © 1992 by Scholastic Inc. Reprinted by permission, (top right) Cover from *Cut from the Same Cloth* by Robert D. San Souci, illustrated by Brian Pinkney, copyright © 1993 by Brian Pinkney, illustrations. Used by permission of Philomel Books, A division of Penguin Young Readers Group, A Member of Penguin Group (USA) Inc., 345 Hudson St., New York, NY 10014. All rights reserved, (bottom left) Cover, © HRW. Illustration by Higgins Bond/American Artist Rep., Inc., (bottom right) Cover from *Adam of the Road* by Elizabeth Janet Gray, illustrated by Robert Lawson, copyright © 1942 by Elizabeth Janet Gray and Robert Lawson, renewed © 1970 by Elizabeth Janet Gray and John Boyd, Executor of the Estate of Robert Lawson. Used with permission of Viking Penguin, a division of Penguin Young Readers Group, a member of Penguin Group (USA) Inc., 345 Hudson St., New York, NY 10014. All rights reserved; **643,** (top left) Cover from *Amos Fortune: Free Man* by Elizabeth Yates. Cover illustration © Lonnie Knabel, 1989. Used with permission from Lonnie Knabel, (top right) From *Shrinking Forests* by Jenny Tesar, used by permission of Blackbirch Press, (bottom left) Used with permission from Dorling Kindersley Publishing, Inc., (bottom right) Used with permission from Grolier Publishing Company; **644–645,** © CORBIS; **654,** Takashi Shima/Photonica; **655,** Dr. E. R. Degginger/Color-Pic, Inc.; **666,** (bottom) © Getty Images; **669,** © Michelle L. Smith; **673,** M. J. Quay/M. L. Falcone; **676,** Lanny Provo/Photonica; **677,** © SuperStock; **679,** © UPI/CORBIS; **681,** © Bettmann/CORBIS; **689,** © Rodica Prato; **690–692,** University of Pennsylvania Museum, Philadelphia; **706,** © Photofest; **719,** © SuperStock; **720,** © Bridgeman Art Library; **722,** © Christie's Images/CORBIS; **723,** © Samantha Loomis Paterson; **730,** Arte Publico Press/University of Houston; **733,** Rollout Photograph #4675 © Justin Kerr, 1990; **734–735,** © Robert Frerck/Getty Images; **735,** The Granger Collection, New York; **739,** © Michael P. Fogden/Bruce Coleman, Inc./PictureQuest; **741,** (top left) Laurie Platt Winfrey, (top right) Chris Costello, (bottom left) © Erich Lessing/Art Resource, NY, (bottom right) © Werner Forman/Art Resource, NY; **743,** © Donne Bryant/Art Resource, NY; **764,** © Photofest; **765,** Courtesy: Special Collections, Carnegie Mellon University Libraries; **782,** (top left) Reprinted by permission of Carus Publishing Company, from *Patakin: World Tales of Drums and Drummers* by Nina Jaffe, art by Christine Ronan, © 2001 by Carus Publishing Company, (top right) Cover © Random House, text copyright © 1996 by Gary Ferguson, Illustrations copyright © 1996 by Douglas Smith, (bottom left) Cover from *The Samurai's Tale* by Erik Christian Haugaard. Copyright © 1984 by Erik Christian

Illustrations

All art by Holt, Rinehart and Winston unless otherwise noted.

Bollinger, Peter   429, 430, 433, 444
Carr, Karen   435
Costello, Chris   741
Deas, Michael J.   267
DiGiorgio, Mike   906, 907, 908
Dill, Jane   160
Ehlert, Lois   528
Geis, Alissa Imre   137, 138, 139, 140, 141, 142
Gil, Mariano   771, 768, 769
Grossman, Myron   525, 526, 542, 819, 832
Haggerty, Tim   265, 285, 286
Hagio, Kunio   747, 755
Halbert, Michael   15
Holland, Brad   445, 453
Hovell, John   82
Kerr, Justin   733
Leister, Brian   146, 147, 151, 155, 159
Leonard, Tom   40, 44, 46, 51, 175
Margeson, John   364, 548
Mattingly, David   84, 86, 89
Ortega, Jose   485, 487
Prato, Rodica   689
Reagan, Mike   50
Riedy, Mark   59–61, 63, 65, 67, 68, 70, 73, 76
Spransy, Tim   272
Steward, Arvis   648
Thompson, John   509–510, 513–515, 517–521

Index of Skills

Boldface page numbers indicate extensive treatment of a subject.

LITERARY SKILLS

Abbreviations key, 636
Academic language, 786
Accuracy, 787
Action, 129
Alliteration, 254, **577**, 585, 593, **601**, 608, 639, 758, 759, 763
Allusion, **174**, 185
Appearance, 128–129
Ars poetica, **609**
Attitude, 766
Author, 204, 437
Author study, 613
    message response chart, 619, 622, 626
Autobiography, **402**, **499**, 505, 637
Basic situation, 2
Biographical narrative, **414**
Biography, **414**, 479, **499**, 637
Boldface, 786
Catalog poetry, **606**, 608
Causal chain, 271
Cause and effect, 271, 282, 294, 686, 842
    causal chain, 271
    chain of events, 686, 842
Chain of events, 686, 842
    flowchart, 271
Character, 50, 135, 136, 144, 162, 172, 185, **190**, 191, 193, 244, 294, **296**, 306, 316, 705, 711, 716, 746, 750, 765, **786**, 814
    action and, 129
    appearance of, 128–129
    character/setting/theme comparison chart, 304, 321
    cluster diagram for, 129
    discovery made by, 237
    dynamic, 296, 304
    imaginary, 84
    main, 204, 437, 484
    motivation, **146**, 162, **174**, 185, 244, 254, 786
    motive, 30, 254
    in narrative poetry, 246
    in nonfiction, 787
    reactions of other characters to, 129
    speech and, 129
    static, 296, 304
    theme and, 237
    thoughts and feelings of, 129
    traits, 132, **136**, 144, **190**, 194, 196, 229, 282, 724
    traits comparison chart, 196, 204, 205
Character/setting/theme comparison chart, 304, 321

Characterization, **128–129**, 135, 172, 229
    direct, **128**
    indirect, **128**
Character traits, 132, **136**, 144, **190**, 194, 196, 229, 282, 724
    comparison chart, 196, 204, 205
Chivalry, 842
Cinderella story, **746**
    comparison chart, 757, 763, 766
Climax, 3, 119, 437, 484, 622
Community, folk tales and, **697**
Comparing literature, 84, 190, 296, 428, 746, 845
    character traits comparison chart, 196, 204, 205
    Cinderella stories comparison chart, 757, 763, 766
    mood/theme comparison chart, 437, 443
    myth comparison chart, 670
    real hero comparison chart, 852, 860
    science fiction story comparison chart, 88, 106
Comparison, 84, 282, 484, 494, 814
Complications, 2, **57**, 78, 484
Conflict, 2, **14**, 30, 162, 204, 299, 437, 613, 621, 622, 763
    external, 2, **484**, 494
    internal, 2, **484**, 494
Contrast, 84, 484, 494, 814
Couplet, **589**, 592
Criticism, 871
Culture, folk tales and, **696–697**
Dialogue, 622
Differences, 626
Direct characterization, **128**
Discovery, character's theme and, 237
Dynamic character, 296, 304
Elegy, **593**, 597
End rhyme, **576**, **586**
Escape story, **697**
Essay, **479**, **527**, 531, **533**, 637
    humorous, **527**
    purpose of, 533
Events
    later, 119
    series of, 2
Everyday language, 613
Exact rhyme, **598**, 600
Exaggeration, **578**, 585
Experience comparison chart, 540
Extended metaphor, **551**, 554
External conflict, 2, **484**, 494
    internal- and external-conflict chart, 102
Fact, 499, 505

Fable, 778
Fantastic situations, 84
Fiction, **478**
    historical, 368, 637
    novel, **478**, **508**, 637
    novella, **478**, **508**
    science, 84, 85
    short story, **478**, **484**, **508**, 637
    See also Poetry.
Figurative language, 106, 621, 787
Figures of speech, **546**, **548**, **609**, 612
    extended metaphor, **551**, 554
    metaphor, 505, **548**, 550, **551**, 609, 613, 619, 626, 639
    personification, **555**, 559
    simile, **548**, 550, 608, 609, 621
First-person narrator, **168**, 172
First-person point of view, **349**, 362, **368**, 380, 469
Flashback, **533**, 536, 540
Folk tale, **696–697**
    community and, **697**
    culture and, **696–697**
    escape story, **697**
    motifs in, **696**
Foreshadowing, 2, **38**, 50, 68, 308, 362, 368
    suspense and, **38**, 50
Forms of poetry, **546**.
    See Poetry.
Forms of prose, **478–479**
    chart, 479.
    See Prose.
Frame story, 831
Freedom, 852
Free verse, **576**, 593, 597, **606**, 608
    alliteration in, **593**, 597
    imagery in, **593**, 597
    onomatopoeia in, **593**, 597
    rhythm in, **593**, 608
Generalizations, 627, 680, 871
Giving/receiving chart, 555
Gods, **647**
    Greek/Roman gods and goddesses chart, 647
Goddesses, **647**
    Greek/Roman gods and goddesses chart, 647
Graphic organizers
    abbreviations key, 636
    chain of events, 686, 842
    chain of events flowchart, 271
    character cluster diagram, 129
    character/setting/theme comparison chart, 304, 321
    character traits comparison chart, 196, 204, 205
    Cinderella stories comparison chart, 757, 763, 766

INFORMATIONAL READING SKILLS

Multiple-meaning words, 122, 874
Mythology, making up words from, 687
Onomatopoeia, **725**
Personification, **671**
Place names, Greek and Roman, **681**
Precise verbs, 663
Prefixes, **163, 663, 815, 832**
    Anglo-Saxon, **815**
    chart for Greek, 663
    Greek, **663**
    Latin, **815**
    word map for, 832
Pronoun references, unclear, **173**
    and antecedents, 173
Roman and Greek place names, **681**
Roots of words, 270
    chart of Greek, 819
    Greek, **819**
    Latin, **270**
Simile, **255,** 671
Specific words, using, **717**
Suffixes, **163, 832**
    word map for, 832
Synonyms, 230, 472, **541,** 780
    word map for, 541
Vivid adjectives, 663
Word analogy, **532**
Word map, 541, 832
Word origins
    Anglo-Saxon, **809**
    etymology, **145**
    French, **843**
    Latin, **809**
Word roots, **163**
    word tree, 163
Word tree, 163, 653
Word web, 363

READING SKILLS

Accurate evidence, **788,** 791
Adequate evidence, **788,** 791
Affixes, Greek and Latin roots and.
    See Greek and Latin roots and
    affixes.
Appropriate evidence, **788,** 789, 791
Author's perspective, analyzing, **350**
    Perspective Wheel, 355
Boldface, 882, 883
Brainstorming map, 682
Causal chain, 271
Cause and effect, **271,** 282, **654,** 662
    causal chain, 271
    cause, **271,** 658, 660
    chain, **726,** 731
    chain chart, 726
    chain-of-events flowchart, 271
    effect, **271,** 655, 660, 661
    recognition of, **271**
Cause-and-effect chain, **726,** 731
    chart, 726

Character
    If—Then strategy, **130,** 135
    motivation of, 244
    plot and, **130**
    theme and, **244**
    tips for understanding, 130
Comparing and contrasting, **84, 190, 296, 428, 484, 746, 845**
    Venn diagram, 484
Conclusions, drawing, **718,** 724
Conflict, 613
Context clues, using, **289**
Details, **393**
Distinguishing fact from opinion, **402,** 408, **499,** 505
"Effects" phrases, 882
Expert testimony, 789
Evidence, evaluating, **788, 791**
    accurate, **788,** 791
    adequate, **788,** 791
    appropriate, **788,** 789, 791
    expert testimony and, 789
    facts and, 788
    inaccurate, **788,** 791
    inadequate, **788,** 791
    inappropriate, **788,** 791
    opinions and, 788
    reliable sources and, 788
Facts, 788
    distinguished from opinions, **402,** 408, **499,** 505
Flashback, **533,** 536, 540
Foreshadowing, 38, 356, 368
Generalizations, making, **508, 613, 675**
    conflict and, 613
    message and, 613
    theme and, **508**
Graphic organizers
    brainstorming map, 682
    cause-and-effect chain chart, 726
    chain-of-events flowchart, 271
    informational text features chart, 887
    Perspective Wheel, 355
    prefixes chart, 652
    Retelling Summary Sheet, 4, **12**
    roots chart, 651
    SQ3R organizer, 415
    suffixes chart, 652
    summarizing diagram, 670
    text features chart, 887
    theme graphics, 245
    Venn diagram, 484
    vocabulary tree, 653
Graphics, 882
Greek and Latin roots and affixes, **650–653**
    prefixes, 650, **652**
    prefixes chart, 652
    roots chart, 651
    suffixes, 650, **652**
    suffixes chart, 652
    vocabulary tree, 653

Headings, 882, 883
If—Then strategy, **130,** 135
Illustrations, 886
Images, **527,** 531
Implications, 393
Inaccurate evidence, **788,** 791
Inadequate evidence, **788,** 791
Inappropriate evidence, **788,** 791
Inferences, **57,** 68, 78, **136, 146,** 162, **168,** 187, 229, 393, 571
Informational texts, reading. *See* Reading informational texts.
Italics, 882
Latin and Greek roots and affixes. *See* Greek and Latin roots and affixes.
Main idea, finding, **393,** 399, **480,** 483
    details and, **393**
    implications and, 393
    inferences and, 393
    reading informational texts and, 885
    topic and, 480
Message, 613
Motivation, 244
Numbered steps, 882
Opinions, 788
    distinguished from facts, **402,** 408, **499,** 505
"Opposite" phrases, 882
Paragraph, 883
    breaks, 885
Perspective, analyzing author's, **350,** 355
    Perspective Wheel, 355
Plot
    character and, **130**
    If—Then strategy, **130,** 135
    theme and, 238, **244**
    topic and, 244
Poetry, reading, **551, 589, 609**
    punctuation and, **589**
    thoughts and, **609**
Predicting, 38, 68, **174,** 185, **356, 368,** 380, 505, **707,** 716
    foreshadowing and, 38, 356, 368
    suspense and, 38
Prefixes, 650, **652**
    chart, 652
Prior knowledge, using, **682**
    brainstorming map, 682
Punctuation in poetry, **589**
Reading informational texts, **882**
    boldface, 882, 883
    "effects" phrases, 882
    features chart, 887
    first paragraph, 883
    graphics, 882
    headings, 882
    illustrations, 886
    italics, 882
    main idea, 885
    numbered steps, 882

WRITING SKILLS

LANGUAGE (GRAMMAR, USAGE, AND MECHANICS) SKILLS

Index of Authors and Titles

Student Authors and Titles